Reporting for the Print Media

Reporting for the Print Media

FIFTH EDITION

FRED FEDLER
University of Central Florida

HARCOURT BRACE JOVANOVICH COLLEGE PUBLISHERS

Fort Worth   Philadelphia   San Diego   New York   Orlando   Austin   San Antonio
Toronto   Montreal   London   Sydney   Tokyo

Editor-in-chief **Ted Buchholz**
Acquisitions editor **Stephen T. Jordan**
Developmental editor **Cathlynn Richard**
Project editor **Steve Norder**
Production manager **Erin Gregg**
Book designer **Brian Salisbury**
Photo/Permissions editor **Sandra Lord**

Literary and illustration credits appear on p. 809.

Library of Congress Catalog Card Number: 92-073519

Address for Editorial Correspondence: Harcourt Brace Jovanovich, Inc., 301 Commerce Street, Suite 3700, Fort Worth, TX 76102.

Address for Orders: Harcourt Brace Jovanovich, Inc., 6277 Sea Harbor Drive, Orlando, FL 32887. 1-800-782-4479, or 1-800-433-0001 (in Florida).

ISBN: 0-15-500602-9

Printed in the United States of America

3 4 5 6 7 8 9 0 1 2 066 9 8 7 6 5 4 3 2 1

PREFACE

This fifth edition of "Reporting for the Print Media" has been rewritten, expanded and brought up-to-date. It has also been extensively reorganized, and many of its exercises are new. The book's primary emphasis has not changed, however; it continues to provide both the instructions and exercises needed to help students become better writers. The book reflects the belief that students learn to write by writing: that students should be given as much practice as possible, and that the practice should be as realistic as possible. Thus, many of the assignments in this book are genuine: actual laws, interviews, speeches, police reports and news releases.

REORGANIZED CHAPTERS

Several chapters have been extensively revised, and four have been rearranged. The material on "Selecting and Reporting the News" has been moved from the seventh to the fourth chapter. The chapters on "Quotations and Attribution," "Interviews and Polls" and "Improving Newsgathering and Writing Skills" have also been moved, so they appear earlier in the book.

Chapter 1 ("The Basics: Format, Spelling and AP Style") combines material that, in previous editions, appeared in several different chapters. Chapter 3 ("Words") is new.

PRO CHALLENGE

Several of the exercises in the chapters about leads and the body of news stories are titled "Pro Challenge." Professionals have completed the exercises so that students assigned the same exercises can compare their work to the professionals'. This is a new feature.

ANSWER KEYS

Students who, after reading several of the chapters and working on their exercises, want additional practice can complete the extra exercises marked "Answer Key Provided," then correct their own work. The answers to those exercises appear in Appendix D.

APPENDIXES

As in previous editions, "Reporting for the Print Media" provides four appendixes: (1) a city directory, (2) a summary of The Associated Press Stylebook And Libel Manual, (3) rules for forming possessives and (4) answer keys.

END-OF-CHAPTER MATERIALS

The material placed at the end of each chapter has been greatly expanded. Such material varies from chapter to chapter, but typically includes: (1) lists of readings, (2) discussion questions, (3) suggested class projects, (4) newsroom bulletins, (5) ombudsmen's commentaries and (6) guest commentaries.

Additionally, this book reprints a half-dozen bulletins titled "Write & Wrong" that were prepared for the staff of the St. Louis Post-Dispatch. These bulletins discuss common errors and provide additional examples of good and bad writing.

This book also reprints several columns written by ombudsmen, the journalists hired to answer reader complaints. This feature, to teach students more about problems involving ethics and good taste, is new.

Another new feature, "Guest Commentaries," also appears at the ends of several chapters. A young copy editor suffering from carpal tunnel syndrome describes her crippling ailment. An attorney in Washington, D.C., advises students on how to avoid libel. And several experts in broadcasting and public relations tell students more about their fields.

HUNDREDS OF EXAMPLES

"Reporting for the Print Media" contains hundreds of examples of writing, some by students and some by professionals. While introducing a new topic or discussing an error, this book typically shows students two or three examples of the error, as well as how to avoid or correct it.

HUNDREDS OF EXERCISES

This book also contains hundreds of exercises. Many of them are both new and genuine. Examples include

- President Bush's speech announcing the war against Iraq.
- The transcript of a 911 call the police in Milwaukee received about Jeffrey Dahmer, the man who admitted murdering 17 young men.
- A verbatim copy of a confession written by John List, who murdered his wife, mother and three children in their home in New Jersey. Students may remember List because he remained a fugitive for 18 years, then was captured with the help of a television program, "America's Most Wanted."

Similarly, the exercises in Chapter 9 ("Interviews and Polls") contain actual interviews conducted especially for this book. Other exercises, although fictionalized, involve topics recently in the news: a dentist with AIDS, predictions of an earthquake along the New Madrid Fault and a debate over controversial exhibits funded by the National Endowment for the Arts.

Many of the exercises also address ethical concerns: four-letter words, the names of rape victims, bloody details and other material that editors may be reluctant to publish.

SAMPLE STORIES

After discussing a particular type of story (obituaries, for example), this book reprints entire stories written by prize-winning professionals. Students can use the stories as models. An example from The Milwaukee Journal shows students how an entire story can be written in chronological order. Many journalists consider Jim Nicholson of the Philadelphia Daily News the nation's best obituary writer; two of his stories appear at the end of Chapter 15 ("Writing Obituaries").

COMPUTER SOFTWARE

Faculty members with access to Macintosh computers can use this book with "Media Writer: Computerized Lessons in News Reporting," also written by Fred Fedler (and coauthored by Lucinda Davenport of Michigan State University). The software, sold separately or with the textbook, provides 32 interactive exercises for the students in reporting classes. The first exercises emphasize the fundamentals of newswriting: spelling, style, accuracy and objectivity. Other exercises teach students how to write more clearly and concisely. Later exercises ask students to write leads and complete news stories. All the exercises test students' news judgment, including their ethics.

A NOTE OF THANKS

Journalists are wonderful people: enthusiastic, interesting and helpful. While working on this book, I wrote to dozens of them. Reporters, photographers and editors from Salt Lake City to Philadelphia, from New York to Miami, answered my letters and provided advice and samples of their work.

I would especially like to thank a colleague, Pat Mills of the Department of Journalism at Ball State University, for updating the chapter on feature stories.

Six professionals, all former students, completed the exercises titled "Pro Challenge": Eric Dentel, Dana Eagles, Geoffrey M. Giordano, Mike Griffin, Lisa Lochridge and Loraine O'Connell.

Other current and former students also helped. Marty Murray describes her apparent death (an "out-of-body" experience). Taylor E. Kingsley, a talented young journalist who suffers from carpel tunnel syndrome, describes her crippling ailment. Barry Bradley describes a story he covered as a young reporter. Diane Taylor suggested revisions in Chapter 16 ("News Releases").

A friend, Jeanne Scafella, suggested revisions in Chapter 12 ("Communication Law").

Other people provided guest commentaries: Frank R. Stansberry discusses careers in public relations; Joe Hall discusses careers in broadcasting; and Alexander Greenfeld, a Washington attorney, advises readers on 30 ways to protect themselves against libel suits.

I would also like to thank the many other professionals who allowed me to quote their work: Donald L. Barlett and James B. Steele of The Philadelphia Inquirer; Mike Clark, reader advocate at The (Jacksonville) Florida Times-Union; Roy P. Clark of The Poynter Institute for Media Studies; Lucille S. DeView, writing coach for The Orange County (Calif.) Register; Harry Levins, writing coach at the St. Louis Post-Dispatch; Henry McNulty, reader representative for The Hartford Courant; Pat Riley, ombudsman for The Orange County Register; and Jim Nicholson, an obituary writer for the Philadelphia Daily News.

Numerous publications and news services gave me permission to quote their stories or republish their photographs: The Associated Press, The Deseret News in Salt Lake City, The Miami Herald, The Milwaukee Journal, The New York Times, The Orlando Sentinel, the Scripps Howard News Service and United Press International.

The following organizations also allowed me to quote them: the American Academy of Pediatrics, American Society of Newspaper Editors, Society of Professional Journalists, National Victim Center and Southern Newspaper Publishers Association.

Several faculty members gave me permission to use their work as exercises in this book: Margaret Vandiver, Michael L. Radelet, Felix M. Berardo and George P. Moschis.

Jill Vejnoska, a prize-winning reporter for The Courier-News in Bridgewater, N.J., provided a copy of a murderer's confession that was used in an exercise in Chapter 21 (''Advanced Reporting Exercises'').

For their insightful comments and useful suggestions during the development process, thanks go to Jim Highland, Western Kentucky University; Rick Jones, Illinois State University; Sharon Smith Pennell, Appalachian State University; and Rick Pullen, California State University-Fullerton.

I would also like to thank the staff at Harcourt Brace Jovanovich—Stephen Jordan, Acquisitions Editor; Cathlynn Richard, Development Editor; Steve Norder, Project Editor; Brian Salisbury, Designer; Sandra Lord, Art Editor; and Erin Gregg, Production Manager—for their part in the publication of this edition.

TO THE STUDENT

Many Americans seem to believe that writing is an easy, glamorous job. The people who think that, says author Elizabeth Lane, "have probably never written anything longer than a check." Lane explains that writing hurts. Moreover, writing does not get any easier as you go along. There is, however, a simple formula for success. "It's this," Lane says. "Fanny on the chair. Elbows on the desk. Fingers on the keyboard. For however long it takes to finish the job."

Like other writers, Lane sometimes asks herself why she got into the business and why she continues to write. "I'm hooked," she answers. "I have a hundred stories in my head and this driving compulsion to put them on paper to read."[1]

Lane is not a journalist. She is a romance writer who has published 10 books. It doesn't matter. Most writers, regardless of their speciality, agree with Lane.

Journalists, too, get hooked. They enjoy the challenge of uncovering important stories and the thrill of being there to watch the stories unfold. Journalists also enjoy the challenge of writing stories quickly, under deadline pressure, and of putting words together in a way that will interest readers. However, their greatest rewards come when they finish a piece: when it appears in print, they see their byline and hear from people who like their work.

Elizabeth Lane adds that writers must also be diligent. Most students realize that athletes and musicians must practice several hours a day. Many fail to realize that writers, too, must practice regularly and systematically. Author Sheila Hailey explains:

> The one thing all professional writers have in common . . . is that they get down to it and write. They don't just talk about it, they don't wait for inspiration, they don't wish they had time to write. They make time and press on. Oh, there's often some pencil-sharpening and desk-tidying that goes on first. But sooner or later, they write, though never knowing with certainty if they are at work on a masterpiece or a disaster.[2]

Other writers agree with Lane's assertion that writing is hard work. One of the nation's most famous and talented sportswriters, Red Smith, once said, "There's nothing to writing. All you do is sit down at the typewriter and open a vein."

Columnist James J. Kilpatrick adds:

> Our task is deceptively simple. It is as deceptively simple as the task of carpenters, who begin by nailing one board to another board. Then other boards are nailed to other boards, and lo, we have a house. Just so, as writers we put one word after another word, and we connect those words to other

---

[1]Elizabeth Lane. "Writing Romance." *WordPerfect Magazine*. August 1989, p. 70.
[2]Sheila Hailey. *I Married a Best Seller*. (Garden City, NY: Doubleday, 1978), p. 95.

words, and lo, we have a news story or an editorial or if it goes badly, a plate of spaghetti.[3]

To avoid a plate of spaghetti, you will need a good editor or teacher: someone who cares about you and who will spend the time needed to evaluate your work critically. For most students, that criticism is the hardest part of all. When they submit a story to a teacher, most students want praise and an ''A.'' Not a critical analysis of their work. Not a dozen corrections. Not a note saying they have to rewrite the entire piece.

If you are serious about becoming a good writer, you will have to learn to accept, even welcome, criticism of your work. However painful the experience, that is how you learn. Too many students fail to realize that. Rather than appreciating such criticism, many students resent it—and take it personally.

For as long as you write, you will have an editor. For the moment, that editor will be your instructor. A good instructor will do everything possible to improve your work, whether it is a news story, an advertisement or a news release. Learn to be grateful and not resentful or thin skinned.

This book, too, will help you learn to write. Its assignments have been made as realistic as possible. While completing them, you will be expected to peform like a professional: to be accurate; to work under deadline pressures; and to produce copy so clear, concise and interesting that your audience will be able, even eager, to read every word.

Many schools require all their journalism students to enroll in a reporting class and to use a book like this one. Why? Because the writing skills emphasized in reporting classes are needed by the professionals in every area of journalism, including those in advertising, public relations and broadcasting. They too must be able to work quickly and to produce material that is clear, concise, accurate and interesting.

This book will also teach you more about the media: about how journalists define news, handle news releases, avoid libel suits and cope with dozens of other problems. And because journalists often deal with problems that involve ethics and taste, exercises throughout this book will challenge your judgment in those areas as well. You will have to decide whether you should use the information provided by anonymous sources; report some bloody details and four-letter words; and identify innocent victims, including the victims of rape.

The early chapters emphasize fundamentals, providing basic, introductory exercises for people with no experience in journalism. They deal with the basic format and style used by newswriters, and with spelling, grammar and vocabulary. Exercises in the following chapters give you a few facts and ask you to summarize them in acceptable newswriting style. Later exercises are more complex and require more sophisticated writing techniques. Still others will send you out of your classroom to gather information firsthand.

Many of the exercises are intentionally disorganized and poorly worded so that you can produce extensive revisions. You will have to develop the habit of critically examining every sentence before using it in a story. To add to the realism, your instructor is likely to impose deadlines that require you to finish your stories by a specified time. And because writing a story in longhand first takes a great deal of time, you may be required to compose your stories on a typewriter or computer.

Students who spend hours working on their first take-home assignments worry about their slowness. This is misperception. As you begin to write, accuracy and clarity are

---

[3]James J. Kilpatrick, ''The Art Of The Craft.'' The Red Smith Lecture in Journalism. University of Notre Dame, Department of American Studies. Notre Dame, Inc.: August, 1985. Reprinted in pamphlet form, p. 2.

more important than speed. Through practice, you will develop speed naturally, over time.

Also remember that few first drafts cannot be improved. You will need to develop the habit of editing and rewriting your own work, sometimes a half-dozen times or more.

Here are some additional guidelines to follow while using this book:

- Unless it mentions another location, assume that every story in this book occurred on your campus or in your community. Also assume that every story will be published by a newspaper in your community.

- Use only the facts that you are given or are able to obtain or verify from other sources. Newswriting is based on fact. Never make assumptions, and certainly never make up facts.

- Verify the spelling of names that appear in the exercises by consulting the city directory in Appendix A. So that you get in the habit of checking the spelling of every name, some names in the exercises are deliberately misspelled. Only the spellings in the city directory are correct.

- To achieve a consistent style of abbreviation, capitalization, punctuation and so forth, follow the guidelines suggested by The Associated Press Stylebook and Libel Manual. This style is used throughout "Reporting for the Print Media," and a summary of the stylebook's most commonly used rules appears in Appendix B. Most newspapers in the United States follow the guidelines recommended by The Associated Press. Copies of the stylebook are available at most bookstores.

Finally, dozens of students and teachers have written to me, telling me what they like and dislike about this book and suggesting new features. I have used many of their ideas, and I would like to hear from you. If you have a suggestion or comment, please write to me.

Fred Fedler
School of Communication
University of Central Florida
Orlando, Fla. 32816

CONTENTS

ISBN 0-15-500602-9

Copyright © 1993 by Harcourt Brace Jovanovich, Inc.
All rights reserved. Printed in the United States of America
ISBN 0-15-500602-9

SPECIAL FEATURES

1. **Checklists and Review Questions**

2. **Exercises With an Answer Key**

3. **Guest Columns**

4. **An Ombudsman's Report: Case Studies**

5. **Pro Challenge (Compare Your Work to a Professional's)**

6. **Quotes (about Journalism)**

7. **Reference Chart for Copy-Editing Symbols**

8. **Tips From a Pro**

Copyright © 1993 by Harcourt Brace Jovanovich, Inc.
All rights reserved. Printed in the United States of America
ISBN 0-15-500602-9

Reporting for the
Print Media

CHAPTER 1

THE BASICS: FORMAT, SPELLING AND AP STYLE

Until the 1970s, newspaper reporters typed their stories on sheets of paper, then used a pencil to correct their errors. Since then, newspapers have experienced a period of rapid technological change. Most reporters now type their stories on computers or word processors. As the stories are typed, they appear on screens above the terminals' keyboards, and reporters can use the keyboards to correct all their errors. When the reporters finish their work, their stories are stored in a computer until an editor is ready to view them on another terminal. Finally, the edited stories are transmitted to other machines, which set them in type. Everything is done electronically, and the system can save a single newspaper millions of dollars a year by eliminating its need for typesetters.

Few typewriters are found in today's newsrooms. Students, however, must still learn newspapers' traditional format and copy-editing symbols, for a number of reasons. First, some smaller companies continue to use typewriters and the traditional format and copy-editing symbols. Second, reporters and editors handle some typed copy from free-lance writers, public relations agencies and a variety of other sources. Third, newspapers' traditional format and copy-editing symbols are helpful in some college classes.

The journalism departments at many colleges have purchased computers, but few require their students to use the computers for every assignment in every class. For many departments, the expense would be prohibitive, especially for large classes. Instead, some students continue to use typewriters, and the traditional format and copy-editing symbols, especially for homework assignments. Others, even after using a computer, may notice an error in their work moments before an assignment is due. In making corrections, they are expected to use the proper format and copy-editing symbols.

NEWS STORY FORMAT

Reporters have developed a unique format for their stories, and each story you write should follow the guidelines suggested here. Although minor variations exist from one newspaper to another, most publications are remarkably consistent in their adherence to these rules.

Type each news story on separate 8½- by 11-inch sheets of paper. Avoid onionskin and other types of glossy or erasable bond paper because it is more difficult to write corrections on such paper.

Type your name, the date and a slugline in the upper left-hand corner of the first page. For example:

Fred Fedler
Jan. 12, 1998
Highway Plans

Editors use sluglines to help them identify and keep track of stories that are being prepared for publication. The sluglines also provide a quick summary of each story's topic. A story that reports a speech by your city's mayor might be slugged "Mayor's Speech"; a story about a fire at an elementary school might be slugged "School Fire." Sluglines should not exceed two or three words and should be as specific as possible. Vague sluglines, such as "Speech" or "Fire," might be used on more than one story, and the stories, their headlines and their placement in the paper might then become all mixed up with one another.

Also avoid jokes, sarcasm and statements of opinion that would cause embarrassment if the slugline were accidentally published, as sometimes happens. A reporter in California became irritated when asked to write about a party given by several prominent women. The reporter thought the story was unimportant and uninteresting. Angrily, he slugged it "Old Biddies." He was almost fired when the slugline inadvertently appeared in print. Similarly, a writer at the Boston Globe wrote an editorial that criticized a speech given by President Carter. Another employee thought the writer's slugline was the headline—and an accurate one. It was set in type, so the lead editorial published the next morning bore the headline, "Mush from the Wimp."

Begin each story one-third to one-half of the way down the first page. When you write for a newspaper, the space at the top of the first page provides room for your byline, a headline and special instructions to your paper's production workers. In class, the space provides room for your instructor to evaluate your work. Leave a 1-inch margin on each side and at the bottom of every page.

Newspapers place a dateline at the beginning of the first line of each news story to indicate the story's geographical source. Datelines normally include the name of the city, printed entirely in capital letters and followed by a comma, the abbreviation for the state in upper/lower case and a dash (for example: LEXINGTON, Ky.— or PORTLAND, Ore.—). The names of major cities that most readers will immediately recognize (such as Boston, Chicago, Miami and Los Angeles) are used alone, without their state. Most newspapers do not use datelines for any stories that originate within their own communities, and most newspapers use only the names of other cities within their own state, omitting the name of the state.

To save time, you will have to learn to type the first draft of every story you write. You will not have enough time to write news stories in longhand first. Type and double-space each story so that it is neat, uniform and easy to read. Use only one side of each page, and do not leave any extra space between paragraphs.

Traditionally, reporters never divided a word at the end of a line, because typesetters might mistakenly assume that the hyphen was part of the word and set it in type. Today, if you use a computer, it will automatically move an entire word to the next line. If you use a typewriter, you will be expected to move the entire word yourself.

If a story is continued on a second page, write the word "more" at the bottom of the first page and circle it to indicate that the word is not part of the story and should not be set in type. Begin the second page and all later pages about 1 inch from the top of the page. Type your last name, the page number and the slugline in the upper left-hand corner. For example:

Fedler
Highway Plans
Page 2

Instead of using the word "paragraph" while communicating with one another, the journalists at some newspapers shorten it to "graf." Similarly, instead of using the word "page," some journalists use "add" or "take." Also, some editors ask their reporters to triple-space rather than double-space their stories.

COPY-EDITING SYMBOLS

Reporters are expected to edit their stories and to correct all their errors before giving the stories to an editor (or instructor).

Most of the stories written for your reporting classes will not have to be typed perfectly, but should be neat and easy to read. If, for example, you make a mistake while using a typewriter, or want to edit a story after typing it, use the copy-editing symbols shown in the following paragraphs. Using the copy-editing symbols is faster, easier and often neater than using an eraser or retyping even a portion of a story.

If several major errors appear in a paragraph or section of a story, you can retype that section and paste it over the original. If your corrections become too numerous and messy, retype the entire story.

Indent every paragraph in a news story, and mark the beginning of each paragraph with the proper copy-editing symbol: |_____ If you want to mark a paragraph to be divided into two shorter paragraphs, you can use either the same copy-editing symbol or this one: ¶

If you indent a line and then decide that you do not want to start a new paragraph, link the lines together with a pencil, as shown here.

The same symbol is used to link the remaining parts of a sentence or paragraph after a major deletion, ~~involving the elimination of a great many words and more than one line of type, or even a complete sentence or two~~, as shown here.

Always use a pencil, not a pen, to correct any errors that appear in your stories. If you make a mistake in correcting your story with a pen, the mistake will be difficult to correct.

Write "OK" or "cq" above facts or spellings that are so unusual that your editors are likely to question their accuracy, and circle the letters (for example: Neil Schneider became a millionaire at the age of 13). (OK) The notations "OK" and "cq" indicate that the information is correct, regardless of how unlikely or bizarre it may appear to be.

If you accidentally type an extra word or letter, cross out the word or ~~or~~ letter, then draw an arc above it to link the remaining portions of the sentence. An arc drawn above a deletion indicates that the remaining segments of the sentence or paragraph should be moved closer together, but a space should be left between them. To eliminate a space within a word, draw an arc both above and below it. To eliminate an unnecessary letter, draw an arc both above and below it, plus a *vertical* line through it.

When two words or letters are inverted, use symbol this to indicate that they should be transposed. If you want to move an entire paragraph, retype that portion of the story. Particularly if the transposed paragraphs are on different pages, several errors are likely to occur if you fail to retype them.

draw three lines under a letter to indicate that it should be capitalized. If a letter is capitalized but should not be, draw a *slanted* line through it. If two words are incorrectly run together, draw a *straight*, vertical line between them to indicate that a space should be added.

If you make a correction and then decide that the correction is unnecessary or mistaken, write the word "stet" alongside the correction to indicate that you want to retain the original version. If you want to add or change a letter, word or phrase, write or type it above the line, then use a caret to indicate where it fits into the sentence. Many punctuation marks, including colons, semicolons, exclamation points and question marks, are added in the same manner (for example: When will she arrive?).

To add a comma, draw a comma in the proper place and put a caret *over* it (for example: He is tall, intelligent and wealthy). If you add an apostrophe or quotation mark, place a caret *under* it (for example: She said, "Don't ignore these rules."). To add a period, draw either a dot or a small "x" and circle it. A hyphen is indicated by the symbol =, and a dash by the symbol |——|.

Never type over a letter. Also, place all corrections above (never below) the typed line and error.

Newspapers never underline, because typesetters do not have a key to underline. However, you can use the symbol shown here to set type in <u>italics</u>, and you can use the symbol shown here to set type in boldface. You can use this symbol to center a line on the page:

⌐ By Marcia Sirota ⌐

⌐ This symbol means flush left.   This symbol means flush right. ⌐

Spell out most numbers below 10 and use numerals for the number 10 and most larger numbers. Consult The Associated Press Stylebook and Libel Manual for more exact guidelines. If you type a numeral but want it spelled out, circle it (for example: He has 8 sisters). If you spell out a number but want to use the numeral, circle it (for example: He has thirteen sisters). Similary, circle words that are spelled out but should be abbreviated (for example: He is from Madison, Wisconsin, and words that are abbreviated but should be spelled out (for example: He is from Minn). Do not use a circle to indicate that a letter should or should not be capitalized.

Below the last line of each news story, in the center of the page, place one of these "end marks":

-30-
###
-0-

As a reporter, you will not normally be expected to write headlines for any of the stories you write, nor to put your own byline on the stories. Newspaper editors write the headlines after they determine the headlines' size and decide where to place the stories in their papers. Editors also control the use of bylines and generally add them only to stories they consider exceptionally good.

THE ASSOCIATED PRESS STYLEBOOK AND LIBEL MANUAL

Most daily newspapers have adopted The Associated Press Stylebook and Libel Manual. The stylebook lists thousands of rules, presented in alphabetical order, for abbreviations, capitalization, punctuation, grammar, spelling and word usage. A summary of the stylebook appears in Appendix B of this book, and you will be expected to study and learn all its rules. If you want to buy a copy of the complete stylebook, it is available at most campus and community bookstores.

The stylebook helps reporters to be more accurate by helping them to avoid misspellings and errors in grammar and word usage. In addition, the stylebook saves reporters time since, in a single volume, it answers most of the questions they are likely to ask about the proper use of the language. Thus, reporters seldom must search through a multitude of reference books or interrupt more experienced colleagues to ask them.

Large newspapers employ dozens, even hundreds, of reporters and editors. By specifying a single set of rules for everyone to follow, The Associated Press Stylebook also encourages consistency. Without a single set of rules, newspapers would publish more errors, and the errors could be both costly and embarrassing. Four or five reporters might use the same word in front-page stories, and each reporter might use a different style. For example: one reporter might spell "percent" as one word ("17 percent"), another might use two words ("17 per cent"), a third might use the percentage sign ("17%"), and a fourth might spell out the number 17 ("seventeen percent"). If the page had already been prepared for publication, it would be expensive for an editor who noticed the inconsistencies to correct all the stories and to order a new printing plate.

In addition to its other uses, the stylebook helps students to prepare for their first jobs. If you learn the book's basic rules while you are enrolled in college, it will be easier for you to begin writing for the media—and to move from one newspaper to another. Since most newspapers have adopted The Associated Press Stylebook, you will not have to learn a new set of rules each time you move to another paper.

A few large newspapers, such as The New York Times and The Washington Post, have published stylebooks of their own. Other large newspapers publish brief supplements that specify the rules for handling unusual problems that arise in their communities. Similarly, some college newspapers publish supplements that specify a standardized set of rules for common usages on their campuses.

ACCURACY OF FACTS AND SPELLING

Responsible editors (and instructors) do not tolerate sloppiness of any kind, and they are particularly critical of spelling errors, since there is rarely any excuse for them.

Be especially careful to check the spelling of people's names. Most misspellings are the result of carelessness, and they anger the victims. Most editors require their reporters to consult a second source, usually a telephone book or a city directory, to verify the way names are spelled.

Use the city directory that appears in Appendix A to verify the spelling of names used in this book, and place a box around the names to show that you have checked their spelling and that they are accurate (for example: Mayor [Sabrina Datolli] has resigned). To avoid inconsistent spellings, check and box a name every time it appears in a news story, not just the first time it is used. Some names in later exercises have deliberately been altered, and you will misspell them if you fail to use the city directory.

Like other city directories, the directory in this book does not list people who live in other parts of the country. Thus, if a story mentions that someone lives in another city, you can assume that the person's name is spelled correctly; because the name will not be listed in the city directory, it will be impossible to check.

Also double-check the accuracy of every fact in every news story. Any factual error will damage a newspaper's reputation and may seriously harm people mentioned in the stories. Because of the serious consequences, your instructor is likely to lower your grade whenever you make a factual error. You will also be penalized for errors in diction, grammar and style. If your instructor accepts late assignments (many do not), your grades on them may also be lowered. Like all the other media, newspapers must meet rigid deadlines, and editors expect work to be turned in on time.

Finally, make and save a copy of each story you write. The copy will be invaluable if a story is lost, if questions arise about its content, or if you want to compare your original story with the edited version published by a newspaper (or returned by your instructor).

COPY PREPARATION CHECKLIST

During this course, as you finish writing each of your news stories, consult the following checklist. If you answer no to any of these questions, your stories may have to be edited or retyped.

1. Have you started typing one-third to one-half of the way down the first page and 1 inch from the top of all following pages?
2. Do you have a slugline (no more than two or three words) that specifically describes your story's content?
3. Is the story typed and double-spaced, with only one story on a page?
4. Is each paragraph indented?
5. Have you used a pencil and the proper copy-editing symbols to correct all your errors?
6. Have you made certain that no words are divided and hyphenated at the end of a line?
7. If the story continues on a second page, have you: typed and circled ''more'' at the bottom of the first page; typed your name, page number and slugline at the top of the second page; and typed ''-30-,'' ''###'' or ''-0-'' at the end of the story?
8. If the story originated outside your community, have you added the proper dateline?
9. Have you used the city directory to verify the spelling of all names used in the story and checked and drawn a box around those names every time they are used?

REFERENCE CHART FOR COPY-EDITING SYMBOLS

1. Abbreviate	She was born on (August) 4 in Urbana, (Illinois.)
2. Boldface	This line should be set in boldface type.
3. Capitalize	An american won the nobel prize.
4. Center	]Continued on Page 10[
5. Change letter	Their hose is expensive.
6. Change word	She received three gifts. four
7. Close up space between words	Their car was totally destroyed.
8. Close up space within a word	Their children ran outside.
9. Continues on next page	(More)
10. Delete letter	They received the monkey.
11. Delete phrase	They did not use any unneeded or unnecessary words.
12. Delete punctuation	They asked, if he was safe. OR: They asked, if he was safe.
13. End of story	### OR: -30- OR: -0-
14. Flush left	[The typesetter will begin this line at the left margin.

15. Flush right   The typesetter will end this line at the right margin.⌋

16. Ignore correction
(Correct as written)   (Stet)

17. Insert apostrophe   It's good you're going home.

18. Insert colon   He set three goals success, health and wealth.

19. Insert comma   The girl lives with her grandmother.

20. Insert dash   The score was 87 to 53 a disaster.

21. Insert exclamation point   "What I don't believe it," she exclaimed.

22. Insert hyphen   The 7 year old girl lives with her mother.

23. Insert letter   Their car filed to sart.

24. Insert period   John C Kefalis received the scholarship
OR: John C Kefalis received the scholarship

25. Insert quotation marks   This is easy, he said.

26. Insert semicolon   Don't go he needs your help.

27. Insert word   He *often* writes *clever* poetry.

28. Italic   Some publications set words in italics for emphasis.

29. Lowercase
(Do not capitalize)   The Mayor failed TO arrive.

30. No new paragraph   To generate more publicity, the candidate announced that he would work at 100 different jobs. He spent the remainder of his campaign picking tomatoes, plucking chickens, hauling trash, digging ditches and driving trucks.

31. Separate words   Journalists are critical of political gimmickry.

32. Spell out numbers or words   She said (8) people will go to (Ala.)

33. Start new paragraph   ¶ Another man campaigned on roller skates. His wife explained: "We met at a roller skating rink, and we thought it would be a fun idea. He's going house to house, subdivision to subdivision on his skates, and people remember him."

34. Transpose letters   Typist often transpose letters.

35. Transpose words   Happily, he accepted the award.

Producing a newspaper: From desktop to doorstep

Newspaper production is a complicated business, with many steps between a reporter's idea and the printed page. News stories and advertising used to pass through several physical forms on the way into the newspaper, from typewritten pages to hand-drawn layout sheets to lead type coming from linotype machines. Newspapers are using new technology to streamline the process.

Pagination

Not so long ago, ads and news stories were written on typewriters, edited on paper, measured with a ruler and blocked out on hand-drawn layout pages. At many newspapers, written material now goes to production without ever leaving the computer.

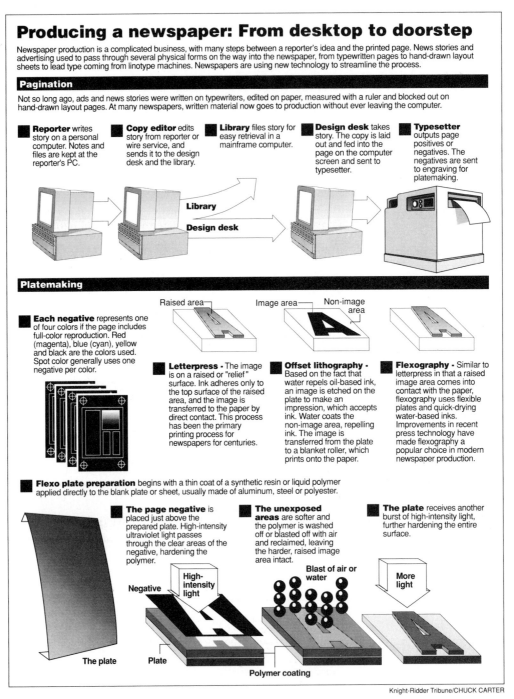

Reporter writes story on a personal computer. Notes and files are kept at the reporter's PC.

Copy editor edits story from reporter or wire service, and sends it to the design desk and the library.

Library files story for easy retrieval in a mainframe computer.

Design desk takes story. The copy is laid out and fed into the page on the computer screen and sent to typesetter.

Typesetter outputs page positives or negatives. The negatives are sent to engraving for platemaking.

Library

Design desk

Platemaking

Each negative represents one of four colors if the page includes full-color reproduction. Red (magenta), blue (cyan), yellow and black are the colors used. Spot color generally uses one negative per color.

Raised area — Image area — Non-image area

Letterpress - The image is on a raised or "relief" surface. Ink adheres only to the top surface of the raised area, and the image is transferred to the paper by direct contact. This process has been the primary printing process for newspapers for centuries.

Offset lithography - Based on the fact that water repels oil-based ink, an image is etched on the plate to make an impression, which accepts ink. Water coats the non-image area, repelling ink. The image is transferred from the plate to a blanket roller, which prints onto the paper.

Flexography - Similar to letterpress in that a raised image area comes into contact with the paper, flexography uses flexible plates and quick-drying water-based inks. Improvements in recent press technology have made flexography a popular choice in modern newspaper production.

Flexo plate preparation begins with a thin coat of a synthetic resin or liquid polymer applied directly to the blank plate or sheet, usually made of aluminum, steel or polyester.

The page negative is placed just above the prepared plate. High-intensity ultraviolet light passes through the clear areas of the negative, hardening the polymer.

The unexposed areas are softer and the polymer is washed off or blasted off with air and reclaimed, leaving the harder, raised image area intact.

The plate receives another burst of high-intensity light, further hardening the entire surface.

The plate

Negative

High-intensity light

Plate

Blast of air or water

Polymer coating

More light

Knight-Ridder Tribune/CHUCK CARTER

St. Louis Post-Dispatch

WRITE & WRONG

By **Harry Levins**
Post-Dispatch Writing Coach

Who says wind is weightless? We load our readers with many burdens, but the heaviest may be windy sentences. Here's an all-too-typical example. It fell short of springing the scale but was needlessly weighty:

> National Airport, opened in 1941 and operated by the Federal Aviation Administration, was the site of a crash by an Air Florida jet in January that killed 78 people.

Grammatical? Sure. Are the words spelled properly? You bet. Are the facts correct? More or less; the crash was a few miles from the airport proper, but the flight originated there.
So what's wrong?
Simple: the sentence meanders through two separate and distinct thoughts. One is the background on when the airport opened and who runs it. The other is the background on the crash. The ideal remains one idea per sentence. Two ideas should get one sentence apiece. Repairing the sentence above would have been a simple matter:

> National Airport opened in 1941 and is operated by the Federal Aviation Administration. In January, an Air Florida jet crashed after taking off from the airport, killing 78 people.

Here's another windy sentence, one that gets tangled up in detail before it can make its point:

> JEFFERSON CITY (UPI)— Gov. Christopher S. Bond's trip to New York City this week is part of a program to promote Missouri as a location for new business, to increase export sales, to bolster the state's stagnant economy and to provide jobs for unemployed workers.

Too many "to" verbs. The sentence has four, which suggests trouble. The writer tried to tell everything but merely produced an eye-glazer. We could have spared the reader by giving him one-idea sentences, leading with the general and then describing the specific:

> JEFFERSON CITY (UPI)— Gov. Christopher S. Bond's trip to New York City this week is part of a three-point program aimed at boosting the state's economy. The governor hopes to:
> —Promote Missouri as a site for new businesses.
> —Increase exports of Missouri's goods.
> —Provide more jobs.

At times, we go out of our way to complicate sentences. Here's an
(continued on next page)

example from The New York Times News Service, a mother lode of complicated sentences:

> WASHINGTON—John W. Hinckley Jr., complaining of restrictions placed by St. Elizabeth's Hospital on his contacts with reporters, has asked the American Civil Liberties Union for help.

The reader dips his toe in—and promptly loses it to the teeth of a nonrestrictive clause. Nonrestrictive clauses (phrases set off by commas) constitute one of the biggest roadblocks to readability. They interrupt the reader's train of thought, sidetracking him into a second idea that may or may not be crucial at that point.

At times, we're forced to use such clauses. But The Coach remains convinced that the nonrestrictive clause often represents a crutch for a writer who lacks the time, talent or inclination to recast his stuff. Sometimes, the sentence can be broken into two, each with its own idea. Sometimes, the information in the clause can be shifted deeper in the story, preferably in a sentence of its own.

And every so often, a two-idea sentence can be recast into something that more nearly meets the ideal of one idea per sentence. For example, that Hinckley lede could have read this way:

> WASHINGTON—John W. Hinckley Jr. wants the American Civil Liberties Union to help him fight what he says are restrictions by St. Elizabeth's Hospital on his contacts with reporters.

Ah, well—at least The Times held itself to a two-idea sentence. Here's a locally produced sentence with *three* ideas:

> Mayor Vincent C. Schoemehl Jr., who asked Hohman

to come to St. Louis, said the study would not be directly related to Homer G. Phillips Center, which the mayor is trying to reopen as a full-service hospital.

Try diagramming *that*. The result looks like the genealogy of a family that practices incest. The writer overloaded the sentence with two nonrestrictive clauses—the ones beginning with "who" and "which." And all of those editors dumped it untouched onto the readers.

Somewhere, somebody could have broken off the first part as a single sentence:

> Mayor Vincent C. Schoemehl Jr. invited Hohman to St. Louis.

One down, two to go:

> The mayor said Hohman's study would not be directly related to Homer G. Phillips Center, an emergency room and clinic on the city's North Side.

Okay, that sentence has 1.6 ideas. Still, we're four-tenths of a point ahead. And now, Strike Three.

> Schoemehl has been trying to re-establish Phillips as a full-service hospital.

But at times, the cure can be as vexing as the ailment. Here's a paragraph that The Coach suspects started life as one sentence:

> The ILO's Committee on Freedom of Association will take up the case when it meets in Geneva, Switzerland, on Nov. 8 and 9, according to Stu Smith. He is executive director of the Capitol Employees Organizing Group.

Somebody deserves praise for making the effort. But somebody also deserves admonishment for doing it so clumsily. The last sentence reads like an afterthought. A bit more work would have made the transition smoother.

> . . . meets in Geneva, Switzerland, on Nov. 8 and 9. The announcement was made by Stu Smith, executive director . . .

***

At least once a week, The Coach runs across a sentence like this:

> Smith, 38, lives in rural Belleville.

What is "rural Belleville"? Or "rural Kirksville" or all the other "rurals" we write about? Presumably, we mean "outside Belleville" or "in a rural area near Kirksville." If so, we ought to say it that way. Otherwise, we are calling Belleville a bucolic village—a description to which 41,000 people might take exception.

***

Some parting shots on words:

Ceremonies. This word almost always appears as a plural; it almost always should be singular. "The awards are to be presented in ceremonies in the rotunda of City Hall." Sorry, but *a ceremony* is all that's planned.

Jobless, joblessness. Here's more headlinese that has crept into copy. The word "jobless" is bad enough in a headline, but a copy editor can plead tight space. No such excuse extends to people who use "jobless" and "joblessness" in copy as substitutes for "unemployed" and "unemployment." We're better off repeating a good word than substituting something from the junkpile of journalese just for the sake of variety.

Plague. Early in the history of journalism, some clever writer seized upon the word as a synonym for "vex," "bother," "trouble," "annoy," "anger," "harass," etc. Very shortly thereafter in the history of journalism, everybody else starting using it. They turned the verb "plague" into a punchless piece of journalese. Let's retire it.

SUGGESTED READINGS

Berner, R. Thomas. *Language Skills for Journalists.* 2nd ed. Boston: Houghton Mifflin, 1984.

Berry, Thomas Elliott. *The Most Common Mistakes in English Usage.* New York: McGraw-Hill, 1971.

Callihan, E. L. *Grammar for Journalists.* 3rd ed. Radnor, PA: Chilton, 1979.

Copperud, Roy H. *American Usage and Style: The Consensus.* New York: Van Nostrand/Reinhold, 1980.

Crump, Spencer. *The Stylebook for Newswriting.* Corona del Mar, CA: Trans-Anglo, 1979.

French, Christopher W., ed., *The Associated Press Stylebook And Libel Manual.* Rev. ed. New York: Dell, 1990.

Hodges, John C., and Mary E. Whitten. *Harbrace College Handbook.* 11th ed. San Diego: Harcourt Brace Jovanovich, 1990.

Holley, Frederick S., ed., *Los Angeles Times Stylebook.* New York: New American Library, 1981.

Jordan, Lewis, ed. *The New York Times Manual of Style and Usage*. New York: Quadrangle, 1976.

Leggett, Glenn, David C. Mead and William Charvat. *Handbook for Writers*. Englewood Cliffs, NJ: Prentice Hall, 1988.

Lippman, Thomas W., ed., *The Washington Post Deskbook on Style*. 2nd ed. New York: McGraw-Hill, 1989.

Mann, Russell A. *Journalism Manual of Style and Format*. Lafayette, LA: Journalism Style Publishers, 1986.

Shaw, Harry. *Punctuate It Right!* New York: Harper & Row, 1986.

Shertzer, Margaret. *The Elements of Grammar*. New York: Macmillan, 1986.

Strunk, William, Jr., and E. B. White. *The Elements of Style*. 3rd ed. New York: Macmillan, 1984.

QUOTES

If you want to say "The hen crossed the street," say "The hen crossed the street," and not "The feathery biped perambulated across the thoroughfare."

(An editor quoted in The Staff Correspondent by Charles Diehl)

The loss of liberty in general would soon follow the suppression of the liberty of the press; for it is an essential branch of liberty, so perhaps it is the best preservative of the whole.

(John Peter Zenger, colonial printer)

The first duty of a newspaper is to be accurate. If it be accurate, it follows that it is fair.

(Herbert Bayard Swope, newspaper editor)

NAME _____ CLASS _____ DATE _____

Exercise 1
FORMAT

INSTRUCTIONS: Using the proper copy-editing symbols, correct the errors in the following stories. If necessary, refer to the reference chart for copy-editing symbols on Page 6.

   Except for some obvious errors, the stories' style (the abbreviations, punctuation and spelling, for example) is correct. There is one exception, however: You will have to form all the possessives. If you need help, see Appendix C, "Rules for Forming Possessives."

GIRL SCOUTS

the countys Girl Scout Council no loonger will acept any checks during its annual cookie sale-a-thon.

During its last sale-a-thon, the council lost $4,284 due to worthlesschecks.

"That may not sound like a lot, but its a serious loss for us," said Linda Goree, the Girl Scoust county executive. "It cuts into our profits, but al so wastes too many hours of our timme."

Next year, Goree said, thecountys Girl Scouts will accept only cash

Two factors agravated the prov problem during the scouts last sale-a-thon, Goree continued. first, more pepople paid by check. Second, a larger percentage of the checks teh Girl Scouts received bounced.

"Some people pay by check because they don't have the cash," Goree said. "Or, they want to place a large order. We have people who place orders for $100 or more, and thosse poeple are especially likely to pay by check. we also receive checks for a little as one or two dollars."

Scout leaders call people who signed the checks that bounce and, in most cases,ask them to mail neW checks to the cty. office. The scout leadesr are unable to reach everyone, however. Smoe People have moved. Other s do not have telephones — or do not seem to answer their tele phones.

"usually its an honest mistake, ad andpeople are embarrassed when we call them,"

Goree said. "THey want to take care of the problem right away. Other people say they want to pay but dont have the money, and

we can usually work something out with them. Unfortunately, there are other people who get mad at us, like its our fault or something, and refuse to pay. Or, they write new checks that also bounce. It puts our leadess in a terrible situaton. A Girl Scout leadershouldn't have to deal with problems like that. Also, its not a good situation or example for our girls, and that's the reason for our ne w policy, why we'll

no longer accept any checks."

###

MEN'S LONGEVITY

Being a middle-aged man and single can be deadly, too sociologists at your college warned today

The sociologists, Margo Matos and LeeAnne verkler, found that middle-aged men who remain single double their chances of dying.

For 10 years, Matos and verkler tracked one thoussand men in the state. All of the men were 40 old years at the start of the study, and half were married. Matos and Verkler fuond that 11.7 percent of the men who remained unmarried died before their 50th birthday, compared to only 5.9 percent of themen who remained married.

Some of the maried men were divorced or widowed during the study, and 7.1 percent of those who remainedd alone for at least half the period also died.

"We arent sure of all the reasons," verkler said. "That's what we'll look at next. WE think poor diet plays a role. Also the use of alcohol, smoking, a lack of exercise and low incomes. Men who live by themselves seem to do more drinking and smoking, and many don't PREprepare good meals for themselves. Plus there's the absence of social support. It ehlps to have someone to talk with, someone who shpares your li fe and is there to provide help when you need it."

Matos and Verkler found that men also live longer if they have a roommate. "It doesn't matter who the persn is, a parent, child orfreind," Verkler said. "We've found, however,that none of the alternatives are as conducive to a long life as a stable marriage. those are the man who live the longest, the men who are happily marrried."

###

OUTSTANDING TEACHER

Wilma DeCastro is an English teacher at Kennedy High Schol and, six months ago, was named the city's "Teacher ofthe Year." Today she resigned.

"All my life I wanted to be a teachher," DeCastro said. "Ive really enjoyed it, but I have two little girls and Can't afford it any longer. I want a good live for may family, and now wecan't afford to buy a decent house in a good neighborhood, a newcar, nice clothes, or so many of the other things we want. wee skimp on everything, even food."

There years ago, DeCastro began to sell real estate during her sumer vacations. For th e last year, she has continued to sell real estate part-time, primarily weakends

"I can't do it any longer," she said. "I can't wrok two jobs, do a good job at both of the jobbs, and a.lso have time for my daughters, so I've decided to into real estate full time. I can triple salary my salary. INN a few years, if I work hard, I should be able to do even better than that. eventually, I'd like togo into businss for myself."

Greg Hubbard, superintendent of the city's school system, said: "Of coures we're sorry to see her leave. We'd like to keep her, to be able to pay all our teachers mr more, espec ially our best teachers. But there's no moneey for higher salaries. NO one wants to pay higher taxes."

DeCastro is 28 and started teaching at the high schoo01 six years ago. she aws named "Teacher OF The Year" because of her popularity, but also because she inspired several studentsto start a literary maga zine that has won adozenprizes

###

NAME _____ CLASS _____ DATE _____

Exercise 2
FORMAT

INSTRUCTIONS: Using the proper copy-editing symbols, correct the errors in the following stories. If necessary, refer to the reference chart for copy-editing symbols on Page 6.

Except for some obvious errors, the stories' style (the abbreviations, punctuation and spelling, for example) is correct. There is one exception, however: You will have to form all the possessives. If you need help, see Appendix C, "Rules for Forming Possessives."

HEROIC GIRL

while walking to school this moningmorning, an 11-year-old girl noticed a gunman robbuing two clerkS in a convence store on Colonial Drive

The girl, Kathryn Kunze of94 Jamestown Drive, raran to a nearby telephone, dialed 911, then returned to the store and noticed an empty car par ked naearby withits motor running. she reachedd inside, shut off the cars motor and took the keys.

"Imagine what the rober thought when he ran out of the storee, jumped into HIS car and realized the keys weregone," said Sgt. Tammy Dow. "she was one smart girl, and Brave, too."

The Gunman went bavck into the stoer and asked the clerks there for the keys to there cars. Bothclerks, however, said that they had walked to work and did not own a car.

The gunman then walked to a near,by park, and the police Aarrested him there five minutse later.

William j. Chuey, 27, of 5710 michigan Ave was charrged with armed robbery.

Polic e officers later questioned the girl at school. "I saw this man with a gun, just like on telivision" she said. "Then I saw thecar. It was running, and I just figured it was the robbers, so I took his keys and ran here."

Kathryn's mother, said she was p' ' 'proud—and frightened—by her daughters actions. "I'Mm proud she thought so quickly," Mrs. Lauren Kunze said. "But I don't wnat her to trfy anything like that ever again."

###

ROADBED TRAILS

RAilroads have abandoned hundreds of m iles of old roadbeds in the state, and the governortoday revealed plans to convert the roadbeds into trawils for bicyclists hikers, horseback riders and runners.

The governor said her budget for nxextt year will include an extra $10 million for the Departmentof natural Resources, which will use the money to ac quire and maintainn the trials

"The initial outlay is modest," the gov. said. "But we hope the program will expand so, in five or 10 years,we'll have hundreds of miles of these trials. Eventually, the people using themshould be able to hike or ride from one end of the state to another."

A representative for the states railrods said that most will probably agree to sell their abandoned roadbeds tothe state, provided they receive a fair pricee,

"We aren't us ing the roadbeds for anything," he said, "and there aren't many other buyers. they were our leasst profitable routes, and that's why we abandoned them."

During a press Conference this mohningthis morning, the governor added: "We need more land for recreation, and this is the perfect solution. wee think we can acquire the roadbeds for a reasonable price, annd we'll start with some of the mmost scenic. We'llalso concentrate, at least initialy, on roadbeds near the state's population centers, os they're conveni ent for a majority of the people using them."

THE governor said the

biggest expense, after acquiri;ng the roadbeds, will be improving their bridges.. "We'll need better flooring and railings to protect the public, and that will cost some money," she said. The railoads havve already tor n up the tracks,o selling them for scrap.

REPOSSESSING CARS

Police Chief Barry Kopperud Wants to ebgin seizing t he cars driven by drunken drivers.

While testifyingbefore a legislative commmittee in the state capital this morning, Kopperud said police oficers in the state need the authority to to seize the vehicles used by motorists convicted three or more times of drunken driving. Kopperuds pproposal would al so apply to motorists convicted of driving with a license suspended or revoked because of drunken drving—and to motorists convicted of driving undre the Influence of drugs.

"Were runninng across too many repeat offjenders," kopperud said. "They ignore the laws now in eff ect, and its time to do something about it. It doesn't do any good to just take away their lcenses. They'll drivewithout one."

Kopperud said some motorists in the statehave been convicted of drunken driving more than a dozentimes . "Weve gott peopel who've served a year in jail, some who've served five years," Kopperud said. "It doesn't seemtodo any good. weather they have a liense or not, they star"t to drink and drive again as soon as they get out. If wetake away their cars, they'll havetostop. U nless they're ultra-rich, there's a limit to howmany cars they can afford to buy."

TOBACCO BAN

Beginning next fall, students in the citys public shcools will have to leave their cigarettes and other tobaco products at home.

The School Board last night voted 6 to 1 to BAN the possession and use of all obacco tobacco products on school grounds.

"The boards policy will apply to evferyone," said gary Hubbard, superintendent of schools. "its not just for ourstudents. The policy will also apply to our teachers, other school personnel and, in addition, to any visitors using our facilities."

Students found smoking on school property will be reprimanded for a firs t ofense, detained for a secnod and su;pended for three days for a third. School personnel will be reprimanded by their principal. Other people wlil be asked to stop using the tobacco products or to leave the school grounds.

"Previously," hubbard said, "we allowed stud ents to smokee inn some designated areas both inside and outside our bldgs.: in our football stadium s, for example. Its badfortheir health, and we decided last night that we weren't being consistent. It doesn't make any sense for us to tell students, in their classes, about the dangers of smoking, andthan to allow them to smokeunder our supervision. Besides, We were getting a lot of complaints from nonsmokesr."

###

NAME _____ CLASS _____ DATE _____

Exercise 3
SPELLING

INSTRUCTIONS: The dozen words listed below are the ones that journalism students misspell most frequently. Some of the words are spelled correctly here, but others are misspelled. Use the proper copy-editing symbols to correct all the misspelled words. If several spellings are normally permissible, use the one recommended by The Associated Press Stylebook.

1. alot	7. it's (possessive)
2. ammendment	8. judgement
3. criticised	9. occured
4. definately	10. recieve
5. develop	11. seperate
6. explaination	12. teenager

Here are 25 more words that journalism students frequently misspell. Use the proper copy-editing symbols to correct the words that are misspelled.

1. accidently	14. liscense
2. adviser	15. magizines
3. alledgedly	16. medias
4. among	17. occasionally
5. apparantly	18. opportunity
6. arguement	19. payed
7. broadcasted	20. practise
8. calendar (for dates)	21. priviledge
9. catagorized	22. reguardless
10. cemetary	23. sophmore
11. conscious	24. suing
12. fourty	25. thier
13. lightning	

Five other words that students often misspell are: "criteria," "data," "graffiti," "media" and "phenomena." All five are plural forms. The singular forms are: "criterion," "datum," "graffito," "medium" and "phenomenon." Thus, it would be correct to say, "The four criteria are adequate" or "The datum is lost," but not, "The media is inaccurate" or "The phenomenon are unusual."

A final point: Journalists tend to be formal in their spelling. For example, they normally use "until" rather than "till" and "although" rather than "though."

NAME _____ CLASS _____ DATE _____

Exercise 4

SPELLING

INSTRUCTIONS: The following list contains 75 words that college students frequently misspell. Some of the words are spelled correctly here, but many others are misspelled. Use the proper copy-editing symbols to correct all the misspelled words. If several letters in a single word need to be corrected, rewrite the entire word. If several spellings are normally permissible, use the one recommended by The Associated Press Stylebook.

1. admited	22. embarrass	43. irregardless
2. alphabet	23. emphacize	44. itinerary
3. attendants	24. employe	45. ketchup
4. baby-sit	25. equipted	46. kindergarden
5. beliefs	26. exagerate	47. leisure
6. believeable	27. existance	48. lieutenant
7. besiege	28. expeled	49. likelyhood
8. catastrophe	29. favortism	50. liveable
9. changeable	30. fiery	51. nickles
10. chauffeur	31. foreigner	52. ninety
11. coller (for dogs)	32. fraternitys (plural)	53. operator
12. controled	33. fulfill	54. patroled
13. cryed	34. goodbye	55. picknicing
14. delirius	35. gray	56. pneumonia
15. descended	36. harrassment	57. prepairing
16. descrimination	37. heros	58. questionaire
17. disasterous	38. housewifes	59. quizes
18. dormitories	39. inaugurate	60. respondent
19. drunkeness	40. indispensible	61. schedule
20. elete	41. innoculate	62. singuler
21. eligable	42. irrate	63. sizeable

64. strangel

65. summerize

66. temperature

67. tenative

68. terrace

69. towards

70. trys

71. useable

72. victum

73. Wedesday

74. wintery

75. worrys

NAME _____ CLASS _____ DATE _____

Exercise 5

SPELLING

INSTRUCTIONS: The following list contains 75 words that college students frequently misspell. Some of the words are spelled correctly here, but many others are misspelled. Use the proper copy-editing symbols to correct all the misspelled words. If several letters need to be corrected in a single word, rewrite the entire word. If several spellings are normally permissible, use the one recommended by The Associated Press Stylebook.

1. accommodate	22. dispise	43. nieghbor
2. advertizing	23. distroyed	44. noone
3. alright	24. forsee	45. noticeable
4. ambulence	25. govermental	46. occurence
5. brocoli	26. grammer	47. paniced
6. bureaucracy	27. illegitimate	48. parallel
7. cannot	28. immitate	49. parties
8. casulties	29. imposter	50. persuasion
9. cautious	30. indorsed	51. poisonous
10. chronicle	31. infered	52. populer
11. committed	32. janiter	53. proceded
12. competition	33. likeable	54. protestor
13. congradulations	34. maintinance	55. pryed
14. contraversial	35. massacre	56. pursued
15. convenient	36. mileage	57. realised
16. defendant	37. miraculous	58. recyling
17. defie	38. mispell	59. refered
18. delagates	39. mosquitos	60. repels
19. desireable	40. munciple	61. repetative
20. deviding	41. necessary	62. resturant
21. dilemas	42. negligence	63. rhythm

64. saleries
65. sandals
66. sandwhich
67. sargeant

68. sattellites
69. sentence
70. skillfull
71. transfered

72. vaccuum
73. villain
74. visability
75. wreckless

NAME _____ CLASS _____ DATE _____

Exercise 6

SPELLING

INSTRUCTIONS: The following list contains 75 words that college students frequently misspell. Some of the words are spelled correctly here, but many others are misspelled. Use the proper copy-editing symbols to correct all the misspelled words. If several letters need to be corrected in a single word, rewrite the entire word. If several spellings are normally permissible, use the one recommended by The Associated Press Stylebook.

1. abdomen	22. canceled	43. hemorrhage
2. absense	23. Caribbean	44. labeled
3. acknowledgement	24. champagne	45. legitimate
4. acter	25. chaos	46. marijuana
5. activitys	26. charitable	47. mathamatics
6. admissable	27. cheif	48. Mediteranean
7. afterwards	28. cigarettes	49. missles
8. aggressor	29. commitment	50. obscenity
9. agreeable	30. compatible	51. optometrist
10. amateur	31. credibility	52. personel
11. amount	32. curcuit	53. possession
12. amuck	33. description	54. proceedures
13. arithmatic	34. desert (food)	55. redundent
14. athletics	35. desparately	56. reelect
15. ax	36. deterant	57. severly
16. backwards	37. diarrhea	58. sherriff
17. basically	38. dieing	59. sking
18. becomming	39. encyclopedia	60. souvenir
19. beginning	40. gubernatoral	61. subpoena
20. benifit	41. handicaped	62. successfull
21. burglars	42. hearld	63. surgary

64. surprizing

65. survivors

66. taxy

67. theives

68. truly

69. untill

70. vacinate

71. valedictorian

72. valiently

73. vicious

74. victorious

75. writen

NAME _____ CLASS _____ DATE _____

Exercise 7

AP STYLE

INSTRUCTIONS: After studying The Associated Press Stylebook in Appendix B, use the proper copy-editing symbols to correct the mechanical, spelling and stylistic errors in the following sentences. Remember that none of the possessives have been formed for you. If you need help in forming the possessives, see the guidelines in Appendix C.

1. The girl, Anne Stockdale, age nine, was carrying 2 small boxes, five cents, and a can of mace.

2. At 12 noon yesterday, the Priest gave the 7 year old girl from Eugene Oregon a bible and five dollars.

3. Forecasters in northern Illinois say the temperature will fall from 0 to -15 by 12 midnight tomorrow evening.

4. The teenager, who lives on Erie Av., is 5′, 6″ tall, weighs 140 pds., and likes both oreos and french fries.

5. During the 20th century, the Federal Govt. spent 4,840,000 million dollars to protect wildlife in the Calif. park.

6. Seven persons, including Mrs. Richard Miehe, will meet the Realtor at 12 noon at the Sherer Realty Company on King Dr.

7. The child, age seven, was sipping a coke and carrying $0.25 as he walked north on Jamestown Blvd. at 8:20 a.m. yesterday.

8. The girl, age 19, will recieve her B.A. in Journalism from a school in Mass., then wants to join the United States Navy.

9. The Governor, a member of the democratic party, said his son earned a Ph.D. in the department of history during the 1960s.

10. The temperature in the Midwest fell below 0 at 12 midnight, then climbed to the 30s as the wind continued to blow from the north.

11. Leaning backwards, the baby sitter in Reno Nevada said she saves 50 percent of her earnings, or about one hundred dollars a month.

12. Mr. Richard Moore works as a reporter in the southwest and, eleven years ago, won a pulitzer prize for a book entitled Tragedy.

13. At 10:00 AM this morning, the Vice-President of the U.S. will meet with three persons, including Rev. James Haloway of Toledo Ohio.

14. The presidential aide said the odds are five to four that the Porsche driven by Movie Star Paul Newman will exceed two hundred miles an hour.

15. Prof. Mildred Berg, a native of Carbondale Illinois, yesterday criticized both Pres. Lyndon Johnson and the United States constitution.

16. He was a member of the Kansas legislature, then the U.S. Senate, and says it will cost from $7 to $9 million dollars to seek re-election.

17. Senator John Glenn, a democrat from Ohio, estimated last Winter that the Federal program will cost from 10 to 20 Billion Dollars.

18. They arrived at 11:00 pm yesterday and, afterwards, revealed that Mrs. Samuel Swauger of 4987 Huron Dr. won the election by a vote of 18732-14011

19. During the 1970s, the Priest was able to xerox a copy for five cents and said it was alright for other persons in the City to xerox additional copies.

20. The F.B.I. agent, who lives at 410 East Lake Dr. in Fort Worth Texas drove South on Austin Blvd., then stopped at the Targill Corporation on Bell Av.

21. The vice-president and two of his advisers said afterwards that they invited 5 outstanding Black teenagers from Wis. to visit the U.S. Capital Bldg. next Fall.

22. The President, Pope, and other dignitaries will meet in the oval office of the white house at 10:00 a.m. tomorrow, then move to room 312 of the senate office bldg.

23. Reverend Alice Caruna held a bible in one hand and a copy of the U.S. constitution in the other as she spoke to members of the Georgia Alumni Assn. yesterday afternoon.

24. While visiting the President in the Oval Office, Senator Edward Kennedy, a Democrat from Massachusetts, warned that the Social Security system will go bankrupt during the 21st Century.

NAME _____ CLASS _____ DATE _____

Exercise 8
AP STYLE

INSTRUCTIONS: After studying The Associated Press Stylebook in Appendix B, use the proper copy-editing symbols to correct the mechanical, spelling and stylistic errors in the following sentences.

1. The girl, age nine, said her Father is a democrat and a capt. in the United States Army.

2. The basketball player is a high school Junior, 17 years old, and six ft., three inches tall.

3. By a vote of 387-322, employes at Wilson Brothers Bakery on Crawford St. rejected the Union.

4. The teenager, Tommy Jones Junior of Bowling Green Ohio, said the building will cost $880 thousand.

5. The Pres., First Lady, and several Presidential Aides will visit the school in San Diego, CA., next Spring.

6. Prof. Lara Ruffenach, a member of the department of english, said her office is in room 311 of the Humanities Bldg.

7. Irregardless of the danger, two Seniors from Colonial High School tackled the theif as he ran South on Colonial Dr.

8. He was born on March 1 1974 in Pittsburgh Pennsylvania, attended high school in Mich., then moved to the northwest.

9. A mass for the lady will be offered at 7:30 p.m. tomorrow evening in the Taylor Brothers Funeral Home, 4960 Hiltgen Rd.

10. It was mothers day, and the 8 yr. old girl, Deborah Nunziata of 1410 1st Avenue, said she had four dollars to buy some flowers.

11. On Oct. 31 1990 the eleven executives met at 500 West Robinson Street and voted 9-4 to pay the bill which totals 1128 dollars.

12. The girl, who is in her early 20's, died at 7:00 p.m. yesterday evening after receiving severe burns in a fire at her home at 2106 North Ninth St.

13. On January 3, the American Federal Insurance Company filed for bankruptcy in Hartford Connecticut, listing debts of 12,640,000 dollars.

14. Afterwards, Andrew A. Vornholt Senior of 10 East Lake Rd. said his number one choice for the position of Mayor is a democrat who works as a realtor.

15. Mr. Jeffrey Logas has a Ph.D. in Economics and estimates that, by the late 1990s, sales at the Larco Corporation will exceed 120,000,000 million dollars.

16. Atty. Pat Keegan Junior works for the Federal Govt. and estimates that, in the next ten years, 3/4 of the states doctors will be sued for malpractice.

17. The boy, age 19, said he enjoys reading USA Today and time magazine, but also enjoys watching 3 television programs: Matlock, Major Dad, and 60 Minutes.

18. Karen McGorwan, President of the Kansas Alumni Assn., said the Fall meeting will be held at 5:00 p.m. Monday October 14th in the Clayton Bldg. at 210 Packwood Drive.

19. Experts in the U.S. said the odds were three to one in the republicans favor, yet only 37% of the voters in the south supported her candidacy for the presidency.

20. Prof. Allison DiLorento, an Associate Prof. who teaches Political Science and, 3 years ago, won a Pulitzer Prize, interviewed the first lady at 2 PM yesterday.

21. Irregardless of the controversy, Asst. Dist. Atty. Leo Friedman said the book, entitled Hope, is protected by the 1st amendment to the United States constitution.

22. The temperature fell from 0 to −12, yet 52% of the citys voters turned out and elected the citys 1st Black Mayor, a member of the University Club on Davenport Av.

23. The thirty year old Okla. man said he paid 6000 dollars for the toyota and was driving south at about 45 m.p.h. when the accident occured at the intersection of Packwood and Erie Streets.

24. Executives at Creative Computers Incorporated, the number one company in the field, predict that the United States congress will buy 40000 of the new computers for the United States army, navy, and air force.

NAME _____ CLASS _____ DATE _____

Exercise 9

Answer Key Provided: See Appendix D

FORMAT AND STYLE

INSTRUCTIONS: Using the proper copy-editing symbols, correct the mechanical, spelling and stylistic errors in the following sentences.

1. Robert j. Curey junior, the Mayorof Eugene Oregon sa id thre media is to bias.d

2. Sandra Oliver, age six, is four feet Tall, weaghs 81 pds, and ivles on Elm boulevard.

3. Oliver Brooks, who ahs a Ph.d., wrote a book entitled Urban Terrorists.

4. After serving in the army he obtairned a B.A. and beCame a citizen of the U.S..

5. The girl, an 18 yearr old blond, sipped a coke, and read Time Magazine

6. The retired col. fought with the united states marines in vietnam durnig the 1960's.

7. The united states congrxess will meet at 10:00 A.M. tues. January 4th in the United States capital bludg.

8. Mr. Richard Harris, an Editor AT Newsweek Magagine, will fly north on Mon. Harris, was born in oct., 1942, and be gan wrok as areporter fr the Chicago Tribune.

9. Sen. Andrews, a democrat from New Hampsire, said hewill spend about fifty percent of his campaign funds—nearly $18,000,000—on radioand telivision advertiznig.

10. Prof. Myron Carey, of 614 North Highla?nd Dr. is Chairman of THE Dept. of Mathematics and hasanoffice in Rm. 407 of thehumanities bldg.

11. the temperature is zero. She is white; he is. Vietnamese.She earns $278.00 a week and spends 4fourty percent of her incgincome on food.

12. Prange Incoporated of Columbia, South carolina manufacsre widgets at a cost of fourty seven cents and sel,ls th hem for two dollars. Normaly, about two % are defective.

13. Ruth, who was borgborn duringg the 1960s will be a Sophmore this Fall and wants to join the republican parTY.

14. 8,000 persons weRe killed when a severe hurrican struck south florida during the eightheenth century.

15. At 10:00 A.M. This morning, the Vice-President said "The Federal Govt. is far too wastefal".

16. A presidential aide sa id its safe to assume that the criteria are so vague tha t neither therepublican nor the democratis parties will object to their content.

17. The source said Eleven College Students—five boys a nd six girls—are likely to attend the city council meetign.

18. 14 members of a Black Congression31 delega a tion visited the President in the Oval Office to day and demandedd that, as his Number One Priority, HE solve the unemployment problem.

19. Mr. Randolph R. Wilcox junior, of Columbus, Ohio a former presidential aide, will speak at the university of N. Carolina at 7:30 P.M. Friday November 6.

20. The senator, an alumnus of Harvard, complained that,he cannot afford to live in the nations capital,

21. He warned that, by the 2020s, the Federal Government will have to transfer $14,800,000,000 billion dollars from general tax revenues to save thw social security system.

22. the retired army sargeant, ag3 43, lives in Sacramento california with his wive and three children James, Randolph and Tricia.

23. Timothy Wagnor, age eight, of 418 Notrth Wilkes Road ATE some french fries and sipped a Coke.

24. A jury awa rded Mrs. Sarah Petersen $1,316,400 after a car was struck and totally destroyed by a van driven by a drunken driver, killing her husband.

NAME _____ CLASS _____ DATE _____

Exercise 10

Answer Key Provided: See Appendix D

FORMAT AND STYLE

INSTRUCTIONS: Using the proper copy-editing symbols, correct the mechanical, spelling and stylistic errors in the following sentences.

1. The consultant was given $125,000 on Feb ruary 7th, 1980 in aust in texas

2. The temperature feyll to −14 aftre a blizzzard struck Denver colorado in december 1982.

3. Tom Becker, a black born in the south during the 1930s was elected Mayor of the Cit.y

4. a senior who will graduate next Spring said "history and english are my favoite subjects".

5. The girls elbow was injjured when ahe fell twelve feat at lincoln park at Noon yesterdy.

6. Susan Majorce, age seven, is five ft. tall and weighs eighty-seven lbs.

7. the caddccident Occurred on Interstate 80, about twleve miles West of Reno Nevada.

8. They moved from 438 North Sunset Drive to 318 Jamestown boulevard.last Thurs.

9. Mr. Carl r. zastrow junior, of Columbus Ohio, a former Presi(dential aide, will speak-at the university Thursday at 7:00 PM. on the 1st of next mnoth.

10. Atty. Martha Dilla, forgmerly liglived at 4062 South EastlanD DRIVE andworks fo r the Westinghouse coporation

11. the companys presidnet said his firm willProvide more than $100,000,000 dollars to develoxpe an electric car able to travel sixty miles per hour.

12. The yout,h a high School Sophomore, said the temperture in Idaho often falls below 0 during the WIntsr.

13. 50 women who met yesterday morning at 11 am said there children are entitled to use the new park on Vallrath Avenue.

14. The 5-member city council wantxxs ot canvass the towns voters to determene weather a large group favors the establishment ov a Civic Orchestra.

15. Dist. Atty. Ramon Hernandez Junior, who was born in Mont. during the 1940s graduated from the Univarsit y ofNebraska.

16. Mrs. Marie Hyde, Asst. Supt. for Public Educatioon for the City, said the 16 year old girls were raised in athens georgia

17. The lady earned her beachelors degree from te university of Kentucky and her masters degr ee froum Indiana Univertiy during the 1960s.

18. The suspects were arrested at 1602 North Highland Avenue, 64 East Wilshire Drive, and 3492 3rd Street.

19. Chris Repanski, of pocatello idaho will enrolled in the college as a Sophmore nxt fall and hopes to become an Attorney

20. The man, whose i n his mid 30s, joined the F.B.I. after Recieving a Ph.D. in Computer Science.

21. Afterwards, the Vice-President sayd hewill need $25 to $30 million dollars to win the Presidential Election next Fall.

22. Reverand Andrew Cisneros estimated that ⅓ of his parishioners contribute att leeast five per cent of their annuall income to the churchs general revenue fund.

23. The cops arrested four kids dirvng North on Michigan Ave. minutes atfer the restaurant was robed of $1640.83 last Friday.

24. The Catholic Priest that was elected to the city council by a vote of 8,437–8,197 said hehad expected to lose the elb electio.

25. the bill of rights was added to the unites states constitution durign the eightheenth century.

26. Since the 1940s, he has livedin five States Ws., Ken., Mass., N.Y., & Ca.

CHAPTER 2

NEWSWRITING STYLE

A sign in the administration building at Valparaiso University stated:

> An oleaginous resin coating has recently been applied to nearby surfaces and is still in an incomplete state of oxidation.
>
> Contact with aforementioned surfaces will cause pigment transference to skin or clothing, compromise the decorative integrity of the coating and invoke ire.

Never write like that! Newswriters are expected to use plain, simple terms that everyone can understand. Thus, a good newswriter could replace the 42 words in that sign with five: "Wet paint. Do not touch."

Newspapers serve a mass audience, and the members of that audience possess diverse capabilities and interests. To communicate effectively—to convey information to a mass audience—newswriters must learn to present that information in as interesting and simple a manner as possible so that almost everyone will want to read and be able to understand it.

Newspapers have consequently developed a distinctive style of writing, and every element of that style serves a specific purpose. Together, the elements enable newspapers to convey information to their readers clearly, concisely and impartially. At first the style may seem difficult and perhaps even awkward. It may also dismay some students because of its emphasis on facts; but newswriters are reporters, not creative writers.

As a first step, reporters must learn to avoid excessive formality. When they begin to write, people often become too formal, and their articles become awkward and pompous. A good writer should be able to present even the most complicated and important ideas simply—in clear, plain language.

Test your stories by reading them aloud to yourself or to a friend. If your sentences sound awkward, or if you would not use them in a conversation with friends, they may have to be rewritten. Be particularly careful to avoid complex phrases and long, awkward sentences that you would not use in a normal conversation.

SIMPLIFY WORDS, SENTENCES AND PARAGRAPHS

To simplify stories, avoid long, unfamiliar words. Whenever possible, substitute shorter and simpler words that convey the same meaning. Use the word "about" rather than "approximately," "build" rather than "construct," "call" rather than "summon" and "home" rather than "residence."

Millions of Americans have heard Andy Rooney's commentaries at the end of the television series "60 Minutes." Fewer Americans know that Rooney is also a talented writer. In one of his books, "Not That You Asked," Rooney says he is suspicious of writers who use the words "launder" when they mean "wash," "inexpensive" when they mean "cheap," "perspiration" when they mean "sweat" and "wealthy" when they mean "rich."

Rooney also complains, "People often replace the simple word 'now' with something that sounds fancier to them. I don't know why they aren't satisfied with just plain 'now.' They say 'currently,' 'presently' or 'at this point in time.'"

In addition to being clearer, simpler words also save space:

He gave assistance to the victims.
REVISED: He helped the victims.

His association with the bank began in 1976.
REVISED: The bank hired him in 1976.

Some women were engaged in conversation with their neighbors.
REVISED: Some women were talking with their neighbors.

Also use short sentences and short paragraphs. Very long or awkward sentences should be rewritten and divided into shorter units that are easier to read and understand. Research has consistently found a strong correlation between readability and sentence length; the longer a sentence is, the more difficult it is to understand. One survey found that 75 percent of the people shown sentences that contained an average of 20 words were able to understand them, but the percentage dropped rapidly as the sentences became longer:

- 62 percent understood stories with 25-word sentences.
- 47 percent understood stories with 30-word sentences.
- 33 percent understood stories with 35-word sentences.
- 17 percent understood stories with 40-word sentences.

Because of the strong correlation between readability and sentence length, publications quite obviously cater to their intended audiences. The sentences in comics contain an average of about eight words, whereas the sentences in publications for the general public contain an average of 15 to 20 words. Publications that contain 20 to 30 words per sentence are much more difficult to understand, and they appeal to more specialized and better-educated audiences. These publications include such magazines as Harper's and The Atlantic, and scholarly, scientific and professional journals.

For some reason, college students tend to write sentences that are much too long. Students are more likely to write sentences that contain 40 or 50 words than sentences that contain four or five. Yet short sentences are clearer and more forceful. Notice, for example, the clarity and impact of the following sentences:

The rain poured. Lightning flashed, and their car stalled.

Every year 17 million Americans try to stop smoking. One million succeed.

Robinson, 40, never studied English in college. He never took writing classes. In fact, this jack-of-all-trades had never shown any interest in writing until 1975.

That's when he was paralyzed.

Mistakenly, critics often accuse newspapers of oversimplifying news stories in the attempt to appeal to the least educated of their readers. However, scientific studies have found that newspaper stories are more likely to be too difficult, rather than too easy, for the public to read. One of these studies revealed that stories disseminated by The Associated Press are written at about a 10th-grade level, and that stories provided by United Press International are written at nearly the 11th-grade level. Together, stories provided by the two news services compose about 40 percent of the news content in most daily newspapers.

Another study found that many newspapers publish stories too difficult for even high school graduates to understand. The Literacy Committee of the American Society of Newspaper Editors examined 10 newspapers to determine whether their stories contained difficult words and concepts. The papers ranged from the Beaver County Times in Pennsylvania to The Washington Post and The New York Times.

The committee members calculated the grade level of stories published by each of the papers. The committee was chaired by a Pulitzer Prize winner, Jane Healy of The Orlando Sentinel. Healy reported: "Our study showed the same grim results that most other readability studies have shown: The newspapers were writing over too many readers' heads. All but three of the 10 papers were writing at a 12th-grade level or higher." The grade levels ranged from a high of 14.5 for The Washington Post and 13.5 for the Yuma (Ariz.) Daily Sun to a low of 10.6 for USA Today.

To make their newspapers more readable, many editors are demanding shorter stories and simpler writing, including shorter sentences and simpler words.

Some critics have charged that newspapers' emphasis on simplicity makes their stories dull, yet the exact opposite is true. When stories are well-written, simplicity makes them clearer and more interesting. Well-written stories contain no distracting clutter; instead, they emphasize the most important facts and report those facts in a clear, forceful manner.

Jerry Ballune, a California editor, has pointed out: "Our goal is to write . . . in short, understandable sentences. We talk in short sentences. Unless we're Einsteins, we think in short sentences. Readers understand our writing in short sentences. Even Einstein, who had less need for it than most of us, advised: 'Keep it simple.'" Harry Levins, a writing coach at the St. Louis Post-Dispatch, noted: "When we play games with the reader, he usually wins. He simply quits reading. Most readers want their information presented clearly and simply. They lack the time and patience to peel off the camouflage of indirection." (Both Ballune and Levins expressed their advice in bulletins written for their newspapers' staffs.)

There's another important reason for using short sentences and short paragraphs in news stories. Newspapers are printed in small type, with narrow columns, on cheap paper. Long paragraphs—large, gray blocks of type—discourage readers. So reporters divide stories into bite-sized chunks that are easy to read. Also, the white space left at the ends of paragraphs helps brighten each page.

Ernie Pyle, a correspondent during World War II, wrote simply, factually and without sentimentalism, and his work might serve as a model for students. Pyle wrote about individuals in the war, and his syndicated column became so popular that many newspapers published it on their front pages. The following column was reprinted in one of his books, "Here Is Your War":

Sergeant Fryer had an experience on one of the last few days of the campaign that will be worth telling to his grandchildren. He was in a foxhole on a steep hillside. An 88mm shell landed three feet away and blew him out of his hole. He rolled, out of control, 50 yards down the rocky hillside. He didn't seem to be wounded, but all his breath was gone. He couldn't move. He couldn't make a sound. His chest hurt. His legs wouldn't work.

A medic came past and poked him. Sergeant Fryer couldn't say anything, so the medic went on. Pretty soon two of Fryer's best friends walked past and he heard one of them say, "There's Sergeant Fryer. I guess he's dead." And they went right on too. It was more than an hour before Fryer could move, but within a few hours he was perfectly normal again. He said if his wife saw the story in print she would think for sure he was a hero.

(Scripps-Howard Newspapers)

The average sentence in that passage contains 10.6 words. Three sentences contain only three words, and two contain only four words.

More recently, Edna Buchanan won a Pulitzer Prize for her work as a police reporter for The Miami Herald. Buchanan has also written several best-selling books, and she describes her work as a police reporter in one of them, "The Corpse Had a Familiar Face." Here is a passage from that book:

Dozens of fires erupted at intersections. Firefighters were forced back by gunfire. Businesses and stores burned unchecked. "It's absolutely unreal," said Miami Fire Inspector George Bilberry. "They're burning down the whole north end of town."

Late Sunday, 15 major blazes still raged out of control. Snipers fired rifles at rescue helicopters. The looting and burning went on for three days. Public schools were closed, and an 8 p.m.–6 a.m. curfew was established.

There are only 8.1 words in Buchanan's average sentence. Several of her sentences contain only five or six words. The longest contains 11.

Compare Pyle's and Buchanan's work with the following sentence taken from William L. Shirer's book "Gandhi: A Memoir":

Clever lawyer that he was, Jinnah took the independence that Gandhi had wrestled for India from the British by rousing the masses to non-violent struggle and used it to set up his own independent but shaky Moslem nation of Pakistan, destined, I believed then, to break up, as shortly happened when the eastern Bengali part, separated from the western part by a thousand miles of India's territory, broke away to form Bangladesh; destined eventually, I believed, to simply disappear.

Because of its length and complexity, this sentence is much more difficult to understand. It contains 80 words. By comparison, the Bible starts simply, "In the beginning God created heaven and earth." The entire Lord's Prayer has only 71 words. The Ten Commandments have 297. The Gettysburg Address has 271. The legal marriage vow has two ("I do").

To succeed as a newswriter, you will have to do more than write short sentences, however. You will also have to write simple sentences, using the normal word order: subject, verb and direct object. Notice how much clearer and more concise the following sentences become when they use this normal word order:

Phillips was invited into the apartment by a woman.
REVISED: A woman invited Phillips into the apartment.

The amount that has been allocated by the city is $42,000.
REVISED: The city allocated $42,000.

Another of the terrorists' demands is that they be given permission to leave the country.
REVISED: The terrorists also demand permission to leave the country.

Notice that, when you use the normal word order, your sentences become more concise:

Her car became engulfed in flames. (6 words)
REVISED: Flames engulfed her car. (4 words)

A jury trial has been requested by the doctor. (9 words)
REVISED: The doctor requested a jury trial. (6 words)

Thousands of dollars could be saved by the school. (9 words)
REVISED: The school could save thousands of dollars. (7 words)

Also be certain that the ideas in each sentence are related. If they are not, even short sentences can become too complicated and unreadable:

Appointed editor of the student newspaper, she likes to swim.

Born in New York on Dec. 21, 1971, he was seriously injured when his car overturned.

She wants to move to California when she graduates and said the book was a gift.

Too many clauses, particularly when they appear at the beginning of a sentence, make the sentence more difficult to understand. The clauses overload sentences, so their main points fail to receive enough emphasis; instead, they are buried amid the clutter:

Left paralyzed on the left side of his body after brain surgery last summer, the 22-year-old is suing his doctor for $6 million.
REVISED: The 22-year-old is suing his doctor for $6 million. He has been paralyzed on his left side since brain surgery last summer.

Echoing parental complaints about the danger to children swimming in the pool, Mayor Sabrina Datolli today closed it.
REVISED: Mayor Sabrina Datolli today closed the pool and explained that she agrees with parents who said it is unsafe.

Other beginners try to pack too many ideas into a single sentence:

She said that just when the new technology is placing greater demands than ever upon journalists to become proficient in grammar, punctuation and spelling, many young people seeking careers in news, advertising, public relations and other communication fields find themselves severely handicapped by today's educational system, which places its priorities elsewhere.
REVISED: She said the new technology is placing greater demands than ever upon journalists to become proficient in grammar, punctuation and spelling. Yet today's educational system places its priorities elsewhere, and that severely handicaps young people seeking careers in news, advertising, public relations and other communication fields.

The meeting between the college president and the Honors Advisory Committee, composed of three students, two faculty members and two deans, came about today after nearly 180 honors students held a sit-in last week in the Office of Undergraduate Studies to protest the firing of the head of the Honors Program, Margaret Chapin.

REVISED: The college president today met with the Honors Advisory Committee. The meeting was scheduled after nearly 180 honors students held a sit-in last week in the Office of Undergraduate Studies. The students were protesting the firing of Margaret Chapin, head of the Honors Program. The advisory committee is composed of three students, two faculty members and two deans.

WRITING CLEARLY AND SIMPLY ABOUT EVEN COMPLEX TOPICS

News stories about even the most complex topics, such as the federal budget, can be written clearly and simply. Read the opening paragraphs of this example, written by Donald L. Barlett and James B. Steele of the Philadelphia Inquirer.

> PHILADELPHIA—A key provision in the federal budget act passed three weeks ago was hailed by Congress as increasing taxes of the country's highest-income individuals and families.
>
> It does not.
>
> In fact, it extends at least one tax benefit to some wealthy households that did not have it before.
>
> Congress boasted that the change would raise $10.8 billion in new tax revenue.
>
> It will not.
>
> In fact, it may raise only $2 billion or $3 billion—if that. In addition, that money would come from the upper middle-income group, not the wealthy.
>
> An analysis of the fiscal 1991 deficit-reduction package by the Philadelphia Inquirer revealed that the provision won't increase taxes one penny for most of the 650,000 individuals and families with incomes of more than $250,000 a year.
>
> How is that possible?

Analyze the story's sentence structure.

* How many words are in the average sentence?
* How many words are in the longest and shortest sentences?

Are the three- and four-word sentences effective? If so, follow these reporters' example and try to use more short sentences in the stories you write.

ELIMINATE UNNECESSARY WORDS

Two of this country's former presidents were models of conciseness. In 1862, President Abraham Lincoln became angry at Gen. George B. McClellan. McClellan's soldiers outnumbered the soldiers in the Confederate Army, yet McClellan was hesitating to seize the offensive. Lincoln sent McClellan a letter that contained a single sentence. "If you don't want to use the army," Lincoln wrote, "I should like to borrow it for a while."

President Calvin Coolidge was known as a tight-lipped New Englander. Coolidge supposedly attended church in Washington one Sunday, without his wife. When he returned home, she asked what the minister had preached about.

"Sin," Coolidge said.

"What did he say about it?" she asked.

"He was against it."

Like presidents Lincoln and Coolidge, newswriters must learn to be concise—to avoid using unnecessary words. However, newswriters must also be more specific, and detailed enough so their stories are informative—more informative than Coolidge's conversation with his wife.

Most newspapers can publish only a fraction of the information they receive each day; for example, an editor for The New York Times has estimated that the Times receives 1¼ to 1½ million words every day but has enough space to publish only one-tenth of that material. By writing concisely, reporters try to present as much information to readers as possible. Brevity also helps readers to grasp quickly the main ideas conveyed by each story, since it eliminates the need to spend time reading unnecessary words. Thus, writers who use two or more words when only one is necessary waste time and space. Moreover, they also exhibit a lack of alertness. Some words are almost always unnecessary: "that," "then," "currently," "now" and "presently," for example. Because the proper verb tells when an action occurred—in the past, present or future—it is redundant to add a second word that reiterates the time, such as "*past* history," "is *now*" and "*future* plans."

Notice how easily several unnecessary words can be deleted from the following sentences without rewriting them or changing their meaning:

> She was able to persuade him to leave.
> REVISED: She persuaded him to leave.
>
> He presently drives a distance of about 80 miles a day.
> REVISED: He drives about 80 miles a day.
>
> At the present time the restaurant opens for business at 6 a.m. every morning of the week.
> REVISED: The restaurant opens at 6 every morning.

Other sentences may have to be more extensively rewritten to eliminate unnecessary words and phrases:

> A pilot said he thinks that the airplane is worth in the neighborhood of between approximately $34,000 and $36,500.
> REVISED: A pilot said the airplane is worth $34,000 to $36,500.
>
> Three drownings occurred in the waters of Crystal Lake this last summer.
> REVISED: Three people drowned in Crystal Lake last summer.
>
> Pointed out in the report is the fact that the problem of alcoholism is not fully understood by most Americans.
> REVISED: The report says most Americans do not understand alcoholism.

Be especially careful to avoid phrases and sentences that are redundant—that unnecessarily repeat the same idea. The following phrases contain only two or three words, yet at least one—the word in italics—is unnecessary:

bodily injuries	*lone* gunman
dropped *downward*	*new* innovation
end result	*now* serves
free *of charge*	*past* experience
helped *along*	*physical* pain

These sentences are also redundant:

Hicks said the damage was considerable and extensive.

The flower is very unique, different and interesting.

She called Wolf's appointment extremely significant and important.

Improving some redundant sentences requires more thought and effort:

Deaths are extremely rare, with only one fatality occurring in every 663,000 cases.
REVISED: One death occurs in every 663,000 cases.

A strong-arm robbery took place Tuesday afternoon when a man in a white Pontiac reached out, grabbed a woman's purse and dragged her across the parking lot.
REVISED: Tuesday afternoon a man in a white Pontiac reached out, grabbed a woman's purse and dragged her across the parking lot.

The problem often arises because writers introduce a topic, then present some specific information about it. In most cases, only the more specific information is needed:

Other injuries the man received include a broken arm.
REVISED: The man also suffered a broken arm.

In an attempt to put out the fire, two men tried to smother it with a blanket.
REVISED: Two men tried to smother the fire with a blanket.

A survey Monday concerning the fairness and accuracy of the news media revealed that four out of 10 students believe the media are unfair and inaccurate.
REVISED: Four out of 10 students surveyed Monday said the news media are unfair and inaccurate.

Repetition is even more common in longer passages that involve several sentences. Sentences that appear near the end of a paragraph should not repeat facts implied or mentioned earlier:

Workers digging a drainage ditch brought up more than dirt. They found the skeletons of three children.
REVISED: Workers digging a drainage ditch found the skeletons of three children.

This is not the first time she has been held up. She has been robbed three times in the past eight months.

REVISED: She has been robbed three times in the past eight months.

A burglary occurred Tuesday afternoon at the home of Clarence Dozier, 2347 Bentley Ave. A .38-caliber revolver and some food were stolen.

REVISED: Burglars took a .38-caliber revolver and some food from the home of Clarence Dozier, 2347 Bentley Ave., Tuesday afternoon.

QUIZ

Are you ready for a quiz? Do not rewrite the following redundant sentences; simply cross out the unnecessary words.

1. She was in a quick hurry and warned that, in the future, she will seek out textbooks that are sexist and demand that they be totally banned.
2. As it now stands, three separate members of the committee said they will try to prevent the city from closing down the park during the winter months.
3. His convertible was totally destroyed and, in order to obtain the money necessary to buy a new car, he now plans to ask a personal friend for a loan to help him along.
4. After police found the lifeless body, the medical doctor conducted an autopsy to determine the cause of death and concluded that the youth had been strangled to death.
5. In the past, he often met up with the students at the computer lab and, because of their future potential, invited them to attend the convention.
6. Based upon her previous experience as an architect, she warned the committee members that constructing the new hospital facility will be pretty expensive and suggested that they step in and seek out more donors.
7. The two men were hunting in a wooded forest a total of 12 miles away from the nearest hospital in the region when both suffered severe bodily injuries.
8. Based upon several studies conducted in the past, he firmly believes that, when first started next year, the two programs should be very selective, similar in nature and conducted only in the morning hours.

Now calculate the number of words you eliminated—and your score. If you need help, the answers appear in Appendix D.

0–30:	Amateur.	Were you really trying?
31–40:	Copy kid.	Time to enroll in Newswriting 101.
41–50:	Cub.	You've still got a lot to learn.
51–60:	Pro.	You're getting there—but can do even better.
61 +	Expert.	Time to ask you boss for a raise—or your teacher for an "A."

REMAIN OBJECTIVE

During the Revolutionary War, American newspapers were journals of opinion and frequently propagandized for or against the British. A colonial editor named Isaiah

Thomas joined the militia that fired on British troops at Lexington, then reported the battle in his paper, the Massachusetts Spy. His story, published on May 3, 1775, began:

> AMERICANS! forever bear in mind the BATTLE OF LEXINGTON!—where British troops, unmolested and unprovoked, wantonly and in a most inhuman manner, fired upon and killed a number of our countrymen, then robbed, ransacked, and burnt their houses! nor could the tears of defenseless women, some of whom were in the pains of childbirth, the cries of helpless babes, nor the prayers of old age, confined to beds of sickness, appease their thirst for blood!—or divert them from their DESIGN of MURDER and robbery!

Some publications, such as Time magazine, continue to use a similar—though usually less inflammatory—style of writing. In addition to reporting the news, Time interprets the news, explaining its meaning. In the fall of 1987, the Dow Jones industrial average plunged 508 points in a single day, dubbed "Black Monday." Time reported that, "What crashed was more than just the market. It was the Reagan Illusion: the idea that there could be a defense buildup and tax cuts without a price, that the country could live beyond its means indefinitely." Time blamed President Reagan, and it explained that:

> . . . he stayed a term too long. As he shouted befuddled Hooverisms over the roar of his helicopter last week, or doddered precariously through his press conference, Reagan appeared embarrassingly irrelevant to a reality that he could scarcely comprehend.

Today, most journalists strive to be as impartial or "objective" as possible. Editors and other newspaper employees can express their opinions in editorials and columns, but not in news stories. Newspaper reporters are expected to be neutral observers, not advocates or participants. Reporters cannot discriminate against any ideas or tell their readers what to think about these ideas.

While working as a reporter, assume that your readers are intelligent and capable of reaching their own conclusions about issues in the news. Your job as a reporter is to gather and report facts that your readers need to make wise decisions—not to make the decisions for them. Avoid adjectives and labels that reflect your opinions. Also avoid loaded words, such as "demagogue," "extremist," "radical," "racist," "segregationist" and "zealot." They are unnecessary, may be inaccurate and may unnecessarily infuriate readers who have opposite views.

In addition to being unnecessary, most expressions of opinion are insulting. Why? Because they state the obvious: the fact that an argument was "heated," a rape "violent" or a death "unfortunate." Thus, the comments waste a newspaper's space and its readers' time. Reporters can eliminate the opinions in some sentences by deleting a single word: "*alert* witness," "*famous* author," "*gala* reception," "*thoughtful* reply." Other examples include:

> The tickets will cost only $19.
> REVISED: The tickets will cost $19.

> The violent explosion injured seven workers.
> REVISED: The explosion injured seven workers.

Other sentences require more extensive revisions:

> Most students were apathetic; only 22 percent voted in the election.
> REVISED: Twenty-two percent of the students voted in the election.

Parnell made an excellent point when he explained that many adults cannot afford to buy their own homes.
REVISED: Parnell said many adults cannot afford to buy their own homes.

To avoid the problem, report factual details as clearly and thoroughly as possible. Avoid labels and avoid drawing any conclusions about the facts:

He drives an expensive car.
REVISED: He drives a $52,000 Mercedes.

The book is long and dull.
REVISED: The book contains 914 pages.

The city was alive with excitement.
REVISED: Police estimated that 80,000 people watched the parade.

Entire sentences sometimes convey opinions rather than facts. In most cases, the opinions are expressed as trite generalities, unsupported by facts. Good editors (and instructors) will eliminate those sentences. Often, deletion is the only way to correct the problem. Here are four examples:

The findings look favorable.

Their answers were thoughtful.

He is a hero to everyone in the city.

This year's program will offer something to please everyone.

As a newswriter, you can report the opinions expressed by other people, but must clearly attribute those opinions to their source. If you fail to provide the proper attribution, readers may think that you are expressing your own opinions (or agreeing with your source):

The family filed a lawsuit because the doctor failed to notice the injury.
REVISED: The family's lawsuit charges that the doctor failed to notice the injury.

For years, Sen. William Proxmire, D-Wis., presented a monthly award to federal agencies that wasted taxpayers' money.
REVISED: For years, Sen. William Proxmire, D-Wis., presented a monthly award to federal agencies that he thought wasted taxpayers' money.

A single word that expresses an opinion can infuriate readers. When a college student was raped, a news story reported that she suffered cuts on her arms and hands but "was not seriously injured." An irate reader asked, "Since when are rape and attempted sodomy, at knifepoint, not enough violence to constitute serious injury?"
Similarly, The Sacramento Bee reported that the state Board of Education endorsed a "power grab," and critics objected to the newspaper's use of the term. Another story in The Bee described a strict anti-smoking ordinance adopted by the Sacramento County Board of Supervisors. The story began, "The tobacco industry's hired guns failed to shoot down the toughest anti-smoking ordinance for workplaces in the state Tuesday." A later paragraph added that the county supervisors "grilled high-powered speakers representing the Tobacco Institute."
A reader complained that this was an editorial, not a story. The Bee employs an ombudsman who responds to reader complaints, and the ombudsman, Art Nauman,

agreed that the term "hired guns" is clearly a pejorative. The speakers, Nauman continued, "didn't have quite the muscle the story would have us believe. They lost. So can we detect a vague little sneer in that description, 'high-powered.'"

Nauman then repeated a bit of advice he received from an old editor: "Eschew adjectives and adverbs. They'll turn around and bite you every time."

AVOID SEXUAL STEREOTYPES

In the past, news stories that mentioned women seemed to emphasize their roles as wives, mothers, cooks, seamstresses, housekeepers and sex objects. During the 1960s and 1970s, women began to complain that such stereotypes are false and demeaning— that women are human beings, not primarily housewives and sex objects.

Fawn Vraze, a writer for The Philadelphia Inquirer, noted, "These are bewildering times for males, especially those who think that old phrases, terms of endearment or jokes—the very ones that women might have shrugged off or smiled at years ago—are still acceptable today." Increasingly, women are offended by such phrases, and complain when they appear in print. The reasons are obvious. Many of the phrases treat women as inferior to men; thus, they are mistaken and insulting.

When you write for the media, you are expected to avoid demeaning comments and sexist stereotypes that will offend many of your readers. Yet it is difficult for some writers to break old ways of thinking, especially the stereotypes they developed in childhood.

As a first step, avoid occupational terms that exclude women: "fireman," "mailman," "policeman" and "workman," for example. Journalists substitute "firefighter," "mail carrier," "police officer" and "worker." Similarly, use the words "reporter" and "journalist" instead of "newsman."

Although some groups favor their use, The Associated Press Stylebook recommends that journalists avoid awkward or contrived words, such as "chairperson" and "spokesperson." Instead, the stylebook advises using "chairman" or "spokesman" when referring to a man or to the office in general. The stylebook recommends using "chairwoman" or "spokeswoman" when referring to a woman. When appropriate, reporters can use a neutral word such as "leader" or "representative."

Also avoid using the words "female" and "woman" in places where you would not use the words "male" or "man" (for example: "woman doctor" or "female general"). Similarly, use unisex substitutes for words such as "authoress" (author), "aviatrix" (aviator) and "coed" (student).

Women object to being called "gals," "girls" or "ladies," and to being referred to by only their first names. News stories do not call men "boys" and usually refer to them by their last names, rarely their first.

Other unacceptable practices include:

- Suggesting that homemaking is not work.
- Identifying a woman solely by her relationship with a man: for example, as a man's wife, daughter or secretary.
- Describing a woman's physical characteristics—her hair, dress, voice or figure—when her appearance is irrelevant to a story. Ask yourself, "Under the same circumstances, would I describe a man's physical characteristics?"
- Mentioning a woman's marital status, especially the fact that she is divorced, unless her marital status is clearly relevant to your story. Again, ask yourself, "Under the same circumstances, would I mention

a man's marital status?" When a woman's marital status is relevant, it seldom belongs in the lead. Avoid stories that begin: "A 35-year-old divorcee. . . ."

Never assume that everyone involved in a story is male, that all people holding prestigious jobs are male, or that most women are housewives. Be especially careful to avoid using the pronouns "he," "his" and "him" while referring to a typical American or average person. Some readers will mistakenly assume that you are referring exclusively to men.

Also avoid the cumbersome and repetitive "he/she" or "he and she." The effort to rid the language of male bias should never become so strained that it distracts readers. There are several techniques that you can use to avoid those cumbersome terms, and the following paragraphs describe them.

A recent headline announced, "Woman Exec Slain in Waldorf-Astoria." Critics said that the slain person's sex was irrelevant to the story, and that few journalists would have written, "Male Exec Slain." Similarly, a headline in The Washington Post said, "School Job May Go to Woman Educator." Critics asked editors at the Post why they used the term "woman educator," since they would never use the term "man educator." Moreover, the headline's wording suggested that it is unusual for a woman to achieve a position of importance.

A story in The New York Times reported that a secretary "wore a full-length blue-tweed coat, leather boots and gold bangle bracelets." Critics responded that the secretary's clothing was neither unusual nor relevant to her involvement in the news. Moreover, the reporter would not have described the attire of a man in the same position.

An obituary that The New York Times published for Nora Astorga, Nicaragua's chief delegate to the United Nations, contained this passage:

> Miss Astorga stood out in her diplomatic surroundings not only as one of the few women in such a position. At 5 feet 11 inches in high heels, she seldom went unnoticed, with her sleek frame fitted in dress-for-success clothes and her hair smartly cropped.

The New York Times has published a newsroom bulletin, called "Winners & Sinners," that cited examples of good and bad writing. The next edition of the bulletin asked how the reporter would have described a man who distinguished himself in a field traditionally dominated by women. The bulletin's editor asked whether, for example, the reporter would have written:

> Mr. Treakle stood out in his stenographic surroundings not only as one of the few men in such a position. At 6 feet 6 inches in wingtips, he seldom went unnoticed, with his sleek frame fitted in pinstripe suits and his hair neatly combed.

The editor concluded, "If it's not appropriate for a man, it's no more appropriate for a woman."

Other comments are even more demeaning, including the following sentence written by a college student:

> Most of her life she has been the typical content housewife. As such she was not motivated to improve herself or even to seek a college degree.

A story published by a campus newspaper referred to women as "chicks." Several female students and faculty members were outraged. They complained that the word implies that women are cute, little, fluffy and helpless.

Some advertisements still contain sexual stereotypes. Radio advertisements have urged women to ask their husbands for money so they can shop at a certain clothing store. Another advertisement urged mothers (not fathers) to take their children to a certain amusement park. You may be more familiar with an advertisement that appeared on television for many years. The advertisement urged women to buy the right brand of laundry detergent so that their husbands would never be embarrassed by "ring-around-the-collar." Critics suggested that men could avoid the embarrassment by washing their own shirts—or their dirty necks.

Here are some specific guidelines and examples of the techniques you can use to avoid sexist writing:

1. Avoid titles that exclude women: for example, titles that begin or end with the word "man."

> Most newsmen are college graduates.
> REVISED: Most reporters are college graduates.

> The Catholic Church is delegating more work to its laymen.
> REVISED: The Catholic Church is delegating more work to the members of its congregations.

2. Substitute an article for the male pronouns "he" and "his."

> To succeed, a gardener must fertilize his crop.
> REVISED: To succeed, a gardener must fertilize a crop.

> A college teacher is expected to serve his community.
> REVISED: A college teacher is expected to serve the community.

3. Substitute plural nouns and pronouns for male nouns and pronouns.

> A reporter must cultivate his sources.
> REVISED: Reporters must cultivate their sources.

> A cautious investor will diversify his portfolio.
> REVISED: Cautious investors will diversify their portfolios.

4. Substitute names, descriptions or job titles for male nouns and pronouns.

> Few men are satisfied with their salaries.
> REVISED: Few Americans are satisfied with their salaries.

> A spokesman for the 300 workmen said they expect a strike.
> REVISED: Union leader Marla McKinney said the 300 truck drivers expect a strike.

5. Use a woman's own name, not just her husband's.

> Mrs. Samuel Rothberg received the award.
> REVISED: Carla Rothberg received the award.

> Alan Vazoff arrived with his wife at 9 p.m.
> REVISED: Margaret and Alan Vazoff arrived at 9 p.m.

AVOID STEREOTYPES OF OTHER GROUPS

Journalists are also expected to avoid stereotypes of all minority groups: blacks, Catholics, Vietnam veterans, Indians and the elderly, for example.

Journalists mention a person's race, religion or ethnic background only when that fact is clearly relevant to a story. Typically, employees at The New York Times are told: "The writer—or the characters quoted in the story—must demonstrate the relevance of ethnic background or religion. It isn't enough to assume that readers will find the fact interesting or evocative; experience shows that many will find it offensive and suspect us of relying on stereotypes."

Both students and professionals often report that a "black" or "Hispanic" committed a crime, even in instances when the criminal's race is irrelevant to the story. Moreover, the stories fail to describe a specific individual whom readers might identify for the police. As a result, the stories cast suspicion upon every member of the race. Henry McNulty of the Hartford Courant recently explained that paper's policy in this regard:

> A long-standing Courant policy states that race and sex alone do not constitute an adequate description. For instance, if the only thing a witness tells police is that a "white woman" or "black man" committed the crime, the Courant will not use any description. Only when such things as height, weight, hair length, scars, clothing and so forth are given will the newspaper print the information.

Follow that policy in the stories you write. If you are writing about a crime, for example, mention a person's race only while describing a specific individual whom some of your readers might be able to identify. For example:

> Witnesses said the bank robber was a white male, about 50 years old and 6 feet tall. He weighed about 250 pounds, was wearing a blue suit and escaped on a Honda motorcycle.

Veterans' organizations have accused the media of encouraging another negative stereotype of the men and women who served in Vietnam as violent and unstable. The media, critics explain, sometimes report that a person charged with a serious crime is "a Vietnam veteran," regardless of the fact's relevance.

Other stories demean Native Americans. Avoid such words as "wampum," "warpath," "powwow," "tepee," "brave" and "squaw" in stories about Indians.

Most stereotypes of the elderly are negative, suggesting that older Americans are all alike: lonely, inactive, unproductive, poor, passive, weak and sick. In fact, more than 50 million Americans are over the age of 50. Most are still active, and some are quite wealthy. When asked to describe their health, a majority respond that it is "good" to "excellent." Yet television programs often portray the elderly as eccentric, foolish, forgetful, sick and unproductive. Similarly, news stories express surprise when older people buy a sports car, fall in love, or remain alert, healthy, innovative and productive.

ARE YOU A SEXIST? DO YOU:

- Mention the marital status of women, but not men?
- Describe women in greater physical detail than the men you write about?
- Refer to adult women as "girls," "gals" or "ladies" but to males as "men"?
- Use the words "female," "lady" and "woman" as occupational modifiers, as in "female doctor," "lady carpenter" and "woman architect"?
- Call women by their first names and men by their last names in similar contexts?
- Call women by their husbands' names (for example: "Mrs. Karl Rudnick")?
- Identify women as "wives" when you do not refer to men as "husbands" in similar contexts?
- Exclude women from occupational categories by using words ending in "man" (business<u>man</u>, con-gress<u>man</u>, repair<u>man</u>)?

REVIEW: WRITING SIMPLY, CLEARLY AND FAIRLY

Before beginning the exercises on the following pages, review these examples and guidelines.

A key to good writing is simplicity. When people speak, they use simple words and simple sentences. Yet many people seem unable to write that way. Instead, their language becomes more formal and stilted when they write. For example:

> Can you afford me the opportunity to visit with you?
> REVISED: Can I visit you?

> He patterned it after programs successfully implemented in Germany.
> REVISED: He copied successful German programs.

Mistakenly, students often begin their sentences with a long clause. The longer the clause, the more unreadable their sentences become because the most important information—the news—is usually buried near the end:

> Scheduled to appear in court at 9 a.m. today for the death of an 8-year-old girl, a man hanged himself in the county jail last night.
> REVISED: A man charged with the death of an 8-year-old girl hanged himself in the county jail last night. He was scheduled to appear in court at 9 a.m. today.

> Calling NASA's practice of flying thousands of guests to Florida to watch its shuttle launches "one of the most expensive and wasteful public relations campaigns in the history of the federal government," Sen. William Proxmire demanded that it be stopped.
> REVISED: Sen. William Proxmire demanded that NASA stop flying thousands of guests to Florida to watch its shuttle launches. He called it "one of the most expensive and wasteful public relations campaigns in the history of the federal government."

Also be certain that you are writing as concisely as possible. Delete words that are repetitious or that state the obvious:

> The boys were in the water swimming together.
> REVISED: The boys were swimming together.

> The police do not have any suspects at this point in time.
> REVISED: The police have no suspects.

You can often substitute a single word for a longer phrase:

> She began to scream at the intruder.
> REVISED: She screamed at the intruder.

> The accident resulted in the death of one man.
> REVISED: The accident killed one man.

Some experts advise writers to present only one idea in each sentence. However, that may be an extreme remedy. Instead, present only a few *related* ideas in each sentence. If a sentence contains too many ideas, eliminate some or start a new sentence:

> Eighty percent of the education majors who took the test last month passed all four parts, with women having an 82 percent passing rate compared to 76 percent for men.
> REVISED: Eighty percent of the education majors who took the test last month passed all four parts. Eighty-two percent of the women passed the test, compared to 76 percent of the men.

> Neighbors said that, at about 5:15 p.m., they heard Thomas Rawl and his girlfriend, Jean Marie Simkell, begin to argue in the front yard of a home

they shared at 3168 Whisper Lake Lane, and they saw Rawl get a gun from his car, shoot Simkell, and then shoot himself, both fatally.

REVISED: Neighbors said they saw Thomas Rawl get a gun from his car and shoot and kill his girlfriend, Jean Marie Simkell, and then kill himself. Rawl and Simkell shared a home at 3168 Whisper Lake Lane. Neighbors said the couple had begun to argue in the front yard at about 5:15 p.m.

Finally, remember to remain objective. Report facts, not your opinion:

The school's athletic program is well-rounded, with 26 sports offered for men and 14 offered for women.
REVISED: The school offers 26 sports for men and 14 for women.

The lengthy 137-page report contains some interesting facts about cancer.
REVISED: The 137-page report discusses cancer.

REVIEW QUESTIONS

As you begin to write news stories, ask yourself the following questions. If you answer "no" to any of the questions, you may have to edit or rewrite your story.

1. Have I used short, familiar words?
2. Have I used short sentences and short paragraphs?
3. Have I eliminated unnecessary words?
4. Have I avoided statements of opinion?
5. Have I avoided overloading my sentences? Does each sentence contain only a few *related* ideas?
6. Finally—and perhaps most important—have I used relatively simple sentences, with the normal word order: subject, verb, direct object?

Newsman Lou Bate and his colleagues on the city desk of the Deseret News in Salt Lake City compiled these examples of wordy phrases which appeared in their newspaper:

held a meeting	should be trimmed to	**met**
was a winner of	should be trimmed to	**won**
voted to appoint	should be trimmed to	**appointed**
was the recipient of	should be trimmed to	**received**
is presently studying	should be trimmed to	**is studying**
made a denouncement of	should be trimmed to	**denounced**
will give a lecture on	should be trimmed to	**will lecture on**
made a $10,000 donation	should be trimmed to	**donated $10,000**
conduct an evaluation of	should be trimmed to	**evaluate**
have come to a compromise	should be trimmed to	**have compromised**
come into compliance with	should be trimmed to	**comply with**
gave its tentative approval	should be trimmed to	**tentatively approved**
several members of the public	should be trimmed to	**several people**

TIPS FROM A PRO

"Some lucky stiffs, whom you will learn to envy if you're not one of them, have the facility for swift, painless writing. Others, the majority I believe—and you may count me in—find writing a labored agony of mental sweat. They figuratively have to flog themselves into starting, and they love it only for the satisfaction of having done it, never for any joy in doing it."

"Of course there is bad newspaper writing. There is terrible newspaper writing, just as there are terrible magazine stories and terrible books. But considering the speed and quantity with which they are produced, newspaper stories deserve a pretty high rating. . . . Some of the finest writing I have ever read has been in newspapers."

"Always, when time permits, read your story before submitting it. If you can't cut out at least a couple of words, you're not doing a sufficiently critical job of reading. One of the toughest things in the writing trade, and one of the best for a writer, is to cut your own copy."

"Don't try to increase your vocabulary, either. Decrease it. The only time a new word is worth using is when it will take the place of three or four others, and then don't try to use it fresh from the dictionary. Wait until you've become familiar with it by hearing or seeing it used. A thesaurus is a curse; don't have one in your desk. If it's handy, it will tempt you to use too many obscure words."

"The new reporter is always prone to use such words as 'contusions and abrasions,' which don't mean as much to the reader as 'cuts and bruises.'"

"One well-chosen verb packs more power than a string of adjectives and adverbs."

(From the book "Newspaperman" by Morton Sontheimer)

SUGGESTED READINGS

Articles

Bourgeois, Bea. "She 'Fainted'; He 'Passed Out': And Other Oddities from the Wonderful World of Language." *The Quill,* Feb. 1990, pp. 40–43.

Bray, Tom. "A Matter of Opinion: On Too Many Newspapers, Too Many Pages Are Editorial Pages." *ASNE Bulletin,* Oct. 1990, pp. 20–21.

Catalano, Kevin. "On the Wire: How Six News Services Are Exceeding Readability Standards." *Journalism Quarterly*, 67, No. 1 (Spring 1990), pp. 97–100.

Healy, Jane. "How Readable Are Our Newspapers?" *ASNE Bulletin,* Oct. 1990, pp. 18–19.

McNulty, Henry. "The Pros and Cons of Using Ethnicity in Police Stories." *Editor & Publisher*, 4 May 1991, p. 28.

Rykken, Rolf. "New Tactics Mark the Push for Accuracy." *Presstime,* July 1991, pp. 6–8.

Shaw, David. "Abortion Bias Seeps into News." *Los Angeles Times,* 1 July 1991. (Reprinted in pamphlet form.)

———. "East Coast Bias Colors the Media." *Los Angeles Times,* 17 Nov. 1988. (Reprinted in pamphlet form.)

———. "Press and Ferraro: A Case Study." *Los Angeles Times,* 5 Dec. 1984. (Reprinted in pamphlet form.)

Books

Barzun, Jacques. *Simple & Direct: A Rhetoric for Writers*. Rev. ed. New York: Harper & Row, 1985.

Bernstein, Theodore M. *Dos, Don'ts, and Maybes of English Usage*. New York: Times Books, 1977.

———. *More Language That Needs Watching*. New York: Atheneum, 1962.

———. *Watch Your Language*. New York: Atheneum, 1981.

Burack, Sylvia K., ed. *The Writer's Handbook*. 5th ed. Boston: The Writer, 1986.

Cheney, Theodore A. *Getting the Words Right: How to Revise, Edit and Rewrite*. Cincinnati: Writer's Digest Books, 1983.

Flocke, Lynne, Dona Hayes and Anna L. Babic. *Journalism and the Aging Population: Covering the Story*. Syracuse, NY: Syracuse University Series in Gerontology Education. Center for Instructional Development, Syracuse University, 1990.

Gibson, Martin L. *The Writer's Friend*. Ames, IA: Iowa State University Press, 1989.

Grey, David L. *The Writing Process*. Belmont, CA: Wadsworth, 1972.

Hohenberg, John. *Concise Newswriting*. New York: Hastings House, 1987.

———. *The Pulitzer Prize Story*. New York: Columbia University Press, 1959.

Newman, Edwin. *A Civil Tongue*. New York: Warner Books, 1976.

———. *Strictly Speaking*. New York: Warner Books, 1974.

Reporting on People with Disabilities. Washington, DC: Disabilities Committee of the American Society of Newspaper Editors, American Society of Newspaper Editors, 1990.

Rivers, William L. *Writing: Craft and Art*. Englewood Cliffs, NJ: Prentice Hall, 1975.

Sale, Roger. *On Writing*. New York: Random House, 1970.

Shaw, Harry. *Twenty Steps to Better Writing*. Totowa, NJ: Littlefield, Adams, 1978.

Yates, Edward D. *The Writing Craft*. 2nd ed. Raleigh, NC: Contemporary Publishing, 1985.

Zinsser, William. *On Writing Well: An Informal Guide to Writing Nonfiction*. 4th ed. New York: Perennial Library, 1990.

QUOTES

The press is the best instrument for enlightening the mind of man, and improving him as a rational, moral and social being.

(Thomas Jefferson)

An Ombudsman's Report

CASE STUDY NO. 1

By **Pat O. Riley**
Ombudsman
The Orange County (Calif.) Register

Mrs. Q. was distressed, angry, incredulous. Her voice trembling, she was unable to control her rage as she complained to the newspaper's ombudsman.

> What gives you people the right to quote my fifth-grade daughter without my permission? Do you realize the harm you've done, the trouble you've caused among the families involved? You have made enemies of former friends.

Well! Another thin-skinned reader unjustifiably accusing the messenger of victimizing the innocent?

Not at all.

A teacher had been accused of molesting students. A judge dismissed two charges against the teacher, and a jury acquitted him of two other charges after several teachers testified that the girls who accused him of the crime were chronic troublemakers. The child was quoted—and named—in a follow-up report.

The follow-up story reported that, "Outside the school Friday, some students and parents also claimed that the four girls were known troublemakers." The story then quoted the fifth-grader indirectly as saying that the girls who made the accusations often talked in class, spoke out without being called on, passed notes and played annoying pranks on other students.

The fifth-grader's mother said she found it difficult to believe that a newspaper would publish the opinions of a child in such a serious matter without asking the child's parents or even school officials whether they had any objections to the interview.

The indirect quotes, she said, had upset the families of the girls who accused the teacher, needlessly creating ill feelings between them and her family.

She felt, in short, that she and her family had been ambushed by the newspaper. A perfectly understandable reaction.

The situation was unusual, of course. Children aren't often quoted on issues of such importance. The question: At what age or grade level does a person become mature enough to offer comment for publication without approval from anyone else?

The answer is necessarily arbitrary, of course, but within hours of the complaint from the fifth-grader's mother, the editor of our newspaper issued a policy statement: children under high school age are not to be quoted on matters of controversy without parental permission.

(continued on next page)

Pat O. Riley has served as the ombudsman at The Orange County Register in Santa Ana, Calif., since 1981. Before that, he says, he lurked in the newsrooms of four papers (two in Texas, one in Ohio, then California), for 25 years, mostly in supervisory positions. He is a past president of the Organization of News Ombudsmen, an international (but small) organization.

That didn't help Mrs. Q. and her family, of course, but it's a positive step to avoid a similar problem in the future.

***

Newspaper readers, after eons of relative passivity, of accepting with minimum grumbling whatever editors dished out, are speaking out, demanding higher standards, seeking to get involved in the process.

And newspapers—at least some of them—are listening. Finally, they're treating readers as valued customers. Some are making an extraordinary effort and investing considerable financial resources to make themselves accessible to their customers. Some—though the numbers are not yet staggering—have hired ombudsmen to hear—and, when appropriate, act on—reader concerns involving accuracy, fairness and balance in the news. A few ombudsmen also deal with complaints regarding advertising and circulation.

Only about 35 newspapers in the United States employ ombudsmen (some are called ''reader representatives,'' ''reader advocates'' or ''public editors''). But, since most newspapers with these offices are quite large, a substantial number of newspaper readers in this country is served by ombudsmen.

Although it's no small expense to add an ombudsman, newspapers can use all the help they can get when the great number and variety of reader complaints are taken into consideration (and taken seriously).

In addition to the normal—and constant—complaints about the inaccuracy of our television magazine (TV stations and networks are forever changing their programming at the last minute) and what readers see as our abysmal ignorance of grammar and spelling, ombudsmen come to expect unusual issues and events. A few at our newspaper:

- We've been victimized by plagiarists (one free-lance writer purloined a story written by Truman Capote and tried to sell it to us and other newspapers as a current travel piece; one of our readers flagged the caper, and we killed the free-lancer's check. He bore no hard feelings and sent us holiday greetings from São Paulo, Brazil.
- We've had to correct corrections. Embarrassing.
- We've had to deal with serious questions of whether to identify a 14-year-old charged with rape and murder (we did) and whether to identify rape victims (we don't).
- Once a feature editor decided to ask readers, in a small headline, to ''Send us your favorite graffiti'' for publication in the paper. Readers were outraged. One said the newspaper might as well invite ''Your favorite vandalism.'' The paper got the message. The next little headline on the subject advised readers: ''Do not send us your favorite graffiti sayings.''
- The owner of a frozen yogurt company denied a quotation attributed to her. The quotation stated that business rivals were envious of her body.

Then there are complaints about suggestive advertisements (bikini contests, ''hot cream wrestling,'' adult gift sales, spas), dropped comics, Pisces missing from the horoscope and, of course, Mrs. Peabody's paper was soaked by the only rain showers we've had in five years, and . . .

Well, call the ombudsman.

Exercise 1

NEWSWRITING STYLE

DISCUSSION QUESTIONS

1. Imagine that you have just been named editor of your city's daily newspaper. Formulate a policy that specifies when your staff can state that a person is "adopted," "illegitimate" or "on welfare."
2. Imagine that your city elected a new mayor today, and that the mayor never met his father, or even knew his identity. Rather, the mayor was raised by his mother, who never married. Would you report that fact while describing the new mayor? Why or why not?
3. If a bank in your city today became the first to name a woman as its president, should your local daily publish a story about her promotion? Why or why not? Should your newspaper publish stories when the first women are named to head a local college, a local hospital and a local police department?
4. If you interviewed the coach of a women's basketball team at your school, and the coach referred to his players as "my girls," would you use the term in your story? Would it matter whether you used the term in a direct quotation?
5. Can you think of any satisfactory, nonsexist substitutes for these words?

    A. fisherman
    B. freshman
    C. gunman
    D. manhole
    E. sportsman

6. Think of your favorite television programs. What percentage of the characters on the programs are elderly, and how are they portrayed—as stereotypes or as individuals?

Exercise 2

NEWSWRITING STYLE

READABILITY

1. Read some of the columns written by the following journalists. Compare the number of words in their average sentences.

   A. Ann Landers
   B. Mike Royko
   C. George Will
   D. William Safire

2. Compare the number of words in *your* average sentence with the number of words in the sentences written by the columnists listed in question 1.

3. Calculate your stories' readability, or grade level. Here are the steps to follow:

   STEP ONE:

   A. Count the first 100 words in your most recent story.
   B. Count the number of sentences. If more than half the final sentence is within the sample, count it as a whole sentence. Also, treat clearly independent clauses as separate sentences.
   C. To determine your average sentence length, divide 100 by the number of sentences in your sample.

   STEP TWO:

   Count the number of words with three or more syllables, including repeated words. Do not count capitalized words, combinations of short, easy words ("bookkeeper") or verbs ending in "ed" or "es."

   STEP THREE:

   Add the figures from steps 1 and 2 and multiply by .4 to determine the approximate grade level for your writing. For greater accuracy, calculate the readability of at least three of your stories.

Average number of words per sentence	+	Number of three-syllable words	× .4 =	Grade level

4. For one week, examine every story published on the front page of your local daily. What percentage of the bylines are men's, and what percentage are women's?

5. For one week, examine every story published on the front page of your local daily. Circle the name of every person mentioned in the stories. What percentage of the people are men, and what percentage are women? Explain your findings.

6. For one week, examine every photograph published on the front page of your local daily. What percentage of the photographs show a woman? Also, what percentage of the photographs show a man by himself, and what percentage of the photographs show a woman by herself? What other differences do you notice in the way the photographs portray men and women?

NAME _____ CLASS _____ DATE _____

Exercise 3

NEWSWRITING STYLE

SEXISM

SECTION I: AVOIDING SEXIST TITLES AND TERMS

Replace these titles and terms with words that include women as well as men.

1. businessman	6. fatherly	11. paperboy
2. chairman	7. founding fathers	12. repairman
3. congressman	8. man	13. salesman
4. craftsman	9. mankind	14. statesman
5. fatherland	10. man-sized	15. workman

SECTION II: AVOIDING EXCLUSIVELY MALE NOUNS AND PRONOUNS

Rewrite the following sentences, eliminating their use of exclusively male nouns and pronouns.

1. A reporter is expected to protect his sources.
2. A good athlete often jogs to build his endurance.
3. Normally, every auto mechanic buys his own tools.
4. No one knows which of the nation's congressmen leaked the details to his wife and friends.
5. If a patient is clearly dying of cancer, doctors may give him enough drugs to ease his pain, and perhaps even enough to hasten his death.

SECTION III: AVOIDING STEREOTYPES

Rewrite the following sentences, eliminating their sexist language and comments.

1. Randy Ortiz married his wife seven years ago.
2. Tom Yapengco and his wife urged their son, James, to act like a man.
3. A male nurse, Richard Diaz, and his wife, an authoress, arrived today.
4. Lois Zarrrinfar, who never married, is 73 and the daughter of a famous poetess.
5. The banks chairman said that the average depositor has $3,248 in his savings account.
6. The two married ladies, both trim redheads, are serving as the programs co-chairmen.
7. The city fathers announced that 10 men and 4 females, all clergymen, will serve on the board.
8. The store sells toys of all types, from guns and chemistry sets for boys to dolls and beauty kits for girls.
9. Although a wife and the mother of four, Mrs. Henry Conaho, a slender blonde, is also president of the community college.
10. A spokesman for the company announced that it has reached a gentlemans agreement with the sportsmen on their use of the woods.

NAME _____ CLASS _____ DATE _____

Exercise 4
NEWSWRITING STYLE

BEING CONCISE

SECTION I: USING SIMPLE WORDS

Substitute simpler and more common words for each of these words.

1. altercation	6. community	11. purchase
2. assistance	7. incarcerate	12. reimburse
3. apprehend	8. intoxicated	13. relocate
4. attempt	9. lacerations	14. request
5. commence	10. ordinance	15. residence

SECTION II: AVOIDING REDUNDANT PHRASES

The following phrases do not have to be rewritten; simply cross out their unnecessary words.

1. are in need of	6. future plans	11. is presently
2. are now	7. hanged to death	12. now costs
3. are presently	8. head up	13. seek to find
4. brilliant genius	9. honest truth	14. totally destroyed
5. first discovered	10. in an effort to	15. whether or not

SECTION III: AVOIDING WORDY PHRASES

Use a single word to replace each of these phrases.

1. absence of danger	6. get underway	11. made a contribution
2. are in agreement	7. in the course of	12. made their exit
3. at present	8. is hopeful that	13. posed a question
4. gave chase to	9. made the ruling	14. proceeded to leave
5. gave their approval	10. made their escape	15. short distance away

SECTION IV: ELIMINATING UNNECESSARY WORDS

Eliminate the unnecessary words from the following sentences. The sentences do not have to be rewritten; simply cross out the excess words.

1. Anyone may participate if they would like to.
2. Before the robbers left, they also took some liquor.
3. At the present time, about 100 students participate.
4. The results showed that only 31 percent passed the test.
5. Firefighters reached the scene and extinguished the blaze.

SECTION V: REWRITING WORDY SENTENCES

Rewrite the following sentences, eliminating as many words as possible.

1. He said the cost of putting on the program will be about $500.
2. The police officer opened fire, shooting six times at the suspect.
3. Sanchez was taken to Memorial Hospital and is in fair condition there.
4. They told the midwife that there was not much time left before the baby was due.
5. Of the 10 stock car drivers interviewed, eight felt like it is inevitable that you are going to have some injuries and deaths among the people participating in their races.

SECTION VI: SIMPLIFYING OVERLOADED SENTENCES

The following sentences are too long and complicated. Divide them into simpler, more concise sentences.

1. Two high school students, Joan Harnish and Sara Courhesne, were driving north on Carpenter Road at 10:20 p.m. when they came around a sharp curve in the road and noticed a wrecked motorcycle and, about 25 feet away, a man, about 20 years of age—apparently seriously injured—sprawled near a telephone pole.

2. In a 122-page report, the Department of Health and Human Services stated that drunken driving causes 28,000 traffic deaths a year, costing the nation $45 billion, and that nearly 9 million persons suffer from alcoholism or lesser drinking problems, a number that represents 10 percent of the U.S. work force.

3. A Colonial High School student, Cynthia Allersen, who was driving the car, a teachers new Buick, was taking four other high school students, including three exchange students from Germany, to a nearby shopping mall when another car smashed broadside into her vehicle at the intersection of Polle Street and Fuller Road, seriously injuring two of the exchange students.

NAME _____ CLASS _____ DATE _____

Exercise 5

NEWSWRITING STYLE

TESTING ALL YOUR SKILLS

SECTION I: AVOIDING REDUNDANT PHRASES

The following phrases are redundant. They do not have to be rewritten; simply cross out the unnecessary words.

1. brand new	6. jail facility	11. right now
2. combine together	7. join together	12. small in size
3. continue on	8. new discovery	13. true facts
4. crowd of people	9. past experience	14. unpaid debt
5. foreign imports	10. personal friend	15. won a victory

SECTION II: AVOIDING SEXUAL STEREOTYPES

Rewrite the following sentences, eliminating their sexist language and comments.

1. A California man and his wife attended the reunion.
2. The bus driver, a divorced lady, was blamed for the accident.
3. While the girls were playing tennis, their husbands were playing golf.
4. While her husband works, Valerie Dawkins raises their children and dabbles in politics.
5. Mrs. John Favata is a widow, 56 years old and a petite grandmother, but she still plays tennis five days a week and today won the citys Senior Women's Tournament.

SECTION III: REMAINING OBJECTIVE

The following sentences do not have to be rewritten. Simply cross out the opinionated words and phrases.

1. Only seven of the 94 people aboard the ill-fated plane were killed.
2. The boy's grief-stricken father says he intends to sue the prestigious school.
3. In an important speech Monday, the governor said the state must adopt needed laws to protect the unfortunate victims.
4. Eighty-six students miraculously escaped injury when an alert pedestrian noticed the flames and quickly warned them to leave.
5. One of the most interesting facts he revealed was that the Chinese replace each barrel of oil with one barrel of water to ensure that all their oil is pumped out of the ground.

SECTION IV: ELIMINATING UNNECESSARY WORDS

Eliminate the unnecessary words from the following sentences. The sentences do not have to be rewritten; simply cross out the excess words.

1. Since the inception of the program it has saved three lives.
2. The boy was submerged under the water for about five minutes.

3. He was pinned in the car for 40 minutes before he could be removed.
4. The engineer said that, in her opinion, relatively few people actually use the road.
5. The center will have a total of eight separate offices for different ministers to occupy.

SECTION V: AVOIDING WORDY PHRASES

Substitute a single word for the wordy phrases in the following sentences.

1. The gunman made off with about $700.
2. Her medical bills are in excess of $35,000.
3. The operation left him in a state of paralysis.
4. The new law will no longer allow tinted car windows.
5. Margaret Van Den Shruck addressed her speech to the Rotary Club.

SECTION VI: SIMPLIFYING SENTENCES

Rewrite the following sentences more simply and clearly.

1. He was the recipient of numerous awards and honors.
2. The police were then summoned to the park by a girl.
3. She said that their farm is in close proximity to the park.
4. Snow-removal vehicles are undertaking a cleanup of the city.
5. They said that a visit to their grandmother's was where they were going.

SECTION VII: TESTING ALL YOUR SKILLS

Rewrite the following sentences, correcting all their errors.

1. They reached a settlement of the debt.
2. Applications must be submitted on or before the deadline date of March 1.
3. A total of eight qualified persons, four men and four females, served on the important committee.
4. They mayor said that, at the present time, she is favorably disposed towards the passage of the important new law.
5. When questioned by the police, the suspect, an unidentified juvenile, maintained that he had been drinking and had no recollection at all of the events that transpired on that tragic Saturday night in question.

NAME _____ CLASS _____ DATE _____

Exercise 6

NEWSWRITING STYLE

TESTING ALL YOUR SKILLS

SECTION I: AVOIDING REDUNDANT PHRASES

The following phrases do not have to be rewritten; simply cross out the unnecessary words.

1. at a later date	6. future goals	11. referred back to
2. abolish altogether	7. hung down from	12. sent away for
3. are currently	8. in order for	13. set a new record
4. first became	9. mental anguish	14. sum of $600
5. free of charge	10. personal habit	15. they both agreed

SECTION II: AVOIDING WORDY PHRASES

Use a single word to replace each of these phrases.

1. adversely affected	4. caused injuries to	7. is in need of
2. came to a halt	5. free of wordiness	8. proceeded to go
3. caused damage to	6. in advance of	9. were aware of

SECTION III: AVOIDING SEXUAL STEREOTYPES

Rewrite the following sentences, eliminating their sexist language and comments.

1. Mike Deacosta, his wife and their two children, Mark and Amy, served as the hosts.
2. Councilman Alice Cycler, the attractive wife of a lawyer and mother of eight girls, is fighting to improve the citys parks.
3. In addition to raising their four children and caring for their home, Nikki Evans has also succeeded as a banker. Today she was promoted to vice president.
4. An attractive young blonde, Elaine Gardepe, seems to be an unlikely person to write a book about the topic, yet her book about auto mechanics has become a best seller.
5. She is a quiet woman, but the 52-year-old divorcee has a reputation for being an aggressive competitor. Last year she sold more homes than any other salesman in the city.

SECTION IV: REMAINING OBJECTIVE

Rewrite the following sentences, eliminating their expressions of opinion.

1. Rudely, the two sullen-looking boys got up and left.
2. His provocative speech was well received, as he was interrupted 17 times by applause.

3. They announced that residents of the city can look forward to the construction of a beautiful new $4.1 million library next year.
4. Another important concept is the author's startling idea that it does not matter whether children begin to read before they are 10 years old.
5. It should be kept in mind, however, that with the interstate highway only 5 miles away, the facility is easily accessible to all the residents of the state.

SECTION V: AVOIDING UNNECESSARY WORDS

Delete the unnecessary words from the following sentences; do not rewrite the sentences.

1. He is currently serving time in prison.
2. The men were in the process of painting a house when they fell.
3. What the group opposed was legislation that would totally ban nudity.
4. The university is currently in the process of building a new stadium.
5. They said that a major problem with the program is that it is now too expensive.

SECTION VI: SIMPLIFYING SENTENCES

Rewrite the following sentences as clearly and simply as possible.

1. They fear that its effects may be detrimental.
2. They extended an invitation to her to join their sorority.
3. Anonymous sources are perceived as unreliable by the public.
4. The enclosed résumé will give you an idea of my training and experience.
5. Another person who saw what was happening said the arrests will serve as a deterrent to other lawless criminals.

SECTION VII: SIMPLIFYING OVERLOADED SENTENCES

Rewrite each of the following sentences, dividing them into two or more shorter, simpler sentences.

1. The injured boy was taken to Mercy Hospital where a spokesman said the youth, who is from Seattle Washington, was in serious condition with a gunshot wound to the chest accidentally fired by a friend with a .22 caliber revolver they found in a box.
2. The man, described by witnesses as about 30, slender, white, and bald, leaped from a blue Ford car at about 3 p.m., grabbed a vinyl bag being carried by Max Butler, then shot him three times, fatally wounding him, before escaping with the bag that contained an estimated $10,000 that Butler, a courier for the First National Bank, had picked up from a Realtor.
3. The chase, which reached speeds of 80 miles an hour, ended when the Pontiac struck two other cars on Holton Drive, where the police arrested the Pontiacs driver, identified as Lynn R. Pryor, and charged her with armed robbery, reckless driving and fleeing to elude capture following an incident in which a convenience store on Mercy Dr. was robbed of less than $20 shortly after 6 a.m. this morning.

NAME _____ CLASS _____ DATE _____

Exercise 7

Answer Key Provided: See Appendix D

NEWSWRITING STYLE

REVIEW

SECTION I: REMAINING OBJECTIVE

Rewrite the following sentences, eliminating all their statements of opinion and other errors.

1. Students may find it worth their time to attend the 15th annual Pre-Law Day scheduled for Nov. 3 at the Student Center.
2. Speaking with great confidence, the attractive young woman did not hesitate to tell the crowd that she favors abortions.
3. The famous school, established 10 years ago, has scheduled a lavish banquet to celebrate its first decade of success.

SECTION II: AVOIDING REDUNDANT PHRASES

The following phrases are redundant. They do not have to be rewritten; simply cross out the unnecessary words:

1. actual facts
2. close down
3. dead bodies
4. dropped downward
5. first began
6. free gifts
7. in order to
8. new innovation
9. past history
10. revert back to
11. right here
12. tracked down
13. very unique
14. winter months
15. young child

SECTION III: AVOIDING WORDY PHRASES

Substitute a single word for each of the following phrases.

1. came to a stop
2. did not pay attention to
3. due to the fact that
4. in advance of
5. in the near future
6. in the vicinity of
7. is in possession of
8. made an investigation of
9. took under consideration
10. united in holy matrimony

SECTION IV: AVOIDING UNNECESSARY WORDS

The following sentences do not have to be rewritten. Simply cross out their unnecessary words.

1. The city council voted to go ahead and sue the builders.
2. The accident occurred when a pickup truck collided with a car.
3. There is a possibility that the sign may be installed sometime later this month.
4. When the police arrived at the scene, they found only an empty box, not a bomb.
5. Police responding to the call found that the assailants had kicked him in the face, head and neck.

SECTION V: TESTING ALL YOUR SKILLS

Rewrite the following sentences, correcting all their errors.

1. He suffered the loss of his right eye.
2. The debt was then not nearly so large as it is today.
3. He criticized the president, calling him inconsistent and unrealistic.
4. The politician extended his appreciation to those who had supported him.
5. The purpose of this article will be to examine the problems of migrant workers.
6. Before a young child reaches the age of 18, he will see a total of 20,000 acts of violence on the tube.
7. The consensus of opinion among participants in the workshop is that it should be up to the governor to decide how to expend the funds.
8. It was brought out at the conference that the terms of the agreement are not in accordance with the desires of the people of Israel.
9. The 62-year-old spinster, the daughter of retired judge Myron Hanson, does not look the part but has become an expert on criminal law.
10. At a party given in her honor on the day of her retirement, co-workers celebrated the occasion by presenting the librarian with a trip to Paris.

CHAPTER 3

WORDS

It can be amusing when a student in elementary or high school makes an error while writing or speaking. Adults are tolerant of such errors because they are seldom serious and only a few people are likely to hear or see them. Many of these errors occur because students are still developing their vocabularies and use the wrong word, as in the following sentences, written by high school students:

Socrates died from an overdose of wedlock.

A horse divided against itself cannot stand.

Floods can be prevented by putting dames in the river.

The following errors are similar but were written by college students:

Education is important, as you well no.

Gothic architecture is distinguished by flying buttocks.

Another method of getting rid of trash is incarceration.

The players returned to the court when the buzzard sounded.

Other errors, as in the following examples, arise because students fail to think and to express their ideas clearly and precisely. As a result, some of their sentences state the obvious (or impossible). Others may have unintended, often comical, meanings:

Rural life is found mostly in the country.

The death of Francis Macomber was a turning point in his life.

Women are the predominant victims of discrimination against their sex.

Ask the dead man if it matters as to what killed him. See what he says. I do not think he will care.

That summer I finally got my leg operated on, and what a relief! It had been hanging over my head for years.

Theodore Roosevelt was saddened when his young wife died and went to a ranch in the Dakotas.

If you could but experience the dirt, the noise and the degradation on the assembly line, then you would understand why the American factory worker is revolting.

People expect better than this from college students—especially from journalism students, whose work requires a mastery of the English language. Moreover, the errors made by college students can be costly as well as embarrassing, as when errors are made by college students who submit their work to a campus newspaper or radio or television station. Instructors also fear that students who develop bad habits in college will continue to make the same types of errors while working for the media after graduation.

The thousands of men and women who devote their lives to journalism develop a respect for the language. They learn to write with precision: clearly, concisely and accurately. They select the exact word needed to convey an idea and place it in a sentence that is grammatically correct.

When those professionals hire a new reporter, they look for someone who has mastered the language: someone who understands the language's usage and treats it with respect; who possesses a knowledge of spelling and grammar; who has developed an extensive vocabulary; and who has learned to write in a clear and interesting manner.

Journalists' emphasis on precision is essential to the media's success. The public expects the media to be accurate and to use the language properly. If a writer is careless, an editor will have to spend extra time correcting that writer's stories. Inevitably, some of the writer's errors will appear in print, and thousands of readers may notice and laugh at them. If the errors become too numerous, they may damage a newspaper's reputation and credibility. The errors may also require the paper to publish costly and embarrassing corrections. To avoid the problem, editors give spelling, vocabulary and writing tests to job applicants and hire only those who score the highest.

BE PRECISE

To communicate effectively, reporters must be precise, particularly in their selection of words. Imprecision creates confusion and misunderstanding. Thomas Berry, author of "The Craft of Writing," explains that the difference between mediocre writing and excellent writing is often the choice of words, and that the perfect choice can change the meaning of an entire sentence. The perfect choice also makes sentences more forceful and interesting.

Some words are simply inappropriate for use in news stories. Few editors permit the use of words such as "cop" or "kid" (unless you are referring to a goat), or derogatory terms about a person's race or religion. Editors allow profanity only when it is essential to a story's meaning and, even then, refuse to publish the most offensive terms. They prefer the word "woman" to the archaic "lady." Many ban the use of contractions, except in direct quotations. Editors also object to nouns used as verbs.

They would not allow you to report that someone "authored" a book, "detailed" a plan, "hosted" a party, "headquartered" a company, "impacted" a community or "gunned" a victim. Nor would they allow you to report that food prices were "upped," plans "finalized" or speeding cars "sirened" to a halt.

Sometimes an error occurs because the reporter is unaware of a word's exact meaning. Few newspapers would report that a car "collided" with a tree, that a "funeral service" was held, that a gunman "executed" his victim or that a child "was drowned" in a lake. Why? Two objects can be said to collide only if both are moving; thus, a car can strike a tree, but never collide with one. The term "funeral service" is redundant. "Executed" means put to death in accordance with a legally imposed sentence; therefore, only a state—never a murderer—can execute anyone. A report that a child "was drowned" would imply that someone held the child's head underwater until the victim died.

Such considerations may seem trivial, but journalists strive for perfection in their choice of words. If they do not, they may confuse or irritate their readers. Thus, your instructors will object if your use of the language is sloppy and inaccurate, as in these examples:

> She turned on her windshield wipers and defroster.

> The youth produced a pistol and threatened the cashier.

> Paramedics took the victim to a hospital with minor cuts and bruises.

A driver may turn on her car's windshield wipers and defroster, but not her own. A robber may "draw" or "display" a pistol, but is unlikely to produce (that is, manufacture) one in the midst of a robbery. Only a victim—not a hospital—can suffer cuts and bruises.

Sentences and paragraphs become awkward and even nonsensical when writers fail to express their ideas with clarity and precision. The worst examples are not only garbled, but inaccurate. Fortunately, that type of error is easy to correct:

> She received a limp.
> REVISED: She suffered a broken leg and now walks with a limp.

> The campus police are open 24 hours a day.
> REVISED: The campus police station is open 24 hours a day.

> The kitchen of a local restaurant caught fire Tuesday but caused little damage.
> REVISED: A fire that started in the kitchen of a local restaurant Tuesday caused little damage.

Before it was rewritten, the third sentence suggested that the kitchen, not the fire, caused the damage.

Other sentences have double meanings that are often difficult to detect. In rare cases, the confusion is deliberate. One example involves an advertisement for a new carburetor guaranteed to improve a vehicle's mileage. The last line in the advertisement promised, "If not satisfactory, money will be returned." Some customers were dissatisfied with the carburetor and asked for their money back. The company refused, and a note it sent to those customers explained: "So far all money we have received has been satisfactory."

In contrast, double meanings in news stories are unintentional. Because reporters have failed to express their ideas clearly and precisely, readers derive a different meaning from the intended one. Double meanings in the following headlines, all of which actually appeared in newspapers, illustrate the problem:

Albany Turns to Garbage

Squad Helps Dog Bite Victim

Milk Drinkers Turn to Powder

Drunk Gets Nine Months in Violin Case

American Sentenced to Life in Scotland

Juvenile Court to Try Shooting Defendant

Death Causes Loneliness, Feelings of Isolation

Readers often consider double meanings humorous. Few editors, however, are amused when the errors appear in their newspapers. Yet they occasionally appear in even the best newspapers. Here is an example from The New York Times:

The State Health Department is surveying hospitals around the state to ascertain whether women patients are being given pap tests to determine if they have uterine cancer as required by law.

Confusion often arises because words look or sound similar. For example, a recent story reported that, "About 40 years ago, she left her native Cypress for New York City and set up a bakery on Ninth Avenue near 40th Street." Few people are born in trees, and an editor wondered, "Could that have been 'Cyprus'?"

College students are more likely to confuse words such as "buses" and "busses," "naval" and "navel," and "reckless" and "wreckless." The word "busses" refers to kisses, not the vehicles people ride in. A "navel" is a belly button, and some motorists drive "wrecks," but are convicted of "reckless" driving.

Are you ready for a quiz? Can you find the misstatements in the following sentences? (If you need help, look at the explanations at the bottom of the page.*)

1. The attorney admitted that his client had an intoxicated driving record.
2. She was given one year in jail, probation and a $1,000 fine.
3. The fire department responded to the call about a small fire, checked it and drove away.
4. Once inside the house, a shotgun and some coins were stolen by the swindler.
5. Although two fire trucks, a rescue squad and a police car arrived within minutes, they were unable to extinguish the flames before the home was destroyed.

USE STRONG NOUNS AND VERBS

To improve their writing, newswriters use strong nouns and verbs. A single verb can transform a drab sentence into an interesting—or even horrifying—one. Notice the

---

*1. The attorney may have admitted that his client had a record of driving while intoxicated; few records, however, can become intoxicated. 2. Judges order criminals to pay fines; they do not give criminals fines. 3. Firefighters are expected to extinguish fires; they do not drive away after simply checking them. Also, change "the fire department" to "firefighters." 4. A criminal, not the shotgun and coins, entered the house. Also, houses are robbed by burglars, not swindlers. 5. Firefighters, rescue workers and police officers may extinguish a fire; cars and trucks cannot.

impact of the word "plunged" in the first example and "danced" in the second, published by the Minneapolis Star Tribune:

> He plunged the blade six inches into his brother's chest.

> While searchlights danced in the sky, thousands of fun-seekers converged on the Mississippi riverfront Wednesday night to mark the beginning of a new year.

The following sentences are also interesting and vivid because the college students who wrote them used descriptive verbs:

> "I love you," he *shouted, throwing* his arms around her and *kissing* her.

> A cargo door *popped* open, *tearing* a hole in the plane's side. Eleven passengers *sucked* out of the hole *plunged* 30,000 feet to their deaths.

> A gunman *jumped* behind the customer service counter of a department store Monday, *grabbed* a handful of money—then *fled* on a bicycle.

By comparison, the following sentences are weak and bland. Yet it is easy to improve them: simply add a strong verb.

> The suspect was gone before police arrived.
> REVISED: The suspect fled before police arrived.

> A man with a gun told her to give him all her money.
> REVISED: A gunman demanded all her money.

Notice that, in addition to making sentences more interesting, active verbs make them more concise:

> There is about $20 in the cash register. (8 words)
> REVISED: The cash register contains about $20. (6 words)

> It is speculated by police that the boy ran away. (10 words)
> REVISED: Police speculate that the boy ran away. (7 words)

Because it lacks a strong verb, the following sentence is vague and bland:

> The girl was on her way home.

The sentence becomes more interesting—and informative—when you substitute a more specific and descriptive verb:

> The girl was *walking* home.

> The girl was *jogging* home.

> The girl was *driving* home.

> The girl was *carried* home.

Changing a single word—the verb—can also change a sentence's impact and meaning:

> His brother *got* an IBM computer.

> His brother *bought* an IBM computer.

His brother *won* an IBM computer.

His brother *stole* an IBM computer.

Be particularly careful to avoid the repeated use of the forms of the verb "to be": "is," "are," "was," "were" and so on. These verbs are overused, weak and dull. Notice that sentences using these verbs are also wordy:

Filing the protest was a history teacher. (7 words)
REVISED: A history teacher filed the protest. (6 words)

A sharp criticism of the plan was voiced by the mayor. (11 words)
REVISED: The mayor sharply criticized the plan. (6 words)

Police officers were summoned to the scene by a neighbor. (10 words)
REVISED: A neighbor called the police. (5 words)

Tips from a Pro

FRESH VERBS SPICE UP STORIES

By Lucille S. deView
Writing Coach
The Orange County Register

Check the verbs in these stories by Francis X. Clines of The New York Times:

- ''An Air Florida jetliner taking off from National Airport in a snowstorm crashed into a crowded bridge this afternoon and broke as it plunged into the Potomac River, leaving at least 10 persons dead and more than 40 missing, according to unofficial police estimates.

"The twin-engine plane suddenly appeared out of the swirling snow over the 14th Street Bridge at the height of an early commuter exodus and sheared open a truck and at least four automobiles, then caromed in pieces into the frigid river.''

- ''The voices of Richard M. Nixon and his inner sanctum people leaked out from the 32 sets of earphones, making the library buzz and burble metallically like the American summer at Locust Pine.''

Crashed, broke, plunged, appeared, sheared, caromed. Leaked, buzz, burble.

Fresh, strong, active verbs are a specialty of this talented writer, who switches gracefully from hard news to features, to profiles, to essays. His verbs help the reader envision the scene; they coax tears or smiles.

Alas, as we churn out stories on deadline it becomes all too easy to lean on the same few, vapid verbs. What, we wonder, happened to those rich words we once prized? What, indeed.

If your copy suffers from verb stagnation, try this remedy:

- Flag your verbs: Before submitting your story, cruise through the copy on your computer and highlight the verbs in bold. Study them.

- Substitute vigorous verbs for weaklings: Consult the dictionary, reference books, colleagues. Jolt your thinking. Get out of that rut.

ISBN 0-15-500602-9

■ Use the active voice: Consult ''Elements of Style'' by William Strunk Jr. and E.B. White, who extoll the active voice as ''usually more direct and vigorous than the passive.''

Examples: Passive—''There were a great number of dead leaves lying on the ground.'' Active—''Dead leaves covered the ground.'' Passive—''The reason he left college was that his health became impaired.'' Active—''Failing health compelled him to leave college.''

■ Eliminate ''there is,'' ''there are'': This inevitably paves the way for descriptive verbs.

Examples: ''There is a deserted house beside the narrow highway.'' Try: ''A deserted house looms above the narrow highway.'' ''There is a lace curtain blowing inside a broken window.'' Try: ''A lace curtain flutters inside a broken window.''

■ Shorten, tighten your copy: The stronger the verbs, the fewer the words needed to tell the story.

■ Keep a verb list: As you read good fiction, non-fiction and poetry, jot down verbs you admire. Keep a running list for future use. The goal is never to be obscure or show off, but to employ the rich vocabulary of verbs at the writer's disposal.

To praise Clines' writing is to praise those who handle his copy, preserving as they do the clarity and power of his carefully chosen verbs. Astute editors and copy editors protect verbs that are simple and clear and do not arbitrarily suppress verbs that are slightly less familiar, so long as they suit the situation.

The gifted editor or copy editor, like the gifted writer, is not above taking a chance. Risk is the name of the good writing game. Risk it. Strengthen those verbs.

WORDS TO AVOID

Newswriters avoid adverbs and adjectives, since they tend to be less forceful, specific and objective than nouns and verbs. The writer Mark Twain warned, "When you catch an adjective, kill it." Similarly, Stanley Walker, editor of the old New York Herald Tribune, advised his staff, "Select adjectives as you would a diamond or a mistress. Too many are dangerous."

Most adverbs and adjectives are unnecessary. They waste space by stating the obvious, and they may unintentionally inject a reporter's opinion into the story. If, for example, you write about a child's funeral, you do not have to comment that the mourners were "sad-faced," the scene "grim," and the parents "grief-stricken." Similarly, there is no reason to report that an author is "famous," a witness "alert" or an accident "tragic."

The adverbs and adjectives in the following sentences editorialize, commenting on the facts rather than simply reporting them:

It was not until 9 p.m. that the police were finally able to find the child.
REVISED: Police found the child at 9 p.m.

After receiving the frightening report, the mayor made it quite clear that she is concerned about the program's outrageous costs.

REVISED: After receiving the report, the mayor said she is concerned about the program's costs.

The use of the word "finally" in the first sentence suggests that the police were negligent: that they should have found the child sooner. Similarly, if you report the facts in the second story clearly and concisely, you should not have to add that the report was "frightening" and the costs "outrageous." Also avoid concluding that the mayor made anything "clear."

AVOID CLICHÉS AND SLANG

Clichés

Because they eliminate the need for thought, clichés have been called the greatest labor-saving devices ever invented. The trouble is that many clichés are so old and so overused that they have lost their original impact and meaning. Clichés no longer startle, amuse or interest the public.

People use clichés automatically, without thinking. Journalists use them as shortcuts or crutches when they do not have enough time (or talent) to be more specific, descriptive or original. A writer for the Chicago Tribune has explained that, "Intelligent men and women working under intense time pressures often have to grab for any metaphor that comes to mind, stale or not."

Journalists may write that a fire "swept through" a building, that an explosion "rocked" a city, that rescue workers "sifted through the rubble" or that a judge "handed down" a sentence. Or they may write that a storm "left a trail of death and destruction"—a cliché so vague that newswriters have used it to describe the damage caused by hundreds of blizzards, hurricanes, thunderstorms and tornadoes. More capable writers might observe and describe specific or unique details about a storm's passage and consequences.

Other clichés exaggerate. Few people are really "blind as a bat," "cool as a cucumber," "light as a feather," "neat as a pin," "straight as an arrow," "thin as a rail" or "white as a sheet."

Political reporting is especially susceptible to clichés. Political reporters write that candidates are nominated in "smoke-filled rooms" or "test the waters" before "tossing their hats into the ring." Other candidates launch "whirlwind campaigns" and "hammer away" at their opponents, usually in an attempt to "take over the reins of government." Some candidates "straddle the fence" on "burning issues of the day." However, few "give up without a fight."

You are likely to be so familiar with clichés that if you are given the first few words of a cliché, you will immediately recognize it and be able to complete it. Want to try? The final word is missing from the following clichés, yet you are likely to have no trouble completing all 10:

a close brush with _____	has a nose for _____
a step in the right _____	last but not _____
could not believe her _____	left holding the _____
evidence of foul _____	lived to a ripe old _____
fell into the wrong _____	lying in a pool of _____

Are you ready for a more difficult challenge? The final three words are missing from each of the following clichés. Can you complete all five?

a bird in the hand is worth two _____ _____ _____ .

between a rock and _____ _____ _____

hit the nail _____ _____ _____

like a bull in _____ _____ _____

some good news and _____ _____ _____

Editors may accept an occasional cliché, but several clichés will make a story sound old and stale. The clichés should be replaced by more specific details:

He said the store's financial losses are a thing of the past.
REVISED: He said the store is no longer losing money.

A picnic ended in tragedy Sunday for two college students.
REVISED: Two college students drowned Sunday afternoon while swimming to a boat anchored about 150 feet from shore.

Other clichés that journalists should recognize and avoid appear in the box on the following page. Unfortunately, clichés may appear anywhere, even in respected dailies. Recently, for example, a story in the Minneapolis Star and Tribune began:

There's some good news in crime statistics for Twin Cities suburbs over the past 15 years.
There's also some bad news.

Slang

Journalists avoid slang, which tends to be more faddish than clichés. Slang may be used occasionally in feature stories and personality profiles, but is inappropriate in straight news stories because it is too informal and annoying. Moreover, slang is likely to baffle some readers who are not of the right age or ethnic group to understand it.

Slang rapidly becomes dated, so that a term used in a story may already be obsolete. During the 1970s and 1980s, young people abused such terms as "cool," "freaked out," "heavy," "like" and "you know." Young people complained that they were unable to "get it together" and did not know "where they were at," yet they wanted to "tell it like it is." They also wanted "a piece of the action" and admired people who were "mellow," "laid-back" and able "to go with the flow."

By the 1990s, young people were abandoning those terms and finding new ones. Some admitted that they had become "health nuts" and "had it in their heads" that vegetarianism was "their bag." Others decided to "put their plans on hold" because money was difficult to "come by." Still others realized that life is "a mixed bag" but hoped to "cut a good deal."

AVOID TECHNICAL LANGUAGE AND JARGON

Reporters must learn to recognize and avoid technical language and jargon. Jargon is the specialized language developed by the people in a particular trade or profession.

CLICHÉS

There are thousands of clichés and slang phrases that reporters must learn to recognize and avoid. Some of the most common are listed here.

a keen mind	few and far between	pitched battle
ambulance rushed	foreseeable future	police dragnet
around the clock	gained ground	pose a challenge
arrived at the scene	gave it their blessing	proud parents
at long last	get a good look	proves conclusively
at this point in time	go to the polls	pushed for legislation
baptism of fire	got off to a good start	quick thinking
bare minimum	grief-stricken	real challenge
beginning a new life	ground to a halt	reign of terror
behind the wheel	hail of bullets	see-saw battle
benefit of the doubt	heated argument	set to work
bigger and better	heed the warning	smell a rat
blanket of snow	high-speed chase	sped to the scene
blessing in disguise	hits the spot	spread like wildfire
called to the scene	in his new position	start their mission
calm before the storm	in the wake of	still at large
came to their rescue	landed the job	stranger than fiction
came to rest	last but not least	strike a nerve
came under attack	last-ditch stand	sudden death
came under fire	left their mark	sweep under the rug
cast aside	leveled an attack	take it easy
caught red-handed	limped into port	talk is cheap
clear-cut issue	line of fire	tempers flared
colorful scene	lingering illness	time will tell
complete stranger	lodge a complaint	tip of the iceberg
complete success	lucky to be alive	tipped the scales
coveted title	made off with	took its toll
crystal clear	made their escape	too late to turn back
dead and buried	made their way home	tower of strength
decide the fate	miraculous escape	tracked down
devoured by flames	Mother Nature	traveled the globe
dime a dozen	necessary evil	tried their luck
doomed to failure	never a dull moment	under siege
dread disease	no relief in sight	under their noses
dream come true	notified next of kin	undertaking a study
drop in the bucket	once in a lifetime	up in the air
dying breed	one step closer	view with alarm
erupted in violence	only time will tell	went to great lengths
escaped death	opened fire	won a reputation
exchanged gunfire	paved the way	word of caution
faced an uphill battle	pillar of strength	words of wisdom
fell on deaf ears	pinpointed the cause	word to the wise

When professionals use jargon to impress or mislead the public, critics call it gobbledygook, bafflegab, doublespeak, legalese or bureaucratese. Most jargon is abstract, wordy, repetitious and confusing. For example, the Occupational Safety and Health Administration defined a stairwell as "that portion of a means of egress which is separated from all other spaces of the building or structure by construction or equipment as required in the sub-part to provide a protected way of travel to the exit discharge." Another government agency warned, "There exists at the intersection a traffic condition which constitutes an intolerable, dangerous hazard to the health and safety of property and persons utilizing such intersection for pedestrian and vehicular movement." The second statement contains 31 words. A good journalist could summarize it in four: "The intersection is dangerous."

Americans expect teachers to set a good example for their students by writing clearly and accurately, but even teachers may succumb to jargon. Some call themselves "educators" and their courses "instructional units." Desks have become "pupil stations," and libraries have become "instructional resource centers." A principal in Houston sent this note home to parents:

> Our school's cross-graded, multi-ethnic, individual learning program is designed to enhance the concept of an open-ended learning program with emphasis on a continuum of multi-ethnic, academically enriched learning using the identified intellectually gifted child as the agent or director of his own learning.

People who use jargon unnecessarily seem pompous. They use long, weighty words that make everything (especially themselves) seem more important. Examples of the words include:

"subsequently" instead of "later"

"in the near future" instead of "soon"

"in view of the fact that" instead of "because"

"eliminate the possibility of" instead of "prevent"

"ingress" and "egress" instead of "entrance" and "exit"

Readers can usually decipher the meaning of jargon but not easily:

> Classic democratic theory holds that voting is the most common behavioral manifestation of a citizen's interest in politics.

Sometimes, however, jargon is almost impossible to understand:

> A workshop on situational leadership is being offered to administrators on Oct. 9 and 10. Participants will learn to diagnose the demands of a situation and determine the amount of task behavior and relationship behavior required to address the needs of the worksite.

> The semiotic perspective promotes a reflective mode of thinking that requires attention to specific contextual clues and relates them to one's understanding of the world with a kind of "informed skepticism" that the authors believe is fundamental to critical thinking.

You may also recognize the following fashionable jargon terms—but have trouble explaining exactly what they mean:

ballpark figure	infrastructure	role model
bottom line	input	role playing
cognitive	interface	scenario
conceptualize	maximize	state of the art
effectuate	ongoing	surrogate
dialogue	optimize	thrust
feedback	parameter	viability
finalize	prioritize	zero growth

Play with these 24 words, using any four or five in a single sentence. They may sound meaningful at first, but they are gibberish. Consider these examples:

The thrust of role playing will help conceptualize the feedback.

Their scenario calls for optimizing and prioritizing the variables to interface the parameters.

This type of technical language may be appropriate in some specialized publications written for the experts in a particular field. It is not appropriate in newspapers written for a mass audience.

Your work as a newswriter will be difficult because you will obtain information from many different sources: doctors, lawyers, business people, press releases, technical reports, and police and court records. Many of those sources use jargon, and you will have to learn to recognize and avoid it. Good reporters reword stories in everyday terms so that their readers can easily understand them. Here are three examples:

JARGON: The official said Montana is in noncompliance with the federal guidelines.
REVISED: The official said Montana is violating the federal guidelines.

JARGON: Identification of the victims is being withheld pending notification of their next of kin.
REVISED: The victims' names are being withheld until their families are notified.

JARGON: Dr. Stewart McKay said, "Ethnic groups that subsist on a vegetarian diet and practically no meat products seem to have a much lower level of serum cholesterol and a very low incidence of ischemic diseases arising from atherosclerotic disease."
REVISED: Dr. Stewart McKay said that peoples who eat little meat have low rates of coronary heart disease and related illnesses.

Journalists are not the only Americans concerned about the problem. Malcolm Baldrige, a one-time cowboy who served as secretary of commerce, argued for plain talk in the federal government. Baldrige said he wanted lean sentences with active verbs and fewer adjectives. To enforce that edict, he had word processors fixed to discourage the use of a list of more than 40 objectionable words and phrases. If someone tried to use them, the word processors stopped and flashed, "Don't Use This Word" on their screens. The forbidden words and phrases included:

as you know	hopefully	ongoing
at the present time	image	orient
bottom line	inappropriate	prior to
contingent upon	input	prioritized
delighted	interface	responsive
different than	is my intention	specificity
effectuated	maximize	therein
enclosed herewith	more importantly	thrust
finalize	mutually beneficial	to optimize

One of the nation's most famous businessmen, former Chrysler Corp. chairman Lee Iacocca, also tried to discourage what he calls "bureaucratic double-talk." In a book titled "Talking Straight," Iacocca commented:

> There are three factors behind the mumbojumbo. First, the almost uncontrollable desire to tell all you know on any given subject. Second, the love of adjectives and adverbs over nouns and verbs. And third, the desire to impress your audience with your depth of vocabulary. I once read a 15-page paper that was tough to understand. I called in the author and asked him to explain what was in the tome he had written. He did it in two minutes flat. He identified what we were doing wrong, what we could do to fix it, and what he recommended. When he finished I asked him why he didn't write that in the paper the way he'd just said it to me. He didn't have an answer. All he said was, "I was taught that way." And he was an M.B.A. to boot.

AVOID EUPHEMISMS

Reporters avoid euphemisms, vague expressions used in place of harsher, more offensive terms. Euphemisms enable people to avoid using words that seem rude, tasteless, embarrassing or ugly. Prudishly, Americans often say that a woman is "expecting" rather than "pregnant," and that they have to "go to the washroom" rather than "go to the toilet." Other examples of euphemisms preferred by Americans are "donkey" for "ass," "intestinal fortitude" for "guts" and "affirmative action" for "minority hiring."

From 1933 to 1941, "Cactus Jack" Garner of Texas served as vice president under Franklin D. Roosevelt. Contrary to legend, Garner never said that the office of vice president is "not worth a pitcher of warm spit." What he actually said was that the vice presidency is "not worth a pitcher of warm piss." Most publishers, especially the publishers of textbooks, prefer the euphemism.

Americans use many euphemisms while talking about death. They say that a friend or relative "passed on" or "is no longer with us," not that their friend or relative has died. Funeral directors object to being called "morticians"—which itself was originally a euphemism for "undertakers." While talking to a dead person's family, funeral directors refer to the dead body as "the deceased" or "the loved one" and offer to incinerate (never to "burn") the remains (never the "corpse") in a crematorium (never a "furnace").

Airlines use their own set of euphemisms before every takeoff. Flight attendants demonstrate the use of seat belts and oxygen masks that will pop from the plane's ceiling "in case of need." Attendants also demonstrate the use of life jackets hidden under each seat and point out the location of emergency exits. Flight attendants explain that all the devices are there for "passenger comfort," not because a plane might crash.

(FOR BETTER OR WORSE, copyright 1991 Lynn Johnston Prod., Inc. Reprinted with permission of UNIVERSAL PRESS SYNDICATE. All rights reserved.)

Americans seem increasingly reluctant to speak candidly or to use unpleasant labels for any of the individuals or groups in our society. Instead, we create more euphemisms. For example:

- Americans no longer become old. Instead, they become senior citizens, the aged, the elderly, retirees or golden-agers.
- Americans no longer are poor. Instead, they are indigent, underprivileged, financially disadvantaged or culturally deprived.
- Americans no longer are fat. Instead, they are heavy, stocky, plump or (in extreme cases) obese. Slim Americans may be lean or slender, but not skinny or scrawny.
- Americans no longer are stupid. Instead, they are exceptional, slow learners or academic underachievers.
- Americans no longer live in slums or ghettos. Instead, they live in substandard housing, inner cities, central cities or depressed areas.
- Americans no longer are fired from their jobs. Instead, they are dehired, de-employed, terminated, furloughed or phased out.

During the recession of the early 1990s, major companies laid off thousands of their employees. Few admitted it, however. Instead, corporate executives announced "cutbacks" and plans to "streamline" or "consolidate" their operations. Others insisted that they were offering their employees "career enhancement opportunities."

Some of the prestigious titles that Americans give themselves also seem to be euphemisms. Garbage collectors call themselves "sanitation workers," prison guards have become "corrections officers" and dogcatchers have become "animal welfare officers." Barbers have become "hair stylists," and salespeople have become "account executives."

Still other euphemisms help businesses enhance their images—and the images of the products and services they offer the public. They sell "pre-owned" rather than used cars, and report their "retained income" rather than their profits. The company that manufactures G.I. Joe calls it an "action figure" rather than a "doll." Why? So little boys will play with it. Miller Brewing Co. manufactures a low-calorie product and, to encourage men to buy it, calls the product a "lite" rather than a "diet" beer. The U.S. Department of Agriculture recently began to permit the sale of hot dogs, bologna and other processed meats containing small bits of bone. However, meat processors did not want to report that their products contain "ground bone." Instead, their labels now report the amount of calcium in an average serving.

Critics charge that people are more willing to accept the horrors of war because armies have invented a clean, sterile language that hides the destruction and the human pain and suffering caused by every war. Airplanes no longer drop high-explosive bombs on enemy soldiers. Instead, they "deliver ordnance to strategic installations." The United States calls its long-range nuclear weapons "Peacekeeper missiles." During the Persian Gulf war, the U.S. military rarely admitted that the American soldiers captured by Iraqi troops were tortured. Instead, briefing officers said, "Allied personnel being forcibly detained appear to be under considerable duress." Finally, modern armies no longer retreat. Instead, they "move to the rear," engage in a "strategic withdrawal" or "occupy new territory in accordance with plan."

Journalists call euphemisms "weasel words." Yet journalists have created some euphemisms of their own. Journalists rarely called presidents Lyndon Johnson and Richard Nixon liars, although both men did lie to the public. Instead, journalists reported "a White House credibility gap." The large corporations that own several newspapers call themselves "groups," not "chains." And editors who give free papers to the public call their publications "controlled circulation newspapers," not shoppers or throwaways.

Are you ready for another quiz? Can you match the euphemisms at the left with their real meanings at the right? If you need help, the answers appear at the bottom of the page.*

1. succumb	a. raped
2. criminally assaulted	b. jail
3. disrobe	c. toilet
4. sex industry workers	d. undress
5. development officer	e. die
6. comfort station	f. commercial
7. beef oil	g. fund raiser
8. water pollution control facility	h. sewage plant
9. message	i. prostitutes
10. correctional facility	j. fat

AVOID JOURNALESE

Critics accuse reporters who abuse the language of writing "journalese." The critics charge that reporters have developed their own vocabulary, and that the vocabulary

---

*Answers: 1e, 2a, 3d, 4i, 5g, 6c, 7j, 8h, 9f, 10b.

distorts, dramatizes and exaggerates. News stories describe fires that "rage," temperatures that "soar," earthquakes that "rumble" and people who "vow." Any new activity is "kicked off." Flooding rivers "go on a rampage." Opponents are "hit" and proposals "killed."

Reporters may write that:

The program is geared toward college students.

The auditorium is tagged for demolition next fall.

City officials gave the go-ahead to the upcoming parade.

Journalese is especially common on sports pages. Because it would be too repetitive, sportswriters are reluctant to report that a team "won" a game. Instead (especially in headlines) they report that one team "ambushed" another. Other words favored by sportswriters are:

blanked	outlasted	spoiled
blitzed	outscored	stunned
bombed	overpowered	swamped
clobbered	ripped	thrashed
crushed	romped	topped
doomed	routed	toppled
flattened	scorched	trampled
humbled	shocked	tripped
marched	slammed	walloped
nabbed	slugged	whipped
nipped	smothered	

Critics of journalese mention other problems discussed in this chapter: journalists' grammatical and vocabulary errors, double meanings, clichés and jargon. In short, they consider journalese a fast, sloppy, careless use of the language.

KEEP RELATED WORDS TOGETHER

In addition to using the right word, reporters must place that word in the proper place in a sentence. Related words and ideas should be placed as close together as possible. For example, modifiers should be kept close to the words they are intended to modify. If the words are separated, the sentence containing them will become more difficult to understand. The sentence's meaning may also change, sometimes comically:

The gunmen tied the victim and left him with his hands and feet taped and lying on the back seat.
REVISED: The gunmen tied the victim and left him lying on the back seat, with his hands and feet taped.

He is making a list of the empty lots in the neighborhood so he can track down their owners and ask if he can plant them next summer.
REVISED: He wants to plant the empty lots in the neighborhood next summer, and is making a list of them so he can track down their owners.

This example appeared in a story transmitted by The Associated Press:

"I want to see if my school is still open," said Mahmoud, a mathematics teacher at a school in Kuwait who gave only his first name.

Placement errors of this type are particularly common in the first paragraph in news stories, and often involve modifiers of time and place, as in the following examples:

A 62-year-old woman was convicted Monday of embezzling $143,000 in Circuit Court.

After spending seven months in jail, Neil Lefforge was taken before Judge Samuel McGregor and sentenced to life in prison for the possession and sale of cocaine Tuesday.

The police said today that Mr. Meest told them he strangled Miss Watson after stabbing her in a marshy, undeveloped area off Meade Avenue.

In the first example, the 62-year-old woman was convicted in Circuit Court; she did not embezzle the money there. The defendant mentioned in the second example was sentenced Tuesday; he did not sell the cocaine then. The murderer mentioned in the third example obviously did not stab his victim "in a marshy, undeveloped area" of her body, as the sentence suggests.

Here are other examples of word-placement problems. The related words appear in italics and are moved together in the revisions:

The police found a broken *bottle* in the back seat *that* was apparently thrown through the windshield.
REVISED: The police found a broken *bottle that* was apparently thrown through the windshield. It was on the back seat.

"I like the idea," *said* Concetta Ciulla of the University of Kansas *in a speech* Tuesday.
REVISED: "I like the idea," Concetta Ciulla of the University of Kansas *said in a speech* Tuesday.

Chris Brown *charges that* as a result of the accident that occurred last summer at the intersection of Star Road and Power Drive *she suffered* a broken leg.
REVISED: Chris Brown *charges that she suffered* a broken leg in the accident that occurred last summer at the intersection of Star Road and Power Drive.

The *parents* of a Kennedy High School graduate, James J. Timms, 18, who was rejected by the Army, Navy, Air Force and Marines, *say* he can neither read nor write.
REVISED: James J. Timms, 18, was rejected by the Army, Navy, Air Force and Marines. Timms graduated from Kennedy High School, but his *parents say* he can neither read nor write.

CLASSICS OF ILLITERATURE

Writers often violate the ideas discussed in this chapter, and their errors are often humorous—for readers, although editors are not amused when the errors appear in their publications. For example, a recent news story reported, "Tucker's father died in 1952, and he left school several months later."

Similarly, an essay written by a high school student insisted, "The difference between a king and a president is that a king is the son of his father, but a president isn't." Other students have written about "navel" battles and about a play "in which the characters are ghosts, goblins, virgins and other mythical creatures."

Insurance forms ask motorists who have been involved in accidents to explain briefly what happened. Their explanations have included:

"I thought my window was down, but I found out it was up when I put my head through it."

"I pulled away from the side of the road, glanced at my mother-in-law and headed over the embankment."

"I had been driving for 40 years when I fell asleep at the wheel and had an accident."

"The telephone pole was approaching. I was attempting to swerve out of its way when it struck the front end."

"To avoid hitting the bumper of the car in front, I struck the pedestrian."

"My car was legally parked as it backed into the other vehicle."

"An invisible car came out of nowhere, struck my car and vanished."

"I saw a slow-moving, sad-faced gentleman as he bounced off the roof of my car."

"I was thrown from my car as it left the road. I was later found in a ditch by some stray cows."

St. Louis Post-Dispatch

WRITE & WRONG

By **Harry Levins**
Post-Dispatch Writing Coach

Good writing draws a clear picture in the writer's mind. When a reader can see a sharp image in his mind, the writing comes alive.

But vague writing blurs the image, throwing it out of focus. Writers who rely on adjectives often blur their images. True, an adjective can evoke a specific image in the *writer's* mind. After all, the writer was on the scene; when he writes of a "giant ice-cream cone," as one reporter recently did, the word "giant" recalls to the writer the three-scoop diet-buster (or whatever it was) that somebody was eating.

But the reader was elsewhere; the reader never *saw* the ice-cream cone in question. As a result, the reader must grapple with a vague word: "giant." How giant is giant? One reader's "giant" ice-cream cone is another's appetizer.

Here's a lede in which the writer made an effort to fix a sharp image in the reader's mind:

> Laurie Ann Oilar of Kahoka, Mo., was a large, red-haired woman who liked to fix autos, tend farm animals and play with her baby daughter.

It worked, except for one word—"large."

What does "large" mean?

Does it mean that Ms. Oilar was fat?

Does it mean that Ms. Oilar was tall?

Does it mean that Ms. Oilar was buxom?

Does it mean that Ms. Oilar was Junoesque?

"Large" could fit any number of attributes. In this case, nobody knows which one—except for the writer (and, of course, Ms. Oilar's acquaintances, who needed no word pictures). We would have served the reader better with precision:

> Laurie Ann Oilar of Kahoka, Mo., was a 325-pound, red-haired woman who . . .

Or:

> Laurie Ann Oilar of Kahoka, Mo., was a 6-foot, 2-inch woman who . . .

Or whatever fits in the context. Even such relatively vague adjectives as "heavy-set" or "plump" or "tall" would have been more precise than "large." Moral: make sure that the picture in *your* mind can be developed in the reader's mind as well.

Sometimes, we're vague because we assume that the reader knows as much as we do—always a dangerous assumption. Here's an example, from a political story in which mayoral contenders were talking about appointing blacks to high-level city jobs:

> Bosley said the number of blacks in such positions should be proportionate to the city's black population.
>
> Jackson would not put a specific number on the percentage of blacks he would place in such posts . . .

And neither would the writer, which was unfortunate. Blacks make up

(continued on next page)

about 47 percent of the city's population. Had we used that figure and the number of jobs in question, the reader would have had some idea of how many blacks Bosley was talking about.

Similarly, a story on the recovery by the police of some stolen goods ended with this paragraph:

> Sgt. Stewart said many of the stolen goods had been sold at tremendous discounts. "For example, we learned that they were selling cigarettes at $30 a case," he said.

But unless we know the retail value of a case of cigarettes, this information is worthless. How much of a discount does $30 represent? Fifty percent? Ninety percent? Who knows? The Coach has few equals as a consumer of cigarettes, but even he has no idea how many packages or cartons of cigarettes make up a case.

At times we're vague through a poor choice of words. A recent lede provides an example:

> A number of major road construction projects in the St. Louis area have been affected by the strike of Teamsters union truck drivers against the Material Dealers Association.

What is "a number of"? Answer: anything from one to infinity. What does "have been affected" mean? Some effects are good, some are neutral, some are bad. Some effects are slight, some are moderate, some are severe. What information did this lede convey? That from one to countless road projects is or are being affected in some way or other to some sort of degree. Conclusion: mush.

On the other hand, the sort of information that readers need was contained in (or perhaps was edited into) a recent AP story on asbestos exposure. The story said current government regulations limited asbestos at places of work "to two fibers for each cubic centimeter of air." Then it added:

> That volume is about the size of a small sugar cube.

Most Americans know little about the metric system. So the sentence about the sugar cube took a hard fact and put it into terms that readers can understand.

Martha Shirk took the same extra step in a story about the sales tax increase proposed in the city. After noting that the increase would add three-eighths of a cent to the tax, she wrote:

> The sales tax increase would add $18.75 to the price of a $5,000 automobile and 37 $\frac{1}{2}$ cents to the cost of a $100 suit.

She needed only a moment to calculate the figures and a few words to convey them. But the beneficial impact can be way out of proportion to the effort. Numbers are abstractions; cars and suits are real.

***

ADDING IT UP

Any newsroom has more than its share of people uncomfortable with mathematics. On election night, their cries ring out: "How do you figure percentages? Is it the big number into the little? Or the other way around?" Still, simple multiplication and division should be within our grasp.

Recently, when Florissant's water supply went bad, Anheuser-Busch gave that community 25,000 cases of canned water—and gave the Post-Dispatch a press release. It spoke of "56,000 gallons in 600,000 cans." The reporter took the brewery at its word, which was unfortunate. The brewery makes good beer but bad numbers.

Six hundred thousand 12-ounce cans equals 7,200,000 fluid ounces. At 128 ounces to the gallon, that comes to 56,250 gallons. The brewery's figure was 250 gallons short. The shortage was caught before the story saw print, but it was a near-run thing.

No big deal, you might say. Two hundred and fifty gallons of beer is one thing, but what's 250 gallons of water?

Well, remember that the vast and anonymous crowd we call "readers" includes people who read every story, notice every detail and catch every mistake. Even if only five or six of them notice that we're 250 gallons short, that's five or six people who wonder whether we know what we're doing.

You may recall the story of the clerk a few years back who was fretting late one Saturday morning because the weather machine had jammed just before the world temperatures moved. The deadline for the early Sunday edition was at hand, and the clerk had nothing to offer but a blank weather form.

Still, he had imagination—not judgment, but imagination. He went to the bound volumes and copied down the temperatures from the preceding week's early Sunday edition. And nobody noticed—nobody except the one reader who follows the world temperatures closely.

That reader found it odd that from Aberdeen to Winnipeg, the temperatures on one Saturday were precisely the same as the temperatures the Saturday before. He found it so odd that he brought it to the attention of the Reader's Advocate.

Moral No. 1: Somebody out there reads *everything*.

Moral No. 2: Recheck the math.

***

TO BE OR NOT TO BE

Here's an all-too common sort of sentence:

> Mrs. Clark's problem is that a city ordinance forced her to run as an independent in a special election last month.

A purist might note that Mrs. Clark ran by choice, not because a city ordinance forced her to. But The Coach had more problems with the writer's use of the verb "is."

Verbs represent the strongest words in English. Verbs propel a sentence. But among English verbs, "to be" in any of its forms is the weakest. With "to be," nothing *happens*; things merely *are*. Nothing *moves*; things merely *exist*.

Naturally, some sentences require "to be." But in many instances, we can replace "to be" with a more active verb:

> Mrs. Clark's problem stems from a city ordinance that barred her from running as a Democrat in a special election last month.

Another example:

> . . . for Tammy Beckham, 16, of St. Louis, who is in need of a liver transplant operation.

The solution:

> . . . For Tammy Beckham, 16, of St. Louis, who needs . . .

***

DEPARTMENT OF NICETIES

• Lazlo Domjan points out that in our election stories, we are using the word "margin" when we mean "ratio." When Smith gets 60,000 votes

(continued on next page)

and Jones gets 40,000, Smith's *margin* of victory is 20,000 votes. His *ratio* of victory is 3–2.

• Be on guard for partial quotes that backfire. We've had a run on bloopers of this sort: *Peach said he "appreciates the offer, but I'm a big boy, and I can do it myself."* George Peach may speak rashly but never ungrammatically. Literally, we have him saying here, "I appreciates the offer." And we appreciates good grammar. Solution: *Peach said that although he appreciated the offer, "I'm a big boy . . ."*

• Now that we are in the waning years of the 20th century, references to the 21st century will appear with increasing frequency. Please remember that the new century starts on January 1, 2001. The year 2000 will be the last year of the 20th century, not the first year of the 21st. (The reason: We had no Year 0. The First Century began on Jan. 1 in the year 1; it ran a full 100 years, ending on Dec. 31, 100. The Second Century began on Jan. 1, 101, and so on.)

• A recent lede told how a line of vicious thunderstorms had raked the metropolitan area, blowing down trees and taking off roofs—and then ended, "according to authorities." Why attribute an event that 2.3 million people witnessed? We can say on our own that it rained.

SUGGESTED READINGS

Articles

Leo, John. "A Glossary of Reporterspeak." *U.S. News & World Report,* 3 Oct. 1988, p. 63.

Morgan, Hugh. "Jargon: Communication Professor Tells Copy Editors Why It's Bad." *Editor & Publisher,* 7 Oct. 1989, pp. 16 and 38.

O'Mara, Richard. "A Terrorist Is a Guerrilla Is a Freedom Fighter." *The Quill,* Oct. 1990, pp. 22–24.

Books

Bernstein, Theodore M. *Dos, Don'ts, and Maybes of English Usage.* New York: Times Books, 1977.

———. *Watch Your Language.* New York: Atheneum, 1981.

Brooks, Brian S., and James L. Pinson. *Working with Words: A Concise Guide for Media Editors and Writers.* New York: St. Martin's, 1989.

Cooper, Gloria, ed. *Red Tape Holds Up New Bridge: And More Flubs from the Nation's Press.* New York: Perigee, 1987.

Hayakawa, S. I. *The Use and Misuse of Language.* Greenwich, CT: Fawcett, 1962.

Kessler, Lauren, and Duncan McDonald. *When Words Collide: A Journalist's Guide to Grammar and Style.* 2d. ed. Belmont, CA: Wadsworth, 1988.

Lewin, Esther, and Albert E. Lewin. *The Thesaurus of Slang.* New York: Facts on File, 1988.

Lutz, William. *Doublespeak.* New York: Harper & Row, 1989.

Neaman, Judith, and Carole G. Silver. *Kind Words: A Thesaurus of Euphemisms.* Expanded and rev. ed. New York: McGraw-Hill, 1990.

Rivers, William L. *Writing: Craft and Art.* Englewood Cliffs, NJ: Prentice Hall, 1975.

Safire, William. *I Stand Corrected: More on Language.* New York: Times Books, 1984.

———. *On Language.* New York: Times Books, 1980.

———. *What's the Good Word?* New York: Times Books, 1982.

Urdang, Laurence. *The Dictionary of Confusable Words.* New York: Facts on File, 1988.

Van Dijk, Teun A. *Communicating Racism: Ethnic Prejudice in Thought and Talk.* Newbury Park, CA: Sage, 1987.

QUOTES

Never write to please the writer. Write to please the reader.

(An editor quoted in King News *by Moses Koenigsberg)*

Why should freedom of speech and freedom of the press be allowed? Why should a government which is doing what it believes to be right allow itself to be criticized? It would not allow opposition by lethal weapons. Ideas are much more fatal things than guns. Why should any man be allowed to buy a printing press and disseminate pernicious opinion calculated to embarrass the government?

(Nikolai Lenin)

As long as a country has no civil liberty and freedom of information and no independent press, then there exists no effective body of public opinion to control the conduct of government.

(Andrei D. Sakharov)

The basis of the First Amendment is the hypothesis that . . . free debate of ideas will result in the wisest governmental policies.

(Chief Justice Fred M. Vinson)

NAME _____ CLASS _____ DATE _____

Exercise 1
VOCABULARY

INSTRUCTIONS: The following pairs or groups of words often cause confusion because, although they may look or sound similar, their meanings differ. In the space provided, define each of the words and explain how its usage differs from that of the other word or words. If necessary, use additional sheets of paper for your answers.

   1. advice/advise _____

   _____

   2. affect/effect _____

   _____

   3. aid/aides _____

   _____

   4. alumna/alumni/alumnus _____

   _____

   5. average/mean/median/mode _____

   _____

   6. because/since _____

   _____

   7. burglar/robber/swindler/thief _____

   _____

   8. capital/capitol _____

   _____

   9. cite/sight/site _____

   _____

   10. compose/comprise _____

   _____

   11. consul/council/counsel _____

   _____

   12. decent/descent/dissent _____

   _____

   13. envelop/envelope _____

   _____

   14. farther/further _____

   _____

15. fewer/less _____

_____

16. fiance/fiancee _____

_____

17. foreword/forward _____

_____

18. hanged/hung _____

_____

19. its/it's _____

_____

20. lay/lie _____

_____

21. loose/lose _____

_____

22. moral/morale _____

_____

23. ordinance/ordnance _____

_____

24. pedal/peddle _____

_____

25. principal/principle _____

_____

26. statue/statute _____

_____

27. than/then _____

_____

28. that/which _____

_____

29. their/there/they're _____

_____

30. to/too _____

_____

31. weather/whether _____

_____

32. who/whom _____

_____

NAME _____ CLASS _____ DATE _____

Exercise 2
VOCABULARY

INSTRUCTIONS: The following pairs or groups of words often cause confusion because, although they may look or sound similar, their meanings differ. In the space provided, define each of the words and explain how its usage differs from that of the other word or words. If necessary, use additional sheets of paper for your answers.

  1. above/more than/over _____

  _____

  2. adapt/adept/adopt _____

  _____

  3. altar/alter _____

  _____

  4. angel/angle _____

  _____

  5. bloc/block _____

  _____

  6. blond/blonde _____

  _____

  7. canvas/canvass _____

  _____

  8. censor/censure _____

  _____

  9. complement/compliment _____

  _____

 10. confidant/confident _____

  _____

 11. conscience/conscious _____

  _____

 12. convince/persuade _____

  _____

 13. elusive/illusive _____

  _____

 14. emigrate/immigrate _____

  _____

15. ensure/insure _____

_____

16. entitled/titled _____

_____

17. foul/fowl _____

_____

18. fourth/forth _____

_____

19. imply/infer _____

_____

20. incite/insight _____

_____

21. liable/libel _____

_____

22. marshal/marshall _____

_____

23. miner/minor _____

_____

24. naval/navel _____

_____

25. pole/poll _____

_____

26. ravage/ravish _____

_____

27. reign/rein _____

_____

28. role/roll _____

_____

29. trail/trial _____

_____

30. trustee/trusty _____

_____

31. who's/whose _____

_____

32. your/you're _____

_____

NAME _____ CLASS _____ DATE _____

Exercise 3
VOCABULARY

INSTRUCTIONS: Words with different meanings often look or sound similar. As a journalist, you should be familiar with the words and use them correctly. Cross out the wrong words from the following sentences, leaving only the correct ones. Also correct errors in style and use of the possessive. If you need help, the rules for forming possessives appear in Appendix C.

1. Three women, all (alumna/alumni/alumnus) of the college, (adviced/advised) the officials to (altar/alter) (their/there/they're) plans.

2. The (principal/principle) said her (role/roll) in maintaining school discipline is (miner/minor).

3. (Fewer/less) than a dozen (statues/statutes) were erected at the (cite/sight/site).

4. Attorneys warned that the city (ordinance/ordnance) is (liable/libel) to cause more (decent/descent/dissent).

5. (Irregardless/regardless) of (weather/whether) the (phenomena/phenomenon) is unusual, the firms stockholders want to protect (their/there/they're) investment.

6. The mass media (are/is) likely to (affect/effect) the teams (moral/morale).

7. The play, (entitled/titled) "Never, Never," was banned by Soviet (censors/censures) until the author (altared/altered) a controversial scene.

8. The mayors (aid/aide) favors the plan but warned that (its/it's) likely (to/too) seem (bazaar/bizarre).

9. A (burglar/robber/swindler/thief) broke into the (principals/principles) garage and took a (canvas/canvass) tent.

10. Each year, thousands of (people/persons) (emigrate/immigrate) (to/too) the United States.

11. The banks (trustee/trusty) said he wants to (ensure/insure) its success (because/since) thousands of (people/persons) depend upon (its/it's) services.

12. They are (confidant/confident) that the enemys (naval/navel) forces will (loose/lose) the battle.

13. A (marshal/marshall) predicted that the evidence will (ensure/insure) the mans conviction for (liable/libel).

14. They want (to/too) know (who's/whose) public opinion (pole/poll) is most reliable.

15. The (forth/fourth) person to (decent/descent/dissent) said he lives in the state (capital/capitol) and objects (to/too) (its/it's) new (ordinance/ordnance).

16. He (hanged/hung) the painting in his home but said (its/it's) larger (than/then) he expected.

17. The student is not (adapt/adept/adopt) at mathematics, and his adviser (implied/inferred) that he is (liable/libel) to fail.

18. He wants to (lay/lie) down for a few minutes, (than/then) address the 1,000 (envelopes/envelops).

19. He accused the schools (trustee/trusty) of (inciting/insighting) a riot among (its/it's) thousands of (alumna/alumni/alumnus).

20. Seventeen (people/persons) obtained copies of the (calendar/calender) before anyone noticed (its/it's) (miner/minor) errors.

NAME _____ CLASS _____ DATE _____

Exercise 4

SPELLING AND VOCABULARY

INSTRUCTIONS: Some words in the following sentences have been placed in parentheses. The words often cause confusion because they look or sound like other words. Decide which of the words is correct here and circle it. Cross out all the other words.

The sentences also contain possessives that need correcting. If you need help, the rules for forming possessives appear in Appendix C.

1. The schools (principal/principle) criticized her two (aids/aides).

2. The story (implies/infers) that the girl (hanged/hung) herself.

3. He (adviced/advised) the city to find another (cite/sight/site).

4. She asked (who's/whose) jacket is (laying/lying) on the floor.

5. His (fiance/fiancee) said (its/it's) unlikely to succeed.

6. They asked (who's/whose) (role/roll) she will be given.

7. He said the (data/datum) eliminated by the (censor/censure) was mistaken.

8. They wondered why (your/you're) being so (elusive/illusive) about the issue.

9. He said the (statue/statute) is likely (to/too) be declared unconstitutional.

10. He is trying to raise more (capital/capitol) to (insure/ensure) the store's

    success.

11. They (complemented/complimented) the architect but want (fewer/less)

    windows.

12. He is (confidant/confident) that the movie, (titled/entitled) "Romance," will

    succeed.

13. They want to (altar/alter) the plans so the buildings are (farther/further) apart.

14. (Their/There/They're) inheritance will total (over/more than) $7 million.

15. The committee is (composed/comprised) of 14 nurses, and they addressed all 5,000 (envelops/envelopes).

16. They (canvased/canvassed) the neighborhood and learned that the problem is (miner/minor).

17. A (loose/lose) wheel (that/which) broke off the trailer caused the accident.

18. Representatives from one (media/medium) said the criteria (is/are) too strict.

19. The (blond/blonde) said that (burglars/robbers/swindlers/thieves) broke into his house.

20. Thousands of the schools (alumna/alumni/alumnus) voiced their (decent/descent/dissent).

21. The banks (trustee/trusty) said she was unable to (affect/effect) the decision.

22. The (trail/trial) began three months after he was charged with (inciting/insighting) the riot.

NAME _____ CLASS _____ DATE _____

Exercise 5
VERBS

SECTION I: AVOIDING USE OF NOUNS AS VERBS

Rewrite the following sentences, eliminating the use of nouns as verbs.

1. She doctored her own illness.
2. They were helicoptered to the site.
3. They are dialoguing with their teacher.
4. They trucked a load of furniture to their new home.
5. They were shotgunned to death, and their bodies will be autopsied Friday.

SECTION II: USING STRONGER VERBS

List three stronger, more active and more descriptive verbs that could replace the verbs in the following sentences.

1. They got a pool for their home. _____
2. About 800 students are in the school. _____
3. The family's scrapbook has many photographs. _____
4. The book should have more information about tennis. _____
5. The editor did a study of newsroom computerization. _____

SECTION III: USING STRONGER VERBS

Rewrite the following sentences, using stronger verbs. Also use the normal word order (subject, verb, direct object).

1. The club is in need of more members.
2. Kathy Tijoriwali is the owner of the hot dog stand.
3. Miller testified that she was visited by Paddock on three occasions.
4. The teacher got a lemon meringue pie thrown in her face by a student.
5. The summer recreation program is set up so that the costs are paid by the city.
6. To obtain more money, she has three college students renting rooms in her house.
7. To make a story interesting a good use of verbs can be extremely effective.
8. A short circuit in the electrical wiring at the church was the cause of the fire.
9. One problem cited in the report was that the mechanic failed to inspect the airplanes engine.
10. It is recommended by the article that the appointment should be temporary, lasting only one year.

NAME _____ CLASS _____ DATE _____

Exercise 6
AVOIDING COMMON ERRORS

SECTION I: AVOIDING GRAMMATICAL AND VOCABULARY ERRORS

Rewrite the following sentences, correcting their wording.

1. Rapists usually attack women that are vulnerable and alone.
2. The school board asked their attorney to help all the students that lost money.
3. Speaking for the highway patrol, Lucas said they would like larger and faster cars.
4. There is not much a student can do to prevent cheating except cover their exam papers.
5. The five men and three ladies that serve on the board predicted that the amount of people seeking help at the clinic will grow to around 500 a month.

SECTION II: KEEPING RELATED WORDS AND IDEAS TOGETHER

Rewrite these sentences, improving the word placement.

1. The girl was taken to a hospital for observation by her parents.
2. Twenty-one students were honored by the high school teachers, two of whom were freshmen.
3. The school board voted to ban seven books from the schools which contain racist statements.
4. A suspect in the burglary case was arrested after a high-speed chase involving two lawnmowers stolen from a hardware store.
5. Robert Allen Wiese was placed on probation after pleading guilty to violating probation by Circuit Court Judge Samuel McGregor.

SECTION III: AVOIDING IMPRECISION

Rewrite the following sentences, making them as precise as possible.

1. Smaller grocery stores usually know their customers.
2. After paying a $325 fine, the dog was free to go home with its owner.
3. A car stopped to help the accident victims, then called the police.
4. A police officer saw a man fitting the description of the suspect he had been given.
5. Minutes after the man left the bar, he collided with a car that totally destroyed his pickup truck.

SECTION IV: AVOIDING JOURNALESE

Rewrite the following sentences, eliminating their slang and journalese.

1. She racked up $30,000 in medical expenses.
2. He gave an OK to spending the $5,000 figure for a car.
3. The program is geared toward helping high school students.

4. The new building will carry a price tag of about $6 million.
5. The proposal met with opposition from three council members.

SECTION V: AVOIDING JARGON

Rewrite the following sentences, eliminating their jargon.

1. He wants to show teachers how to utilize computers as an instructional tool in their classrooms.
2. The university president said he is looking to the private sector for funds with which to construct the cafeteria.
3. Teresea Phillips, a/k/a Marie Phillips, testified that she entered the store and helped the defendant steal an unknown quantity of jewelry from the premises on or about the 9th day of last month.
4. Brown's lawsuit charges that, as a result of the auto accident, he suffered from bodily injury, disability, disfigurement and mental anguish. Browns lawsuit also charges that he has lost his ability to earn a living and that the accident aggravated a previous condition.

NAME _____ CLASS _____ DATE _____

Exercise 7

TESTING ALL YOUR SKILLS

SECTION I: RECOGNIZING EUPHEMISMS

List five euphemisms for each of these words.

1. Drunk _____
2. Lie _____
3. Mistake _____
4. Steal _____
5. Toilet _____

SECTION II: USING DESCRIPTIVE VERBS

List three stronger, more active and descriptive verbs that can replace the verbs in the following sentences.

1. The newspaper will be made weekly. _____
2. The committee has had several meetings. _____
3. He is asking for $250,000 for the land. _____
4. The robber told her to give him her purse. _____
5. Students made the lowest scores in mathematics. _____

SECTION III: IMPROVING VERBS AND SENTENCE STRUCTURE

Rewrite the following sentences, using stronger verbs and the normal word order (subject, verb, direct object).

1. It is estimated by police that the car was traveling 90 mph.
2. Raising the ministers salary to $48,600 a year was approved by the churchs trustees.
3. The decision as to which student will be named editor will be made by the newspapers adviser.
4. Another goal of Fidel Castro was for Cuba to emerge as a leader of developing Third World countries.
5. A lack of interest in the tennis tournament resulted in a vote by the club members to cancel it in future years.

SECTION IV: TESTING ALL YOUR SKILLS

Rewrite the following sentences, eliminating all their errors.

1. They are products that the public has come to know and trust
2. He said an investigation of the swindle is being conducted by the police.
3. She succeeded in spite of sexual prejudices due to her talent as a writer.
4. Both the speech and the breakfast are free to the public which begins at 7 a.m.
5. After robbing the convenience store, a waiting vehicle sped east on Northrup Road.

ISBN 0-15-500602-9

6. He said the primary reason EDB is used is because it is the most effective pesticide.
7. The law will increase the fines given to every motorist convicted of speeding by 50 percent.
8. Foods sold in vending machines with a high sugar content will be replaced by foods considered more healthy.

NAME _____ CLASS _____ DATE _____

Exercise 8

Answer Key Provided: See Appendix D

REVIEW

SECTION I: AVOIDING SLANG AND CLICHÉS

Rewrite the following sentences, eliminating their slang and clichés.

1. The club president said he plans to call it quits.
2. She said the student has a long way to go before he can graduate.
3. The mayor painted a rosy picture of the city's financial situation.
4. The bank vice president admitted coming up $43,000 short in her accounts.
5. The exercise trail is geared toward the average adult citizen who is serious about getting into good shape.

SECTION II: IMPROVING VERBS AND SENTENCE STRUCTURE

Rewrite the following sentences, using stronger verbs and the normal word order (subject, verb, direct object).

1. The governor's goal is to raise teachers salaries.
2. The woman had her purse snatched by a boy, about 16.
3. The bike path is used by other people as an exercise track.
4. Their lawsuit complains that the bottle had an insect in it.
5. The cost of the chapel is estimated by church officials to be $320,000.

SECTION III: KEEPING RELATED WORDS AND IDEAS TOGETHER

Rewrite the following sentences, moving the related words and ideas as close together as possible.

1. He was charged with shooting his girlfriend, Saundra Marrston, 33, a waitress at Freddy's Inn, 410 Lakemont Ave., in the throat.
2. She married her high school sweetheart, David Garner, in Greenville, North Carolina, on Jan. 3, 1975, who works as a tennis instructor.
3. To help the crippled children, she begged her parents and other responsible adults in a speech at the church to donate the money they need for medical care Sunday evening.
4. The good samaritan, described by witnesses as a white male, approximately 35 years old, 5 feet 8 inches tall, with black hair, brown eyes and a bandage on his forehead, was driving a honda civic.
5. She said that if a student fails two or more subjects, is frequently absent, has discipline problems, and shows signs of low self esteem, loneliness or stress, that youngster is at high risk for dropping out of high school.

SECTION IV: TESTING ALL YOUR SKILLS

Rewrite the following sentences, correcting all their errors.

1. He said the book is a good read.

2. The plan was deemed illegal by the city attorney.
3. The teacher does not get her ideas across very well.
4. The council chairman cast a strong no vote against the proposal.
5. The purpose of the new program is to provide medical services to the indigent.
6. The plan of the youths was never to tell their parents about how they obtained the money.
7. It was stated in the report that water skiing is a sport that can be enjoyed by anyone regardless of their age.
8. The consensus of opinion among participants in the workshop is that a pay raise of 15 to 20 percent should be received by the nurses.

NAME _____ CLASS _____ DATE _____

Exercise 9

Answer Key Provided: See Appendix D

SPELLING AND VOCABULARY

INSTRUCTIONS: Correct all the errors in the following sentences, which contain a number of words that cause confusion because they look or sound like other words. You were asked to define many of the words in Exercises 1 and 2.

The sentences also contain possessives that need correcting. If you need help, the rules for forming possessives appear in Appendix C.

1. He adviced the city to adopt the ordinance.

2. The concept was to illusive to insure success.

3. Its rules were altered, but the affects were minor.

4. The blonds fiance said there new home was robbed.

5. Who's statue was laying near you're construction cite?

6. Rather than dissenting, he agreed to study their advise.

7. The alumna, all men, said the dissent became to violent.

8. He censured the aides behavior and ignored their descent.

9. A prison trustee said its two miles further down the road.

10. The council was confidant that his advice would insure success.

11. The data was placed in envelops and sent to all the news medias.

12. The governors two aids were given offices in the capitol building.

13. The man was hung because he insited a riot which caused three deaths.

14. The portrait hung in his brother-in-laws office in the state capital building.

15. Six of the schools alumnus said there childrens curriculum should be altered.

16. The principle is liable to lose his students respect if he blocks their proposal.

17. The phenomenon were unusual and affected their son-in-laws roll in the

    family.

18. The board is composed of seven alumnus rather than seven students or teachers.

19. He sited three precedents and implied that the councils decision could be altered.

20. Thomas Alvarez, a tall blonde from California, said the governments data is false.

21. The councilor was confidant of victory but said his roll in the matter was minor.

22. The church alter lay on its side, less than a dozen feet from the broken statutes.

23. His insight, conscience and high principles ensured an excellent performance.

24. The schools principle threatened too censure the newspaper if it tries to publish an article advicing students on how to obtain an abortion.

25. Merchants, fearing that they would lose thousands of dollars, complained that the governments criteria is to difficult to implement.

CHAPTER 4

SELECTING AND REPORTING THE NEWS

Newspapers do not have enough reporters, time or space to report everything that happens. Moreover, their subscribers could not afford to pay for all the news and would not have enough time or interest to read it. Instead, journalists serve as filters, or "gatekeepers." They evaluate potential news stories, then determine their fate. If journalists consider a story newsworthy, they may open the gates that allow the story to flow into the nation's news channels and, as a consequence, to reach the public. If, however, journalists consider a story unimportant, they may cut or kill it.

The selection process is subjective: an art, not a science. Journalists do not have any scientific tests or measurements to help them judge a story's newsworthiness. Instead, they rely on their instincts, experience and professional judgment. For most journalists, the process becomes automatic. They look at a story and instantly know whether it is news.

If you asked journalists to define the term "news," many would be unable to respond. Some might say definitions are unimportant. Others might say news is impossible to define because almost anything can become news. Faced with a similar dilemma, Supreme Court Justice Potter Stewart once confessed that he could not define the term "hard-core pornography." But, Stewart added, "I know it when I see it."

Journalists have tried to define news, but no single definition has won widespread acceptance. Also, no definition acknowledges all the factors that affect the selection process. Typical definitions include:

> News is a report of an event, containing timely (or at least hitherto unknown) information which has been accurately gathered and written by trained reporters for the purpose of serving the reader, listener or viewer.
>
> *(Phillip H. Ault and Edwin Emery,* Reporting the News*)*

> News is an account of an event which a newspaper prints in the belief that by so doing it will profit.
>
> *(Curtis MacDougall,* Newsroom Problems and Policies*)*

> News is an account of a current idea, event or problem that interests people.
>
> *(Laurence R. Campbell and Roland E. Wolseley,* How to Report and Write the News*)*

> The news—what happens and what men think, do and feel about it—this is the first concern of the press.
>
> *(James Wiggins in "Journalism Quarterly")*

News . . . is current information made available to the public about what is going on—information often of vital importance to men and women trying to make up their minds about what to think and how to act. News is a timely, concise, accurate report of an event; it is not the event itself.

(Mitchell V. Charnley, Reporting)

News has also been defined as "anything you didn't know yesterday," "what people talk about," "what readers want to know," "what a well-trained editor decides to put in his or her paper," "anything timely," "the report of an event" and "tomorrow's history."

TYPES OF NEWS

There are two major types of news: "hard" and "soft." The term "hard news" usually refers to serious, factual and timely stories about important topics. The stories may describe a major crime, fire, accident, speech, labor dispute or political campaign.

Hard news may also be called "spot news" or "straight news." A similar label, "breaking news," refers to events occurring, or "breaking," at the present moment.

The term "soft news" usually refers to feature or human-interest stories. Their topics may be old and unimportant—but never dull. Soft news is written primarily to entertain rather than inform and appeals to its readers' emotions more than to their intellect. Such stories may make readers laugh or cry, love or hate, envy or pity. Such stories may also use a more colorful style of writing, with more anecdotes, quotations and descriptions.

Most Americans are more familiar with the terms "good" and "bad" news. Critics frequently charge that the media report too much bad news. One of those critics, Howard K. Smith of ABC News, said the media do not "give the public a rounded, whole picture of the times they live in." Smith explained that journalists generally become interested in stories "only when things go wrong," and that a steady diet of negative news about the United States, whose history has been mainly successful, creates a false picture of life in the country.

Chet Brinkley of ABC News has also criticized local newscasts for their emphasis on bad news. Brinkley complains that:

There's a tired old cliché that news is about a man biting a dog. That's silly. News is something worth knowing, something you didn't know already. I don't look at local news much. I'm tired of seeing stories about crime on the sidewalk: blood, knives, guns, death and destruction. I don't like the stories about bodies on sidewalks. It's of no interest except, of course, to the family of that body on the sidewalk.

Another journalist, Al Neuharth, served as chairman of the Gannett newspapers, a chain that owns more than 90 of the nation's dailies. Neuharth agrees that too much of the news is negative. Neuharth adds that journalists could learn something by listening to Charles Kuralt's "On the Road" segments on CBS. Neuharth explains that:

Kuralt has a message for all of us in print or on the air: The country I see on my television screens and on my newspaper front pages is not quite the country I see with my eyes and hear with my ears or feel in my bones.

Neuharth's autobiography, "Confessions of an S.O.B.," adds that too many editors practice a "journalism of despair." They are skeptics, Neuharth says. They believe that good news is no news, that "their mission is to indict and convict rather than inform and educate." Neuharth insists that the editors are wrong and that their stories are driving readers away, not drawing them in. Neuharth established USA Today and says that it, by comparison, practices a "journalism of hope."

Systematic studies have found that most readers exaggerate the amount of crime and violence reported by the media. Dozens of studies have examined the issue and found that individual newspapers devoted from 2 percent to 35 percent of their space to violence. On the average, one-tenth of newspaper content is concerned with violence.

Because of the public's complaints, journalists have tried to report more good news, but without much success. A retired journalist started a special service, called "Good

Photographs taken for The Associated Press show President Ronald Reagan as he was struck by a bullet while walking to his limousine just three months after taking office. The second photograph shows Reagan glancing toward his assailant, and the third shows him being shoved into the limousine. Doctors who saved his life at the George Washington University Hospital in Washington, D.C., found that the bullet struck Reagan under his left arm, then tore a 3-inch furrow through his left lung.

News from Everywhere." He sent customers—about 200 newspapers, radio and television stations—10 "good news stories" a week. Many of the stories were about good Samaritans and animals. One story reported that a cat earned $7 a day by tasting cat food. Another described a law that would have required cats to wear bells so they could not quietly stalk and kill birds. The news service failed because its stories became too repetitious. Many of the stories were also unimportant, and editors wanted to devote their resources to stories they considered more newsworthy.

A Miami paper once tried to eliminate all the violence from its editions for one day. It killed every violent feature, including three comics, and news stories about two armed robberies, a bloody campus riot and a boxing match. The newspaper's editors almost abandoned the experiment when a fugitive sought for murdering a policeman was captured in a shoot-out that morning, but instead, the paper's front page featured a strike by garbage workers and a waiter who had been awarded $3 million.

One of the newspaper's editors wrote a front-page explanation that concluded: "This de-emphasis of violence for this one day may demonstrate that we, as readers, would not receive from our paper an accurate and complete picture of the world around us if the paper practiced such deliberate selectivity every day and tried to shield us from reality."

Nevertheless, the criticisms continue. The Reagan administration accused the media of prolonging a recession by constantly reporting bad news about the nation's rising unemployment rate. Journalists responded that it was absurd to believe that a few news stories could affect anything so complex and massive as the nation's economy. But President Reagan urged the television networks to devote a week to good news; "then, if the ratings go down, they can go back to the bad news." CBS news anchor Dan Rather responded that Reagan was blaming his administration's difficulties on "the people who call attention to the problems."

THE CHARACTERISTICS OF NEWS

Although journalists cannot easily define news, most agree on its characteristics. Stories that get printed or broadcast are likely to possess the following characteristics:

Timeliness

Journalists stress current information—stories that occurred today or yesterday, not several days or weeks ago. Moreover, journalists try to report the stories ahead of their competitors. If a story occurred even one or two days earlier, journalists will look for a new angle or development to emphasize in their leads. If some background information is necessary, they usually keep it to a minimum and place it near the end of the story.

Importance

Reporters also stress important information: stories that affect, involve or interest thousands of readers. A plane crash that kills 180 people is more newsworthy than an automobile accident that kills two. Similarly, an increase in your city's property taxes is more newsworthy than an increase in the license fees for barbers and beauticians because the property tax increase would affect many more residents of your city.

As you evaluate potential news stories, you must consider their importance or magnitude. Ask yourself whether a story is about a *severe* storm, a *damaging* fire, a *deadly* accident, a *major* speech or an *interesting* organization. Also, you should usually consider stories with serious consequences more newsworthy than stories about more frivolous topics.

Prominence

Stories about prominent individuals, such as your mayor and governor, are more newsworthy than stories about people who play a less important role in civic affairs and who have less power to make decisions that affect your readers' lives. Because he is the nation's leader, almost everything the president does is news. The president may veto a bill, fly to Europe, go fishing or seek a divorce. Because of his prominence, the media would report all four stories.

You may object to journalists' emphasis on celebrities, but the American public seems to have an insatiable appetite for information about them. People magazine, to take just one example, has been phenomenally successful because it is filled with facts and photographs about the lives of famous people.

Proximity

Journalists consider local stories more newsworthy than stories that occur in distant places. Editors explain that readers are most interested in stories about their own communities because they are more likely to be affected by those stories and because they may know the people, places or issues mentioned in them. However, proximity may be psychological as well as physical. Two individuals who share a characteristic or an interest may want to know more about each other even though they are separated by thousands of miles. An American mother may sympathize with the problems of a mother in a distant country; American college students are likely to be interested in the concerns of college students elsewhere.

Oddities

Deviations from the normal—unexpected or unusual events, conflicts or controversies, drama or change—are more newsworthy than the commonplace. The fact that two people were killed in an automobile accident is more newsworthy than the fact that thousands of other commuters reached their destinations safely. Similarly, the fact that your mayor is squabbling with another city official is more newsworthy than the fact that two other officials are good friends.

Journalists must be alert for the unusual twists in otherwise mundane stories. Thus, most newspapers would not report a minor auto accident; but if journalists noticed that a car involved in the accident was driven by a 6-year-old girl, a robot or a police chief, the story could become front-page news.

Critics charge that the media's emphasis on the unusual gives their audiences a distorted view of the world—that the media do not accurately portray the life of normal people on a typical day in a typical community. Again, editors respond that, because they cannot report everything, they report problems that require the public's attention. Also, routine events are less important to, and therefore of less interest to, the public.

Other Characteristics

Dozens of other factors affect journalists' selection of news. However, most definitions of news acknowledge only a few of those factors. Journalists look for humorous stories—anything that will make their readers laugh. Journalists also tend to report simple events—fires, storms, earthquakes and assassinations—partly because such events are easier to recognize and report. Journalists are less adept at reporting complex phenomena: for example, the causes and consequences of crime, poverty, inflation, unemployment and racial discrimination. Journalists also have difficulty reporting stories that never culminate in obvious events. It would be difficult for anyone, journalists included, to assess the quality of education provided by your city's schools, the quality of life in the city, or the effectiveness of its judicial system.

Systematic studies have also found that journalists are most likely to report whatever stories they receive first. Why? Because they have more time and space to handle stories they receive at the beginning of the day. Other studies have found that many editors rely on the recommendations of the nation's news services, using whichever stories they say are most newsworthy. Other editors follow the examples set by larger, more prestigious newspapers.

Definitions of news often vary from one medium to another. Daily newspapers emphasize events that occurred in their communities during the last 24 hours. Weekly newsmagazines report events of national interest, often in more depth, and try to explain the events' significance. Television reports headline news: a few details about the day's major stories. Former CBS news anchor Walter Cronkite observed, "In an entire half-hour news broadcast, we speak only as many words as there are on two-thirds of one page of a standard newspaper." Television journalists also look for visual stories that can be shown rather than read to viewers: colorful stories filled with action, drama and excitement.

A newspaper's selection of news is affected by its size and by the size of the community it serves. A newspaper in a small town may report every local traffic accident; a newspaper in a medium-sized city may report only the accidents that cause a serious injury; and a newspaper in a large city may have enough space to report only the accidents that result in death. Similarly, newspapers in small cities often publish all wedding announcements and obituaries, whereas newspapers in larger cities are able to publish only those of prominent citizens.

If two stories are of approximately equal importance, newspapers are more likely to report the story that is easiest to obtain—the one that occurs nearby and can be covered during normal working hours, when reporters are easily available. The day of the week is important because newspapers publish more advertisements on Wednesdays, Thursdays and Sundays and consequently have more space for news stories on those three days. (Most newspapers attempt to maintain a specific ratio of advertisements and news, often about 65 percent advertisements to 35 percent news. So on the days they publish more advertisements, the newspapers also publish more news.)

Newspapers are also most likely to publish the types of stories that they have traditionally published. The Daily News in New York City has traditionally placed a greater emphasis on crime, sex, sports and photographs than The New York Times, which appeals to a more sophisticated audience and places a greater emphasis on political, business and foreign news. Similarly, some newspapers diligently investigate the problems in their communities, whereas others hesitate to publish any stories that might offend their readers or their advertisers.

Few publishers admit that they favor any individuals or organizations, yet most newspapers develop certain "dos and don'ts" that reporters call "policies" or "sacred cows." Sacred cows reflect the interests of a newspaper's publisher, editors and other executives; unfortunately, some use their power to distort the news. Publishers who are deeply involved in politics sometimes order their staffs to print only positive stories about their favorite candidates and political parties. Other publishers order reporters to suppress unfavorable stories about their friends and their advertisers.

It is difficult for people to detect all of a newspaper's sacred cows unless they actually work for it. Readers can see that a newspaper has published certain stories but seldom know why it did so, or whether in doing so it has deliberately left out any facts. Even in newspaper offices, sacred cows are never written down. Instead, reporters learn about them through more indirect means, often by talking to more experienced colleagues, by observing and listening to their editors and by noticing the changes made in the stories they have written.

Few journalists rebel against their newspapers' policies. Most like their jobs, respect their editors and are preoccupied with the task of gathering the news. Moreover, they want to advance in their profession. So they accept the sacred cows as a part of the job. Clearly, however, newspaper policies—especially political biases—are becoming less common.

THE CONCEPT OF OBJECTIVITY

A previous chapter noted that news stories must be objective, or free of bias. Journalists are expected to gather information and then to report that information as factually as possible. They cannot comment, interpret or evaluate. If an issue is controversial, journalists interview representatives for the opposing sides, then include all the conflicting opinions in a single story. Some of the representatives may be mistaken, and some may lie, but journalists cannot call their statements lies.

Journalists traditionally assumed, perhaps mistakenly, that if they reported all the conflicting opinions, their readers would think about these opinions and be able to determine which ones were most important and truthful. Because that has not always worked, newspapers now publish separate stories that analyze major issues in the news. The stories may be labeled "commentary" or "interpretation," and they critically evaluate the news in an effort to help readers better understand it.

No human can be totally objective. Like everyone else, reporters are influenced by their families, educations, personal interests and religious and political beliefs. Nevertheless, editors believe that objectivity is a worthwhile goal and that journalists can be taught to be more objective.

Also, news stories rarely are the work of a single individual. Normally, an editor assigns a story and a reporter writes it. Several other editors may then evaluate and correct it. Each serves as a check on the others. If one slips and expresses an opinion in a story, another is likely to detect and eliminate that opinion.

THE CHANGING NATURE OF NEWS

Definitions of news are constantly changing. The newspapers published in Colonial America served rich and well-educated white males. Because the newspapers were expensive, only the rich could afford to buy them. Because the newspapers emphasized serious stories about business, politics and foreign affairs, they interested only the educated elite. Because women could not attend college, could not vote and had little or no money of their own, the newspapers ignored them.

On Sept. 3, 1833, Benjamin Day revolutionized American journalism by publishing the New York Sun for the city's workingmen. To appeal to workingmen, Day had to report the types of stories that would interest them. He began to discuss the problems of workingmen, to emphasize humor and local news, and to publish stories about crime, sex and sports. Day also published one of the most famous hoaxes in journalism history. A series of stories in the New York Sun reported that an astronomer using a powerful new telescope could see plants and amphibious creatures living on the moon. The most sensational story added that the astronomer saw men and women living on the moon, and that those men and women had wings and were flying about the moon's surface.

Fifty years later, Joseph Pulitzer began to publish the New York World and again changed journalists' definitions of news. To attract more readers, including women, Pulitzer emphasized lively news: sensational stories about crime, sex, disasters, gossip, scandals, oddities, monstrosities and sports. Pulitzer also published front-page illustrations of gruesome murders and stories about children and animals, two topics that also attracted more readers.

On Feb. 17, 1898, a single story filled the front page of William Randolph Hearst's New York Journal. The story reported that the USS Maine had been destroyed and 260 seamen killed. Hearst wanted the United States to declare war against Spain and immediately suggested the Spaniards were responsible for the explosion. A Navy Court of Inquiry found that the explosion was caused by something outside the ship—but was unable to determine who was responsible for it.

If they were published today, many of the stories that appeared in the New York World would be considered sensational and irresponsible. The American public has become better educated and wants more serious and reliable information. Journalists also are better educated and, more than ever before, are dedicated to the task of informing citizens so they can govern themselves more wisely.

Journalists continued to modify their definitions of news during the 1970s and 1980s. To help their readers lead more comfortable and enjoyable lives, they began to publish more expert advice, consumer news, and what-to-do and how-to-do-it articles. Similarly, newspapers' society and women's pages have been replaced by new sections that appeal to a broader audience. Many of the sections have been renamed: "Outlook," "Emphasis," "People" or "Entertainment." Traditional stories on the women's pages discussed health and beauty hints, engagements, anniversaries, charities, clubs, recipes, fashions, homes and other society news. The new sections contain more stories about current issues and social problems. They discuss the problems of working mothers, the aged and the handicapped. Other stories concern modern families, personalities, medicine, the arts and entertainment.

DETAILS NEWSPAPERS ARE RELUCTANT TO PUBLISH

Reporters must learn to recognize the types of information that are not considered newsworthy and that newspapers rarely publish. Some of those types of information have been briefly described in previous chapters. Newspapers rarely mention routine procedures, such as the fact that a city council met in a city hall and began its meeting with a prayer and the Pledge of Allegiance. Newspapers rarely report what has not happened—the fact that no one was injured or arrested. They delete the obvious and the irrelevant: the fact that police officers were called to the scene of a traffic accident, and the fact that an ambulance was used to transport the injured to a hospital.

Newspapers also hesitate to publish stories congratulating anyone. Journalists are in the business of reporting the news, not recognizing or praising people who deserve to be honored. If editors published all the stories submitted to them by publicity seekers, the stories might not only bore their readers but might completely fill their papers, leaving no space for the news.

The Problem of Good Taste

Generally, editors omit material that is obscene or in poor taste, usually on the grounds that their newspapers are family publications that are read by children as well as adults. Newspapers refuse, for example, to publish gruesome photographs, particularly when those photographs lack significance or show the body of someone killed in their community (someone their readers might know). Newspapers report accidents, but not all their bloody details.

Thus, the following sentence may shock you. Why? Because it is gruesome and bizarre—the type of detail that newspapers rarely publish.

> The man's right hand was ripped apart, his right foot was cut almost completely off, his left leg was fractured and his skull split open.

Never include that type of bloody detail in your stories.

A journalism student wrote the sentence. She enrolled in an advanced reporting class and, for one of her first assignments, visited a local police station. One of the reports she read there described the man's death. Witnesses said the man seemed to be drunk and was standing alongside some railroads tracks, "tapping" boxcars as they went by. A latch caught the man's hand, throwing him under the train.

The student was not yet familiar with the newspaper policy of avoiding nonessential details that might offend the public.

The Problem of Sensationalism

Most newspapers avoid sensationalism, though not sensational stories. Historically, the word "sensationalism" has been used to describe an emphasis on or exaggeration

A 13-year-old boy in Lakeland, Fla., was electrocuted while climbing a tree. The boy lost his footing, reached out and grabbed a high-voltage electric line. A Lakeland newspaper, The Ledger, published this photograph showing the victim's body being lowered from the tree, with his legs visible over the side of the bucket. Another photograph showed the boy's mother weeping and embracing a friend.

The Ledger's executive editor, Louis M. "Skip" Perez, defended the photos—but wondered how the mother felt. "Nothing you did made me angry," she told Perez. Nor was she offended by the photos. "I appreciate having them now," she said. "They are the only photos I have of that day. You really couldn't see my son's face."

of stories dealing with crime, sex, oddities, disasters and sports. However, some stories are inherently sensational: stories about presidential assassinations, wars and other disasters. The media do not make those stories sensational and should not be accused of sensationalism when they report them. Because of their importance, such stories must be reported.

Journalists evaluating a potentially scandalous or sensational story must weigh several conflicting considerations and may ask themselves the following questions: "How seriously will this story harm the people it mentions?" "How will readers react to the information?" "Is the story newsworthy?" "Does the public need and have a right to this information?"

Newspapers' policy of avoiding anything tasteless or sensational can make it more difficult for them to report the news. Two recent controversies illustrate this point. The first controversy involved the rap group 2 Live Crew. A federal judge ruled that some of the group's lyrics were obscene. The judge's decision in the case contributed to a national furor that remained in the news for weeks. Newspapers reported that the lyrics were "sexually graphic" and that some Americans agreed that they should be suppressed. Other Americans—including some journalists—sided with 2 Live Crew. They complained in columns and editorials that the judge's ruling was a form of censorship.

Ironically, it was impossible for most readers to decide for themselves whether the lyrics were offensive and obscene because newspapers refused to print the lyrics. Thus, John Leo, a columnist for U.S. News & World Report, commented that, "The general tone of coverage was: Censorship is stupid, but we can't show or tell you what it is that we think shouldn't be censored." The lyrics referred to women as "bitches" and mentioned forcing anal sex on a girl, forcing a girl to lick feces and "busting" the walls of a vagina.

The second controversy involved the work of photographer Robert Mapplethorpe. Newspapers reported that some people objected to exhibits of Mapplethorpe's photographs because some of them were "homoerotic." Editors were hesitant to be more specific: to report that one of the photographs showed a man urinating into another man's mouth; that a second photograph showed a finger inserted into a penis; and that three other photographs showed men with various objects inserted in their rectums.

In either example, would you want to see such details printed in your local daily? Would you want your family to see them printed in your local daily? There are no right or wrong answers to the questions; rather, it is a matter of individual judgment (one that you may want to discuss with your classmates and instructor). Both examples, however, reflect journalists' dilemma. Journalists are reluctant to report graphic details that are likely to offend the public. Yet readers denied those details may be unable to understand some stories.

Newspapers are becoming less squeamish about the use of four-letter words, however. For years, newspapers referred to syphilis and gonorrhea as "social diseases" and used the terms "streetwalker" for "prostitute" and "operation" for "abortion." Editors also changed "damn" to "darn" or deleted it entirely. As society has become more candid, editors have begun to leave previously objectionable words in news stories, provided that they are needed to help readers understand an event or a person's character.

Rumors

Newspapers are reluctant to report rumors, especially harmful ones. Yet a newspaper's failure to report some rumors may confuse, frighten or alienate the public. As a rumor spreads through a community, more and more people are likely to become interested in it and to believe it. More and more people are also likely to believe that journalists are deliberately suppressing the story.

Some rumors involve important issues, such as racial problems, and therefore cause widespread anxiety. Normally, responsible editors will investigate the rumors and, if they find no evidence that the rumors are true, conclude that there is no story. If a rumor becomes widespread, however, editors may decide to publish a story that emphasizes the fact that the rumor is not true.

Editors will consider the rumor's effects upon the community, and especially upon innocent victims. In some cases, editors may decide that a story exposing even a harmful rumor will be more helpful than their newspapers' continued silence. A story exposing a rumor can help clear the subject's reputation. Newspapers helped a popular restaurant, for example, by exposing rumors that it mixed spiders (and, later, kangaroo meat) in its ground beef. Newspapers also exposed rumors, perhaps started by a competitor, about a small but successful company in Brooklyn that manufactured an inexpensive brand of soda. One rumor insisted that the Ku Klux Klan owned the company, and another held that its soda contained an ingredient to sterilize black men.

Some rumors are examples of urban folklore. People throughout the United States repeat the rumors, often insisting that the incidents occurred in their city. For example, you may have heard rumors that a woman in your city was bitten by a poisonous snake while rummaging through the imported rugs (or sweaters) at a department store. Or you may have heard rumors that a stranger grabbed a boy in a department store, dragged him into a restroom and cut off his penis. Another tale describes an angry woman whose philandering husband asked her to sell his Porsche for him; she sold it for $50. Yet another concerns a teen-age girl with a beehive hairdo; bugs living in her hair supposedly ate through her skull to her brain, killing her.

There are dozens of similar tales. Jan Brunvand, a professor at the University of Utah, describes them in two books: "The Choking Doberman" and "The Vanishing Hitchhiker."

Other Details Reporters Avoid

Most newspapers refuse to identify juvenile delinquents or the victims of rape, even when they have a legal right to do so. Newspapers constantly search for humorous stories, but few make fun of another person's misfortune. When fire damaged the home of a minister in California, one journalist wrote this headline for the story, and an editor promptly ordered him to rewrite it:

Pastor's Study
Goes to Blazes

Newspapers rarely mention lotteries because the U.S. Postal Service can refuse to deliver any publication that advertises or promotes them. A lottery is any contest that involves a prize awarded by chance in exchange for a financial consideration, such as the price of a ticket. Because of the postal regulations, newspapers seldom report that a charitable organization will raffle off a television set or that a new car will be given to a ticketholder at a county fair. However, newspapers can mention a lottery after it has become newsworthy: for example, if a local teacher wins $50,000 in some sweepstakes or if a state legislature debates the establishment of a government lottery to raise money for education.

Newspapers also hesitate to mention trade names, usually on the grounds that the publication of trade names is unnecessary and provides free advertising for the products.

When two cars collide, reporters rarely mention the fact that one of the cars is a Chevrolet and the other a Buick; their identity is irrelevant to the main point of the story—the accident and its consequences. When the types of products involved are important, reporters often substitute generic terms for trade names. They may report that someone bought a "soft drink" rather than a "Coke," "tissue paper" rather than "Kleenex," a "vacuum bottle" rather than a "Thermos bottle" or a "photocopy" rather than a "Xerox copy."

Manufacturers encourage journalists to use trade names properly. They place advertisements in magazines read by journalists to remind them to capitalize all trade names and to use trade names to describe only the products made by their companies, not similar products made by their competitors. If the public begins to use a trade name to describe every product within a certain category, the manufacturer will lose its exclusive right to use that trade name.

However, if carried to an extreme, the media's policy of avoiding trade names can have unfortunate results. When a small airplane crashed during a snowstorm in a mountainous area of Northern California, a family aboard the plane survived for three days by drinking melted snow and eating boxes of Cracker Jack carried by a child. In reporting the family's ordeal and rescue, some newspapers pointlessly substituted the term "candied popcorn" for Cracker Jack. A copy editor, disgusted because his paper refused to allow him to use the trade name "Jeep" in a story about several hundred people who had formed a caravan of Jeeps for a weekend camping trip (called a "Jeep Jamboree"), substituted the phrase "small truck-type four-wheel-drive vehicles of various manufacture." He did not expect his newspaper to print this circumlocution, but it did.

Common sense should dictate whether or not a reporter uses a trade name. If you believe a trade name is pertinent, include it in your story.

Some trade names have become generic terms. Their manufacturers lost the right to the words' exclusive use because the public began to use the words to describe every product of their type, not just the manufacturer's product:

aspirin	escalator	raisin bran
brassiere	kerosene	shredded wheat
cola	lanolin	tollhouse cookies
cornflakes	linoleum	trampoline
cube steak	mimeograph	yo-yo
dry ice	nylon	zipper

The following words remain trade names and should be capitalized and used only while referring to the specific product or brand:

Astroturf	Jacuzzi	Realtor
Baggies	Jeep	Saran Wrap
Band-Aid	Jell-O	Scotch tape
Caterpillar	Jockey (shorts)	Scotchgard
Coca-Cola	Kleenex	Styrofoam
Coke	Kool-Aid	Technicolor
Dacron	Life Savers	Teflon
Dictaphone	Liquid Paper	Vaseline
Ditto	Minute Rice	Velcro
Fiberglas	Muzak	Weight Watchers
Fig Newtons	Ping-Pong	Xerox
Formica	Plexiglas	Ziploc

THE IMPORTANCE OF ACCURACY

Accuracy in Facts

The information that appears in newspapers is more accurate than most Americans believe. Newspapers are managed by professionals who do their best to report the news as fairly and as accurately as possible, but journalists are not always able to convince the public of that fact. When reporters Bob Woodward and Carl Bernstein of The Washington Post investigated the Watergate scandals, they were required to confirm every important fact with at least two sources before reporting it. This policy is not uncommon among American newspapers. Editors insist on accuracy, and reporters will place a long-distance telephone call to check a minor detail.

Errors occur, but less frequently than is generally imagined. Unfortunately, some have been stupendous. On Nov. 7, 1918, the president of the United Press Association, Roy Howard, reported that an armistice ending World War I had just been signed in France. United Press relayed the story to newspapers throughout the United States; schools and factories closed and thousands of people paraded down their cities' main streets. Yet Howard was mistaken. The armistice was not signed until Nov. 11.

In a rush to be first with another story, columnist Jack Anderson announced that Sen. Thomas Eagleton of Missouri had been arrested several times and charged with drunken driving. It was 1972, and Eagleton was the Democratic Party's vice-presidential candidate. Anderson had not yet seen the traffic citations but thought his source was reliable. Anderson never was able to verify the story and later apologized for it. At about the same time, other journalists revealed that Eagleton had been treated for a mental illness, and he was forced to withdraw in the middle of the campaign. All the stories, right and wrong, contributed to the Democrats' landslide defeat by Richard M. Nixon that fall.

The Saturday Evening Post lost $460,000 in a libel suit because of its unprofessional handling of another story. The story charged that Wally Butts, athletic director at the University of Georgia, had conspired to fix a football game between Georgia and the University of Alabama. Despite the seriousness of the charge, journalists at the Post failed to look at the notes taken by its source (a man who had been placed on probation), to interview a second person who was supposed to have been with the source or to screen films of the game to determine whether the information it received was accurate.

Other factual errors are more embarrassing than costly. A daily newspaper in Iowa was forced to publish a correction after one of its reporters mistakenly quoted a dead sheriff. The reporter had called the sheriff's office to obtain some information about an accident and assumed that the man who answered the telephone was the sheriff. He was the sheriff, but a new one; his predecessor had died a few weeks earlier. In writing a story about the accident, the reporter—who failed to ask the sheriff his name—attributed all the information to his dead predecessor.

Most factual errors, like those just described, are caused by carelessness. After finishing a news story, reporters must learn to recheck their notes to be certain that the story is accurate. If reporters lack some information, they should consult their source again. If the source is unavailable, or is unable to provide the information, reporters may have to delete portions of their story or, in extreme cases, kill the entire story. Reporters should never guess or make any assumptions about the facts; they are too likely to make an error.

Reporters must also be certain that they understand a topic before they begin to write about it. Too often, when asked about a fuzzy sentence or paragraph, beginners respond, "I really didn't understand that myself." If you do not understand a topic, never try to write about it. Instead, go back to your source and ask for a better explanation. If that source is unable to help, find another.

Journalists anxious to meet their deadlines—and to beat their rivals—sometimes guess at a story's outcome. In 1948, editors at the Chicago Tribune were certain that Thomas Dewey would defeat President Harry Truman. They rushed copies of this early— and mistaken—edition to the city's newsstands.

To emphasize the need for accuracy, journalism teachers who find a factual error in a story usually lower its grade. At many schools, stories containing factual errors receive an automatic F.

Accuracy in Names

Newspapers are particularly careful in their handling of names. Spelling errors damage the papers' reputations and infuriate their readers, particularly when the misspelled names appear in wedding announcements and other stories that are likely to be clipped and saved. Consequently, many newspapers require their reporters to verify the spelling of every name that appears in local news stories by consulting a second source, usually a telephone book or city directory.

Most errors occur because reporters fail to consult a second source and to check their stories' internal consistency:

Raymond Foote, editor of the newspaper, said minority groups often want publicity but do not know how to obtain it. Foot said he tries to be fair but does not have enough space to publicize the activities of every group in his community.

Of the 10 men and women who were interviewed, five favored the proposal, three opposed it and three said they had not reached any decision.

Other errors arise because of reporters' carelessness. A source may say his name is "Karl" and, mistakenly, reporters may assume his name is spelled with a "C" rather than with a "K." Dozens of other common American names have two or more spellings, including, for example: Ann (Anne), Cathy (Cathie, Kathy), Fredric (Fredrick, Frederic or Frederick), Gail (Gayle), John (Jon), Linda (Lynda) and Susie (Suzy).

Obstacles to Accuracy

Some errors may be inevitable. Because of the need to meet strict deadlines, reporters must work quickly and often lack the time needed to perfect their stories. Reporters are also vulnerable to misinformation. They obtain much of their information from other people, yet some of those people may be mistaken, and reporters may unknowingly report their misstatements. If a prominent person discusses a matter of public importance, that discussion is news and must be reported, regardless of any doubts that journalists might have about the comments' validity. This definition of news required journalists to report President Lyndon Johnson's claims of victory in Vietnam and President Richard Nixon's claims of innocence in Watergate. Other news stories written by journalists questioned the accuracy, and even the truthfulness, of both presidents, but those stories were not read by everyone and lacked the impact of the presidential speech or proclamation.

Historians can often be more accurate than journalists because they see more of a story before they begin work. Journalists deal with isolated fragments; they obtain stories piece by piece and cannot always predict their outcome or ultimate significance. For example, journalists failed to recognize immediately the significance of the break-in at the Democratic Party's headquarters in Washington in 1972. At the time, no one knew the break-in would lead to the resignation of President Nixon and the imprisonment of his top aides. Historians have the advantage of knowing the consequences of that break-in from the outset of their work.

In the past, many errors arose when stories were set in type. The word "house" might be typed "mouse," "friend" became "fiend" and typesetters occasionally left the "r" out of "shirt." One popular tale concerns a retired Army colonel who stormed into a newspaper office because a news story had accidentally called him "battle-scared" instead of "battle-scarred." The newspaper's editor apologized and published a correction—which called the colonel "bottle-scarred." Whole lines of type from different stories were sometimes mixed together. One sentence about a wine festival in California appeared in a story about a new supermarket and suggested that the supermarket's theme would be "wine, women and song." Today, fortunately, computers that give journalists more control over the typesetting function in newspaper offices eliminate many errors.

Journalists might eliminate even more errors by giving the people named in news stories an opportunity to read and correct those stories before they are published. The idea has been discussed most seriously by science writers and by other journalists who deal with complex issues and have more time to write in-depth articles. However, most editors prohibit the practice; they fear that it would consume too much time and that people shown the stories would argue about matters of judgment and try to change all the statements they disagree with, not just factual errors.

Some newspapers give copies of their stories to sources *after* the stories have been published, then ask the sources to evaluate their accuracy. Researchers who have analyzed the sources' corrections have found that sources believe about half the stories contain an error. However, many of the perceived errors are judgmental rather than factual. Sources may interpret some facts differently from reporters or want to include, emphasize or de-emphasize different facts. Sources also may complain that they have been misquoted or that a headline distorts a story. Only about one-third of the errors marked by sources are typographical or factual errors. Most involve misspelled names and inaccurate times, dates, numbers, addresses, locations and titles.

APPLYING THE PRINCIPLES OF NEWS SELECTION

Most students seem to understand the ideas discussed in this chapter but have difficulty applying them. Journalism teachers often ask all the students in reporting classes to find and write about a newsworthy topic on their campus. Several students in a typical class return empty-handed, especially the students without any practical experience on high school or college newspapers. Other students, even if given a week to complete the assignment, return with stories likely to interest only a few other people on their campus.

How can you find a good topic? Ken Fuson, an award-winning reporter for The Des Moines Register, suggests, "Whenever you find yourself laughing at a situation, or shaking your head, or saying to someone, 'Listen to this,' you've probably got a story." Fuson adds that if your idea for a story is not a good one, "no amount of solid reporting or pretty writing can salvage it."

Think about your own experiences. What on your campus is new? What is planned for next week, next month or next year? What is needed? What do you like? What do you dislike? What interests you and your friends? What puzzles or troubles you and your friends? Who is your most interesting friend or faculty member? If something is new, needed, interesting, troubling or confusing, it may be worth a story.

Also approach other people. Ask them about ideas for news stories that are new, different, interesting and important. You may have to approach a dozen friends, secretaries, faculty members and other people before finding a good topic. That type of digging is part of a reporter's job, perhaps the most important part.

AUDIENCES' RESPONSE TO THE NEWS

A recent survey found that 54 percent of the nation's adults said that they read a daily newspaper regularly and 43 percent said they had read a daily paper the day before. By comparison, 74 percent said they watch television news regularly, and 52 percent said they had watched television news the day before. Other studies have found, however, that only 18 percent watch a network newscast on the average day.

Similarly, about 50 percent of the nation's adults listen to radio news each day, and about 28 percent read a magazine. However, only 5 percent read a news magazine such as Time, Newsweek or U.S. News & World Report.

Researchers have also found an "all-or-none principle." Adults who use one source of news are likely also to use several others. Typically, one study revealed that 75 percent of the adults who watched a television news program on a particular day also read a newspaper. By comparison, only 59 percent of the adults who did not watch a television news program read a newspaper that day.

The adults most likely to read a daily newspaper are middle-aged, married and registered to vote. In addition, they have attended college, hold white-collar jobs and have household incomes of $50,000 or more. Newspapers' best readers tend to live in cities rather than rural areas, and to have lived in their cities a long time.

Journalists do not expect every story they write to interest every reader. The average reader spends only 20 to 30 minutes a day looking at a paper. Many are in a hurry and

ISBN 0-15-500602-9

read their papers on the run: while riding a bus, eating lunch, watching television or talking with friends. They skim each page, looking for stories of particular interest. They may pause to read a headline or lead. But if they encounter an obstacle—a dull or confusing paragraph—they quickly move on to another story.

Thus, one study found that only 56.7 percent of readers who start a story that contains just five paragraphs will finish it. The percentage declines as stories become longer. Only 39 percent will finish a story that contains 10 paragraphs, and only 28 percent will finish a story that contains 20 paragraphs.

Readership surveys have also identified the most popular types of stories. However, newspapers continue to publish many of the stories that attract only a few readers. Editors explain that, although unpopular, the stories are important or of great interest to those few readers.

A typical man looks at about 20 percent of all the items published by a newspaper. Younger men read fewer items, about 15 percent. Women read almost the same number of items as men and generally enjoy reading the same types of stories, except sports. A national survey involving 130 daily newspapers found that comics, the most popular item published by the newspapers, attracted 58.3 percent of their readers. The most popular news stories concerned wars, major crimes and disasters, the weather, human interest features, consumer information and scientific discoveries. The least popular news stories concerned business, agriculture, religion, minor crimes, state government, and art, music and literature.

NEWSPAPERS' DWINDLING AUDIENCE

The greatest crisis facing the newspaper industry is its loss of readers. For years, newspapers were the nation's leading medium of communication. Now they seem to have lost that lead to television. The crisis is forcing editors to improve their newspapers' appearance and to reexamine their definitions of news. The changes, however, may fail to help newspapers regain their position as the public's primary source of news.

Some Americans believe that newspapers are obsolete and will eventually disappear. That seems highly improbable. Rather, newspapers are likely to reach a smaller and increasingly specialized segment of the market. Fortunately for the industry, newspapers reach a segment that advertisers like: the wealthy and well educated.

Newspapers reached their peak of popularity during the early decades of this century. In 1920, daily newspapers sold an average of 134 papers for every 100 households in the United States. Virtually every household subscribed to at least one newspaper, and some subscribed to two or three. Today, daily newspapers' "penetration rate" (the percentage of households that subscribes) has fallen almost 50 percent to 68 percent. In other words, nearly one-third of the nation's households no longer receive a daily paper.

Here are the circulation statistics for the last 40 years:

Year	Total Number of U.S. Dailies	Total Daily Newspaper Circulation	Total U.S. Population
1950	1,772	53,829,072	151,300,000
1960	1,763	58,881,746	179,300,000
1970	1,748	62,107,527	203,300,000
1980	1,745	62,201,840	226,500,000
1985	1,676	62,766,232	238,200,000
1990	1,611	62,324,156	248,700,000

The statistics show that the circulation of U.S. dailies is stagnant. It was 62.1 million in 1970 and has not risen significantly since then. Yet the country's population has risen by more than 45 million.

Since 1950, the country's population has increased 62.5 percent. If the circulation of daily newspapers had increased as rapidly, publishers would be selling 87.5 million papers every day, not the current figure of 62.3 million.

Thus, while the total circulation of the country's daily newspapers is stagnant, the *percentage* of households that receive a daily paper is declining. Even 20 years ago, many daily newspapers sold subscriptions to 80 or 85 percent of the households in their communities. Today, many dailies reach only 55 to 65 percent of their local households. In some cities, the figure has dropped below 50 percent. As a result, advertisers who want to reach everyone in a community are turning to other media, especially television and direct mail.

Why are circulations stagnant? One reason is competition. Millions of Americans say they obtain their news from other media, especially television. Other Americans say they do not have time to read a paper. Yet, on average, they spend three hours a day watching television. When they call to cancel their subscriptions, people also complain about delivery problems. Few say that they did not like their paper or thought it was a bad paper.

In the past, it was also easier for people to subscribe to several daily newspapers, often to one paper published in the morning and to another published in the evening. Today, fewer than 50 cities in the entire country support two or more competing dailies. Occasionally, a single company publishes one newspaper in the morning and another in the afternoon. But for economic reasons, most companies that once published both a morning and an evening paper have merged the two, preserving only their more popular edition (usually the morning edition).

That trend largely explains the decline in the number of daily newspapers in the United States. Fifty years ago, most large cities had several daily newspapers. In most cities, only one has survived. The decline now seems to be ending.

Studies have consistently found that the declines in readership are greatest among young adults aged 18 to 30 or 35. Why? More and more young people come from homes that never received a daily paper, so they never developed the habit of reading a paper. Young people are also more mobile than ever before and often fail to develop strong ties to their community. In addition, the cost of subscriptions has increased, and young people with low-paying, entry-level positions complain that they cannot afford to buy a daily paper. Others consider newspapers old-fashioned and believe that reading newspapers is "an old people's habit."

Young adults seem to be uninterested in the news, not just in newspapers. Recent surveys have found that only 37 percent of Americans aged 18 to 30 say they regularly read a daily newspaper, compared to 49 percent of the people 30 to 49 and 64 percent of the people 50 and older. Similarly, only 62 percent of the Americans 18 to 30 watch television news, compared to 69 percent of the Americans 30 to 49 and 83 percent of those 50 and older. A study conducted by the Times-Mirror Center for the People and the Press concluded that young adults "know less and care less about news and public affairs than any other generation of Americans in the past 50 years."

To attract more readers, newspapers are experimenting with dozens of new ideas, including changes in their definitions of news. Newspapers are also trying to improve their content, appearance and delivery and to promote themselves more aggressively.

Newspapers have eliminated material that no longer seems to interest many readers: old comics, social news and bureaucratic government news. They are covering new topics of more interest to today's readers: shopping malls, health and fitness, and the workplace, for example. You may also notice new sections devoted to news for youths or for senior citizens.

Following the example of USA Today, newspapers are improving their packaging. They are making their stories shorter and simpler, and using more color; more photographs; more white space; and other graphics, such as charts and maps.

The News, a daily newspaper in Boca Raton, Fla., recently unveiled a new design that is attracting national attention. Its format includes shorter stories, a ban on jumps (stories continued on another page), more eye-catching graphics, and more stories about topics important to families and neighborhoods. The paper's other new features include:

- Today's Hero: "a mini salute to a worthy local resident."
- Keeper pages that present useful information for readers to pull out and save.
- An improved business section that provides more stories about topics of immediate help to readers: stories about personal finance and consumerism, and features on earning, saving and spending money.

During the first year after its redesign, the News increased its circulation by more than 20 percent. Other newspapers in Charlotte, Long Beach, Akron, Boulder, San Jose and St. Paul are adopting similar innovations.

Yet all the changes may not help newspapers regain their position as the nation's most important medium of communication. Donald L. Shaw of the University of North Carolina, one of journalism's top scholars, explains that no medium can remain at the top indefinitely. New competitors always challenge, and eventually surpass, established leaders. As an industry begins to decline, its leaders always try to return to their old position of dominance. "That always fails," Shaw says. "No medium, once it has lost its dominant position, has ever returned to the top." Media can adapt, but can never come back.

Shaw explains that industry leaders initially assume that people have become dissatisfied with their medium's content, and they think that they can regain their old audience simply by adjusting and improving their content. Shaw has found, however, that changes in content alone will not help a medium regain its old audience. Why? Because people's decisions to use a medium are influenced by other factors such as convenience, habit and interest.

"The challenge," Shaw concludes, "is to innovate, to find new ways to serve (and make money from) a loyal segment of the market and perhaps win new friends."

SUGGESTED READINGS

Articles

Breed, Warren. "Social Control in the News Room." *Social Forces,* 33 (May 1955), pp. 326–35. (Reprinted in *Mass Communications,* ed. Wilbur Schramm. Urbana: IL: University of Illinois Press, 1960.)

Gieber, Walter. "Across the Desk: A Study of 15 Telegraph Editors." *Journalism Quarterly,* 33 (1956), pp. 423–32.

Goltz, Gene. "Reviving a Romance with Readers Is *the* Biggest Challenge for Many Newspapers." *Presstime,* Feb. 1988, pp. 16–22.

Leo, John. "Ugly Truths Untold by the Press." *U.S. News & World Report,* 2 July 1990, p. 15.

Rykken, Rolf. "Readership Decline Brings Newspapers to Crossroads." *Presstime,* March 1989, pp. 22–31.

Schorer, Jane. "The Story of a Rape." *The Quill,* May 1990, pp. 14–19.

Shaw, David. "The AP: It's Everywhere and Powerful." *The Los Angeles Times,* 3 April 1988. (Reprinted in pamphlet form.)

Shaw, Donald L. "The Rise and Fall of American Mass Media: Roles of Technology and Leadership." Roy W. Howard Public Lecture in Journalism and Mass Communication. No. 2. Bloomington, IN: School of Journalism, Indiana University, 4 April 1991.

White, David. "The 'Gate Keeper': A Case Study in the Selection of News." *Journalism Quarterly,* 27 (1950), pp. 383–90. (Reprinted in *People, Society, and Mass Communications,* ed. Lewis A. Dexter and David M. White. New York: The Free Press, 1964.)

Will, George F. "America's Slide into the Sewer." *Newsweek,* 30 July 1990, p. 84.

Books

Abel, Eli, ed. *What's News: The Media in American Society*. San Francisco: Institute for Contemporary Studies, 1981.

Bogart, Leo. *Press and Public: Who Reads What, Where, and Why in American Newspapers*. 2d ed. Hillsdale, NJ: Erlbaum, 1989.

Broder, David S. *Behind the Front Page: A Candid Look at How the News Is Made*. New York: Simon and Schuster, 1987.

Brunvand, Jan. *The Choking Doberman and Other "New" Urban Legends*. New York: Norton, 1984.

Brunvand, Jan. *The Vanishing Hitchhiker: American Urban Legends and Their Meaning*. New York: Norton, 1981.

Dunn, Delmer D. *Public Officials and the Press*. Reading, MA: Addison-Wesley, 1969. (See especially Chapter 3, "What Is 'News'?")

Fishman, Mark. *Manufacturing the News*. Austin, TX: University of Texas Press, 1980.

Gans, Herbert J. *Deciding What's News*. New York: Random House, 1980.

Gaunt, Philip. *Choosing the News: The Profit Factor in News Selection*. Westport. CT: Greenwood Press, 1990.

Manoff, Robert Karl, and Michael Schudson, eds. *Reading the News*. New York: Pantheon, 1987.

Mayer, Martin. *Making News*. Garden City, NY: Doubleday, 1987.

Modern Media Institute. *Making Sense of the News*. St. Petersburg, FL: Poynter Institute, 1983.

Neuharth, Al. *Confessions of an S.O.B.* Garden City, NY: Doubleday, 1989.

Rose, Tom. *Freeing the Whale: How the Media Created the World's Greatest Non-Event*. New York: Birch Lane Press, 1989.

Roshco, Bernard. *Newsmaking*. Chicago: University of Chicago Press, 1975.

Schudson, Michael. *Discovering the News: A Social History of American Newspapers*. New York: Basic Books, 1978.

Seib, Philip. *Who's in Charge? How the Media Shape News and Politicians Win Votes*. Dallas: Taylor, 1987.

Stephens, Mitchell. *A History of News: From the Drum to the Satellite*. New York: Viking, 1988.

Tuchman, Gaye. *Making News: A Study in the Construction of Reality*. New York: Free Press, 1978.

Weinberg, Steve. *Trade Secrets of Washington Journalists*. Washington, DC: Acropolis Books, 1981.

An Ombudsman's Report

CASE STUDY NO. 2

By **Henry McNulty**
Reader Representative
The Hartford (Conn.) Courant

Imagine this scene:

You are a newspaper editor. One afternoon, leaving the newspaper office, you meet one of the paper's photographers, and you both stand chatting on the street. All of a sudden, a friend rushes up to you and says, "Come home quickly! Your child has just been killed in a terrible plane crash."

You are stunned. For a few seconds you can't move—you can't even think. But the photographer quickly raises a camera and snaps off several frames—pictures that show clearly the panic and agony on your face.

The photos are news, the photographer says. They tell the human story, and report reaction to an event of importance.

Would you, the editor, want these used in your newspaper? If it were in your power to stop publication of them, would you permit them to be used? I have asked a number of editors these questions many times over the years. Not even one has answered, "Yes, I would want them used." Most have told me that the moment was too private—too personal, intimate and shattering—to share with the reading public.

Yet newspapers run photos like this all the time.

After Pan Am Flight 103 was blown up over Lockerbie, Scotland, the Bergen (N.J.) Record printed a photograph of a grief-stricken mother lying on the ground at New York's JFK International Airport clutching a Rosary. The National Press Photographers Association elected it as one of the "Pictures of the Month." (Interestingly, the photographer said her editors were "squeamish" about putting the photo on Page 1, so it went on Page A16.)

At my newspaper, we occasionally poll readers about how they would have handled tricky ethical situations. Once, we asked readers what they would do with a photo of a man who had just been told that his son died in a fire.

About three-quarters of the readers answering the question said such a picture should not be printed. At the same time, the newspaper's editors were asked whether they would print the picture. A majority said they would.

In the face of overwhelming public sentiment against these tragedy-reaction shots, and in light of editors' statements that they wouldn't want themselves to be the subjects of such photos, why do they keep being used?

The most common answer is that these pictures fulfill the public's right to know. This answer, in my opinion, doesn't hold up well.

There's no question that the First Amendment gives newspapers the *right* to print this type of picture. But photographs are not needed to fully inform the public, or to fulfill the right-to-know doctrine. For nearly 150 years, my newspaper informed its readers without using a single photograph. Saying "the mother fell to the floor when she heard her child was dead'' may not be elegant, but *it tells the news*.

Of course, it's obvious that photos tell the news in a way that even the most carefully crafted words cannot. Pictures have an immediacy, an intimacy and an impact far beyond that of text. But how related are such matters to the public's right to know? To inform is one thing, but do newspapers have an obligation to let the public *feel* the news, as well as to know it?

Another common answer to the question ''Why run this photo?'' is that pictures of this type can be a valuable teaching tool. They can, for instance, warn about playing with matches, or leaving your children unattended for even a minute, or going swimming with no lifeguard.

There are several problems with this answer. One is the question of whether there's any lasting teaching effect. Many people can recall the so-called ''scare films'' that were shown in schools at the time teen-agers were getting their driver's licenses. I'm unconvinced that these had any meaningful impact on the teen-age car-crash statistics of any generation.

Another problem is whether newspapers really have a commitment to such teaching or whether editors simply haul out this answer to defend using an intrusive photo. Would the paper be willing to devote news space on a regular basis to teaching its readers about auto, plane, fire and boat safety? I'd say not, but newspapers frequently open up space for photos of grieving relatives after crashes, fires or drownings.

Perhaps the most common reason for using such pictures is what I call ''the reality argument.''

Every day, photographers and editors have to deal with what are basically set-up shots. From the well-known ribbon-cuttings, proclamation-signings, check-passings and trophy-receptions to portraits, press conferences and parades, lots of what photographers deal with is posed. It is ''set up'' for them to shoot.

And when it isn't, it's likely to be impersonal: car crashes, sports action shots, driving-in-a-snowstorm, and so forth.

Real life, so to speak, seldom plays a part.

But occasionally, there is a moment when all pretense and posing are swept aside and the naked emotion is revealed. To the photographer, this is the rare time when reality and truth are present, with no formality, no time to say ''cheese.'' It is what photographers dream of.

Is this a compelling argument for using intrusive photos? Perhaps, except it speaks too much of the newspaper's needs, not the needs of readers.

I find myself frequently asking photographers, on behalf of readers, why this photo, or that photo, was taken. Quite often, the answer has been ''because it was something different.'' In many cases, I think what this really means is, ''Because I'm so bored taking pictures of smiling mayors, beauty queens and politicians.''

Journalists should have a problem with turning our boredom into an excuse for violating someone's basic right to privacy.

Exercise 1

SELECTING AND REPORTING THE NEWS

DISCUSSION QUESTIONS BASED ON THE READINGS

1. What do you think is "news"? Can you devise a good definition of the term?
2. Do you agree with Howard K. Smith and Al Neuharth that the media report too much bad news? If so, how would you correct the problem?
3. Chet Brinkley of ABC News said that he does not watch much local news on television because he is tired of seeing stories about blood, knives, guns, death and destruction.

    A. Do you think that Brinkley is right in saying that local newscasts devote too much time to crime and violence?
    B. If so, why do you think that local newscasts devote so much time to that type of story?
    C. Is the public inconsistent? Many Americans complain that the media report too much bad news. But would television stations broadcast that type of story if it didn't help boost ratings?

4. If you edited your local daily, would you have printed the controversial lyrics sung by 2 Live Crew? Why?
5. If you edited your local daily, how would you have handled the Mapplethorpe controversy? Specifically, how would you have described the photographs?
6. Assume that you edited your local daily and received the photographs reprinted in this chapter. Which of the photographs would you publish? Why?
7. Should newspapers devote more space to worthwhile causes and organizations in their communities, recognizing and promoting their good work?
8. In your work have you encountered any "sacred cows," policies that reflected the interests (or prejudices) of your editor or publisher?
9. Do you believe that journalists are objective? If so, would you want them to abandon the concept of objectivity? Why?
10. Do you read your local daily? Why?

    A. If you don't, is there anything that its editor could do to improve the paper so that you would read it?
    B. If you (or a classmate) said you do not have time to read a daily newspaper, do you also lack the time to watch television?
    C. If editors fail to interest young adults in reading newspapers, will that generation of Americans ever begin to read a paper? If not, how can newspapers survive?

11. A recent study concluded that young adults "know less and care less about news and public affairs than any other generation of Americans in the past 50 years." Do you believe that conclusion is an accurate one? Why?
12. Do you agree that newspapers are obsolete and that reading newspapers is an old people's habit? Why?

Exercise 2

SELECTING AND REPORTING THE NEWS

OTHER DISCUSSION QUESTIONS

1. Normally, newspapers report every birth, death, divorce and bankruptcy in their community.

    A. Do you agree with that policy? Why?
    B. As editor, would you include the births to unwed mothers?

2. As editor, would you report every local suicide? Why?

3. As editor of your local daily, you normally avoid publishing pictures of scantily clad young women. But a student on your campus has won the Miss America preliminaries in your state and has flown to Atlantic City for the national finals. During the first day of competition there, your paper received only one photograph, and it shows her and two other contestants in bikinis at a beach. Would you publish the photograph? Why?

4. Assume that your mayor has often criticized the city's welfare system and the fact that some recipients are able-bodied adults without children. If you learned that your mayor's 27-year-old son (who does not live at home) was broke because of a business failure and had applied for welfare, would you publish the story?

5. Assume that three local high school students, each 15 years old, have been charged with arson; they started a fire that caused $80,000 in damage at their high school, closing it for a day.

    A. If you obtained the students' names, and it was legal to do so, would you identify them in your story?
    B. Before publishing the story, would you call and warn (or interview) the students or their parents?

6. Reporters are forced to make difficult decisions about which elements of a story are most newsworthy. Assume that, earlier today, two men robbed a local restaurant and shot a customer. Then, during a high-speed chase through the city, a police car skidded out of control and struck a pedestrian, a 34-year-old nurse. Both the customer and the pedestrian have been hospitalized in serious condition.

    Which element would you emphasize in your lead: the customer shot by two robbers, or the pedestrian struck by police chasing the robbers?

7. If a member of the American Nazi Party spoke in your community and criticized blacks, Jews and immigrants, would you report the story? How would you justify the story's publication or suppression?

8. Imagine that a member of your city council, a Democrat, offered to give you information proving that store personnel had caught your mayor, a Republican, shoplifting. The store's owner declined to prosecute. Morever, the Democrat insists that you never identify him as your source. The Democrat is a potential candidate for mayor and an obvious rival of the current mayor. Yet the information is genuine. How would you respond?

9. Assume that a local woman today announced her candidacy for mayor. Which—if any—of the following facts about her personal life would you include in a story about her candidacy?

   A. She is 57 years old.
   B. She is a millionaire.
   C. She is the mother of four children.
   D. She is 5 feet, 1 inch tall, has gray hair and weighs 180 pounds.
   E. Her first husband died, and she divorced her second.
   F. Her first husband committed suicide two years after their marriage.
   G. After her husband's death, she transformed a small restaurant they established into one of the largest and finest in the city.
   H. She now lives with a bank executive.
   I. The bank executive is 36 years old.
   J. One of her sons is a high school teacher. Two help her in the restaurant. The fourth is in prison, convicted of selling cocaine.

10. Which of the details you want to publish about the candidate described in question 9 would affect her performance if she was elected mayor?

    A. If some of the details about her private life would not affect her performance as mayor, how can you justify their publication?
    B. Would you publish the same details about a male candidate?

CHAPTER 5

BASIC NEWS LEADS

The first paragraph in a news story is called the "lead." The lead (some people spell it "lede") is the most important part of a story—and the most difficult part to write. Traditionally, the lead summarizes an entire story so that readers can decide at a glance whether they want to read it. In this way, readers do not have to waste any time or effort. And—even if they read only the lead—they will receive a capsule account of the entire story.

Newspaper editors prefer the use of summary leads because their readers tend to be skimmers who glance from one story to another and read only what interests them. If a lead fails to interest readers—if it is confusing or dull—they will move on to another story rather than read any of the following paragraphs. Thus, a lead must do more than simply summarize the story; it must also arouse readers' interest and lure them into the story.

Before reporters can write an effective lead, they must first learn to recognize what is news. Leads that fail to emphasize the news—the most interesting and important details—cannot be used, regardless of how well they are written. After deciding which facts are most newsworthy, a reporter must then summarize those facts in sharp, clear sentences, giving a simple, straightforward account of what happened. On the night Abraham Lincoln was shot, a correspondent for The Associated Press wrote the following lead. Typically, it is concise and to-the-point:

> WASHINGTON, FRIDAY, APRIL 14, 1865—The President was shot in a theater tonight, and perhaps mortally wounded.

Other leads have also provided clear, concise summaries of momentous events in the nation's history:

> TOKYO, Dec. 8—Japan went to war against the United States and Great Britain today with air and sea attacks against Hawaii followed by a formal declaration of hostilities.
>
> *(The Associated Press)*

> DALLAS, Nov. 22—A sniper armed with a high-powered rifle assassinated President Kennedy today. Barely two hours after Mr. Kennedy's death, Vice President Johnson took the oath of office as the thirty-sixth President of the United States.
>
> *(The Associated Press)*

> WASHINGTON, D.C.—Richard Milhous Nixon announced his resignation last night as President of the United States, the first chief executive to resign in the Republic's 198-year history.
>
> *(San Francisco Chronicle)*

CAPE CANAVERAL—Space shuttle Challenger exploded into a gigantic fireball moments after liftoff today, apparently killing all seven crew members, including schoolteacher Christa McAuliffe.

(The Associated Press)

THE QUESTIONS A LEAD SHOULD ANSWER

In the past, every lead was expected to answer six questions: *Who? How? Where? Why? When?* and *What?* Newspapers have abandoned that rigid style because leads that answered all six questions became too long and complex. Also, answers to all the questions were not always important. Because few readers in large cities know the people involved in routine stories, the names of those people do not have to appear in leads. The exact time and place at which a story occurred may also be unimportant.

Today, leads emphasize answers only to the most important of the six questions, which vary from one story to another. The following examples, although slightly exaggerated, are traditional leads that attempt to answer all six questions. Their revisions, following the currently preferred style, answer only the most important questions:

Andrew A. Kernan, 18, a student at Central High School and the son of Mr. and Mrs. Harry Kernan of 1432 Hillmore Lane, died at about 3:30 p.m. Tuesday when his car overturned near a sharp curve on State Road 12.
REVISED: An 18-year-old student was killed Tuesday when his car overturned while he was driving home from high school.

Samuel Alston, assistant district attorney for Hennepin County, announced during a press conference in the Blackhawk Hotel at noon today that a prisoner, whom he did not identify, has confessed to the murder of a local liquor store owner seven years ago.
REVISED: A prisoner in the county jail has confessed to the murder of a local liquor store owner seven years ago.

To determine which questions are most important for a story you have been asked to write, consider the following points:

1. What is the most important information—what is the story's main point or topic?
2. What was said or done about the topic—what happened or what action was taken?
3. What are the most recent developments—what happened today or yesterday?
4. Which facts are most likely to affect or interest your readers?
5. Which facts are most unusual?

Each of the following leads emphasizes the answer to only one of the six basic questions—the question that seems to be most important for that particular story:

WHO: Three teen-agers, including a 14-year-old who is eight months pregnant, today were sentenced to 20 years in prison for robbing and murdering a cab driver.

HOW: A 15-year-old boy in the county jail ripped part of a sheet from his bedding and used it to hang himself from a coat hook in his cell.

WHERE: Turbulent air 35,000 feet above the state jolted an American Airlines jet last night, injuring 23 passengers and three flight attendants.

WHY: Desperate over the breakup of his marriage and financial problems, Teddy Bruce Flichum killed his 2-year-old son, then committed suicide in a motel room Wednesday.

(The Orlando Sentinel)

WHEN: Moments after two young women left a jewelry store Monday afternoon, a salesman discovered that four gold bracelets valued at $1,840 were missing from a display case he had opened for them.

WHAT: PROVIDENCE, R.I.—Teen-age children in one out of 10 American families hit, beat, stab or shoot their parents, according to a survey released Monday by a University of Rhode Island sociologist.

(The Associated Press)

SENTENCE STRUCTURE IN LEADS

Most leads consist of a single sentence, and that sentence must follow all the normal rules for punctuation, grammar, word usage and verb tense. If an event occurred in the past, the lead must use the past, not the present, tense. Leads must be complete sentences and should include all the necessary articles (the words "a," "an" and "the"). Mistakenly, inexperienced reporters often use incomplete sentences and the present, rather than the past, tense. Some beginners also eliminate the articles, particularly when they appear at the beginning of a lead, a practice that is distracting and unnecessarily brusque:

Man dies on railroad tracks.
REVISED: A 19-year-old Detroit man was killed early Tuesday when he was hit by a train while lying on some railroad tracks just south of Nova Road.

Party ends in tragedy as two die.
REVISED: Two 7-year-old girls attending a friend's birthday party suffocated Monday after climbing into an unused freezer during a game of hide-and-seek.

Most leads contain only one sentence. Two- or three-sentence leads often become wordy, repetitious and choppy, particularly when all the sentences are very short. Like most multisentence leads, the following examples can be combined more concisely into a single sentence:

The federal government issued a report about welfare recipients today. The report stated that the number of welfare recipients in the United States has risen to 14.4 million, a record high.
REVISED: The federal government reported today that the number of welfare recipients in the United States has risen to 14.4 million, a record high.

Two women robbed a shopper in a local supermarket Tuesday. One woman distracted the shopper and the second woman grabbed her purse, which contained about $50.

REVISED: One woman distracted a shopper in a local supermarket Tuesday, and another woman grabbed her purse, which contained about $50.

The original leads were redundant. Before describing the report's content, the first lead said—unnecessarily—that the report was issued. The second lead reported that two women robbed a shopper, then described the robbery. Yet if a lead says that one woman distracted a shopper and another woman grabbed her purse, it is redundant to add that "two women robbed a shopper."

Reporters use two-sentence leads only when the need to do so is compelling. Often, the second sentence is used to emphasize an interesting or unusual fact of secondary importance. It may also be impossible to summarize all the necessary information about a complex topic in a single sentence. The following examples, both transmitted by The Associated Press, use a second sentence to summarize an unusual or secondary highlight:

ST. MARY'S, W. Va. (AP)—Fifty-one construction workers plunged screaming to their deaths Thursday when a scaffold inside a power company cooling tower collapsed and crashed 168 feet to the ground. Nine of the victims were members of one family.

OSSINING, N.Y. (AP)—Joseph and Edna Reyes were buried Wednesday beside their teen-age son, reunited in death with a beloved only child. They had chosen not to go on living without him.

Some problems with sentence structure arise because beginners confuse a story's lead with its headline. The lead is the first paragraph of a news story. The headline is a brief summary that appears in larger type above the story. Most headlines are written by editors, not reporters. To save space, the editors use only a few key words in each headline. However, that style of writing is not appropriate for leads.

While writing leads, reporters use a relatively simple sentence structure. Most leads begin with the subject, which is closely followed by an active verb and then by the object of the verb. Reporters deviate from that style only when they want to emphasize some other element of a story. Leads that begin with long qualifying clauses and phrases lack the clarity of simpler, more direct sentences. Long introductory clauses also clutter leads, burying the news amid a jumble of less significant details. Because they begin with clauses, the following leads fail to emphasize the most important facts and to report those facts clearly and immediately:

While on a routine patrol, a police officer discovered that burglars had pried open the back door of a liquor store on Pennsylvania Avenue and stolen more than 100 cases of whiskey Thursday night.
REVISED: Burglars pried open the back door of a liquor store on Pennsylvania Avenue and stole more than 100 cases of whiskey Thursday night.

While a 42-year-old man was dropping off two women on West Jackson Street Tuesday night, he was robbed and punched in the face by three youths who opened a car door and took his wallet.
REVISED: Three youths opened the door of a car stopped on West Jackson Street Tuesday night, robbed its driver and punched him in the face.

Before it was revised, the first lead emphasized the commonplace—the fact that a police officer discovered a burglary "while on a routine patrol." The second lead delayed the news—information about the robbery—until its 18th word.

GUIDELINES FOR WRITING EFFECTIVE LEADS

Be Concise

Newspapers' concise style of writing makes it easier for the public to read and understand leads, but more difficult for reporters to write them. Typically, leads written by correspondents for the nation's two major news agencies, The Associated Press and United Press International, contain an average of only 18 to 20 words. Some journalists insist that no lead should exceed 30 words, but that limit is too rigid and forces reporters to stop and count the number of words in every lead. Slightly longer leads are acceptable if they are easy to read and understand. It is easier to count the number of typed lines in leads instead of the number of words. Most leads contain about two typed lines, and some contain three. A lead that exceeds three typed lines is probably too long and should be critically examined to determine whether it is wordy or repetitious or contains facts that could be shifted to a later paragraph. A lead that exceeds four lines should always be rewritten and shortened.

Reporters shorten leads by eliminating unnecessary background information and the description of routine procedures; a lead should report a story's highlights, not all its minor details. Even more important, reporters must eliminate unnecessary words, always expressing their ideas as concisely as possible:

> A county education official Wednesday said she favors spanking elementary school children but admitted the practice should not be used on high school students.
> REVISED: A county educator Wednesday said she favors spanking elementary school children, but not high school students.

> A police officer shot and seriously wounded Robert R. Chuey, 25, of 624 Church St., who fled from the scene of a robbery, then fired at the officer during a foot chase in an alley in the 1600 block of N. 35th Street early this morning.
> REVISED: A police officer shot and seriously wounded a 25-year-old man who fired at him while fleeing the scene of a robbery early this morning.
> The shooting occurred in an alley in the 1600 block of N. 35th Street, and police identified the man as Robert R. Chuey of 624 Church Street.

The revision summarizes the story in its lead. It places details of secondary importance in the next paragraph—an option always available to you.

Reporters can shorten leads by deleting unnecessary names, dates and locations. Leads should not contain too many names, particularly obscure names that readers are unlikely to recognize, or the names of people who played minor or routine roles in a story. If you include someone's name in a lead, you may also have to identify that person, and the identification will take up even more space. Reporters can often substitute descriptive phrases for names (for example: "a 16-year-old girl," "an Austin teacher," "a retired nurse"). Similarly, instead of reporting a story's precise time and location, a lead might mention only the day and city; the specific hour and street address could be reported in a later paragraph.

Thus, most leads should contain no more than two or three typed lines, and reporters can save space by eliminating minor details, unnecessary names and precise times and locations. However, there is no *minimum* length for leads; an effective lead may contain only four or five words (for example: "The president is dead" or "Americans have landed on Mars"). Despite their brevity, editors at The New York Times have praised the following leads, written by members of their staff:

Smallpox is about to be eradicated from the earth.

Howard R. Hughes died today as mysteriously as he had lived.

Be Specific

Good leads contain interesting details and are so specific that readers can visualize the events they describe. As you read the following leads, you should be able to imagine the dramatic scenes they describe:

MIAMI (UPI)—A "grandmother-type" 71-year-old woman, who became annoyed when a teen-ager blew cigarette smoke in her face on a city bus, whipped out a can of Mace Friday and chased the youth down the aisle, her spray can going full blast.

TAMPA (AP)—The parents, two lawyers, a doctor and a nurse looked on in tears as the respirator was unplugged. Forty minutes later, 14-month-old Andrew James Barry died in his mother's arms.

The following leads are less interesting because they are abstract and contain vague generalities. However, reporters can easily transform them into more interesting leads by adding more specific details:

A Clark County woman is suing her former employer, charging sex discrimination.
REVISED: A Clark County receptionist who says she was fired because she became pregnant is suing an optometrist for sexual discrimination.

Several agencies handle the large number of animals killed or injured on city and county roads.
REVISED: Each week, the Humane Society picks up about 50 animals killed or injured on city streets, and county employees bury hundreds of others at the spots where they are found.

A secretary whose child was born handicapped is suing a medical laboratory for what she says was negligence.
REVISED: A secretary whose child was born blind and deaf is suing a medical laboratory which failed to detect her exposure to measles. Because of the negative test results, she decided to continue her pregnancy.

A related (and lazy) way of summarizing a story is also too vague. Instead of presenting any specific details about a topic, some reporters write that "a step has been taken," or that someone has moved "one step closer" to a goal. These are vague, dull clichés:

The City Commission has taken a step to combine the city's police and fire departments under one boss.
REVISED: The City Commission voted to appoint a director of public safety to head both the police and fire departments.

The state is one step closer to the adoption of a tourism tax that will add $30 million to its promotional budget.

REVISED: A House subcommittee Monday passed a bill authorizing the establishment of an 11-member tourism commission. The commission will impose a tax on tourism-related businesses and use the $30 million it raises each year to promote tourism.

Also avoid "iffy" leads. In addition to being too vague, "iffy" leads are too abstract, tentative and qualified. Avoid, for example, reporting that one thing may happen if another happens. Rather, report the story's more immediate and concrete details:

The Board of Regents will meet at 2 p.m. Friday, and students will have to pay higher tuition next year if the regents approve the first item on their agenda.
REVISED: The Board of Regents will vote Friday on a proposal to raise tuition 8 percent.

Alcohol sales in restaurants may be restricted if a charter amendment approved last night by the City Council is passed by voters in a March referendum.
REVISED: The City Council last night approved a charter amendment that would restrict the sale of alcohol in restaurants.
The charter amendment must also be approved by voters and will be placed on a March referendum.

Use Strong, Active Verbs

A single word—a descriptive verb—can transform a routine lead into a dramatic one. As you read the following lead, for example, you may be able to sense the drama of a wounded deputy struggling to his feet:

PAHOKEE, Fla.—A deputy sheriff who was shot four times on a street in this town on Lake Okeechobee struggled to his feet and shot his assailant, who was trying to escape in the officer's patrol car.

(United Press International)

The following lead contains several colorful verbs, and they make the lead more interesting, even exciting:

BUDAPEST, Hungary—Thousands of East German refugees—cheering, laughing and crying—poured into the West today after Hungary agreed to let them flee across its border with Austria.

(USA Today)

Avoid weaker, nondescriptive verbs, especially forms of the verb "to be," such as "is," "are," "was" and "were." Strong, active verbs are more colorful, interesting and dramatic:

Nearly 300 irate citizens *were* at the School Board's meeting Tuesday night and *said* it *is* not right for the board to *raise* taxes by more than 20 percent.
REVISED: Nearly 300 irate citizens *stormed* into the School Board's meeting Tuesday night, *demanding* that the board *abandon* its plans to *raise* taxes by more than 20 percent.

One person *was killed* and four others *were injured* Sunday morning when their car, which *was traveling* west on Interstate 80, *hit* a cement bridge pillar and *was engulfed* in flames.

REVISED: A car *traveling* west on Interstate 80 *swerved* across two eastbound lanes, *slammed* into a cement bridge pillar and *burst* into flames, *killing* one person and *injuring* four others Sunday morning.

If you write a passive lead, you can easily convert it to the active voice. Simply rearrange the words, so that you begin by reporting: (1) who . . . (2) did what . . . (3) to whom. Instead of reporting that "Rocks and bottles were thrown at firefighters," report that "Rioters threw rocks and bottles at firefighters." Similarly, instead of reporting that "The contract was approved by teachers," report that "Teachers approved the contract."

Emphasize the Magnitude of the Story

If a story is important, reporters emphasize its magnitude in the lead, often by revealing the number of dollars, buildings or other objects it involves. When describing a major storm, reporters may emphasize the amount of rain or snow that fell. When describing a major fire, they may emphasize the amount of damage, the number of people left homeless or the number of injuries:

PENSACOLA (AP)—A Boeing 727 carrying 60 people plowed into Pensacola Bay on a landing approach late Monday night, killing at least one.

A power failure plunged New York City and Westchester County into darkness last night, disrupting the lives of nearly nine million people.

(The New York Times)

Most good leads emphasize the impact that stories have on their participants or readers. For example: the fact that a person was injured is considered more important than the fact that a car was destroyed or that a store was robbed. Thus, the following leads also emphasize the fate of people involved in the news:

Two gunmen shot a customer in the chin while robbing a restaurant at 944 W. Colonial Drive Wednesday night.

A police officer suffered a broken leg and a concussion when his motorcycle collided with a car Monday afternoon.

Stress the Unusual

Leads also emphasize the unusual. By definition, news involves deviations from the norm. Newspapers are sometimes criticized for emphasizing the unusual, but the fact remains that the unusual is more interesting than the routine and is therefore more likely to attract and hold readers' attention. The unusual or unexpected also tends to be more important. The fact that someone was born, married, divorced, arrested, robbed, injured or honored is more interesting and more important than the fact that, on the same day, someone else did nothing out of the ordinary. Similarly, the fact that an airplane crashed is more important (and more interesting and unusual) than the fact that hundreds of other airplanes had routine flights.

Leads about a city council meeting should not report that the council met at 8 p.m. in the city council chambers in city hall and that the council began its meeting with a prayer and the Pledge of Allegiance. Those facts are routine and consequently not newsworthy. Most city councils meet at least once every week, usually at the same time and place, and many begin all their meetings with a prayer and the Pledge of Allegiance. Leads should emphasize the unique—the action that follows those routine formalities.

Normally, for example, newspapers do not report minor crimes, yet in one instance a $20 robbery became front-page news. A reporter learned that an attorney had gotten a client released from jail by convincing a judge that the man was a thief. The man had accepted $20 from an undercover officer and promised to give him some cocaine. Instead of delivering the cocaine, the man fled. He was arrested several days later and charged with the unlawful delivery of cocaine: a felony. Because the man did not have enough money for bail, he was locked in the county jail. During a preliminary hearing, his attorney argued that the man was a thief: that he never possessed any cocaine and never intended to deliver any. Instead, he had simply stolen the officer's $20. Because the theft of $20 is a less serious crime—a misdemeanor—the man was freed without bond.

Similarly, bank robberies are so common in big cities that newspapers normally devote only a few paragraphs to them. Yet a robbery at the Burlington National Bank in Columbus, Ohio, became a front-page story, published by newspapers throughout the United States. A story transmitted by The Associated Press explained that:

> A 61-year-old man says he robbed an Ohio bank with a toy gun—he even told the FBI ahead of time when and where—because he wants to spend his golden years in federal prison.

After his arrest, the bank robber insisted that he did not want a lawyer. Instead, he wanted to immediately "plead guilty to anything." The man explained that he recently was divorced, had no family ties and was disabled with arthritis. He had spent time in at least three federal prisons and wanted to return to one of them. "I knew what I was doing," he insisted. "I wanted to get arrested, and I proceeded about it the best way I knew how."

To make the following leads more interesting, both have been revised to emphasize the unusual:

> A restaurant was robbed of $62 early Tuesday morning.
> REVISED: An elderly woman with a knife robbed a restaurant of $62 early Tuesday morning and explained that she needed the money to buy Christmas presents for her grandchildren.

> Judge Marlene Ostreicher today sentenced a bank robber to five years in a federal prison.
> REVISED: A man who robbed four banks, once while disguised as the Joker from the movie "Batman," was sentenced today to five years in a federal prison.

Stories may involve other kinds of unusual details that reporters must learn to recognize and emphasize in their leads. Here are three examples. The first, written by a college student, describes a Hollywood stunt man:

> Kim Kahana has broken his arms 60 times and broken his back twice, but calls the injuries "just part of my job."

Trials for motorists caught speeding by Highway Patrol radar units in Dade County have been postponed because the devices were proven inaccurate—in one case clocking a tree at 86 mph.

Despite a tearful plea from his pregnant wife, a 20-year-old man today was sentenced to life in prison for selling drugs within 1,000 feet of an elementary school.

(The Associated Press)

Similarly, other leads emphasize the unexpected:

MIAMI (AP)—Nineteen-year-old Jose Pico thought he was doing a good deed when he chased down a hit-and-run driver and held him at gunpoint until police arrived.
He still can't understand why he was arrested and the driver was set free.

GAINESVILLE, Fla. (AP)—When Eddie Lasco pulled a gun on Julie Black and robbed the hair styling parlor where she worked, she was impressed by his thoughtfulness and manners.
A few months later, she married him.

Localize and Update Your Lead

Reporters are trained to localize and update their leads whenever possible by emphasizing their communities' involvement in stories. Editors explain that readers are most interested in stories that affect their own lives and the lives of other people they know. To satisfy their readers' interests, newspaper editors emphasize stories that occur within their own communities and that mention people, places and events that their readers are familiar with. Consequently, when an editor in Kansas City was asked to define news, he replied, "The farther it is from Kansas City, the less it is news."

Reporters also try to localize stories that arise in other parts of the world. If Congress grants federal employees a raise, reporters may localize the story by reporting the number of federal employees in their communities who will benefit from the congressional action. Similarly, when the FBI reports on the number of violent crimes committed in the United States, reporters stress the statistics for their local communities:

The FBI reported today that the number of violent crimes in the United States rose 8.3 percent during the last year.
LOCALIZED: The number of violent crimes committed in the city last year rose 5.4 percent, compared to a national average of 8.3 percent, the FBI reported today.

Eighty-three people were killed today when their jet plunged into a field two miles south of an airport in Tokyo.
LOCALIZED: Eighty-three people, including three from this area, were killed today when their jet plunged into a field two miles south of an airport in Tokyo.

Reporters update a lead by stressing the latest developments in the story. Often, even a story that occurred only a few hours earlier can be updated. Instead of reporting that a fire destroyed a local store the previous day, reporters may stress the fact that subsequently authorities have learned the fire's cause, identified the victims, arrested an arsonist or estimated the monetary loss. Stories are updated so they offer the public something new—facts not already reported by other newspapers or by local radio and television stations.

Major stories about such topics as economic trends, natural disasters, wars and political upheavals often remain in the news for several months and must also be updated. Reporters must always emphasize the latest developments so that readers are given new facts that they have not already heard from other sources:

> Two men robbed the First National Bank, 1841 Main St., of about $20,000 yesterday and shot a police officer in the chest.
> UPDATED: A police officer shot during a bank robbery is reported in critical condition today at Memorial Hospital.

> Sheriff's deputies raided a "nickel and dime" poker game at a retirement home yesterday and charged eight men with gambling.
> UPDATED: Eight men charged with gambling after sheriff's deputies raided a poker game at a retirement home said today that they will plead guilty to the charge.

Not every lead can be updated or localized. If a story has no new or local angles, report it in a simple, straightforward manner. Do not distort the story in any way or attempt to create any new or local angles that are fictional.

Be Objective and Attribute Opinions

Leads of news stories, like their bodies, must be objective. Reporters are expected to gather and to convey facts to their readers, not to comment, interpret or advocate. There is rarely any justification for calling the people involved in news stories "alert," "heroic" or "quick-thinking," or for describing facts as "interesting" or "startling." These comments waste space and, when they are accurate, usually state the obvious. Leads composed entirely of opinion or interpretation must be rewritten to provide more factual, comprehensive accounts of the news:

> An afternoon fishing trip turned into tragedy Wednesday.
> REVISED: A 41-year-old mechanic drowned Wednesday after he apparently suffered a heart attack while fishing in Clear Lake and fell out of a small boat.

> Speaking to the Downtown Rotary Club last night, Emil Plambeck, superintendent of the City Park Commission, discussed a topic of concern to all of us—the city's park system.
> REVISED: Emil Plambeck, superintendent of the City Park Commission, wants developers to set aside 5 percent of the land in new subdivisions for parks.

> It pays to be a friend. That is what Clarence and Edith Grafton of Birmingham, Ala., have learned.
> REVISED: A retired minister has left his entire estate, valued at $280,000, to two friends: Clarence and Edith Grafton of Birmingham, Ala.

The first lead states the obvious by calling a 41-year-old man's sudden death a "tragedy." The second lead is weak because it refers to "a topic of concern to all of us." The reporter does not identify "us" and is wrong to assert that any topic concerns everyone. The third lead contains a cliché as well as opinion, and thus fails to give a clear report of what happened.

Here are other examples of leads that state an opinion or conclusion:

> Whether competing or just hitting the ball back and forth, it is hard to find a person who doesn't enjoy a good game of table tennis between friends.

> Adult entertainment establishments have fallen victim to another attempt at censorship.

> Recycling does not pay, at least not economically. However, the environmental benefits make the city's new recycling program worthwhile at any cost.

To demonstrate the fact that all three leads are statements of opinion—controversial and perhaps mistaken—ask your friends and classmates about them:

- Do *all* your friends and classmates enjoy table tennis?
- Do *all* your friends and classmates agree that the regulation of adult entertainment establishments is "censorship"?
- Do *all* your friends and classmates agree that recycling programs are "worthwhile at any cost"?

To avoid infuriating or offending your readers, never express your opinions in the leads and stories you write. Simply report the facts. Then your readers can reach their own conclusions about them.

Although reporters cannot express their own opinions in stories, they often include the opinions of people involved in the news. A lead that contains a statement of opinion must be attributed so that readers clearly understand that the opinion is not the reporter's.

Often, beginners misplace the attribution in leads, use attribution when it is not necessary and fail to use attribution when it is needed. Attribution is usually necessary in leads that contain a quotation, charges or criticism of any kind, or other statements of opinion. The attribution should be expressed as concisely as possible and should be placed near the end, rather than at the beginning, of the lead. Leads should begin with the news—important details that reporters want to emphasize—as in the following examples:

> NEW YORK—More American workers are dissatisfied with their jobs now than at any other time in the past 25 years, according to a survey released Tuesday.
>
> *(The Associated Press)*

> WASHINGTON, D.C.—Working wives are drawing better salaries, but they still earn only 57 percent as much as their husbands, says a report issued Tuesday by the Census Bureau.
>
> *(Scripps-Howard News Service)*

Reporters often use "blind leads" that do not specifically name their source. So they can devote more attention to the news, reporters use only a brief descriptive phrase (such as "leading doctors") in the lead, and present most of the attribution in the second or third paragraph. The attributions in the following leads are also brief, with the sources identified more fully in the subsequent paragraphs. Notice that only the biochemist's title is used in the first lead; his name appears in the second paragraph:

> The mysterious process by which green plants turn sunlight into chemical energy can certainly be harnessed to help man solve the energy crisis and world hunger, a University of Kansas biochemist said Friday.
> "When sunlight hits a leaf, it makes a small chemical battery," said Ralph Christoffersen. "If we knew the details of how that process occurs, there's no reason why we couldn't build a copy of the leaf."
>
> *(The Associated Press)*

> Childbirth is far more dangerous than generally believed and may be the 11th leading cause of death to women 15 through 44 years of age, a new federal study has disclosed.
> The study, conducted in Georgia by the national Centers for Disease Control, supports earlier findings that deaths associated with pregnancy and childbirth may be 50 percent higher than currently reported.
>
> *(The Chicago Tribune)*

Similarly, the following lead contains only seven words of attribution. More information about the source appears in the fourth paragraph:

> WASHINGTON, D.C.—Teen-agers are more than twice as likely as adults to be victims of rape, robbery and assault, according to a government report issued Sunday.
> The study shows that more than 60 of every 1,000 teen-agers are victims of violent crime each year, compared to just 27 of every 1,000 adults.
> The study also found that teen-agers were nearly twice as likely as adults to be victimized by theft. The teen-age rate for theft was 123 per 1,000 compared to 65 per 1,000 for adults.
> The report by the Justice Department's Bureau of Justice Statistics was compiled from twice-a-year surveys of 49,900 households. . . .
>
> *(The Associated Press)*

A lead that contains an obvious fact or a fact that the reporter has witnessed, or can verify by some other means, generally does not require attribution. An editor at The New York Times, instructing reporters to "make the lead of a story as brief and clear as possible," has noted: "One thing that obstructs that aim is the inclusion of an unnecessary source of attribution. . . . If the lead is controversial, an attribution is imperative. But if the lead is innocuous, forget it." Thus, if a lead states a fact that no one is likely to question, you can place the attribution in a later paragraph because none is necessary in the lead:

> Seven children and both their parents were killed when their van slammed into the back of a truck parked along an Arizona highway late Friday night.

> WASHINGTON (AP)—Children who murder their parents will no longer be able to collect Social Security survivors' benefits.

Strive for Simplicity

While employing these techniques, also strive for simplicity. Every lead you write should be clear, simple and to the point. Here are two examples from USA Today:

> Bad news for 450,000 taxpayers: Your refund checks aren't in the mail.

Children of women who smoke during pregnancy continue to suffer physical and mental deficiencies at age 3, a new study shows.

The following leads were written by students. Again, all three of the leads are so clear, concise and simple that you can grasp them at a glance:

A jury deliberated for only 30 minutes Friday before deciding that a woman was guilty of kicking dents in a car.

An Arkansas couple filed a lawsuit today, charging that a pest control company killed their cat.

Jose Young, a student who has been comatose since a fight on Oct. 7, is showing signs of improvement.

If your leads are not this simple, rewrite them:

The mayor said she wants the City Council to approve an ordinance that would require the city to begin paying for burials for people unable to afford them.
REVISED: The mayor wants the city to pay for the burial of indigents.

Two police officers checking on reports of a commotion and a possible prowler at a sorority house Sunday night were surprised when, while searching the basement, they found a family of five, all raccoons, living there.
REVISED: Police officers found that five raccoons, not a prowler, caused the commotion in a sorority house's basement Sunday night.

AVOIDING SOME COMMON ERRORS

The following pages discuss the errors that appear most often as students begin to write leads.

Emphasize the News

Mistakenly, some leads emphasize whatever occurred first. Yet the first events rarely are the most newsworthy. As you begin a story, decide which facts are most interesting and important, then begin your leads with those facts regardless of whether they occurred first, last or in the middle of the story:

A pollster who spoke to political scientists meeting today began by welcoming them to the city and by describing his accuracy in recent surveys.
REVISED: No woman is likely to be elected president of the United States during the next 50 years, pollster Lester Marshal predicted during a speech today.

The prosecution this morning opened its case against a 19-year-old man charged with murdering a cab driver.
REVISED: Two police officers testified today that they observed a 19-year-old man driving a stolen cab and found the cab driver's watch and wallet in the man's jacket pocket.

Other leads place too much emphasis on the time and place at which stories occurred:

> A country-and-western bar on Benson Avenue was the scene of a fight last night that left one man critically injured.
> REVISED: A 41-year-old man is in critical condition after being stabbed by his brother-in-law outside a country-and-western bar on Benson Avenue.

> At 9 a.m. Monday in Room 240 of the General Classroom Building, university administrators will meet with about 100 students who are demanding a tuition refund because a journalism teacher came to only 17 of their 48 classes last semester.
> REVISED: About 100 students are demanding a tuition refund because a journalism teacher came to only 17 of their 48 classes last semester.
> University administrators will meet with the students at 9 a.m. Monday in Room 240 of the General Classroom Building.

Until it was revised, the first lead emphasized the story's location rather than the victim's critical condition (and the unusual fact that the injuries were inflicted by his brother-in-law). The second lead emphasized the place where university administrators were scheduled to meet with the students rather than the students' unusual grievance.

If you are uncertain about what to emphasize, look for a story's action or consequences. The following lead, as revised, does more than report that four shotgun blasts were fired at a house; it also summarizes the consequences or damage caused by those shotgun blasts. Similarly, the second lead, as revised, stresses the consequences of the accident.

> Four shotgun blasts were fired into a home at 205 E. Mason Drive at 2 a.m. today.
> REVISED: Four shotgun blasts fired into a home at 205 E. Mason Drive at 2 a.m. today shattered several windows and damaged some furniture but did not injure the home's five occupants.

> A 15-year-old boy learning to drive his family's new car struck a gasoline pump in a service station on Hall Road late Tuesday afternoon.
> REVISED: A 15-year-old boy learning to drive his family's new car struck a gasoline pump in a service station on Hall Road late Tuesday afternoon, causing a fire that blocked traffic on the road for three hours.

Here are two more examples of leads that fail to report the news (the stories' outcome or consequences):

> Last weekend the women's volleyball team participated in the regional playoffs.
> REVISED: The women's volleyball team won five of its seven games and placed second in the regional playoffs last weekend.

> An argument between three men turned into a shoot-out at a nightclub at 1:45 a.m. Sunday.
> REVISED: One man was killed and another shot in an ear outside a nightclub at 1:45 a.m. Sunday.

Begin with the News

Be particularly careful to avoid beginning with an attribution. Names and titles are dull and often unimportant. Moreover, if every lead begins with the attribution (or with the time and place a story occurred), all the leads will sound too much alike. Place the attribution at the beginning of a lead only when it is unusual or significant and deserves that emphasis:

At a press conference in Washington, D.C., today, Neil A. Schuster, a spokesman for the U.S. Bureau of Labor Statistics, announced that last month the cost of living rose 2.83 percent, a record high.
REVISED: The cost of living rose 2.83 percent last month, a record high, the U.S. Bureau of Labor Statistics reported today.

In a speech before a statewide convention of the National Education Association in the state capital today, Gov. Ronald A. Harris revealed plans to raise the state sales tax by one penny and to use most of the money to improve the state's school system.
REVISED: The governor plans to raise the state sales tax by one penny and to use most of the money to improve the state's school system.

Originally, the two leads devoted more space to the attribution than to the news. The first lead, as revised, emphasizes the news—the information revealed by the Bureau of Labor Statistics. The attribution has been condensed and can be reported more fully in a later paragraph. The second lead, as revised, stresses the governor's plans to raise the state sales tax, an idea that would affect virtually all of a newspaper's readers. The fact that the governor revealed the plans at a teachers' convention is less important and can be reported later.

Avoid "Label" Leads

Leads should report the substance of a story, not just its topic. A good lead will do more than report that a group met, held a press conference, issued a report or listened to someone speak. The lead will reveal what the group did at its meeting, or summarize what was said at the press conference, in the report or during the speech.

An introductory paragraph that fails to report the news—that mentions a topic but fails to reveal what was said or done about that topic—is called a "label" lead. Because they use similar words and phrases, label leads are easy to recognize and avoid. Many of the leads report that an issue "was the subject of" a speech or "the main topic of discussion." Other label leads report that people "spoke about," "delivered a speech about" or were "interviewed about" an issue. Typically, then, label leads emphasize the topic under consideration but fail to summarize the statements made about the topic or the action provoked by it. Here are three examples:

The City Council last night discussed ways of regulating a new topless club in the city.

Faculty and staff members and other experts today proposed strategies to recruit more minority students.

Administration officials and student body leaders are considering a variety of plans to solve the parking problem on campus.

The first lead should summarize the city council's discussion, clearly explaining how the council plans to regulate the topless club. The second lead should summarize the experts' strategies for recruiting more minority students. Similarly, the third lead should summarize the plans to solve your school's parking problems.

Here are more examples of the problem, along with a correction for each of them:

LABEL LEAD: Reporter Mike Griffin spoke on Monday to a group of students about what it takes to become a journalist.
REVISED: If you want a job in journalism, finish your college degree and complete an internship or two before you graduate, reporter Mike Griffin advised students here Friday.

LABEL LEAD: The Department of Health and Human Services issued a report on alcoholism today.
REVISED: Alcohol is the major drug problem in the United States, and one out of 10 working Americans suffers from alcoholism or a lesser drinking problem, the Department of Health and Human Services reported today.

LABEL LEAD: A police lieutenant spoke to the Methodist Women's Club last night about the danger of firearms.
REVISED: People who own guns are more likely to shoot themselves or members of their family than to shoot a prowler, a police lieutenant said last night.

Avoid Unfamiliar Terms

Make your leads as clear, simple and readable as possible. If your readers are unlikely to recognize a name or term, place it in a later paragraph, not the lead—or avoid it altogether. A lead that contains several unfamiliar names or terms is likely to be especially dull:

Police Officer Bruce Esterling told Prosecuting Attorney Leslie Hess on Monday that he spotted the defendant, Charles McLockland, 820 Randall St., attempting to flee from a store.
REVISED: A police officer testified Monday that he saw a young soldier running from a convenience store moments after a clerk was robbed and raped.

Health care for the poor is substandard in this county, according to medical health care experts who met at an AMA conference here. They hope that Vertical Integration Systems will help reverse that trend.
REVISED: To improve medical care in the county, experts want to establish eight clinics in poor neighborhoods and to refer only the most serious cases to specialists at County Hospital.

Avoid Lists

Avoid placing any lists in your leads. Most lists, like names, are dull. If you *must* use a list, place an explanation before it, never after it. If you begin with a list, your readers will not immediately understand its significance. The following example, published by a Denver newspaper, delays starting the explanation until the 20th word:

BOULDER, Colo.—Complaints about bicycle racing fans urinating on lawns, perching on the roofs of private homes and trampling flower beds may lead city officials to ask Coors Classic organizers to find a new setting next year for their Boulder criterium.

If you place the explanation before a list, your readers can immediately understand its meaning:

> The family home, a new Cadillac, $2,500 a month, and a 50 percent interest in the family business were awarded to Claire Marcial, who sued her husband for divorce.
> REVISED: As part of the divorce settlement, a judge awarded Claire Marcial the family home, a new Cadillac, $2,500 a month and a 50 percent interest in the family business.

> The company that made it, the store that sold it and the friend who lent it to him are being sued by a 24-year-old man whose spine was severed when a motorcycle overturned.
> REVISED: A 24-year-old man whose spine was severed when a motorcycle overturned is suing the company that made the motorcycle, the store that sold it and the friend who lent it to him.

Avoid Stating the Obvious

Avoid stating the obvious, and avoid emphasizing routine procedures in your leads. If you write about a crime, you do not have to begin by reporting that police "were called to the scene" or that ambulances "rushed" the victims to a hospital "for treatment of their injuries." This problem is particularly common on sports pages, where many leads have become clichés. For example, most coaches and players express optimism at the beginning of every season; news stories then report that the coaches and players want to win most of their games. Here are two examples, both from college newspapers:

> Coming into the new season, the women's soccer team wants to make the playoffs.

> The football team is beginning its new season with a few pesky questions and a host of high expectations.

Both leads suggest that readers are so dumb that they have to be told that teams want to win. Unfortunately, the problem of leads that state the obvious is common. Here are several additional examples:

> Police are looking for a man who fled after robbing a bank Friday.

> Homecoming is the time when alumni reunite with old friends at their alma mater.

> Saturday was no ordinary day for running back James Schwartz. After all, it's not every day that a guy gains more than 100 yards, scores a touchdown and asks a girl to marry him.

The police look for every bank robber. That's routine: a normal part of their job. Similarly, alumni reunite at every homecoming. The third lead contains some newsworthy details, but begins with a comment that states the obvious. As you read the third lead, you may have also been distracted by a word that seemed jarring: The word "guy" is slang and therefore inappropriate in most news stories.

The following leads are ineffective for the same reason: they state the obvious or emphasize the routine. The first lead may be difficult to rewrite. If the placement center is not doing anything new, the story lacks a newsworthy angle. If, however, the placement center is offering a new service, the lead should describe that service:

> The college's Placement Center has a wide variety of information and facts to help prepare students for their future careers.
> REVISED: On Monday, the college's Placement Center will install computers in every building to inform students about new jobs and job interviews.

> It can be a frightening experience to wake up and find an armed intruder in your bedroom. Just ask 20-year-old Stacy Hidde. It happened to her Tuesday.
> REVISED: A 20-year-old college student was awakened at 2 a.m. Tuesday and saw a prowler, with a knife in one hand, searching her bedroom.

Avoid the Negative

When you write a lead, report what happened—not what failed to happen or what does not exist:

> Americans over the age of 65 say that crime is not their greatest fear, two sociologists reported today.
> REVISED: Americans over the age of 65 say their greatest fears are poor health and poverty, two sociologists reported today.

> A 20-year-old woman was not seriously injured Tuesday night when a shotgun accidentally discharged in a pickup truck.
> REVISED: A 20-year-old woman seated in a pickup truck bent down to light a cigarette Tuesday night just as a shotgun accidentally discharged two inches above her head, shattering a rear window and temporarily deafening her.

Avoid Exaggeration

Never exaggerate in your lead. If a story is weak, exaggeration is likely to make it weaker. A simple summary of the facts can be more interesting (and shocking) than anything you might contrive:

> A 78-year-old woman has left $3.2 million to the Salvation Army but only 2 cents to her son.

> A jury today found a restaurant innocent of serving a man and his wife a dead rat in a loaf of bread.

> ST. PETERSBURG, Fla.—Saying it was "outrageous" that a man's body fell out of a casket before startled pallbearers, a jury awarded a widow and her family $240,000 in their suit against a funeral home and cemetery.

Avoid Misleading Readers

Every lead must be accurate and truthful. Never sensationalize, belittle or mislead. In addition to being factually accurate, a lead must also set a story's tone—accurately revealing, for example, whether the story that follows will be serious or whimsical. Most of the stories that you write as a beginning reporter will be routine, and many of their topics may not interest you. Yet, as a service to readers who *are* interested in them, report such stories as you would any others: as well as you possibly can.

Breaking the Rules

Occasionally, it pays to use your imagination, to try something a little different, perhaps reporting the facts more cleverly than any of your competitors. Two journalism students wrote the following leads. Both summarize the same story, yet the second lead is more effective. Why?

> FIRST STUDENT: A young woman was robbed of $2 Thursday on her way to work by a young man with a knife.
> SECOND STUDENT: After a man threatened her with a pocket knife, a young woman gave him all her money—all $2 of it.

The following are also factual summaries, but reported with more imagination than most:

> When a masked man walked into a convenience store and pounded a hammer on the counter, demanding money, clerk Brenda Kay Casey didn't argue with him. She handed it over.

> BOSTON (AP)—Here's a strategy for long life: Avoid the elevator and take the stairs. Each stair climbed could increase lifespan by about 4 seconds.

REMEMBER YOUR READERS

While writing every lead, remember your readers: the general public. If you want people to read your work, you will have to be clear and interesting. The following leads fail both tests:

> Two policy resolutions will come before the Student Senate this week.
> REVISED: The Student Senate will vote this week on two proposals that would raise parking and athletic fees by a total of more than $100 a year.

> The County Commission approved various exemptions and other items at Monday's meeting.
> REVISED: The County Commission voted Monday to allow a computer programmer to build a 6-foot fence around his property to protect his children from wild dogs.

Did the original leads interest you? Why not? The first lead emphasized the number of resolutions that the Student Senate was scheduled to consider. Yet almost no one would care about the number of resolutions or, from the lead, understand their significance: the fact that they would affect every student at your school. More than a dozen students attended a County Commission meeting, and one of them wrote the second lead: a vague, bland lead. Another student found a more interesting angle— one that almost every reader would understand and perhaps sympathize with: A father wanted to build a fence to protect his children from wild dogs that roamed their neighborhood.

Here are two more examples of leads unlikely to interest most readers:

> Bit by bit, the city's elementary schools are incorporating computers into their classroom curricula as auxiliary learning tools.
> REVISED: The city's elementary schools are using computers to help their students overcome weaknesses in grammar, punctuation, spelling and arithmetic.

> A proposal to rezone 722 acres for use as a planned unit development has been placed on the agenda of the County Commission's work session.
> REVISED: County commissioners will review plans for a 722-acre development that will house 1,800 families and provide land for an elementary school, an 18-hole golf course and four parks, each with its own tennis courts and swimming pool.

Again, the revisions emphasize the information most likely to *interest* or *affect* readers, not routine or bureaucratic procedures.

Rewriting

Finally, critically examine every lead you write, and rewrite it as often as necessary. First drafts are rarely so perfect that they cannot be improved. Even experienced professionals often rewrite their leads three or four times (or more).

BECOMING A GOOD LEAD WRITER

If you are diligent in applying these guidelines, you can become an excellent writer. You can learn to write good leads even while working under deadline pressures.

Below are six more examples of good leads. All six are likely to arouse your interest in their topics. Thus, you may find yourself rereading them, pondering their details and wondering about the stories' outcomes. If so, the leads succeed. They make you want to learn more by reading the stories.

Notice that these leads do not use gimmicks. Rather, they report the facts: specific details, not generalities or opinions. Moreover, they present the details simply, clearly and concisely—always emphasizing the details most likely to interest readers:

> NEW YORK—American men are mean, manipulative, oversexed, self-centered and lazy. At least that is what many American women think, a survey released on Wednesday says.
>
> *(The Associated Press)*

> FORT LAUDERDALE—Strong and healthy, Mollie Hawley died because a fire ant pricked the middle toe of her left foot.
>
> *(The Miami Herald)*

> For his first murder, James Leo Dodd was sentenced to 20 years in prison and got out in nine. For his second murder, Dodd was sentenced Wednesday to 40 years. He'll probably serve 16.
>
> *(The Orlando Sentinel)*

While state and federal agencies have shuffled papers for the past five months, an unemployed, destitute and nearly deaf man has hobbled around without the lower part of his left leg.

(The Orlando Sentinel)

USAir Flight 188 from Washington to Cleveland had a perfect record in November. It was never on time.

(The New York Times)

Once a week here on the evening news, television viewers are making the acquaintance of a man with AIDS, hearing first hand about his fears and frailties and watching his jaunty passage toward death.

(The New York Times)

APPLYING THE GUIDELINES TO OTHER KINDS OF LEADS

All the guidelines presented in this chapter are guidelines for effective writing of all kinds of openings, not just leads for news stories. Good writing does not vary from one medium to another. You may want to work in the field of public relations, to write for a radio or television station, to become a columnist or to write a book. Regardless of your goal, the guidelines will help you achieve it.

Begin to analyze everything you read. You are likely to find some surprising similarities among books, magazines and newspapers. Also watch the opening scenes in movies and on television. Most, like a good lead, begin with a detail (or a story or scene) likely to capture your attention.

These, for example, are the opening sentences of two newspaper columns:

On Feb. 11, Terry Shapiro put "Bambi" on the VCR, picked up a pistol and fired five bullets into her sleeping husband's body.

(Kathleen Parker)

'Twas the night before Christmas when Gerald Williams shot his wife, Alice, in the head.

(Clarence Page)

Similarly, these are the opening sentences in two books:

The small boys came early to the hanging.

(Ken Follett, "The Pillars of the Earth")

On the 26th of July, my best friend decided he wanted to kill me.

(Wyatt Wyatt, "Deep in the Heart")

CHECKLISTS FOR WRITING LEADS

Use the following checklists to evaluate all the leads you write. If you answer "no" to any of these questions, your leads may have to be rewritten.

Writing Style

1. Is your lead specific rather than vague and abstract?
2. Have you avoided stating the obvious or the negative?
3. Have you emphasized your story's most unusual or unexpected developments?
4. Have you emphasized your story's most interesting and important developments?
5. Have you emphasized your story's magnitude—and its impact on its participants and readers?
6. Have you used a complete sentence, the proper tense and all the necessary articles ("a," "an" and "the")?
7. Is your lead concise? (If it exceeds three typed lines, examine the lead critically to determine whether it is wordy or repetitious or contains some unnecessary details. If your lead exceeds four typed lines, rewrite it.)
8. Have you avoided writing a label lead that reports your story's topic but not what was said or done about it?
9. Did you begin your lead with the news—the main point of the story? (If you began with attribution or the time and place your story occurred, rewrite it.)
10. Have you used a relatively simple sentence structure, exercising particular care to avoid beginning the lead with a long phrase or clause?
11. Have you used strong, active and descriptive verbs rather than "to be" verbs such as "is," "are," "was" and "were"?
12. Is every name that appears in the lead essential? (Avoid unfamiliar names—and names that require lengthy identification that could be reported in a later paragraph.)
13. If a lead contains a quotation or a statement of opinion, is it properly attributed?
14. Has the lead been localized, and does it emphasize the latest developments, preferably what happened today or yesterday?
15. Have you eliminated statements of opinion, including one-word labels such as "interesting" and "alert"?
16. If you have used two sentences, can you justify their use? Have you checked to be certain that they are concise and nonrepetitive?
17. Have you remembered your readers? Have you written a lead that is clear, concise and interesting—that emphasizes the details most likely to affect and interest your readers?
18. Have you read the lead aloud to be certain that it is clear, concise and easy to understand?

Checklist for Format and Accuracy

1. If the story originated in a distant city, did you begin with a dateline?
2. Is the lead typed and double-spaced, and have you used the proper copy-editing symbols to correct all your errors?
3. Have you double-checked the facts to be certain that they are accurate, and have you used a telephone book or city directory to check the spelling of every name? (If the lead is mistaken, exaggerates, sensationalizes or misleads, rewrite it.)

St. Louis Post-Dispatch

WRITE & WRONG

By **Harry Levins**
Post-Dispatch Writing Coach

Those file cards posted daily on the bulletin board near the newsroom door have a two-day life out in the open. On the third day, they're filed under headings that range from "Abbreviations" to "Word Order."

And after a month's worth of filing, The Coach can report with pleasure that the thickest single category, by far, is the one marked "Hits"—those gems of good writing that brighten so many of our pages.

Most of the clippings are ledes, the make-or-break part of the story that determines so often whether a reader will stay with the rest.

A few samples of note, and the reasons why:

Specific nouns: *ST. CLAIR, Mo.—It was the kind of heat that could fry a piece of bologna on the hood of a Buick.* (Bill Smith)

Not just any kind of food (especially not the egg of cliché), but "a piece of bologna." Not just any kind of car, but "a Buick," an especially massive, solid and square car. Specific nouns focus the images in the reader's mind.

Vivid verbs: *Higher education officials sighed with relief this week when the Missouri Legislature approved higher taxes to stave off deep budget cuts for colleges and universities.* (Virginia Hick)

Face it: A story on education budgets can easily turn into what Ben Bradlee calls "a real room-emptier." But Hick's lede used bright verbs to help the reader over the hump of abstraction.

Perfect quote: *JOPLIN, Mo.—Johnny Lee Wilson, described by his lawyer as a person who "was not dealt the proper cards in life," went to court Tuesday in a bid to end his life prison term.* (Jim Mosley)

Rather than bog the reader down up front about the specifics of Johnny Lee Wilson's case, Mosley used a quote that cuts to the heart of things, giving the reader a keen sense of what this story is going to be about without snagging the reader in needless detail. Not all stories offer this kind of quote—but when they do, the smart writer grabs them.

Imaginative phrasing: *As the flight carrying Velda Village Mayor Lottie Mae Williams and other U.S. mayors approached the west coast of central Africa recently, she decided to dump any preconceptions of the African people in the Atlantic Ocean.* (Harry Jackson)

Jackson's image speaks for itself.

Straight-to-the-point English: *Creston Austin says it was his life or hers in November 1987, when he shot to death a graduate student at Lindenwood College on a secluded parking lot in the West Port Plaza Area.* (Bill Lhotka)

"It was his life or hers . . ." Lhotka translated the abstract concept of self-defense into the simple Anglo-Saxon English that real people use in real life.

Key detail: *A car taking a 12-year-old girl to meet her grandparents for a summer visit was struck broadside by a pickup Tuesday night at a highway intersection in St. Charles County, killing the girl and her 8-year-old cousin.* (Kim Bell)

Bell's inclusion of the victim's plans for a summer visit to her grandparents lifted this lede above mere news by adding a poignantly human touch.

The human touch: *Barbara Moore figures that what she doesn't know might hurt her.*
The Aug. 8 ballot carries eight proposals to increase fees for various St. Louis County services, but the ballots don't say what the new fees would be.
So Moore, a retired teacher from Creve Coeur, said that if she had to vote on what she saw earlier this week on a sample ballot, she would vote no. (Virgil Tipton)

A reader heading into a typical election advance finds tough going—a swamp of facts, figures and government officials speaking in bureaubabble. But here, Tipton introduced the reader to a kindred soul, pondering the election issue in the terms that real people use.

Clear compression: *Missouri has started filling its excess prison space by renting beds to Illinois and Colorado.*

It hopes to make $10 million to $13 million a year until its own prisoners fill the space. (Fred Lindecke)

In the paper, this lede came out as five lines of clear, simple English in which the reader learns (a) what's happening, (b) why it's happening, and (c) how long it will last. Lindecke wasted nary a word but still conveyed his information smoothly.

Clever word play: *Beverly Hotchner ended her discussion on s-e-x with a four-letter word: "T-a-l-k."* (Lorraine Kee Montre)

That sort of lede grabs a reader's attention, but Montre refused to tease the reader for more than one brief sentence. Having grabbed the reader with a brief flash, she went on in the next graf to the substance of the story, leading the reader in gently by repeating the last word from her lede:

Talk to your children about the pleasurable and not-so-pleasurable aspects of sex, Hotchner, a sex therapist, told a group of about 20 people at a Parenting Fair seminar.

Maximum use of the facts: *FREDERICKTOWN, Mo.— Cindy Box jumped anxiously each time her telephone rang Monday evening, hoping that someone had spotted her little girl.*
No one had—not since 10:30 p.m. Saturday, when 13-year-old Gina Dawn Brooks disappeared just six blocks from her modest clapboard house. (Dan Browning)

(continued on next page)

That's a second-day story about a day in which, in hard-news terms, nothing happened. But staying strictly within the facts, Browning found a touch of drama that made a compelling lede.

In a class by itself: *Enough already on title-insurance offices and concrete plazas. Clayton wants some snazzy storefronts.* (Sue Brown)

That lede came out of—get this—a *zoning hearing*, the dullest of all possible events. Brown has thus set the zoning-hearing-lede standard for generations to come.

SUGGESTED READINGS

Brooks, Brian S., George Kennedy, Daryl R. Moen and Don Ranley. *News Reporting and Writing.* 3d ed. New York: St. Martin's, 1988.

Cappon, Rene J. *The Word: An Associated Press Guide to Good News Writing.* New York: The Associated Press, 1982.

Charnley, Mitchell V., and Blair Charnley. *Reporting.* 4th ed. New York: Holt, Rinehart and Winston, 1975.

Garrison, Bruce. *Professional News Writing.* Hillsdale, NJ: Erlbaum, 1990.

Harriss, Julian, and B. Kelly Leiter. *The Complete Reporter.* 5th ed. New York: Macmillan, 1985.

Hohenberg, John. *The Professional Journalist.* 5th ed. New York: Holt, Rinehart and Winston, 1983.

Hough, George A. *News Writing.* 4th ed. Boston: Houghton Mifflin, 1988.

Izard, Ralph S., Hugh M. Culbertson and Donald A. Lambert. *Fundamentals of News Reporting.* 5th ed. Dubuque, IA: Kendall/Hunt, 1990.

Metz, William. *Newswriting: From Lead to "30."* 3d ed. Englewood Cliffs, NJ: Prentice Hall, 1991.

Metzler, Ken. *Newsgathering.* 2d ed. Englewood Cliffs, NJ: Prentice Hall, 1986.

Stephens, Mitchell, and Gerald Lanson. *Writing and Reporting the News.* New York: Holt, Rinehart and Winston, 1986.

Ward, Hiley H. *Professional Newswriting.* San Diego, CA: Harcourt Brace Jovanovich, 1985.

QUOTES

There is a great disposition in some quarters to say that the newspapers ought to limit the amount of news they print; that certain kinds of news ought not to be published. I do not know how that is. I am not prepared to maintain any abstract position on that line; but I have always felt that whatever the divine Providence permitted to occur, I was not too proud to report.

(Charles A. Dana, newspaper editor)

When there are no papers, there is no agitation. That is why we imposed censorship.

(Indira Gandhi)

Exercise 1

LEADS

EVALUATING GOOD AND BAD LEADS

INSTRUCTIONS: Critically evaluate the following leads. Select the best leads and explain why they are effective. Point out the flaws in the remaining leads. As you evaluate the leads, look for lessons—"dos and don'ts"—that you can apply to your own work.

1. Even after 34 years on the police force, 63-year-old Chief Barry Kopperud has not lost sight of his goal to "protect and serve."
2. The city's public schools have come under fire since it was revealed that student test scores are declining. Now, the superintendent of schools has responded to the criticism.
3. The school board will offer a $30,000 settlement in exchange for the resignation of a teacher acquitted of sexually molesting two fifth-grade girls.
4. A new health insurance plan will pay city employees for staying well.
5. A man who admitted slashing his neighbor with an 8-inch kitchen knife was acquitted today of aggravated assault. A jury decided that the man acted in self-defense.
6. Local schools have a lot of holiday activities planned for their youngsters.
7. A college student was left bound and gagged in her dormitory room last night after being robbed by a man who answered her advertisement in the campus newspaper.
8. A motorcyclist involved in an accident at about 5 p.m. Sunday suffered multiple injuries.
9. Carbon monoxide sucked into an air conditioning duct spread through a house at 105 Crown Point Drive early today, killing a couple and their five children.
10. The School Board has voted to give Greg Hubbard a 12 percent raise and to extend his contract as superintendent of schools for another three years.
11. Two people remain hospitalized after a collision on State Route 419 at 2:30 a.m. Thursday.
12. After 25 years as an undercover agent, retiring Drug Enforcement Administration agent Daniel Sweers is speaking out against the way the government is fighting the drug war.
13. A local man was beaten and robbed Monday, losing both his pants and wallet.
14. A 32-year-old man described Tuesday how he and another man robbed a tavern.
15. Transfer students often have problems adjusting to their first semester here. There are ways to make it easier.

Exercise 2

LEADS

EVALUATING GOOD AND BAD LEADS

INSTRUCTIONS: Critically evaluate the following leads. Select the best leads and explain why they are effective. Point out the flaws in the remaining leads. As you evaluate the leads, look for lessons—"dos and don'ts"—that you can apply to your own work.

1. Circuit Court Judge Marilyn Picott today refused to allow James Roger Carrig to attend the funeral services for his parents, whom he is accused of murdering.
2. A school bus carrying 46 pupils to an elementary school was involved in a collision on Jefferson Avenue at 8:10 a.m. today.
3. Kennedy High School is the only school in the city that has a school-community liaison counselor.
4. Syndicated columnist Jack Anderson spoke Tuesday evening to a crowd of about 350 people in the Student Union.
5. A 42-year-old man was arrested and charged with cultivating marijuana Monday after his landlady discovered more than 300 plants in a house he rents from her.
6. One man fell 40 feet and another was left dangling from a drainpipe yesterday after a scaffold collapsed while they were painting a house at 48 Par Ave.
7. A small fire, started by a 13-year-old baby sitter, caused more fear than harm Monday afternoon.
8. Children in this area will join more than 30 million other trick-or-treaters across the United States this Halloween in a night of make-believe and masquerade.
9. The first-degree murder trial of Eldred L. Tontenot continued Thursday with testimony from the assistant county medical examiner, Dr. Guillermo Ruiz.
10. Members of the city's Ministerial Alliance charged today that church members "spend more money on beer and cigarettes than on charity."
11. In a nationally televised speech to the American public last night, the president explained why he will not run for reelection.
12. The university's president, Amy Clayton, told the Alumni Association that she is proud of what her administration has already accomplished, "but no one can afford to relax."
13. Perestroika came to the university Monday in the form of Russian telejournalist Dr. Boris Nodkin. Referred to as the Walter Cronkite of Russian news, Dr. Nodkin talked with professors and students for two hours in the President's Dining Room.
14. A student wanting to stress a point in his small-group interaction class brought Toni, a one-year-old owl, in for a show-and-tell session.
15. Toxic waste chemicals at the university are going down the drain—literally.

Exercise 3

LEADS

IMPROVING WEAK LEADS

SECTION I: CONDENSING LENGTHY LEADS

Condense each of these leads to no more than two typed lines (about 20 words).

1. Maggie Baile, 28, of 810 N. Ontario Ave., an employee at the Halstini Manufacturing Plant, 810 Hall Road, suffered second- and third-degree burns at 2:15 p.m. yesterday when sparks from her welders torch started a fire that quickly spread through the factory, causing nearly $1 million in damage and totally destroying the facility.
2. During a regularly scheduled meeting that began in its chambers at 8 p.m. last night, the City Council voted 5 to 2, after nearly 3 hours of debate, in favor of a proposal which, for the convenience of pedestrians, will require developers to construct a sidewalk in front of every new home and subdivision in the city.
3. At its annual awards banquet last night, the citys Chamber of Commerce named Marlene P. Gianangeli, the founder and owner of the citys largest pest control firm, the citys "Business Person of the Year," then proceeded to elect Destiny Schifini, a vice president at Sun Bank, to a two-year term as chamber president, to begin on the 1st of next month.

SECTION II: USING THE PROPER SENTENCE STRUCTURE

Rewrite the following leads, using the normal word order (subject, verb, direct object). Avoid starting the leads with a long clause or phrase. You may want to divide some of the leads into several sentences or paragraphs.

1. Saying that he had concluded that no benefit would come to anyone from the imprisonment of a 51-year-old woman who killed two teenagers while driving while intoxicated last summer, Circuit Court Judge Bruce R. Levine today suspended the womans drivers license for five years and sentenced her to one year in the county jail, then suspended her jail sentence on the conditions that she seek professional help for her chronic alcoholism and pay all the teenagers medical and funeral expenses.
2. Although the world has plenty of food due to great advances in agricultural techniques in recent years, especially in the United States, the World Bank reported today that about 700 million people in developing countries do not have enough to eat, primarily because they do not have sufficient funds to buy the food that is available.
3. Because the victim, Bobby Correia, contributed in large measure to his own death by refusing medical attention that might have saved his life after the incident, James K. Arico, the 47-year-old man accused of stabbing him in the chest during an argument seven months ago, was allowed to plead guilty to assault today and was sentenced to six months in the county jail. He had been charged with murder.

SECTION III: EMPHASIZING THE NEWS

Rewrite the following leads, emphasizing the news, not the attribution. Limit the attributions to a few words and place them at the end, not the beginning, of the leads.

1. During a meeting in her office in Washington, D.C. today, the secretary of Health and Human Services told a group of health care specialists that American men and women who practice "wellness," a program of health promotion and disease prevention, can expect to live 11 years longer than people who neglect their health.

2. According to Tracy R. Edwards and John W. Robitzsch, psychiatrists hired to testify for the defense at the murder trial of Tommy Ahrens in your community today, Ahrens was temporarily insane—emotionally upset and too distraught to think clearly—when he shot and killed his former wife and her boyfriend last year.

3. Tracy Tibitts, Lisa Drolshagen and Dorothy Brayton, all members of the Delta Delta Delta sorority at Iowa State University, appeared in a local courtroom this morning and testified that the defendant, Steven House, appeared drunk when he got into his car to leave the party moments before he struck and killed a pedestrian.

SECTION IV: COMBINING MULTISENTENCE LEADS

Rewrite each of the following leads in a single sentence, leaving out unnecessary information.

1. Acting on a tip, four detectives staked out a restaurant at 12:50 a.m. this morning and foiled an armed robbery. While posing as customers and employees, they observed two men with guns approach a cashier. The detectives captured both men.

2. Two city officials resigned today. Both had been criticized for abusing their positions. Mechanics at the city garage complained that both officials had them repair and wash and wax their private cars during working hours. One of the city officials was the mayor. The other was her assistant. They never paid for any of the services.

3. The parade is scheduled for 9 a.m. tomorrow. The citys annual Memorial Day parade will proceed down Main Street to Wildwood Cemetery. Services there will honor the men and women killed in Twentieth Century wars. The mayor will be the guest speaker.

Exercise 4

LEADS

Pro Challenge

WRITING BASIC NEWS LEADS

INSTRUCTIONS: Write only a lead for each of the following stories. As you write your leads, consult the checklists on pages 160–61. When you finish, you can compare your work to a professional's. A professional journalist has been asked to write a lead for each of these stories, and these leads appear in a manual available to your instructor. You may find, however, that you like some of your own and your classmates' leads better than the professional's.

1. There was an accident occurring in your city at 7:10 this morning at the intersection of Post Road and Rollins Avenue. Charles R. Lydon was driving north on Post Road and proceeded to enter the intersection in his van at a speed estimated at 40 mph. His van struck a fire engine responding to an emergency call, with its lights and siren in operation. Two firemen aboard the vehicle were hospitalized; however, their condition is not known at this point in time. Lyden was killed instantly in the serious and tragic accident. Authorities have not yet determined who was at fault. The truck was traveling an estimated 25 mph and responding to a report of a store fire. However, it was a false alarm. Lyden's van was totally destroyed. Damage to the truck was estimated at $50,000.

2. There was a report issued in Washington, D.C. today. It came from the Highway Loss Data Institute, an affiliate of the Insurance Institute for Highway Safety. It shows that there are advantages to driving big cars. A study by the institute found that small two-door models and many small or midsize sport or specialty cars have the worst injury and repair records. Many of these small cars show injury claim frequencies and repair losses at least 30 percent higher than average, while many large cars, station wagons and vans show 40 percent to 50 percent better-than-average claim records. According to the analysis, a motorist in a four-door Oldsmobile Delta 88, for example, is 41 percent less likely than average to be hurt in an accident.

3. An article appeared today in the Journal of the American Medical Association. The article concerns the dangers of hot dogs. "If you were trying to design something that would be perfect to block a child's airway, it would be a bite-size piece of hot dog," says a researcher. He concluded that children under 4 should "never be given a whole hot dog to eat," and that hot dogs should never be cut crosswise. The hot dogs are so dangerous that every five days, it is estimated, someone, somewhere in the United States, chokes to death on them. Other risky foods for young kids up to 9 years of age include: candy, nuts, grapes, apples, carrots and popcorn.

4. The family of Kristine Belcuore was grief-stricken. She was 51 years old and died of a heart attack last week. She left a husband and four children. Because her death was so sudden and unexpected, an autopsy had to be per-

formed before the funeral last Saturday. It was a big funeral, costing more than $7,000. More than 100 friends and relatives were in attendance. Today, the family received an apologetic call from the county medical examiner. Mrs. Belcuor's body is still in the morgue. The body they buried was that of a woman whose corpse had been unclaimed for a month. The error was discovered after the medical examiner's office realized the month-old corpse had disappeared. Someone probably misread an identifying tag, they said. Also, the family never viewed the remains; they kept the casket closed throughout the proceedings. A relative said, "We went through all the pain and everything, all over the wrong body, and now we have to go through it again."

5. It's another statistical study, one that surprised researchers. For years, researchers thought that advanced education translated into greater marriage stability. Then they discovered that marital disruption is greater among more highly educated women than any other group (except those who haven't graduated from high school). Now a sociologist at Ohio State University has conducted a new study which explains some of the reasons why women with graduate degrees are more likely to be graduated from their marriages as well. The key fact seems to be timing. Women who married early, before they began graduate school, are more likely to have established traditional family roles which they find difficult to change. When the wife goes back to school and no longer wants to handle most of the housework, it causes resentment on the part of husbands. If the husband refuses to pitch in and do his share, it creates tension. Such unhappiness on both sides often leads to divorce. Indeed, a third of the women who began graduate school after they were married ended up separated or divorced. By comparison, only 15.6 percent of those who married after they had finished an advanced degree ended up divorced or separated. They seem more likely to find husbands supportive of their educational goals.

6. The Department of Justice, as it often does, conducted a crime-related survey. It questioned long-term prisoners. It found that new laws limiting the ownership of guns do not discourage handgun ownership by career criminals. The report concludes, however, that even though curbs on legitimate retail sales of guns have failed to attain the goal of keeping weapons out of the hands of criminals, the laws still may serve other useful functions. The report explains that criminals get their weapons most often by theft or under-the-counter deals. The department surveyed 1,874 men serving time for felonies in 11 state prisons and found that 75 percent said they would expect little or no trouble if they tried to get a handgun after their release from prison. Fifty-seven percent had owned a handgun at the time of their arrest. Thirty-two percent of their guns had been stolen, 26 percent acquired in black market deals, and others received as gifts from family and friends. Only 21 percent had been bought through legitimate retail outlets.

7. Thomas C. Ahl appeared in Circuit Court today. He pleaded guilty last week to robbing and murdering two restaurant employees. In return for pleading guilty, prosecutors promised not to seek the death penalty. He was sentenced today. Ahl is 24 years old, and the judge sentenced him to two life terms, plus 300 years. It is the longest sentence ever given anyone in your state. Ahl will be 89 before he can be considered for parole. The judge explained that Ahl had a long history of violence and brutality, and that the public deserved to

be protected from him. There had been no reason for him to shotgun the two employees to death. Ahl himself admitted that they had not resisted him in any way.

8. The International Standardization Organization, which is composed of acoustics experts, today opened its annual convention. The convention is meeting in Geneva, Switzerland. Delegates from 51 countries are attending the convention, which will continue through Sunday. An annual report issued by the organization warned that noise levels in the world are rising by one decibel a year. If the increase continues, the report warned, "everyone living in cities could be stone deaf by the year 2020." The report also said that long-term exposure to a noise level of 100 decibels can cause deafness, yet a riveting gun reaches a level of 130 decibels and a jet aircraft 150.

9. The city's Human Rights Commission lost a battle last night. It wanted the City Council to ban a history book that it claims "deals erroneously and disparagingly" with American Indians. City Council members said they did not want to start banning books and refused to endorse the commission's efforts and refused to order school officials to remove the book from city schools.

10. Ramon Hernandez was charged with evading income taxes some time ago. The Internal Revenue Service said that he has not filed a tax return since 1986 and that he owes $76,144 in back taxes. Hernandez is 37 years old. He appeared in U.S. District Court this morning and pleaded guilty to the charges against him. The judge delayed sentencing until next week. Hernandez has been district attorney in the city since 1978. He resigned five weeks ago.

11. A 19-year-old shoplifting suspect died last Saturday. Police identified him as Timothy Milan. He lived at 1112 Huron Avenue and was employed as a cook at a restaurant in the city. A guard at Panzer's Department Store told police he saw Milan stuff 2 sweaters down his pants legs, then walk past a checkout line and out of the department store. The guard then began to chase Milan, who ran, and 3 bystanders joined in the pursuit. They caught up with Milan, and, when he resisted, one of the bystanders applied a headlock to him. A police officer who arrived at the scene reported that Milan collapsed as he put handcuffs on him. An autopsy conducted to determine the cause of death revealed that Milan died due to a lack of oxygen to the brain. Police today said they do not plan to charge anyone involved in the case with a crime because it "was a case of excusable homicide." The police said the bystanders did not mean to injure Milan or to kill him, but that he was fighting violently—punching and kicking at his captors and even trying to bite them—and that they were simply trying to restrain him and trying to help capture a suspected criminal, "which is just being a good citizen."

12. Several English teachers at your city's junior and senior high schools require their students to read the controversial book, "The Adventures of Huckleberry Finn." The book was written by Mark Twain. Critics, including some parents, said last week that the book should be banned from all schools in the city because it is racist. After considering their complaints and discussing them with his staff, the superintendent of schools, Gary Hubbard, announced today that teachers will be allowed to require reading the book in high school English classes but not in any junior high school classes. Furthermore, the superintendent said that it will be the responsibility of the high school teachers

who assign the book to assist students in understanding the historical setting of the book, the characters being depicted and the social context, including the prejudices which existed at the time depicted in the book. Although the book can no longer be used in any junior high school classes, the school superintendent said it will remain available in junior and senior high school libraries for students who want to read it voluntarily. The book describes the adventures of runaway Huck Finn and a fugitive slave named Jim as they float on a raft down the Mississippi River.

Exercise 5

LEADS

Pro Challenge

WRITING BASIC NEWS LEADS

INSTRUCTIONS: Write only a lead for each of the following stories. As you write the leads, consult the checklists on pages 160–61. When you finish, you can compare your work to a professional's. A professional journalist has been asked to write a lead for each of these stories, and these leads appear in a manual available to your instructor. You may find, however, that you like some of your own and your classmates' leads better than the professional's.

1. The man is Herman Weiskoph of 4817 Twin Lakes Boulevard in your city. The woman involved is Sharon Meyer of 810 Kalani Street. She is pregnant with his child. However, they are not married. At 9 a.m. next Monday morning, a judge in your county will hear his plea. The judge, JoAnne Kaeppler, today issued a temporary restraining order to prevent Meyer from having an abortion. The judge issued the order in response to a suit filed by Weiskoph. On Monday, the judge will decide whether to make the order permanent or to dissolve it. In his lawsuit, Weiskoph offers to marry Meyer, to pay all her medical expenses, and/or to take custody of the child after it is born. He bases his suit upon a claim "that a natural father has rights to the life of his child."

2. At its meeting last night, the Muncie city council in Indiana made another important but controversial decision. Not everyone agrees with it. After hearing from interested citizens during a 60-minute hearing, the council voted by a narrow margin, 4–3, to stop donating cats and dogs from the city pound to Indiana University. Proposed experiments there caused some controversy earlier this year. The controversy erupted when one researcher proposed suspending cats from their legs to test the effects of spaceflight on bones. Another controversy erupted when a researcher proposed drowning dogs to test methods of saving human drowning victims. Last year, the city donated about 1,400 cats and dogs picked up on the city's streets and held 10 days at the pound without being claimed. Now, instead, it will put the cats and dogs to sleep, as it does with other unclaimed animals. University officials said they are unhappy, and one researcher explained, "People don't understand, but our experiments with animals have resulted in great advances for mankind, providing life-saving medicines and other innovations that make all our lives healthier and safer."

3. There is a new study out, one conducted by your city's police department. The department questioned a random sample of 350 people living within your city and announced the results during a press conference held at 9 a.m. this morning. The chief of police made the announcement. He said the survey revealed that 65 percent of all the crimes occurring in your community are not reported to the police because the victims consider the incidents unimportant or believe that nothing can be done about them. About half the violent crimes of rape, robbery and assault seem to be reported, he said. The rates for reporting crimes ranged from 25 percent for household larceny to 69 percent for motor

vehicle theft. Forty percent of those who reported crimes gave economic reasons, either to recover property or collect insurance money, for doing so. Thirty-five percent cited a sense of obligation.

4. Pollsters have asked a random cross-section of American adults their attitudes toward the nation's federal income taxes, and the results are contained in a 12-page report. The study was financed by the Internal Revenue Service, which released the results to reporters in the federal capital today. In general, the report concluded that the average American's respect for the federal income tax system is declining. A similar study conducted just 10 years ago found that, when Americans were asked to describe the tax they thought was most unfair, most mentioned their local property tax. But now, the new study released today found that a majority of the nation's adults consider their federal income tax most unfair. Guaranteed that their identities would not be revealed by the pollsters, 27% of the respondents said they themselves had cheated on their federal tax returns on at least one occasion during the past five years.

5. Your city's fire chief today released copies of his proposed annual budget for next year. He will present the proposal to your City Council at its next regular meeting. Chief Tony Sullivan wants $4,943,612, a 19.8 percent increase, which he says is needed primarily to beef up protection on the east side. If fully funded, it would raise property owners' taxes for fire protection to 6.41 mills, or $6.41 for every $1,000 of taxable property value. Sullivan said he needs to hire eight new firefighters. The eight new firefighters would fill two round-the-clock positions. The department also wants to buy several pieces of equipment. "We are a manpower-intensive operation," he explained. "And some very expensive equipment is necessary to outfit these people." Sullivan added that, within the next five years, the city will have to build a new fire station and purchase at least three new trucks.

6. For 10 years, researchers at the University of Washington in Seattle have been studying a sample of 5,000 adult males. The researchers received a federal grant totalling $720,000 in amount to conduct the study, and they announced the results today. It was a study of heart attacks: who gets them, when and with what results. All the men were aged 50 to 60 at the time the study began 10 years ago. Now, many have retired. The researchers found that those who retired were more likely to suffer and die of a heart attack. "We found an 80 percent higher rate of death from coronary disease among those who had retired compared with those who had not," one of the medical researchers said. The researchers had set up the long-term study to determine men's physical and mental responses to retirement, and the results announced today were the first phase of their study. Other results will be announced next year. Another of the researchers added: "For some people, retirement is a reward for a lifetime's work, and they look forward to it. But for other people, it is a punishment for growing old. Those who feel that way perhaps might be the ones who are most likely to suffer bad health, but we don't have that breakdown yet."

7. Sonya Barlow was born brain-dead. She lived about a month. Today, her mother, Mrs. Janet Barlow, 23, 2886 Moore Street, was charged with her death. Mrs. Barlow, who has two other daughters, is in jail. She is accused of being responsible for her infant daughter's death by taking drugs, consuming alcoholic beverages and recklessly disregarding medical instructions during preg-

nancy. Legal experts say this is the state's first criminal action for the crime, sometimes known as "fetal abuse." Prosecutors say the case will "foster a greater sense of parental responsibility for prenatal care."

8. Two researchers at your school, both psychologists, have studied births in your state for the past 10 years. They were particularly interested in children born to parents who live under airport landing patterns. Today, they finally issued their report. The report, which examines the frequency of birth defects, uncovered some interesting differences. The psychologists found that the rate of abnormal births is 42 percent higher among parents who live near airports. The researchers explained that the cause is stress suffered by pregnant women who are repeatedly exposed to the noise of loud jet aircraft overhead.

Exercise 6

LEADS

Pro Challenge

CAMPUS STORY LEADS

INSTRUCTIONS: Write only a lead for each of the following stories. Assume that all the stories occurred on your campus. As you write the leads, consult the checklists on pages 160–61. When you finish, you can compare your work to a professional's. A professional journalist has been asked to write a lead for each of these stories, and the leads appear in a manual available to your instructor. You may find, however, that you like some of your own (and your classmates') leads better than the professional's.

1. A journalism professor at your school has sparked a heated debate. She teaches a course titled "Communication Law." During her class last week Friday, she took her class outdoors and burned a small American flag. She said the flag was "a teaching tool." The class was discussing Supreme Court cases that defined flag burning as protected speech. The teacher, assistant professor Denise Beall, said she hoped her action would spark debate in the classroom about free-speech issues. "It was not a personal act," she said. "It was a pedagogical one." This morning, about 250 students, led by veterans groups on your campus, gathered to protest the flag burning. They marched to the building where Beall was teaching the course. The protesters entered the building, stood outside the room where the class was in session, and sang the national anthem. The students also said the Pledge of Allegiance and chanted "U.S.A." In a statement issued soon thereafter, the president of your school said Beall had used "extraordinarily bad judgment" in burning the flag. But, your president said, it would be inappropriate for the school to do anything further to question or punish her teaching techniques.

2. At first, it seemed like a wonderful idea! Your schools president learned that the wife of the President of the United States was going to be in the area. He proceeded to invite her to deliver your schools commencement address for this springs graduating class—and she accepted. Now opposition is arising. About a week ago, a half-dozen senior women began circulating a petition opposing her delivering the commencement address and, thus far, more than 300 of their classmates have signed the petition. "To honor the First Lady as a commencement speaker," says the petition, "is to honor a woman who has gained recognition through the achievements of her husband, which contradicts what we have been taught over our years of study—that women should be honored for their own achievements, not their husbands." The president of your institution has scheduled a meeting for late Friday to discuss the issue with members of the graduating class.

3. College students have an unusual problem that has gone largely unnoticed in the past. Some call it "freshman fat." Others call it "the Freshman 5," "the Freshman 10," "the Freshman 15" or even "the Freshman 20." Now, a specialist at your school is studying the issue and finding some truth to the folklore. Freshmen women, she found, are more than twice as likely to gain a significant

amount of weight as similar women who don't go to college. Of your schools incoming freshmen last year, 26% gained weight. By comparison, 9% of a group of comparable young women in your community who did not enroll in college gained weight. Freshman Fat isn't considered a serious health threat. Five or 10 extra pounds don't make a big difference for most people. The best remedy, in fact, may be to ignore the extra weight: sooner or later, your eating habits are bound to settle down. A constellation of factors lies behind Freshman Fat: sudden freedom from parental rules; overabundance of choices; erratic, late hours; a more sedentary life; a social life that revolves around eating and drinking. And stress. Food is the age-old comforter. Linda Kasparov, a licensed dietitian at your school, conducted the study and released all the information about the results of it today.

4. There's a heated, controversial debate at your school. The school has a foundation that invests its money in various stocks, bonds and properties. A reporter for your student paper last week uncovered the fact that some of the money is invested in tobacco companies. Now some people want the foundation to eliminate those stocks from its investment portfolio. The editor of your student paper advocates the elimination of such stock and, in an interview with you today explained quite persuasively that, "Cigarettes have been responsible for millions of deaths, and owning shares in the companies that produce them sends a conflicting message to both students and the public. Furthermore, the foundation, and thus our school, is benefiting from those deaths: from the sale of a product known to kill its users." The Board of Regents met at 8 a.m. this morning, and the topic was one of several on its agenda. It voted 8–1 that the foundation should not be ordered to sell any of its tobacco stocks.

5. Last week a group of medical researchers conducted an unusual survey of the women on your campus. As part of an effort to learn more about students needs and ways of improving student health care, doctors at your student clinic conducted a survey, personally contacting and interviewing a random sample of 1,044 women. The women were interviewed in person and were also asked to complete anonymous questionnaires developed by the researchers. The researchers found that almost 1 in 10 had had an abortion at some point in her life. "I was shocked, to be quite frank," said Robert Einhorn, the clinics director. "We have some students who come to us, learn they're pregnant, and ask about their options. Some want a referral to a clinic that performs abortions, and there are a number of names that we give them. But I never thought we were talking about this number of students. Of course, some reported having their abortions years ago—as young as the age of 12." More specifically, 9.41 percent of the women students surveyed said they have had an abortion. 1.7% of the women students have had two abortions.

6. Five students on your campus, all members of a fraternity, Sigma Kappa Chi, have been arrested as the result of a hazing incident. The investigation began after one SKC pledge was hospitalized Saturday with serious internal injuries and another with a sprained back. Each of the five was charged with two counts of battery. The incident occurred during a fraternity meeting Friday at which members "beat pledges with wooden paddles and canes and subjected them to other forms of physical and verbal punishment," according to Detective Sgt. Albert Wei, who headed the investigation. One of the two injured students, sophomore Roland Dessaur, was hospitalized for kidney damage and de-

hydration. Another sophomore, Eddie Muldaur, was treated for a sprained back and bruised buttocks. State laws require hospital officials to report injuries that appear to be the result of a crime. Thus, hospital officials notified the police and, as the investigation continued, four other pledges were taken to the hospital and also examined, then released. Several suffered contusions, Wei said. A university spokesman said both university and national fraternity officials are investigating to determine what disciplinary action, if any, should be taken against the fraternity.

7. There was a shooting on your campus at the end of your last term. It involved an English major, Alan Daniel Sulsenti, a senior, who had hoped to graduate next spring. As one of his course requirements, a requirement of every student who enrolls as a freshman at your institution, Sulenti is required to enroll in and pass college algebra. He put it off until his senior year. There were three tests in the class. He flunked the first two and, later, his third test was returned with a third "F." He went to the professors office, Prof. Mark Pearson, apparently to plead with him for a passing grade, even a "D," so he could graduate as planned. The professor, however, said Sulsenti would receive an F for the course. Sulsenti then returned with a handgun. He fired three shots, killing Pearson. He was arrested and charged with first-degree murder. During a two-day trial, several mental health experts testified that Sulenti was temporarily insane at the time of the killing: heavily in debt, experiencing great pressure to succeed and graduate, and to stop requiring money from his parents for whom it was a financial hardship to keep him in school. He pled innocent by reason of insanity. Last week a jury found him guilty. At 9 a.m., today, he appeared before Judge Marlene Ostreicher for sentencing. The sentence she handed down was life in prison. He will be eligible for parole in 25 years.

8. There was an accident on your campus yesterday. Fortunately, no one was killed. Three men were working on the roof of what is to be the first-floor lobby of the new Jabil Dormitory. About 15 minutes after concrete for the roof was poured onto support beams, the roof buckled and "the men rode it down," said project developer Randy Whitlock of the Wagnor Development Corp. The three construction workers were scratched, bruised, and shaken, but otherwise unhurt. They were rushed by ambulance to Mercy Hospital, examined, and released several hours after the 2 p.m. accident. Campus police and campus construction supervisors said they were not certain what caused the collapse. The lobby juts out from the nine-story building. Its roof was shored up with lumber, which acts as temporary support for the concrete until it dries. The workmen were identified as Jason Perez, Donald Collen, and Michael Romisak, all of your city. Opening of the dorm is scheduled for the start of classes next fall and is not expected to be delayed by the mishap.

Exercise 7
LEADS

Pro Challenge

CITY, STATE AND NATIONAL LEADS

INSTRUCTIONS: Write only a lead for each of the following stories. As you write the leads, consult the checklists on pages 160–61. The first set of stories involves events in your city; the second set involves events in your state; and the third set involves events in the nation. When you finish, you can compare your work to a professional's. A professional journalist has been asked to write a lead for each of these stories, and the leads appear in a manual available to your instructor. You may find, however, that you like some of your own and your classmates' leads better than the professional's.

CITY BEAT

1. The restaurant is located at 480 Parkside Dr. and specializes in Chinese cuisine. It is owned by Fred Lee, who also does all the cooking. City health inspectors suspended its license late yesterday. They complained of poor food handling and storage. "The condition of the licensed premises was so serious that it was condemned as posing an immediate threat to public health," the city's emergency license suspension order states. Chester Garland, a city health inspector, said the city suspends licenses only when there are serious violations. "It has to be something that is a major problem," Garland said. "We don't just do it on minor stuff." Garland added that the restaurant has consistently failed to comply with city health codes. Violations cited yesterday by city inspectors include rodent and roach infestations. The inspectors found rodent droppings strewn about storage areas and on canned goods. Garlands report adds: "A mouse was seen running across the dining room. A live mouse was spotted in the pantry. Another mouse jumped on an inspector. Toxic materials were stored in food-preparation and dish-washing areas. Food was found improperly stored in a janitors closet as well as in uncovered containers and in locations less than 6 inches off the floor."

2. Marlene Holland is a junior at Colonial High School. She was enrolled in a biology class there last term and objected when, as part of her class assignments, she was asked to dissect worms, frogs, and a fetal pig. She said the assignments violated her religious beliefs. The teacher then gave her a grade of "F" on the assignments, and she flunked the course as a result. Her parents sued the school district, and the trial was supposed to begin at 8 a.m. next Monday. The lawsuit charged that the Board of Education violated her freedom of religion by giving her failing grades for refusing to participate in dissection experiments. There was a settlement today. "I learned that it's worth it, in the end, to act on your convictions," the girl said when interviewed after the settlement. The boards attorney, Karen Bulnes, said the district decided to settle, giving her a passing grade based upon her other work, a grade of "B," because Marlene would have proven in a trial that her refusal to cut up dead animals stemmed from sincere religious beliefs. The district also agreed to pay $12,500

in legal fees, which will go to the American Civil Liberties Union, which represented her. Marlene said her spiritual doctrine bars her from harming animals or cutting them up. They also keep her from wearing leather or wool, eating meat, or drinking milk. She also shuns makeup, which is often tested on animals.

3. Todd Lefforge is an orthodontist who has been working in your community for 11 years. His is 36 years old and lives at 537 Peterson Place. He has a practice of about 750 current patients. He has treated approximately 5,000 more in the past. Today he announced that he has AIDS. He was diagnosed with AIDS three days ago. He immediately closed his practice. He also wrote a letter to all his patients, mostly children, and their parents. His letter, which parents began to receive today, says, "I am very sorry for any anxiety this may cause to anyone." The city's Department of Health has set up an emergency center at its downtown office where, starting today, his patients can be tested for the AIDS virus and counseled about their fears. Leforge, who decided to immediately close his practice, said he tried to be reassuring in his letter. "I have always followed the CDC [Centers for Disease Control] guidelines regarding infection and sterilization procedures," he wrote. "I feel no patients could have been infected by me." Dr. Cathleen Graham, M.D., head of the citys Health Department, agreed that: "The risk is minimal. But the long odds don't lessen the fears of a parent. Since we're dealing primarily with children, its more emotional. Its going to be a traumatic time."

4. Your police department arrested a thief at 11 p.m. last night: Mark Johnsen, 43, of 2463 Pioneer Road. After his arrest, Johnson promptly confessed. Talking to a reporter, he said: "I worked construction, but it was hard and I didn't like it, so I quit. I could make better money stealing, and it only took an hour or two a day." Johnson estimates that he broke into about 300 homes during the last 12 months. "I'd make $2,000, maybe $3,000, a week," he said. He sold his loot, mostly jewelry, to fences, pawnshops, and flea markets. He was arrested shortly after 11 p.m. after leaving a house with a VCR and jewelry, Detective Karen Sweers said. Neighbors called the police after seeing him enter the house. Detectives later found about $10,000 in rings, watches, coins and other jewelry in his car and at his girlfriends apartment. Johnsen was released from prison about two years ago after being convicted of strong-armed rape, robbery and kidnapping. "He's a career criminal," Sweers said. "He has spent 15 of the last 17 years in the prison system." He is being held without bail on charges of burglary and grand theft. Investigators are trying to track down the owners of dozens of stolen coins, rings and necklaces.

5. The accident occurred yesterday at your citys airport. A plane crashed on takeoff. Gusty crosswinds were at least partly to blame, said airport officials. The plane was a single-engine Cessna 172 Skyhawk. It crashed shortly after 4 p.m. yesterday afternoon. The Federal Aviation Administration has been notified and is investigating the crash. The pilot was Joel Fowler, age 23, of 2606 Hillcrest Street. The identity of his 3 passengers was not immediately available. All survived the crash. "It was a miracle we only got scratches," said Fowler, who added that they were "out cruising" in the rented plane, and that he was practicing a few touch-and-go landings. A touch and go is where the plane hits the runway for a split second and then goes airborne again. As the craft touched the runway it was going about 70 mph and being tossed by the wind,

Fowler said, "It was real tough." He gave it full throttle to climb back into the air, but in an instant the plane veered right, a wing struck the pavement and it turned upside down, "spewing pieces everywhere." The four, stunned but not seriously hurt, unbuckled their seat belts and piled out of the plane immediately. The passengers were taken to Regional Medical Center for examination and treatment of cuts, bruises, and shock.

6. Its a war against your citys stray cats. No one knows the exact number. Some estimate hundreds. The cats are making people angry. People complain the furry felines screech outside windows at night, defecate in flower beds and saunter across the roofs of cars. Animal Control officers are especially concerned this year because they recently captured three sick cats, which can harbor rabies. The tests have not been completed. Residents are helping reduce the cat population by signing up to use one of 100 traps available to them: lent, free of charge, by the citys Office of Animal Control. There is a one month waiting period to receive a trap. Residents keep the trap for three days. If they capture a cat, they can keep the trap another three days. The trap is returned if no cat is caught, and the next person on the list is called to pick one up. Besides cats, residents have captured rats, dogs, possum and raccoons, which are picked up by Animal Control officers. A majority of the stray cats are found in apartment complexes and low-income areas, but they can be found in almost any neighborhood where people have either moved away and abandoned their cats or where cats have not been spayed or neutered. Captured cats are kept at a shelter for five days, then destroyed, if they are not picked up by their owners or adopted.

STATE BEAT

1. It was an interesting little idea proposed today by a state senator from your city: Neil Iacobi. Today Iacobi made a proposal that would affect most newspapers in your state, or at least those that publish editorials. Iacobi said he is drafting legislation that would require newspapermen to sign the editorials they write so people know the writers identity. "It's one of the most blatant attempts at press-bashing in recent memory," responded Tony DiLorento, executive director of the State Press Association. Iacobi said he has already found 32 co-sponsors for his bill. Violations would be punishable as second-degree misdemeanors. "It doesn't say you can't write something—only that you have to sign what you write," Iacobi said. "Editorialists should be accountable to their readers. They can attack you and tear you apart and do anything to you, and no one even knows who they are. That's not right or fair. Only cowards would do something like that."

2. Each year, there is a Miss America contest in your state, and the winner goes on to compete in the Miss America contest in Atlantic City, New Jersey. The producers of your state pageant announced a new policy today. They have decided to ban high heels and skimpy swimwear. "Our contestants are nice girls, not hookers," explained state contest coordinator Shannon Basa. This years contest will be held on the first Saturday of next month, with 96 contestants from throughout your state. They will walk barefoot wearing Esther Williams swimsuits: halter tops with waist-high bottoms cut straight across the top of the leg. Color: snow white. "We're going back to the glamorous movie star days of Betty Grable and Marilyn Monroe. Less skin, but still sexy," said

Basa. "Only hookers and Playboy centerfolds wear high heels with swimsuits," she added. "That's not the right direction for us."

3. State Senator Karen Simmons proposed another new law today. She introduced it in the state senate. To protect the environment she wants to ban disposable diapers but expects strong opposition among working mothers and day-care centers. "We're running out of landfill space," Simmons, a Democrat, said. "But there are young mothers who are going to scream and holler." Many day-care centers will not accept children who wear cloth diapers instead of disposable diapers. "You just cannot handle cloth diapers as sanitarily," said Denise Abdondanzio, a spokesman for the states day care centers. Simmens filed her bill (SB 1244) to ban disposable diapers effective Jan. 1. Without a ban, she said, disposable diapers will fill up landfills, "causing problems long after the babies have babies."

4. Richard Clair, head of your states Department of Corrections, testified before a legislative committee in your state capital today. He reported that, 10 years ago, 4.5% of the people in the states prisons were women. Five years ago it was 6.4%. Today women are 8.7 per cent of the inmates in state prisons "and the percentage seems certain to continue to increase." There are also more older inmates: inmates age 51 and older. The percentage has jumped from 3.8% to 4.6% during the last 10 years, Clair said. Women and the elderly present special problems for a prison system historically geared toward young men. Medical costs for women and older inmates are higher than for young men. And because there are fewer women in the system, there are fewer facilities for them, prompting charges of unequal treatment. Women tend to commit drug-related and economic crimes rather than crimes of violence. Yet in prison they have less access than men to programs that could help them, such as drug treatment, education, and job training programs.

5. Merchants in the state say they are delighted with a new law the governor signed today. It will go into effect on the 1st of next month. Basically, it stiffens check-bouncing penalties. Amy Woods, director of the State Federation of Independent Businesses, said the bill will send a stern message to the writers of bad checks. "We're delighted," Wood said. "SFIB has 15,000 members in the state, and we've lobbied hard for a bill like this." The bill makes check-bouncers liable for paying three times the face value of each bad check if they fail to make good on their bills within 30 days after receiving a written demand for payment. It also requires the writer of a bad check to pay all service charges, court costs and attorney fees incurred in the collection effort. Damage awards are limited to a total of $2,500 per check.

6. Last spring, Rachel Young was named the states "Outstanding Teacher." She is a high school economics teacher. She was invited to give a speech today at the annual convention of the National Education Assn. in the state capital. The main thrust of her speech was to criticize the fact that many high school students hold part-time jobs. She called minimum wage jobs "the silent killers of quality education," and explained that too many teens jeopardize their futures by working part time in high school. She continued in her speech: "Flipping burgers and running a cash register teach youngsters next to nothing and leave them scant time to study, keep up on current events, or participate in extra curricular activities. If you look at these students, few have to work to help support their families, put food on the table, or save up for college. Instead, most

working teens are middle class students who labor to buy themselves flashy cars, pay car insurance premiums or clothe themselves in the latest fashions. They are trapped in seeking material goods, and they come to school truly tired, truly burned out. They're sacrificing their future earnings and career satisfaction because these jobs compromise their ability to make the most of their high school years."

NATIONAL BEAT

1. The Census Bureau issued a report today concerning the problem of illiteracy. The Census Bureau set out to determine how many people currently living in the United States are literate or illiterate in the English language. It administered literacy tests to 3,400 adults in the United States. It found the illiteracy rate for adult Americans whose native language is English is 9%. For adults whose native language is not English, the illiteracy rate climbed to 48%. A large portion of those people are, by their own account, probably literate in their native language, according to the study. Of the native English speakers who failed the test, 70% had not finished high school. The test has a sampling error of 1 to 2 percentage points.

2. A controversy in Hegins Pennsylvania is attracting national attention—and making some people very angry. Fistfights have broken out. As tempers continued to flare, state troopers arrested 25 people, and three of the troopers suffered injuries, all minor, during the ensuing scuffles. The controversy involves pigeons. To raise money for a charity, people shoot birds—pigeons—released from cages. The proceeds are used to maintain a park in this east-central Pennsylvania town. Competitors compete for prizes of up to $1,000 and use shotguns. They stand 20 yards from the birds which are released one at a time from metal cages. Dead birds are put in barrels for use in fertilizer. An estimated 4,800 birds were killed Sunday, and more will be killed when the event concludes this coming weekend. Several fistfights broke out last Sunday. Fourteen people ran on the field at different times in attempts to free the birds. "It was just getting out of control," state police spokesman Clay Bulnes said. He and 40 other officers have been assigned to the park. The 14 people who rushed the field were charged with criminal trespass. Eleven other demonstrators were charged with disorderly conduct. About 150 people, some from as far away as Florida, California, and Texas, continue to picket the event, billed as the largest live pigeon shoot in the world.

3. The Centers for Disease Control issued a report Friday that, for many, will be pleasing. It concerns Americans' consumption of hard liquor. That consumption has fallen to its lowest level since 1959. The average American drank 0.85 gallons of spirits last year, compared with 0.84 gallons in 1959, according to the Alcohol Drug Abuse and Mental Health Administration. Distilled spirits are hard liquors such as whiskey, rum, vodka, or gin. Beer and wine, which are fermented but not distilled, are considered separately. CDC statistics, however, show that consumption of alcoholic beverages as a whole is on the decline. The statistics indicate that some drinkers are switching to lower-alcohol drinks such as wine coolers and light beers as a result of their concern for physical fitness, nutrition and alcohol abuse. Two out of three American adults drink. But just 10 percent of those adults drink half of all the alcohol consumed in the nation.

4. The President lost a battle in Congress today. Congress decided against spending $12 million for a cause the president favored. The project involved huge dish-shaped antennas which listened for radio signals from outer space. It was cut from NASA's budget. The House today approved a $14.29 billion budget for NASA in a 355–48 vote. If the Senate agrees with the House, the space agency budget for next fiscal year will be $2 billion above current spending levels but $800 million below what the president requested. The president wanted included in the budget $12 million for the alien-search project. NASA's search for extraterrestrial intelligence, a project known as SETI, was to cost $100 million over 10 years. Its sophisticated radio antennas have picked up only static since the program began last year. "Our country can't afford this," said Rep. Ronald Machtley, R-R.I., who suggested that the money be spent on education. "I'd rather see a search for terrestrial intelligence in our schools," he said.

5. The Department of Veterans Affairs today admitted that its made a little mistake. The mistake cost an estimated $5.7 million a year. Each year, the Veterans Affairs Department pays more than $14.7 billion in disability compensation and pension benefits to more than 2.8 million veterans and to nearly 1 million surviving spouses and other dependents. An audit of those payments revealed that the Department of Veterans Affairs has been paying benefits to more than 1,200 veterans who are dead. The exact total was 1,212 veterans who were reported dead. About 100 of the veterans have been dead a decade or more. Auditors said the department could have reduced the erroneous payments by matching VA benefit payment files with death information maintained by the Social Security Administration. In the past, the department relied on voluntary reporting of deaths as a basis for ending benefits.

6. The nations homebuilders are concerned about a problem that affects young adults—but also the entire nation (and its economy as well). The problem is affordable housing. At its annual convention, currently being held in Las Vegas Nevada, the National Homebuilders Assn. revealed that a survey it commissioned shows a drop in homeownership rates over the last 10 years among young families—and a rapidly dwindling stock of low-cost rental housing. The associations members expect the problems to continue. The homeownership rate among families in the 25-to-34 age group has fallen to 45%, largely because they don't have the cash for a down payment or the income to qualify for a loan. At the same time, rents are at record high rates in much of the country, making it harder for young families to accumulate the money needed for a down payment. Wayne Doyle, the associations President, offered no concrete solutions to the problem, which has sent the homebuilding industry into the doldrums, with fewer sales and higher unemployment rates. "Young families face a difficult situation," Doyle concluded. "They must accumulate enough savings to make a down payment but they are finding it harder to obtain good jobs, and also find that more and more of their money is going for rent, so its harder to save anything for a house." By comparison, the homeownership rate for 65-to-74 year olds is 78.2%.

Exercise 8

LEADS

SPECIAL PROBLEMS (THE UNUSUAL, LOCALIZING AND UPDATING)

INSTRUCTIONS: Write only the lead for each of the following stories, following the guideline that precedes each group of stories. Some stories contain highly unusual facts that should be emphasized in their leads. Other stories will have to be localized or updated. Again, consult the checklists on pages 160–61.

PART I: STRESS THE UNUSUAL

1. Daniel J. Silverbach is a policeman in your community. Last year, because of his heroic rescue of seven persons held at gunpoint during a robbery, Police Chief Barry Kopperud named him the department's Police Officer of the Year. Kopperud fired Silverbach when he reported for duty at 7 a.m. today. The department adopted certain grooming standards, and Kopperud said Silverbach's mustache was a quarter inch too long and his sideburns a half inch too long, and he refused to trim them. Kopperud added that he warned Silverbach a month ago to trim his hair, then ordered him to do so at the first of last week. He fired him for failing to obey the order of a superior officer.

2. Terri Snow of 3418 Hazel St. is a nurse at Mercy Hospital. She is married to Dale Snow, a former eighth-grade science teacher at Mays Junior High School. Snow was crippled after a diving accident three years ago, when his arms and legs were paralyzed. He met his wife at the hospital, where he was a patient, and they were married last month. Now state officials have suggested that they get a divorce. Before his marriage, Snow received $345 a month from the state's Department of Social Services and a monthly $792 federal Supplement Security Income payment. Because of his wife's income, he no longer is eligible for the payments, and the couple says without the payments they cannot afford to pay for Snow's continuing medical treatments and special diet. State officials have advised them that Snow will again become eligible for the aid if they get a divorce. The officials refused to talk to reporters, however.

3. Cremation is rising in popularity. Nearly 30 percent of the people who die in your state are now cremated. The Funeral Directors Assn. in your state met at noon yesterday and discussed a growing problem. The ashes of nearly 50 percent of those people they cremate are never claimed by family members, friends or anyone else, so they are stored in the funeral homes, and the directors want to dispose of them but are uncertain of their legal right to do so. They voted to ask the state legislature to pass a bill that spells out disposal procedures. The bill they propose would require funeral homes to make every possible effort to settle with the family of the deceased the desired disposal method. Families would have up to 90 days to pick up the remains or to specify what they want done with them. After 90 days, the funeral homes would be free to get rid of them either by burying them, even in a common container (in a properly designated cemetery) or by scattering them at sea or in a garden, forest or pond.

4. A home at 2481 Santana Avenue was burglarized between the hours of 1 p.m. and 4 p.m. yesterday afternoon. The owner of the home is Dorothy R. Elam, a sixth-grade teacher at Madison Elementary School. She said no one was home at the time. Neighbors said they saw a truck parked in the driveway but thought some repairmen were working at the home. The total loss is estimated at in excess of $5,000. The items stolen from the home include a color television set, a videocassette recorder, stereo, sewing machine, electric typewriter, 2 pistols and many small kitchen appliances. Also, a stamp collection valued at about $1,000, some clothes, silverware and lawn tools were taken. Roger A. Elam, Mrs. Elam's husband, died 2 days ago. The robbery occurred while she was attending his funeral at 2:30 p.m. yesterday at the Powell Funeral Chapel, 620 North Park Avenue. Elam died of cancer after a long illness.

5. A city health inspector today inspected several restaurants in the Colonial Mall, and his reports show that he found everything in those restaurants satisfactory. But while in the mall, the inspector, Randall Tillmann, said in a separate report that he noticed a popcorn stand which did not meet various city requirements for an establishment selling food to the public. As a consequence of his inspection and the deficiencies he noted in its operations and facilities, he ordered the popcorn stand closed. His report explains that it does not have a washroom or sink for its patrons. The stand is owned and operated by Mr. and Mrs. Herbert J. MacDonald, who pay the sum of $100 a month for the right to operate the popcorn stand in one corner of the mall. The MacDonalds were not available for comment. They closed the stand immediately after Tillman's inspection early today.

6. Gladys Anne Riggs is 81 years old. Her husband, George, died 10 years ago. She is retired and normally receives about $600 a month in Social Security benefits. She complains she has not received her benefits for the past 4 months. When she inquired as to the reasons for the troubles, officials at a Social Security office in your city today explained that she is dead. Four months ago, her check was returned and marked "deceased," so all her benefits were canceled. Because of the error, Mrs. Riggs fears that her check for next month may also be late, and she says she needs the money to buy food and to pay her rent. She lives alone in a one-bedroom apartment and says she has already fallen behind in her rent and is afraid she will be evicted. Social Security officials said that they will correct the problem as soon as possible and that she will receive a check for all the benefits she has missed during the past 4 months, but that it may take several weeks to issue the check. They suggested that she apply for welfare until the check arrives.

PART II: LOCALIZE YOUR LEAD

1. The state Department of Transportation today announced plans for next year. It will spend a total of $218 million to build new roads and to improve old ones. The amount represents a $14.5 million increase over last year's total. The money comes from a state gasoline tax amounting to 4 cents per gallon sold. The department allocates the money on the basis of need, with the most congested and dangerous areas receiving the most help. Included in the allocations for next year are $7.8 million, allocated to widen from two to four lanes state highway 17–92, which runs through the southeastern part of your city for a distance of approximately three miles. Construction work on the highway

project is expected to begin in four months and to be completed within one and one-half years.

2. Three persons have been killed in the crash of a single-engine plane. Police have identified the victims as Mr. and Mrs. Joel Skurow of Atlanta, Georgia, and Melville Skurow of 4138 Hennessy Court in your community. Joel and Melville are brothers. The plane, flown by Joel, crashed on the outskirts of Atlanta at 7:30 a.m. today. Cause of the crash is unknown. No one on the ground was injured. Friends said Melville Skurow was visiting his brother, an attorney in Atlanta. Skurow is a carpenter and was thirty-seven years of age. The plane, valued at $14,800, was fully insured.

3. The annual Conference of U.S. Mayors is being held in New York City this week. Mayors from throughout the United States hold an annual convention to discuss problems of mutual interest. At the closing session today they elected their officers for the forthcoming year, and they elected your mayor, Sabrina Datolli, first vice president. Approximately 1,460 mayors were in attendance at the convention, which next year will be held in Las Vegas.

PART III: UPDATE YOUR LEAD

1. William MacDowell, 28, a housepainter who lives at 1429 Highland Drive, is being tried for the murder of a cocktail waitress, Ethel Shearer. His trial opened last Thursday, and witnesses last Friday said a ring found in MacDowell's home belonged to the murder victim. MacDowell took the stand today and said he knew the victim and had bought the ring from her for $60 for a girlfriend. If convicted, MacDowell could be sentenced to life in prison. He is currently on parole after spending 8 years in prison on an armed robbery charge.

2. There was a grinding head-on collision on Cheney Road yesterday. Two persons were killed: Rosemary Brennan, 27, and her infant daughter, Kelley, age 2, both of 1775 Nairn Dr. The driver of the second car involved in the accident, Anthony Murray, 17, of 1748 North 3 Street, was seriously injured, with multiple fractures. Police today announced that laboratory tests have confirmed the fact that Brennan was legally drunk at the time of the accident.

3. The state Legislature passed a law which prohibits doctors from performing abortions on girls under the age of 16 without the consent of their parents or guardians. The law specifies that doctors found guilty of violating the law can be fined up to $5,000 and can lose their licenses to practice medicine in the state. The law, which has been signed by the governor, will go into effect at midnight tonight. The Legislature adopted the law after news media in the state revealed that girls as young as the age of 11 had been given abortions without their parents' knowledge or consent. The law is intended to prevent that. The parents' consent must be in writing. The law stipulates that the girl who is pregnant must also agree to the abortion so that her parents cannot force her to have one unwillingly.

CHAPTER 6

ALTERNATIVE LEADS

The previous chapter described basic summary leads. That type of lead is more common than any of the alternatives—and probably easier to write. While reading your local daily, you may find that 95 percent of its stories begin with a summary lead. Yet increasingly, experienced reporters are using newer and more controversial types of leads.

The alternatives are called "soft leads." There are at least a dozen variations, but most soft leads begin with a story's most interesting details—often a question, quotation, anecdote or description. A summary of the story's most important details may appear later, perhaps in the third or fourth paragraph. Or the soft lead may move directly into a story without any attempt to summarize it.

Writing an alternative lead requires thought and imagination: the ability to recognize and convey an interesting idea in a unique manner. It does not require an unusual story. In one instance, all the students in a class were given the same assignment: to rewrite a news release. Most of the students started with a good but routine summary. A young woman in the class was more imaginative:

> TYPICAL SUMMARY: A free seminar about how to cope with depression caused by the Christmas season will be held Dec. 16 at Mercy Hospital on Central Boulevard.
> ALTERNATIVE LEAD: Mercy Hospital will offer a seminar to help residents who may not be so jolly this holiday season.

Here are two other examples of routine stories made more interesting by imaginative leads:

> Bobby Thomas reeled in 22 speckled perch from Lake Monroe on his day off Thursday. But his final catch of the day was a real lifesaver.
>
> *(The Orlando Sentinel)*

> FORREST CITY, Ark.—A thousand criminals will descend on this little town 25 miles from the Mississippi River. Folks couldn't be happier.

The first story went on to explain that Thomas rescued a 69-year-old man who fell out of a boat and lost consciousness. The second story explained that the federal government had announced plans to build a prison in Forrest City. People there were happy because several local factories had closed, and the city's unemployment rate was the worst in Arkansas. The federal prison would be a new, large and stable employer.

When reporters finish a story, their editors expect it to be well written: clear, concise, accurate and interesting. If a story meets these criteria, editors are unlikely to object if its lead does not use the conventional summary form. However, beginners should use the alternative forms sparingly. Beginners who try to use the alternative forms before they have mastered the basic summary lead run the risk of making too many serious errors.

THE CONTROVERSY

During the 1940s, The Wall Street Journal became one of the first daily newspapers to use soft leads. Since then, a few other dailies, such as the Los Angeles Times, The Miami Herald and The Boston Globe, have become known as "writers' newspapers." These dailies give their reporters more freedom to experiment with newer styles of writing. Many of their reporters use soft leads, and reporters at other dailies are following their example.

Proponents of soft leads argue that it does not matter whether a lead is hard or soft—only whether it works. They disparage the traditional summaries as "suitcase leads." In the past, they explain, newspapers tried to jam too many details into the leads. They argue that summary leads and the inverted pyramid style are unnatural, making it more difficult for reporters to write a good story. They further explain that summary leads eliminate the possibility of surprise and make all their stories sound alike.

Reporters using soft leads see their stories as hourglass-shaped, with three parts: (1) an introduction; (2) a turn or transition; and (3) a narrative which tells the story, usually in chronological order. Roy Peter Clark, a proponent of more experimentation in writing, insists that the hourglass form is a more natural way to tell a story. Like good storytellers, the reporters start at the beginning of a tale and proceed to the end, thus presenting the facts in a normal, logical sequence. Clark adds that the key to a good story is the turn—the transition from the lead to the narrative.

The more literary style of soft leads may also help newspapers compete with television. The style's proponents explain that television can report the news more quickly than newspapers but that, by using soft leads, newspapers can make their stories more interesting.

Critics—primarily other reporters and editors—call the style "Jell-O Journalism." They complain that soft leads are inappropriate for most news stories: too artsy, literary, dangerous and unprofessional. Critics add that the soft leads are too long and fail to emphasize the news. If a story begins with several paragraphs of description or quotations, for example, the story's most important details may be lost: buried somewhere in a later paragraph. Critics also complain that some reporters seem to be straining to write fine literature, and that many lack the necessary ability. Their leads seem fashionable but dull. Some soft leads begin with minor but misleading details. Others "turn to mush."

Critics believe the traditional summary leads are clearer and more straightforward—and more appropriate for hard news stories. They do not expect reporters to begin every news story with a summary lead, but do not want the delays (the introductions) to be excruciatingly long.

Thus, some editors are trying to discourage soft leads: to limit the number of stories that start with color instead of the news. These editors are particularly critical of front-page stories that begin with soft leads that fail to deliver their main point until after the jump (the continuation on an inside page). Editors fear that, if readers have not learned the stories' main points by then, few will turn to the inside page.

The following lead is an example of the problem: an alternative lead that is poorly written and is thus likely to make you impatient. You have to read more than 100 words before getting to the news: the main point of the story.

For most of his life Ronald Hensley was the All-American boy: an Eagle Scout, a star football player and honor student in high school, and president of the student body at his community college.

Hensley went on to study management at Notre Dame and graduated in 1986. After serving two years in the Peace Corps, he returned here and was hired as a financial analyst by the Elton Corp.

Hensley joined the Downtown Rotary Club and, in months, was elected its president. Then he was married, and his wife is expecting their first child.

At 3 p.m. Monday, a clean-cut, stocky and executive-looking Hensley was sentenced to 16 years in prison. His crime: aiding and abetting the distribution and sale of several pounds of cocaine.

The writer's intention was good: contrasting Hensley's successful start in life with his sudden and unlikely involvement with cocaine. The introduction would have been more effective, however, if it was cut in half.

The following pages describe all the different types of alternative leads, and show good examples of them.

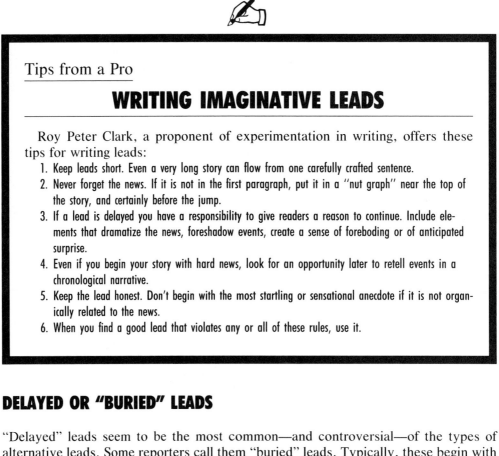

Tips from a Pro

WRITING IMAGINATIVE LEADS

Roy Peter Clark, a proponent of experimentation in writing, offers these tips for writing leads:

1. Keep leads short. Even a very long story can flow from one carefully crafted sentence.
2. Never forget the news. If it is not in the first paragraph, put it in a "nut graph" near the top of the story, and certainly before the jump.
3. If a lead is delayed you have a responsibility to give readers a reason to continue. Include elements that dramatize the news, foreshadow events, create a sense of foreboding or of anticipated surprise.
4. Even if you begin your story with hard news, look for an opportunity later to retell events in a chronological narrative.
5. Keep the lead honest. Don't begin with the most startling or sensational anecdote if it is not organically related to the news.
6. When you find a good lead that violates any or all of these rules, use it.

DELAYED OR "BURIED" LEADS

"Delayed" leads seem to be the most common—and controversial—of the types of alternative leads. Some reporters call them "buried" leads. Typically, these begin with an interesting example or anecdote that sets a story's theme. Then—perhaps in the third or fourth paragraph—a "nut graf" summarizes the story and provides a transition to the body. Thus, the nut graf moves the story from a single example or anecdote to the general issue or problem. Like a traditional lead, it summarizes the topic. In addition, it may explain why the topic is important.

Here are three examples of delayed leads. As you read them, notice that you can start a story about a complex or abstract problem by showing how the problem affects a single individual: someone your readers may know or identify with. Or you can use an anecdote that illustrates the problem and is likely to arouse readers' interest in the topic.

WASHINGTON—He exists only in snapshots and the memories of aging relatives. His last known words were whispered to a buddy in a Japanese prison. No one knows how he died or where he was buried.

Harry Younge, a B-29 tail gunner shot down over Japan in 1945, was one of 78,000 U.S. servicemen from World War II whose remains have never been found or are buried in graves marked "unknown." Many of the servicemen were lost at sea.

(The Associated Press)

MOSCOW—On a recent morning at Moscow's Ryzhsky Market, a middle-aged man in a padded workman's coat did a brisk business selling burned-out light bulbs for a ruble apiece.

His pitch was simple: "Take one of these to work, unscrew a good bulb, put this one in its place and take the good one home."

As the Soviet economy stumbles and consumers face shortages of more and more items—from light bulbs to coffee, paint and drinking glasses—petty theft has become the national sport of the workers' paradise.

(The Associated Press)

BRENTWOOD, Pa.—Shana Racquel owns a mink coat, a dozen custom-made outfits (including a dress trimmed with ostrich feathers and a London Fog raincoat), gold bracelets; her own seamstress, chauffeur, nanny and beautician.

Unusual for a 13-year-old. Even stranger for a dog.

"This is the little girl I never had," Suzanne Brandau says of the brown-and-white English springer spaniel. "She always has the best—the best food, the best clothes, the best baby sitters."

Brandau is one of a growing number of pet lovers across the USA who are spoiling their animals to the hilt—and willing to pay for it.

(USA Today)

Some delayed leads, such as the following example, contain even more of an "O. Henry touch," surprising their readers with an unusual twist. The following story begins in chronological order, delaying its twist until the fifth paragraph:

SAN JOSE, Calif.—The man who called the state Employment Development Department last week said he wanted to hire 70 or 80 people to tear down a vacant house in East San Jose in a hurry.

He got action.

About 75 men, jobless and hungry for the job, offered $5 an hour, set about the task with zeal. By Tuesday morning, only the foundation and the floor remained—and the floor was disappearing fast.

That's when the owner, Mark Campbell, showed up.

"He asked us, 'Who gave you permission to tear my house down?' " said Robert Robinson, one of the workers. "He told us to get the hell off his property. We didn't know we were tearing down somebody's house we weren't supposed to."

(Knight-Ridder Newspapers)

If a story is only three or four paragraphs long, journalists may save the twist for the last line. If a story is longer, they use the twist to lure readers to the nut graf, and it provides a transition to the following paragraphs.

MULTIPARAGRAPH LEADS

Other newswriters think of a lead as a unit of thought. Their summary leads consist of two or three paragraphs, as in the following examples:

> LEOMINSTER, Mass. (UPI)—Two teen-age girls opened a bottle of champagne, shared it and left behind letters about how happy they were about to be.
> Then they took out a 12-gauge shotgun and killed themselves.

> Eugene W. Phillips stumbled and fell from his porch, punctured his back with a stick and slammed his head against the ground. It was about the nicest thing that ever happened to him.
> Phillips had been blind most of the past 16 years. The accident a week ago helped him to partially regain his eyesight.

> Rafael Morales promised he would show up for trial. His father promised. His mother promised. And his two sisters promised. His boss promised, too.
> Morales, 33, a Hialeah salesman charged with cocaine trafficking, did not keep his promise. He jumped $75,000 bail and skedaddled. So Dade County Circuit Judge Margarita Esquiroz sent his father, mother, two sisters and his boss to jail Thursday for 30 days.
>
> *(KNT News Service)*

> Hopelessly lost in an underwater cave with only minutes of air left in his scuba tank, Jason Tuskes wanted to say goodbye to his family.
> So the 17-year-old took out his knife, pulled off his tank and carved a note to his parents and younger brother on the aluminum cylinder.
> "I love you Mom, Dad and Christian," it said. His message complete, Tuskes discarded his diving gear and drowned.
>
> *(The Orlando Sentinel)*

USING QUOTATIONS

Reporters sometimes use quotations in leads—but sparingly. Reporters use a quotation only when a source has said something so effectively that the statement cannot be improved on. A quotation used in a lead should: (1) summarize the entire story, (2) be brief, and (3) be totally self-explanatory:

> "Congress should immediately ban the sale of all tobacco products, especially cigarettes," the president of the American Cancer Society declared in a speech here last night.

> "Indian education is a failure and a national disgrace," a California educator told teachers here today.

> "He made me mad, so I grabbed an ax and chased him," a 72-year-old woman said after capturing a prowler in her back yard Tuesday.

Never use a quotation simply because it is sensational and likely to startle your readers. A quotation used in a lead should summarize the entire story, not just a small part of it. If the quotation summarizes only a sensational detail, the main point of the story is likely to be unclear, and later paragraphs are likely to seem disorganized—unrelated to the sensational detail presented in the lead. If the quotation is not self-explanatory, it may confuse and discourage your readers. If the quotation is too long, your entire lead may become too long and complicated.

Be particularly careful to avoid quotations that begin with words that must be identified or explained in a later paragraph: words such as "he," "we," "it" and "this." If "he" or "we" is the first word in a story, readers have no way of knowing to whom the word refers. When the subject's identity is revealed later in a story, readers may have to stop, go back and reread the quotation to understand its meaning. Here is an example of that type of error:

> "If you don't cooperate, I'll blow your brains out," he told her as she walked to work this morning.
> REVISED: Lisa Vantorini was walking down Princeton Street when a young man approached her from behind and threatened to kill her unless she helped him rob a bank where she works as a cashier.

Leads that use a quotation can often be rewritten with a brief introduction placed *before* the quotation to enhance its clarity:

> "It was saucer-shaped and appeared to have a glass window section running around the center." That's how a woman described the flying object she saw hover above Crystal Lake on Monday and Tuesday nights.
> REVISED: A woman who saw a flying object hover above Crystal Lake on Monday and Tuesday nights said, "It was saucer-shaped and appeared to have a glass window section running around the center."

> "Forget it" is the advice a 20-year-old gave in an interview Monday to other youths who want to drive race cars.
> REVISED: A 20-year-old, who was crippled when his stock car collided with two other cars and struck a wall, Monday warned other youths who want to drive race cars to "forget it."

Instead of using a full quotation, reporters often quote only a key word or phrase in a lead:

> LONDON—Cigarette smoking can lead to "smoker's face," a wrinkled, weary, haggard look that will give you away every time, a British doctor says.
>
> *(The Associated Press)*

> A police chief, speaking here today, accused sociologists of being "impractical, blind, maudlin sentimentalists," with unrealistic attitudes toward crime and criminals.

> WHEATCROFT, Ky.—Methane gas ignited and flashed "like a flame thrower" through a coal mine Wednesday, killing 10 miners in the nation's worst coal mine disaster in five years.
>
> *(The Associated Press)*

USING QUESTIONS

Questions also make effective leads but, again, are most appropriate for light, humorous stories—not serious news stories. In one case, members of a college psychology class disguised a student as an old man, placed him in a booth on campus and watched as he tried to give away dollar bills. Most passers-by refused to accept money from the "old man." A journalism student asked to write a story about the experiment came up with this lead:

> Students in a psychology class tried to give away dollar bills Friday but found that most of their classmates were unwilling to accept them.

Another student, given the same assignment, wrote this question lead:

> Would you accept free dollar bills from an old man?

To be effective, question leads must be brief, simple, specific and provocative. The question should contain no more than a dozen words. Moreover, readers should feel absolutely compelled to answer it. Thus, the question should concern a controversial issue that readers are familiar with: an issue that interests and affects them. Avoid abstract or complicated questions that would require a great deal of explanation.

The following questions are ineffective because they are too abstract, long and complicated. Moreover, they fail to ask about issues that everyone is certain to care about:

> Would you like to have a say in the physical and mental health care facilities offered in your city?

> If you were on vacation miles from your house, and you thought the mechanic at a service station deliberately damaged your car, then demanded an exorbitant fee to repair it, would you be willing to file criminal charges against the mechanic and return to the area to testify at his trial?

The following questions, although more provocative, are too long and complicated:

> Is severe mental retardation reason enough to justify the involuntary sterilization of a young woman who has been institutionalized and has a sexually mature body but the mind of a 5-year-old?

> You may think that you are honest but, if you were certain that you would never be caught, would you cash a check that, by mistake, your auto insurance company made out to you for $3,740,000 instead of $374?

The following questions also fail, but for different reasons. The first question asks about an issue unlikely to concern most readers. The second question is flippant, treating a serious topic as a trivial one, and unanswerable:

> Have you thought about going to prison lately?

> Someone was swindled today. Who'll be swindled tomorrow?

The following, more effective leads are short and specific, and concern topics more likely to affect or interest large numbers of readers:

Why do people lie?
Are you a playaholic?
Why do some children become delinquents?
Do college professors give too many As and Bs?
Do you have what it takes to become a millionaire?
At what age should children start learning about sex?

You may also like the following leads. Notice that, immediately after asking a question, they answer it:

Do you want to hear something really disgusting about the president of the United States? The man who brought you Tabasco sauce with pork rinds is now indulging in another strange food combination: Butter-finger candy bars crumbled onto oat bran.

(The New York Times)

Would you like to live near a power plant, a state prison and a mound of garbage almost as tall as a 15-story building?
Developer Glen Irving thinks you would. He is asking regional planners for permission to build 800 apartments, an office park and a shopping center in a cow pasture just west of the county landfill.

The second question is longer than most, 23 words, but succeeds because it is clear, provocative and to the point.

Some editors prohibit the use of both quotation and question leads. The editors explain that most quotations lack clarity and, when used in leads, are too long and complicated. Some editors also believe that news stories should answer questions, not ask them.

SUSPENSEFUL LEADS

Some leads are written to arouse readers' curiosity, create suspense or raise a question in their minds. By hinting at some mysterious development explained in a later paragraph, this type of lead compels readers to finish a story:

Three weeks ago Sue McCrady bought a stack of guidebooks to national parks, planning a cross-country trip she and her husband were to begin today. Two days later she bought a coffin.

(The New York Times)

It seemed like a normal day, until Seminole County jail chief Thomas Welke learned that a dead woman was on his telephone line.

(The Orlando Sentinel)

It was a broken music box that got 4-year-old Meara Taylor into trouble. But it was climbing into her baby brother's crib that got her killed.

(Houston Chronicle)

The second story went on to explain that Welke knew the woman on his phone was dead because he had given her son, a guard in the county jail, a week off to attend her funeral. Welke had also contributed money for flowers sent to the guard's house. The third story quoted a woman who explained why she had killed her daughter.

DESCRIPTIVE LEADS

Other leads begin with descriptive details and move gradually into the action. The description should be colorful and interesting, so that it arouses readers' interest in the topic. The description can also help summarize a story:

> There were no screeching tires or slamming doors, just the hum of an approaching car's engine.
> A blue Oldsmobile had come up behind the armored car in the parking lot of the First State Bank of Eden Prairie. A gray van pulled in front. Three masked gunmen appeared. They carried M-16 rifles, an Uzi submachine gun and a box that looked like a bomb.
> In less than a minute, almost without a word, the largest heist in Minnesota history was over.
>
> *(Minneapolis Star Tribune)*

> There were row after row of gravestones—and they were knocked over, lying flat, more than 500 of them, under a chill sun yesterday at Mount Hebron Cemetery in Flushing, Queens.
> Ruth Kart, whose father-in-law's stone had been among those overturned and, in some cases, cracked by vandals during the night, remembered how she had been sickened when she saw a monument in Israel to the six million Jews who were murdered by the Nazis in World War II. The new sight, she said, "turned my stomach again."
> Jewish graves have not been the only target of cemetery vandals. . . .
>
> *(The New York Times)*

> It's Thursday morning, and the back room of the restaurant is filled with neatly dressed men holding earnest conversations over eggs and pancakes.
> Mimeographed pamphlets are handed out. A sex-education book is passed around, causing heads to shake negatively. A rousing prayer is delivered.
> The Decency in Education Committee of Lee County is holding its weekly meeting.
>
> *(The Associated Press)*

The following leads, which appeared on the front page of The New York Times on the same day, demonstrate the effectiveness of descriptive leads. The first lead *summarizes* a major story. The second lead *describes* the story. As you read the second lead, notice its effective use of descriptive verbs: "hit," "glided," "skidded" and "sank."

> An Air Florida jetliner taking off from National Airport in a snowstorm crashed into a crowded bridge this afternoon and broke as it plunged into the Potomac River, leaving at least 10 people dead and more than 40 missing, according to unofficial police estimates.
>
> It hit the bridge with a deafening roar and then, suddenly, there was silence. There was no sound at all, those who watched said later, as the Air

Florida 737 jetliner glided into the river, skidded across the gray ice and sank slowly into the icy waters.

SHOCKING LEADS—WITH A TWIST

Reporters also like "shockers"—startling leads that immediately capture the attention of readers. The following examples, written by students, have an unusual twist that adds to their effectiveness.

A freight train carrying toxic chemicals smashed into a bus Thursday, killing two teen-agers. "It was fun," said one 17-year-old. "I'd like to do it again next year."

Sharon Handler, a high school senior, could talk about her "death" because she and 59 other high school students volunteered to be the victims of a mock disaster.

An Edgewood patrolman today said that he would like to shoot people all day long if it would make the streets any safer.

"It's easy. Take the gun, aim and shoot—whammo, you've nailed 'em," said patrolman L. E. Dobbins.

He spends about two hours a day hidden in bushes or behind a building, waiting for the unsuspecting speedster to cross the sights of his radar gun.

IRONIC LEADS

Closely related to shockers are leads that present a startling or ironic contrast—again, details likely to arouse readers' curiosity, as in the following examples:

Civil Defense officials estimate there are 300 handicapped residents in the county who will need help during an emergency. So far, the officials have located only 50.

RALEIGH, N.C.—Velma Barfield, who crocheted dolls for her grandchildren and slipped fatal doses of arsenic to her mother and three other victims, was executed by lethal injection early today.

Wearing pink cotton pajamas and strapped to a stainless-steel gurney, Barfield became the first woman executed in the United States in 22 years shortly after 2 a.m. when a powerful muscle relaxer was pumped into her veins.

(The Orlando Sentinel)

DIRECT-ADDRESS LEADS

Reporters occasionally use a form of direct address, speaking directly to their readers:

If you are convicted of drunken driving after Jan. 1, you will be fined $1,000 and sentenced to three days in prison.

If you live another 50 years, you are likely to be a millionaire. The Social Security Administration predicts that an average worker will earn $656,000 a year. However, a loaf of bread will cost $37.50, a car $281,000 and a home $3.4 million.

UNUSUAL WORDS USED IN UNUSUAL WAYS

If you are clever and have a good imagination (or a good grasp of literature), you can use a common word or phrase in an uncommon manner:

> Parole may be an idea whose time has gone.
>
> *(The New York Times)*

> Two veteran motion picture industry executives were chosen today by the board of Walt Disney Productions to head the troubled company a mouse built.
>
> *(The New York Times)*

> The home of the brave may soon become the land of the fee. The Immigration and Naturalization Service is drafting a plan to charge people who enter the United States on foot or by car.
>
> *(United Press International)*

However, this style is difficult because what seems funny or clever to one person may seem corny or silly to another.

Also, the subjects may be too serious for such a light touch:

> A man who punched a highway patrolman in the face will pay through the nose for the blow.

> A 15-year-old boy's errant throw at a baseball tryout landed him in court, but the jury found him safe and pitched the lawsuit.

> Mark Mazur, once in a pickle over a cucumber, was a free man Wednesday after a judge suspended his six-month jail sentence and placed him on probation.

The first story went on to explain that a man had been ordered to pay $40,000 to a state trooper he punched in the face during a routine traffic stop. The trooper suffered a broken nose. The second story explained that a 15-year-old had been sued for $178,000 after a baseball he threw from first base struck an airline mechanic watching the game from near home plate. The mechanic claimed that the baseball shattered his glasses, destroying 50 percent of the vision in his right eye. The third story described a man arrested and charged with theft after he ate a cucumber, raw hamburger and bacon bits at a supermarket.

CHRONOLOGICAL ORDER

As mentioned in Chapter 5, many journalists like to tell some stories—even serious news stories—in chronological order. They consider chronological order the natural way to tell a story. Here's an example from The Milwaukee Journal:

> June Shore, 71, was getting ready to leave for church when the smoke alarm began to blare in her apartment building at 3414 W. Wisconsin Ave.
> "All of a sudden, people were running around in robes yelling, 'There's a fire! There's a fire!' " Shore said in a telephone interview. "It was a horrendous thing, but everyone tried to help everyone else."

Although most of the building's 23 residents were at home when the three-alarm fire broke out about 8 a.m. Sunday, no one was injured. The fire caused about $170,000 in damage to the three-story brick building and its contents, Battalion Chief Dennis Michalowski said.

OTHER UNUSUAL LEADS

The following leads are difficult to categorize. All the leads are unusual, yet effective. Notice their simplicity, brevity and clarity. The average sentence contains fewer than nine words. Also notice the leads' emphasis on the interesting and unusual. The first lead describes the failure of some unusually large frogs to win the annual Calaveras County (Calif.) frog-jumping contest. The second lead describes the birth of quadruplets.

They came. They croaked. They choked.

(Los Angeles Times)

It's a boy!
It's another boy!
It's a girl!
It's another girl!
"That's enough!" exclaimed Carol Abella of Tempe. "What more does he need for Father's Day?"
"Diapers," answered David Abella.

(The Arizona Republic)

Ashley Benham, 17, was mourned Wednesday. Richard Ross, 16, was recovering from surgery to reconstruct his face.
Friday night the two teen-agers from neighboring high schools met in a crush of steel on a winding road.
Richard wore his seat belt. Ashley didn't.

(The Orlando Sentinel)

Every week millions of drivers encounter trains at crossings nationwide. Hundreds of them never get across the tracks.
The winners who beat the trains get no prizes. The losers show up as statistics: 7,280 accidents, 649 deaths and about 2,900 injuries. . ..

(Journal of Commerce)

Save your sympathy, Glenn Stephens says. His blindness doesn't bother him. But ignorant clerks and waiters do.

(St. Petersburg Times)

NEW YORK—Police horses, police dogs and now—police seals?
Three harbor seals, taught to retrieve guns, tools and other objects and to enter a diving bell to take a breath, showed off their skills Wednesday before police and other public officials at a private research institute.

(Knight-Ridder Newspapers)

The man who stumbled out of the Miami Beach paddywagon into the county's alcoholic referral center at about 10 p.m. wore filthy, ragged dungarees.
He smelled of dirt and beer.
He was loud.
He was obnoxious.
He was a cop.

(The Miami Herald)

St. Louis Post-Dispatch

WRITE & WRONG

By **Harry Levins**
Post-Dispatch Writing Coach

Bob Koenig wrote some lovely stuff out of Berlin as the wall came down, but this lede may have been the loveliest:

BERLIN—On the night after the Berlin Wall opened, the hundreds of thousands of East and West Berliners who gathered in a plaza to celebrate suddenly looked skyward when they heard bells toll.

The ringing came from the tower next to the bombed-out ruins of the Kaiser Wilhelm Memorial Church, which stands in West Berlin as a reminder of the world war that led to Germany's division in 1945.

"When those bells rang, I felt history move," said Werner Schumann, 25, an East Berliner who had just crossed the wall to the West for the first time. "I felt two Germanys coming together."

But after the initial euphoria of that night, Nov. 10, cold reality began to strike Germans, and others across the world. Some asked for whom—and for what—did those bells toll?

"The rebirth of a single Germany could mean a funeral for the stable order we've had [in Europe] for 40 years," said Oskar Brandt,

46, a teacher in West Berlin. "It's not the reunification of Germany I fear; it's the potential for instability."

Forty-four years after the Allies crushed Adolf Hitler's Third Reich, the "German Question" that has haunted Europe for more than a century has returned to the fore.

What made it work? Let's take a closer look.

1. Verbs. Koenig's opening sentence runs to 32 words—and in most cases, a 32-word sentence goes past the point that readers want to follow. But here, Koenig peppered the sentence with verbs, five of them: "opened," "gathered," "celebrate," "looked" and "heard." Elsewhere through the opening grafs, Koenig gives us vivid verbs ("strike," "crushed," "haunted"). And where others might have been content with a dead "to be" verb and written that the bombed-out church "is in West Berlin," Koenig wrote that it "stands" in West Berlin.

2. People. In the first five paragraphs, Koenig introduces the reader to two ordinary Germans, one from each side of the Berlin Wall. Ordinary people—and most of our readers live ordinary lives—find news more compelling when we tell it in terms of other ordinary people.

3. Quotes. "When those bells rang," says Schumann, "I felt history move." What a vivid image—and what a feat of writing to organize the story in a way that hits the reader with this quote as soon as possible.

4. Thematic unity. The tolling bells gave Koenig a literary glue that holds this lede together. The lede has "bells," the next graf says "ringing," the third graf says "rang" and the fourth says "toll." That fourth graf let him echo John Donne and glide smoothly into the basic question that the story sets forth: Are the bells tolling for the wedding of the two Germanys? Or for the funeral of European stability?

***

As long as we're talking about nicely done ledes, we ought to credit Jo Mannies for this one:

> Sen. Edward M. Kennedy, D-Mass., says he is out to help the Ed and Paige Hoffmans of this country—hard-working families overwhelmed by what the senator calls "a national health-care system in crisis."

As published on Page One, that lede took up only seven lines of type. But in those seven lines, Mannies:

- Spotlighted a national problem.
- Put that national problem in a local framework.
- Found two people to humanize an abstraction.

Score that lede as a hat trick.

Take note also of what the lede *lacks:*

- A time element. This story appeared in a Thursday paper, describing events that took place on a Wednesday. Sure, the writer could have slipped a "Wednesday" into her lede—"Sen. Edward M. Kennedy, D-Mass., said Wednesday that he was out to help," etc.—but to what end? It would have added a word whose time had not yet come, and it would have forced the narrative into the past tense, even though, as a general rule, readers find the present tense more comfortable. (The past tense for "said" also introduces all of those sequence-of-tenses complications. In this case, anyway, they can wait until the second graf.)

- A place. Without a past-tense "said," the writer lacked a good place to insert a "here" or an "on a visit to St. Louis." So she did the smart thing. She held it until the second paragraph, along with the time element.

Did the lede answer all of the journalism-school W's? No.

Was it a better lede for that? You bet.

The writer distinguished between facts that are important and facts that are for the record. She used her lede for the important facts, and put the for-the-record later, wherever it fit.

***

One more piece of lovely wordsmanship, this one from John McGuire's profile of Calvin Trillin:

> Trillin moves about the land picking up morsels of indigenous foodstuffs and local lore, much like a man in a blue serge suit walking through a sheep-shearing barn.

As usual, McGuire wins the simile-of-the-year award with his wonderfully whimsical image. OK, hard-news stories rarely offer an opening for this kind of simile. But when they do . . .

***

The managing editor recently got a letter from a reader who said in part:

> A recent Post-Dispatch headline declared that something gave the city "a shot in the arm." I've occasionally noted use of the phrase in the paper's news columns, sports columns, etc.

(continued on next page)

Of course, the phrase derives from drug use. To equate "a shot in the arm" with some desirable pick-me-up does not sound appropriate when drugs are a matter of such grave concern.

This isn't a matter of great moment. But among those of us who care about language and what it implies, the phrase should be shunned. I would urge your splendid newspaper to exorcise it.

The letter goes to prove that out there among the anonymous mass we call readers, any wording that *can* be read pejoratively *will* be read pejoratively. The moral: Be careful.

***

Here's a tail-end tack-on of some problem words that crop up with dismaying frequency:

apprehend: An awful piece of cop's jargon, and key evidence that most law-enforcement people are guilty of police brutality when it comes to English. Replace "apprehend" with "arrest."

citizen: Sometimes, we use it when we mean "resident," as in "Joe Smith, a *citizen* of Kirkwood." Remember:

One is a "citizen" of a nation but a "resident" of anything smaller. At other times, we use "citizens" in an unintentionally limiting sense, as in, "Citizens are wary of industrial emissions." Many resident aliens call the United States home, and they worry about the same things that citizens fret about. When citizenship is beside the point, avoid the word: "People are wary of industrial emissions" or "The public is wary of industrial emissions."

comprehensive: Typically, we use this stuffy and windy word in overstated fashion: "a comprehensive plan for development." In such cases, use "detailed" and save "comprehensive" for something that's encyclopedic, even exhaustive in scope.

in order to: Wasted words, as in "He kicked the door down in order to get in the house." The Coach has yet to see the usage in which the words "in order" couldn't be junked without loss: "He kicked the door down to get in the house."

language: Often misused, as in, "He objected to the language of the bill." We presume that the *language* is English; what's being objected to is the *wording*.

SUGGESTED READINGS

Brooks, Terri. *Words' Worth: A Handbook on Writing and Selling Nonfiction.* New York: St. Martin's Press, 1989.

Clark, Roy Peter. "A New Shape for the News." *Washington Journalism Review*, March 1984, pp. 46–47. (Reprinted in *Best Newspaper Writing 1985*, ed. by Roy Peter Clark and Donald Fry. St. Petersburg, FL: Modern Media Institute, 1985, pp. 90–95.)

———. "Plotting the First Graph." *Washington Journalism Review*, Oct. 1982, pp. 48–50.

Lanson, Gerald, and Mitchell Stephens. "Jell-O Journalism: Why Reporters Have Gone Soft in Their Leads." *Washington Journalism Review*, Apr. 1982, pp. 21–23.

Exercise 1

ALTERNATIVE LEADS

EVALUATING ALTERNATIVE LEADS

INSTRUCTIONS: Critically evaluate the following leads, each of which uses one of the alternative forms discussed in this chapter. Select the best leads and explain why they succeed. Point out the flaws in the remaining leads. As you evaluate the leads, look for lessons—"dos and don'ts"—that you can apply to your own work.

1. Are you afraid of snakes?

2. Could you swim 40 miles, jog 100 miles or bike 400 miles in one month?

3. Brenda DeVitini got up at dawn to jog. She planned to use a high school track two blocks from her house, a track she had used every morning for the last four years.
   A paper carrier found her body there an hour later.

4. She is young, beautiful and a good athlete—but confined to a wheelchair.

5. "I'll let you guys have it with both barrels," a member of the state Legislature told members of the Association of Secondary Teachers, who held their state convention in the city today.

6. A 16-year-old girl who said she "considers abortion murder" was placed in jail today because she refused to obey her mother and have an abortion.

7. Should America's 1 million excess dairy cows be donated to impoverished nations or destroyed as ordered by the federal government to maintain the price of dairy products?

8. With tears forming in his eyes, Albert Chmielewski whispered goodbye to his mother.
   Moments later, Chmielewski was handcuffed and led from the courtroom on his way to prison. A jury of nine men and three women had just found him guilty of burglary.

9. On July 8, Rhonda Harmon attended a birthday party at a lounge on Princeton Street. She left at about midnight, and friends saw her get into a light-colored van.
   No one has seen or heard from her since.

10. An off-duty police officer thought she would take her family into a Kentucky Fried Chicken restaurant for a bite to eat.
    But what she walked into was the middle of an armed robbery.

11. "You've had enough contact with the legal system." That's the message that Judge Bruce R. Levine today gave a man appearing before him for the third time this year.

12. Stopping for a picnic lunch Friday, Cindy Lowry began walking her horse toward a field off the trail. In seconds, they were covered with hundreds of stinging bees.
    Cindy survived. Her horse, Dan, did not.

13. "I didn't come here to make you come to your feet," the Rev. Tyrone Burns told about 100 students Tuesday. "I came here to make you come to your senses."

14. Merit pay for teachers is beginning to look like a flawed idea whose time has gone.

15. Todd Gill faces life in prison with no possibility of parole for 25 years for what one prosecutor called "the most deliberate, brutal murder I've ever encountered."

Exercise 2

ALTERNATIVE LEADS

WRITING LEADS WITH QUOTATIONS

INSTRUCTIONS: Use a full or partial quotation while writing a lead for each of these stories.

1. The senior United States senator from your state gave a speech in your community early today and, in the speech, he criticized the federal government's college student loan program. The program is designed to help young people get a higher education. He complained that the program "teaches many student loan recipients to become deadbeats," since 21 percent of the students in your state, on the average, fail to repay their loans. Your senior senator added that the amount of student loans in default in your state alone "exceeds by 76% the total amount stolen in all bank robberies in the entire United States last year." The senator added, "It is truly disturbing that such a high percentage of the young, college-educated people in our state take a major financial obligation so lightly."

2. Ralph R. Palomino, 42, of 374 Douglass Road is a local businessman. He is also a candidate for mayor. He issued his campaign platform to the news media today. He promises, if elected, to hold taxes at their present level—or even to reduce them—by attacking the problem he considers most severe at the moment, the problem of mounting welfare costs. Palomino said, "Most people who receive welfare checks are bums and chiselers too damn lazy to work. Hard-working, decent Americans should not be forced to support these parasites."

3. Dr. Guy Alvarez gave a speech at a meeting of the county medical society last night. Alvarez works in Washington, D.C. for the Department of Health and Human Services. He said: "Thousands of Americans die every year because their diseases are not profitable. The country's major pharmaceutical firms refuse to conduct research and to produce drugs to combat serious diseases that strike only a small percentage of the American public because those drugs are not profitable. Instead, the drug companies are looking for types of medicines, such as tranquilizers, that 30 or 40 million people will take. Their approach is hard-hearted and mistaken. What's more, they admit to the practice but say it is necessary to recoup the cost of their research and development for new medicines."

4. Scientists at the Nielsen Institute in Oregon issued a report about marijuana today. It said: "There are 15 million regular marijuana smokers in the United States, and the use of marijuana has become part of America's cultural mainstream. Like alcohol, marijuana is an intoxicant, and the greatest danger in its use involves the operation of motor vehicles rather than the more widely publicized alarms about biological damage. There is little evidence to support charges that marijuana causes brain damage, chromosome breakage and adverse effects in the body's immune response and hormone levels. But as marijuana becomes more acceptable to society, more users are likely to drive cars

under its influence, and that is the most serious problem. Our studies have shown that 39 percent of the drivers involved in fatal accidents in this state were intoxicated on alcohol, and 16 percent had recently used marijuana."

5. Marilyn Kubik is an English teacher at North High School and today she went to the police department and charged three students with vandalism: Herman Krueger, 16, Stephen Reeves, 15, and Fred Albertson, 15, all sophomores at the school. Kubik explained: "For years, students have been vandalizing the school and have gotten away with it. They've caused thousands of dollars of damage, and no one's had the guts to do anything about it. We're not going to allow it anymore. We teachers have gotten together and have agreed that, whenever we see any vandalism, we're going to file criminal charges against the students responsible for it. It's not enough to just make them stay after school or pay for the damage. Money doesn't mean anything to some of these kids, and most of their parents don't give a damn, so they're no help."

6. The president of your state's medical association, Dr. Leonard Holmann, made a speech to your state Legislature in the state Capitol today. The speech concerned the topic of boxing and the medical risks incurred by the people who engage in that sport. He warned that, "New evidence shows that 15% of all boxers suffer brain damage. So nationwide, thousands of amateur and professional boxers wind up suffering from memory loss, slurred speech, tremors and abnormal gait. In the worst cases, boxers become punch-drunk. Their speech and walk become unsteady, their memories fade, and they lose their grasp of reality." The association's president added that: "Boxing is barbaric. The only purpose is to hurt someone—to knock him unconscious or to injure him so badly that he is physically incapable of continuing a fight." Dr. Hollman recommended that the state Legislature "immediately ban boxing to protect athletes from serious and permanent harm and possibly death."

7. A report released by researchers at the Annenberg School of Communications at the University of Pennsylvania today warned that "watching television can hurt your health." Their report explains that: "People who watch television many hours a day are likely to adopt the nonchalant, careless outlook of the characters who populate prime-time TV. The more people watch television, the more complacent they are about health and exercise, and the more confidence they have in the medical profession. There is an unrealistic belief in the magic powers of medicine. They say, 'If anything goes wrong, the doctor will take care of it.' " The characters shown on TV eat, drink or talk about food eight times an hour. They grab a fast snack almost as often as they eat breakfast, lunch and dinner combined. Despite these poor eating habits, less than 6 percent of the male TV characters and 2 percent of the female characters were overweight. The study also found that "the most common beverage on the tube is alcohol." Thirty-six percent of the characters drink, but only 1 percent are alcoholics.

8. It is a bright red sticker. It says, in large white letters: "Convicted DUI: Restricted License." The letters "DUI" stand for "Driving Under the Influence." Today a judge in your community announced that, effective immediately, he will require every person convicted of drunken driving in his courtroom to attach one of the stickers to the rear bumper of his car, and another to the front bumper. An attorney who opposes the idea responded that the notion is il-

legal, "like putting somebody in a pillory." A second judge, who also favors the idea, responded that, "The public deserves to be protected from these people—to know who they are and to be able to avoid them." Other proponents add that the stickers will serve as a deterrent "since most people would be embarrassed, so embarrassed that they'd be more careful about driving after drinking, and the ones convicted of drunken driving might stay off the roads to avoid being seen and identified as drunks." Even after their convictions nowadays, many drunk drivers are given "restricted licenses" that allow them to drive, but only to and from work. The proposal would apply mainly to them.

Exercise 3

ALTERNATIVE LEADS

WRITING ALTERNATIVE LEADS

INSTRUCTIONS: Write only the leads for the following stories—but not routine summary leads. Instead, write the types of alternative leads described in this chapter.

1. There was a strange party in Los Angeles yesterday. The honoree wasn't there, however. He is Richard ("Dick") Hoglinn, a former employee of the Hughes Aircraft Co. Friends and former colleagues hold an annual party on behalf of Hoglinn, who worked as an aircraft engineer. He went to lunch one day and never came back. The party yesterday was held at Tequila Willie's Saloon & Grill. People at the party said the disappearance seven years ago of Hoglinn "symbolized rebellion against the corporate world." Some added that they themselves have sometimes thought of disappearing when the pressures of family and job begin to get to them. But Dick really did it. Some party-goers wore "Dick" masks. Hoglinn, still in his early 30s, left behind a wife of 12 years and two young children. Another employee reported spotting him at the Los Angeles International Airport around midnight the day he disappeared. Every year since the disappearance, Hughes employees celebrate the anniversary of his flight. The parties attract people who didn't even know Hoglinn.

2. Jill Laszlo is a psychologist at Michigan State University. She talked to you today about her primary area of research: how people spend their time. People are always talking about how busy they are, says Prof. Laszlo, but that may be bunk—a convenient excuse. For 25 years, she has been studying the way Americans spend their waking moments. She has found a steady increase in the amount of their free time. People feel that the work week has been increasing and leisure time has been decreasing. "In fact, since 1965," Laszlo reports, "men have gained seven hours of free time in a week, to 41 hours from 34 in a week. Women have gained six hours of free time, to 40, from 34." Yet people feel starved for time. Women, Laszlo adds, "have more free time than they did two decades ago, all of which has gone into watching television." TV now consumes 37% of the free time of American women and 39% of the free time of American men. There has always been a large segment of the population that feels rushed, she continued. But only in recent years has lack of time become a valid excuse, "a convenient cover-up." In response to a question you asked, Laszlo further stated, "Many people say they don't have time to read newspapers, but it's just another way of saying they'd rather be doing something else."

3. For years, children everywhere have been hearing and reading "Little Red Riding Hood." Now, the story has become involved in a controversy in your city. As a result, it has been pulled from the recommended reading and discussion lists for all elementary school children. The book will remain in school libraries, but teachers will no longer read and discuss the tale with their students nor encourage their students to read it on their own. Why? The heroine has wine in the basket of goodies that she is bringing her ailing grandmother. "It gives the younger ones the wrong impression about alcohol," said Karen Johnsen, your school districts assistant superintendent for elementary instruc-

tion. "If they should refrain, why give them a story saying it's OK?" School Board member Jane Tribit agreed, saying, "I don't think the basket of wine is a good concept for kindergarten or first grade." She said she would rather see "a nice thing like cookies and cakes."

4. Two youngsters in your city have a pet rabbit. They are Shannon Simmons, 9, and her brother, Chris, 7. They are the children of Rachel and Wayne Simmons of 708 E. Lisa Lane. The rabbit, which they've named "Jimmy," lives in a cage in their fenced backyard. Occasionally, they let Jimmy out to play in their house or yard. Most of their neighbors like Jimmy, too. But one of them lodged an anonymous complaint, saying Jimmy should go. Your citys Code Enforcement Board agrees. The Simmons were told today that they have 15 days to get rid of the rabbit. Mr. Simmons then got in touch with their county commissioner, Anne Chen, who says the order "is preposterous." Todd Drolshagen, head of your citys Code Enforcement Board, said: "We received a complaint, and we're required to enforce the law. It states that a family can't keep farm animals in a residential neighborhood, and a rabbit is listed in the definition of farm animals. The problem is, where do you draw the line? One rabbit? Two rabbits? Six rabbits? Two dozen rabbits?" Chen said, "I have a great appreciation for the circumstances, and I'm going back and trying to see what the intent of the Planning and Zoning Commission was way back when the ordinance was passed. Another option is getting the zoning regulations changed—modifying the ordinance to allow a family to keep a single pet rabbit in their home." Chen then added that, "The two children here paid for the rabbit with money their grandma sent them two Easters ago. The fact that they have had the rabbit for over two years makes them responsible owners. My Easter bunnies always ran away in six months."

5. The U.S. government's Census Bureau issued some statistics today. In a report from Washington, it discussed the net worth of the richest Americans. It found that, by last year, 1 out of every 100 American families had a net worth of $1,000,000 dollars or more. That does not mean the families have an income of $1,000,000 dollars or more, but only that if they sold everything they owned and then paid their debts that they would have that amount left over. The report also drew a profile of the average American millionaire. The average millionaire, it found, is an entrepreneur: a white male in his early 60s, married to his first wife, with a business "catering to the ordinary needs of his neighbors." Most millionaires are from middle-class or working-class backgrounds and worked hard to get their money: 10 to 12 hours a day, six days a week, for 30 years or more. Washington, D.C. was tops, with 1.7 millionaires for every 100 households. The state of Connecticut was next, with 1.6.

6. It was one of those crazy contests that you sometimes read about. Everyone seems to enjoy them and lots of people buy tickets for them, hoping to win the grand prize. The grand prize was 3 minutes in a supermarket. The Optimist's Club in your city sponsored the contest. It wanted to raise money to buy playground equipment for a park. To raise the money, they had a charity raffle. They charged $1.00 a ticket. They said the winner would be allowed in a supermarket just before it normally opened for the day and would be allowed 3 minutes. In that time, the winner could keep everything he could pile into grocery carts. The winner's name was drawn last Tuesday night: Allison Hesslin. She got her chance just before 9 this morning. In three minutes, she filled four carts with groceries. Club officials are shocked. Her bill was $1,024.91. "There goes

the kids' money right out the door," said the club president. "We raised $980 and thought that was a lot. We figured the winner might get a few hundred dollars, but that'd still leave us a good profit. Now, we'll have to dig into our treasury to make up the difference, and there's nothing left for the playground." Mrs. Heslin filled the carts primarily with costly meats, cheese and wines that cost up to $29.99 a bottle. "I planned this out with my husband," she said. "We visited the store in advance, so I knew where everything was. You don't get a chance like this very often." The contest planners never specified that the winner could take only one of each thing; normally, that limits the bill to about $100 a minute.

7. Two college students, David Kaeppler and Michael Hosokawa, dreamed of rafting down the Mississippi River, all the way from their homes in Minneapolis south to New Orleans. Using materials they said they "scrounged," they built the raft from old oil drums, lumber and inner tubes. They built a lean-to on its deck and added two stuffed chairs and a red sail. They estimated that the entire raft cost only $100 to construct. The two youths attended high school together in Minneapolis and plan to enroll in the University of Minnesota next fall. Both are 18 years old. Their sailing plans were reported in Minneapolis newspapers, and some Coast Guardsmen apparently read the news stories in the paper. They nabbed the two youths only a few miles into their journey this morning. The Coast Guardsmen said the 22-foot raft needs life preservers, electric lights, river charts and a radio so the two youths can communicate with other boats using the Mississippi River in order to avoid a serious collision. The Coast Guardsmen also complained that the raft does not have a motor, only two paddles. The youths were ordered to go ashore immediately and to remain ashore until they are equipped to obey all the Coast Guard orders. Because they have a small gas stove, they also need a fire extinguisher. Because they plan to live on the raft, they also need a toilet.

8. Niklas H. Romain is a 47-year-old welder. He has been unemployed for a total of 8 months. He went to a state employment office in your city early yesterday and was in line when the office opened at 8 a.m. Because he has been out of work for so long, he says, he has had to put his boat and even his pickup truck up for sale in order to buy food for himself, his wife and his four children. After waiting in line for about 3 hours yesterday morning, he finally reached the clerk, whom police identified as Beth Snowden. Everyone agrees that she told Romaine that he was in the wrong line and would have to start over at the back of another line. Romaine complains that she was "real snotty-like" and that, "Something just snapped, and I just got so I couldn't take it anymore." Instead of getting in the second line, Romain tore up his computer card and went to a nearby supermarket and spent $4.79 for a lemon meringue pie. He hurried back and threw the pie in Snowdin's face. Snowdin said she is used to short tempers but that there are strict rules in the office, and that she is not supposed to deal with people in the wrong line. A good sport, she added that she understands his frustrations and would not charge him with assault, although for a moment she considered doing so.

Exercise 4
ALTERNATIVE LEADS

PRO CHALLENGE

INSTRUCTIONS: Professionals have written alternative leads for the following stories. Write an alternative lead for each of the stories. When you finish, you can compare your work with the professionals'. Their leads appear in a manual available to your instructor. You may find, however, that you like some of your own and your classmates' leads better than the professionals'.

1. In many ways, it was a rather common robbery. Fortunately, the police succeeded in capturing the apparent perpetrator. This is the story. Employees at the First Union Bank, 3720 Kohlar Boulevard, pushed an alarm button at 2:38 p.m. yesterday after a lone man came into the bank and demanded money. The man said he had a sawed-off shotgun under his raincoat. A teller gave him money in a paper bag he carried. She also slipped in an exploding dye pack. Just as the man left the bank the pack detonated, and the man tossed the bag containing the money into the bushes. Witnesses said he then fled on foot. Officers started combing the area, looking for a man in a yellow shirt, blue jeans, and raincoat. They lifted the lid of a trash bin behind the McDonald's at 3782 Kohlar Blvd. and found him there. He was crouched among the half-eaten burgers and fries. Police identified him as Alan Franklin, age 23, of 820 Apollo Drive, Apartment #223.

2. Judge Samuel McGregor performed the unusual wedding Monday. He married Sunni McGrath and Wallace A. Svec. It wasn't a fancy wedding. There was no cake or dress or hugs, not even a kiss. They weren't allowed. Why? Because McGregor performed the wedding in his courtroom, minutes after sentencing McGrath to a years probation for drunken driving. Immediately after the wedding ceremony, the bride was ordered back to prison. She is serving time there for other crimes. Thus, their honeymoon will be delayed. "It was real different. But I feel really good because I love him to death," McGrath said from her jail cell yesterday afternoon. The two have dated for three years and said they wanted to marry to avoid problems with prison visitation rights and requirements. McGrath is scheduled to be released in three months, and the couple has plans for a traditional wedding—flower girl and all, at that time. At yesterdays ceremony a blue jail uniform served as her wedding gown. For security reasons—so they could not pass anything to one another (notes, drugs, weapons, or anything)—an attorney stood between the couple as they exchanged vows. The couple longed to kiss. The judge suggested that they wave instead. They did. They also blew kisses. McGrath said she planned to spend her wedding night watching television. Svec wasn't certain what he would do. Because McGrath was already on probation for burglary, grand theft and possession of cocaine, the arrest for drunken driving resulted in her being returned to jail. She said she committed the other crimes to support a drug habit which she said she has kicked.

3. It was 12:40 a.m. today and the incident occurred at a home located at 4772 E. Harrison Ave. Two men were involved: Michael Uosis and Edward Beaumont, 40. Uosis lives in the home and, a few weeks ago, was robbed. This morning

Uosis heard someone banging at a window of his home. He thought it was the man who had robbed him, coming back to rob him again. So Uosis went to a closet, got out a .38-caliber revolver and fired a single shot at the window. Uosis said he didn't see anyone and didn't mean to shoot anyone and only fired the gun to scare away whoever was outside. "I didn't mean to shoot him," Uosis said. "He was a good friend, and I didn't know it was him outside. I didn't even see who it was outside." Neither the police nor Uosis know why Beaumont, who used to work with Uosis, both as postal workers, until Uosis retired three years ago, had gone to the house at 12:40 a.m. Beaumont is in serious condition in the intensive care unit at Regional Medical Center. Hospital officials said that Beaumont may be paralyzed as a result of the gunshot wound to his head. Police charged Uosis with aggravated battery, and he was released from the city jail after posting $2,500 bail. If convicted, he could be sentenced to as much as 15 years in prison and fined up to $10,000. Under state law, it is illegal for a resident to use unnecessary force against an intruder unless the resident is defending himself or another occupant of the home against death or great bodily harm.

4. There was another burglary in the city. A pair of burglars struck VFW Post #40 at 640 Sherwood Dr. Both burglars appeared to be teenagers. Janitor Steven Cowles heard them. Cowles, age 70, didn't catch them, however. He said, "I'm getting old, and it would have been a chore catching up with them. They lit out." Cowles went to work at the VFW post at about 5 a.m. today and almost tripped and fell over two knapsacks filled with expensive liquor and cigarettes from the post. "I knew something was funny. Then here's those two kids coming around the corner by the popcorn machine," he said. "I let out a big noise and said a few things. I had two loaves of stale bread for the ducks I feed every morning and an old box of Entenmann's sticky buns. I started hitting them with the bread, and then I threw the buns at them. That's when they dropped everything and ran. I went to a phone and called the cops."

5. The drama started when Lillian Sodergreen parked her car and ran into the supermarket to buy a gallon of milk and other groceries. She told her son in the back seat to sit still and be quiet while she was gone. Her daughter was already sleeping. She said it is the last time she will leave the children alone. The admitted criminal is Troy Dysart, 21. Troy is a car thief and admits it. He insists, however, that he is not a kidnapper. He wanted a car to steal for a joyride and, at approximately 8:30 a.m. Tuesday, noticed a car left running, with the keys in the ignition, parked outside a supermarket: Albertsons at 4240 Michigan Street. Normally, he's careful. "There are rules to follow," he explained in an interview with you in his cell in the city jail. "My number one rule is: 'Make sure you don't get more than you bargained for.' " But he was "moving too fast," he said. So he didn't see the children in the back seat: Troy Sodergreen, age 4, and his little sister, Jena, age 8 months. "I saw the keys and got in, but I didn't notice the kids," he continued. He peeled out of the supermarket's parking lot. "When I turn around the corner, I looked to my side and saw the little girl lying on the seat, and then another kid. I saw the kids and say, 'Oh, damn.' I freaked out and parked the car." Dysart is now charged with grand theft and kidnapping. He added, "I didn't want nothing to do with the kids. I didn't touch the kids. My wife has three kids. I don't need no more kids. I'm going to tell the judge the same thing. He can charge me, but I didn't know they were there. Why would I want more kids?" The children were unharmed.

6. Renee Patzel, 17, was a student at Colonial High School in your city. She excelled as a student, placing near the top of her class, and was named by the senior class the "Most Likely to Succeed." She was to have graduated next June. She planned to begin classes at your college next fall. While driving home from work two weeks ago, she lost control of her car, police said. It ran off the highway and hit a tree. She has been in a coma since then. She had a dream: a dream of being elected homecoming queen at her school. She wanted it more than anything else, she often told her parents. Earlier, she had twice served on the homecoming court. Last week Wednesday morning, as she was in a coma at Mercy Hospital, her classmates elected her homecoming queen. The dance was last Saturday night. Her parents went to the hospital to tell Renee that her dream had come true: that she had been elected homecoming queen at her high school. On Saturday night they pinned a corsage to her hospital bed, then went to the dance and received the crown for her. They then took the crown to her hospital room and told her all about the dance. "The doctors said she couldn't hear us, but we never believed it," her parents, Bruce and MaryAnn Patzel said. This morning Renee died without ever regaining consciousness after the tragic accident.

CHAPTER 7

THE BODY OF A NEWS STORY

The portion of a news story that follows the lead is called the "body," and it normally presents facts in descending order of importance. After reporters summarize a story in the lead, they normally place the story's most important details in the second paragraph. They continue to add details in decreasing order of importance, until only the least important remain. Those details may be discarded or, if they are used, may be placed in the final paragraph.

THE INVERTED PYRAMID STYLE

Reporters call this form of writing the "inverted pyramid" style. The lead in an inverted pyramid story summarizes the topic, and each of the following paragraphs presents some additional information about it: names, descriptions, quotations, conflicting viewpoints, explanations, background data and so forth. Most paragraphs are self-contained units that require no further explanation, and the only summary of the entire story appears in the lead. News stories end with their least important details—rarely with any type of conclusion.

The primary advantage of the inverted pyramid style is that if someone stops reading a story after only one or two paragraphs, that person will still learn the story's most important details. The inverted pyramid style also ensures that all the facts are immediately understandable. Moreover, if a story is too long, editors can easily shorten it by deleting one or more paragraphs from the end.

The inverted pyramid style has several disadvantages. First, because the lead summarizes facts that later paragraphs discuss in greater detail, some of those facts may be repeated in the body. Second, a story that follows the inverted pyramid style rarely contains any surprises; the lead immediately reveals every major detail. Third, the style makes some stories more complex and more difficult to write. Despite these problems, reporters use the inverted pyramid style for most news stories.

If two cars collided, injuring several people, an inverted pyramid story about the accident might contain the following sequence of paragraphs:

Lead	Summarizes the story
Paragraph 2	Identifies the injured
Paragraph 3	Explains how the accident occurred
Paragraph 4	Reports one driver was charged with speeding
Paragraph 5	Quotes one driver, a police officer or witness
Paragraph 6	Describes unusual damage to the cars
Paragraph 7	Describes traffic problems caused by the accident
Paragraph 8	Background: reveals that several other accidents have occurred at the same location

214

Normally, news media emphasize either the role that people play in a story or the story's impact on the lives of those people. As a consequence, paragraph 2 identifies the people who were injured. Damage to the cars—much less important—is reported later. Notice that if the damage was not unusual, the story might not mention it. Paragraph 3 describes the accident itself—the recent action and main point of the story. Quotations, such as the one used in paragraph 5, add detail and color as well as a pleasing change of pace. Paragraphs 6, 7 and 8 are less essential and might be deleted if little space is available for the story.

Not every reporter would present all the facts in exactly the same order; some variation is inevitable. However, most reporters would begin with a summary lead and then would present whichever of the remaining facts they considered most important—usually the victims' identity, particularly if they were seriously injured, and a description of the accident.

As another example of the inverted pyramid style, imagine that the police in your community arrested three high school students and charged them with auto theft. A newspaper reporter might write the following story:

1. Three students have been charged with the theft of a dozen cars from a faculty parking lot at Wilson High School.
2. Police arrested the youths last night after noticing a stolen car parked near a theater on Palmer Avenue.
3. The youths were apprehended when they returned to the car at 11:15 p.m. after watching a movie.
4. Police said the youths, all sophomores at the school, admitted stealing 12 cars from the faculty parking lot during the past year.
5. Each youth was charged with 12 counts of auto theft and was released to the custody of his parents. They are scheduled to appear in Juvenile Court at 11 a.m. Monday.
6. All the other cars were recovered within a week of being stolen. However, one had been involved in an accident and was badly damaged, and some parts had been stripped from the others.
7. Police did not identify the youths because they are juveniles.

Typically, the lead summarizes the story, and each of the following paragraphs presents some additional details about it, beginning with the most important: the youths' arrest and confessions (the action and the most recent developments). Later paragraphs report more routine details and background information. For example, paragraph 6 reports that all the cars stolen weeks or months earlier were recovered, and paragraph 7 reports that the youths' names were not revealed because they are juveniles, a common practice. If little space was available, both paragraphs 6 and 7 could be deleted.

The inverted pyramid style is most appropriate for short, simple stories that have only one source and one main topic. Notice how the leads in the following stories summarize their topics, and how the second and third paragraphs present their most important details. Neither story ends with a summary or conclusion; instead, the final paragraphs present the least important details. The stories are cohesive because their leads summarize their main topics and because each of the subsequent paragraphs presents additional information about those topics:

> Burglars took an estimated $3,000 worth of appliances and jewelry from a home at 1424 Balchner Drive late Sunday morning.
> The owners, Linda and Henry Ruiz, returned home at noon after taking their four children to church. They found a back door pried open and the house ransacked.

"I didn't know what to think," Mrs. Ruiz said. "The house was a mess, and we were afraid the burglars were still inside. It was really quite scary."

The burglars took a television set, a stereo, two cameras, jewelry and several kitchen appliances.

Neighbors said they saw an unfamiliar car parked in the driveway of the home at 11 a.m.

A new survey has found that Americans believe that a happy family life is more important than a good income or satisfactory sex life.

Newsweek magazine conducted the survey and found that 48 percent of its respondents said that a happy family is essential to their lives.

By comparison, 29 percent said that a good income is essential, and 24 percent said a satisfactory sex life is essential.

Twenty-one percent rated a clean and healthy environment a top priority, 17 percent mentioned their friends, and 15 percent mentioned their home.

"We were surprised at the results," one of the pollsters said. "They seem to reflect a change from the self-centeredness of the 1980s. Today's adults seem to realize that not everyone can climb to the top of the career ladder. And once you're there, it's not necessarily as satisfying as people expect."

The respondents were asked six questions and given four options for answering each question: "essential," "very important but not essential," "somewhat important" or "not important at all."

The results are based upon a telephone survey of 1,240 adults in all 50 states.

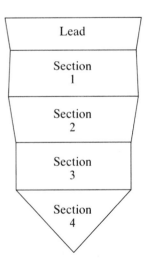

Because many of the facts reported in longer news stories are of approximately equal importance, those stories are more likely to resemble the diagram shown at the left rather than the perfect triangle shown on Page 214. Immediately after the diagram's summary lead, Section 1 presents several paragraphs that contain information of roughly equal importance. Those paragraphs may present some additional information about a single topic or information about several different, but related, subtopics. Section 2 presents other details in descending order of importance, and Section 3 presents more facts of approximately equal importance—but of less importance than the facts in Section 1. Section 4 contains the least important details, perhaps routine procedures, background information or a reminder of some related incidents that occurred in the past.

WRITING THE SECOND PARAGRAPH

The second paragraph in a news story is almost as important as the lead—and as difficult to write. Like the lead, the second paragraph should emphasize the news. In addition, the second paragraph should provide a smooth, logical transition from the lead to the following paragraphs.

While writing their stories' second paragraphs, some reporters fail to emphasize the news. Other reporters fail to provide smooth transitions. As a result, their stories may seem dull or disorganized. The following pages discuss both problems, and their solutions.

Avoid Leapfrogging

Reporters often refer to an individual in their lead and begin their second paragraph with a name. However, many reporters fail to clearly link the two: to state that the individual referred to in their lead is the person named in their second paragraph. Readers are forced to guess, to make that assumption. They will usually be right—but not always.

The problem is so common that it has been given a name: "leapfrogging." To avoid the problem, provide a one- or two-word transition from the lead to a name in the second paragraph:

> LEAPFROGGING: A 55-year-old man wept Wednesday after a Circuit Court jury found him innocent of burglary and sexual battery.
> Gary Lee Phillips was arrested two months ago.
> REVISED: A 55-year-old man wept Wednesday after a Circuit Court jury found him innocent of burglary and sexual battery.
> *The defendant*, Gary Lee Phillips, was arrested two months ago.

> LEAPFROGGING: The Norfolk City Council has denied a former mayor's request for the annexation and re-zoning of 19 acres located along Highway 50.
> E. E. "Sparky" Dawson threatened to sue the city.
> REVISED: The Norfolk City Council has denied a former mayor's request for the annexation and re-zoning of 19 acres located along Highway 50.
> *The former mayor*, E. E. "Sparky" Dawson, threatened to sue the city.

Continue with the News

After providing a smooth transition between the lead and the second paragraph, continue with the news: more information about the topic summarized in your lead. Mistakenly, some reporters shift to a different topic, a decision certain to confuse their readers:

> CORVALLIS, Ore.—The police spend more of their time responding to domestic squabbles than to any other type of call.
> Merritt Tendall has been the police chief in Corvallis for 15 years. He has seen a lot of wrecks and a lot of crimes, but says he never wanted any other job.
> REVISED: CORVALLIS, Ore.—The police spend more of their time responding to domestic squabbles than to any other type of call.
> "We hate those calls," says Police Chief Merritt Tendall. "You never know what to expect. We settle most of the disputes in a few minutes. But people get angry and irrational, and some take their anger out on us. I've been the police chief here for 15 years, and it's my biggest problem."

> "I worry about my sons getting crippled," Sara Capiello told the School Board last night. "They're all football players, and their school can't afford new equipment."
> Because of budget problems, the Board voted 4–3 to lay off 64 teachers and discontinue all of the district's art and music classes.
> REVISED: "I worry about my sons getting crippled," Sara Capiello told the School Board last night. "They're all football players, and their school can't afford new equipment."

Capiello gave the board a petition signed by the parents of 47 players on the football team at Kennedy High School. The petition complains that the team is using helmets and other safety equipment that is old and worn.

Before revision, the first story seems to discuss two different topics. The lead summarizes a problem that confronts police officers everywhere: family disputes. The second paragraph shifts to the police chief's career and goals. It fails even to mention the problem of family disputes. The second story also changes topics. Before revision, the lead summarizes a mother's fears about her sons' safety, and the second paragraph shifts to the board's decision to eliminate 64 jobs.

Names, Names—Dull, Dull

Reporters sometimes place too much emphasis on their sources' identity. As a result, their second paragraphs fail to convey any information of interest to readers. The following examples have been revised to emphasize the news—what the sources said, saw or did, not who they are:

A construction worker was killed Monday afternoon when a gust of wind toppled the frame for a new apartment building on Conway Road.

Julian Prevatte, a carpenter for John McCormack & Sons, was an eyewitness to the accident.

REVISED: A construction worker was killed Monday afternoon when a gust of wind toppled the frame for a new apartment building on Conway Road.

Julian Prevatte, a carpenter at the site, said he tried to warn the victim when the frame began to collapse, but the noise made by a saw drowned out his shouts.

Three gunmen who took $4,200 from a Safeway Supermarket at 1010 S. Broadway Ave. Friday were captured in a nearby motel room 20 minutes later.

Kathy Laxalt, 21, of 1842 S. Gayle Road was one of two cashiers on duty when the men entered the store.

REVISED: Three gunmen who took $4,200 from a Safeway Supermarket at 1010 S. Broadway Ave. Friday were captured in a nearby motel room 20 minutes later.

Kathy Laxalt, a cashier at the supermarket, said the men stood near the entrance for five minutes before they came in, drew their pistols and forced an assistant manager to open the safe.

Background: Too Much, Too Soon

Avoid devoting your entire second paragraph to background information. That information is rarely interesting. The second paragraphs in the following stories are dull because they emphasize that type of old, routine or insignificant detail:

On a typical day, Meals on Wheels delivers 720 meals to the city's shut-ins.

Lucinda Nankin, community relations director for Meals on Wheels, said, "Providing services and identifying resources to enable the homebound and elderly to remain independent has been the role of Meals on Wheels for 20 years."

"Rape is the most difficult crime to solve because of the insensitive treatment given to victims," District Attorney Russell Grant said during a seminar held last night at the YMCA.

The seminar, the fourth presented in the county during the last year, was sponsored by the Rape Prevention Center, 1015 Fifth Ave., which offers counseling to rape victims and encourages them to prosecute their assailants.

The first example shifts from the news—the number of meals that Meals on Wheels delivers to your city's shut-ins—to the organization's purpose. Yet that purpose has not changed since Meals on Wheels was established 20 years ago. Thus, the second paragraph says nothing new, nothing likely to retain readers' interest in the story.

The second example fails to emphasize the district attorney's comments about rape. Instead, its second paragraph presents background information about the sponsor's identity and goals. Yet the same background information might have been reported in stories about the group's first, second and third seminars, held months earlier. Again, the background information should have been placed after an account of the news: a thorough summary of the district attorney's remarks.

Fortunately, the problem is easy to correct, as in these examples:

Six hundred children in the state needed foster homes last month, but only 220 new homes were licensed to care for them.

Karen Hudgins of 2406 Eastbrook Road coordinates the program. She studied sociology in Tennessee and, after earning her master's degree there, moved here in 1984. She is married and has three children.

REVISED: Six hundred children in the state needed foster homes last month, but only 220 new homes were licensed to care for them.

Why? "With more women working, fewer are home and able to care for children, especially problem children," an expert explained. "Also, it's a lot of work with no pay. The only reward is sharing a part of a child's life and knowing it's important—something that has to be done."

Two men robbed a restaurant on Kirkman Road early Sunday after holding a knife to one employee's throat and forcing another employee at gunpoint to let them into the restaurant's office.

The amount of money stolen from the McDonald's Restaurant at 5400 S. Kirkman Road is unknown.

REVISED: Two men robbed a restaurant on Kirkman Road early Sunday after holding a knife to one employee's throat and forcing another employee at gunpoint to let them into the restaurant's office.

The two men, who seemed to have been drinking, then tore out the telephones and locked seven employees and four customers in a restaurant freezer.

Before revision, the first story shifts from a topic in the news (the shortage of foster homes) to background information about the person who administers the program. That information should be moved to a later paragraph, preferably the story's final paragraph. The second example moves from an exciting description of a robbery to a routine, minor detail. When robbers seize all the money in a cash register, it often takes several hours for the victim to determine exactly how much is missing.

The second paragraphs in the following stories are much stronger. They continue with the news: the main points summarized in the leads (the stories' action and other important details). The stories' second paragraphs contain no minor details, unnecessary names or background information:

The School Board has unanimously approved an exchange program with three cities in China.

The program will enable 32 high school students to spend next summer studying in China.

Laura Goldfarb wiped the tears from her eyes Wednesday as she told a judge and jury how she was tied up and robbed in her home two years ago.

Mrs. Goldfarb said she was drinking a cup of tea after lunch when she heard a knock at the back door. As she unlatched the door, a man pushed it open, pointed a gun at her chest and ordered her to remain silent.

One high school student was killed and three others seriously injured in an accident that blocked traffic on Kirkman Road for three hours last night.

The students were returning from a basketball game when their Honda was hit from behind, overturned and burst into flames.

Tips from a Pro

DON'T "WRITE YOUR NOTEBOOK"

By **Lucille S. deView**
Writing Coach
The Orange County Register

The first draft of a story began:

"One-thousand students gathered Thursday outside Cocoa (Fla.) High School to pay tribute to 1st Lt. Clyde Wayne Plymel, a 1976 graduate killed Oct. 23 in the bloody bombing of the Marine headquarters in Beirut."

Nothing wrong, but what impressed the reporter was the solemnity of the students, a scene he failed to share with readers. After some urging, he wrote:

"It was a silence like no other. The 1,000 high school students were hushed, not one of them stirring as they stood for a quarter of an hour at the foot of a hill waiting for the memorial service to begin, and another quarter-hour listening to the eulogies.

"More looked down than up at the blue sky and the sun, so at variance with the sadness and somberness of the occasion.

"They had come to pay tribute to one of their own—a fallen soldier who had once studied, laughed and dreamed in the same classrooms where they now study and laugh and dream.

"They gathered Thursday outside Cocoa High School to pay tribute to 1st Lt. Clyde Wayne Plymel, a 1976 graduate killed . . ."

The writer opted for storytelling instead of formula journalism.

Here's a method to help you break from tradition and go to the heart of a story:

1. **Examine your work habits:** Do you take accurate but spare notes? Listen, think, pause, analyze, memorize?

    Wean yourself from taking notes on the computer. Fingers fly, then the temptation is to rearrange your notes instead of writing a story that sparkles and flows like a stream in springtime.

If you use the computer for telephone interviews, don't take down every little word. Print out your notes to avoid switching screens from notes to story-in-progress, a process that makes the writing as jerky as a car chugging to life on a cold morning.

2. **Rely on memory, observation:** Use your senses; gather details—colors, mannerisms, weather, moods, sounds.

3. **Begin writing during the interview/event:** When you write down a good quote or fact, circle it or fold back the page so you can find it quickly. Shape your story even as you gather data.

4. **Write the lead or outline before leaving the scene:** Save the first part of your notebook for this purpose. Write while impressions are fresh.

5. **Rehearse en route to the newspaper:** Talk the story through as you drive. This is your most valuable time-saver.

6. **Maintain concentration:** Hit the computer fast. Avoid conversation, phone calls, distractions.

7. **Close your notebook:** Write your first draft without it. Race through. Use xxx's for names, dates. Make notes—"Smith's quote here," "stats here." Don't wait for that clever phrase, perfect lead, graceful transition; they'll come in the rewrite.

8. **Stay focused on storytelling:** Good cooks aren't afraid to mess up the kitchen. Your first draft is messy but you clean it up from your notes on the second draft.

9. **Enjoy rewriting:** If you spend three-fourths of your time on a first draft and one-fourth on rewrites, reverse your timetable. Use the bulk of your time to craft your story after your first draft. Print out the first draft, the better to see it whole.

10. **Read aloud:** Mumble, pace, rock in your chair as you write. Read aloud. Listen to your words and the cadence of your sentences. Does your story have the breathless quality of a first telling? If it's stilted, you may have tinkered too much. Know when to stop.

11. **Have you met your deadline?** This storytelling method should increase your speed and help you write simple, conversational sentences with a rich vocabulary and vigorous verbs. Best of all, it should lead you to a writing style uniquely your own.

IMPROVING YOUR LATER PARAGRAPHS

Each paragraph, regardless of its placement in a story, should present only one idea or unit of thought. When reporters shift to a new topic or a new phase of the same topic, they should start a new paragraph. Because the quotation in the following example introduces a new idea—a fact unrelated to the topic of American norms—it should be placed in a new paragraph. At the same time, the topic of American norms might be expanded to explain or illustrate it more clearly:

Living with his cousin has helped Faisal adjust to American norms. He added, "We often cook Middle Eastern dishes and invite our American friends over to our apartment."

REVISED: Faisal said living with his cousin has helped him adjust to American norms. He explained: "Life is so much freer here than in the Middle East. My cousin explains your ways to me and shows me what to do."

They often cook Middle Eastern dishes and invite American friends to their apartment.

Avoid generalities that have to be explained in a later paragraph. If you focus on a story's specific details, the generalities often become unnecessary. The following paragraphs illustrate that principle. Until they were revised, they emphasized general topics rather than any specific information that sources provided about those topics:

> She described the life she observed in New Zealand.
> REVISED: She said life in New Zealand is relaxed and carefree.

> He also talked about the economic hardships faced by unwed mothers.
> REVISED: He said 80 percent of unwed mothers under the age of 18 drop out of high school, and 84 percent become dependent on welfare.

If you are specific—if you report that someone said life in New Zealand "is relaxed and carefree"—you do not have to add that someone described the life in New Zealand. Similarly, if you report the specific problems of unwed mothers, you do not have to add that your source described the hardships they face. The following examples contain similar problems. Until they were revised, they presented only dull generalities:

> Two high school students managed to get a description of the gunmen's car.
> REVISED: Two high school students said the gunmen escaped in a white Chevrolet driven by an elderly woman.

> A neighbor witnessed the explosion.
> REVISED: A neighbor said she was walking to a park with her two children, heard "a terrible explosion" and saw the garage burst into flames.

Also avoid reporting the details within each paragraph in chronological order, especially if you are not reporting the overall story in chronological order. Instead, emphasize the news. Too many times, a paragraph reports that a topic was discussed, then slowly proceeds to the results. Consequently, the most important details are buried in the final line.

If you begin at the beginning of each new topic, then proceed to the news (the results), many of your readers are likely to lose interest in the topic and turn to another story.

Here are one-paragraph examples of the problem:

> The second witness called by the prosecutor was Norman Chrzan, a private investigator. Chrzan testified that Mrs. Ehren hired him to follow her husband. "She thought her husband was seeing another woman," Chrzan said. "She wanted me to find out who she was." Chrzan said he never found another woman. But just two weeks before her husband's murder, Mrs. Ehren asked Chrzan for a gun.
> REVISED: A private investigator, Norman Chrzan, testified that Mrs. Ehren asked him for a gun just two weeks before her husband's murder.
> Chrzan said Mrs. Ehren hired him to follow her husband. "She thought her husband was seeing another woman," he testified. "She wanted me to find out who she was." But Chrzan never found another woman.

> Next on its agenda, the City Council opened bids to determine who would receive a contract to construct the recreation center. The lowest bid was $1.5 million. The budget for the center was only $1,240,000. "It was very disappointing," the mayor said. "Now we'll have to go back over the plans with our architects and eliminate some of the options to lower its cost. It'll delay construction six to nine months."
> REVISED: The construction of a recreation center will be delayed six to nine months because the bids were $260,000 over the amount budgeted for the work.

The city had allocated $1,240,000 for the work, but the lowest bid was $1.5 million. The mayor said that city officials will "have to go back over the plans with our architects and eliminate some of the options to lower its cost."

Here is a longer passage, also reported in chronological order:

Defense attorneys then called psychologist Tony Salcido, who said he examined Preston last summer. Salcido said Preston told him of his long history of drug abuse, beginning at the age of 10.

"He described a typical day to me as waking up, smoking marijuana, drinking wine, then taking an injection of PCP," Salcido testified Friday. "This is the same pattern he followed the day Carmen Tran was killed."

Salcido concluded that Preston's judgment was impaired at the time he committed the murder.

REVISED: Another witness, psychologist Tony Salcido, testified Friday that Preston's judgment was impaired by alcohol and drugs at the time he committed the murder.

Salcido said he examined Preston last summer, and that Preston told him of his long history of drug abuse, beginning at the age of 10.

"He described a typical day to me as waking up, smoking marijuana, drinking wine, and then taking an injection of PCP," Salcido said. "This is the same pattern he followed the day Carmen Tran was killed."

IMPROVING YOUR SENTENCES: A BRIEF REVIEW

Write naturally, the way you talk. Be clear and direct. No one would use the following sentences in a casual conversation with friends, yet beginners used them in news stories:

Killed in the accident was a 7-year-old girl.
The vehicle damage is estimated to be $4,000.
Angry words were exchanged between the two drivers.

The sentences are awkward because they fail to use the normal word order: subject, verb and direct object. Moreover, all three use passive verbs: "was," "is" and "were." Here are two more examples and their revisions:

The team's victory was witnessed by only 17 spectators.
REVISED: Only 17 spectators witnessed the team's victory.

Editors are looking for qualities in a reporter that include creativity and aggressiveness.
REVISED: Editors want reporters who are creative and aggressive.

Shorten Your Sentences

Beginners use sentences that are too long and complicated. Yet the longer a sentence, the more difficult it is to understand. Moreover, when too many ideas are crammed into a sentence, none receives the clarity and emphasis it deserves.

As you read the following sentences, you are likely to stop and to start again, because both sentences contain more ideas than most readers can absorb at a glance. As you reread each sentence, count the number of ideas it contains:

UNICEF officials, who have found that 40,000 children die each day, mostly in developing countries, call the death toll "the greatest single stain on our civilization today," and are asking for an unprecedented world summit to save the lives of an estimated 100 million children in the next decade by, during each of the next 10 years, taking the money spent in a single day on the world's military forces and reallocating that money to feed the hungry.

Number of ideas in sentence:_____

Judge Marilyn Picott today threw out a manslaughter charge halfway through the trial of a teen-age girl accused of killing her stepfather, Fritz Walker, as he beat her mother, ruling that the girl had every right to shoot him after coming home from high school and seeing her parents in a bloody knife fight and her younger brothers and sisters screaming in terror.

Number of ideas in sentence:_____

Readers may count as many as 12 ideas in the first sentence, and 10 in the second. To make your sentences more readable, shorten them:

A mother of three children—two daughters ages 27 and 22, and a son age 16—and the grandmother of three, Mrs. Johns explained that she opposes abortion because, since abortions have become legal, Americans next "might try to do away with the aged."

REVISED: Mrs. Johns said she opposes abortion because, since abortions have become legal, Americans next "might try to do away with the aged." Mrs. Johns has two daughters, 27 and 22, and a son, 16. She also has three grandchildren.

A sentence does not have to be long to be overloaded. If the ideas it contains are unrelated, as in the following examples, even a very short sentence may have to be divided.

Born in New Hampshire, he has red hair.

Petrowski, who has a wife and six stepdaughters, was elected mayor by only 27 votes: 382,917 to 382,890.

Avoid Choppy Sentences

A few writers go to the opposite extreme, using a series of very short, simple sentences. Although a typical sentence or paragraph should be short and simple, some variety is necessary to keep paragraphs from becoming too choppy and repetitive, as in the following example:

The youth was sentenced to prison at 9:45 a.m. today. The judge was C. R. Revere. The youth's attorney immediately appealed his conviction. The state Court of Appeals reversed the sentence. The youth was freed at 4:45 p.m.

REVISED: Judge C. R. Revere sentenced the youth to prison at 9:45 a.m. today, but his attorney immediately appealed the conviction. The state Court

of Appeals reversed Judge Revere's decision, and the youth was freed at
4:45 p.m.

Vary your sentence length. Remember, however, that even the longer sentences
should be uncomplicated, and it is better to make them too short than too long.

Also vary your wording so that sentences and paragraphs do not begin with the same
words, or with very similar words. When writing a story about a government report,
for example, it may be tempting to begin several paragraphs with the words: "The
report said. . ." "The report added. . ." "It said. . ." "The report also said. . ." "It
continued. . ." and "The report concluded. . ." But if every sentence or paragraph
begins with the same words, your story will be dull and repetitious.

TRANSITIONS

Transitions help stories move from one fact to the next in a smooth, logical order.
Reporters introduce new ideas by relating them to ideas reported earlier in a story.
Often, the natural progression of thought, or sequence of facts and action, is adequate.
Or reporters may repeat a key name or pronoun:

> The company's president, Mark *Stoudnaurer*, opposed the plan.
> *Stoudnaurer* said the company cannot afford to construct a new plant.

> *Lt. Lee Marey* said the Navy is a small, elite force that offers an effective
> deterrent to nuclear war.
> *He* added that submarines have become more important than battleships
> and aircraft carriers.

The first example repeats the name of the company president. In the second example,
the pronoun "he" refers to the lieutenant mentioned in the preceding paragraph.
Reporters can also repeat other key words, ideas or phrases:

> The company borrowed $52 million to pay for the *machinery*.
> The *machinery* arrived in July and was operating by November.

> Richard *Nolles*, editor of the Weekly Outlook, said the *newspaper* tries to
> report the truth even when its *readers* do not want to hear it.
> "A *newspaper* that reports only what its *readers* want to hear is dodging
> its moral obligations," *Nolles* said.
> In a speech Wednesday, *Nolles* added that many *readers* want to avoid un-
> pleasant news and threaten to cancel their subscriptions when *he* reports it.
> "But if a problem exists, *they* need to know about it so *they* can correct
> it," *he* said. "Ignorant citizens can't make wise decisions."

Here is another example. Again, notice the repetition of several key words. Moreover,
every sentence continues to discuss the topic summarized in the lead—downtown
trees:

> *Sycamore trees* are sprouting along *Main Street* in the first phase of an effort
> to make the downtown shopping district more attractive and comfortable for
> pedestrians.
> The *trees* will line *Main Street* for five blocks between Jefferson and Jackson
> Avenues, according to Daisy *Lemkuehl* of the Downtown Development Board.

"We chose *sycamore trees* because they're deciduous," *Lemkuehl* said. "In the summer they'll provide shade. In the winter they'll lose their leaves and let the sun warm the streets."

Lemkuehl said the City Council provided the money, and all the *trees* will be planted within a week.

In addition to the trees, *Lemkuehl* said the sidewalks in the five-block stretch of *Main Street* will be widened and paved with red *brick*.

"We expect to start with the *brick* sidewalks in a month or so," *Lemkuehl* said.

Transitional Words

You can sometimes use a single word to lead your readers from one idea to the next. Many of your transitional words are likely to refer to the time: words such as "earlier" and "later," "before" and "after," "promptly" and "tardy." Other transitional words that refer to the time are:

TIME TRANSITIONS

delayed	meanwhile	once
eventually	next	seldom
finally	now	sometimes
formerly	occasionally	soon
frequently	often	then

Or you may provide a transition by using the hour, day of the week, month, season, year, decade or century ("an hour later," "the previous Saturday" and so on).

Other types and examples of linkage words include:

ADDITIONS

again	beyond	new
also	extra	other
another	furthermore	together
besides	moreover	too

CAUSATIONS

accordingly	hence	then
because	since	therefore
consequently	so	thus

COMPARISONS

agreeing	hostile	opposite
conflicting	identical	related
contrary	inconsistent	separately
different	like	similarly
diverse	objecting	unlikely

CONTRASTS

although	however	still
but	if	until
conversely	nevertheless	yet
despite	simply	while
exactly	solely	without

There are also dozens of phrases that you can use to move from one idea to another. Examples include:

along with	in an earlier accident
as a result of	in another case
aside from	in contrast
at last	in other action
at the same time	in other business
due to	on the contrary
for example	on the other hand
for instance	until then
for that reason	years earlier
in addition	with the exception of

Transitional Sentences

Transitional sentences link paragraphs that contain diverse ideas, but the sentences should do more than report that another idea was "introduced" or "discussed." They should present some interesting details about the new topics so readers will be motivated to finish the story. Mistakenly, beginners often use vague generalities, such as:

> There were other developments as well.
> She also mentioned a drainage problem.
> Two people spoke in opposition to the resolution.

A good transitional sentence often summarizes the topic it introduces, revealing whatever was said or done about it. The following paragraphs can then discuss the topic in more detail:

> He also discussed the television coverage of the president's funeral.
> REVISED: He said the television coverage of the president's funeral was misleading.

> He also talked about the city's schools.
> REVISED: He said the city's schools are too old and overcrowded.

> Later, he discussed the other advantages of living in the South.
> REVISED: Later, he said that people living in the South enjoy a milder climate, lower taxes and newer, less crowded cities.

Here are three more examples of weak transitions, which fail to say anything likely to retain readers' interest in the topic:

> The board also heard the concerns of a school bus driver.

> She then presented information about the cost of maintaining the museum.

Traffic and growth are not the only problems that O'Hanlon has had to deal with.

Here are three stronger transitional sentences, which are more specific and interesting:

Only the recycling program is losing money.

Teen-agers said the media are too critical of the president.

Three college students, all women, said they have experienced sexual discrimination.

Questions as Transitions

Like leads, transitional sentences occasionally take the form of questions. The questions should be short and, as in the following examples, should be immediately followed by their answers—the new details or topics that reporters want to introduce:

Where does she get the ideas for her books?
"People," she said. "Most people can give you a good story. And I talk to everyone."

Forty-seven percent of the students enrolled in the university will earn a degree within the next six years, according to Dr. Robert McMahon, director of the Office of Institutional Research.
What about the other 53 percent? They will drop out or transfer to another institution.
Why? A study just completed by the Office of Institutional Research found that most students who drop out of school accept full-time jobs, get married, have children or say they lack the money needed to continue their education.

Did the rehabilitation program change their lives?
"Yes, it has," Kathy said. "I started to grow up. I feel so much older than other kids my age."
"Yes," Ellen agreed. "I realize now that I had better start controlling my life better."
"No," Jill said. "I can't say that it has changed my life, although my life has changed. I'm going to be married soon, and I'm very happy."

CONCLUSIONS

Experienced reporters present a story's least important details in the final paragraph and, if they have nothing more to add, stop. Reporters rarely place any important information in the final paragraph because too many readers will stop before they get that far. Reporters also know that, if their editor does not have enough space for an entire story, the editor is most likely to discard the story's final paragraphs. So the information placed at the end of a story is least likely to be published or read.

Avoid Stating Opinions and Mentioning Additional Topics

Reporters must resist the temptation to end news stories with a summary, conclusion or opinion of any kind. The following conclusions are inappropriate:

Is Miss Roth a good teacher? We certainly believe so.

The remainder of the meeting was concerned primarily with the gripes and comments of those present about conditions at the hospital. Also discussed were some suggestions on ways those conditions could be resolved.

The first example contains an opinion rather than a fact. If the story was well written, and if it clearly described Miss Roth, her performance and her students' reaction to her, readers should not have to be told she is a good teacher. The facts reported earlier in the story should have made that obvious. The second example summarizes facts never discussed in the story. It fails to describe specifically the conditions that disturbed people and the suggestions made to resolve those conditions. Every topic mentioned in news stories must be fully explained, including topics mentioned in final paragraphs.

The second problem is a common one. As students approach a story's concluding paragraphs, many simply *mention* the story's final topics without reporting what was said or done about them. Here are two additional examples:

Zoning was the final topic on the council's agenda.

After concluding his speech, Nader answered the audience's questions.

Again, remember your readers. As a newswriter, you have an obligation to inform, not confuse. If a topic is important enough to mention, provide enough detail to inform your readers about it. These examples fail to do so. The first example mentions "zoning," but fails to present any specific details about it or to summarize the council's discussion and action. The second example reports that "Nader answered the audience's questions," but fails to report the specific questions and answers and thus does not present any meaningful information to readers.

Ignore the Routine and Unimportant

Other stories end by reporting what did not happen. A list of everything that did not happen today would be endless; by tomorrow, the list would be dull and repetitious. Thus, as you write a story's final paragraphs, avoid the temptation to report that:

No one was killed.
No charges were filed.
No one else was injured.
The burglar has not been caught.
No one saw the car's license number.
No one was able to describe the thief.
Police searched the area but found nothing.

Similarly, an alert reporter or editor would eliminate the following conclusions because they state the obvious:

Police are looking for the thief.
The victim said she hopes to get well soon.
City officials said they are proud of the program's success.

Don't End Your Story Too Soon

Some stories end too quickly. When you write a news story, be thorough. Assume that your editor has enough space to report every important detail. If you are uncertain about whether a fact is important enough to be included in a story, place that fact in the story's final paragraph. If your editor (or instructor) considers the fact unimportant, it can easily be deleted. If you fail to include an important fact, it is difficult for your editor (or instructor) to find you and for you to retrieve your notes, return to your typewriter or computer and add the missing information.

ALTERNATIVES TO THE INVERTED PYRAMID

Although, as noted at the beginning of this chapter, most news stories follow the inverted pyramid style, several alternatives are available.

Chronological Order

Reporters tell some stories in chronological order, and this natural sequence of events creates a smooth, logical flow of ideas. This passage appeared in a news story that Newsday, a daily on Long Island, published about the Challenger space shuttle disaster.

> . . . But then at 11:38 a.m., the gleaming ship rose from a new launch pad, a majestic 700-foot stream of snow-white vapor trailing behind. Onlookers cheered, as is the custom at space shots, and a NASA spokesman described the progress of the flight.
>
> Challenger reached a speed of 1,977 mph—three times that of sound—and was 10.4 miles over the Florida terrain. Mission Control in Houston sent the routine order: "Challenger, go throttle up."
>
> Commander Francis (Dick) Scobee increased power to the main engines as planned and then spoke what proved to be his final words: "Roger, go throttle up."
>
> At that point, officials said, Challenger, one of four U.S. space shuttles, was to enter a period when maximum force would be brought to bear on the vehicle by atmospheric condition and wind force.
>
> Television viewers then were able to see flames racing toward the space vehicle from an aft section, in the area of the craft's solid-fuel booster rockets. Almost immediately there was a titanic explosion, and Challenger, which had been carrying 526,000 gallons of highly volatile propellant, began rapid disintegration.
>
> A space center employee watching the flight said in horror: "It's too soon. It's too soon. It can't be separation (of the boosters)." Another said simply: "I can't believe it. . . ."

Here is a second example, from a story about a man charged with manslaughter. The man's van struck a teen-ager lying injured on a road. While covering the man's trial, a reporter for The Orlando Sentinel reported that day's events in chronological order.

> Goss . . . testified that on the day of the accident he and a co-worker left work at 3 p.m. to repair a leaky roof on Goss' father's house in the Ocala National Forest.
>
> On the way, Goss said, they stopped at a store and bought hot dogs and a six-pack of beer. He said that by 5 p.m. they had consumed three beers apiece.

About 5:45 p.m., after the roof was repaired, Goss said they started back home, and on the way bought another six-pack. He said he was drinking a beer as he drove his Ford van along S.R. 44 toward Eustis.

It was almost dark by that time, he said.

Goss said he saw a car signal and then pull off the road 500 to 600 feet ahead. He said that as he approached that car, the lights of an oncoming car temporarily blinded him.

"When my eyes readjusted, there was an object in the road," Goss said. The object was only a few feet away, he said, and veering off the road would have meant colliding with cars on either side.

"I hit my brakes and slid," he said. Goss testified that he never realized the object was a person. . . .

Especially when writing a brief, dramatic story, you can begin with a summary lead, provide a short transition, then report all the remaining details in chronological order. The transition can be brief: only four or five words, as in these examples:

Witnesses gave this account:
A passenger described the accident:

Here is a complete story that uses this technique. All the students in a reporting class interviewed a young woman who witnessed a shooting, and one of the students wrote the following account. Notice that she summarizes the story in the lead, provides a brief transition, then tells the remainder of the story in chronological order:

A sheriff's deputy shot and killed a young man outside a Pizza Hut on Thomasville Avenue Monday afternoon.

The shooting occurred in front of dozens of witnesses in the restaurant. One of the witnesses, 28-year-old Lillian Dysart, described the events this way:

"I was having dinner with my boyfriend in the Pizza Hut when I noticed two men and a woman talking with two sheriff's deputies in the parking lot. The men were being loud and boisterous, and the deputies were trying to get them to leave. My boyfriend, Mike, recognized one of the deputies and went out to see if he could help.

"Suddenly, one of the men pulled a knife and cut a deputy in the face. I went to help and, when I got outside, I could see the other deputy had drawn his gun and was pointing it at the man, saying, 'Stay back and drop the knife.' The man lunged at the deputy, who then shot him in the chest."

The assailant was pronounced dead at Memorial Regional Medical Center. The Sheriff's Department did not immediately identify him.

The injured deputy, Laurie Anne Slater, was released from the hospital Tuesday morning.

As another alternative, you can write a summary lead, then simply report the remaining details in chronological order. The following example does not use the same type of transition from the lead to the body:

A gunman robbed a McDonald's restaurant at 2604 Forest Road Thursday night of $430 and 10 fish sandwiches.

An employee said a man in a blue van appeared at a drive-through window and ordered the sandwiches, then paid for them with a $20 bill.

When the employee opened a cash register to get some change, the gunman pointed a pistol at her and said: "I want all the money, and fast. Put it all in a bag, and don't forget my sandwiches. I want them, too."

The employee put the money in a white paper bag and handed it to the gunman.

The gunman then demanded the money in a second cash register at the drive-through window. When the employee showed him that it was empty, the gunman drove away.

Witnesses said he was about 20 years old, 6 feet tall and weighed about 220 pounds. His van had a Nebraska license plate and a bumper sticker that said, "I read banned books."

The following stories are more unusual. Neither has a summary lead. Instead, both begin with the initial event and proceed in chronological order:

MIDDLEBURG, Fla. (AP)—Samuel Warren Jr. was sitting in his kitchen about to eat breakfast when he heard a loud roar and then saw a Navy attack jet bearing down on the house.

"We looked out the window and saw the plane coming toward us," the 17-year-old recalled. "My dad tried to get my aunt to the ground. The blast (from the jet) knocked everyone down."

When it was all over Sunday, the charred wreckage of a single-engine A-7E Corsair 11 attack jet lay 30 feet from Warren's front door.

The pilot, Lt. j. g. Scott S. Scheurich, 25, of Excelsior, Minn., parachuted from the plane after it developed engine trouble six miles from its destination, Naval Air Station Cecil Field in Jacksonville, said Navy spokesman Nick Young.

The pilot's parachute was snared in a pine tree 300 yards from the crash site, and neighbors helped the pilot down, Young said. Scheurich was taken to Navy Regional Medical Center in Jacksonville for observation.

LAKE WORTH, Fla. (UPI)—Police patrolman Richard Marks was dispatched to a physician's clinic to make out a routine report on the death of a heart-attack victim.

"About 30 minutes after I got to the clinic, I went into the examination room with the guys from the funeral home," Marks said.

"As I walked in, the guy on the table started gasping, then quit, then gasped again."

Funeral home attendant Pat Leach, who had been sent to pick up the corpse, rushed forward at Marks' yell. The husky Leach had worked for three years as an aide in a hospital emergency ward. He shouted to a co-worker to call an ambulance.

Leach then began administering mouth-to-mouth resuscitation and massaging the elderly man's heart. A flicker of life returned to Ramon E. Lawrence, 68, and he was rushed to the intensive care ward of a nearby hospital.

Complex Stories

Stories that contain several major subtopics may be too complex to summarize in a brief lead. Each week it is in session, for example, the U.S. Supreme Court announces all its decisions on a single day, and several of those decisions may be very important. To save space, most newspapers report all the decisions in a single story. However, reporters can mention only one or two of the most important decisions in their leads, so they often summarize the remaining decisions in the second, and sometimes the third, paragraphs of their stories:

> WASHINGTON—The Supreme Court today upheld a controversial federal law that requires banks to report to the government large cash transactions made by their customers.
>
> In other decisions, the Supreme Court said an Iowa newspaper reporter can be forced to disclose the notes she used while writing about a divorce, and it removed the last barrier to oil and natural gas exploration in the Atlantic Ocean off the East Coast.
>
> The court refused to question the authority of states to ban homosexual acts between consenting adults.

After summarizing all the major decisions, reporters can then discuss each of them in more detail, starting with the most important. By mentioning all the decisions in the story's opening paragraphs, reporters alert readers to the entire content so that readers interested in the second or third decision immediately learn that it will be discussed later in the story. If, in contrast, the lead and following paragraphs mentioned only the most important decision, readers might mistakenly assume that the entire story concerned that one decision, and many might stop reading before reaching the discussion of other decisions that might be of greater interest to them.

The following Associated Press story begins by summarizing the Supreme Court's most important decision and then, in subsequent paragraphs, summarizes other decisions announced the same day.

High Court Keeps Ban on Teacher-Supervised Prayer at School

> WASHINGTON (AP)—The Supreme Court shunted aside arguments by 24 U.S. senators on Monday and refused to let teacher-supervised student groups pray in public schools at Lubbock, Texas.
>
> The justices, without comment, let stand a ruling that a prayer-accommodation policy devised for Lubbock schools crosses the constitutionally required separation of church and state.
>
> At issue was whether Lubbock school officials could allow students to "gather at school with supervision either before or after regular school hours on the same basis as other groups . . . for any . . . religious . . . purposes so long as attendance at such meetings is voluntary."
>
> A federal appeals court said no earlier this year, and the Supreme Court refused to disturb that ruling, despite the senators' urgings. They had submitted an extraordinary "friend-of-the-court" brief to the justices.
>
> In other matters, the court:
>
> • Refused by 7 to 2 to consider letting students at two Orthodox Jewish high schools in Chicago wear yarmulkes while playing basketball against other schools. The Illinois High School Association bars all headgear by basketball players, and the two Jewish schools say that rule violates their students' religious freedoms.
>
> • Agreed to decide in a Minnesota case whether its Miranda rule protecting criminal suspects when questioned by police also applies when probation officers do the asking.
>
> • Refused by 7 to 2 to speed up the review of a ruling against the government's continued collection of billions of dollars under the . . . windfall profits tax on oil. . . .

• Agreed to hear the appeal of a Nebraska man who wants custody of his illegitimate child and is trying to prevent its mother from putting the baby up for adoption in Texas.

• Refused to free South Carolina officials from paying nearly $5 million to women illegally denied unemployment benefits because of pregnancy.

Reporters often use lists in news stories that involve a number of diverse ideas, subtopics or examples. If all the ideas or examples are of roughly equal importance, reporters may begin a news story by summarizing one or two main points, adding a brief transition, and then presenting the other ideas or examples in a simple, orderly list:

NEW YORK—"We seem to have turned the corner in the epidemic of heart disease," Dr. Robert T. Levy, director of the National Heart, Lung and Blood Institute, said at a recent American Heart Association meeting. He cited some impressive statistics:

• Since 1968, the death rate from heart and blood vessel disease has been declining in both men and women, blacks and whites.

• The 30 percent decline in the cardiovascular death rate since the early 1960s is nearly double the drop in deaths from other causes.

• Two years ago, despite an increasingly older and larger population, the total number of deaths from cardiovascular diseases dropped below 1 million for the first time since 1967.

(New York Times Dispatch)

Three women have been attacked in the college's parking lots, and Police Chief Alvin Schwab today warned other students that the attacks may continue.

To protect themselves, Schwab recommended that women:

• Avoid dark areas.
• Park in areas that will be lighted when they return.
• Tell friends where they are going and when they will return.
• Keep their car doors locked and windows rolled up when driving alone.
• Check their car's floor and back seat for intruders before getting into the vehicle.
• Report any suspicious activities they see to the campus police.

Later in a story, reporters can discuss each of the points in greater detail. Of course, the initial summary may contain all the essential information about a topic; in that case, it may never again be mentioned.

Each item in a list must be in parallel form. If one item begins with a noun and uses an active verb and a complete sentence, then every item in that list must do the same. For example, each item in the story at left below is an incomplete sentence that begins with a verb. Each item in the story at right is a complete sentence that begins with "You" or "Your":

The governor said he wants to raise the state's sales tax and to increase state spending on education.

He told the National Education Association he would use the money to:

• Raise teachers' salaries.
• Test new teachers to assess their competence

Financial advisers say there are certain warning signals that you are about to experience a financial crisis and possibly bankruptcy:

• Your checkbook balance gets lower each month.
• You are behind on one or more installment payments.

ISBN 0-15-500602-9

- Place more emphasis on English, science and math.
- Reduce the number of students in each class.
- Give schools more money to education gifted students.

- You don't know how much money you owe.
- You must obtain new loans to pay your debts.
- Your savings account is slowly disappearing or has already disappeared.

Reporters also use lists to summarize less important details placed at the end of news stories. Lists are particularly useful when the details are minor and concern a number of diverse topics that would be difficult to organize in any other manner. During the question-and-answer session after a speech, a celebrity may be asked to discuss a dozen unrelated topics:

Donald M. Schoen, Republican candidate for governor, last night promised to cut the state's budget and taxes by a "minimum of 10 percent."

Schoen, mayor of Madison for the past eight years, also promised to dismiss 10 percent of the state's employees.

"People complain that the government has become too big and that it imposes too many taxes and places too many restrictions on their lives," he said at a fund-raising dinner held last night at Pine Hills Country Club.

On other subjects, Schoen said:

EDUCATION—School budgets should be frozen until educators trim administrative costs and improve students' test scores.

CRIME—Only 19 percent of the serious crimes committed in the state are solved, and fewer than 2 percent of the criminals responsible for those crimes are convicted and sentenced to prison. Penalties should be harsher, and criminals should be kept in jail until they have served their full terms, without parole.

MEDIA COVERAGE—News media devote too much attention to staged campaign activities and "have failed to critically analyze candidates' qualifications and positions on major issues."

Similarly, after voting on one or two major proposals, a city council may act on several less important matters that may be summarized in a list:

After a 5½-hour debate, the City Council last night voted 8 to 1 to fire Police Chief Walter M. Durrance and two of his aides.

All three men have been accused of misusing Police Department funds.

The aides are Capt. Anthony Escalon, who started as a patrolman 24 years ago, and Lt. Raymond Krellar, a 17-year veteran with the department.

Criminal charges have been filed against all three men, but their trials have not yet been scheduled.

The council appointed Capt. James R. Bolack acting police chief.

In other action last night, the council:

—Approved the establishment of a branch library in a rented building at 5801 Shoals Drive.

—Approved the hiring of seven additional firefighters, including one lieutenant, and the purchase of two rescue vehicles that will cost $38,400 apiece.

—Refused to reconsider a motion, defeated last week, to remove the parking meters along Jamestown Drive.

—Delayed until next week consideration of a proposal to require all elected officials to file copies of their income tax returns with the city clerk in an attempt to reveal possible conflicts of interest.

Some newspapers number each item in a list. Others mark each item with a dash, bullet, asterisk, check mark or some other typographical symbol.

THE NEED TO BE FAIR

Regardless of how you organize a story, it must be balanced and fair as well as accurate. Reporters who write about a controversial issue have an obligation to present every significant viewpoint fully and fairly, and they must exercise particular care when their stories might harm another person's reputation. A reckless or irresponsible charge may destroy an innocent person's reputation, marriage or career.

If a story contains information critical of an individual, that person should be given an opportunity to respond. It is not enough to call the victim after a story has been published and to report the person's response in a later story. Because not everyone who read the original criticism will see the second story, the victim's rebuttal should always be included in the original story. Typically, The New York Times has adopted a policy which requires that: ". . . a person mentioned derogatorily or critically in a story should immediately be given a chance to respond. If the person is unreachable, consideration should be given to holding the story over. If holding it over is deemed inadvisable, mention should be made in the story that efforts to reach the person were unavailing, and the efforts should be renewed the next day. . . . This is a cardinal, unbreakable rule."

For example, a story might report:

> The Better Business Bureau today warned consumers about "free inspections" offered to homeowners by Doss Furnace Repair Inc.
>
> An employee at the bureau said it has received more than 200 complaints from homeowners during the past month. Some homeowners said they received bills for more than $300 after the company's representatives offered to inspect their furnaces for free.
>
> A vice president at the company said some customers apparently failed to read and understand its contracts. He said customers are always told that the inspections are free, but that they will be charged for necessary repairs, labor and replacement parts.

If the subject of a negative story is unavailable or refuses to respond, that fact should also be mentioned. A brief sentence might explain:

> Attempts to reach a company employee were unsuccessful.
> OR: A vice president at the company declined to comment about the charges.
> OR: Company officials did not return eight phone calls made by reporters.

THE FINAL STEP: EDIT YOUR STORY

After finishing a story, edit it ruthlessly. Author Kurt Vonnegut recommends that, "If a sentence, no matter how excellent, does not illuminate your subject in some new and useful way, scratch it out." Vonnegut also urges writers to have mercy on their readers. Vonnegut explains: "Our audience requires us to be sympathetic and patient teachers, ever willing to simplify and clarify—whereas we would rather soar high above the crowd, singing like nightingales."

Thus, good reporters—if not writing on deadline—will reread and edit their stories. Mistakenly (and lazily), less competent reporters immediately submit their stories to an editor. Those reporters may think their stories are so good that they will not need any editing. Or, those reporters may expect the editor to correct all their errors. That attitude involves some risks, however. If the editor fails to notice several errors, the reporters will be embarrassed when the errors appear in print. Moreover, the reporters—not the editor—will be held responsible for the errors.

Or, an editor may decide that the stories require extensive changes, perhaps even total rewriting. When that happens, reporters often complain about the changes made in their stories.

If reporters correct their own errors, editors will not have to make extensive changes in their stories. Moreover, the reporters will develop reputations as good writers and be rewarded for their efforts: given better assignments, raises and promotions.

Tips From a Pro

ALTERNATIVE STYLES

The following stories were written by professional reporters for The Associated Press and The Milwaukee Journal. Both stories are effective, yet neither uses newspapers' traditional inverted pyramid style.

The first story is presented informally, and as a series of unfortunate coincidences. The second story is reported in chronological order. It appeared in a special section published by The Milwaukee Journal. "Each year," The Journal explained, "hundreds of thousands of people die of heart disease. Many of those deaths could be prevented by timely treatment using medical techniques not available until recent years."

HOMESTEAD, Fla.—Hey, Luther Germantown said to his family, why don't we all take a nice drive to Disney World for Christmas? Great idea, everybody said. We'll have a fine time.

It didn't exactly work out that way.

Germantown and eight family members started out Friday in two cars hauling two campers for a Christmas weekend at Disney World. Then:

• The bolts holding the transmission onto his car fell out.

• He lost some of the replacement bolts.

• The drive gear went, and the car was towed to a Fort Pierce transmission shop.

• The transmission shop, Germantown learned the next day, was closed for the weekend. While trying to recover the keys he had slipped under the door, he set off a burglar alarm.

• After explaining the situation to suspicious police officers, he had the car towed to another transmission shop. But after workers told him it couldn't be fixed for days, he took the limping car back on the highway.

• It caught fire.

(continued on next page)

• The car was towed again (this is the third time, if you're counting) to another shop, and this time it was fixed, sort of.

• Back on the highway, the muffler fell apart, and the radiator hose, weakened by the small fire, ruptured.

• Giving up, Germantown and family returned home. The car was towed there (fourth time).

• They found that the house had been burglarized of more than $400 worth of tools.

***

Joseph Krushas awoke at 4 a.m. The day that almost became the last day of his life.

"I just didn't feel right," the 55-year-old assistant principal at Forest Home Avenue elementary school recalled of that morning, Sunday, Feb. 1.

"I just felt uncomfortable. There was no burning in my chest or shortness of breath or sweating. I lay down but I couldn't get comfortable. I woke up my wife and told her to take me to the hospital."

She drove him to Community Memorial Hospital of Menomonee Falls, where initial tests did not disclose any problems. He was admitted to the intensive care unit as a precaution.

About 8 a.m., he began to die. His face suddenly got hot. A severe, crushing chest pain followed. His face turned gray, he began to sweat profusely, and his blood pressure began dropping. His blood pressure dipped to 60; normally it would be twice that high. It was well below the level of shock.

Tests showed he was in the throes of a massive heart attack affecting his heart's left pumping chamber. David E. Engle, a cardiologist who happened to be in the hospital at the time, took over the case. The entire front and side of the chamber showed an acute injury pattern, Engle said.

"I brought his wife into a room and frankly told her he was in the middle of a heart attack, that things were not going well and that he might die," Engle recounted.

At the same time, he ordered that Krushas get intravenous streptokinase, a drug that can dissolve blood clots. The aim was to break up the presumed clot in one of the three coronary arteries feeding his heart.

Exactly 30 minutes later, Engle noticed evidence on the electrocardiogram that Krushas' heart was getting normal blood flow.

"I turned to him and asked him how he felt," Engle said. "He said at that moment the chest pain began to ease. His blood pressure at that point began to rise and came back to normal. We did an EKG a short time later and found it was normal."

Engle had Krushas transferred to St. Joseph's Hospital, which has a complete catheterization laboratory and backup surgery team. Within a few hours after the heart attack began, a thin tube was being threaded into his heart through an artery in his groin.

After injecting dye, Engle confirmed that the streptokinase had dissolved a clot in the left anterior descending coronary artery. That artery is so crucial to the survival of the heart that physicians have macabrely dubbed it the "widow maker" because clots that develop in it often are lethal.

An X-ray examination of the artery showed Engle that at the site of the clot, the artery had been narrowed to only 5 percent of its normal diameter by a buildup of fatty deposits. Without further treatment, Krushas would be at risk of a future heart attack if another clot formed there or if further buildup of plaque completely choked off the flow of blood.

So Engle inserted another tube with a small sausage-shaped balloon at the end, guided it into place at the site of the narrowing and inflated it. The rigid, inflated balloon flattened the deposits against the inner walls of the artery, widening the channel and restoring normal blood flow.

Less than five hours had elapsed since that first crushing pain in the hospital.

On Feb. 8, a week after he first woke up feeling uncomfortable, Krushas went home. Less than three weeks later, he was back at work.

Without the treatment with clot-dissolving drugs and balloon angioplasty, Engle said, "I think he would have died."

Did you notice the second story's sentence structure? Almost every sentence, beginning with the lead, uses the normal word order: subject, verb, direct object.

Reread the fifth paragraph. Do you like its opening sentence: "About 8 a.m., he began to die." What makes that sentence so effective? Notice its simplicity: it contains no unnecessary adverbs or adjectives, only a simple statement of the facts. The sentence also helps demonstrate the principle that understatement is usually more effective than exaggeration.

Count the number of words in the story's average sentence, then compare the sentence length to that of a recent sample of your work.

CHECKLISTS FOR WRITING NEWS STORIES

Use the following checklists to evaluate all your stories. If you answer "no" to any of the questions, your stories may have to be rewritten.

Inverted Pyramid Style

1. Have you summarized the story in your lead, then presented the details in the order of their importance, beginning with the most important?
2. Have you emphasized the most newsworthy details, the ones most likely to interest and affect your readers?
3. Does your story's second paragraph continue to discuss the topic summarized in your lead?
4. Does your story's second paragraph continue to emphasize the news, rather than swerving into minor details, names or background information?

5. Are you guilty of leapfrogging? If your lead mentions an individual, and your second paragraph begins with a name, have you provided a transition that makes it clear you mean the same person?
6. Does each of your paragraphs present a single idea or unit of thought?
7. Have you avoided reporting the details within each paragraph in chronological order, especially if you have not reported the overall story in chronological order?
8. Are your sentences clear, concise and to-the-point? (Have you avoided passive verbs and used the normal word order of subject, verb, direct object?)
9. Have you occasionally varied your sentence structure?
10. Have you avoided overloading your sentences?
11. Have you provided transitions to lead your readers from one sentence or paragraph to another in a smooth, logical manner?
12. Are your transitional sentences specific, and do they say something interesting that will help retain your readers' interest in the topic?
13. If you have used a question as a transition, is it clear, short and simple?
14. Have you avoided generalities that have to be explained in a later sentence or paragraph?
15. Have you resisted the temptation to end your story with a summary, conclusion or opinion of any kind?
16. Have you reported only what happened, omitting what did not happen?
17. After finishing your story, have you critically edited and rewritten it?
18. How many words are in your average sentence? How many words are in your longest sentence? (Critically examine sentences that contain more than 25 words. Consider rewriting your story if your average sentence contains more than 20 words.)

Alternative Styles

1. If you reported your story in chronological order, have you provided a transition from the lead to the body? Is your transition concise?
2. If your story discusses several major subtopics, have you mentioned all the major subtopics in your story's opening paragraphs so your readers know what to expect?
3. If you used a list, is each item in the list written in parallel form?
4. After finishing your story, have you critically edited and rewritten it?
5. How many words are in your average sentence? How many words are in your longest sentence? (Critically examine sentences that contain more than 25 words. Consider rewriting your story if your average sentence contains more than 20 words.)

St. Louis Post-Dispatch

WRITE & WRONG

By **Harry Levins**
Post-Dispatch Writing Coach

Remember the words that always signaled a happy ending?

> *"Who was that masked man?"*
>
> *"I don't know—but he left a silver bullet."*

Our own "bullets"—those typographical black boxes at the beginning of paragraphs—often amount to ammunition we can use when we shoot to make things easier for the reader.

Here's an example, from a story by Nordeka English:

> *Bridgeton officials are marshaling their forces to fight a proposal to extend Lambert Field into their city.*
>
> *The battle plan calls for officials to:*
>
> • *Pass the word to all of the city's boards and commissions, which have more than 100 members.*
>
> • *Give moral support to a residents' group that is forming to fight the expansion.*
>
> • *Ask officials of municipalities near the airport to join the opposition.*
>
> • *Hold a "town hall" meeting to generate support from residents and from the state and federal officials who have been invited.*
>
> *That meeting is scheduled for . . .*

Bullets allow us to give readers lists, and readers like lists, for several reasons:

1. Lists break a complicated world down into easily digestible bites. In effect, lists make a complicated world make sense.

2. Lists have a beginning and an end. The bullet typography tells a reader up front, "We're not leading you into an endless swamp of facts. We're pulling you into a tunnel that really *does* have a light at the end." (We're also telling readers, in effect, that they are free to skip over the list to the point where the narrative resumes. But when we give readers a list in the painless form that bullets allow, most readers will read it.)

3. Lists give readers lots of verbs, at least when the lists are compiled by writers who grab the opportunity to enliven their writing by starting each item with a verb. Note how English used verbs to open each item: "Pass," "Give," "Ask" and "Hold." Verbs make up the heavy firepower of any language; they propel the narrative.

4. Lists give readers plenty of "air"— the white space that fills out the last line of a paragraph. Contrast English's sample with this sample of English:

> *The old plan called for expanding City Hall to the east and providing major increases in parking to serve both City Hall and commercial outlets;*

(continued on next page)

acquisition of new park land; expansion of Jackson Park and a pedestrian-bicycle pathway linking major park areas; relocation of dislocated businesses and residents; development of apartments for older adults; and moving the Post Office to North Hanley Road.

No air there, right? Count the semicolons; that sentence has five. Any sentence with more than one semicolon can almost certainly benefit from being torn apart with bullets.

For example:

The old plan called for the municipality to:

- *Expand City Hall to the east.*
- *Provide more parking for City Hall and businesses.*
- *Buy new park land.*
- *Expand Jackson Park and connect it to other parks with a pedestrian-bicycle pathway.*
- *Relocate businesses and residents pushed out by the redevelopment.*
- *Develop apartments for older adults.*
- *Move the Post Office to North Hanley Road.*

True, the bullet version gains two more lines of space. But it also gains a lot of punch (with verbs), a lot of air (with white space) and very probably a lot more readers.

Sometimes, we provide the air by breaking our lists into paragraphs. But we fail to use the bullets that would clearly mark our list as a list. Here is an example:

The research turned up revealing characteristics of pregnant women who smoke.
They are young. The high-

est percentage of smokers is 18 or 19 years old.

They are poorly educated. Half of the women who smoke during pregnancy have not completed high school. Only 15 percent of women who have attended college smoke during pregnancy.

They are overwhelmingly single. Nearly half the women who smoke are unmarried.

Altogether, about 30 percent of pregnant women in Missouri smoke.

Although we gave the readers air, we failed to let them know that this particular list had an end as well as a beginning—that the tunnel had a light at the end. We could have done the same paragraphs this way:

The research turned up revealing characteristics of pregnant women who smoke:

- *They are young. The highest percentage of smokers are 18 or 19 years old.*

- *They are poorly educated. Half of the women who smoke during pregnancy have not completed high school. Only 15 percent of women who have attended college smoke during pregnancy.*

- *They are overwhelmingly single. Nearly half the women who smoke are unmarried.*

Altogether, about 30 percent of pregnant women in Missouri smoke.

That small touch pays big dividends in making things clear.

Moral: Don't bite the bullet. Use it.

***

Herewith, a Christmas stocking's worth of problem words:

another: Often misused, as in this case: *Delta placed firm orders to buy 50 MD-90s and took options on another 110.* You can't have "another 110" unless you had an original 110—and here, the original number was 50. Try: *Delta placed firm orders to buy 50 MD-90s and took options on 110 more.*

create: A word of awe and majesty. It ought not to be wasted like this: *The committee was created partly in response to state audits criticizing St. Louis Treasurer Larry Williams.* Let politicians "form" or "set up" committees, and reserve the act of creation to God, artists and nature.

curb: Fit for headlines only, at least in the sense of "limit" or "restrict": *The House has approved a measure designed to curb portrayals of violence on television.* Readers speak English, not headlinese.

currently: Almost always redundant when used with a verb in the present tense (*Pippa and Susan McNary currently have joint legal custody*) and *always* redundant when used with "is."

each other/one another: "Each other" applies to two; "one another" applies to three or more. We get it wrong a lot, as in this case: *Eight bidders offered prices within $300,000 of each other* . . .

estimated . . . about: "About" is redundant, because the verb "estimated" already contains the sense of approximation. Avoid this sort of error: *Chambers estimated that the woman's ordeal lasted about 30 minutes.*

fail/refuse: "To fail" suggests either an obligation or an effort to do whatever wasn't done, but we tend to use it interchangeably (and erroneously) with "refuse." For example: *Local 3 of the Mailers Union failed to approve the company's offer.* The union had no obligation to approve the offer, nor did it set out to approve the offer but fall short of its goal. The union simply *refused* to approve the offer.

ironically: This word comes from "irony," which always involves subtly sarcastic humor. To say something ironically means to say the opposite of what you mean, as when we say to a friend in torn blue jeans, "Geez, you're certainly well-dressed." But we often use the word when we really mean "By odd [or eerie] coincidence." For example: *Ironically, the trial was held in the same courtroom in which the elder Lucas had argued cases.* Moral: When you're tempted to use "ironically," look it up first.

possible: Our logic fails us when we use "possible" in contexts like this: *The boy's mother says the possible publication of the photos adds to her belief that her son has been victimized.* The very existence of photographs makes their publication "possible"; in fact, almost anything is "possible." What we mean in such cases is: *The boy's mother says the possibility that the photos might be published adds to her belief* . . . Remember: If the syntax wouldn't accommodate "impossible," it won't take "possible" either.

senior citizen: A dreadful euphemism for "old people," "the elderly," "the aged," "older adults," etc. Think about it: Our meaning has nothing to do with citizenship; many of the people we write about are resident aliens. And even if it did have something to do with citizenship, citizenship in the United States has no gradations of seniority. We're all created equal, with nobody "senior" to anybody else.

white stuff: With winter coming on, we can sponsor a contest to guess not when the first snow will fall but rather when the first writer will use the cliché "white stuff" to describe it.

SUGGESTED READINGS

Anderson, Douglas A. *Contemporary Sports Reporting*. Chicago: Nelson-Hall, 1985.

Best Newspaper Writing. St. Petersburg, FL: Poynter Institute for Media Studies. (This book, published every year since 1979, contains prize-winning articles, followed by an editor's comments, and question-and-answer sessions with the writers.)

Brooks, Terri. *Words' Worth: A Handbook on Writing and Selling Nonfiction*. New York: St. Martin's Press, 1989. (See Chapter 2, "Transitions.")

Cappon, Rene J. *The Word: An Associated Press Guide to Good News Writing*. New York: The Associated Press, 1982.

Garrison, Bruce. *Professional News Writing*. Hillsdale, NJ: Erlbaum, 1990. (See Chapter 4, "News Story Organization").

Ghiglione, Loren, ed., *Improving Newswriting: The Best of the Bulletin of the American Society of Newspaper Editors*. Washington, DC: American Society of Newspaper Editors Foundation, 1982.

Hohenberg, John. *The Professional Journalist*. 5th ed. New York: Holt, Rinehart and Winston, 1983.

Hough, George A. *News Writing*. 4th ed. Boston: Houghton Mifflin, 1988. (See Chapter 5, "News Story Organization.")

Izard, Ralph S., Hugh M. Culbertson, and Donald A. Lambert. *Fundamentals of News Reporting*. 5th ed. Dubuque, IA: Kendall/Hunt, 1990. (See Chapter 6, "The Structure of Writing.")

Kelsch, Mary Lynn, and Thomas Kelsch. *Writing Effectively: A Practical Guide*. Englewood Cliffs, NJ: Prentice Hall, 1981.

Metz, William. *Newswriting from Lead to "30."* 3rd ed. Englewood Cliffs, NJ: Prentice Hall, 1991. (See Chapter 5, "Putting Things in Order.")

Murray, Donald. *Writing for Your Readers: Notes on the Writer's Craft from the Boston Globe*. Chester, CT: Globe-Pequot Press, 1983.

Scanlan, Christopher, ed., *How I Wrote the Story*. Rev. ed. Providence, RI: Providence Journal, 1986.

Sims, Norman, ed., *The Literary Journalists*. New York: Ballantine, 1984.

Sloan, William D., Valarie McCrary, and Johanna Cleary. *The Best of Pulitzer Prize News Writing*. Columbus, OH: Publishing Horizons, 1986.

Synder, Louis L., and Richard B. Morris, eds., *A Treasury of Great Reporting*. 2nd ed. New York: Simon and Schuster, 1962.

Tarshis, Barry. *How to Write Like a Pro*. New York: New American Library, 1982.

Teel, Leonard R., and Ron Taylor. *Into the Newsroom: An Introduction to Journalism*. 2nd ed. Chester, CT: Globe-Pequot Press, 1988.

QUOTES

When you can't find anything wrong with the story you've written, there is something wrong with you. There never has been a story that couldn't be improved upon. When you're having trouble finding fault with your own stuff, reflect how easy it is to criticize anyone else's.

(Morton Sontheimer, "Newspaperman")

Whoever would overthrow the liberty of a nation must begin by subduing the freedom of speech.

(Benjamin Franklin)

Exercise 1

THE BODY OF A NEWS STORY

SECTION I: TRANSITIONS

Critically evaluate the following transitions. Which transitions provide a smooth, specific, informative and interesting introduction to the next idea?

   After evaluating the transitions, give each of them a grade from A to F.

1. Why would a former nurse open a hot dog stand? (Grade: _____)
2. He went on to provide guidelines and hints by which journalists might hone their skills. (Grade: _____)
3. The council heard representatives of the Coalition for the Homeless, a non-profit organization, explain why the city needs a new shelter. (Grade: _____)
4. Asian students said they expected Americans to be friendlier. (Grade: _____)
5. The problem library officials are most concerned about is smoking. (Grade: _____)
6. Only 23 percent of the women said they would like to give up their jobs and stay home full-time to raise their children. (Grade: _____)
7. Frank Yamer, a business major, also encountered a number of problems when he transferred from another school. (Grade: _____)
8. The university's math department awards the lowest percentage of As (14.1 percent) and the highest percentage of Fs (15.6 percent). (Grade: _____)
9. Officials explained how the plan will ease overcrowding at the three schools. (Grade: _____)
10. A man who lives across the road was working outside at the time and saw the accident. (Grade: _____)
11. Forty percent of the teen-agers said they never worry about catching AIDS. (Grade: _____)
12. Dr. Kostyn said there is a shortage of about 2,200 certified math and science teachers in the state. (Grade: _____)

SECTION II: SECOND PARAGRAPHS

Critically evaluate the second paragraph in each of the following stories. Which of the second paragraphs are most successful in: (1) providing a smooth transition from the lead, (2) continuing to discuss the topic summarized in the lead and (3) emphasizing the news: details that are new, important and interesting?

   After evaluating the transitions, give each of them a grade of from A to F.

1. Jewel C. Harris, 42, of 2245 E. Broadway Ave. was arrested and charged with aggravated battery after her car struck a bicyclist, police say.
   Jerry R. Harris, 24, also of 2245 E. Broadway Ave., was transported to Memorial Hospital with cuts, bruises and a broken leg. (Grade: _____)
2. The School Board has expelled eight more students for using drugs, bringing the total this year to 81.
   Only one of the eight students appeared before the board last night to defend herself. She was accused of selling marijuana to a classmate. (Grade: _____)
3. The new Alcohol Information Center on campus acknowledges a slow start with its responsible drinking program. But program coordinators have plans to change that.

Karen Dees is one of the program's coordinators. She wants to make sure that students understand the philosophy of responsible drinking. "We're not affiliated with any religious sect," she said. "Our main goal is to keep heavy drinkers off the streets and keep them from harming themselves and others." (Grade: _____)

4. County Commissioner Anne Chen wants pornographic movies banned from cable TV.

In an interview Friday, Chen said that watching pornography can be psychologically damaging to children. "I'm not talking about R-rated movies," she said. "I'm talking about hard-core stuff that shows animals, whips and chains used in sexual acts." (Grade: _____)

5. A man claiming to have a bomb tried to rob the First Federal Savings and Loan Co. at 9:05 a.m. today.

A man carrying a brown paper bag told a teller that it contained a bomb and that he would kill everyone in the bank unless she gave him $10,000. (Grade: _____)

6. A 22-year-old auto mechanic and his wife delivered their triplets at home Monday because there was no time to drive to a birthing clinic.

Barbara and Paul Wyman of 2020 Lorry Lane delivered their triplets at 4:30 a.m. The babies and their mother are reported in excellent condition. (Grade: _____)

7. Complaining that college administrators are insensitive to their needs, 50 handicapped students, some in wheelchairs, picketed the Administration Building Friday.

About 10 percent of the student population is handicapped, but there is no way of determining how many there really are. When the Rehabilitation Act of 1973 was passed, the disclosure of information about handicapped students was prohibited. The law is intended to ensure that a handicapped student is not discriminated against and denied entrance into a college. (Grade: _____)

8. The police in Reno, Nev., feel safer and more confident since the PR-24 Baton replaced their night stick.

Officer Jim Balliet said the concept of a baton was derived from a martial arts weapon called the tonfa. Lon Anderson, a New Hampshire police officer, developed the baton and brought the idea to a company to manufacture it, Balliet said. (Grade: _____)

9. Two soldiers who were abducted, robbed and tied in a woods said their captors apologized, saying they became robbers in order to feed their children.

The young couple told the soldiers that they had also abducted several other people but never enjoyed it. (Grade: _____)

10. Peter Laguna, a 24-year-old Alabama man, went on trial Wednesday on charges of armed robbery.

The first witness was Lynita Sharp, a clerk who was working at the convenience store when it was robbed on July 18. (Grade: _____)

11. The School Board voted Tuesday to construct an elementary school on Grant Avenue.

Two years ago, the Meadow Woods Subdivision offered to give the board land for the school. (Grade: _____)

12. A 22-year-old man today pleaded innocent to violating his probation, arguing that his poor education made it impossible for him to understand the instructions given by his parole officer.

The defendant, Henry Forlenza, told the judge that he dropped out of high school and never learned to read.

Exercise 2

THE BODY OF A NEWS STORY

Pro Challenge

WRITING COMPLETE STORIES

INSTRUCTIONS: Write complete news stories based on the following information. Be thorough; include most of the information provided for your stories. Because much of the material is wordy, awkward and poorly organized, it will have to be extensively rewritten.

When you finish, you can compare your work to a professional's. Experienced reporters have also been asked to write stories for each set of facts, and their work appears in a manual available to your instructor.

1. The announcement is a major one. It was made at a press conference this morning in the office of Enrico Lowdes, director of the Regional Medical Center. The announcement is that the hospital is one of 10 medical facilities located throughout the entire United States selected to participate in an important new study the purpose of which is to determine whether or not a new technique will be successful in helping smokers stop smoking. The hospital will not accept volunteers to participate in the experiment. Rather, Lowdes said, doctors in the city will be asked to refer a total of 800 of their patients who smoke and want to stop smoking to the hospital for participation in the experiment. Lowdes noted that nicotine is as addictive as cocaine or heroin. That may explain why 28% of adult Americans smoke. Experts estimate that as many as 90% of those who now smoke say they would like to quit. Many have tried to kick the habit many times but failed. The most difficult part of kicking the habit, Lowdes said, is acute withdrawal symptoms ranging from physical cravings, nervousness, irritation, difficulty concentrating, difficulty sleeping, and changes in appetite. That is why the Regional Medical Center sought to be one of 10 medical facilities in the United States to test a new nicotine patch that may help smokers who want to discontinue the habit ease the pain of withdrawal. Lowdes explained that smokers asked to participate in the study will be prescribed adhesive patches. They will be instructed that, as soon as they get up in the morning, they are to apply one of the patches to their upper body. The patch releases a steady level of nicotine throughout the day. It is less nicotine, however, than that provided by cigarettes, but is thought to be enough to alleviate withdrawal symptoms. Nicotine gum is designed to work in much the same way, but some evidence indicates that the patch may be more effective because some people find the gum hard to chew, chew it improperly, or don't use it in sufficient quantity. The 800 patients will be monitored monthly for an entire year in an attempt to determine how many are helped by the patches: how many succeed in stopping smoking over a period of 1 year. Lowdes added finally that the patch may also help smokers quit smoking without gaining as much weight as sometimes happens to smokers who quit the habit.

2. There's a totally new idea starting to be implemented in your city. Some call it "a pilot program." Others call it "a satellite school." Your School Board likes

the idea because it saves the board money. Businesses like it because it helps them attract and retain good employees. There was a meeting of your citys School Board last night. Greg Hubbard, superintendent of your citys school system, recommended the idea, and the School Board then proceeded to vote 6–1 in favor of trying the new idea. What's the idea? Its to mix companies and classrooms. Recently, plans were announced to construct a major new General Electric manufacturing plant in your city. The plant will employ a total of more than 600 employees, many of them women who will work on assembly lines, helping make small appliances for the new General Electric plant. To attract and retain qualified women, many of whom have young children, the plant wants a school to be located on its premises. It offered to provide, free of charge, free space: to construct a separate building on its premises with 3 rooms built according to the School Boards specifications. Its the wave of the future, Hubbard told the School Board last night. Its a win-win situation, he added. He explained that it is a good employee benefit, and it helps ease crowding in the districts schools if some students go elsewhere. The details are being negotiated. To start with at first, the school will have three rooms and serve about 60 kindergarten and first-grade children of employees. The school district will equip the classrooms and pay the salaries of a teacher and a teachers aide for each classroom. At this point in time there are only approximately 20 school districts in the entire country trying the idea. Students will eat in the factorys employee cafeteria and play on a playground also provided by the new factory. Parents will provide transportation to and from the facility. Equipping each classroom will cost in the neighborhood of approximately $10,000. The price is about the same as for a regular classroom. Hubbard said if the program is successful, it will expand to other companies. A company will have to supply a minimum of 20 children to justify the cost of the program which could, if successful, serve young students in 2nd and possibly 3rd grades as well. The program is thought to attract and retain more employees—to reduce the rate of attrition, thus saving companies the cost of training new employees. That is especially important in industries with many low-paying positions in which there is often a high turnover. Its also a solution to working parents who feel there is never enough time to spend with their children. Hubbard said one of the nice things is that many will have the opportunity to ride to and from work and also have lunch with their children.

3. They're all heroes, but no one knows exactly how many of them there are, nor all their identities. They were shopping late yesterday evening at the Colonial Mall in your city. The mall closes at 10 p.m., and it was about 9:50 pm when the incident occurred. There was a serious incident: a robbery. Among the other stores in the mall is a jewelry store: Elaine's Jewelry. An unidentified man walked into the store and, before anyone could respond, pulled out a hammer, smashed two display cases, and then proceeded to scoop up with his hands handfuls of jewelry, mostly watches and rings. Elaine Benchfield is the owner of the store, and also its manager, and she was present at the time and began screaming quite loudly. People heard her screams, saw the man flee, and, according to witnesses, 8 or 10 people began pursuing the man through the mall. As the chase proceeded, the posse grew in number. "Things like that just make me mad," explained Keith Holland, one of the shoppers who witnessed the crime and joined the posse. The chase ended in one of the shopping malls parking lots. Once outside in the parking lot, even more people started joining the posse, yelling at and chasing the man. Asa Smythe, a jogger who says he jogs a distance of 20 miles a week, said he knew the man might out-

sprint him for a short distance, but that he also knew he was going to follow
the man to hell if he had to. "He couldn't lose me, no way he could lose me,"
Smythe said. Smythe is a former high school football player and Marine. He
succeeded in catching up with and tackling the man. More shoppers, an estimated 15 or 20 by police, then surrounded the man, holding him there in the
parking lot until police reached the scene. The people stood in a circle around
the man, threatening him, but also applauding and shaking hands among themselves, proud of their accomplishment. The suspect has since then been identified by police officers as Todd Burns, age 23, of 1502 Matador Dr., Apt. 302.
He has been charged with grand theft and is being held on $25,000 bond at the
county jail. Police officer Barbara Keith-Fowler, the first officer to reach the
scene, said she thinks Burnes was happy to see her. Burnes was not armed,
and was apparently frightened, police said, by the crowd. At one point in the
chase he threw them the bag of loot, apparently hoping they would stop following him. A bystander retrieved the bag and returned it to Blancfield, who said
it contained everything stolen from her store. A grateful Blanchfeld then proceeded to tell you, when you called her on the phone, that the people who
helped her were a super bunch of people and made her feel wonderful. Blanchfeld added that she thinks people responded as they did because they are sick
and tired of people getting ripped off.

4. Its a most unusual controversy. It involves an act at a circus the Shriners in
your city put on to raise money for their charitable activities. In addition, the
Shriners, who put the circus on every year at this time in your city, invite free
of charge hundreds of the citys ill and retarded and needy children. One of
everyones favorite acts involves six cats that look like rather typical household
pets. The circus opened last Friday, with shows to continue every nite at 8
p.m. this week through this coming Saturday evening. There will also be a
show at 2 pm Saturday afternoon. After seeing the first shows last weekend,
some people began to complain about an act put on by Sandra Kidder of Farmers Branch, Texas, a suburb of Dallas. Kidder travels from city to city with the
circus and explains that she enjoys traveling and loves her animals, all cats.
The cats dive through flaming hoops, and that's what people have complained
about. Her cats do it for love, Kidder said when you interviewed her today.
They'll do anything for her, she said, because she loves them and they love
her. Someone, however, filed a complaint with the citys Humane Society. The
complaint charges that Kidder terrifies and starves her cats, endangering their
lives to get them to do the trick. Annette Daigle, who filed the complaint, re-
sides in her home at 431 E. Central Blvd. Her complaint states that the cats
are forced to perform highly unnatural behaviors for them—that the last thing a
cat wants to do is go near fire. Diagle said she is not the only one concerned
about the cats welfare but that other people who also feel the way she does
that the cats are being starved, terrorized, endangered, and abused don't want
to get involved in the controversy. Kidder responded to you that she feeds her
cats one good meal a day at the end of their performance. She couldn't do it
sooner, she said, because, if they had just eaten, her cats would fall asleep in
the middle of their act. Kidder then went on to add that she would never do
anything to hurt or endanger her cats. In addition to jumping through flaming
hoops, her cats during each act also leap from stool to stool; jump high in the
air; stand on their hind legs; stand on their front legs; sit on their haunches in
the begging position like dogs; and walk across a stretched wire, like tight-rope
walkers. She calls them her "fabulous flying felines." They're professionals,
she concluded. Finally, in addition, Kidder added that its easier for her cats to

jump through the flaming rings than to master many of the other, simpler-looking tricks. They're not scared of the flaming hoops, she insists. They're only scared if someone is mean to them. They need to feel that you love them. The hardest thing for them to learn to do is to stand up on their hind legs. Its not natural for them, but they'll do it for her. She also further revealed that they're not special cats. Friends gave her some. She picked up others at a pound. Renee Chung-Peters, head of your citys Humane Society, said she is in the process of investigating the complaint. Chung-Peters said she will watch tonights show and hopes to examine all the cats immediately after the show. When you contacted Kidder, she said that she has no objections to that.

5. Gus DiCesare, your countys sheriff, appeared before the County Commission today. He made an unusual and unique proposal that he says will save the county money and help beautify it, all at the same time. He proposed that trustees in his county jail should be taken from the jail six days a week, Monday through Saturday, to clean the countys roadways of trash and other debris. He said all he needs is a truck to take several inmates to roadsides in need of cleaning and to haul away the debris. The trusties will wear their regular jailhouse uniforms: bright orange in color. They will work in crews of 8 or 10 and will be guarded by two armed officers with radio communication. Sheriff DeCesare admitted, "Any time you work prisoners outside the institution, there is always a slight risk of escape. So we're not going to put Jack the Ripper out there." He said that he's not worried about escapes, however. He thinks they are highly unlikely. He explained that inmates on the road crews will be trustees carefully chosen by this staff. Corrections officers will screen inmates who have been sentenced, weeding out sex offenders and those guilty of assaults and other serious crimes. Likely candidates will be those convicted of theft, fraud, drunken driven, writing bad checks, and petty larceny, for example. DeCesare added, while seeing how the program works initially, the crews will work in more remote areas of the county. He further explained that all the trusties will be serving sentences of less than a year and, if they escape, they would be liable for sentencing of up to five more years in a state prison. The county used road crews until the 1970s. Officials abolished them then because some people began to complain that the county was exploiting the prisoners and that it was degrading for them to work along roadways where everyone could see them and know they were criminals. The sheriff said he was a deputy then, and many inmates were unhappy when the county abandoned the practice. Now, they will be paid about 25 cents an hour for their work. Also, for each month they work, four days will be taken off their sentence. The sheriff said he does not expect a problem finding volunteers. Most inmates like to work, he said. It makes their time go faster. A lot of them would work seven days a week if you let them, anything to get out of their cells, he said. Prisoners inside the jail, helping with the cleaning and cooking there, are also paid 25 cents an hour, and money for some prisoners salaries is already budgeted in the Sheriffs Departments annual budget. Kerwin Dawkins, head of the countys Public Works Department, was also at the meeting and supported the idea. He agreed to provide all the necessary trucks. He said he likes the idea because the county needs crews to clean both roadways and parks and, since the labor costs are low, the plan will save his department money as well as benefit the public. Dawkins further stated that he firmly believes that the program will also be popular with the public because people will like to see the jails inmates work. If successful, the program will expand to include more inmates and more trucks.

6. An estimated 12,000 people in your city and surrounding area will be affected by the news. A chain of health spas called "Mr. Muscles" is closing. It is the areas largest spa, with 6 clubs located throughout the city. It closed without warning. The company is owned by Mike Cantral of 410 South Street. Normally, the spas open at 6 a.m. and, when people went to them today, they found a simple notice taped to the doors at all 6 saying, "Closed Until Further Notice." Cantral was unavailable. His attorney, Jena Cruz, said the company is bankrupt and she doesn't expect it to reopen. She said she will file a bankruptcy petition for the spas in federal court, probably early next week. Hundreds and hundreds of regular members showed up at the clubs today and found the doors locked, the lights out, and the equipment inside sitting unused. Employees, estimated to total 180 in number, were also surprised. They said they did not know the spas were in trouble and had no inkling they were about to close. Several said they are worried about whether or not they will be paid for their work during the last two weeks. They are paid every two weeks, and their normal payday is tomorrow. Some members paid up to $499 a year for use of the facilities. Some have paid for 3 or 5-year memberships. An undetermined number bought lifetime memberships for $3,999. The clubs have been open for more than 10 years. The state Department of Consumer Affairs is investigating the closing. Kim Eng, director of the department, said she did not know if any members could get refunds on their memberships but said if the company goes bankrupt that seems unlikely. Cruz said the clubs were losing a total of $3,000 a week. She added that there is no money left to return to members. The state attorneys office is also investigating members complaints. The company opened its first spa in 1981, then began an aggressive expansion program. Atty. Cruz said the company borrowed money to buy land for its spas and to build the spas, each of which cost a total of well over $1.2 million to build and equip, and that it has not been selling enough new memberships in recent months to make the payments on all its loans.

7. It was a dreadfully tragic incident and involved a 7-year-old girl in your city: Tania Abondanzio, the daughter of Anthony and Deborah Abbondanzia. The girl was admitted to Mercy Hospital last Friday morning. She was driven to the hospital by her parents. She was operated on later that morning for a tonsillectomy. She died Saturday morning. Hospital officials investigating the death announced, during a press conference this morning, that they have now determined the apparent cause of death: that the girl was given the wrong medication by a pediatric nurse. They did not identify the nurse, saying only that she has been suspended, pending completion of the investigation. The girls parents were unavailable for comment. Tania was a 2nd grade student at Washington Elementary School. Her physician, Dr. Priscilla Eisen, prescribed a half milligram of a pain reliever, morphine sulphate, after surgery. Hospital records show that, somehow, by mistake, the nurse gave the girl a half milligram of hydromorphone, a stronger pain reliever commonly known as Dilaudid. The victim was given the drug at 2:30 p.m. Friday afternoon and developed severe respiratory problems at 2:40 p.m. She also complained of being hot and went into an apparent seizure. An autopsy conducted over the weekend to determine the cause of her problems showed results, also announced during the press conference today, that were consistent with the hospitals report, police said. Police are treating the death as accidental. After developing respiratory problems, the girl was immediately transferred from the medical facilitys pediatrics ward to the intensive care ward and remained in a coma until Saturday morning, when doctors pronounced her brain dead. She was then taken off a respirator and died min-

utes later at 9:40 a.m. Saturday morning. The nurse involved in the unfortunate incident noticed she had apparently administered the wrong drug during a routine narcotics inventory when the shifts changed at midnight Friday. She immediately and promptly notified her supervisor. The two drugs are kept side by side together in a locked cabinet. Hospital officials said a dosage of a half-milligram of hydromorphone is not normally considered to be lethal, not even for a child. Dr. Irwin Greenhouse, hospital administrator, said in a statement released to the press today that, "Our sympathy goes out to the family, and we will stay close to them to provide support." He declined to comment further. Hydromorphone, a narcotic used to treat pain, is six to seven times more potent than morphine. Children sometimes are given a half milligram of hydromorphone to control coughing, a druggist you consulted said. The druggist added that the dosage did not sound outrageous to her, but rather sounded very reasonable, as a matter of fact. The drug is generally used for pain relief after surgery or as medication before an operation, the druggist also informed you, asking that she not be identified by name, a request that you agreed to honor.

8. A lone man robbed a bank in the city. He entered the Security Federal Bank, 814 North Main Street, at about 2:30 p.m. yesterday. Bank officials said he first went into the bank with the excuse of obtaining information about a loan, talked to a loan officer and then left. When he returned a few minutes later, he was brandishing a pistol and demanded money from the bank's tellers. Gladys Anne Higginbotham, the bank's manager, said he forced two tellers to lie on the floor. He then jumped behind a counter and scooped up the money from five cash drawers. As the gunman scooped up the money, he also scooped up a small exploding device disguised to look like a packet of money and stuffed it into his pockets along with the rest of the cash. The device contains red dye and tear gas and automatically explodes after a specified amount of time. The length of time before the explosion is determined by each individual bank using the device. The device is activated when someone walks out of a bank with it. As the gunman left the bank, he ordered four customers to lie down on the floor. Most of the customers were unaware of the robbery until told to get down on the floor. Witnesses believe the gunman sped away from the scene in a pickup truck parked behind the building. Police say they found a red stain in the rear parking lot and surmise that the device exploded just as the robber was getting into the truck. An eyewitness told police he saw a late-model black pickup truck a few blocks away with a red cloud coming out the window a few moments after the robbery but was unable to get the license number. Detective Myron A. Neeley said, "That guy should be covered with red. The money, too. Just look for a red man with red money. You can't wash that stuff off. It just has to wear off. It explodes all over the place—in your clothes, in your hair, on your hands, in your car. It's almost like getting in contact with a skunk." An FBI agent on the scene added that many banks now use the protective devices in an effort to foil bank robbers and that the stain will eventually wear off humans but stays on money forever. He estimated that the man will be covered with the red dye for at least the next two or three days. The man was described as a white man. He is between the ages of 25 and 30 years of age. He is about 6 feet tall. He weighs about 180 pounds. He has long blond hair. His attire includes wire-rimmed sunglasses, a gold wedding ring, a blue plaid shirt, blue jeans and brown sandals.

Exercise 3

THE BODY OF A NEWS STORY

WRITING COMPLETE NEWS STORIES

INSTRUCTIONS: Write complete news stories based on the following information. Be thorough: include most of the information in your stories. Because much of the material is wordy, awkward and poorly organized, it will have to be extensively rewritten.

1. Under state law, it is a second-degree misdemeanor to publish or broadcast information that identifies rape victims or to cause such information to be published. The law is relevant to this case, which involves a daily newspaper: The Daily Courier in your city. The newspaper was sued by the victim of a rape. She is Paula Andrews, 52, of 4030 New Orleans Avenue. On the 20th of October, two years ago, the victim was raped, and she reported the crime to your city's police department. On the 22nd, The Daily Courier published the story, identifying her as the victim. She sued. A jury of 8 men and 4 women began to hear the case one week ago. At 4 p.m. yesterday, the presentation of evidence ended, and Circuit Court Judge Julian Strickland ordered the jury to find the newspaper negligent and to determine whether the victim deserved any financial damages. After a break for dinner, the jury immediately began its deliberations and, at 8:35 p.m., announced its verdict. The jury awarded the woman $75,000 compensation and an additional $250,000 in punitive damages. The publisher of the newspaper, Ricky Becker, testified during the trial that one of his newspaper's reporters had violated the newspaper's policy and published the woman's name by mistake in a police briefs column, and that no one else noticed the error until after its publication. Becker said he "was amazed and dumbfounded" by the jury's verdict. "We'll appeal, of course," he said. "There's no justification for awarding anyone that kind of money. We were well within our First Amendment rights; the Constitution is supposed to protect us from this kind of harassment. Normally, we don't publish the name of a woman who's been raped, but the information's non-publication is a voluntary matter. The government can't mandate it." An attorney for the newspaper added that the state law is unconstitutional because it is equivalent to a prior restraint on the publication of truthful, legally obtained information that was part of a public record. The newspaper reporter obtained the information from a police report. Andrews, a widow, told reporters that she considers the award fair and hopes that it will discourage publication of rape victims names by other newspapers.

2. It began with a routine inspection. Health inspectors in your city inspect every restaurant and bakery, normally twice a year. The inspections are a surprise. They are not announced in advance. Rather, the inspectors drop in by surprise. Last Friday, they dropped in at a bakery on Moore Street: the Kalani Bros. Bakery. It is one of the largest in the city, with 40 employees. It supplies more than 100 grocery stores and restaurants with bread, pies, cakes and other pastries. After the inspection Friday, the Health Department proceeded to suspend the baker's license, effective immediately. The Kalani brothers, Charles and Andrew, say they will appeal to the city council, which meets at 8 p.m. to-

night. During an inspection a year ago, health inspectors found cockroaches, mice droppings, flour beetles and other health problems. There have been two inspections since then, and they found that some problems were corrected, but new problems—such as inadequate refrigeration and garbage thrown on floors—had arisen. The inspectors returned again last Friday—a fourth time—to determine whether all the problems had been corrected. Under emergency provisions of city health laws, a business can be closed immediately—its license temporarily suspended—to protect the public health if a dangerous situation exists. After a hearing, the license can be permanently revoked. City inspectors said, despite their repeated warnings, the problems had not been corrected; some had gotten worse. So Friday, they temporarily suspended the license. Attorney Margie Allen, who represents the brothers, said she does not believe the sanitation problems are as bad as city officials allege and that most have been corrected and that the remainder are in the process of being corrected. She adds that the brothers are losing $13,000 a day in lost business and may permanently lose some customers, who are getting their bakery goods from rivals during the shutdown. "There has been no hearing here," Allen says. "Their business is being destroyed by an edict, without proper legal safeguards. We'll appeal tonight to the city council and, tomorrow, to the courts, if necessary."

3. It's an idea being tried in many places. County commissioners want an impact fee. The county has been growing so rapidly, they point out, that it is impossible, without some additional sources of income, to provide the necessary services. The county needs more fire stations and more firefighters and sheriff's deputies. The county needs a bigger sewer system, a bigger jail, better roads, new schools and more teachers to accommodate all the new residents moving to the county. A task force of 12 county officials has been looking into the matter during the past three months, and they revealed their report at a press conference at 9 a.m. today. The county commissioners will consider the report at their next meeting: next Tuesday night at 8 pm. The task force recommends that new people moving to the county should be required to pay for the expanded services they want and need. Taxes should not be raised. Rather, each time a new house is built, an "impact fee" should be assessed. The money would be used for needed capital improvements. New businesses would also be assessed: 5% of the cost of their construction. The plan is expected to raise about $18 million dollars a year. The impact fee for hooking up to the county sewage system for a single-family home would cost $2,500. The impact fee for a water connection would be $1,000. The fees for apartment units would be $1,800 and $750, respectively. There would be other fees for roads, education and police protection. The county would then issue $260 million worth of bonds during the next five years to build three new sewer plants, a new water treatment plant, a jail, two fire stations, and several new schools, including a brand-new high school. The impact fees would be used to repay the bonds. Developers object to the idea, saying that the proposed fees would raise the price of each new home more than $5,000 and that many people could not afford that kind of money. The county's goal is to get ahead of growth and to maintain a high quality of life for the countys residents. There will be a series of public hearings, the task force said, but no dates or locations have been set. The task force warns that, without new fees, growth will have to stop. The county will be forced to stop granting any new building permits because it will not have the water and sewage capacity to hand future growth. Roads and

schools will become overcrowded, forcing double sessions at the schools. Police and fire protection will deteriorate.

4. There was a meeting of scientists at the University of Oklahoma today. They talked about dangers of nuclear war. The scientists represented many different fields, from biology to physics and meteorology. They concluded that the results of a nuclear war would be much worse than believed. Survivors may envy the dead. "We have very good reason to be scared," said one scientist about the long-term effects of nuclear war. More than 500 scientists from around the world—including Russia and China—attended the conference. Some concluded that a major nuclear war would result in the extinction of the human race. One said that even a relatively small nuclear war would trigger major changes in climate, which would destroy crops and endanger millions of people. A major nuclear war, they estimated, would kill more than 1 billion people and critically injure at least that number. A huge cloud of dust could be thrown into the atmosphere, cutting off sunlight and causing temperatures to drop well below freezing for weeks—possibly months or even years, so the world would be plunged into a new ice age. Much of the world's farmland would be covered with ice. People would freeze or starve in a dark, smoggy world. In a full-scale nuclear war, the Northern Hemisphere would be destroyed. Everyone there would suffer, not just the citizens of the warring nations. In fact, everyone there would be likely to die. The effects would spread across the equator to the Southern Hemisphere, so the entire globe would be affected. The predictions are based upon statistics concerning a nuclear war involving 5,000 megatons of explosives. The consequences would be more or less severe, depending upon the amount of weapons used and how they were used. A less severe war, a 3,000-megaton war, would lower the global average temperature by 8 degrees, which would be sufficient to wipe out all the worlds grain production. The scientists said a Civil Defense program would save peoples lives, but only for a few miserable weeks or months. Instead of being killed by the initial blasts, the survivors would die more slowly: of starvation, radiation, cold and disease. There would be no electricity or means of communication or transportation. Medicine and medical care would be unavailable. In parts of the United States, even water might be difficult or impossible to obtain.

5. It was an unusual case. It reached the Supreme Court in the State of New Hampshire, and the judges there reached their decision today. They ruled in favor of the doctor, not in favor of the couple filing the lawsuit. The couple are Wilbur and Martha Yantorini of Keene. Wilbur, the father of two other children, underwent a vasectomy two years ago to keep from fathering any more children, as he felt that was all that he could reasonably afford to raise. A year later, his wife, Martha, became pregnant. Three months ago, she gave birth to a third child, Fred. Wilbur then underwent a second vasectomy, as medical tests showed the first had been unsuccessful. The couple subsequently filed suit upon the doctor who performed the first operation, Dr. Richard Z. Abberger. They are demanding the costs of rearing the third child—a normal, healthy male. It is the first case of this kind to be filed in the state of New Hampshire, and perhaps the first in the nation. The couple demanded $500,000, calculated at the rate of $25,000 for 20 years to raise and educate Fred. They also demanded all their legal expenses. The court reached its decision today. It ruled against the family and in favor of the doctor. The vote of the court was narrow: 4 to 3. The majority explained that, "Litigation cannot answer every

question, and every question cannot be answered in terms of dollars and cents. We are convinced that the damage to the child will be significant: that to be an unwanted or 'emotional bastard' child who will someday learn that its parents did not want it and, in fact, went to court to force someone else to pay for its raising, will be harmful for that child. But we must also consider a ruling that could undermine societys need for a strong and healthy family relationship. Families have always been responsible for the care and upbringing of their children, and we are reluctant to alter that centuries-old tradition so basic to our society." If damages are to be awarded because an unwanted child was born, the court said, the state Legislature should take action, enacting a new law to settle the issue. The judges who dissented said forcing the issue on the legislature was a cop-out. They also said a policy of denying benefits in such cases would encourage abortion or adoption.

Exercise 4

THE BODY OF A NEWS STORY

WRITING COMPLETE STORIES

INSTRUCTIONS: Write complete news stories based on the following information. Be thorough; include most of the information in your stories. Because much of the material is wordy, awkward and poorly organized, it will have to be extensively rewritten.

1. A new law that goes into effect next fall will affect elementary, junior high and high school students throughout the state. The state Legislature enacted the law, and the governor signed it today. Basically, the law prohibits the sale of so-called junk food at public schools. So, as a result of the laws passage, the content of all school vending machines will undergo a drastic change. The machines no longer will contain any candy bars, gum, soda or other foods with a high sugar content. Instead, they will be replaced by foods which are considered by many to be more healthy, foods such as canned soups and juices, jerky, toasted soy beans, sunflower seeds, yogurt, nuts, cheese, popcorn, pretzels, ice cream and milk. The law was supported by physicians, dentists and educators, who testified in legislative hearings that many students bought snacks and soft drinks from machines instead of eating the more nutritous meals served in school cafeterias. Other persons, primarily food manufacturers and vending-machine operators, opposed the law. Students, too, generally opposed it, claiming that their rights were being violated and that they were old enough to make their own decisions about what they want to eat. Some school principles also opposed the law, pointing out the fact that the law will be costly since they recieve a percentage of the receipts of the vending machines located in their buildings. Some big high schools earn up to $20,000 a year from machines and use the money to buy materials that would not otherwise be available, such as supplemental textbooks, library materials, calculators for their mathematics laboratories, television cameras for their communications classes, and athletic equipment. School bands and athletic programs will be hurt most severely by the loss of revenue. The practice of showing free movies at some schools may also come to a quick end, since many were financed by vending machine revenues. Critics said it was inconsistent for schools to teach good nutrition in classes and then make food with a high sugar content easily available. The ban will be in effect only during school hours, so the junk food will still be able to be sold after school hours, such as during school dances and sports events, so schools can continue to earn a limited amount of money from their sale. One proponent added, "There's simply no sense in talking to kids about dental care and good nutrition and selling them junk food at the same time." Opponents responded that students will buy candy anyway, simply going off campus to buy it.

2. Thomas E. Richardson is 28 years old and a city policeman and alive today because while on duty he wears a bullet-proof vest supplied free of charge by the city. He lives at 5421 Jennings Road with his wife, Inez, and two children: Mary, 8, and Suanne, 5. He has been a policeman since leaving the Army 4 years ago. Without the vest, he might have died last night. Richardson went on duty at 4 p.m. and shortly after 10 p.m. the police received an anonymous phone call about a suspicious person loitering behind a restaurant at 640 Aloma

Avenue. Responding to the call, Richardson spotted a man matching the description he was given and, when he pulled his patrol car to the curb and got out, he said without warning the man drew a .38-caliber revolver from a jacket pocket and without saying anything fired four shots at him. Two shots struck Richardson. Two struck his patrol car. The first two shots hit Richardson in the chest, and he was spun around and knocked against the car door by the impact of those two shots. A third bullet shattered a left rear window of the patrol car and the fourth bullet entered the left rear door of the patrol car. After catching his breath, Richardson returned fire, blasting six shots at the suspect, who fell to the ground. Richardson was treated at Mercy Hospital for severe bruises on the chest, including one bruise that doctors say is directly above his heart, in a hospital emergency room. The suspect, who was killed in the exchange of gunfire, has not yet been identified. A police spokesman said they do not yet know why he opened fire at Richardson. The police department purchased bullet-proof vests for all its outside policemen last year, but wearing them is voluntary and many officers do not because they are heavy and uncomfortable, particularly during the hot summer months.

3. The police today celebrated the first anniversary of an innovative program. The program is for senior citizens—usually persons 65 and older, although any person who lives alone and is over the age of 55 can participate if that person wants to do so. The program is called "Project Reassurance." Each day, elderly persons who participate in the program call Dorothy Morovchek, a clerk, and two aides at the police department between the hours of 7 and 9 a.m. If they do not call by 9:15 a.m., Miss Morovchek will dispatch a police officer to the person's home to determine whether the person is safe, and the officers have keys to each participants home so they do not have to break their way in. Since the program started a year ago, Miss Morovchek says it has saved three lives, including the life of a woman who police officers found lying on the kitchen floor of her home after having suffered a heart attack before she was able to call the police that morning. Altogether, a total of 318 persons in the city participate in the program at the current time, and police say they will not impose any limitations on the number of participants in the future. Miss Morovchek adds that the elderly like the program for a second reason as well, since many feel alone, and it gives them someone to talk to every morning. One elderly person who uses the service says, "Its a thrill to hear a voice. My wife died four years ago, and I don't have anyone else to talk to. I also feel now like I have some security. I know someone's there to help if I need it."

4. The case involves another unusual lawsuit. As a result of it, if you are blind, or going blind, you may have to wait longer to receive cornea transplants. Your states supreme court ruled on the matter today. It issued a decision saying that medical examiners can no longer remove corneas from the eyes of a deceased without the permission of relatives. A state law, adopted in 1979, gave medical examiners the right to remove corneas without permission of the family of the deceased. The law applied to bodies under the jurisdiction of medical examiners, such as victims of accidents, murders, suicides and other unexplained deaths. Since then, attorneys opposed to the law have argued that it violates a familys right to decide the disposition of a loved ones remains. There was a test case. It involved a woman who died two years ago, at the age of 31. She has not been identified, in part because she committed suicide. During the autopsy of her body, both corneas were removed from her eyes. Later, when her relatives learned of that action, they objected on the grounds of their reli-

gious beliefs. Your State Supreme Court, ruling on the case today, said the state law violates a familys right to decide the disposition of a loved ones remains. The ruling is expected to be appealed to the U.S. Supreme Court. People at an eye bank in your state say the decision could drastically affect cornea procurement. The director of the eye bank said the ruling could extend the waiting period for the sight-restoring surgery from a week or two to a year or longer. "I think this will have a disastrous effect on our ability to obtain an adequate number of corneas to serve our patients," said the medical director of the eye bank. On the other hand, presenting the other point of view, parents have complained that they did not even know about the law until after the corneas of their deceased children were removed. The law permitted the removal of the corneas, the transparent tissue forming the outer coating of the eye and covering the iris and pupil, as long as the family didn't object. The law did not require the medical examiner to notify the family of the procedure. So many families may not have objected because they did not know what was being done. About half of the 50 states have similar laws governing the procurement of corneas. In states where there is no law giving medical examiners the authority to remove corneas, the typical wait for a transplant is from three to six months. "In every state where there's a similar law, the waiting list is very small," a doctor said.

5. It was an unusual situation. Two police officers responding to an emergency call were involved in an automobile accident on the 14th of last month. Today they were fired. They were not fired for causing the accident, although they did. The chief of police announced their firing during a press conference in his office at 8 a.m. this morning. The chief complained that the two officers had lied in their official report about the accident and continued to lie to their superiors during subsequent and questionings. That's why they were fired. The officers were Kevin Barlow and Wesley Zozuli. Barlow had been with the department for 3 years and Zozuli for 7. The chief said he reached his decision after receiving a report from his Internal Affairs Division, which had been in charge of the investigation. Since the accident—during the investigation—the officers have been assigned to the department's Traffic Patrol Division, directing traffic and checking parking violations. At the time of the accident, the two officers were responding to a report of a "burglary in progress, with officers in foot pursuit." They were situated about 2 miles from the scene and, upon notification that they were needed at the scene, informed the dispatcher that they were en route. All agree that they activated their lights and siren while proceeding to the scene. At the intersection of Vine Street and Twin Lakes Boulevard, their squad car collided with a second vehicle. Fortunately, no one was injured in the collision, as everyone was wearing their safety belt. However, both vehicles were totally destroyed. A state trooper initially cited the driver of the other vehicle, a Toyota Celica, with failure to yield the right of way to an emergency vehicle but, upon further investigation and complaint from the driver of that vehicle, the charge was dropped. City police officers who conducted a routine investigation into the accident subsequently decided, from skid marks and other evidence at the scene, including the comments of four eyewitnesses to the collision, that the cruiser driven by Barlow had failed to stop as it was supposed to according to police department rules for cruisers entering an intersection against a red traffic signal. It is now estimated that the cruiser was traveling 30 to 35 mph when it entered the intersection. In their initial written account of the accident, the officers said they came to a complete stop. Chief Barry Kopperud, at his press conference this morning, revealed that both offi-

cers failed polygraph tests about the accident. When questioned about the accident and about the chiefs decision after his press conference this morning, Barlow declined to comment. Zozula commented: "I don't think its right. We were trying to help another officer in need of assistance. There was no way we were going 30 mph, no way. We may not have come to a complete stop, but when another officer is chasing someone, and needs help, we try to get there as quick as possible. Everyone knows that. If we didn't, we wouldn't be good officers. We were doing our jobs, and the chief hasn't supported us like he's supposed to. That's his job. Sure, this collision was unfortunate, but that's a chance we take. Things like that happen. People would complain even more if we didn't get there fast when they needed help. Its the least we can do for another officer."

Exercise 5

THE BODY OF A NEWS STORY

REPORTING CONTROVERSIAL STORIES
(QUOTING OPPOSING VIEWPOINTS)

INSTRUCTIONS: Write complete news stories about the following controversies. As you write the stories, present both sides of each controversy as fully and as fairly as possible. Also, try to integrate those conflicting viewpoints. Instead of reporting all the opinions voiced by the first source, and then all the conflicting opinions voiced by the second source, try—when appropriate—to report both opinions about the story's most important issue, and then both opinions about the second, third and fourth issues.

Story 1: Police Response Time

FACTS: Two armed gunmen robbed the Jewelry Shoppe at 1118 Main Street at about noon yesterday. They escaped with about $1,200 in cash and with jewelry valued at about $35,000 to $40,000. The two gunmen, described as being in their mid-20s, wore business suits when they entered the store and said they wanted to look at a watch, then drew their handguns and forced the owner, Thomas Hoequist, to empty several cash registers and to open several display cases containing watches, rings, pearl earrings and necklaces, which they scooped up. "They knew what they wanted," Hoequist said. "They took only the best." Two clerks and five customers in the store at the time were made to lie face down on the floor.

ONE SIDE: Hoequist told reporters covering the robbery: "I'm very upset, very upset. The first police car didn't arrive until 10 minutes after I pushed a silent alarm button we have in the store, and its connected directly to the police station. I pushed it as soon as I saw their guns, but the men escaped before the police arrived. We've had some false alarms in the past. I've pushed the button by mistake once or twice myself, and so have the employees. Then two or three police cars would come screeching into our parking lot in a minute or two. The officers would all jump out of their cars holding shotguns and revolvers. Yesterday, the only guns I saw were the ones pointed at me."

THE OTHER SIDE: Police Chief Barry Kopperud, interviewed in his office late yesterday, said: "Our records show that 9 minutes elapsed before the first police car arrived on the scene, but all the units in that district were extremely busy on other calls. We aren't required to respond to calls within a specified length of time, and sometimes we can't. Its not uncommon for us to reach the scene of a complaint within 2 or 3 minutes, and that's what we try to do when its a real emergency. That didn't happen yesterday because there was a four-minute delay before the first patrol car was dispatched to the store because all the cars in the district were extremely busy. It took another 5 minutes for the car to get there because it was miles away in another district at the time. We had a problem because, at the same time the call was received, several patrol cars were chasing a man driving a stolen car. Another car had just arrived at Midtown Park, where a young woman who had been severely beaten had just been found. It was a long dispatch time, but there are times when we are extremely busy.

Every day, our heaviest volume of calls comes between 11 a.m. and midafternoon. It really comes down to a problem of money. Without more money, we can't put more cars on the road, but people say their taxes already are too high. It really wasn't a big factor here, but you've also got to consider that we've had 10 false alarms from this store in the last year. After a while, its like crying wolf; you just don't believe them anymore. It makes you more reluctant to move an officer from where he's really needed."

Story 2: Housing Project

FACTS: Your City Council voted last night on a proposal to locate a low-income housing project in the 4200 block of Forest Boulevard, which is part of the Creekside Village subdivision. The project would consist of 14 two-story brick buildings. Each building would house 6 to 8 families. The project would cost $6 million and would be federally subsidized. It would serve the elderly, the handicapped and low-income families. After last nights meeting, at which many people loudly and vigorously objected to the plans, the City Council vetoed the proposal by a unanimous vote of 7 to 0. The plans were presented to the City Council by the Tri-County Housing Authority, which is a semi-autonomous public body but which needs the approval of local governing boards to locate its projects within the boundaries of their jurisdictions.

ONE SIDE: The director of the City Housing Authority, Tom Chinn Onn, told the City Council before the vote: "I'm really disappointed in the opposition here tonight. We have a backlog of over 900 applicants waiting to find public housing. This would go a long way toward meeting that need. Low-income people are the ones who'll be hurt, badly hurt, if this isn't approved. Everyone seems to be saying they want to help the poor, but no one wants them in their own neighborhoods. Everyone complains when we try to place them in a nice neighborhood. And a lot of what you're hearing tonight about this project is emotional rather than factual. Its all scare tactics. Studies done by Don Brame (the city's traffic operations engineer) show that the project would add only 600 to 800 additional vehicles on the areas roads on a daily basis, and that's a very liberal estimate considering that about a third of the units would be occupied by older people who probably wouldn't drive much. The elderly also wouldn't need other city facilities, like schools. Now, we've already spent more than $160,000 planning this project, and all the money will be wasted, just totally wasted, if you reject this proposal, and we've got nowhere else to go with it. Everyone says they want to help the poor, but they want to help them somewhere else. That's real hypocrisy. This is a chance for the members of this council to be real statesmen and do some real good for some needy people. This means a lot to them, so I ask you to approve these plans."

THE OTHER SIDE: Residents of the neighborhood voiced the following complaints during the council meeting. Frank D. Shadgett of 8472 Chestnut Drive said, "This thing would cause all sorts of problems: crowded roads, crowded schools, more kids in the streets. We don't have enough parks, and there's only one junior high school and one high school that serve our neighborhood, and both have been filled for years. Now, if you dump this project on us, you'll have to bus some of our children out of their neighborhood schools, or you'll have to bring in some portable classrooms. There are other places that could handle the project better. It just doesn't fit in our neighborhood. You should come out and look at the area before coming up with an idea like this. A lot of our homes cost $100,000 or $150,000 or more. You put this project in the middle of them, and it'll hurt our property values." Another person, James Lasater of 374 Walnut Drive, said: "The area is zoned for single-family homes, and that's why we invested here. We've got our life savings in our homes, and this will hurt us. We've got no lack of compassion for the cause, but it just doesn't belong here. We want to protect our neighborhood and keep our neighborhood the way it is. We object to this bunch of bureaucrats coming in and changing its character. Its a good area to live in, and we don't want that to change." An attorney representing the neighborhood, Michael Perakis, said: "The area is one of the most stable and beautiful single-family neighborhoods in the city, and these people are only interested in maintaining that status. Right now, you're in danger of violating your own laws if you put this project in Creekside Village. There's been no proper hearings to rezone the land, and this project doesn't fit its current zoning restrictions. The zoning laws are intended to prevent this very kind of thing, this invasion of a residential neighborhood with a nonconforming project of any type."

Story 3: School Attendance Incentive Program

FACTS: Greg Hubbard, superintendent of schools in your city, has adopted a unique but controversial pilot program. Last year, the citys school district lost $1,132,000 in state funds because it had an overall 6.4 percent absenteeism rate, compared to a statewide average of 5.3%. To try to solve the problem, Hubbard persuaded the members of the school board to set up a $25,000 fund to pay students at Roosevelt High School the equivalent of 25 cents a day—a maximum of $5 a month. Last fall, students in the school began getting a coupon worth 25 cents for every day of attendance. Students can exchange their tokens in the schools student bookstore for school supplies such as notebooks and pencils. Since then, the absentee rate at the 1,410-student school has averaged about 13.7%, compared to 15.2% for the same period last year, when it had the worst attendance in the city.

ONE SIDE: In an interview in his office today, Supt. Hubbard said: "We're trying this program out in one high school where our worst truancy problems exist. Then if it works, we may expand it to other schools. Under this program, a student can earn the equivalent of $5 a month just for being there—for attending school and compiling a perfect attendance record. They are credited with the equivalent of 25 cents for every day they make it to school and to all their classes on time. They don't actually get any cash. They get coupons they can use in the school store. We mark up the prices of goods sold in the store about 50%, so it really costs us a lot less than the students receive. So far as I know, the idea has been tried in only two or three other school districts, including one in San Diego, and I just thought we might try it here. We've really got nothing to lose. Some students just don't see any other reason to attend school. My responsibility is to give teachers an opportunity to teach the students, and getting them to attend class is a necessary first step. We already can see the results. Attendance is up, and inquiries have been pouring in from other school districts from all over the state and from news organizations as far away as England and Japan. There's a tremendous curiosity about it. It sort of shocks some parents to pay children to go to school, but nothing else has worked. If this works, it could save us thousands of dollars a year in lost state aid, and certainly the students are better off being in school."

THE OTHER SIDE: Stephen I. Wong is chairman of the citys School Advisory Committee, which is composed of one parent representative from each school in the city. Wong is opposed to the program. Today he said: "The program gambles with taxpayers money. The 25 cents they give student's comes out of our tax money. If attendance improves by 25 percent or more over a full year, we'll recover the money in increased state aid. But if the attendance figure remains low, we'll lose money. So we're gambling, and that just doesnt seem right. Its also materialistic and amounts to bribery. We shouldn't have to pay our children to do something as basic as going to school because then they expect to get paid for everything. Already, we've got some students in that high school complaining they aren't being paid enough, and students in other schools are demanding that they get paid, too. These kids are winding up with some very unrealistic ideas about how the world works and about what education is all about. Besides, the whole thing is cosmetic. It doesn't solve our real problems. The long-term remedies for truancy lie in more fundamental changes. I'll admit attendance is up so far this year, but not very much, and we don't know the real reason. It could be the money, or it could be something totally different. You also have to recognize that, once these students get to high school, they don't have to do well. They can flunk all their classes and still get paid. Some of these students also could be disruptive, so it may be better for other students if they don't come to school. Its a hell of a mess."

Story 4: Banning Handguns

FACTS: In a close vote at a City Council meeting in your community last night, the council members voted 4 to 3 to ban the sale and possession of handguns, except by law enforcement officers and by those persons holding a permit issued by the chief of police. The law goes into effect on Jan. 1 of next year, and those persons now possessing handguns will, according to the law, have to dispose of them by that time. First-time offenders of the law will face a fine of $50 to $500. A second offense carries maximum penalties of up to six months in jail or a fine of up to $500, or both.

ONE SIDE: Councilman Luis Ramirez, who spoke and voted in favor of the law, said during last night's meeting: "There's no question, the law is valid and doesn't infringe on an individuals constitutional rights. We recognize the deep-seated convictions of a number of persons that they should be permitted to possess handguns for the purpose of protecting themselves and their families and property. But in this case the public interest outweighs the claim of personal interests. We're adopting this law for the overall good of the entire city, to help protect all its citizens from the careless and lawless use of handguns. I'm sure that hundreds of other cities are going to follow our example and consider similar measures. If they do, a lot of lives could be saved. There's no sense to the current slaughter. People can't use handguns to hunt with. Their only purpose is to shoot people. They're used mostly by criminals and, in this city alone, we have 8 or 10 people killed by guns every year and many more seriously injured. There also are hundreds and hundreds of robberies committed with handguns. This law will help put a stop to that. If people want to hunt, they can still buy a rifle or shotgun, and they can use a rifle or shotgun to protect themselves in their homes if they want. But its harder for a criminal to conceal a weapon that large when he goes into a grocery store or restaurant with the intention of robbing it."

THE OTHER SIDE: Margaret Ungarient, an attorney representing the citizens opposed to the ban, said at the meeting: "We plan to appeal. The law infringes on citizens constitutional right to keep and bear arms. Its also a matter of self-defense. Criminals do use some handguns in committing crimes. But that doesn't mean the solution is to take away everyones gun. Law-abiding citizens would comply with this law, but criminals never would. So the criminals would be the only ones with guns, and everyone else would be at their mercy. The council has, in effect, ruled in favor of a minority element that has for a long time been trying to deny the rights of other individuals. We won't rest until this gets reversed in a court of law. If we have to, we'll take this all the way to the Supreme Court."

CHAPTER 8

QUOTATIONS AND ATTRIBUTION

Reporters obtain much of their information by listening to other people, and they can convey that information to readers in the form of (1) direct, (2) indirect or (3) partial quotations. Direct quotations present a source's exact words and consequently are placed entirely in quotation marks. Indirect quotations do not use a source's exact words and consequently are not placed inside quotation marks; instead, reporters use their own words to summarize, or paraphrase, the source's remarks. Partial quotations use key phrases from a source's statement and quote them directly.

> INDIRECT QUOTATION: Mrs. Ambrose said journalism students should deal with ideas, not mechanical techniques.

> PARTIAL QUOTATION: Mrs. Ambrose criticized the "trade school atmosphere" in journalism schools and said students should study ideas, not mechanical techniques.

> DIRECT QUOTATION: Mrs. Ambrose said: "Journalism students should be dealing with ideas of a social, economic and political nature. There's too much of a trade school atmosphere in journalism schools today. One spends too much time on minor technical and mechanical things, like learning how to write headlines."

WHEN TO USE DIRECT, INDIRECT AND PARTIAL QUOTATIONS

Reporters use direct quotations when their sources say something important or controversial and state their ideas in an interesting, unusual or colorful manner. To be quoted directly, sources must also state their ideas so effectively that their wording cannot be improved. For example, many Americans were amused by one of George Bush's first statements after he became president, and many of the nation's news media quoted the statement. Bush said:

> I do not like broccoli. I haven't liked it since I was a little kid and my mother made me eat it. And I'm president of the United States, and I'm not going to eat any more broccoli.

If you listen carefully, you will find that other sources, including people less prominent than George Bush, also provide quotations that will fascinate your readers. When you hear one of those statements, record its exact wording, then quote it in your story. Here are four examples:

> Atkin said she got into her parked car and drove about a block, then realized that someone was in the back seat.

"I heard a noise and saw a shadow in the rear-view mirror," she said. "I screamed hysterically and pulled off the road. I tried to get out, but he held onto me, wouldn't let me go. He was saying something, but I wasn't listening. I was trying to escape."

Before dismissing the case, Judge Ostreicher turned to Griffin and said, "You have a serious drinking problem, and three things can happen: you can spend your life in a state prison, be put in a mental institution or die young."

"One of my roommates had to have an abortion," Katie said. "She went through hell—all bummed out and depressed. As her best friend, I really felt badly, too."

Kim, a junior majoring in nursing, said: "It's my job to care for the sick. I may have to take care of an AIDS patient someday, and it scares the hell out of me. I'm not satisfied with what's known about AIDS, about how AIDS is transmitted. I'm afraid of bringing it home to my family—my children."

Direct quotations bring sources to life, clearly reporting their opinions in their exact words, with all the original flavor, emotions, color and drama. Quotations also help reveal the sources' character and give readers a sense of rapport—a sense that they have talked directly with the sources. The following quotations also help reveal the sources' humor:

Mark Twain said: "Always do right. This will gratify some people and astonish the rest."

Will Rogers said, "What the country needs is dirtier fingernails and a cleaner mind."

Direct quotations do not have to be long. Four words spoken by President Richard M. Nixon during the Watergate scandals fascinated the American public not only because of what the president said but also because of the fact he felt a need to say it: "I'm not a crook."

Reporters use indirect quotations when their sources have not stated their ideas effectively. By using indirect quotations, reporters can rephrase their sources' remarks, stating them more clearly and concisely. Reporters can also emphasize the sources' most significant remarks and reword or eliminate remarks that are unclear, irrelevant, libelous, pretentious or otherwise unprintable:

ORIGINAL STATEMENT: He said, "I fully intend to resign from my position as mayor of this city."
PARAPHRASED: The mayor said he plans to resign.

ORIGINAL STATEMENT: "The president's plan has put confusion into the nation's farmers," she said.
PARAPHRASED: The president's plan confuses farmers, she said.

ORIGINAL STATEMENT: Mrs. Czarski said, "Women do not get the same tax and insurance benefits that men receive, and they do not receive maternity benefits that even start to cover what they should."
PARAPHRASED: Mrs. Czarski said women do not receive the same tax and insurance benefits as men, nor adequate maternity benefits.

Reporters generally avoid partial, or fragmentary, quotations. Most partial quotations are awkward, wordy or unnecessary. Sentences that contain several partial quotations are particularly distracting. The phrases should be paraphrased or used in indirect constructions, with the quotation marks simply eliminated:

> FRAGMENT: Andrews said he expects to finish the job "sometime within the next month."
> REVISED: Andrews said he expects to finish the job next month.

> FRAGMENT: He said the press barons "such as William Randolph Hearst" created "an amazingly rich variety" of newspapers.
> REVISED: He said the press barons such as William Randolph Hearst created an amazingly rich variety of newspapers.

Reporters also avoid using "orphan" quotes—placing quotation marks around an isolated word or two used in an ordinary way. The addition of quotation marks to emphasize individual words is inappropriate. Similarly, there is no reason to place quotation marks around profanities, slang, clichés or grammatical errors:

> He complained that no one "understands" his problem.
> REVISED: He complained that no one understands his problem.

> She said that having to watch her child die was worse than "hell" could possibly be.
> REVISED: She said that having to watch her child die was worse than hell could possibly be.

Reporters use partial quotations only for statements that are particularly controversial, important or interesting. The use of partial quotations also helps attribute the statements more clearly to their sources:

> He called the welfare recipients "lazy, no-good bums."

> Hendricks said he killed the girls "because they laughed at me."

> Phil Donahue accused the television critic of "typing with razor blades."

> The petition urged the City Council to ban the sale of Penthouse and Playboy magazines "for the sake of our wives and children."

USING DIRECT QUOTATIONS EFFECTIVELY

Direct quotations should be used to illustrate a point, not to tell an entire story. Stories composed entirely of quotations become too tiresome and often seem poorly organized because they lack natural transitions. The following two stories contain a pleasing combination of quotations and paraphrases:

> Zukowski said he did not see the car because he had opened his van's glove compartment and was looking for a cigarette.
> "It was a dumb move, yeah," he said. "But just because I drove into a parked car doesn't mean I was drunk."
> Zukowski challenged the accuracy of a breathalizer test administered by the police. "Those things aren't reliable," he said. "I've heard of people taking mouthwash and then being recorded as drunk."
> Witnesses said he had consumed six to eight beers, but Zukowski said he had "only a few, maybe three at the most."

She started dancing six months ago after a friend told her about the job. Debbie (who does not want her last name used) said: "I knew my friend was dancing topless, but I didn't think I could ever do it. At the time, though, I was desperate to find a job, so I agreed to try it."

Debbie said she felt guilty the first time she appeared topless in front of other people but "after the first time, it seemed there was nothing to hide anymore."

Now, after dancing topless for half a year, Debbie says: "I really enjoy it because there is no actual work involved. I love to dance anyway and I can pick my own hours around my class schedule and, with tips, earn $1,400 a week."

Few of Debbie's classmates know about her job. She explains, "It's not that I'm ashamed of what I do. It just makes it easier for me to know that no one in the audience will be sitting beside me in a class the next morning. I know the general public thinks that what I do is pretty low, and I don't want other students to say, 'There goes that topless dancer.' "

Be careful to use quotations only when they provide some additional information about a topic. Reporters often summarize a major point, then use a direct quotation to explain the idea or to provide more specific details about it:

Medically, he was dead for three or four minutes. "His pupils were fixed and dilated. There was no pulse, no respiration and he had turned blue," Dr. Holman said.

Karcher's girlfriend was instructing a class of lifeguards and asked him to help administer their final test. Karcher said: "My job was to go out in the lake and act like I was drowning. I was to bite, scratch, tear—anything to try to keep them from rescuing me."

A quotation should not repeat facts reported earlier in a story, as in these examples:

Company officials said they are not worried about the upcoming audit. "We're not expecting anything to worry about," treasurer Peter VanNeffe said.

A 6-foot-10-inch guard who graduated from Kennedy High School, he will likely be a starting guard on the college's varsity basketball team next fall. "He is an outstanding player and a strong candidate to start at the point guard position," Coach Lopez said.

Quotations can also help describe a story's dramatic moments. Because of their importance, those moments should be described in detail, and that description should be placed near the beginning of a story. The following quotations are so interesting and dramatic that they would compel most readers to finish the entire story:

As the grease and flames spread, she panicked and poured water on them. "That just made the flames go higher," she cried. "I knew the whole house was going to burn down, so I picked up my baby and ran outside."

"After the accident I must have passed out for a minute," she said. "Then I woke up and realized the car was on fire. I thought I was going to die. I wasn't badly hurt, but I couldn't get out. I couldn't move."

"I was confused," the girl said. "I woke up at about 2 a.m. and saw this strange man standing near my bed. I didn't know why he was there, and at first I thought my parents had visitors or something. Then I realized he was a prowler."

Quotations help to reveal the personalities of people mentioned in news stories, showing them to be unique, interesting individuals. A story about a middle-aged woman who returned to college included this revealing quotation:

"Very practically, I came back to college to get my degree in education because I wanted to be busy and couldn't quite see myself as a 40-year-old checkout clerk in some supermarket. Fifteen years of my life consisted of runny noses and coffee klatches with the neighbors. Now my kids wipe their own noses and the neighbors are still having their coffee klatches, and I'm going to be a senior next term."

Using Exact Words and Ellipses

Some reporters (the "pragmatists") insist that their only responsibility is to convey a source's thought and meaning—not the source's exact words. The pragmatists explain that people rarely speak with precision in clean, complete sentences. Rather, they pause, stutter and repeat themselves. To eliminate the errors (and anything else they dislike) the pragmatists will "improve" a statement's wording. The pragmatists will also correct obvious factual errors. They call it "doctoring," "massaging" or "cleaning up" a quote. The pragmatists explain that reporters should use their common sense and correct obvious slips of the tongue: quotations that would make a source look foolish or would make their readers' job more difficult.

The pragmatists are most likely to clean up quotations from people unaccustomed to dealing with the press. Even the pragmatists, however, may quote the clumsy statements of sources who could be expected to do better, such as the president and other prominent sources whose language seems careless or inappropriate for their position or for the issue they are discussing.

Other reporters (the "purists") insist that quotation marks are sacrosanct—that every word placed inside quotation marks should be a source's exact words. They fear that if they alter a quotation, they may be accused of fictionalizing or lying to their readers. The purists add that the practice of doctoring quotations destroys their richness and originality and may make sources sound more eloquent than they really are. Moreover, the purists fear that readers do not understand the practice, and that the changes made in quotations make it easier for sources to claim that they were misquoted.

To avoid these problems, use your source's exact words. Most editors will insist that you do so. If you are uncertain about the source's exact words (or think a statement needs rewriting), use an indirect rather than a direct quotation. If you try to doctor a quotation and make a mistake, you may seriously injure your source's reputation as well as your own.

There are only a few exceptions to the principle of using a person's exact words in direct quotations. Those exceptions usually involve the deletion of unnecessary words, grammatical errors and profanities. Even the purists delete unnecessary words, provided that their deletion does not change the meaning of what has been said:

ORIGINAL STATEMENT: He said, "Look, you know I think nuclear power is safe, absolutely safe."
QUOTATION: He said, "Nuclear power is safe, absolutely safe."

ORIGINAL STATEMENT: Dr. Tausche said, "Uh, all the problems will be solved, you know, and, uh, solved effectively, when the new hospital is completed."

QUOTATION: Dr. Tausche said, "All the problems will be solved, and solved effectively, when the new hospital is completed."

If they delete a significant number of words (entire phrases or sentences), reporters may add an ellipsis (three periods). An ellipsis that appears at the end rather than in the middle of a sentence uses four periods when the phrase preceding the ellipsis is a complete sentence. However, policies vary from newspaper to newspaper, and some journalists—as in the previous examples—do not use ellipses in reporting ordinary interviews. However, they may use them in quoting from longer and more formal statements.

Correcting Grammatical Errors

Normally, reporters correct the grammatical errors in direct quotations. An editor at The New York Times has explained that: "Cultured people are not expected to maintain in conversation the rigid grammatical standards normally applied to writing, so we delete their false starts and grammatical lapses. Failing to do so would make those we quote seem illiterate by subjecting their spoken language to the standards of writing." Similarly, The Associated Press Stylebook explains, "Quotations should be corrected to avoid the errors in grammar and word usage that often occur unnoticed in speech, but are embarrassing in print." For example:

GRAMMATICAL ERROR: The woman said, "The fire kept spreading, and my husband and me couldn't put it out."

REVISED: The woman said, "The fire kept spreading, and my husband and I couldn't put it out."

GRAMMATICAL ERROR: An usher said, "The people started pouring in, and there weren't no way to stop them."

REVISED: An usher said, "The people started pouring in, and there wasn't any [or was no] way to stop them."

Deleting Profanities

Reporters also delete most profanities. Editors explain that newspapers are family publications that go into their readers' homes and are seen by a variety of people. Some children read daily newspapers, but even some adults are likely to be offended by the publication of four-letter words. Newspapers are becoming more candid, and many now publish mild profanities that are essential to a story. However, most forbid the publication of casual profanities—those used habitually and unnecessarily by many people:

PROFANITY: The youth told police, "Hell, that man tried to cheat me."
REVISED: The youth told police, "That man tried to cheat me."

PROFANITY: "Shit, I wasn't going to try to stop that damned idiot," the witness testified. "He had a knife."
REVISED: "I wasn't going to try to stop that idiot," the witness testified. "He had a knife."

Using Dialogue

With practice, writers can begin to use dialogue to let the characters in their stories reveal more information about themselves and about their most newsworthy experiences. For example: after a major airline crash, federal investigators usually release a transcript of the crew's final conversation. Reporters may publish the transcript as a separate story, or they may quote the crew members in a conventional news story. Because a storm dumped a heavy coating of snow onto the plane's fuselage and wings, Air Florida's Flight 90 crashed into the Potomac River during takeoff. As the plane began speeding down a runway at Washington's National Airport, co-pilot Roger Pettit noticed that they did not seem to have enough power. A story about that moment quoted the conversation between Pettit and Capt. Larry Wheaton:

> "God, look at that thing," Pettit said, apparently referring to a needle gauge that displayed the power being developed by the engines. "That don't seem right, does it?"
> "Yes it is," Wheaton said.
> "Naw, I don't think that's right," Pettit said. "Maybe it is, I don't know."
> The plane rose into the air 1,900 feet farther down the runway and 15 seconds later than normal. Moments later, it began to shudder, lose speed and fall.
> "Larry, we're going down, Larry," Pettit said.
> "I know it," Wheaton replied.

This story, transmitted by The Associated Press, also relies heavily—and effectively—on dialogue:

> CAMDEN, N.J.—A 26-year-old woman pleaded guilty Tuesday to murdering her four children, describing how she placed them into a rain-swollen, polluted river.
> . . . Though Wright did not explain her motive, she described for the first time how the drownings occurred as she sat Nov. 10 with her children along a railroad track beside the Cooper River.
> "It was about 11:30 or 12 o'clock at night. I was sitting on a wooden plank. I sat there for quite a few hours trying to think. I did away with them," she said.
> "How?" Superior Court Judge Rudolph J. Rossetti asked.
> "By them drowning," she said.
> "Did you throw them into the river?" the judge asked.
> "I laid them," she answered. "I was sitting at the edge of the river, and put them in one at a time."
> Wright said her children—aged 11 months to 7 years—had fallen asleep near the river and were still asleep when she put them in the water. . . .

Stressing Answers, Not Questions

When reporters quote someone, they normally stress their source's answers, not the questions the source was asked. The use of both the questions and the answers is usually unnecessary, repetitive and dull. Reporters can either omit the questions or incorporate them into the answers:

> He then asked her, "What's your name?" She said, "Mary Delaveux."
> REVISED: She said her name is Mary Delaveux.

The president was asked whether he plans to seek a second term, and he responded that he will not announce his decision until next winter.

REVISED: The president said he will not announce his decision regarding a second term until next winter.

OR: In response to a question, the president said he will not announce his decision regarding a second term until next winter.

OR: During a question-and-answer session after his speech, the president said he will not announce his decision regarding a second term until next winter.

Explaining Quotations

Harry Levins, writing coach for the St. Louis Post-Dispatch, has complained about another problem: the fact that some reporters present a quotation and then provide the information that readers need to understand the quotation. In a sense, Levins says, those reporters put the punchline before the joke. Here's an example:

"It's a good group for people who are going through a divorce," Immer said of the group for divorced Catholics.

Levins notes that:

Only when the reader has slogged through the quote and gotten into the attribution does he understand exactly what group Immer is talking about. One tipoff to this backward construction is the words *said of*. They're usually a sign that the writer started writing without thinking the sentence through. Having chosen to start the sentence with a quote, the writer falls back on the *said of* construction. And at that point, the reader gets stuck with the mess that results.

To avoid the problem, Levins suggests turning the sentence around and using a partial quotation:

Immer called the organization for divorced Catholics "a good group for people who are going through a divorce."

Now, says Levins, readers know what Immer is talking about as he talks about it.

Thus, if a quotation requires some explanation, place that explanation before, not after, the quotation so that your readers will immediately understand what is being said. Here are two more examples of the problem:

"Without them, we might have been hit by another vehicle," she said. "Everyone should carry a half dozen in their car." She was referring to flares.

REVISED: She said everyone should carry a half dozen flares in their car. "Without them, we might have been hit by another vehicle," she said.

"Many of our neighbors have had accidents because of it, and my son almost was killed when a truck hit his bike," said one homeowner complaining that State Route 15A is too narrow.

REVISED: A homeowner complaining that State Route 15A is too narrow said, "Many of our neighbors have had accidents because of it, and my son almost was killed when a truck hit his bike."

If the information needed to clarify a quotation is brief, it can be inserted in parentheses:

> An attorney said, "He (Mayor Wilson) is almost certain to be indicted by the grand jury."

> Dr. Harold Termid, who performed the operation, said, "The technique dates back before the 20th century, when it was first used by the French to study ruminants (cud-chewing animals)."

> "He's working on (recuperating from) his third heart attack," the doctor said. "Usually people on their third heart attack have a better chance of survival than they had on their first, so his chances are good."

Reporters use such parenthetical matter sparingly, however. If reporters peppered their stories with parenthetical explanations, the stories would become more difficult to read. Each bit of parenthetical matter is an obstacle that forces readers to pause and absorb some additional information. Most stories will become more readable if reporters rewrite the sentences:

> "They (members of the school board) have strong objections to the plan," he said.
> REVISED: He said school board members "have strong objections to the plan."

> She said, "They (police) are the last line between us and chaos."
> REVISED: She said the police "are the last line between us and chaos."

Avoiding Weak Quotations

In an effort to brighten their stories, some reporters use whatever quotations happen to be available. Yet a weak quotation is worse than none. If a quotation bores or confuses people, many will immediately stop reading a story. The following quotations, for example, are too dull and vague to use in a news story:

> "We're currently in the process of change and transition here," she said.

> "We hired her because we heard a lot of good things about her," he said.

Reporters can never justify a weak quotation by responding, "But that's what my source said." The quotations used in a story reflect the reporter's judgment and interviewing techniques. Thus, use only strong quotations—quotations that are clear, concise, dramatic and interesting.

Sometimes a source will give you only routine, boring quotations such as, "I really love to play football." Continue your interview, asking better questions, until you get a better response. Here's the type of quotation you want:

> "I really love football," Joe Lozado said. "I've been playing since I was 7 years old, and I would feel worthless if I couldn't play. There's no better feeling than just before a game when you run out on the field with all your buddies and see the crowd. You can feel the excitement."

Avoid quotations that state the obvious: something your readers already know. The following quotations are likely to sound familiar, because they appear dozens of times every year. You may see these quotations in newspapers or hear them on radio and television:

> "We really want to win this game," Coach Riley said. (Readers already know this. Does any coach want to lose?)

> "We want to win so bad we can taste it," Joe Taskin said. (Readers already know this too. Additionally, it is a cliché. Avoid clichés, even in direct quotations.)

> "If we can score some points, we can win this game," Tran Ogbondah said. (Another boring and uninformative quotation.)

Finally, avoid quotations that are vague and self-serving—quotations that enable sources to praise themselves and their programs.

> Lyons called her program a success. "We had a terrific crowd and a particularly good turnout," she said.

> The director of the school's library said she is "very excited and confident about the library's direction."

THE NEED FOR ATTRIBUTION

Identifying Your Sources

Reporters are expected to identify their sources as fully as possible. Normally, reporters provide a source's name, occupation or position and other identification relevant to a story. Some reporters, especially those in Washington, attribute their stories to anonymous sources—to "government employees," "congressional aides," "reliable sources in the State Department" and "high government officials." Asked to justify that practice, reporters might respond: "If we identified all our sources, some would be embarrassed by the publication of their statements, and some would lose their jobs. But if we protect their anonymity, the sources will speak more freely and give us more information. So by protecting our sources, we obtain more information and can do a better job of informing the public."

Two reporters for The Pittsburgh Press relied on anonymous sources to uncover a major story about airline safety. The reporters, Andy Schneider and Matt Brelis, found that pilots who abused drugs and alcohol continued to fly commercial jets.

Pittsburgh is the hub for USAir, the nation's sixth busiest airline, and more than 7,000 of the airline's employees live in the area. Schneider and Brelis interviewed doctors and nurses at six hospitals and found that their emergency room staffs recalled 20 cases "of flight crew substance abuse" involving cocaine, heroin, Valium and alcohol. Yet, because of patients' right to confidentiality, the doctors and nurses were unable to notify the airline and keep the crew members from returning to their jets.

One of Schneider's stories began:

> Doctors and nurses at six Pittsburgh area hospitals say they have treated members of USAir flight crews for cocaine overdoses but are forbidden by law from reporting the potential safety hazards to officials who would prevent the personnel from flying.

> The most recent incident occurred shortly before midnight on Sept 10, when Rubin Lavine, a 30-year-old USAir pilot, blue-faced and near death from a

cocaine overdose, was brought by friends to the parking lot of Mercy Hospital. "He wasn't breathing and was far more dead than alive," said a doctor.*

The stories attracted national attention and led to major reforms by the Federal Aviation Administration.

Generally, editors are becoming more critical of anonymous sources, including those who "leak" information to the press. Leaks occur when someone who wants to remain anonymous reveals some confidential information. Some leaks are unsolicited and provide important stories. Reporters dig for other leaks, but officials can misuse them. The officials can leak information that will help their own careers and policies—or harm their rivals'.

Some sources provide anonymous information to launch "trial balloons." They may announce a plan anonymously, then watch the public's response. If the response is favorable, the officials will publicly endorse the plan and take the credit for its success. If the response is unfavorable, the officials will abandon or even publicly denounce the plan. No one (except reporters) will know that the officials are denouncing their own plan. Reporters are helpless because they cannot identify their source. Thus, reporters cannot hold the officials accountable for their statements: not if the officials are wrong, and not even if they lie.

Because the practice is so easy to exploit, reporters are becoming more reluctant to quote anonymous sources unless the information they provide is obviously factual and important. Critics believe that if reporters placed more pressure on their sources by threatening to ignore all the information provided by anonymous sources, more sources would agree to the publication of their names. If some still refused, reporters might seek the same information from other sources who *were* willing to be identified.

George Blake, editor of The (Cincinnati) Enquirer, discourages the use of anonymous sources and does not allow his staff to quote them on the Enquirer's front pages without his approval. Because of that policy, the Enquirer missed several big stories: reports that baseball player Pete Rose was being investigated on charges that he bet regularly and heavily on the game. Most of the revelations came from people unwilling to be identified: bookmakers, cocaine traffickers and FBI agents. Other newspapers in the state reported all the details, and Blake criticized them, saying they were "needlessly rushing things into print" and "throwing credibility to the wind."

Other editors agree that the use of anonymous sources threatens the media's credibility. If reporters fail to identify their sources, readers may wonder whether the sources really exist. Readers may also wonder whether the "informed sources" mentioned by reporters are truly informed, and whether the information they provide is accurate, important and objective. A bulletin published for employees of The Miami Herald commented:

> Why do we so often use the phrase "who refused to be identified"? Because of lazy and sloppy reporting, that's why.
>
> There are exceptions, sure. But it is a bad habit. Every time we print the phrase, we suggest to others that they, too, can use it. It is for weasels. We hurt our own credibility, not someone else's.
>
> When a reporter grants a source anonymity in type, he is asking for trouble. To the source, anonymity can be an invitation to embroider, embellish, take the cheap shot.
>
> Most of the time it is not necessary. An astute reporter should be able to persuade the source to say what he thinks up-front. If not, go elsewhere.

---

*We have substituted a pseudonym for the pilot's name, for two reasons: the story is no longer new, and the pilot may since have sought help, completed a rehabilitation program and returned to work.

Similarly, Benjamin Bradlee called the continued abuse of unattributed information "a professional disgrace." Bradlee, former executive editor of The Washington Post, added: "Why, then, do we go along so complacently with withholding the identity of public officials? I'm damned if I know. I do know that by doing so, we shamelessly do other people's bidding; we knowingly let ourselves be used. . . . In short, we demean our profession."

On the rare occasions when there is some justification for the use of anonymous sources, the editors at several major dailies have instructed their staffs to follow these guidelines:

- Consult an editor and give your source's name to the editor. The editor will determine whether the information provided by your source is important to your newspaper's readers, and whether you could obtain the same information from a source willing to be identified.
- Identify sources as specifically as possible without revealing their identities so that readers can judge their importance and reliability. For example, instead of attributing information to "an informed source" or "a key official," you might attribute it to "an elected city official."
- Explain in your story why the source does not want to be identified.
- Try to corroborate the information with at least one other source.

It is also a good rule never to allow a source to engage in anonymous attacks on other individuals or groups. A bulletin published for reporters and editors at The New York Times explains:

People who have nice things to say about someone will usually not mind being named in a story, but those who attack someone often request anonymity. It is the anonymous detractors that we—as editors as well as reporters—must, as a matter of fairness, keep out of stories whenever possible. It may not be possible when the attack is crucial to the story. But in all other instances, we should strive to identify the attacker at least by his position or his relationship to the attacked person. If we cannot do that, the attack should not be reported.

Statements That Require Attribution

Reporters do not have to attribute statements that report undisputed facts, such as the fact that World War II ended in 1945, that Boston is in Massachusetts or that three people died in an accident. Attribution is also unnecessary in stories that reporters witness. However, reporters must attribute the information given to them by other people, especially: (1) statements about controversial issues, (2) statements of opinion and (3) all direct and indirect quotations. If reporters fail to attribute such statements, they will seem to be presenting their personal opinions rather than the opinions of their sources. Two or three words of attribution are usually adequate:

Insurance companies cannot lower their rates because they are not making enough money.
ATTRIBUTED: Vail-Summerville said insurance companies cannot lower their rates because they are not making enough money.

The Birthing Center is an alternative for pregnant women who prefer more personalized care.

ATTRIBUTED: Director Sally Malone said the Birthing Center is an alternative for pregnant women who prefer more personalized care.

Attribute statements that criticize a person or organization. Again, clearly indicate that you are reporting what someone else said, not expressing your own or your newspaper's opinion:

Congress has failed to deal effectively with the problem of unemployment.
ATTRIBUTED: The Republicans said Congress has failed to deal effectively with the problem of unemployment.

He is cocky, aggressive and hot-tempered, but most of all, he is unpredictable.
ATTRIBUTED: The coach said he is cocky, aggressive and hot-tempered, but most of all, he is unpredictable.

Attribute statements that assign blame. For example:

The girl rode her bike directly into the car's path.

Acting in self-defense, the deputy shot the teen three times in the chest.

The workers were fooling around while they were loading the hay.
Suddenly Frey's jacket sleeve became tangled in the machinery, and his hand was crushed.

Who said the girl rode her bike into the car's path, implying that she was responsible for the accident? By failing to attribute the statement, the reporter seems to be expressing his or her own opinion. Similarly, was it the deputy who said he or she shot the teen three times in self-defense? If so, attribute his or her version of the incident. The statement would be even more credible, however, if you could attribute it to someone not involved in the shooting: to several witnesses, the coroner or a police review board. Attribution is particularly important in the third example because the statement implies that the workers were careless. Most editors would delete the phrase "fooling around."

Attribution helps readers determine the credibility of statements reported by news media. Readers may accept the statements made by some sources but distrust others. For example, although each of the following statements reports the same basic allegation, American readers would be least likely to believe the second statement and most likely to believe the third:

The U.S. government is ignoring millions of hungry and jobless citizens.

The Chinese newspaper People's Daily charged Tuesday that the U.S. government is ignoring millions of hungry and jobless citizens.

During a congressional hearing, former President Jimmy Carter testified Tuesday that the U.S. government is ignoring millions of hungry and jobless citizens.

Three Recent Failures of Attribution

The need for journalists to be wary of unattributed statements and anonymous sources has been demonstrated in dozens of cases. You are likely to remember the following episodes and to wonder why journalists failed so badly.

FAILURE I: *The Attica Prison Revolt.* In 1971, inmates at Attica Prison in New York rioted and took a number of hostages. After crushing the revolt by storming the prison, state troopers and corrections officers found 10 hostages and 29 inmates dead. Prison officials explained that the inmates had slashed several of the hostages' throats and beaten and stabbed others to death. At first, reporters accepted and reported the officials' version of everything that occurred that day.

A later investigation revealed that the inmates had seriously wounded only two hostages and that no hostage's throat had been cut. It was the state troopers and corrections officers who had killed the 10 hostages and 29 inmates.

FAILURE II: *The USS Iowa Explosion.* In 1989, an anonymous source in the Navy slandered a hero. That April, a gun turret on the battleship USS Iowa exploded, killing 47 sailors. A month later, an anonymous source (apparently a Navy investigator) leaked to the media the information that the Navy was investigating two young sailors: Gunner's Mate Clayton Hartwig, 24, and Gunner's Mate Kendall Truitt, 21.

Hartwig died in the explosion. Witnesses said that Truitt had acted heroically, climbing through the smoke, debris and bodies to reach switches that flooded the burning turret with water. Because of Truitt's heroism, the fire never reached another 2,000 pounds of gunpowder, which would have been enough to destroy the ship.

The anonymous source told journalists that the two young men may have had a homosexual relationship. Either Truitt may have blown up the turret to kill Hartwig and collect on a $100,000 insurance policy (Hartwig had named Truitt the sole beneficiary), or Hartwig may have blown it up to kill himself because Truitt had rejected him and gotten married.

After a four-month investigation, the Navy officially announced that the disaster had probably resulted from sabotage perpetrated by Hartwig. Since he was dead, Hartwig was unable to defend himself. Truitt was never charged with a crime. Yet both men were tried in the media, and their reputations were destroyed.

Truitt's attorney charged that the Navy was trying to hide its own negligence in storing the gunpowder on barges under a hot Virginia sun. Some journalists speculated that the Navy was also trying to protect its battleships from being declared too old and unsafe for continued use.

Two years later, the Navy apologized, publicly stating that both Truitt and Hartwig were innocent. A segment on "60 Minutes" charged that the Navy had always known that the men were innocent and had engaged in a coverup to hide its own negligence. Now Truitt is suing several media outlets for libel.

FAILURE III: *The Murder of Carol Stuart.* Also in 1989, a young couple, Charles and Carol Stuart, attended a childbirth class at a Boston hospital. The couple had been married for four years, and Mrs. Stuart was pregnant with her first child.

Shortly after the couple left the hospital, Charles Stuart, 30, used a car phone to call the police. Stuart told the police that a mugger had just shot his wife and critically wounded him in the abdomen. Stuart remained on the phone for 13 minutes, apparently trying to fight off unconsciousness and driving aimlessly, looking for help. He could not identify street signs, he said. A police dispatcher instructed officers in the area to turn on their cars' sirens. By listening to them, Stuart was able to direct the officers to his car.

Before Carol Stuart died, doctors delivered the baby by Caesarean section. The baby was two months premature, however, and died 17 days later.

Stuart told police that the robber was a raspy-voiced black man dressed in a jogging suit. The man had forced his way into their car and ordered Stuart to drive to the neighborhood where the shooting took place.

Time magazine reported that Stuart was showered with sympathy and that the media treated the couple "as starry-eyed lovers . . . cut down by an urban savage." Both the

the beginning or end of the first sentence or after the first meaningful clause in that sentence. The attribution should not be delayed until the end of the second or third sentence. Similarly, if a quotation contains only one sentence, but that sentence is long, the attribution should be placed at or near the beginning of that sentence—not at the end:

> "Of each dollar spent on personal auto liability insurance, only about 45 cents end up in the hands of accident victims, while 30 cents are used to pay insurance companies' selling and administrative costs, and more than 20 cents on the premium dollar are burned up in legal battles," Quinn said.
> REVISED: "Of each dollar spent on personal auto liability insurance," Quinn said, "only about 45 cents end up in the hands of accident victims, while 30 cents are used to pay insurance companies' selling and administrative costs, and more than 20 cents of the premium dollar are burned up in legal battles."

> "However close we sometimes seem to that dark and final abyss, let no man of peace and freedom despair. For he does not stand alone. If we all can persevere, if we can in every land and office look beyond our shores and ambitions, then surely the age will dawn in which the strong are just and the weak secure and the peace preserved," the president said.
> REVISED: "However close we sometimes seem to that dark and final abyss," the president said, "let no man of peace and freedom despair. For he does not stand alone. If we all can persevere, if we can in every land and office look beyond our shores and ambitions, then surely the age will dawn in which the strong are just and the weak secure and the peace preserved."

A direct quotation should be attributed only once, regardless of the number of sentences it contains:

> "I planned to shoot them and then shoot myself," Horwitz told the judge. "They kept telling me lies," he explained. "They were plotting to get rid of me, to take away my job, and I made up my mind I wouldn't let them," he continued.
> REVISED: "I planned to shoot them and then myself," Horwitz told the judge. "They kept telling me lies. They were plotting to get rid of me, to take away my job, and I made up my mind I wouldn't let them."

> "I'm opposed to any laws that prohibit the sale of pornography," the attorney said. "The restriction of pornography infringes on Americans' First Amendment rights," he explained. "I like to picture myself as a good guy defending a sleazy thing," he concluded.
> REVISED: "I'm opposed to any laws that prohibit the sale of pornography," the attorney said. "The restriction of pornography infringes on Americans' First Amendment rights. I like to picture myself as a good guy defending a sleazy thing."

Even quotations that continue for several paragraphs need to be attributed only once:

> Capt. Bonventre eliminated the police department motorcycle squad. "The main reason is that there are more injuries to motorcycle officers," he said. "I want to protect my officers. They think there's no danger on a cycle.
> Well, that's just optimistic thinking; there's a real danger.

"Officers have much more protection in a car. I think that's pretty obvious. If an officer gets in a hot pursuit and crashes, he stands a better chance of escaping injury when he's in a car.

"Also, almost any situation, even traffic, can be handled better in a patrol car than on a motorcycle. There are some places a motorcycle can go more easily, but a car certainly commands more respect."

A single phrase may unnecessarily attribute a quotation twice. For example, the first of the following sentences reports that a fire chief made an announcement, then adds that he "said":

In making the announcement, the fire chief said arsonists caused 20 percent of the blazes reported in the city last year.

REVISED: The fire chief said arsonists caused 20 percent of the blazes reported in the city last year.

"We need to raise the speed limit," R. L. Wirtz said, speaking at a meeting Thursday night.

REVISED: "We need to raise the speed limit," R. L. Wirtz said at a meeting Thursday night.

Reporters must learn to avoid "floating" quotations: a summary followed by a direct quotation which appears in a separate sentence and is not attributed. Every direct quotation must be attributed, even when the speaker is identified in a previous sentence. If a quotation is not clearly attributed, readers may be momentarily uncertain about its source. The source may be the person mentioned in the last sentence, but some readers may assume that the source is some other person who will be identified in the following paragraph. The attribution also provides a smooth transition from one sentence to the next. In short, quotations should be attributed even when readers already know or can guess who is speaking:

Columnist Jack Anderson said investigative reporters dig up what government officials are trying to hide. "I've never known a government official who'd admit mistakes."

ATTRIBUTED: Columnist Jack Anderson said investigative reporters dig up what government officials are trying to hide. He added, "I've never known a government official who'd admit mistakes."

The sociologist said there is a trend toward vocationalism on college campuses.

"Many students now demand from college not a chance to think, but a chance to become qualified for some job."

ATTRIBUTED: The sociologist said there is a trend toward vocationalism on college campuses.

"Many students now demand from college not a chance to think, but a chance to become qualified for some job," he said.

Another practice causes even more confusion. Some reporters use a quotation, then attribute it in the following paragraph:

"I was scared to death. I knew I was hurt, and I needed help."

These were the words today of an 18-year-old student trapped in her wrecked car.

REVISED: An 18-year-old student trapped in her wrecked car said: "I was scared to death. I knew I was hurt, and I needed help."

"All a lottery would do is take money from the poor. Poor people would spend every dollar on lottery tickets instead of buying a loaf of bread. They would risk everything for that one-in-a-million chance."

The Rev. Arthur K. DeZego voiced that opinion today during a speech to the Rotary Club.

REVISED: Speaking to the Rotary Club today, the Rev. Arthur K. De-Zego said: "All a lottery would do is take money from the poor. Poor people would spend every dollar on lottery tickets instead of buying a loaf of bread. They would risk everything for that one-in-a-million chance."

Reporters must also provide transitions between statements made by different people, particularly when the statements are contradictory or appear in succeeding paragraphs. If reporters fail to attribute and separate the statements, readers may not understand which of the two people is speaking:

The newspaper's editor said he no longer will accept advertisements for X-rated movies. He explained: "These movies are worthless. They contribute nothing to society and offend our readers. They're depressing and pornographic."

"Newspapers have no right to pass judgment on matters of taste. If they do, they should also ban the advertisements for other products considered harmful: cigarettes, liquor and pollutants like automobiles," a theater owner responded.

These two paragraphs are confusing. People beginning the second paragraph might mistakenly assume, at least momentarily, that the editor has suddenly begun to contradict himself—to criticize newspapers and the position he just endorsed. The confusion can be easily avoided by placing a brief transition at the beginning of the second paragraph. The paragraph might begin: "However, a local theater owner responded that: 'Newspapers have no right to pass judgment on matters of taste. . . .' "

Even more attribution is necessary for indirect quotations than for direct quotations. Every idea or opinion in an indirect quotation—sometimes every sentence—must be attributed. Moreover, the attribution should be varied because paragraphs might become too clumsy and repetitive if reporters simply added the words "he said" at the end of all the sentences they contain:

The police chief insisted that the death penalty must be retained. The death penalty, harsh as it may seem, is a form of justice designed to protect the lives and rights of law-abiding citizens. Without it, criminals' rights are overly protected. Because of the almost endless mechanisms of the appeal system, it is unlikely that an innocent person would be put to death.

REVISED: The police chief insisted that the death penalty must be retained. He said the death penalty may seem harsh, but it is a form of justice designed to protect the lives and rights of law-abiding citizens. Without it, he added, the criminals' rights are overly protected. Because of the endless mechanisms of the appeal system, he said, it is unlikely that an innocent person would be put to death.

Journalists cannot attribute the police chief's remarks by placing the entire paragraph within quotation marks because they have no way of knowing for certain that the remarks they have been given are his exact words—they may be someone else's summary of what the police chief said. Similarly, editors cannot convert an indirect quotation (a paraphrase) written by a newspaper reporter into a direct quotation. However, editors can take a statement out of quotation marks and then reword it, provided they do not change its meaning.

GUIDELINES FOR CAPITALIZING AND PUNCTUATING QUOTATIONS

Quotations must be capitalized and punctuated properly. The first word in a quotation that is a complete sentence is capitalized, but the first word in a partial quotation is not capitalized:

> He said, "life is just one damned thing after another."
> REVISED: He said, "Life is just one damned thing after another."

> He called journalism "Literature in a hurry."
> REVISED: He called journalism "literature in a hurry."

If the attribution is placed before a quotation that contains one full sentence, the attribution should be followed by a comma. If the attribution is placed before a quotation that contains two or more sentences, the attribution should be followed by a colon. The attribution is not followed by a period in either case:

> James Thurber said: "It is better to know some of the questions than all of the answers."
> REVISED: James Thurber said, "It is better to know some of the questions than all of the answers."

> Mark Twain said, "I apologize for writing a long letter. If I'd had more time, I'd have written a shorter one."
> REVISED: Mark Twain said: "I apologize for writing a long letter. If I'd had more time, I'd have written a shorter one."

When reporters place the attribution after a quotation, they use a comma (not a period) after the last word in the quotation:

> "I'm feeling better." she said.
> REVISED: "I'm feeling better," she said.

> "He was always trying to help somebody." his wife said.
> REVISED: "He was always trying to help somebody," his wife said.

The comma or period at the end of a quotation should always be placed *inside* the quotation marks. There are no exceptions to this rule:

> Benjamin Franklin said, "A penny saved is a penny earned".
> REVISED: Benjamin Franklin said, "A penny saved is a penny earned."

> "Nothing can now be believed that is seen in a newspaper", he said.
> REVISED: "Nothing can now be believed that is seen in a newspaper," he said.

While attributing most statements, journalists place the words of attribution in their normal order, with the subject appearing before the verb. That is the way people talk, and it is usually the most graceful way to write:

> Said Ronald Reagan, "I've noticed that everybody who's for abortion has already been born."
> REVISED: Ronald Reagan said, "I've noticed that everybody who's for abortion has already been born."

"Hard work is good for you. Nobody ever drowned in sweat," insisted the executive.
REVISED: "Hard work is good for you. Nobody ever drowned in sweat," the executive insisted.

However, if you place a long phrase between the subject and verb, the normal word order can be awkward. In that case, place the verb first and the subject second:

"It will cost $2 million," Smith, a 29-year-old architect employed by the California firm, said.
REVISED: "It will cost $2 million," said Smith, a 29-year-old architect employed by the California firm.

"It wasn't our fault," Pauley, director of communications and marketing for the new company, said.
REVISED: "It wasn't our fault," said Pauley, director of communications and marketing for the new company.

Only the quotation—never the attribution—should be placed inside the quotation marks:

"Mrs. Johnson said, A politician should be born an orphan and remain a bachelor."
REVISED: Mrs. Johnson said, "A politician should be born an orphan and remain a bachelor."

"The motorcycle slid sideways and skidded about 100 feet, she said. The driver was killed."
REVISED: "The motorcycle slid sideways and skidded about 100 feet," she said. "The driver was killed."

If a quotation continues for several sentences, all the sentences should be enclosed within a single set of quotation marks; quotation marks do not have to be placed at the beginning and at the end of every sentence in the quotation:

The report said: "The land is too expensive." "Its price doubled in five years."
REVISED: The report said: "The land is too expensive. Its price doubled in five years."

"I did not see the car when I stepped out onto the street." "But when I saw the headlights coming at me, I knew it was going to hit me," she said.
REVISED: "I did not see the car when I stepped out onto the street. But when I saw the headlights coming at me, I knew it was going to hit me," she said.

Like any other part of a news story, a long quotation should be divided into short paragraphs to make it easier to read. Reporters divide long quotations at natural breaks, usually changes in topic, however slight. The paragraphs' lengths should vary, with few exceeding five or six typed lines. Reporters place a quotation mark at the beginning of a long quotation and before every new paragraph. However, they place a closing quotation mark only at the end of the entire quotation—not at the end of every paragraph:

The senator added: "Perhaps the most shocking example of the insensitivity of the Bureau of Indian Affairs' educational system is the manner in which boarding school dormitories have been administered.

"Psychiatrists familiar with the problems of Indian children have told us that a properly run dormitory system is the most crucial aspect of boarding school life, particularly in the elementary schools.

"Yet, when a 6-year-old Navajo child enters one of the boarding schools and becomes lonely or homesick, he must seek comfort from an instructional aide who has no training in child guidance and who is responsible for as many as 100 other unhappy children.

"This aide spends most of his time performing custodial chores. At night, the situation worsens as the ratio of dorm aides to children decreases."

When a quotation appears within another quotation, the first is enclosed in double quotation marks, and the second is enclosed in single quotation marks (use an apostrophe for a single quotation mark):

Mrs. Veen said: "My breathing was shallow, my heartbeat weak and my pulse faint. That's when the doctor told my husband, 'I think she may die.' "

During his 1960 presidential campaign, John F. Kennedy joked, "I got a wire from my father that said: 'Dear Jack, Don't buy one vote more than necessary. I'll be damned if I'll pay for a landslide.' "

SOME FINAL GUIDELINES FOR ATTRIBUTIONS AND QUOTATIONS

Reporters can attribute information to people, but not to places or institutions. For example, reporters can quote a hospital official, but not a hospital:

The hospital said the epidemic has ended.
REVISED: A hospital spokesperson said the epidemic has ended.

Atlanta announced that all city offices will be closed next Monday.
REVISED: The mayor of Atlanta announced that all city offices will be closed next Monday.

To avoid awkward combinations, separate partial quotations from complete sentences that are also being quoted. You can solve the problem most easily by (1) placing some attribution between the partial quotation and the full-sentence quotation or (2) by paraphrasing the partial quotation:

His mother said life is "a simple matter. I told all my children that if they really believe in God, they have nothing to fear."
REVISED: His mother said life is "a simple matter." She explained, "I told all my children that if they really believe in God, they have nothing to fear."
OR: His mother said life is a simple matter. "I told all my children that if they really believe in God, they have nothing to fear," she explained.

Ross said he expects to find a job "within a few weeks. And when I do get a job, the first thing I'm going to buy is a new car."
REVISED: Ross said he expects to find a job "within a few weeks." He added, "And when I do get a job, the first thing I'm going to buy is a new car."
OR: Ross said he expects to find a new job within a few weeks. "And when I do get a job, the first thing I'm going to buy is a new car," he added.

Reporters rarely add that a source "told reporters" or "informed this newspaper." Most news is transmitted through reporters, and it is unnecessary to say so. If reporters included the phrases in all their stories, they would become too repetitious and consume too much space:

> He told reporters that the city is bankrupt.
> REVISED: He said the city is bankrupt.

> During an interview today, she informed this newspaper that the city must release some prisoners because its jails are overcrowded.
> REVISED: During an interview today, she said the city must release some prisoners because its jails are overcrowded.

Avoid unintentional editorials. If worded carelessly, partial quotes, and even attribution, can express an opinion:

> The mayor made it clear that the city cannot afford to give its employees a raise.
> REVISED: The mayor said the city cannot afford to give its employees a raise.

> Each month, Sen. William Proxmire presented the Golden Fleece Award "for the biggest, most ironic or most ridiculous example of wasteful government spending."
> REVISED: Each month, Sen. William Proxmire presented the Golden Fleece Award for what he considered "the biggest, most ironic or most ridiculous example of wasteful government spending."

Before revision, the first sentence editorialized by saying that the mayor "made it clear"—that she stated a fact in a convincing manner. The second sentence reported as fact Proxmire's claim that all the recipients of his "award" wasted the government's money, yet many of the recipients disagreed, and some provided convincing evidence that Proxmire was wrong.

Finally, do not attribute a direct quotation to more than one person. Instead, eliminate the quotation marks. Two or more people rarely use exactly the same words.

CHECKLISTS FOR QUOTATIONS AND ATTRIBUTION

Consult the following checklists when using quotations and attribution. If you can answer "no" to any of these questions, the quotations or attribution in your stories may have to be revised.

Quotations

1. Have you used quotations sparingly—for emphasis and for a change of pace rather than to tell an entire story?
2. Are all the words that you have placed in quotation marks your source's exact words?
3. Does each quotation serve a purpose? Does it help reveal the source's character; explain, describe or emphasize an important point; or present additional details about that point?
4. Are all the direct quotations clear, concise, relevant and effective? If not, they should probably be paraphrased or discarded.
5. Have you reported only the source's answers, not the questions the source was asked?

6. If a quotation includes several sentences, have you placed quotation marks only at the beginning and the end of the entire quotation—not at the beginning and end of every sentence?

7. Have you divided long quotations into shorter paragraphs, with quotation marks appearing at the beginning of every paragraph and at the end of only the final paragraph?

8. Do quotations that appear within other quotations use single quotation marks?

9. Have you avoided the use of orphan quotes?

10. Are you certain that none of the quotations repeat facts reported elsewhere in your story?

Attribution

1. Have you attributed second-hand information, criticisms, statements about controversial issues, other statements of opinion and all direct and indirect quotations—but not undisputed facts?

2. Have you punctuated the attribution properly? Have you used a comma before one-sentence quotations and a colon before quotations that contain two or more sentences? Also, have all the commas and periods been placed inside the quotation marks?

3. Have you capitalized the first letter in all full sentences—but not sentence fragments—that are quoted?

4. Has the attribution been placed at or near the beginning of all long quotations?

5. If the attribution appears in the middle of a sentence, does it appear at a natural break in the sentence rather than interrupt a thought?

6. Have you varied your sentences and paragraphs so most do not begin with the attribution?

7. Have you placed the attribution outside the quotation marks?

8. Have you attributed direct quotations only once?

9. Have you attributed each separate statement of opinion expressed in indirect quotations?

10. Have you quoted only people, not places or institutions?

11. Have you avoided awkward combinations of partial and complete quotations?

12. Have you provided transitions to separate the statements made by different people, particularly if one of those statements is quoted immediately after the other?

13. Have you selected the proper words of attribution—words that accurately convey the speaker's actual meaning and behavior?

14. Have you avoided words of attribution such as "hopes," "feels," "believes," "laughs," "coughs" and "cries"?

15. Is the attribution as concise as possible?

If you would like more practice using these rules, complete Exercises 3 and 4, then compare your answers with the answers provided in Appendix D.

An Ombudsman's Report

CASE STUDY NO. 3

By **Mike Clark**
Reader Advocate
The Florida (Jacksonville) Times-Union

The item was brief, apparently routine, tucked inside the local news section of The Florida Times-Union.

In matter-of-fact style, readers were informed of a murder in a Jacksonville working-class neighborhood.

On a Friday night, Thomas C. Maynard left home to run an errand for his family. Eight weeks earlier, his wife had given birth to a baby boy.

Maynard, 31, stopped at an automatic teller machine in a strip shopping center to get some money. While there, he was accosted, robbed and murdered. Early the next morning his body was found in a front yard in his neighborhood.

That was the story on the surface. The article inside a local news section was so brief and nondescript that the reporter's name was not printed.

But that little article caused shock waves. Joyce Maynard, his wife, was suddenly alone and coping with her husband's death. She picked up the Sunday newspaper and received another scare. The story listed her address.

Since the killers were still at large, they could find her by simply reading the newspaper. Mrs. Maynard called the newspaper to complain. There was determination, fear and anger in her voice.

"I don't know who edits your newspaper, but they should not have run that, especially with a wife and baby at home," she said to the newspaper's reader advocate.

"I know you guys have a job to do, but for God's sake, you don't know what you have done. Your reporters don't know when to stop.

"I'm afraid you have put my baby in jeopardy and my baby is all I have left. I can't believe my address showed up in the paper. Somebody should have been more sensitive."

On the following Wednesday, the day of her husband's funeral, the arrest of four suspects in the murder was reported. Incredibly, the exact address of the victim's house was printed again. Apparently the wife was no longer in jeopardy, yet by printing the address again, it looked like another example of insensitivity.

The reason for printing the address: There was a new editor and a new police reporter on duty that night, and neither had heard of the original complaint.

Now put yourself in the position of a top editor at the newspaper. What would you do?

Here is what the reader advocate did:

1. He took the original complaint and passed it along to the editor responsible for police reporters.

(continued on next page)

2. When the address was printed a second time, he called Mrs. Maynard to apologize. Then he informed all the top editing staff at a daily news meeting.
3. He attended the funeral to show the support of the newspaper.
4. He wrote a column for the following Sunday's newspaper that outlined the situation and called for a change in the newspaper's policy toward victims. He visited Mrs. Maynard and read her the column to make sure it did not worsen the situation.

    The column ended this way: "As a father of two daughters, one born prematurely, I grieve for Mrs. Maynard. As a journalist, I deeply regret the additional suffering this newspaper caused, however unintentionally."
5. He promised Mrs. Maynard that he would take steps to expose the staff to the emerging concern for victims of crime. That included a seminar featuring two nationally-known speakers on victims' rights. The seminar was held several months after the Maynard story.
6. Newspaper editors then changed their policy so that exact addresses would not be used when referring to homes of crime victims.

Other related changes in policy have also occurred:

• In a Question-&-Answer feature that included a brief quote on a topical question and a photo, the newspaper used to identify people by full name and street name (Joe Smith, Oak Street). That made it easy to find that person's telephone number. After some women received obscene phone calls, the newspaper removed the street name and replaced it with the person's occupation.

• Wives of sailors at the Navy bases in Jacksonville are asked permission to use their names when interviewed in connection with a departing ship. Often, their husbands must be away for extended periods of time.

• Coeds interviewed and photographed after recent mass murders near the University of Florida campus were not named in follow-up stories after readers objected that they might be vulnerable to a killer on the loose.

• The address of a shelter for battered women is not used out of concern that abusive spouses could find it.

• Photographers are careful not to intrude on families when covering funerals. Generally, the minister at the church is consulted.

Names of rape victims have not been used as a matter of course, though Florida law makes identifying rape victims illegal.

As Mrs. Maynard said, news personnel sometimes do not understand the impact of their stories. One of the jobs of a newspaper ombudsman is to keep the staff aware of the impact of their work on the lives of their readers.

One important lesson is that readers are less likely to care about their "right to know" if published information threatens to endanger another human life or cause suffering to families in mourning.

SUGGESTED READINGS

Cunningham, Richard P. "A Suggestion for Handling Offensive Quotes." *The Quill*, June 1990, pp. 4–5.

Isaacs, Norman E. "Only Editor Should Decide Whether to Grant Anonymity." *Presstime*, Sept. 1988, pp. 12–13.

Lehrer, Anrienne. "Between quotation marks." *Journalism Quarterly*, Winter 1989, pp. 902–906+.

Matera, Fran. "A Blast of Bad Journalism?" *Editor & Publisher*, Sept. 2, 1989, p. 52.

McManus, Kevin. "The, Uh, Quotation Quandary." *Columbia Journalism Review*, May/June 1990, pp. 54–56.

Mowrer, Richard Scott. "The Press Is in Danger of Manipulation When It Quotes Anonymous Sources." *Presstime*, June 1987, p. 74.

Stein, M. L. "Anonymous Sources." *Editor & Publisher*, Oct. 24, 1987, p. 17.

Weiss, Philip. "Who Gets Quote Approval?" *Columbia Journalism Review*, May/June 1991, pp. 52–54.

Winternitz, Felix. "When Unnamed Sources Are Banned." *The Quill*, Oct. 1989, pp. 38–40.

QUOTES

The function of the press is very high. It is almost holy. It ought to serve as a forum for the people, through which the people may know freely what is going on. To misstate or suppress the news is a breach of trust.

(Justice Louis D. Brandeis, U.S. Supreme Court)

Since I write a humor column, I have a vested interest in a free press. I don't seem to have any problem making fun of the President of the United States, the Cabinet, Congress, the CIA and the FBI. I don't know if our leaders read the column or not, but since I've been writing it, I have had no visits from anyone in a raincoat telling me I better knock it off.

The people who attempt to do the same thing I am doing in 95 percent of the world are either in gulags, under house arrest or are jobless. For some reason not too many governments can handle satire. My heroes in the world are the men and women in these countries who, knowing the consequences, persist in holding up their leaders to ridicule.

The problem, if there is a problem in this country, is because we have a free press, people have no idea what it's like to live in a country that doesn't.

(Art Buchwald)

The press is like the peculiar uncle you keep in the attic—just one of those unfortunate things.

(G. Gordon Liddy, Watergate co-conspirator)

Exercise 1

QUOTATIONS AND ATTRIBUTION

IMPROVING QUOTATIONS AND ATTRIBUTION

SECTION I: PARAPHRASING WEAK QUOTATIONS

Rewrite the following quotations more simply as paraphrases.

1. "To tell you the truth, I would, uh, I'd be disinclined to recommend buying any shares of General Motors at this, uh, present moment in time," the financial planner said.
2. "I want to tell you that, like, uh, you know man, what we're aiming for is to get everybody to realize that, uh, suicide is never an acceptable option for anyone under any circumstances, not even like, uh, the terminally ill," she said.
3. "My brother was driving down this road and, uh, at first I didn't know what happened. Like I wasn't watching the road or nothing and didn't know what the hell it was. Then, uh, so I looked out the back window and saw this kid lying all bloody and dead on the road. Then I knew what we'd hit," he said.

SECTION II: AVOIDING DOUBLE ATTRIBUTION

Rewrite the following sentences, attributing them only once.

1. A report issued Tuesday by the U.S. Department of Justice said the number of serious crimes committed in the U.S. declined 3% last year.
2. Speaking to more than 3,000 people in the Municipal Auditorium, she continued by stating that only the Democratic Party favors universal health care.
3. The Census Bureau issued a report today stating that, according to data it gathered last year, 5.2 million people in the U.S. are homeless, including 620,000 children.

SECTION III: CORRECTING PLACEMENT ERRORS

Correct the placement of the attribution in the following sentences.

1. People under 18, she said, should not be allowed to drive.
2. Another important step is to, she said, lower the books' prices.
3. "The average shoplifters are teen-age girls who steal for the thrill of it, and housewives who steal items they can use. They don't have to steal; most have plenty of money, but they don't think it's a crime. They also think they'll get away with it forever," Valderrama said.

SECTION IV: CONDENSING WORDY ATTRIBUTION

The attributions in the following sentences are too wordy. They appear in italics and contain a total of 76 words. How many of the words can you eliminate? Rewrite the attribution, if necessary.

1. *She concluded her speech by telling the scouts that* the jamboree will be held August 7–13.

2. *He was quick to point out the fact that, in his opinion,* the president has "failed to act effectively to reduce the federal deficit."

3. *She expressed her feelings by explaining that she believes that* all those convicted of drunk driving should lose their licenses for life.

4. *She also went on to point out the fact that the results of federal studies show that,* by recycling 1 ton of paper, you can save 17 trees.

5. *In a speech to the students Tuesday, he first began by offering them his opinion that* their professors should emphasize teaching, not research.

6. *He continued by urging his listeners to remember the critical point that* the country's energy policy has failed: that the U.S. is not developing alternative fuels, nor conserving existing fuels.

SECTION V: IMPROVING ATTRIBUTION

Correct the attributions in the following quotations.

1. He said: "after a certain number of years, our faces become our biographies".

2. Andy Rooney declared "if dogs could talk, it would take a lot of fun out of owning one".

3. "Because that's where the money is" Willie Sutton answered when asked why he robbed banks.

4. He continued by claiming that there are "two" types of people who complain about their taxes: "men" and "women."

5. "Blessed is he" said W. C. Bennett "who expects no gratitude, for he shall not be disappointed". explained Bennett.

6. Mother Teresa then spoke to the youths, telling them that. "The most terrible poverty is loneliness and the feeling of being unwanted."

7. Andy Rooney was also the individual who once announced that: "For those who don't get killed or wounded, war is a great experience."

8. He went on to also state that, getting older is doing "less and less" for the first time and "more and more" for the last time.

9. "My views on birth control" said Robert F. Kennedy "Are somewhat distorted by the fact that I was the seventh of nine children".

10. Being a police officer is not always fun and exciting, says Hennigan. "Some things you'd just as soon forget." "Some things you do forget."

11. "The art of taxation." claimed a French statesman long ago "Consists in so plucking the goose as to obtain the most feathers with the least hissing".

12. When asked why she wants to do it, she said she "loves it. My friends think I'm a little crazy, but this is what I want to do with my life—be a highway patrolman."

13. Howe, a junior majoring in nursing, announced that he dislikes the tests. "You have to study differently for multiple choice tests. You have to memorize instead of learn."

14. Dr. Hector Rivera said they test for AIDS at the clinic "but do not treat the disease." "People come in to be tested scared to death." "Some leave the clinic relieved, and some don't." he said.

15. Her friendships, home, and family are the most important things in her life. "My husband is my best friend." "Maybe that's why we've lasted so long." "You really need to be friends before you're lovers".

16. "I cheat because professors give too much work." It's crazy, he said. "They don't take into consideration that some people have jobs, families and other outside interests." continued the history major. He then continued by adding that he's never been caught.

17. "My son thinks I'm old." "But I'm actually in good health for my age." "Of course, I have the usual aches and pains of an 80-year-old." "But I can still take care of my own house, and I still enjoy it." "My son thinks I should move into one of those retirement apartments and watch Wheel of Fortune all day." said he.

18. Jo Ann Nyez, a secretary, grew up in Milwaukee and described a childhood fear: There was this house at the end of my street and none of us would dare go near it on Halloween. It was supposed to be haunted. The story was that the wife had hung herself in the basement and the husband killed and ate rattlesnakes.

Exercise 2

QUOTATIONS AND ATTRIBUTION

MISCELLANEOUS EXERCISES:
IMPROVING YOUR QUOTATIONS AND ATTRIBUTION

SECTION I: AVOIDING WORDY ATTRIBUTION

Condense each of these phrases to two or three words.

1. She want on to say that
2. She told the audience that
3. She concluded by saying that
4. She said that, in her opinion
5. She expressed her belief that
6. He also made mention of
7. He also pointed out that
8. He revealed the fact that
9. They were quick to point out that
10. The author made the remark that

SECTION II: AVOIDING DOUBLE ATTRIBUTION

Mistakenly, each of these statements is attributed twice. Rewrite the statements, attributing them only once.

1. In her speech, she also said the city has dozens of beautiful old homes.
2. In a report issued today, the researchers revealed that the disease is spreading.
3. In a speech to the community, the senator announced that he will seek federal funds to repair the bridge.
4. According to the mayor in a speech she gave Wednesday, it would cost too much to widen the highway.
5. Slater said that, in his opinion, he is convinced that no one could have prevented the girl's death.

SECTION III: PLACEMENT

Correct the placement and punctuation of the attribution in the following sentences.

1. "Nice guys" Leo Durocher said "finish last."
2. Said Gen. William Sherman: "War is hell".
3. "Another important step" she said "is to proofread everything you write".
4. "People under 18," she insisted "should never be allowed to drive".
5. "The federal government is like an alcoholic who has to hit rock bottom before he decides to seek help." Anders said in reference to the federal deficit.

SECTION IV: ADDING ATTRIBUTION

Provide the proper attribution for the first statement, which is paraphrased, and for the second, which is a direct quotation. Also divide each statement into several shorter paragraphs.

1. Republican Eugene McIntry said tuition rates at the state's colleges and universities are too low, and he went on to make all of the following points as well. The tuition rates that students are charged cover only one-fifth the cost of their college educations, and taxpayers are forced to make up the difference. No taxpayer struggling to support a family should have to help subsidize healthy young college students; students should pay their own bills. What we have, in effect, is a form of welfare, since other citizens are forced to help college students pay their bills. It's unjust. Students can work full-time summers and part-time during the school year and take out loans that they can repay when they graduate and find high-paying jobs.

2. The teen-ager said: "We were at the beach, and suddenly it began to rain. The lightning was falling, hitting all around us. There was no place to go, nowhere to hide, and I was absolutely terrified. All of a sudden I felt something hit me. I turned around because I thought my boyfriend had thrown something at me. I thought he had thrown a rock because it hurt so bad. From the small of my back down to the bottom of my feet I felt pain, like somebody had slapped me. The pain moved downward and concentrated in my feet. It was lightning, and it hit me. I think the only reason it didn't kill me was because I was wearing rubber track shoes."

SECTION V: MISCELLANEOUS ERRORS

Correct the errors in the following sentences.

1. Ball, 20, said the Jeep was crushed to about half its normal size. "It was just a box of metal". he said. "Everything in the Jeep was totally crushed," he added, "except for the two front seats".

2. He said, "We're hoping it (the water level) will increase back (to normal).

3. Margaret Hamill, a senior, claimed that she often went home and cried after the algebra class. "I wanted to quit." she said. "There wasn't enough time to ask questions," she explained. "Each day I got more and more confused."

4. He described himself as, "A church-going person who neither smokes nor drinks."

5. "I think it's kind of ridiculous." he explained about the high cost of a new home.

6. A specialist said: "in one third of all heart attack fatalities, the first symptom is death."

7. "Patriotism is the last refuge of a scoundrel," argued Samuel Johnson.

8. "I'm doing better." "Not hitting as many spectators." Former president Gerald Ford announced today while describing his golf game.

9. More women are becoming alcoholics, according to two sociologists who spoke at your school Friday.

10. He urged his listeners to remember one critical point: that high schools do not exist for the purpose of preparing every student to enter college.

Exercise 3

Answer Key Provided: See Appendix D

QUOTATIONS AND ATTRIBUTION

WORDING, PLACEMENT AND PUNCTUATION

Make any changes necessary to improve the attribution in the following sentences and paragraphs, and correct matters of style.

1. "Our goal is peace". claimed the president.
2. Benjamin Franklin said: "death takes no bribes".
3. She said her son refers to her literary endeavors as, "mom's writing thing".
4. He is a scuba diver and pilot. He also enjoys skydiving. "I like challenge, something exciting."
5. "The dangers promise to be of indefinite duration." the president said referring to the Mideast crisis.
6. "Freedom of the press is not merely freedom to publish news." "It is also freedom to gather the news. We cannot publish what we cannot gather." said columnist Jack Anderson during a speech last night.
7. Jesse Owens expressed the opinion that "I think that America has become too athletic." "From Little League to the pro leagues, sports are no longer recreation." "They are big business, and they're drudgery." he continued.
8. The man smiled, "It's a great deal for me." "I expect to double my money," he explained.
9. When asked what she likes most about her job as a newspaper reporter, the woman responded by saying—"I'm not paid much, but the work is important. And it's varied and exciting." She grinned: "Also, I like seeing my byline in the paper."
10. The librarian announced to reporters that the new building "will cost somewhere in the neighborhood of about $4.6 million."
11. "Thousands of the poor in the United States," said the professor, "die every year of diseases we can easily cure." "It's a crime," he said, "but no one ever is punished for their deaths."
12. Thomas said students should never be spanked. "A young boy or girl who gets spanked in front of peers becomes embarrassed and the object of ridicule."
13. The lawyer said, "He ripped the life-sustaining respirator tubes from his throat three times in an effort to die. He is simply a man" the lawyer continued "who rejects medical treatment regardless of the consequences. He wants to die and has a constitutional right to do so."
14. Bobby Knight, the basketball coach at Indiana University, said. "Everyone has the will to win." "Few have the will to prepare." Knight added that. "It is the preparation that counts."
15. She said she firmly believes that the federal government "must do more" to help cities "support and retrain" the chronically unemployed.

Exercise 4

Answer Key Provided: See Appendix D

QUOTATIONS AND ATTRIBUTION

PLACEMENT AND PUNCTUATION

INSTRUCTIONS: Make any changes necessary to improve the attribution in the following sentences and paragraphs. Not every sentence necessarily contains an error. You can correct your own work by comparing your answers with the answers printed in Appendix D.

1. "We can't wait any longer." he said.
2. He said: "no one was seriously injured".
3. Smith said he is "not very happy. My wife is divorcing me," he explained.
4. He found the plane in a woods a half mile away and saw two people inside, both "dead".
5. "At least two he said and perhaps three people will be charged with fraud."
6. The girl smiled, "Yes, I'll marry you." She explained, "I've always loved you."
7. "I know I shouldn't smoke," the girl coughed. "But I can't help myself."
8. She said she hates college. "The teachers make us memorize." "They don't teach us how to think".
9. Thompsen, asked about her feelings as she received the award as the school's outstanding journalism student, said "its the biggest surprise of my life."
10. When asked whether he would teach next year, the art professor responded, "I think so. I like having a steady income, and I haven't been able to earn enough from the sale of my paintings," he explained.
11. The student grinned. "I really don't enjoy college, but I don't know what else to do." "Perhaps I should just quit school and look for a job."
12. The woman claimed that "only a few" of her friends are happy as full-time homemakers and that "most want to find a job. They want to make some money and become less dependent on their husbands."
13. The city council voted 7 to 2 against a proposal to give police officers a 12 percent raise. "It's just too much," Mayor Sabrina Datolli said. "Policemen are already overpaid." She added that "police officers just aren't worth $25,000 a year."
14. "My daddy will give me a dime." the girl declared as she ran home.
15. When asked whether he planned to run for another term, the governor responded, "I'm not going to speculate about that now." It's too early," he said.
16. Tests showed that "low" or "moderate" speed, rear-end collisions involving the car resulted in "massive" fuel leaks and fires, the magazine reported.

Exercise 5

QUOTATIONS AND ATTRIBUTION

USING QUOTES IN NEWS STORIES

INSTRUCTIONS: Write complete news stories based on the following information. Use some quotations in each story to emphasize its highlights, but do not use quotations to tell the entire story. Use the most interesting, important and revealing quotations, not just those that happen to appear first.

1. Carlos Vacante is a police officer who has worked 3 years for your city's police department. Last night he had an unusual experience. This is his story, as he told it to you in an interview today: "I remember his eyes. They were cold, the eyes of a killer. He was pointing a gun at me, and it fired. I smelled the gunpowder and waited for the pain. I thought I was dead. The whole thing had started at about 11 p.m. This man was suspected of stealing from parked cars, and I'd gotten his description by radio. Then I spotted him in a parking lot. This morning we learned he's wanted in the robbery and murder of a service station attendant in Tennessee. There's no doubt in my mind he wanted to kill me last night just because I stopped him. I was an object in his way. I'd gotten out of my car and called to him. He started turning around and I spotted a handgun in his waistband. As he drew the gun and fired, I leaned to the right and dropped to one knee. It was just a reflex that saved my life. When I heard the shot, I thought he hit me. I couldn't believe it was actually happening to me. I thought I was going to cash everything in. Then I was running—zig-zagging—behind some cars. He fired another shot, but my backup arrived, and he fled. Maybe 60 seconds had passed from the time I spotted him. Five minutes later, we found him at the back door to a house, trying to break in and hide. I ordered him to stop, and he put his hands up and said, 'You got me.' I still smell the gunpowder this morning. I thought I was dead."

2. Judge Edward Johnson provided this story during an interview this morning. This is what he said: "I sentenced 42 men and one woman to jail yesterday, all for not making their child support payments. They've all been found in contempt of court. The jail's just bulging now. We're expecting more, so the sheriff is bringing in extra mattresses and wood cots. I'm scheduled to hear 40 more cases tomorrow. Normally, I hear about a dozen of these cases a month, and three to four are sentenced to jail. But the problem's been getting worse, and we decided the only way to deal with it was to crack down on these people. We've got hundreds of people in this county behind on their child support. Nothing's usually done about it, so people figure they can get away with it. Then their families starve or go on welfare. This is the last resort to get these people to place first priority on their children's support and care. We find that most of the offenders could have made their payments. They have the money. The maximum penalty is 179 days, but most are sentenced to pay what they owe or serve 90 days in jail. I'm told that yesterday seventeen of the defendants, including the woman, made all their back payments and were released. Others are in the process of raising the money they owe and will be released today. We decided to start with the worst offenders, the people farthest behind in their payments, so the majority of the offenders being brought in are $1,000 or more behind. There was one yesterday who was in arrears by $40,000. I

think in general I've tried to be very firm and fair to get across to these people that this has to be their first priority, ahead of car payments or anything else. They have to take care of their children. I'm not really trying to punish them. I'm just trying to get their attention, and I believe the system works. I can't see how anyone can neglect their children."

3. There was a trial yesterday. It was a rape trial that lasted 6 hours and that ended in the conviction by an 8-man, 4-woman jury of Lonnie T. Ward, 20, who was then sentenced to a term of 28 years in prison. The main witness against him was the victim, Ashley Deyo. This is what she told the court: "I was alone in my apartment that night and had been asleep when I woke and found this man standing by my bed. He was nude, and I think I tried to scream because I opened my mouth, but nothing came out. He slapped me. Then he put his hand over my mouth and told me not to talk. He said if I cooperated, he wouldn't hurt me, but he had a knife. Then he touched me and raped me, using all kinds of nasty, filthy, four-letter words. He said he had done it lots of times before. I was scared to death, so that I literally could not move. He threatened to stab me if I resisted. I was petrified. I thought he was going to kill me. I just didn't think he'd do what he did and let me live to tell about it. It's ruined my life. My marriage has fallen apart, and I've had to move to another city, but I never forget. Never, not for a day, not for an hour. Never."

4. At their meeting last night, your city commissioners shut down a pet store: Kim's Pets located in the Colonial Mall. The commission revoked the owner's occupational license. They had received numerous complaints from customers, police and Humane Society officials that the store sold sick animals and did not take proper care of its animals. During a hearing before the commission, representatives of the County Humane Society, police officers and several unhappy customers complained about the store and its owner, Kim Rybinski. Rybinski claimed she has never knowingly sold sick animals or improperly cared for them. She said the Humane Society has been harassing her, and that its harassment "has been unbelievable." Serving as a spokesman for dissatisfied customers and other complainants, Michael Jeffries, director of the Humane Society, said: "She's not running her business in the fashion that other pet stores are being run. We have about 40 documented cases of improper business practices, including the sale of sick animals and improper care. We're also investigating complaints that she sold animals which she claimed were registered with the American Kennel Club. After selling the animals, she's been unable to deliver registration papers to the pets' owners. She's allowed sick pets to remain in cages with healthy pets, and she keeps large animals in small cages. We had to sue her over a sick cat that was for sale. It's in our custody now, and we're trying to find a home for her. At first, we were trying to help her, but she's never cooperated with us and orders me out of her store. We get more complaints about her than any other pet store in the area. We get complaints about other pet stores, but they're generally unfounded or involve passing conditions that can be corrected. We got a complaint the first month Rybinski opened, and we're still getting complaints about her. The problem is, she's looking at the almighty dollar and not at the welfare of her animals."

5. The city's Ministerial Alliance spoke out today against the death penalty. A copy of a resolution it adopted will be sent to the governor and to every member of the state legislature. As its spokesman, the Rev. Stuart Adler declared: "None of us is soft on crime. There must be just punishment for those who

commit violent crimes, but what we are saying is we stop short of taking another person's life. We object because several independent studies have concluded that the death penalty is no deterrent to crime, rather the violence of the death penalty only breeds more violence. Also, the method of sentencing people is inconsistent. There is a great disparity between the victim being black or white. Defendants accused of killing black victims often are not sentenced to death, but when the victim is white, the death penalty is often imposed. People are frightened by the amount of violence in our society, and they've been sold a bill of goods. They've been told that the death penalty is a deterrent, and yet every major study disproves that reality. We're not getting at the deeper causes. We're a violent society, and getting more violent. Half the households in this city have guns, and it's inevitable some are going to use them. If we're really serious about stopping crime and violence, we have to recognize and correct its root causes: poverty, racial and sexual discrimination, broken homes and unloved children. Also drugs and alcohol. That's what's responsible for most crimes. And television. Studies show the average child in America witnesses, on television, 200,000 acts of violence by age 16. So we're against the death penalty. It's not going to solve our problems, and it's not fair, not fairly applied. It'll take time, but we intend to abolish it, and we'll persist. We're already beginning to stimulate discussion, and we expect that discussion to spread."

6. Tommy Crosby, 16, and Richard Picardo, 15, are sophomores at Grant High School in your community. Yesterday they were water-skiing on Elkhart Lake. Crosby, whose family owns the boat, was pulling Picardo, who was water-skiing. This is what Crosby said in an interview describing Picardo's death: "We were taking turns water-skiing, and lightning hit him. He's my best friend, and I saw him die. It was about 4 o'clock, and we could see a storm east of us. It never did rain, so we thought the storm would miss us. Dick was on one ski—he's pretty good at that. Then, uh, at first, I didn't know what happened. I was looking ahead, uh, watching for other boats. There was a flash, a bright flash, but at first it was like I still didn't know what was happening. I didn't hear any thunder then. Nothing. When I turned around, Dick was in the water. At first, I thought he had fallen, but he was face down."

BACKGROUND: The force of the lightning bolt shredded the youth's bathing suit and caused first- and second-degree burns from his chin to his navel. When firefighters arrived, the victim had been pulled into a boat and taken to shore. An off-duty firefighter tried to revive him there. County firefighters applied advanced life-support procedures, but he was pronounced dead a short time later at Park Regional Hospital. Deaths caused by water-related lightning strikes run second only to those in open fields. Usually, however, the victims are in boats at the time the lightning strikes. Authorities in the county said they can't remember lightning ever hitting anyone else on water skis.

7. Marcia Baugh, a consumer advocate employed by the state, spoke at Kennedy High School this morning and discussed the problem of fat. She told an assembly of students at the school that: "Americans spend $10 billion a year to fight fat. It's estimated that 70 million Americans are overweight, and they seem willing to try almost anything to shed some pounds. But they want it to be easy. Every year, they spend millions of dollars on appetite suppressants, anti-obesity prescriptions, reducing pills, diet books, mechanical devices, health spas and all sorts of related items, much of it outright quackery. Women constitute 90 percent of the weight-reducing market, and much of their money is

wasted. Dieters need more will power, not more pills. The best way to lose weight is simply cut down on the amount you eat and to eat more nutritious types of food. Fewer sweets and smaller portions. And exercise, lots of exercise. Doctors estimate that obesity is a secondary cause in the deaths of 50,000 people every year. But people who are overweight usually don't go to see their family doctors because they're embarrassed about the problem. Instead, they buy over-the-counter products, 90% of these diet products are sold in supermarkets and drugstores, which makes them super-easy to get."

Exercise 6

QUOTATIONS AND ATTRIBUTION

USING QUOTES IN NEWS STORIES

INSTRUCTIONS: Write complete news stories based on the following information. Use some quotations in each of your stories to emphasize its highlights, but do not use quotations to tell the entire story. Use the most interesting, important and revealing quotations, not just those that happen to appear first.

1. Gus DiCesare is the county sheriff. During an interview in his office this morning he discussed the problem of motorists who leave self-service gasoline stations without paying their bills. DiCesare made the following remarks: "It's a growing problem and getting worse every year. We're getting at least 30 complaints a week from gas stations about the problem. How often a station is cheated depends a great deal on its location and popularity. The larger stations, especially those located near major highways and those with transient customers, are hit most frequently since drivers can quickly lose themselves on the highways. The small, neighborhood service station gets hit least often because its attendants know their regular customers. Stations owners are trying to solve the problem, but there's only a limited number of things they can do. Most require employees who let a customer get away without paying to pay the bill out of their own pockets, and the employees at some large stations lose as much as $60 a week from their salaries because of customers leaving without paying. It gets busy at these big stations, and the employees just can't watch everyone. Some drivers speed away even when the employees are watching. A lot of the self-service stations are beginning to make you pay first, before you get your gas, and that cuts down on the thefts. We also recommend a number of other safeguards. We suggest that they service only one vehicle at a time, and that employees keep a pencil and paper handy to write down license numbers and a description of the drivers for later identification purposes. Attendants should pay closer attention to cars, and owners should do a better job of lighting their stations at night. But as the price of gas increases, we expect that the number of thefts will also continue increasing."

2. Norma J. Holtzclaw is a local realtor, and she spoke to the Rotary Club last evening. During the speech, she focused on the growing trend for single people to buy property. She told the club members: "The singles market in some areas now exceeds 25% of all home sales, but the trend isn't that pronounced in this area. Locally, about 10% of all the homes being sold are sold to singles, and that percentage seems to be increasing. It includes the sale of co-ops and condominiums as well as detached single-family dwellings. A lot of my clients say they're buying property for the tax benefits and as an investment. Usually, by the time they buy a house, singles are in their 30s or 40s, although I've had a few in their middle and late 20s. Other factors are contributing to the upswing in these sales. Because of the baby boom after World War II, there are a lot more people in the home-buying age range. More people seem to be living alone; many are divorced. More people also are getting married later in life, and more people 65 and older are living alone. Overall, townhouses are the most popular type of housing for singles, since their owners don't have to worry as much about the upkeep and maintenance; it's all done for them.

Condominiums rank second with single buyers. Single-family homes are third, and mobile homes a poor fourth."

3. The American Medical Association issued a report in Philadelphia today. It concerns the results of a three-year study of medical treatment in United States jails. The American Medical Association surveyed one thousand inmates at thirty jails across the country. Its report states: "Although these are only preliminary findings, they are indicative of a high percentage of undetected illnesses among the jail population of the country. Only 37% of the jails surveyed had medical clinics, and only 13 percent of the jails gave all their inmates routine physicals on admission. Treatment facilities for mentally ill offenders were available in 43% of the jails. As examples of our findings, 15% of the inmates examined in an Indiana jail had positive tuberculosis skin tests, and in a small jail in Washington state, 15% of the prisoners examined had positive X-ray readings for TB. 66% of the inmates in a Georgia jail had abnormal urinalysis tests. The initial findings show a shocking lack of medical manpower and services throughout the country. The ultimate objective of the program is the collection of information to be used for the development of a national certification system for jail medical programs, using approaches similar to those applied to the certification of hospitals and medical schools." Each of the thousand prisoners was given a physical examination as part of the American Medical Association study, and the prisoner's medical history was taken. The study is financed by a federal grant and will run for an additional two years. The grant provides an annual budget of $497,652. It started one year ago.

4. A rise in insurance rates is being blamed for a rise in hit-and-run motor vehicle accidents within the state. Richard Byrum, state insurance commissioner, discussed the problem during a press conference in his office today. He said, "The problem is serious. At first, we thought it was a police problem, but police in the state have asked my office to look into it. There has been a dramatic increase in hit-and-run accidents in the state, particularly in big cities where you find the higher insurance rates. I'm told that last year we had nearly 28,000 motor vehicle accidents in the state, and 4,500 were hit-and-run. People are taking chances driving without proper insurance coverage, or they're afraid of a premium increase if they have insurance and stop and report an accident. They seem to think, 'What the heck, no one saw it, and I won't get caught,' and they just bug out of there. If you look at the insurance rates in the state, it's practically impossible for some people to pay them, and as insurance rates go up, the rate of leaving the scene of an accident increases. Drivers with the worst records—those with several accidents and traffic citations—pay as much as $3,600 a year in insurance premiums, and they may pay even more than that if they are young or have a high-powered car. Even good drivers found at fault in an accident may find their rates going up several hundred dollars for the next three to five years. So leaving the scene of an accident is definitely tied to the economic situation, yet the insurance company people I've talked to say they can't do anything about it. It's just not realistic to expect them to lower their rates; they aren't making that much money. Right now, I'm not sure what we'll do about the situation. In the meantime, we can expect more hit-and-run accidents and more drivers going without any insurance coverage because of its high cost."

Exercise 7

QUOTATIONS AND ATTRIBUTION

USING QUOTES IN NEWS STORIES

INSTRUCTIONS: Write complete news stories based on the following information. Use some quotations in each story to emphasize its highlights, but do not use quotations to tell the entire story. Use the most interesting, important and revealing quotations, not just those that happen to appear first.

1. Michael Ernest Layoux, 22, is a clerk at a convenience store at 1284 East Forest Boulevard. He was robbed late yesterday. Here is his account of the incident: "First, you have to understand where the store is. It's located in a remote area in the northeast corner of town. There's nothing around that's open at night, so I'm all alone in the store. I started carrying a gun to work last year after I read where two clerks at another convenience store in the city were robbed and killed. Carrying a gun is against company policy, but I figured I had to protect myself. We're open 24 hours, and the store has a history of holdups, particularly at night when there aren't any customers in the store. But it never happened to me personally before. Just after 11, when the store was empty except for me last night, this guy walks in and asks for a pack of Winston cigarettes. I handed him a pack, and then he pulled a gun and says, "You see what I got?" He had a pistol, and he held it low, level with his hip, so no one outside the store could look in and see it. Then he asked me for the money, and I gave it to him. We never have more than $30 in cash in the register. It's company policy. We put all the big bills we get into a floor safe we can't open. So he didn't get much, maybe $20. Then he motioned for me to move toward the cooler. We have a big cooler in the back for beer and soda and other stuff we have to keep cold. When he started shoving me toward the cooler I really got scared. There's no lock on the cooler, so he couldn't lock me in while he was getting away. There's no reason for him to put me in the cooler; I could walk right out. The only thing I could figure was that he wanted to shoot me, and he wanted to do it in some place where no one could see what was happening. That's where the two other clerks were shot last year, in a cooler in their store. Since they were killed, I've kept a .25-caliber pistol under the counter, and when he motioned for me to get into the cooler I shot him. He'd started turning toward the cooler, and then he must have heard me cocking the pistol because he started jerking his head back around toward me. I shot him 3 times in the chest and side, but I didn't know right away that I hit him. He just ran out through the front door. He didn't even open it. He ran right through the glass. I called the police, and they found his body in a field about 200 yards away. He was dead, and now I've lost my job. But I wouldn't do it any different. The police talked to me for almost two hours, and they said it was OK, that I acted in self-defense. Then this morning, just after 8, I got a call at home from my district manager, and he said I'm fired because it's against company policy to have a gun in the store. It's a real shame, because I'm still a college student, and I need the job. I can attend classes during the day and then work at night at the store. I've been doing it for 4 years now, and I want to graduate in a couple more months. But I can understand the company's rules. Most people don't know how to handle guns. I do. I've been around them and using them all my life."

   Company officials refused to comment about the robbery or the firing.

2. Lillian Shisenaunt is a pharmacist. She was elected president of your County Pharmacists Association at a meeting held last year. During an interview with you today, she talked about an issue of concern to pharmacists, one that the pharmacists talked about at their meeting last night, along with possible solutions. She said: " We find that we've got an awful lot of older people taking three or four or five different drugs all at once. If they think that's going to do them any good, they're fooling themselves. We find that, in many cases, the medicine—the dosage and the way its taken—are all wrong. Patients, especially the elderly, sometimes get all their different drugs confused, and then they take two of one and none of the others. Even when the elderly take all the right pills, sometimes the different drugs nullify each other. Different doctors these people see give them prescriptions without knowing what else a patient is taking for some other problem. So some of these oldsters become real junkies, and they don't even know it. As they get older and have more problems, they take more and more medication. After a few years, their children think their minds are going because they're so heavily sedated all the time. But if they get a good doctor, or a good druggist, they probably can stop taking some of the medicines, and then they don't actually have all the problems people think they have. A lot of these older people aren't senile; they just take too many different drugs, and then it hits them like senility. Drug companies don't help. If you look at most drug companies, they test their products on healthy young adults, a 25-year-old, 180-pound male. Then the companies set a normal adult dosage based on the clinical tests with these young adults. But the things that determine how drugs affect you change with age, so what the drug companies set as a normal daily dosage doesn't always fit an older person with a number of conditions. If you look at studies of hospital emergency rooms, you'll find that people over 60 are admitted twice as often for adverse drug reactions as the young. Most people don't know that. They think about all the problems of the young, not the old. But most of the problems can be solved, and without too much effort. People should talk to a good pharmacist or physician. Unfortunately, we find that most people are scared of their doctors and don't ask them enough questions and don't understand what their pharmacists have to offer. Patients also should make a list of all their different medicines and dosages each time they go to a doctor and tell him what they're taking. Then when they get a new prescription, they should write down the doctor's instructions, and they should get all their prescriptions from just one pharmacist so the pharmacist knows everything they're taking and can watch for any problems. If they ask, the pharmacist can color code their pill bottles so they can't be confused. But patients also have a responsibility for their own health care. Each morning, they should sort out all that day's pills ahead of time, and then they'd be less likely to make a mistake."

CHAPTER 9

INTERVIEWS AND POLLS

Reporters interview people to learn their opinions and to obtain factual information about events in the news. Reporters like interviews because they provide a fast, easy way to obtain the news. Often there is no alternative. Reporters cannot personally observe every newsworthy event that occurs in their communities. There are too many events, and some occur unexpectedly. So reporters interview other people who witnessed the events, who became involved in them or who are concerned about their consequences.

Unfortunately, interviews are notoriously unreliable. Sources may fail to notice important details or may misunderstand or forget the details. Other sources may want to promote a cause or gain recognition for themselves. Thus, they reveal only their side of an issue and present it as favorably as possible.

Like their sources, the reporters conducting an interview may fail to recognize the importance of some details and may misunderstand or forget others. Reporters may also fail to consult a second source to verify the details and may make some factual errors while writing their stories.

Regardless of their training, it is difficult for reporters to be totally neutral observers during the interviewing process. Some personal prejudices may be unconscious but still affect what the reporters see, remember and consider important. Even the reporters' ages and physical characteristics may affect their sources. For example, older sources may not respect young reporters, regarding them as inexperienced and unreliable. Conversely, younger sources may be more responsive to young reporters. Researchers have also found that if a black and a white interviewer ask the same questions, they are likely to receive different answers.

The way reporters word questions also affects their sources' responses. Children are particularly susceptible to suggestion and often give the answers that interviewers seem to expect. Adults are more cautious and, to avoid embarrassment, sometimes give the answers that are socially acceptable. A source who is unaware of a fact may pretend to know it to avoid seeming uninformed.

Through months and years of practice, perceptive reporters improve their interviewing skills. By studying the advice provided by more experienced reporters, beginners can avoid many of the problems likely to arise during interviews. This chapter will discuss those problems and recommend solutions to them.

ARRANGING AN INTERVIEW

Normally, reporters call in advance to make appointments for formal interviews. The reporters identify themselves and the newspapers they work for and explain why they want to conduct an interview. Then their source can prepare for the interview, perhaps by gathering information the reporters specifically requested.

Reporters try to arrange most interviews with top officials, such as the presidents of businesses and the mayors of cities, rather than with subordinates, such as secretaries, assistants or public information officers. Reporters want to interview people who have first-hand knowledge of their topics and can immediately answer all their questions. Also, because top officials have more power, their opinions are more important than those of their subordinates.

In-depth interviews require a minimum of one hour and often take two or three hours. Reporters usually offer to go to the sources' homes or offices because, if the sources are in familiar surroundings, they are more likely to be comfortable and thus to speak more freely. Perhaps even more important, the site of an interview should be private, free of interruptions and distractions. If other people are present, they may interrupt or inhibit a source.

Reporters rarely schedule major interviews in their newsrooms. Most newsrooms lack privacy and seem too noisy and chaotic, especially for strangers. Reporters also avoid luncheon appointments because they want to talk during an interview, not eat. Luncheon meetings require too much time, create too many distractions and can be unnecessarily expensive.

PREPARING FOR AN INTERVIEW

To prepare for an interview, reporters may spend several hours learning all they can about their source and about the topics they want to discuss with that source. Reporters must be prepared to ask the right questions—meaningful, intelligent questions—and to understand their source's answers.

If reporters are well prepared, they will not waste any time by asking unnecessary questions about issues that have already been widely publicized, questions that might bore their source and reveal their own ignorance. They are also more likely to recognize significant statements and are better able to ask intelligent followup questions about them. Reporters who prepare for an interview also are more likely to notice if their sources are avoiding certain topics or are presenting only one side of a controversial issue. Moreover, if reporters obviously understand an issue, their sources are likely to be more trusting and to speak more freely.

Reporters who fail to prepare for an interview are less likely to uncover interesting and important new information. Because of their ignorance, the reporters may be forced to rely on the source for guidance and may be unable to detect the source's biases. Reporters will not know what to ask, nor what is new, important or controversial. Inevitably, some sources will detect the reporters' ignorance and try to take advantage of it. The sources may avoid complex topics that they fear the reporters would not understand, or they may try to promote a cause or to hide their errors. If reporters are obviously unprepared, a source may lose interest in an interview and provide only perfunctory responses to the reporters' questions. A few sources will immediately end the interview—and scold the reporters.

Thus, the preparation of good questions may be the single most important step in the interviewing process. Sources rarely reveal startling new information without some prompting. They may not want to discuss some issues or may be hesitant to speak freely with reporters whom they do not know. So reporters must pry the information (and more colorful quotations) from them.

Good interviewers write their questions in advance, then check off each question as they ask it so that they do not repeat any questions or forget to ask an important question. All the questions should be arranged in a logical order, so that a source's answer to one question leads to the following question.

Some reporters like to list their most important questions first so that if they run out of time, only their least important questions will remain unanswered. Depending on the situation, reporters may also save their most embarrassing and difficult questions for the end of interviews. By then, their sources should be more trusting and accustomed to answering their questions. If a source refuses to answer the embarrassing questions and abruptly ends an interview, reporters will have already obtained most of the information needed for their stories.

At some time during your life, you are likely to be interviewed for a consumer survey or public opinion poll. When the pollsters call you, notice that they usually begin with a few easy questions. Their last question will be the most personal—perhaps, "What is your annual income?" Even then, pollsters rarely ask for the exact amount. Rather, they list several income ranges and ask in which range your income falls. If such a question came first, people might immediately hang up their telephones or walk away. But if that is the last question, people are more likely to answer it, as well as all the preceding questions.

As you prepare for an interview, ask yourself, "What questions would my readers want to ask?" and "Which facts are new, important and likely to interest or affect the public?" After deciding exactly what you want to know, ask your source about those specific points. If a fact is particularly important, begin with a general question about it, then prepare several followup questions designed to elicit more information about it.

The best questions tend to be short, simple and clearly relevant. They are also specific. Vague questions elicit vague answers: abstract generalities rather than specific, factual details. Sources may not answer long, complex questions because they do not understand them. Moreover, long questions will consume too much of the time allocated for the interview.

Reporters try to avoid asking questions that can be answered with a simple "yes" or "no." They want lively responses—colorful quotations and interesting details—and consequently ask questions that require sources to give more detailed answers. They may ask the sources to "describe" or to "explain" or to tell "how" or "why" some event occurred.

CONDUCTING AN INTERVIEW

After scheduling an interview, reporters should arrive promptly and should be appropriately dressed. Too many college students dress informally, regardless of the circumstances, then wonder why their sources fail to give them much time, information, trust or respect.

Reporters often begin important interviews by chatting quietly with the sources. They may mention a subject of mutual interest or ask about something interesting or unusual they noticed in the source's home or office. The reporters want to put the source at ease and to establish a friendly relationship so the source will be more willing to answer their questions. That is especially important when a source is not used to answering reporters' questions.

When the serious questioning begins, reporters should take control of the interview—and then remain in control. They should decide which matters are most important, then encourage the source to discuss those matters. If the source lapses into generalities, reporters should ask more specific questions. If the source strays from the topic, reporters should immediately ask additional questions to return the conversation to it. Reporters cannot let a source waste time or evade important questions.

Thus, good interviewers must be careful listeners. They must listen carefully to ensure that a source has answered their questions—and that they understand the answers. Reporters must ask the source to repeat or to explain any comment that is unclear. If the source fails to provide some important information, reporters must ask followup questions. If the source raises an interesting point that the reporters are not expecting or do not know about, they must ask for more details, temporarily setting aside their remaining prepared questions. Reporters must also ask the source to spell names and to repeat important numbers. Later, the reporters should verify the accuracy of these spellings and numbers.

Reporters occasionally ask a source to repeat important facts two or three times. Each time a source recalls a fact, he or she may add a new and sometimes important detail. However, reporters should not argue or debate with a source. Instead, they should encourage the source to express his or her opinions as fully and freely as possible. Few sources will continue to speak freely after reporters disagree with them.

After asking all their prepared questions, reporters should ask the source whether there is any other information that should be included in the story. Although some sources will have nothing to add, others will provide their interviews' most valuable information. A source may mention related issues, new developments of great importance or facts of personal interest about which the source may begin to speak more candidly and enthusiastically.

Before ending an interview, reporters also should be certain that they understand everything that has been said. As a precaution, they should also ask how and where they can reach the source if a question arises while they are writing the story.

Good reporters will interview a second and third, and possibly even a fourth and fifth, person for a story. When they interview one person, reporters typically learn only what that person wants them to know or perceives to be the truth. By interviewing several other people, reporters can verify the source's remarks and obtain a fuller account of the topic. The additional interviews are essential when reporters are writing about controversial issues.

During interviews, reporters observe their sources so that they can describe as well as quote them. Reporters may, when appropriate, describe a source's height, weight, posture, hair, voice, gestures, facial expressions, clothing, jewelry, home, car, office or family.

Some experts say reporters should also analyze and respond to their sources' nonverbal behavior. A cough, grin, shaking fist or nod of the head may reveal that a source is nervous or relaxed, sympathetic or angry, deceitful or truthful. Researchers have found that people speak more rapidly when they are anxious about a topic, and that they begin to stutter, repeat words, leave sentences unfinished and look away from their interviewers. Few beginning reporters possess the knowledge necessary to interpret accurately and take advantage of all these nonverbal cues. However, experienced reporters may begin to watch their sources' physical reactions to difficult questions and to consider those responses as they continue the interview.

Reporters should specify the rules they intend to follow at the beginning of an interview. If a source says that an interview is "off the record," reporters should ask what is meant by that term, since the source may be confused and really mean something else. Normally, information provided off the record cannot be published. Reporters may try to change the source's mind. If that fails, they may cancel the interview, then seek the same facts elsewhere.

If a source grants an interview and—at the end of the interview—says it was off the record, reporters are not obligated to cooperate. Most reporters probably would feel free to report all the information they received under those circumstances.

Other sources will want to review stories before they are published. Most newspapers prohibit this practice. Editors fear that it would take too much time, that some stories might be lost and that some people shown the stories would want to edit them. Then the reporters, their editors and the sources might spend hours haggling over the

ISBN 0-15-500602-9

changes. To avoid the problem, reporters can tell their sources that deadline pressures make the practice impossible, or that it violates their newspapers' policies. If a source persists, reporters should tell that source to call an editor.

Dealing with Hostile Sources

Most people cooperate with reporters because interviews are mutually beneficial, enabling sources to achieve their goals at the same time they enable reporters to obtain the information necessary for a story. Sources may enjoy seeing their names in print, welcome the opportunity to tell their side of a story, hope to promote some cause or inform the public about an issue they consider important. Sources may also cooperate because they are flattered that reporters consider their opinions important or are curious about how the media operate.

However, some people are hostile and refuse to talk to reporters. They may distrust the media and fear that a topic is too complex for reporters to understand or that the story will be inaccurate or sensational. Hostile sources frequently complain—sometimes justifiably—that reporters have misquoted them and made other embarrassing errors in previous stories. Some people are too nervous to talk to reporters. Others may consider a topic unimportant, may dislike a particular newspaper or may fear that any story, regardless of its accuracy, may harm them.

When reporters encounter a hostile source, they may try to learn why the source is hesitant to speak to them. After learning the reason, they may be able to overcome that specific objection. Reporters may also try to convince sources that they will benefit from a story's publication—for example, that favorable publicity will help them and the organizations they represent. Reporters may argue that it would look bad if they had to say the source refused to comment about an issue, or that a story would be less damaging if the source explained his or her side of an issue.

At a last resort, experienced reporters may try to threaten or bluff a hostile source. Reporters usually begin by obtaining as much information as possible from other people, including the source's critics. Then they confront the source and ask for a comment on the information. Alternatively, reporters may pretend that they want to talk about an unrelated issue or that they have already obtained all the information they need for a story. Then the reporters may ask the hostile source to explain a few details or to respond to some minor allegations. By responding, the source may unintentionally provide more information and confirm the information's accuracy.

The Problem of Note Taking

Another major problem, especially for beginners, is note taking. A few experienced reporters do not take any notes during interviews. Instead, they try to remember everything their sources say and write their notes later. Those reporters fear that, if they take notes during an interview, their sources will become nervous and speak less freely. They may find it too difficult to think of questions, listen to a source's answers and take thorough and accurate notes all at the same time.

While writing the book "In Cold Blood," about the murder of a Kansas family, Truman Capote was afraid that a tape recorder would inhibit the people he wanted to interview. So Capote trained himself to remember everything they said. He practiced by talking to a friend or reading for a while, then writing down everything he had heard or read. Later, he would compare his record with a recording of the conversation or with the actual reading material. Capote said, "Finally, when I got to be about 97 percent accurate, I felt ready to take on this book."

Unless they have photographic memories, most newspaper reporters need to take detailed notes. Traditionally, reporters have used paper and pencil to record their notes in longhand, and most continue to do so. A recent survey found that 68 percent never use tape recorders and that only 12 percent use them frequently.

Good interviewers take copious notes, writing down much more information than they can possibly use. At the time they take the notes, reporters often do not know which facts they will need or which facts they will want to emphasize in their stories. If they record as much as possible, they are less likely to forget an important point or to make a factual error. Later, they can discard the unimportant and irrelevant items.

Few reporters know shorthand. Few, if any, schools of journalism in the United States teach or require it. However, many reporters develop a shorthand of their own. Because they cannot record everything a source says, they leave out some words and abbreviate others. They may take notes only on the most crucial points—key words, phrases and ideas—then fill in the details later. Reporters also write down every name, number and good quotation. Reporters can learn to recognize good quotations and key statements as they are spoken and train themselves to remember those quotations long enough to write them down, word for word.

If a source speaks too rapidly, reporters can ask the source to slow down or repeat an important statement. Reporters might say: "Could you wait a minute? That's an important point, and I'd like to write it down." Then, to be certain that they have recorded it accurately, reporters can read the statement back to the source. If a source is talking too rapidly for reporters to record an important statement, they ask the source an unimportant "dummy" question, then catch up on their notes while the source answers it.

If their note taking makes a source nervous, reporters can stop and explain that the notes will help them write more accurate and thorough stories. Reporters can also show or read their notes to the source.

After completing an interview, reporters should review their notes as soon as possible, while everything is fresh in their minds. They may want to fill in some gaps or be certain that they understand everything a source said. Finally, reporters should write their stories as soon as possible after the interview. The longer they wait, the more likely they are to forget some facts and to distort others.

The use of tape recorders enables reporters to concentrate on the questions they want to ask and on their sources' responses to those questions. Tapes also provide verbatim and permanent records, so reporters make fewer factual errors and their sources are less likely to claim that they were misquoted. Moreover, when reporters replay the tape, they are likely to find some important statements that they had not noticed during the interviews.

Despite these advantages, few reporters use tape recorders, especially for routine stories, because the use of tape recorders requires too much time. After taping a one-hour interview, reporters would have to replay the entire one-hour tape at least once, and perhaps two or three times, before writing their stories. It might also be difficult to find a particular fact or quotation in the tape. By comparison, reporters can read their handwritten notes in a few minutes and find a particular fact or quotation in a few seconds.

In the past, reporters also feared that their sources might freeze at the sight of a tape recorder and that the recorders might break or run out of tape. Modern tape recorders are more reliable, unobtrusive and able to play for longer periods of time. Tape recorders have also become small enough to hide in a pocket—but they should be used openly. If reporters intend to record an interview, they have an obligation to inform their source of that fact.

As a final alternative, reporters may record major interviews and augment the tapes with written notes. The reporters can consult their notes to write the stories, then use the tape recordings to verify the accuracy of important facts and quotations.

Telephone Interviews

Reporters conduct most of their interviews by telephone, often without having had time to prepare their questions. People who have stories they want published in a newspaper often call reporters unexpectedly, and the reporters may want to interview them immediately. Reporters may also be instructed to call immediately and interview people involved in spot news stories, such as crimes, accidents and fires.

Telephone calls save enormous amounts of time, since reporters do not have to leave their newsrooms, drive to a source's home or office, wait until the source is free, conduct the interview, then walk back to their cars, drive to their offices, find new parking places and return to their desks. Experienced reporters will cradle a telephone on one shoulder and type their notes directly onto a computer. When they hear the noise and realize that reporters are typing everything they say, some sources become upset; they begin to speak more cautiously and try to end the interview as quickly as possible. Reporters can try to reassure them and, if the noise continues to upset a source, can begin to take their notes more quietly in longhand. Sources used to dealing with reporters become accustomed to the noise.

Reporters for the nation's largest news media obtain many of their stories by calling sources throughout the United States. If your telephone rang and a reporter said, "This is CBS News," "The Washington Post" or "Time magazine," you would probably give the reporter your full attention and cooperation.

Telephone calls, however, are not a very satisfactory means of obtaining in-depth interviews about controversial or complex issues and personalities. It is difficult to cultivate sources known only by telephone and never seen face-to-face, and therefore difficult to persuade those sources to talk for a long time and to answer questions about embarrassing or personal matters. Thus, telephone interviews tend to be brief and superficial. If reporters want to conduct longer, in-depth interviews, they try to visit the source in person.

WRITING THE STORY

As they begin to write, reporters must examine critically all the information they have gathered, decide which facts are most newsworthy and then concentrate on those facts. In doing so, they must discard clichés, platitudes and self-praise, as well as the repetitious, the irrelevant and the obvious. This task is more difficult than it may seem. A student interested in the U.S. space shuttle interviewed a representative of the National Aeronautics and Space Administration but lost control of the interview and was overwhelmed by facts promoting NASA. Because the student included much of that information in her story, it sounded more like a news release for NASA than a news story:

> NASA has two major purposes: to develop transportation through the use of the space shuttle and to transfer technology from previous space programs into common use.
>
> A representative for NASA gave several examples of technological innovations that resulted from projects such as the Apollo and Skylab programs. These innovations include the development of Teflon, artificial limbs, global weather forecasting, communication satellites and computer technology.
>
> The representative added that many of the computer systems that Americans take for granted today are a direct result of the Apollo project. He said the computers were developed for use in the Apollo program and that the technology learned as a result affects almost everyone in every day of their lives.

All the information in the story is accurate, but much of it is several years old and irrelevant to the student's topic, the U.S. space shuttle. (NASA depends on annual appropriations from Congress and, to win support for the space program, attempts to emphasize its benefits for the American public.)

While writing your story, also remember to use quotations judiciously. Try not to tell the entire story in quotations, only its highlights. After shadowing a police reporter, a journalism student began her report as follows:

> Karen Kaeppler, the night police reporter for The Daily Telegraph, could teach dignitaries a thing or two about diplomacy. In the course of her job she has been refused information, hung up on, yelled at, ignored, sexually harassed and called every name in the book. In each case she smiles, politely says, "Thank you very much" and almost always manages to walk away with the information she needs.

Later in her report, the student used this mix of quotations and paraphrases:

> Kaeppler has worked the evening police beat at The Daily Telegraph for almost two years. She is scheduled to move to another beat—a daytime beat—next month. She does not know what she will be covering, but is anxious to move on.
>
> "This job is really wearing on me hard," Kaeppler said. "It's ugly. It's all death and destruction. Nobody wants to help you or give you any information. Those in trouble don't want to jeopardize their cases, and most of the police just don't like reporters."
>
> According to Kaeppler, the only thing tougher than being a reporter in the midst of a bunch of cops is being a woman reporter.
>
> "I've devised my own way to deal with it, though," Kaeppler said. "At first I had a really hard time. The police wouldn't take me seriously. They would say condescending and sexist, harassing things to me just because I'm a woman. Some of them even went so far as to come on to me. At first it really bothered me. Then I realized the only way I could get them to take me seriously was to prove to them that I am serious about what I do. So, when I ask a question about a case and they reply by telling me how pretty I am, I ignore the remark and repeat my question."

Reporters try to make their sources come alive through the use of quotations and description. After a newspaper editor spoke to a class of journalism students, one student effectively described the manner in which the editor answered questions as well as his exact words:

> Lewis answered questions quickly and sharply, speaking in short, clipped sentences, never wasting a word. Sometimes, anticipating questions, he interrupted the students with his answers.
>
> At one point, he told the students: "I don't know why you would want to get into the newspaper profession. There are long hours, low pay, hard work and lots of pressure and strain."
>
> Why is he in the profession?
>
> "I like it all," he said.

Do not expect your sources to be totally candid, especially not while talking about themselves, their work or their programs. Rather, sources are likely to praise themselves:

> According to Wang, the program has become the best in the state.

"We've worked hard," Levcenko said. "But it's been worth it. People really like what we're doing, and it's obviously helping our clients."

Never allow a source to use or manipulate you in order to engage in self-praise. Either ignore the self-praise or, if the topic is important, ask your source for evidence—specific facts—to support the claim. Even better, interview people using the program. They're the experts, the ones who truly know whether or not a program works. The people using a program are also likely to be more candid about its strengths and weaknesses.

The use of unidentified sources, particularly outside Washington, D.C., is greatly exaggerated. However, if reporters believe that there is a legitimate need to withhold a source's name—to protect that source from undeserved embarrassment or retaliation, for example—they can identify the source by an initial, a first name, a fictitious name or a descriptive phrase. If you do not identify a source, tell your readers why:

> The woman, whose identity is being withheld to protect her daughter, told police that Johnson fondled and kissed her 7-year-old for weeks before she learned what was happening.

> Like many other homeless people, Jason feels the police harass the homeless. He agreed to talk if he did not have to give his last name. He fears the police would remember it.
> "I think they pick on the homeless because we're helpless," Jason said. "It's getting on their nerves to see us. It's really bad for us because we've got no place to go, nowhere to hide, and they think we're all crooks and winos."

FEATURE-STORY INTERVIEWS AND PRESS CONFERENCES

Reporters interview people for personality or feature stories that describe people in the news. Personality and feature stories go into more depth than most news stories, and they are more colorful and descriptive. Reporters writing such stories usually want to reveal someone's personality, mannerisms, accomplishments or opinions. Reporters may talk to that person for several hours; talk to that person's family, friends and business associates; and then return to interview the source a second or third time. Reporters may also observe the source in action for several days, both at home and at work.

Press conferences are less personal and rewarding for journalists than one-to-one interviews. Most press conferences, including the president's, are more convenient for sources than for reporters. Press conferences enable sources to speak to dozens of reporters at once. It is usually impossible for a single reporter to ask several questions or to obtain any exclusive information at a press conference. Also, people used to dealing with the media may find it easier to manipulate reporters at a press conference. They may begin with long statements that consume much of the allotted time and that present only their side of an issue, then avoid recognizing reporters who are likely to ask hostile questions. If reporters are not given an opportunity to ask followup questions, press conferences make it easier for the sources to evade some questions.

Newspaper reporters rarely use a question-and-answer format in writing their stories; this format requires too much space and makes it more difficult for readers to grasp a story's highlights. Instead, reporters begin most interviews with a summary lead, then present their story's highlights in the following paragraphs. All the information is presented in the order of its importance, not the order in which it was provided by a source. Background information is kept to a minimum and presented in later paragraphs. Also, reporters vary their style of writing so that every sentence and every paragraph does not begin with the source's name.

CONDUCTING AN INFORMAL POLL

Reporters often conduct polls to learn people's opinions of issues in the news. To conduct a truly accurate public opinion poll, reporters must interview a random sample of all the residents in their community. Because that is difficult, some newspapers hire professionals to conduct their polls, especially during elections.

Reporters also conduct less formal surveys. They may interview local experts or simply people they meet on a street. Those reporters, however, learn only the opinions of the individuals they interview. They cannot generalize from the results. Still, the informal surveys are often interesting and enable reporters to localize issues in the news.

If you are asked to conduct an informal survey—to ask a dozen people whether they favor a new tax, for example—encourage people to respond with more than a simple "Yes" or "No." Ask people why they favor or oppose the tax. If they respond with vague generalities, ask them to be more specific. The responses you obtain are vital; if the responses are dull, vague or unclear, your story will be just as uninteresting.

Your lead should summarize your findings—the opinion expressed by a majority of the people you interviewed. The lead must do more than report that you conducted a poll or that the people you interviewed were "divided" about an issue. People are divided about every controversial issue, and the fact that you conducted a poll is not newsworthy; only the results are likely to interest your readers. Leads should also be as specific as possible. Instead of reporting that a "majority" of the people you interviewed favored or opposed an issue, report that majority's exact size. Was it 51 percent, 84 percent or 99.7 percent? For these reasons, three of the following leads need to be revised. Only the fourth is well-written:

> One hundred college students were polled Tuesday about the nation's pornography laws. (This lead fails to report the news—the results of that poll.)

> One hundred college students responded with varied answers Tuesday when they were asked, "Should Congress legalize the sale of pornography?" (This lead states the obvious—the fact that people disagree about a controversial issue.)

> One hundred college students were interviewed Tuesday, and a majority said the sale of pornography should be legalized for adults, but not for children. (This lead is too vague—it fails to reveal the size of that majority.)

> BETTER: Sixty-eight out of 100 college students interviewed Tuesday said the federal government should legalize the sale of pornography to adults, but not to children.

After the lead, present two or three paragraphs of introductory material before you begin to quote specific individuals. The second and third paragraphs in your story might summarize other highlights or trends, and the fourth paragraph might quote the exact question that you asked each respondent. Shifting directly from the lead to a quotation will be too abrupt a transition and will make your story seem disorganized.

Also, if the quotation placed in the second paragraph reflects the opinion of a single individual, it is probably not important enough to merit that position in the story.

Fully identify every person you quote. In addition to their names, identify students by their major and year in school, faculty members by their rank and department, and nonacademic employees by their jobs. If some people refuse to identify themselves or to answer your questions, ask them why they are reluctant to respond and try to identify them by some other means, such as their age.

You do not have to quote everyone you interview, only the people who say something colorful, important or unusual. Paraphrase or discard responses that are awkward, wordy, unclear or repetitious. If two people make similar replies, combine their responses in a single sentence or paragraph. However, because two people are unlikely to use exactly the same words, you cannot attribute a direct quotation to both of them. Instead, paraphrase their responses or indicate that several people expressed the same opinion, then quote one of those people to illustrate that point of view. For example:

> Lionel Jackson and Eugene Bushnell, both seniors majoring in political science, said the state's sales tax discriminates against the poor.

> Three students said they had dropped out of college for a year or more. Marsha Dilte, a senior, explained: "I was running out of money, and I really wasn't certain what I wanted to do. After two years of working as a secretary, I had enough money to finish college and knew I wanted to be a nurse."

Organize all the quotations in a logical order, grouping similar responses together and placing transitions between those groups. Look for trends—perhaps consistent differences between the responses of men and women, young and old, students and nonstudents. First quote people who expressed the majority viewpoint, then people who expressed opposing viewpoints. Some quotations may be divided into even smaller groups. For example: if the respondents who favor an issue give four reasons for their beliefs, you might begin by quoting respondents who mentioned the most popular reason, then quote respondents who cited the second, third and fourth most popular reasons.

Transitions should be interesting. Many summarize the viewpoint of the group of quotations that reporters are about to present. The following transitions appeared in a poll about high school students' opinions of the Army. The paragraphs following each of these transitions quoted students who expressed the viewpoint that the paragraph summarized:

> Fourteen students said they consider service in the Army a patriotic duty.

> Seven students said they plan to join the Army because they want to travel but cannot afford to go overseas by themselves.

> Four women said the Army offers higher salaries than civilian employers and is more willing to promote women.

Vary your sentence structure and avoid beginning every sentence and every paragraph with the name of the respondent you are quoting. Also decide which of the people you interviewed made the most interesting statements, then devote several paragraphs to their remarks. If you quote 10 or 20 people but devote only one paragraph to each of their remarks, your story will seem too choppy and superficial.

Avoid repeating the words "yes" and "no" when reporting the opinions expressed by your respondents. If the fourth paragraph in your story repeats the question that each respondent was asked, and the 10th paragraph reports that, "Mary Alton responded 'yes,' " readers may not understand that she was responding to the question presented six paragraphs earlier:

> Mary Alton responded, "Yes."
> REVISED: Mary Alton agreed that the president's relationship with Congress is deteriorating.

> None of them said "yes" when asked if the women's movement has affected their lives.
> REVISED: None of them said the women's movement has affected their lives.

Be specific and clear, even if it means that you must briefly restate an idea:

> Gayle Prince echoed the opinions expressed by Drucker.
> REVISED: Gayle Prince agreed that apartment complexes have a right to reject couples that have children.

> Sandy Roach more or less agreed with Miss Hass.
> REVISED: Sandy Roach agreed that government workers are overpaid but said it is the fault of politicians, not of the unions representing government workers.

Never criticize or attach any labels to your respondents' answers. Do not refer to any answers as "interesting," "thoughtful" or "uninformed." Simply report whatever your respondents said, and let your readers judge their remarks for themselves (your readers' conclusions may be quite different from your own). Also avoid making comments about the manner in which people responded to your questions, and be especially careful to avoid trite generalities. For example, do not report that one person seemed "sincere," or that another seemed "apathetic." However, you can report specific details, such as the fact that one person paused for nearly a minute before answering your question and then talked about the question for more than 30 minutes.

Some of the people you attempt to interview may be undecided on or unfamiliar with your topic. People who are undecided or uninformed usually constitute a small minority and can be mentioned in your story's final paragraphs. In the final paragraphs you might also describe the methods you used to conduct your poll: the exact number of people you interviewed and the way you selected those people. Never summarize or comment on your findings in the final paragraphs; a news story contains only one summary, and it belongs in the lead.

Newspapers often conduct informal polls of this type, because they are fast and cheap, but they are often inaccurate. The polls are so notoriously inaccurate that newspapers have begun to conduct more systematic studies, using techniques developed by social scientists. In the past, when reporters interviewed 50 or 100 people on a street corner, they could not generalize about the results of their poll because those 50 or 100 people were unlikely to be typical of everyone in their community. For that reason, you can report only the opinions of the 10 or 20 people you interview; you cannot suggest that other people on your campus share their opinions. Using more scientific techniques, reporters at many newspapers now conduct their polls by selecting a random sample of the people living in their communities—usually a sample of several hundred people. Because of their more scientific procedures and carefully worded questions, the reporters can accurately determine the public's opinions about important issues and the way people will vote in elections.

St. Louis Post-Dispatch

WRITE & WRONG

By **Harry Levins**
Post-Dispatch Writing Coach

—Get to chronological order as soon as your story, your editor and your conscience will allow.

—Every reader sighs with relief when he gets to that point in an article where the journalism ends and the story finally begins.

—Charlie McDowell,
Chief Washington correspondent,
Richmond (Va.) Times-Dispatch

The Coach dug into his back files to revive those quotes after reading Jim Dustin's Page 1 piece on Sunday, Dec. 5, on the flooding in Old Monroe, Mo.

You'll recall that Jim got through the journalism in a hurry, and then set out—in strict chronological order—what was happening in Old Monroe as the water rose, inch by inch, hour by hour. The result was a fine story. The suspense went up along with the river, holding the reader's attention throughout.

Not all stories lend themselves to this approach. But whenever chronological order can be used, it ought to be. After all, that's the narrative tradition, the way most of us tell stories. Novelists begin at the beginning: "It was the best of times, it was the worst of times." Tale-spinners at a newspaper tavern do the same thing: "It all began when . . . And then . . . And finally . . ."

In all too many stories, we ignore chronological order. We weave back and forth in time, like a movie that depends on flashbacks. Characters are introduced out of sequence; events occur in a pattern of our making rather than in a natural flow. The result: a patchwork narrative that confuses when it should inform.

The nature of the Old Monroe story—a disaster in slow motion—let Jim use a simple technique. He led into each segment with the time and date set in boldface. This approach struck The Coach as ideal, although only the special circumstances of the story made it possible.

Still, writers working on complicated, highly detailed stories about events that stretch over a period of time can shift after the lede paragraphs to straight chronological order, even without typographical devices. The reader is helped greatly by a sequence of paragraphs that start with phrases like these:

"The problem began when . . ."

"The next sign of trouble was . . ."

"When officials heard that, they . . ."

"Things came to a head when . . ."

☆ ☆ ☆

But in speaking of chronological order, The Coach is reminded of a phrase someone once set forth as the unofficial British motto: "Moderation in all things, including moderation."

The phrase comes to mind most often when reading the Police/Courts report. There, chronological order tends to run amok. Here's an example:

Two young women were robbed of $3,000 in jewelry and cash at a downtown park-

(continued on next page)

ing lot. Authorities said Tammie Smiley, 23, and Sandra Clem, 26, were leaving their pickup truck about 1 a.m. Sunday in a parking lot at 914 North Third Street when two men approached. One man grabbed Ms. Smiley and the other hit Ms. Clem on the head with a revolver, police reported. After the women gave the assailants jewels and money, the men fled north on foot. Both victims refused medical attention, authorities reported.

How much scene-setting do we need in a police item? Certainly not so much as this example offers. The writer and editors could have jumped over some of the events and written a tighter account:

Two women were robbed of $3,000 in jewelry and cash about 1 a.m. Sunday in a parking lot at 914 North Third Street, police said. One man grabbed Tammie Smiley, 23, while the other struck Sandra Clem, 26, on the head with a revolver. The men ran away; both women refused medical attention.

The Coach deleted the notice that robbers ''approached.'' The approach is obvious in the context. After all, how many robbers stand 20 yards away and holler at the victims to hand over their money? (The same thinking applies to sentences that begin ''The robbers entered the bank . . .'' Very few bank robbers operate from the sidewalk.)

In the example above, The Coach deleted ''young'' from ''young women,'' figuring that the ages conveyed the sense. At any rate, some people would argue that a woman of 26 is past ''young.''

The writer followed his chronological nose to note deep in the item that the women handed over the cash and the jewelry. But the first sentence had already said precisely that. Why repeat it?

The Coach eliminated some details—the pickup truck, for example. In this item, what difference does the type of vehicle make? Parking lots are parking lots. And The Coach struck the direction in which the robbers fled. Does anybody think that by the time we printed the item, the trail still led north?

(Note that robbers seem always to ''flee on foot.'' Can't they simply ''run away'' from time to time? In burglaries, the bad guys ''gain entry'' by breaking windows or a door. Every so often, The Coach would like to see them simply ''get in.'')

Finally, The Coach struck the attribution from the final sentence. Victims who refuse medical treatment are neither rare nor controversial. When the sentence contains mundane facts, take the plunge and let the facts stand by themselves.

☆ ☆ ☆

BACK TO THE BASICS
(PART OF A CONTINUING SERIES)

Some of us ignore basic grammar by tossing a comma into copy every time we see a sentence bisected with the words ''and'' and ''but.'' The Coach sees at least one example of this every day. Here's an example:

Jett returned the money when questioned on the subject, but has refused to make a specific account of its use.

Whoever inserted the comma fashioned a compound sentence that isn't a compound sentence. A compound sentence is two sentences in one, joined by a conjunction—"and" or "but," for example. Each of the two parts must have its own subject and verb. Without a second subject, the sentence isn't compound—and the use of the comma is wrong. Here are some hypothetical examples:

Right: He took the money, and he ran away to Buffalo, N.Y. (Two subjects, "he" and "he," and two verbs, "took" and "ran.")

Even More Right: He took the money and ran away to Buffalo, N.Y. (It's even more right because it's smoother. Commas mean stop signs to readers. We must use them when necessary, but we ought to avoid erecting more stop signs than we need.)

Wrong: He took the money, and ran away to Buffalo, N.Y. (The sentence has only one subject—"he." That makes "took the money and ran" a single verb phrase, indivisible under God and the rules of English grammar.)

☆ ☆ ☆

Bad weather brings out the clichés in all of us. What do tornadoes and flooding rivers do? They *rampage*, of course. The Coach suspects that the word *rampage* lost its impact years ago. But even so, we seem to use it automatically, just as the wire services refer by reflex to the House Ways and Means Committee as *the powerful House Ways and Means Committee*. One of these days, the committee's secretary is going to answer the telephone by saying, "Good morning—powerful House Ways and Means Committee."

We are heading into winter, when The Mercury starts to Plummet. The Coach is thinking of starting a pool—everybody kicks in a buck and picks a date on which the words "white stuff" will first appear as a synonym for "snow."

The White Stuff is, of course, "dumped." By whom? By Old Man Winter. And when Old Man Winter Dumps White Stuff, what happens to us? If we're at home, we Dig Out. But if we're on the highway, we Get Snarled, even though Weary Highway Crews Are Working Around the Clock.

Clichés like that have a life all their own. Ten minutes after they become clichés, they are incorporated into standard newspaper usage, as if our computers were programmed to insert them.

Take, for example, fires. What do they do? They invariably "sweep through" buildings, like some sort of semantic broom.

The wire services like clichés. They are fond of calling any military post "sprawling." All calm is "an uneasy calm," and it almost always "prevails." Labor reporters write of "grueling" or "marathon" negotiating sessions, aimed at "hammering out" a "new" contract. (Does anybody hammer out an *old* contract?)

Adjectives—"marathon" and "grueling"—are the tools of weak writers. Good writers rely on colorful nouns and, most important, on strong verbs. Once upon a time, "hammering out" was a strong verb. Now, it's a cliché. Here's a hypothetical labor-story sentence that sags with those clichés:

Both sides met in a marathon 12-hour negotiating session in an effort to hammer out a new contract.

And here's the same sentence stripped to its basics:

The session dragged on for 12 hours as negotiators tried to agree on a contract.

(continued on next page)

We must learn:

1. To recognize clichés, and
2. To replace clichés with standard English.

A writer who sits down to recount a fire may be unable to come up with a vivid replacement for "swept through." After all, fires are one of the things we write about most often. But the writer ought to recognize "swept through" for what it is—weary and stale formula writing. The readers will be better served with a story that starts flatly, "A fire destroyed . . ." or "A fire heavily damaged . . ."

SUGGESTED READINGS

Articles

Arlen, Michael J. "The Interview," *The New Yorker,* Nov. 10, 1975, p. 141.

Fletcher, Connie, and Jon Ziomek. "How to Catch a Star." *The Quill,* Dec. 1986, pp. 32–36.

Hentoff, Nat, et al. "The Art of the Interview." *(More),* July 1975, p. 11.

Johnson, James W. "If You Take Super Notes, Skip This." *The Quill,* May 1990, pp. 29–31.

Johnson, James W. "What's Wrong with Pre-Publication Review?" *The Quill,* May 1990, pp. 26–28.

Joseph Barbara. "Interviewing Grieving Sources." *Editor & Publisher,* Jan. 28, 1989, p. 48+.

Books

Best Newspaper Writing. St. Petersburg, Fla.: Poynter Institute for Media Studies. (This book, published every year since 1979, contains prize-winning articles, followed by the editors' comments and question-and-answer sessions with the writers. Several of the writers have published exceptional interviews, and some discuss their interviewing techniques.)

Biagi, Shirley. *Interviews That Work: A Practical Guide for Journalists.* Belmont, CA: Wadsworth, 1985.

Brady, John. *The Craft of Interviewing.* Cincinnati: Writer's Digest, 1977.

Donaghy, William C. *The Interview: Skills and Applications.* Glenview, IL: Scott, Foresman, 1984.

Killenberg, George M., and Rob Anderson. *Before the Story: Interviewing and Communication Skills for Journalists.* New York: St. Martin's Press, 1989.

McCombs, Maxwell, Donald Lewis Shaw and David Grey. *Handbook of Reporting Methods.* Boston: Houghton Mifflin, 1976.

Metzler, Ken. *Creative Interviewing.* Englewood Cliffs, NJ: Prentice Hall, 1977.

Rivers, William L. *Finding Facts: Interviewing, Observing, Using Reference Sources.* Englewood Cliffs, NJ: Prentice Hall, 1975.

Sherwood, Hugh C. *The Journalistic Interview.* 2nd ed. New York: Harper & Row, 1972.

Sincoff, Michael Z., and Robert S. Goyer. *Interviewing.* New York: Macmillan, 1984.

Stewart, Charles J., and William B. Cash, Jr. *Interviewing Principles and Practices.* 3rd ed. Dubuque, IA: Brown, 1985.

Turkel, Studs. *Working: People Talk About What They Do All Day and How They Feel About What They Do.* New York: Pantheon, 1974.

Yates, Edward D. *The Writing Craft.* 2nd ed. Raleigh, NC: Contemporary Publishing, 1985.

QUOTES

The basis of our government being the opinion of the people, the very first object should be to keep that right; and were it left to me to decide whether we should have a government without newspapers, or newspapers without a government, I should not hesitate a moment to prefer the latter. But I should mean that every man should receive those papers and be capable of reading them.

(Thomas Jefferson)

It is never pleasant to read things that are not agreeable news, but I would say that it is an invaluable arm of the Presidency—to check really on what is going on in the administration. And more things come to my attention that cause me concern or give me information. So I would think that . . . there is a terrific disadvantage not to have the abrasive quality of the press applied to you daily, to an administration, even though we never like it, and even though we wish they didn't write it, and even though we disapprove, there isn't any doubt that we could not do the job at all in a free society without a very, very active press.

(John F. Kennedy)

The First Amendment . . . presupposes that right conclusions are more likely to be gathered out of a multitude of tongues, than through any kind of authoritative selection. To many this is, and always will be, folly; but we have staked upon it our all.

(Learned Hand, American jurist)

Exercise 1

INTERVIEWS AND POLLS

DISCUSSION QUESTIONS

1. How would you respond to a source who, several days before a scheduled interview, asked for a list of the questions you intended to ask?
2. Do reporters have an obligation to inform their sources when they plan to record an interview?
3. If a story's publication is likely to embarrass a source, do reporters have a responsibility to warn the source of that possibility? Does it matter whether the source is used to dealing with reporters?
4. Would you be willing to interview a woman whose son just died? Would it matter whether her son drowned in a swimming pool, was murdered or was a convicted killer executed in a state prison?
5. Imagine that you wrote a front-page story about students' use of marijuana on your campus. To obtain the story, you promised several sources that you would never reveal their identities. If, during a subsequent legal proceeding, a judge ordered you to identify your sources, would you do so, or would you be willing to go to jail to protect them?

CLASS PROJECTS

1. List 10 interviewing tips provided by other sources.
2. Interview an expert on body language or nonverbal communication, perhaps someone in your school's psychology or speech department, then report on the information's usefulness to journalists. You might also invite an expert to speak to your class.
3. Interview an expert on interviewing, perhaps a faculty member in your school's psychology department. You might also invite the expert to speak to your class.
4. Interview government officials who frequently deal with reporters. Ask those officials what they like and dislike about interviews and how they try to handle interviews and the reporters who conduct them.
5. Ask several government officials which local reporters are the best interviewers, then interview those reporters about their interviewing techniques. You might also invite one of those reporters to speak to your class.
6. Ask every student in your class to write one paragraph about each of the three most newsworthy experiences in his or her life. Select the students with the most interesting experiences and have your entire class interview them, one by one, and write news stories about their experiences.

Exercise 2

INTERVIEWS AND POLLS

INTERVIEW WITH A YOUNG HERO

INSTRUCTIONS: Write a news story based on the following interview with Jason Jaco, a 7-year-old boy. The interview provides a verbatim account of an incident that occurred earlier today. "Q" stands for the questions that Jason was asked during an interview this morning, and "A" stands for his answers, which may be quoted directly. Jason is the son of Robin and Milan Jaco of 2202 S. 8th Street in your city. Tanya Willging, 5, is the daughter of neighbors, Judie and Jurgen Willging of 2204 S. 8th Street.

Q: Can you tell me what happened?
A: I was playing with Tanya, and she turned colors, red and then blue. My mother was screaming at me to get away from her.

Q: What did you do then?
A: I ignored her. I knew what to do. I said to my mother, "I saw this on TV."

Q: What did you see on TV?
A: Some program, I don't remember what it was. This guy was choking. His cheek was blown up like a balloon and a different guy went behind him, put his arms around, squeezed him, lifted him up and saved him.

Q: How did you save Tanya?
A: I got back of her and lifted her up and banged her on her feet. She bended over and she coughed and it plopped out.

Q: What came out? What was she choking on?
A: Some hard candy we had in a dish. We were both eating it.

Q: Is she OK now?
A: Yeah. She wanted to play some more, but her Mom is making her take a nap. We were talking and everything afterward. It was exciting.

Q: What's happened since then?
A: We had some firemen here, sirens and everything. Now everyone's calling me. When I'm watching cartoons its brring, brring, brring. The phone keeps going brring, brring, brring.

Q: How do you feel?
A: I saved a little girl's life. I feel good.

Q: How old are you?
A: Seven. Almost seven and a half.

Q: What do you want to do when you grow up?
A: Be a fireman or a policeman. Or maybe a plumber like my dad.

Mother's Comments

"I was in the bedroom and heard Jason ask Tanya if she was choking, so I went into the room to see why he was asking her that. I looked at her, and her face was red, bright red. Jason got behind her. I screamed at him to get away from her. I started to go into a panic. But then, before I could dial 911 or anything, it was all over. He's pretty strong. He takes karate and everything. He's overly confident, but thank God for that. Anyway, I went ahead and called 911 just in case, and the paramedics and everyone came. They didn't even take her to a hospital or anything. She's OK, and now it just won't end. We've been getting calls, people stopping at the house, photographers and everything. We've even gotten calls from England, and one from Australia."

Exercise 3

INTERVIEWS AND POLLS

INTERVIEW WITH A ROBBERY VICTIM

INSTRUCTIONS: Write a news story based on the following interview with Michele Schipper, a sophomore majoring in journalism at your college. The interview provides a verbatim account of a robbery that occurred yesterday. "Q" stands for the questions Ms. Schipper was asked during an interview this morning, and "A" stands for her answers, which may be quoted directly. (This is a true story, told by a college student.)

Q: Could you describe the robbery?

A: I pulled up into the parking lot of a convenience store on Bonneville Drive, but I pulled up on the side and not in front where I should have, and I was getting out of my car, and I was reaching into my car to pull out my purse when this guy, 6 foot tall or whatever, approached me and said, "Give me your purse." I said, "OK." I barely saw him out of the corner of my eye. And then, I, um, so I reached in to get my purse. And I could see him approaching a little closer. Before then, he was 4 or 5 feet away. So I turned around and kicked him in the groin area, and he started going down, but I was afraid he wouldn't stay down, that he would seek some kind of retribution. So when he was down, I gave him a roundhouse to the nose. I just hit him as hard as I could, an undercut as hard as I could. And I could hear some crunching, and some blood spurted, and he went on the ground, and I got in my car, and I went away. I called the cops from a motel down the street. They asked where he was last I seen him, and I said, "On the ground."

Q: Did the police find him?

A: No, he was gone.

Q: Had you taken judo or some type of self-defense course?

A: No, but I used to be a tomboy, and I used to wrestle with the guys, my good friends, when I was young. It was a good punch. I don't know, I was just very mad. My dad, he works out with boxing and weightlifting and everything, and I've played with that, so I've got the power.

Q: Could you describe the man?

A: I didn't see him well enough to identify him, really, but I hope he thinks twice next time.

Q: What time did the robbery occur?

A: This was about 4 in the afternoon, broad daylight, but there were no other cars parked around, though.

Q: Did you see the man when you drove up, or was he hiding?

A: There was a dumpster, and I guess he came from behind the dumpster, like he was waiting there, just like he was waiting there. And I guess he was waiting around the dumpster, because no one was standing around when I pulled up, I remember that.

Q: Were there any witnesses who could describe the man?

A: There was no one around, there were no cars parked. The clerks were inside the store. I didn't see any pedestrians around and, after I did it, I didn't wait to find if there were any witnesses because I wanted to leave right away.

Q: Was the man armed?

A: Out of the corner of my eye I realized I didn't see any weapon. And I guess I thought he was alone. You register some things; you just don't consciously realize it.

Q: What was your first reaction, what did you think when he first approached and demanded your purse?

A: I didn't think of anything, really, you know. I just reacted. I was very, really indignant. Why, you know, just because he wanted my purse, why should he have it? There was really only $10 in there, and I probably wouldn't really do it again in the same situation. And my parents don't know about it because they would be very angry that I fought back.

Q: Had you ever thought about being robbed and about what you would do, about how you would respond?

A: It just came instinctively, and after the incident, you know, I was shaking for about an hour afterwards.

Q: About how long did the robbery last?

A: It really only lasted a second, just as long as it would take for you to kick someone and then to hit them and then drive away in the car. It really only lasted a second.

Exercise 4

INTERVIEWS AND POLLS

INTERVIEW WITH A YOUNG KILLER

INSTRUCTIONS: Write a news story based on the following interview with Kyle Hana, an 18-year-old. The interview provides a verbatim account of an interview conducted this morning. "Q" stands for the questions that Hana was asked during the interview in his prison cell, and "A" stands for his answers, which may be quoted directly. Hana is the son of Jena and Edward Hana of 134 Eisen Avenue in your city.

BACKGROUND INFORMATION:

Yesterday afternoon Hana appeared in a local court and pleaded guilty to the murder of a convenience store clerk 2 months ago. Hana pleaded guilty to first-degree murder after prosecutors agreed not to seek the death penalty against him. Hana will have to serve at least 25 years before he will be eligible for parole. As part of his deal with prosecutors, he agreed to testify for the state in the first-degree murder trial of Alan Macco, 19, and Charlotte Jones, 17. Macco and Jones are also accused of killing Terry daRoza, 23, during a robbery of the Jiffy Food Store, 8230 Star Road. Their trial will be held next month. Hana turned himself in two days after the murder. The other two suspects were caught by sheriff's deputies. DaRoza was killed by five gunshot wounds. Four of the bullets pierced either his heart or lungs, and one passed through his neck, according to the county medical examiner. He suffered stab wounds that would also have been fatal.

A fourth defendant in the case, Macco's 15-year-old brother, Lloyd, will be tried as a juvenile.

Q: You called the newspaper yesterday and said you wanted to talk to a reporter. Why?
A: Same reason I confessed. I just couldn't live with myself, knowing what happened and all. I want to get it all over with.

Q: Why did you shoot daRoza?
A: Alan and his girlfriend needed money to run away. They were going to Colorado.

Q: So you planned it together?
A: Not the murder. We never intended to shoot anyone. We only wanted to rob him.

Q: So you planned the robbery together?
A: Yeah! We thought we'd tie him up and take the money.

Q: What went wrong?
A: Everything, just everything.

Q: Can you be more specific? Exactly what happened?
A: Lloyd was supposed to go into the store and distract the guy by talking to him. Lloyd had been in the store before and knew the guy. Then he was supposed to signal us when it was safe, when no one else was in the store.

Q: What were you supposed to do?
A: Alan and I were waiting outside until Lloyd signaled that it was OK to go ahead.

Q: Where was Charlotte?
A: She stayed in the car. She was our lookout.

Q: Then what happened?
A: Lloyd chickened out. Lloyd came outside and told us to forget it.

Q: And then?
A: Alan didn't hear what he said. He thought it meant, when Lloyd came out, that, uh, we should start the thing, the robbery. So we rushed in through the door.

Q: Why did Alan shoot the clerk?
A: The clerk made a sudden move. After that, it was a chain reaction. Alan started shooting. It was more or less total chaos. Charlotte came running in, and I just started screaming. Charlotte started crying.

Q: Why did you stab daRoza?
A: It was a mistake, a stupid mistake, that's all. I was afraid he recognized us. I didn't know if he was dead or nothing, so I stuck my knife in him. It was awful. There was so much blood, blood everywhere, and Charlotte was crying, and Alan, it was like he went crazy or something.

Q: How much money did you get?
A: It was $120, about $120.

Q: What did you do after the robbery?
A: I threw my knife against the wall. I couldn't believe a man died for that. It was hardly nothing for the four of us.

Q: What did you do with the money?
A: I never saw it. I mean, after what happened I didn't want it. I went home and watched for it on television.

Q: When did you decide to go to the police?
A: When I saw it on TV. The body and blood and everything again. Mostly his family crying and all that. I didn't know he had two little kids. Mostly seeing them kids on television, I guess.

Q: Did you realize you'd go to jail?
A: So what? I feel like, man, I mean, so what? After what I've done to my family and all, and his family, it's what I deserve. I know we did wrong, bad wrong. I deserve it, but I don't want to die. I'm only 18.

Exercise 5

INTERVIEWS AND POLLS

INTERVIEW: MURDER TRIAL

INSTRUCTIONS: Write a news story based on the following transcript from a murder trial. "Q" stands for the questions of District Attorney Ramon Hernandez, and "A" stands for the answers of Frank Biegel, one of the defendants. The questions and answers are the men's exact words and may be quoted directly.

BACKGROUND INFORMATION

Biegel, 43, of 782 12th Ave. and Eric A. Knapp, 27, of 2314 N. 11th St. are accused of robbing a service station of $83 last July and of abducting and murdering the attendant, Larry Totmann, age 17. Biegel testified this morning, the second day of the trial.

Q: Well, let me ask you this. Did you commit a robbery at a service station on Baytree Road last July 14?

A: Yes, I did.

Q: And did you help take the attendant, Larry Totmann, out to a campground somewhere away from that station?

A: Yes, sir.

Q: And did you personally see Eric Knapp, your co-defendant, shoot and kill that attendant?

A: Yes, sir.

Q: Describe for us how you and Knapp went about robbing and murdering Totmann.

A: It wasn't me. It was Knapp that shot the kid, not me. We had gone up to the gas station, got my car filled with gas. While I was . . . I went in the bathroom. While I was in the bathroom some other people drove up in a car, young kids it sounded like, and they had an argument with the attendant about using the telephone. When it was all over, I came out, and I got back in the car while Knapp put a gun on him.

Q: All right. Did the young people who had driven up, did they leave before you got back into the car?

A: Yes, sir.

Q: Then what happened?

A: I started the car, and Knapp made the kid take all the money out of the register, and he found a gun hidden under the counter and put it in a box with the money.

Q: Tell us what happened after that.

A: Well, sir, Knapp told the kid to get into the car with us, and, uh, I drove out of town about five miles.

Q: Where was Knapp all that time?

A: He was in the back seat with the kid. He had his gun on him, and the box with the money.

Q: And then what happened?

A: I was driving out toward a campground I use sometimes, and Knapp told me to stop. He told the kid to get out of the car and lay down in some bushes along the road. I didn't know he was going to shoot the kid, I swear. The kid hadn't caused us any trouble, and I thought we'd just dump him there so he couldn't call the cops right away.

Q: But Knapp shot him, didn't he?

A: Yes, sir.

Q: How many times?

A: Four. He fired four shots. I don't know how many times he hit him.

Q: Did Knapp shoot him in the head?

A: Well, sir, I couldn't see that. It was dark, and they were off the side of the road. I just heard the shots and saw like blue flames coming out of his gun.

Q: Uh, how far away from Totmann was Knapp when the shots were fired?

A: Not over three or five feet. He was standing right over him.

Q: Did Totmann say anything or try to run away?

A: No, he just kept lying there. He'd done everything we said, and I don't think he expected it. He just lay there; he never moved.

Q: What . . . well, what did you do after that?

A: I drove Eric home. We had a couple beers at his apartment and divided the money. There wasn't much, not even a hundred dollars.

Q: What did you do with the gun?

A: The next night we went out and threw both guns down a sewer. It was over on the other side of town, near a ballpark.

Q: Do you know why Knapp decided to kill Totmann?

A: He told me the kid recognized him, that the kid had seen him before. And he . . . he was afraid the kid might've seen my license number, the license number on my car.

Q: Why didn't you try to prevent the murder?

A: How could I? I didn't know he was going to shoot anyone, I really didn't. We'd never talked about that. I thought we'd just drop the kid there and leave.

Q: Can you tell us why you've decided to confess?

A: The murder wasn't my idea; I didn't pull the trigger. I didn't know Eric was going to shoot the kid. I don't think I should die, and I thought maybe if I cooperated, I wouldn't get the death penalty.

Q: Have the police or anyone else promised you anything in return for testifying against Knapp?

A: No, sir. No one's promised me anything, nothing at all. I wish they would.

Exercise 6

INTERVIEWS AND POLLS

INTERVIEW WITH A MURDER WITNESS

INSTRUCTIONS: Write a news story about the following interview with a bookkeeper at the North Point Inn. "Q" stands for the questions she was asked during an interview at her home this morning, and "A" stands for her answers, which may be quoted directly. (The interview is based on an actual case: a robbery and murder at an elegant restaurant.)

Q: Could you start by spelling your name for me?
A: N-i-n-a C-o-r-t-e-z.

Q: You work as a bookkeeper at the North Point Inn?
A: Yes, I've been there seven years.

Q: Would you describe the robbery there yesterday?
A: It was about 9 in the morning, around 7 or 8 minutes before 9.

Q: Is that the time you usually get there?
A: At 9 o'clock, yes.

Q: How did you get in?
A: I've got a key to the employee entrance in the back.

Q: Was anyone else there?
A: Kevin Blohm, one of the cooks. He usually starts at 8. We open for lunch at 11:30, and he's in charge.

Q: Did you talk to him?
A: He came into my office, and we chatted about what happened in the restaurant the night before, and I asked him to make me some coffee. After he brought me a cup, I walked out to the corridor with him. That was the last I saw him.

Q: What did you do next?
A: I was just beginning to go through the receipts and cash from the previous night. I always start by counting the previous day's revenue. I took everything out of a safe, the cash and receipts, and began to count them on my desk.

Q: About how much did you have?
A: $6,000 counting everything, the cash and receipts from credit cards.

Q: Is that when you were robbed?
A: A minute or two or less, a man came around the corner, carrying a knife.

Q: What did you do?
A: I started screaming and kicking. My chair was on rollers, and when I started kicking, it fell. I fell on the floor, and he reached across my desk and grabbed $130 in $5 bills.

Q: Did he say anything?
A: No, he just took the money and walked out.

Q: Was he alone?

A: I don't think so. I heard someone—a man—say, "Get that money out of there." Then someone tried to open the door to my office, but I'd locked it. Three or four minutes later, the police were there.

Q: Is that when you found Mr. Blohm?

A: I went into the hallway with the police and saw blood on a door in the reception area. It was awful. There was blood on the walls and floor. Kevin was lying on the floor, dead. He had a large knife wound in his chest and another on one hand.

Q: Can you describe the man who robbed you?

A: He was about 5 feet 10, maybe 6 feet tall, in his early 20s, medium build.

Q: What was he wearing?

A: Blue jeans, a blue plaid button-up shirt and blue tennis shoes.

Q: Did you see his face?

A: He had a scarf, a floral scarf, tied around the lower part of his face, cowboy style. It covered the bottom half of his face.

Q: Did the man look at all familiar, like anyone you may have known or seen in the restaurant?

A: No.

Q: Did you notice anything unusual that day?

A: I saw a car in the parking lot when I came in, one I didn't recognize. It didn't belong to anyone who worked there, but that's all I remember.

Q: Do you have any idea why someone stabbed Blohm?

A: No. Kevin might have gotten in his way or tried to stop him or recognized him or something. I don't know. I didn't see it. I don't know anything else.

Exercise 7

INTERVIEWS AND POLLS

INTERVIEW: "OUT OF BODY" EXPERIENCE

INSTRUCTIONS: Write a news story about the following interview with Marty Murray. Assume that she returned to work today after recovering from surgery. "Q" stands for the questions you asked during an interview at her office this morning, and "A" stands for her answers, which may be quoted directly. (Again, this is a true story: a verbatim transcript of an interview taped with Mrs. Murray. Moreover, she consented to the use of her real name. While writing the story, assume that she works in your community.)

Q: Could you begin by describing what happened during your surgery?

A: I went into the hospital for surgery—tonsil and adenoid removal. I came out of my body and could look down on the operating table. I never exactly saw my body lying on the operating table, but I saw the people all around me, and I knew it was me on the operating table. I saw the attendants and the nurses and the person who was handling the anesthesia and the attending physician standing right there. Then I went like a corkscrew, right through the top of the hospital. I heard a very loud noise, like a rush of wind, and it was almost like a train going through a long tunnel. The noise was very loud. I don't recall being frightened, but was perplexed and puzzled by it. It didn't scare me in the least, mainly because the place where I wound up was so peaceful and quiet, and I remember it was kind of cold too. I remember the sensation of coldness. I don't know whether to call them people or beings, but the people communicated with one another. I couldn't understand it, but they understood each other.

Q: Other people have had similar experiences at times they were near death. Did you feel that happened to you—that you nearly died during the operation?

A: I don't know. I was never told, but I was under a general anesthesia and could have been.

Q: The people you saw, what did they look like?

A: They were beings. I don't remember seeing them. I only remember being aware of their presence.

Q: What else do you remember?

A: I remember a light. It seemed like the light came after the loud noise, the whoosh and the very fast trip. I mean it was just—the speed the trip took—it was just incredible. It was just an incredibly quick journey that defied everything I had ever known about and, what was so convincing about it was that, in my wildest imagination, I never could have dreamed this up. That is why I am so convinced that it actually happened, because I am a practical person. I am a very practical, down-to-earth person, always wanting to find the scientific proof for this or that, and I have no explanation for what did happen except that it really did happen.

Q: Was it a frightening experience?

A: No, it was not frightening. It was not frightening at any time. Even though it was a strange and bizarre experience, it was never frightening. And it really was out of this world.

Q: It was off in space somewhere?
A: Somewhere away from here. Far away.

Q: Can you describe where it was?
A: It was up in the atmosphere. It wasn't on earth. It wasn't on clouds. It was in space.

Q: Have you ever met anyone who had a similar experience?
A: No, but when I've told people, I've had them tell me, "Well, my grandmother had that happen to her," or "I know someone that happened to." I've never actually spoken to anyone else who had the experience.

Q: Were you always able to look down—even when you were off in space—look down into the operating room and see all those people around the table?
A: It seemed like the table itself went up. The whole insides of the operating room: the table, myself, the persons attending me and myself, out of the body, looking on the whole scene, were transported to a different place.

Q: The doctors and all went off in space with you?
A: Yes.

Q: Suddenly . . . and then you went back to sleep?
A: I woke up. I didn't see that scene anymore. I was in the recovery room trying to tell about the experience.

Q: Did you have any sense of time?
A: No, I really didn't. I had no concept of the time or of the distance traveled. It could have been one second, or it could have been an eternity.

Q: Has the experience changed your feelings about death?
A: Absolutely! I would not fear death. It was not a frightening thing. It was kind of a comforting thing and, I guess if I had to think about what death might be like, it was not anything to be frightened of. I would not want to leave two children—I have two children now—I would like to see the children raised to be adults themselves, but I would not be afraid to die. I'll never think that a person just dies with his body. There's much more to it than that. Basically, it made me not be afraid to die.

Q: And you seem to remember everything?
A: Yes, I sure do. It's something that a person could never forget. Never! Once something like that has happened to you, you could never forget the emotions. I'm kind of at a loss to express myself because so many of the things that happened to me—because we don't have those concepts on earth, we don't even have the words to describe what happened, and so the words themselves fail to describe the entire experience because it was so different from anything I have ever encountered.

Exercise 8

INTERVIEWS AND POLLS

INTERVIEW WITH A HOUSEWIFE

INSTRUCTIONS: Write a news story based on the following interview with Irene Barber, a woman arrested for stealing her own clothes. Assume that you interviewed Mrs. Barber today and that she lives in your community.

This is a true story, and Mrs. Barber was interviewed especially for this book. Because this is a verbatim account of the interview, you can use direct quotations. Assume that the incident occurred today and that the clerk and the owners of the shop declined to talk to you.

The interview is more complicated than most because Mrs. Barber quotes other sources, and one of those sources is profane. Thus, before beginning to write your story, you may want to discuss the problems with your classmates and instructor. You may also want to discuss the issue of polishing direct quotations—for example, of eliminating words such as "uh" and "you know."

Being new in the area, I needed to find a dry cleaner's to take clothing to, and there was one that was convenient in a little shopping center, and uh, so, I went in there, took six pieces of clothing, two shirts of my husband's, two pairs of his pants and two of my blouses. And I went back a couple of days later and found that the pants were OK, but his shirts were not even pressed under the arms or anything, and my blouses, one of them was stained on the front, and the pockets were all wrinkled and, and did not look like what I would want to take home and wear. So she said, well, we can redo them. I said, all right. So, about a week later, I had to go to the pharmacy next door and, while I was waiting for the prescription, I thought, I'll run next door and pick up my clothing. And so I went in, and the two shirts of my husband's were pressed and in better shape, but my blouses were in worse shape than they were the first time they sent them in. The stains were still in front of the white one, and the other one, the pockets were pressed, but nothing else seemed to be pressed. So I told the girl I would just take them home. She said, I can send them back again, and I said, well, obviously you can't get them right, so I'll just take them with me. So she proceeded to ring up the amount and told me it was eight dollars and sixty cents. And I looked at her and I said, you're charging me for those blouses? She said, yes, I have to. And I said, I'm not going to pay you for ruining my blouses. She said, you have to. My boss will fire me if you don't. And I said, well, tell you what, let me talk to him on the phone. So she got him on the phone and, uh, he told me that I had to pay for it, and I said, well, I'm paying you for a service that obviously you did not perform. And he said that if I did not pay for it he would have me arrested and charged with merchandise theft plus assault, which I thought, what in the world is he thinking about? So, uh, he, uh, proceeded to tell me that, uh, he was going to call the police, and I told him, don't bother, I will. And he proceeded to call me an asshole. So I hung up the phone and picked up the phone and called the police and said that I was at the dry cleaner's and that I was going to walk out with my clothes. And, uh, the lady said it would be a while, and I said that was OK, I'll wait. So I went back and sat on the bench they had there. But, uh, the phone rang again, and it was the owner, and I heard him talking to the girl. And she said, I'm not going to get myself hit, and I thought, what is he telling her to do? So anyway, I looked, and sitting on the stool behind the counter was my blouses, and she was in the back on the phone, and so I went over and picked up my blouses and walked out the door with them. Not with intending to leave, but just to get out, to get my blouses, I guess. Uh, so I walked down to the corner, and I thought, I have to get my husband's prescription. So I put the, I went into the pharmacy, still shaking, still upset. And, uh, got the prescription and, uh, I went back out, put my clothes, prescription in the car and stood on the corner and waited to see if the police would get there, and I didn't see them, didn't see them, assuming it would be a while like the dispatcher told me. And, uh, so I went back to the phone and I called, and I said, yes, I'm waiting at the dry cleaner's. She said, the police officer is there. You'd better go back down there. So I walked back down there, and they had already started to file a report saying that I had stolen my blouses and, uh, so I walked in, and the police officer said, yes, they called the police, and I said, no, I did. And he sort of looked at me funny, and I said, my blouses were not clean. I left with them. And he set me down, and he said, now, when you stepped over the threshold you broke the law because when you turn items over to be repaired or to be worked on, uh, cleaned, they are their possessions. So, he said, do you have any ID, and I said, in the truck, and he said, OK, let's go get it. So we walked out there, and he said, you have to pay them first, then go after them in court. This is the law, you know, and he said, not that I always agree with it, but this is the law. So he said, are you willing to make restitution? Do you have the money to pay for it? I said, of course I have the money to pay for it. You know, I didn't walk out knowingly stealing them. And so he said, OK. So we walked back in there, and he said to the girl, she's willing to make restitution, you know, will you accept that? The girl said, I don't know, I have to talk to the owner. It's a husband and wife combination and, so, they got ahold of the owners, and they said, no, don't accept one penny from her, have her arrested. So the police officer said, I'm sorry, he said, put your purse up on the counter. And I said, you are going to handcuff me, and he said, yeah, I have to. So he handcuffed me, and walked me out to the cruiser. They took me down to jail, and they chained me to the wall. So then, while we were sitting there, the sergeant came walking by and said, what did she steal, and the officer that arrested me said, her own clothes. So they, they found this comical, and yet here I was in the process of being booked on merchandise theft. So the sergeant went over and got a book, and he was trying to figure out how we could lower it, and uh, he went through the book and found out that there is such a law as service theft, which is lower than merchandise theft. So anyway, he decided to write that in there, and the phone rang. They asked for the lieutenant, I believe he was, that arrested me, and he got on the phone, and he put it on hold and said, it's the lady who owns the shop. She wants to talk with you. I said, I'm not going to barter with her, you know, this is, at that point I was angry, and I wasn't sure what to do. I wasn't to a point of being afraid yet. It was the point. It was eight dollars and sixty cents, and it was the point that the man—usually service-oriented companies will do whatever they can to accommodate you—I guess, um, so anyway, the wife got on the phone, and she wanted to talk to me. So here I am, with my arm chained to the wall, talking to this woman, and she said, where do you stand, and which I thought was the funniest line, because I said, what do you mean where do I stand? I stand in jail being booked on merchandise theft, and she said, well, we want to know, you know, what you plan on doing, and I said, at this point I don't know. She said, well, not always can you see stains on clothing when you take them in. If you're not a trained eye, you don't know that it's on there before. And I said, well, I heard the girl on the phone tell you and your husband that the stains were not on those blouses when I brought them in. She said, well, they don't always see everything, they don't find things in pockets, and so I said, you hire incompetent people? She didn't have anything to say to that. And then she said, we're not animals here, we are human beings. And I said, yes, that's why I'm chained to the wall, and she said, how barbaric, and I said, yes ma'am, it is, thanks to you. And she said, well if you promise not to pursue it any further we will come down and drop the charges. And with that I didn't, I couldn't, even answer that. I handed the officer back the phone because I thought, how dare you, you know, I'm not going to barter with you. So anyway, they started to get more things out, and they were preparing to fingerprint me, and to photograph me, and the phone rang again, and it was the husband this time. And he got on the phone, and the officer said, well, you need to get down here shortly, because after I'm done fingerprinting her and photographing her we will take her in the back, strip search her, and take her down to the county jail. So, uh, at that point, you know, they said, they, they want to talk to you. And I said, I don't want to talk to 'em. Anyway, at that point the officer said, you know, let's make you more comfortable. At that point he took me off of the wall and said, come over here and sit down. He started filling out the paperwork. And, uh, before he was finished the owner came in and, and I told the officer, I don't want to talk to him. I don't want to, you know, he needs to sign that release, and I'll give him his eight dollars and sixty cents. So that was, that was the finale of it. But he just, he is a very cocky man as far as the way he carries himself. I don't understand how he can be in a service-oriented business but, uh, anyway, I paid my eight dollars and sixty cents.

Exercise 9

INTERVIEWS AND POLLS

POLLS

INSTRUCTIONS: Interview a minimum of 10 people, about half of them men and half of them women. Ask them a single question concerning a controversial issue; then write a news story about their opinions. The respondents may be students, professors, nonacademic employees, visitors or anyone else you encounter on your campus. Conduct your interviews separately, not simultaneously with other members of your class—if only because it is disconcerting to be approached by two or three people, all asking the same controversial question. Identify yourself, explain why you are conducting the poll, then ask the single question selected by your instructor or class. You may want to use one of the following questions:

1. Do you believe that newspapers and radio and television stations in the United States report the news fairly and accurately?
2. Should faculty members be allowed to date their students, or should your institution adopt some rules prohibiting the practice?
3. Would you want your state legislature to adopt a law making it legal—or illegal—for women to serve as surrogate mothers: to have and sell babies to childless couples?
4. If you saw another student cheating on a test, would you try to stop the student or report the student to your teacher? Why?
5. If the administrators at your school learned that several students had AIDS, would you want them to allow the students to attend classes with you? Why?
6. Do you favor the execution of criminals convicted of murder and other serious crimes?
7. Should the government prohibit the sale of pornographic magazines or the showing of pornographic movies?
8. Should churches and other religious organizations be required to pay property taxes for the municipal services, such as police and fire protection, they receive?
9. Should women under the age of 18 be allowed to obtain abortions without their parents' knowledge or consent?
10. Should married women be allowed to obtain abortions without their husbands' knowledge or consent?
11. Do you think that movies and television programs place too much emphasis on crime, sex and violence?
12. Should the government do more to limit the sale and possession of handguns?

Your instructor may ask you to conduct the interviews and to write your story within a single class period, or you may be allowed to complete the assignment outside class. However, if you do the work outside class, you may be asked to interview more than 10 people.

CHAPTER 10

IMPROVING NEWSGATHERING AND WRITING SKILLS

When a major event occurs, dozens and sometimes hundreds of journalists rush to the scene, gather information and then transmit that information to the public. All the journalists write about the same event, but some of their stories are much better than others. Why?

Some reporters are particularly adept at gathering the information needed to write exceptional stories. They go beyond the superficial, critically examine all the information they are given and ask probing questions. They also search for alternative sources of information and are good observers. These reporters notice and record minor details that help reveal the truth and make their stories more colorful, descriptive and interesting.

Other reporters produce exceptional stories because of their mastery of the English language. Their language is vivid and forceful, and their stories are written so clearly and simply that everyone can understand them. These reporters describe the people, places and events involved in news stories and use quotations that enable those people to speak directly to the public. Their stories are so descriptive and specific—their images so vivid—that readers are able to picture in their minds the scenes the reporters describe.

Skilled reporters can transform even routine events into front-page stories. A reporter who is unimaginative about or indifferent to a topic may write a three-paragraph story that, because of its mediocrity, will not be used. Another reporter, excited by the same topic, may go beyond the superficial—may ask more questions, uncover some unusual developments and inject more color into the story. The second reporter may write a three-page story about the topic and, because of its excellence, the story may be published at the top of page 1.

A young reporter named Barry Bradley uncovered and wrote an exceptional front-page story. Asked to describe his coverage of it, Bradley said:

> Sometimes the best news stories are those you might have missed had you not done a little extra snooping or asked that one extra question. The old saying 'leave no stone unturned' applies to no business as much as it applies to the news business.
>
> I picked up a press release at the local police station. These releases contain the barest essentials regarding police activities that might be of interest to reporters. Many times a set of facts on a press release may seem dull. But a little effort can turn these facts into an interesting story.
>
> The facts said an elderly man was robbed at knife-point. I did some nosing around and found out the man lived in a nursing home. How did the robber get into a nursing home? And why did the robber choose such an unlikely

spot? I also discovered the man was 71 years old and in a wheelchair. The story looked much better now than it did when I first looked at the bare facts.

Then I found out the man lost $4 and a pocketknife in the robbery. To make matters worse, that was about all he had. That little tidbit was enough to warrant front-page space.

I went to the nursing home, interviewed him and took some pictures. I found out he beat the mugger soundly with his cane before the mugger got away with his cash and belongings. He was a feisty gent who had been in three wars and wounded in two. This made the story good enough for my editors to submit it to an annual writers' contest sponsored by the local press club. I didn't win any awards, but it was still a good story. And I would have missed it if I hadn't been nosey enough that day.

Bradley's lead reported that:

> Seventy-one-year-old Joseph L. Hill has been through a lot during his last 32 years confined to a wheelchair, but he never expected to be robbed at knife-point while watching television at a nursing home.

The same principles might be applied to any type of story—to stories about the awarding of a scholarship, the celebration of an anniversary or retirement, the construction of a school, the election of a mayor or the damage caused by a storm. A good reporter will always begin by obtaining as much information about a topic as possible. The reporter may interview witnesses, consult experts, visit the scene or examine some documents, always observing and recording details of even minor significance—details that will help readers understand the topic and make it more interesting.

To help you improve your newsgathering and writing techniques, this chapter will discuss those techniques in more detail.

BE SPECIFIC, DETAILED AND THOROUGH

Good writing is specific, and good writers fill their stories with illustrative details. Generalities are less interesting and a sign of hasty writing. To be specific, reporters must take time and be perceptive in gathering information and in presenting that information in their stories.

Here are two good examples of paragraphs filled with specific details. USA Today published the first paragraph in a story about jockey Bill Shoemaker, who retired at the age of 58. The second paragraph appeared in a story about an athlete's chances of becoming a professional. Count the specific details in each paragraph:

> In 41 years of riding, Shoemaker won a world-record 8,833 races and his horses earned more than $120 million. He won 11 Triple Crown races, including four Kentucky Derbies—the first when he was 23 years old, the last when he was 54.

> In a typical year, about 500,000 students play for their high school basketball teams, and 12,000 play for their college teams. The National Basketball Association will draft about 160 players, and 50 will be employed in the NBA—for an average of three years.

Good reporters avoid vague sentences and qualifiers, words such as "young" and "old," "big" and "little," "early" and "late," "high" and "low," "fast" and "slow." Other vague qualifiers are: "rather," "very," "much," "quickly," "awhile" and "a lot." Entire phrases may be too vague, as in the following examples:

at an early age	only recently
in a lot of pain	too time-consuming
for several years	within a short time
in her later years	traveled extensively
he rested for a while	never finished his formal education

What is "an early age," for example? Readers are forced to guess, and one reader might guess two months and another eight years. Similarly, one reader might assume that "a short time" means five minutes, whereas another might assume that it means 10 days. And someone who "never finished his formal education" might have left school after the sixth grade or after his junior year of high school.

The following sentences also need to be rewritten because they are too vague and consequently fail to convey any meaningful information to their readers:

One of the men was short.	They traveled extensively.
Police were on the scene quickly.	He led a controversial life.
Many of the students were involved.	The loss was kept to a minimum.
The customers were cooperative.	She attended school erratically.
The response to the exhibit was great.	The mayor instituted numerous reforms.

When more specific details are added to sentences, the sentences become not only clearer but more interesting:

They said the land used to be cheap but now is at a premium.
REVISED: They said speculators bought the land for $320 an acre and are now selling it for an average of $280,000 an acre. A bank paid $240,000 an acre for a corner lot, and developers paid $350,000 an acre for the land to build a shopping center.

He had not traveled very far when his troubles began.
REVISED: The youth paid $3,795 for his first car, a 7-year-old convertible, and began to drive it home. A tire went flat two miles from the used car lot. The youth quickly changed the tire, but the brakes failed when he tried to stop at the next intersection. Two days later, the car's transmission failed.

Reporters who understand a topic sometimes forget that their readers know less about it than they do. Consequently, they sometimes fail to provide a clear explanation:

A reporter covering Indiana's U.S. senators devoted all the coverage to the senior senator because the senator had done a favor for the reporter concerning a drunken-driving incident.
REVISED: Goligoski said the reporter for an Indiana newspaper was charged with drunken driving and put in a Washington, D.C., jail.
The senior senator from Indiana quietly arranged for the reporter's release, and the reporter began to publish a great many favorable stories about the senator.

"It was obvious that the reporter was paying back the favor," Goligoski said.

Before the paragraph was revised, it failed to explain the incident adequately. The paragraph mentioned "a favor" but did not specifically describe it. It also mentioned "a drunken-driving incident" but failed to provide any meaningful information about that incident.

News stories should be so detailed and so thorough that all the questions readers might logically ask about their topic are answered. As pointed out in Chapter 5, reporters no longer attempt to answer six major questions in leads: "who," "how," "where," "why," "what" and "when." Nevertheless, the answers to all six questions should be presented somewhere in every story. Reporters must also answer all the questions raised by their stories' subtopics. Yet stories that contained the following statements failed to answer the questions they obviously raise:

She said the institution of marriage should be abolished. (Why?)

She said women should not be given the same opportunities as men. (Why?)

He retired from undercover work after he was thrown out a second-story window. (When? Where? Why? By whom? And with what result?)

Rue said he encountered only one problem while living on campus: finding the right roommate. "My first roommate tried to strangle me," Rue said. "I got out of there real quick." (When? Why?)

Kahana said the best advice he could give college students interested in becoming part of the movie industry was to "keep your eyes and ears open and mouth shut." (Why?)

Sentences and paragraphs should be so thorough and phrased so clearly and specifically that they do not require any later explanation. Notice how easily the following sentences can be rewritten to clarify their meaning:

Tipton remarked that he has never had a problem like this before.
REVISED: Tipton said it is the first time he has been accused of shoplifting.

The girl and her boyfriend tried to obtain a marriage license but were turned down because of the age requirements.
REVISED: The girl and her boyfriend tried to obtain a marriage license but were turned down because neither is 17, the minimum age for marriages in the state.

Before they were revised, the first sentence vaguely referred to a "problem like this," and the second sentence mentioned "the age requirements." Neither sentence explained the terms' meaning.

The same problem arises when stories report that a topic was "mentioned" or "discussed." If a topic is important enough to be included in a news story, that topic should be fully explained. Stories should reveal what was said—the substance of the discussion—not just the fact that a discussion took place. The error appears often in leads but may arise anywhere in a news story:

He said blood donors must be 17 to 65 years old. Also, he mentioned a checklist of diseases that a potential donor may not have had.

REVISED: He said blood donors must be 17 to 65 years old. He added that the blood bank rejects donors who have had malaria, hepatitis, diabetes or venereal diseases.

He also discussed the federal tax structure.
REVISED: He said the federal tax structure places too heavy a burden on middle-income families.

As an alternative, you may be able to delete the portions of a sentence or quotation that are too vague:

He said the county fair will feature 25 rides and various other activities.
REVISED: He said the county fair will feature 25 rides.

The YWCA counselor said, "We have 800 girls in the program, and it's meeting with a large measure of success."
REVISED: The YWCA counselor said, "We have 800 girls in the program."

Mistakenly, students often begin their paragraphs with a generality, then present more specific details in the following sentences. If you begin with the specific details, the generality may become unnecessary:

Mrs. Harris was also active in the community. She served as president of the PTA at Roosevelt High School and as vice chair of the League of Women Voters. She was a member of the Democratic Party and attended St. Paul's Episcopal Church.
REVISED: Mrs. Harris served as president of the PTA at Roosevelt High School and as vice chair of the League of Women Voters. She was a member of the Democratic Party and attended St. Paul's Episcopal Church.

He called the conditions in the cafeteria "critical and hazardous." He explained that the cafeteria's french fry bins are fire hazards, its refrigerators often break and its storeroom is infested with roaches and mice.
REVISED: He said the cafeteria's french fry bins are fire hazards, its refrigerators often break and its storeroom is infested with roaches and mice.

IDENTIFY, DEFINE AND EXPLAIN

Reporters should never assume that their readers are familiar with a topic. Newspapers may have published earlier stories about the topic, but not every reader will have seen those stories. Consequently, reporters must always identify, define and explain unfamiliar topics. The information should be expressed as simply and briefly as possible; often, it can be stated in a short phrase or sentence.

Reporters identify virtually all the people mentioned in news stories, and they usually present the identification the first or second time a person is mentioned. Readers should not be forced to guess a person's identity nor wait until the end of a story to learn who the person is. Newspapers identify most people by reporting their ages, occupations and addresses. However, they report specific street addresses only for the people who live in their communities. If someone lives outside the area in which a newspaper circulates, the paper will report only the person's hometown.

Reporters use a variety of other descriptive phrases to identify the people mentioned in news stories. Military papers use soldiers' ranks, and college papers list students' years in school, majors and hometowns. Stories that mention a child usually identify the child's parents, since readers are more likely to know them. Other stories describe people's achievements, goals and physical characteristics.

If a title is short, reporters place it before a name. For example: "Sheriff Keith Kirby" or "Sen. Claire Valle." If reporters refer to the same person later in a story, they use only the person's last name; they do not repeat the title. If a title is longer, reporters place it after a name or in the following sentence:

Associate Superintendent for Planning and Government Relations Gordon Marinelli said Friday the school is unsafe.
REVISED: Gordon Marinelli, the associate superintendent for planning and government relations, said the school is unsafe.

Assistant Deputy Commander for District II Ralph Phillips said the American Legion's membership is declining.
REVISED: An American Legion official, Ralph Phillips, said the organization's membership is declining. Phillips is the assistant deputy commander for District II, which includes California, Arizona and New Mexico.

If a person has several titles, place no more than one before a name, regardless of how short the titles may be:

Dr. and Human Resources Committee chair Ruth Heebner said she opposes the fee.
REVISED: Dr. Ruth Heebner said she opposes the fee. Heebner chairs the Human Resources Committee.

Junior medical technology major and former Peace Corps volunteer Susan Glenn said she expects to graduate next June.
REVISED: Susan Glenn, a junior majoring in medical technology, said she expects to graduate next June. She served with the Peace Corps in Africa.

Reporters have several reasons for identifying so specifically the people mentioned in news stories. Because some sources are more believable than others, a source's identity may affect a news story's credibility. Some people are more interesting than others, and reporters may attract more readers if they identify a prominent or popular person involved in a story. Reporters also identify the people involved in news stories to protect the innocent from adverse publicity. Because it failed to adequately identify the man mentioned in several stories, a newspaper in Orlando, Fla., was forced to publish a separate story to exonerate an innocent man. The first stories reported that a man named Kenneth Bray was remodeling a famous hotel in the city and that the hotel would appeal to a homosexual clientele. Angry citizens began to call Kenneth Lee Bray, a U.S. probation officer living in Orlando, yet the hotel was owned by another man, Kenneth Edward Bray. The newspaper had failed to fully identify Kenneth Edward Bray—to report his middle name, age or address—in all its earlier stories.

In extreme cases, proper identification protects newspapers from libel suits. If newspapers report that a man named Ralph Ussery has been charged with rape, but fail to provide any further identification, the papers may libel every local resident named Ralph Ussery, and the Ralph Usserys who have not been charged with rape might sue the papers for libel. But if the newspapers report that Ralph Ussery, 47, of 481 Georgia Ave. has been charged with rape, they identify a single individual, the Ralph Ussery who is 47 years old and who lives at that address.

Reporters must also identify or define unfamiliar places and locations. They should try to avoid words that are not used in everyday conversation. When an unfamiliar word is necessary, reporters must immediately define it. Stories that fail to define unfamiliar terms may annoy as well as puzzle readers. A story about a 19-year-old football player who collapsed and died before a practice session at the University of South Carolina reported that he died of clinical terminal cardiac arrythmia. The story placed the term in quotation marks but failed to define it. Yet many readers would be interested in the death of a college football player and would wonder why an apparently healthy young athlete had died. Because the story failed to define the term, it failed to satisfy their curiosity about the cause of the young man's death.

Here are three of the techniques reporters can use to define or explain unfamiliar terms:

1. Place a brief explanation in parentheses:

> The university employees 620 full-time faculty members and 338 adjunct (part-time) instructors.

> The law would ban accessory structures (sheds, pool houses and unattached garages) in new subdivisions.

2. Place the explanation immediately after the unfamiliar name or term, setting it off with a colon, comma or dash:

> While shopping at the mall they saw some furniture made from polyvinyl chloride: commonly called pipe furniture.

> Ralph and Suzanne Hargis of 1574 Carlton Drive filed for bankruptcy under Chapter 13, which allows them to repay their creditors in monthly installments over a three-year period.

> About 800 foreign students at the university are on F-1 student visas— which means that they are allowed to stay in the United States only until their educations are complete.

3. Place the explanation in the next sentence:

> LeClaire failed the sobriety tests, and a breathalizer test indicated that she had a blood alcohol level of .29. The legal limit for blood alcohol levels is .10.

> The major banks raised their prime rate to 12.5 percent. The prime rate is the interest rate that banks charge their best customers.

Instead of using an unfamiliar term and then defining it, it's often better to eliminate the term and use the definition or explanation instead:

> He wants to improve the student-teacher ratio to 1:18.
> REVISED: He wants to provide one teacher for every 18 students.

> She said the school will have K–6 facilities.
> REVISED: She said the school will accept children from kindergarten through the sixth grade.

Another story reported that a new hospital had "138 private rooms, 72 semi-private rooms and 15 ICU-CCU units distributed over two patient floors." Most readers might know the difference between a private and a semi-private room. Some would not, however, and others would stumble over the terms "ICU/CCU" and "two patient floors." All four terms can easily be avoided:

> The hospital has 138 rooms that contain one bed, 72 rooms that contain two beds, and 16 intensive-care and critical-care units. All rooms for patients are located on two floors.

Reporters using these techniques can make even the most complicated stories understandable for their readers. For example, after President Ronald Reagan was shot, Newsweek magazine provided this clear description of his treatment:

> The first order of business was peritoneal lavage, a procedure to double-check for injuries in the abdominal cavity. Giordano [the surgeon] made a small incision under the navel and pumped a clear liquid into the abdomen. The liquid that drained back out seemed free of blood, showing that no organs had been damaged.

Similarly, an environmental reporter for The Arizona Daily Star in Tucson wrote about several wells contaminated by trichloroethylene. The topic was complex, yet reporter Jane Kay's stories were clear and dramatic. Kay explained that the chemical, also called "TCE," is an industrial degreaser that may cause cancer in humans. The wells contaminated by TCE were closed, and government officials assured people that their drinking water was safe. But after hundreds of interviews, Kay discovered that, "For 10 to 30 years, many southside Tucson residents unknowingly got minute quantities of TCE almost every time they turned on the water tap." As many as 20,000 people "drank TCE at home, inhaled it in the shower and absorbed it through their skin when they washed the dishes."

Kay added that:

> TCE is a tasteless, odorless, colorless—and very toxic—chemical. It is volatile, meaning that it evaporates quickly, much like common household cleaning fluids.
> Only a teaspoon of it poured into 250,000 gallons of water—about the amount used by five people in an entire year—would create a taint slightly beyond the 5 parts per billion suggested as a guideline for safety by the state Department of Health Services.

Apparently as a result of the TCE contamination, residents of Tucson's south side suffered from an unusual number of serious illnesses, including cancer.

Explain large numbers: millions, billions and trillions. For example, if you saw a story reporting that the savings and loan crisis will cost the nation $500 billion, would you really understand that number? As a reporter, you can help your readers understand large numbers by converting the numbers into something more familiar, perhaps something related to their own lives:

> The county's residents and businesses produce about 2,200 tons of garbage each day, or 6.7 pounds per resident.

> Last year in this state, a serious crime was committed every 29 seconds, and a violent crime every 3 minutes, 29 seconds. Every citizen had a 1 in 11 chance of being a victim.

> About 59 billion pieces of junk mail get sent through the U.S. Postal Service each year: 250 for every man, woman and child in the land, or 1,000 a year for a family of four.

The national debt exceeds $2.6 billion and is increasing by $7,927 every second. How big is that? "So big," the (Pasadena, Calif.) Star-News explained, "that if you tried to pay it off without interest at a dollar a second, it would take 75,000 years. So big that a stack of $1 bills representing the debt would reach 200,048 miles high—almost to the moon."

Similarly, The Washington Post reported that an investment bank offered to pay $20.6 billion to take over RJR Nabisco Inc., the conglomerate that makes Oreos, Life Savers and Camel cigarettes. RJR Nabisco rejected the offer, saying it wasn't big enough. If $20.6 billion cannot buy a cookie company, what is it good for? A writer at The Post calculated that it could:

- Provide shoes for every American for a year.
- House 2 million criminals in prisons for a year.
- Sponsor 80 million destitute children around the world for one year.
- Match the combined fortunes of the six richest men in the United States.
- Cover the cost of every movie ticket bought in the United States in the past 4.5 years.
- Buy every advertisement in every magazine published in the United States for the past four years, or every radio ad for the past three years.

THE IMPORTANCE OF EXAMPLES

Specific examples make stories more interesting, personalize them and help readers understand them more easily. If you wrote about a teen-ager who became an alcoholic and flunked out of college, you might describe specific examples of the problems she experienced:

> She said school became unimportant, adding that: "I can remember staying up all night before my public health final. When I took the test I was smashed. And if that wasn't bad enough, then I ran the entire 10 blocks back to my apartment so I could drink some more. Of course, I flunked public health."

Specific examples are especially important in stories about abstract issues. If you wrote about the lives of people who drop out of college, you would have to report the percentage of students who drop out of college nationally, their reasons for dropping out and what they do afterward: join the military, get married, find a job or enroll in another school. In addition to reporting the general trends, a good writer would illustrate the story by describing the lives of two or three dropouts—specific examples of the trend. Similarly, The New York Times began a story about the chemical contamination of fish by describing the story's impact on a single person:

> Sitting in his Fulton Market office one morning, Abe Haymes swallowed his shot of scotch from a paper cup, slapped his chest and declared:
> "I've been eating fish every day of the week for the past 40 years. Do I look sick?"
> Like the rest of the city's fish dealers, Abe Haymes is angry about recent publicity concerning mercury . . . contamination of fish.

Following the same style, Fortune magazine began a story about the interstate highway system by describing the system's impact on a single truck driver. Notice the story's use of specific details:

> Five days a week, Cecil Irvin swings up into the cab of his truck, carefully fits his sunglasses and leather gloves, and then starts the heavily loaded twin trailers behind him down the narrow streets of St. Louis.
>
> Six blocks later, he turns up a ramp leading to Interstate 70 and then, shifting up through 10 gears, he gradually picks up speed toward Kansas City.
>
> In Irvin's 250-mile trip westward, one sees in capsule form much of the impact, good and bad, of the $70 billion interstate highway system.

The following story, published by The Miami Herald, uses three examples to illustrate the impact of a paralyzing disease. Ironically, the disease was caused by a vaccination program intended to protect Americans from a dreaded strain of influenza:

> WASHINGTON—At first none of them believed anything significant was happening. Their fingers tingled because the weather was bad. They were "coming down with something." That's what caused the tender areas on their heads.
>
> Then the symptoms came with savage swiftness.
>
> • Judy Roberts of Lakeland, Fla., tried to wiggle her toes in a tight-fitting pair of sandals and found she couldn't feel them. She took off her shoes—and found she couldn't feel her feet.
>
> • Maryalice Beauton of Chula Vista, Calif., was eating a hamburger. Astonished, she realized she hadn't tasted anything.
>
> • Herman Bauer of Pittsburgh was shopping with his wife when his legs began to buckle. Confused and embarrassed, he grabbed onto a wall and called for help.
>
> They didn't know it yet, but for these people and hundreds of other Americans, the preliminary stages of a paralyzing disease known as Guillaine-Barré syndrome had just begun. . . .

THE USE OF DESCRIPTION

Descriptions, like quotations, make stories more interesting and help readers visualize scenes more easily. But many reporters are reluctant to use descriptive phrases; they summarize whatever they hear but are less likely to describe what they see, feel, taste and smell. Typically, a student who attended a speech by a controversial priest handed her instructor a note that said:

> The question-and-answer period was very brief. Father Groppi answered only three questions because he had to catch a train because the State of Wisconsin would only let him leave Wisconsin for a brief time until the legal charges against him are settled.

Despite the unusual circumstances, the student failed to describe Father Groppi's legal problems and early departure in her story.

When students begin to use descriptive phrases, most rely too heavily on adverbs and adjectives. Verbs and nouns are more effective. Their impact is demonstrated in "The Death of Captain Waskow" by Ernie Pyle, a correspondent during World War II. The story describes the death of Henry T. Waskow, a popular company commander who was killed in Italy. Pyle won a Pulitzer Prize in 1944, with this among his entries:

> One soldier came and looked down, and he said out loud, "God damn it!" That's all he said, and then he walked away.
>
> Another one came, and he said, "God damn it, to hell, anyway." He looked down for a few last moments and then turned and left.
>
> Another man came. I think he was an officer. It was hard to tell officers from men in the dim light, for everybody was bearded and grimy. The man looked down into the dead captain's face and then spoke directly to him, as though he were still alive, "I'm sorry, old man."
>
> Then a soldier came and stood beside the officer and bent over, and he too spoke to his dead captain, not a whisper but awfully tenderly, and he said, "I sure am sorry, sir."
>
> Then the first man squatted down, and he reached down and took the captain's hand and he sat there for a full five minutes holding the dead hand in his own and looking intently into the dead face. And he never uttered a sound all the time he sat there.
>
> Finally he put the hand down. He reached over and gently straightened the points of the captain's shirt collar, and then he sort of rearranged the tattered edges of the uniform around the wound, and then he got up and walked away down the road in the moonlight, all alone.
>
> (Scripps-Howard Newspapers)

Adverbs and adjectives are more opinionated than verbs and nouns, and are often redundant. After Pyle's description, there is no need to add that war is unfortunate, tragic, deadly or wasteful. Nor is there any reason to state that the men were upset or that they loved and respected the captain.

William L. Laurence won two Pulitzer Prizes for his work at The New York Times. Laurence was aboard the plane that dropped an atomic bomb on Nagasaki during World War II, and he wrote a story that contained this description of that event:

> Captain Bock swung around to get out of range; but even though we were turning away in the opposite direction, and despite the fact that it was broad daylight in our cabin, all of us became aware of a giant flash that broke through the dark barrier of our arc welder's lenses and flooded our cabin with intense light.
>
> We removed our glasses after the first flash, but the light still lingered on, a bluish-green light that illuminated the entire sky all around. A tremendous blast wave struck our ship and made it tremble from nose to tail. This was followed by four more blasts in rapid succession, each resounding like the boom of cannon fire hitting our plane from all directions.
>
> Observers in the tail of our ship saw a giant ball of fire rise as though from the bowels of the earth, belching forth enormous white smoke rings. Next they saw a giant pillar of purple fire, ten thousand feet high, shooting skyward with enormous speed.

Reporters who want to describe an object must learn to use concrete, factual details as opposed to trite generalities. When a black man and his white wife applied for an apartment, a journalism student reported that the rental agent "seemed nervous," yet in her story the student failed to provide any facts to support her conclusion. Later, she explained in class that the rental agent lit a cigarette, tapped a pencil against her desk and began to speak more rapidly, frequently repeating herself, after the couple entered her office. The rental agent also insisted that she had no vacancies.

Tips From a Pro

STORIES NEED A SENSE OF PLACE

By **Lucille S. deView**
Writing Coach
The Orange County Register

Schoenecker was held in a 12-man jail in the center of Mineral County, a remote 600,000 acres of rolling hills, brisk creeks and snowcapped peaks that is home to about 1,500 residents.

About 1,000 of them live in Superior, which along with the 1920 jail has four bars, two markets, a brick courthouse and a Chevrolet dealership with just one car on display.
—Janine Anderson from Superior, Mont.

Creating a sense of place is essential to good writing. Some novelists, poets, journalists do this so well that we speak of Isak Dinesen's Africa, Carl Sandburg's Chicago, Bobbie Ann Mason's South, Joan Didion's Los Angeles.

To create a sense of place, imagine yourself as a camera focusing on detailed close-ups or capturing the broader scene with a wide-angle lens.

CLOSE-UPS:

Use your senses. What do you see—skyscrapers, hovels, meadows, cement? What do you hear—birds, sirens, whistles, waves? What do you smell—chemicals, flowers, garbage, perfume? What do you feel—nostalgia, alarm?

Who are the people? What ages? Backgrounds? What do they do with their days? Don't see people as quaint; to do so is to overlook their truth, however much it may differ from yours. What distinguished Anderson's description of Superior, Mont., was her respect for the town and its residents.

Hang out where people hang out. Robert Frank received a good tip for a story about Garden Grove police officers by hanging out at a restaurant they frequent. Charlie Finnie found a mission for the homeless when he methodically combed every street on his beat, looking for stories.

Take along your Polaroid and snap candid shots of streets, parks, cemeteries, industries to augment your notes. Look for contrasts—the ugly and beautiful, the soft and the tough.

What are the architectural styles, the costs of buildings? What does the presence or absence of lawns, trees, flowers say? What is the local history? The prospect for change?

DISTANCE SHOTS:

Characterize the entire town, the entire neighborhood within a region. What is typical, what not? Is it like any other place on Earth?

YOU CAN'T TELL ALL:

A sense of place need not be lengthy but your research should be thorough, the better to help you select telling details and weave them into exciting prose.

Be the writer. The camera.

The following sentences, written by students who were asked to describe their campus, are also too vague:

> The library casts a knowledgeable shadow.

> The art complex appears to be a temporary structure.

> Here man has altered nature, but he has not destroyed it.

> The campus is a lesson in harmony between man and his natural surroundings.

> The students seemed relaxed as they studied under the trees on the large lawn.

> Most of the buildings have few windows. Those few windows are small and cleverly designed.

The first sentence presents an opinion rather than a verifiable fact; it's also absurd. How can a shadow be "knowledgeable"? The second sentence calls the art complex "a temporary structure" but fails to explain why the reporter reached that conclusion. Another sentence concludes that students studying beneath some trees "seemed relaxed" but fails to provide any specific details to support that observation. The same sentence refers to a "large lawn" but never estimates its exact size.

To be effective, description must be so factual and detailed that readers can visualize the scene in their minds:

> VAGUE: A 6-foot fence surrounds the construction site.
> BETTER: The construction site is surrounded by a 6-foot chain-link fence topped by three strands of barbed wire.

> VAGUE: There were about 50 men working in the area.
> BETTER: About 50 men were working in the area, and most wore hard hats, some yellow, some white and others red. Four of the men had tied nail pouches around their waists. Others smoked cigarettes and looked weary in their dirty white T-shirts, jeans and sunglasses.

The same problems arise when reporters attempt to describe other people. Instead of presenting factual details, some reporters mistakenly present generalities or their personal impressions of those people's appearance and character, as in the following (often contradictory) examples, written about a man and a women:

He spoke with authority.
He gave a cool, casual speech.
He was frank about his duties.
He appeared comfortable and relaxed.
He appeared unprepared for the occasion.
He immediately took control of the situation.

Her eyes lit up.
Her face has a healthy glow.
She is a very animated speaker.
Kay gestured freely with both hands.
There was an awkwardness to her appearance.
She seemed to enjoy talking about her work.

None of these sentences is an actual description. The first sentence concludes that the man spoke "with authority" but fails to explain why the writer reached that conclusion.

The second sentence reports that he gave a "cool and casual" speech but does not specifically describe either the speaker or his speech.

Generalities are often inconsistent. One student reported that a woman "seemed relaxed and very sure of herself." Everything about her "conveyed calmness." Yet another student concluded that, "She seemed nervous, perhaps embarrassed." The students could have avoided the problem by reporting specific details as opposed to their impressions, opinions and conclusions.

Reporters must learn to observe and describe specific details, including a person's height, weight, age, clothing, voice, mannerisms, facial expressions, hair, glasses, jewelry, posture, gestures, family and surroundings. Each factor can be described in detail; for example, a reporter describing a person's hair might mention its color, length, thickness, neatness and style. Thus, when you are asked to describe another person, look at the person carefully, then report specific facts about that person. Avoid generalities and conclusions:

> VAGUE: He is a large man.
> BETTER: He is 6 feet tall and weighs 210 pounds.

> VAGUE: Butler was dressed casually.
> BETTER: Butler was dressed in a maroon shirt that was left unbuttoned
> near the collar, striped pants and black shoes. He wore no jewelry, not even
> a watch or ring.

Reporters can include a descriptive word or phrase almost anywhere in a news story, or they can devote an entire sentence or paragraph to description:

> The audience applauded Dutton, a tall, gray-haired man.

> Mrs. Ambrose, a former newspaper editor, arrived breathless and five minutes late for her speech.

> He leaned back in his chair, laced his fingers together across his round belly and clenched the cigar in the corner of his mouth.

> They sat across the table from each other. The girl, who had long, blonde hair, picked at her hamburger, tearing it into bite-sized bits. Her boyfriend, who was wearing a gold shirt and brown shorts, was nibbling french fries from a bag.

> She is 70 years old, but her thick brown hair is only slightly graying. As she spoke, she leaned back on a pillow and nervously smoked a cigarette. She has only a small table and a cot in her living room, and both are covered with knickknacks. She takes her guests into her bedroom to sit and talk.

Study the following examples. Both help reveal the character of the people they describe. The first example, reprinted from The Miami Herald, describes a 79-year-old city commissioner. The second example, reprinted from a Louisville paper, describes the city's mayor. An editor who praised the second example explained that: "Those details paint a picture. They show the reader Harvey Sloane. They add life and meaning."

> She has white hair, red lips, clip-on earrings, good manners and a dog named Muffy. She sews, has arthritis, says "dear," and points her finger when she talks.

He wore Nike running shoes, mud-splattered pants and the Santa-red parka that's been his insignia since his walk to win election as mayor of Louisville. . . .

Sloane is physically slight. His dark hair is lightly streaked with gray. He is about 45 but looks younger. He is a millionaire by inheritance. He jogs. He has three little children, a chic wife and a classy renovated home in Old Louisville staffed with servants.

THE USE OF HUMOR

Editors constantly look for humorous stories and often place those stories on page 1. But for most writers, humorous stories are particularly difficult to write. Reporters should not try to inject humor into stories that are not obviously humorous. If a story is funny, the humor should be apparent from the facts themselves. Reporters should not have to exaggerate or point out the humor by labeling it "funny" or "comical." Author and economist John Kenneth Galbraith has explained: "Humor is an intensely personal, largely internal thing. What pleases some, including the source, does not please others." Thus, although some people may laugh at a story, others are likely to see nothing funny in it.

When columnist James J. Kilpatrick wrote an article about conservative William Buckley, he did more than report that Buckley "had a good sense of humor." He gave a specific example of Buckley's wit. Kilpatrick reported that Buckley had once run for mayor of New York City and, when asked what he would do if he won, replied, "Ask for a recount."

Similarly, a story about the peculiar laws still in effect in some cities never called the laws "peculiar" or "funny." Instead, it simply listed them so that readers could judge the humor of the laws for themselves. The laws made it illegal to:

- Hire a neighbor's cook
- Take a cow on a school bus
- Allow a fly into a motel room
- Roll a barrel down a city street
- Take a bath without a bathing suit
- Break more than three dishes in a single day
- Ride a horse that had not been equipped with a horn and taillight

If you were writing about Ann Landers, you might give an example of her famous wit so that readers could judge for themselves:

While attending an embassy reception, Landers was approached by a rather pompous senator.

"So you're Ann Landers," he said. "Say something funny."

Without hesitation Landers replied, "Well, you're a politician. Tell me a lie."

There are dozens of stories about England's wartime leader, Winston Churchill. Many of the stories will amuse readers and reveal aspects of Churchill's wit and character. Here are two examples:

An American woman married to a British aristocrat visited Churchill's home and talked about women's rights. Churchill disagreed with the woman

on this and several other topics. In exasperation, she said, "Winston, if I were married to you, I'd put poison in your coffee."
Churchill responded, "And if you were my wife, I'd drink it."

Churchill argued with a woman at a dinner party one evening. Scornfully, the woman remarked, "Mr. Churchill, you are drunk."
Churchill replied: "And you, madam, are ugly. But I shall be sober tomorrow."

Try to include some humor in your stories when appropriate, but remember that understatement is more effective than exaggeration. Simply report the facts that you think are humorous, then hope that your readers will laugh.

NEWSWRITING HABITS TO AVOID

Avoid Stating the Obvious

Dull, trite remarks are called "platitudes," and reporters must learn to avoid them. News stories should not state obvious facts that readers already know. Platitudes that have appeared in news stories include:

As it has in most areas of modern life, science has entered the profession of firefighting in recent years.

Superhighways, high-speed automobiles and jet planes are common objects of the modern era.

The second example appeared in a story about technological changes that had occurred during the life of a 100-year-old woman. The sentence would have been more interesting if it had described the changes in more specific detail and clearly related them to the woman's life, such as:

Mrs. Hansen, who once spent three days on a train to visit relatives in California, now flies to California in three hours every Christmas.

A student writing about attempts to control the birth rate of pigeons began the story this way:

Pigeons are common in large cities and even in small towns across the country. They are social birds and establish stable communities.
It seems acceptable that they are social and stable. However, citizens are annoyed by the messiness of pigeons and would rather not have so many around.

A more interesting lead would have avoided the obvious—the fact that pigeons are common and messy—and immediately emphasized the latest developments and main point of the story:

Cities are experimenting with the use of drugs to prevent pigeons from breeding.

Other students have included these platitudes in their stories:

Counselors help students with their problems.

The mayor said he was pleased by the warm reception.

The sponsors hope the art show will attract a large crowd.

She said she is looking forward to the challenge of her new job.

The principal said he has a staff of hard-working, dedicated teachers.

The university is constantly changing to meet the needs of its students.

The sources in these stories stated the obvious (what they were expected to say). Their statements sound familiar because these platitudes have been used before, perhaps millions of times.

Other platitudes appear in direct quotations. However, that does not justify their use. Such dull quotes should be deleted:

The newly elected mayor said, "I hope to do a good job."

A secretary said, "My boss is very kind and hard-working."

The athlete said, "I owe a lot of my success to my father and my coach."

The committee chair said, "Homecoming is going to be big and exciting."

The teacher said, "My students are a great bunch of kids and have a lot of enthusiasm."

When people stop reading a story, they rarely think about the reasons it bored them. If people re-examined the story, they might find not just one, but a series of platitudes. The following platitudes (and a half-dozen others) appeared in an interview with a football coach:

"College is a great experience—an education," Coach Smith said. "Everybody should have the opportunity to experience college life."

Smith added that it is important for a person to go to college and learn how to interact with other people, even if he does not pass all his courses.

Even if some athletes do not get a degree, Smith said, they will still learn a lot on a college campus.

To avoid platitudes, reporters must be alert, particularly when conducting interviews. Sources often give obvious, commonplace answers to the questions they are asked. If a bartender is robbed at gunpoint, there is no reason to quote him as saying that he "was scared." Most people confronted by gunmen are scared, and they often say so. If reporters wanted to quote the bartender—or any other source—they would have to ask more penetrating questions and to continue their interview until they received more specific, interesting or unusual details.

Avoid Personification

Avoid describing inanimate objects as if they were human. Objects such as buildings, cars, stores and trees cannot hear, think, feel or talk. Yet some writers treat them as people. The writers see (and repeat) the error so often that they no longer recognize it and continue to personify almost everything, from committees to cities. Here are two examples that appeared in The New York Times:

> His chief accusers are friends who have told the courtroom of seeing a dead classmate only hours after a pep rally.

> China has decided "in principle" to accept Peace Corps volunteers for the first time, Foreign Minister Wu Xueguian told a luncheon meeting at the National Press Club.

An editor at The Times criticized the first sentence. "People who talk to rooms, even courtrooms," he commented, "are not very credible witnesses." The editor suggested a correction for the second sentence: ". . . Foreign Minister Wu Xueguian said at a luncheon meeting at the National Press Club."

Similarly, students have written that:

> Memorial Hospital treated her for shock and a broken arm.

> Ecologically concerned car washes are filtering and reusing their water.

> She was driving west on Hullett Avenue when two cars in front of her slammed on their brakes.

Can a hospital treat patients, or is that the job of a hospital's staff? Similarly, can a car wash be concerned about the environment, and can a car slam on its own brakes? Of course not! Such personification errors are easy to correct:

> The store said it will not reopen.
> REVISED: The store's owner said it will not reopen.

> The intention of the road was to help farmers transport their crops to market.
> REVISED: The road was built to help farmers transport their crops to market.

Personification contributes to two other problems. First, it handicaps readers. Readers cannot determine a story's credibility if reporters fail to identify their source. Readers can assess the credibility of a statement attributed to their mayor or governor, but not the credibility of a statement attributed to their city or state.

Second, personification allows people to escape responsibility for their actions. Officials cannot be held responsible for their actions if reporters attribute their actions to a city or state, for example.

Avoid the Negative

For clarity, avoid the negative. Your sentences should be constructed in positive, rather than negative, form, as in the following examples:

> The student did not often come to class.
> REVISED: The student rarely came to class.

> It was not the first time the plane's engine failed.
> REVISED: It was the third time the plane's engine failed.

> The defense attorney tried to disprove his client's sanity.
> REVISED: The defense attorney tried to prove that his client was insane.

ISBN 0-15-500602-9

Sentences that contain two or three negatives are even more difficult to decipher. As you read the following examples, you may have to pause and struggle to determine their meaning:

> The women said they are not disinclined to use butter.
> REVISED: The women said they may use butter.

> The senator said he will not accept any campaign contributions from people who do not live in his district.
> REVISED: The senator said he will accept campaign contributions only from people who live in his district.

In most cases, you can correct the problem by changing a word or two:

> Most people are not careful readers.
> REVISED: Few people are careful readers.

> The financial planner said she can help people not go into debt.
> REVISED: The financial planner said she can help people avoid debt.

Avoid an Echo

Avoid an echo: the unnecessary repetition of a word, as in these examples:

> He was succeeded by his successor, Todd Fong.

> They will pay the mortgage in monthly payments of $1,281.

> In Japan, cancer patients are usually not told they have cancer.

Writers sometimes repeat a key word or phrase for emphasis or to demonstrate an important similarity. If the repetition is needless, however, the result is likely to be awkward, distracting or confusing.

Avoid Gush

Reporters also avoid "gush"—writing with exaggerated enthusiasm. They write news stories to inform their readers, not to please their sources. Thus, news stories should report useful information. They should not praise nor advocate.

Because it is fast and easy, too many reporters obtain all their information from a single source, often an official responsible for the issue being discussed. Officials try to use reporters. They would be foolish not to. Few officials are foolish enough to criticize their own programs. Instead, most try to impress or manipulate reporters in an attempt to obtain more favorable publicity, and often they succeed. They reveal only the information that makes them, their policies and their institutions look good.

To avoid this problem, reporters must talk to several sources to obtain a variety of viewpoints and to verify statements made by officials. Reporters must also prepare for each interview so that they can ask more knowledgeable questions and recognize evasive responses. Perhaps even more important, reporters must learn to ask for more specific details that support the officials' claims. The following statements lack those details and consequently enable the officials to engage in self-praise:

> "Our program is very respected and well-run," the director said.

"We feel we are providing quality recreational programs for both adults and children," Holden said.

Police Chief Barry Kopperud said the city's mounted horse patrol, which began one year ago, has become a great success.

When a reporter finishes an article, it should sound like a news story, not a press release. One travel story gushed that Mexico is "a land of lush valleys and marvelous people." Another story reported that some films "are in great demand, and the school is fortunate in being able to offer them to the community." Other examples of gush include:

The fair will offer bigger and better attractions than ever before.

The event will provide fun and surprises for everyone who attends.

Free beer will be provided, along with contests and games that will add to the excitement.

This gush cannot be rewritten, because there is nothing of substance to rewrite. It should simply be deleted.

There is a second type of gush: an escalation in modifiers. Columnist Donna Neely explains that what used to be called "funny" is now called "hilarious" and what used to be "great" is now called "fantastic" or "incredible."

These new words appear everywhere: in news stories, press releases, advertisements and everyday speech. Sportswriters call athletes not just "stars," but "superstars." Advertisers call their inventories "fabulous" and their sales "gigantic." Teen-agers like the word "awesome." Some call almost everything that impresses them "awesome," or even "totally awesome."

Avoid Contrived Titles and Labels

Some students attach their own labels to subjects, yet most of those labels are unnecessary, opinionated and awkward. Many are also ridiculous. One writer referred to a young girl with an unusual illness as "the diseased student." Other students have referred to "a preliminary plant plan," "a two-motorcycle, three-person accident" and "the county's school bond-financed building program." If a label is so artificial that you have never heard or used it before, and would not use it in a conversation with friends, do not use it in a news story.

Here are other examples of awkward, contrived labels:

a black-clad man
the young gun-holder
an ambulance collision
the Washington County-owned car
the shopping center developer's
  request

the well-patrolled parking lot
the tentatively approved program
the estimated $3.6 million building
the Plymouth County Fair Queen
  Beauty Contest
the newly named university annual
  fund drive committee

Such labels—also called "false titles"—often appear as a jumble of modifiers piled before a name:

Twenty-year-old Seminole Community College business major Nina
Thomas won the $5,000 prize.

ISBN 0-15-500602-9

REVISED: Nina Thomas, a 20-year-old business major at Seminole Community College, won the $5,000 prize.

The German measles vaccination program aimed at adolescent girls will begin Monday.
REVISED: A vaccination program intended to protect adolescent girls from German measles will begin Monday.

Labels are even more difficult to understand when reporters try to use their possessive forms:

The fleeing 22-year-old robbery suspect's red sports car was found abandoned near his home.
REVISED: The 22-year-old robbery suspect fled, and police found his red sports car abandoned near his home.

The American Association of Political Scientists' annual summer convention will be held in San Diego.
REVISED: The American Association of Political Scientists will hold its annual summer convention in San Diego.

Inexperienced reporters use the time as a label, treating it as if it were a significant factor that could be used to distinguish one event from another. Thus, they may describe "a 10:05 a.m. fire," "an 11:20 a.m. drowning" or "a 2:15 p.m. storm."

Avoid Vague Time References and the Present Tense

Unless your instructor suggests otherwise, do not use the words "yesterday," "today" and "tomorrow" in news stories; you are too likely to mislead your readers. Instead, use the specific days of the week: "Sunday," "Monday," "Tuesday" and so forth. Many of the stories that appear in newspapers are written the day before their publication or even earlier. For example, the reporters employed by morning papers often work until midnight and, if a fire destroyed a home at 5 p.m. Tuesday, the reporters would write a story about the fire later Tuesday night. The reporters could not say the fire occurred "today" because readers who received the papers Wednesday morning would assume that "today" meant that day—Wednesday. Thus, even though the fire occurred on Tuesday and reporters wrote the story on Tuesday, they would have to tell readers the fire occurred "yesterday." To avoid the confusion and errors that invariably arise, always use the name of the day of the week instead of "today," "yesterday" and "tomorrow." Because it is too vague, reporters also avoid the word "recently."

Because many of the events that newspapers report end before readers receive the papers, newswriters avoid the present tense and terms such as "at the present time." Even though it is true, a reporter working at deadline should not say, "A fire at the Grand Hotel threatens to destroy the entire block." Firefighters would almost certainly extinguish the blaze before readers received the paper hours later. For the same reason, a reporter covering a fatal accident should not say, "The victim's identity is not known." Police might learn the victim's identity in a few hours, and local radio and television stations might broadcast the person's name before subscribers received their papers. Consequently, reporters must use the past tense, clearly indicating that the situations they are describing existed at some time in the past:

A fire at the Grand Hotel threatens to destroy the entire block.
REVISED: At 11:30 p.m. Tuesday, a fire at the Grand Hotel was still threatening to destroy the entire block.

The victim's identity is not known.
REVISED: Police were unable to learn the victim's identity immediately.

Other Problems to Avoid

Reporters avoid exaggeration and excessive punctuation, and use words such as "it," "this," "these," "those" and "that" with caution.

Exaggeration in news stories is artificial, wordy and ineffective. It also tends to be trite and to state the obvious. There is no need to report that an explosion was "violent," that a murder was "brutal" or that an ambulance "rushed" someone to a hospital. The adjectives waste newspapers' space and readers' time.

Sweeping generalizations, another form of exaggeration, are impossible to verify and often wrong. Consequently, few good reporters will claim that everyone in a community considers an issue important, that everyone mourns the death of a prominent person or that everyone is celebrating a holiday.

Reporters avoid excessive punctuation, particularly exclamation points and parentheses. Exclamation points are rarely necessary and should never be used after every sentence in a story, regardless of that story's importance.

Reporters avoid parenthetical matter because it creates an obstacle that makes reading more difficult. Parentheses interrupt the flow of ideas and force readers to pause and assimilate some additional, often jarring, bits of information:

> She (the governor) said that, during the last 20 years, the elderly population (people 65 and older) has grown twice as fast as any other segment of the state's population.
> REVISED: The governor said that, during the last 20 years, the percentage of people 65 and older has grown twice as fast as any other segment of the state's population.

> "I wish they (school administrators) would quit fooling around," she said. "They say they don't have enough money (to hire more teachers), but I don't believe that. I know they have it (the money); it's just a matter of priorities—of using their money more wisely."
> REVISED: She said the school administrators should "quit fooling around." They say they do not have enough money to hire more teachers, but she does not believe that. "It's just a matter of priorities—of using their money more wisely," she said.

Because their meanings are often unclear, reporters use words such as "it," "this," "these," "those" and "that" with caution. Reporters must be particularly careful to avoid starting a sentence or paragraph with one of these words unless its antecedent is obvious. To avoid unnecessary confusion, reporters can repeat a key word or phrase or rewrite a foggy sentence to clarify its meaning:

> He said: "Only childless couples will be admitted, so there won't be any noise and the trailer park won't affect schools in the area. We expect the average trailer in the park to cost $50,000, and some will cost twice that much."
> Some members of the audience disagreed with this.
> REVISED: He said: "Only childless couples will be admitted, so there won't be any noise and the trailer park won't affect schools in the area. We expect the average trailer in the park to cost $50,000, and some will cost twice that much."

Some members of the audience disagreed, saying the trailer park would be too noisy and would lower the value of property in the area.

Commissioner Ben Benham, who represents Scott County on the Transit Authority, said the bus system is no longer losing money. He attributed this to the elimination of routes that had consistently shown losses.
REVISED: Commissioner Ben Benham, who represents Scott County on the Transit Authority, said the bus system is no longer losing money because routes that had consistently shown losses have been eliminated.

For clarity, new stories should be emphatic. Facts that are important should never be slipped into stories as minor clauses or phrases that receive little emphasis:

James Loach admitted that he robbed Anders of $170 and said he tied the Vanguard Theater employee's hands with a rope, but he denied that he killed the son of Central High School Principal Robert Anders.
REVISED: James Loach admitted that he robbed Anders of $170 and said he tied Anders' hands with a rope, but he denied that he killed the youth.
Anders, the son of Central High School Principal Robert Anders, worked at the Vanguard Theater.

The first sentence began by mentioning Anders but later referred to "the Vanguard Theater employee" and to "the son of Central High School Principal Robert Anders." The sentence failed to make it clear that Anders himself was the theater employee and the son of the high school principal. At best, the inclusion of these facts was confusing. At worst, it was misleading, since readers might assume that the story was describing three different people.

MORE ON GRAMMAR AND WORD USAGE

To become an effective writer, you will have to do more than master the basics of grammar and word usage. You will have to become an expert, understanding—and avoiding—all the following problems.

Use Parallel Form

Every item listed in a series must be in parallel form. If the first verb in a series uses the past tense, every verb in the series must use the past tense. If the first verb ends in "-ing," all must end in "-ing."

The woman was running from the dog, crying and bled.
PARALLEL FORM: The woman was running from the dog, crying and bleeding.

Police said the plastic handcuffs are less bulky, less expensive and no key is needed to remove them from a suspect's wrists.
PARALLEL FORM: Police said plastic handcuffs are less bulky, less expensive and less difficult to remove from a suspect's wrists.

The executive said common mistakes in job interviews include failing to show initiative, vague responses, being overly concerned about pay, not having any questions and having no career goals in mind.

ISBN 0-15-500602-9

PARALLEL FORM: The executive said common mistakes in job interviews include failing to show initiative, giving vague responses to questions, being overly concerned about pay, failing to ask any questions and failing to express any career goals.

Use the Articles Correctly

Use the articles "a," "an" and "the" correctly. The words "a" and "an" are indefinite articles, used to refer to one member of a broad category or class of objects (for example, "They want to buy a table"). The word "the" is a definite article, used to refer to a specific person or object (for example, "That is the table they want to buy"). As a general rule, use an indefinite article when referring to a person or object that has not been mentioned earlier in a story. Use the definite article when referring to a specific person or object that your readers are familiar with, because it was mentioned earlier in a story.

If it is misused, the definite article may mislead readers, since it often suggests that the object being referred to is the only such object in existence. If, for example, a story reports that three people were taken to "the hospital," yet the story's earlier paragraphs never mentioned the hospital's name, the sentence implies that the area has only one hospital, the one at which those people are being treated. Similarly, if you reported that someone ate lunch at "the McDonald's in Chicago," your sentence would imply, wrongly, that there is only one McDonald's in the entire city.

Use Strong Verbs

Again, use strong, active and descriptive verbs:

He has a bike that is insured for $2,400.
REVISED: He owns (rides, rents, won, borrowed) a bike that is insured for $2,400.

The Girl Scouts did a survey of 500 homes.
REVISED: The Girl Scouts conducted (organized, financed, supervised) a survey of 500 homes.

Use "Who," "Whom" and "That" Correctly

Use the words "who" and "whom" only when referring to a person or to an animal with a proper name. Use the words "that" and "which" when referring to inanimate objects and to animals without names.

Check for Subject-Verb and Noun-Pronoun Agreement

If your subject is singular, use a singular verb, and if your subject is plural, use a plural verb. Similarly, if a noun is singular, use a singular pronoun, and if a noun is plural, use a plural pronoun:

A team of researchers have been gathering the information.
REVISED: A team of researchers has been gathering the information.

The group failed in their attempts to obtain more money.
REVISED: The group failed in its attempts to obtain more money.

Some nouns are confusing: nouns such as "committee," "family," "group," "jury" and "team." The Associated Press Stylebook explains that all those nouns take singular verbs and pronouns, because they denote a single unit:

The team won their third game in a row.
REVISED: The team won its third game in a row.

The jury reached their verdict at 11:10 p.m.
REVISED: The jury reached its verdict at 11:10 p.m.

Collective nouns refer to a group or quantity regarded as a single unit and also take singular verbs and pronouns. For example: "A thousand bushels is a good yield"; "The data is sound."

Avoid Convoluted Sentences

As your sentences become more complicated, they become more likely to contain errors. These sentences, written by students, illustrate the problem:

She said advice for a swimming pool with the algae would be not swim in the pool.

Primarily a rental area, the commission wants to rezone the neighborhood and encourage single-family ownership over rental properties.

Paramedics reported no signs of life in the children and began administering CPR and oxygen. Still unable to find a heartbeat in either victim, they were transported by ambulance to Mercy Hospital.

The first sentence warns swimming pools not to swim in the pool. The second sentence calls the commission a rental area. The third sentence, the most confusing of all, seems to report that the paramedics unable to find a heartbeat (not the victims) were taken to Mercy Hospital.

SOME FINAL GUIDELINES

1. Begin by obtaining a good, solid foundation for your story: all the information that your readers might want to know about the topic. To add to your story's credibility and depth, consult several credible sources, not just one, and report every viewpoint.
2. If your story is complicated, prepare an outline. Decide which facts are most important and decide how you want to organize them. Plan the transitions between different ideas and the point at which you want to end the story.
3. Emphasize the human element in every story: the people involved in the story (or the people affected by it). Readers are interested in other people: their interests, values, habits, jobs, eccentricities, families, problems, triumphs and tragedies.
4. Ken Fuson, an award-winning reporter for the Des Moines Register, suggests that reporters look for unexpected or unusual ways to present the facts in their stories. For example, while writing about a town's isolation, Fuson began:

"State Center is 45 miles from Des Moines, 15 miles from Ames and 13 miles from the nearest McDonald's."

5. Place the information you want to emphasize at the beginning or end of a sentence. Avoid burying it in the middle of a sentence, since it receives less emphasis there. Because readers are most likely to remember whatever they saw last, many experts believe that information placed at the end of a sentence is likely to have the greatest impact on readers.

6. When you mention several objects or numbers in a story, always check their arithmetical consistency. For example, if you report that seven people received awards and list their names, count to be certain that you have listed seven, not six or eight, recipients.

7. When you list several items in a sentence, place an explanation before the list, not after it. If the explanation does not appear before the list, readers may not immediately understand the relationship among the items or the significance of the list:

Attempting to elude a police officer, no driver's license, fleeing the scene of an accident and driving while intoxicated were the charges filed against the mayor.
REVISED: The mayor was charged with attempting to elude a police officer, driving without a license, fleeing the scene of an accident and driving while intoxicated.

To obtain a better salary, better hours and not so few opportunities for advancement are the reasons the woman gave for changing jobs.
REVISED: The woman said she changed jobs to obtain a better salary, better hours and more opportunities for advancement.

8. Be consistent in your description of, or reference to, topics. If you write about a hospital, use the hospital's full name the first time you mention it. Later in the story, refer to it as "the hospital" (you do not have to repeat the hospital's full name). Do not call the building a "hospital" the first time you mention it and later refer to it as a "structure," "building," "medical facility" and "health center." The different labels might confuse readers.

9. Except in extraordinary circumstances, reporters should remain neutral bystanders. They should not mention themselves in news stories. Reporters should not have to use the words "I," "me," "we" or "us," except in direct quotations (when they are quoting some other person). When they appear outside quotation marks, the words are likely to confuse readers. Reporters who use the word "we" rarely explain who they are referring to, yet their subject is not always clear. Moreover, it is a mistake for reporters to assume that all their readers will fit into the category they mean when they use "we":

He said we must work harder to improve the city's schools.
REVISED: He said parents must work harder to improve the city's schools.

The governor said we are being hurt by inflation.
REVISED: The governor said residents of the state are being hurt by inflation.

10. If you use a specific figure, such as 41 or 471, do not use approximations such as "about." Use approximations only with round numbers, as in, "About 700 people attended the concert."

11. Avoid loaded words that might prejudice your readers for or against a subject. When they attribute statements, reporters avoid the word "claim" because it im-

plies doubt, suggesting that the statements may be false. The word "only" is even more troublesome. If a reporter comments that, "Only three people were killed," the use of "only" suggests that those deaths were unimportant.

12. Avoid contractions: "doesn't," "hadn't" and so on. Many papers prohibit their use except in direct quotations.

13. Avoid overusing the words "that" and "then"; both words can usually be deleted. "Then" is especially troublesome, since some writers habitually add it to most of their sentences.

14. Avoid using too many pronouns in a sentence. They become confusing and repetitive, as in these examples:

    She said she would be happy to help him if they could finish the work after the test.

    He said he had a bomb in the bag he was carrying, and he threatened to blow up the bank if he did not get their money.

15. Tell your readers how or where you obtained the information presented in each story: from a press conference, speech, interview or telephone conversation. The source does not have to be emphasized or placed in a story's lead, but it should be included somewhere, perhaps in a brief phrase or sentence (for example, "During a press conference in her office, the governor said she opposes legalized gambling in the state.").

16. If you are unable to obtain an important fact or some information that your readers might expect or need, explain why you did not include that information in your story:

    University officials said it will take several days to calculate the average faculty member's salary.

    Company officials said it would be impossible to determine how the food became contaminated.

    Rescue workers said they will not know how many people were killed until all the water is pumped out and they are able to search the entire mine.

17. Never create or manufacture any information; report only the facts you obtain from reliable sources. If you need some additional information, research your topic more thoroughly; never make up any information. News stories are based on fact, not fiction.

18. Be original. Go out and personally gather the information you need for a story. Do not rewrite information that has already been reported by other media. By the time you copy it, the information is likely to be old, and many of your readers may have seen or heard it before. Moreover, some readers may accuse you of plagiarism.

CHECKLIST FOR IMPROVING NEWSGATHERING AND WRITING SKILLS

1. Are the words in your story used properly, and are they descriptive, specific and interesting?
2. Have you started any sentence with the words "it," "this," "these," "those" or "that"? If so, is the antecedent clear?

3. Have you eliminated generalities and vague qualifiers, such as "young," "big," "late," "fast," "very" and "a lot"?

4. Have you used the articles "a," "an" and "the" correctly?

5. Do you use the words "who" and "whom" only in referring to people and to animals that have a proper name?

6. Have you used strong, colorful, descriptive verbs?

7. Is your reference to topics consistent, and have you avoided loaded words and opinionated or artificial labels?

8. Have you avoided mentioning yourself in the story? Have you avoided using the words "I," "me," "we," "us" and "our," except in direct quotations?

9. Have you used singular verbs with singular subjects, and plural verbs with plural subjects? Similarly, have you used singular pronouns with singular nouns, and plural pronouns with plural nouns?

10. Do the items listed in series appear in parallel form?

11. Have you placed the explanation before rather than after items in lists?

12. Is your story so detailed and thorough that it answers all the questions that readers might logically ask about the topic?

13. Have you identified everyone mentioned in your story, defined unfamiliar words and explained unfamiliar concepts? Also, have you identified people only once—normally, the first time you mentioned them in your story?

14. If you have used a large number—millions, billions or trillions—have you defined it for your readers, converting the number into something more familiar, perhaps something related to their lives?

15. Have you emphasized the human element: the people involved in (or affected by) your story? Have you used examples to personalize topics and to explain abstract concepts?

16. If you have described the objects or people mentioned in your story, have you provided specific, factual details as opposed to generalities and personal impressions?

17. If you included some humor, did you present that humor in a clear, straightforward manner, without labels or exaggeration?

18. Have you avoided misleading statements about the time the story occurred? Did you use the specific day of the week (not "yesterday," "today" or "tomorrow") and avoided suggesting that your story will continue indefinitely?

19. Have you avoided gush, exaggeration, contrived labels, excessive punctuation and unnecessary parentheses?

20. Have you avoided personification: any suggestion that inanimate objects can talk, think or feel?

21. Have you avoided an echo: unnecessarily repeating the same word in a sentence?

22. Have you avoided platitudes: stating the obvious, such as the fact that a government official was happy to be elected?

23. Have you buried important facts in the middle of a sentence or paragraph?

24. Are your sentences worded in positive rather than negative form?

25. Have you revealed how or where you obtained your information? If you were unable to include some important information, have you explained the reason for its omission?

26. Is your story original and based entirely on facts that you were able to verify—not "facts" you have made up?

St. Louis Post-Dispatch

WRITE & WRONG

By **Harry Levins**
Post-Dispatch Writing Coach

How do you organize a story so that it flows smoothly from its beginning through its middle to its end?

In an effort to find out, The Coach chatted with four writers whose work he admires. From these conversations came three common themes:

- *The written outline doesn't exist, at least not here.*

- *Quotes play a big part in drawing the blueprint.*

- *Writing is like sex: We do most of it by instinct, and we all do it a little bit differently.*

☆ ☆ ☆

Pam Schaeffer wrinkled her nose at the mention of the word "outline."

"I hate them," she said. "I find them cumbersome."

Does Tom Uhlenbrock use an outline? "Never."

How about John McGuire? "No."

And Bill Smith? "No. Well, maybe in my head a little."

Well, maybe in my head a little . . .

Think of a reporter as an odd combination of technician (like, say, a carpenter) and creative artist (like an architect). The carpenter needs the architect's blueprint before he starts hammering and sawing.

Most reporters draw that blueprint in their heads, often in their cars.

"Driving back from the assignment," Smith said, "I generally figure out what my top quote and top piece of information are—and then the second, and then the third, and so on."

McGuire recalled that in his city desk days, "I would organize the story in my head on the way back from the assignment—the lede, and then the things I really wanted to get in."

Uhlenbrock said that when time allowed, he liked to let the facts bubble and stew inside his head until something floated to the top. "If I can do the interviews one day and have a night to think about it," he said, "I can get in at 9:30 the next morning, and it'll write itself."

But when time runs short, Uhlenbrock follows a time-tested pattern:

"First, my lede graf. The second graf is a killer quote. The third graf is the nut graf, the one that sums up the story."

Schaeffer prefers to do her organizing at the keyboard. "One helpful aid," she said, "is to ask yourself: What does the reader want to know *next?*"

☆ ☆ ☆

Quotes play a surprisingly big part for all four writers as they organize their stories.

"It's important to get a good quote up high, if you've got one," Smith said. "Nothing breathes life into a story like a good, strong quote—especially if it's a quote that summarizes the nut of the story."

McGuire said, "Past the lede, I start thinking of quotes. If I organize in any way, it's by quote."

But finding what Uhlenbrock called "a killer quote" means talking to a lot of people.

(continued on next page)

Uhlenbrock recently covered a flash flood at a campground. "I had time to talk to 40 or 50 people," he said, "and I *knew* I had good quotes. But when you talk to 40 or 50 people, you'll *always* have some good quotes.

"After the story appeared, some people told me I got great quotes." His words trailed off, but his expression said it all: The people who congratulated him never saw his reams of so-what quotes.

Smith said, "Sometimes, it takes 15 or 20 minutes of talking to somebody to get one good quote. For a color story the last time the Cubs came to town, I got one really good quote—a restaurant owner said he'd have to back a Brinks truck up to his place every night—and I *knew* as he said it that it would be my lead quote."

☆ ☆ ☆

Schaeffer does much of her interviewing by phone, taking notes on the VDT. When she sits down to write, she splits the screen and calls up her notes—sometimes in the order of interest or importance, but occasionally in the order in which they appear on the VDT list.

From these notes, she does a first draft. On a long story, she said, "The first draft is like giving birth: I'm miserable until it's done.

"But when it's done, I have clay that I can shape the way I want it."

How does she shape the clay?

"I rewrite and rewrite and rewrite.

"I'm striving for a good, clear read. Is it logical? Is it clear?" To get that logic and clarity, she uses the computer's magic to shuffle paragraphs around.

In the pre-VDT days, she said, she would often use scissors to cut a story into paragraphs, then rearrange them with glue. Such rearranging "is a good way to get things in logical order," she said.

"Maybe stories that are unorganized are missing only a couple of rewrites."

Like Schaeffer, McGuire often has the luxury of time to rewrite. Does he, too, split his screen?

"I never learned how," he said with a grin. "I'm old enough to still like *paper,* so I use printouts a lot. Sometimes I take printouts home at night to look at them, scribble notations, move stuff around.

"With a printout in your hand, you can really *see* the excess baggage."

(McGuire recalled that John Archibald also used a paper system. Archibald would tear the sheets out of his notebook, put them on the desk beside him and shuffle them around until an order emerged.)

Uhlenbrock, an old wire-service warhorse, tends to arrange his stories in his head. After his patented opening of lede–killer quote–nut graf, "I start from the beginning—chronological order."

And if the story doesn't lend itself to chronological order?

"I start scaling things from the top down, in order of importance."

Like the three other writers, Uhlenbrock is articulate. But like the three others, he had some difficulty in articulating what he does and why he does it. That's because he operates in large part on a combination of experience and instinct.

After doing the reporting on a recent story about construction problems at the Arch, he said, "I knew before I wrote that after my opening, it would be a three-part story: the problem, the solution, the results."

And how did he know?

He doesn't know.

☆ ☆ ☆

Smith said that chronological order "is clearer. It's the way most people think." So when his facts allow, he said, he gets to chronological order as quickly as he can.

Schaeffer said that chronological order helped to speed her writing.

"The last time I used it," she said, "I had only an hour to write the story. So I wrote a lede and then went straight into chronological order. That was the bulk of the story. It went *fast*—and it came out fine."

When McGuire was asked whether he liked to use chronological order, he replied with another grin, "The copy desk would say that I don't. That's a weakness. Sometimes, I start out that way—but then a third of the way or halfway through, I change my mind and start flopping paragraphs." So much for chronological order.

Still, as Smith noted, chronological order is the way most people think. To Western people, time moves in a straight line, starting on the left at the beginning and moving toward the right, the end.

Stories that fit on that straight line tend to read more easily than stories that bend or break the line. Good storytellers start at the beginning: "Once upon a time . . ." "In the beginning . . ."

To repeat an oft-cited quote from a writer with a lovely style, Charlie McDowell of the Richmond (Va.) Times-Dispatch:

"Get to chronological order as soon as your facts, your editor and your conscience allow. Readers sigh with relief when they get to the point in an article where the journalism ends and the *story* begins."

☆ ☆ ☆

The technician side of the reporter uses a notebook as a tool kit. The key question put to the four: *When* do you use your notebook?

Schaeffer has her electronic notes on the split screen, like a notebook open and at hand. Uhlenbrock said he kept his notebook open and at hand but referred to it only sparingly, mainly to check quotes.

McGuire gave the answer that The Coach was hoping for: "When I really get on a roll, I don't refer to it at all, except to go back and check.

"Once, in my city desk days, I lost my notes for some story, and I was horrified. But somehow, I wrote a story—and it turned out to be the tightest, most concise story I had ever written."

Smith said his use of the notebook "depends on the story. If I'm using a lot of quotes, I refer to the notebook a lot."

He paused, then said: "Sometimes, I think I can be more creative and feel better about what I'm doing if I push the notebook aside while I write, then use it only afterward to double-check.

"But the notebook is a security blanket."

The Coach suspects that Smith's creative instinct is the right one. The artist side of the reporter knows instinctively how to tell a *story*. Maybe we'd tell better stories if we gave the artist the first shot at doing the telling—if we kept the notebook closed, kept the technician out of the way.

The artist will usually leave holes—numbers that need inserting, say, or quotes that need verifying. Fine. At that point—*after* the artist has told the story—we can open the notebook and turn the technician loose to add the details and verify the quotes.

Would this artist-first method work for everybody? Of course not. Schaeffer writes fine stories without it, and Smith is reluctant to shed his security blanket.

But on a day when you feel as if your story is drowning in data, try closing your notebook and starting

(continued on next page)

again as a simple storyteller. You just may find yourself on a roll.

☆ ☆ ☆

Uhlenbrock said stories deserved to end snappily, not just peter out. "That's what you *leave* the reader with," he said. He said he liked a kicker quote as an ending.

So does McGuire. "I try to end with a great quote—an ironic or incredible quote that underpins everything you've tried to do with the story," he said.

(In fact, he said, "After the lede, the ending is the hardest part. I'll change it quite a bit if I have time.")

Smith expressed some wariness about deliberate endings. "Basically, I don't like them," he said. "First, there's the risk that some editor will cut them off."

(On this point, Schaeffer said endings could be protected by staying within the negotiated length. And Steve Kelley noted that when pagination arrived, endings would no longer automatically fall victim on the composing room floor.

("With pagination," Kelley said, "the preferred way to trim four or five lines is to find four or five grafs that end in a line with only one or two words. Then, you tighten those grafs a little, and you've made up your four or five lines.")

But Smith's wariness had more than mechanics behind it. "I don't think we're in the business of writing stories with beginnings, middles and ends," he said. "We're in the business of providing information."

As The Coach struggled to hide a frown, Smith added:

"But I look for a good quote to end with."

SUGGESTED READINGS

Articles

Brown, Karen F., and Don Fry. "Taking Risks for Readers: The 1990 ASNE Writing Award Winners." *ASNE Bulletin,* July/Aug. 1990, pp. 20–23.

Fry, Don. "What Do You Mean, 'Make My Prose Brighter'?" *ASNE Bulletin,* Oct. 1989, pp. 12–15.

Gailbraith, John Kenneth. "Writing, Typing and Economic$." *The Atlantic,* March 1978, pp. 102–105.

Shaw, David. "The Use and the Abuse of Language." *The Los Angeles Times,* Apr. 19, 1981. (Reprinted in pamphlet form.)

Spear, Michael M. "The Man Who Would Not Freeze: And Other Tales That You Ought to Tell." *The Quill,* July/Aug. 1988, pp. 26–29.

Books

Armour, Richard, ed., *How to Write Better.* Boston: Christian Science Publishing Society, 1980.

Berkman, Robert I. *Finding It Fast: How to Uncover Expert Information on Any Subject.* Updated and Expanded Version. New York: Perennial Library, 1990.

Bernstein, Theodore M. *The Careful Writer.* Boston: Atheneum, 1965.

Berry, Thomas Eliott. *The Craft of Writing*. New York: McGraw-Hill, 1974.

Dembers, David P., and Suzanne Nichols. *Precision Journalism, A Practical Guide*. Newbury Park, CA: Sage, 1987.

Fensch, Thomas. *The Hardest Parts: Techniques for Effective Nonfiction*. Austin, TX: Lander Moore Books, 1984.

Fensch, Thomas. *Writing Solutions: Beginnings, Middles and Endings*. Hillsdale, NJ: Erlbaum, 1989.

Ghiglione, Loren, ed., *Improving Newswriting*. Washington, DC: American Society of Newspaper Editors Foundation, 1982.

Hall, Donald. *Writing Well*. 5th ed. Boston: Little, Brown, 1985.

Hohenberg, John. *Concise Newswriting*. New York: Hastings House, 1987.

————. ed., *The Pulitzer Prize Story II*. New York: Columbia University Press, 1980.

Keir, Gerry, Maxwell McCombs, and Donald L. Shaw. *Advanced Reporting: Beyond News Events*. New York: Longman, 1986.

Kessler, Lauren, and Duncan McDonald. *Uncovering the News: A Journalist's Search for Information*. Belmont, CA: Wadsworth, 1987.

Kilpatrick, James J. *The Writer's Art*. Kansas City, MO: Andrews, McMeel & Parker, 1984.

McIntyre, Bryce T. *Advanced Newsgathering*. New York: Praeger, 1991.

Murray, Donald M. *Writing for Your Readers: Notes on the Writer's Craft from The Boston Globe*. Chester, CT: Globe-Pequot, 1983.

Nicholas, David, ed., *Ernie's War: The Best of Ernie Pyle's World War II Dispatches*. New York: Random House, 1986.

Rivers, William L., and Alison R. Work. *Writing for the Media*. Mountain View, CA: Mayfield, 1988.

Sloan, William David, Valarie McCrary, and Johanna Cleary. *The Best of Pulitzer Prize News Writing*. Columbus, OH: Publishing Horizons, 1986.

Strentz, Herbert. *News Reporters and News Sources*. Ames, IA: Iowa State University Press, 1989.

Tarshis, Barry. *How to Write Like a Pro*. New York: New American Library, 1982.

War, Jan, and Kathleen A. Hanson. *Search Strategies in Mass Communication*. New York: Longman, 1987.

Zinsser, William K. *On Writing Well*. 4th ed. New York: Harper & Row, 1990.

QUOTES

Give 'em a show, laughs, tears, wonders, thrills, tragedy, comedy, love and hate.

(Harry Tammen, co-owner of The Denver Post)

When the press is free and every man able to read, all is safe.

(Thomas Jefferson)

The theory of a free press is that the truth will emerge from free reporting and free discussion, not that it will be presented perfectly and instantly in any one account.

(Walter Lippmann)

Exercise 1

IMPROVING NEWSGATHERING AND WRITING SKILLS

RECOGNIZING AND CORRECTING NEWSWRITING ERRORS

SECTION I: DESCRIBING PEOPLE

Which of the following descriptions are most effective? Rank them from best (No. 1) to worst (No. 5), then discuss them with your instructor and classmates.

1. She is an attractive blonde: young, slender, articulate and intelligent. (Rank: _____)
2. He walked into the courtroom wearing a blue suit, dark glasses, a gold bracelet and five gold chains. (Rank: _____)
3. It was a dreary scene: ugly and unpleasant, and that may have contributed to their illness. (Rank: _____)
4. Jorge cried when a bailiff snapped handcuffs on his wrists after the jury foreman read the verdict of guilty. (Rank: _____)
5. Linn is an 18-year veteran of the Police Department. His tall, heavy-set appearance and no-nonsense attitude befits a man in his position. (Rank: _____)

SECTION II: AVOIDING PERSONIFICATION

Rewrite the following sentences, eliminating all their examples of personification (and other errors).

1. Slamming on its brakes, the car turned to the left, then skidded off the road and collided with a tree.
2. The corporation, which denied any responsibility for the deaths, will appear in court next month.
3. The committee issued their report Monday, saying they will discuss the problem in a press conference at 11 a.m. Monday.

SECTION III: AVOIDING FALSE TITLES

Rewrite these sentences, eliminating their false and contrived titles.

1. Assistant Solid Waste Disposal Director Carlos Alicea said he opposes the fee.
2. President of the Michigan Avenue Boat Shop Robert Ellerbee discovered the 7:05 a.m. fire.
3. The door of the 1213 Ashland Avenue home of the two female senior college students was pried open.
4. The typical 1990s American family spends 37 percent of its weekly food-budgeted dollars in restaurants.
5. The Seventh Avenue lawn furniture manufacturing company damaged by the 7:10 a.m. Tuesday fire hopes to reopen next week.

SECTION IV: AVOIDING THE NEGATIVE

Rewrite the following sentences in positive form.

1. He cast a no vote for the proposal to raise property taxes.

2. Not until late August did she finally receive the check for $820.
3. The mayor said he would not be disinclined to vote against the bill.
4. The students do not have any limitations on which songs they can choose.
5. She said she does not feel the decision will have a negative impact on the town.

SECTION V: USING PARALLEL FORM

Rewrite these sentences in parallel form.

1. He said the gunman is white, about 20, had a moustache and almost bald.
2. She suffered a concussion, broken nose and required 45 stitches in her left arm.
3. The man was described as being 35 to 40 years old, black hair, brown eyes, 6 feet tall and 160 pounds.
4. She said the other advantages of owning her own business include being independent, not having a boss, flexible hours and less stress.
5. The writer advised journalism students to keep their writing simple, don't use jargon, writing should also be precise, be concise and don't use clichés.

SECTION VI: IMPROVING SENTENCES

Rewrite the following sentences, correcting all their errors. Some sentences contain more than one error.

1. He said the book were a good read.
2. The article went on to add that none of todays most popular comedians are women.
3. Two guitar players, a lute player, strolling minstrels and jugglers will provide the nights entertainment.
4. He wants to establish a program where convicted juveniles would be required to perform some sort of community service and not go to jail.
5. The latest fire occurred Sunday night in a basement room used by the school band, causing an estimated $30,000 damage and destroyed 80 of their uniforms.

Exercise 2

IMPROVING NEWSGATHERING AND WRITING SKILLS

RECOGNIZING AND CORRECTING NEWSWRITING ERRORS

SECTION I: DEFINING AND EXPLAINING

Define or explain each of the large numbers or unfamiliar terms in the following sentences.

1. Their son has meningitis.
2. A single B-2 Stealth bomber costs $800 million.
3. Pioneer 10, a satellite launched on March 2, 1972, is 4.2 billion miles from the sun.

SECTION II: AVOIDING UNNECESSARY PARENTHESES

Eliminate the parentheses (and other errors) from the following sentences.

1. She (the mayor) said (in response to a question about property taxes) that she opposes any such proposal (to increase them).
2. Despite the loss (now estimated at $4.2 million), he said the company should be able to pay all their debts before the deadline (Dec. 30).
3. The governor predicted that, "They (members of the Legislature) will approve the proposal (to increase the sales tax) within 60 days."

SECTION III: AVOIDING THE NEGATIVE

Rewrite the following sentences in positive form. Also correct any other errors.

1. The restaurant is not far away.
2. He does not like candy as much as he likes fruit.
3. High school students are not as likely to watch newscasts as entertainment programs on television.
4. Due to the danger of rabies, students are being encouraged not to approach any animals they do not know on campus.
5. The more physically fit one is the less likely they are to injure themselves while engaging in a sporting activity.

SECTION IV: USING PARALLEL FORM

Rewrite these sentences in parallel form.

1. He was charged with drunk driving and an expired drivers license.
2. Her injuries include a broken left arm, permanent blindness in her left eye, an 84-day hospital stay and bills exceeding $40,000.
3. To join the club, one must be a sophomore, junior or senior; studying journalism; be in good academic standing; and demonstrated professional journalistic ability.
4. The purpose of the paper is to summarize the basic writing skills for all good writers, whether they be journalists, writers of prose or the simple task of writing a letter.

5. Under the conditions of his probation, the teen-ager must obey his parents, complete his high school education, not possess drugs or associate with people who do, and he is restricted from drinking alcohol.

SECTION V: IMPROVING SENTENCES

Rewrite the following sentences, correcting all their errors. Some sentences contain more than one error.

1. The respondents agreed that the only crime serious enough to receive capital punishment as a penalty are those involving murder.
2. John Adles said the possible deformity of the child is the only circumstance in which he feels that abortion should be legal.
3. He said that before marijuana is legalized, there has to be more extensive research pointing in the direction of its being a harmless drug.
4. Academic reputation, school location, and cost were the three major items listed by college students as their reason for attending the school in which they are currently enrolled.
5. Assistant director for instruction and research in the Division of Computer Services Abraham Cohen said that every elementary school should teach their students how to use a computer.

Exercise 3

IMPROVING NEWSGATHERING AND WRITING SKILLS

WRITING NEWS STORIES

INSTRUCTIONS: Write complete news stories based on the following information. Critically examine the language and organization of the information, improving it whenever possible. To provide a pleasing change of pace, use some quotations in your stories. Go beyond the superficial; unless your instructor tells you otherwise, assume that you have enough space to report every important and interesting detail.

1. It was almost like a popular movie titled "Home Alone" that you may have happened to see in a theater or on a tape at home on your VCR. It involved an 11-year-old boy in your city, Andrew Jones of 4851 Edmee Cir. When you interviewed him today, Andy said he doesn't feel much like a hero. "I was scared," he said. "I thought he was going to see me and beat me up or something if he got in, so I tried to hide at first." In fact, Andy used his imagination—and a baseball bat—to thwart a would-be burglar who tried to break into his familys home when he was home alone. The incident began when Andy was home alone, watching television at approximately 6 p.m. last night. His parents and 3 sisters had left the house to go pick up a pizza for dinner. They had been gone for only a few minutes and were due back very shortly. Andy told you that he was watching television and heard a noise. "I saw a man at the window and ran to my bedroom to hide in the closet," he said. "Then I remembered the bat there. I went back into the dining room and saw this guy opening the window. He put his hand in first. He was coming in the window, and had his left hand on a table there. I took the bat and hit it as hard as I could. I, uh, really smashed it hard. He screamed like real loud, man, and ran away. Then, uh, I called 911." Police Detective Jack Noonan was at the scene and, when questioned by you, commented on the case, stating that: "Preferably, we would like to see someone in an incident like this call 911 first. It's safer that way. Someone could get really hurt in a situation like this. In this case, the boy was lucky. He kept his head, and he was really brave about it. He was home alone and decided he should protect himself and his house. He must have really walloped the guy. There's a lot of blood on the window and table, so now we're looking for someone who's injured." Police found the bad guy later last night. After the break-in, they notified hospital emergency wards to be on the lookout for a man suffering from trauma to his left hand and, shortly after 1 a.m., received a call from the Regional Medical Center, where a man matching a description Andy gave the police came in for treatment of a very badly cut, broken, swollen, and painful left hand. He has been arrested and charged with attempted burglary. Police identified the man as Steven Jabil, 23, of 800 Crestbrook Loop, Apt. 314.

2. It was a fatal accident and involved two small planes. They collided at an estimated height of 800 feet above your city shortly after 8:30 a.m. today. Three people were aboard the planes. No one on the ground was seriously hurt, although the wreckage fell on and near several homes. "It could have been a lot worse," Police Chief Barry Koperud said. "People living in the area were very fortunate." The dead include the pilot of one plane, identified as Sharon Noruse of 4740 Valley View Lane. She was flying a single-engine Piper Cub. It col-

lided in the air with a single-engine Cessna 172. The Piper, which was towing a banner, belonged to Aerial Promotions, Inc., said police. The pilot, Nouse, had worked for Aerial Promotions, Inc. for three months. The Cessna, carrying a flight instructor and his student, belonged to the Pratt Air Academy. The names of the two deceased individuals in the Cessna were withheld pending notification of their next of kin. Both businesses are located at the Municipal Airport. The Cessna crashed into the roof of the house owned by Bobby and Dawn Correia of 9542 Holbrook Dr. Some members of the family—Mrs. Correia and their youngest child, a boy named Sean, age four—were home at the time and ran out when the Cessna slammed into their home. They were not injured at all. The Correias retired to the home of a neighbor who said they were too distraught to be interviewed. Other family members later joined them there. A block away, Mr. and Mrs. Elton Amanpour and their two children, Casey and Carmen, were eating dinner when the Piper fell in front of their house at 823 E. Pierce Av. A fuel tank from the Cessna smashed into the ground in front of Trina Greenhouse, who was smoking a cigarette on her front porch at 9557 Holbrook Dr. She was taken to Regional Medical Center after she complained that fuel got into her eyes and was burning them. According to other eyewitnesses, the two planes were very close to each other. People at the airport said the planes apparently tried to land at the same time. They are in the process of reviewing air traffic control tapes to determine which plane had been given clearance to land. Some witnesses said they heard a dull thud moments before the planes plummeted to the ground. Ronald Lin said he was standing in his back yard at 6287 Airport Boulevard when the collision occurred. "It was a loud, dull impact," he said. "There was no explosion. It was more like a blunt impact. I looked up and couldn't believe what I was seeing. There was a moment when both planes just seemed to stop in midair for a second, and then they both fell to the ground." Lori Kaeppler of 9540 Holbrook Dr., a neighbor of the Correias, said, "When it first hit, it sounded like a car hit our house or something. I ran to the front door and yelled to my husband, 'Call 911, we have a plane in the Correias house.' There wasn't any fire or anything, and I went in the house to see if I could help. I spotted this one guy in the wreckage in the kitchen, almost cut in half. Before our children were born, I worked as a nurse, and I reached in to feel his pulse but couldn't find it. Later, I saw the other guy sprawled on our roof. He must have been thrown there and, obviously, he was dead." Witnesses said it appeared the Cessna clipped the wing of the banner plane, then got caught up in the banner, sending both to the ground.

3. Some said she shouldn't be charged with murder. She wasn't. She's a doctor. She had a patient with leukemia. She admitted helping her patient commit suicide. Today she was cleared by a state board of charges of misconduct. The 7-member board—your states Board for Professional Medical Conduct—could have revoked her license to practice medicine. Instead it concluded that the actions of Dr. Catrina Lowrie were "legal and ethically appropriate." Lowrie is an internist at the Regional Medical Center in your city. No one might have known what she did, but she described it in a public speech sponsored by your citys chapter of the Hemlock Society, and an anonymous caller called the police about what she said. In the speech she described how she prescribed barbiturates for a patient and made sure the patient knew how many to take to kill herself. The patient, who has since been identified as Irma Cain of 427 Hidden Lane, was 37 years old and, her husband and parents said, in terrible, hopeless pain. They supported the doctor in the matter, their attorney said, but they

refused to talk to you about it. Cain decided to commit suicide rather than undergo chemotherapy which would have given her only a 25% chance of survival. Her death occurred six months ago. Last month, a grand jury investigated the matter and then cleared the doctor of criminal responsibility for the womans death. Now the board, which issued it's ruling late yesterday, said that the doctor did nothing medically improper in prescribing the barbiturates because "she could not have known with certainty what use a patient might make of the drug she prescribed, and which was totally appropriate and needed by her patient." Lowrie said in a statement that the ruling "seemed like a very thoughtful decision." The members of the board stated that they were not condoning "so-called assisted suicide." They added that this case differed from other recently publicized cases in that Lowrie had a longstanding relationship with her patient. In addition, she did not directly take part in ending her patients life. Rather, she prescribed pills needed to alleviate the patients pain, and the patient, by herself, took them all at once in a successful attempt to terminate her own life and very painful suffering from the deadly disease.

4. Its an unusual case. Sara Zerwin is a 33-year-old woman. She was arrested several weeks ago and charged with burglarizing a house. After her arrest, she went on to confess to robbing, in addition, "about 200 other houses" in your city during the past two years. She is divorced. She said she has no other skills or job and that her husband, a dentist, who was ordered by a court as part of their divorce decree to pay her $600 a month in child support and $500 a month in alimony disappeared without ever paying her a penny. She was raising their three children, ages 12, 11 and 8. Because of their ages, the three children have not been identified. In court today, Zerwin tearfully pleaded guilty to all the charges against her: both burglary and 3 counts of contributing to the delinquency of a minor. She admitted to the judge today that she trained her children to help her commit the burglaries but said it is not the childrens fault and that they should not be punished: that it was all her fault. "I taught them that it was OK," she said, "that we were professionals, and that it was a good way for us to make some money. I tried to make it fun, like a game, and I let them keep any of the small stuff they saw and liked, games and stuff. It was exciting, and we were always together, working together. Then we'd go to a flea market on weekends and sell the stuff, and that was fun too." The burglary for which she was caught occurred about six blocks from her home at 2021 Dyan Way. She was arrested when an officer searching the neighborhood after the burglary saw her and her children walking from their van to their garage with armloads of appliances and other pieces of their loot. The officer detained the family, then phoned the victim of the burglary. She came to the scene and identified the appliances as the ones just stolen from her house. Zerwin further testified in court today that she and her children were often able to find an open window in the rear of a house. If no window was open, they would break one, and then she would lift her 11-year-old son inside. He would try to unlock a back door and then let the other family members inside. If that was impossible, he would hand items to them out the window. "We were good," Zerwin said. "I trained the kids what to look for so we could go through a house in five minutes. Then we'd go home and celebrate. The children never thought they were doing anything wrong. I told them that other people didn't deserve to have that much: that we needed it and had a right to take it from people richer than us." Her children—2 girls and 1 boy—have been turned over to the custody of the State Department of Social Services. A

spokesman for the department said investigators are currently looking into the case and trying to decide what to do with the 3 kids.

5. Janet C. Herholtz is a professor of sociology at the University of Wyoming. She was in town today to give a speech at the annual convention of the American Association of Sociologists. During her speech, she discussed the topic of murder, about which she wrote her Ph.D. dissertation. She is also in the process of writing a book about murder and, at the University of Wyoming, teaches an unusual course titled "The Epidemic of Murder." She explains that each year one out of every 10,000 Americans is murdered, and that in five years more Americans are murdered than were killed during the entire war in Vietnam. Yet, she said, many popular stereotypes about murder are false, totally without foundation. "The most likely murderer is a victim's relative," she explained. "Almost a third of all victims are related to their killers. The murderers are husbands, wives, lovers, neighbors, friends and acquaintances—people who can no longer endure chronic frustrations. Most murders are committed by men in their 20s—often because they blame other people rather than themselves for their problems. In two-thirds of the murders, they use guns. I should mention the fact that the probability of being murdered varies from one area of the country to another and from one race to another. People in the South are three times more likely to be murdered than people living in New England, and people who live in a large city are twice as likely to be murdered as people living in a suburb or rural area. Also, black men are 10 times more likely to be murdered than white men, and black women five times more than white women. In 90 percent of the cases, blacks are murdered by blacks, and whites by whites. When racial lines are crossed, it is usually a white who kills a black." Dr. Herholtz blames the use of alcohol for many murders, along with drugs, rising frustrations, permissive parents, joblessness and marital instability.

6. What can you do to maximize the span of your life? Raymond W. Herron, author of a book titled, "Centenarians," autographed copies of his book at area bookstores today and, during a press conference at 9:30 a.m. today, answered the questions of local reporters from newspapers and radio and television stations in the area. In response to their questions, he said a major factor is work. "Old age is not a time to be sedentary, but to be active. Work is an invaluable remedy against premature old age—hard work. If you study the background of people who live to be 100, you'll find few of them are lazy. Most worked hard all their lives, and many are still working." Herron noted that the Soviet Union claims to have almost 20,000 centenarians, many more than any other country in the world, and that the highest age claimed by the Soviet Union is 167, attained by Shirali Mislimov, who passed away in the year 1972. Herron noted that the Soviet Union reports that healthy old people seem to have several characteristics in common. Most live in rural areas. More than 99 percent are married. Most have large families. All are moderate eaters and drinkers and stick to a regular diet of plain foods. Much of their work is physical. Other studies, Herron continued, have found that people seem to live longer if they live in high places, drink well water and talk a lot. In the United States, he continued, researchers often note the effects of "pension illness"—the fact that people who retire deteriorate quickly in health and mind and often die within a few years after reaching their 65th birthdays, whereas people who continue to work maintain a better health and enjoy considerably longer lives. What are

the average American's chances of living to be 100? Less than 1 out of 50,000, responded Herron.

7. Roger and Carolyn Nuñez say it is outrageous. Their son, Bobby, 14, says it is not fair. Fifteen other neighborhood children who helped Bobby build a treehouse in his front yard at 2280 Norwell Ave. are also upset. It was an elaborate split level 8 × 15-foot treehouse, painted green with a white frame. Bobby's father helped the children build the treehouse three years ago, but it was not until last month that a neighbor complained. He called a county building inspector and said the treehouse is an eyesore in the neighborhood and that all the kids make too much noise, especially late at night. A building inspector who visited the site and inspected the treehouse called it a "nonconforming structure." He said it does not meet the city's building code, which requires the same standard of construction in playhouses as in wood frame residences. He ordered it torn down by noon Saturday. If it is not torn down, Mr. and Mrs. Nuñez, the property owners, can be hauled into court and fined up to $500. Mr. Nuñez, an engineer, told reporters that the treehouse "is as sturdy as any house on the block." His son, Bobby, says, "I don't think it's fair. The city should have better things to do than mess with our clubhouse." The county building inspector, Walt Straiton, responds that the structure was built without a building permit and that the building code is clear and designed to protect the public from any structure that would be damaged by a heavy wind and collapse into "deadly flying missiles." Straiton also noted that, if the playhouse did collapse, anyone inside it at the time might be seriously injured. The playhouse is about 12 feet off the ground. Straiton adds, "I've explained the problem to the Nuñez family at least a half dozen times during the past month, and we've suggested they take the playhouse down and rebuild it elsewhere. We've even offered to help with the plans. But as it stands now, the building is in violation. It's nonconforming, and it has to come down. So I've given them a Saturday deadline." Bobby and other children in the neighborhood begged scrap lumber from neighbors and built the playhouse with about $40 worth of paint, nails and glass. It has three windows. Bobby Nuñez added: "At first, we were going to build it in a vacant lot, but we thought somebody might come in and take it down. We never thought they'd come in our own front yard and tear it down. It's a playhouse for kids around here. When you get bored at home, there's always something to do in it."

8. The Department of Health and Human Services issued a 121-page report today. Congress recently passed a law which requires the department to issue a report on alcoholism each year, and this was the first such report. The report was prepared by a committee of 11 within HHS. The report said losses caused by alcoholism are high. It said alcohol causes 23,000 traffic deaths a year, and the deaths cost the nation a total of $15,000,000,000. Nearly 9 million people suffer from alcoholism or lesser drinking problems, and they constitute 10% of the work force within the United States. The report also contained some statistics about the use of alcohol. It said that in the last year, the average American drinker drank the equivalent of 44 fifths of whiskey. The report concluded that alcohol is "the major drug problem in this country." It said HHS will spend $500,000 next year to pay for advertisements to warn the public about the dangers of excessive drinking. The liquor industry has endorsed the campaign. The advertisements will be used on radio and television and in newspapers and magazines. But an official added: "We will not tell people not to drink. That is a personal decision. What we are saying is that citizens have a responsibility not

to destroy themselves or society." The 121-page report suggests that the problem of alcoholism is not adequately understood by most Americans, who seem more concerned about other drugs, such as cocaine and heroin, even though those drugs do not cause as many problems as alcohol. To prove that point the report pointed out that New York City has an estimated 600,000 alcoholics but only 125,000 heroin abusers. Yet the city spends 40 times more to fight narcotics addiction than it does to fight alcoholism. The report explained that most people do not know much about alcoholism and do not consider alcohol a serious problem. People are also reluctant to admit they have a drinking problem or are alcoholics. Alcoholism is a particularly serious problem among certain groups. For example, the report said that on some Indian reservations alcoholism has reached epidemic proportions. On some reservations 10 percent of the residents are alcoholics, twice the national average, and the rate of alcoholism rises to as much as 25 percent on some reservations.

CHAPTER 11

CAREERS IN JOURNALISM

Journalism continues to attract a record number of students. In some years when enrollment in the nation's colleges and universities has grown by only 1 percent, the enrollment in journalism (including mass communications) has grown by 6 to 7 percent. As recently as 1960, only 11,390 undergraduates in the United States were majoring in journalism. By 1970, the number had increased to 33,106, and by 1980 it had reached 75,000. Today, about 140,000 undergraduates are studying journalism, and about 33,000 graduate every year.

Thousands of students have decided to major in journalism because the curriculum helps prepare them for specific jobs. Other students select journalism because they like to write and believe that journalism is an important profession that provides an opportunity to serve the public. Students also explain that they enjoy working with people, that the media are interesting and that journalism is a creative field.

There are more than enough journalism students to replace every reporter and editor currently employed by the nation's daily and weekly newspapers. The numbers are deceiving, however. The term "journalism" covers more than just newspaper work. It also includes advertising, public relations, broadcasting and photography, for example, and many students hope to make careers in those fields.

Of the roughly 140,000 undergraduates in journalism, only 13.2 percent are majoring in their schools' reporting and editing (news/editorial) sequence, and that percentage has been declining for years. Moreover, not every news/editorial major wants to work for a paper.

One professor has explained that: "Journalism continues to attract a number of young people who see such education as an excellent preparation for other endeavors, and it is simply not correct to assume that all persons majoring in journalism are going to seek media-related positions upon graduation." Some students go on to graduate or law school. Others enter the military, become teachers or seek jobs in sales or management.

Each year, Lee B. Becker of Ohio State University studies the nation's journalism students, and his most recent study revealed that 19.5 percent are majoring in advertising, 15.1 percent in public relations, 13.2 percent in news/editorial, 10.2 percent in broadcasting, 8.2 percent in mass communication, 8.1 percent in journalism, and 7.7 percent in public relations. Other students are majoring in a combination of advertising and public relations. Still others are majoring in magazine, film or agricultural journalism. A few students in other sequences—especially in journalism and mass communication—may also want to work for newspapers.

Twenty-five years ago, most students graduating with degrees in journalism were male. Today, 66 percent are women. The percentages of women studying advertising and public relations are even higher.

EDUCATIONAL PHILOSOPHY OF JOURNALISM

More than 400 American colleges and universities offer bachelor's degrees in journalism. Ninety-four of their programs are accredited by the Accrediting Council on Education for Journalism and Mass Communication (ACEJMC). Upon request, ACEJMC will send a team of educators and media professionals to examine an entire unit (a department, division, school or college); it no longer accredits individual sequences within a unit. Typically, the accreditation team will ask about the number of faculty members who teach in the unit, their qualifications and course requirements. The team will also examine the unit's budget, physical facilities and graduates' success in finding jobs.

Other accreditation standards are more controversial. The ACEJMC recommends that only 25 percent of a student's courses should be in journalism or communications, with most of the remaining 75 percent in the liberal arts. So if a college student takes a total of 40 courses, only 10 are likely to be in journalism. The ACEJMC also recommends that the journalism courses should be concentrated in the last two years of a four-year program and that the number of academic credits granted for media internships should be limited.

These accreditation requirements encourage students to obtain a broad liberal arts education so that they will learn how their communities function and will be able to understand and write knowledgeably about a variety of topics. Traditionally, journalism majors have taken elective courses in economics, English, history, philosophy, political science, psychology and sociology. Some editors also recommend courses in business administration, explaining that graduates who want to become news executives should be prepared to handle budgets and to supervise other employees.

The ACEJMC does not rate the schools it accredits, nor rank them in any order. Rather, "That a program is listed as accredited demonstrates that the administration and faculty of the school have passed a thorough examination by their peers." One member of the accrediting group has added that: "Accreditation is a guarantee that a school has been reviewed by a body of peers and professionals and meets certain standards. It does not necessarily mean that non-accredited schools are not good. Some just don't seek accreditation. Perhaps they don't believe in it or can't afford it."

Some educators and newspaper editors argue that students should be required to take more journalism classes than the ACEJMC recommends in order to sharpen their professional skills. Other critics charge that the accreditation requirements discourage diversity and experimentation—that, to be accredited, every program must conform to the same standards.

Most departments require journalism students to take several reporting and editing classes and to study the history of American journalism and communication law and ethics. The curriculum exposes students to the history and traditions of their profession. It also encourages students to learn something about the media's problems; the media's relationship to government; and the media's effects, responsibilities and functions within a democratic society.

Some good reporters and editors never took a journalism course, and some editors (a declining number) argue that students interested in journalism should get a traditional liberal arts education, then learn newspaper work on the job. These editors say they prefer graduates who majored in English, history, political science or economics rather than in journalism, and who have obtained some practical experience by working for their college paper and completing an internship or two.

Trying to become a journalist through on-the-job training involves some risks, however. Today, fewer newspapers hire non-journalism majors, and few provide formal training programs for new employees. If busy editors notice a mistake in a reporter's story, it is easier for the editors to correct the mistake themselves than to find the reporter, explain the error and wait for the reporter to correct it. Even summer interns and regular staff writers complain that they do not receive enough constructive criticism or feedback from their editors. Newcomers trying to learn the work on the job would need even more help—and most are likely to be disappointed.

Moreover, some topics—the history, law and ethics of journalism, for example—cannot easily be taught on the job. As a consequence, non-majors may be unprepared for some of the problems they encounter. Occasionally, an experienced reporter or sympathetic editor will teach a beginner some fundamentals of these topics, but many of the people trying to learn journalism through on-the-job training are likely to flounder.

WHAT EDITORS WANT IN JOB APPLICANTS

Newspaper editors are often asked to describe ideal applicants for the jobs on their staffs. Most editors say they want applicants who are intelligent and well-informed. Editors also wanted talented writers: good grammarians who can spell and who can write clearly and accurately. In addition, they look for applicants who are honest, curious, aggressive and able to act on their own initiative.

Newspaper editors also seek applicants who are dedicated: clearly committed to careers in journalism, willing to sacrifice and likely to stay in their jobs for several years. As evidence of that commitment, editors look for applicants who show a long-term interest in journalism: who have worked for student publications and who have sacrificed to obtain some additional experience, possibly in a summer internship.

Before retiring as executive editor of The Washington Post, Benjamin Bradlee said he looked first for energy, for commitment to the news business and for a willingness to take work home. After that, he looked for knowledge, ability and judgment.

Asked to list applicants' major shortcomings, editors usually begin with the failure of many applicants to master the English language. Editors complain that many applicants cannot write effectively and know too little about grammar, spelling and punctuation. Editors also complain that many applicants are unfamiliar with city and county governments; cannot cope with deadline pressures; and lack an adequate background in economics, history, literature, philosophy and science.

A committee of the American Society of Newspaper Editors recently asked editors to rate the characteristics they consider most important in applicants seeking their first full-time job at a newspaper. The following list begins with the characteristics the editors said are most important:

	Very Important	**Important**
Writing skills	86%	14%
Spelling and grammar	73	25
Newspaper internships	51	31
Knowledge of journalism ethics	35	46
Broad background in arts and sciences	33	48
Typing or word-processing skills	20	44
Journalism skills courses	19	47
Work on a school paper	21	40
Grade point average	6	47
Knowledge of media law	11	35
Business and economics courses	6	39
Hands-on experience with computers	6	31
Familiarity with communication theory	4	16

Many reporters use portable word processors to write their stories, and telephone lines to transmit the stories to their offices, whether across town or across the country.

Thus, editors said their No. 1 priority is finding applicants with good writing skills and a knowledge of spelling and grammar.

The editors were also asked to rank the most useful courses for journalism students. Fifty-two percent listed ethics. Thirty-two percent listed media law.

Many editors add that more than enough students are majoring in journalism, and that schools should begin to place more emphasis on the quality, not the quantity, of their graduates. Many schools are limiting their enrollments, not only to weed out the least fit, but also because they simply cannot handle the thousands of students seeking admission to their programs. The nation's largest undergraduate program, at Michigan State University, has more than 3,100 students. California State University at Fullerton is second, with 2,257. Pennsylvania State University is third with 1,980. Other universities with 1,500 or more undergraduates are Syracuse, Boston, Alabama and Purdue.

To be admitted as a journalism major, you may be required to pass an entrance examination—usually a grammar and spelling test. Some schools require prospective majors to have earned at least a C in several basic writing courses. Others require journalism majors to be juniors and to have a 2.5 or even a 3.0 (B) grade point average— and to maintain that average while completing their journalism courses.

WHO ACTUALLY GETS NEWSPAPER JOBS?

Newspapers hire about 8,600 new reporters and editors every year. The largest percentage—48.5 percent—comes from other newspapers. Newspapers like to hire reporters from other newspapers because those reporters have already been trained; they are experienced, productive professionals. Journalism schools provide about 28.5 percent of newspapers' new employees. Twelve percent come from other media jobs, 6 percent from other college majors and 4 percent from miscellaneous sources. These statistics reflect two major trends. First, newspapers no longer hire many people without a college degree. Second, journalism majors are getting more and more of the available jobs.

In 1970, only 10 percent of the new reporters and editors hired by the nation's daily newspapers did not have a college degree. Today, the percentage of new employees being hired without a degree has fallen so low that it is barely measurable.

A journalism degree gives graduates an obvious edge over non-majors trying to find their first job. Journalism majors also seem to obtain more rapid promotions. Three out of four news executives—76 percent—are journalism majors.

Why do newspapers hire so many journalism majors? Professor Warren W. Schwed suggests several reasons:

- Journalism majors apply for the jobs at newspapers.
- Journalism majors obtain newspaper internships, then are hired for full-time jobs because of the experience they obtained as interns.
- Journalism majors do not require as much training, can show editors more writing samples and know how to operate the electronic equipment used in newsrooms.
- Journalism majors are motivated and understand what is expected of them.
- After moving into executive positions, journalism majors tend to hire other journalism majors.

Thus, the students who find jobs are the ones who prepared most intensively for them, and that trend seems to prevail in every field of journalism. The media also tend to hire the graduates who earned the highest grades. In every field of journalism, graduates who maintained B+ or higher averages are more likely to find jobs than are students who earned lower grades.

Many daily newspapers are hiring more specialists, so editors are impressed by new graduates who have developed an interest or expertise in some area of specialization. Partly for that reason, many of the students who major in journalism minor in another field. Editors at smaller newspapers often hire applicants who can operate a 35mm camera and who can develop their own film, so that they can also serve as photographers. Editors also look for good copy editors. Most newspapers pay their copy editors more than their reporters and are more likely to promote their copy editors; nevertheless, there seems to be a persistent and widespread shortage of copy editors, so it may be easier for journalism graduates to obtain jobs as copy editors than as reporters.

Employing More Women

Newspapers continue to lag behind other industries in the percentage of women they employ and promote. About 39 percent of the people employed by newspapers are women, compared to 48 percent of the total U.S. civilian work force. Similarly, 28

A features editor works at her desk at the Detroit Free Press.

percent of newspapers' executives and managers are women, compared to an average of 37 percent in other industries.

Women are also discriminated against in their salaries. About 56 million women are in the work force and, on average, they earn just 72 cents for every dollar earned by a man. That compares with 64 cents 10 years ago. Newspapers seem to be doing a bit worse than average.

Newspapers' record is improving, however. Sixteen percent of their top editors are now women, and the figure is rising by about 1 percentage point a year.

The problem of sexual discrimination is not confined to the newspaper industry, however. Rather, it seems to be a societal problem. Women in virtually every industry complain about a "glass ceiling" of subtle discrimination that limits their opportunities for advancement. A recent study conducted by the U.S. Department of Labor found that the glass ceiling is much lower than expected: that most women never get past the ladder's first rung or two. The Labor Department found that 37.2 percent of the employees in large corporations are women, yet only 16.9 percent of the corporations' managers and 6.6 percent of their very top executives are women.

Employing More Minority-Group Members

The American Society of Newspaper Editors has adopted a resolution urging the industry to employ more members of minority groups so that, by the year 2000, newspaper staffs will have the same percentage of racial and ethnic minorities as the U.S. population. However, newspapers seem unlikely to reach that goal, or even to come close. Recent surveys have found that 51 percent of the nation's daily newspapers still do not employ a single minority professional in their newsrooms.

A reporter and editor discuss a story.

Of all the minorities, blacks seem to be having the least success. During a recent five-year period, the number of blacks employed in the nation's newsrooms increased by 44 percent. By comparison, the increase for American Indians was 59 percent; for Hispanics, 74 percent; and for Asian-Americans, 113 percent.

Minorities now make up 22 percent of the U.S. population, but only 18 percent of the people employed by newspapers. The greatest number of newspapers' minority employees—25 percent—work in their circulation departments. Newsrooms have the lowest percentage. Minorities compose 5 percent of newsroom supervisors, 9 percent of copy editors, 9 percent of reporters, 11 percent of photographers and artists, and 19 percent of their clerical and administrative support staff.

Again, there is evidence of progress. A recent survey found that of the 55,700 professionals who work in the nation's newsrooms, 4,900 (8.72 percent) are minorities. That compares to 4.22 percent in 1980 and 5.76 percent in 1985. Also, 22 percent of the professionals most recently hired by newspapers were minorities, and 34 percent of newspapers' most recent interns were minorities.

Schools of journalism are also trying to attract more minorities. Six percent of their most recent graduates were blacks, 2.3 percent Hispanics, 2 percent Asians and 1.7 percent other minorities.

What difference does it make whether women and minorities are offered more and better opportunities in journalism? Dave Lawrence, an executive with the Knight-Ridder newspapers, explained in a recent speech: "My vision is both moral and practical: Moral in the sense that what is proposed in the hiring, advancement and retention of minorities and women is simply a matter of being fair. Practical in the sense that what is proposed is absolutely crucial to the future of our business."

Lawrence added that people bring different perspectives to their work, and that: "No matter how progressive and sensitive and thoughtful, a newspaper staff and management predominantly male and white cannot fully serve a genuinely diverse readership and a genuinely diverse nation. . . . Ultimately, the very best and most successful newspapers in our business will be those reflecting the full rainbow of human experiences."

Although newspapers are trying to hire more minorities, they are not always successful in retaining them. Several studies have found that the minorities employed by newspapers are more likely than whites to become dissatisfied and quit. When asked why they intend to quit, minorities are most likely to mention their lack of opportunities for advancement. Whites are most likely to mention boredom or low pay.

Many newspapers have affirmative action plans, and some (the Gannett chain, for example) have succeeded in hiring and promoting both women and minorities. Other newspapers have not, and some editors explain that they have been unable to find qualified applicants. Minority journalists respond that the applicants exist if only editors would look for them.

As the racial and ethnic makeup of the country's population continues to change, the employment of minorities becomes more than a matter of social justice. It also becomes a matter of good business. Because of immigration and higher birth rates, the minority population in the United States is growing seven times faster than the white population. As a result, the country's nonwhite population will exceed the white population sometime during the last quarter of the 21st century. In other words, whites will become a minority in the United States. The 1990 Census found that whites are already a minority in 52 cities with a population of 100,000 or more.

The media will suffer if they fail to satisfy that market's needs. Advertisers want to reach every American, including minorities. Editors who want to increase their newspapers' circulations will also have to do a better job of appealing to the minorities in their communities. The newspapers in New York City, for example, are already trying to reach the newest members of that city's melting-pot population: Koreans, Haitians and Salvadorans.

FINDING A JOB IN JOURNALISM

The early 1990s were a difficult period for journalism graduates. There was a serious recession, advertising revenue was declining and some newspapers imposed a freeze on hiring. Others laid off some of their employees and encouraged older employees to retire early. It was difficult, then, for new graduates to find jobs.

Each year, several organizations help pay for a national survey of journalism graduates. The most recent survey found that 20.7 percent of the graduates did not look for a job when they finished school because they already had a job lined up. Almost 12 percent accepted a job they had found before graduation, 6.3 percent continued working in a job they held while in school and 2.3 percent accepted a position that had been held open for them until graduation. Other new graduates entered the military. Another 9.2 percent delayed looking for a job. Thus, only 70 percent of the journalism students who received a bachelor's degree entered the job market upon graduation.

The following statistics show more specifically where the graduates who found media jobs went:

Public relations department	8.7%
Daily newspaper	7.9
Television station	7.4
Advertising agency	7.1
Radio station	5.4
Weekly, biweekly, triweekly newspaper	5.3
Advertising department	4.4
Public relations agency	4.3
Magazine company	3.5
Cable television	2.7
Book publisher	1.9
Wire or news service	0.9

During a typical year, the news services and daily and weekly newspapers hire about 3,270 journalism majors. The number has not changed significantly during the last 25 years. Moreover, it accounts for only 42.7 percent of the news/editorial graduates. News/editorial graduates, however, are unusually successful at obtaining jobs in other media fields, probably because of their writing skills. One study found that 8 percent of schools' news/editorial majors obtain jobs in public relations, 4.4 percent at magazines, 3.5 percent at radio and television stations, and 2 percent at advertising agencies. About 5 percent become free-lancers or find other media jobs.

Some graduates encounter a situation called "the journalism merry-go-round." Newspaper editors refuse to hire the graduates because they do not have any experience. The graduates respond that they cannot get any experience because editors will not

Until the 1960s, newspapers set their stories in lead type and arranged the type in narrow columns on their pages. Newspapers now save time and money by using computers to type their stories and by pasting the typed stories on dummy sheets. They make printing plates from a photographic image of the page.

hire them. When journalism graduates apply for jobs, editors want to see samples of their work: clippings of stories that they wrote and published in newspapers or magazines.

Most journalism students obtain some experience while still in school. They start by working for campus publications. Later, they may free-lance or work part-time for a local paper. Summer internships are even more valuable, enabling students to acquire more professional experience and to become better acquainted with the editors who hire a paper's regular staff members. All that experience provides a variety of benefits. It demonstrates students' commitment to journalism. It improves their professional skills. It also provides the "clips" they need to obtain jobs when they graduate.

About 18 percent of the reporters hired by daily newspapers have worked as interns at the same papers. Overall, the statistics are even more dramatic. Nearly three-fourths of the journalism graduates who find media-related jobs have worked somewhere as interns. When asked what advice they would give future journalism students, graduates with media jobs are most likely to suggest that students obtain an internship or some other practical experience while still in school.

Summer Internships

A newspaper editor has explained that: "It's just not enough to have a degree. We look for someone who has interned, worked for the school newspaper and who has a pile of clips so we don't have to play journalism school." Another news executive added: "Somehow, some way, the real gutsy students will find a summer newspaper job. We are impressed with them. They show us that they are actively pursuing a journalism career. And they can offer us something other than a journalism degree—experience."

The media employ thousands of interns every summer. Most internships are sponsored by individual newspapers, magazines, news services and radio and television stations. However, too many students seek internships with a few prestigious media. Typically, The Washington Post receives thousands of applications for the internships it offers each summer. Other big dailies receive hundreds of applications. Students are more likely to obtain internships with their hometown newspapers or with smaller newspapers in their area. To obtain the internships, students should get an early start and, in case they are rejected by one newspaper, should apply at several. Large dailies often set an early deadline, in November or December, for applications for their summer internships.

Most schools encourage their students to obtain internships, and some require them to. But it is difficult to ensure that every intern will benefit from the experience. Some interns are badly supervised, and some internships turn out to be routine clerical or secretarial jobs. Schools that grant students academic credit for their internships normally appoint a faculty adviser who may visit the students on the job, conduct weekly seminars and consult their employers. The advisers try to eliminate internships that fail to develop students' professional skills.

Some newspaper editors expect interns to work for nothing. Other editors exploit interns, using them as free labor, often to replace vacationing employees. Still others say that they cannot afford to employ paid interns or that the work performed by interns does not merit a regular salary. Some editors also insist that they are giving the interns valuable professional experience and that, when they were students, they too were expected to accept unpaid internships. Many schools encourage students to accept such internships because of the experience they provide. Others do not, and their administrators insist that interns should be treated (and paid) as professionals.

The best internships include formal training programs: orientation sessions, seminars with news executives, and regular reporting and editing duties. They also pay students the same salaries paid beginning reporters.

Newspapers may provide internships because their editors feel an obligation to support journalism education or because they want to help students get ahead in the field. Editors also use internships to observe talented young journalists whom they might want to employ some day.

Seeking Your First Job

New graduates looking for their first permanent jobs should set realistic goals for themselves. Most metropolitan newspapers and radio and television stations do not hire beginners, but look for people with several years of solid professional experience. Those that do hire beginners are likely to assign them rather menial tasks. New graduates should concentrate their search on weekly newspapers or small dailies, which receive fewer applications and are more likely to accept applicants with little experience. Moreover, jobs at smaller newspapers often provide better experience, since their reporters and editors are given a variety of assignments and greater responsibilities. Graduates who want to work in a metropolitan area are more likely to find jobs there after they have obtained some experience in the smaller markets.

Graduates seeking jobs in another state can consult Editor & Publisher, a weekly magazine that publishes several pages of help-wanted advertisements for newspaper reporters and editors, as well as some ads for jobs in public relations.

Writing Your Résumé

Your résumé should be neat, thorough and well-written. Even more important, every résumé should contain the types of information that employers consider most important. If, for example, you are applying for a job at a newspaper, never forget that fact while writing your résumé. Continually emphasize your qualifications for a job on a newspaper's staff, whether as a reporter, photographer or copy editor.

To develop a good résumé, begin working on it while you are a freshman or a sophomore. Then you can begin to develop the skills and practical experience that editors look for in applicants. Think about a minor (or double major), begin to work for your student newspaper and obtain an internship. If you want an internship at a large daily, get some practical experience before applying for it: at your student paper, working part-time for your local paper, or stringing for a news service.

An expert estimates that: "The sad fact is that about one out of every 250 résumés that lands on someone's desk will result in an interview. That means your résumé has to dazzle editors or news directors—and it had better dazzle quickly because chances are that they see hundreds of résumés a year and give each one about 90 seconds."

Normally, a résumé is short: only one or two pages. In the past, many applicants began with personal data that included their age, height, weight and marital status. Today, many consider that information irrelevant.

Because of its importance, an applicant's experience in the field of journalism should be presented early in a résumé. A good résumé will begin with the applicant's current or most recent experience, including work on student publications, internships and part-time jobs. An applicant might also describe the publications' circulations and his or her duties there.

Employers are also interested in an applicant's education: in the applicant's major and minor, and the college he or she attended. In addition, an applicant might list his or her grade point average, both overall and within the major.

Another portion of the résumé might list any honors or awards an applicant has received—anything that helps demonstrate the applicant's capabilities. An applicant might also list other skills and interests helpful in a career as a reporter or editor. For example: Can the applicant type? Use a camera and develop photographs? Operate the electronic equipment used in newsrooms? Speak a foreign language?

Many students also state their goals in applying for a job. This statement is important, and many students place it at the top of their résumé. But few students do a good job of writing the statement. Few are specific and realistic. Here are two bad examples:

> My objective is to utilize my communication abilities, writing skills and management experience to enhance the growth of an organization.

> I am always looking for positive ways to share my abilities and experiences with others to whom they may be useful. I have proven to my previous employers that I am trustworthy, honest and dependable.

Both statements fail to mention a desire to work as a reporter, or even a desire to work for a newspaper.

Other applicants say they want to work for a newspaper, but fail to mention the specific position they want:

> I want to obtain a job in the field of journalism.

> My goal is to find a permanent position with a daily newspaper. I want to put my training, experience and creativity to work for you.

Here are two better—more specific and realistic—statements of goals:

> I want to find an entry-level position as a sports writer for a daily newspaper.

> My goal is to obtain a job as a religion writer: a job that will allow me to use and improve my talents in newsgathering and writing.

Select your references carefully. Your references should be familiar with your work and able to comment on it immediately. Then list your references' names, titles, addresses and telephone numbers. It is a mistake simply to say that your references "are available on request." If you fail to list your references, editors inundated by hundreds of résumés are unlikely to call and ask for their names.

Here are some additional ideas to consider while writing your résumé:

- Keep it simple. Avoid fancy formats, flowery language and colored paper.
- Give your full name, address and telephone number.
- While describing your work experience, start with your current job and work backward. Include all other work experience, but begin with and emphasize your media experience.
- List your memberships and the offices you have held, especially in media-related organizations.
- List other interesting or unusual experiences: years abroad, special programs, seminars and workshops.
- List your date of graduation and the dates on which you will be available to have an interview and to begin work.

Gail Anne Flemming

408 Langdon Street
Madison, Wis. 53706
608-262-1446

CAREER OBJECTIVES: To work as a newspaper reporter for several years and then to become a newspaper editor.

EDUCATION: Currently a senior majoring in journalism (news/editorial sequence) at the University of Wisconsin, Madison. Will graduate Dec. 12.
Minor: Sociology
GPA: 3.68 (Overall)
3.81 (In major)
Graduated with honors from Plymouth High School, 12th in a class of 684. High school GPA: 3.86

MEDIA EXPERIENCE: Two summer internships covering county government for The Sheboygan Press.

Sold free-lance feature stories to seven daily newspapers in Wisconsin, including The Milwaukee Journal.

Worked four years as a reporter and editor for the university newspaper, the Daily Cardinal. Editor-in-chief during senior year.

Editor of high school newspaper and co-editor of the yearbook.

WORK EXPERIENCE: Office of Public Affairs, University of Wisconsin. Duties included writing articles for a faculty newsletter and an alumni magazine, writing press releases and arranging publicity for university events.

Wendy's Old Fashioned Hamburgers, Plymouth, Wis. Duties included serving as a cashier and all-purpose employee. Took customers' orders, operated a cash register, helped prepare each day's supply of food, made sandwiches and cleaned after closing time.

HONORS:	Phi Kappa Phi National Honor Society Regents' Scholar High School Honor Society
MEMBERSHIPS:	Vice president, campus chapter of the Society of Professional Journalists Member, Phi Beta Kappa Member, the National Federation of Press Women Member, Dean's Journalism Advisory Council

REFERENCES:

Prof. Myron Nelson
School of Journalism
University of Wisconsin
Madison, Wis. 53706
Phone: 608-262-3691

Prof. Linda Duane
School of Journalism
University of Wisconsin
Madison, Wis. 53706
Phone: 608-262-3691

Sandra James, Editor
Sheboygan Press
420 Michigan Ave.
Sheboygan, Wis. 53081

There are some deadly errors to avoid in preparing a résumé. Many students list some of the necessary information—their skills and experience, for example—but fail to present it in parallel form. If the first item in a list begins with a verb, the following items should also begin with a verb. Similarly, if the first item in a list uses the present tense, the following items should also use the present tense.

Another error applicants make is to leave gaps, failing to explain what they did for one- or two-year periods in their lives. Editors are skeptical of these as well as of résumés that list too many former jobs, suggesting that the applicant rarely stays anywhere more than a year or two.

Still another mistake is to be unrealistic. While stating their goals, students say they want "to learn every facet of the newspaper industry" or that they want to become the editor of a daily newspaper within five years. No one can "learn every facet of the newspaper industry." Similarly, few new graduates are likely to become top editors in five years.

After preparing the final draft of your résumé, proofread it several times, then ask your friends to proofread it. A single error—a cliché, grammatical error or misspelled word—will destroy its effectiveness.

There are a number of helpful guides to writing résumés, and some colleges and universities offer résumé-writing seminars through their placement offices. Students preparing their first résumé would do well to use such services.

The sample résumés reprinted on these pages illustrate the format and content of an effective résumé.

Thomas J. Wilke

Campus Address
1505 Yates Crescent, Apt. 42
Lexington, Kentucky 40505
Telephone: 606-257-2786

Home Address
1014 22nd Avenue
Morehead, Kentucky 40351
Telephone: 606-783-2649

GOAL: To begin my newspaper career as a police reporter. After gaining more experience as a professional (and learning more about the community), I would like to become a political reporter.

JOURNALISM EXPERIENCE

Lexington Leader
(daily)

Clerk responsible for delivering editorial material to and from newspaper editors; answering newsroom telephones; and writing obituaries, news briefs and weather forecasts. Extensive training on the newspaper's video display terminals. Worked 20 hours a week during junior and senior years of college.

The Wildcat
(campus daily)

Managing editor during senior year, responsible for staff management, story assignments, editing and page layout. Earlier, worked as news editor, entertainment editor and general assignment reporter.

United Press International

Campus stringer for three years.

Roseville Outlook
(weekly)

Summer reporter/intern.

High school yearbook

Editor-in-chief. Also worked as photo editor and staff writer.

OTHER WORK EXPERIENCE

Custom Painting & Decorating.
Job as house painter, three summers.
J.C. Penney Co., Inc.
Stockboy during high school.

EDUCATIONAL BACKGROUND

B.A. University of Kentucky.
Major: Journalism
Minor: Political Science
Grade point average in major: 3.54 on a 4.0 scale; Overall grade point: 3.48
Graduated Cum Laude

AWARDS AND HONORS	Alumni Scholarship, two years. Member, Phi Kappa Phi National Honor Society Reader's Digest Grant for reporting project during junior year Honorable mention in national Hearst newswriting contest, feature category
ACTIVITIES, HOBBIES	Member, Sigma Phi Epsilon social fraternity Member, Society of Professional Journalists (Campus chapter) Tennis, swimming, bowling, chess, reading
OTHER SKILLS	Typing: 55 words per minute Photography: Own two 35mm Minolta cameras with wide angle and telephoto lenses and can develop black-and-white prints Languages: Can speak and write Spanish (studied Spanish for three years in high school and for two years in college)

REFERENCES

Prof. Louis Murphy
School of Journalism
University of Kentucky
Lexington, Kentucky
Phone: 606-257-2786

Alice Stearman
City Editor
Lexington Leader
Lexington, Kentucky
Phone: 606-241-3765

Mike Tipton, Editor
Roseville Outlook
411 N. Lakeview Blvd.
Roseville, Kentucky
Phone: 606-365-6974

Writing Your Cover Letter

In addition to writing your résumé, you will also be expected to write a cover letter that introduces yourself and that expresses an interest in working for a particular newspaper. Your cover letter may be even more important than your résumé, especially if you are applying for a job as a reporter. Your cover letter gives you an opportunity to demonstrate your talent as a writer, and most editors will read it first. If your cover letter is interesting and well written, the editors may then look at your résumé.

Modify your cover letter for each job you seek. As clearly and specifically as possible, explain what you want to do and why you want to do it at a specific paper.

Begin by addressing your cover letter to an editor (not the director of personnel). In the newspaper business, editors hire their staffs. Also be certain to address your letter to the right editor, and to mention that editor by name. *Never* address a cover letter to "Dear Editor" or to "Dear Sir/Madam." That salutation is a sign that you failed as a reporter: that you lack the common sense and initiative needed to learn the editor's name. If you use a reference book (such as Editor & Publisher Yearbook) to learn an editor's name, remember that the yearbook may be outdated. Call the newspaper to be certain that the editor still works there and that the editor's name is spelled correctly.

Your opening paragraph in a cover letter is especially important. Avoid stating the obvious:

> I am a senior majoring in journalism, and my interests lie in a career with a newspaper.

> I am currently enrolled in my last semester in college, where I am finishing a journalism major. I am really interested in beginning work as a reporter on your staff.

Here are some better beginnings: more specific, interesting and imaginative.

> In today's magazine business, qualified young professionals can be found easily. All may be literate, many may be talented, but few have the background for your specialized publication.

> Every morning with my first cup of coffee, I open my daily newspaper and read as many stories as I can before hurrying to my first class. I have always enjoyed reading and writing, and have dreamed of covering important stories for a daily newspaper.

> To prepare for a career as a writer, I have majored in journalism and worked for my campus paper, rising to the position of managing editor. Now, I feel that I am ready to begin work as a reporter on your staff.

> This letter is in response to your advertisement for a reporter. Are you looking for someone who:
> —Has a passion for news?
> —Is dynamic and hardworking?
> —Is excited about the city's future?

After introducing yourself, avoid repeating too many of the details in your résumé. You might, however, briefly summarize your strengths:

> I have a strong background in reporting and editing, and practical experience that gives me the ability to perform efficiently and effectively in high-pressure, deadline situations.

> Please consider the following highlights:
> Strong writing and research skills
> Strong camera skills and black-and-white film processing experience
> Understanding of Associated Press style
> Resourcefulness and thoroughness in uncovering information
> Ability to organize tasks and meet deadlines
> Willingness to work long hours to get the job done

You might also describe yourself. Tell prospective employers something unique about yourself. What are your greatest strengths or most interesting or unusual experiences? For example:

> I have studied politics, theater and American literature. I like racquetball, travel, ethnic food and books by P.J. O'Rourke.

During the past 12 years, I have studied journalism, skydived, been certified as a fitness instructor, improved my photography skills, raised a family and held a full-time job. Now, I am determined to find a position as a reporter at a daily newspaper I admire.

Mistakenly, many cover letters are too formal and stilted, as in these examples, all written by students applying for internships or full-time jobs:

It is my desire to begin work in journalism.

I would like to express my interest in working for you as a reporter.

I will readily meet with you at any time that you have open to interview me.

Attached please find my résumé in response to your search for an individual to fill a position in your News Department.

That is not the way you talk, and it is not the way reporters are expected to write. Thus, it is not an appropriate way to write a cover letter.

If you want a job as a reporter, you will also be expected to include copies of your best clips (copies that do not have to be returned). Briefly mention them in your cover letter. Similarly, if you want a job as a photographer, attach copies of your best photos.

Finally—and perhaps most important—do not try to be cute in your cover letter. That type of letter seems to offend, not impress, editors.

Several days after mailing an application for a job, you might call the editor and request an interview. If the editor says the newspaper does not have any vacancies, you might still try to arrange an interview and offer to travel to the newspaper's office at your expense. That type of persistence may impress an editor. Also, because reporters are constantly moving to other jobs, a vacancy may develop a few days or weeks later. However, don't pester the editor with too many phone calls, and never walk in unannounced and expect an interview.

Preparing for Your Interview

If your cover letter, résumé and clips impress an editor, you may be invited in for an interview—the critical step in obtaining most jobs. When you appear for the interview, bring evidence of your commitment and experience: additional copies of your clips or other samples of your work.

An applicant's appearance is important. Every applicant should be well-groomed: neat, clean and properly dressed. Applicants should be neither overdressed nor underdressed. For women, a coordinated jacket and skirt or a simple daytime dress with low-heeled shoes is most appropriate; makeup, if any, should be applied discreetly. Men should wear a dark suit or jacket and tie with slacks (no jeans) and well-polished shoes (no sneakers or running shoes). One college student wore shorts when he came in to pick up an application for a summer internship, and editors remembered his gaffe for years. Another student appeared for an interview dressed in a T-shirt inscribed, "Start a Movement—Eat a Prune." Neither student got the job.

During a typical interview, you are likely to meet several members of a newspaper's staff, including its managing editor and the editor of the department in which you would work: the city, suburban, sports or photo editor. The editors will want to learn more about you: your strengths, personality, interests and intelligence. They will be aware of how well prepared you are. Can you answer the editors' questions—and ask them intelligent questions?

Editors will want to know more about your expectations and understanding of journalism. Are you realistic about the salary you might be offered, and do you understand that you may have to work evenings, weekends and holidays? If you want to be a columnist, editorial writer or Washington correspondent, do you realize that it may take many years to achieve that goal? If you want to be a foreign correspondent, have you learned several foreign languages?

These are the types of questions that editors are likely to ask:

- Tell me about yourself.
- What books and magazines have you read during the last month or two?
- Why do you want to be a journalist?
- Why should I hire you?
- What are your short- and long-range goals?
- What are your primary strengths and weaknesses?
- Why do you want to work here? What is it that you like about this particular newspaper?
- What would you like to know about us, this newspaper and the company that owns it?
- Why do you want to leave your present job?

With one exception, none of these questions has a right or wrong answer. The final question is the tricky one. Few employers like applicants who criticize their current employer. As for other questions, employers look for students who, while answering them, are able to provide some evidence of their commitment, intelligence and initiative.

Interviewers are also impressed by applicants who ask good questions: questions that are thoughtful and informed. You may want to ask about your probable hours, salary, assignment or opportunities for advancement. Or you might ask:

- Exactly what would I do here?
- Who would edit my stories, and how much feedback would I receive about them?
- Who would evaluate my work, and how?
- Can I meet the editor I would work for?
- Can I talk with other reporters?

After the interview, write a letter thanking the editors and expressing a continued interest in the job. If you are not hired immediately, continue to write to the editors every few months, submitting fresh clips or other samples of your work.

If you are offered a job, be certain that you understand the offer. Is it a full-time position? Will you start on probation? If so, how long will you remain on probation, and will your salary increase when you complete your period of probation? Also, will you be expected to own a car? If so, will your employer pay your mileage and other expenses?

To save money, some newspapers give college graduates jobs as correspondents, stringers, interns or part-time employees. Typically, these positions pay less than other jobs on newspapers' staffs—and do not include medical insurance, paid vacations and other benefits.

Job Testing

Increasingly, newspapers test the applicants for jobs on their staffs. Some newspapers also test current employees who want a promotion. The tests range from simple typing exams to more elaborate tests of an applicant's personality, mental ability and management skills. Newspapers everywhere are also testing applicants for drug abuse.

Barbara J. Hipsman and Stanley T. Wearden, faculty members at Kent State University, surveyed 350 U.S. dailies and found that 55.8 percent test applicants for jobs on their news staffs. Moreover, the percentage seems to be increasing.

What types of tests should you expect? Hipsman and Wearden found that 95 percent of the daily newspapers that give entry-level tests want to learn more about applicants' ability to spell. Ninety-two percent test for grammar skills, 88 percent for punctuation skills, 77 percent for writing ability, 37 percent for reporting skills and 24 percent for coping skills. To test applicants' writing skills, editors often give them some rough notes, then ask them to write a news story that summarizes the information. The tests are similar to many of the exercises in this book. Thus, it will pay to take the exercises seriously—and to be sure that you understand your instructor's suggestions for improving your work.

A growing number of major dailies ask applicants to come in for tryouts: to spend a day or two working in their newsrooms so editors can see how they handle everyday assignments. Most dailies pay the applicants for this work, but editors may try out three or four applicants before deciding which one will get the job. Hipsman and Wearden found that 26 percent of the papers they surveyed used tryouts. Very large dailies (those with circulations of more than 100,000) seem most likely to use tryouts, and some of the tryouts last a week or more.

ON THE JOB: CONDITIONS IN THE NEWSROOM

Journalists encounter a number of problems, from low salaries to crippling new injuries. Still, most journalists are satisfied with their jobs. They like their work, think it is important and enjoy numerous opportunities for advancement. Moreover, they are in the midst of an exciting revolution: an electronic revolution that is transforming the industry.

Job Satisfaction—and Dissatisfaction

Studies have found that about 80 percent of the journalism graduates hired by newspapers say they are moderately to very satisfied with their jobs. Only 10 percent are very dissatisfied.

Why are so many journalists satisfied with their work? One reason, they explain, is that their jobs are varied, creative, important and challenging. Perhaps more than anyone else, journalists witness a kaleidoscope of the life within their communities: the good and the bad, the joyous and the tragic, the significant and the mundane. They are admitted everywhere and meet everyone. And, wherever they go, journalists share some of the power and prestige of the institutions they represent.

From a broader, more philosophical perspective, journalists represent the public when they cover a story. By providing citizens with the information they need to be well-informed, journalists perform a vital function within our democratic society.

In addition, newspaper jobs give journalists an opportunity to write. And writing a good story—being able to select the important facts, the correct words, the proper organization—is a highly creative process. It is also challenging. Within a few minutes, journalists may have to summarize a complex topic in a clear, accurate story that will interest the public. Within hours, the story (and the journalists' bylines) may appear on the front page of a newspaper read by thousands of people.

More systematic studies have found that journalists also like their jobs because they like their colleagues and have opportunities to learn something new every day, acquire new skills and play a role in improving their communities.

However, careers in journalism have several disadvantages as well. Reporters complain about their long, irregular hours; deadline pressures; and dull assignments. Much of their work is more routine than most people realize. For every reporter covering a major story, dozens of others are writing obituaries or covering meetings of their local Rotary Clubs.

When asked about their problems, reporters are more likely to complain about inept management than low salaries. Several studies have found that newspaper reporters are most dissatisfied with the way their stories are handled and with poor management practices, especially with a lack of direction from and communication with their editors. Reporters complain that too many of their stories are severely edited: that their stories are chopped and rewritten, and that they are rarely consulted beforehand or given an opportunity to correct their own errors. Reporters want more time to write their stories, more praise, more opportunities to talk with their editors and more opportunities for advancement.

Some of these problems arise because few editors are trained in personnel management. Good reporters are offered jobs as copy editors, and the best copy editors become department editors. The editors are taught new professional skills, such as newspaper design, but few are taught how to supervise other people. Also, because of deadline pressures, editors may not have enough time to let reporters rewrite their own stories, nor to explain the changes they make in reporters' stories.

Starting Salaries

Generally, people with better educations earn higher salaries. That trend intensified during the 1980s, especially among men. In 1979, white males who were 25 to 34 years old and college graduates earned 18 percent more than high school graduates. By 1987, the gap had widened to 41 percent. No one knows exactly why.

There are quirks, however. Many jobs that seem to require roughly comparable intellectual skills offer much different salaries. And the best workers do not always receive the highest salaries.

Some industries simply pay higher salaries than others, generally industries dominated by large companies that have little competition. Salaries in the oil industry are about 50 percent higher than the nationwide average. Salaries in the tobacco industry are 40 percent higher, and salaries in public utilities are 30 percent higher. More competitive industries with smaller profits tend to pay lower salaries. Thus, clothing manufacturers and retail stores pay about 15 percent below average. Restaurants are nearly 30 percent below average.

The newspaper industry seems to be an exception to the general rule. Today, most cities have only one daily newspaper, so the industry is less competitive than ever before. In addition, the industry's profits are unusually high. Yet its salaries remain low.

Why? No one seems to know for certain. Some newspaper editors say they cannot afford to pay higher salaries. That seems implausible, however, since newspapers are far more profitable than many other types of businesses. It may be a matter of tradition, since newspaper salaries have always been low. Or it may be a matter of high supply (of job applicants) and low demand. Melvin Mencher, a professor at Columbia University's School of Journalism, speculates, "The supply of young people seems unlimited, and they will battle for even the lowest-paid jobs." In addition, the news business is not highly unionized. Finally, many people go into the field knowing that its salaries are low but willing to accept the salaries because they like the work.

In 1990, the Southern Newspaper Publishers Association surveyed the journalism schools in 14 Southern states and determined the entry-level salaries paid the schools' graduates. For comparative purposes, the schools were also asked to list the entry-level salaries paid to beginning teachers and to the graduates in business administration at their schools. Here are the fields' average beginning salaries:

Business administration	$22,300
Teaching	19,666
Public Relations	17,220
Advertising	16,262
News/editorial	15,415
Broadcasting	13,950

A national survey of 1990's journalism graduates found that salaries in the rest of the nation were somewhat higher. The median weekly salary for graduates with a bachelor's degree was $346. Public relations agencies and departments paid the highest median starting salary, $378. That compared to advertising agencies and departments, $356; daily newspapers, $348; weekly, biweekly and triweekly newspapers, $300; television, $289; and radio, $254.

Other studies have found that employers pay higher salaries to beginners who had internships and who earned high grades. Typically, those graduates earn $1,000 a year more than graduates who had B − or lower averages and no internships.

Many good reporters double their salaries in five years, especially if they move to larger papers. Daily newspapers often hire their new reporters on a probationary basis, then raise their salaries when they complete the probationary period satisfactorily. Also, many young journalists receive rapid promotions. It is not unusual for an ambitious and talented reporter to become a copy editor in two or three years, a department editor within four or five years and a city or managing editor by his or her late 20s or early 30s, receiving a raise with each promotion.

Few journalists make it that far, but the salaries paid by the nation's leading news media are phenomenally good. Journalists employed by the media in the nation's largest cities, by newsmagazines and by the nation's major radio and television networks can earn $100,000 or more. A few nationally known journalists, such as Dan Rather, earn millions of dollars a year.

Typically, however, reporters begin their careers at small dailies, and officials at the Society of Professional Journalists (SPJ) have complained that the low salaries offered by those newspapers are driving students away. The situation is so serious that the society has discussed the idea of changing its Code of Ethics to allow entry-level journalists to hold second jobs.

"Hundreds of small papers are paying salaries that are just miserable," explains Sara Mantooth, SPJ's vice president in charge of campus chapters. "Over a period of time they will lose the bright people who would have gone into the business."

Similarly, Maurine Beasley, a professor at the University of Maryland, complains that college instructors are not preparing their students for the economic realities they are likely to face after graduation. Beasley, too, warns, "The low salaries and harsh working conditions of entry-level journalism jobs are keeping the brightest and most talented students out of journalism schools altogether, or else are causing them to pursue other work after earning journalism degrees."

Some educators fear that journalism is becoming another low-paying "pink ghetto." They explain that salaries remain low in fields traditionally dominated by women (nursing and teaching, for example). Thus, as more and more women enter the field of journalism, its salaries may be depressed even further. If so, the problem will affect everyone in the field, men as well as women.

Trevor Brown, dean of the School of Journalism at Indiana University, worries about a related problem: students' ability to repay their college loans. More and more college students are borrowing money to complete their educations, partly because the salaries they receive for college jobs have not increased as fast as college costs. Also, journalism majors are expected to work for their campus paper "and it pays even less than other campus jobs, if at all."

Brown studied a recent group of journalism graduates at Indiana University and found that 32.8 percent had taken out loans from state or federal funds administered by the university. The students' loans ranged from $500 to $40,000, with an average indebtedness at graduation of $8,242. (Brown did not look at other loans—from local banks, insurance policies or mortgages—that the students' families may have taken out.)

College students must begin repaying their government loans six months after graduation at monthly rates ranging from $30 to $500, with an average monthly payment of $112. Brown concluded that for a student earning a reporter's entry-level salary, the monthly payments would be difficult.

The results of a national survey are even more discouraging. The survey found that 76.5 percent of the students graduating with a bachelor's degree in journalism worked an average of about 20 hours a week during their last year of college. Despite that work, 47.2 percent of the new graduates were in debt.

Robert P. Clark calls newspapers' salaries "pretty disgraceful," and warns that low salaries and its emphasis on profits threaten the newspaper industry. Clark, a retired vice president at Harte-Hanks newspapers, also worked as executive editor of The (Louisville, Ky.) Courier-Journal and of The Florida Times-Union in Jacksonville.

Clark explains that some newspapers earn a profit of 40 percent, and the average is about 20 percent: nearly double the average rate of other manufacturers in the United States. To maintain their high profits, editors may try to cut their newspapers' costs by publishing less news, by eliminating some employees or by keeping their employees' salaries low.

"Think how many more bright young people we could attract, and keep, if we paid decent salaries, and how much better our newspapers would be," Clark says. The answer, he adds, is for newspaper owners to realize the lessons learned the hard way by American carmakers and others: quality pays. Clark explains, "If newspaper publishers will invest in their products, will look at the salaries of their employees, will give their readers more and better news, not less, I am convinced they will enhance their chances for a successful bottom line."

Newsroom Organization and Procedure

Most journalism graduates who go to work for newspapers begin as reporters. As new reporters, they may spend the first several weeks in their newspapers' offices. There, they are given a variety of minor assignments: answering telephones, writing obituaries and rewriting news releases. Such work enables newcomers to become better acquainted with their newspapers' policies, and it enables editors, who are always nearby, to supervise their work more closely. Or, to become better acquainted with a city, newcomers may follow experienced reporters on their beats. Or, they may begin work in a suburban bureau.

Because it requires less expertise than other areas, the police beat is often assigned to a newspaper's newest and least experienced reporter. Police officers write reports about most of the calls they answer, and reporters are allowed to read most of those reports. In the past, police departments in large cities also provided special rooms for reporters and equipped them with typewriters, telephones and police radios. Today, reporters are likely to bring their own computers.

Typically, when reporters arrive at a police station, they page through all the reports filed during the past 24 hours and take notes on the most newsworthy. In addition, reporters may ask whether any major crimes or accidents are being investigated at that moment. Because police reports contain all the information needed for routine stories, reporters do not have to drive to the scene of every crime and accident, nor personally interview every person involved.

Most newsrooms contain a police radio, and reporters listen to it while writing other stories. If a major story arises later in the morning, reporters for afternoon dailies will cover it themselves; they cannot wait for a police report, since it may not be completed until long after their newspapers' final deadlines. To save time, reporters try to cover the stories by telephone. If a store is robbed, they may call and ask a clerk to describe the robbery. If a student is injured, they may call the student's school and ask a teacher or principal to describe the injury. Reporters drive to the scene of major stories but, again to save time, may organize the facts in their minds, then call their offices and dictate their stories to a clerk, thus saving the 20 or 30 minutes it might take to return to their offices.

This method of police coverage is not ideal, but it is efficient. Police officers complain that newspapers use the police beat as a training ground, forcing them to deal with a succession of novices who remain on the job only a few months before they are transferred to other beats. Some police officers are reluctant to trust inexperienced reporters and complain that the novices do not understand how police departments operate, are too inaccurate and sensational, and are not even good writers. But critics charge that newspapers obtain too much of their information from the police and other government officials and, as a result, emphasize the official version of events.

More experienced reporters also are assigned beats, often a specific building such as the city hall, the county courthouse or the federal building. Other beats involve broader topics rather than a geographical location. The most common of those beats are business, education and religion. Larger newspapers establish dozens of more specialized beats, ranging from agriculture to art, from medicine to consumer affairs. This system promotes efficiency, since reporters become experts on the topics they cover and are able to cultivate important sources of information. Reporters often remain on the same beats for years, become friends with their sources and obtain information from them more easily than they could from strangers.

Each beat involves a topic that is especially newsworthy or a location where news is likely to arise or be reported. When a serious problem arises, citizens often report it to one of the government offices regularly visited by reporters: to police stations, firehouses or the city hall.

On a typical day, the reporter assigned to cover, say, the city hall for a medium-sized afternoon daily will begin work at about 8 a.m. and may spend the first hour in the paper's newsroom, writing minor stories left from the previous day, scanning other newspapers published in the area, rewriting minor news releases or studying issues in the news. The reporter is likely to confer with an editor about major stories expected to arise that day, then go to the city hall at about 9 a.m.; few important sources are likely to be in their offices before that time. During the next hour or two, the reporter will stop in all the major offices in the city hall, especially those of the mayor, council members, city clerk, city treasurer and city attorney. The mayor is the most newsworthy individual in most communities and may meet with reporters in his or her office at a specified time every morning to disseminate information about current developments (and to generate favorable publicity for himself or herself and the policies he or she favors).

The city hall reporter will return to the daily's newsroom at about 11 a.m. and, during the next hour or two, will quickly write all the stories that must be published that day. Other reporters, meanwhile, will have gathered information from the remaining beats; for example, the reporter covering the federal building may have seen the postmaster, the federal marshal, federal court officials, the county agricultural agent, employees of the Internal Revenue Service and recruiters for the armed forces. News stories written by all the reporters may be due at noon, a common deadline for afternoon dailies. The deadline is rarely later than 1 p.m., since stories must be edited and printed, and a newspaper transported to subscribers' homes, by 3 or 4 p.m. The deadline at some afternoon dailies is as early as 9 or 10 a.m., especially for early editions that must be transported to readers in distant areas.

Morning papers are becoming more popular than evening editions, and their reporters typically work from 3 or 4 p.m. to midnight. Then workers in the newspapers' other departments have several hours to print and deliver their final product to subscribers' doorsteps by 5 or 6 a.m.

Some experienced writers are given jobs as general-assignment reporters, and they cover stories that arise outside their newspapers' regular beats. The stories are more varied, often unexpected and often highly important. General-assignment reporters might write about a presidential candidate campaigning in the area, a train wreck, a speech given by a celebrity invited to the area, or a circus arriving in town.

Reporters compete for a number of other assignments, including jobs as columnists and as feature and editorial writers. Most of these jobs are given to a newspaper's most experienced writers. Some daily newspapers also hire correspondents to work in their state capitals, and larger dailies hire correspondents to work in Washington, D.C. The number of such jobs is limited, and they too are given to experienced professionals.

Because they enjoy the work, some journalists remain reporters until they retire. Other journalists are promoted to the position of copy editor, and a few begin their careers as copy editors. Most copy editors check the stories written by reporters, write headlines for those stories and help arrange the stories on a page. Copy editors tend to be anonymous; they receive few bylines and spend most of their time working at a desk. Consequently, journalism students know less about their jobs and are less likely to seek such positions. Yet jobs as copy editors are often more plentiful than jobs as reporters, and copy-editing experience is essential for people seeking further promotions.

Newspapers appoint subeditors to supervise the various departments in their newsrooms, and many of those appointments are given to people who have learned the necessary editing skills by working as copy editors. The city or metropolitan editor (the most important of a newspaper's subeditors) is responsible for the coverage of local news and supervises the paper's staff of reporters. The city editor may assign the reporters' topics, edit their stories and design the pages that contain local news.

Another major figure, the news or wire editor, handles stories transmitted by the news services, deciding which of the stories to use, editing them and arranging their placement in the paper. Small and medium-sized dailies also employ subeditors to supervise the following departments: sports, business, religion, entertainment, arts, suburban news and Sunday news. Larger dailies employ many more subeditors, and each of them may have several assistants.

The managing editor at most newspapers coordinates the subeditors' work and supervises a paper's day-to-day operations. Editors are responsible for budgets, policies, long-range planning and, at many smaller newspapers, writing all their papers' editorials (larger dailies employ specialists to write their editorials). The publisher, the chief executive in a newspaper office, supervises the work of all the paper's major divisions, including the advertising, circulation and production departments. In the past, many publishers owned their own papers. Today, most publishers are appointed by groups that own the papers.

The Electronic Revolution in Newsrooms

During the past 30 years, an electronic revolution has transformed the way news stories are written, edited and published. Previously, reporters wrote their stories on typewriters, then used pencils to correct them. After proofreading a story, reporters pasted all its pages into one long strip, so none of the pages could be misplaced, and placed the story in a basket or impaled it on a sharp metal spike on their editor's desk. Editors used pencils to edit the story. Then typesetters operating Linotype machines used molten lead to set the story in type, line by line, and proofreaders checked the type for errors. Other skilled workers arranged the lead type in page forms and used those forms to make heavy metal plates that fit onto a newspaper's printing press.

Today, you may not be able to find any typewriters, typesetters, proofreaders or printers in a newspaper office. Instead, reporters type their stories on video display terminals (VDTs) that have keyboards like a typewriter's, plus a TV-like screen that displays stories as quickly as they are typed. The VDTs resemble the computers that many Americans are buying for their homes, but are part of a larger system or network.

When a reporter finishes writing a story, it is stored in a computer until the editor is ready to retrieve it. Working at another VDT, often a more sophisticated model, the editor can correct the story, trim it, write a headline, then set the story's width, measure its precise length and transmit it to a machine that types it in narrow columns. Other employees paste the typed story onto a page form, photograph the entire page, and make a lightweight printing plate from the negative.

Even newer equipment enables editors to assemble entire pages on a computer

Newspapers use computers to write and edit their stories, and now also to help with their layout. An editor using this combination of standard-size and large-screen monitors can edit and make up a full page before it is typeset and printed.

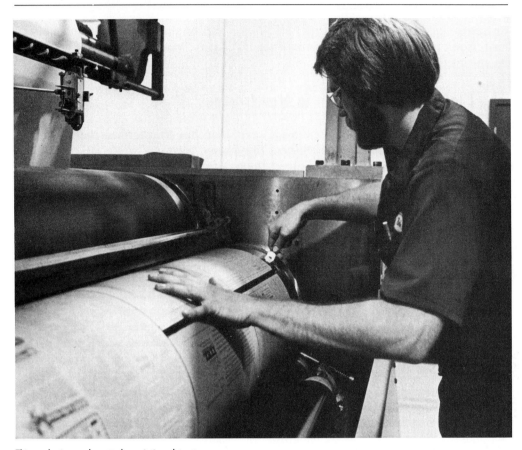

This production worker attaches printing plates to a press.

screen: news stories, headlines, illustrations and advertisements. These new machines allow editors to see what an entire page will look like before it is set in type. The machines also eliminate the need for hand-drawn page dummies.

The new electronic systems save millions of dollars in production costs, primarily because they eliminate the need for printers and other skilled workers. News stories are typed only once, by reporters. Thirty years ago, The Washington Post employed more than 500 printers, and The New York Times employed about 800. Imagine how much money each of those newspapers saved by eliminating most of these positions, along with all the machinery, space, power and supplies needed by their hundreds of printers.

The new systems are also faster and more accurate. A good Linotype operator could cast six to eight lines of type a minute. Keypunch operators who replaced them could punch a tape that enabled Linotypes to set 14 lines a minute. The newer machines type hundreds of lines a minute. Moreover, because stories no longer have to be retyped by production workers after being typed and edited by journalists, they contain fewer errors, thus eliminating the need for proofreaders.

Because of their speed, the new systems enable editors to get more late-breaking stories into their newspapers—and give journalists more control over their papers' production processes.

Carpal Tunnel Syndrome: The Journalists' Disease

More than 15 million Americans work at VDTs, and millions of other Americans use computers in their homes. Some blame their machines for ailments ranging from sore necks, wrists and backs to cataracts, miscarriages and birth defects.

Suffering from CTS

A YOUNG WOMAN'S ORDEAL

By **Taylor Kingsley**

Carpal tunnel syndrome may have killed my journalism career.
And I'm only 26.

An "A" student, I earned my bachelor's degree in journalism and promptly landed a paying internship at a daily newspaper. Three months later, I was hired as a permanent copy editor. After working for about six months, I felt a nagging pain in my right wrist.

I figured it was nothing serious, perhaps a muscle ache, but mentioned it to my chiropractor, who treats me for unrelated back problems. He took an X-ray and said, "Looks like you've got a precursor to carpal tunnel syndrome, but maybe we can nip it in the bud." I didn't report it as a work-related injury yet because my chiropractor was optimistic it would be quickly cured. But after four months of chiropractic treatment and more nights of work, pounding away at my keyboard, my pain worsened considerably. I was feeling shooting pains up my forearms and around both wrists.

One night while performing my usual duties, I also felt horrendous searing pain in my hands. I could barely move my fingers. I thought, "This is serious." I nearly did not make it home safely because my hands were either numb or felt like they were in a vise. Try steering a car like that.

I went to two orthopedic hand surgeons. They performed numerous tests on my hands and said I had a classic case of CTS.

Within a week of that night of agony, I reported my CTS to my employer. I know my injury was caused by my work on a computer keyboard, and my doctors agree, yet under pressure from my paper, the insurance company denied my claim for worker's compensation. The insurance company didn't even send me to a doctor or examine my medical records before it denied my claim. So far, I've had to spend about $5,000 for my own treatment, and I haven't had a real paycheck in four months.

Some administrators at my paper are claiming I'm making the whole thing up. (Presumably, so are all of my doctors.) But, believe me, you can't get rich off worker's compensation. This injury has drained me financially as well as physically and emotionally. So I have been forced to hire a lawyer and file a claim against my employer and the insurance company to try to get the benefits I'm entitled to under state law: 100 percent medical coverage for my CTS and two-thirds of my lost wages. My attorney believes I have a strong case. The law is on my side, and I haven't given up hope for justice.

A cortisone injection reduced the pain in one of my wrists somewhat, but cortisone shots aren't a long-term cure. For about two months, I continued to work, with splints on both wrists, and popped pain killers nearly every night. The pain continued, so my doctor and I decided it was time for surgery.

My doctor explained that the procedure is very simple and safe, requiring only a local anesthetic. He cut the swollen ligaments in the wrist and palm, releasing pressure on the nerve. He said that 95 percent of his patients feel marked improvement after the surgery. For some of that 95 percent, though, the pain returns when they return to the same job.

I had my left wrist done first, then the right two weeks later, so I'd have the use of one hand at all times. The worst part about the operation, performed at a surgery center, was the 6-inch (yes, 6-inch-long) needle used to administer the anesthetic. The surgery took only five minutes. The best part? I didn't feel a thing. I was in and out of the surgery center in 2½ hours.

The aching and itching I felt after the surgery were less painful than the CTS itself, so I felt immediate relief. I consider my surgery a definite success.

For six weeks I remained home, resting my hands and allowing them to heal. Then I returned to my job. But within hours of sitting down at my keyboard, I felt pain again: the same pain as before the surgery. I worked for three nights, hoping the pain would lessen each night but, alas, it got progressively worse.

My doctor said I need to stay off the keyboard for several more months at least. My newspaper put me on indefinite medical leave.

It can take three months or longer for some patients' hands to fully heal.

No one knows when or even if I'll ever be able to work as a copy editor again. I left my job and moved to another state to pursue work outside the newspaper business. As long as I don't work on a keyboard, my hands feel pretty good. Maybe someday my hands will be able to tolerate a keyboard so I can return to the field I love.

Meanwhile, life goes on as I look for the light at the end of the carpal tunnel.

Hundreds, perhaps thousands, of journalists suffer from repetitive strain injuries, or "RSI." The problem is also called "cumulative trauma disorder" and "repetitive motion injury."

RSI is common among workers whose jobs require constant, repeated hand movements. Its victims include meatpackers, garment workers and grocery clerks who flick items across electronic scanners. RSI also strikes office workers. In newspaper offices, it can strike anyone who uses a VDT.

Victims complain that their arms, wrists, necks, backs and shoulders hurt, and that their eyes burn. The victims may be advised to wear splints, braces, gloves or bandages or to use cushioned keyboards. Because of the pain, some victims cannot sleep. Others cannot work for several days. A few are permanently disabled and must leave their jobs. Perhaps 10 percent require surgery to correct nerve damage to their hands and wrists—now one of the nation's most common operations.

One of the most severe forms of the ailment is called carpal tunnel syndrome (CTS), or "the journalists' disease." CTS is caused by damage to or pressure on a nerve that travels through a portion of the wrist called the carpal tunnel. Repeated stress or trauma can cause tendons that also travel through the carpal tunnel to swell and press painfully on the nerve. Symptoms include a tingling or burning sensation in the fingers and wrists. A victim's fingers, even an entire hand, may go numb. Over time, victims lose their ability to grip objects or even to use their hands. Thus, some cannot drive.

People using typewriters rarely experience the problem. Typewriters are designed to be slow so their keys will not jam. Moreover, typists often stop striking their machines' keys to insert new sheets of paper, to correct errors and to perform other manual chores. By comparison, people using VDTs can type as fast and long as they can, until pain and injury slow them down.

Imagine, for example, that you typed 60 words per minute. You would strike your VDT's keyboard 18,000 times an hour, or 144,000 times during an eight-hour day. Without adequate rest, the tendons in your fingers, hands and wrists might become inflamed and swell, compressing the surrounding nerves. Then, you would become another victim of CTS.

What's the solution? Ideally, your VDT screen should be at or below eye level, your wrists should be straight and your elbows at a 90-degree angle. You should be equipped with a comfortable, adjustable chair under proper lighting.

To help them avoid CTS, some newspapers teach their staffers how to sit, adjust their screens and type with a lighter touch. In addition, they provide regular breaks.

VDT Radiation: A Second Danger?

VDT users in a dozen locations have reported high rates of miscarriages for which they at first blamed the low levels of radiation emitted by their VDTs. However, repeated studies have not found any causal link between the two.

Researchers in the San Francisco Bay area questioned 1,583 women and found that those who spent more than 20 hours a week in front of a VDT screen had an 80 percent increased risk of miscarriages compared with women who worked but did not use VDTs. The researchers admitted, however, that other factors could be responsible for the miscarriages, ranging from the women's deadline pressures to the fact that they sat in cramped positions.

Two other studies found no statistical link between VDTs and "adverse pregnancy outcomes." In one, researchers in Denmark gathered information from more than 214,000 women, then narrowed their study to 6,212 who became pregnant while working at VDTs. The researchers found no connection between "negative pregnancy outcomes" and work on VDTs. They defined "negative pregnancy outcomes" as late spontaneous abortions, birth defects, premature birth, babies with low birth weights, stillbirths or death within the first year of life.

In the other study, the National Institute of Occupational Safety and Health conducted a four-year investigation of 2,430 telephone operators in the United States. About half the telephone operators worked on VDTs, and half did not. Seventeen percent of the VDT operators who became pregnant suffered miscarriages during the first three months of their pregnancy, compared with 16 percent of the telephone operators who never worked at VDTs. The difference was not statistically significant.

To protect workers, a few cities and counties have enacted laws that regulate companies' use of VDTs. For example: Long Island's Suffolk County requires employers to pay 80 percent of the cost of an employee's annual eye exam. Suffolk County also requires companies to give VDT users a 15-minute break every three hours and to provide adjustable chairs and desks, detachable keyboards and special lighting.

FREE-LANCE WRITING

College students often dream of becoming free-lance writers. As free-lancers, the students imagine, they will be able to set their own hours, write about topics that interest them, pursue those topics in greater depth, sell their stories to prestigious national magazines and live comfortably on their earnings.

Some journalists supplement their income by writing for other publications, but free-lancing is more difficult than most people realize. It's been estimated that 25,000 Americans call themselves free-lance writers, but that only a few hundred earn a living at it. Most free-lancers hold another job or depend on a spouse's income. To supplement their incomes, some free-lancers write speeches and books or work part-time in public relations.

Why is it so difficult to make a living doing free-lance work? One reason is that many of the big magazines that once bought articles from free-lancers have folded. They have been replaced by smaller, special-interest magazines that pay much lower rates. Other magazines no longer accept any articles from free-lancers, instead relying exclusively on full-time staff writers. Editors can assign specific topics to staff writers and may consider them faster, more dependable and more talented than free-lancers.

The competition among free-lancers is intense. Major publications receive hundreds of manuscripts for every one they accept. Even the best-written manuscripts may be rejected because they are inappropriate for a particular magazine or because the magazine has already accepted or published another article about the same topic or has received a similar article from a more famous writer whose byline will generate more publicity.

Free-lancers may spend days, weeks or even months working on an article, only to have it rejected by a dozen editors. As a consequence, the free-lancers may collect enough rejection slips (usually impersonal, printed forms) to paper every wall in their offices. Even if an article is accepted, it may be severely edited, or the free-lancer may be asked to rewrite it.

Free-lancers complain that magazines pay too little and too late. After submitting an article, a free-lancer may have to wait several months until it is accepted. The free-lancer may then be told that the magazine pays "on publication," which means that the free-lancer will not receive any income from the article until it is published months later.

Hundreds of magazines pay by the word: often 5 to 10 cents for each word they publish. Other magazines pay a specified flat fee, often less than $100 per article. Relatively few magazines pay more than $500 an article. There are exceptions: Good Housekeeping pays up to $1,500 for an article, Playboy pays a minimum of $3,000 for articles of 3,000 to 5,000 words, and Harper's pays 50 cents to $1 a word for articles of 4,000 to 6,000 words. Some major publications also pay a "kill fee," usually about 25 percent of their normal rate, for articles they ask free-lancers to write, then decide not to publish.

In addition to all the other problems, free-lancers must provide and equip their own offices. A few large magazines pay some of their expenses, but most magazines do not. Travel is expensive. Even telephone, postage, computer and supply bills can total thousands of dollars a year. Many magazines prefer articles that are accompanied by illustrations, so successful free-lancers may also have to be skilled photographers— which involves spending even more money for cameras, film and developing costs. Moreover, free-lancers receive no fringe benefits: no medical or life insurance, no paid vacations, no pensions. On the plus side, they can take an income tax deduction for many of their expenses, including part of their rent and utility bills.

Few literary agents are willing to take on beginning free-lancers as clients. Typically, the Scott Meredith Literary Agency in New York has advised potential clients, "If you are selling fiction or articles regularly to major national magazines, or have sold a book or screenplay or teleplay to a major publisher or producer within the last year, we'll be happy to discuss handling your output on a standard commission basis of 10 percent on all American sales and 20 percent on British and all foreign sales." If you are a beginner, however, you may have to pay an agent to handle your articles. Again, the Scott Meredith Agency has explained, "As recompense for working with beginners or newer writers until you begin to earn your keep through sales, our fee, which should accompany material, is $100 minimum charge per magazine story or article under 5,000 words."

Most literary agents prefer to handle book authors. After spending two or three days selling a book proposal to a publisher, the agents may collect 10 percent of a $50,000 fee. With articles, they may work two or three days, then collect 10 percent of a $3,000 fee.

Despite all these problems, free-lance writing can be an enjoyable hobby or part-time pursuit. It provides another outlet for people who like to write and enables them to supplement their incomes from other jobs. However, beginners are most likely to sell their articles to smaller, less prestigious publications. Those publications may not pay as much as Harper's or Playboy, but they receive fewer manuscripts and are much less demanding. Aside from a typewriter or computer, a successful free-lancer's indispensable tool is a book titled Writer's Market. This guide, updated annually, lists thousands of markets for free-lance writers and describes the types of articles that each publication wants to buy and the fees it pays. Copies are available at most bookstores.

Guest Column

THE BROADCAST ALTERNATIVE

By **Joe Hall**

I began my career at a medium-sized television station in the Midwest, and the sports director there, a man named "Will," was fond of telling the following story. Shortly after accepting his first job as an "on-air" sports anchor, Will was attending a Big Ten basketball game. A young boy approached him and asked for his autograph. Will's first reaction was that either someone had put the boy up to it as a joke or that the boy had mistaken him for someone else: someone "really" important. An irate parent saw that Will was reluctant to give the boy his signature, and quickly convinced him that not only was this no joke—but also that he wasn't yet *so* important that he could refuse his adoring public. Thus, Will learned what every reporter or anchor from Paducah, Ky., to New York City eventually learns. TV conveys a degree of celebrity status to those appearing on its channels: a status that isn't enjoyed by people in print journalism or, for that matter, by TV's electronic cousin, radio.

Unfortunately, it is frequently the appeal of instant celebrity that attracts students to a major in broadcast journalism. This is unforunate for two reasons. First, the number of "on-air" jobs is only a small percentage of the total number of jobs in broadcast news. Therefore, realistically, few students will have a chance to realize this goal. Second, for those individuals who do work "on-air" as TV journalists, the instant celebrity status frequently becomes a negative rather than a positive aspect of the job. After all, how many people really enjoy going grocery shopping and having total strangers take an abnormal interest in the contents of their shopping cart? At any rate, aspiring broadcast journalists can rest assured that life
(continued on next page)

behind the scenes can be just as exciting, challenging or rewarding for those seeking a career in broadcast news as life in front of the camera every night on the evening news.

Entry-level jobs in broadcasting are typically more abundant in radio than TV. About 11,000 radio stations and 1,500 full-power TV stations are on the air. An additional 1,000 low power TV stations (LPTV's) are also in operation. However, many of the LPTV's employ only a token news staff, and a significant number have no news staff at all.

The typical radio station has a news staff of only one or two people, and at least one of those persons probably has additional responsibilities in another area besides news. Small stations and stations that place little emphasis on news typically rely heavily on the news services and, in some cases, their local newspapers for news. These stations usually involve all their on-air people (DJ's, announcers, air personalities) in the re-writing and delivery of brief news updates. Larger stations, or stations with an "all-news" format, will employ from five to 50 people in a comprehensive news operation.

An entry-level job that involves some announcing (even if the station is small and most of the news is "rip and read") might seem attractive. But a job as a news assistant at a station committed to news will almost always be the better career choice. News (or desk) assistant positions usually involve a lot of general office duties (answering phones, distributing wire copy, etc.), and sometimes people in that position earn the unofficial title of "gofer," but the positions also offer newcomers a chance to work alongside experienced journalists. Ambitious (and talented) news assistants will usually find an opportunity to write some news copy, record phone

interviews, or in other ways demonstrate their untapped potential. Of course, an entry-level job as a reporter with a small-market station committed to its own coverage of the news is a challenging, if not rare, opportunity.

Although the number of TV stations in operation is significantly smaller than the number of radio stations, the size of the average TV news staff is substantially larger. The number of employees at a TV station may range from as few as eight to as many as 100. The typical TV station with a news operation has a staff of 20 or more. The variety of jobs in a TV news operation is also broader than that of a radio station.

In addition to the very visible on-air anchors and reporters, TV stations also employ producers, assignment editors, writers, photographers and production assistants. And, of course, overseeing the entire operation is the news director and possibly an assistant news director. In smaller markets and at smaller stations, one individual may assume a number of different roles. For example, reporters may double as photographers and possibly even work as part-time, on-air anchors. For this reason, the medium and smaller markets provide excellent opportunities for gaining valuable experience and perfecting skills. However, the need to be a "jack-of-all-trades" in many of these entry-level jobs places a premium on students who have developed a wide range of skills. Students who can write, shoot and edit their own stories have a much greater chance of employment than students who are great "readers" but lack these other abilities.

Just as with other media employers, broadcast stations have increasingly come to expect potential employees to have a college degree. However, a high premium is also placed on practical experience. Therefore, internships and part-time jobs are a big plus for students entering the job market. Many stations have allocated a certain number of internships and part-time jobs for minority students. This is part of the overall industry effort to improve minority employment. Women and Hispanics made significant employment gains in broadcast news during the 1980s. However, gains for blacks were modest. The employment outlook for women and all minority groups should improve steadily throughout the 1990s.

In addition to a written résumé, a "résumé tape" is expected of any aspiring reporter or photographer. Most college programs give students an opportunity to put together such a tape, but an internship or part-time job at a station should give you an even greater opportunity to do so. Résumé tapes should be kept short (fewer than 10 minutes), with the strongest material placed at the beginning of the tape.

Broadcasting magazine is the primary industry publication and publishes a substantial number of job listings. However, you will find that most of these jobs require several years of experience. Even advertisements for positions at smaller stations frequently include the phrase "no beginners please." Broadcasting is a highly competitive field, and finding your first job will probably require a combination of perseverance, aggressiveness and luck. Broadcasting Yearbook provides a comprehensive listing of all stations, including information on market size and programming. A copy should be available in the reference section of most libraries. Using the yearbook as a source, you can identify potential markets and stations to target in your job search. An introductory letter followed by a personal visit to hand-deliver a

résumé tape has proven to be one of the more successful approaches.

While broadcast news may appear glamorous, students owe it to themselves to carefully evaluate both the positive and negative aspects of a broadcast career. In addition to the low starting pay and difficulty in finding an entry-level job, several other job characteristics are usually mentioned as drawbacks. Long and irregular hours, including work on major holidays, are generally the norm, and career advancement usually requires relocation—sometimes to a station thousands of miles away. Job security is sometimes only slightly better than that of a college football coach. Radio stations may change formats and let the entire staff go overnight. The jobs of TV news producers, reporters, and especially anchors, are usually only as secure as the latest rating book. There is also a degree of risk associated with many broadcast journalism jobs. The danger inherent in providing on-the-scene coverage of a hurricane or war is self-evident, and most news directors allow reporters or photographers to decline these assignments if they choose. Also, broadcast journalists and photographers are more visible than their print counterparts, and sometimes become the target of violence by an unruly crowd or misguided individual.

These potential drawbacks to a career in broadcast news are offset by the advantage of a career that puts you in the center of what is happening in your community. A career that provides an opportunity to meet an amazingly wide variety of people and to face a new challenge every day. Broadcast news certainly isn't for everyone, but it's a career alternative that might be perfect for you.

The author is an assistant professor in the Radio-TV Division of the School of Communication at the University of Central Florida. His career in broadcasting has spanned 16 years, including work as a television news producer and director.

SUGGESTED READINGS

Articles

American Society of Newspaper Editors Committee on Education for Journalism. *Journalism Education: Facing Up to the Challenge of Change.* Washington, DC: American Society of Newspaper Editors, April 1990.

Beasley, Maurine. "Journalism Schools Do Not Prepare Their Students for the Realities They Will Face After Graduation." *The Chronicle of Higher Education,* May 23, 1990, p. B1.

Becker, Lee B., and Thomas E. Engleman. "1988 Grads Like First Jobs; Median Salary Increases." *Journalism Educator.* Spring 1990, pp. 22–27.

Bissinger, Debra. "Let Your Résumé Do the Talking." *The Quill,* Feb. 1986, pp. 19–22.

Clabes, Judith G. "Cutesy Cover Letters Are Like Bricks." *The Quill,* Apr. 1988, pp. 20–21.

Endres, Fred, and Stanley Wearden. "Career Choices, Perceptions of Work by Undergrads." *Journalism Educator,* Spring 1990, pp. 28–35.

Fowler, Giles. "Rating the Internships." *The Quill,* Sept. 1991, pp. 35–36.

Hembree, Diana, and Sarah Henry. "A Newsroom Hazard Called RSI." *Columbia Journalism Review,* Jan./Feb. 1987, pp. 19–24.

Hipsman, Barbara J., and Stanley T. Wearden. "Skills Testing at American Newspapers." *Newspaper Research Journal,* Winter 1990, pp. 76–89.

Mills, Kay. "New Perspectives, Different Voices: And Better Newsrooms." *The Quill,* Apr. 1989, pp. 22–24.

Moore, Sandy. "Tips for Scaling the Job-Hunt Wall." *The Quill,* Oct. 1988, pp. 11–18.

Pease, Ted, and J. Frazier Smith. "The Newsroom Barometer: Job Satisfaction and the Impact of Racial Diversity at U.S. Daily Newspapers." *The Ohio Journalism Monograph Series,* No. 1. Bush Research Center, E. W. Scripps School of Journalism, Ohio University, July 1991.

Peterson, Paul V. "Enrollment Up 7 Percent in '86, Outstripping University Growth." *Journalism Educator,* Spring 1987, pp. 4–10.

Rowe, Chip. "Learning on the Cheap: Low or No-Pay Internships Teach Some Hard Economic Lessons." *The Quill,* Sept. 1991, pp. 33–34.

Rykken, Rolf. "Repetitive Strain Injury." *Presstime,* June 1989, pp. 6–10.

Schwed, Warren W. "Hiring, Promotion, Salary, Longevity Trends Charted at Dailies." *Newspaper Research Journal* 3, no. 1 (Oct. 1981): pp. 7–8.

"Trouble at the Top: A U.S. Survey Says a 'Glass Ceiling' Blocks Women From Corporate Heights." *U.S. News & World Report,* June 17, 1991, pp. 40–48.

Books (Historical)

Abbot, Willis J. *Watching the World Go By.* Woodstock, NY: Beekman, 1974.

Hohenberg, John. *Foreign Correspondence: The Great Reporters and Their Times.* New York: Columbia University Press, 1967.

Kendrick, Alexander. *Prime Time: The Life of Edward R. Murrow.* New York: Avon, 1969.

McPhaul, John J. *Deadlines and Monkeyshines.* Englewood Cliffs, NJ: Prentice Hall, 1962.

Mencken, H. L. *Newspaper Days.* New York: Knopf, 1941.

Murray, George. *The Madhouse on Madison Street.* Chicago: Follett, 1965.

O'Connor, Richard. *The Scandalous Mr. Bennett.* Garden City, NY: Doubleday, 1962.

Ross, Isabel. *Ladies of the Press: The Story of Women in Journalism by an Insider*. New York: Harper, 1936.

Salisbury, William. *The Career of a Journalist*. New York: Dodge, 1908.

Smith, H. Allen. *The Life and Legend of Gene Fowler*. New York: Morris, 1977.

St. John, Robert. *This Was My World*. New York: Scribner's, 1961.

Swanberg, W. A. *Citizen Hearst*. New York: Scribner's, 1961.

————. *Luce and His Empire: A Biography*. New York: Scribner's, 1975.

————. *Pulitzer*. New York: Scribner's, 1967.

Walsh, Justin E. *To Print the News and Raise Hell*. Chapel Hill, NC: University of North Carolina Press, 1968.

Books (Current)

Baker, Russell. *The Good Times*. New York: Morrow, 1989.

Belford, Barbara. *Brilliant Bylines: A Biographical Anthology of Notable Newspaper Women in America*. New York: Columbia University Press, 1986.

Bernstein, Carl, and Bob Woodward. *All The President's Men*. New York: Simon and Schuster, 1974.

Biagi, Shirley. *News Talk I: State-of-the-Art Conversations with Today's Print Journalists*. Belmont, CA: Wadsworth, 1987.

————. *News Talk II: State-of-the-Art Conversations with Today's Broadcast Journalists*. Belmont, CA: Wadsworth, 1987.

Brendon, Piers. *The Life and Death of the Press Barons*. New York: Atheneum, 1983.

Broder, David S. *Behind the Front Page: A Candid Look at How the News Is Made*. New York: Simon and Schuster, 1987.

Brownfield, Janice. *Reporter vs. Publisher: What Journalism Professors Don't Tell You*. Santa Ana, CA: Alpenstock, 1986.

Buchanan, Edna. *The Corpse Had a Familiar Face*. New York: Random House, 1987.

Chancellor, John, and Walter R. Mears. *The News Business*. New York: New American Library, 1983.

Craft, Christine. *Christine Craft: An Anchorwoman's Story*. Santa Barbara, CA: Capra Press, 1986.

Creedon, Pamela J., ed., *Women in Mass Communication: Challenging Gender Values*. Newbury Park, CA: Sage, 1989.

Crouse, Timothy. *The Boys on the Bus: Riding with the Campaign Press Corps*. New York: Ballantine, 1976.

Donaldson, Sam. *Hold On, Mr. President!* New York: Random House, 1987.

Edwards, Julia. *Women of the World: The Great Foreign Correspondents*. Boston: Houghton Mifflin, 1988.

Elwood-Akers, Virginia. *Women War Correspondents in the Vietnam War, 1961–1975*. Metuchen, NJ: Scarecrow Press, 1988.

Halberstam, David. *The Powers That Be*. New York: Knopf, 1979.

Kuralt, Charles: *A Life on the Road*. New York: Putnam, 1990.

Mills, Kay. *A Place in the News: From the Women's Pages to the Front Page*. New York: Dodd, Mead, 1988.

Modgel, Leonard. *Making It in the Media Professions: A Realistic Guide to Career Opportunities in Newspapers, Magazines, Books, Television, Radio, the Movies and Advertising*. Chester, CT: Globe-Pequot Press, 1988.

Neuharth, Al. *Confessions of an S.O.B.* Garden City, NY: Doubleday, 1989.

Phelan, James. *Scandals, Scamps and Scoundrels: The Casebook of an Investigative Reporter*. New York: Random House, 1982.

Copyright © 1993 by Harcourt Brace Jovanovich, Inc.
All rights reserved. Printed in the United States of America
ISBN 0-15-500602-9

Prichard, Peter. *The Making of McPaper: The Inside Story of USA Today,* Kansas City, MO: Andrews, McMeel & Parker, 1987.

Ricchiardi, Sherry, and Virginia Young. *Women on Deadline*. Ames, IA: Iowa State University Press, 1981.

Safer, Morley. *Flashbacks: On Returning to Vietnam*. New York: Random House, 1990.

Salisbury, Harrison E. *A Journey for Our Times: A Memoir*. New York: Harper & Row, 1983.

Sevareid, Eric. *Not So Wild a Dream*. New York: Atheneum, 1976.

Swann, Phil, and Ed Achorn. *How to Land a Job in Journalism*. White Hall, VA: Betterway Publications, 1988.

Talese, Gay. *The Kingdom and the Power*. New York: Dell, 1981.

Wagner, Lilya. *Women War Correspondents of World War II*. Westport, CT: Greenwood Press, 1989.

Waters, Enoch P. *American Diary: A Personal History of the Black Press*. Chicago: Path Press, 1987.

Weaver, David H., and G. Cleveland Wilhoit. *The American Journalist: A Portrait of U.S. News People and Their Work*. Bloomington, IN: Indiana University Press, 1986.

White, Theodore H. *America in Search of Itself*. New York: Harper & Row, 1982.

—— *In Search of History: A Personal Adventure*. New York: Harper Row, 1978.

Wolseley, Roland E. *The Black Press, U.S.A.,* 2nd ed. Ames, IA: Iowa State University Press, 1990.

CAREER AND SCHOLARSHIP INFORMATION

For more information about careers in journalism, write to the Dow Jones Newspaper Fund, P.O. Box 300, Princeton, N.J. 08540. The Dow Jones Newspaper Fund is a foundation that encourages young people to consider careers in journalism. Its programs include awards, scholarships, internships, workshops and career information.

Each year, the Newspaper Fund lists millions of dollars in scholarships available to journalism and communications majors. The latest edition of its Career and Scholarship Guide includes a College Search Questionnaire for students interested in finding the colleges and universities that would best suit their needs and interests.

QUOTES

One human being had killed another, and I was happy because this was what I had been training for; reporting murders was my business. Now I could get a story into the paper, get recognition!

(Robert St. John, This Was My World*)*

Those who expect to reap the blessings of freedom must undergo the fatigue of supporting it.

(Thomas Paine)

Freedom of conscience, of education, of speech, of assembly are among the very fundamentals of democracy and all of them would be nullified should freedom of the press ever be successfully challenged.

(Franklin D. Roosevelt)

Exercise 1

CAREERS IN JOURNALISM

DISCUSSION QUESTIONS

1. Do you think it is true that the nation's brightest and most talented students avoid journalism because they believe its salaries are low and working conditions are harsh?

2. Do you agree that journalism is becoming a "pink-collar ghetto," and that women's entry into the field has contributed to its low salaries? What percentage of the students in your class (and school) is female?

3. Imagine that you owned your local daily and set its policies. Would you be willing to increase your employees' salaries if you knew that you would not have to do so and that the increase would reduce your profits?

4. Imagine that you edited your local daily, and that four applicants for jobs on your staff listed these goals on their résumés. Which applicant would you be most likely to interview and hire? Why?

   A. To work as a newspaper reporter or copy editor.
   B. To obtain an entry-level job as a reporter at a good daily newspaper.
   C. To obtain a job as a police reporter at a daily newspaper and to improve the knowledge and skills I've developed while minoring in criminal justice and working for three years as a reporter for my student paper and as an intern for two dailies.
   D. To find a career position that would readily accept my imaginative thinking and work-related energies and help me transform them into acceptable print for my employer.

Exercise 2

CAREERS IN JOURNALISM

CAREER PROJECTS

1. Study the sample résumés in this chapter, then prepare your own résumé and cover letter.
2. Write a three- to four-page paper that compares the appearance, content and style of four major journalism magazines: Editor & Publisher, Columbia Journalism Review, Journalism Quarterly and The Quill.
3. Obtain a copy of Writer's Market, then describe the types of articles published by 10 magazines that interest you. Also list the amount each magazine pays for articles.
4. Critically analyze the content of the help-wanted ads that Editor & Publisher magazine publishes for newspaper reporters and editors. Which types of jobs seem to be most plentiful? What are the requirements for those jobs? In what parts of the country are the jobs available? Write a two- to three-page paper that summarizes your findings.
5. Conduct a survey of all the daily newspapers in your state to determine which newspapers hire summer interns and how many interns they hire. Ask the editors at each paper for additional information, such as the name and title of the person to whom applicants should write, what the newspaper's deadline is, and how much it pays interns. After gathering and summarizing the information, distribute copies of your report to journalism students in other classes and schools.
6. Conduct a survey of all the daily newspapers in your state to determine how many of them give tests to applicants for their reporting and editing jobs, what types of tests they give, and whether they ask applicants to try out for several days before offering them jobs.
7. Conduct a survey of all the media in your state to learn their starting salaries for college graduates. Also ask how many new reporters they hire during a typical year, and where the reporters come from.
8. Conduct a survey of last year's graduates from your school. Where are they now, and what do they like and dislike about their new jobs? What were their starting salaries?
9. Invite several editors to your school to describe their publications' internships. Or, invite several editors to your school and ask them to:

   A. Tell you what they look for while interviewing applicants for the jobs on their staffs.
   B. Describe the qualifications they consider most important for interns.
   C. Describe the type of college degree and experience they like job applicants to have.

CHAPTER 12

COMMUNICATION LAW

Congress shall make no law respecting an establishment of religion, or prohibiting the free exercise thereof; or abridging the freedom of speech, or of the press; or the right of the people peaceably to assemble, and to petition the Government for redress of grievances.

(The First Amendment)

Although the First Amendment to the U.S. Constitution declares that "Congress shall make no law . . . abridging the freedom of speech, or of the press," these freedoms are not absolute. Some restrictions are necessary because they sometimes conflict with other rights that are also protected by the Constitution. For example: the Constitution protects Americans' reputations and privacy, yet some news stories may damage their reputations and invade their privacy.

Each time a conflict between two constitutional rights arises, it is up to the courts to try to balance them. The courts determine which right should be the preferred or dominating right in a particular case, and their decisions provide guidelines that can be applied in other cases.

The Constitution has been amended only 26 times. Nevertheless, the law is constantly evolving. As our society changes, its needs also change, and courts reinterpret the Constitution and apply it in new ways. Interpretations of the Constitution are also affected by new appointments to the U.S. Supreme Court. The court's decisions may change significantly from one decade to another because of the appointment of new justices whose philosophies are more liberal or more conservative than those of their predecessors.

This chapter will examine recent decisions involving the First Amendment and the effect of those decisions on journalists. The decisions involve six legal issues of particular interest to journalists: libel, privacy, the free press/fair trial dilemma, the government's use of subpoenas to obtain information, the adoption of shield laws to protect journalists, and censorship.

LIBEL

Every reporter and editor is expected to understand the problem of libel and to help newspapers avoid it. However, generalizations about libel laws are difficult. Libel laws

are adopted by the 50 states, not by the federal government, and consequently vary from one area to another. Moreover, as new cases reach the Supreme Court, its decisions change, often dramatically. A series of favorable decisions that began in 1964 encouraged journalists to believe that the laws of libel were being repealed—that it had become almost impossible for responsible journalists to lose a libel suit. In an effort to encourage a free and vigorous discussion of public issues, the Supreme Court protected even news stories that contained obvious factual errors, so long as the errors were not malicious. However, a series of more recent decisions has created new guidelines that now make it easier for individuals, especially private citizens, to sue the media for libel.

Filing a Libel Suit

Libel has been defined as written communication that exposes people to hatred, ridicule or contempt, that lowers them in the esteem of others, that causes them to be shunned, or that injures them in their ability to carry on their business or profession. More simply, a libel is a written statement that damages a person's reputation. The libel may appear anywhere in a newspaper: in a news story, headline, photograph, advertisement, editorial or letter to the editor. Depending on the circumstances, citizens can also sue the broadcast media for slander, which is oral rather than written. Because it is less permanent, slander is usually considered less serious than libel.

An individual who believes that a printed statement has damaged his or her reputation can file a civil lawsuit against the publication. The court that hears the suit will balance two conflicting rights: the media's right to gather and report the news and the individual's right to protect his or her reputation. If the court finds that the individual's reputation was indeed damaged unfairly, it usually awards that person a sum of money to be paid by the publication to compensate for the damage.

The person who claims to have been libeled (the plaintiff) usually files a suit against a newspaper's publisher and against the company that owns the paper, since they can afford to pay the largest possible settlements. However, each person who handles a story can be held personally liable for its content, so a suit may also name the reporter who wrote the story and the editor who checked it.

The Five Elements of Libel

To win a libel suit, a plaintiff must be prepared to prove the five elements of libel: (1) publication, (2) identification, (3) defamation, (4) fault and (5) injury.

Publication. The first proof requirement in libel suits, publication, occurs when a potentially libelous story appears in a newspaper and that newspaper is distributed to readers. If the newspaper discovers a possible libel quickly enough, it may be able to protect itself by recalling and destroying all the copies that contain it.

Identification. In order to win a libel suit, the plaintiff does not have to be identified by name if other facts in a story enable even a few readers to guess his or her identity. However, only the person who is identified can file a libel suit; the victim's relatives cannot, even though they may be embarrassed by a story's publication. If the victim is dead, usually no one can file a suit for libel—so both journalists and historians are free to criticize the dead.

Reporters can avoid some libel suits by not identifying people who might be embarrassed by a story's publication. Thus, a reporter who wants to write about a humorous event or minor incident likely to interest readers may report that "a local woman" lost her dentures while diving into a public pool, or that "a young father" suffered a broken nose while teaching his 4-year-old son how to box. Such stories do not libel anyone because they do not reveal the participants' exact identities.

However, journalists cannot always protect themselves so easily. The identity of people involved in the news is usually important, and their names must be included in stories. For example, newspapers normally identify people who have been arrested and charged with serious crimes; their identities are news and a matter of public interest.

Defamation. The plaintiff cannot win a libel suit simply because a story is false. To be actionable, the falsehood must damage the plaintiff's reputation. For example, courts have ruled that it is usually not libelous to report mistakenly that a married woman is pregnant, nor to report mistakenly that a person is dead. Judges have explained that it is not a disgrace for a married woman to become pregnant, nor for anyone to die. However, it would be libelous to report falsely that an unmarried woman was pregnant.

Fault. The plaintiffs in libel suits are required to prove some level of fault on the part of the newspaper or magazine that published a defamatory item. The level of fault can vary from simple negligence to actual malice, depending on just who the plaintiff is. According to recent Supreme Court decisions:

> Most private citizens suing the media for libel are required to prove at least some level of fault, usually only simple negligence on the part of the media.

> Public officials and public figures suing the media for libel must prove a very difficult level of fault: that the media acted with actual malice. This means the plaintiff must prove that the media published the information knowing it was false, or published it with reckless disregard as to its truth or falseness.

The court has explained that because private citizens have not volunteered for public scrutiny, they deserve more protection than public persons. Also, private citizens may be more vulnerable to injury and less able to defend themselves.

Thus, one of the first steps in a libel suit is to determine whether the plaintiff is a private citizen or a public person (either a public official or a public figure such as a public activist or even a movie star).

Private citizens who are involved in matters of public interest must also prove that a defamatory statement is false. The Supreme Court noted in its 1986 decision in *Philadelphia Newspapers* v. *Hepps* that the First Amendment protects speech about both public figures and matters of public concern. While proving actual malice in their libel suits, public officials and public figures have to prove falsity. Justice Sandra Day O'Connor said that since private plaintiffs have to prove fault anyway, usually negligence, their burden will not increase that much. Again, this ruling by the court was limited. It does not apply to all private persons, only to those involved in matters of public interest.

Injury. Finally, the plaintiff must prove that he or she suffered some damages: some actual injury or financial loss.

Tips from a Pro

THIRTY WAYS TO PROTECT YOURSELF AGAINST LIBEL LAWSUITS

By **Alexander Greenfeld**

1. When you are starting a highly sensitive story or an investigative story which contains allegations of illegal or unethical acts, have the editor and writer go over the parameters of it with an attorney so that he can point out potential problems.

2. The best protection always is to get an interview or comment from a subject who is being pictured in a bad light. You may learn you have errors, learn about other sources, and deflect a lawsuit by giving the person his say and showing him a balanced picture.

3. Ask these questions: Is the story accurate? Is it fair? Is it based on credible or authoritative sources or documents? Is it written according to the ordinary standards of a writer on this subject matter? Do you have any serious doubts, or even plain doubts, about statements in the story? What would you do if the story were written about you?

4. An editor and your counsel should know the names, credentials and ability to have the information of the sources.

5. Be prepared to attempt ultimately to defend on the basis of truth if you are using confidential sources and there is no chance they would testify.

6. If there might be a difference in judgment whether an act is illegal or immoral, have your sources make the accusation and not the writer. For example: "Lawyers in the SEC say such activities are illegal," as opposed to the writer, who is not a legal expert in the field, asserting that certain activities are illegal.

7. Avoid guilt by association. If you have accurate, well-based information that Smith is a crook, do not mention his prominent friends when there is no evidence that they are involved in or are aware of his illegal activities.

8. Editors should play lawyer with a sensitive story. Editors should ask the reporter for sources and documentation. If the reporter will not reveal the names, tell him to publish the story in his own newspaper. Confidentiality of sources is not damaged by giving the names to editors as well as to lawyers.

Alexander Greenfeld is former corporate and libel counsel of The New York Times and U.S. News & World Report. He is currently in private practice in Washington, D.C.

9. Do not play with legal concepts you may have heard of, prior to publication, such as whether the subject is a public or private figure or whether the writing is negligent or reckless. These concepts are useful only for litigators. It can be quite difficult to predict how a court will rule on such questions.

10. A corporation, union, association, product or group can be libeled just as well as an individual; but not a government.

11. When a group has 25 or fewer members, do not print that the group are crooks or psychopaths. Any unnamed single member of such a small group can sue.

12. Make sure every word of a sensitive story is read for libel and invasion of privacy. Problems pop up in unexpected places.

13. Avoid defamatory labels. A defamatory statement is one which injures someone's reputation. Stick to the subject's actions. Moreover, in many jurisdictions, opinions must be based on facts. Make sure there are facts to back up opinions.

14. Make sure your lawyer reads documents which are the bases for allegations of illegality or unethical behavior. In some cases, this may be boxfuls.

15. Double-check the spelling of names and identity of pictures of convicted, indicted, and arrested persons.

16. Have photographers get written permission from parents for pictures of minors, particularly when they are in correctional, medical, or mental institutions.

17. Be sure that advertising and press releases accurately reflect statements in a story.

18. Neither reporters nor editors should make private disparaging remarks about a story's subjects.

19. Beware of remarks about the competency of professionals such as doctors, lawyers, and educators. They sue.

20. You have a privilege to report false and defamatory statements made in a court or legislative body or by a public official or by anyone in a public meeting discussing public matters. Make sure the quotes or statements of what was said are accurate.

21. Make sure that information has been obtained from, or double-checked with, original sources—particularly court records—and is not based on news clips alone.

22. Be especially vigilant for the main categories and kinds of language which, when not based on facts, have led to libel judgments: allegations of crime, mental problems, professional incompetence, sexual aberration, abhorred political affiliations, conflict of interest, the wrongful use of a public, corporate, or union office.

23. Editors should decide whether characterizations and interpretations are supported by facts.

24. When a reporter is using a confidential source, a source which cannot be named, have the reporter ask the source if he would testify in the event of a lawsuit.

25. It is always best to name sources. This will deter an aggressive lawyer from filing suit.

26. You cannot rely on the distinguished history or awards of a writer. Every writer should be sourced out. The most successful and famous want to be. They want an accurate story and they do not want to get involved in a lawsuit.

27. Do not print a questionable story because you think the subject will not sue. There is no way to predict who will sue. Ensure that stories are accurate, fair, and based on credible sources or on documents. (My experience is that many people who sue do so because they are angry.)

(continued on next page)

28. Reporters should keep all their notes and tapes.

29. If, prior to publication, you are informed by a story subject or an attorney that you have false informa-tion, check the claim and respond to the complainer.

30. Denials should go into a story to show fairness and that care has been taken to be objective and accurate.

Primary Defenses in Libel Suits

Traditionally, newspapers have relied on three primary defenses in libel suits: (1) truth, (2) fair comment and (3) qualified privilege.

Truth. In many ways, truth is the best defense in a libel suit, but it may be difficult to prove to a judge or jury that the facts reported in a news story are true. In many states, truth alone is an adequate defense. If a newspaper in those states can prove that the statements it published are true, it will win a libel suit. Newspapers in the remaining states must prove not only that the statements they published are true but also that they published those statements for good reason—on a proper occasion and for some justifiable purpose. Truth in those states is not an adequate defense if a newspaper published a story needlessly or maliciously. For example, a newspaper in those states could not report that a prominent individual committed a crime 10 or 20 years earlier unless something that person did recently made the past record a matter of public interest.

Newspapers cannot defend themselves in a libel suit by proving that they attributed a statement to someone else, nor by proving that they accurately quoted someone else. Newspapers that rely on the defense of truth must prove that a statement is true in and of itself, not just that the statement is an accurate account of what someone else said. Thus, if a police officer accused someone of committing a crime, a newspaper that reported the accusation would have to prove that the person actually did commit the crime, not just that the police officer said the person did.

To win a libel suit, the proof of truth must be as broad as the statements published. Newspapers that accuse the plaintiff of a crime must also prove that the plaintiff is guilty of the specific crime they mentioned, not of any other crimes. Moreover, newspapers usually cannot protect themselves by saying that a story is "reportedly" or "allegedly" true. To win a libel suit, they must prove that it *is* true.

Thus, newspapers are legally responsible for everything they publish. It does not matter whether a libelous statement was provided by a reporter, advertiser, news service, press release or police officer, nor that it was published in a direct quotation or letter to an editor. The fact that a newspaper published a libelous statement accidentally or unknowingly (or that its reporter obtained the libelous material from another person) will not absolve it of guilt.

Fair Comment. "Fair comment and criticism" is a legal doctrine that enables newswriters to express their opinions about matters of public interest. Because of that doctrine, newswriters are free to criticize public figures and public officials, including politicians, actors and actresses, inventors, writers, astronauts and athletes. Newswriters are also free to criticize the work of public figures, including radio and television programs, speeches, plays, movies, books, paintings and athletic events. Even the meals served by restaurants and the cars manufactured in Detroit are subject to public criticism. Courts have explained that people who deliberately go before the public, who seek the public's approval, and whose own actions invite public interest in their lives, must be willing to accept unfavorable as well as favorable publicity.

Newswriters are also free to comment on the actions and lives of people who are thrust into the news unwillingly. Those people may be involved in an accident or other newsworthy event that makes them public figures, however fleetingly.

A writer's criticisms may be unpopular and harsh. A review of the book "Always on Sunday" by Peggy Whedon began: "This is a remarkably dreadful book . . . Actually, it is a mish-mash of unrelated trivia and girlish revelations." Similarly, a movie review began:

> They say that if a million monkeys sat down at typewriters, one of them would eventually produce "War and Peace." Well, one of them—bearing the name of Jeremy Joe Kronsberg—seems to have written *Every Which Way But Loose,* a Clint Eastwood "comedy" that could not possibly have been created by human hands.

When you think of harsh criticism, Richard Nixon may come to mind. Nixon left the White House in disgrace and, for years afterward, seemed to be trying to restore his reputation and become a respected elder statesman. Under the doctrine of fair comment, journalists have been free to continue criticizing Nixon. Some, in fact, have called him "the greatest con man in American history," "a scheming sleazeball," and "a sewer rat" who trashed the Constitution.

You may also remember Leona Helmsley, who controlled a chain of hotels and, according to some estimates, has a fortune that totals several billion dollars. When Helmsley was convicted of cheating on her income taxes, news stories called her "a disgrace to humanity," "a rich bitch" and "the wicked witch of the West." An article in Newsweek magazine stated that Helmsley was stingy, mistreated her employees, and possessed "a stevedore's mouth and the compassion of a cluster bomb."

Qualified Privilege. Government officials (presidents, legislators and judges, for example) enjoy an absolute privilege while acting in their official capacities. Regardless of whether their statements are true or false, defamatory or not, the officials cannot be sued for libel. Everyone participating in a judicial proceeding, such as a trial, also enjoys an absolute privilege. Courts grant that privilege because they believe it is important that certain people be allowed to speak freely and fearlessly.

Reporters enjoy a "qualified privilege" to report the statements made during those official government proceedings. To be protected by that privilege, their stories must be full, fair and accurate. Courts grant reporters immunity from libel suits in instances when the need to inform citizens about public affairs is more important than the need to protect an individual's reputation.

However, reporters can invoke the defense only while reporting official government proceedings. The proceedings include almost everything the president says and does, congressional and legislative sessions, and trials. However, the qualified privilege does not protect statements that government officials make outside those proceedings—the statements a police officer makes at the scene of a crime, for example. It also excludes statements made at the meetings of private organizations.

Two Additional Defenses. As two additional but less common defenses, newspapers may try to prove that the plaintiff consented to a story's publication or that the statute of limitations has expired. The statute of limitations varies from state to state. In most states, libel suits must be filed within one, two or three years of a defamatory story's publication.

Secondary Defenses in Libel Suits

Some secondary defenses are available to newspapers sued for libel. However, those defenses are used less frequently and normally offer less protection than truth, privilege and fair comment. The secondary defenses do not absolve newspapers of guilt but may lessen the amount they are required to pay in damages.

Newspapers will do everything possible to show that they did not injure a victim intentionally—that they made an honest error, that they sincerely regret the error, and that they have retracted or corrected it. Newspapers may try to show that they obtained their information from a normally reliable source, had no way of knowing that it was false, were at least partially correct, innocently republished a statement that had already been printed elsewhere, or accidentally identified the wrong person.

As another defense, newspapers may attempt to prove that a plaintiff's reputation was already so bad that it could not be damaged any further by the story they published.

Types of Damages

Normally, juries award successful libel plaintiffs "compensatory" or "general" damages to compensate for damage to their reputations and for their financial losses. On occasion, they may also award damages for emotional suffering.

Juries can award "special" damages to plaintiffs able to prove that they suffered some additional or specific losses to their reputations or businesses.

Juries award "punitive" damages to punish publications found guilty of irresponsible conduct and to discourage the conduct's recurrence. To win punitive damages, the plaintiff must prove that the publication acted with malice. Both special and punitive damages can be awarded in addition to compensatory damages.

New York Times v. *Sullivan*

In 1964 the U.S. Supreme Court made it virtually impossible for public officials to sue the media for libel. The Supreme Court ruled that a public official cannot be awarded any damages, not even for a story that contains obvious factual errors, so long as the publication has not acted with *actual malice*. The court defined the term as "publishing information knowing that it was false, or publishing with reckless disregard of the truth of falseness of the information."

The New York Times had published an advertisement for a civil rights group, and the advertisement charged that police officers armed with shotguns and tear gas had ringed an Alabama campus. The advertisement did not name L. B. Sullivan, the commissioner for public affairs in Montgomery, but Sullivan was responsible for the city's police department. He complained that the advertisement contained several errors, sued The New York Times for libel and was awarded $500,000. The Alabama State Supreme Court upheld the decision, but the U.S. Supreme Court ruled against Sullivan.

The U.S. Supreme Court said it considered the case "against the background of a profound national commitment to the principle that debate on public issues should be uninhibited, robust, and wide-open, and that it may well include vehement, caustic and sometimes unpleasantly sharp attacks on government officials." Justice William Brennan Jr., in writing the majority opinion, added:

> We are required for the first time in this case to determine the extent to
> which the constitutional protections for speech and press limit a state's power

to award damages in a libel action brought by a public official against the critics of his official conduct. . . .

The constitutional guarantees require, we think, a federal rule that prohibits a public official from recovering damages for a defamatory falsehood relating to his official conduct unless he proves that the statement was made with "actual malice," that is, with the knowledge that it was false or with a reckless disregard of whether it was false or not.

This ruling remains in effect today: To win a libel suit, a public official must prove that the publication acted with "actual malice." This doctrine has become known as the "New York Times rule." The Supreme Court adopted the rule to encourage debate on public issues. The court feared that if the media could be punished for honest mistakes, they would become more hesitant to discuss important issues and to publish even truthful criticisms of public officials.

Expanding the Media's Freedom

In 1967 the U.S. Supreme Court declared that the New York Times rule applied to public figures as well as to public officials. Combining two cases, on June 12, 1967, the Supreme Court ruled on both *Butts* v. *Curtis Publishing Co.* and *Associated Press* v. *Walker*. The Curtis Publishing Co. owned the Saturday Evening Post, which reported that Wallace Butts, the athletic director at the University of Georgia, had conspired to fix a football game. The Post charged that Butts had given his team's plays and defensive patterns to the University of Alabama. Butts sued the Curtis Publishing Co. for libel, and a jury awarded him $60,000 in general and $3 million in punitive damages.

The Supreme Court ruled that Butts was a public figure but upheld the award because the Saturday Evening Post had acted with a "reckless disregard for the truth"—a violation of the New York Times rule. The court explained that the story was not "hot news," and the magazine's editors could have taken time to conduct a more thorough investigation but failed to do so. The editors knew that their source was on probation for bad-check charges but failed to examine his notes, failed to interview a second witness and failed to screen films of the game to determine whether the source's information was accurate. The editors also failed to determine whether Alabama changed its game plans after allegedly receiving the information. Moreover, "The Post writer assigned to the story was not a football expert, and no attempt was made to check the story with someone knowledgeable in the sport." The court concluded, "In short, the evidence is ample to support a finding of highly unreasonable conduct constituting an extreme departure from the standards of investigation and reporting ordinarily adhered to by responsible publishers." Butts eventually settled for $460,000.

In the other suit, however, the Supreme Court ruled against Walker, a former Army general. The Associated Press reported that Walker had assumed command of some students and led a charge against federal marshals trying to help James Meredith, a black student, enter the University of Mississippi. The story also reported that Walker encouraged the rioters to use violence and instructed them on ways to avoid the effects of tear gas. The court found that the story contained some factual errors, but it concluded that, "Under any reasoning, Gen. Walker was a public man in whose conduct society and the press had a legitimate and substantial interest." Moreover, an AP reporter was at the scene, seemed to be trustworthy and competent, and wrote a story that required immediate dissemination. The court found that: "Nothing in this series of events gives the slightest hint of a severe departure from accepted publishing standards. We therefore conclude that Gen. Walker should not be entitled to damages from The Associated Press."

Gertz v. *Welch*

In 1974 the Supreme Court made it easier for private citizens to sue the media for libel.

A Chicago policeman shot and killed a youth, and the victim's family hired attorney Elmer Gertz to file a civil suit against the policeman. American Opinion, a monthly magazine published by the John Birch Society, called Gertz a "Communist-fronter," implied that he had a criminal record and said that he had designed a national campaign to discredit the police. Gertz sued for libel, and a jury awarded him $50,000. The Supreme Court upheld that award by a vote of 5–4.

In the Gertz case, the Supreme Court said that private citizens deserve more protection than public officials and public figures. Public officials and public figures must prove actual malice because they have given up some of their privacy voluntarily. The court ruled that Gertz was a private citizen, not a public official or public figure, because he did not have "general fame or notoriety in the community" and did not "thrust himself into the vortex of this public issue, nor did he engage the public's attention in an attempt to influence its outcome."

The court added that private citizens are entitled to damages if they can prove that a statement was false and defamatory and published as the result of negligence or carelessness. It defined the criterion for negligence as whether a "reasonable person" would have done the same thing as the publisher under the same circumstances.

Thus, private citizens who sue for libel have to prove some level of fault on the part of the media. Different states have adopted different standards. Most use "negligence," which simply means failure to act as a reasonable person would in similar circumstances. In libel law, it means whether the reporter used due care.

The Supreme Court also announced a radical new rule on damages. Previously, few states required plaintiffs to prove that they had suffered a loss. If someone was libeled, courts assumed that the victim was injured and awarded that person some money as compensation for the injury. In *Gertz,* the court ruled that private citizens who prove that the media were mistaken can be compensated only for their actual damages. Thus, private citizens now have to prove that they suffered an injury, such as a financial loss, harm to their reputation, or mental anguish and suffering. A jury will then decide how much the citizen deserves as compensation for the injury.

Anyone (either a private citizen or a public figure) seeking punitive damages must prove actual malice. Moreover, the court warned lower courts that punitive damages should be reasonably related to the injury a plaintiff suffered, and should not be excessive. Thus, the court seemed to be trying to curb exorbitant awards for damages.

The 1980s: Applying *Gertz* and *Sullivan*

The outcome of three major cases heard during the 1980s depended on rules formulated during the 1960s and 1970s. The media seemed to win two of the cases. However, both victories were expensive—and controversial.

Dun & Bradstreet, Inc.* v. *Greenmoss Builders. During the 1980s, a closely divided court ruled that nonpublic figures seeking punitive damages do not have to prove that the media acted with malice—if the libelous material concerns *private* matters. The vote was 5–4, but the justices wrote four separate opinions. Only three signed the prevailing opinion.

Dun & Bradstreet issued a credit report stating that Greenmoss, a building contractor in Vermont, had filed for bankruptcy. Dun & Bradstreet obtained the information from a part-time employee, a 17-year-old high-school student. The student misinterpreted a bankruptcy petition filed by a former Greenmoss employee. The student thought that

Greenmoss itself had filed for bankruptcy. After receiving the information, Dun & Bradstreet failed to follow its own rules about verifying the data.

Dun & Bradstreet sent its credit report to five subscribers, and Greenmoss learned about it while talking to a banker. Greenmoss asked Dun & Bradstreet for a correction and for the names of everyone who received the report. After checking and determining that it was mistaken, Dun & Bradstreet sent a corrective notice to the subscribers. Greenmoss was dissatisfied with its correction and again asked for the five names. Because Dun & Bradstreet again refused, Greenmoss sued for libel.

A Vermont jury awarded Greenmoss $50,000 in compensatory damages for the harm it suffered and $300,000 in punitive damages to punish Dun & Bradstreet for its handling of the matter. Dun & Bradstreet appealed, insisting that under the *Gertz* rule, it should not have to pay anything because it had not acted with malice. In *Gertz,* the Supreme Court had ruled that a nonpublic plaintiff could recover some damages by proving that he or she had been harmed by a defamatory statement made negligently. To collect punitive damages, a nonpublic plaintiff had to prove that a statement had been made with actual malice.

The Supreme Court based its decision on what was said. The court ruled that a jury can award punitive damages, without proof of malice, if the libelous material does not involve a "matter of public concern." Justice Lewis F. Powell, who wrote the court's decision, explained: "We have long recognized that not all speech is of equal First Amendment importance. It is speech on 'matters of public concern' that is 'at the heart of the First Amendment's protection.' . . . Speech on matters of purely private concern is of less First Amendment concern."

Thus, the court upheld the punitive damages against Dun & Bradstreet because its credit report was not in the public interest. Rather, it was "solely in the individual interest of the speaker and its specific business audience." The court failed to define "public concern," and its decision alarmed journalists. They fear that other judges will begin to second-guess their news judgment and rule on whether other stories they publish truly involve matters of public concern.

Ariel Sharon v. *Time, Inc.* Israel's former defense minister, Ariel Sharon, filed a $50 million libel suit against Time Inc. A story in Time had reported that Christian Phalangist militiamen killed 700 Arabs two days after the assassination of Lebanese President-elect Bashir Gemayel. The Phalangists drove into Palestinian refugee camps in West Beirut, supposedly searching for terrorists but instead massacring hundreds of unarmed men, women and children.

The Israeli government appointed a commission to investigate the massacre, and it found that Sharon bore an "indirect responsibility" for the deaths. The commission explained that Sharon allowed Phalangists into the Arab camps, despite warnings that they might seek revenge.

Time also reported that, after Gemayel's assassination, Sharon visited the Gemayel family to express his condolences. Time added that a classified appendix to the commission's report indicated that during Sharon's visit, he discussed the Phalangists' need for revenge.

Sharon admitted meeting with the Gemayel family but insisted that he never discussed revenge. Sharon also insisted that the secret appendix did not, as Time claimed, say that he had talked about revenge. He sued Time, charging that its story implied that he had deliberately encouraged the massacre—an accusation well beyond the commission's public findings.

As a public figure, Sharon had to prove actual malice. Sharon's lawyers charged that David Halevy, Time's correspondent in Jerusalem, was unreliable and prejudiced against Sharon. The lawyers accused Halevy of inventing portions of his story, and they accused Time's staff in New York of failing to verify the details. Halevy responded that he had relied on four sources, including an Israeli intelligence officer who took notes during Sharon's condolence call.

At first, the Israeli government refused to let Time's lawyers examine the secret appendix. Israel later relented, and attorneys for both sides looked at it. The appendix never mentioned a conversation about revenge, so Time was forced to admit—in court—that it had been mistaken. However, Time continued to insist that its error had been a minor one.

The trial lasted six weeks. Sharon called only 13 witnesses, and Time did not call any defense witnesses.

The judge instructed the jury to reach its verdict in three steps. First, the jury had to decide whether Sharon was defamed. Did Time say that Sharon encouraged the massacre, or only that he knew it might occur? The jury concluded that Time defamed Sharon.

Second, the jury had to decide the question of truth or falsity. Was Time accurate when it described Sharon's condolence call? The jury concluded that Time was mistaken. Thus, the jury found Time guilty of both defamation and falsehood. However, Time continued to hope that the jury would rule in its favor on the third question: whether it acted with malice. For Sharon to win, the jury had to answer all three questions in his favor.

The jury criticized Time for acting "negligently and carelessly" while reporting and verifying its information, but nevertheless ruled in its favor. Sharon had failed to prove that Time acted with a reckless disregard for the truth. Thus, the jury concluded that Time's story was defamatory and false, but that Time was careless rather than reckless.

Both sides claimed victory. Sharon did not receive any money but said that he had filed the libel suit to clear his reputation and to prove that Time had lied. Time won the legal battle, but its reputation suffered. Many Americans could not understand—or agree with—the jury's verdict. Sharon proved that he had been defamed and that Time had reported false information, yet he still lost.

***Gen. William Westmoreland* v. *CBS News*.** In 1982, the CBS television network broadcast a 90-minute documentary titled "The Uncounted Enemy: A Vietnam Deception." It charged that Gen. William Westmoreland, who commanded the U.S. forces in South Vietnam from 1964 to 1968, had engaged in a deliberate conspiracy to mislead his superiors, including President Lyndon Johnson, about the number of enemy soldiers in Vietnam and about his success in defeating them. The documentary accused Westmoreland of telling President Johnson and the Joint Chiefs of Staff that there were about 300,000 Viet Cong, yet many intelligence officers believed there were 500,000, or perhaps even 600,000. The documentary also charged that Westmoreland and his staff failed to report that nearly 25,000 North Vietnamese troops were infiltrating the South each month.

The war in Vietnam was America's longest and costliest war—and a war of attrition. There seemed to be only one measure of success: the "body count," or number of Viet Cong killed each month. Westmoreland was trying to kill the Viet Cong faster than they could be replaced.

The documentary charged that Westmoreland minimized the enemy's strength to make it appear that he was winning the war. CBS added that Americans learned the truth—the enemy's real strength—during the Tet offensive in January, 1968. The offensive showed that the Communists were able to strike anywhere in South Vietnam, including Saigon.

Westmoreland sued CBS for $120 million, although he was counseled that it would be difficult for him to win. Like Sharon, he would have to prove malice. Westmoreland charged that CBS news producer George Crile and CBS correspondent Mike Wallace were wrong, and that they knew they were wrong. Westmoreland also claimed that he had been "ambushed." He charged that CBS tricked him into the interview by promising a fair and educational study of the Tet offensive. Westmoreland's lawyers also tried to show that CBS failed to present a balanced account.

CBS seemed to be in trouble even before the trial started. Critics—including other journalists—accused CBS of treating Westmoreland unfairly: of taking some quotes out of context, of ignoring facts that conflicted with its own conclusions, and of retaping an interview with a source critical of the general. Because of the criticisms, CBS conducted an internal investigation, and it revealed that people working on the documentary had violated the network's own rules.

In court, Westmoreland testified that there was no deceit or conspiracy. He insisted that CIA and military analysts genuinely disagreed about whether they should count the Viet Cong's irregular, self-defense forces. Westmoreland's count did not include those forces, and he explained that they were part-time and often untrained civilians: mainly old men, women and youths. He considered them a home guard with no offensive capability: poorly armed and badly organized, not dangerous fighters to be killed.

The trial ended abruptly, just a few days before it was scheduled to go to the jury. Westmoreland withdrew, and the two sides issued a joint statement saying, in part, "CBS respects Gen. Westmoreland's long and faithful service to his country and never intended to assert, and does not believe, that Gen. Westmoreland was unpatriotic or disloyal in performing his duties as he saw fit."

Westmoreland claimed that he had won, yet he received no money and no retraction: only the statement saying that CBS did not think he was disloyal. Westmoreland called it an apology that affirmed his honor, yet CBS never admitted that its documentary was mistaken. Moreover, CBS had reportedly offered to make a similar statement a year earlier.

Why did Westmoreland withdraw? It appeared that CBS was proving, in court, that its documentary was basically true. Several of Westmoreland's subordinates from his tour of duty in Vietnam and CIA officials testified that estimates of the enemy's troop strength had been tainted by politics. Even Westmoreland's former intelligence chief, a retired major general, testified that Westmoreland had withheld information because it would cause a "political bombshell" in Washington. Some testimony was even more harmful for Westmoreland than the statements aired during the CBS documentary.

As the testimony turned against Westmoreland, his supporters seemed to become confused and demoralized. Some feared the jury would rule that CBS had not acted with malice and, even worse, might rule that the documentary was accurate—that Westmoreland had lied to his superiors. The Capital Legal Foundation, a conservative public-interest firm based in Washington, D.C., had offered to represent Westmoreland and to pay most of his legal expenses. But it began to run out of money, and may have been reluctant to invest any more in a case that it seemed to be losing. (During interviews conducted after the settlement, the jurors indicated that they would have voted in favor of CBS.)

Westmoreland had filed the libel suit to vindicate himself; instead it vindicated CBS. Thus, he turned a publicity victory into a courtroom defeat. He was worse off after the trial than before it. Stories published before the trial favored him, charging that CBS had acted unfairly. If Westmoreland had never filed his lawsuit, millions of Americans might have continued to believe that CBS had been both unfair and mistaken.

It seemed to be a major victory for CBS—but an expensive one. CBS spent about $250,000 to produce the documentary and millions to defend it. The network never revealed its legal expenses, but experts estimated that the two sides spent $7 million to $9 million in legal fees. Of that, Westmoreland's costs were estimated at $3.5 million. Moreover, some of the testimony harmed CBS, suggesting that, although accurate, the documentary may not have been fair.

The Legacy of the 1980s. Another major case, *Philadelphia Newspapers* v. *Hepps,* arose after the (Philadelphia) Inquirer published a series of articles that linked the plaintiffs to organized crime. The case reached the Supreme Court and, in writing its decision, Justice Sandra Day O'Connor declared that private citizens involved in matters of public interest must prove that the stories written about them are false. Public officials and public figures must prove falseness as part of their showing of "actual malice" by the media.

Thus, to win a libel suit and collect general damages, private citizens involved in matters of public interest must now prove: (1) that the libel has been published, (2) that they have been identified, (3) that they have been defamed and (4) that the story is false and the media are at fault; and (5) that they suffered damages—some kind of actual injury or out-of-pocket loss. To collect punitive damages, every plaintiff must prove that the media acted with actual malice.

Libel Trends in the 1990s

During the early 1990s, the U.S. Supreme Court ruled on three more cases that involved the media, and journalists clearly lost two of the cases. Some journalists consider the court's decision in the third case a partial victory.

Milkovich v. *Lorain Journal Co.* In a 1974 decision, Supreme Court Justice Louis F. Powell Jr. had stated, "There is no such thing as a false idea." Lower courts concluded that, because opinions cannot be proven true or false, they should be immune to libel. In 1990, the Supreme Court clarified this conclusion in its ruling in *Milkovich* v. *Lorain.*

Ted Diadun was a sportswriter and columnist for the Willoughby (Ohio) News-Herald and wrote a column suggesting that a high school coach had lied. The coach, Michael Milkovich, worked with wrestlers at Maple Heights High School in suburban Cleveland, and a brawl broke out at one of the team's matches. The Ohio High School Athletic Association placed the team on probation. Several wrestlers and their parents appealed to a court, and it ruled that the team had wrongly been suspended.

Diadun had seen the brawl and charged that Milkovich lied. "Anyone who attended the meet," Diadun wrote, "knows in his heart that Milkovich . . . lied at the hearing after . . . having given his solemn oath to tell the truth." Milkovich sued Diadun, his paper and its owner, the Lorain Journal Co., complaining that Diadun's column accused him of perjury. The Ohio Court of Appeals dismissed the lawsuit and explained that Diadun's words were opinion, not fact.

In 1990, the U.S. Supreme Court overturned that decision by a vote of 7–2. Chief Justice William H. Rehnquist explained that the Constitution does not provide any wholesale exemption from libel "for anything that might be labeled opinion." Thus, Diadun's statements were not protected merely because they appeared in a signed column.

Rehnquist added that the court's earlier ruling that "there is no such thing as a false idea" was not intended to exempt the press from libel suits for everything that might be labeled opinion. Even an opinion, he explained, might imply a false assertion of fact. As an example, Rehnquist said the statement, "In my opinion Jones is a liar," can cause as much damage to reputation as the statement, "Jones is a liar." The court made it clear that simply calling a factual statement an opinion does not make it so. Writers should be careful to distinguish between the two.

The court sent the case back to Ohio for trial, and the Lorain Journal Co. decided to settle it and pay Milkovich $116,000. The case was already 15 years old, and the company's lawyer called the settlement a victory for the paper. He explained that it would have cost more than the $116,000 to continue the legal battle.

Cohen v. Cowles Media Co. In 1991, the U.S. Supreme Court ruled against the media in two major cases. The first case, *Cohen* v. *Cowles Media Co.*, involved two newspapers that revealed the name of a confidential source. Dan Cohen was a public relations practitioner in Minnesota and worked as a consultant to a Republican candidate for governor. During the last days of the campaign, Cohen gave four journalists copies of court records showing that a Democratic candidate for lieutenant governor had been convicted of shoplifting for leaving a store without paying for $6 worth of sewing materials. In return for the information, the reporters agreed to keep Cohen's identity a secret.

Independently of one another, editors at two newspapers, the St. Paul Pioneer Press and the Minneapolis Star Tribune, decided to overrule their reporters and identify Cohen by name. The editors explained that Cohen's identity was an important part of the story. They considered his leak a dirty trick and thought readers should know the derogatory information came from a Republican campaign worker.

The Associated Press also received and used the story, but did not identify Cohen. A television station that received the story never used it.

Cohen lost his job when he was identified as the reporters' source and sued the two newspapers for misrepresentation and breach of contract. A jury in Minnesota ruled in Cohen's favor, awarding him $200,000 in compensatory and $500,000 in punitive damages. The state Court of Appeals upheld the $200,000 in compensatory damages, but not the punitive damages. The Minnesota Supreme Court dismissed the compensatory damages, too. It explained that "enforcement of the promise of confidentiality . . . would violate defendants' First Amendment rights."

By a vote of 5–4, however, the U.S. Supreme Court ruled that news organizations can be held liable for damages when they break their promises and reveal the names of confidential sources. Justice Byron White wrote the court's decision and explained that the First Amendment does not grant the press any special right to break its promises. Also, Minnesota's breach-of-contract law did not unfairly target or single out the news media, but applied equally to everyone.

Masson v. The New Yorker Co. In 1991, the U.S. Supreme Court ruled that the Constitution does not protect journalists who deliberately change or falsify quotations in a way that changes their meaning and harms a person's reputation.

Writer Janet Malcolm recorded 40 hours of conversation with a psychoanalyst, Jeffrey M. Masson, then wrote a critical profile that appeared as a series in The New Yorker magazine. Malcolm later expanded the series into a book.

Masson filed a $10 million libel suit against Malcolm, charging that she had made up some quotations attributed to him. They were boastful, arrogant statements. In one, Masson supposedly called himself an "intellectual gigolo." In another, he supposedly called himself "the greatest analyst who ever lived."

Malcolm denied that she had made any significant changes in Masson's words, but the quotations were not on her tapes. Masson said they came from unrecorded conversations during which she took notes.

Lower courts dismissed Masson's suit on the grounds that the quotations, even if invented, were a rational interpretation of Masson's views. The U.S. Supreme Court disagreed. It ruled that the First Amendment does not protect writers who deliberately fabricate quotations that are materially different from a speaker's actual words. The court explained that writers do not have "the freedom to place statements in their subjects' mouths without fear of liability."

The court added, however, that not every misquotation is libelous. While writing the court's decision, Justice Anthony Kennedy explained, "Writers and reporters by necessity alter what people say, at the very least to eliminate grammatical and syntactical infelicities."

Thus, the court's ruling protects journalists who make honest errors and even deliberate changes that do not cause a "material change" in a quotation's meaning. Because the court condemned only altered quotes that "differ materially" from the speaker's meaning, some journalists viewed its ruling as a victory for the press.

Libel's Chilling Effect

The high cost of libel suits has a chilling effect on the media. Even the threat of a libel suit may make the media more timid. While larger media, such as the CBS television network, are able to protect themselves, smaller newspapers and broadcasting stations are more vulnerable. A single libel suit could force the smaller media into bankruptcy. To avoid this, some editors now censor themselves. They avoid publishing investigatory stories or remove the stories' most controversial details. Even book publishers seem frightened by the threat of libel. Many now edit their manuscripts to avoid anything even potentially dangerous.

Twenty years ago, the jury in a successful libel case awarded the plaintiff an average of $20,000. The first million-dollar verdict was awarded in 1976. By the 1990s, the *average* award was close to $2.2 million.

However, plaintiffs rarely collect that much. Recent studies show that 74 percent of all the libel suits filed against the media never reach a jury. Newspapers lose 64 percent of the libel suits that do reach a jury; but at least 75 percent of the jury awards are overturned on appeal. Another 10 percent are substantially reduced, to an average of about $60,000.

The media can protect themselves by purchasing libel insurance, but it is expensive. Many libel policies have deductibles that require newspapers to pay the first $20,000 or $30,000. Due to rising legal costs, some insurance companies also require newspapers to pay 20 percent of *all* their legal costs, even beyond the $20,000 or $30,000 deductibles.

The Alton (Ill.) Telegraph, a daily with a circulation of 37,831, was forced into bankruptcy in 1981 by a libel suit resulting from a memo that it never published. Two of the newspaper's reporters sent a Justice Department lawyer a memo which said that their sources linked a local building contractor to the underworld. The charge was never substantiated, and the newspaper never published a story about it. However, when the contractor learned about the memo, he sued the Telegraph, and a jury awarded him $9.2 million, the largest amount a daily newspaper had ever been ordered to pay in a libel suit. The case was settled out of court for $1.4 million. Bankruptcy laws allowed the Telegraph to continue publication throughout the litigation, and the settlement enabled it to remain in business.

Similarly, a California jury ordered the National Enquirer to pay actress Carol Burnett $1.6 million. The newspaper reported that:

> At a Washington restaurant, a boisterous Carol Burnett had a loud argument with another diner, Henry Kissinger. She traipsed around the place offering everyone a bite of her dessert. But Carol really raised eyebrows when she accidentally knocked a glass of wine over one diner and started giggling instead of apologizing. The guy wasn't amused and "accidentally" spilled a glass of water over Carol's dress.

Miss Burnett complained that the story was false, and the National Enquirer published a correction. Nevertheless, she sued the newspaper for libel, and a jury awarded her $300,000 in actual damages and $1.3 million in punitive damages. Witnesses testified that Miss Burnett had not been boisterous, had not argued, had not traipsed around and had not offered "everyone" a bite of her dessert. Moreover, she is a teetotaler, and the story implied that she was tipsy.

Many Americans consider the National Enquirer a sensational, even a disreputable, newspaper, and its story obviously contained several errors. But should any newspaper, regardless of its popularity, be ordered to pay $1.6 million because of the publication of a single story? Columnist James J. Kilpatrick said he was not concerned about the National Enquirer, "a penny-dreadful magazine that has grown fat on journalistic garbage." But he feared that "an award of $1.6 million is simply grotesque. The Enquirer's earnings reportedly are slightly under $2 million a year. Two or three such verdicts, and it's goodbye Enquirer." (A judge later reduced the award.)

Even newspapers that win libel suits may find their victories prohibitively expensive. Consider The Milkweed, a monthly newsletter that reports on the milk marketing industry for dairy farmers. The Eastern Milk Producers Cooperative filed a $20 million libel suit against the newsletter, which had only 1,200 subscribers. Eastern, one of the largest dairy cooperatives in the Northeast, charged that the newsletter contained defamatory and inaccurate statements, including a prediction that the cooperative would lose more than $10 million. A federal judge dismissed the suit, but the newsletter's editor and publisher, Peter Hardin, feared that he was "in danger of winning the war but losing the peace." His legal expenses and other defense costs were nearly $20,000, or more than half the newsletter's annual income.

Journalists are most concerned about the huge sums that some juries continue to award in punitive damages. In 1990, the Philadelphia Inquirer lost a $34 million libel suit: $2.5 million in compensatory and $31.5 million in punitive damages. If upheld, it will become the largest amount a news organization has ever been ordered to pay a defendant. The Inquirer plans to appeal, but the process is long and costly.

The largest damage award to be upheld on appeal is $2.77 million. A former judge named Richard DiSalle sued the Pittsburgh Post-Gazette after it reported that he had conspired to falsify a client's will. DiSalle won the case, and the Post-Gazette was ordered to pay the $2.77 million to DiSalle, his wife and their lawyer. The award included $210,000 in compensatory damages and 10 times that much—$2 million—in punitive damages, plus $561,000 in interest.

The Post-Gazette tried to appeal the verdict to the U.S. Supreme Court. The newspaper wanted the court to declare that punitive damages in libel cases are unconstitutional under the First Amendment. The court, however, declined to review the case.

The Post-Gazette said it would have to borrow money to pay DiSalle. "We just don't keep that kind of money lying around," said the paper's general manager. "It's certainly going to take some belt-tightening." Nevertheless, the newspaper's editor vowed that he would not let the size of the verdict hurt the newspaper's coverage of the news.

Why Are the Media So Often Sued for Libel?

Americans seem to believe that the media are too large, powerful, arrogant, sensational, inaccurate and irresponsible. Consequently, people are more willing to sue the media for libel. But libel suits are part of a trend toward more litigation. More Americans are also suing doctors for malpractice and manufacturers for injuries caused by defective products. Even lawyers are experiencing rising malpractice insurance costs as their own clients sue them.

People are outraged when the media publish stories critical of them. They file most libel suits to restore their reputations and to obtain some compensation for the harm they have suffered. In court, the plaintiffs usually claim that their reputations were ruined or their careers destroyed. Jurors seem to sympathize with the plaintiffs, especially when a story is obviously mistaken or unfair. The plaintiffs may hope to win millions of dollars and feel they have nothing to lose. They can engage attorneys to represent them on a contingency basis. If their cases fail, the plaintiffs pay their attorneys nothing. If they win, the attorneys receive a share of their award or settlement.

Other libel suits—a growing number—are being filed by public officials. The officials may realize that public opinion is shifting in their favor (and against the media). Also, some officials may want to punish or intimidate the media.

City council members, legislators, judges, mayors, governors and other public officials are increasingly bringing suits against the media, sometimes for amounts far greater than the net worth of those media, in litigations that can drag on for eight to 10 years, even before the appeal process starts.

However, the media are not the only victims. More libel suits—perhaps 1,000 a year—are being filed against private citizens and other institutions, often by public officials. Anyone can be sued: a citizen who accuses the police of brutality, an environmental group that accuses a developer of pollution or a politician who accuses a rival of corruption.

Avoiding and Discouraging Libel Suits

Journalists can avoid libel suits by striving to be fairer and more accurate. When they do make a mistake, they should admit their error and publish a correction as quickly as possible. Researchers at the University of Iowa interviewed plaintiffs involved in libel suits during a 10-year period and found that more than half of the suits could have been avoided. The plaintiffs said that when they first went to the media to complain, they were insulted or ignored. The Iowa study also found that many plaintiffs did not care about the money they might win. They filed the suits to protect or restore their reputations or to punish the media.

Some newspapers assign a single individual, called an "ombudsman" or "reader representative," to handle all the complaints they receive. The ombudsman is usually an experienced and impartial editor who investigates the complaints and has the power to publish a correction or retraction whenever a newspaper has erred.

To discourage libel suits, newspapers are also filing more countersuits. As a matter of policy, The Charleston (W. Va.) Gazette files a countersuit whenever it considers a libel suit frivolous or an attempt to intimidate it. After countersuing for malicious prosecution, the Gazette received a $12,500 settlement from a lawyer. In another countersuit, also filed against a lawyer, the Hollywood (Fla.) Sun-Tattler won $25,097 in legal fees and court costs.

A third countersuit, filed in California, was even more successful for the media. The Port Reyes Light, a weekly with a circulation of 3,100, won a Pulitzer Prize for a series of articles about Synanon, a drug rehabilitation center. Synanon responded by suing the Light's publisher, David Mitchell, and his former wife, Cathy. Four libel suits filed against the Light demanded a total of more than $1 billion. The Mitchells countersued, charging that Synanon's libel suits were attempts at harassment and intimidation. Synanon settled out of court, reportedly paying the Mitchells $100,000 for "defamation, abuse of process and malicious prosecution." As part of the settlement, both sides dropped their lawsuits.

To avoid libel suits and to protect the reputation of innocent persons, reporters rarely suggest that anyone mentioned in a news story was negligent or guilty of a crime. Reporters can say that a person has been arrested and charged with a crime (a fact that is easily proved), but not that the person actually committed the crime. If an automobile accident injured several people, journalists would report only that two cars collided; few would attempt to determine which driver was responsible for the collision. That is the job of the police and the courts. Even if several witnesses said one driver was drunk and sped through a stop sign, journalists normally would not report their allegations. The driver must be presumed innocent until convicted in a court of law, not by the people standing on a street corner:

> LIBELOUS: Thomas was drunk when his car sped through the stop sign and struck the van.
> REVISED: Police charged Thomas with failure to stop for a red light, speeding and drunken driving.

If the police did not file any charges against Thomas, the allegations could not be reported. Similarly, newspapers could not safely report:

> Sheriff Gus DiCesari said he caught two thieves, William Johnson and Marvin Wilke, both of 2107 N. Ninth St., red-handed as they broke into a service station at 802 Jefferson Ave. last night.

The sentence calls the men thieves, yet the only proof of that is the sheriff's statement. The men are not public figures, there has been no official governmental proceeding, and they have not been convicted by a judge or jury. If the men sued a newspaper after it reported the sheriff's allegations, the newspaper would be required to prove that the men were thieves, not just that the sheriff said they were. Yet the sheriff might be mistaken, charges against the men might be reduced or dropped, or a jury might find the men innocent. Reporters could avoid a libel suit by reporting only that the suspects had been arrested and charged with the crime:

> Sheriff Gus DiCesari charged William Johnson and Marvin Wilke, both of 2107 N. Ninth St., with breaking into a service station last night.
> DiCesari said a service station at 802 Jefferson Ave. was broken into and $80 was taken from a cash drawer.

As rewritten, the story no longer reports that Johnson and Wilke are guilty, only that a service station was broken into and that they have been charged with the crime—again, facts that are easily proved.

Newspapers will not usually report the charges that one private citizen makes about another. The charges are likely to be libelous and, in most cases, of little interest to the public. Charges voiced during family disputes, including divorces, are among the most common examples. Women beaten by their boyfriends or husbands often call the police and, if newspapers reported their allegations and were later sued for libel, they would be forced to rely on the women's testimony. Yet the men would be likely to deny their charges, making the situation one person's word against another's; moreover, some women might be afraid to testify against the men.

Thus, reporters who write stories that damage another person's reputation must exercise extreme caution. They might ask themselves: "Is this story true, and can I prove its truth in a courtroom?" "Is the person involved a public figure or a public official?" "Was the person involved in an official governmental proceeding, such as a trial or a legislative session?" If reporters are unable to answer "yes" to at least one of those questions (that is, if they are unable to rely on the defenses of truth, privilege or fair comment), they should eliminate the libelous comments from their stories or kill the stories.

Alternatives to Libel Suits

Many journalists would like the courts to order the losers in every libel suit to pay the winners' legal fees. Journalists believe that fewer people would file frivolous suits if, after losing, they were ordered to pay the media's legal fees.

Other journalists would like the courts to make it impossible for any public official to sue the media for libel. A few justices on the U.S. Supreme Court—but never a majority—have advocated this sweeping doctrine.

Journalists have also proposed less costly alternatives to libel suits. The legal system might be changed so that plaintiffs sue not to recover damages, but only to determine a story's truth or falsity. The plaintiffs who won their cases would be entitled to a retraction and their legal costs, but not huge damage awards. However, none of the plaintiffs—not even public ones—would have to prove that the media acted with malice.

Other journalists and legal scholars want judges to negotiate more pretrial settlements, or to have more libel cases taken out of courtrooms and arbitrated by some other means. Again, the emphasis might be on retractions and the correction of errors rather than on the award of damages. By avoiding the legal system, cases might be decided in a few weeks rather than years. Moreover, neither side would have to pay thousands of dollars in legal fees.

Other journalists are turning to their state legislatures for help. For example, the South Carolina Press Association supported a bill that would have limited punitive damages in the state to $250,000. However, that type of remedy seems unlikely to succeed. People libeled by the media believe they have a right to some compensation for the harm to their reputations, and other Americans sympathize with them. Americans are unlikely to support legislation that seems to favor the media rather than the citizens they libel.

A few trials have already ended with verdicts that cleared the plaintiffs' reputations but awarded them only a token sum. In 1956, William Shockley shared the Nobel Prize for physics. Shockley's interests later shifted to genetics, and he concluded that overbreeding among the "genetically disadvantaged" was responsible for a general decline in intelligence. Shockley also concluded that blacks are genetically inferior in intelligence to whites. To improve the population, he proposed a voluntary sterilization plan. Shockley suggested that people with low IQs might be paid as an incentive to be sterilized. Shockley also proposed sterilizing people with genetically transmitted disorders, such as hemophilia and sickle-cell anemia. In 1980, a health and science writer for the Atlanta Constitution wrote that "the Shockley program was tried in Germany during World War II." Shockley called the comparison a "damnable, evil lie," and filed a $1.25 million libel suit against the Constitution and its writer, Roger Witherspoon. Shockley charged the Constitution with malice, arguing that it knew, at the time it published Witherspoon's story, that it was false. After deliberating 3½ hours, the jury concluded that Shockley had been libeled—but awarded him only $1 for the harm to his reputation.

PRIVACY

Americans' right to privacy has been defined as "the right to be let alone." Writer Bruce W. Sanford explains, "Whereas the law of libel protects primarily a person's character and reputation, the right of privacy protects primarily a person's peace of mind, spirit, sensibilities and feelings."

The right of privacy is relatively new and, like the nation's libel laws, requires courts to balance two conflicting values: newspapers' right to gather and report the news, and citizens' right to prevent the unwarranted and unauthorized publication of facts about their private lives.

For years, there was no legal right to privacy in the United States. When sensational news stories about his private social affairs angered Samuel D. Warren, a Boston attorney, he and his law partner, Louis D. Brandeis (who later became a Supreme Court justice), submitted an article to the Harvard Law Review in 1890. The article denounced sensational "yellow journalism," charging that, "The press is overstepping in every direction the obvious bounds of propriety and decency." The article argued that individuals have a right to privacy and that invasions of their privacy subject them "to mental pain and distress, far greater than could be inflicted by mere bodily injury." After publication of this article, courts slowly began to recognize a right to privacy, and some states adopted new laws to protect that right.

In 1902, however, a young woman in Albany, N.Y., learned that her picture was being used without her consent on posters for Franklin Mills flour. She sued for an invasion of her privacy but lost. A court of appeals explained that she could not collect any money from the company because there was no law or precedent which established a right of privacy. In 1903, New York adopted the nation's first privacy law, but the law simply prohibited the use of a person's name or likeness for advertising.

The right of privacy is not mentioned in the U.S. Constitution, but the Supreme Court has recognized a constitutional right to privacy. Writers Harold L. Nelson and Dwight L. Teeter explain:

> Although privacy was not mentioned by the Constitution by name, its first eight amendments, plus the Fourteenth Amendment, include the right to be secure against unreasonable search and seizure and the principle of due process of law. Taken together with the Declaration of Independence's demands for the right to "life, liberty and the pursuit of happiness," it can be seen that the men who founded the nation had a lively concern for something like the "right to be let alone."

Types of Violations of Privacy

The law of privacy has been divided into four separate areas of law, called "torts" or "civil wrongs." What may be a proper defense for the news media in one area of privacy may not work in another. For example, publishing private facts about a person's life is not a wrong until publication occurs, but in intrusion the wrong occurs at the time of an intrusive act by the media.

The four tort areas of privacy are: (1) intrusion, (2) publication of private information, (3) false-light privacy and (4) appropriation.

Intrusion. Reporters cannot intrude on an individual's private affairs or property. Intrusion often involves some type of physical surveillance: the use of tape recorders, wiretaps, telephoto lenses and other electronic eavesdropping devices to spy on individuals in private places, such as their homes or offices. The offense occurs at the moment of intrusion, so it may not involve the actual publication of any information. Most intrusion cases do not involve the media because they are unlikely to use wiretaps and other surveillance devices.

Publication of Private Information. The media cannot publish embarrassing information about the life of a private citizen, regardless of whether that information is true. For example, they cannot publish facts about an individual's health, idiosyncrasies or sexual habits. The media are freer to discuss the private lives of public figures and public officials.

False-Light Privacy. Courts have ruled that the media cannot publish anything that would mislead the public about an individual or place an individual in a "false light."

Falsity may occur when reporters fictionalize a true story in an effort to make it more interesting or dramatic. The story does not have to harm an individual's reputation. If it suggests that an individual said or did something the person never actually said or did, it casts that person in a false light.

Appropriation. Finally, the media cannot use an individual's name or image in advertisements, nor for any other commercial purposes, without that individual's permission.

Defenses Against Privacy Suits

Truth is not an adequate defense in privacy cases; however, newspapers sued for an invasion of privacy can defend themselves by proving that a story was newsworthy or that the plaintiff consented to its publication.

The primary defense in privacy cases is "newsworthiness." Courts are reluctant to punish newspapers for reporting the truth and have been quite liberal in defining the term. So newspapers normally enjoy a broad freedom to publish whatever they want about people, so long as they can show that the topic interests the public.

Newspapers are also free to publish the names and photographs of public officials and public figures and even to discuss their private lives. Private citizens who become involved in newsworthy events or in other matters of public interest, whether willingly or unwillingly, also forfeit their right to privacy. In addition, newspapers normally have the right to take photographs in any public place and to publish those photographs, regardless of whom or what they show.

Finally, people who consent to an invasion of their privacy cannot later sue the media for an invasion of privacy. However, it may be difficult for the media to obtain an individual's consent or to prove that an individual gave that consent. People may consent to publication of a story or photograph but later revoke that consent, or they may attach certain restrictions to publication of a story or a photograph.

Court Decisions

Few privacy cases have reached the U.S. Supreme Court, but state courts have ruled on several cases. In 1972, for example, Jacqueline Kennedy Onassis, widow of President John F. Kennedy, sued photographer Ron Galella for intrusion, and a New York court found that his constant surveillance and interference in her daily life violated her privacy. For years, Galella had followed Mrs. Onassis everywhere. Her lawsuit charged that he had once jumped from behind a wall, frightening her young son and causing the boy to lose control of his bike; had pursued Mrs. Onassis into the lobby of a friend's apartment building; had chased her at dangerous speeds in a car; had fired flashbulbs suddenly on lonely black nights; and had cruised so close as she was swimming that she feared being cut by his boat's propeller. The court found that:

> He was like a shadow: everywhere she went he followed her and engaged in offensive conduct; nothing was sacred to him, whether plaintiff went to church, funeral services, theatre, school, restaurant or aboard a yacht in a foreign land. While defendant denied so deporting himself, his admissions clearly spell out his harassment of her and her children.

As a result of the lawsuit, the court ordered Galella to keep at least 25 feet away from Mrs. Onassis and 30 feet from her children and to keep from blocking their movements or from doing anything else that might harm or endanger them.

An earlier privacy case involved a former child prodigy. William James Sidis had attracted national attention when he graduated from Harvard in 1910 at the age of 16. In 1937, The New Yorker magazine published a brief biographical sketch describing Sidis' life since then, revealing that he had held several menial jobs. The article was accurate, but Sidis sued The New Yorker for invading his privacy. The court ruled against Sidis, explaining that:

> He had cloaked himself in obscurity but his subsequent history containing as it did the answer to the question of whether or not he had fulfilled his early promise, was still a matter of public concern. The article . . . sketched the life of an unusual personality, and it possessed considerable popular news interest.

However, in another invasion of privacy suit, a woman sued a newspaper after it published a picture showing her leaving the fun house at a county fair. A photographer took the picture the moment a jet of air blew her dress up over her head. She charged that publication of the picture caused her immense embarrassment and that it was only minimally newsworthy. The court found in her favor (*Daily Times Democrat* vs. *Graham*, 1962).

Another woman won a $3,000 privacy suit against Time magazine. The woman had been admitted to a Kansas City hospital because of an unusual disease: she ate constantly but still lost weight. A photographer took her picture against her will in the hospital. Time published the picture and called her a "starving glutton" (*Barber* vs. *Time, Inc.*, 1948).

Other privacy cases have involved fictionalization. A newspaper legally published a photograph showing a 10-year-old girl who had been struck by a careless motorist. Twenty months later, the Saturday Evening Post used the same photograph to illustrate a story about children injured because of their own carelessness. The Saturday Evening

The Albuquerque Tribune published this photograph along with a series of articles titled, "Gallup: A Town Under the Influence." The series explored the problem of alcoholism among Indians who live in or near Gallup, N.M., and this photo shows a 15-year-old girl who died in a car wreck after a six-day drinking binge, a beer can still clasped in her hand. Mike Davis, The Tribune's picture editor explains, "The decision to run this photo was an easy one, once we determined the focus of the story: to show the effects of alcohol on the population in and around Gallup. Lots of publications had done passing reportage on the place but none sought to expose the effects to the extent that we did. When the loss of human life is at the heart of a story, a publication has to somehow depict the loss." Legally then the newspaper was free to publish this picture. It involves a topic that is newsworthy, and it accurately depicts the scene.

Post was found liable for damages because it placed the child in a false light as a careless pedestrian (*Leverton* vs. *Curtis Publishing Co.,* 1951).

The U.S. Supreme Court ruled on its first privacy case involving the news media in 1967 but was closely split. James J. Hill, his wife and children were held hostage in their home by three escaped convicts but were released, unharmed, after 19 hours. Less than a year later, a novel titled "The Desperate Hours" described a family of four held hostage in its home by three escaped convicts. However, the convicts in the fictional story treated the hostages more violently. The book was made into a play and then into a movie.

Life magazine reported that the play described the Hill family's ordeal. Moreover, Life published several photographs staged in the Hills' former home. Hill sued for invasion of privacy, charging that the article "was intended to, and did, give the impression that the play mirrored the Hill family's experience, which to the knowledge of the defendant . . . was false and untrue." Attorneys representing Life responded that the topic was of legitimate news interest; however, a jury disagreed and awarded the Hills $75,000.

On appeal, the Supreme Court weighed the family's right to privacy against the media's First Amendment right to publish. Justice Brennan, who wrote the court's majority opinion, said that truth is a complete defense for reports about newsworthy people or events, and that Hill was a newsworthy person "substantially without a right to privacy" regarding his hostage experience. However, Brennan added that Hill was entitled to sue for an invasion of privacy if he could prove that Life fictionalized and exploited the story for commercial benefit. The court then applied the malice rule from *New York Times* v. *Sullivan,* and Hill lost the case because the court found no evidence of malice. Justice Brennan explained:

> We hold that the constitutional protections for speech and press preclude the application of the New York statute to redress false reports of matters of public interest in the absence of proof that the defendant published the report with knowledge of its falsity or in reckless disregard of the truth.

Justices Hugo Black and William Douglas concurred with the majority and were even more outspoken in their defense of the press' freedom:

> Life's conduct here was at most a mere understandable and incidental error of fact in reporting a newsworthy event. One does not have to be a prophet to foresee that judgments like the one we here reverse can frighten and punish the press so much that publishers will cease trying to report news in a lively and readable fashion as long as there is—and there always will be—doubt as to the complete accuracy of the newsworthy facts. Such a consummation hardly seems consistent with the clearly expressed purpose of the Founders to guarantee the press a favored spot in our free society.

THE FREE PRESS/FAIR TRIAL DILEMMA

Another constitutional dilemma arises when journalists report local crimes. Journalists believe that the public has a "right to know," and that the news media have an obligation to keep citizens fully informed about important events that occur in their communities. The media report local crimes because they are important and because they interest readers. In addition, citizens are entitled to know whether their local judicial systems are working properly—whether honest citizens are being protected and whether criminals are being apprehended, convicted and given appropriate punishments.

This photograph demonstrates the dangers of fictionalization. The original cutline accurately described its content, explaining that, "When parents reach old age, they and their children (like this 98-year-old man and his daughter) sometimes experience a sharp role reversal as children take care of their parents." However, the woman shown in the picture sued a national magazine that later used the photograph to illustrate an article about Alzheimer's disease.

However, attorneys and other court officials are concerned about the effect of news stories on the reputations of defendants in criminal cases and on the minds of potential jurors. The Sixth Amendment to the U.S. Constitution guarantees that "in all criminal prosecutions, the accused shall enjoy the right to a speedy and public trial by an impartial jury." Jurors should not be influenced by the content of news stories, nor by anything else said or done outside a courtroom. But news stories about a sensational crime may convince some potential jurors that a suspect is guilty. Moreover, the stories may contain information that would not be admissible as evidence during a trial—for example, a description of a suspect's prior criminal record or the results of a lie detector test.

Journalists call this conflict between the public's right to know and a defendant's right to a fair trial the "free press/fair trial" controversy.

Supreme Court Decisions

In 1961, for the first time in U.S. history, the Supreme Court overturned the conviction of a criminal in a state court solely because prejudicial publicity had made it impossible for him to obtain a fair trial. Justice Thomas Clark, who wrote the majority decision, declared that jurors do not have to be totally ignorant of the facts and issues in a case: "It is sufficient if the juror can lay aside his impression or opinion and render a verdict based on the evidence presented in court." But in *Irvin* v. *Dowd,* the buildup of prejudice was clear and convincing.

Parolee Leslie Irvin had been arrested and charged with six murders. A government prosecutor issued press releases calling him "Mad Dog Irvin" and reporting that he had confessed to all six murders. The court called 430 people as potential jurors, but 375 said they already believed Irvin was guilty. Of the 12 jurors selected to hear Irvin's case, eight said they believed he was guilty even before the trial began. Not unexpectedly, the jury convicted Irvin, and he was sentenced to death. Irvin was granted a new trial after the Supreme Court overturned his conviction. He was convicted for a second time but was sentenced to life imprisonment rather than to death.

A second case involving prejudicial publicity became even more notorious. Dr. Samuel Sheppard, a Cleveland osteopath, was accused of murdering his pregnant wife, Marilyn, on July 4, 1954. Sheppard told police he was sleeping on a couch in their lakeside home, heard his wife scream and went upstairs to help. According to Sheppard, he struggled with his wife's assailant but was knocked unconscious. When Sheppard regained consciousness, he found his wife on a bedroom floor, bludgeoned to death.

News stories reported that Sheppard refused to take a lie detector test, and editorials charged that someone was "getting away with murder." Other editorials asked why Sheppard was not in jail. Authorities held the inquest in a school gymnasium, and local television stations broadcast it live. At the start of Sheppard's trial, newspapers published the names and addresses of all his jurors, thus exposing them to the public.

Much of the space inside the courtroom during Sheppard's trial was set aside for journalists, including a large area inside the bar. Normally, that area is reserved for the defendant, attorneys and other court officials. The presence of journalists inside the bar made it difficult for Sheppard to talk confidentially with his attorney. Noise created by the journalists moving in and out of the courtroom also made it difficult for everyone to hear. Moreover, almost everyone involved in the case talked to journalists outside the courtroom. Some of the information journalists received and published incriminated Sheppard but never was introduced as evidence during his trial. The judge, who was running for re-election, did nothing to correct these problems.

Sheppard was convicted of murder and sentenced to life in prison. An appellate court called his trial a Roman holiday and an orgy of press sensationalism. In 1966, the case reached the U.S. Supreme Court, which threw out Sheppard's conviction, declaring that massive and highly inflammatory pretrial publicity had violated his right to a fair trial. Justice Thomas Clark noted: "Newsmen took over practically the entire courtroom, hounding most of the participants in the trial, especially Sheppard." The Supreme Court blamed the judge for allowing such a "carnival atmosphere" to prevail during Sheppard's trial.

In 1963 the Supreme Court reversed the conviction of a Louisiana defendant whose interrogation was filmed, then broadcast by a local television station. The defendant, Wilbert Rideau, was charged with robbing a bank, kidnapping three bank employees and killing one of them. The morning after Rideau's arrest, he was interrogated by the sheriff, and television station photographers filmed the 20-minute session. Rideau admitted the robbery, kidnapping and murder, and a television station broadcast his confession three times during the next three days. Three of Rideau's jurors saw and heard the confession; two other jurors were deputy sheriffs. Rideau was convicted and sentenced to death, but the Supreme Court overturned his conviction, saying, "Any subsequent court proceeding in a community so pervasively exposed to such a spectacle could be but a hollow formality."

Attempts to Resolve the Dilemma

Since the Sheppard case, judges in dozens of cities have met with journalists and attorneys to formulate and adopt voluntary guidelines to prevent the publication of prejudicial information. Judges, prosecutors and defense attorneys can question potential jurors to determine whether they are impartial or whether they have been influenced by the content of news stories. After jury selection, judges can instruct the

Reporters and photographers smoked, played cards, and swapped yarns as they lounged in the courtroom, waiting for the jury to finish its deliberations in the trial of Dr. Samuel Sheppard.

jurors to avoid news stories and conversations about the cases they are scheduled to hear.

Judges can take several additional precautions to minimize the impact of prejudicial publicity, but each precaution creates new problems. Judges can postpone sensational trials until the emotions inflamed by prejudicial publicity have subsided. But if a trial is postponed, the defendant will not receive a speedy trial and may have to spend several months in jail. Judges can grant a change of venue, moving sensational trials to distant locations that did not receive as much prejudicial publicity. But a change of venue is expensive, since the government must pay for some participants' transportation, room and board. As another alternative, judges can sequester a jury. That is, if a trial is likely to attract extreme publicity, judges can lock up the jury so that during the entire trial, the jurors eat and live together, usually at a hotel near the courthouse. Their telephone calls, even visits from their families, may be monitored by court officials. Court officials also screen all the news media they receive, eliminating any stories about the trial. This procedure, too, is expensive. In addition, it may anger jurors to be kept away from their families and jobs for weeks or months.

During the 1970s, journalists began to complain that some judges were going too far in their efforts to avoid prejudicial publicity. Because of the Supreme Court's apparent mandate in the Sheppard case—because the court clearly stated that judges have a responsibility to protect defendants—judges began to issue "gag orders" forbidding journalists to report some facts.

In 1976, for example, police charged a suspect with murdering six members of a Nebraska family, and Judge Hugh Stuart instructed journalists covering the case not to publish any information about: (1) a confession, (2) statements the suspect had made to other people, (3) a note the suspect had written, (4) some medical testimony at a preliminary hearing and (5) the nature of a sexual assault and the identity of its victim.

In a unanimous decision, the U.S. Supreme Court ruled that the judge had exceeded his authority and that the gag order was unconstitutional. Chief Justice Warren Burger explained, "Any prior restraint on expression comes to this court with a 'heavy presumption against its constitutional validity.' " In writing the majority opinion, Burger added:

> We reaffirm that the guarantees of freedom of expression are not an absolute prohibition under all circumstances, but the barriers to prior restraint remain high and the presumption against its use continues intact. We hold that, with respect to the order entered in this case prohibiting reporting or commentary on judicial proceedings held in public, the barriers have not been overcome; to the extent that this order restrained publication of such material, it is clearly invalid. To the extent that it prohibited publication based on information gained from other sources, we conclude that the heavy burden imposed as a condition to securing a prior restraint was not met and the judgment of the Nebraska Supreme Court is therefore reversed.

Despite that decision, journalists continue to complain that courts are closing more and more judicial proceedings to the public and are gagging other people (not journalists) involved in those proceedings. Some proceedings, such as juvenile and divorce hearings, have long been closed to the public. But recently, judges have also closed preliminary hearings in some criminal cases because they feared that publication of information revealed at those hearings would make it more difficult for the defendants to obtain fair trials. Judges have ordered police officers, prosecutors, defense attorneys and other court officials not to speak to journalists outside a courtroom about some cases. Anyone who violates the orders can be cited for contempt of court.

JOURNALISTS AND THE SUBPOENA

Until the 1960s, government officials rarely subpoenaed journalists. But the 1960s and 1970s were decades of social unrest caused by the civil rights movement, the movement opposing the Vietnam War, women's struggle for equality, changes in the lifestyles of young adults, the growing use of drugs and a variety of other tumultuous transformations in our society. Journalists witnessed those changes and interviewed their participants, including some people suspected of violating state and federal laws.

Government officials began to subpoena reporters to ask for the identity of their sources, and to ask for copies of information they gathered in the form of notes, tape recordings and photographs. Some prosecutors also asked reporters to testify at trials and to describe crimes they had witnessed. The prosecutors were often unable to obtain information in any other way, and they insisted that reporters who possessed information necessary to find, identify or prosecute criminals had an obligation, as citizens, to give that information to the appropriate law enforcement officials.

Journalists disagreed, insisting that their right to gather and report the news is protected by the First Amendment and that such subpoenas interfere with their responsibility to inform the public. Journalists explain that they must protect their sources to obtain confidential information. If they are forced to reveal sources' identities, fewer people will talk to them, thus curtailing the flow of information to the American public. So a new conflict has arisen between reporters' desire to protect their sources and the judicial system's desire to obtain information.

The journalists' demands are not unique. Spouses cannot be required to testify against each other. The relationship between attorneys and their clients is privileged. Relationships between doctors and their patients, and between ministers and penitents, are also privileged in many states. Yet journalists who disobeyed subpoenas and other court orders have been found guilty of contempt of court and sentenced to prison terms—usually indeterminate, with judges saying that the journalists would have to remain in prison until they were ready to identify their sources or to provide other information demanded by prosecutors. In reality, however, few journalists have been kept in jail more than 30 days.

In 1972, a case involving reporter Earl Caldwell reached the U.S. Supreme Court. Caldwell was assigned to The New York Times' bureau in San Francisco and often wrote about the Black Panthers, a militant black organization. Because of his knowledge of the Panthers, Caldwell was ordered to appear before a grand jury investigating the organization and to bring his notes and tape recordings of some interviews. Caldwell refused to appear, saying that even if he did not answer any questions, simply entering the grand jury room would destroy his credibility with the Black Panthers because they would never know what he said or did in the privacy of that room.

In a 5–4 decision, the Supreme Court ruled that journalists can be forced to provide information about criminal activities. It explained that, "The great weight of authority is that newsmen are not exempt from the normal duty of appearing before a grand jury and answering questions relevant to a criminal investigation." Justice Byron R. White, in writing the majority opinion, added:

> The sole issue before us is the obligation of reporters to respond to grand jury subpoenas as other citizens do and answer questions relevant to an investigation into the commission of crime. Citizens generally are not constitutionally immune from grand jury subpoenas; and neither the First Amendment nor other constitutional provisions protects the average citizen from disclosing to a grand jury information that he has received in confidence.

SHIELD LAWS

Journalists do not enjoy many special legal privileges, but "shield laws" are an important exception. Most shield laws are new, adopted because of the recent conflicts between journalists and the nation's judicial system. Courts ruling on those conflicts have said that either state legislatures or the U.S. Congress could adopt new laws to protect a journalist's privilege to withhold information from government officials. At least 26 states have adopted shield laws, and those laws usually protect only journalists, not any other citizens.

The shield laws vary from state to state. Most shield laws are limited; they declare that reporters cannot be forced to reveal the identities of confidential sources. Some shield laws offer more protection, declaring that reporters cannot be forced to reveal the identities of confidential sources, nor to give government officials any other information or materials, such as notes or photographs.

Congress has failed to adopt a federal shield law, perhaps because too many questions remain unanswered. For example: Who is a "journalist"? Should a federal shield law protect only people employed by newspapers and by radio and television stations? Or should it also protect free-lance writers, authors of books and other writers? Also, what should a federal shield law protect—only the identities of sources, or all information journalists gather, including information about serious crimes? Similarly, if Congress adopts a federal shield law, should it apply to every court, or should it be limited to federal courts?

Journalists themselves are divided, and their disagreement may have made Congress more hesitant to act. Some journalists favor a qualified shield law. Others favor an absolute shield law. Still others do not want Congress to adopt any laws involving the news media. They fear that if Congress adopts one law to protect journalists, it later may adopt other laws that limit journalists' freedom. Some journalists insist that a federal shield law is unnecessary because the First Amendment already protects the media. They argue that, despite the Supreme Court's decision in the Caldwell case, the First Amendment protects reporters, and its protection is absolute. Proponents of that argument add that it would be foolish to endorse a qualified shield law if the First Amendment already grants journalists absolute protection.

CENSORSHIP

Another recent decision, *Hazelwood School District* v. *Kuhlmeier,* gave administrators a broad power to censor high school newspapers. In 1988, the U.S. Supreme Court decided, by a vote of 5–3, that administrators can censor high school publications so long as the censorship has a "valid educational purpose."

As part of a journalism class, students at Hazelwood East High School in Missouri wrote about student pregnancies and about the children of divorced parents. Their principal, Robert Reynolds, complained that the first story failed to adequately disguise the identity of several pregnant students, and that the story's references to sexual experiences and birth control were inappropriate for the school's younger students. Reynolds complained that the second story failed to adequately disguise the identity of a parent who was getting divorced. He deleted two pages from the student paper and explained that, because of a printer's deadline, he did not have enough time to ask the students to rewrite their stories.

The Supreme Court's decision, written by Justice Byron White, declared that, "Educators do not offend the First Amendment by exercising editorial control over the style and content of student speech in school-sponsored expressive activities so long as their actions are reasonably related to legitimate pedagogical concerns." Thus, the court will allow school officials to impose "reasonable restrictions on the speech of students, teachers and other members of the school community."

White distinguished between a school's obligation to *tolerate* student speech and its obligation to *promote* such speech. In this case, the school funded and published the paper. Under those circumstances, White said, school officials had a right to set and maintain standards—especially since the paper was produced by a class that was subject to the supervision of teachers and administrators.

A dissenter, Justice William Brennan, called Reynolds' conduct an act of "brutal censorship." Brennan complained that Reynolds "violated the First Amendment's prohibitions against censorship of any student expression that neither disrupts classwork nor invades the rights of others." Furthermore, Brennan warned that the majority decision could convert public schools into "enclaves of totalitarianism. . . ."

Journalists who agreed with Brennan's dissent complained that the majority decision turned students into second-class citizens. Journalists said the decision seemed to say that students can study the First Amendment in high school, but cannot practice it there. Journalists also complained that the decision gave school administrators too much power, and that it would encourage the administrators of other schools to censor controversial stories.

But many daily newspapers, including The New York Times, agreed with the court's decision. Daily newspapers explained that the decision provided a realistic lesson for students. The First Amendment has never given reporters and editors the right to print stories that their publishers do not want to print. The men and women who own the press—not their employees—decide which stories should be published. Newspapers supporting the court's decision added that school boards are no different from other publishers, and that high school students are not entitled to more freedom than working journalists. Thus, students have no right to demand that their stories be printed without editing.

Moreover, newspaper publishers—not their employees—are held responsible for their papers' content. School boards serve as the publishers of student newspapers and can be held responsible for their content. If, for example, a school paper libels someone, the victim is likely to sue the school board, not a poor student.

The case seems unlikely to affect college papers, however. College students are adults, and courts have usually granted them the full protection of the First Amendment.

SUGGESTED READINGS

Articles

America, Anna. "Anatomy of a Libel Suit." *Presstime,* May 1991, pp. 6–10.

Anderson, Mary A. "Access to Information: In the Realm of Media Law, Attention Has Been Slowly Shifting from Libel to Closed Civil Court Proceedings and Sealed Documents." *Presstime,* March 1989, pp. 6–8.

Novak, Viveca, and William E. Francois. "Fighting Back on the Libel Front." *Columbia Journalism Review,* March/Apr. 1989, pp. 46–50.

Ridge, George W. "Under Oath: Reporters Can Prepare for the Day They're Called to the Witness Stand." *Presstime,* Dec. 1985, pp. 18–20.

Salisbury, Bill. "Burning the Source: The St. Paul Pioneer Press Reporter Tells How He Promised Dan Cohen Confidentiality, Then Exposed Him on Orders of an Editor. The Case Wound up in the Supreme Court." *Washington Journalism Review,* Sept. 1991, pp. 18–22.

"Trying to Gain Access to Information Is Replacing Libel as Newspapers' Leading Reason for Going to Court." *ASNE Bulletin,* Dec. 1988, pp. 8–12.

Books

Adler, Renata. *Reckless Disregard: Westmoreland v. CBS et al.; Sharon v. Time.* New York: Knopf, 1986.

Bezanson, Randall P., Gilbert Cranberg, and John Soloski. *Libel Law and the Press: Myth and Reality.* New York: Free Press, 1987.

Campbell, Douglas S. *The Supreme Court and the Mass Media: Selected Cases, Summaries and Analyses.* New York: Praeger, 1990.

Denniston, Lyle W. *The Reporter and the Law: Techniques of Covering the Courts.* New York: Hastings House, 1980.

Devol, Kenneth S., ed., *Mass Media and the Supreme Court.* 4th ed. New York: Hastings House, 1990.

Diamond, Sidney A. *Trademark Problems and How to Avoid Them.* 2nd ed. Chicago: Crain Communications, 1981.

Dill, Barbara. *The Journalist's Handbook on Libel and Privacy: The Most Comprehensive and Up-to-Date Guide to Avoiding Lawsuits.* New York: Free Press, 1986.

François, William E. *Mass Media Law and Regulation.* 5th ed. Ames, IA: Iowa State University Press, 1990.

Franklin, Marc A., and David A. Anderson. *Cases and Materials on Mass Media Law.* 4th ed. Westbury, NY: Foundation Press, 1990.

Galvin, Katherine M. *Media Law: A Legal Handbook for the Working Journalist.* Berkeley, CA: Nolo, 1984.

Gerald, Edward J. *News of Crime: Courts and Press in Conflict*. Westport, CT: Greenwood Press, 1983.

Gillmor, Donald M., Jerome A. Barron, Todd F. Simon and Herbert A. Terry. *Mass Communication Law: Cases and Comment*. 5th ed. St. Paul, MN: West, 1990.

Hixson, Richard F. *Mass Media and the Constitution: An Encyclopedia of Supreme Court Decisions*. New York: Garland, 1989.

——— . *Privacy in a Public Society: Human Rights in Conflict*. New York: Oxford University Press, 1987.

Holsinger, Ralph. *Media Law*. 2nd ed. New York: McGraw-Hill, 1991.

Hopkins, W. Wat. *Actual Malice: Twenty-Five Years after Times v. Sullivan*. New York: Praeger, 1989.

Ingelhart, Louis E. *Freedom for the College Student Press: Court Cases and Related Decisions Defining the Campus Fourth Estate Boundaries*. Westport, CT: Greenwood Press, 1985.

Littlewood, Thomas B. *Coals of Fire: The Alton Telegraph Libel Case*. Carbondale, IL: Southern Illinois University Press, 1988.

Middleton, Kent, and Bill F. Chamberlain. *The Law of Publication Communication*. 2nd ed. White Plains, NY: Longman, 1991.

Nelson, Harold L., Dwight L. Teeter, and Don R. Le Duc. *Law of Mass Communications: Freedom and Control of Print and Broadcast Media*. 6th ed. Westbury, NY: Foundation Press, 1989.

Pember, Don R. *Mass Media Law*. 5th ed. Dubuque, IA: Wm. C. Brown, 1990.

——— . *Privacy and the Press*. Seattle: University of Washington Press, 1972.

Sanford, Bruce W. *Libel and Privacy Litigation: Prevention and Defenses*. New York: Law & Business/Harcourt Brace Jovanovich, 1985.

Schuetz, Janice, and Kathryn Holmes Snedaker. *Communication and Litigation: Case Studies of Famous Trials*. Carbondale, IL: Southern Illinois University Press, 1988.

Watkins, John J. *The Mass Media and the Law*. Englewood Cliffs, NJ: Prentice Hall, 1990.

Zuckman, Harvey L., Martin J. Gaynes, T. Barton Carter and Juliet Lushbough Dee. *Mass Communications Law in a Nutshell*. 3rd ed. St. Paul, MN: West Publishing, 1988.

QUOTES

The First Amendment does not speak equivocally. It prohibits any law "abridging freedom of speech or of the press." It must be taken as a command of the broadest scope that explicit language, read in the context of a liberty-loving society, will allow.

(Justice Hugo L. Black, U.S. Supreme Court)

Whenever you start nibbling away at freedom of the press, it's hard to know when to stop. We've got to have a free press, whether it's responsible or not.

(Bernard Kilgore, newspaper publisher)

In my opinion, the newspapers are equal to the courts—and sometimes ahead of the courts in our system—in protecting the people's fundamental rights.

(U.S. Sen. Robert F. Kennedy)

NAME _____ CLASS _____ DATE _____

Exercise 1

LIBEL

INSTRUCTIONS: Decide which of the following sentences and paragraphs are potentially libelous. Place a "D" in the space preceding each statement that is dangerous for the media, and an "S" in the space preceding each statement that is safe.

1. _____ The police officers said they shot and killed Ira Andrews, a 41-year-old auto mechanic, because he was rushing toward them with a knife.

2. _____ Testifying during the second day of his trial, Mrs. Andrea Cross said her husband, Lee, never intended to embezzle the $70,000, but that a secretary, Allison O'Hara, persuaded him that their actions were legal. Her husband thought they were borrowing the money, she said, and that they would double it by investing in real estate.

3. _____ Store employees told the police that they detained Martha Jacbos, 23, 1889 32nd St., after she attempted to leave the supermarket with $8 worth of groceries that she allegedly failed to pay for.

4. _____ A 72-year-old woman, Kelli Kasandra of 9847 Eastbrook Lane, has been charged with attempting to pass a counterfeit $20 bill. A convenience store clerk called the police shortly after 8 a.m. today and said that she had received "a suspicious-looking bill." The clerk added that she had written down the license number of a car leaving the store. The police confirmed the fact that the $20 bill was counterfeit and arrested Mrs. Kasandra at her home about an hour later.

5. _____ Margaret Dwyer said a thief, a boy about 14, grabbed her purse as she was walking to her car in a parking lot behind Memorial Hospital. The boy punched her in the face, apparently because she began to scream and refused to let go of her purse. She said he was blond, wore glasses, weighed about 120 pounds and was about 5 feet 6 inches tall.

6. _____ Sheriff's deputies said that Terry Smythe "appeared to have been exceeding the 45 mph speed limit." They also suspect that he may have been drinking. The results of his breath and urinalysis tests are expected in a week.

7. _____ Four police officers teamed up yesterday to arrest a man who sold them crack cocaine. The police arrested Michael Allen, 32, and charged him with the possession, sale and delivery of cocaine.

8. _____ The manager of the Plaza Book Shoppe announced today that it is bankrupt and will close permanently at 5 p.m. Saturday. The store's manager explained: "We still don't know exactly how she managed to do it, but one of our clerks embezzled more than $100,000. In three months since we hired her, she drained all our accounts, so we can't buy any new merchandise; we can't pay for it. We've turned the matter over to the district attorney and are asking other merchants in the area to consider hiring our six other employees. They're good, hard-working people and shouldn't have to suffer like this. It's awful."

9. _____ Police said the victim, Catherine White of 4218 Bell Ave., was too intoxicated to be able to describe her assailant.

NAME _____ CLASS _____ DATE _____

Exercise 2

LIBEL

INSTRUCTIONS: Decide which of the following sentences and paragraphs are potentially libelous. Place a "D" in the space preceding each statement that is dangerous for the media, and an "S" in the space preceding each statement that is safe.

1. _____ "I've never lived in a city where the officials are so corrupt," Joyce Andrews, a Cleveland developer, complained. "If you don't contribute to their campaigns, they won't do anything for you or even talk to you. You have to buy their support."

2. _____ The political scientist said that Americans seem unable to elect a competent president. "Look at who they've elected," she said. "I'm convinced that Lyndon Johnson was a liar. Nixon was a crook. Carter was incompetent, and Reagan was the worst of all: too lazy and senile to be even a mediocre president."

3. _____ The newspaper's restaurant reviewer complained: "I've had poor service before, but nothing this incompetent. The service at The Heritage Inn wasn't just slow; it was awful. When she finally did get to us, the waitress didn't seem to know what was on the menu. Then she brought us the wrong drinks. When we finally got our food, it was cold and tasteless. I wouldn't even feed it to my dog. In fact, my dog wouldn't eat it. The stuff didn't even smell good."

4. _____ Police Chief Barry Kopperud said: "We've been after Guiterman for years. He's the biggest drug dealer in the city, but it took months to gather the evidence and infiltrate his operations. His arrest last night was the result of good police work, and we've got the evidence to send him away for 20 or 30 years."

5. _____ Dennis A. Shatuck, 20, of 532 Third St. was arrested at 1 a.m. and charged with trespassing and possession of a controlled substance. A deputy said he spotted Shatuck parked behind a shopping center, and found him with a small amount of marijuana in his possession.

6. _____ George Adcock reported that he was robbed while withdrawing $50 from an automatic teller outside the First National Bank late Monday. A man, about 20, had been waiting in line behind him. When Adcock withdrew the money, the robber opened his jacket, revealed a shotgun strapped to his shoulder and asked Adcock whether he wanted to die. After taking the $50, the robber ordered Adcock to begin walking south along Grand Avenue.

7. _____ A police officer in your city, George Ruiz, today filed a $100,000 personal injury suit against Albert Tifton, charging that Tifton punched him in the nose last month while the police were responding to a call about a domestic dispute at Tifton's home. "It's the third time I've been hit this year," Ruiz said. "I'm tired of being used as a punching bag by these criminals, and I'm doing what I can to stop it."

8. _____ There was an emergency meeting of about 100 angry parents at the Wisconsin Avenue branch of the YMCA at 8 p.m. yesterday, with its director, Marty Willging, presiding. Willging said he called the meeting to calm the parents' fears and to respond to rumors. A parent asked whether it was true that the YMCA's janitor had been dismissed for molesting several boys. Willging

responded that there had been some unfortunate incidents and the janitor had been discharged, but some of the allegations were exaggerated. When asked whether the police had been called in, Willging answered that they had, and that their investigation is continuing. He assured the parents that the YMCA will see that the matter is resolved appropriately.

Exercise 3

LIBEL

INSTRUCTIONS: The following stories contain information that is potentially libelous. Write a news story for each set of facts, carefully avoiding the danger of libel. Remember that you can report that an individual has been *charged* with a crime, but cannot normally report that an individual is guilty until after that person has been convicted by a judge or jury.

Thus, you should describe each crime, but avoid saying that the person charged with the crime is the person who committed it.

1. Andrew J. Herman, an unemployed accountant, is in jail. The police have charged him with robbing a convenience store of $83. A store clerk, Vivian Hoffman, said Herman entered the store while she was alone shortly after 7 a.m. today and asked for a pack of cigarettes. He then drew a revolver. When he began firing the revolver, she ran into a back room and locked herself in it. The gunman then proceeded to scoop all the money from a cash register and fled on foot. Police arrested Herman driving north on Parkway Drive about 3 miles from the store and charged him with armed robbery.

2. Mildred R. Thistel is a counselor at Roosevelt High School. On Sunday afternoon, she was charged with shoplifting at a local department store. Two clerks told the police that they personally saw Thistel, 41, place a bottle of perfume valued at $32 in her purse and then leave without paying for it. A security officer apprehended Thistel outside the store and held her until police arrived. She was charged with shoplifting and released on $100 bond. School officials declined to immediately comment on her case, saying they need more time to gather information about the matter but that she might be suspended, with pay, until her case is cleared up.

3. Moments after reaching your office today, you received a call from an irate mother: Lisa Kopez of 1067 Eastland Avenue. Mrs. Kopez complained that, yesterday afternoon, her 8-year-old son, Brandon, was beaten by Florence Hendricks, a teacher at Risser Elementary School. "He was spanked and slapped," Mrs. Kopez said of her son. "And he was slapped hard. He was crying when he came home, and you could still see the ruler marks on his buttocks. What his teacher did was against the law; no one has a right to beat children, not even their teachers." Mrs. Kopez further added that she complained to the principal, and if nothing is done about the matter she fully intends to go to the police. When you called the principal, Collette Mejia, she responded: "Mrs. Kopez did call me, and I'm looking into the matter. At this point, it wouldn't be appropriate for me to make any other comments about the matter. I'll be meeting with the teacher involved later today—when she's got a free period. That's all I can say about it at this point in time."

4. Thieves entered a clothing store at the Colonial Shopping Center early today. A report filed by patrolman Wayne Warniky says: "I noticed the suspect, James Wilke, now incarcerated on charges of burglary, at the shopping center, sitting in a parked car in a suspicious manner at 3 a.m. As I drove up, Wilke started to drive away, with his car's headlights still turned off. I proceeded to force Wilke to stop his vehicle and asked him to step out. Several articles visible in the back seat of Wilke's car were identified as items stolen from a cloth-

ing store in the mall, and other perpetrators are also thought to have been involved, since more merchandise is missing from the store. Wilke's accomplices may have escaped while I was questioning him. We think there was also a second vehicle involved and are following several leads in the case."

5. Jack R. Denboar, 40, of 1415 Idaho Avenue, was arrested at 9 p.m. yesterday. The police have charged him with spouse abuse, aggravated assault on a police officer, and resisting arrest with violence. Police reports show that Denboar's wife, Anne, called for help. She told a dispatcher that her husband had beaten her and was threatening to set their house on fire. Officers responding to her call said her husband came to the door, ordered them to leave, and slammed the door shut. He then poked his fist through the window portion of the door, cutting his right fist. While the officers were attempting to subdue Mr. Denboare, Mrs. DenBoare ran out a back door. The officers said that, after entering the premises, they had to wrestle a butcher knife from her husband and subdued him with a chemical spray. They then allowed Mrs. Denboare to return to the house to pick up some clothing, as she was dressed only in a nightgown.

6. The police arrested Russell Kernan, 59, of 168 Lake Street at 3:20 p.m. and charged him with aggravated assault. The police were responding to a call from a 17-year-old boy. The youth said he had been struck by a BB pellet on his left cheek, causing it to bleed. When Officer Allison Biaggi turned onto Lake Street, a group of about 10 juveniles waved at her and informed her that a man in a nearby garage had confronted them with a gun. Biagi then questioned Kernan, and the victims identified him as their assailant. Kernan admitted that he had argued with the juveniles about their behavior and the loud music on their radios, but denied pointing or firing a BB gun at them. Kernan, who is on parole, is being held in the county jail. He was unable to post a $1,000 bond.

7. Police say that a trio of three men broke a 2- by 4-foot hole in the back of a convenience store. An official police report said that two of the men, Marvin Kehoe, 26, 182 West Broadway Road, and Thomas Murhara, 23, 40 West Hiller Avenue, were crawling out of the hole as the police officers responded to an anonymous call reporting a burglary in progress. The two men admitted to the officers that they had been robbing the store and also admitted that there was another person involved who was waiting in a van a short distance away. The third man, Grady Smith, 8213 Perch Street, drove away before the police were able to apprehend him. He was arrested at his home a short time later. The men had 18 six-packs of beer piled outside the hole. Next to the beer were a tire iron, screwdriver, sledge hammer and other burglar tools used to assist in the crime. All three men were charged with burglary.

Exercise 4

LIBEL

INSTRUCTIONS: The following stories contain information that is potentially libelous. Write a news story for each set of facts, carefully avoiding the danger of libel. Remember that you can report that an individual has been *charged* with a crime, but cannot normally report that an individual is guilty until after that person has been convicted by a judge or jury.

Thus, you should describe each crime, but avoid saying that the person charged with the crime is the person who committed it.

1. Police have charged the estranged husband of an elementary school teacher with trying to forcibly kidnap her at gunpoint. The teacher, Tina Marie Alvarez, 28, told the police that her car was parked in a school parking lot, and she was approaching her car—leaving work for the day—at about 3:40 p.m. yesterday afternoon. Her husband, Harold Alvarez, 47, confronted her, she told investigating officers, and ordered her to get into his car, which was parked in the same parking lot. Mrs. Alvarez said she refused, and her husband then proceeded to produce a gun and said, "Get in or I'll blow your head off." Mrs. Alvarez tried to flee, but her husband grabbed her and knocked her down, police said. Mrs. Alvarez told police that her husband held the gun to her ribs and told her that he was going to take her away and that she would learn to love him again. Another teacher, Nancy Webber, 62, 44 East Princeton Street, witnessed the struggle and alerted a school secretary, who immediately called the police. A patrol car happened to be in the neighborhood and reached the school in less than a minute. Apparently hearing their siren as they approached, Alvarez threw his wife to the ground and fled, alone, in his car. His wife's purse, containing $70, was in the car when he fled. He is still at large.

2. There was a public hearing last night in the fellowship hall at Redeemer Lutheran Church, 6400 Hall Road. About 300 people were in attendance, primarily residents of the Deer Run Estates subdivision on Hall Road. They met with developer Richard Haselfe, who last week revealed plans for a shopping center, business park, and apartment complex directly adjacent to the subdivision's northern boundary. Haselfe told the residents that his development would not affect them adversely: that he would leave a 25-foot buffer between the subdivision and his development. "This should be an asset to the neighborhood," he said. "It's going to be a high-class, high-rent development, with a park-like atmosphere and establishments—stores and fine restaurants—that you people will be anxious to patronize." Residents accused him of lowering their property values and destroying the neighborhood. "You developers are all alike," one homeowner said. She identified herself as Bev Haslo. "You come in, bulldoze everything in sight, and slap together a shopping center no one wants, with a huge, ugly asphalt parking lot. That's not a park. That's crap." Another resident, Anne Abare, said: "We're tired of your lies. We work hard for our money, and then you developers come in and cheat us. When we moved in, our developer said all the land around us was zoned for single-family homes, and we believed and trusted him. He lied to us then, and you're lying to us now. This won't help our neighborhood. It'll destroy it. You're all a bunch of crooks."

3. Two police officers in your city arrested a 53-year-old woman at a supermarket at 4340 North Howell Drive at 4:20 p.m. yesterday. This is exactly what the officers' reports say: "We were called to the store by an assistant manager, Richard E. Propes. Mr. Propes explained to us that he saw the woman leave the store without paying for two pizzas, which cost $4.99 each. He followed her to the parking lot and asked her to pay for them. She refused, according to Propes, and shoved him to the ground while attempting to flee. Mr. Propes and two other store employees then stopped and detained the woman until we arrived. Identification she produced for us revealed her identity: Gumersinda Sanchez, 19, of 173 Burgass Road. We brought her in on charges of shoplifting. She was released on $500 bond."

4. Another couple seemed to work as a team. A security officer at a department store in your community reported that a man tried to steal five dresses last evening. The security officer, Margaret Hammar, said she observed a man and a woman, each about 30, select five dresses from a rack of clothing and put them in a shopping bag. The man and woman then split up, and he allegedly left the store carrying the bag. A second security officer stopped the man outside the store after he left without paying for the merchandise. The two security officers then held the man, whom the police arrested and charged with grand theft. He is 33-year-old Jonnie Lewis, 1840 Maldrin Avenue. The police do not know the identity of his accomplice, who escaped.

5. Patrolman Roger Temple was on a routine patrol shortly after 1 a.m. today when he noticed a shattered rear window at a restaurant, The Heritage Inn, 310 North Park Avenue. Temple summoned help, and other officers arrived with a K-9 unit. A dog was sent into the building and, when it began to bark, the police officers proceeded to enter the premises and found a man attempting to hide in a washroom. After being handcuffed and read his rights, the man was arrested on charges of burglary. Police said they found burglar tools in his possession and about $1,000 worth of liquor in his car, which was parked in the restaurant parking lot. The suspect was unarmed. Other restaurant supplies, including more liquor, were piled up inside the restaurant, very near the broken window. This morning, his bail was set at $8,600. The suspect is Ralph Beasley, 23, 810 Howard Street.

6. James D. Allen of 28 Rio Grande Road has been charged with the possession, delivery and sale of cocaine. Allen's problems began last night when he flagged down a car containing two undercover police officers. One of the officers told Allen that he needed a $20 "piece." According to a report filed by the officers, Allen took their money, which was marked, and returned with the cocaine. The officers took the cocaine and met with Sgt. Bill Jacobs and Officer Jeffrey Haille. Jacobs and Haille returned to the scene of the sale and arrested Allen. They reported finding in his possession the marked $20 bill given him by the other two officers. In addition, they reported finding and confiscating cocaine valued at more than $5,000 in his car, which was parked nearby. The police told reporters they did not know why Allen had such an unusually large amount of the drug in his possession.

CHAPTER 13

ETHICS

Ethical problems arise at every step in a journalist's work. Editors must decide which stories their reporters should cover, how their reporters should cover the stories and how the stories should be presented to the public. Reporters may ask the editors for permission to discuss a rumor or quote an anonymous source. A photographer may want to use a picture of a mother grieving over a dead child. A minister charged with drunken driving may call and plead that she is innocent and that a story about the charge (not yet proven) would destroy her career.

No matter what the editors decide, some readers are likely to criticize their decision. Readers have a wide range of complaints: the media have become too big, powerful, arrogant and insensitive; the media are too critical and report too much bad news; the media are too sensational and are more interested in their profits than in serving the public.

Readers also question the techniques that reporters sometimes use to obtain the news. Rude, aggressive reporters seem willing to do anything to get a story: invade people's privacy, invent some details and interview the victims of crimes and accidents while they are still in shock.

A surprising number of readers remember Janet Cooke, a Washington Post reporter who won a Pulitzer Prize for a story about a young heroin addict, which she later confessed she had fabricated. Other readers remember the reporters and photographers who chase everyone—the jurors, witnesses and attorneys—involved in famous trials. Or they may remember R. Foster Winans, a writer for the Wall Street Journal. Winans was assigned to "Heard on the Street," an influential stock column published by the Journal. Winans began to leak information before it appeared in the column to a stockbroker, who then bought or sold stocks to make illegal profits. As a result, Winans and two other men were charged with insider trading. Prosecutors said that one of the brokers grossed $675,000 and that Winans and a roommate received $31,000 as their share of the profits. Winans was convicted, fined $5,000 and sentenced to 18 months in prison.

Journalists have defended their profession by responding that these were isolated incidents, the regrettable acts of a few individuals, and that they should not be used to condemn the entire profession.

Unfortunately, other problems compound the public's misunderstanding and criticisms of the press. Journalists want to report stories that the public needs to know, not just stories that the public wants to read. Journalists feel an obligation to inform the public about every important event occurring in their communities. Many Americans, however, worry about the effects of some stories. They want journalists to be more sensitive and to suppress stories that are unpleasant or sensational or likely to harm people involved in the news.

Journalists reject the notion that they have a responsibility to suppress any stories. John Chancellor of NBC News explains, "Too much of the public doesn't understand

A 5-year-old boy drowned while swimming in Bakersfield, Calif., and this controversial photograph shows a rescue worker trying to console the victim's mother and siblings. The victim's father is on his knees. Robert Bentley, managing editor of The Bakersfield Californian, said, "I ran the picture because it was a powerful photograph, and it was news, and I'm a newsman." The picture also appeared in other newspapers, from Salt Lake City to Boston and Tampa.

   The Californian received more than 400 telephone calls and 500 letters. A bomb threat forced employees to evacuate their office, and 80 readers canceled their subscriptions. People complained that the photograph showed a callous disrespect for the victim, and that it invaded the family's privacy at a moment of grief and shock. Bentley apologized, admitting that he had made a mistake. Photographer John Hart disagreed. "The picture should have run," Hart said. "It was a very good picture. This was an area where there have been a lot of drownings, and the photograph will have long-term benefits in making people aware of water safety and swimming safety."

that just because we report a story does not mean that we are in sympathy with what we are reporting." Katharine Graham, publisher of The Washington Post, has added:

> To say the press ought to suppress some news if we deem it too bad or too unsettling is to make the press into the censor or the nursemaid of a weak and immature society. We cannot serve ourselves and our heritage by running away from our troubles. . . . National security does not rest on national ignorance. This is hardly the faith of a free people.

Columnist Andy Rooney, too, has commented on this issue. After describing a controversial story, Rooney concluded: "Whether a journalist is reporting a war or a grocery store holdup, it is not his business to consider whether the story will do good or harm. He has to have faith that, in the long run, the truth will do good."

   Despite the public's criticisms, journalists in general are acting more ethically and professionally than ever before. They are better educated and better paid. They are also doing more to raise their ethical standards.

In the past, reporters slanted some stories and invented others. Some reporters stole pictures from the homes of people involved in the news. Other reporters impersonated police officers or accepted expensive gifts from the people they wrote about. Today, those reporters would be fired, just as The Washington Post fired Janet Cooke. The public, however, rarely remembers that part of the story: the fact that it was other journalists who exposed and denounced Cooke.

Today's journalists generally agree that it is unethical to fabricate a story or to accept anything of value from a source. Other issues are more complex because of conflicting journalistic values. A journalist may want to report an important story but fear that it would intrude on an individual's privacy. Or, a journalist may want to publish an important document, but hesitate because a source stole the document or because a government official insists that it is a "state secret."

Each problem is unique, and journalists must consider each individually, trying to balance the conflicting values or to decide which value is most important. While covering one story, journalists may decide to protect an individual's privacy. While covering another story, journalists may decide that a community's need to be informed about an issue is more important than any individual considerations. Regardless of what they decide, it is impossible for them to convince every reader that they made the right decision. Thus, some criticisms are inevitable.

DECEIT: WHEN IS IT JUSTIFIED?

Journalists want everyone to believe in and trust them. But to obtain some stories, journalists feel compelled to lie. Occasionally, there seems to be no alternative.

Many journalists insist that anonymity is essential to their job. They may not lie about their identities, but simply fail to reveal them. For example: restaurant reviewers would be ineffective if everyone knew their identities. Restaurant owners, anxious to obtain more favorable publicity, would cater to the reviewers, offering them special meals and special service. As a result, the reviewers would be unable to describe the meals served to the average customer.

Other reporters may want to shop anonymously at a store whose employees have been accused of misleading customers. Or, reporters may want to visit a fortune-teller or attend a protest rally. If protesters realized that several reporters were present, they might either act more cautiously or perform for the reporters, behaving more angrily or violently to ensure that they got into the news. Other protesters might harass or attack the reporters.

Depending on their needs in gathering the information for a story, reporters may sometimes lie about their identities. The reporters may pose as patients while gathering information about a mental hospital. Or, they may pose as laborers while writing about migrant workers and their exposure to the chemicals sprayed on farm crops.

A reporter for The Milwaukee Journal posed as a high school student. The Journal had covered more routine stories about the area's schools, but its metropolitan editor, Patrick Graham, wanted to get closer to the students: to learn "what they're thinking, what they're saying, what their likes and dislikes are, what their cherished aspirations might be." Graham also hoped to learn: "What do they really think about drugs and alcohol? About sex? About going to college? About what they'll be doing or want to do after school?" Reporter Vivian S. Toy agreed to enroll in a suburban high school. Toy, who was 25 but looked much younger, explained: "There's a natural wariness of any adult. I couldn't have broken through that." A suburban school board gave the Journal permission to go undercover, provided the school's principal and teachers were notified. Later, while writing her story, Toy felt ethically obliged not to identify the individual students she talked to.

An Ombudsman's Report

CASE STUDY NO. 4

By **Henry McNulty**
Reader Representative
The Hartford (Conn.) Courant

Ask an editor whether newspapers ought to expose racial discrimination in the community, and the answer doubtless will be yes. Will the answer be the same if reporters must lie to uncover the discrimination?

That was the dilemma facing me last May when, as The Hartford Courant's reader representative, I examined a package of stories reporting racial bias among some Hartford-area real estate firms. The central question was: In this case, did the end justify the means?

For years, many of us at the paper had suspected that black people and white people are not treated the same when they look for homes. On May 21, The Courant provided the evidence. In some cases, real estate agents gave blacks tougher financial scrutiny than they did whites. Other times, blacks were "steered" to towns that already have significant minority populations.

Courant reporters had shown up at various real estate agencies apparently looking for a house. Two black and two white "testers" appeared to be nearly identical in every financial and personal detail—except race. They followed testing guidelines in a manual approved by state and federal fair-housing agencies. When they were with real estate agents, the reporters used altered names and provided other false information that masked their identities.

The investigation was meticulously prepared, carefully written and clearly presented. Immediately after it appeared, Connecticut's governor ordered a statewide investigation of real estate discrimination. This led many Courant editors to argue that the reporters' deception had been worth it.

With regret, I disagreed, and I said as much in my June 4 column. We had to lie to get the story, and for me, that was a fatal flaw. I don't think a news story, however important, can be based on deception.

It was not an easy conclusion to reach. There's a long history of reporters disguising themselves to root out corruption. And this investigation struck a strong blow for justice and equality.

But I can't think of a case in which such deception would be justified. Even when the goals are noble, as these certainly were, and even when the results are positive for the community, I think journalists must not lie.

The Courant's policy states: "We do not misrepresent ourselves" in pursuing a story. But that's quickly followed by the statement that "From time to time, legitimate stories in the public interest might involve a conflict with (this policy)."

The escape clause essentially means we have a policy that permits deception. It flatly prohibits only casual or willy-nilly misrepresentation—but it lets us lie to get a story whenever we think we should. The real estate probe wasn't even an exception to the rules, since an exception is already built in.

(continued on next page)

To our credit, the testing procedure and the newspaper's policy were explained in a sidebar headed "How, Why the Test Was Done." At least we didn't hide the deception.

Saying, "Journalists shouldn't lie" opens up a host of questions. What about restaurant reviewers who pretend to be ordinary customers when in fact they intend to report on their dining experience? Aren't they misrepresenting themselves, too?

Perhaps. But there are many facets to the question of deceiving sources, and I feel each case must be examined closely. I make a distinction, for example, between actively giving a false name and passively letting someone assume a reporter is just an average consumer. Admittedly, not everyone is willing to make that distinction.

Could we have done the real estate story without telling lies? Maybe, but it would have been an arduous task. Executive Editor Michael E. Waller, who approved the project, thinks it would have been more difficult than that.

"To have an outside group . . . do the testing would still have posed problems," he said. "They would have had to misrepresent themselves—and I see little ethical difference between us misrepresenting ourselves and asking someone else to do it for us.

"Asking real home buyers . . . to be the testers posed, in my mind, insurmountable problems. The first would be finding the people to fit the test criteria and getting them to do it simultaneously and in a timely manner. The second would be keeping any reasonable control of accuracy, and assurance that they faithfully would follow all the testing guidelines."

He's probably right. So I say, with deep regret, that we couldn't—and so, we shouldn't—have done this investigation, despite its social importance.

After my column appeared, a handful of readers called me to support my position. For the most part, I had no way of knowing whether they had any stake in matters involving real estate, although one caller was a former Realtor. Another caller said he had just finished a course in journalism ethics at a local college, and a third amazed me by identifying himself as an investigative reporter at a competing newspaper!

There was moderate reaction inside the newspaper. A couple of reporters agreed with me; most didn't, saying that our deception was benign in comparison to the illegal activity we disclosed.

Credibility is our most important asset. And if we deceive people in order to do our job, we've compromised that credibility before a word is written.

A Chicago paper lost a Pulitzer Prize because other journalists objected to its use of a more elaborate disguise. To expose corruption in the city, the Sun-Times bought a tavern and, appropriately, renamed it the Mirage Bar. With the help of the Better Government Association, the Sun-Times used the bar to photograph and tape record city inspectors who, in return for payoffs, ignored the bar's violations of city health and safety standards. A panel nominated the Sun-Times for a Pulitzer Prize. Benjamin C. Bradlee, then executive editor of The Washington Post, served on a board that selected that year's prize winners, and Bradlee opposed the Sun-Times' nomination. Bradlee and other critics charged that the Sun-Times had created the story and that its reporters had become participants in it. Critics agreed that there was a need to expose the city's corruption, but insisted that the Sun-Times did not have to buy a bar to obtain the story.

Other disguises are more obviously unethical. Two reporters for a tabloid dressed as priests during Bing Crosby's funeral. While pretending to comfort Crosby's widow, the "priests" were actually trying to get an exclusive story from her.

Typically, editors allow their reporters to use a disguise only when a story is very important and there is no other way to safely obtain it. While writing their stories, the reporters are expected to admit their use of deception and to explain why it was necessary. The reporters are also expected to call everyone criticized in their stories and give them an opportunity to respond.

Journalists are more reluctant to secretly record their conversations, since the tactic may seem devious and unfair. Journalists also fear that, if sources learn that reporters secretly record some conversations, they may become more reluctant to speak candidly, if at all.

Journalists in most states can legally record their conversations. Or, they can ask someone else to record a conversation and to give them a copy. Imagine, for example, that several women complained of sexual harassment while applying for city jobs. An editor might want to send out an attractive female reporter with a hidden recorder to document the allegations.

Other reporters use tape recorders to protect themselves in case they are accused of lying. The reporters fear that, after giving them some information, a source might claim that the reporter had misquoted him or her or even had fabricated the entire interview. Some sources honestly forget what they said. Others are shocked by how awful their statements appear in print. Then, to defend themselves, they claim that the statements attributed to them are inaccurate.

If reporters record their interviews, they can prove that their stories are accurate. They can also protect themselves more easily in libel suits. In the rare cases when reporters do record a conversation, however, most try to do so openly, with their sources' permission.

INVASIONS OF PRIVACY

Newspapers sometimes intrude on the privacy of other individuals. They usually have a legal right to intrude, but do they have the moral or ethical right?

Newspapers report the important events occurring in their communities, typically including every birth, engagement, marriage, divorce and bankruptcy. When people die, newspapers publish their obituaries, and some newspapers include everyone's age and cause of death. Many Americans consider the publicity embarrassing. They do not want anyone to know their age, nor that they are bankrupt or divorced. People are also embarrassed when the media publish the cause of a relative's death, especially when the cause is suicide or an illness with a social stigma, like AIDS.

Other events are more obviously newsworthy: major lawsuits, crimes and accidents. Anyone who becomes involved in such an event, even unintentionally, may expect to appear in a news story about it.

Other decisions are more difficult. Newspapers normally do not identify juvenile delinquents. But if several teen-agers are arrested and charged with committing a series of rapes and burglaries that terrorized a neighborhood, editors may feel a need to identify the teen-agers, and perhaps their parents as well. Editors may decide that their obligation to calm people's fears by informing the neighborhood about the arrests outweighs their normal obligation to protect the teen-agers and their families.

Journalists are often criticized for their treatment of government officials and other public figures. Most Americans seem to agree that journalists should expose government officials who abuse their power or who have personal problems, such as alcoholism,

Gary Hart withdrew—but only temporarily—from the 1988 presidential election after newspapers revealed his relationship with Donna Rice, a Miami actress. The National Enquirer published two photos that showed Hart and Rice vacationing together in Bimini.

After his death, Americans learned that John F. Kennedy also enjoyed the company of attractive young women, even after his election as president. Some journalists knew about Kennedy's relationships but, at the time, considered them a private matter.

that affect their work. However, many Americans object to stories that expose politicians' personal weaknesses, especially weaknesses that do not affect their work (their sexual habits, for example). Critics insist that journalists have become too zealous and moralistic in their pursuit of stories and should stop prying into other people's private lives.

In the past, journalists were more reluctant to discuss people's personal lives, even the lives of public officials. The officials' personal lives may have seemed irrelevant to their fitness for public office. Thus, journalists ignored the fact that some officials were profane, liked to gamble or told dirty jokes. Even after his election as president, journalists never reported on President John F. Kennedy's womanizing, nor (until the Watergate scandal broke) on President Richard Nixon's profanity.

Journalists are still hesitant to intrude on the lives of private citizens. However, they are becoming more aggressive about reporting on the lives of public figures and public officials. They are most likely to publish details that can be verified and that might affect the officials' work or that help reveal their character. Increasingly, journalists believe that a candidate's character is more important than his or her stand on the issues. Thus, journalists are examining politicians' character (and their spouses') more openly and critically than ever before.

When Geraldine Ferraro became the Democratic candidate for vice president in 1984, journalists reported that her husband, John A. Zaccaro, had been appointed the legal conservator of an estate and had improperly borrowed $175,000 from it. Other stories claimed that Zaccaro had conducted some business with people involved in the Mafia.

Some editors said that the stories were a relevant part of their coverage of Ferraro's campaign, especially since she might someday become president. Others, however, avoided using the words "mob" and "Mafia." Some also deleted details that were never clearly substantiated. Critics considered publication of the details to be irrelevant, irresponsible, unproven and unfair. Months after Ferraro's defeat, journalists also reported the fact that her son had been charged with selling drugs.

Four years later, reporters were criticized for "staking out" Gary Hart and ending his presidential campaign. Hart's wife was standing at his side when he announced his candidacy, promising "the very highest standards of integrity and ethics, and soundness of judgment." Polls showed that Hart was the leading Democratic candidate, and likely to receive 65 percent of the votes cast in Iowa's early caucuses. But questions were arising about Hart's character, including discrepancies concerning his age and a revelation that he had changed his last name to Hart from Hartpence.

For years, there had also been rumors that Hart was a womanizer. Then The Miami Herald received a telephone call from a woman who said Hart was having an extramarital affair. One of the Herald's reporters flew to Washington, and a colleague joined him outside Hart's home there. They saw Hart leaving his house with a young woman, subsequently identified as Donna Rice. The couple returned later that evening and apparently spent the night together. The Herald published the story, and the ensuing furor caused Hart to withdraw from the presidential campaign.

After Hart's withdrawal, the National Enquirer published two photographs showing him with Rice during a trip to Bimini. In one, the pair was cuddling on a dock, with Rice sitting on Hart's lap. The second photo showed Hart, Rice and another couple partying at a Bimini nightspot. The National Enquirer obtained the photos from one of Rice's friends, paying a reported $25,000 for them.

Was that good journalism—or an invasion of Hart's privacy?

Some Americans were outraged by the publication of these stories. They complained that journalists had gone too far in following a presidential candidate and invading his personal life. Critics, including some journalists, were especially scathing in their evaluations of The Herald's stakeout techniques. Yet The Herald admitted that its stakeout was imperfect—that its reporters had not watched every door, nor stayed outside Hart's home all night—and many Americans supported the paper. They thought that Hart himself was responsible for The Herald's surveillance because of his comments, behavior and "flagrant flaunting of fundamental rules of our society."

Hart knew that he was being observed and that his personal life was an issue in the campaign. Under the circumstances, journalists considered his behavior reckless and arrogant. Why would any presidential candidate (especially a married man) openly continue his relationship with an attractive young woman? And why would he pose for the photographs in Bimini?

Thus, Americans disappointed by Hart's behavior concluded that he had betrayed his family, staff and supporters. For them, the issue was not just Hart's morality, but his attitude toward women, his self-discipline and his sense of responsibility toward other people. They were also disappointed by Hart's belligerence toward reporters and his failure to accept any responsibility for his own actions and their consequences.*

During the 1988 campaign, the media were critical of Republican George Bush's nominee for vice president, Sen. Dan Quayle of Indiana. The media reported allegations that Quayle was lazy and dishonest, a coward, hypocrite and draft-dodger. Clearly, Quayle was a conservative and a militant anti-Communist. He had supported the war in Vietnam but, instead of fighting there, joined the National Guard. Positions in the National Guard were scarce, and the media also reported allegations that Quayle had used his family's influence to obtain his position.

Other stories and columns accused Quayle of being a spoiled rich kid: a poor student and lazy congressman who got by on his connections, wealth and good looks. There were also rumors and stories (never substantiated) about his career as a law student. One of the rumors accused Quayle of plagiarism. Another said that he had hired someone to take the bar exam for him.

Journalists quoted (but never identified) a professor who charged that Quayle "was vapid, ordinary and relied on his personality to cut corners." Journalists also quoted (but never identified) a fellow congressman who said: "You cannot dislike Dan. He's personable, he's fun to be with, and he's about a quarter of an inch deep."

The attacks continued even after Quayle was elected vice president. In 1991, the Doonesbury comic strip ran a series suggesting that Quayle had used cocaine while he was a law student and a U.S. senator. The strip's fictional reporter, Rick Redfern, learned that the federal Drug Enforcement Administration (DEA) had a file containing the allegations about Quayle. In real life, DEA officials admitted that they had investigated such allegations but had concluded that they were false. Some newspapers refused to run the series. Others added a note explaining that the allegations had never been proven. Several major news organizations, including "60 Minutes," had already investigated the allegations and, like the DEA, found that they were groundless.

Journalists have become involved in similar controversies after overhearing—and reporting—remarks not meant for publication. Their victims were outraged and accused the journalists of invading their privacy and acting unfairly and unethically. Journalists responded that the remarks were newsworthy: that they revealed the speakers' true feelings, character and behavior. Some journalists have added that public officials should be more cautious about what they say, not saying anything in public that they would be ashamed to see in print.

When President Ronald Reagan joked about bombing the Soviet Union, journalists reported the story. Reagan told the joke just before a radio broadcast, and it was accidentally transmitted to a pressroom. During Jesse Jackson's campaign for the presidency, journalists also overheard—and reported—derogatory remarks he made about Jews.

The media's probing may have the unfortunate result of making some potential candidates reluctant to run for public office because they do not want to be exposed to the media's scrutiny. In Seattle, John Jamison was asked to run for mayor and declined because he did not want to surrender his privacy nor that of his family. "I was not willing to make myself a target for the hostility of the press," Jamison said. He complained that political leaders are perpetually under attack and that he did not

---

*For a firsthand account of the Herald's stakeout and coverage, see: "The Gary Hart Story: How It Happened," The Miami Herald, May 10, 1987, p. 1.

A furniture store owner in St. Louis, Ron Olshwanger, received the Pulitzer Prize for spot news photography for his photo showing a fireman giving mouth-to-mouth resuscitation to a child pulled from a burning building.

want to spend his time "defending this or that two-bit issue" dredged up by the press. Jamison added that he found other people—men and women across the country—making similar decisions. He concluded that the country may be losing some of its best leaders because of their fear of the press.

The same issue arose in 1992. Several of the nation's leading Democrats seemed hesitant to seek their party's nomination for the presidency, and some people speculated that it was because they did not want the press prying into their personal lives.

Has the press gone too far? Does the public really benefit from its scrutiny of public officials such as Ferraro, Hart and Quayle? The press never discussed President

Franklin Roosevelt's troubled marriage, nor the fact that he had a mistress. Would the country have been better off if the press had revealed that relationship? Would the public also have benefited if reporters had caught John F. Kennedy with a girlfriend and forced him to withdraw from the 1960 campaign for the presidency?

The fact is that journalists cannot predict the consequences of their stories and are not in the business of hiding facts from the public. Moreover, readers would complain even more vehemently if they discovered that journalists were deliberately withholding some stories.

DECIDING WHEN TO NAME NAMES

Normally, journalists want to identify fully everyone who is mentioned in their stories. Generalities are difficult, however, and editors make their decisions on a case-by-case basis. Certain types of stories present especially thorny problems.

Rape Victims

Most newspapers withhold the names of all rape victims. Editors explain that there is a stigma attached to rape, and that the victims have already suffered enough. Editors do not want to add to the victims' suffering. Also, victims might be more reluctant to report rapes to the police if they thought their names would be revealed to the public.

People critical of newspapers' policy respond that newspapers have adopted a dual standard: that they identify the people charged with rape (usually men), but never their accusers. Critics add that the policy is an old-fashioned and paternalistic means of protecting women.

Increasingly, some victims want to be identified, because they want to discuss the crime openly and to help other victims. That, however, is usually a decision made by a victim, not an editor.

Typically, most editors never printed the name of a 29-year-old jogger who was brutally beaten and gang-raped in New York City's Central Park in 1990. Newspapers throughout the United States reported only that the victim was an investment banker who had attended Wellesley and Yale. Newspapers also described the woman's remarkable recovery and the fact that she returned to work after seven months of intensive rehabilitation.

While withholding the victim's identity, newspapers repeatedly published the names and photographs of her alleged attackers, all of whom were black or Hispanic. One of the youths' lawyers complained: "The press is inconsistent. They protect the wishes of the jogger because of all she's been through. But they don't care at all about the consequences for my client, who's been branded a gang-raper. . . ."

An editor responded that people who are arrested do not have a right to privacy. The woman, however, was an innocent victim. She was not accused of committing a brutal crime.

The Palm Beach rape case of 1991 also created controversy. A young woman said she was raped by William Kennedy Smith, a nephew of Sen. Edward Kennedy. A tabloid published in Boca Raton printed the woman's name. Prosecutors in West Palm Beach County immediately charged the tabloid with violating a 1911 law that makes identifying a rape victim in Florida a second-degree criminal misdemeanor. The New York Times and NBC News also identified the woman. Why? Michael Gartner, president of NBC News, explained, "The immediate issue is, I'm in the business of disseminating news, not suppressing it." Normally, when one news organization breaks a story that others have been withholding, all the media then report the story. In this case, that did not happen. Other journalists thought that The New York Times and NBC News were wrong, and they continued to withhold the woman's name.

Homosexuals

Newspapers are also in a quandary about the exposure of homosexuals. Many homosexuals prefer to keep their sexual preferences private. But some prominent Americans—entertainers, politicians and military leaders, for example—are being exposed by gay activists using a controversial tactic called "outing."

These activists explain that, by exposing other homosexuals, they are increasing the number of role models for young gays. They also hope to eliminate the stigma attached to being gay and to eliminate the curse of secrecy from homosexual life.

One of the most controversial stories appeared after the death of Malcolm Forbes, the publisher of Forbes magazine. Forbes had led a lavish and flamboyant life. He enjoyed riding in hot-air balloons, was linked romantically with Liz Taylor and gave millions of dollars to charity. To celebrate his 70th birthday, Forbes had invited hundreds of friends to a highly publicized $2 million party in Tangier, Morocco. A few months after Forbes' death, another magazine described his secret life as a homosexual. Some mainstream newspapers and magazines reprinted the details.

Prostitutes and Their Customers

In the past, most newspapers published the names of women arrested for prostitution, but not the names of men arrested for patronizing them. Today, an entire neighborhood may become concerned when prostitutes begin doing business there. In some cities, coalitions of local merchants, homeowners and government officials have been organized to combat the problem. They encourage the police to make more arrests, and they encourage newspapers to publish the names of both prostitutes and "johns," or customers. Some people add that more than community service is involved. It is also a matter of fairness, since newspapers were practicing a form of discrimination when they identified only the women.

REPORTING (OR EXPLOITING) GRIEF

A recent public opinion survey found that 47 percent of the nation's adults believe that the media do not care about the people they report on. An even greater number—73 percent—believe that the media have no regard for people's privacy. Readers are especially critical of the media's coverage of death and grief: of photographs of and interviews with grieving relatives.

Some journalists insist that the interviews are necessary because they are the only way reporters can confirm important facts, learn more about the victims and obtain the survivors' stories.

Anantha Babbili and Tommy Thomason, professors at Texas Christian University, studied an example of the problem. When the space shuttle Challenger exploded, television cameras were focused on the parents of Christa McAuliffe, a teacher and passenger aboard the Challenger. Journalists wanted to record the parents' proud reaction to the launch. Instead, they recorded the parents' horror as they watched their daughter die. Babbili and Thomason wondered:

> Is the reaction of a mother to her daughter's tragic death of such public importance? The Constitution certainly implies that the public has a right to

This series of prize-winning photos shows a Boston firefighter trying to rescue a young woman and a little girl. The fire escape collapsed just as he reached them, and the young woman died in the fall. Some readers objected to the photographs' publication.

know. But do we have a right to intrude upon private sorrow of private individuals—even if they happen to be related to public figures? Was the constant replaying of those seconds of grief really necessary?

On Dec. 21, 1988, Pan Am flight 103, an American jet traveling from London to New York, crashed in Lockerbie, Scotland, killing 270 people, including 38 students from Syracuse University. Some television stations broadcast a tape showing a mother collapsing to an airport floor, screaming in grief after learning that one of the students, her daughter, was dead.

Increasingly, the media are becoming more sensitive to the problem. The St. Louis Post-Dispatch no longer covers funerals unless they are of great public interest. The Post-Dispatch has also stopped taking pictures without the permission of the family of the deceased. "Funerals are private events," an editor at the Post-Dispatch explains. "It's an intrusion for the press to attend as a rule."

Similarly, the Chicago Sun-Times announced that it would not cover the funerals of U.S. soldiers killed during the war against Iraq, nor seek out their relatives without invitations. Editor Dennis A. Britton explained: "We have decided that the Chicago Sun-Times will not intrude upon the private moments of grief and mourning of those who have lost a loved one in the war. We will afford family and friends the opportunity to talk with us if they'd like, but we will not bother them with phone calls, nor camp out on their front steps, nor invade the privacy of funerals."

VICTIMS' RIGHTS

The National Victim Center prepared this set of guidelines to help the victims of violent crime deal with the media. The center was established in 1985 to lead the fight for victims' rights. It is located in Fort Worth, Texas, and was formerly called the Sunny Von Bulow National Victim Advocacy Center.

As a journalist, you may disagree with some of the guidelines. They are likely to make your work as a journalist more difficult. The guidelines, however, reflect a growing concern about the victims of violent crime. The guidelines also reflect concern about journalists' treatment (or, in some cases, mistreatment) of victims.

1. **You have the right to say "no" to an interview.** Never feel that because you have unwillingly been involved in an incident of public interest that you must personally share the details and/or your feelings with the general public. If you decide that you want the public to be aware of how traumatic and unfair your victimization was, you do not automatically have to give up your right to privacy. By knowing and requesting respect for your rights, you can be heard and yet not violated.

2. **You have the right to select the spokesperson or advocate of your choice.** Selecting one spokesperson—especially in multiple-victim cases—eliminates confusion and contradictory statements. You also have the right to expect the media to respect your selection of a spokesperson or advocate.

3. **You have the right to select the time and location for media interviews.** Remember, the media are governed by deadlines. However, nobody should be subjected to a reporter arriving unannounced at the home of a victim. When you are traumatized, your home becomes your refuge. If you wish to protect the privacy of your home, select another location such as a church, meeting hall, office setting, etc. It helps if you are familiar and comfortable with the surroundings.

4. **You have the right to request a specific reporter.** As a consumer of daily news, each of us identifies with or respects a reporter whom we may never have met. We often form personal opinions about reporters whom we feel are thorough, sensitive, compassionate and objective. If a newspaper, radio station or television station contacts you for an interview, don't hesitate to request the reporter you feel will provide accurate and fair coverage of your story.

5. **You have the right to refuse an interview with a specific reporter even though you have granted interviews to other reporters.** You may feel that certain reporters are callous, insensitive, uncaring or judgmental. It is your right to avoid these journalists at all costs. By refusing to speak to such reporters you may help them recognize their shortcomings in reporting victim-related stories. However, recognize that the reporters may write the story regardless of your participation.

(continued on next page)

6. **You have the right to say "no" to an interview even though you have previously granted interviews.** It's important to recognize that victims often ride an "emotional roller coaster." You may be able one day to talk with a reporter, and be physically or emotionally unable to do so the next. Victims should never feel "obliged" to grant interviews under any circumstances.

7. **You have the right to release a written statement through a spokesperson in lieu of an interview.** There may be times when you are emotionally incapable of speaking with the media, but you still wish to express your point of view. Writing and distributing your statement through a spokesperson allows you to express your views without personally granting interviews.

8. **You have the right to exclude children from interviews.** Children already suffering from the trauma of crime are often retraumatized by exposure to the media. Children often lack the means to verbalize their emotions and may be misinterpreted by both the media and the public. You have a responsibility to protect the interests of children at all costs!

9. **You have the right to refrain from answering any questions with which you are uncomfortable or that you feel are inappropriate.** You should never feel you have to answer a question just because it's been asked.

10. **You have the right to know in advance what direction the story about your victimization is going to take.** You have the right to know what questions reporters will ask you, along with the right to veto any questions. This places you in a partnership with the reporter who is covering the story.

11. **You have the right to ask for review of your quotations in a story prior to publication.** Articles are reviewed and revised by editors who have neither seen nor spoken to you. All too often, victims' statements and the intended impact of their remarks are misinterpreted or inaccurate. To protect your interests and the message you wish to convey, you have the right to request a review of direct quotations attributed to you in the story.

12. **You have the right to avoid a press conference atmosphere and speak to only one reporter at a time.** At a time when you are in a state of shock, a press conference atmosphere with numerous reporters can be confusing and emotionally draining. If a press conference is absolutely unavoidable, you have the right to select one reporter to ask questions for the majority present.

13. **You have the right to demand a retraction when inaccurate information is reported.** All news media have methods of correcting inaccurate reporting or errors in stories. Use these means to correct any aspect of media coverage which you feel is inaccurate.

14. **You have a right to ask that offensive photographs or visuals be omitted from airing or publication.** If you feel that graphic photographs or visuals are not the best representation of you or your loved one, you have the right to ask that they not be used.

15. **You have the right to conduct a television interview using a silhouette or a newspaper interview without having your photograph taken.** There are many ways for reporters to project your physical image without using your photograph or film footage of you, therefore protecting your identity.

---

16. **You have the right to completely give your side of the story related to your victimization.** If you feel that a reporter is not asking questions which need to be addressed, you have the right to give a personal statement. And if the alleged or convicted offender grants interviews which are inaccurate, you have the right to publicly express your point of view.
17. **You have the right to refrain from answering reporters' questions during trial.** If there is any chance of jeopardizing your case by interacting with the media during judicial proceedings, you have the right to remain silent.
18. **You have the right to file a formal complaint against a reporter.** A reporter's superior would appreciate knowing when his or her employee's behavior is unethical, inappropriate or abusive. By reporting such behavior, you will also protect the next unsuspecting victim who might fall prey to such offensive reporters or tactics.
19. **You have the right to grieve in privacy.** Grief is a highly personal experience. If you do not wish to share it publicly, you have the right to ask reporters to remove themselves during times of grief.
20. **You have the right to suggest training about media and victims for print and electronic media in your community.** Resources are available to educate media professionals about victims, how to deal with victims, and how to refrain from traumatizing victims. You will be suggesting a greatly needed public service to benefit not only victims and survivors, but all members of the community who interact with the media.
21. **You have the right at all times to be treated with dignity and respect by the media.**

PHOTOGRAPHS: WHAT'S NEWSWORTHY, WHAT'S SENSATIONAL?

Newspaper editors usually decide to publish a photograph because it seems important and helps tell a story. Readers upset by the editors' decisions accuse them of acting sensationally and of being more interested in selling papers than in helping people in distress. Readers are also more concerned about the photographs' effects: about whether the photographs are too unpleasant, tasteless and upsetting.

Some photographs are so compelling—so filled with fresh, hard news—that editors publish them regardless of the criticisms they are certain to arouse. This problem often arose during the war in Vietnam. Editors used pictures that portrayed the horrors of the war. One of the pictures showed a Buddhist monk burning himself to death on a Saigon street. Another showed a South Vietnamese police chief shooting a prisoner in the head at point-blank range.

Stanley Forman of Boston's Herald-American snapped a series of horrifying photos that showed a young woman and a little girl about to be rescued from a burning building. The fire escape collapsed while the two were still standing on it, and Forman's photos showed the two in midair, falling to the ground. The woman died, yet newspapers throughout the world published the riveting photographs, and Forman was awarded a Pulitzer Prize for his work. Predictably, some readers accused the newspapers of sensationalism: of poor taste, insensitivity, an invasion of the victims' privacy, and a tasteless display of human tragedy to sell newspapers.

Journalists in Pennsylvania faced a similar dilemma. The state treasurer, R. Budd Dwyer, shot and killed himself during a press conference. Dwyer, 47, had been

Copyright © 1993 by Harcourt Brace Jovanovich, Inc.
All rights reserved. Printed in the United States of America
ISBN 0-15-500602-9

Would you publish these photographs in a daily newspaper? Does it matter that the man was a state official and killed himself during a press conference attended by about 35 reporters and photographers? Some newspapers used these photographs, but not a fourth taken after the official fired a single shot into his mouth.

convicted in a bribery scandal and faced up to 55 years in prison. He began the press conference by insisting that he was innocent and by accusing other government officials of conspiring against him. Near the end of a rambling 30-minute account, Dwyer also began to attack the press. Then he opened a manila envelope, pulled out a gun and fired one shot into his mouth. The entire episode—from the moment Dwyer pulled out the gun until he shot himself—took only 21 seconds. There were about 35 witnesses, primarily reporters and photographers.

WHTM-TV in Harrisburg broadcast the entire videotape, and so did two stations in Pittsburgh. Some parents complained that their children saw the suicide before they were able to change channels. Newscasters responded that the media should not sugarcoat reality. Another journalist explained: "The feeling was, this was a major news event and it was at a public press conference. It captures the horror of the story in terms everyone can understand and see. Pictures are part of the story." Stations elsewhere generally edited or discarded the videotape. Their edited versions showed Dwyer holding the gun, but not putting it into his mouth and pulling the trigger.

A California paper, the San Jose Mercury News, recently asked its readers "to grapple with some of the same questions editors face daily." Two of its questions involved controversial photographs. Readers were asked whether they would have used a photograph taken after a devastating earthquake. The photograph showed a woman, her legs horribly shattered, in agony as rescuers pulled her from the wreckage of a building.

The second photograph was a close-up of a 15-year-old boy who had lost his footing while trying to climb a 6-foot fence. As the boy fell, an iron fence post pierced his face. The boy hung from the fence, still conscious, and the picture captured his agony "as rescue teams used cutting torches to free him." Editors who printed the photograph called it "compelling" and "spellbinding." Those who rejected the photograph called it "gruesome," "grotesque" and "ghastly."

Seventy-four percent of the reporters and editors at the Mercury News, but only 52 percent of their readers, said that they would publish the photograph showing the injured woman being pulled out of the wreckage. Why? John Connell, the paper's religion and ethics editor, explained, "The earthquake was a horrible event, and no matter how unpleasant the image, they say the newspaper must mirror that reality. And this photo was one that made the whole story human."

There was less disagreement between journalists and readers about the photograph of the impaled boy. Only 26 percent of the newspaper's reporters and editors, and 23 percent of their readers, said they would publish it.

WHEN IS A JOURNALIST A CITIZEN?

After beginning to work for the news media, you may find that your job occasionally conflicts with your normal responsibilities as a citizen. Journalists believe that their primary responsibility is to report the news. To do so, they may have to set aside some rights and responsibilities that conflict with their work. When journalists in Vietnam photographed a Buddhist monk burning himself, readers wondered why the journalists failed to lay down their cameras and extinguish the flames. Readers also wondered why the journalists failed to notify the authorities so they could prevent the suicide.

Journalists are reluctant to become involved in the stories they cover. They want to remain neutral bystanders, not preventing, encouraging, or changing a story. Yet this puzzles and sometimes outrages other citizens, who believe that journalists should help people in distress, cooperate with the police and support the president.

Other citizens also want journalists to suppress stories that may harm innocent people.

Suppressing Stories

Journalists occasionally do suppress a story, but only in extreme cases: most commonly, when a life is in danger. The police in El Paso, Texas, asked journalists there to suppress news of a kidnapping until the victim was rescued. The journalists agreed, and an editor explained, "No story is worth the lives of children." Other journalists knew that some Americans were hiding in the Canadian Embassy in Iran while the Iranians were holding 52 other Americans as hostages. No one reported the story.

However, "NBC Nightly News" decided to broadcast a film taken by a free-lancer who lived with Communist guerrillas in the Philippine countryside. The free-lancer, Jon Alpert, showed the guerrillas pointing to a map and explaining how they planned to ambush a convoy of Philippine soldiers. Alpert's film also showed the actual ambush. Fifteen soldiers were killed, and some viewers called NBC to ask whether the film was real. Others wanted to know why Alpert referred to the government soldiers as "the enemy." Still others wondered why Alpert failed to prevent the killings by warning the soldiers of the danger. Yet, when other journalists slipped into Afghanistan, no one objected when they showed rebels there killing Soviet troops.

Eddie Adams, a photographer for The Associated Press, won a Pulitzer Prize for this photograph, which shows the chief of the South Vietnamese National Police executing a captured Viet Cong officer on a Saigon street. Adams took the photograph during the 1968 Tet offensive, and it has become one of the most widely circulated photographs in history. Some newspaper editors were reluctant to publish this and other controversial photographs taken during the Vietnam War. Other editors decided to publish photographs of violence and human suffering, but not on their newspapers' front pages.

Witnessing Crimes (and Interviewing Criminals)

Reporters occasionally learn about a crime that is about to be committed. They might either go to the police or watch the crime and interview the criminal.

Reporters in San Diego received a call from a "Billboard Bandit" who said that he had scrawled graffiti on 26 billboards that advertised cigarettes but that no one seemed to have noticed his work. The "Bandit" then invited a reporter and photographer from the paper to accompany him. He stipulated, however, that the newspaper could not use his name and that the photographer could not show his face. The "Bandit" said he wanted to be arrested, but not quite yet. A reporter and photographer from the Union did watch the "Bandit" on one of his night-time raids.

Readers criticized the resulting story and photographs. They complained that the paper had abetted an illegal act and turned a petty criminal into a folk hero. Letters addressed to the newspaper's editor ran 3-to-1 against the "Bandit."

Similarly, a reporter for The Sacramento (Calif.) Bee secretly interviewed two women who were members of an animal-rights group and admitted committing a string of crimes, including theft and vandalism. The women arranged to meet the reporter secretly at a motel. To hide their identities, the women wore ski masks throughout the interview. The women said they were members of the Animal Liberation Front, a militant national animal-rights group whose members raided medical research facilities to rescue animals from lab experiments they considered cruel and inhumane.

NBC was criticized even more vehemently after it broadcast an interview with a suspected terrorist, Abul Abbas. Three countries were looking for Abbas after the hijacking of a ship and the murder of an American tourist. NBC agreed to conceal his location; it seemed to be the only way to persuade him to talk. During the interview, Abbas said the Palestinians now consider the United States, not Israel, their chief enemy. Abbas then threatened to conduct his next terrorist operations in the United States.

An official at the State Department called NBC's decision "reprehensible," charging that the network had become an accomplice to terror. Another government official complained that the publicity NBC gave Abbas "encourages the terrorist activities we're all seeking to deter."

The Chicago Tribune called NBC's story "an abysmal disgrace to journalism." An editorial written by Tribune editor James D. Squires argued that Abbas' location was the only new and important element of the story, yet NBC had agreed to keep his location a secret. Squires added that, "If the Chicago Tribune could find Abbas we would turn him in." The Tribune said it would accept Abbas' offer for an interview, then tell the government his location.

Other journalists also criticized NBC, but were even more critical of the Chicago Tribune's plan to betray Abbas. They feared that, if a newspaper broke its word with Abbas, other sources would become more suspicious of every journalist and more reluctant to talk with them. Sources in other countries might also feel freer to harm journalists, especially if they seemed to be cooperating with their governments.

CONFLICTS OF INTEREST

After years of confusion and contradictory standards, there seems to be a growing consensus about what constitutes a conflict of interest.

Accepting Gifts

Most journalists agree that financial corruption is unethical and that they should not accept money or anything else of value from the people they write about. An editor at The Washington Post has explained that: "It is rather generally accepted among newspaper people that financial corruption is probably sinful, that editors and reporters ought not take money or other things of value from people and organizations that are in the news. On some newspapers (this one included), the acceptance of a bribe—for that is what it is—is a firing offense."

In the past, reporters often readily accepted gifts, considering "freebies" to be fringe benefits. They received free tickets to every attraction in their communities. Each Christmas, a political reporter might receive a carload of gifts from the officials in city hall. After writing about a jewelry store, a reporter might receive a watch from the store's owner.

Free trips, called "junkets," were also common. Fashion writers were invited to New York, and television critics to Hollywood, with all their expenses paid. Sportswriters might accompany their local teams to games in distant cities, with the teams paying all the writers' expenses.

Journalists accepting the gifts insisted that they could not be corrupted because they were trained to remain objective. They also explained that most of the gifts were insignificant: small tokens of appreciation for their work. They added that they would be less willing to accept the gifts if they were better paid and could afford to buy the items for themselves. Journalists who accepted the junkets also insisted that the main issue should be the public's right to know. Smaller newspapers and broadcasting stations could not afford to send their reporters to distant cities, and the junkets helped them obtain stories that would otherwise be unavailable.

Most newspapers now prohibit their reporters and editors from accepting anything of value. Other newspapers allow their newspeople to accept small items worth only a few dollars: a cup of coffee or souvenir T-shirt, for example. Some newspapers also allow their newspeople to accept free tickets to sports events, plays and movies. However, newspapers generally prohibit their newspeople from calling a press agent to ask for the tickets.

Participating in the News

Increasingly, newspapers prohibit outside work and activities that might conflict with their reporters' objectivity. Editors explain that reporters' first obligation should be to their primary employer, and that the reporters continue to represent their employers even after they leave work for the day.

Editors generally agree that reporters should not hold any public office, either elected or appointed. Most editors also agree that reporters should not serve as party officials or help with anyone's campaign. Editors want to avoid even the appearance of a conflict. For example, there might not be a direct conflict if a business writer ran for city council; a business writer might never cover the city council. But the newspaper's readers might suspect that other writers slanted the news in favor of their colleague's campaign.

Yet reporters who feel strongly about an issue often want to speak out on it. The problem arose during the war in Vietnam, and some editors quickly drew up guidelines that prohibited any political activism. Now, the problem is arising once again, this time over the issue of abortion rights. More and more journalists say they feel compelled to take sides, yet their newspapers' policies discourage or even prohibit any such advocacy.

A reporter for Florida's Vero Beach Press-Journal was fired after she sent letters and small copper coat hangers to all 160 members of the state Legislature. The legislators were meeting in a special session to consider the adoption of tougher abortion laws.

The reporter, Vicky Hendley, 26, said she did not think her job as a reporter required her to give up her personal involvement in a cause she believed in. Also, she had been covering education for two years and said the abortion issue never came up on that beat.

Darryl Hicks, the newspaper's general manager, said Hendley was fired not because of her beliefs about abortion, but because she had violated company policy. In addition to writing the letters, Hendley had given interviews to other papers. "In all those she was clearly identified as a reporter for the Press-Journal," Hicks said. "We were drawn into it right away—clearly a conflict."

Similarly, a reporter at the (Troy, N.Y.) Times Record was fired for failing to give up her post as an alternative delegate to a Democratic National Convention. The reporter, Susan O'Brien, said her firing was unfair. "I had absolutely no dealings with any political figures in my position at the paper," she said. "I wrote a three-times-a-week hot line column, typed up bowling scores, put together a weekend calendar and sat in for the receptionist when she was out to lunch."

The paper's executive editor responded, "When we found out, we told her that in the newspaper business, politics and reporting don't mix. We told her she would have to give up one or the other and gave her a week to make her decision. After a week, she told us she still had not decided. We consulted on the matter and decided we had no choice but to let her go."

The reporters at most newspapers are free to accept other types of second jobs, provided that they do not create any conflicts. Typically, reporters and photographers can work as free-lancers, but cannot sell their work to their employers' competitors, such as other media in the same market. Similarly, newspapers may allow their sportswriters to teach at a community college, but not to serve as scorekeepers at the games they cover. As scorekeepers, the writers would become part of the stories they

This photo, perhaps the most famous taken during the war in Vietnam, shows a 73-year-old Buddhist monk protesting government policies he considered oppressive. The monk's self-immolation on a Saigon street succeeded in turning the world's attention to the issue.

were covering. Their decisions might be controversial and might determine the outcome of some games. Thus, the writers would have to report on their own actions. Similarly, newspapers might tell a sports editor to stop serving as the host of a local radio program and to avoid appearing on local television programs, especially for pay.

Pillow Talk and Cronyism

Increasingly, journalists also face a newer conflict: their spouse's employment or position. To avoid the conflict, editors rarely allow reporters to cover any story in which their spouse is involved.

Another problem, called "hobnobbery journalism," arises when journalists become good friends with their sources. Walter Lippmann, one of the nation's most respected columnists, insisted that: "Newspapermen can't be the cronies of great men. There always has to be a certain distance between high public officials and newspapermen." The problem often arises in Washington and was especially common during the Kennedy administration. Some journalists became the president's friends and, because of that friendship, may have been reluctant to criticize him.

Other Conflicts of Interest

A survey conducted by the Ethics Committee of the American Society of Newspaper Editors revealed that 30 journalists were suspended and 48 fired because of their unethical behavior during a recent three-year period. The two most common problems involved: journalists' social contacts with newsmakers and journalists' rewriting of their competitors' stories without first verifying the details. Other ethical violations involved plagiarism, the fabrication of stories, the use of unpublished material for financial gain, and the acceptance of discounts from companies the journalists wrote about.

Some conflicts have affected an entire state or industry. In 1972, The Newspaper Guild endorsed George McGovern, the Democratic candidate for president. The Guild is a union that represents thousands of the nation's journalists. After its endorsement, critics asked whether the Guild's members would be able to remain impartial while covering that year's presidential election. Because of the controversy, the Guild did not endorse a candidate in 1976 or 1980. In 1984, however, it endorsed Walter F. Mondale.

In 1978, Florida's large daily newspapers opposed a proposal to legalize casino gambling in the state. The newspapers used their editorial pages to denounce the proposal. In addition, they contributed up to $25,000 apiece—a total of almost $150,000—to a campaign to defeat the proposal. The proposal was defeated, but reappeared on Florida's 1986 ballot. In 1986, the dailies declined to donate any money to help defeat it, partly because of the controversy caused by their earlier donations.

A Disney Bribe?

Walt Disney World invited thousands of journalists to fly to Orlando to celebrate its 15th anniversary and, supposedly, to celebrate the 200th anniversary of the U.S. Constitution. Each journalist was allowed to bring one guest.

More than 5,000 people accepted Disney's invitation. Some were disc jockeys or worked in management, advertising or promotion. They flew to Orlando from all 50 states, and were joined by several hundred Canadians, about 200 Europeans and 20 Japanese.

The junket cost about $7.5 million, but Disney contributed only $1.5 million. Seventeen airlines offered their services free or at reduced rates. Hotels donated 5,000 rooms and free breakfasts. The state of Florida and several local groups, all established to promote tourism, contributed an additional $350,000 apiece. They spent $600,000 on a single party in downtown Orlando. The visiting journalists were also treated to a concert and a fireworks display, and had Disney's Magic Kingdom to themselves for an entire evening.

The Disney organization insisted that there were no strings attached: that the journalists were not under any obligation to give the theme park any favorable publicity. Moreover, Disney said, it had offered the journalists three options:

- They could accept the free trip.
- They could pay $150 a day to cover a portion of their expenses.
- They could accept Disney's offer but pay the entire cost of their travel, food and lodging.

Disney refused to provide a list of the journalists who accepted its invitation. However, about one-third seemed to be employed by newspapers and magazines, and about two-thirds seemed to be employed by the broadcast media. Their acceptance renewed a controversy that many journalists thought had ended years earlier. Hundreds of newspapers and broadcasting stations have adopted codes of ethics that prohibit the acceptance of anything of value. Almost every major organization in the field of journalism has adopted a similar code. Yet, when offered a junket that violated their codes, thousands of journalists accepted it. Why?

Journalists employed by small newspapers and broadcast stations explained that they would have been unable to cover the story without Disney's subsidy. Larger newspapers may have accepted Disney's subsidy because a travel writer's expenses for one year could total $100,000 or more. Other journalists said they accepted Disney's offer because they were not required to do anything in return. Still others insisted that, as trained professionals, they would remain objective: they would not be corrupted by Disney's subsidy.

A writer for The Orlando Sentinel responded that: "This generosity is no better than a bribe to get puffy coverage, and the so-called journalists who accept it are a disgrace." A second critic complained that Disney "exposed dramatically the seamy side of the journalism profession." Disney's offer seemed to prove "that a great deal of favorable publicity is, without question, for sale by a significant percentage of the country's media."

Even the critics overlooked a more fundamental issue. Was the party newsworthy? Was Disney's 15th anniversary important enough to justify coverage by 5,000 media employees? Or, did the recipients use Disney's anniversary as an excuse to accept a free vacation in Florida?

Disney obviously wanted publicity. Why else would it invite so many journalists to Orlando? Moreover, it succeeded. A Disney representative called it "the biggest marketing project we have ever undertaken." Within three months, Disney estimated that it had received $9 million worth of free publicity. Television stations broadcast 186 live reports during the extravaganza, and radio stations provided 1,000 hours of live coverage. Even major networks covered the story. Both ABC's "Good Morning America" and NBC's "Today" broadcast live from Disney World.

Publicists at Disney collected a two-foot stack of press clippings. The extravaganza was also supposed to have observed the 200th anniversary of the signing of the U.S. Constitution, but most of the stories described Disney World. Moreover, the Constitution was only 199—not yet 200—years old.

Thus, Disney exploited journalists' greed. It was up to journalists, however, to decide to accept the offer. Moreover, Disney World repeated the offer on its 20th anniversary, when it threw another gigantic party. Once again, it sent invitations to thousands of news organizations, offering their employees free trips to Orlando. A Disney representative explained: "The sole purpose is to let people see the shows we offer the public, the same as they do a movie, play or sporting event. The only way you can review a travel destination is to travel to the destination. . . . You can't do it by remote."

Perhaps because of the controversy surrounding its first celebration, Disney declined to reveal the cost of its second celebration—or to reveal the identities and number of guests who accepted its invitations to the second celebration.

Speaking Fees

Increasingly, the nation's leading journalists have become celebrities who can earn thousands of dollars for a single speech. Richard Harwood, an ombudsman at The Washington Post, estimates that columnist Jack Anderson earns $500,000 a year for his speeches. William Safire of The New York Times earns an estimated $200,000 a year for his speeches and for appearances on television's public affairs programs.

There may not be a conflict if a journalist speaks to a group of journalists or at a university, for example. But should any journalist be allowed to accept $20,000 or $30,000 to speak to a corporation or trade association? If that organization later became involved in the news, would the journalist be able to cover the story objectively?

Some journalists have also criticized Linda Ellerbee, a newswoman and author, for making several television commercials for Maxwell House coffee. Weatherman Willard Scott made similar commercials for Maxwell House coffee but was not criticized because he is considered more of an entertainer than journalist.

Critics maintain that journalists are hypocrites, reporting on and exposing the methods of others, but rarely their own. To expose conflicts of interest, journalists expect members of Congress and other top government officials to reveal their sources of outside income. But journalists rarely reveal their own sources of income. Similarly, journalists complain about the thousands of dollars that some members of Congress earn from speeches, but rarely mention their own speaking fees.

Journalism Contests

Journalists also worry about another conflict: a proliferation of contests. Editors do not want their employees to accept gifts from the people they write about. Yet each year journalists enter hundreds of contests, including some that offer thousands of dollars in prizes.

There are an estimated 500 contests for journalists—so many that Editor & Publisher magazine publishes an annual directory of journalism awards and fellowships. The latest edition needed 60 pages to describe all of them.

Typically, the Thoroughbred Racing Association gives "Eclipse Awards" for the best coverage of thoroughbred horse racing. The Korea National Tourism Corp. has given "Heavenly Horse Awards" for travel writing about the Republic of Korea. The National Multiple Sclerosis Society gives $1,000 prizes "for stories improving understanding about multiple sclerosis."

Some sponsors specify that, to be eligible for a prize, a story must be favorable. For years, the International Association of Fire Fighters honored "news media for reporting and photography that best portray the professional and hazardous work of the firefighters in the United States and Canada." Similarly, the Mexican Government Tourist Office has given cash, silver trophies and trips for articles "that promote travel to Mexico."

Some of the contests are aimed at college students. For example, the Laymen's National Bible Association awards cash prizes and a trip to New York City for the best editorial that a student enrolled in a U.S. college writes about the Bible.

Associated Press photographer Nick Ut took this picture of Vietnamese children fleeing a napalm bomb attack.

Why do journalists enter these contests? Some obviously want the money. Also, editors may feel that their newspapers and staffs benefit when other people recognize their best work. In addition, the contests and prizes may help to boost their staffs' morale—and provide an incentive to do a better job.

Critics charge that the prizes corrupt newspapers. Some editors seem to be preoccupied with the contests and look for stories that will win awards, especially the prestigious Pulitzer Prizes. To obtain those stories, editors may neglect other stories, even stories that are more important to their communities. Also, reporters eager to win the cash prizes may be tempted to write only favorable stories. Then, after winning the prizes, reporters may find it difficult to remain objective while continuing to cover the same groups.

To avoid the problems, many editors are becoming more selective. They avoid contests sponsored by trade associations and other special interest groups: contests designed to promote a product or organization. The editors allow their employees to enter contests sponsored by press associations. They also allow their employees to enter contests sponsored by commercial groups that use an outside, or objective, panel of judges. The editors want to be certain that sponsors want to honor excellence in journalism, not stories that happen to cover or promote a certain topic.

Thus, before allowing their employees to compete for any of the prizes, many editors now ask:

- Who is sponsoring the contest?
- Must the publicity be favorable?
- How do journalists benefit from the contest?
- Who are the judges?
- Who selects the judges and screens the initial entries?

RUMORS: GOSSIP OR NEWS?

Journalists are supposed to publish facts, but are often tempted to publish some rumors. If everyone in their community seems to be talking about a rumor, journalists may want to report on it. Yet some rumors are impossible to verify, and journalists should be aware that, by discussing a rumor, they may be encouraging its repetition. News stories may explain that the rumor is "unconfirmed," but some readers may fail to notice or remember that disclaimer.

Some rumors are little more than gossip. They may insist that a celebrity is gay, getting divorced or dying of AIDS. Or, they may wrongly insist that a celebrity has died. One rumor insisted that the governor of New York had had a facelift (a charge he vigorously denied).

A book published after President Ronald Reagan left office reported that his wife, Nancy, had enjoyed long lunches in the White House with Frank Sinatra. Moreover, the book implied that Sinatra and Mrs. Reagan may have enjoyed more than just lunch with each other. Tens of thousands of people bought the book, and some were discussing it with friends. Most of the nation's news media then reported the gossip. Some news stories added that journalists were unable to confirm the details. Some news stories also criticized the author's investigative techniques. Still, all the stories helped publicize the book, thus increasing its sales—and spreading the gossip.

Some rumors concern topics that might affect an entire community. They may claim that a new building is unsafe, that a local business is owned by the Mafia, or that a major employer plans to move out.

Journalists have tried to expose rumors that were obviously false and harmed innocent victims. For example, dozens of news stories tried to refute a rumor that Procter & Gamble Co.'s old trademark, stars and the moon inside a circle, was a symbol of Satanism. Some Americans, however, continued to believe the rumor and to boycott the company. People repeating the rumor usually claimed that a Procter & Gamble official had appeared on a nationally televised talk show and admitted that he had agreed to work for the devil in return for the devil's help in making him a millionaire. To stop the rumor, Procter & Gamble began to file libel suits against the people reprinting the rumor as fact. The company also eliminated the symbol from its packages.

Another rumor confronted Stanley Dearman, editor of The Neshoba Democrat in Philadelphia, Miss. Dearman said he heard persistent rumors that three local men—a businessman, a law enforcement official and a pilot—had been arrested with a planeload of cocaine. Dearman investigated the story and found that it was false, yet readers continued to call him and ask why he failed to report it. Some readers suspected that Dearman had been paid off. The callers were certain that the story had been broadcast by a television station; however, none had actually seen it. Finally, Dearman published an editorial offering a $500 reward to anyone able to prove that the story was true. He also promised to publish all the details. No one claimed the money, and the rumor died.

CENSORING ADVERTISEMENTS

Many Americans oppose censorship of any type, and journalists are especially vigilant in their efforts to combat it. Yet journalists themselves regularly censor the advertisements submitted to them. Journalists clearly have the legal right to do so. Courts have consistently ruled that the First Amendment gives editors the right to reject any advertisement that they dislike, regardless of the reason.

For almost 200 years, newspapers published virtually every advertisement submitted to them. Editors rarely felt responsible for the content of advertisements. Rather, the editors' philosophy was *caveat emptor:* "Let the buyer beware."

During the 1800s, newspapers in both the North and the South published advertisements for slaves. Perhaps unknowingly, some also published advertisements for prostitutes. Advertisements for quack medicines were even more common. Some medicines contained enough alcohol to inebriate the people using them. Others contained enough heroin, opium and morphine to make the people using them addicts. Even the "soothing syrups" sold for babies were spiked with drugs, so that some babies may have died of overdoses.

A single medicine might be advertised as the cure for dozens of ailments, including headaches, tuberculosis, malaria, poison ivy, ulcers, varicose veins, cancer, syphilis, hay fever and diarrhea. People felt better after taking some of the medicines, but only because they contained narcotics or alcohol.

During the 1800s, a few periodicals began to protect their readers from fraudulent advertising. When Cyrus H. K. Curtis took over the Saturday Evening Post in 1897, he began to reject advertisements for liquor and patent medicines. During the 20th century, newspapers began to reject advertisements for patent medicines and for get-rich-quick financial schemes, especially schemes that required large down payments. The St. Louis Post-Dispatch was a leader in the campaign to clean up newspapers' advertising columns. It lost thousands of dollars in revenue, but its publisher never objected.

Most editors now reject advertisements that seem distasteful or that promote products that seem illegal, immoral or harmful. The editors want to act ethically. Some explain that they have always felt responsible for the content of their news columns, routinely deleting anything that seemed tasteless, inaccurate, unfair, libelous or obscene. Now, the editors say, they are accepting a similar responsibility for the content of their advertising columns. Many readers agree with the editors' decisions. Others accuse them of censorship.

Policies vary from newspaper to newspaper and from magazine to magazine. They also change over time. Historically, for example, television stations banned advertisements for contraceptives. Television stations recently began to lift that ban, especially their ban on advertisements for condoms, because condoms can help deter AIDS.

More than 100 daily newspapers reject advertisements for alcoholic beverages, especially hard liquor. Other dailies reject advertisements for X-rated movies, sexual aids, mail order goods, hair restorers and fortune tellers. A few dailies reject advertisements for abortion services and handguns. Some also reject advertisements for massage parlors and escort services, which in some cities have been fronts for prostitution.

Of the nation's 1,600 daily newspapers, only a dozen or two reject advertisements for cigarettes. Scientists have proven that tobacco causes cancer, and the U.S. Surgeon General has called smoking "the chief single avoidable cause of death in our society and the most important public-health issue of our time." Since 1965, manufacturers have been required to place health warnings on cigarette packs. In 1971, Congress banned cigarette advertisements on radio and television. Since then, the tobacco industry has turned to other media, especially newspapers and magazines. U.S. Rep. Mike Synar advocates a law that would limit print advertisements for tobacco products, and he explains that: "Tobacco is more than unhealthy—it is deadly. It is the only product that, when used as intended, can kill you." Also, tobacco cannot legally be sold to children in most states, yet 90 percent of all smokers begin as teens. Moreover, many of the advertisements for tobacco products seem to be aimed at teens. Typically, the advertisements show healthy, athletic young people engaged in pleasurable, glamorous activities.

Why do most newspapers and magazines continue to accept the advertisements for cigarettes? A few journalists may not believe that smoking causes cancer. Others seem reluctant to offend smokers or the tobacco industry. The industry still spends more than $2 billion a year on advertising in the United States. Most editors explain that it would be unethical or irresponsible for them to reject the advertisements. The editors say they are hesitant to withhold information from the public simply because they happen to disagree with it. As long as the tobacco industry's advertisements are truthful and legal, the editors add, they want to protect Americans' freedom to make their own decisions, however good or bad. Editors also warn that any new law that banned the advertisements would infringe on the freedom of the press.

David Shaw of the Los Angeles Times adds that, "Only 1 percent of newspaper advertising revenue comes from tobacco companies, but it is not that loss that worries newspapers; it is the much larger loss they would suffer if a ban on cigarette advertising established a precedent, and advertisements for other, more lucrative products were subsequently banned as well." Advertisements for handguns might be the next target, or advertisements for alcohol or fast cars.

New censorship issues are constantly arising. Some newspapers, concerned about their readers' health and safety, no longer accept advertisements for "happy hours" (for cheap or free drinks). Bars usually advertise the "happy hours" during the late afternoon and evening, when people begin to drive home after work. Editors fear that the advertisements will contribute to heavy drinking and drunken driving.

Newspapers in the Northeast have been troubled by advertisements for babies. Typically, the advertisements promise to pay $10,000 or more for "a white newborn." Because of contraceptives and legal abortions, and because many unmarried mothers are keeping their babies, few healthy white infants are available for adoption. Couples unwilling to take several years to work with a conventional adoption agency may turn to a newspaper's classified advertising columns. To persuade mothers to put their babies up for adoption, couples promise to give babies loving and secure homes. In addition, they promise to pay the mothers thousands of dollars.

The advertisements have also begun to appear in the Midwest, and newspapers there have no standard policy for handling them. Some newspapers publish the advertisements, but others do not.

DO JOURNALISTS ENCOURAGE TERRORISM?

Striking at random, terrorists kidnap tourists, assassinate diplomats and hijack airplanes. Their causes may seem obscure, yet the terrorists seem willing to die for them. They also seem willing to kill hundreds of other people. Because of their fanaticism, entire nations seem helpless against them.

The terrorists usually want publicity and have learned to create news so compelling that television is unable to ignore it. The terrorists provide genuine drama: hijackings, demands, deadlines and the threat of mass murder. They can add to the drama by moving from one place to another and by releasing or murdering a few of their hostages.

To attract even more publicity, the terrorists have learned to conduct press conferences. Some allow journalists to photograph and interview their helpless captives. Others make videotapes of their captives, typically showing the captives pleading for their lives, reading the terrorists' demands, and warning that they will be killed if the demands are not met.

Critics insist that television does more than cover the terrorists: that it also encourages them. They believe that if the media ignored terrorists, they would become discouraged and abandon their acts of violence. Former British Prime Minister Margaret Thatcher

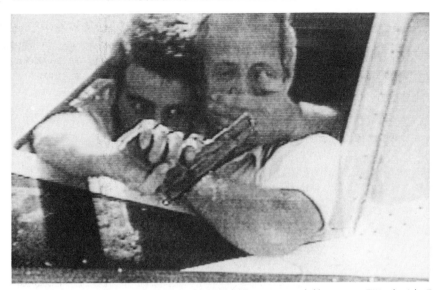

Most terrorists want publicity—and succeed in obtaining it. Here, a terrorist holds a gun on TWA pilot John Testrake as he was interviewed after the plane was hijacked to Beirut. One passenger was killed, but Testrake, his crew and the remaining passengers were released after days of negotiations (and intensive television coverage).

urged journalists to stop covering terrorists, to starve them of the "oxygen of publicity." The critics want journalists to adopt a voluntary code that would limit coverage of terrorists. But that may be impossible. No one seems able to develop a code acceptable to thousands of journalists in dozens of countries. It also seems impossible to develop guidelines that would cover every possible situation.

Moreover, most journalists are reluctant to accept guidelines that would limit their coverage of an important story—and their freedom. Journalists add that Americans have a right to know what is happening in the world, and that a news blackout might be worse because rumors about the terrorists' activities might become more frightening than the truth. Journalists also fear that, if the terrorists were ignored, some would escalate their violence. Instead of hijacking one plane, they might hijack two or three. Instead of using a small bomb to kill a single individual, they might use a larger bomb to kill hundreds. Eventually, the media would be forced to cover them.

Thus, journalists seem both unable and unwilling to censor themselves. Some governments might censor the media, but in the United States, government censorship is illegal. Journalists add that it would also be unwise. To censor the media would be to limit the freedom—that is, the free access to knowledge—of the people the government was trying to protect.

CODES OF ETHICS

Every major organization in the field of journalism has adopted a code of ethics, but there is little evidence that any of the codes are effective. They are seldom enforced, and some organizations adopted their codes merely for self-protection: to convince the public that they are doing a good job of regulating themselves and that government regulation is unnecessary.

The American Society of Newspaper Editors (ASNE) adopted one of the industry's first codes, the Canons of Journalism, in 1923. The Canons did not prohibit anything; rather, they told newspaper editors what they should do. Among other things, they

A photographer practiced for a month before secretly taking this picture of Ruth Snyder as she was electrocuted for murdering her husband. The photo appeared in a sensational tabloid, the New York Daily News. A mask was placed over Snyder's head after she was strapped into Sing Sing's electric chair on the night of Jan. 12, 1928. To avoid detection, the photographer—who posed as a reporter—tied a miniature camera to one ankle. He lifted a pants cuff and used a remote control to snap one photo as the first jolt of electricity surged through Snyder's body, and to snap another photo at the second jolt.

declared that newspapers should act responsibly: that they should be truthful, sincere, impartial, decent and fair. However, the Canons were so vague that even the most sincere journalists might disagree about their meaning.

In fact, the ASNE rejected attempts to enforce the Canons. During President Warren G. Harding's administration, Frederick Bonfils, co-publisher of The Denver Post, accepted a bribe to ignore the Teapot Dome scandal. When the ASNE learned about the bribe, it considered expelling Bonfils, but abandoned the idea. Instead, the ASNE decided to encourage editors to comply voluntarily with the Canons of Journalism. Its members were divided over the issue and feared that if they tried to expel Bonfils, the organization might be destroyed.

Another group, the Society of Professional Journalists, adopted a revised code at its national convention in 1973. The code declares that journalists must seek the truth and that they have a responsibility to "perform with intelligence, objectivity, accuracy and fairness." The code adds that journalists should accept "nothing of value" because gifts and special favors might compromise their integrity. The code also recommends that journalists avoid second jobs and political involvement that might cause a conflict of interest.

The code's most controversial section stated that journalists who violated the code should be censured. The section explained that, "Journalists should actively censure and try to prevent violations of those standards, and they should encourage their observance by all news people." Yet few violators were censured, and the society never adopted any formal procedures for censure.

During the 1980s, journalists began to call for an end to the hypocrisy. They wanted to eliminate the SPJ code's censure clause or to adopt the procedures necessary to

Society of Professional Journalists

CODE OF ETHICS

SOCIETY of Professional Journalists, believes the duty of journalists is to serve the truth.

We BELIEVE the agencies of mass communication are carriers of public discussion and information, acting on their Constitutional mandate and freedom to learn and report the facts.

We BELIEVE in public enlightenment as the forerunner of justice, and in our Constitutional role to seek the truth as part of the public's right to know the truth.

We BELIEVE those responsibilities carry obligations that require journalists to perform with intelligence, objectivity, accuracy, and fairness.

To these ends, we declare acceptance of the standards of practice here set forth:

I. RESPONSIBILITY:

The public's right to know of events of public importance and interest is the overriding mission of the mass media. The purpose of distributing news and enlightened opinion is to serve the general welfare. Journalists who use their professional status as representatives of the public for selfish or other unworthy motives violate a high trust.

II. FREEDOM OF THE PRESS:

Freedom of the press is to be guarded as an inalienable right of people in a free society. It carries with it the freedom and the responsibility to discuss, question, and challenge actions and utterances of our government and of our public and private institutions. Journalists uphold the right to speak unpopular opinions and the privilege to agree with the majority.

III. ETHICS:

Journalists must be free of obligation to any interest other than the public's right to know the truth.

1. Gifts, favors, free travel, special treatment or privileges can compromise the integrity of journalists and their employers. Nothing of value should be accepted.

2. Secondary employment, political involvement, holding public office, and service in community organizations should be avoided if it compromises the integrity of journalists and their employers. Journalists and their employers should conduct their personal lives in a manner that protects them from conflict of interest, real or apparent. Their responsibilities to the public are paramount. That is the nature of their profession.

3. So-called news communications from private sources should not be published or broadcast without substantiation of their claims to news values.

4. Journalists will seek news that serves the public interest, despite the obstacles. They will make constant efforts to assure that the public's business is conducted in public and that public records are open to public inspection.

(continued on next page)

5. Journalists acknowledge the newsman's ethic of protecting confidential sources of information.

6. Plagiarism is dishonest and unacceptable.

IV. ACCURACY AND OBJECTIVITY:

Good faith with the public is the foundation of all worthy journalism.

1. Truth is our ultimate goal.

2. Objectivity in reporting the news is another goal that serves as the mark of an experienced professional. It is a standard of performance toward which we strive. We honor those who achieve it.

3. There is no excuse for inaccuracies or lack of thoroughness.

4. Newspaper headlines should be fully warranted by the contents of the articles they accompany. Photographs and telecasts should give an accurate picture of an event and not highlight an incident out of context.

5. Sound practice makes clear distinction between news reports and expressions of opinion. News reports should be free of opinion or bias and represent all sides of an issue.

6. Partisanship in editorial comment that knowingly departs from the truth violates the spirit of American journalism.

7. Journalists recognize their responsibility for offering informed analysis, comment, and editorial opinion on public events and issues. They accept the obligation to present such material by individuals whose competence, experience, and judgment qualify them for it.

8. Special articles or presentations devoted to advocacy or the writer's own conclusions and interpretations should be labeled as such.

V. FAIR PLAY:

Journalists at all times will show respect for the dignity, privacy rights, and well-being of people encountered in the course of gathering and presenting the news.

1. The news media should not communicate unofficial charges affecting reputation or moral character without giving the accused a chance to reply.

2. The news media must guard against invading a person's right to privacy.

3. The media should not pander to morbid curiosity about details of vice and crime.

4. It is the duty of news media to make prompt and complete correction of their errors.

5. Journalists should be accountable to the public for their reports and the public should be encouraged to voice its grievances against the media. Open dialogue with our readers, viewers, and listeners should be fostered.

VI. MUTUAL TRUST:

Adherence to this code is intended to preserve and strengthen the bond of mutual trust and respect between American journalists and the American people.

The Society shall—by programs of education and other means—encourage individual journalists to adhere to these tenets, and shall encourage journalistic publications and broadcasters to recognize their responsibility to frame codes of ethics in concert with their employees to serve as guidelines in furthering these goals.

CODE OF ETHICS
(Adopted 1926; revised 1973, 1984, 1987)

enforce it. Other journalists opposed the idea. They wanted to encourage, not enforce, ethical conduct. Journalists seemed reluctant to infringe on their colleagues' freedom, to tell them how to act, or to publicly condemn their decisions. In 1987, delegates at the society's national convention voted to eliminate that section of the code.

Recent surveys have found that at least half the nation's daily newspapers and broadcasting stations have adopted codes to govern the conduct of their employees. Most of these codes are designed to prevent conflicts of interest, and many are strictly enforced. Typically, they prohibit the acceptance of anything of value, including gifts, favors, tickets and trips. Most also prohibit any outside work, political involvement or other activities that would conflict with their coverage of the news.

A recent poll of 34 newspapers in the Northeast revealed that 51 percent had adopted a written code, and that:

- 90 percent did not allow their newsroom employees to accept gifts.
- 90 percent did not allow their newsroom employees to become involved in politics.
- 79 percent did not allow their newsroom employees to accept tickets to dinners.
- 63 percent did not allow their newsroom employees to accept tickets to artistic events.
- 57 percent did not allow their newsroom employees to accept tickets to athletic events.
- 27 percent did not allow their newsroom employees to accept books for review.

Some reporters have responded that the codes infringe on their freedom and that, as citizens, they have a responsibility to become involved in their communities. Reporters have also complained of a double standard in journalism. The codes limit their freedom, yet many editors and publishers continue to do as they please, heading charities and serving on the boards of local schools and businesses. Similarly, a publisher can write editorials that endorse a politician's candidacy, but reporters cannot sign petitions, march in rallies or provide any other help for a politician's campaign.

All in all, the professional standards in journalism are improving. Journalists are becoming better educated, more responsible and more ethical. But it is difficult for them to convince the public of that fact. Journalists are forced to make too many controversial decisions, and the decisions are more complex than most people imagine.

Also, journalists and their readers often disagree about which stories the media should report and about how those stories should be presented to the public. Journalists are reluctant to suppress any stories. Readers, however, worry about the effects of some stories on the people involved, and on other readers.

Journalists are adopting codes of ethics to eliminate the most obvious abuses, especially conflicts of interest. But the codes cannot solve every problem. There are too many problems, and the problems are too diverse. Thus, decisions will always vary from one newspaper to another—and that may be one of our system's greatest strengths. Every journalist is free to decide what is right or wrong, ethical or unethical. Inevitably, some journalists will be mistaken. But any effort to change the system— to force every journalist to conform to a predetermined standard—would limit the media's diversity and freedom. It would also limit Americans' access to some information.

YOU BE THE EDITOR

The Miami Herald published these hypothetical cases. After reading the cases, decide what your decision would be if you were the editor. Check the most appropirate box in each example. You may make additional comments in the space provided or on a separate sheet of paper.

1. A woman on the county commission is raped. The afternoon paper reports she was hospitalized following an assault but does not indicate it was a sexual attack. A conservative and anti-feminist, she has blocked the expenditure of public monies for a rape crisis center at the county hospital. This has been a much publicized local controversy for the past six months. But now she tells you that she plans to rethink her position on the crisis center. She also makes clear the deep personal trauma she is suffering as a result of the assault and asks that you not say she was raped.

☐ Do you go ahead with the story, including her change of mind, recognizing that the shift is a significant public policy development?

☐ Do you say no more than the afternoon paper did?

☐ Do you refer to the attack simply as an assault but report that the convalescing commissioner is rethinking her position on the crisis center, thus suggesting the nature of the attack?

☐ Do you report the assault and say nothing about the rape now, but decide that when she actually votes for the rape crisis center you will report the reasons for her change of mind, whether or not she wants to talk about it?

2. The mayor is a hardliner on crime. He has made local drug enforcement a major issue. You learn that his 19-year-old son, who lives at home and attends a local community college, has been arrested for possession of a small quantity of marijuana, a misdemeanor if convicted.

(a.) Would you run a story on the arrest?
☐ Yes.   ☐ No.

(b.) Would you run a story if the arrest were for selling a pound of marijuana?
☐ Yes.   ☐ No.

(c.) Would you run a story if the arrest were for selling cocaine?
☐ Yes.   ☐ No.

3. A prominent businessman identified with United Way and many other charitable causes is discovered to have embezzled $25,000 from one of the charities he heads. There is no question about his guilt, although charges have not yet been filed. The story is yours alone. When your reporter contacts him for comment, the man says there are extenuating circumstances he cannot go into and that he will make full restitution if given a chance. He pleads that no story be written, saying his wife suffered a serious heart attack, is in critical condition at a local hospital and he fears that public disclosure of what he has done could kill her.

☐ Would you run the story, now?

☐ Would you wait until you have had an opportunity to talk with the hospital's doctors and are confident the woman is out of immediate danger, then run the story?

☐ Would you give him an opportunity to make restitution and, if this is done, write nothing?

4. A businessman donates $5 million to the University of Miami to build a new football stadium. Checking his background, you learn that the man was arrested at age 18 for armed robbery and avoided prison only by volunteering for military duty in World War II. His record, as far as you can discover, has been spotless since. He refuses to talk about the incident, says he has never even told his closest friends and threatens to withdraw his contribution to the university if you print the story. University officials are shocked and urge that you write nothing.

☐ Do you print the information on the arrest as one element in an over-all profile of the man and who he is?

☐ Do you hold off on the arrest information until the UM has the money?

☐ Do you take the position that the information is not relevant and discard it?

SUGGESTED READINGS

Articles

Brill, Steven. "Corrections Policies: Why Can't Editors Just Do the Right Thing?" *NewsInc,* March 1990, pp. 41–43.

Davis, Foster. "Did Joseph Pulitzer Succeed Too Well? Are Newspapers Paying Too Much Attention to Too Many Prizes?" *ASNE Bulletin,* May/June 1990, pp. 22–23.

Gup, Ted. "Identifying Homosexuals: What Are the Rules?" *Washington Journalism Review,* Oct. 1988, pp. 30–33.

Hess, John L. "Who's Conning Whom? The Sins of Journalists Are More Imagined Than Real." *The Quill,* May 1989, pp. 29–33.

Palmer, Nancy Doyle. "Going After the Truth—In Disguise: The Ethics of Deception." *Washington Journalism Review,* Nov. 1987, pp. 20–22.

Quine, Frank. "What Editors Think About Journalism Contests: Who Are the Judges? What About the Sponsor? Do Journalists Write and Edit for Awards?" *Washington Journalism Review,* Jan./Feb. 1990, pp. 47–57.

Rambo, C. David. "Tough Calls: In the Newsroom, There Often Is No Single Right or Wrong Answer to Ethical Questions about What to Print." *Presstime,* Dec. 1989, pp. 30–33.

Saul, Stephanie. "Judgment Call: Do Reporters Have a Right to March?" *Columbia Journalism Review,* July/Aug. 1989, pp. 50–52.

Shaw, David. "Newspapers Draw Foggy Line on Ads." *Los Angeles Times,* Feb. 15, 1987. (Reprinted in pamphlet form)

"Special Report: Ethics in Journalism." *The Quill,* March 1991, pp. 20–38.

Steele, Bob. "Pointed Question: Publish This Photo or Pass?" *The Quill,* Sept. 1989, pp. 38–40.

Taylor, John G. "Views from the Other Side: Two Veteran Journalists Recount How People Close to Them Became Victims of Violence—and of the Media." *ASNE Bulletin,* Oct. 1989, pp. 16–20.

Vernois, Christine Reid. "J-Schools Beef Up Ethics Teaching." *Presstime,* Sept. 1989, pp. 30–33.

Wisnia, Saul E. "Private Grief, Public Exposure: In Covering a Disaster, How Intrusive Is Too Intrusive?" *The Quill,* July/Aug. 1989, pp. 28–30.

These publications also discuss ethical issues in journalism:
Columbia Journalism Review
FineLine
Journal of Mass Media Ethics
The Quill
Washington Journalism Review

Books

Christians, Clifford G., Kim B. Rotzoll, and Mark Fackler. *Media Ethics: Cases and Moral Reasoning.* 2nd ed. New York: Longman, 1983.

Day, Louis A. *Ethics in Media Communications: Cases and Controversies.* Belmont, CA: Wadsworth, 1991.

Dennis, Everette E., and John C. Merrill. *Media Debates: Issues in Mass Communication.* New York: Longman, 1991.

Elliott, Deni, ed., *Responsible Journalism.* Beverly Hills, CA: Sage, 1986.

Fink, Conrad C. *Media Ethics: In the Newsroom and Beyond.* New York: McGraw-Hill, 1988.

Goldstein, Tom. *The News at Any Cost: How Journalists Compromise Their Ethics to Shape the News.* New York: Simon and Schuster, 1986.

Goodwin, H. Eugene. *Groping for Ethics in Journalism,* 2nd ed. Ames, IA: Iowa State University Press, 1987.

Hanson, Jarice, and Alison Alexander. *Taking Sides: Clashing Views on Controversial Issues in Mass Media and Society.* Guilford, CT: Dushkin, 1991.

Hulteng, John L. *The Messenger's Motives: Ethical Problems of the News Media.* 2nd ed. Englewood Cliffs, NJ: Prentice Hall, 1985.

———. *Playing It Straight: A Practical Discussion of the Ethical Principles of the American Society of Newspaper Editors.* Chester, CT: Globe-Pequot Press, 1981.

Klaidman, Stephen, and Tom L. Beauchamp. *The Virtuous Journalist.* New York: Oxford University Press, 1987.

Kreig, Andrew. *Spiked: How Chain Management Corrupted America's Oldest Newspaper.* Old Saybrook, CT: Peregrine Press, 1987.

Lambeth, Edmund B. *Committed Journalism: An Ethic for the Profession.* Bloomington, IN: Indiana University Press, 1986.

Meyer, Philip. *Ethical Journalism: A Guide for Students, Practitioners and Consumers.* New York: Longman, 1987.

Olen, Jeffrey. *Ethics in Journalism.* Englewood Cliffs, NJ: Prentice Hall, 1988.

Patterson, Philip, and Lee Wilkins. *Media Ethics: Issues and Cases.* Dubuque, IA: Brown, 1991.

Pfaff, Daniel W. *Joseph Pulitzer II and Advertising Censorship, 1929–1939.* Journalism Monographs, No. 77. Columbia, SC: Association for Education in Journalism and Mass Communication, 1982.

Pippert, Wesley G. *An Ethics of News: A Reporter's Search for Truth.* Washington, DC: Georgetown University Press, 1989.

Rivers, William L., and Cleve Mathews. *Ethics for the Media.* Englewood Cliffs, NJ: Prentice Hall, 1988.

Schmuhl, Robert, ed., *The Responsibilities of Journalism.* Notre Dame, IN: University of Notre Dame Press, 1985.

Shaw, David. *Press Watch: A Provocative Look at How Newspapers Report the News*. New York: Macmillan, 1984.

Swain, Bruce M. *Reporters' Ethics*. Ames, IA: Iowa State University Press, 1978.

Thayer, Lee. *Ethics, Morality and the Media*. New York: Hastings House, 1980.

Winans, R. Foster. *Trading Secrets: Seduction and Scandal at The Wall Street Journal*. St. Martin's Press, 1986.

Wulfemeyer, K. Tim. *The News Blues: Problems in Journalism*. Dubuque, IA: Kendall Hunt, 1989.

QUOTES

Whatever else one may say about the newspaper business, self-examination is one of its virtues. Searching questions about right conduct or wrong conduct are put whenever journalists gather.

(Marquis W. Childs, newspaper columnist)

The media can, and should, be much better. The media need to care about values. I've had some very sharp disagreements with First Amendment absolutists who say that all the media have to do is report; values are somebody else's business.

I don't believe that's true. And the choice of what we say and how we say it, what we report—we do have an impact, and we need to care what that impact is. Journalists need to be more committed to objectivity and thoroughness and accuracy and fairness. We need to respect people's privacy, whether those people are public figures or private figures. . . . We need to do these things because they are decent and because they are right and because if we don't, people are going to reject the very rights that are essential to their own freedoms.

Media can't correct all the problems that are faced by families and individuals, but what we can do is bring those problems into the open where they can be discussed, examined and dealt with. That is the media's job. And I would rather have it done by all those separate voices called the media than by any single voice called government.

(Jean Otto, editorial page editor, Rocky Mountain News*)*

Exercise 1

ETHICS

DISCUSSION QUESTIONS

1. Reread the list of rights prepared by the National Victim Center (see page 475), then discuss the list with your classmates. Do you agree with the center's guidelines? Also, how will the guidelines affect you as a reporter—or as a consumer of the media?

2. If you were a journalist, and Disney World offered you and a companion a free trip to Orlando for its 25th anniversary celebration, would you accept? Why or why not?

3. If you served on the board that awards Pulitzer Prizes, would you have given a prize to the Sun-Times for its exposure of corruption in Chicago? Or, would you have objected to the Sun-Times' purchase of its own tavern to obtain the story?

4. Imagine that you worked as the news director at a Pennsylvania television station on the day the state treasurer, R. Budd Dwyer, shot and killed himself during a press conference. If one of your photographers returned with a 21-second videotape of his suicide, what would you do with it?

5. The Newspaper Guild, a union that represents thousands of newspeople, endorsed a candidate in several presidential elections. Do you agree with its policy? Why or why not?

   If newspaper owners can endorse candidates on their editorial pages, why shouldn't reporters be able to endorse candidates through their unions?

6. Imagine that, as the editor of your local daily, you learned that one of your copy editors, working at home during her spare time, had written an article about a local celebrity. Would you allow her to sell the story to a magazine published in your city?

7. If you were the editor of your campus newspaper, would you accept and publish the advertisements submitted by companies that sell term papers? From discussions with friends, you know that some students submit the papers as their own work.

8. As the editor of a daily newspaper, would you report every birth, death, marriage, divorce, lawsuit and bankruptcy in your community? Would you also report every suicide, and every arrest and conviction for drunken driving?

9. Normally, the newspaper you edit avoids pictures of human grief. But imagine that a driver was killed during a stock car race at your county fair. More than 10,000 people saw the crash, and your photographer snapped a picture showing the driver's wife, holding his hand and crying as his body was cut from the wreckage. It is not a bloody scene, but you can see much of the driver's body and face. Would you publish the picture? Why?

10. Each year, you send a photographer to the graduation ceremonies at a local high school. Your photographer noticed several students misbehaving, and you published a picture of them because it seemed interesting and unusual. School administrators complained that the picture was not representative of the entire graduating class and that it may encourage other students to misbehave during next year's ceremonies. As a newspaper editor, you want to be fair but wonder whether it is your responsibility to encourage high school students to behave at their graduation ceremonies. What instructions, if any, would you give the photographer who covers next year's ceremonies?

11. You have just become the news director at a local television station and give each of your leading newspeople an allowance of $5,000 a year to purchase their wardrobes. The manager of a clothing store calls and offers to provide all their clothing free. In return, the manager wants a brief "credit" broadcast at the end of each program. By accepting, you would be able to save $50,000 a year and could use the money to hire another newscaster and raise the salaries of your other employees. Would you accept the store's offer? Why or why not?

12. Your police reporter has learned that a prominent minister has been charged with shoplifting, a crime that you normally report. The police reveal that it is the minister's third arrest during the last year, but charges were dropped by the stores. The minister has learned that your reporter is working on the story. He calls and warns you that, if you publish the story, he will be forced to kill himself. How would you handle the situation?

Exercise 2

ETHICS

SETTING YOUR NEWSPAPER'S POLICIES (WHAT WOULD YOU PERMIT?)

1. If you published your city's daily newspaper, would you accept advertisements for all these products? If not, which ones would you ban, and how would you explain that ban to your readers? Similarly, how would you explain your decision to publish the other advertisements?

   A. X-rated movies.
   B. Massage parlors.
   C. Abortion clinics.
   D. Some or all alcoholic beverages.
   E. Cigarettes and other tobacco products.

2. As the editor of a daily newspaper, you have been asked to write a code of ethics for your reporters. You want to be fair, but you also want to prevent any conflicts that might affect your staff's coverage of the news or that might harm you paper's credibility. Would you allow:

   A. Your science writer to date the mayor?
   B. Your science writer to run for the city council?
   C. Any of your reporters to sign a petition urging the mayor to resign?
   D. Your publisher to write an editorial endorsing the mayor's campaign for re-election?
   E. Your publisher to donate $1,000 to the mayor's re-election campaign?
   F. Your political reporter to volunteer his time each Saturday to help supervise a fund drive for the Salvation Army?
   G. Your political reporter to volunteer his time each Saturday to write publicity releases for the Salvation Army?
   H. Your political reporter to accept $100 for occasional appearances as a panelist on a Sunday-morning television program?

3. Normally, your newspaper reports every birth, death, divorce and bankruptcy in your community. You also identify everyone charged with drunken driving, and your obituaries include everyone's age and the cause of their death. You rarely approve any exceptions to the policies. You want to protect your paper's reputation and avoid charges of favoritism. As editor, would you agree to help any of these people?

   A. A 74-year-old woman mails you a letter explaining that she is dying of cancer and does not want you to report her age in her obituary. Her friends think she is 65. She is embarrassed by the matter and does not want them to know that she lied.
   B. A man's family calls and asks you to not report the cause of his death: cirrhosis of the liver. They admit that he was an alcoholic but see no reason to inform the entire community of that fact.
   C. A local couple with four children asks you to not report their marriage. Their children have always thought that they were married, and the news that they are finally getting married would upset and embarrass everyone in the family.

D. A minister charged with drunken driving pleads that he is innocent, that he was taking a prescription drug that made him dizzy. He insists that, in three or four days, breath and urinalysis tests conducted by the police will prove his innocence. Normally, you report everyone's arrest at the time of their apprehension, and later report the outcome of each case.

4. Assume that you edit your local daily and that a reporter on your staff receives a tip that your city airport's security system is defective. Moreover, airport officials know about the problem and have failed to correct it. How would you respond if the reporter proposed to walk through several airport checkpoints with a toy (but realistic) pistol in her purse?

   A. Would you approve her plan?
   B. Would you approve her plan, but instruct her to notify the police and other appropriate law enforcement agencies beforehand?
   C. Would you order the reporter to abandon the idea and to obtain the story through more conventional means?

5. Which of the following cases of deception do you think are justified? If you edited your local daily, would you agree to let a reporter:

   A. Pose as a bag lady while researching a story about the plight of the homeless?
   B. Join the Ku Klux Klan and remain a member for several months while preparing a story about the Klan's activities in your city?
   C. Obtain a job as a janitor in a nursing home suspected of abusing its patients, causing several deaths?
   D. Attend a church to investigate allegations that the church's minister has been making bigoted attacks on other races in the city? Your reporter would never identify himself as a journalist. Rather, to avoid detection, he would pretend to be a new member of the congregation. Also, since he could not openly take notes, your reporter would use a hidden tape recorder during the sermon.

6. Robbers entered a local jewelry store just before 9 a.m. today, shot one clerk and seized seven hostages. Police have surrounded the store and cordoned off the entire block. It is your biggest story in years. As the news director at a local television station, would you instruct your staff to:

   A. Call and interview the hostages' relatives?
   B. Call the store and try to interview the robbers?
   C. Televise the confrontation live from across the street?
   D. If the robbers requested it, agree to let your leading newscaster serve as an intermediary between them and the police?
   E. In return for the robbers' promise to surrender and to release all seven hostages, agree to let them appear on the air—live and unedited—for three minutes after their surrender?

7. The police have shot a 15-year-old boy who broke into a liquor store. Police officers responding to a silent alarm surrounded the store and ordered the intruder to come out. At the time, they did not know his age. The intruder fired a .22-caliber pistol at the officers. They returned the fire, killing him. As a reporter, which of the following details would you include in your story?

A. The boy was an Eagle Scout, the highest rank in scouting.
B. Other teen-agers—the boy's friends—say he was often drunk and may have been an alcoholic; however, the boy's parents deny it.
C. The boy had committed dozens of other crimes, starting when he was 8, and had spent three years in a home for delinquents.
D. The boy's parents are separated but not divorced. He lived with his mother and her boyfriend.
E. The boy's father is unemployed and an admitted alcoholic, fired from at least a dozen jobs. Relatives say he rarely saw his son.

Exercise 3

ETHICS

WHAT'S YOUR DECISION? (SOLVING THE MEDIA'S ETHICAL DILEMMAS)

1. Imagine that you are a political reporter for your local daily and, while at a Saturday-night party given at a friend's home, you see your mayor and over-hear him listening to and telling several sexist jokes that degrade women. You are attending the party as a guest, and the mayor does not know you are there (or that anyone can overhear the group he is with). What would you do?

   A. Not publish the jokes.
   B. Not publish the jokes but warn the mayor that, in the future, you will feel obligated to report that type of story. Then, to prevent additional conflicts, immediately sever all your social contacts with the mayor and other sources.
   C. Publish a story about the jokes but attribute them to a "city official," without identifying the mayor.
   D. Instruct a reporter to call other participants in the conversation and to get the story from them.
   E. Inform the mayor that you overheard the jokes and feel obligated to report them. Then ask the mayor to respond and include his response in your story, even if he insists that you are mistaken or lying.

2. Late Saturday morning, an aide for the Democratic candidate for mayor gave your political reporter evidence clearly proving that the Republican candidate has been treated twice for an addiction to cocaine. In return for the evidence, your political reporter promised never to reveal its source. The election is next Tuesday, and it is only a half hour before your Saturday deadline: too late to find and question the Republican. Moreover, you do not publish a Sunday edition. As editor, what would you do?

   A. Ignore the story as unfair and a political smear.
   B. Because of its importance, publish the story immediately. Then, on Monday, publish a second story reporting the Republican's response.
   C. Publish the story immediately, but overrule your political reporter and identify its source, so your readers understand that it is a political smear.
   D. Wait until Monday—the day before the election—and then report both the charges and the Republican's response, all in the same story.
   E. Publish the story immediately, but in a column on your editorial page, identify and denounce its source, pointing out that he seemed to have deliberately waited until the last minute so the Republican would be unable to respond.

3. The crime rate in your city's downtown shopping district has been rising along with an increase in prostitution. Customers are hesitant to visit the area, especially at night, and merchants are demanding better police protection. A major developer is considering a proposal to invest millions of dollars to revitalize the area, but is worried about its sordid reputation. The police and other city officials ask your newspaper for help. In the past, your paper has reported the names of women arrested for prostitution. Now, to discourage their customers, the police want you to also publish the names of the prostitutes' customers, their "johns." Which of these policies would you adopt?

A. Respond that you sympathize with the officials' problems, but that your newspaper is not an arm of the police, with an obligation to help enforce the city's laws. Thus, you will not publish the men's names.

B. Decline to publish any names, but publish news stories and editorials about the problem, encouraging the legal system (the police and the courts) to solve the problem.

C. Publish a warning, an editorial announcing your new policy: that in one week, you will begin to comply with the officials' request to publish the name of every john arrested in the area.

D. Announce that you plan to begin publishing everyone's name, but not because the police asked you to. Explain, truthfully, that you discussed the problem with your staff, and that several reporters pointed out that it was discriminatory to publish the women's names but not the men's. (Or, as an alternative, announce that you will no longer publish any names.)

E. Respond that the campaign is senseless, and that the prostitutes and their johns will simply move to another part of the city. Thus, the proposal will not solve the problem of prostitution in your community.

4. Normally, your newspaper never reports suicides. As editor, you consider suicides a personal and private matter. Moreover, you are reluctant to add to a family's grief and embarrassment. But during the past year, three teen-agers—all high school students in your community—have killed themselves. Last night, a fourth teen-ager (a well-known athlete) shot himself. There were no witnesses. What would you do?

A. Ignore the fourth suicide, just as you ignored the first three.

B. Assign a reporter to write a story about the problem of teen-age suicides and to mention the four local deaths, but without using any of the teen-agers' names.

C. Report the story as fully as possible, but identify only the latest victim, the prominent athlete.

D. Call the teen-agers' parents and ask for their permission to report the story as a warning to other parents and teen-agers. Then write a story about the problem and identify only the teen-agers whose parents are willing to cooperate with you.

E. Report the story as fully as possible, identifying all four victims.

5. As a reporter/photographer, you are invited inside a welfare office seized by its clients. The protesters want you to report their grievances and encourage you to interview and photograph everyone there. As you leave, police who surrounded the building ask you how many people are inside, whether they are armed, and whether they seem likely to use their weapons. What would you do?

A. Decline to answer any of their questions.

B. Tell the police that you cannot answer their questions, but that your story and photographs will appear in the next morning's paper.

C. Give the police only the information that you plan to publish in the next morning's paper.

D. Answer all the officers' questions.

E. Answer all the officers' questions and give them copies of all your pictures.

6. A photographer on your staff has covered a series of major fires during the past month. The police and firefighters want to see all the photographer's pic-

tures, including dozens never published by your newspaper. They explain that the fires were set by an arsonist, and that the arsonist probably returned to watch them. Thus, he may appear in the pictures. As editor, would you cooperate with the authorities?

At what point, if any, would you change your mind?

A. The police say they have no other leads.
B. The police insist that you have a civic duty to help them and that, if you refuse, they will publicly denounce you and your newspaper.
C. Many of your readers fear that their homes and businesses may be the next to be burned.
D. The arsonist has sent letters to the local media, threatening to destroy the entire city.
E. A fire set last night caused the deaths of two children.

7. You produce the evening news for a local television station, and one of your photographers has filmed a fire that destroyed a famous old apartment building. The film shows a woman, her clothing in flames, running out the front door, screaming in pain. Before anyone can reach her, the woman collapses and dies. No one knows who she is, and her identity may never be known. The building was supposed to be vacant; the city condemned it because of numerous fire, health and safety violations. However, transients and other homeless people lived in it and continue to live in many of your city's other condemned and abandoned buildings. Some of their occupants even build small fires to cook with and keep warm. The city has been criticized for failing to help the homeless, and this story seems to illustrate their plight. What would you do?

A. Have a newscaster describe the story and then show the fire, but never the woman.
B. Use only the first few seconds of the film, showing the woman alive and running out of the building, but not collapsing and dying.
C. Warn your viewers that you are about to show something unpleasant but important. Then broadcast the entire film, hoping that it will warn other viewers of the danger and encourage the city to help them.
D. Broadcast only a portion of the film on your 6 p.m. newscast, but broadcast the entire film at 11 p.m., when fewer children are watching.

8. As a reporter, you regularly cover an environmentalist group in your city. Frustrated by their past failures, the environmentalists are becoming more militant. You discover that they plan to kidnap a 7-year-old girl, the daughter of a local developer. They intend to hold the girl hostage until her father agrees to stop polluting a river. You have covered the environmentalists for years, and they confided in you because you never betrayed their trust. What would you do?

A. Say nothing.
B. Warn the environmentalists that, because an innocent child's life is in danger, you cannot remain silent. You will have to notify the police if they do not change their plans.
C. Call the developer and warn him that his family is in danger, but without identifying the kidnappers.
D. Call the police and inform them that someone plans to kidnap the girl, but without identifying the kidnappers.
E. Call the police and tell them everything you know.

CHAPTER 14

SPECIALIZED TYPES OF STORIES

In addition to the news stories discussed in previous chapters, reporters write more specialized types of stories, including brights, followups, roundups and sidebars.

BRIGHTS

Brights are short, humorous stories that often have a surprise ending. Some brights are written in the inverted pyramid style; they begin with a summary lead, then report the remaining details in the order of their importance, with the most important details appearing first. Other brights have unexpected or bizarre twists, and reporters may try to surprise their readers by withholding those twists until the stories' final paragraphs. Brights that have a surprise ending are called "suspended interest stories" and, to keep their endings a surprise, usually begin with an interesting or suspenseful fact—some detail likely to interest readers. Because it would reveal their surprise endings, suspended interests stories cannot begin with summary leads.

Editors are always searching for humorous stories and publish the best on page 1. Brights entertain readers, arouse their emotions and provide some relief from the seriousness of the world's problems. Here are four examples of leads for brights:

Many young children know they come from their mommy's tummy, but others say babies come from pictures, toys and boxes of Cheerios.

What's the worst gift you ever received for Christmas? Does the word "fruitcake" strike fear in your heart?

It's nice to be young, but most people think life is happier after 40.

DAVENPORT, Iowa (AP)—Two Davenport men were arrested Wednesday on charges of riding a horse on a sidewalk, riding a horse without lights and failure to pick up manure.

The suspended interest story that follows begins so routinely that at first it may mislead readers; its bizarre twist is not revealed until the final paragraphs:

Police killed an intruder after he set off a burglar alarm in a clothing store on Main Street shortly after 1 a.m. today.
Police entered the store after customers in a nearby tavern heard the alarm and surrounded the building until the officers arrived.
Police found the intruder perched on a counter and killed it with a fly swatter.
"It was my third bat this year," declared a police officer triumphantly.

508

Here are two more brights. The one on the left begins with a summary lead. The one on the right does not, and its ending may surprise you.

College students often complain about sloppy roommates, and Oscar—the first pig to be evicted from an apartment in the city—may be the sloppiest of all.

Oscar is a 6-week-old, 20-pound Hampshire pig. His owners claim that Oscar is only slightly different from other pets that live in the Colonial Apartments on University Boulevard. But the complex's owners say Oscar has to go.

"He's dug up the entire back yard," co-owner Sean Fairbairn said. "Besides that, he's noisy, and he stinks. We've gotten all sorts of complaints."

Oscar has lived in an old hay-filled refrigerator in Todd Gill's patio for a week. The patio is fenced in, but neighbors complained to the owners. The owners then told Gill and his roommate, Wayne Brayton, that Oscar has to go by noon Saturday.

"I don't think it's fair," Gill said. "People love Oscar. He runs around and grunts and squeals, but nothing too obnoxious. We've only let him out a couple times, and he's dug a hole under the fence once or twice, but no one's complained to me."

Gill and Brayton bought Oscar last week at a livestock auction.

The briefcase was on the floor near the Police Department's information desk for about 45 minutes. A clerk got suspicious. Maybe it contained explosives, she thought.

She called the department's bomb squad, and it evacuated the building. Members of the bomb squad then carried the briefcase outside and blew it up in a vacant lot.

That's when they learned that the briefcase belonged to their boss: Police Chief Barry Kopperud. He left it at the information desk while visiting the mayor.

"It's my fault," Kopperud said. "I should have mentioned it to someone. My officers did a good job, and I'm proud of them. They did what they were trained to do: to be alert and cautious."

Kopperud added that his son is likely to be upset, however. Today is the boy's seventh birthday, and Kopperud had his present in the briefcase.

FOLLOWUPS

"Followups," which are also called "second-day" and "developing" stories, report the latest developments in stories that have been reported earlier. Major stories rarely begin and end in a single day, and newspapers publish fresh articles about the topics each time a new development arises. So stories about a trial, legislative session, political campaign or flight to the moon may appear in the media every day for weeks. Other stories remain in the news for years: stories about wars, inflation, terrorism and federal deficits, for example. However, each followup and its lead emphasize the latest developments. Followup stories may also summarize some previous developments, but that information is presented as concisely as possible and placed in a later paragraph.

Followup stories about disasters are especially common. On Monday, newspapers may report that an explosion trapped 47 miners in a West Virginia coal field. The papers will report later developments on Tuesday, perhaps that rescuers have found 21 bodies. On Wednesday, the papers may report that seven miners have been found alive. Followup stories published on Friday may describe funeral services held for the known dead.

Rescue workers may find all the remaining bodies on Saturday, and work in the mine may resume the following Tuesday. Weeks later, another followup story may report that state and federal investigators have determined the cause of the explosion. Months later, the final followup may report that lawsuits filed against the mine's owners have been dropped in return for payments of $260,000 to each victim's family.

As is typical of followups, the following leads would appear on successive days, and each lead emphasizes a new development in a continuing story:

> 1. The principal of Roosevelt Elementary School was arrested Monday and charged with shoplifting $12.72 worth of food from a supermarket.

> 2. The School Board on Wednesday suspended with pay an elementary school principal charged with shoplifting $12.72 worth of food from a local supermarket.

> 3. Margaret Soole, the suspended principal of Roosevelt Elementary School, pleaded innocent Friday to a charge of shoplifting.

> 4. Shoplifting charges filed against an elementary school principal were dropped Friday after she agreed to seek counseling and to pay a supermarket for the food she was accused of stealing.
> Assistant District Attorney Helen Wehr explained: "We didn't feel a need to take this case to trial. The amount involved is rather small. We've also considered the fact that all the adverse publicity this case has attracted and the possible loss of her job seem to be a harsh enough penalty for the defendant to pay."

> 5. Margaret Soole, who was charged with shoplifting and was suspended from her job as principal of Roosevelt Elementary School, will return to work next fall but has been reassigned to an administrative job in the School Board office.

Again, each of the following leads emphasizes a new development in a continuing story:

> 1. A 17-year-old junior at Kennedy High School collapsed and died while playing basketball during a physical education class Tuesday.

> 2. An autopsy Wednesday revealed that a junior who collapsed during a physical education class at Kennedy High School died of a heart attack.
> The student, Brandon R. Cogeos, had passed his physical examination for the school's football team the day before his death.

> 3. The School Board has appointed five doctors to a committee that will study sports injuries and the sudden death of an athlete at Kennedy High School.

> 4. The physical examinations given athletes enrolled in the city's public schools are "generally inadequate and ineffective in detecting many pre-existing medical problems," five doctors told the School Board Monday night.

> 5. To prevent injuries and deaths, the School Board on Wednesday voted to require athletes in the city's junior and senior high schools to take more thorough physical examinations.

Followup stories are becoming more common, and some publications have established regular columns for them. You may also notice some followup stories on television news broadcasts. In the past, critics complained that journalists, like firefighters, raced from one major story to the next, devoting most of their attention to momentary crises. Critics added that when one crisis began to subside, reporters moved on to the next, so older stories disappeared from the news before they were fully resolved. To solve the problem, both newspaper and magazine reporters now regularly return to important topics and tell readers what has happened since the topics dropped out of the headlines. Followups may relate that an area devastated by a hurricane has been rebuilt, or that the victims of an accident are still suffering from its consequences.

ROUNDUPS

To save space, newspapers publish roundup stories that summarize several different but related events. Traffic roundups are most common; instead of publishing separate stories about each traffic death that occurs during a single weekend, newspapers summarize a dozen or more fatal traffic accidents in a single story. Newspapers may also report all the weekend crimes, fires, drownings, graduation ceremonies or football games in a single roundup.

Another type of roundup story deals with a single event but incorporates facts from several sources. Reporters may interview half a dozen people to obtain more information about a single topic, to verify the accuracy of facts they have obtained elsewhere or to obtain new perspectives. For example, if your mayor resigned unexpectedly, you might interview the mayor and ask him why he resigned, what he plans to do after leaving office, what he considers his major accomplishments and what problems will confront his successor. You might then: (1) ask other city officials to comment on the mayor's performance and resignation, (2) ask the city clerk how the next mayor will be selected and (3) interview leading contenders for the job. All this information would be included in a single roundup story.

The lead in a roundup story emphasizes the most important or unique developments and ties all the facts together by stressing their common denominator, as in the following examples of roundup leads:

> Eleven people, including three teen-agers who were driving to the state fair, were killed in traffic accidents reported in the region last weekend.

> Gunmen who robbed four service stations during the weekend escaped with a total of $3,600. All four stations are located along Highway 141 on the west side of the city.

Subsequent facts in roundup stories should be organized by topic, not source. After the lead, roundup stories usually discuss the most important topic—the most newsworthy accident, crime, fire or drowning—then move on to the second, third and fourth most important topics. As they discuss each topic, roundup stories usually report what every source said about it. If roundup stories report first every fact provided by one source, then every fact provided by the second, third and fourth sources, the stories will become too disorganized and repetitious, since each source is likely to mention the same topics, and their comments about similar topics will be scattered throughout the stories.

SIDEBARS

Sidebars are related to major news stories but are separate from them and are usually of secondary importance. The sidebars are set apart for clarity—so that the main stories do not become too long or complicated. Sidebars give readers some additional information about the main topic, usually from a different source or perspective. They may provide background information, explain a topic's importance or describe the scene, emphasizing its color and mood. If fire destroys a nightclub, newspapers may publish a sidebar that quotes several survivors and describes their escape. If a prominent person is given an award (or arrested or injured), a news story will describe that award, arrest or injury, and a sidebar may describe the person's character or accomplishments. Similarly, when a new pope is selected, sidebars may describe his personality, past assignments, philosophy and previous trips to the United States. Other sidebars may describe his new home in the Vatican and problems confronting Catholic churches throughout the world.

Sidebars are usually briefer than the main news stories and are placed next to them. If, for some reason, the sidebars must be placed on a different page, editors will add tielines (a brief note) telling readers where they can find the related stories. Because some people read only the sidebars, most briefly summarize the main stories even when they are placed alongside them.

QUOTES

A dog fight on Sixteenth Street is a better story than a war in Timbuktu.

(Frederick J. Bonfils, co-owner of the Denver Post*)*

There are very few friends of a free press in the world. Year by year those countries which enjoy a free press grow fewer in number. Because a free press is the deadliest enemy of tyrrany, it is the first target of tyrranical governments everywhere.

(Mark S. Fowler, chairman, Federal Communications Commission)

Exercise 1

SPECIALIZED TYPES OF STORIES

BRIGHTS

INSTRUCTIONS: Use the following information to write "brights," a series of short, humorous stories. Write some brights that have a summary lead and others that have a surprise ending.

1. Have you ever heard anyone say that people who drive red cars get more speeding tickets than anyone else? Two researchers at your university decided to determine, once and for all, whether or not that common belief is really true. To conduct the study, the two researchers counted the first 1,000 cars traveling on Main St., beginning at 8 a.m. yesterday morning, to determine the typical colors of cars on the road. They then looked at the last 1,000 speeding tickets given by the citys policemen, keeping track of car colors. The bottom line: the red-car theory fizzled. Red cars, they discovered, accounted for 14 percent of the vehicles on Main St. and about 15% of the speeding tickets given in the city. The difference is not statistically significant. The researchers did find that white cars get fewer tickets, proportionately, than other cars. White cars accounted for 25 percent of the vehicles on the street but only 19% of the tickets. "You are just as apt to see a silver Cadillac come by at an excessive speed as a red Porsche," said Lt. Vicki Perez, adding that police officers treat red cars "the same as anything else."

2. The results of a survey of the bartenders in your community were announced today. They were asked a single question: Who are their best and worst tippers? To conduct the survey, the bartenders were asked to rank 20 categories of persons on a "tipping scale" of from zero to 10. A "zero" is a certain "stiff" (that's bartender-talk for a nontipper), and a "10" is the best tipper. They were also asked to name the states from which the best and worst tippers come. Bartenders said the best tippers come from the Northeast and the worst come from the South and Midwest. Customers from New York were ranked the no. 1 tippers, and Georgians were the worst. Here is a list of the 20 categories of tippers and their ranking:

   1. Bartenders: 9.82%
   2. Waiters/waitresses: 9.49%
   3. Regulars: 7.83%
   4. Lawyers: 7.53%
   5. Males: 6.88%
   6. Ages 21–35: 6.34%
   7. Prostitutes: 6.23%
   8. Ages 36–55: 6.22%
   9. Salesmen: 5.66%
   10. Working women: 5.49%
   11. Tourists: 5.02%
   12. Females: 4.98%
   13. Doctors: 4.84%
   14. Secretaries: 4.57%
   15. Bankers: 4.52%
   16. Teachers: 3.44%
   17. Senior citizens: 3.15%
   18. Housewives: 2.87%
   19. Under 21: 2.31%
   20. Students: 2.13%

3. Rhonda and Tim Andrews operate a farm in northern Wisconsin. Each fall, they complain that deer hunters overrun their property, causing damage to their fences, crops, and livestock. In the past, two of their cows have been shot, apparently by hunters who thought they were deer. This year the Andrews got humorous revenge. They bought a stuffed deer and put it in a field,

about 50 feet from Buckneer Rd. Then they listened and watched. "We could hear the shots," Rhonda said, "dozens and dozens of them. We've got binoculars, and we'd watch from our kitchen window. Hunters driving by would slam on their brakes, pile out of their cars and start shooting, sometimes three or four of them all at once. Some emptied their guns, reloaded and shot some more. Usually it'd take 'em a couple minutes before they figured out something was wrong, but we saw 2 or 3 hunters who climbed over the fence, walked up to the deer, and shot it another four or five times, anything to knock it down. One even kicked it. We had to stop after three days. We had so many bullet holes in the thing that we couldn't count 'em all, and it was falling apart. By the third day we had to prop the deer up on a stool. Then its head fell off and we decided it was time to quit."

4. For a class project, two psychology students at your school conducted a little experiment about the honesty of the people living in your community. The students, Larry Patzel and Anne Capiello, presented the results in a class this morning. What they did was to collect a total of $25 in coins, plus some $1 and $5 and $10 bills from their classmates and friends, a total of $60. Then they stuffed all the money in a clear plastic purse. Then they went out into the city and approached a total of 100 persons: fifty men and fifty women. Then they showed each of the 100 persons the purse stuffed with money, said they had just found the purse, and asked the subjects of their interesting little experiment what they should do with the purse and the money it contained. 81 people said the money should be turned over to the nearest authorities. 12 said the students should keep the money for themselves. 3 refused to speak to the students. Others gave miscellaneous answers. One of the two students, Anne, said: "People were basically honest and concerned that someone had lost the money. Women were easier for us to approach, and I got the impression they were a little more honest. 43 of the women said we should turn in the purse, compared to 38 of the men." A shabbily dressed man in his late forties was one of the subjects in the experiment and he told the 2 students, "Go out and buy yourselves a case of Jack Daniels and celebrate." A husky young man chewing a cigar gave similar advice, saying, "If there is no identification, its yours, and nobody can take it away from you. But if you keep asking people somebody will swear its theirs. So keep it cool!"

5. Joseph R. DeLoy told the judge today that he's in love. DeLoy, 26, said he loves a 29-year-old woman, Patty McFerren. DeLoy met McFerren while they were both shopping at a supermarket in the city. DeLoy asked McFerren for a date. McFerren refused. "But she was wonderful, and I could tell she really liked me, so I called her," DeLoy said. In fact, DeLoy tried to call McFerren more than 200 times, sometimes in the middle of the night. However, it wasn't really her number that he called. By mistake, he got the wrong number and called Patrick McFerren instead. The two McFerrens are unrelated and do not know each other. Their listings in the phone book are very similar. Patty is listed as "P. McFerren." Patrick is listed as "P. J. McFerren." Patrick informed DeLoy that he was dialing the wrong number. DeLoy said he didn't believe him and continued to call. "I was hoping that she'd answer," DeLoy said in court today. Patrick installed an answering machine so he could screen the calls, and the machine got a heavy workout. Finally, Patrick called the police, and they told DeLoy to stop making the calls, but no charges were filed against him. So Patrick sued, accusing DeLoy of intentional infliction of emotional duress and invasion of privacy. The calls were a costly mistake for DeLoy. In

ISBN 0-15-500602-9

court today, DeLoy's attorney explained that his client was acting "on his heart and hormones, not his head." A jury of 5 men and 7 women decided that his calls were worth $25 each—for a total of $5,000. The jury ordered DeLoy to pay that sum—$5,000—to Patrick. "I'm satisfied," Patrick said.

6. Charles Todd Snyder was charged with drunk driving following a traffic accident in your city one week ago. He was also charged with driving without a driver's license in his possession. He was scheduled to appear in court at 9 a.m. this morning. He failed to appear in court. As a consequence, Judge Edward Kocembra ordered police to go to Snyder's home and to haul Snyder into court. Police went to the address Snyder had given officers at the time of the accident: 711 Broadway Avenue. The police returned to the court at approximately 10:15 a.m. and appeared before Judge Kocembra with Snyder. Snyder was in his mother's arms. He is a 13-month-old child, and his mother insisted that he drinks only milk and that the only vehicle he ever drives is a stroller. So the judge apologized for the inconvenience and told the officers to give Snyder and his mother a ride back to their home. Snyder, apparently frightened by the unfamiliar surroundings and people, cried. Police said that whoever was stopped had falsely given the arresting officers Snyder's name and address when he signed the drunk driving ticket and the ticket for driving without a driver's license in his possession. They told the judge that they have no idea who that person might be.

Exercise 2

SPECIALIZED TYPES OF STORIES

BRIGHTS

INSTRUCTIONS: Use the following information to write "brights," a series of short, humorous stories. Write some brights that have a summary lead and others that have a surprise ending.

1. Nude Man

A vacationing couple was driving a pickup camper through Phoenix, Arizona, yesterday. When a traffic light suddenly turned red, the woman slammed on the camper's brakes, coming to a very fast stop. Her husband was sleeping in the camper at the time, nude, as he says he always sleeps, and the sudden stop threw him off a cot. Half asleep and thinking they had been involved in an accident and forgetting his lack of attire, the husband threw open the back door of the camper and jumped to the ground. At that moment, the light turned green and his wife, not knowing he had jumped from the camper, drove on. So as a consequence, her husband was left standing naked in the middle of the intersection, in broad daylight, without any identification, without anything. Police at first charged him with indecent exposure but dropped the charges when he was able to convince them of the truth of his story. Highway patrolmen stopped his wife 78 miles away. She returned to Phoenix to pick him up at a police station. The police did not release the couple's names.

2. Political Dinner

Reid R. Wentila is a candidate for governor. Last night he had an unusual fund-raising dinner in the city. It was a great success and raised a total of $17,800 for his statewide political campaign. Wentila and his aides got the idea after they noticed how reluctant people are to buy tickets for fund-raising dinners and to take an evening off to attend them. Worse, many people who buy tickets give them to someone else, and those people come and eat everything available, thus increasing a candidate's expenses. "The overhead is something terrible," one of Wentila's aides said. So they implemented a new idea. They sold tickets for a dinner scheduled for last night. They charged guests $25 if they promised not to attend and $50 if they planned to attend. No one bought any of the $50 tickets, and no one appeared at the dinner last night. "That's just the way we wanted it," Wentila said. "We raised more money this way, and we didn't impose on anyone's time."

3. Lie Detector

Some people just don't trust lie detectors. To prove a point, a psychology professor on your campus, Ahmad Aneesa, Ph.D., conducted an unusual experiment. Using funds provided by a small grant, he sought 10 volunteers to serve as subjects. He asked each of the subjects some questions about their backgrounds and interests and college majors and grades. He instructed each subject to tell a lie about one of those facts in their background and offered each subject a sum a money as a reward or incentive if the subject could stay with the lie and register "normal" on a highly sophisticated lie-detector. Local police agreed to cooperate with the experiment. The city's police department has its own lie detector, and a sergeant is trained to use that detector. The police chief allowed Aneesa to bring 10 students, all psychology majors from your school, to the police department last Saturday. The lie detector normally is not used for regular police business on Saturday. The sergeant, who normally does not work on Saturdays, volunteered to come in on his normal day off to administer the tests without pay. Dr. Aneesa then offered to pay each student $50 for a successful lie. He announced the results today. He found that the sergeant, who asked that his name not be used, was unable to detect the lies of 7 of the 10 students even though he was given a list of questions to ask each student and was told, in advance, that each student was going to give a lie in response to one of those questions.

4. Truck Theft

There was a motor vehicle theft which occurred in the city at some time in the middle of last night. The vehicle was taken from a building located at 7720 Avonwood Dr. The building was unlocked at the time, and 12 occupants sleeping in an upstairs room said they heard nothing unusual. They were all in bed by midnight and the first got up at 6 a.m., discovering the theft at that time. Police describe the missing vehicle as a bright canary-yellow fire truck, marked with the name of the city fire department. The custom-made truck cost a total of $92,000 and was delivered to the city just three months ago. Firemen said it had a full tank of gas, about 50 gallons. However, it gets only 1½ miles to the gallon. It contained enough clothing and equipment for six firefighters, a dozen oxygen tanks, 1,000 feet of hose, four ladders (each up to 60 feet tall), plus miscellaneous other equipment. The people sleeping upstairs were all firefighters and the building was a fire station. The firefighters suspect that someone opened the station's main door, then either pushed or towed the truck silently outside and started its engine some distance away from the building. It is the first time in its history that the city fire department has reported that one of its trucks has been stolen. It was not insured. The keys are always left in the truck to reduce the response time when firefighters receive a call for help.

5. Inheritance

The will of a local man, Benjamin Satterwaite, 74, of 307 E. King Boulevard was filed in Probate Court today. Satterwaite died on the twentieth of last month of cancer. He had lived alone in his home, neighbors said, for at least the past 20 years. He was a retired postal clerk. According to the will, Satterwaite left a total estate of $1,071,400.38. Much of the money was earned in the stock market. Neighbors said they were surprised by the amount. Satterwaite was not a miser but lived frugally, and neighbors said they did not suspect that the deceased was a millionaire. Satterwaite left the entire estate to the U.S. government, explaining that, "Everybody seems to be living off the government, so maybe someone ought to help it out." He had no known relatives.

6. Bank Regulations

Abraham Burmeister is president of the First National Bank, the largest bank in your community. Each year, in accordance with new federal laws, the bank is required to send all its customers copies of some complex new federal rules concerning the regulation of banks and the procedures followed for money transfers by means of electronic banking. Consequently, the First National Bank prepared a 4,500-word pamphlet describing and summarizing those new federal rules and then sent copies of the rules to all its 40,000 regular depositors and customers. Like many other bankers, Burmeister objected to the federal law, saying it imposed a needless burden and needless expense on bankers since the federal laws that banks are being forced to explain are too complicated for the average person to understand and too dull and uninteresting for people to spend time trying to read. To prove his point, on the last page of 100 of the 40,000 copies of the rules he took a gamble and inserted a special extra sentence. That sentence said, "If you return this pamphlet to any of the bank's tellers within the next 30 days, they will give you $25." The 30 days passed yesterday, and not one person turned in a single copy of the 100 special pamphlets and requested the $25 due on demand, apparently because no one read the pamphlets. Bank officials calculated that it cost somewhere in the neighborhood of $15,000 to prepare, print, address and mail the pamphlets to the 40,000 bank customers, and they said that is a waste of money, yet they must do it every year, even though obviously no one reads the things, as they have just proven with their interesting little experiment.

Exercise 3

SPECIALIZED TYPES OF STORIES

FOLLOWUP STORIES

INSTRUCTIONS Write a story summarizing the initial set of facts and then just the lead for each of the later developments. Your instructor may instead ask you to write a complete news story about each day's developments.

Original Story

A big chunk of the U.S. heartland is nervous. Tony Pasquin, a Ph.D. in oceanography who works at the Cruz Institute in Philadelphia, attracted alot of attention when he called a press conference at 8 AM this morning to announce a startling prediction of his: an earthquake on the New Madrid fault. The fault runs through several states, from Arkansas north into the southern tip of Illinois. Pasquin explained that there are often small earthquakes, up to 200 a year, below cities stretching from Cairo Illinois south to Arkansas. This morning, Pasquin predicted a 50–50 chance of a major earthquake, one of at least 7.5, perhaps even 8.0 on the Richter scale, in the 48 hours on either side of noon next week Tuesday. The earthquake, if it occurred, would affect an estimated 40 million people in the region. The reason that Pasquin is focusing on next week Tuesday is because that's when tidal forces will reach a 100-year high for much of the Northern Hemisphere. Pasquin said the tidal forces will "pull the trigger" on earthquakes and volcanoes around the world. During his press conference at the Cruz Institute today, Pasquin told newsmen he also predicted the 1980 eruption of the Mount St. Helens volcano in Washington State and the last major earthquake in San Francisco.

Experts at the Federal Emergency Management Agency contacted by you in Washington, D.C. said the New Madrid is due for a major quake "sometime in the next 30 years," but called Pasquins prediction of a quake on a specific day next week "bunk."

Scientists have long predicted that the region is due for another severe quake. The fault was the site of three monster quakes in 1811–1812. The experts in Washington add that, in the eventuality of a major quake, major cities like Memphis, Little Rock Arkansas, and Evansville, Indiana are built on soft soil that could literally liquify in a temblor. Brick buildings could collapse. Roads buckle. The Mississippi River flood and, in addition, permanently change its course. Damage could exceed $50 billion.

Day 2

Experts throughout the U.S. today scoffed at the prediction by Tony Pasquin. They say he is an oceanographer, not an expert in earthquakes, that there are no indications of an earthquake occurring on the New Madrid fault, and that no one, at this point in time, knows how to accurately predict earthquakes anywhere in the entire world. The states that might be affected, however, are preparing for an earthquake. Late yesterday, city officials in St. Louis ordered fire trucks parked outside for the duration so, if the cities fire stations collapse, the trucks won't be destroyed in them. Government disaster plans are being dusted off, hospitals have drawn up emergency plans, and water, gas, and electric utilities have scrambled for backup systems should the need arise. Police and fire dept. leaves have been canceled in some cities, and the governor of Kentucky has placed the National Guard in that state on standby.

"It's a crime," said Diana Gant, a geologist at your school. "This is causing outright panic, and there's no basis for it, no reason to expect an earthquake. People are gullible about things they don't understand, and this is an example of that. There was another prediction, quite similar to this one, back in the spring of 1990 or 1991, and people believed it, too. Of course, there wasn't an earthquake then, and I don't expect one next week."

Day 3

As the nation's heartland approaches zero hour for the predicted quake, some people fear that, if it occurs as predicted, the tremor could disrupt everything from the course of the Mississippi River to Elvis Presley's grave. The school systems in dozens of cities have announced a holiday next Tuesday, so students will have a vacation. Businesses are closing. Police are standing by. Earthquake insurance is selling like hotcakes. Kent Hernandez, the superintendent of schools in Memphis, said, "Yes, we've declared a holiday. It may be uncalled for, but I'd rather be criticized for being too cautious than have a building collapse with our students inside." In Arkansas, earthquake drills are slated for Monday at schools in a dozen cities. "You have never seen the kind of damage we could be faced with," explained Thomas Moy, the mayor of Little Rock, where some conventions scheduled to start next Monday have been canceled, and airlines report a record number of last-minute travelers booking flights out of town. People in many of the cities throughout the region have also been reported to be currently in the process of stocking up on emergency supplies: batteries, bottled water, food, and the like.

When questioned about the scare, Martin Singh, a seismologist at the University of Arkansas, said, "I'm worried about the hysterical tone that's coming out of this. Its totally uninformed, totally ridiculous. I blame the media and stories they've broadcast about Pasquins prediction. Its sensationalism of the worst sort, absolutely irresponsible, but they'll do anything to sell more papers."

Next Wednesday

There has not been a big earthquake, not even a little quiver. Thus, life is returning to normal. Interviewed at his office in Philadelphia, Pasquin said: "I don't understand what's happening, why people are upset. Some people seem almost disappointed and are mad at me, almost like they wanted an earthquake or something. All I was trying to do was warn them that an earthquake was likely. That there was a 50–50 chance of an earthquake, and that they should prepare for it. Now that nothing's happened, they should be happy. It could have been a real disaster."

Exercise 4

SPECIALIZED TYPES OF STORIES

FOLLOWUP STORIES

INSTRUCTIONS Write a story summarizing the initial set of facts and then just the lead for each of the later developments. Your instructor may instead ask you to write a complete news story about each day's developments.

Background

Years ago, tuberculosis ranked among the worlds most lethal diseases, and it remains a serious health problem in developing countries. The number of Americans with tuberculosis has declined dramatically over the last half century. Only approximately 23,000 new cases were reported in the U.S. last year, about 1000 of them in your state. Basically, TB is a bacterial infection. It usually affects the respiratory system. It is spread through coughing, sneezing, and singing. Because of advances in the field of medicine, it is rare for a death to occur because of TB. Modern treatment succeeds virtually 100 percent of the time. Doctors can prescribe medications to stop the disease if the infection is detected early enough. However, TB can be fatal if undetected. Symptoms include a prolonged and unexplained cough, night sweats, and sudden weight loss. To test for TB, a small amount of dead bacteria is injected into the skin of the upper arm of a person. Health workers know there is an infection when natural antibodies, formed to fight the illness, respond to the dead bacteria, and harden the skin around the test area.

Original Story

Maureen Verdugo, principal of Kennedy High School, called a special assembly at the beginning of classes at the school today and made a startling announcement. Verdugo revealed to the students that a 16 year old student enrolled at the school whose exact identity she in no way revealed, other than as a tenth grader, has been diagnosed as suffering from the disease tuberculosis. Verdugo continued on by announcing that city health officials were notified by the students doctor and will be available at the school all five days of classes next week to give free TB tests to every student enrolled in one the 16 yr. olds classes, as well as to students known to be the victims friends. "Anyone else—students, faculty members, and school personnel—who fear they may have been infected will also be tested free of charge. The tests will be administered in the school clinic, and students will be excused from their study halls and other free periods to be tested," Verdugo said. The clinic will be open from 7 am to 5 pm and people can also visit it before or after their classes. "I've been working in high schools for 30 years," Verdugo went on to say, "and this is the first time I've had a problem like this. But I want to reassure you that there's no reason for panic. We're taking all the necessary precautions and have the situation well under control."

Saturday of the Next Week

On Monday and Tuesday of this week the citys Public Health Dept. had its personnel at the school, busily testing students that may have come in contact with an infected 16 yr. old student enrolled in Kennedy High School. Initial tests were given free of charge at the school clinic. About 250 of the schools students were singled out by school authorities as having had regular contact with the infected teen, either by being enrolled in the kids classes or by having some other close contact with the guy. Other students and teachers went in on their own. The testing is continuing and the final results will be announced sometime during the course of next week.

Of approximately three hundred students tested Monday and Tuesday, six showed signs of infection and were advised to have more testing done on them. "Infected students are being advised to undergo chest X rays and possibly sputum tests to determine whether they have developed TB," said Cathleen Graham, head of the citys Public Health Dept. "Those who are merely infected with the bacteria will be prescribed an antibiotic to prevent the onset of the disease. If the disease has progressed further, students will have to undergo more extensive drug therapy."

Some parents were frightened and dissatisfied. Tanaka Holland, mother of Sophomore Andrea Holland, said during an interview today: "When I called the school with some questions they were totally uncaring, and their procedures stink. Every student in the whole school should be tested. Just because a child wasn't in a class with the carrier doesn't mean they didn't come in contact with the disease," Mrs. Holland said. A second parent, James R. Waundry, agreed, adding, "This isn't anything to mess with. I've heard that people can die of tuberculosis, and how do we know that, uh, it's not going to come back? We've told our son, Paul, to stay home this week, and we're thinking of putting him in a private school."

Saturday of the Following Week

In all, 581 Kennedy High School students were tested after learning that a 10th grade schoolmate had TB, Kennedy High School Principal Maureen Verdugo announced today. A total of 23 of the 581 students have tested positive for exposure to tuberculosis but none of the 23 have developed the disease. "The students are not contagious but must take antibiotics for six months to prevent the disease," said Joseph Perez, a health official employed by the city.

Greg Hubbard is the citys superintendent of schools. Hubbard said during a press conference today that he believes that this TB outbreak was the worst in the citys entire history. Hubbard said there is nothing the district can do to prevent occasional health problems like this one. "You're always subject to this kind of thing with the number of kids we have," he said. Health officials added that no one will ever know exactly how the outbreak started.

Exercise 5

SPECIALIZED TYPES OF STORIES

FOLLOWUP STORIES

INSTRUCTIONS: Write a story summarizing the initial set of facts and then just the lead for each of the later developments. Your instructor may instead ask you to write a complete news story about each day's developments.

Day 1

Twelve people have been selected to hear the murder trial of Sara Kindstrom, 27, of 4828 North Vine Street. She is charged with murdering her live-in boyfriend, Frederick C. Taylor, 25. Kindstrom is charged with first-degree murder. If convicted of the charge, she could be sentenced to life imprisonment and would have to serve at least 25 years before becoming eligible for parole. Taylor's death occurred last summer, on the 4th day of August, at about 7 p.m. in the evening. Taylor was shot and killed by shots from a .22 caliber pistol. This morning, assistant county attorney Donald Hedricks and Kindstrom's attorney, assistant public defender Marilyn Cheeseboro, spent several hours questioning 42 potential jurors before selecting an 8-man, 4-woman panel to hear the case. The trial is scheduled to begin at 9:00 a.m. tomorrow before Circuit Court Judge Randall Pfaff.

Day 2

Jurors seemed to be spellbound as they listened to the fascinating testimony of Sara Kindstrom today. She told a tearful story of bloody beatings and verbal, physical and sexual abuse at the hands of her live-in boyfriend, whom she is accused of killing. During her 5½ hours of testimony today, Kindstrom said: "He was going to kill me. It wasn't a matter of whether he'd kill me, but when he was going to do it. I met him a year ago, and he moved right in with me, and at first it was really nice. Then he lost his job and got sicker and sicker. We could sleep together for a month and not have sex. Then we'd fight and he'd force himself on me. I work as a waitress, and when I got home Aug. 4 he was waiting for me. He started calling me names and hitting me and accused me of running around with other men, and that's not true. I'd never do that, but he was jealous. He was always jealous. I tried to keep quiet and make supper, but he started drinking. Later, we started arguing again. He was telling me how dumb I was, that if I left, he'd move someone nice in. I said it was my house, and he said I'd be dead and then it would be his house. He was hitting me really hard, hitting my face, and I was bleeding. Then we were in the bedroom, and I just couldn't take it anymore. He kept a pistol in a bedroom closet, and I had it in my hand. I don't remember getting it out, but I must have, and it started going off. I don't remember pulling the trigger. He looked surprised and then he just fell to the floor without saying anything. I knew I'd hurt him, but I didn't think he was dead. I didn't mean to kill him."

Day 3

A neighbor, Martha Rudnick, testified: "My husband and I heard her screaming, but that wasn't unusual. They were always fighting over there, and everyone in the neighborhood heard it. The police had been there a dozen times, but it never seemed to do any good. This time I heard the gun. Right away I knew they were shots, but I thought he was shooting at her. He was always threatening to kill her. My husband picked up the telephone and called the police, and I ran next door to see if I could help Sara. But when I got outside, Freddy was crawling out their front door, and she was coming after him with the gun, still shooting him. She was shooting him in the back, and he was just lying there, bleeding on the sidewalk. She kept pulling the trigger, but the gun must have been out of bullets and was clicking every time she pulled the trigger. Then the police came and arrested her. I could see her face was all red and swollen and bleeding where he'd hit her, and it wasn't the first time I'd seen her like that."

Day 4

Police Sergeant Michael Barsch said: "I interrogated her as soon as we got her to the police station. She told me she'd shot him and that she hoped she'd killed him. It was his gun, but we checked and found that she'd used it before. He'd taught her how to shoot it. He'd taken her target shooting and hunting with him. We also found a box of shells in her purse, with 9 shells missing, and found that she'd bought the box herself at a sporting goods store near her home about a week earlier, so she'd apparently been planning to use the gun."

Day 5

In his closing arguments, the prosecuting attorney said: "The defendant did not have to murder Fredrick Taylor. She could have called the police for protection. She could have charged Taylor with assault, and she could have forced him to leave her house. But she never sought help and consistently returned to the man who beat her. She may regret it now, but she killed him. She shot him, and she did it deliberately. If she only wanted to protect herself, she could have shot him once, possibly twice, and escaped. But she fired 9 bullets, and all 9 hit him—mostly in the back. She continued firing those bullets even after Taylor was obviously helpless and down on the ground, trying to crawl to safety. That's murder in the first degree."

In her closing arguments, the public defender said: "This woman is a victim who acted in self-defense. She was repeatedly and brutally beaten by Frederick Taylor during their 12-month relationship. We also know that Taylor was an extremely dangerous man, a brutal woman-hater who eventually would have killed Sara Kindstrom. She killed him to protect herself from rape and murder. Imagine yourself in that situation. You're being beaten, badly beaten. Dazed, confused, in need of protecting yourself, you pick up a gun and begin to shoot. You're acting in self-defense, to protect your own life, and you may not be entirely rational at a moment like that."

Day 7

After two days of deliberation, the jury returned with a verdict. The jury announced that it found the defendant guilty. However, the jury found the defendant guilty of murder in the second degree rather than of murder in the first degree. The maximum penalty for a conviction of that type is from 5 to 18 years in prison.

Day 10

The judge today sentenced the defendant, Sara Kindstrom. He sentenced her to a term in a state prison of the minimum sentence of 5 years. In sentencing Kindstrom to the minimum prison term the judge noted the extenuating circumstances in the case, including her brutal treatment at the hands of her victim and her apparent effort to defend herself. However, the judge complained that she used excessive force in that defense. She will be eligible for parole in as short a time as a period of 18 months, with time off for good behavior.

Exercise 6

SPECIALIZED TYPES OF STORIES

FOLLOWUP STORIES

INSTRUCTIONS: Write a story summarizing the initial set of facts and then just the lead for each of the later developments. Your instructor may instead ask you to write a complete news story about each day's developments.

Original Story

To supplement their incomes, Herman Ansel and Cecil LaCette scavenge for aluminum cans, which they sell to recycling plants. Ansel is 20 and LaCette 23. Both live at 2814 Ambassador Drive in apartment number 61. They were looking for aluminum cans in a dumpster behind the Colonial Shopping Center at 8 p.m. last night. When LaCette looked inside a bag that had been dumped into the dumpster, he found a dead baby. Later, he talked to the police who responded to his call and he said to them: "Sometimes we find cans and other valuable stuff in all sorts of containers, so we open everything. So I started to tear open this bag, and at first I thought it was a doll inside, a baby doll. Then I got scared, real scared, and called you." Police said it was the body of a white male infant. It apparently was only a few hours old. An umbilical cord was still attached. The bag was a plain grocery bag. The baby was taken to Memorial Hospital, where it was pronounced dead. The county coroner will conduct an autopsy to determine the cause of death. However, detectives said it might be as long as a week before the cause of death can be determined unless there are some visible signs of abuse or maltreatment. A detective added that: "We're trying to determine if there was life before death. The baby could have died after birth, or it could have been born dead. So we may have a murder case here, but at this point we just don't know. The dumpster was emptied at 2 p.m. yesterday afternoon, so we do know the body had to be put in there sometime after that."

One Day Later

Detective Larry Chevez has been placed in charge of the case. During a press conference in his office today he revealed the following developments: "We've got nine men working on this case full time, and a lot of citizens who've heard about the baby are calling us with information, and we're tracking down all the leads they're giving us, but we don't have anything really substantial yet. It's a slow, tedious process. We've got some possibilities, some things to check on, but nothing that I could consider real good information. But we are working on the assumption the baby was murdered; there was some evidence it was beaten, but the autopsy hasn't been completed yet. Next Sunday, we've got 18 officers who've volunteered to come in on their own time to help check the neighborhood. We think the mother lives in the vicinity. There are about 2,500 homes in the area and, if we have to, we're going to knock on the door of every one of them." Chevez urges anyone with information about the baby or its mother to call the police department. His number is 841-4111.

The Following Monday

An autopsy was conducted, and the results were announced today by the coroner, Dr. Marlene Stoudnour, who held a press conference in her office at 8 a.m. today. Detective

Chevez was present. At the press conference, she released copies of her autopsy report, then answered the questions asked by reporters. The autopsy report reveals that the baby was "murdered by repeated blows to the back of the head with a blunt instrument." Also, the autopsy adds that the white male infant was newborn and "lived for less than 24 hours before he was beaten to death." The baby was definitely alive before he was killed and thrown into the dumpster. He was slightly premature—probably the product of a seven- or eight-month pregnancy. Also, Detective Chevez said the house-to-house check of the neighborhood by police Sunday and the pursuit of leads phoned in by private citizens has thus far been fruitless. His office still requests any assistance possible from the public which might lead to the identification of the baby's mother. "People have called in, but we haven't gotten nowhere near the response we hoped we'd get," Chevez said. "We have a few leads, but none are promising." At the present time, Chevez said police officers are contacting all hospitals, clinics and other medical facilities in the area to learn the identities of women who have received prenatal care in recent months. He said all the women will be contacted by the police in an effort to find a woman who was pregnant but doesn't have a baby to show for it. The dead baby's remains are being held in the county morgue.

Two Weeks Later

Police officers report they are continuing to investigate the case. Three officers are working on it full time. They have no solid clues. The officers are continuing to knock on doors and question pregnant women for leads. Literally hundreds of pregnant women have been eliminated from consideration. The officers have begun to consider the possibility that the mother may have been a transient, in which case there will be no local records of her pregnancy and it will be much more difficult to successfully identify and prosecute her. Detective Chavez said, "We're a long way from quitting, I can tell you that." He said the investigation is focusing on the mother because "Whoever and wherever she is, we believe that either she killed the kid herself, or she knows who did it and can lead us to the guilty party."

One Year Later

Police officers say the case is still "open." It has not been shelved, and officers occasionally look into it when they have free time. No one is regularly assigned to the case. Officers have not been able to obtain any firm clues regarding the identity of the mother. They are now certain that she is not from the local area, since "It would have been impossible for a woman to hide a seven- or eight-month pregnancy from everyone she knew—her family and friends and neighbors and doctor and everyone else she ran into."

Exercise 7

SPECIALIZED TYPES OF STORIES

ROUNDUPS—MULTIPLE SOURCES

INSTRUCTIONS: Write a single news story that summarizes the following information. Organize the information in a clear, logical, cohesive manner. As you write the story, correct the spelling, style, grammatical and vocabulary errors. Also be thorough; report every issue in depth. Notice that the sources' comments appear in quotation marks, so you can quote them directly.

Background

There were two votes in the United States House of Representatives today. The first motion was to eliminate the entire $170 million dollar budget of the National Endowment for the Arts. That motion was defeated. The vote was 251–173 against. There was then a second motion which the House of Representatives proceeded to consider. The vote was 361–65 in favor of the second motion, which therefore was passed by the House. The 2nd resolution was to trim the National Endowment for the Arts budget by $45,000. That is the amount that the NEA provided, indirectly, for two controversial exhibits. In essence, the vote in the House of Representatives was in retaliation for 2 NEA grants that were used to fund the exhibits.

One of the 2 exhibits included a set of photographs showing nude men posed in ways described by critics as homoerotic and sadomasochistic. The photos of nude men were taken by Robert Mapplethorpe, who died of AIDS just a few years ago. A Philadelphia art center spent a total of $30,000, with the funds coming from a grant provided by the NEA, to finance an exhibition of Mapplethorpe's work. Mapplethorpe's photographs were also scheduled for a subsequent exhibit in a gallery in Washington, D.C., but it was canceled after public protests.

The second controversial exhibit included a photograph of a plastic crucifix submerged in a jar of the artists urine. According to the artist, his work protested the commercialization of Jesus. He got a total of $15,000 in payment for the exhibit from an art center in Winston-Salem, N.C. The art center, in turn, had received a grant from the NEA.

These were some of the comments made during the debate before the two votes in the House of Representatives today.

Rep. Daniel Kissick (R-Calif.)

"This is filth, not art. But that's not the issue we're voting on. The real question is not whether adults should be allowed to view art that sexually explicit. No one is trying to censor art or repeal the First Amendment. The issue here is whether or not a taxpayer should be forced, through his taxes, to subsidize this kind of so-called art. My answer to that is a definite 'No.' "

Rep. Margaret Doyle (R-Utah)

"Representative Kissick is right about this. The issue isn't simply good taste, or even pornography, which I believe this is. The issue here is the waste, the absolute waste, of our constituents money. We wonder, sometimes, why people don't respect Congress. I can tell you why. Its because we spend the publics money on garbage like this. If anyone wants to see this stuff, let them pay for it. We shouldn't be spending a penny of the federal government's money on it."

Rep. Jeff Izquierdo (D-Minn.)

"Ultimately, these resolutions take a piece out of America. The price we're being asked to pay is our freedom of expression. The NEA is a worthwhile cause. Every modern government in the world supports the arts. Its a sign of a civilized nation. But once Congress has allocated the money, we should let the NEA decide how to spend it. We shouldn't look over its shoulder, second-guessing the identity or value of any of its recipients. That's censorship—government interference in the arts. This issue before us today calls for tolerance, not a lynch mob."

Rep. Alan Schwab (D-Fla.)

"We should be honest about this. These two exhibits are pornographic and offensive and sacrilegious, and the people responsible for them should be in jail. They're not just immoral, they're in clear violation of the law. The NEA comes to us every year and asks us for millions of dollars, then spends it on garbage like this. What we need to do isn't just shut down these exhibits. What we really need to shut down is the NEA."

Exercise 8

SPECIALIZED TYPES OF STORIES

ROUNDUPS—MULTIPLE SOURCES

INSTRUCTIONS: Write a single roundup story that quotes the following sources:

Background

Ronald James Smitkinns, a 16-year-old youth, appeared in Circuit Court in your community today. He is charged with rape. His address is 417 Huron Avenue. He is the son of Marlene and Myron Smitkinns, also of 417 Huron Avenue. His victim is a junior high school teacher. Police have not identified her or the junior high school at which she teaches. Last Sept. 3, Smitkinns asked the woman for help in her classroom after the end of the day's classes, police said. Then he turned out the lights, locked the classroom door and, brandishing scissors, raped her several times. Last Friday, he pleaded guilty to a charge of sexual battery, and today the judge had to decide whether to sentence Smitkinns as a juvenile or as an adult. As a juvenile, he could be sentenced to a maximum of three years at a youth facility, to be followed by two years of probation. The range of sentences for an adult convicted of the same offense, sexual battery, is 30 years to life imprisonment. The following remarks were made at a hearing which preceded the sentencing this morning. Under new state laws, the victim was allowed to testify about the crime and about the assailant at the presentence hearing.

Ronald Smitkinns

"I'm sorry for what I did. I can't explain why I did it, but I know it's wrong, and it'll never happen again, I promise. I made a bad mistake, and I've learned from it. I want to repay society and the victim. All I need is another chance. I'm doing good in school, and I've never been in bad trouble like this before, you know. So you wouldn't ever have to worry about me again. It's just one dumb crazy thing I did and, hey, you know, it wouldn't ever happen again."

The Victim

"It was the most horrible, absolutely horrible, degrading experience of my life. I've needed psychiatric treatment and surgery, and I'm still not done with the counseling. I don't know if I can ever be done with it. My marriage has suffered, and I don't enjoy teaching any longer. All my life I wanted to be a teacher, and I was a good one. Now I'm nervous and afraid of the students, and I don't want to leave my home in the morning. But I'm not here today because I want vengeance. I just want protection. I want protection for me and for all the other women who work in the city's schools. You can't let this happen, especially in a school, and you can't let this rapist go free with a slap on the wrist. Rapists do it again because they get off on the violence, and he did."

Marlene Smitkinns, the Defendant's Mother

"I beg you, he's sorry. He's only 16, just a boy, and he didn't know what he was doing. If you send him to prison now, you'll destroy him. You'll ruin his whole life.

You send a nice young boy like him, a good son, to prison for 30 years, and he'll never have a chance for a real, normal life. He'll be thrown in there with a lot of criminals, and they'll be a terrible influence on him."

Joel Greene, Defense Attorney

"This boy has no criminal record, had good grades in school and went to church. I agree there's a need to protect this victim and other potential victims, but the way to do it is not to send such a young boy to a state prison. In 10 years he'll come out 10 years older and stronger and full of hatred for society. That's not justice, that's not going to help society, and that's not going to help the victim. This young boy needs help, and he's not going to get it in prison. He's not a criminal now, but you put him in prison for 10 or 20 years, and you'll have a criminal on your hands when he gets out, and maybe a bad one. That just doesn't make sense."

Marlene Ostreicher, Judge

"I think those who are involved in the education and upbringing of young people should have some assurance that these matters will not be taken lightly by the court. Teachers are entitled to protection and some guarantee of their personal safety, and that thought is uppermost in my mind. This defendant is 16 years old, almost 17, and he's old enough to know better, to know right from wrong. Therefore I've decided to sentence him, as an adult, to a term of 30 years in the state prison. I recognize that he may suffer, but it's also obvious that he inflicted a great deal of undeserved suffering upon his victim, and that she may continue to suffer for years to come, perhaps for the rest of her life. Our society has to put a stop to this kind of behavior and maybe, just maybe, sentences of this nature will make some other youths pause and think about the consequences of their action and know we're not going to let them engage in this kind of behavior and then come into our courtrooms and say they were too young to know what they were doing and that they are too young to be punished for their crimes."

Followup

Smitkinns and his attorney said they will appeal the sentence. If the appeal fails, Smitkinns must serve three years and nine months before he can be considered for parole. However, in cases of this kind parole is usually granted after the offender has served between 8 and 15 years; but Smitkinns may serve longer because he used the scissors as a deadly weapon in the commission of the felony. After the judge pronounced sentence, the victim said she felt like justice had been done. "I feel as if someone lifted a ton or two off me," she said. "Now I can stop worrying that he's coming back and that it'll happen again."

Exercise 9

SPECIALIZED TYPES OF STORIES

ROUNDUPS—MULTIPLE SOURCES

INSTRUCTIONS: Write a single news story that summarizes the following information. Organize the information in a clear, logical, cohesive manner. As you write the story, correct the spelling, style, grammatical and vocabulary errors. Also be thorough; report every issue in depth. Notice that the sources' comments appear in quotation marks, so you can quote them directly.

Background

The Sunnyview Retirement Home is an 8-story brick building located at 410 Hillcrest Street in your community. The building is a former hotel. Ten years ago it was renovated and turned into apartments for retirees. It is privately operated, for profit, with 110 apartments, including 30 for a single resident and 80 for two residents, often married couples, sharing an apartment. About 175 people were living there when a fire broke out at approximately 7:10 a.m. this morning. As many as 150 firefighters from throughout your region, including nearby communities, were called in for assistance in battling the blaze and assisting in rescuing all the victims from their peril.

Fire Chief Tony Sullivan

"It's the worst damn fire I've ever seen. We've got seven dead we know of and maybe 20 more that've been taken to hospitals with various injuries, some pretty serious. We just can't tell for sure. There could be lots more in the building, people who couldn't get out. I can't send my men in yet to look for them, not at this point, because its not safe. We've got the fire out, but it was a fierce one, and some floors and walls were weakened and are liable to collapse at anytime. It may be another day before we're able to make a thorough search and recover all the bodies."

Rescue Worker John Charlton

"People I've talked to say the fire started on the first or second floor. The fire itself wasn't so bad, except on the first couple of floors. Everything on those floors is gone. The fire didn't spread to the upper floors, but most of the deaths occurred up there. It was the smoke that did it. People said they couldn't breath, and then a lot of them were old and in bad shape to begin with. We've taken the survivors that weren't hurt none to a church just across the street, and they're mostly resting there now. I don't know where they'll go tonight, where they'll sleep. The Red Cross is setting up an information center for relatives at the church. We've, uh, got all sorts of relatives that've been in and out all morning, looking for their people and apparently bringing them home with them, so we don't know who's missing or dead or home safe with their families."

Director Mildred Anchall

"We don't know how the fire started, just that it started somewhere on the second floor, and our alarms sounded at 7. It happened so fast, it spread to fast, that all we could do was try and get everyone out. No one had time to stop and get a list of all our residents, and now they've been taken a half-dozen different places. We don't have any way of knowing who's safe and who's missing. Besides our residents, I've got my staff to worry about, and some visitors who were in the building. It's a tragedy, a real tragedy, something like this. You hear about things like this happening but never think it could happen at your home."

Building Inspector Ralph Schweitzer

"We inspected the building just a couple weeks ago, and it satisfied all our codes. When it was remodeled 10 years ago we didn't require sprinklers, and they would have saved everyone, would have put the fire out in a minute or two, so they would have really prevented a tragedy like this. Anyone building a nursing home today is required to put in sprinklers, and this is what we have in mind to prevent, a real serious tragedy like this one."

Survivor Steven Minh

"I'm 82, and I've been living here since it opened 10 years ago. Nothing like this ever happened here before. Its like I was back in World War II or something. I live on the eighth floor, and people up there were screaming for help. The smoke was real bad, and some of us don't move so quick anymore. The firemen got up there real fast and led us down the stairs. There were some real heroes up there. I saw firemen carrying a half-dozen people down 6 or 8 flights of stairs when they could hardly breath themselves, and a lot of us would be dead without them. We couldn't have lasted much longer, with the smoke and all. I'd just like to know what started the fire because it spread so fast. One minute everything was OK, then we were all choking on the smoke."

Survivor Betsy Aaron

"It was terrible in there. We began hearing fire alarms, but they weren't loud enough. By the time we realized what it was and went out into the hall it was full of smoke. I have a third-floor apartment, so I was able to get right out. I just took an elevator downstairs. Other people said they weren't working, but that must have been later, after I was out, that the elevators stopped working. When I got out on the street and looked up I saw people I knew leaning out their windows and shouting, 'Help me! Help me!' I couldn't do anything for them, not anything at all."

Fire Marshal R.J. Hilton

"We haven't pinpointed the cause of the fire yet. It's too early, but my personal feelings are, strictly on a preliminary basis, it seems to have been an accidental fire that started in one of the apartments. It'll be at least a day or two before we have anything official on that."

Exercise 10

SPECIALIZED TYPES OF STORIES

ROUNDUPS—MULTIPLE EVENTS

INSTRUCTIONS: Write a single roundup story that summarizes all three of the following traffic accidents.

Accident 1

One car was driven by T. J. Ortsen, 51, of 810 N. 14th St. The other car was driven by Sara Anne Talbertson, 34, of 3214 Riverview Drive. The two vehicles collided at the intersection of U.S. 141 and Carlton Avenue. The accident was reported to police at 12:35 a.m. today. The accident was investigated by Patrolmen Julius Tiller and Manuel Cortez. They reported that Ortson and his wife, Martha, 53, suffered head and chest injuries. An ambulance rushed the couple to Memorial Hospital, where both are reported in serious condition. Miss Talbertson was not injured. The officers charged Miss Talbertson with running a red light. Both cars were demolished.

Accident 2

Officers were called to the 4200 block of Wymore Road at 6:30 a.m. today. Patrolman Cecil Roehl filed a report concerning the accident. The report said: "I arrived at the scene at 6:34 a.m. and, upon arrival, found the victim's motorcycle in the eastbound lane of traffic. The victim has been positively identified as Leon Merritt, 17, of 301 Wymore Road. Skid marks indicate that his motorcycle was traveling at excessive speeds and went out of control just past a dip in the road. Road signs warn of the dip. The posted speed limit is 45 miles an hour. The subject's motorcycle is estimated to have been traveling in excess of 60 miles an hour. The motorcycle went off the road and struck a telephone pole and then seems to have bounced back onto the road. The victim's body was thrown into a field and was lying 47 feet from the roadway. The coroner pronounced Merritt dead at the scene. His motorcycle was totally destroyed."

Accident 3

The accident occurred at 8:20 a.m. today. Two vehicles were involved. A van driven by Jay Gable of 1701 Woodcrest Drive and a car driven by Jean Janvier, 27, of 1883 Hope Ter. Gable was alone in his vehicle. A passenger in the Janvier vehicle has been identified as Reba Carvel. She was 23 years old. Miss Janvier and Miss Carvel taught at Colonial Elementary School, and they apparently were on their way to school when the accident occurred. Patrolman Nego, who investigated the accident, reported that: "Gable suffered a broken leg and possible head injuries and has been taken to Memorial Hospital. He seemed in shock so I couldn't talk to him. Gable had stopped to pick up another man who works with him, Melvin McCaully, 47, of 540 Osceoloa Blvd. The accident occurred directly in front of his house. McCaully said he heard Gable stop and honk and then heard the crash. From skid marks at the scene, it appears that Gable hadn't pulled off the road and the Janvier vehicle rammed square into the back of his van. The van was pushed off the road and into a ditch, where it overturned. The car remained upright on the highway. Skid marks and the extent of the damage indicate

that the car was traveling about fifty miles an hour. The speed limit on Osceola Blvd. at that point is fifty-five miles an hour. Both women were dead when I got to them and it took more than a half hour for the rescue squad to pry their bodies out of the wreckage. Charges of manslaughter will probably be filed against Gable later today. The district attorney is looking at the evidence now."

Exercise 11

SPECIALIZED TYPES OF STORIES

ROUNDUPS—MULTIPLE EVENTS

INSTRUCTIONS: Write a single roundup story that summarizes all three of the following fires.

Fire 1

Two police officers patrolling Main St. reported a fire at Frishe's Bowling Alley, 4113 Main St., at 3:32 a.m. today. They smelled smoke, got out of their squad car and traced the smoke to the bowling alley. Firefighters said the fire was confined to an office, where it caused an estimated $10,000 damage. Firefighters found evidence of arson and notified police that the office apparently had been set on fire after it was burglarized. Two cigarette machines, a soft-drink machine and a door leading to the office had been pried open. Police said the thieves probably set the fire to hide the robbery. Art Mahew, manager of the bowling alley, estimated that $20 was missing from the three machines and $50 was taken from a cash box in the office. He added: "That's all the money we keep in the building at night. Except for some change for the next day's business, we just don't keep any money in the building at night. It's too risky. This is the third robbery we've had since I started working here four years ago."

Fire 2

Firefighters were called to 1314 Griese Drive at 8:23 a.m. today. They found a fire in progress on the second floor of the two-story home. The home is owned by Mr. and Mrs. Timothy Keele. Mr. and Mrs. Keel and their four children escaped from the home before firemen arrived. Firefighters extinguished the blaze within 20 minutes. The fire was confined to two upstairs bedrooms and the attic. Smoke and water damage were reported throughout the house. No one was injured. Damage was estimated at $20,000. Mrs. Keel told firemen she had punished one of her children for playing with matches in an upstairs closet earlier in the morning. Fire marshals said the blaze started in that closet and attributed the fire to the child playing with matches. Mrs. Keel added that she was not aware of the fire until a telephone repairman working across the street noticed smoke, came over and rang her doorbell. When she answered, he asked, "Do you know your house is on fire?"

Fire 3

Firefighters responded to a call at the Quality Trailer Court at 10:31 a.m. today after neighbors were alerted by screams from a trailer occupied by Mrs. Susan Kopp, age 71. Flames had spread throughout the trailer by the time firefighters arrived at the scene. The firefighters had to extinguish the blaze, then wait for the embers to cool before they were able to enter the trailer. They found Mrs. Kopp's body in her bedroom in the trailer. A spokesman for the Fire Department said she had apparently been smoking in bed, then awoke when her bedding caught fire. She died of suffocation before she could get out. Neighbors who heard her screams were unable to enter the trailer because of the flames, smoke and heat.

Exercise 12

SPECIALIZED TYPES OF STORIES

SIDEBARS

INSTRUCTIONS: Use the following information to write two separate stories: first a news story reporting the fire, then a sidebar based on the interviews with Mrs. Noffsinger.

Main Story

The Grande Hotel is located downtown at the corner of Wisconsin and Barber Avenues. It is a seven-story structure with a total of 114 rooms. It was constructed and opened for business in the year 1924. In recent years the hotel has been in an obvious state of decline, unable to compete with new facilities in the city and with the convenience of motels located along highways which now bypass the city. Many of the hotel rooms have been rented on long-term leases, often to elderly persons who like its downtown location, which is more convenient for them, since many facilities they use are in walking distance and buses are easily available for other trips they want to make. Three persons died in a fire at the hotel last night. The cause of the fire is undetermined. It started in a third-floor room. It spread and also destroyed the fourth, fifth, sixth and seventh floors before it was brought under control at 4:30 a.m. today. At about 11 p.m. a guest called the lobby to report the odor of smoke. A hotel employee used a passkey to enter the third-floor room where the fire originated and found it totally engulfed in flames. The room is believed to have been vacant at the time. The employee sounded a fire alarm in the hotel and called firefighters. It was the first five-alarm blaze in the city in more than 10 years. Every piece of fire equipment in the city was rushed to the scene, and off-duty firefighters were called in to assist. Fortunately, said Fire Chief Tony Sullivan, no other fires were reported in the city at the same time or he would have had to send a truck and men from the scene of the hotel blaze. Hotel records indicate that 62 persons were registered in the hotel at the time the blaze initiated; 49 had long-term leases and 13 were transients. All the transients were located on the second floor and escaped safely. The dead, all of whom had long-term leases, have been identified as Mildred Haserot, age 58; Willie Hattaway, age 67; and Pearl Petchsky, age 47. The bodies of all three victims were found on the fourth floor, where they lived. Fire Chief Tony Sullivan said this morning the hotel is a total loss and that some walls are in danger of collapse. He said: "The fire was already out of hand when our first units reached the scene. I was called from home, and by then the flames were breaking out through the third- and fourth-floor windows. We were really lucky there weren't more people killed, but the hotel people knocked on the door of every room that was occupied to get everybody out. Most guests used a back stairway, and we were lucky the elevators kept working for awhile even after my men got into the building, otherwise the loss would have been worse. I'm also told that the top two floors were empty, and that helped keep down the loss of lives."

The Red Cross is caring for survivors, finding them new rooms and providing clothes and emergency allocations of cash, a total of $250 per person. Five people were injured, including one fireman who suffered from smoke inhalation. The others suffered from burns, some serious, and also from smoke inhalation. Three are being treated at Mercy Hospital. Two have been released, including the fireman. Their names and conditions are unknown at this time.

Sidebar

Nora Noffsinger, 74, has been a resident of the Grande Hotel for the past nine years. She paid $580 a month rent for one room on the fifth floor. A retired bookkeeper, she said afterward: "It was dreadfully expensive, but it was a charming old building and I had lots of good friends living there. I was asleep last night when I heard someone pounding on my door. I don't know who it was, but he told me to get out fast, and I did. All I had on were my pajamas and a robe, but I could see the smoke, even up there on the fifth floor, and I was scared; I knew right away that it was bad. Everyone else was scared too, but we all knew what to do. We'd talked lots about what we'd do if there was ever a fire because you hear so often about fires in old hotels, and we wanted to be prepared. We all kept flashlights in our rooms and planned to go down the back stairway unless the fire was there, and it wasn't. The lights were still on, so we didn't even need our flashlights. Now the Red Cross put me in a motel room a few blocks away, and I guess I should be happy I'm safe, but I lost everything—my clothes, a little money I'd kept hidden in a secret place, all my photographs. My husband's dead, you know, and I lost all my pictures of him. I don't know what I'll do now; I don't have any children. I'm all by myself, except for my friends, and they all lived at the hotel with me."

Exercise 13

SPECIALIZED TYPES OF STORIES

SIDEBARS

INSTRUCTIONS: Use the following information to write two separate stories: first a news story reporting the Senate's action, then a sidebar based on the interview with the sheriff.

Main Story

The state Senate today approved a bill overwhelmingly. The bill has already been approved by the house and now goes to the Governor, who has indicated that he will sign it. The bill was passed almost unanimously by angry lawmakers who want inmates housed in jails throughout the state to help pay the costs of their room and board. There were only 2 votes against the measure in the senate and none against in the house. The bill will go into effect next January 1st. It will require persons housed in a jail within the state to reveal their incomes and, if they can afford it, to pay the entire cost of their room and board behind bars, or whatever share of the cost they can reasonably afford. The bill requires the State Department of Offender Rehabilitation to draw up guidelines on how prisoners will disclose their finances and how much they will be required to pay. The department will consider a number of relevant variables, such as whether a prisoner must support a family and devote all his or her income to that family. The idea of the bill arose a number of months ago when lawmakers touring a state prison were told that some inmates received Government benefits (mostly Social Security and veterans' benefits). The lawmakers were told that some prisoners opened bank accounts in the prisons and that the money they received piled up so they had thousands of dollars accumulated in the accounts when they were released. A subsequent survey requested by legislative leaders found 19,000 inmates in the state and that, of that total, 356 received government payments of some type. The same survey found that the inmates had a total of $3.1 million in inmate accounts at state prisons. Prison officials cautioned that the prisoners may have more money deposited in banks outside the prison system and that it would be difficult to locate those accounts. To enforce the new bill, lawmakers stipulated that prisoners who refuse to disclose their finances cannot be released early on parole. Officials have not yet determined how much each prisoner will be charged. Lawmakers also noted that some inmates may have other assets, such as farms, homes, automobiles, and stocks and bonds, and that those prisoners can also be expected to help defray their prison expenses.

Sidebar

Gus DiCesare is the county sheriff. He has held that position for 11 years. To retain the position, he must run for reelection every four years. As sheriff, DiCesare is in charge of the county jail, which has a capacity of 120 inmates, mostly men but also a few women. Criminals sentenced to terms of less than one year in prison are usually sentenced to the county facility rather than to a state prison. Despite its capacity of 120 persons, the county jail usually holds 140 to 150 persons—20 or 30 more than its rated capacity. When interviewed today about the legislature's approval of the bill in question, DiCesare said: "Hey, I think it's a great idea. Some of these prisoners got more money than I'll ever have. When we pick them up, they're driving fancy cars, living in big homes and carrying a thick wad of money. Not most of them, but there're always a few in here, mostly drug dealers. We sentence them to jail as punishment, but it punishes honest taxpayers who pay to keep them in here—pay for this building, their food, clothes, jailers and all the rest. A couple of years ago, we calculated that it cost about $35 to keep one prisoner here one day. Hell, if they can afford it, prisoners should help pay for it all; that could be part of their punishment. I'll bet our costs are up to nearly $80 a day apiece now, and they're still rising. It'd help me too. I've got a damned hard problem trying to run this place on the budget the county gives me. With a little more money, I could improve the food, come up with some more recreational facilities and maybe even try to rehabilitate a few prisoners—bring in some teachers and counselors and that type of thing. Now, all I really do is keep them locked behind bars all day, and that's not going to rehabilitate anyone."

CHAPTER 15

WRITING OBITUARIES

Obituaries are newspaper reports that people have died. Typically, obituaries announce a person's death, briefly describe the person's life, then summarize the funeral arrangements.

That information is more important and popular than most people realize: as popular as a newspaper's comics. Several readership surveys have found that 40 to 50 percent of a newspaper's readers look at its obituaries. Moreover, the percentage increases with age. About 45 percent of the readers 18 to 24 express "at least some interest" in obituaries, compared to more than 60 percent of the readers over 60.

One study compared the popularity of obituaries with the popularity of other features in newspapers. The study found that, on average, about 45 percent of a newspaper's readers say they look at its obituary page every day. By comparison, about 87 percent look at a newspaper's front page; 66 percent at its local news; 47 percent at the weather; and 44 percent at the comics, sports and food pages. Forty-one percent look at their newspaper's editorial page and 37 percent at its business page.

One reason for the popularity of obituaries is that only newspapers provide them. Radio and television stations mention the deaths of a few celebrities. Only newspapers, however, have the time, space and staff necessary to publish obituaries for everyone in their communities, not just the rich and famous. Moreover, few stories are so important to the people involved—and so likely to be clipped, pasted in scrapbooks and mailed to friends.

Unfortunately, most obituaries are cold and impersonal. Few convey the impression that any of the people they describe possessed unique personalities and sets of experiences. The primary reason is that few newspapers devote enough time, space or reporters to obituaries. Newspapers often assign a single reporter to write all their obituaries and, in a few hours each day, that reporter may have to write the obituaries for 10 or 15 people. Another reason is that newspapers traditionally have assigned obituaries to their newest and least experienced reporters. Some newspapers even hire people without any journalistic training to write obituaries, thus freeing experienced reporters for assignments thought to be more important. Obituaries are considered an ideal assignment for beginners because they seldom require any specialized knowledge; rather, most obituaries are brief, simple, and easy to write. Moreover, reporters can write the obituaries without leaving their desks—or the close supervision of their editors.

Some newspapers expect experienced reporters to help write obituaries, but few reporters like the assignment. Reporters rarely know the people who died and complain that the assignment is unexciting and unimportant. Many also consider it unpleasant. Like most other Americans, reporters are uncomfortable with death and reluctant to call the friends and relatives of people who just died. In the past, reporters also realized that they were unlikely to receive many rewards for writing good obituaries.

Today, that may be changing. A few newspapers have begun to devote more attention to their obituaries, and some reporters have begun to win prizes for their work—even to become nationally famous for it.

Typically, newspapers in small towns try to publish an obituary for everyone who dies in their geographical area. However, all the obituaries may have to fit into a limited amount of space, perhaps two or three columns (about 40 to 60 inches). Because some of that space is filled by headlines, only 3 to 4 inches are left for each obituary. Increasingly, larger newspapers publish the obituaries for noncelebrities only in their regional or suburban editions. A few newspapers in very large cities no longer print everyone's obituary because they simply do not have enough space. Like radio and television stations, those papers report only the deaths of the most prominent members of their communities.

Some people confuse the obituaries with news stories. If a newsworthy individual dies, or if someone's death is unusual, newspapers will publish a news story about the person's death. Newspapers may also publish an obituary, but the obituary may appear a day or two later. Also, the obituary will emphasize the person's life, not death.

People sometimes confuse obituaries with paid funeral notices. While obituaries are separate stories written by reporters and published at no cost, some newspapers do not have enough space to publish everyone's obituary. Instead, funeral directors will often place paid funeral notices in those newspapers. Most funeral notices are only one paragraph long and are published in alphabetical order among the newspapers' classified advertisements. The notices are written by funeral directors, and the fee for having one published is added to the cost of the funeral. Funeral directors often place these paid notices in newspapers that also publish free obituaries.

Funeral homes give newspapers all the information they need to write most obituaries. The funeral homes, eager to have their names appear in the newspapers as often as possible, obtain the information when families come in to arrange funeral services. Some funeral homes have the families fill out special forms provided by their local newspapers, and immediately deliver the completed forms to the papers. Just before their daily deadlines, reporters may call the funeral homes to be certain they have not missed any obituaries.

If the person who died was prominent, reporters may learn more about the person by going to their newspaper's library and reading previous stories published about him or her. Reporters may also call the person's family and business associates to obtain some additional information and a recent photograph. Most people willingly cooperate with reporters; they seem to accept requests made by the reporters as part of the routine that occurs at the time of death. Many people also cooperate with reporters because they want their friends' and relatives' obituaries to be accurate, thorough and well written.

THE CONTENT OF OBITUARIES

Most obituaries begin with a lead that identifies the person who died, typically revealing the person's name and identification and at least one unique or outstanding fact about the person's life, usually the person's major accomplishment. The inclusion of some unique or outstanding fact is essential; it makes obituaries more interesting and keeps them from all looking alike. For example:

Dr. Catherine Mekdeci of 4112 N. Lakeview Drive died of a heart attack at St. Nicholas Hospital Monday. She was 72.
REVISED: Catherine Mekdeci, who delivered more than 10,000 babies during the 40 years she worked as an obstetrician at St. Nicholas Hospital, died at the hospital Monday.

Russell C. Johnson, 73, of 4578 Davisson Ave., a retired businessman, died Monday at his home after a lingering illness.

REVISED: Russell C. Johnson, who began work as a mailroom clerk for the nation's largest insurance company and 30 year later became the company's president, died Monday at the age of 73.

The original leads stressed dull, routine facts: the people's ages, addresses and causes of death. The revisions contain more interesting facts about their lives and accomplishments. Other good leads might describe an individual's interests, goals, hobbies, philosophy or personality. Here are two examples, written about more famous individuals:

WASHINGTON, D.C.—William O. Douglas, a mighty force for individual freedom during almost four decades as a Supreme Court justice, died Saturday at the Walter Reed Army Medical Center.

(The Associated Press)

COLUMBUS, Ohio—Woody Hayes, who for 28 seasons ruled his Ohio State University football teams like one of the generals he so admired, died in his sleep Thursday at home. He was 74.

(The Associated Press)

After the lead, an obituary should provide a chronology of the individual's life. The information commonly presented in obituaries, and its approximate order of inclusion, includes:

1. Identification (full name, age, address, major accomplishment);
2. Time and place of death;
3. Occupation and employment history;
4. Other major interests and accomplishments;
5. Honors, awards and offices held;
6. Educational history: schools attended and graduated from;
7. Membership in churches, clubs and other civic organizations;
8. Military service;
9. Years and places of birth and marriage;
10. List of surviving relatives;
11. Religious services;
12. Other burial and funeral arrangements.

Reporters are trained to avoid eulogies, euphemisms and sentimentality. They report that people have "died," not that they have "passed away," "departed," "expired" or "succumbed." Obituary writers must also avoid the flowery language used by funeral directors and by grieving friends and relatives—terms such as "the remains" and "the loved one." Yet, as a sign of respect, newspapers often use a person's full name the first time he or she is mentioned in an obituary and, in later references, use a courtesy title, referring to the person as "*Mr.* Jones" or "*Mrs.* Smith."

If time and space are available, and if an individual merits a lengthy obituary, reporters may include some anecdotes about the person's life and the recollections of friends and relatives, as well as other biographical highlights.

Normally, information about the religious services, burial and surviving relatives is placed at the end of an obituary. The information should be as specific as possible so that mourners will know when they can call on the person's family and when and where they can attend the funeral and burial. The list of survivors normally includes only an individual's immediate family. It begins with the names of the person's husband or wife, followed by the names of parents, brothers and sisters, and children. Newspapers may list the number (but not the names) of grandchildren and great-grandchildren. Few newspapers list more distant relatives, such as nieces, nephews and cousins, unless they are the only survivors or are themselves people of note. Recently, some newspapers have also begun to list the names of other survivors: nonrelatives, including live-in friends who played an important role in the person's life.

Newspapers usually report the specific street address of survivors who live in their local communities, but only the home towns (not the street addresses) of people living elsewhere.

The following obituaries illustrate newspapers' typical format:

David C. Curnutte, who owned and managed a downtown bookstore after serving as a fighter pilot in two wars, died at his home Monday. He was 75.

Mr. Curnutte opened the Classics Bookstore at 410 N. Main St. in 1966 and operated it until his retirement in 1983.

He was born in Seattle, Wash., and was an All-American basketball and football player in high school. He attended Duke University on a football scholarship and majored in philosophy.

Mr. Curnutte joined the Army Air Corps before Pearl Harbor was attacked in 1941 and flew 132 combat missions in the South Pacific. He was recalled to active duty during the Korean War and flew 81 missions during that conflict. He retired from the Air Force in 1963.

He was a member of the Quiet Birdmen, the Retired Officers Association, the University Club and the American Association of Retired Persons.

Survivors include his wife, Helen; sons Leroy of 4810 N. Highley Road and Jason of Fresno, Calif.; daughter, Mrs. Paul (Mary) White of Des Moines, Iowa; and seven grandchildren.

Memorial services will be conducted at 2 p.m. Thursday at the First Congregational Church, with the Rev. Randolph Schultz officiating. Burial will be in Evergreen Cemetery.

Margaret Joan Holleanna, 69, a teacher at Hawthorne Elementary School for 37 years, died at the Elder Kare Nursing Home early today.

She was offered several jobs as an elementary school principal but never accepted them. She once explained: "I always loved the children in my classroom, and they're the only children I ever had. I never want to leave my children."

She was born in Holland, Mich., and received her bachelor's and master's degrees from the University of Michigan.

She was a member and a past president of the City Women's Club and a past president of the State Federation of Women's Clubs.

She was also a member of St. Andrew's Catholic Church, the Sunshine Society, Chaminade Club and Daughters of the American Revolution.

Miss Holleanna never married. Survivors include a niece, Marlene Sanders of 4827 N. Garland Ave.

Funeral services will be held at 1:30 p.m. Saturday at the Pine Garden Chapel, with Father Robert Kurber of St. Andrew's Catholic Church officiating. Interment will follow in Greenwood Cemetery.

Friends may call from 2 to 4 and from 7 to 9 p.m. Friday at the Pine Garden Chapel, 430 N. Kirkman Road.

In lieu of flowers, memorial contributions may be made to the American Cancer Society.

Some newspapers also try to report the cause of every death. However, others do not, often because that information is difficult to obtain. Many people are reluctant to reveal the cause of their relatives' deaths, particularly if they died of a dreaded disease, such as AIDS, or of a humiliating disease, such as cirrhosis of the liver (which may be caused by alcoholism). For years, people were also reluctant to mention cancer, so obituaries used the euphemism that people "died after a long illness." A similar euphemism—"died after a lingering illness"—continues to appear in many papers.

Newspapers are most likely to report the cause of a celebrity's death. Because it is unexpected, they are also more likely to report the cause of a young person's death.

Some newspapers report suicides in separate news stories, particularly when the suicides are bizarre, occur in public or involve prominent individuals. Other newspapers mention the cause of death, even when it is suicide, in routine obituaries rather than in news stories. Still other newspapers consider suicide a private matter, never to be reported in any manner. When newspapers do report suicides, they carefully attribute the determination of the cause of death to some authority, usually the coroner. Few newspapers describe in detail the methods used to commit suicide or any bloody details about the deaths. If you work for a newspaper, you will be expected to follow the policies set by its executives; in other cases, use your own judgment.

It often takes authorities several days to announce the official cause of death. When that problem arises, an initial story or obituary may report that the cause of death has not yet been determined, or that, "An autopsy will be conducted Thursday." A later story may report the results of the autopsy or inquest.

IMPROVING THE OBITUARIES YOU WRITE

You can easily improve the obituaries you write. It takes surprisingly little time or effort to transform routine obituaries into sparkling ones.

Obituaries become more interesting when reporters go beyond the routine and do more than list the events in a person's life: when they take the time to include additional details and to explain their significance. To produce a good obituary, however, you need to be a good interviewer as well as a good writer: to call two or three friends or relatives and ask them about the deceased. Then, while interviewing the friends and relatives, you must obtain specific details, not generalities.

For example, instead of simply reporting that a woman served in the Army and graduated from college, an obituary might tell what the woman did in the Army, where she attended college and what she studied. Similarly, instead of simply reporting that a man retired 10 years earlier, an obituary might explain what the man did after retiring. If someone mentions a person's sense of humor, ask for an example of it. Or, if a friend said the deceased "cared a lot about people," ask for two or three examples of the person's caring.

After gathering the specific details needed for a good obituary, begin by summarizing the most important, interesting or unique factor in the person's life:

> Tania Ladizco, a 21-year-old journalism student who hoped to become a professional sports writer, died of cancer Thursday morning at her home.

> Bruce R. Horwitz, 72, a plumber who played a violin in the Municipal Orchestra for 41 years, died Sunday of a heart attack.

Mistakenly, beginners quickly shift to chronological order and, in their second paragraph, report their obituaries' least interesting details: a collection of dates. For example:

Carlos Diaz, a doctor who specialized in caring for the victims of AIDS, died Thursday.

Dr. Diaz was born in San Antonio, Texas, in 1943, attended the University of Texas and began his practice here in 1973.

David Dinnen, 48, a history professor for the last 21 years, died of a heart attack at his home Tuesday.

Mr. Dinnen was born in Hamilton, Ohio, in 1940 and received his bachelor's degree from Cornell in 1962 and his doctorate from Indiana University in 1968. He served in the U.S. Navy from 1962 to 1965.

Instead, an obituary's second and third paragraphs should immediately develop the primary idea summarized in the lead. If, for example, your lead reports that the deceased was a plumber who played the violin, immediately begin to describe that person's work and hobby.

Here are three examples of more cohesive and interesting obituaries. Notice that the second and third paragraphs immediately develop the primary idea summarized in the lead:

Alan Lieber, 31, a devoted guitar player, died Tuesday at his home.

Mr. Lieber began playing the guitar when he was 12, and a friend, Diana Roon-McNally, said: "Music, his guitar, became the most important thing in his life. He worked night and day on that guitar and even wrote some music."

For 10 years, Mr. Lieber traveled around the country, working as a professional musician. At the age of 30, he decided to enroll in college and study to become a music teacher. . . .

Anne Cochran, a college student who dreamed of becoming an artist, died Monday.

"Anne was a fun-loving gal who wanted to make a career out of something she really enjoyed," said her boyfriend, Larry Cooper. "She wanted to be an artist ever since third grade, when she won a prize in a poster contest."

Miss Cochran's favorite pastime was drawing portraits of her family and friends. "She would spend hours trying to get their color and features just right," Cooper said. . . .

Ronald Dimitiri, an attorney who won more than 70 motorcycle races, died of AIDS Wednesday at home with his family. He was 54.

Wendy Chin, a partner in Dimitiri's law firm, talked about his racing career.

"He loved to race his motorcycle," Chin said. "He said the concentration that racing demanded forced him to really concentrate, to clear his mind of everything else. Plus, he loved the competition."

Dimitiri's trophies filled five shelves in his office.

"Of course, he had to give it up," said his son, Michael. "When he stopped winning, he realized he was getting too old for it and quit. But he still loved his bike and to go out for a weekend ride with one of us kids on the back seat. . . ."

If the person who died was young, you might report his or her goals:

Allaski was majoring in English and dreamed of writing a best-selling novel.

A political science major, she wanted to become an international lawyer and work in England or France.

Regardless of a person's age, you might also describe his or her hobbies:

She loved to sail, ski and dance.

He began to play tennis while he was in high school and, for the next 40 years, continued to play two or three times every week. He also enjoyed swimming, traveling, and playing poker and chess.

In addition, describe the person's character and physical appearance:

White's friends described him as a big man—he stood over 6 feet tall and weighed 205 pounds.

Tony Rodriguez, a friend and classmate, said: "He was one of the smartest people I've ever known. We studied together all the time. If I was having trouble understanding something, he would always help."

"She was a quiet person and loved animals," said a friend, Dina Coe-Levcenko. "She was also very kind and never had a bad thing to say about anyone."

OBITUARIES FOR CELEBRITIES

Newspapers publish more colorful obituaries for celebrities, such as politicians, athletes and entertainers. The Associated Press and other news services provide the obituaries for national celebrities. Some newspapers localize the news-service obituaries and also prepare the complete obituaries for local celebrities.

Some celebrity obituaries are prepared in advance, then brought up-to-date periodically so that if, for example, the president dies, his obituary is ready for immediate dissemination. Similarly, if a celebrity becomes seriously ill, newspapers may prepare that person's obituary and even set it in type. Then, when the celebrity dies, only the obituary's lead has to be written.

The Content of Celebrities' Obituaries

Typically, the obituaries for celebrities are longer than the obituaries written for other people and emphasize different types of information. Because few readers are likely to know a national celebrity and to attend that celebrity's funeral and burial, the obituary may not mention those services. Instead, it will emphasize the celebrity's personality and accomplishments.

Here are some typical leads for obituaries of famous people:

WASHINGTON—Werner von Braun, a dreamer whose love was the heavens and whose wizardry sent men to explore them, is dead.

He died of cancer at 3 a.m. Thursday in Alexandria Hospital in suburban Virginia.

HONOLULU—Arthur Murray, the immigrant baker's son who danced his way to fame and fortune as the world's best-known teacher of ballroom dancing, died Sunday at his home. He was 95.

(The New York Times)

NEW YORK—Andy Warhol, the pale prince of pop art who turned images of soup cans and superstars into museum pieces, died Sunday of a heart attack.

(The Orlando Sentinel)

GENEVA—Richard Burton, the Welsh actor who juggled a spellbinding stage and screen career with alcoholism and a volcanic love life that included two marriages to Elizabeth Taylor, died Sunday. He was 58.

(The Associated Press)

To reveal a celebrity's character or philosophy, an obituary may reprint the person's most interesting or controversial statements. Obituaries for artist Andy Warhol quoted a book he wrote. ''In the future,'' Warhol predicted, ''everyone will be world famous for 15 minutes.'' An obituary for actress Ava Gardner reported that she had been married three times and said of her husbands, ''I loved them all but I never understood any of them, and I don't think they understood me.'' Similarly, obituaries for Richard Burton revealed that he had said, ''I rather like my reputation, actually, that of a drunk, a womanizer; it's rather an attractive image.'' Burton had also said, ''If I had a chance for another life, I would certainly choose a better complexion.''

Obituaries for actor John Wayne noted that he had been a patriotic figure and once said, ''I am proud of every day in my life I wake up in the United States of America.'' Wayne rarely received good reviews for his performances, and obituaries also reported that he had said, ''Nobody likes my acting but the public.'' Other quotations reprinted at the time of his death include:

I'm 53 years old and 6 feet 4. I've had three wives, five children and three grandchildren. I love whiskey. I still don't understand women, and I don't think there is any man who does.

Hell, I'm no saint. Never said I was. I thought of three things when I had the cancer operations. My wife, my kids and death. I was butchered. One lung gone, some of the other cut away. When the doctor came in to give me the news, I was in the bed trying to be John Wayne and I gruffly said, ''Doctor, you trying to tell me I've got cancer?'' What a shock. I couldn't believe I was dying.

Obituaries for television star Michael Landon described him as ''an athletic man with thick, curly hair.'' Landon was 54 when he died of inoperable cancer of the liver and pancreas, and obituaries also described his battle against the disease. ''If I'm gonna die,'' Landon had told reporters, ''death's gonna have to do a lot of fighting to get me. I'm not just gonna lie down and let it happen.''

Other obituaries quote people who knew the celebrities. The following quotation appeared in an obituary for Louis Armstrong, jazz trumpet player, singer, composer and orchestra leader:

Armstrong's fourth wife, Lucille, once said of him:
''Life with Louis is a laugh a day. Why, that man even wakes up happy. I

tell him sometimes, 'Louis, it's against the law of averages for you to be so happy all the time.' But he always finds something to laugh about just the same.''

(The Associated Press)

Obituaries may describe the hurdles that celebrities overcame. Richard Burton was a coal miner's son, born in South Wales. Entertainer Sammy Davis Jr. was born in Harlem, joined his father's vaudeville act when he was 3 and never attended school. Davis lost an eye in a car wreck and worked in clubs and hotels that refused to serve him meals or let him stay overnight because he was black. Arthur Murray had been a shy, gangling wallflower who found that he had a flair for ballroom dancing. Murray's success as a dancer helped him gain self-confidence. He began giving lessons, then built a network of more than 300 franchised dance studios. By the time Murray stepped down as president, the studios were grossing $25 million a year.

Comedian Lucille Ball was the daughter of an electrician and left home at the age of 15 to study acting. A drama teacher in New York City told Ball that she had no talent and advised her to return home. Ball was so poor that she stole the tips left on coffee-shop counters. She eventually found work as a model and chorus-line beauty, then went on to Hollywood and made about 75 movies. Ball and her husband, Ricky Ricardo, became famous, however, as a result of the television series "I Love Lucy."

Even on the day a celebrity dies, reporters may recall anecdotes that will make readers laugh or reveal more about the person's life and character. Actress Bette Davis died of cancer at the age of 81 and had once said that she did not care about aging. Obituaries, however, reported that she had celebrated her 70th birthday "by hanging a black wreath on her door and needlepointing a pillow that read, 'Old age ain't no place for sissies.' "

Similarly, when Newsweek magazine published an obituary for Eddie Rickenbacker, a World War I ace who later became head of Eastern Airlines, the magazine reported that Rickenbacker had been badly injured years earlier when a DC-3 crashed as it approached Atlanta:

> In the hospital, he heard the radio voice of Walter Winchell announce that he was dying. "I began to fight," Rickenbacker recalled later. "They had me under an oxygen tent. I tore it apart and picked up a pitcher. I heaved it at the radio and scored a direct hit. The radio fell apart and Winchell's voice stopped. Then I got well."

Obituaries also explain how the celebrities died. Sammy Davis Jr died of throat cancer at the age of 64. Supreme Court Justice William O. Douglas entered a hospital on Christmas Eve, "suffering from pneumonia, and was treated for progressive respiratory and kidney failure." A publicist attributed pianist Liberace's death "to cardiac arrest due to congestive heart failure," but some obituaries reported rumors that Liberace died of AIDS.

The best obituaries combine all the different techniques in an attempt to reveal more about the celebrity. Typically, an obituary for Alfred Hitchcock began:

> HOLLYWOOD—Sir Alfred Hitchcock, the master director who probably frightened more moviegoers than anyone in history with his 54 suspense-packed movies, died peacefully Tuesday at his home.

(The Los Angeles Times)

The obituaries for Hitchcock also quoted him, quoted his friends and revealed interesting details about his personality and life. Hitchcock, who frightened millions

Should newspapers have reported the cause of Liberace's death?

of moviegoers, was himself a fearful man; he was afraid of burglars, crowds, darkness, Sundays, heights, closed spaces, open spaces and, above all, false accusation and arrest. Obituaries explained that Hitchcock feared the police because, as a youth, he had been taken to a police station and locked in a cell as an example of "what we do to naughty boys."

Newsweek also described Hitchcock's attitude toward sex, even quoting one of his statements about it:

> Sex has never interested me much. I don't understand how people can waste so much time over sex: sex is for kids, for movies—a great bore.

Although most newspapers apply all these principles only to the obituaries for celebrities, you can apply them with equal success to obituaries for other people as well: to the obituaries written for the students on your campus and for everyone else in your community.

Reporting the Good—and the Bad

Most journalists insist that celebrities' obituaries should not simply praise the individuals, but should report both the good and the bad about their lives. The obituaries for Andy Warhol described his unhappy life as a youth, including three nervous breakdowns. In 1968 an actress waylaid Warhol at his office and shot him. Bullets punctured his lungs, spleen, liver and stomach. After that, Warhol was believed to have sent lookalikes to some public events.

After Harry Reasoner's death, Andy Rooney, a colleague at CBS, reminisced:

> In pure intellect, Harry was the smartest of all the TV correspondents—but he did more dumb things than any of them. He would not have died at the age of 68 if this were not true. He smoked three packs of cigarettes a day. He drank martinis, a lot of them. Four years ago, he had his cancerous left lung removed and continued to smoke heavily.
>
> "I can stop drinking if I have to," he said to me one day two years ago, "but I can't stop smoking." That was the last time I ever said anything to him about smoking.

He died of almost everything. His other lung, his liver and his kidneys had deteriorated, and in early June he had brain surgery. . . .

An obituary for Liberace reminded readers that a 27-year-old chauffeur had filed a $113 million palimony suit, charging that Liberace had promised to support him in exchange for sexual favors. The obituary added that the suit was settled out of court for $95,000, with Liberace insisting that the chauffeur was just a vengeful ex-employee. Similarly, the obituaries for boxer Joe Louis reported that he won the heavyweight crown and held it for 12 years, defending his title a record 25 times. The obituaries also reported that Louis had married three times, used cocaine, spent some time in a Denver mental hospital and spent the last year of his life working in a Las Vegas hotel, shaking hands and posing for pictures with gamblers, "a sad figure in a crumpled suit and golf cap."

In some cases, it may be impossible to avoid the unpleasant, controversial and negative. For example, some Americans remember Gen. Curtis LeMay as an ultraconservative and possibly a mad bomber. The obituaries for LeMay explained that he helped the United States win World War II and, in 1964, retired as Air Force chief of staff. Then, during the war against North Vietnam, LeMay suggested that the United States might "bomb 'em back to the Stone Age." LeMay also suggested that, as a final option, the United States might use nuclear weapons in Vietnam.

Controversy was a part of Billy Martin's life: so much a part of his life that no obituary could ignore it. Martin, a former manager of the New York Yankees, died at the age of 61 when a pickup truck skidded off a road and fell into a gully. Obituaries reported that Martin had been known for his fiery personality and was nicknamed "Battling Billy." Martin himself had admitted: "You know me. I could get in trouble in church." An obituary added that, as a player and manager, "Martin seemed to have as many fights as Muhammad Ali."

Owner George Steinbrenner fired Martin five times as manager of the Yankees. Yet, even after his fifth firing, Martin had insisted, sadly:

> I'm still the best manager in baseball. I'm a proud Yankee. I'm a Yankee, and I'll leave like a Yankee. I'll try to handle it as best I can, but how many times can a man have his heart broken? I'm not a good loser. I never have been.

Newspapers that publish negative information in obituaries do not have to fear lawsuits. A person who has died cannot sue the newspapers for libel; nor, in most cases, can the person's relatives. Thus, the decision to publish or to suppress critical information is influenced by the information's newsworthiness, good taste or impact on the community, not by any legal considerations.

Newspapers are more likely to publish negative information about public figures than about private citizens. Also, large dailies are more likely than smaller daily and weekly newspapers to mention a person's indiscretions. Smaller newspapers tend to be more protective of their communities and of the people living in them. Journalists in smaller cities may know the people who died and fear that the critical information would anger the people's friends and relatives and be disturbing for the entire community.

ADDITIONAL GUIDELINES AND PROBLEMS

Obituary writers must be especially careful and accurate, because obituaries are usually the last stories written about a person. If a reporter makes an error, it is likely to infuriate the person's friends and relatives. The error may also be difficult to correct.

An Ombudsman's Report

CASE STUDY NO. 5

By **Henry McNulty**
Reader Representative
The Hartford (Conn.) Courant

Father James Curry had been pastor of a church on the Connecticut coastline. Several years ago, he had been accused by a parishioner, in a civil suit, of sexual assault of an 11-year-old girl. The matter, which had been reported in my newspaper, was settled out of court.

Then Father Curry died, and we published his obituary. In the obit, the newspaper reported that he had founded a parish, told something of his background, and mentioned the civil suit.

I have never received such abuse from readers as I did on the days following our publication of the priest's obit. In my years as the newspaper's ombudsman I have spoken with literally tens of thousands of readers, some of them quite upset. But I have never heard such cursing, screaming and crying as I did after Father Curry's obit was printed.

The readers' complaints are familiar to anyone who has worked in the press. The vast majority of those who called and wrote said an obituary is no place to discuss a person's past misfortunes—especially when the person is a priest, a man of God, someone whose life in other ways apparently was a model of piety and goodness.

Of all the dilemmas facing reporters and editors, I can think of few more difficult than the matter of how to write a sinner's obituary. What is to be done? I have never spoken to an editor or a reporter who enjoyed staining a person's reputation for all time. Yet that is what the callers accused us of doing.

You can't always rely on calls made and letters written by angry readers. Do they really represent the views of most readers, or are they a biased minority? On this issue, we have some answers.

Once or twice a year, my newspaper runs a ''you-be-the-editor'' poll, inviting readers to send in their solutions to some knotty journalism problems. At the same time, our editors are asked, anonymously, how they would solve the same problems.

After the priest died, we asked our readers and editors how they would have handled his obit. Would they have mentioned the lawsuit and its outcome, or would they gloss over it? (In our example, we changed the name and altered the facts in minor ways to avoid identifying the priest all over again.)

Hundreds of people responded. The results were astonishing.

About 80 percent of readers told us they would *not* mention the lawsuit involving the charge of child molestation. About 80 percent of the editors, on the other hand, said they would have no trouble including the lawsuit in the obit.

Of the dozens of questions posed in these columns over the years, there has never been such a split of opinion. Why is this so? Should anything be done about it? If so, what?

Here are some of my answers.

Journalists and readers have quite different ideas about what an obituary really is. Editors, I've found, are quite willing to give lip service to the idea that obits are important, and to agree with you if you say they ought to be handled with care and taste.

But when it comes down to it, most journalists really consider obits to be just another news story. As for what makes better reading or more worthwhile journalism, a good scandal or a political story will beat an obit every time. We tip our hats to obits, but when push comes to shove we are willing to push and shove obituaries into a dark corner.

Readers take nearly the opposite point of view.

To them, obits are often the summation of a life's worth. They are precious bits of family history to be saved in heirloom Bibles and passed down to the next generation. They are public statements about the worth of a human life. Among the sentiments I hear countless times are the maxims: "Let the dead rest in peace" and "If you can't say anything good about someone, don't say anything at all."

Those, of course, fly in the face of what reporters and editors believe.

Journalists have frequently told me that obits, like other news stories, must tell the truth. To conveniently forget the rough spots in someone's life, they say, is journalistic prostitution, practically an affront against the First Amendment. I am frequently told that we have a "responsibility" to bring up such matters as past lawsuits when writing a person's obit.

I have been asked whether readers would be willing to see an obit for Al Capone that didn't mention his criminal activity. And should we be nice in writing Hitler's obit?

Another factor is the way most obituaries come to be written. Let's say John Doe, a fairly prominent businessman, dies one afternoon and the newspaper gets wind of it. What happens? Most likely, an editor assigns a new or young reporter to go to the files, dig out some facts on the deceased, and put together something from the clips and with information supplied by the funeral home.

More often than not, newspaper files hold a motley collection of outdated stories, heavily weighted toward any scandal, trouble, controversy or mishap in the person's life.

So it was with our file on Father Curry. According to the clips, he founded a parish and was accused of molesting a child. That was it; nothing more.

So in most cases, the reporter splices together an obit based on what can be found at the time of death. Add a file photo and the deed is done. Is it any wonder that obituaries are frequently incomplete, or are dangerously tilted toward the unpleasant part of a person's life?

How can this situation be improved? Here are my suggestions.

First, recognize their importance. This probably means devoting more news space to obits, and making an equivalent commitment of personnel. Obituaries are well read; they are one of the few parts of the daily paper that are a "must" for a large percentage of readers.

(continued on next page)

Second, assign prepared obits months or even years before they are likely to be used. This will allow reporters to do more than simply rely on whatever clips happen to be in the files. If possible, see that seasoned reporters write the advance obits.

Third, the tough part. How do you write a sinner's obituary?

Since the death of Father Curry, I have changed my mind on this question. At first, my response was just what I'd said for years: Too bad, facts are facts, we must be honest, we can't whitewash, the truth sometimes hurts. I now think these knee-jerk answers—the ones traditionally given by reporters and editors—are too simplistic.

For one thing, they arrogantly and perhaps wrongly assume that we newspaper people are able to determine the truth about someone's life, and to render it fairly. It's too convenient to think that a person's file equals his or her life, and that whatever we happen to have reported during life is worth repeating at death.

For another, these stock answers have little compassion, little human understanding, little charity and little discretion. In other words, they fail to approach a death the same way our readers do. This is yet another way we are out of touch with the people we're supposedly trying to reach.

Al Capone? Hitler? Of course we will tell all about their crimes in their obits. We'd be fools not to.

But that's not the issue here; that's a red herring pulled across the trail by defensive reporters and editors. In almost every case we're not talking about out-and-out villains.

We're talking about sinners: ordinary people who, at one time or another, may have been involved with some sort of misstep, some controversy, a brush with the law, an accusation settled privately, a rumor, and so forth.

Naturally, each case must be examined and decided individually. But when we make the examination, we need to keep in mind what 80 percent of readers think is proper: forgive and forget, let bygones be bygones, and bury the dead without a final, permanent jab delivered in the daily newspaper.

Even the information provided by funeral directors should be checked for errors. Friends and relatives are likely to be upset at the time they make the arrangements for a funeral and may be mistaken about some of the information they give to funeral directors. The friends and relatives may not know or remember some facts and may guess at others. The funeral directors may make some mistakes while recording the information and may misspell some names, especially the names of unfamiliar individuals and cities.

Other problems encountered by obituary writers are unique. Many people are reluctant to reveal their relatives' ages, particularly if they falsified them or kept them a secret during their lifetimes. Obituary writers will report that someone died in a hospital, but many do not identify the hospital. Editors explain that deaths are rarely a hospital's fault, and that if obituaries repeatedly mentioned a specific hospital, they might unfairly harm its reputation. Because the statement might offend florists who advertise in their newspapers, many editors and publishers also hesitate to report that, "The family requests no flowers." However, some permit the publication of more positive statements, such as, "The family requests that gifts be sent to the Heart Fund."

Readers often call newspapers and ask reporters to write obituaries for other people, and the callers usually provide all the necessary information. The callers may explain that they have not yet made any arrangements with a funeral home, and some have no intention of ever dealing with a funeral home, particularly if the body is to be cremated, disposed of by a private burial society or used for scientific or medical purposes. Other callers explain that the person they are describing died in another city but formerly lived in the local area, had many friends there or is related to a prominent person there.

People described in the obituaries occasionally call newspapers the next day, insisting that they are not dead. Because it is not uncommon for pranksters to call newspapers and give them obituaries for living people, editors often require their reporters to call a second source and confirm every obituary before it is published.

Author Mark Twain experienced the problem while traveling in Europe. After learning that newspapers in the United States had reported that he was dead, Twain wrote a cable insisting that, "Reports of my death have been greatly exaggerated."

A European experienced the same problem and, because of it, is remembered as a great benefactor of mankind. Alfred Nobel was born in Stockholm in 1833 and became a chemist and engineer. Nobel invented dynamite and other explosives, became an armaments manufacturer and accumulated an immense fortune. In 1888, Nobel's brother died, and a newspaper in Paris published Alfred's obituary by mistake. The obituary called Alfred "a merchant of death." Nobel was so shocked by the obituary's description of him that, when he died in 1896, he left the bulk of his estate in trust to establish the Nobel Prizes for peace, literature, physics, chemistry and physiology or medicine. Thus, Nobel used his wealth to honor people who have done the most to enhance people's lives "rather than simply kill them off, as his products had done."

Finally, here are a few other guidelines to consider while writing obituaries:

- A man is said to be survived by his wife, not his widow. Similarly, a woman is survived by her husband, not by her widower.
- A Catholic funeral Mass is celebrated, not said, and the word "Mass" is capitalized.
- Many editors object to reporting that a death was "sudden," explaining that most deaths are sudden.
- Because burglars sometimes break into surviving relatives' homes while they are attending a funeral, some newspapers no longer print survivors' addresses in obituaries.
- Medical experts often conduct autopsies to determine the cause of death. When that happens, simply report that, "An autopsy will be conducted." If you report that, "An autopsy will be conducted to determine the cause of death," you will be stating the obvious—and thus wasting your readers' time and newspaper's space.
- Finally, avoid suggesting that one relationship is inferior to another. Unless the family requests that you do so, do not create separate lists of natural children and adopted children, and of brothers and half-brothers, for example.

JIM NICHOLSON: NO. 1 IN OBITUARIES

In 1983, Jim Nicholson started a unique obituary page for the Philadelphia Daily News. Earlier, Nicholson had worked as an investigative reporter and had been nominated for a Pulitzer Prize. Now, while working for the Daily News, Nicholson has become famous and has repeatedly been honored as the nation's best obituary writer.

While most newspapers publish long obituaries only for celebrities, Nicholson writes "richly detailed, colorful obituaries of ordinary Philadelphians." Nicholson writes about bus drivers, school crossing guards, sanitation workers and retirees. He calls these people the real heroes in our society and explains that:

> Most people never make the paper because they never murdered anybody, dealt in narcotics, got locked up or elected to public office. But what I write about are the most important people in the world—[those] who make your water run, your street cars and buses operate, deliver the vegetables. Who would you miss more when he goes on vacation, the secretary of state or your garbage man?

A colleague at the Philadelphia Daily News adds:

> On Jim's obit page, you read about laborers, plumbers, pastors, housewives, you read about their pride and their small kindnesses. You read about the security guard who died with no survivors and few possessions who was a World War II hero. You read about the elderly storekeeper who gave away as much as she sold, and listened to her customers' troubles.

Nicholson calls his job "the most rewarding I've ever had." He explains that, as an obituary writer, he has "touched more lives positively than I have with anything else I've done." He adds:

> The obit page can provide the purest and most complete form of public service in the newspaper—aside from the weather and box scores. . . . It is the last—and sometimes only—time we can say someone lived a life and their being here mattered. . . .
>
> Any one of my obits will outlive any investigative thing I've ever done. People save these forever. Some people will Xerox 200 to 300 copies and take them to the funerals. They'll put them next to the register and people will sign in and take a copy. People laminate my obits and give them to friends.

Some of Nicholson's guidelines for writing obituaries, and two examples of his work, appear on the following pages.

Tips From A Pro

NICHOLSON'S GUIDELINES FOR WRITING OBITUARIES

By **Jim Nicholson**

Jim Nicholson, the famed obituary writer for the Philadelphia Daily News, prepared the following guidelines to help journalists write better obituaries.

I. WHAT DOES A GOOD OBITUARY CONTAIN?

    A. **Basic facts:** Name, age, occupation, area of residence, organizational memberships, awards, survivors, services, memorials.

B. **Character portrait:** Draw from quotes from friends and family. The reader should be able to see the outlines of a personality in the subject and perhaps relate the subject to someone the reader knows or the reader himself or herself. The ultimate acclaim may be when a reader thinks, "I wish I had known this person."

C. **Quotes:** Quote people the way they talk—fragmented sentences, dangling prepositions. Anyone who has read grand jury or court testimony or tape transcripts knows this is how most of us talk.

D. **Warts and wrinkles:** Cleaning up someone's act after they have died really does not serve the cause of the deceased or loved ones. A sanitized portrait is indistinguishable from any other. It is the irregularities of personality and human shadings of temperament which give us all identity. A person described as being a strict parent, impatient with unprofessional conduct, and openly hostile toward insurance salesmen becomes real to the reader. The subject is no longer an oil portrait of George Washington hanging on the wall. The subject is in a Polaroid snapshot, caught in the act of living.

E. **Historical notes:** Sometimes, in a few sentences or paragraphs, you can put the subject in his youth or childhood, and thus place the reader in another era of the city's or town's history. For example: "Bob Smith was raised in the east end of town in the early 1920s, when Zeke Clayton's blacksmith barn was still standing only a few hundred yards from the Smith family's clapboard house. Years later, Bob would tell his grandchildren how he would wake up most mornings to the hard ping of a hammer bouncing against an anvil."

II. THE INTERVIEW

A. The funeral director, who has had time to deal with the family and evaluate the members, can usually point the reporter to the most articulate or together family member or friend. He will gladly furnish the home phone number.

B. Sometimes it is best to open the interview with known facts that the interviewee can recall and re-cite easily. Some facts, such as services, etc., may already be known to the reporter, but the object is to get the individual talking. The subject may be delved into through the professional side. For example: "Why did your father choose to become a tree surgeon?" The response may be: "Well, after his father was gunned down by the Capone mob for holding back numbers receipts, my dad had to quit school in the ninth grade and support the family."

C. Remember, you are not writing about death, you are writing about life. The interview can go as any feature-style interview would progress. The fact that the subject is dead is almost incidental, al-though how some people face death can be an important part of an obituary because it may re-veal how they handled the previous 70 or 80 years of their life.

III. WHAT TO LOOK FOR AND REPORT IN AN OBITUARY

One writer can sometimes step out of the pack and stand alone by including what I call important insignificant details. Those details include:

1. Name
2. Nickname (why that nickname?)
3. Height and weight
4. Build
5. Hair (color and style)
6. Dress
7. Occupation (how long, what before?)
8. Education (where?)
9. Residence (where, how long?)
10. Previous residence
11. Raised where
12. Smokes (what brand?)
13. Drinks (what kind?)
14. Marital status
15. Age
16. Family
17. Military background
18. Tone of voice

(continued on next page)

19. Gestures
20. Temperament
21. Religious
22. Hobbies/outside interests
23. Clubs/organizations
24. Voice cadence
25. Values
26. Introvert/extrovert
27. Eye contact
28. Smile
29. Sudden change (voice, smile, eye contact)
30. Excess jewelry
31. No jewelry (watch, ring, etc.)
32. Makeup (heavy, light, none)
33. Hat
34. Speech connectors ("and, uh. . ." "ya' know. . ." "like, a. . ." "Well uh. . .")
35. Scene indicators ("orange sofa with thread-bare cushions")
36. Weather/lighting

IV. EXAMPLES OF NICHOLSON'S WORK

Jack Weinstein, M.D., a gruff and loving doc

Jack Lewis Weinstein, a doctor who cared enough to stay behind when affluence fled Strawberry Mansion, died Monday. He was 83 and lived in Bala Cynwyd.

He was a doctor for 56 years, starting out in a time when his all-white, mostly Jewish neighborhood was the place to be for a young, ambitious Jewish doctor. Neighborhoods changed and the money left. A lot of merchants and professionals followed the money.

Jack Weinstein followed the Hippocratic Oath, the part that says, "With purity and with holiness I will pass my life and practice my art."

He was the pure warrior who could fight on any ground, disdainful of any obstacles, supremely confident of his own skills—the pure practitioner who did not quibble over whether the sickness and suffering were couched in genteel surroundings or whether his patients had taken a shower that morning.

His office was at 33rd and York streets, where the tire meets the mud.

His daughter, Susan Marks, said: "He loved life and he loved people and he liked to have fun. His office was a three-ring circus. His vocabulary was every other word a four-letter word.

"My father was a diamond in the rough. He was well educated, but he was a man of the people," Marks said. "He was not a world-famous man, but the people who knew him appreciated him. A flock of people would be there by the time he got to the office at 8:30 a.m. He never worked by appointment. He wasn't that kind of guy. You sat and you waited for him."

They didn't mind waiting. Jack Weinstein was the kind of doctor some people wait a lifetime just to find. He would burst into an examining room, all 5-foot-5, wired with energy and pumping vinegar. "What the hell is the matter with you?" he'd bellow.

"He was an aggressive personality, assertive," his daughter said. "When he walked into a room, you knew he was there. You'd smile and feel better because he was there. He had a way of curing people."

People did feel better in Jack Weinstein's sure hands. Sick people who were weak, worried and confused knew that this man was in charge and moving out. If he couldn't get a person well, he knew who could. He was highly regarded in the profession as an expert diagnostician. He also served on the staffs at Jefferson Park Hospital, Hahnemann University Hospital and Roxborough Memorial Hospital.

He didn't forget his patients from the early days. They were up in years, so he'd visit them in Olney, the Northeast or the suburbs. He did this into his late 70s, even when he suspected he was experiencing the onset of Alzheimer's disease. "His car knew the way," Marks said, evoking the image of the country doc, nodding off in the carriage as the horse went on to the next stop by memory.

"Jack Weinstein to me was just an old-fashioned doctor everyone grew up with 30, 40, 50 years ago. The family doctor who really cared about his patients. If you had a problem and he came to see you, he remembered what bothered you in the past," said Larry Cooper, who married into the extended family.

The son of immigrants who ran a grocery at Fifth and Porter streets, Jack was the youngest of eight children and the only son. In a Jewish home, that virtually anointed him to the throne from birth. It was easy for a child to gain confidence and a sense of self when parents and seven older sisters practically heralded his arrival at the breakfast table each morning.

"He was a god to them [parents]," Marks said. "They were proud of all their children, but he was the king." She said his success and occupation were pre-ordained. As the only boy in the Jewish family, he would become a professional. Turning out to be quite smart, he would become a doctor. He graduated from South Philadelphia High School in 1924 and was a 1928 graduate of the University of Pennsylvania. He graduated from Hahnemann Medical College in 1932.

He chose Strawberry Mansion to open his practice, Marks said, because "he wasn't dumb" and knew he could make a good living there. But money didn't matter that much to Jack. He didn't have any hobbies. He tried golf when he was younger, but it didn't take. When he got bored around the house, he drove to the hospital. He never failed to find something worthwhile to do with his time at the hospital because that's where sick people were who needed help and that's what he did best.

Mealtimes at the Weinsteins' were not sedate affairs. "My father had a loud strong voice," Marks said. "Dinners at our house, if you wanted to be heard, you had to speak louder than the next person. It was animated and a lot of yelling."

Jack Weinstein was all bark. He could lose his temper in a flash and forget about it before the last word got out. He didn't carry grudges.

Four years ago, just before he retired, the neighborhood threw him a big luncheon in his office. Cold cuts, home cooking. Neighborhood children handed him cards with crayoned sentiments.

Some had a four-letter word that fit Jack Weinstein.

Love.

In addition to his daughter, he is survived by his wife of 55 years, the former Jean S. Cottler; a son, Dr. Saul F. Weinstein; a sister, Minnie Weinstein; and six grandchildren.

Services will be held at 2 p.m. today at Joseph Levine & Son, 7112 N. Broad St. Burial will be in Haym Salomon Memorial Park, Frazer, Chester County.

Chef Charles A. Brown, walked tall through life

Charles A. Brown Sr., a chef and restaurateur who was a hard worker and an easy touch, died Saturday. He was 79 and lived in West Philadelphia.

Charlie Brown had moved in a lot of interesting circles in his 79 years. In Philadelphia restaurant circles he
(continued on next page)

was known as a man who could come in and put a place back on its feet. He knew how to handle people, could organize, was a perfectionist around pots and pans, and, as his son Bob Brown said, "He could cook in any language."

Over the years he variously chefed, helped manage or had an interest in the Pub Tiki at 18th and Walnut streets, a couple of Pub Tikis on Chestnut Street and one at the Airport Circle in Pennsauken. He also chefed and helped run the Franklin Inn Club on South Camac Street.

Brown finally retired in 1989 and spent more time than he ever did in life sitting in a chair, taking naps and watching soap operas on television. But no soap on TV could shade the life Charles Brown had lived.

He also moved in music and sports circles from the 1930s to the 1950s. In those days they were the two main avenues of upward movement for blacks, and it wasn't that big of a world. So a man like Charlie could get a reputation quick and meet most of the heavies in those industries.

In the late 1930s, on an introduction from Louis Armstrong, Charlie met a rising middleweight boxer who would become an icon to later generations—Sugar Ray Robinson. The Sugar Man traveled with an entourage that at times numbered 50 and Charlie was his personal "dietitian." He also was dietitian for Henry Armstrong, world lightweight champion in 1938.

In those days, when Charlie was working long hours on the road, Bob Brown, whose godfather was Robinson, said he anxiously watched the Gillette Friday Night Fights on TV because he would be sure of catching a glimpse of Dad and maybe Mom too, sitting at ringside. In the 1950s, when the years had claimed Robinson's ring magic, Sugar Ray tried to earn enough money to maintain his lifestyle with a nightclub act. Before leaving for Paris one year, he asked Charlie to go along, but Charlie's wife, the former Catherine Amanda Robbins, said no.

Away from the kitchen, Charlie dressed to the nines. The family used to say he looked like a stockbroker. In his closet were dozens of pairs of shoes, the $100 to $175 kind. Bob once asked why his father bought more shoes than any one man needed.

"When I walked to Philadelphia I didn't have any shoes," he said.

Only a few people close to Charlie knew about that great walk from Miami to Philadelphia more than 60 years ago. It took five months. And only Charlie would ever know what it was like in that personal crucible on the road.

The Miami of 1927 was noted not for neon and nightlife but for unrestrained redneck bigotry. Charlie was working in his Aunt Eva Davis' diner on Third Street in a section now called Liberty City. One night, a few blocks from the diner, a black man stared too long at a white woman who had looked at him. He did not cast his eyes downward—as was demanded by the white supremacist culture. The black man was lynched and his body dragged through parts of town.

A few hours later, Charlie's mother, Mary, told the 15-year-old boy to leave Miami and go north, to Philadelphia, to where his Aunt Eva had a house. She didn't want her youngest son growing up in a town like that. She gave him about three dollars, and that same night he started walking north.

"He hoboed and lived in hobo camps and took jobs along the way," said his son, "whatever he could to make an honest living until he got to Philadelphia. When he came to her [Aunt Eva's] door five months later, he was so dirty she didn't recognize him."

He went right to work at various jobs and never continued school past the eighth grade. He was a young man who would rivet total attention to a book or a person or anything that could teach him.

He learned baking from a German while going to baking school in the Navy during World War II. Charlie's cakes were beyond description, said his son, and when Charlie tasted any cake that didn't come up to par, he'd deride it as "nothing but sweet bread."

He learned to cook Chinese from a man named Choy Lee. For a time Charlie and Bob were cooking in a Chinese restaurant. Bob still laughs when he thinks of how the customers raved about the food, unaware that "black people were the cooks." He said his father's shrimp-fried rice was without equal.

He was a man who never raised his hand or voice to his children. But a disapproving glance could cut like a laser. They held him in awe. He and his wife of 57 years plied their children with religion, the arts and music, exposing them to what life can offer. But he let them know they would have to work for what was out there.

Charlie himself came from humble, but not dirt-poor surroundings. His parents, Mary and John Brown, started as sharecroppers in the Buck Swamp area of Brunswick, Ga. Charlie was one of 12 sons. His tallest brother was Big Jake at 7-foot-3, Big Frank was 6-foot-10, and down the line to the runt of the litter, Charlie, who was six-one. The Browns brought in so much to the landowner that he eventually gave them their own land, and 300 acres are still in the family.

In his time Charlie moved in an out of the fast lane and drank, worked, laughed and played with the people who got their pictures in the newspaper. But the glitter never covered the Georgia clay. He lived fast without getting slick and endured early hardship without getting hard.

"He was the type of guy if you saw him on the street and he had five dollars in his pocket and you asked him for four, he would give you the five, sometimes to the point of being ridiculous," Bob said.

"My father was a Mason," said his son. "He was a 'Travelin' Man.' You walk along life's road, you help every other man along the way, and ask nothing in return. He liked everybody on the street. He didn't find fault. He thought there was good in everybody."

If Bob or anyone else lost their cool, Charlie would squelch it with a raised hand and say, "Back off, back off, I don't need no hard guys in here." His son said Charlie believed "you caught more flies with honey than vinegar." He liked to joke and tease, but not to the point of hurting anyone's feelings.

Charlie's favorite line when life occasionally collapsed on his head or a loved one's was: "Now let's turn the page and go on to the next chapter."

Bob Brown believes that is what his father has done.

In addition to his wife and his son, he is survived by two daughters, Rosemary Cameron and Valerie McCall; a sister, Eva Davis; three brothers, Jake, Elmo and Frank; and six grandchildren.

Services will be at 11 a.m. tomorrow at the Johnson Funeral Home, 4617 Woodland Ave., where friends may call two hours before the service. Burial will be in Eden Cemetery, Springfield Road, Collingdale, Delaware County.

Contributions may be made to the Fox Chase Cancer Center, 7701 Burholme Ave., Philadelphia, Pa. 19111.

SUGGESTED READINGS

Caughey, Bernard. "The Popularity of Obituaries." *Editor & Publisher*, Apr. 23, 1988, pp. 46 and 146–47.

Duffy, Glen. "Death Takes a Job: How Reporter Jim Nicholson Learned to Relax and Love Writing Obits." *Philadelphia*, Dec. 1988, pp. 131–32.

Lippman, Thomas W., ed., *The Washington Post Deskbook on Style*. 2nd ed. New York: McGraw-Hill, 1989. (See Chapter 4: "The Craft of the Obituary.")

Nicholson, Jim. "Obituary Writing" in *Best Newspaper Writing 1987*, ed. by Don Fry. St. Petersburg, FL: Poynter Institute for Media Studies, pp. 227–63.

Rambo, C. David. "Obits Provide Lifelong Reading Appeal: Subtle Changes Are Afoot, Although Getting It Right Remains Rule No. 1." *Presstime*, June 1990, pp. 46–48.

Storm, Bill. "A Different Type of Obit Page: Jack Nicholson of the Philadelphia Daily News Writes Obituaries Not Only about the Upper Class, but Also about the 'Common' Man and Woman." *Editor & Publisher*, June 6, 1987, pp. 100 and 149.

QUOTES

Newspapers are the schoolmasters of the common people. That endless book, the newspaper, is our national glory.

(Henry Ward Beecher)

Freedom of the press is the staff of life for any vital democracy.

(Wendell Willkie)

Freedom is always the exception, never the rule. Of all human beings, who have lived on this earth, only a few have lived in freedom. For the anonymous millions living private lives in this country today, the First Amendment, above all else, is the constitutional expression in their behalf of the greatest of all human values: Freedom of the mind.

(Philip Kerby, editorial writer, Los Angeles Times*)*

Exercise 1

OBITUARIES

DISCUSSION QUESTIONS

1. If you became the editor of your local daily and had to set its policies for obituaries, would you:

   A. Report the cause of everyone's death?
   B. Report that a family does not want flowers?
   C. Report that the deceased was survived by his or her *second* spouse?
   D. List an adult's roommate among his or her survivors?
   E. Report that the deceased never married?
   F. Report every suicide in your community? If so, how would you report the suicides: (1) in separate news stories or (2) in obituaries?

2. When it comes to including controversial information in an obituary, do you agree with Jim Nicholson, the obituary writer for the Philadelphia Daily News, or Henry McNulty, the reader representative for The Hartford Courant?

   A. If you were assigned to write an obituary for a local teacher, would you report everything, including all the teacher's "warts and wrinkles"?
   B. If you were assigned to write the obituary for Father James Curry, would you mention the fact that he had once been accused of assaulting an 11-year-old girl? (See Case Study No. 5: An Ombudsman's Report.)

Exercise 2

WRITING OBITUARIES

WRITING CHALLENGING OBITUARIES

INSTRUCTIONS: Your teacher may ask you to write one or more of the following obituaries. As you work on the obituaries, you will find that each one presents several unusual problems.

Obituary 1: Helen Veit

FULL NAME:	Reverend Helen Lynn Veit
ADDRESS:	184 Nelson Avenue
AGE:	55
TIME OF DEATH:	Yesterday evening
PLACE OF DEATH:	Home
CAUSE OF DEATH:	Suicide by asphyxiation. According to an official coroner's report, she died of carbon monoxide poisoning while seated in her car, which was running in a closed and locked garage. Friends said she suffered from bouts of depression and was receiving medical help and counseling and medication for it.
TIME OF FUNERAL:	Services will be held at 8 p.m. Friday. Visitation will begin an hour before the services and will also be held at the church.
PLACE OF FUNERAL:	First Covenant Church
PLACE OF BURIAL:	Park Memorial Cemetery at 10 a.m. Saturday
OFFICIATING CLERGY:	Samuel R. Graumann
PLACE OF BIRTH:	Family farmhouse in Minnesota
PREVIOUS RESIDENCES:	Reverend Veit grew up on a farm near St. Cloud, Minnesota. She served in churches in Moline, Illinois, Iowa City, Iowa, Chicago, Illinois, and then here (in your city).
EDUCATION:	She graduated from the University of Wisconsin—Eau Claire and also graduated from the Moody Bible Institute in Chicago, being the first woman ever to do so.
OCCUPATION:	She became minister of visitation at First Covenant Church here 11 years ago and has held the position here ever since then.
MEMBERSHIPS:	A member of the American Association of University Women, the Women's National Democratic Club, the ACLU and Overeaters Anonymous
SURVIVORS:	No known survivors. Reverend Veit never married and had no children. Her only sibling, a brother, Ralph Veit, was an officer in the Army and was killed during the war in Vietnam.

Her parents, Abby and Gerhardt Veit, preceded her in death.

COMMENTS: "Everyone who knew her loved her," said Wendy Tai, a member of the church. "If anyone was sick, she'd be there to take you to the hospital, talk to you, help care for your family, and then helped you get back on your feet and all." Diana Nyez, another member of the church said, "Uh, you've never met anyone so kind. You didn't have to ask. She'd just appear with her arms full of food. If you were sick—or needed help for any reason—she'd be there. She'd even do your shopping or cleaning—anything you needed, just anything."

Obituary 2: Tony Guarino

FULL NAME: Tony Allen Guarino

ADDRESS: 6139 Eastland Drive

AGE: 53

TIME OF DEATH: Late yesterday afternoon

PLACE OF DEATH: The emergency room of Memorial Hospital

CAUSE OF DEATH: He collapsed at home after jogging. An autopsy showed that his death was caused by arteriosclerosis. His son, Chuck, said he jogged at least 3 miles every day after school but yesterday wasn't feeling well and had to stop and walk home, then collapsed and was found by a friend there, Jo-Anne Shoemucker.

TIME OF FUNERAL: 4 p.m. tomorrow afternoon

PLACE OF FUNERAL: Pieper Brothers Funeral Home

PLACE OF BURIAL: Park Memorial Cemetery immediately following the services. Burial will be with full military honors.

OFFICIATING CLERGY: Reverend Stuart Adler

PLACE OF BIRTH: Los Angeles, California.

PREVIOUS RESIDENCES: The deceased was born in Los Angeles, California, then brought here and raised by an aunt after his parents died in an automobile accident when he was an infant. He lived here his entire life, except for 3 years he served in the U.S. Army after graduating from Colonial High School. He then attended college here (at your school) on the GI Bill.

OCCUPATION: A biology teacher at Colonial High School for 26 years. He taught sophomore biology and field biology in the school's international baccalaureate program, an advanced placement program for 11th and 12th graders. He coached varsity boys' baseball, with a win/loss record over the years of 186–104, the best record compiled by any of the present coaches at the school, but he never won a state championship. He received an M.A. in Educational Administration and Supervision and wanted to become a high school principal, applied numerous times, but was never selected for any of the jobs that became available.

OTHER: He served in the Army Reserves, rising to the rank of Lieutenant Colonel before finally retiring from it. He was a former leader of Boy Scout Troop 122. During the summers, when he was not employed as a teacher, and also some weekends and holidays, he worked as a driver for Safe-T-Cab Company to supplement his income as a teacher.

SURVIVORS: His wife, Anne, from whom he was separated. Two adopted sons, Charles of Oakland, California and Tony Junior of St. Louis, Missouri. A daughter, Linda Guarino in the St. Stephens Home for the Mentally Retarded, 8420 Hamilton Road. The aunt who raised him, Belva Guarino of 84 Lakeland Avenue.

COMMENTS: "He was extremely popular among students and faculty at Colonial," said Jeanette Weinstein, a teacher who shared a classroom with Guarino for years. "His classes were always full. Students liked him. He was always a kidder and a joker. But if you really got to know him, he took his job very, very seriously, and he was terribly disappointed that he wasn't made at least an assistant principal. He never understood why."

Instead of flowers, the family asks that remembrances be contributed to the Boy Scouts of America.

Obituary 3: Wesley Saleeby

FULL NAME: Wesley Saleeby

ADDRESS: 1916 Elizabeth Lane

AGE: 58

TIME OF DEATH: Last evening

PLACE OF DEATH: Memorial Hospital

CAUSE OF DEATH: Cirrhosis of the liver

TIME OF FUNERAL: 2 p.m. Sunday

PLACE OF FUNERAL: Gramkow Funeral Home Chapel with visitation from 7 to 9 pm Friday and 3–5 pm Saturday

PLACE OF BURIAL: Oaklawn Cemetery immediately after the funeral services.

OFFICIATING CLERGY: Reverend Stuart Adler

PLACE OF BIRTH: Here

PREVIOUS RESIDENCES: None. He was a lifelong resident of the city. Also, he and his wife have lived in their home at 1916 Elizabeth Lane for 36 years

OCCUPATION: Retired police chief. He served in the city's police department 23 years before the City Council promoted him to the rank of chief at the age of 47. He served as chief for 4 years, then retired.

EDUCATION: Graduated from Grant Elementary School and Central High School. Attended numerous law enforcement workshops but never attended or graduated from college.

MEMBERSHIPS: The Kiwanis Club. Eastside Bowling League. Masonic Lodge 240. Associated Masons. Post 82 of the American Legion. Volunteer driver for Meals on Wheels.

SURVIVORS: Wife, Olivida Gray Saleeby. Son, Edward Saleeby of Washington, D.C. Sisters: Kathy Saleeby Vermell of 1010 Vermont Avenue and Julie Anne Saleeby Stevens of 624 N. 3rd Street. Two brothers, John of 626 N. Third Street and Henry of 84 Sunnyvale Road.

COMMENTS: "He loved his work," his wife said. "He really loved it. He wanted to help people, and, oh, it was so exciting for him. He really enjoyed helping people in trouble, and then he was made chief. I was so proud of him."

LIBRARY FILE: News stories published years earlier and stored in your newspaper's library reported that he was fired from his position as the city's chief of police after members of the City Council concluded that his apparently heavy drinking, including at least two instances in which he was reported to have appeared in public in a drunken state, made his removal from office an immediate necessity, although he always vigorously denied all the allegations against him.

Obituary 4: Samuel Pinckney

FULL NAME: Samuel Pinckney

ADDRESS: 976 Grand Avenue

AGE: 82

TIME OF DEATH: Sometime early this morning. His corpse was found by a nurse at 6 am this morning.

PLACE OF DEATH: Regional Medical Center

CAUSE OF DEATH: Lung cancer (friends say he was a heavy smoker, smoking an average of two or three packs of Camel cigarettes a day all his adult life). He entered the Regional Medical Center for treatment of terminal cancer a month ago and, last week, he and his family asked doctors to stop giving him medicine (except for painkillers) and to let him die so his suffering would end.

TIME OF FUNERAL: 11 a.m. Saturday at the First United Methodist Church

PLACE OF FUNERAL: The First United Methodist Church

PLACE OF BURIAL: No burial. The body will be cremated.

OFFICIATING CLERGY: Reverend Audrey Wagnor-VanPelt

PLACE OF BIRTH: Cleveland, Ohio

PREVIOUS
RESIDENCES: He moved here with his family at the age of five and always lived here thereafter.

EDUCATION: Attended Colonial High School but dropped out after the 10th grade and never graduated.

OCCUPATION: Owner and retired president of Sam's, a chain of 17 supermarkets in the area. He and a friend opened a small corner grocery store as teenagers, when both were 19, and, 2 years later, Pinckney won his partner's 50% share of the store in a poker game. He subsequently transformed that one small store into the largest independent chain in the area. In 1956, he also opened a second business, Sam's Restaurant, but it went bankrupt and was closed in 1961.

OFFICES HELD: President of the local school board from 1958 to 1964. Past president of the County Tax Levy Board. Past vice president of the Chamber of Commerce. Former trustee of the Public Library.

MEMBERSHIPS: A president of Junior Achievement for five years. Past president of the city's Council of Civic Clubs. A member and past president of the Downtown Rotary Club.

SURVIVORS: His third wife, Terese. A son, William of Columbia, S.C. Daughters, Alice Pinckney DeBecker of Providence, Rhode Island, Iris Pinckney Stovall of 7402 Southland Boulevard and June Pinckney Meeske of Tucson, Arizona. 17 grandchildren and 8 great-grandchildren. Another son, David, preceded him in death.

OTHER: The family does not want any flowers. Rather, it asks friends and relatives to donate to the Cancer Society.

Exercise 3

WRITING OBITUARIES

INSTRUCTIONS: Many newspapers give blank obituary notices to local funeral homes and ask the people working there to complete the forms when friends and relatives come in to arrange a funeral. The system enables newspapers to easily obtain all the information needed to write most obituaries. Use the information in these forms to write obituaries for the four individuals they describe.

OBITUARY NOTICE

Please supply the information asked for below and send to the newspaper office as quickly as possible after the death. Relatives, friends and neighbors of the deceased will appreciate prompt reporting of this news so that they may attend funeral services or send messages of condolence.

Full Name of Deceased _Robynn Anne Richter_

Address _42 Tusca Trail_

Age _Exact age unknown—estimated by friends to be about 65_

Date of Death _Late yesterday afternoon_

Place of Death _St. Nicholas Hospital_

Cause of Death _Injuries suffered during a fall at her home last week, including a broken hip._

Time and Date of Funeral _The authorities are still trying to contact all her relatives._

Place of Funeral _Unknown—to be determined by her relatives._

Place of Burial _Unknown_

Officiating Clergy _Unknown_

Place of Birth _Reidsville, N.C._

Places and Lengths of Residences _After graduating from the University of South Carolina in 1948, where she majored in political science, she worked briefly in Charleston and in Boston. She moved here in 1951._

Occupation _Retired stockbroker. After moving here in 1951, she taught civics and history at Roosevelt High School, working summers as a clerk at the local office of Merrill Lynch Pierce Fenner & Smith, Inc. In 1957, she became the first woman stockbroker employed at the office, rising to the position of office manager 7 years ago._

Did Deceased Ever Hold Public Office (When and What)? _Long active in the Democratic party, she was appointed to the city's Library Board in_

1954 and served 2 4-year terms. She was elected to the city council in '62 and re-elected to a second 3-year term in '65. At the time of her death, she was a member of the Mayor's Advisory Committee.

Name, Address of Surviving Husband (or Wife) ___ Friends think she was separated or divorced when she moved here in 1951, but it was a topic she never discussed. Since 1953, she shared her home here with a friend, Patricia Richards.

Maiden Name (if Married Woman) ___

Marriage, When and to Whom ___ Unknown

Names, Addresses of Surviving Children ___ None

Names, Addresses of Surviving Brothers and Sisters ___ A sister, Alvia Dey of Phoenix, Ariz. Three brothers, George of Reno, Nev., Robert of Stanhope, N.J. and Thomas of Modesto, Calif.

Number of Grandchildren (Great, Great-Great, etc.) ___ None

Names, Addresses of Parents (if Living) ___ Her father, Melvin, preceded her in death in 1958. Her mother, Sara, preceded her in death in 1973, both of Reidsville, N.C.

Additional Information ___ A member of the Board of Directors of the Kenmore Home for Unwed Mothers. A member of the University Club, the ACLU and Amnesty International. The first woman to join this city's Rotary Club. Also a member of the County Democratic Executive Committee, and chairwoman of the committee, serving 3 2-year terms, from 1964–65 and from 1968–71. Actively involved in the campaigns for John F. Kennedy in 1960, Robert Kennedy, George McGovern and Eugene McCarthy, serving as Robert Kennedy's county campaign coordinator and as McGovern's state campaign coordinator. She once told a reporter: "I've never had any children, but then I've never had to change any diapers or wipe any noses. It's politics and travel that I love—that make me alive, and I've enjoyed the time I needed for both."

OBITUARY NOTICE

Please supply the information asked for below and send to the newspaper office as quickly as possible after the death. Relatives, friends and neighbors of the deceased will appreciate prompt reporting of this news so that they may attend funeral services or send messages of condolence.

Full Name of Deceased _Jeffrey R. Ahson_

Address _49 Groveland Ave._

Age _Born August 4, 1923_

Date of Death _Sometime last evening_

Place of Death _Home_

Cause of Death _A lifelong smoker, he died of emphysema._

Time and Date of Funeral _Funeral service to be at 10 a.m. Saturday_

Place of Funeral _At the Littleton Mortuary, to be immediately followed by burial. Viewing at the mortuary from 4-5:30 and 7:30-9 Friday._

Place of Burial _Memorial Park Cemetery_

Officiating Clergy _The Rev. Billy Lee West_

Place of Birth _Chico, Calif._

Places and Lengths of Residences _Moved here after leaving the Navy in 1946_

Occupation _City firefighter, 1946–1966. After retiring from the fire department, he became a new car salesman for Romero Buick. At the age of 62, he retired from sales._

Did Deceased Ever Hold Public Office (When and What)? _No_

Name, Address of Surviving Husband (or Wife) _Wife, Theresa Ahson_

Maiden Name (if Married Woman) _____

Marriage, When and to Whom _1947, Therese Alpert_

Names, Addresses of Surviving Children _Three adopted children: son, Richard D. of Phillipsburg, Kan.; daughters Angela Molino of Omaha, Neb. and Lela Stalling of Pipe Creek, Texas._

Names, Addresses of Surviving Brothers and Sisters ___Brother Henry of San Francisco. Sisters Judith Eaker of Reidsville, N.C. and Shirley Solomon of Newark, N.J.___

Number of Grandchildren (Great, Great-Great, etc.) ___Five grandchildren and five great-grandchildren___

Names, Addresses of Parents (if Living) ___All deceased.___

Additional Information ___Member VFW Post 4206. Served aboard a destroyer in the Pacific during World War II. Also a member of the Elks Lodge, the National Checkers Association and Gideons. Member and usher at John Calvin Presbyterian Church. Past commander of American Legion Post 702. During the 1950s, after becoming a fireman, he became interested in the history of firefighting in the city. He began to research the topic and to gather memorabilia, including a 1924 fire truck he restored with friends and used to carry his exhibits to the city's elementary schools. He was well known by young school children in the city, speaking to thousands of them about the history of firefighting, until overtaken by the illness that subsequently claimed his life. Two years ago, he donated his firefighting collection to the city's public library, and all are now on permanent display there—including the fire truck. (The family wants no flowers.)___

Copyright © 1993 by Harcourt Brace Jovanovich, Inc.
All rights reserved. Printed in the United States of America
ISBN 0-15-500602-9

OBITUARY NOTICE

Please supply the information asked for below and send to the newspaper office as quickly as possible after the death. Relatives, friends and neighbors of the deceased will appreciate prompt reporting of this news so that they may attend funeral services or send messages of condolence.

Full Name of Deceased _Ellen Jean Koch_

Address _4214 Azalea Court_

Age _Approximately 65_

Date of Death _Last night_

Place of Death _Memorial Hospital_

Cause of Death _A recurrence of cancer for which she had been receiving medical treatment for the past 3 years._

Time and Date of Funeral _10 a.m. Friday. A mass will be said at 8 p.m._

Place of Funeral _St. John Vianney Catholic Church_

Place of Burial _St. Andrews Cemetery_

Officiating Clergy _The Reverend John Carey_

Place of Birth _Philadelphia_

Places and Lengths of Residences _Miss Koch resided at her family home in Philadelphia until graduating from the Philadelphia Musical Academy, then spent 3 years living in Europe. She returned to Philadelphia for 3 years, attending law school there, then moved here._

Occupation _Attorney_

Did Deceased Ever Hold Public Office (When and What)? _Appointed to the city's Human Relations Commission, nonpaid, voluntary position. Served from 1966 until her death._

Name, Address of Surviving Husband (or Wife) _Never married_

Maiden Name (if Married Woman) ____

Marriage, When and to Whom _Never married_

Names, Addresses of Surviving Children _None_

Names, Addresses of Surviving Brothers and Sisters _Two brothers: Warren and Richard, both of Philadelphia._

Number of Grandchildren (Great, Great-Great, etc.) _None_

Names, Addresses of Parents (if Living) _Both are dead._

Additional Information _Moving here in 1958, Miss Koch worked for the law firm of Ellis, Ballard, Searl and Associates. In 1960, she opened the Neighborhood Law Office at 818 Pershing Avenue, dispensing free legal aid to the poor from a donated office furnished with borrowed furniture. Clients were asked to donate what they could but she supported herself mainly from an inheritance from her parents and donations from foundations, a few law firms and other sources in the city. Served an estimated 250 needy clients and fielded more than 1,000 telephone calls for assistance monthly. She was also involved in the Democratic party. In 1962–63 she spent 14 months as a Peace Corps attorney in Addis Adaba, Ethiopia, where she said she found parallels between America's poor and the poor and their problems in Africa. During her absence, about two dozen colleagues in the city each volunteered their presence one day a month to continue her office's operations. In recent years, some also provided donations to it. Since 1971, the office has received some government grants and grown to a full-time staff of seven. In recent years, she urged the elderly to political activism and was a key organizer for the Gray Panthers and other older-citizen advocacy groups. Received dozens of awards for her work, and named to the boards of a dozen neighborhood and community organizations. (In lieu of flowers, friends are asked to make donations to the Neighborhood Law Office.)_

OBITUARY NOTICE

Please supply the information asked for below and send to the newspaper office as quickly as possible after the death. Relatives, friends and neighbors of the deceased will appreciate prompt reporting of this news so that they may attend funeral services or send messages of condolence.

Full Name of Deceased Beryl Anne Goetz

Address 1010 McLeod Road

Age 63

Date of Death Yesterday

Place of Death At home. She was transported from Mercy Hospital to her home 5 days ago at her insistence after being told she would soon die.

Cause of Death Breast Cancer

Time and Date of Funeral 4 p.m. tomorrow

Place of Funeral Faith Baptist Church

Place of Burial Evergreen Cemetery

Officiating Clergy The Rev. Harley O. Marchese

Place of Birth Boulder, Colo.

Places and Lengths of Residences Moved here with her husband in 1960.

Occupation Dentist/Authoress/Mother

Did Deceased Ever Hold Public Office (When and What)? No

Name, Address of Surviving Husband (or Wife) Separated after 22 years of marriage from her husband, Gerald Roy Goetz, now of Portland, Ore.

Maiden Name (if Married Woman) Beryl Anne Shenuski

Marriage, When and to Whom Married in 1957 at West Point to Lt. Gerald Roy Goetz, then a new graduate of the military academy.

Names, Addresses of Surviving Children Daughters Patricia Anne Cooper of Buffalo, N.Y., Elaine Marie McElhenny of Lexington, Ky., Betty Anne Dawsun of Kansas City, Mo. and Grace Stoops of Chicago, Ill. Sons Patrick M. of Dallas, Texas, Frederick W. of Midlothian, Va., Anthony Roy of San Antonio, Texas, Christopher of Seattle, Wash. and Charles of Minneapolis.

Names, Addresses of Surviving Brothers and Sisters Stepbrothers Steven and Richard, both of Boulder, Colo. Stepsister Linda, of Denver.

Number of Grandchildren (Great, Great-Great, etc.) Seventeen grandchildren.

Names, Addresses of Parents (if Living) Mother, Gertrude, and stepfather, Ernie, of Boulder.

Additional Information Graduated from the University of Colorado, receiving both her B.S. and dental degrees there. All 9 children born here. Worked at dentistry part-time, mornings only, until her youngest, Christopher, was in high school, then opened her own office at 702 East Broadway Avenue. Started writing as a hobby, as she created stories to entertain her own children and later began to write them down for others. Began to write children's books and published a total of 37. In 1974, she received the Newberrry Medal, the highest honor awarded to the author of books for children. A Baptist and member of Faith Baptist Church. Told an interviewer several years ago: "I get up at 5 and write until 7 every morning. It's a habit I started when all 9 children were still at home. With 9 children, it was the only time the house was quiet. Now they're gone, but that's still when I write. It's a bad habit."

Exercise 4

WRITING OBITUARIES

A.

Write the obituary for another student in your class. Assume that the student died of unknown causes early today, and that the student's funeral arrangements have not yet been made. Do not write a news story about the student's death, but an obituary about the student's life. Include the student's philosophy and goals and interesting experiences or major accomplishments. You might also describe the student's physical traits. Avoid generalities and clichés.

B.

During a two-hour class period, go out onto your campus and look for two people together, both strangers to you. Write an obituary for one of those persons and question the second about the "deceased." Continue the interview until you obtain some good (specific) quotations about the deceased. Then return to your classroom and complete the obituary before the end of the period. Assume that the person died of unknown causes early today and that the person's funeral arrangements have not yet been made.

As an alternative, write an obituary for one of your teachers, and interview several of the teacher's colleagues and students.

C.

Write an in-depth obituary for one of the following celebrities. Briefly report that the person died of unknown causes at home last night and that the person's funeral services have not yet been scheduled. Do not make up any other facts, nor report only what you remember about the person. Instead, use your campus library to *thoroughly* research the person's character and accomplishments. (Consult and, on a separate page, list a minimum of 10 sources you used while writing the obituary.)

After your lead, immediately report additional highlights—interesting and important details—that help describe the person's life, character and accomplishments. Avoid dull lists, and avoid reporting the information in chronological order. More routine details (such as the person's place of birth, education and survivors) should be placed near the end of the obituary, not near the lead.

People about whom you might write an obituary include:

ATHLETES AND ENTERTAINERS

Henry Aaron	Joe Montana
Muhammad Ali	Eddie Murphy
Woody Allen	Martina Navratilova
Roseanne Barr	Jack Nicholson
Johnny Carson	Leonard Nimoy
Howard Cosell	Arnold Palmer
Mike Ditka	Pete Rose
Jane Fonda	Brooke Shields
Dustin Hoffman	Don Shula
Magic Johnson	Barbra Streisand
Billie Jean King	Lee Trevino
Paul McCartney	Vanna White
Bette Midler	

AUTHORS AND JOURNALISTS

Jack Anderson
Patrick Buchanan
Art Buchwald
William Buckley
Walter Cronkite
Sam Donaldson
Katharine Graham

Charles Kuralt
Norman Mailer
Bill Moyers
Andy Rooney
A. Solzhenitsyn
Barbara Walters
George Will

POLITICAL FIGURES

Spiro Agnew
Jerry Brown
Barbara Bush
Rosalyn Carter
Fidel Castro
Bill Clinton
Mario Cuomo
Robert Dole
David Duke
Betty Ford
John Glenn
Barry Goldwater
Mikhail Gorbachev
Gary Hart
Saddam Hussein
Jesse Jackson
Thomas Jefferson
Lady Bird Johnson

Jack Kemp
Edward Kennedy
Henry Kissinger
Edward Koch
Nelson Mandela
Eugene McCarthy
George McGovern
Robert McNamara
Walter Mondale
Daniel Patrick Moynihan
Sam Nunn
Dan Quayle
Nancy Reagan
Margaret Thatcher
George Washington
Boris Yeltsin
Andrew Young
Your mayor, governor or senator

OTHERS

F. Lee Bailey
Jim Bakker
Tammy Bakker
Cesar Chavez
Princess Diana
Dale Earnhardt
Jerry Falwell
A.J. Foyt
Billy Graham
Anita Hill

Lee Iacocca
Coretta King
G. Gordon Liddy
Ralph Nader
Oliver North
Sandra Day O'Connor
Pat Robertson
Gloria Steinem
Clarence Thomas
Donald Trump

CHAPTER 16

NEWS RELEASES: WORKING WITH PR PRACTITIONERS

Newspapers are besieged by individuals and organizations seeking publicity. Even the daily newspapers published in small towns are likely to receive hundreds of news releases in their mail every day. In addition, 20 people may call each of the papers, and another 10 may stop at their offices. Larger dailies receive thousands of requests for publicity each day.

Business firms issue news releases to describe their growth, to report their latest dividends and to solicit more customers. Charities issue news releases to plead for money and volunteers, politicians to win votes, colleges to attract more students, and parents to obtain recognition for their children—and often for themselves as well.

Similarly, individuals and groups seeking publicity besiege campus papers. Moreover, many of the people seeking publicity seem to believe that every newspaper has a responsibility to provide it. Journalists disagree. They believe that their primary obligation is to their readers. Thus, they reject news releases that seem unlikely to interest many of their readers.

Yet, for most papers, news releases are an important and convenient source of information. No newspaper can afford to employ enough reporters to uncover every story occurring in its community. Instead, newspapers depend on the people involved in some stories to notify editors about them: about church and school activities; business and medical news; art, music and theater schedules; speakers; and festivals, for example.

JOURNALISTS' SKEPTICISM ABOUT PUBLIC RELATIONS

Diane Taylor, a PR practitioner for a public school system, has observed that, "The relationship between public relations practitioners and journalists often has been described as love-hate." To do their jobs well, Taylor explains, the two groups must rely on each other for information or coverage. Yet they do not seem to like each other, and that can make everyone's job more difficult.

Many Americans, not just journalists, seem to fear the power of public relations. Perhaps exaggerating that power, Americans seem to believe that skilled PR practitioners can manipulate public opinion. Some Americans fear and resent that manipulation. Others seem to believe that public relations is unnecessary and even wasteful—that it fails to contribute anything to the nation's productivity.

In addition, newspaper reporters and editors believe that their jobs are more important than those in public relations. Journalists also believe that their jobs are more honorable, noble and pure. Journalists explain that they serve the public,

informing people about important issues and watching over the government. Many journalists view PR practitioners, in contrast, as promoters who project only positive images for their clients—and who attempt to shield their clients from negative publicity.

In the past, some journalists called the people in public relations "flacks" and "propagandists." Other journalists complained that the people in public relations were "hired guns" who seemed to be willing to promote anyone who would pay their salaries, regardless of the cause. Even today, some journalists argue that PR practitioners are an unnecessary hindrance rather than a help.

Journalists are also critical of the news releases they receive. They complain that most news releases are self-serving: written for the benefit of the practitioners' clients rather than for the media or the public.

In addition, journalists maintain that many news releases are poorly written and concern subjects that are obviously not newsworthy: that are likely to interest only the people paying to have them written. Other news releases promote or praise rather than report. Journalists discard those and explain that it is not their job to promote or praise even the most outstanding individuals and organizations in their communities.

There may be another reason for journalists' antagonism toward PR practitioners. Some journalists seem to resent former colleagues who "sold out" and accepted higher-paying jobs in public relations. Inconsistently, however, many of the reporters and editors who decide to leave the newspaper business—perhaps as many as 45 percent—accept jobs in public relations.

PR practitioners respond that they provide a valuable service for both their clients and the public. And they complain that journalists generalize from a few bad experiences with practitioners who are ineffective or unprofessional: practitioners who do not understand how the media operate, nor the media's need for information that is clear, concise, accurate and objective.

Whatever its cause, journalists' skepticism about public relations develops early. Several studies have found that even the students majoring in their colleges' news/editorial sequences are critical of public relations. News/editorial majors admit that careers in public relations offer higher salaries and more job opportunities, but insist that their own work as reporters and editors is more important and enjoys a higher status in our society.

HANDLING NEWS RELEASES

Newspaper reporters handle news releases like any other type of story. Reporters critically examine whatever information the news releases provide, then summarize that information as clearly, concisely and objectively as possible. Their task is often difficult because some news releases fail to emphasize the news. Others contain clichés, jargon, puffery and platitudes. Moreover, most fail to use the proper style for capitalization, punctuation and abbreviations.

Typically, editors discard 100 news releases for every three or four they accept. Some editors do not even open all the news releases they receive in the mail every day. Rather, they glance at the return addresses on the envelopes and immediately throw away those from sources that regularly submit trivia. For example: the major automakers often send out news releases announcing the promotions of executives in Detroit, yet few newspapers print stories about those promotions because they are of little interest to people living in other cities and states. Editors reject other news releases because they are unimportant, poorly written and obvious advertisements.

The worst news releases, usually those submitted by local groups unfamiliar with the media, fail to provide all the information that reporters need to write complete stories. They also fail to include the names and telephone numbers of people whom reporters might call to obtain more information or explanations of facts that are unclear. Or, the news releases give telephone numbers that reporters can call during the day, but not during the evening, when the reporters employed by morning dailies often work. Still other news releases are handwritten and submitted days after the events they describe have taken place. By then, journalists no longer consider the events news.

Many editors, especially those at large dailies, refuse to publish any news releases verbatim. The editors may decide to use some news releases but, as a matter of principle, instruct their reporters to rewrite them. The editors may be reluctant to use anything submitted by publicists. Or, the editors may want the stories in their newspapers to be distinctive. In addition, most editors believe that every news release can be improved: that the reporters on their staffs are better writers than the publicists who submit news releases.

Other editors use news releases primarily as a source of ideas. If the editors like an idea provided by a news release, they will assign a reporter to gather more information about the topic, then to write a story about it.

A rewriteman at New York's Herald Tribune estimated that he rewrote 110,000 news releases during his 24-year career at the paper:

> About one in 10,000, he judged, had been suitable for publication as received. Almost all were written to satisfy the clients of public relations firms rather than the needs of the newspapers to which they were ostensibly directed, and almost none contained the home telephone number of the author-flack, of whom a rewriteman for a morning paper might want to make inquiry in the evening.*

Other editors are less critical. News releases are most likely to be reprinted verbatim at smaller papers that lack the necessary staff and sometimes the stricter standards of metropolitan dailies.

It may be unfair, however, for journalists to be so critical of the news releases they receive. Many of the people who send news releases to the media know that journalists are likely to rewrite their stories. Thus, those people do the best they can to provide all the facts that journalists will need, but do not try to present the facts in perfectly written stories.

Also, journalists deal with two distinctly different groups of publicists: professionals and amateurs. Amateur publicists who represent small clubs and churches, for example, often know little about the media and their requirements and are unable to write

---

*Richard Kluger. *The Paper: The Life and Death of the New York Herald Tribune* (New York: 1989), Vintage Books, pp. 719–20.

polished stories. Their news releases are still useful, however, since they help inform journalists about all the activities occurring in their communities. Journalists who criticize news releases sometimes forget that so many come from amateurs. Or, after receiving a terrible news release from a professional, they begin to generalize, criticizing every professional.

This chapter will show you how to rewrite news releases that are imperfect, regardless of their source.

The No. 1 Problem: Lack of Newsworthiness

Reporters obviously prefer news releases about topics that satisfy their definitions of news: that are new, local, interesting, unusual, relevant and important. Reporters also look for topics likely to affect or interest hundreds or even thousands of readers. Action is more newsworthy than opinions, and a genuine or spontaneous event is more newsworthy than a contrived one. Increasingly, for example, newspapers refuse to publish news releases about ribbon-cutting and ground-breaking ceremonies. They also refuse to publish photographs showing people handing over a check or a gavel.

Newspapers might use the following news releases because they describe topics likely to interest some readers. However, all three news releases would require some rewriting to make them conform to the style—especially the type of lead—suitable for newspapers:

> This season's first rollicking musical comedy by the Lake Street Players is "How to Succeed in Business Without Really Trying." The hit musical spoof of big business will play the State Theatre on the 9th thru 12th and 16th thru 19th of next month. For your convenience, information and reservations are available through the Lake Street Players' 24-hour phone, 357-7777. Make your reservations now!
>
> REVISED: Lake Street Players' first musical comedy of the season, "How to Succeed in Business Without Really Trying," will play at the State Theatre two weekends next month.

> All eyes will be skyward this Saturday and Sunday when the U.S. Navy Blue Angels, World Aerobatics Champion Leo Loudenslager and others take to the air. More than 20,000 people are expected to attend the 22nd Annual State Air Fair sponsored by the Rotary Club. The exciting weekend show will feature three acres of aviation displays and eight thrilling aerobatics acts.
>
> REVISED: The 22nd Annual State Air Fair this Saturday and Sunday will feature three acres of aviation displays and eight aerobatics acts, including the Navy's Blue Angels.
>
> More than 20,000 people are expected to attend the fair, which is sponsored by the Rotary Club.

> Programs making war violence exciting and fun entertainment are said to lead the new Fall programs, according to the National Coalition on Television Violence (NCTV). NCTV has just released its most recent monitoring results of prime-time network programs. Violence remains about seven violent acts per hour, with new programs taking three of the top four violent spots. ABC continued to be the most violent network for the fourth quarter in a row.
>
> REVISED: Prime-time network programs contain about seven acts of violence every hour, and this fall's new programs are among the most violent, according to the National Coalition on Television Violence.

Newspapers would be less likely to use the following news releases, because their topics would not interest many readers—except, of course, members of the organizations they mention. Those organizations can use other means, such as newsletters, to communicate with their members. That is not the job of a newspaper.

> The list of bus companies registered for the fifth annual American Bus Marketplace in Cincinnati, Nov. 30–Dec. 4, literally spans the alphabet (from Adirondack Trailways of Kingston, N.Y., to Zanetti Bus and Fast Express, Inc., of Rock Springs, Wyo.)

> Poland's Commissar of Elections Jerzy Adam Stephen is attending the annual conference of the International Association of Clerks, Recorders, Election Officials and Treasurers (IACREOT), in Little Rock, Arkansas, being held June 22–27.

> The American Society of Civil Engineers East Central Branch—Younger Member Forum was awarded Chapter of the Year by the National ASCE. The local branch has been awarded this distinction 3 times within the past 5 years. Dan Spindler, P.E. of Westinghouse Environmental and Geotechnical Services, Inc., is the current President.

> The State Chiropractic Association is holding its annual Fall Convention and Exposition August 24–26 at the Peabody Hotel. This year's convention offers 20 hours of license renewal education for doctors of chiropractic (DCs), a 12-hour license renewal program for certified radiologic technicians (CRTs) and 12 hours of instruction for chiropractic assistants (CAs).

Similarly, reporters are likely to discard the following news releases because they announce contrived events:

> WASHINGTON—The President has joined with the blood bank community in proclaiming January as National Volunteer Blood Donor Month and is urging everyone who is healthy to donate blood to help others.

> The governor has proclaimed Nov. 14–20 American Education Week in the State. The theme of this year's event, observed since 1921, is "A Strong Nation Needs Strong Schools."

Every week and every month of the year is dedicated to some cause, and often to dozens of different causes. For example, May is Arthritis Month, National High Blood Pressure Month, National Foot Health Month, Better Speech and Hearing Month, National Tavern Month and American Bike Month. Furthermore, the two news releases above tend to state the obvious. Most responsible adults would urge "everyone who is healthy to donate blood to help others." Most adults also recognize the importance of good schools. Thus, stories about such proclamations are trite, dull, repetitive and of little news value.

Journalists use—but must rewrite—news releases that contain some newsworthy details, but fail to emphasize those details. Typically, the following news releases (all issued by an ambitious state official) tend to sound alike because they all begin in the same manner, with the official's name:

> State Insurance Commissioner Bill Gunter has fined seven insurance companies a total of $48,750 for alleged violations of the state statutes and rules of the Department of Insurance.

> State Insurance Commissioner Bill Gunter today announced he will file an administrative complaint against the state's largest private passenger auto in-

surer—State Farm Mutual Auto Insurance Co.—charging that a recent rate increase filed by the company would circumvent the state's law against excess profits.

State Insurance Commissioner Bill Gunter this morning announced the issuance of warrants for five people, including an attorney, an insurance adjuster and an administrator of a medical treatment clinic, each charged with insurance fraud, first-degree grand theft and conspiracy.

News releases issued by former Sen. William Proxmire, D-Wis., usually started in the same way—with his name. Proxmire was unusually adept at attracting favorable publicity. Every month until his retirement, Proxmire issued a Golden Fleece Award for what he considered "the biggest, most ironic or most ridiculous example of wasteful spending." It was a clever gimmick that attracted publicity for Proxmire because it appealed to an almost universal value: Americans' opposition to government waste. Moreover, many of the examples that Proxmire cited seemed to be truly wasteful.

A student asked to write a story about one of Proxmire's monthly awards began with this lead:

Sen. William Proxmire, D-Wis., has given his Golden Fleece of the Month Award for wasteful government spending to the National Aeronautics and Space Administration.

The lead is dull because it emphasizes the routine: the fact that Proxmire gave another of his awards for wasteful government spending, something he did 12 times every year. Moreover, the lead contains three names: Proxmire's, NASA's and the award's. The lead should have emphasized the news—a specific description of the latest recipient:

The Golden Fleece Award for February has been given for a $14 million to $15 million project designed to find intelligent life in outer space.

Sen. William Proxmire, D-Wis., has complained that the project "is a low-priority program that at this time constitutes a luxury that the country can ill afford."

Proxmire presents the Golden Fleece Award each month to what he considers "the biggest, most ironic or most ridiculous example of wasteful spending." The project to find intelligent life in outer space was proposed by the National Aeronautics and Space Administration.

Notice that the revision mentions Proxmire in the second paragraph rather than in the lead, and that NASA is not mentioned until the third paragraph. Also, the introductory paragraphs do not present Proxmire's claims as fact; rather, they are carefully attributed. However, the most important point is that the lead did not have to begin with Proxmire's name, since it is not the newest, most interesting or the most newsworthy aspect of the story.

The problem is a common one. Many of the people writing news releases seem to be more interested in pleasing their bosses than in satisfying the media and informing the public. To please their bosses, they begin with their bosses' names.

Other news releases show even less understanding of the media and their definitions of news. They are actually editorials that philosophize or praise rather than report. Typically, a news release submitted by a state's beef producers declared that, "Red meat makes a contribution to America's health and vitality and should be saluted." The news release continued:

We often overlook the fact that American meat products are known throughout the world for their quality, wholesomeness and delicious flavor.

This week is National Meat Week, and it is an excellent opportunity to recognize the important contribution red meat makes to the diets of more than 250 million Americans who have made meat one of the country's favorite foods. Meat is more than a satisfying meal—it's part of a healthy, well-balanced diet.

Most journalists would respond that the media do not have a responsibility to salute the importance of red meat—nor of anything else. That is not their job. Moreover, it is not the type of story that the people who buy newspapers seem eager to read.

The No. 2 Problem: Lack of Objectivity

A second major problem with news releases is their lack of objectivity. Too many news releases are puffery, promoting rather than reporting. They contain laudatory adverbs and adjectives, not facts. The worst news releases are blatant advertisements, obviously intended to help sell commercial products. Most journalists would reject the following releases for that reason:

A briefcase that can't be lost, can't be stolen and prevents others from secretly recording your conversations is one of several new security devices now available from Hammacher Schlemmer, the internationally famous New York emporium of luxurious, unusual and useful gadgetry.

SportaRub, a new Aloe Vera product, will be test marketed this fall by Warren Bridges, Inc. SportaRub is the amateur athlete's answer to weekend aches and pains.

Joggers, golfers and tennis players alike appreciate SportaRub's soothing qualities. . . .

Another news release promoted a state lottery, claiming, "This game offers players lots and lots of cash prizes that can be claimed at any Lottery retailer, with excellent overall odds." Similarly, a release for a phone system stated: "We have successfully achieved our goal of combining hassle-free procedures with a fine user-friendly product in order to save HERTZ/Phone Link customers time and energy, and assure customer satisfaction. . . . Additionally, our phone system is more convenient and, for most users, less expensive than the competition's."

That type of news release offends journalists. No journalist is going to report anyone's claim that a lottery offers "lots and lots of cash prizes . . . with excellent overall odds." Journalists are also going to throw away any news release that claims a company offers "a fine user-friendly product" that assures customer satisfaction and is more convenient and less expensive than its competitors'. Those are advertisements, not news stories.

Yet newspapers continue to receive that type of news release, and it contributes to journalists' criticisms of the people who write them. Here's another example of a release that promotes a company's product, in this case baby shoes:

One memory parents cherish is baby's first step. Another memory is one which leads to baby's first step: baby's first shoe fitting. One of the most respected baby shoe companies brings local parents a free keepsake of this special occasion.

Altamonte Mall invites parents of young children to Stride Rite's "First Fitting" on June 23 in front of Sears at the mall.

The free program will educate parents on the importance of proper fitting shoes and give them the free keepsake. Each baby's photo will be taken and inserted into a commemorative "My First Fitting" magnet for parents to display on the refrigerator at home.

Reporters also eliminate laudatory adjectives. Every speaker does not have to be called a "guest speaker," and none should be labeled "famous," "prominent," "well-known" or "distinguished." If a speaker is truly famous, readers will already know the person and will not have to be told of his or her fame.

No news story—or news release—should call a program "wonderful," "successful," "timely" or "informative." Similarly, nothing should be called "interesting" or "important." Reporters also avoid phrases such as "bigger and better," "the best ever" and "back by popular demand."

Such puffery often appears in leads:

NEWS RELEASE: Michael R. Zaslow, a nationally recognized and respected forecaster in the field of economics and financial investments, will speak in the city November 15.

REVISED: Michael R. Zaslow will speak about financial investments—gold, stocks and real estate—at 8 p.m. Nov. 15 in the Municipal Auditorium.

NEWS RELEASE: The Creative Art Gallery, devoted exclusively to fine art photography, proudly announces an event of international significance in the photographic community: an exhibition of the works of Jerry N. Uelsmann and Diane Farris.

REVISED: The Creative Art Gallery, 324 N. Park Ave., will exhibit the photographs of Jerry N. Uelsmann and Diane Farris from Jan. 4 to 29.

Instead of reporting any news, other news releases urge the public to act: to donate their time and money, to buy new products, to attend events, to join organizations. For example:

Come and enjoy the fair.

Get into the "Spirit of the Season" by joining in the celebration.

Please be generous. Send your contributions of $25, $50, $100 or more to help the needy.

Reporters delete such editorial comments or rewrite them in a more factual manner. One approach is to summarize a story and then, in the final paragraph, tell readers how they *can* respond. Reporters will not tell readers that they *should* respond, only how those who want to do so can:

NEWS RELEASE: Everyone should bring their familiy to the picnic.
REVISED: The picnic is open to the public and will be held from 10 a.m. until 8 p.m. at Central Park. Admission is $3 for adults and $1 for children.

NEWS RELEASE: Tickets for the program are available to the public for $5 each at the Performing Arts Center and by calling 422-4896. Seating will not be reserved, so the public is urged to arrive early and to hear this most important message on the subject of women's rights.
REVISED: Tickets cost $5 and can be obtained at the Performing Arts Center or by calling 422-4896.

Other Problems with News Releases

Journalists rewrite some news releases because they state the obvious, especially in their leads:

> For years, elderly Americans have worried about the rising cost of medical care.
>
> The state fire marshal today urged people to observe simple fire safety precautions.
>
> The Muscular Dystrophy Association expects this year's MDA Jerry Lewis Labor Day Telethon to be the most spectacular in the history of the event.

The cost of medical care has been rising for years, and most Americans are already aware of that fact; thus, it is not news. Similarly, people expect a fire marshal to encourage fire safety. That is a routine part of any fire marshal's job, and is not news. It would, on the other hand, be news if the Muscular Dystrophy Association warned Americans that Jerry Lewis' annual telethon was going to be an intolerable bore, the worst ever. Instead, the MDA's news release contains a common (and unsubstantiated) claim that Lewis' telethon will be "the most spectacular in the history of the event."

The real news is often buried in a news release's second—or 22nd—paragraph. Here are two examples:

> Choosing a college or a career can be a pretty traumatic experience. It's a major decision which will impact on an individual for the rest of their life.
>
> Recognizing this, the Jewish Community Center, located at 851 North Maitland Ave., has organized a professionally led two-day seminar beginning on Jan. 4, titled "Exploring Your Future." Open to the community, the program is geared to assisting high school juniors and seniors plus college students.
>
> REVISED: The Jewish Community Center at 851 N. Maitland Ave. will conduct a two-day seminar to help students select a college or a career.

> "It's not easy to raise kids in today's fast-paced society, but that's all right," according to the Program Director of the Regional Medical Center's Child Protection Team. Doreen Mayer asserts that levels of stress inherent in child-rearing are normal.
>
> Mayer is among several child abuse professionals who will address a community service program titled "Help! My Kids Are Driving Me Crazy," which will be conducted next Wednesday from 7 to 9 p.m. in the RMC Auditorium.
>
> REVISED: The Regional Medical Center will offer a program to help parents who are having difficulty raising their children. The program, titled "Help! My Kids Are Driving Me Crazy," will begin at 7 p.m. Wednesday.

Some sentences in news releases contain no facts, only generalities, platitudes and self-praise. While rewriting the releases, reporters will eliminate every one of those sentences. Here are three examples:

> It will be an exciting musical celebration.
>
> An impressive lineup of speakers will share their expertise.
>
> The library has a reputation as a friendly, pleasant place to visit.

Such gush often appears in direct quotations, but that never justifies its use. If a quotation lacks substance, reporters will discard it too:

Blosser-Hitt said, "The colorful costumes will make a memorable impression at this once-in-a-lifetime experience."

Jaitt stated, "The fair is the best ever, with a dazzling lineup of new entertainment."

"We're very excited about the opening of the new store," said Mark Hughey, president. "The store represents a new direction for us and extends our commitment to provide customers with the highest-quality products at the lowest possible prices."

The platitudes and generalities sound familiar because they are used so often. For example, the following platitudes are similar but appeared in news releases that four different companies used to describe new employees:

We are fortunate to have a man with Russell's reputation and background as a member of the team. His knowledge and experience will be invaluable as we broaden our sales and marketing base.

We are extremely fortunate to have someone of his background and expertise join our program. He's joining our program at a most opportune time, when we are preparing to move forward with new vigor and emphasis.

Dave Harrier is the consummate industry professional. We're proud of Dave, and proud to have him move into this important position in our company.

We were impressed with Belmonte's accomplishments and his professionalism. We're extremely pleased with our good fortune in having him join us.

Other problems are more difficult to resolve. People and organizations submit news releases to the media because they hope to benefit from the stories' publication. As a result, almost all their news releases are one-sided. They present only their sources' opinions, and present those opinions as fact. The news releases that do mention an opposing view usually try to show that it is mistaken.

Because it is fast and easy, reporters may be tempted to accept the information provided by a news release. Reporters who do so—who fail to check the facts—are likely to make a serious error. For example, a college newspaper missed a major story because it received and immediately published a news release announcing that eight faculty members had been granted tenure or promotion. The news release failed to reveal the real story: the fact that a dozen other faculty members, including some of the college's most popular teachers, had been denied tenure or promotion because they were not good researchers. Moreover, the faculty members denied tenure had, in effect, been fired. A single telephone call to a faculty representative would have uncovered the story.

Some news releases encourage controversy. Here, too, newspapers that publish those releases allow themselves to be used. For example, Paul N. Strassels, a former tax-law specialist for the Internal Revenue Service, has charged that the IRS uses the media to scare taxpayers. Each year, stories about tax evaders who have been sentenced to prison begin to appear in the media shortly before the April 15 deadline for filing income tax returns. Strassels explains: "It's the policy of the IRS public affairs office to issue such stories at the time when you are figuring your taxes. The service knows that prison stories make good copy. It's simple manipulation."

Because of these and all the other problems that reporters encounter while handling news releases, they regularly condense four- and five-page handouts into three- and four-paragraph news stories. The following news release has been reduced by half:

News Release

Joyce Jones, organ virtuoso and concert artist, returns to perform her second concert on the Trexler Memorial Organ of St. Paul Lutheran Church at 8:00 P.M., Friday, November 19.

Her dazzling technique left the audience calling for more at her first performance in the Trexler Memorial Concert Series in 1980. Long before that appearance and certainly many times since, she has thrilled audiences all over the United States and Europe.

"Utterly charming . . . dazzling bravura mingled with intelligence," said the Los Angeles Times. The Stuttgarter Nachrichten hailed her performances in Germany as displays of "phenomenal technique . . . played magnificently."

Studying piano at age 4 and composing by age six, her seemingly boundless energy and talent have earned her a wall full of accolades of international recognition. When she is not touring, she is organist in residence at Baylor University, Texas.

Her program will include: Toccata on "Loge den Herren," Fantasia and Fugue in G minor, Twilight at Fiesole, Sonata: The Ninety-fourth Psalm, In Paradisium and Pageant.

Like all Trexler Memorial Concerts, her performance will begin promptly at 8:00 P.M. Tickets are $10.00 each and are available at the Concert Series Office, 300 E. Church St. Telephone number is 425-6060, Ext. 7117, between the hours of 1:00 and 5:00 P.M. weekdays.

News Story

Organist Joyce Jones will perform at St. Paul Lutheran Church at 8 p.m. Nov. 19 as part of the Trexler Memorial Concert Series.

Tickets cost $10 and are available at the Concert Series Office, 300 E. Church St. or by calling 425-6060, extension 7117, from 1 to 5 p.m. on weekdays.

Her program will include: Toccata on "Loge den Herren," Fantasia and Fugue in G minor, Twilight at Fiesole, Sonata: The Ninety-fourth Psalm, In Paradisium and Pageant.

Ms. Jones is the organist in residence at Baylor University in Waco, Texas. She also performed here during the 1980 concert series.

GOOD PR: A JOURNALIST'S VIEW

What do journalists want from public relations people? Journalists respect PR practitioners with good writing skills: practitioners able to translate complicated information into clear, readable stories. Journalists also respect PR practitioners who

Guest Column

A PRACTITIONER'S VIEW

By **Frank R. Stansberry, APR**

Research has shown that journalists have a low regard for public relations people in general, yet have a high regard for PR practitioners they know well or with whom they have a good working relationship. This might indicate that journalists have a healthy skepticism of PR people until a PR person's usefulness (or lack thereof) is established.

Ethical PR people see part of their mission as being a news source to journalists. Content analyses of major newspapers show that as much as 50 percent of the news in their business sections, for example, originates with PR people.

PR people do seek publicity for their clients or employers, but ethical practitioners define publicity as "information from an outside source used by journalists because of its news value." An honest, ethical PR person knows that news value is the linchpin of successful publicity.

There may have been a time, decades ago, when unethical PR people were able to influence equally unethical journalists with gifts and favors. If those days ever existed, they are over now. Today ethical journalists and PR people know that their relationship can be, and must be, one of pure professionalism. For both, this means being honest, available and informed.

An ethical PR person will be honest with a reporter, providing the journalist with information, access or interviews in a truthful and timely manner. One of the canons of the Code of Ethics of the Public Relations Society of America holds that members will not obstruct channels of communications in any way, and honest, ethical PR practitioners will honor that commitment.

The ethical journalist has a similar responsibility. Reporters should be up-front about their mission and not mislead news sources about the direction or tone of the reporting. The ethical PR person will honor that honesty by being as cooperative as possible.

"Availability" means that both the PR professional and the reporter should be available to each other whenever possible. Being available can be as simple as accepting or returning a call or as complex as gathering information as deadlines approach. The PR professional should respond as quickly when the news is not favorable as when the news is good. Reporters, likewise, need to listen to a news idea from the PR professional, even if the idea later proves to lack news value. Neither person benefits from a one-way relationship.

Finally, both the journalist and the PR practitioner need to be informed about the other's profession. For PR people, this means understanding not only their employers' business, but also the news business.

Frank R. Stansberry, an accredited member of the Public Relations Society of America, has a bachelor's degree in journalism from the University of Tennessee and a master's degree in communication from the University of Central Florida. He has 10 years of media experience with daily newspapers and Business Week magazine, and 20 years of agency and corporate PR experience.

A knowledge of the news process begins with an understanding of what the media consider news—and with an understanding of the media's deadlines and special requirements. It also includes an ability to produce tight, concise writing in a style suited to the medium. A public relations person who understands the news process can do a better job of serving both an employer and a journalist.

Journalists, too, need to understand the companies or agencies they cover. What does the company produce? Is it successful? Why? How? A journalist who understands how a news source does business will conduct a better interview and write a better story.

The first article in the Public Relations Society of America Code of Ethics says members will operate in the public interest at all times. Thus, the ethical PR professional is frequently trying to serve three masters: the employer, the journalist and the public interest. But not everyone operating as a PR person subscribes to these ethical and professional standards.

PR people, like journalists, are not all alike. Some are good; some are incompetent. Experience quickly enables a journalist to separate those who deliver information with true news value from those who come seeking only to improve their image at the expense of the news process.

understand the media's definitions of news. Journalists want to be informed about major stories, not to be bothered with stories that are obviously not newsworthy.

Good public relations people are also available and cooperative. To help journalists meet their deadlines, they respond quickly, no matter what the question, and do their best to provide accurate and complete information at all times.

They also send their news releases to the right editor and regularly update their files so their news releases are not addressed to editors who moved (or died) 10 years earlier. By sending their news releases to the right editor, PR practitioners can significantly increase the likelihood that they will be used. At the same time, PR practitioners will *decrease* the likelihood that they will waste other editors' time—and harm their own reputations in the process. For example: most editors would discard a news release about an employee's promotion. However, a newspaper's business editor might report the promotion in a weekly column devoted to local promotions. Similarly, most editors would discard a news release about a Christmas program at a church. Yet a newspaper's religion editor might mention the program in a roundup about Christmas activities in the community.

The best PR people are also well informed about their own companies and industries. They can find information quickly and will arrange interviews with experts and top executives. When an important issue arises, some anticipate journalists' questions and make sure that the right corporate officials are available to answer them.

Moreover, the news releases they submit are excellent. The best are so good that it is difficult to distinguish between them and the stories written by a newspaper's own staff. Here are three examples:

Tina Delgado, assistant professor of music at Rollins College, will present a piano recital at 4 p.m. Sunday, Feb. 18, in the Annie Russell Theatre.

Women Alone, a growth group for women who are divorced, widowed or separated, will meet at noon on Friday, July 13, at the Center for Women's Medicine in the Medical Plaza at 2501 N. Orange Ave.

Philomene Gates, the author of "Suddenly Alone: A Woman's Guide to Widowhood," will speak about widowhood at the Public Library at 10:30 a.m. Saturday, May 19.

Analyze those leads. Notice that all three emphasize the news and are clear, concise and factual.

The following news releases are also unusually good, perhaps as good as or even better than the stories written by most reporters. All three news releases were submitted by the same source, the University of Florida's Health Science Center:

While many Americans may be eating less red meat to lower cholesterol and fat levels, researchers at the University of Florida are investigating the possibility that older Americans should, in fact, be eating more.

Doctors have some unseasonal advice for pregnant women heading outdoors to enjoy this summer's warm weather: Bundle up.

Although the risk is small, they could get bitten by ticks carrying Lyme disease, a rare but disabling illness that University of Florida physicians say can be transmitted by infected mothers-to-be to their unborn babies.

Schoolteacher Dawn Flanegan doesn't have to whisper to her class any more, thanks to a new surgical procedure performed on her vocal cords by a University of Florida surgeon.

Just a few months ago, the 40-year-old kindergarten teacher could speak only in a hoarse, breathy whisper. She now speaks in tones clearly audible over the telephone, and she no longer struggles to communicate, although her vocal volume remains slightly weaker than it was previously.

The loss of Flanegan's voice was caused by a paralysis of her right vocal cord, which occurred last November when surgeons found it necessary to sever a nerve during the removal of a noncancerous tumor. The tumor was wrapped around the nerve.

Raising her voice to be heard above a room full of noisy 5-year-olds became so physically exhausting that Flanegan had to quit teaching. The vocal cord paralysis also made it difficult for her to cough, and when she attempted to swallow, food would frequently enter her windpipe instead of the esophagus.

"My voice is very important in managing 24 children from 8 a.m. to 2 p.m. every day," said Flanegan, who has three children of her own. "I couldn't read stories to them; I couldn't help teach them sounds because I couldn't even make some sounds myself after the tumor surgery."

Flanegan's voice loss was evaluated last December at the University of Florida's Voice Disorder Clinic. . . .

The first of the three news releases discusses blood cholesterol levels, a topic that concerns many adults, but also points out an unusual or unexpected twist—the fact that older Americans may need to eat more, not less, red meat. The second release concerns another unusual topic: the fact that pregnant women need to bundle up, even in summer, to protect their unborn babies from Lyme disease (a disease often in the news). Notice that the third news release emphasizes the human element: a woman's struggle to overcome an unusual medical problem. Moreover, all three news releases are factual and localized. Thus, all three emphasize the news: facts likely to interest the public. They mention their source, but are not blatant advertisements for it.

Conversely, people at companies with reputations for bad public relations seem to be unfamiliar with newsroom procedures and uninformed about their own companies and industries. Some are unable or unwilling to arrange interviews with their top executives. They fail to return phone calls and refuse to answer questions or respond "no comment." They are also defensive, trying to hide unfavorable information. Some deliberately mislead journalists—a tactic that often backfires. Moreover, the news releases they send to the media are unusable. Instead of emphasizing the news, they gush, promote or editorialize.

ADDITIONAL GUIDELINES

First, whenever possible, localize the news releases you handle. A recent news release distributed by the U.S. Forest Service began:

> WASHINGTON—An estimated $342 million will be shared by 43 states and Puerto Rico as their portions of this year's National Forest System receipts, according to estimates released today by the U.S. Department of Agriculture.

This release ended with a list of the 43 states and the amount that each state would receive. Perceptive reporters would localize their stories' leads, emphasizing the amounts their own states would receive.

Second, a surprising number of news releases mention raffles and lotteries, and reporters must delete every reference to them. Most newspapers distribute some subscriptions by mail, and postal regulations prohibit using the mail to promote lotteries. Also, many references to lotteries are linked to promotional gimmicks:

> Brinks Home Security will be passing out lights to the walkers, and people can sign up for the raffle of a Brinks Home Security system valued at $530.

> Americans who recycle aluminum play a large role in the protection of their environment. Now those recyclers can be rewarded with as much as $100,000 for their efforts in Reynolds Aluminum Recycling Company's "Great American Outdoors Game."
> "Every time consumers recycle at a Reynolds center between May 1 and October 31, they could possibly win instant prizes from $1 to $1,000," said Mike Brinkley, Regional Manager of Reynolds Aluminum Recycling Company (RARCO). "In addition, they can also become eligible for the grand prize of $100,000."

Third, avoid unnecessary background information, especially statements about a group's philosophy, goals or organization. The information is rarely necessary. Moreover, it would become too repetitious and waste too much space if reporters included it in every story about a group:

> MDCA is a private, nonprofit arts organization dedicated to the presentation and advancement of the fine arts in our area.

> Throughout the year volunteers give unselfishly of their time as Big Brothers and Big Sisters. "The lives of boys and girls in this community are enriched by their caring," said Joe Midura, Executive Director, in announcing the Volunteer Appreciation Week event.

> Habitat for Humanity of the Greater Metropolitan Area has as its goal the fulfillment of the dream of decent housing for hardworking but poor and un-

derprivileged members of our community. We are an independent affiliate of Habitat for Humanity International, headquartered in Americus, Georgia.

REPORTING COURSES FOR PR MAJORS

To help solve the problems discussed in this chapter, many schools require every student majoring in public relations to enroll in a reporting course. The course teaches public relations majors about the media's definitions of news, style of writing, deadlines and other characteristics and policies.

PR professionals agree on the course's importance. A survey of 200 members of the Public Relations Society of America found that professionals consider a news reporting course more important for public relations majors than any course in public relations. The professionals were asked to select 13 courses for a public relations major from a list of 38 possible courses. Ninety percent listed "Basic News Reporting." The second choice, "Introduction to Public Relations," was listed by 85 percent.*

Finally, some people believe that the hostility between the people working in journalism and those who work in public relations is slowly dissipating. That may be true. However, some conflict seems inevitable—and perhaps healthy.

CHECKLIST FOR HANDLING NEWS RELEASES

1. Is the news release newsworthy?
   A. Is it new?
   B. Does it involve an issue likely to interest or affect many of your newspaper's readers? (If the topic will interest only the members of a single organization—the organization that submitted the news release—discard it.)
   C. Does it involve a genuine rather than a contrived event, such as a proclamation, ground-breaking or ribbon-cutting ceremony?
2. Does the news release need rewriting?
   A. Does every paragraph—especially the lead—emphasize the news, or is the news buried in a later paragraph?
   B. Does the lead begin by stating the obvious?
   C. Does the lead begin with an unnecessary name?
   D. Does the lead need to be localized?
   E. Is the story clear and concise?
   F. Does the story contain every necessary detail?
   G. Does the story contain any clichés, jargon, gush, platitudes, generalities or self-praise? Even if they appear in direct quotations, eliminate them.
   H. Is the story objective?
      • Does it contain any puffery: words such as "best," "exciting," "famous," "interesting," "important," "successful" or "thrilling"?
      • Does it promote a private company or commercial product?
      • Does it make any unsubstantiated claims about being the "cheapest," "biggest" or "best"?
      • Does it urge the public to act?
3. Does the news release contain any unnecessary background information?
4. Does the news release present every side of a controversial issue? Even if it does, are its presentations adequate: fair and thorough?
5. Does the news release contain any references to a raffle or lottery?

---

*Mike Shelly. "PR Professionals Pick News Writing as Priority Course," *Journalism Educator*, January 1981, p. 16.

SUGGESTED READINGS

Articles

Arnoff, Craig. "Credibility of Public Relations for Journalists." *Public Relations Review*, 1, 1975, pp. 45–56.

Bishop, Robert L. "What Newspapers Say about Public Relations." *Public Relations Review*, 14, 1988, pp. 50–52.

Fedler, Fred, Tom Buhr and Diane Taylor. "Journalists Who Leave the News Media Seem Happier, Find Better Jobs." *Newspaper Research Journal*, 9, no. 2, Winter 1988, pp. 15–23.

Feldman, L. "The Public Relations Man as City Editors See Him." *The Quill*, 49, 1961, pp. 16–17.

Kopenhaver, Lillian Lodge, David L. Martinson and Michael Ryan. "How Public Relations Practitioners and Editors in Florida View Each Other." *Journalism Quarterly*, 61, Winter 1984, pp. 860–65+.

Poorman, Paul. "Public Relations: The Newsman's View." *Public Relations Journal*, 30, no. 3, 1974, pp. 14, 16, 40.

Rees, Clair. "Avoiding the Hot-Air Syndrome: Writing for Publication: News Releases and Newsletters." *WordPerfect Magazine*, May 1989, pp. 25–27.

Ryan, Michael, and David L. Martinson. "Journalists and Public Relations Practitioners: Why the Antagonism?" *Journalism Quarterly*, 65, Spring 1988, pp. 131–40.

Sanoff, Alvin P. "Image Makers Worry about Their Own Image." *U.S. News & World Report*, Aug. 13, 1979, pp. 57–59.

Smith, Ron F. "A Comparison of Career Attitudes of News/Editorial and Ad/PR Students." *Journalism Quarterly*, 64, Summer/Autumn 1987, pp. 555–59.

Stegall, Sandra Kruger, and Keith P. Sanders. "Coorientation of PR Practitioners and News Personnel in Educational News." *Journalism Quarterly*, 63, Summer 1986, pp. 341–47+.

Books

Bivins, Thomas. *Handbook for Public Relations Writing*. 2nd ed. Lincolnwood, IL: NTC Business Books, 1991.

Brody, E. W. *The Business of Public Relations*. New York: Praeger, 1987.

Brody, E. W. *Public Relations Programming and Production*. New York: Praeger, 1988.

Brody, E. W., and Dan L. Lattimore. *Public Relations Writing*. New York: Praeger, 1990.

Cantor, Bill, and Chester Burger, eds., *Experts in Action: Inside Public Relations*. 2nd ed. New York: Longman, 1989.

Goff, Christine Friesleben, ed., *The Publicity Process*. 3rd ed. Ames, IA: Iowa State University Press, 1989.

Haberman, David A., and Harry A. Dolphin. *Public Relations: The Necessary Art*. Ames, IA: Iowa State University Press, 1988.

Hiebert, Ray Eldon, ed., *Precision Public Relations*. New York: Longman, 1988.

Olasky, Martin N. *Corporate Public Relations: A New Historical Perspective*. Hillsdale, NJ: Erlbaum, 1987.

Oxley, Harold. *The Principles of Public Relations*. London: Kogan Page, 1987.

Seitel, Fraser P. *The Practice of Public Relations*. 4th ed. Columbus, OH: Merrill, 1989.

Simon, Raymond. *Public Relations: Concepts and Practices*. New York: Macmillan, 1986.

Weiner, Richard. *Professional's Guide to Public Relations Services*. 6th ed. New York: American Management Association, 1988.

Wood, Robert J., with Max Gunther. *Confessions of a PR Man*. New York: New American Library, 1988.

QUOTES

If all printers were determined not to print anything till they were sure it would offend nobody, very little would be printed.

(Benjamin Franklin)

Liberty of circulating is as essential to that freedom as liberty of publishing; indeed without the circulation, the publication would be of little value.

(Justice Stephen J. Field, U.S. Supreme Court)

Every bit as important as improving the credibility of the press is the need to foster greater understanding of the concept of freedom of the press. It is not . . . a special privilege granted to those few who own printing presses. Rather, it is a right granted to the people for their protection against the vicissitudes of government and all other sources of power and influence. . . . The newsman is but the surrogate for the people in a never-ending search to uncover the truth.

(Stanford Smith, former general manager,
American Newspaper Publishers Association)

Exercise 1

NEWS RELEASES

EVALUATING NEWS RELEASES

INSTRUCTIONS: Critically evaluate the newsworthiness of the following leads. Each lead appeared in a news release mailed to a daily or weekly newspaper. Rate each news release's newsworthiness on a scale of "1" (Not Newsworthy) to "10" (Extremely Newsworthy), then discuss the ratings with your class.

1. Nail polish remover is still being dropped into the eyes of conscious rabbits to meet insurance regulations, infant primates are punished by electric shocks in pain endurance tests and dogs are reduced to a condition called "learned help-lessness" to earn someone's Ph.D.

   With the theme "Alternatives Now," People for the Ethical Treatment of Animals (PETA) is sponsoring a community rally on Friday—World Day for Laboratory Animals—at 1 p.m.

   RATING:_____ EXPLANATION:_____

2. A new device that alleviates pain by allowing each patient to administer his own medication is now available at Memorial Hospital.

   The hospital has purchased Harvard's Patient-Controlled Analgesia (PCA) Pumps that allow patients to safely and effectively control pain by pressing a button at their bedside.

   RATING:_____ EXPLANATION:_____

3. Dr. Paul Becton, who recently retired after 35 years with the U.S. Department of Agriculture, has assumed his new duties as Chief of the Bureau of Brucellosis and Tuberculosis with the State Department of Agriculture and Consumer Services, Commissioner Doyle Conner announced today.

   RATING:_____ EXPLANATION:_____

4. Demand for gas energy in the United States could, under the right conditions, increase as much as 50 percent to approximately 30 trillion cubic feet (Tcf) by the year 2010 according to a study by the American Gas Association (AGA).

   RATING:_____ EXPLANATION:_____

5. An eye disease that affects only diabetics nonetheless has such vision-destroying potential that it now ranks among the country's leading causes of blindness. The National Society to Prevent Blindness warns that all diabetics are at risk from the disease, diabetic retinopathy, that blinds some 4,700 of them each year. Right now, a million diabetics have eye changes that can lead to blindness if not treated—10 percent of the country's estimated 10 million diabetics.

   RATING:_____ EXPLANATION:_____

6. The Crime Prevention Commission has produced a brochure of crime prevention and safety tips that every child should know. This free brochure contains

a handy list of home and bicycle safety guidelines as well as rules regarding "dangerous strangers" that should be taught to all youngsters. The cheerful yellow leaflet also includes a panel of emergency numbers for posting near the telephone.

RATING:_____ EXPLANATION:_____

7. The State Supreme Court has suspended an attorney from the practice of law for three months and one day, effective immediately. The discipline resulted from action brought by the State Bar.

RATING:_____ EXPLANATION:_____

8. High interest rates, coupled with low prices for most agricultural commodities, are causing serious "cash flow" problems for farmers, pushing some toward bankruptcy, according to a study by the Institute of Food and Agricultural Sciences (IFAS) at your state university.

RATING:_____ EXPLANATION:_____

9. General Electric Company will establish the worldwide headquarters for its new Automation Systems Department near your city, James A. Meehan, General Manager of the Automation Systems Department, announced today.

Automation Systems markets industrial robots designed for parts assembly, arc and spot welding, spraying, material handling, and process applications such as grinding, polishing, and deburring.

RATING:_____ EXPLANATION:_____

10. "The Changing Face of Men's Fashion" will be illustrated in a fashion presentation in Robinson's Men's Shops at 5:30 on Thursday. A special feature of the event will be commentary of the distinctive directions in men's designs by Pieter O'Brien, a fashion editor of Gentlemen's Quarterly magazine.

RATING:_____ EXPLANATION:_____

11. Fire safety education in the state's public schools should be stepped up, according to the State Fire Marshal.

RATING:_____ EXPLANATION:_____

12. Women have made much progress against discrimination through social and legal reforms, but they are still the victims of a very disabling form of discrimination that largely goes unnoticed: arthritis.

Of the more than 31 million Americans who suffer from arthritis, two-thirds are women, according to the Arthritis Foundation.

RATING:_____ EXPLANATION:_____

13. Parents who refuse to let children believe in Santa Claus may be doing them harm, today asserted a Mt. Sinai School of Medicine psychologist.

Mr. David M. Kelley stated in the current issue of Parent's magazine, "Being the only one in the classroom who knows for sure that there's no such guy could make a child feel very different, very strange." He said it "would be unusual" if the denial led to a sense of strength.

RATING:_____ EXPLANATION:_____

14. Pregnant women throughout the state are finding it more difficult to locate an obstetrician willing to deliver their baby because of the number of obstetricians—80 last year alone—who are discontinuing this practice because of the high cost of malpractice insurance, according to a survey by the State Obstetric and Gynecologic Society.

RATING:_____ EXPLANATION:_____

Exercise 2

NEWS RELEASES

ELIMINATING PUFFERY

INSTRUCTIONS: Rewrite the following sentences and paragraphs more objectively, eliminating all their puffery.

1. The entry deadline is Friday, March 16th, so hurry and sign up!

2. As a proponent of innovative hiring practices, the company's president has worked diligently to hire older workers, disabled workers and the homeless.

3. The outrageously funny British farce, RUN FOR YOUR WIFE!, will romp across the Lake Street Players stage May 25–27 and May 31–June 2. It will be a fun-filled evening for the entire family, with each hilarious performance starting promptly at 8 p.m.

4. The governor has not wasted any time. Today the governor announced the selection of a special blue-ribbon search committee for the state's university system. This important group is composed of 12 distinguished members with a broad range of interests and will immediately begin its vital task of seeking a new chancellor to head the system.

5. If you're looking for something out of the ordinary for an evening's entertainment, the Center for Arts is the place to be at 7 p.m. Friday and Saturday and at 2 p.m. Sunday. Director Chris Allen will introduce "Love, Love, Love," an exciting new musical comedy certain to please the entire family— and at the low price of only $9.50 a ticket.

6. Johnson is committed to his work and, while serving as head of the Chamber of Commerce in Houston, succeeded in increasing its membership by 41 percent. His goal when he assumes the presidency of the chamber here next week is to achieve the same type of rapid growth. Johnson has already prepared a detailed plan of action outlining the tasks to be accomplished in the months ahead.

7. The stellar cast includes such renowned performers as Hans Gregory Ashbaker as Rodolfo and Elizabeth Holleque as Mimi. Holleque has become one of America's most sought-after sopranos since winning the 1983 Metropolitan Opera National Council Auditions. She thrilled audiences here with her portrayals of Marguerite in Faust last season and is sure to do the same with her rendition of Mimi.

8. County residents have many opportunities to register to vote, and Supervisor of Elections Diedre Morsburger likes to make it as easy as possible for them to do so. Kicking off "Voter Registration Month" in the County on the 1st of next month will be a voter registration drive. There will be no need to travel far, Morsburger says. Deputized personnel from her office will fan out to special booths at every major shopping mall in the county to make it easy for residents to register to vote. Morsberger said she has set as her goal next month the registration of 5,000 new voters.

9. Torey Pines is home to a new community of luxury custom homes with lot sizes starting at 1/2 acre and prices from $300,000. In stark contrast to the surrounding properties, which are built on former farmland, Torey Pines stands out as a forest of extremely tall pines and offers a distinctly different skyline. Built by twelve of the area's most renowned custom builders, Torey Pines homes feature floor plans and elevations that are strikingly individual. Eighteen of the finest luxury models will open for the public's inspection and appreciation at noon this Sunday.

10. Guest conductor Richard Hayman and the Symphony Orchestra will bring all the bright lights and excitement of New York's famous theatre district to the stage of the Carr Performing Arts Centre as they present "Broadway Bound," the final concert of the current series, at 8 p.m. Saturday. One of this country's most sought-after "pops" conductors, Hayman is re-invited, season after season, to conduct leading orchestras across the continent. In his usual exuberant style, he will conduct selections from some of Broadway's most beloved musicals, including South Pacific, The Sound of Music, My Fair Lady, Cabaret, Cats and Les Miserables.

Exercise 3

NEWS RELEASES

INSTRUCTIONS: These are actual news releases mailed to daily or weekly newspapers. Only the locations and the names of some individuals have been changed. Your instructor may ask you to write only the lead for each news release or to write the entire story.

1. Recovered Anorexic to Speak

"Understanding the Anorexic/Bulimic Family Member" will be the subject of a meeting sponsored by Memorial Hospital's Eating Disorders Unit Monday, Nov. 3, at 6:00 p.m. in the hospital auditorium.

Karen Balliet, a recovered anorexic and the president and director of the state chapter of the American Anorexia/Bulimia Assn., Inc., will be the speaker.

Anorexia nervosa, which is characterized by an intense fear of becoming obese, affects over 100,000 people in the U.S. alone. Bulimia, characterized by recurrent episodes of binge eating often followed by attempts to purge food by vomiting or laxative abuse, is especially prevalent in female high school and college students.

The Memorial Hospital Eating Disorders Unit has been open for two years. It is unique to this area in that it offers both in-patient and out-patient programs. Its staff is available to answer questions concerning these life threatening disorders and to assist patients and family members in coping.

For information about Balliet's talk or the Eating Disorders Unit, call the hospital at 767-2267.

2. Beauty Contest Entries

Mr. Carlos Zumbado, General Manager of the County Fair, announced that this year's County Fair Queen Beauty Contest will be held on October 22 at the Fashion Square Mall at 6:30 pm. The contestant must be a student and a resident of the county between the ages of 16–20.

The prizes will be as follows:

FIRST: $150.00 cash, free modeling course from MDM Studios, beautiful crown, banner and trophy, and two VIP tickets good for every fair concert, general admission and midway rides and many nice gifts from the Fashion Square Mall Merchants.

SECOND: $50.00 cash, two VIP tickets for any two concerts and free general admission every day and a gift from the Fashion Square Mall.

THIRD: $25.00 cash, two VIP tickets for any two concerts and free general admission every day and a gift from the Fashion Square Mall.

Entry forms can be picked up at any high school, Fashion Square Mall business office and the County Fair office at 500 Friday Road.

Contestants must have their entry forms returned to the Fashion Square Mall office by October 10. The preliminary judging and interviewing will be held on October 15 at the Fashion Square Mall. The finals will be open to the public. For further information, contact Bonnie Whidden at 452-3270.

3. Annual "Stop, Drop & Shop" Program

The city Parks & Recreation Dept. and the Public Library invite you to spend an afternoon of Christmas Fun, Sunday, December 14, 1 p.m.–5 p.m.

Parents can begin by *Stopping* off at the Public Library, *Dropping* off their school age children and *Shopping* for the holidays with their free time, knowing that their children are being well cared for and having fun.

The Public Library's annual *Stop*, *Drop & Shop* program will be held at the library from 1 to 5 p.m. Sunday, December 14. Games, films, stories and other activities for school age children will be featured to add to their holiday fun. It's all completely free of charge.

4. First Community Respite Care Weekend

Alzheimer's, the fourth leading cause of death among adults in the U.S., has a profound impact on the entire family, thus leaving the primary care giver in a "high risk" category for stress related illnesses. Any time off, regardless of how little, is essential in helping reduce that stress.

Next week, on Saturday and Sunday, Sand Lake Hospital will offer the area's first "Community Respite Care Weekend," a new concept. Volunteers will offer time and loving care the entire weekend.

The Community Respite Care Project offers rest or relief to those families who are continually caring for an Alzheimer's loved one. This weekend will give those family members the opportunity to have a weekend off to do just as they please while their loved one is safe and in the caring hands of trained volunteers and nursing professionals.

After this weekend's respite, similar respite care will be offered on the first weekend of each month at the Sand Lake Hospital facility. The new program also offers in-home volunteer help and subsidized adult day care.

"Anyone who has an interest in volunteering their time is greatly needed," says Charlotte McFarland. "Our program relies solely on volunteer power to staff both the in-home and hospital respite. We realize many people may find this type of volunteerism difficult, however, the devoted people we do have find much personal satisfaction and reward once they see how much they help and the difference they make to these families."

For more information, call Charlotte McFarland, Respite Project Director, at 425-2489.

5. Blood Donors Needed During Summer Months

Come roll up your sleeve and give a lifesaving gift to a patient who needs you.

The summer is a time for enjoyment and relaxation, but for many local hospital patients who are ill or injured, the summer won't be so much fun. The Blood Bank asks that you help these patients return to good health by donating blood.

"The community blood supply traditionally decreases during this time of the year because many regular donors are on vacation or busy with other activities," said Linda Wallenhorst-Zito, director of communications and marketing at the Blood Bank. "However, accidents and emergencies increase during the summer, and many patients wanting elective surgery are forced to postpone it until more blood becomes available."

Any healthy person at least 17 years old may donate and there is no upper age limit. Donors complete a brief medical questionnaire and health screening that many find a good way to regularly monitor such factors as their heart rate and blood pressure.

For additional information, call your local Blood Bank branch. Come help save a life. Someday, someone may save yours.

Exercise 4

NEWS RELEASES

Using News Releases

WRITING NEWS BRIEFS

INSTRUCTIONS: Assume that you have been asked to write a column of news briefs that will be published tomorrow in your local daily. Summarize each of the following news releases in a separate story or brief. The news releases are genuine; only a few names and dates have been changed.

1. Help SunBank Alleviate the Year-Round Problem of Hunger

Nearly one-fourth of the children in this state must go to bed hungry every night. That's no way to let our future generations grow and take shape.

In order to help alleviate the growing concern of hunger in our local state, SunBank has announced that it will begin their seventh annual SunSanta food drive next June 14. Residents of the state are encouraged to bring any canned or nonperishable food items to their nearest SunBank office for distribution to the needy. When the food drive ends on Friday, July 6, the Christian Service Center will pick-up and distribute all donated items to local, needy families and individuals.

For the first time, SunBank is hosting their statewide food drive in the summer months. "When we first began the program seven years ago, there were few food drives during the winter holidays," explained Sara Curtis, Senior Vice President of Marketing. "However, as more and more organizations sponsored year-end food campaigns, we have rescheduled our program for the summer months to help replenish depleted food banks."

Last year, residents of the state donated over 78,000 items to 55 different charities. Clearly, you "can" make a difference. So when composing your vacation packing list, don't forget to drop off your canned goods at your local SunBank office.

2. "Buggy Exhibit"

The Dodd Science Center is preparing for an invasion of insects. Beginning with a Members Preview Party at 2 p.m. Sunday, DSC hosts the highly successful "Insect Zoo, Arachnids Too" developed and circulated by Great Explorations, Inc. of Boston, Massachusetts. The exhibit celebrates the diversity and splendor of the world of insects. Over 20 species of live arthropods including tarantulas, a bird-eating spider, walking sticks, praying mantises, grasshoppers and native and exotic cockroaches, including the giant hissing cockroaches from Madagascar, will be in residence at DSC during this exhibit, which opens to the public on Tuesday and will continue for 6 weeks. The staff will conduct daily feedings and demonstrations at 10:00 a.m. and 1:00 p.m.

DSC's hours are:

Tuesday–Saturday	9 a.m. to 5 p.m.
Sunday	12 p.m. to 5 p.m.
Monday	Closed

Admission is $3.00 for adults and $2.00 for children ages 3–17. Children under 3 and members of DSC are admitted free. Group rates and programs are available. Call DSC at 259-5572 for further information.

The Center's unique gift shop has a wide variety of books, posters, games, and much more. Don't forget to stop in and buy your favorite glow-in-the-dark critters and insect t-shirts.

3. News Release

Metro Life Church welcomes internationally known Christian leader, author, and speaker Terry Virgo. Terry will be our special guest in our weekly Worship Celebration both this Sunday and the following Sunday.

Terry leads the unusually large Clarendon Church in Brighton, England. In addition, he leads an apostolic team in close relationship with more than 70 churches in the United Kingdom and throughout the world in five other countries.

An acclaimed Bible teacher, Terry has ministered at major national and international conferences. He and his wife Wendy have also authored a number of books, including the popular *Restoration in the Church*.

Senior Pastor Danny Jones invites you to join us for the ministry of Terry Virgo. Children's ministry will be available for the ages 1–9. Services are at 9 and 11 a.m. each Sunday with Bible Study at 7 p.m. The Virgos will appear at all 3 services both Sundays.

4. Calling All Winners!

It's time to gear up for the competition, fun, and prizes at the 87th edition of the State Fair. Although the State Fair is not until June, now is the time to prepare for the state's most competitive event.

The theme of next June's Fair is "Carry on the Tradition" and there are plenty of contests to enter. Whether your interest is sewing, baking, tropical fish, photography, horticulture, fine arts, wood-carving, fashions, cheerleading, wine, or championship livestock, there's a place for you at the Fair. This is your opportunity to showcase your talents to nearly one million people. All entries will be judged by professionals in their field.

To enter most Family Living Events, you must be a resident of the state and entries must be received by the State Fair Authority by Friday, April 1. Wine entries must be submitted by April 15. Livestock deadlines are May 5.

5. Women and Depression

MERCY HOSPITAL is sponsoring a free presentation on Women and Depression. Participants will be taught to:

- identify the symptoms of depression
- explore the dynamics of depression
- learn treatment alternatives, including individual and group therapy
- define issues unique to women which impact on identification and treatment of depression

The seminar will be held in the hospital auditorium next Wednesday with registration beginning at 6:30 p.m. The presentation will be from 7–9 p.m. To make a reservation call **MERCY HOSPITAL** at 767-0152 or 1-800-221-4223.

Speakers: Marie Lozando, M.D.—Dr. Lozando is Clinical Director of **MERCY HOSPITAL'S** Women's Issues Program.
Deborah L. Carter, Ph.D.—Associate of the Lovell Psychiatric Association.
Phyllis Williams, A.R.N.P., M.S.W.—Associate of Lovell Psychiatric Association

6. *"Inventing Your Life" Seminar*

On Friday evening of next week, the county's Mental Health Association and the Center for Women's Medicine will present a two-hour seminar designed to provide simple, practical techniques to help women achieve greater success and happiness in every area of their life. Through a combination of lecture and audience participation, participants will be given the tools to "Invent Your Life" the way they want it to be. The featured seminar leader will be Joyce Reynolds from the Swan Center for Intuitive Living in Atlanta, Georgia. Ms. Reynolds states, "When you know how to create what you want, you can be more productive and motivated, and have an excitement for life. You can make your life what you want it to be." The seminar will also include a discussion of how physical health is directly affected by the level of stress in life. Scheduled to begin at 7 PM, the workshop will be held in the Great Hall of the Cathedral of St. Luke's, 130 Dakota Avenue. Pre-registration is encouraged. "Early Bird" registration fees for the seminar are $10 per person for M.H.A. members and $12 for non-members. Registration at the door will be $15 for everyone. Refreshments will be provided. For more information or to register by telephone, please call the Mental Health Association at 843-1563.

Exercise 5

NEWS RELEASES

INSTRUCTIONS: The following are actual news releases that have been mailed to newspapers. Only the locations and the names of some individuals have been changed. Write a complete story for each news release. Or, your instructor may ask you to write only the leads.

The exercises contain numerous style, spelling and punctuation errors. Some are even inconsistent from one paragraph to the next.

news release news release

AMI Brookwood Community Hospital

Beat the Holiday Blues

Loneliness, depression, suicidal thoughts. These feelings do not belong in the festive Christmas season that's about to begin. Yet it is common knowledge among mental-health professionals that the months between Thanksgiving and New Year can bring not so happy times.

Feeling like you don't belong, marital or family problems, overspending and the high expectations that usually accompany the holidays can bring stress to any of us. Bad past experience during the holidays, such as the death of a loved one, also can make the season a sad one, psychologists say.

To help area residents better cope with the "holiday blues," Brookwood Community Hospital and Mental Health Services are sponsoring a free seminar on December 6.

The 1½-hour program will deal with ways to cope with stress, loneliness in the elderly, family and marital problems and how to spot depression or suicide tendencies in children. The seminar includes a 30-minute question-and-answer period.

Although there are no hard statistics about the so-called "holiday blues," the number of "suicide and mental-health admissions peak during December and June," said Jane Dudley, a spokesperson for the American Psychological Association in Washington, D.C. She said there's usually a 20 percent increase in the number of admissions to mental-health agencies during this period.

"The number of depressed people who call us threatening to commit suicide jumps substantially during the holidays," adds Kathy Joanakait, spokesperson for "We Care," a non-profit organization which serves our local community with a suicide crisis hotline.

The free seminar will be held on Saturday, December 6, at the Public Library on Central Boulevard. Speakers will include doctors, psychologists, family therapists and other counselors

For more information on the "Holiday Blues" seminar, or to register, please call Brookwood's Marketing Department at 295-5161, extension 40.

Crimeline Program Inc.

FOR IMMEDIATE RELEASE

This week's CRIMELINE case comes from the files of the County Sheriff's Office.

It was a relatively quiet night last October 18, while Sgt. David Aneja was riding in patrol. He normally worked in the Internal Affairs Section of the County Sheriff's Office, but he liked riding on the street periodically; so when he had the chance to fill in for a friend and fellow sergeant who was on medical leave, he readily volunteered.

Just a few minutes after midnight, Sgt. Aneji spotted a black Chevrolet Nova parked on a dead-end street north of Beville Road directly across from the Forest Lake subdivision.

The vehicle was jacked up in the rear, had wide tires and a Duval County tag. Both the lights and the engine were turned off.

Sgt. Aneji pulled his unmarked police car behind the Nova and got out. At the same time, a male in his mid 20's, 6' tall, 180 pds. got out of the other car. Even though Sgt. Aneja was in uniform, he wanted to make sure that there was no doubt that the man knew he was a police officer, so he reached back in his car to turn on the blue lights. When he stood back up, he heard a shot and felt a sharp pain in his left chest. The bullet struck the deputy's badge and, thankfully, his bulletproof vest. Sgt. Aneja fell to the ground behind his car door. The suspect fired five more rounds through the door, narrowly missing the deputy.

The gunman then jumped into his car and sped off, heading west on Beville Road, with Sgt. Aneja returning fire. Through the whole gun battle, not one word was spoken!

Who was this man, and why was he so bent on killing Sgt. Aneji? If you know, you could earn a reward of up to $1,000 by calling CRIMELINE at 423-TIPS. And, of course, you don't have to give your name. When only _you_ know, we keep it that way.

FRIENDS OF FATHER MARTIN

431 E. Central Boulevard, Suite 250

Your City

TO: ALL MEDIA

FROM: Friends of Father Martin/Jackie Lewis, President

RELEASE: Immediate

RE: FATHER MARTIN TO SPEAK AT CARR ON "ALCOHOLISM AND THE FAMILY"

Author and internationally acclaimed educator on alcoholism, Father Joseph Martin, will speak for one night only at the Carr Performing Arts Center next Monday and will address the problem of "Alcoholism and the Family" in a practical manner, offering guidelines for recovery from alcoholism.

Father Martin, who has lectured on alcoholism in all fifty states and several foreign countries, received national acclaim for his film, "Chalk Talk." The film, initially used by the armed services, has become a standard for use in government and private alcoholic rehabilitation centers throughout the United States. He received the first annual Marty Mann Award for Outstanding Achievement in Alcoholism Communications, presented by the "Alcoholism/The National Magazine" and his book, "No Laughing Matter" has just been released by Harper & Row, Publishers.

It has long been recognized that the alcoholic is not the only person affected by his disease. Drinking affects the family deeply, and reaches out to affect the alcoholic's relationships with his employer and fellow workers, friends and social habits. Alcoholism is quickly approaching being the number one concern in the nation, not only for the individual, but for the death and destruction caused as a result of the disease.

Friends of Father Martin in the area, realizing the need for information to combat the spread of alcoholism, organized this special appearance as a benefit for his rehabilitation center, Ashley, a non-profit, tax-exempt effort in Maryland, that will be utilized by alcoholics and their families from throughout the United States.

Tickets for the Father Martin appearance are available to the public at the Carr Performing Arts Center, and by calling 422-4896, for $5.00 each. Groups wishing to attend should call Friends of Father Martin in advance to arrange for blocks of tickets. Seating will not be reserved, so the public is urged to arrive early to hear this most important message on the subject of alcoholism.

-30-

NEWS RELEASE

BETTER BUSINESS BUREAU

For Immediate Release

As the film and modeling industries continue to make inroads in the area, more businesses preying on young hopefuls and their lack of industry knowledge are making their presence known. One look at the employment section of local newspapers confirms this.

Ads are glamorous and exciting; however, all too often many of the dreams are shattered by "promoters" and "con men" who hustle the naive with promises of fame and fortune.

The Better Business Bureau takes the position that no modeling or talent agency should advertise under "Help Wanted" unless they are hiring people to work for them. We urge consumers to be wary of any modeling or talent agency requiring a purchase or investment when responding to an advertisement for employment.

If you are considering employment in this area, you might contact employment managers who hire people in this field and possibly obtain their opinions on your chances of success as well as the requirements for employment.

A number of hopeful models have reported to the Better Business Bureau after responding to the "Help Wanted" ads in local newspapers, they learned that the firms were offering training on how to become a model or an actor and that there were no positions open. Other consumers have reported that in response to such ads some firms required them to pay for photographs to be put in a portfolio, which in turn would be sent to companies who may or may not be in the market to offer the consumer some kind of employment.

Therefore, we offer these guidelines to potential models and actors in dealing with such agencies:

1. Determine if the company actually has jobs available or if it's just a ploy to enroll you in a training course or to sell you photographs.

2. If the agency offers training, are they licensed by the State Board of Education? Ask to see a current license.

3. Determine whether the agency has an established reputation with reputable retailers, advertising agencies, and other persons and organizations who would be knowledgeable in this area.

4. Is the agency offering to serve as an agent? Real agents make their money on the amount of work they secure for their talent . . . not on the sheer number of models they represent.

5. Will the agent use the photographs from another agency or photographer? Be wary if they will only accept their own photographs or portfolio.

Facts for Consumers
from the Federal Trade Commission
BUREAU OF CONSUMER PROTECTION   •   OFFICE OF CONSUMER EDUCATION   •   WASHINGTON, D.C. 20580

Vacation Certificates

Immediate
Release

"Gift vacation for two. Have an exciting fun-filled holiday.
Deluxe room accommodations for two days and three
nights." Sometimes it's in Las Vegas. Or Reno. Or Miami.
Or it might be in some other vacation spot.

It sounds too good to be true. And it sometimes is. Las Vegas
law enforcement officials are warning consumers about
vacation certificate promoters who make these claims.

Phone and
Mail Sales

According to these officials, about 100 firms make these
offers either directly to consumers—through telephone
or mail solicitations—or to businesses who use these
vacation certificates as part of their own sales
promotions. Consumers don't always get what they
expected.

However, the files of Nevada Consumer Affairs
Commissioner David Cook are filled with complaints from
unhappy people who took the certificate promoter up on
the "free vacation" offer. Cook tells of people who traveled
to Las Vegas only to find out that—even though they had
"confirmed" reservations—the hotel staff had never
heard of them.

Deposits
Made in
Advance

Vacation certificates usually cost from $15 to $25. If you
buy one—or a local merchant gives you one it bought—
you would typically be entitled to a three-day, two-night
vacation to Las Vegas or Reno or Miami. According to the
conditions on the certificate, you would have to contact
the promoter—not the hotel—to make your reservation
and would probably have to make a deposit to "hold" it.
You might even have to make another deposit when you
confirm the reservation.

In some cases, the promoter has a good relationship with
the hotel, and the hotel agrees to set aside a block of
rooms so the certificates can be redeemed.

However, in some cases vacation certificate promoters get rooms from the hotel **only if the hotel is not already booked up**. If it is already booked up, consumers who want to redeem their certificates may not get their first choice of hotel. They may find promised "first class accommodations" aren't all that classy or that their "vacation site" may be some distance from the main attractions of the resort community.

In fact, as Commissioner Cook indicates, some promoters sell vacation certificates without reserving **any** rooms. They issue counterfeit certificates that are not honored by the hotel, restaurant, or casino indicated. These promoters rake in the money, go out of business overnight, and leave you holding the casino chips.

Some companies, more sophisticated in their sales techniques, simply make it virtually impossible for you to **use** your certificates. They do this by repeatedly refusing your requests for a specific vacation date. You may never get a confirmed reservation. They figure that after a while you'll just give up.

If you do get a date and take the vacation (one promoter said they figure fewer than 2% of the recipients actually do), you might have some unpleasant surprises. You will usually have to pay travel costs and the cost of your meals. Also, your "bonus coupons" for free meals, drinks, discount gambling, show tickets, or golf may not be a bargain at all. For example, an offer of free meals may be limited to the hours of 2 a.m.-5 a.m., and the free tickets for gambling might be available only from certain casinos at odd hours. Very often you'll have to spend your own money first; then the promoter will match it with an equal sum.

The Better Business Bureau of Southern Nevada released a typical standard vacation certificate coupon package showing that you would have to spend as much as $50 of your own money to get a $13.50 value in coupons.

Some vacation certificate offers are completely above board and plainly disclose any limitations they may have. But before you fly off to your free vacation, invest some time checking the reputation of the company. If you can't get straight answers to the questions you ask, don't go.

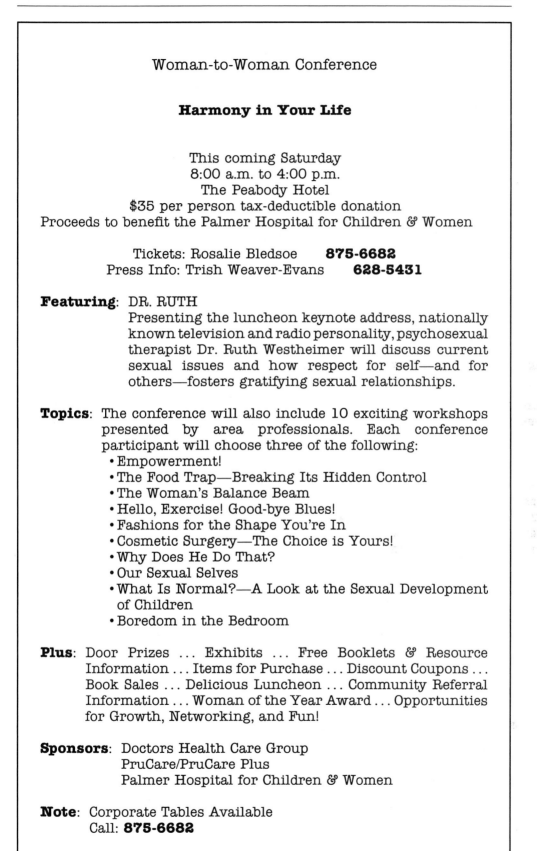

Woman-to-Woman Conference

Harmony in Your Life

This coming Saturday
8:00 a.m. to 4:00 p.m.
The Peabody Hotel
$35 per person tax-deductible donation
Proceeds to benefit the Palmer Hospital for Children & Women

Tickets: Rosalie Bledsoe   **875-6682**
Press Info: Trish Weaver-Evans   **628-5431**

Featuring: DR. RUTH
Presenting the luncheon keynote address, nationally known television and radio personality, psychosexual therapist Dr. Ruth Westheimer will discuss current sexual issues and how respect for self—and for others—fosters gratifying sexual relationships.

Topics: The conference will also include 10 exciting workshops presented by area professionals. Each conference participant will choose three of the following:
• Empowerment!
• The Food Trap—Breaking Its Hidden Control
• The Woman's Balance Beam
• Hello, Exercise! Good-bye Blues!
• Fashions for the Shape You're In
• Cosmetic Surgery—The Choice is Yours!
• Why Does He Do That?
• Our Sexual Selves
• What Is Normal?—A Look at the Sexual Development of Children
• Boredom in the Bedroom

Plus: Door Prizes ... Exhibits ... Free Booklets & Resource Information ... Items for Purchase ... Discount Coupons ... Book Sales ... Delicious Luncheon ... Community Referral Information ... Woman of the Year Award ... Opportunities for Growth, Networking, and Fun!

Sponsors: Doctors Health Care Group
PruCare/PruCare Plus
Palmer Hospital for Children & Women

Note: Corporate Tables Available
Call: **875-6682**

FROM: Madison Pancake Festival   News Release
        P.O. Box 5029
        Madison

MADISON PANCAKE FESTIVAL

MADISON'S Seventeenth Annual Pancake Festival takes place this Saturday and Sunday.

The Festival has always been non-profit, sponsored by the Betterment Association of the Madison Area, Inc. and for the past three years, has been co-sponsored with the Madison Area Jaycees.

Civic organizations, churches, school children, City Hall employees, inmates from the Copeland Road Prison, local businesses and residents from surrounding areas all work together to stage a smooth-running two-day event that over the past 16 years has drawn almost a million people to this small town of 3,200.

From last year's proceeds, money was donated to the city of Madison to be used for park improvements. Monies also were donated to the Madison Volunteer Fire Department and the Gateway Ambulance Service. Also a portion of the proceeds were set aside for scholarships for local high school students.

The volunteers' successful efforts to stage the Festival show what communities can do on their own—with ingenuity, determination, and effort. *Nobody gets paid. All work is volunteer.* Chief lure of the Festival is the picturesque and historic town itself.

The menu consists of pancakes with your choice of delectable toppings such as nuts, berries (blueberries, raspberries or strawberries), jams, syrups, bananas, and much, much more. These Pancake Plates will be served both days, from 7 AM to 9 PM on Saturday and Sunday. A Pancake Plate will cost $12 for adults and $6 for children 12 and under. That one low price includes the cost of admission to the festival and free refills for an entire day.

Visitors will also be able to purchase tickets for a drawing on a 16-foot boat, a trailer, and a 45 HP outboard motor sponsored by the Madison Volunteer Fire Dept.

There will be over 100 booths to display a large selection of the finest arts and crafts. Booths manned by local clubs and residents will also offer other special foods.

Country music is played continuously both days. The Festival will feature Country and Western artist "Lionel Cartwright" on Sunday at 1:00 and 3:00 PM. Also featured will be clogging, kiddie and carnival rides, hot dogs, ice cream, popcorn, pies, soft drinks, coffee, iced tea and cold beer served in Festival mugs that the purchaser gets to keep as souvenirs of his visit to our event.

Madison has campgrounds and motels for guests who would like to spend the weekend. There are many other attractions in Madison and the surrounding areas: swimming, fishing, camping, hiking, horseback rides, boat tours, glider and plane rides, an observation tower to climb and shopping at the town's many fine antique stores. In addition, there will also be a gigantic flea market with bargains galore. Visitors are welcome to set up a table of their own. The registration fee for the flea market is $10 per table.

For those planning to come by plane, the City has an airport with a 2400-foot runway. There is no charge for landing your plane. Volunteers handle plane parking. There is also an area close to the Festival at which arrivals in RVs may park for overnight stays for a modest fee.

CHAPTER 17

SPEECHES AND MEETINGS

Many newspaper stories summarize the content of speeches and the actions taken at meetings. Even in small towns, there are likely to be dozens of speeches and meetings every week. In large cities, there may be hundreds. Some speeches and meetings involve government agencies. Others are sponsored by clubs, schools, churches, and business and professional organizations. Journalists attend only the most newsworthy: the speeches and meetings likely to affect or involve large numbers of people.

Newspapers normally publish at least two stories about major speeches and meetings: an "advance" story before the speeches and meetings take place and a "follow" story afterward. Advance stories notify readers about future events, often helping them to prepare for events that they may want to attend, support or oppose. Most advance stories are published the day speeches and meetings are announced, or shortly thereafter. As a reminder to their readers, newspapers may publish a second advance story a day or two before the speeches and meetings are scheduled to take place.

Newspapers may publish a dozen advance stories about events of unusual importance. If, for example, the president of the United States announced plans to visit your city, your local newspapers would immediately report those plans. As more information became available, newspapers would publish additional advance stories about the president's schedule, companions and goals. Other stories might describe the security measures, presidential plane and limousine, visits by previous presidents and opportunities the public will have to see the president.

Most advance stories emphasize the same basic facts: what will happen, when and where it will happen, and who will be involved. Advance stories for speeches identify the speakers, report the times and places they will appear, and describe their topics. Advance stories for meetings identify the groups scheduled to meet, report the times and places of their meetings, and describe the topics on their agendas. In addition, advance stories may mention the events' purpose or sponsor: why the speeches and meetings are important. Advance stories are also likely to tell readers whether the public is invited, whether those who attend will be given an opportunity to participate, and whether there will be a charge for admission.

The leads for advance stories should be as specific and interesting as possible. Leads should emphasize the important and the unusual, not just the fact that someone has scheduled a speech or meeting. Often, leads mention celebrities who will be involved in the events, or the topics that will be discussed. For example:

> Singer and actress Barbra Streisand has agreed to perform in Washington, D.C., at a dinner expected to raise more than $5 million for the Cancer Society.

> Members of the American Civil Liberties Union will meet at 8 p.m. Friday at the YMCA to discuss charges that the Police Department refused to hire an applicant because he is a homosexual.

Advance stories are generally short, containing no more than two or three paragraphs. Typically, a complete advance story might report that:

> Sen. Charles Kulify, who has introduced a constitutional amendment that would force the federal government to balance its budget and repay the national debt, will discuss the amendment during a speech at 8 p.m. Saturday in the Municipal Auditorium.
>
> His appearance is being sponsored by the Republican Council of 1,000. The public is invited, and there will be no admission charge.
>
> Kulify, a Texan elected to the Senate four years ago, introduced the amendment earlier this month and says that it will curb wasteful federal spending and eliminate the problem of inflation.

To save space, some editors summarize an advance story in a single paragraph and combine a number of them in roundups or digests (often called "Community Calendars"). Typically, roundups list all the newsworthy events scheduled in the community during the coming week.

Follow stories are usually much longer than advance stories—and more difficult to write, because many follow stories involve a multitude of issues and participants. Seven members may attend a council meeting, hear a dozen witnesses, then vote on four issues. Many of the issues may be complex. Yet, to save space, reporters will summarize all the issues in a single story.

Inevitably, follow stories will repeat some of the facts reported in advance stories because some basic facts, such as the identity of a speaker, must be reported in both.

Reporters assigned to cover a speech or meeting usually try beforehand to learn as much as possible about its participants and issues. As a first step, reporters may go to their newspaper's library and read previous stories written about the topic. Reporters can obtain agendas prior to many meetings and may, if they are lucky, obtain advance copies of some speeches. Then, instead of having to take notes, they can simply follow the printed texts, checking to be certain that the speakers do not depart from their prepared remarks.

To attract more publicity, groups often schedule press conferences immediately before or after the speeches they sponsor so that reporters will have an opportunity to obtain additional information. If that is not done, reporters may arrange to see speakers for a few minutes immediately after their appearances.

Reporters who cover a meeting should learn all the participants' names beforehand so they will always know the identity of the person who is speaking. So that they understand everything that is said, reporters should also learn as much as possible about every item on the agenda. In case any unexpected or confusing issues arise, reporters may arrange to see the leading participants after a meeting adjourns.

While writing speech and meeting stories, you will have to apply many of the lessons learned in earlier chapters. You can and should use some color in your stories: quotations and descriptions. Because follow stories are likely to be complex, you will also have to be creative in organizing your stories.

To help you with the special concerns of speech and meeting stories, the following pages briefly review guidelines discussed in earlier chapters. While reviewing those guidelines, the following pages apply them specifically to speech and meeting stories.

WRITING EFFECTIVE LEADS

The leads for follow stories must do more than simply repeat the information reported in advance stories. The leads for follow stories should summarize a speaker's comments about a topic or a group's actions at a meeting:

ADVANCE STORY LEAD (SPEECH): Former President Jimmy Carter will speak in the Municipal Auditorium at 8 p.m. Friday about housing for the poor.

FOLLOW STORY LEAD (SPEECH): Every American has a right to a decent home, and the federal government should do more to help people obtain one, former President Jimmy Carter said here Friday night.

ADVANCE STORY LEAD (MEETING): The Student Senate will meet at 4 p.m. Thursday to discuss the university's decision to dismiss history professor Albert Calley.

FOLLOW STORY LEAD (MEETING): After learning the reasons for his dismissal, the Student Senate voted 27 to 2 Thursday not to support Albert Calley, a history professor whose contract for next year has not been renewed by the university.

Mistakenly, students often begin their follow stories for a speech by reporting that a speaker "discussed" or "voiced an opinion" about a topic. Mistakenly, others may begin their follow stories for a meeting by reporting that a group "considered" or "dealt with" a topic. Be more specific. If you write about a speech, summarize the speaker's comments. If you write about a meeting, summarize its outcome.

FOLLOW STORY LEAD (SPEECH): The president of the Chamber of Commerce discussed the dangers of higher taxes in a speech Tuesday night.

REVISED: If the city continues to raise its property taxes, major businesses will begin moving elsewhere, throwing thousands of people out of work, the president of the Chamber of Commerce warned Tuesday night.

FOLLOW STORY LEAD (MEETING): At its meeting Tuesday, the City Commission discussed the need for a traffic light at the intersection of Maple Boulevard and Jay Road.

REVISED: The City Commission decided Tuesday to spend $52,000 for the installation of a traffic light at the intersection of Maple Boulevard and Jay Road. Twenty-one accidents and two deaths occurred there last year.

STORY ORGANIZATION

Reporters use the inverted pyramid style to write most follow stories. Consequently, the stories present information in the order of its importance—not the order in which it arose during a speech or meeting. Reporters can move statements around and may begin their stories with a statement made at the end of a one-hour speech, then shift to a topic discussed midway through the speech. If topics discussed during the first half-hour of a speech are unimportant, reporters may never mention them at all.

Problems of Organizing Speech or Meeting Topics

If a speech or meeting involves several important topics, briefly summarize all the topics in your story's opening paragraphs. Then report each of the topics in detail, starting with the most important. If you fail to do so, your story may mislead your readers. If your story's opening paragraphs mention only one topic, your readers may assume that the entire story concerns that topic. If the topic fails to interest readers, they may immediately turn to another story.

Here are three solutions to the problem of organizing a speech or meeting story:

SOLUTION 1: If a speech or meeting involves several major topics, select the single most important topic and summarize it in your lead. Or, summarize the two most important topics in your lead. Briefly summarize your story's remaining topics (rarely more than two or three) in your second paragraph. Then discuss the topics in the order of their importance. For example:

> The County Commission voted Monday to fine motorists $50 a day if they leave unoccupied vehicles marked "For Sale" parked along county roads.
> The Commission also passed ordinances regulating billboards, skateboards and the cable television industry.

> The School Board has adopted a $14 million program designed to reduce the high school dropout rate from 24 percent to 10 percent.
> In other action Thursday night, the board voted to build an elementary school on Hattz Drive and to require every new teacher to pass a series of competency tests.

SOLUTION 2: If a speech or meeting involves several major topics, select the most important and summarize it in your lead. Provide a brief transition. Then, using numbers, bullets or some other typographical device, briefly summarize the speech's or meeting's other major topics. Remember that, if the first element in a list is a complete sentence, the following elements must also be complete sentences. Similarly, if the first element is an incomplete sentence, the following elements must also be incomplete sentences.

Normally, reporters will later return to each of the topics, discussing it in more detail. Here are two examples:

> Despite angry protests, the City Council voted to impose a 10 percent tax on every utility bill issued to residents of the city.
> In other action Monday night, the Council:
> ONE: For the convenience of people who need to do business there, decided to open the City Hall a half-hour earlier (at 7:30 a.m.) and to keep it open a half-hour later (until 5:30 p.m.) every weekday.
> TWO: Instructed city planners to determine the cost of requiring utility companies to lay all their new telephone and electric lines underground.
> THREE: Debated a resolution that would require every new employee of the city to be tested for drugs, alcohol and AIDS.

> Carlos Diaz, a Democratic candidate for governor, promised last night "to cut the state's taxes by at least 20 percent."
> Diaz said the state can save billions of dollars a year by:
> • Eliminating at least 10 percent of the state's employees.
> • Hiring private companies to build and operate the state's prisons.
> • Establishing a "workfare" system that will require every able-bodied adult on the state's welfare rolls to either work or go to school.
> • Reforming the state's school system by abolishing tenure and reducing the number of administrators.

SOLUTION 3: If a speech or meeting involves one major topic and several minor topics, begin with the major topic and, after thoroughly discussing it, use the bullet technique to briefly summarize the minor topics in your story's final paragraphs:

In response to questions asked after her speech, LeClarren said:
- Most colleges are still dominated by men. Their presidents, deans, department chairs—and most of their faculty members, too—are men.
- A subtle, often unintentional, discrimination steers women away from fields traditionally dominated by men: from mathematics, business and engineering, for example.
- When two college students marry, the husband rarely drops out to support his wife. Rather, the wife drops out to support her husband.
- Some parents discriminate against their college-age children by giving more help and encouragement to their sons than to their daughters.

In other action, the Commission:
- Proclaimed Feb. 17 to 24 "Future Farmers of America Week."
- Voted to pay $62,400 for an engineering study to determine whether Keller Road needs to be widened from two to four lanes.
- Voted to give the Public Library an emergency allocation of $118,000 to repair its leaky roof.
- Approved the installation of a street light at the corner of Clark Drive and State Road 426.

Never, in a story's final paragraph, simply report that a speaker or group "discussed" or "considered" another topic. If a topic is important enough to mention, give your readers some meaningful information about it. As specifically as possible, summarize the group's discussion or action:

Before adjourning, the council members also discussed two other problems: next year's budget and problems involving the Water Department.
REVISED: Before adjourning, the council members agreed to begin work on the city's budget for next year and asked city auditors to investigate allegations that the Water Department cannot account for almost $40,000.

Finally, Commissioner Cycler expressed concern about the Senior Citizens Center on Eisenhower Drive.
REVISED: Finally, Commissioner Cycler said several people have called her and complained that the staff at the Senior Citizens Center on Eisenhower Drive is arrogant and unhelpful.

Problems of Sequence and Attribution

Two other problems often arise in speech and meeting stories. First, some beginners report events in the order in which they occurred, as if the sequence of the events was somehow important to readers. Second, beginners tend to start every paragraph with the attribution: with the speaker's name. As a result, their stories become dull and repetitious. When you finish a story, look at your paragraphs. If you see either of these patterns, your paragraphs need rewriting:

City Manager Faith An-Pong began by discussing the problems that recycling is creating for the city.
Next, An-Pong said . . . .
Turning to a third topic, An-Pong said . . . .
She then went on to add that . . . .
Continuing, An-Pong said . . . .
In conclusion, she added . . . .

Weider-Abbot said . . . .
Weider-Abbot added that . . . .
Weider-Abbot also stated that . . . .
She said . . . .
Weider-Abbot warned, however, that . . . .
Weider-Abbot concluded that . . . .

Transitions

When you shift from one idea to another, provide a transition. A good transition will show readers the relationship between two ideas. It will also arouse readers' interest in the topic you are introducing.

Remember that your transitions should be brief. They may ask a question; shift to a new time or place; or repeat a key word, phrase or idea. If the change in topic is more abrupt, provide a transitionary sentence. Do not, however, simply report that a speaker or group "turned to another topic." Instead, treat the transition as a secondary lead. Briefly summarize the topic you are introducing, giving its most specific, interesting and important details:

> The board also considered two other topics.
> REVISED: The board also considered—and rejected—proposals to increase students' health and athletic fees.

> Hunt then discussed the problem of auto insurance.
> REVISED: Hunt then warned that the cost of auto insurance rose 9.6 percent last year and is expected to rise 12 percent this year.

> Commissioner Hatfield expressed concern about a related issue.
> REVISED: Commissioner Hatfield warned that the city also needs more money to maintain its parks.

REMEMBER YOUR READERS

Everything you write should be so clear that your readers will be able to understand it at a glance—and so interesting that they will want to read every word. In addition, try to show how your stories will affect your readers, their neighborhood, city or state.

One story about a city council meeting began by reporting that three employees received awards for working for the city for 25 years. That type of award is common and, although important to the recipients, is unimportant to almost everyone else. The story's later paragraphs discussed a topic more likely to interest readers: plans to help people with low incomes buy their own homes.

Here are other examples of leads that fail to emphasize the information most likely to interest or affect readers. Mistakenly, the leads emphasize routine, abstract or bureaucratic procedures:

> The City Council has approved issuing $12 million in bonds for improvements at the Regional Airport.
> REVISED: The City Council will spend $12 million to expand the Regional Airport's parking lots and to construct an observation tower and restaurant for visitors.

City commissioners unanimously approved the zoning for West Town Center, an 820-acre planned unit development to be located on Chapman Road.

REVISED: The City Council unanimously approved the zoning for West Town Center, an 820-acre development that will include an 18-hole golf course, a major shopping center and 3,100 new homes and apartments.

The County Commission will spend $64,800 for a preliminary engineering study involving Hillcrest and Kerner avenues and County Road 432.

REVISED: Would you like the county's busiest roads widened from two to four lanes?

The County Commission voted Tuesday to spend $64,800 for a study on the need to widen Hillcrest and Kerner avenues and County Road 432.

Be Specific

So that your readers can understand every word you write, be as specific as possible. The following sentences appeared in stories about meetings and, until they were revised, failed to convey any meaningful information to readers:

VAGUE: Commissioner Peters then addressed the developer.

MORE SPECIFIC: Commissioner Peters told the developer that he will have to pay for every streetlight in the subdivision.

VAGUE: Lydia Willard, an attorney representing the property owners, provided the commissioners with a packet of documents to convince them to approve the plan.

MORE SPECIFIC: Lydia Willard, an attorney representing the property owners, gave the commissioners maps of the subdivision and a petition signed by more than 100 residents who favor the plan.

VAGUE: A fire last month destroyed more than 80 percent of the restaurant. If it is rebuilt, it will have to abide by certain rules.

MORE SPECIFIC: A fire last month destroyed more than 80 percent of the restaurant. If the restaurant is rebuilt, its owner will have to follow new building codes that require a parking space for every customer.

Avoid Jargon

Avoid jargon, especially the bureaucratic language used at government meetings. The students attending one meeting reported on their county's plans to regulate "adult congregate living facilities." Only two of the students approached a county commissioner after the meeting and asked her to define the term. Those students were then able to use a term that their readers could understand: "nursing homes."

Another story reported that the county commissioners "passed the preliminary plat for the third section of the Deer Run subdivision." Do you understand that? If you don't, would your readers? Instead of reporting that type of jargon, get more specific details. In this case, the commissioners approved plans to build another 82 homes in the subdivision.

Unfortunately, even some leads contain that type of jargon, as in these examples:

The City Council will request proposals for the city's Organization and Operation Study at its meeting at 7:30 p.m. Monday.

The City Council unanimously approved a comprehensive plan and moratorium at its Thursday night meeting.

Neither of those leads says anything that the average reader is likely to understand or care about.

ADDING COLOR

Report What You Hear

Use some direct quotations to provide emphasis and a change of pace and to reveal more about your sources' personalities and manner of speaking.

Before the fall of communism in the Soviet Union, a school board considered an exchange program that would allow 32 high school students to spend a semester studying and traveling in Russia. Two men objected to the program, complaining that the students would be exposed to Soviet propaganda. By using direct quotations, a student allowed the participants in the debate to speak for themselves:

> "This is a sneak attempt at changing the students' values," said LeRoy DeBecker of the John Birch Society. "The students will never be shown any of the negative aspects of communism, only propaganda promoting the system."
>
> Erik Lieber, chair of the Pro-Family Forum, agreed that the program should be rejected. "Russia wants only one form of peace," Lieber said. "It wants to completely dominate the world, and this trip will help it."
>
> Catrina Weinstein, a teacher at Colonial High School, disagreed. Weinstein said that she has led students from other high schools on similar trips, and that the trips made the students more patriotic, not pawns of the Communists.
>
> "When the students got home they realized how fortunate they were, so they were more motivated to study our political system," Weinstein said. "All these other comments you've heard are nonsense. These trips introduce students to the Soviet people, not Soviet ideology. The closest we ever came to propaganda was a guide's speaking with pride of his country's accomplishments."
>
> The board voted 6 to 1 to establish the program, and board member Anna Nemechek explained: "If we're going to be afraid every time our children cross a border, than perhaps we should lock them up in cages and make sure they're well fed."

Describe What You See

Describe the speeches and meetings you attend: their participants, audience and setting. The description can appear anywhere, even in your leads:

> Nearly 100 irate parents stormed into Tuesday's School Board meeting, demanding that the board abandon its plans to stop teaching art and music.

> Dozens of people in the audience cheered Tuesday night when the County Commission rejected plans to rezone a golf course and permit the construction of a 720-unit apartment complex on the site.

> A public hearing on an animal control ordinance drew a standing-room-only crowd to a County Commission meeting Thursday.

only crowd to a County Commission meeting Thursday.

"I have never seen an issue that's received such attention in years," chair Linda Chapin said. "Pet control is an issue that raises emotions akin to abortion and capital punishment."

Some of the spectators wore T-shirts inscribed with pictures of their pets, primarily cats and dogs.

Later paragraphs can also describe the speeches and meetings:

People poured in throughout the meeting, filling all the seats and standing along the walls.

About a dozen people stood in the back of the room, holding signs that said, "I'm behind our mayor" and "We support the mayor."

To make your stories even more interesting, use a combination of quotations and descriptions:

The spectators cheered and waved cardboard axes in boisterous support. "Ax the tax," they chanted. "Ax the tax."

Baker loudly objected to each vote in favor of the project.
"We're citizens," she yelled. "You should consider us."
After all the votes were cast, she threw her petition to the floor and stormed out of the room, shouting: "This is not a dictatorship! You should listen to us."

Spectators shook their heads in disagreement as Johnson said: "I've spent $400,000 in planning this development. I'm not trying to make a fast buck on it. I want to make the development a good place to live, and these people here don't have any reason to complain."
Commissioner Anne Chen interrupted Johnson, saying, "The public has a right to have their say."
Homeowner Ray Taub then walked to the podium. "That man isn't telling you the whole story," he said, pointing at Johnson. "The place is a mess. Besides that, he wants to put in more houses and put them on smaller lots. He's already started work on his plans even before you've approved them."
Amid bursts of applause and cries of approval, Chen recommended that the commission deny Johnson's application to build 42 homes on land originally set aside for a park.
Her motion passed by a vote of 7 to 0.

ISBN 0-15-500602-9

Exercise 1

SPEECHES AND MEETINGS

EVALUATING SPEECH AND MEETING LEADS

INSTRUCTIONS: Critically evaluate the following leads, giving each of them a grade from A to F. Then discuss the leads with your teacher and classmates.

1. The County Commission voted unanimously Tuesday against raising the county tourism tax one cent to pay for a new baseball stadium. (Grade: _____)

2. A spokesperson for Citizens Against Crime warned parents Wednesday night about violent crime and its impact on families in the city. (Grade: _____)

3. By a vote of 5 to 4, the City Council rejected Monday night a proposal to build an apartment complex near Reed Road and State Road 419. (Grade: _____)

4. A heated debate took place at the City Council meeting Thursday night over the need for police dogs. (Grade: _____)

5. Fifty percent of the drug abusers who enter treatment centers go back to using drugs within a year, Mimi Sota told an audience here Monday. (Grade: _____)

6. The Student Health Fee Committee voted unanimously Friday to increase fees by $6 in fall and spring semesters and $4 in the summer. (Grade: _____)

7. During a speech to the American Legion last night, former Marine Lieutenant Colonel Oliver North discussed his work in the Reagan White House. (Grade: _____)

8. County commissioners heard testimony from more than 20 people Tuesday morning on plans to license and regulate snowmobiles. (Grade: _____)

9. The County Commission reviewed a resolution Wednesday to create a committee that will identify conservation and recreation lands within the county. (Grade: _____)

10. Blasting opponents of the plan, Mayor Sabrina Datoli last night defended a proposal to establish a police review board. (Grade: _____)

11. Traveling by airplane has never been more dangerous, Roman Madea charged in a fiery speech Sunday night. (Grade: _____)

12. The City Council voted unanimously Monday to change the zoning along three streets from residential to commercial. (Grade: _____)

13. The business before the School Board flowed smoothly Tuesday night as the board proceeded through their agenda. (Grade: _____)

14. The County Commission continued to struggle with the issue of protecting the water quality in Butler Lake at their meeting Monday. The commissioners eventually denied a petition to build a new boat ramp on the lake. (Grade: _____)

15. The County Commission unanimously passed an ordinance that makes it illegal for anyone to possess an open container of alcohol in a vehicle. A previous law made it illegal to drive while drunk, but legal to drink while driving. (Grade: _____)

Exercise 2

SPEECHES AND MEETINGS

SPEECHES

INSTRUCTIONS: Write separate advance and follow stories about each of the following speeches. Because these are verbatim accounts, you can use direct quotations.

1. Firefighter Concerns

INFORMATION FOR ADVANCE STORY

Tony Sullivan is scheduled to speak to the Downtown Rotary Club Monday of next week. The club meets every Monday noon at the Blackhawk Hotel. Lunch is served and costs $6.50 per person. The public is invited to the lunch, which begins promptly at noon, or the public may come for just the speech, which will begin promptly at 1 p.m. Tony Sullivan is your city's fire chief, and he will speak to the club members about the major concerns of today's firefighters.

SPEECH FOR FOLLOW STORY

Some of you don't know me. My name is Tony Sullivan. When I was 22 years old and had just been discharged from the Army, I didn't know what I wanted to do with the rest of my life. Two of my best friends wanted to join the Fire Department, and they talked me into taking all the physical and written tests along with them. I passed, but they didn't, and I've been associated with the Fire Department for the past 28 years. For the past 6 years, I've been chief.

The Fire Department is much different today than it was when I joined 28 years ago, and we've got much different problems today. I've been asked to talk to you about those problems. Our biggest problems, as you might expect, are low pay and long hours. But we're also concerned about the problems of arson and outdated gear. Now I'd like to talk to you about each of those problems, and in much more detail. As local business people, all of you are affected by the problems, and I hope that you'll be able to help us solve them.

First, the problem of arson. It's gotten completely out of hand. Property owners in this state alone lost at least $500 million in damaged and destroyed property due to arson last year. We'd estimate, conservatively, that right here in this city 10 to 20 percent of our fires are arson. It's hard to control because the conviction rate for arson is low. And that's because fires oftentimes destroy the evidence. You, as business people, lose money because arson causes higher insurance premiums for everyone. It also causes lower profits, lost wages to workers and lost tax revenue to the city.

Another big problem we face involves the gear we use in fighting fires. A good truck these days costs $200,000. If we want a good ladder truck, one that can reach some of the taller downtown buildings, it may cost twice that much. The city can't afford many, but if we don't have the trucks, then we can't rescue people trapped on the upper floors of those buildings.

Even the protective gear worn by our firefighters is getting terribly expensive. Until recently, all our protective clothing has been made of a highly flammable cotton coated with neoprene, usually black. Black is bad because it absorbs heat and because firefighters can't be seen if they fall and get into trouble inside a dark building or a building filled with smoke. Then take a look at our helmets; they're far from being the state of the art. They melt in temperatures above 700. In your average fire, the floor temperature is 200 and the ceiling is 1,800. The state-of-the-art helmets can resist heat up to 2,000 degrees, but they cost three times what we're paying now.

One reason why the injury and death rate among firefighters is so high—more firefighters die annually than police—is because our gear is so expensive, and cities won't buy it. They seem to think it's easier to replace firefighters than to outlay the money for better gear.

The heavy physical labor and working conditions also contribute to the high injury rate. When you send people into a fire, and you've got intense heat, broken glass, the danger of whole walls and floors collapsing, and the danger of explosions from unknown chemicals stored in these buildings, it's almost inevitable that you're going to have some injuries and possibly even some deaths. With the proper equipment, we could reduce the number and severity of injuries, but there's no way to completely eliminate them. Danger's a part of our job. We accept that.

Despite the fact we have a higher death rate than the police, firefighters start out earning $1,000 to $2,000 a year less than they do, and we object to that. It's not fair. When we ask the City Council why, they say because it's always been that way and it would cost too much to pay firefighters as much as the police. We don't think that's right, especially when you consider that the police work only 40 hours a week. Firefighters work 24-hour shifts and an average of 56 hours a week. So they work longer hours for less money.

The next time you hear anyone talking about these problems, and the next time you see us going to the City Council, requesting a larger budget, we'd appreciate your support. With your support, we'll be able to offer you, and everyone else in the city, better fire protection. It's already good, but with your help we can make it even better, and that benefits everyone.

2. Abortion Critic

INFORMATION FOR ADVANCE STORY

John F. Palladino is an outspoken critic of abortion. He is scheduled to speak at a prayer breakfast next Sunday at the First Baptist Church, 412 North Eastland Ave. in your city. His topic will be, "Abortion: Our Greatest Sin." The public is invited free of charge for both the breakfast and speech. The prayer breakfast will be held in the church's social hall, starting at 7:30 a.m. Palladino is a Republican and unsuccessful candidate for governor in the last election in your state. He was defeated in the Republican primary. Previously, he served three terms in your State Senate. Currently, he lives in the state capital and operates his own real estate firm there. He is chairman of your state's Right to Life Committee, which opposes abortion.

SPEECH FOR FOLLOW STORY

I appreciate your invitation to speak to you today. I also appreciate the help that many of you have given our Right to Life Committee. I recognize that some of you have given us very generous financial donations, and that others of you have helped man our telephone lines and distribute our literature.

I'd like to begin this morning by telling you something of my personal views. Personally, I cannot understand how a woman can achieve sexual liberation by taking the life of her unborn child. I believe that abortion basically is a very selfish, self-centered remedy to those that think the birth of a child is an inconvenience. I think it is an inconvenience for only nine months. After that, there are 3- or 4-year waits to adopt children. I know of many families who go down to El Salvador to adopt children.

I have other friends who adopted little babies from Korea and from many other countries of the world. So no child is unwanted; there's a loving home in this country for every child.

Now some people ask, "What about cases where the mother's life is threatened, or where the mother is impregnated through rape or incest?" My main concern is with the 99 percent of the abortions that do not deal with that, but merely with inconvenience. When the mother's life is in question, and it's a true case of the life of a mother vs. the life of an unborn child, certainly the life of the mother should take precedence— the reason being that there is a good possibility that the mother is already a mother of other children. To say that we're going to deprive these already-born children of their mother to protect the life of an unborn child is improper.

But I find it difficult from a personal standpoint to say that I would agree to abortion in the case of rape or incest because, again, it's an innocent child no matter whether it's the product of a legitimate or illegitimate sexual union. So if I had the authority to stop all abortions, except those that involve the endangerment of the mother's life, then certainly I would agree to that.

Now, in talking about this issue, you have to remember one critical point. Life begins upon fertilization of the egg. If you don't agree with that, certainly at least you have the potential for life at that point, and therefore it should be jealously guarded as life itself.

The federal and state laws that permit abortion are wrong, absolutely and totally wrong. Abortions are a crime and a sin. When governments adopt these laws, they're saying that life doesn't exist, or that some forms of life aren't as important as others and don't deserve the same protection as others. So even from a political view, abortion is wrong because it allows governments to judge the value of life—to say that there's a point or condition under which some lives can be ended. I think that's a very dangerous position for government to be in. And you have to ask where it'll stop. What other lives will governments decide we can end? Next it could be the sick, the elderly, the insane, or the criminals from all our jails. That's not the kind of decision government should be making. All life is precious. All life should be protected by the government—and by us, as individuals.

Thank you.

3. City Parks

INFORMATION FOR ADVANCE STORY

The city's University Club meets at 8 p.m. every Monday night at its own building located at 428 Michigan Ave. During its regular meeting next Monday, the guest speaker will be Emil Plambeck. Plambeck is superintendent of the City Park Commission. He has said that he will talk about the city's park system. All members of the club are urged to attend the meeting, which is sure to be interesting and informative. The public is also welcome. Admission is free to all club members and their families and is $1 for all other people.

SPEECH FOR FOLLOW STORY

I'm pleased to be here this evening and intend to discuss a topic of concern to all of us—the city's park system. All of you, as business people, know the value of an attractive community. It promotes growth and helps attract both new residents and new industry. An attractive community with a good park system also improves the quality of life for those of us already living here.

Members of this community long have boasted of one of the finest park systems in the United States. But now, because of financial problems, we are beginning to fall behind. We simply are not getting enough money to expand our park system to meet the needs of a growing community or even enough money to maintain our old system properly. As a result, the parks are becoming overcrowded and all the people utilizing them every weekend are endangering the vegetation and wildlife we've worked so hard to preserve.

We used to feel that we were among the top-ranking communities in the United States, but now there definitely are several other cities that have gone ahead of us, even within this very state. We still look pretty good on paper, but some of the statistics are misleading. Neighborhood parks in the new suburbs are lagging badly behind our needs. We do have several excellent parks, with a lot of acreage, but they're concentrated in the older sections of the city.

City planners recommend that we provide one acre of playground for each 100 people living in the city. We now have 1.3 acres—30 percent more than the minimum requirement. But that lead is slipping. Just five years ago we had 1.45 acres per 100 residents. And you have to keep in mind the fact that 1 acre for every 100 people is a minimum—not an ideal. An ideal ratio would be 1.5 acres for every 100 people, and we're falling farther and farther away from that goal.

We need some laws to force developers to provide property in new subdivisions for schools and playgrounds. My office is working on a new code to help the city obtain land for parks in each new suburb constructed around the city. I haven't revealed that fact before, but we expect to submit the proposal to the City Council within a few days. If the council accepts it, the developers will be required to set aside 3.5 percent of their land for miniparks. That way we'll be able to have wooded areas in every neighborhood, maybe with baseball diamonds or a few tennis courts.

The city hasn't been totally inactive in this area since I took office five years ago. We have acquired three parks. One of them—near Ridgeview School—has two ball fields and a large picnic area. The other new areas include Petersen Park, on West Dover Court and Hillandale Road, and Riverview Park. In the case of the Ridgeview and Petersen Parks, the land was purchased by the park board with funds provided by the City Council. The city inherited the land for Riverview Park. Altogether, the city now has 27 parks and playgrounds, which include 1,168 acres valued at more than $25 million. But I'd like to see the city develop at least a half-dozen more parks, all in the newer subdivisions.

Exercise 3

SPEECHES AND MEETINGS

FIRE MARSHAL'S SPEECH: THE NEED FOR CPR TRAINING

INSTRUCTIONS: Assume that Steven Chen, the training officer for your city's fire department, gave this speech to the Rotary Club at a breakfast meeting in your city today. Write a story that summarizes his comments. Because this is a verbatim copy of his comments, you can use direct quotes.

I've been asked to talk to you this morning about CPR: cardiopulmonary resuscitation. What we'd like to happen is for everyone to learn CPR themselves instead of counting on paramedics to revive someone in an emergency. A few weeks ago, we had a man drown in a hotel pool just a few blocks from here. He was pulled from the water by a woman sitting by the pool, but he died because no one knew CPR. When paramedics arrived, it was too late. The situation is a typical one, repeated somewhere almost every day. You can't fault the paramedics. They respond as quickly as possible.

Rarely can we save a victim that has not had CPR done to them before we arrive. Depending on the location, it takes our rescue squad from 1 to 10 minutes to respond to a call. The American Heart Association recommends that CPR be done in no more than 4 to 6 minutes to keep the person alive. After 10 minutes, we don't even try to start CPR. After 10 minutes, the brain damage is too severe for the person to lead a normal life if he were resuscitated.

There are exceptions to the 10-minute rule. Last winter, you may have read, a small boy was successfully resuscitated after 45 minutes. But he had been submerged in icy water. That rescue was possible because the cold temperature slowed down the boy's body responses enough so that no brain damage was done. If it's summer and hot and humid, the heat and humidity quicken the body's responses and make it impossible to survive without brain damage.

Most of our calls where we have to use CPR are near drownings. The more swimming pools people build in their backyards, the more calls we get. Statistics show that people have a better chance of drowning in their own backyard pool than in public swimming areas. The statistics show the safest place to swim is a patrolled beach, since all the lifeguards there are required to know CPR. Also, help gets to them quicker, and the lifeguards prevent trouble—horseplay and roughhousing—that could lead to serious accidents.

I would like to see us follow the footsteps of Seattle, where 1 out of every 3 people knows CPR, the highest rate in the country. Here, classes are offered by various schools and medical organizations, and at least once a year at each of the city's fire stations. Classes usually take about 4 hours to complete.

That's all I have to say, but I'll be happy to answer your questions.

Q: Do the classes cost anything?
A: No, just $4.99 for a workbook.

Q: What can you do to help if you don't know CPR?
A: The most important thing is to call for help and then to stay calm until help arrives.

Q: If you use CPR and there's a problem, if something goes wrong, can you be sued?
A: The state has a good Samaritan law, and it covers possible lawsuits for injuring someone while trying to revive them. So if you've had the proper training and try it, you're fully protected. It's nothing to worry about.

Exercise 4

SPEECHES AND MEETINGS

SPEECH TO SPJ

INTRODUCTION: Following a dispute between your city's reporters and police department, Police Chief Barry Kopperud agreed to speak at 7:30 last night at a meeting of your local chapter of the Society of Professional Journalists. This is a verbatim transcript of his comments and can be quoted directly.

You all know who I am and why I'm here. We've had a problem, and I'm trying to handle it as best I can. I have a responsibility to the residents of this city to maintain law and order. I've also got to run my department as efficiently as possible.

Some unfortunate things have happened during the last year, and they caused us to take a good look at the information we make available to the public. On the 1st of this month we instituted a new policy. Before then, we let any member of the public look at our daily events list: the blotter. It not only listed the events—the names and addresses of where they took place—but also included the officers' narrative. Since the 1st, people can still look at it, but the blotter now lists only the time, case number, patrol car number, event and a code for the disposition of the case. Narratives describing what happened are available to legitimate news people, but a clerk has to get them from the files for you. We don't want other people abusing them. That's the problem.

About a year ago, we started getting complaints from burglary victims. Private security agencies were checking our blotter every day to determine which homes were burglarized and picking up the victims' phone numbers—in some cases, unlisted numbers. Then they would call and try to sell burglar alarms to the victims. Other law enforcement agencies in the state report the same thing happening there.

That's not all of it. Insurance people were using our blotters for all sorts of things, and other people too. A few months ago, we had two burglars who confessed to a whole string of crimes. They told us they felt safe because one of their friends had come in and looked at a burglary report for them and learned we hadn't gotten their description. We also suspect that we had some ambulance chasers—lawyers looking for clients. So now we limit the blotter to the information required by state law. I've tried to explain that to our regular police reporters, but we're getting all sorts of complaints, and one editor called and threatened a lawsuit.

I've always thought I had a friendly relationship with reporters. It's been my philosophy that reporters have, as their primary vocation, to write a story. It's been my policy to do everything I can to help you. That hasn't changed.

Now, let me answer your questions.

Q: A lot of us didn't know what was happening. Why didn't you tell everyone before you started?

A: I thought if I told the regulars, they'd tell their editors and the others. I admit, if I had it to do over again, I'd do it different.

Q: If your clerk doesn't know us, what sort of identification will she want?

A: A press card or anything showing that you work for the media.

Q: Last week some of us had to wait 10 minutes until a clerk was there to help us.

A: That shouldn't happen, and I'll see that it's corrected. Thank you for listening to me. My department is anxious to work this out with you. There's nothing to get upset about.

Exercise 5

SPEECHES AND MEETINGS

SPEECH: SELF–DEFENSE AGAINST RAPE

INSTRUCTIONS: Write separate advance and follow stories about the following speech.

Information for Advance Story

Albert Innis is a lieutenant in the Detective Bureau of the city's police department. He will speak at the YWCA Friday about the topic of rape. The speech will be open to the public free of charge. Women, particularly, are urged to attend the meeting by the sponsor, the YWCA Young Adults Section. The speech will begin at 8 p.m. in Room 12. Innis has agreed to answer questions from the audience at the conclusion of his speech. Members of the Young Adults Section will hold their monthly business meeting after the conclusion of the speech, and the public is also welcome to attend the meeting. To be eligible for membership in the section, women must be between the ages of 18 and 35. The Young Adults Section is sponsoring the presentation because of public interest in the topic of rape and its importance to women, a club representative said. According to some estimates, there are 10 rapes for every one reported to the police.

Speech for Follow Story

I've been asked to come here tonight to talk to you about rape. I'd like to begin by discussing three myths about rape. Two concern the victim, another the rapist. According to one myth, the victim is always young and attractive; movies and television programs perpetuate this myth. The truth is that every woman is a potential victim. Last year, the victims in this city ranged in age from 2 to 91 years. A second myth is that the woman provokes the attack. But sexual assault isn't provoked by a woman's behavior or by the way she dresses. The truth is that the rapist selects his victim on the basis of opportunity. Most rapists select as their victims women who appear vulnerable and alone. Third, it's also a myth to think that rape is committed for sexual gratification. Sex is not the motivating factor. Rapists have feelings of hostility, aggression and inferiority, and they enjoy overpowering and degrading their victims; it raises their self-esteem.

Rape can occur virtually anywhere, but it is most likely to occur in the victim's home or in the home of the assailant. Often, the assailant is someone the victim knows either closely or by sight.

Most rapists are emotionally unstable, and all rapists have the potential to be violent. Outwardly, they appear to be normal, but most have difficulty relating to other people and establishing lasting relationships.

No one can predict how a woman will react when actually confronted with the threat of sexual assault. Panic and fear are perfectly normal responses. The first few moments you may be too terrified to utter a sound. That's perfectly normal. But if you have thought in advance about the possibility of sexual assault, the shock won't be as great. And if you mentally prepare yourself in advance and think about what you might do, you may be able to react more quickly and effectively.

One tactic available to women is making noise. Sometimes screaming "Fire!" or "Call the police!" or blowing a whistle if you have one with you may frighten away your assailant or bring help. But it may antagonize him. All the alternatives involve some dangers, and screaming can make an assailant angrier, and he may beat you or try to strangle you to keep you quiet. You have to weigh the odds, depending on the situation, of this tactic being successful.

A second tactic is trying to run to safety. But unless you are reasonably certain you can get a good lead and reach safety before he overtakes you, this may be too risky. Make sure you have a place to run where someone will help. If you try running away and your assailant overtakes you, it may make him even more violent.

A third tactic is trying to gain a psychological advantage. Try to defuse your assailant's anger and give yourself time to think. If you do something the rapist doesn't expect, it may stop or delay him because rapists want to be in control, and many can't cope with actions they don't expect. This tactic can take many forms—going limp, sinking to the ground and eating grass, hiding your face to stick your fingers down your throat and cause yourself to vomit, making yourself belch, even urinating on your attacker. Crying might be effective in some instances.

You should understand that rapists don't understand or recognize the rights of women as individuals. So it's important to teach them in a way that breaks their fantasies and allows them to see you as an individual with honest feelings and concerns—not as an object. Many of these men put women on a pedestal and, through sexual assault, feel they're cutting women down to size.

You might try to speak calmly and sincerely as one human being trying to reach out to another. Don't beg, plead, cower or make small talk. That's what these assailants expect to hear, and it may antagonize them even more. Talk about something that interests you—anything you can talk about comfortably—a pet, a recent movie you've seen, a book you're reading, a recent death in the family. The important thing is to convince your assailant you're concerned about him as a person.

The last tactic available to you is fighting, but you should keep in mind the fact that all rapists have the potential for inflicting serious harm; they are all potentially violent, so fighting is the last tactic to try if all the others have failed. And if you use this tactic, you have to be willing and able to inflict serious injury. If you try fighting and fail to completely incapacitate your assailant, your risk of receiving serious injury is greatly increased. Most studies show that about half of all rapists carry some weapon, and you have to always assume they're willing to use the weapons. If you are going to fight, use surprise and speed to your advantage. For instance, gently put your hands on the assailant's face and get your thumbs near his eyes, then press his eyeballs suddenly with your thumbs as hard as you can. This will put the assailant into shock and could blind him. Or grab his testicles, squeeze as hard as you can and jerk or pull to inflict immobilizing pain.

There is no universal prescription for foiling sexual assaults. No one can tell you what specific tactics to use. What worked for one woman may not work for you. It all depends upon the circumstances, your basic personality and your perceptions of the rapist. The way you react may depend upon your physical condition. The very thought of sexual assault makes some women so angry that they would rather face the risk of serious injury. Other women may want to escape with the least possible injury or may be more concerned about the safety of other members of their families than with rape or other injury to themselves.

Thank you.

Exercise 6

SPEECHES AND MEETINGS

SPEECH: PREVENTING SHOPLIFTING

INSTRUCTIONS: Write separate advance and follow stories about the following speech.

Information for Advance Story

There will be a breakfast meeting of the Chamber of Commerce at 7 a.m. next Monday. The speaker will be Loretta Hemphill, director of security for the State Alliance of Businesspeople. Anyone is welcome to attend. Cost of the breakfast will be $8.50. However, persons who come only for the speech, which will begin at approximately 8:15, will be admitted free of charge. The affair is being held at the Downtowner Motel. Ms. Hemphill has been asked to talk about shoplifting, a continuing problem for merchants in the city and especially appropriate for this meeting, since most members of the Chamber of Commerce are merchants in the city.

Speech for Follow Story

U.S. retailers lose nearly $5 billion a year to thieves, and the losses at some stores now exceed their net profits. The problem is growing worse, and arrests of shoplifters in the state are rising an average of 15 percent a year. There are no easy solutions. The only sure way to eliminate shoplifting is to lock your stores and to fire all your employees.

The worst shoplifters are white, middle-class suburban girls. Housewives are next most likely to be shoplifters. We've found that a lot of the younger people, people under 18, are shoplifting because of peer pressure or are attempting to buy friendships by stealing gifts for their friends. Teenage girls often steal in groups, sometimes just for the thrill of it, and they usually take merchandise they can use: records, clothing, cosmetics, recreational items and furnishings for their rooms. Many of these young people consider shoplifting a minor thing that doesn't hurt anyone. Most are under the impression that, if they're caught, they'll be lectured and released.

Professionals take smaller, more expensive items they can quickly resell. True kleptomaniacs—people who steal because of psychological disorders—are rare.

Few people shoplift because they are poor. We've found that 95 percent of the persons arrested for shoplifting in the state either have the money or the means, such as a credit card, to pay for the things they've stolen.

As merchants, there are a number of things you can do to cut down on the problem. We think the best answer is to prosecute more offenders—and to let your customers and employees know about it. Shoplifters avoid stores with a reputation for tough prosecution and good security.

Another important step is to pay attention to your customers; never turn your backs on them. True customers will be flattered by the attention, and shoplifters will leave if they know they're being watched and never come back. Train your sales staffs to look for people with unusual clothing—people who wear baggy clothes, long dresses, heavy outer garments out of season, and raincoats when the sun's been out all day. Some thieves wear special hooks or straps to conceal merchandise. Others wear a dummy cast or sling. Also watch for shoppers carrying bags, boxes, briefcases, topcoats, umbrellas, oversized purses, and other possible hiding places for stolen items.

Some mothers hide things in their children's clothing, and other thieves work in pairs—they move merchandise to other areas so their accomplices can pick it up later without suspicion. Items such as jewelry are often stashed in dressing rooms. So keep your dressing rooms free of merchandise, and watch for people who frequent the dressing rooms and your stores' restrooms. Also watch for people who continually refuse service and seem on the alert or defensive.

It's a good policy to have shoppers check all their packages when they enter your stores, or at least to seal their packages. If they buy something in your stores, seal the packages you sell them so they can't put anything else in them.

There are lots of other safeguards, some more expensive than others. It's a good idea to buy price tags that can't be switched, even though they're somewhat more expensive. Magnetized or electronically sensitive tags that can be attached to merchandise are especially effective. Clerks can remove the tags when the merchandise is sold. If someone tries to carry an article out of your store with the tag still on, it'll sound an alarm. Of course, your clerks have to be conscientious about it; if they forget to clip off a tag or to demagnetize an item, one lawsuit for false arrest will wipe out all your profits.

You can also hire more security people, install two-way mirrors and try closed-circuit TV systems. Tie down display items and eliminate narrow, cluttered aisles where it's hard to observe customers. Keep everything as open and neat as possible, and set up cash registers so your clerks can see your display areas. If the merchandise you're selling comes in pairs, only show one of a pair. Keep valuable merchandise away from doors, and limit the number of entrances and exits to your store. Where possible, use separate doors for entering and exiting.

Another problem is proving that the shoplifters you've caught intended to steal the items found in their possession. When they appear in court, defendants often say they forgot to pay for the items. There's an average wait of two months between an arrest and a trial, so you should write or dictate as much as you remember about shoplifting incidents immediately after they occur. A lot will happen between the time of the incident and the trial, and you need to remember all the details.

But not all the thefts in your stores are caused by shoplifters. It's estimated that 75 percent of all the losses in some industries, especially restaurants and hotels, are due to stealing by employees, and many companies are resorting to lie detector tests. Most companies give the tests to new job applicants, but some companies require all their employees to take a test once a year.

Exercise 7

SPEECHES AND MEETINGS

BLOOD, TOIL, TEARS AND SWEAT

By **Winston Churchill**

On Friday evening last I received His Majesty's commission to form a new administration. It was the evident wish and will of Parliament and the nation that this should include all parties, both those who supported the late Government and also the parties of the Opposition. I have completed the most important part of this task. A War Cabinet has been formed of five Members, representing, with the Opposition Liberals, the unity of the nation. The three party leaders have agreed to serve, either in the War Cabinet or in high executive office. The three fighting services have been filled. It was necessary that this should be done in one single day, on account of the extreme urgency and rigor of events. A number of other key positions were filled yesterday, and I am submitting a further list to His Majesty tonight. I hope to complete the appointment of the principal Ministers during tomorrow. The appointment of the other Ministers usually takes a little longer, but I trust that, when Parliament meets again, this part of my task will be completed, and that the administration will be complete in all respects.

I considered it in the public interest to suggest that the House should be summoned to meet today. Mr. Speaker agreed and took the necessary steps, in accordance with the power conferred upon him by the Resolution of the House. At the end of the proceedings today, the adjournment of the House will be proposed until Tuesday, May 21, with, of course, provision for earlier meeting if need be. The business to be considered during that week will be notified to Members at the earliest opportunity. I now invite the House, by the Resolution which stands in my name, to record its approval of the steps taken and to declare its confidence in the new Government.

To form an administration of this scale and complexity is a serious undertaking in itself, but it must be remembered that we are in the preliminary stage of one of the greatest battles in history, that we are in action at many points in Norway and in Holland, that we have to be prepared in the Mediterranean, that the air battle is continuous and that many preparations have to be made here at home. In this crisis I hope I may be pardoned if I do not address the House at any length today. I hope that any of my friends and colleagues, or former colleagues, who are affected by the political reconstruction, will make all allowance for any lack of ceremony with which it has been necessary to act. I would say to the House, as I said to those who have joined this Government: "I have nothing to offer but blood, toil, tears and sweat."

We have before us an ordeal of the most grievous kind. We have before us many, many long months of struggle and of suffering. You ask what is our policy? I will say: It is to wage war, by sea, land and air, with all our might and with all the strength that God can give us: to wage war against a monstrous tyranny [the Nazi regime of Adolf Hitler in Germany], never surpassed in the dark, lamentable catalogue of human crime. That is our policy. You ask, What is our aim? I can answer in one word: Victory—victory at all costs, victory in spite of all terror, victory, however long and hard the road may be; for without victory, there is no survival. Let that be realized; no survival for the British Empire; no survival for all that the British Empire has stood for; no survival for the urge and impulse of the ages, that mankind will move forward towards its goal. But I take up my task with buoyancy and hope. I feel sure that our cause will not be suffered to fail among men. At this time I feel entitled to claim the aid of all, and I say, "Come, then, let us go forward together with our united strength."

(Delivered May 13, 1940, to the House
of Commons, three days after he
became Prime Minister of England)

Exercise 8

SPEECHES AND MEETINGS

REQUEST FOR A DECLARATION OF WAR

By **Franklin D. Roosevelt**

Yesterday, December 7, 1941—a date which will live in infamy—the United States of America was suddenly and deliberately attacked by naval and air forces of the Empire of Japan.

The United States was at peace with that nation and, at the solicitation of Japan, was still in conversation with its Government and its Emperor looking toward the maintenance of peace in the Pacific. Indeed, one hour after Japanese air squadrons had commenced bombing on Oahu, the Japanese Ambassador to the United States and his colleague delivered to the Secretary of State a formal reply to a recent American message. While this reply stated that it seemed useless to continue the existing diplomatic negotiations, it contained no threat or hint of war or armed attack.

It will be recorded that the distance of Hawaii from Japan makes it obvious that the attack was deliberately planned many days or even weeks ago. During the intervening time the Japanese Government has deliberately sought to deceive the United States by false statements and expressions of hope for continued peace.

The attack yesterday on the Hawaiian Islands has caused severe damage to American naval and military forces. Very many American lives have been lost. In addition American ships have been reported torpedoed on the high seas between San Francisco and Honolulu.

Yesterday the Japanese Government also launched an attack against Malaya. Last night Japanese forces attacked Hong Kong. Last night Japanese forces attacked Guam. Last night Japanese forces attacked the Philippine Islands. Last night the Japanese attacked Wake Island. This morning the Japanese attacked Midway Island.

Japan has, therefore, undertaken a surprise offensive extending throughout the Pacific area. The facts of yesterday speak for themselves. The people of the United States have already formed their opinions and well understand the implications to the very life and safety of our nation.

As Commander-in-Chief of the Army and Navy, I have directed that all measures be taken for our defense.

Always will we remember the character of the onslaught against us.

No matter how long it may take us to overcome this premeditated invasion, the American people in their righteous might will win through to absolute victory.

I believe I interpret the will of the Congress and of the people when I assert that we will not only defend ourselves to the uttermost but will make very certain that this form of treachery shall never endanger us again.

Hostilities exist. There is no blinking at the fact that our people, our territory and our interests are in grave danger.

With confidence in our armed forces—with the unbounded determination of our people—we will gain the inevitable triumph—so help us God.

I ask that the Congress declare that since the unprovoked and dastardly attack by Japan on Sunday, December seventh, a state of war has existed between the United States and the Japanese Empire.

(Delivered Dec. 8 before Congress,
which responded that same afternoon,
declaring war on Japan without a dissenting vote)

Exercise 9

SPEECHES AND MEETINGS

INAUGURAL ADDRESS

By **John F. Kennedy**

Mr. Chief Justice, President Eisenhower, Vice President Nixon, President Truman, reverend clergy, fellow citizens, we observe today not a victory of party, but a celebration of freedom—symbolizing an end, as well as a beginning—signifying renewal, as well as change. For I have sworn before you and Almighty God the same solemn oath our forebears prescribed nearly a century and three quarters ago.

The world is very different now. For man holds in his mortal hands the power to abolish all forms of human poverty and all forms of human life. And yet the same revolutionary beliefs for which our forebears fought are still at issue around the globe—the belief that the rights of man come not from the generosity of the state, but from the hand of God.

We dare not forget today that we are the heirs of that first revolution. Let the word go forth from this time and place, to friend and foe alike, that the torch has been passed to a new generation of Americans—born in this century, tempered by war, disciplined by a hard and bitter peace, proud of our ancient heritage—and unwilling to witness or permit the slow undoing of those human rights to which this Nation has always been committed, and to which we are committed today at home and around the world.

Let every nation know, whether it wishes us well or ill, that we shall pay any price, bear any burden, meet any hardship, support any friend, oppose any foe, in order to assure the survival and the success of liberty.

This much we pledge—and more.

To those old allies whose cultural and spiritual origins we share, we pledge the loyalty of faithful friends. United, there is little we cannot do in a host of cooperative ventures. Divided, there is little we can do—for we dare not meet a powerful challenge at odds and split asunder.

To those new States whom we welcome to the ranks of the free, we pledge our word that one form of colonial control shall not have passed away merely to be replaced by a far greater iron tyranny. We shall not always expect to find them supporting our view. But we shall always hope to find them strongly supporting their own freedom—and to remember that, in the past, those who foolishly sought power by riding the back of the tiger ended up inside.

To those peoples in the huts and villages across the globe struggling to break the bonds of mass misery, we pledge our best efforts to help them help themselves, for whatever period is required—not because the Communists may be doing it, not because we seek their votes, but because it is right. If a free society cannot help the many who are poor, it cannot save the few who are rich.

To our sister republics south of our border, we offer a special pledge—to convert our good words into good deeds, in a new alliance for progress, to assist free men and free governments in casting off the chains of poverty. But this peaceful revolution of hope cannot become the prey of hostile powers. Let all our neighbors know that we shall join with them to oppose aggression or subversion anywhere in the Americas. And let every other power know that this hemisphere intends to remain the master of its own house.

To that world assembly of sovereign states, the United Nations, our last best hope in an age where the instruments of war have far outpaced the instruments of peace, we renew our pledge of support—to prevent it from becoming merely a forum for invective—to strengthen its shield of the new and the weak—and to enlarge the area in which its writ may run.

Finally, to those nations who would make themselves our adversary, we offer not a pledge but a request: that both sides begin anew the quest for peace, before the dark powers of destruction unleashed by science engulf all humanity in planned or accidental self-destruction.

We dare not tempt them with weakness. For only when our arms are sufficient beyond doubt can we be certain beyond doubt that they will never be employed.

But neither can two great and powerful groups of nations take comfort from our present course—both sides overburdened by the cost of modern weapons, both rightly alarmed by the steady spread of the deadly atom, yet both racing to alter that uncertain balance of terror that stays the hand of mankind's final war.

So let us begin anew—remembering on both sides that civility is not a sign of weakness, and sincerity is always subject to proof. Let us never negotiate out of fear. But let us never fear to negotiate.

Let both sides explore what problems unite us instead of laboring those problems which divide us.

Let both sides, for the first time, formulate serious and precise proposals for the inspection and control of arms—and bring the absolute power to destroy other nations under the absolute control of all nations.

Let both sides seek to invoke the wonders of science instead of its terror. Together let us explore the stars, conquer the deserts, eradicate disease, tap the ocean depths, and encourage the arts and commerce.

Let both sides unite to heed in all corners of the earth and the command of Isaiah—to "undo the heavy burdens and to let the oppressed go free."

And if a beachhead of cooperation may push back the jungle of suspicion, let both sides join in creating a new endeavor, not a new balance of power, but a new world of law, where the strong are just and the weak secure and the peace preserved.

All this will not be finished in the first 100 days. Nor will it be finished in the first 1,000 days, nor in the life of this administration, nor even perhaps in our lifetime on this planet. But let us begin.

In your hands, my fellow citizens, more than in mine, will rest the final success or failure of our course. Since this country was founded, each generation of Americans has been summoned to give testimony to its national loyalty. The graves of young Americans who answered the call to service surround the globe.

Now the trumpet summons us again—not as a call to bear arms, though arms we need; not as a call to battle, though embattled we are; but a call to bear the burden of a long twilight struggle, year in, and year out, "rejoicing in hope, patient in tribulation"—a struggle against the common enemies of man: tyranny, poverty, disease, and war itself.

Can we forge against these enemies a grand and global alliance, North and South, East and West, that can assure a more fruitful life for all mankind? Will you join in that historic effort?

In the long history of the world, only a few generations have been granted the role of defending freedom in its hour of maximum danger. I do not shrink from this responsibility—I welcome it. I do not believe that any of us would exchange places with any other people or any other generation. The energy, the faith, the devotion which we bring to this endeavor will light our country and all who serve it—and the glow from that fire can truly light the world.

And so, my fellow Americans, ask not what your country can do for you: Ask what you can do for your country.

Finally, whether you are citizens of America or citizens of the world, ask of us the same high standards of strength and sacrifice which we ask of you. With a good conscience our only sure reward, with history the final judge of our deeds, let us go forth to lead the land we love, asking His blessing and His help, but knowing that here on earth God's work must truly be our own.

(Delivered Jan. 20, 1961)

Exercise 10

SPEECHES AND MEETINGS

SURGEON GENERAL'S SPEECH

INSTRUCTIONS: Write a news story that summarizes the following speech given by the surgeon general of the U.S. Public Health Service. Assume that the surgeon general spoke at a state PTA convention in your city at 8 p.m. yesterday. This is a verbatim copy of a speech actually given by the surgeon general and can be quoted directly. As you write the story, assume that it is just two days before Halloween.

I am pleased to be here today with representatives of several organizations who recognize that alcohol is the nation's number one drug problem among youth and who share my concern that the alcohol industry has targeted Halloween, a traditional holiday for children, as their latest marketing opportunity.

Just as Saman, the ancient Celtic Lord of the Dead, summoned the evil spirits to walk the earth on October 31, America's modern-day distilleries, breweries and vineyards are working their own brand of sorcery on us this year. On radio and television and even at supermarket check-out counters we are being bombarded with exhortations to purchase orange and black 12-packs and even "cocktails from the Crypt."

Well, as your surgeon general I'm here today with my own exhortation: Halloween and hops do not mix.

Alcohol is the number one substance abuse problem among America's youth. In fact, it is the only drug whose use has not been declining, according to our most recent National High School Senior Survey. The National Institute on Alcohol Abuse and Alcoholism reports that, currently, 4.6 million teenagers have a drinking problem.

Why do so many of our young people drink? There are no easy answers to this question, but clearly the availability of alcohol and its acceptance, even glamorization, in our society are factors. The National Coalition on Television Violence reports that before turning 18, the average American child will see 75,000 drinking scenes on television programs alone.

In just two days many of our young people will be celebrating Halloween. Many children look forward to this day as much as they do Christmas and Hanukkah. Who among us can forget the excitement of dressing up as ghosts and goblins and going from door to door shouting "trick or treat," and coming away with a fistful of candy?

Trick or treat.

This year the alcohol industry has given new meaning to those innocent words of childhood. They are serving up new treats—and new tricks.

They are saying: "It's Halloween, it's time to celebrate, it's time for a drink!" Beer companies offer free Halloween T-shirts, bat sunglasses, and glowing cups. Halloween parties sponsored by a major brewer are being held in nearly 40 cities.

What I say is scary is the possibility of increased carnage on our highways, the real specter of more binge drinking by our young people, and the absolute reality of those smaller, less dramatic cases of health and emotional problems caused by alcohol consumption.

Last year alone, we lost 3,158 young people in alcohol-related crashes, over 60 in every state in the union. Fully 40 percent of all deaths in young people are due to crashes—6,649 last year, and, as you can see, about half are related to alcohol.

What is also scary to me is the encouragement of "binge drinking" by our young people. Some of these Halloween ads encourage the purchase of 12 or 24 packs of beer, and who will drink all that beer? 43 percent of college students, 35 percent of our high school seniors and 26 percent of 8th grade students have had five or more drinks in a row during the past two weeks. And beer and wine coolers are their favorite alcoholic beverages.

I also find it scary that we continue to think of beer and wine as "soft liquor." There's nothing "soft" about ethyl alcohol. And there's just as much ethyl alcohol in one can of beer or one glass of wine as there is in a mixed drink. That is the hard fact.

Finally, as the nation's doctor and as a pediatrician, what I find scariest of all is that alcohol affects virtually every organ in the body. Alcohol consumption is associated with medical consequences ranging from slight functional impairment to life-threatening disease states—among them, liver disease, cancer of the esophagus, and hypertension. Where the organs of the body are concerned, alcohol is an equal opportunity destroyer.

The alcohol industry and its hired guns, the advertisting agencies, know these facts. I hope that parents and other concerned adults do too. For if the alcohol industry has chosen to be part of the problem, it is up to you to be part of the solution.

In closing I would like to speak on behalf of those who have no voice in this debate—America's children and adolescents. Let us not make this year, the year they robbed the kids of Halloween. For their sake and our own, let us keep Halloween sane, safe—and sober.

Exercise 11

SPEECHES AND MEETINGS

IRAQI WAR SPEECH

By **President George Bush**

INSTRUCTIONS: This is a transcript of President George Bush's address to the nation on Jan. 16, 1991, the night that allied planes began to bomb Iraq. Assume that the president presented his speech last night. Write a news story that summarizes its content. Because this is a verbatim copy of the president's speech, you can quote it directly.

Five months ago, Saddam Hussein started this cruel war against Kuwait; tonight the battle has been joined. This military action, taken in accord with United Nations resolutions and with the consent of the United States Congress, follows months of constant and virtually endless diplomatic activity on the part of the United Nations, the United States and many, many other countries.

Arab leaders sought what became known as an Arab solution, only to conclude that Saddam Hussein was unwilling to leave Kuwait. Others traveled to Baghdad in a variety of efforts to restore peace and justice. Our Secretary of State James Baker held an historic meeting in Geneva only to be totally rebuffed.

This past weekend, in a last-ditch effort, the secretary-general of the United Nations went to the Middle East with peace in his heart, his second such mission, and he came back from Baghdad with no progress at all in getting Saddam Hussein to withdraw from Kuwait.

Now, the 28 countries with forces in the gulf area have exhausted all reasonable efforts to reach a peaceful resolution, have no choice but to drive Saddam from Kuwait by force. We will not fail.

As I report to you, air attacks are under way against military targets in Iraq. We are determined to knock out Saddam Hussein's nuclear bomb potential. We will also destroy his chemical weapons facilities. Much of Saddam's artillery and tanks will be destroyed.

Our operations are designed to best protect the lives of all the coalition forces by targeting Saddam's vast military arsenal.

Initial reports from General Schwarzkopf are that our operations are proceeding according to plan.

Our objectives are clear. Saddam Hussein's forces will leave Kuwait. The legitimate government of Kuwait will be restored to its rightful place and Kuwait will once again be free.

Iraq will eventually comply with all relevant United Nations resolutions and then when peace is restored, it is our hope that Iraq will live as a peaceful and cooperative member of the family of nations, thus enhancing the security and stability of the gulf.

Some may ask, "Why act now? Why not wait?" The answer is clear. The world could wait no longer.

Sanctions, though having some effect, showed no signs of accomplishing their objective. Sanctions were tried for well over five months, and we and our allies concluded that sanctions alone would not force Saddam from Kuwait.

While the world waited, Saddam Hussein systematically raped, pillaged and plundered a tiny nation—no threat to his own. He subjected the people of Kuwait to unspeakable atrocities, and among those maimed and murdered—innocent children. While the world waited, Saddam sought to add to the chemical weapons arsenal he now possesses an infinitely more dangerous weapon of mass destruction, a nuclear weapon.

And while the world waited, while the world talked peace and withdrawal, Saddam Hussein dug in and moved massive forces into Kuwait. While the world waited, while Saddam stalled, more damage was being done to the fragile economies of the Third World, the emerging democracies of Eastern Europe, to the entire world, including to our own economy.

The United States, together with the United Nations, exhausted every means at our disposal to bring this crisis to a peaceful end.

However, Saddam clearly felt that by stalling and threatening and defying the United Nations, he could weaken the forces arrayed against him.

While the world waited, Saddam Hussein met every overture of peace with open contempt. While the world prayed for peace, Saddam prepared for war.

I had hoped that when the United States Congress, in historic debate, took its resolute action, Saddam would realize he could not prevail and would move out of Kuwait in accord with the United Nations resolutions. He did not do that. Instead, he remained intransigent, certain that time was on his side. Saddam was warned over and over again to comply with the will of the United Nations—leave Kuwait or be driven out. Saddam has arrogantly rejected all warnings. Instead, he tried to make this a dispute between Iraq and the United States of America.

Well, he failed. Tonight, 28 nations, countries from five continents—Europe and Asia, Africa and the Arab League—have forces in the gulf area standing shoulder to shoulder against Saddam Hussein. These countries had hoped the use of force could be avoided. Regrettably, we now believe that only force will make him leave.

Prior to ordering our forces into battle, I instructed our military commanders to take every necessary step to prevail as quickly as possible and with the greatest degree of protection possible for American and allied servicemen and women. I've told the American people before that this will not be another Vietnam.

And I repeat this here tonight. Our troops will have the best possible support in the entire world. And they will not be asked to fight with one hand tied behind their back.

I'm hopeful that this fighting will not go on for long and that casualties will be held to an absolute minimum. This is an historic moment. We have in the past year made great progress in ending the long era of conflict and Cold War. We have before us the opportunity to forge for ourselves and for future generations a new world order, a world where the rule of law, not the law of the jungle, governs the conduct of nations. When we are successful, and we will be, we have a real chance at this new world order, an order in which a credible United Nations can use its peacekeeping role to fulfill the promise and vision of the U.N.'s founders.

We have no argument with the people of Iraq. Indeed, for the innocents caught in this conflict, I pray for their safety. Our goal is not the conquest of Iraq. It is the liberation of Kuwait.

It is my hope that somehow the Iraqi people can even now convince their dictator that he must lay down his arms, leave Kuwait and let Iraq itself rejoin the family of peace-loving nations.

Thomas Paine wrote many years ago: "These are the times that try men's souls." Those well-known words are so very true today.

But even as planes of the multinational forces attack Iraq, I prefer to think of peace, not war. I am convinced not only that we will prevail, but that out of the horror of combat will come the recognition that no nation can stand against a world united, no nation will be permitted to brutally assault its neighbor.

No president can easily commit their sons and daughters to war. They are the nation's finest. Ours is an all-volunteer force, magnificently trained, highly motivated. The troops know why they're there. And listen to what they say, for they've said it better than any president or prime minister ever could. Listen to Hollywood Huddleston, Marine lance corporal.

He says, "Let's free these people so we can go home and be free again." And he's right. The terrible crimes and tortures committed by Saddam's henchmen against the innocent people of Kuwait are an affront to mankind and a challenge to the freedom of all.

Listen to one of our great officers out there, Marine Lieutenant General Walter Boomer. He said, "There are things worth fighting for. A world in which brutality and lawlessness are allowed to go unchecked isn't the kind of world we're going to want to live in."

Listen to Master Sergeant J. K. Kendall of the 82nd Airborne. "We're here for more than just the price of a gallon of gas. What we're doing is going to chart the future of the world for the next 100 years. It's better to deal with this guy now than five years from now."

And finally, we should all sit up and listen to Jackie Jones, an Army lieutenant, when she says, "If we let him get away with this, who knows what's going to be next?" I've called upon Hollywood and J.K. and Jackie and all their courageous comrades in arms to do what must be done.

Tonight America and the world are deeply grateful to them and to their families.

And let me say to everyone listening or watching tonight: When the troops we've sent in finish their work, I'm determined to bring them home as soon as possible. Tonight, as our forces fight, they and their families are in our prayers.

May God bless each and every one of them and the coalition forces at our side in the gulf, and may he continue to bless our nation, the United States of America.

Exercise 12

SPEECHES AND MEETINGS

COUNTY COMMISSION MEETING

INSTRUCTIONS: Write a news story that summarizes the comments and decisions made at this meeting. Assume that your county commission held the meeting at 2 p.m. yesterday.

The members of your county commission began their meeting by listening to plans for a luxury condominium development on Elkhart Lake. The new development will be called "SunCrest." The property is owned by The Roswell Development Corporation, headquartered in Pittsburgh. Carlos Rey, a spokesman for the company, said: "We are planning a series of 10-story buildings overlooking the lake. None will exceed 100 feet in height. They will contain a total of 715 units. Estimated selling price of a unit will be $100,000 and upwards, perhaps to a top of $500,000 for the larger penthouse units. The development is about 5 miles from the nearest town, and we intend to promote it as a vacation and recreation center. We'll have our own well and our own sewer system, with an extensive recreation system centered around the lake. We know that fire protection is a concern. The township fire department serving the area doesn't have a ladder truck capable of reaching the top of a 10-story building. We'll donate $320,000 for the purchase of one." The commission voted 5–2 to approve the plans and to rezone the land from agricultural to PUD: Planned Unit Development.

Next, at 3 p.m., the commission honored and presented plaques to two 15-year-old girls. The girls, Doreen Nicholls and Pamela DeZinno, were walking along a river in a county park last week and saw a young child fall from a boat. Both girls dove into the river and pulled her out. While Doreen then proceeded to administer CPR, Pamela called for help, thus saving a life.

Appearing next before the commission, Sheriff Gus DiCesare asked it to require a three-day wait before a pistol could be bought from any gun dealer in the county. "I do not think that 72 hours is too long for someone to wait to buy a handgun," Sheriff DiCesare said. "There are a lot of cases where people went out and bought a gun with criminal intent and used it right away to shoot or rob someone. We want a cooling off period." Under the proposed ordinance, a customer would also have to provide the dealer with his name, address, date of birth and other information, then wait 72 hours before picking up the pistol. The dealer would mail the information to the sheriff's department, where it would be kept on a computerized file. Sheriff DiCesare said it would speed the identification of the owner of a pistol found at a crime scene. A majority of the commissioners said they favor such a proposal but want to get more information and possibly hold a public hearing to give every citizen an opportunity to speak his mind. They promised to seriously consider it at their next meeting.

The commissioners then decided not to give themselves a raise, rejecting a proposed pay raise on a 4–3 vote. It has been five years since the last pay raise for them. Then their salary went from $42,500 to $46,000 a year. Yesterday, the majority, led by Commissioners Roland Graumann and Anita Shenuski, argued that a raise was "inappropriate." Faith Ellis argued a proposed increase to $52,500 was not out of line because commissioners in other counties earn more. "This is not asking too much," she said. "The county is getting a good deal for the time we put in." Anne Chen responded, "Our work should be done for community service, not just for how much we make."

Exercise 13

SPEECHES AND MEETINGS

SCHOOL BOARD MEETING

INSTRUCTIONS: Write a news story that summarizes the comments and decisions made at this meeting. Assume that your school board held its monthly meeting at 7:30 p.m. yesterday.

The board opened its meeting by honoring seven retiring teachers: Shirley Dawsun, Carmen Foucault, Nina Paynich, Kenneth Satava, Nancy Lee Scott, Lonnie McEwen, and Harley Sawyer. Paynich worked as a teacher 44 years, longer than any of the others. Each teacher was given a framed "Certificate of Appreciation" and good round of applause.

The school board then turned to the major item on its agenda: the budget for next year. The budget totals $324.4 million, up 5% from this year. It includes $3.2 million for a new elementary school to be built on West Madison Ave. It will be completed and opened in two years. The budget also includes a 4.5% raise for teachers and a 6% raise for administrators. Also, the salary of the superintendent of schools was raised $10,000, to $88,000 a year. The vote was unanimous: 9–0.

The school board then discussed the topic of remedial summer classes. Board member Umberto Vacante proposed eliminating them to save an estimated $820,000. "They're just too expensive, especially when you consider we serve only about 900 students each summer. A lot of them are students who flunked their regular classes. Often, if they attend the summer classes, they don't have to repeat a grade. If we're going to spend that kind of money, I think we should use it to help and reward our most talented students. They're the ones we ignore. We could offer special programs for them." Supt. Greg Hubbard responded, "Some of these summer students have learning disabilities and emotional problems, and they really need the help. This would hurt them terribly. Without it, they might never graduate." The board then voted 7–2 to keep the classes one more year, but to ask its staff for a study of the matter.

During a one-hour hearing that followed, about 100 people, many loud and angry, debated the issue of creationism vs. evolution. "We've seen your biology books," said parent Claire Sawyer. "I don't want my children using them. They never mention the theory of creationism." Another parent, Harley Euon of 410 East Third Street, responded: "Evolution isn't a theory. It's proven fact. Creationism is a religious idea, not even a scientific theory. People here are trying to force schools to teach our children their religion." A third parent, Roy E. Cross of 101 Charow Lane, agreed, adding: "People can teach creationism in their homes and churches. It's not the schools' job." After listening to the debate, the board voted 6–3 to continue using the present textbooks, but to encourage parents to discuss the matter with their children and to provide in their individual homes the religious training they deem most appropriate for their families.

Finally, last on its agenda, the board unanimously adopted a resolution praising the school system's ADDITIONS: adult volunteers who contribute their spare time to help and assist their neighborhood schools. Last year, Supt. Greg Hubbard reported, there was a total of 897 ADDITIONS, and they put in a total of 38,288 hours of volunteer time helping the schools.

Exercise 14

SPEECHES AND MEETINGS

CITY COUNCIL MEETING

INSTRUCTIONS: Write a news story that summarizes the comments and decisions made at this meeting. Assume that your City Council held the meeting at 8 p.m. yesterday.

BACKGROUND

For 10 years, a downtown church in your city (the First United Methodist Church at 680 Garland Avenue) has provided a shelter for the homeless, allowing them to sleep in the basement of its fellowship hall every night and feeding them both breakfast and dinner. The church can house 180 people each night and relies on a staff of more than 200 volunteers. In recent years, they've been overwhelmed, and the church is unable to continue to afford to shoulder the entire burden. It has asked for help: for donations and for more room, especially in winter, for the homeless to sleep. Civic leaders have formed the Coalition for the Homeless, Inc., a nonprofit organization, and hope to build a new shelter. The coalition has asked the city to donate a site, valued at $500,000. Coalition leaders said they will then raise the $1.5 million needed to construct the shelter. The coalition leaders say they will also then operate the shelter, relying on volunteers; a small, full-time professional staff; and donations from concerned citizens.

First Speaker: Ida Levine, President, Coalition for the Homeless, Inc.

"As you know, uh, what we're trying to do here is raise $1.5 million to build the shelter. We're approaching everyone that might be able to help and, so far, have collected about $200,000 and have pledges of another $318,000, and thats just the beginning, in two months. So we're certain that if you provide the land, we'll be able to, uh, come up with all the money for this thing. The site we have in mind is the old fire station on Garland Avenue. The building is so old that its worthless, and we'd tear it down, but its an ideal location for our purposes."

Second Speaker: Lt. Luis Rafelson

"I'm here officially, representing the police department, to say that we're all for this. It costs the taxpayers about $350,000 a year to arrest homeless people for violating city ordinances like trespassing on private property and sleeping at night in parks and such. During the average month last year we arrested 300 homeless people, sometimes more. It takes about 2 hours to arrest a person and do all the booking and paperwork, while taking five minutes to transport them to a shelter. So you're wasting police time, time we could be spending on more important things. So if the city spends $500,000 on this deal, it'll save that much in a year, maybe more."

Third Speaker: Irvin Porej, Banker

"The people who stay in shelters are just like you and me. The difference is that we have a place to go. They're good people for the most part, just down on their luck. This would provide a temporary shelter for them, help them get back on their feet. Until now, we've had churches doing this, and the Salvation Army has a shelter, too, but we should put an end to the church shelters. Its not fair to them because the churches are burdened by a problem that everyone should be helping with, and the problem is getting too big for them to handle."

Fourth Speaker: Council Member Sandra Bandolf

"We have to address this problem. It's not going to go away. And with this solution, it really won't cost the city anything. No one's asking us for money or anything, only for a piece of land that's been lying unused for years."

Fifth Speaker: Council Member William Belmonte

"I suppose I'm going to be the only one who votes against this. Why should taxpayers suddenly start paying for this, people who work hard for their money and are struggling these days to support their families? And what happens if the coalition don't raise all the money it needs for the shelter, what happens then? What happens if they breach the agreement? Then we'll be left holding the bag, expected to pay for this damn thing and to support it for years. That'll add a whole new bureaucracy to the city, and where'll the money come from then?"

Sixth Speaker: Trina Guzman, President, Downtown Merchants' Assn.

"The members of my association are strongly opposed to this. We agree that the city needs a shelter, that we have an obligation to help the people who are really homeless and needy, but not on Garland Avenue. That's just a block from downtown, and we've been having trouble with these people for years. Some of them need help, have all sorts of problems like alcoholism and mental illness that no one here's talking about. Remember too that these people aren't allowed to stay in the shelters during the day. Theoretically, they're supposed to go out and work, or at least look for work. What some of them do is hang around Main Street, panhandling and annoying people and using our parking lots and alleys for toilets. We've got customers who tell us they won't come downtown any more because they're afraid of being approached and asked for money and being mugged or something. Let's feed these people and help them, but put them out somewhere where they can't hurt anyone."

OUTCOME

The council voted 6–1 to donate the land. Belmont cast the single vote against the proposal.

Exercise 16

SPEECHES AND MEETINGS

ADVANCE AND FOLLOW STORIES: CITY COUNCIL MEETING

INSTRUCTIONS: Write separate advance and follow stories about the following city council meeting. Assume that the meeting was held in Roseville, a suburb of your community.

Information for Advance Story

City Clerk Wilma Durbin said: "There are three issues on the agenda for next Monday's meeting, but you never know. If the council wants to, it can consider other issues that come up. And then they always give everyone in the audience a chance to speak. The issues we've got listed now include a proposal to give city employees an 8 percent raise. That comes from the city manager's office. Then they will open bids and award a contract for the operation of concession stands at the Civic Center. Number 3 on the agenda, the council will vote on a proposal to limit the number of dogs that anyone can have in a home in a residential area without a permit. The proposal would limit the number of adult dogs in a household to four. That's a controversial topic. Everyone gets excited about dogs."

Information for Follow Story

TOPIC 1

The first issue on the city council's agenda last night was the city budget for next year. City council members debated the size of the raise that city employees will receive. City Manager W. E. Knowles started the discussion, saying: "I recommend an 8 percent across-the-board raise for city employees. Every employee deserves at least that much. We've got a total of 275 employees, and an 8 percent raise would cost the city a total of $320,000. The annual payroll is about $4 million, and this would increase it to $4,320,000. It's really a catch-up raise. If you look at the salaries the city pays today, and you compare those salaries with the salaries we paid 10 years ago, and then you compare them with the rise in the cost of living over those 10 years, then you'll find that city employees have fallen behind; they've lost 11.5 percent of their salaries to inflation. In constant dollars, they're earning 88.5 percent of what they did 10 years ago. We've also got to give them a good raise to maintain a competitive position in the local labor market. They haven't gotten a decent raise for years, and if we don't give them one this year, we'll begin to lose some key employees. Last year, they got a 3 percent raise, and the year before that they got 4 percent. That's not enough."

Mayor Brad Freeman said: "Eight percent is too much. Everyone agrees they're underpaid and deserve a raise. I don't question that. The real issue is whether we can afford to give them 8 percent. Where would the money come from? We'd have to raise property taxes, but they're already too high. We just don't have the money."

Council member Stacy Ruskiewicz said: "I don't know enough about the budget to say what we can and can't afford. Tax revenues might go up next year, or we might cut back somewhere else. I think this is important, but let's get some more information before deciding anything. I move that we ask the city treasurer to look into this and report back to us at our meeting next week." Her motion passed by a vote of 9–0.

TOPIC 2

The council then opened 14 bids for the right to operate concession stands at the city's Civic Center. The high bidder, Dehuer Catering, agreed to give the city 21.3 percent of its gross receipts if it was awarded the exclusive contract to operate all the concession stands at the Civic Center, and it was granted the contract. The next highest bidder offered the county 18.61 percent of its gross receipts. The low bid was 12 percent. It is estimated by Civic Center authorities that the total receipts at the concession stands may exceed $1.5 million on an annual basis. The contract is for a five-year period of time.

TOPIC 3

City Zoning Director Mack Felino offered a new ordinance that specifies that no homeowner in an area zoned for single- or multiple-family residences could keep more than four dogs that are older than 6 months without a license from the city. To obtain a license, dog owners would have to demonstrate that they have ample room and facilities for the dogs and that the dogs would not be a nuisance to neighbors. A license would cost $100.

Felino then added: "We have found that many city residents receive additional income from breeding and selling these animals, dogs especially, and it's often a nuisance for neighbors. We need to place some restrictions on the breeding of dogs. People shouldn't be allowed to have commercial kennels in residential neighborhoods. We don't permit any other kinds of businesses in residential neighborhoods, and we shouldn't permit these kennels."

City Commissioner Willie Ralph said: "I agree with all that's being said. We're going to have a lot of people angry with us if we adopt this law, but we need some guidelines for the number of animals kept in homes. I'd say this is my number 1 problem as a city commissioner. Every week, I've got people calling and complaining about barking dogs and strange dogs running loose in their yards, and I know the police get hundreds of these calls."

City Commissioner Duwayne Tutone said: "This isn't something we should rush into. I'm not convinced it's necessary, or even a good thing. There are lots of people living in this city that hunt and that raise dogs for show, and they have a right to as many dogs as they want. How many dogs someone has isn't any of our business. We've already got enough other laws, so if there's a real problem with noise or anything, it can be taken care of."

The City Commission approved the proposal, thus limiting people living in residential areas to a maximum of four dogs aged 6 months and older. The vote was 7–2 with Commissioners Duwayne Tutone and Larry Raftis voting against the proposal.

TOPIC 4

James Gracie is the city attorney. He has been the city attorney for the past nine years. He submitted his resignation at the end of the meeting. His resignation was a surprise. No one expected it. He said he wants to go into private law practice and has been offered a good job as a partner with a major law firm in the city. City commissioners asked him to continue working until his replacement can be found. He agreed. The job will be advertised, with a deadline for applications on the last day of next month. The job currently pays $45,600 per year and is a full-time position.

CHAPTER 18

PUBLIC AFFAIRS REPORTING

Previous chapters described the system of beats that reporters use to gather local news. Normally, the most important beats are government offices: police stations, city halls, courthouses and federal buildings, for example. Reporters assigned to those offices visit them daily, gathering information and cultivating sources among the people who work there.

New reporters are often assigned to their cities' police and fire departments. The stories that arise there tend to be simple, requiring little expertise. After a year or two, small dailies may transfer their police reporters to more complex beats, perhaps a city hall or county courthouse. At larger dailies, the reporters covering those beats are seasoned professionals. City hall and county courthouse reporters must be familiar with their communities and with the people who live there. They must also know their local officials and understand how cities work.

In addition, the reporters covering major beats must be able to write good stories about complicated issues. The best public affairs reporters do more than describe events, however. They also explain why the events occurred and how they are related to other issues in the news.

Thus, the stories you write as a public affairs reporter will challenge all your skills. To succeed, you will have to understand what is (and is not) news, and then continually emphasize the news in every sentence and paragraph. You will also have to work hard to make every story as interesting as possible. In addition, you will have to understand and avoid a multitude of problems, some unique to public affairs reporting. The following pages discuss those problems and show you how to avoid them.

THE LEADS OF PUBLIC AFFAIRS STORIES

Every lead should emphasize the news—a story's latest and most interesting, unusual and important developments. The following rules repeat some guidelines presented earlier, but are especially important while writing stories about public affairs:

- Be specific.
- Emphasize the news—the substance of a story—not routine procedures.
- Emphasize the human element: the people involved in a story or the story's effects on other people in your community.
- Avoid jargon and descriptions of bureaucratic procedures.
- Report facts, not your opinions or interpretations of the facts.
- Write so clearly—so vividly—that your readers will be able to visualize every scene.

Unfortunately, some of the stories written about public affairs are so flat and lifeless that readers avoid them. A weak lead might report that:

> A development firm is being sued for breach of contract by its partner in a joint venture.

> The opening arguments were heard in Circuit Court in the trial of Willie Keaton of 4909 Leonard Drive on charges of burglary and petty theft.

> A special task force appointed by the mayor has recommended the establishment of a central management group to coordinate housing programs, establish support services such as job placement, and develop and support legislation that addresses the problems of the homeless.

These leads are dull and unintelligible because they contain unfamiliar terms and abstract generalities.

Some topics are less interesting than others, but that is never a valid excuse for writing a dull lead. Some reporters write dull leads because they do not understand a topic or fail to notice (and emphasize) its most interesting details. Good leads require considerable thought about what is interesting and important. Good leads also require thought about how those details should be presented to the public. Here are three more successful—more interesting—leads:

> The residue in an empty barrel exploded Monday, severely burning a 37-year-old man who was sawing the barrel in half to make a barbecue pit.

> A 73-year-old widow lay bound and gagged on a bed for nearly two days after burglars ransacked her home.

> City commissioners voted Monday to rename a ballfield in memory of a 13-year-old Little League shortstop killed by lightning.

Good leads are not an accident: a result of luck or a good assignment. Rather, good leads are written by good reporters. You are likely to notice that principle in your class. When your instructor gives everyone in your class the same assignment, some students will consistently write leads that are better than their classmates'. Similarly, reporters from competing dailies often cover the same stories, and the leads written by some are dull and unimaginative while those written by their competitors sparkle. Here are three examples:

> FIRST REPORTER: Burglars robbed the home of a 36-year-old man while he was sleeping.
> SECOND REPORTER: Burglars entered a home occupied by a man, a dog and a talking parrot, and—without causing an alarm—managed to steal almost $3,000 worth of cash and household goods.

> FIRST REPORTER: Donna Sokoler, 17, 5810 Cascade Way, was sentenced to three consecutive life terms after being convicted of three counts of murder, despite the defense of insanity.
> SECOND REPORTER: A 17-year-old high school senior who pleaded that television violence drove her insane has been convicted of poisoning her mother and two brothers.
> She was sentenced to three consecutive life terms.

> FIRST REPORTER: A local couple has filed suit against Sears, Roebuck and Co., charging that a single-mantle propane lantern malfunctioned and caused the death of their son.

SECOND REPORTER: A local couple is suing Sears, Roebuck and Co., charging that their son died of carbon monoxide poisoning because a propane lantern malfunctioned in an old school bus he used as a camper.

The following story illustrates the same principle. The first account emphasizes a squabble between government agencies. The second account emphasizes the story's impact on teen-age girls:

FIRST REPORTER: The "squeal rule," the newest proposed amendment to the Public Health Service Act, comes into direct conflict with the philosophy of the County Health Department, according to its director, Kurt Scorse.

The squeal rule, introduced in Congress Monday, would require federally funded public health clinics to notify parents within 10 days if their children have been given prescription contraceptives.

SECOND REPORTER: County health officials fear that a new federal rule "will cause an epidemic of teen-age pregnancies."

Why are some reporters better than others? The best reporters write leads that are specific and that emphasize important and unusual details. The best reporters also remember their readers, emphasizing the facts that are most likely to interest or affect them. Moreover, they present the facts so clearly that everyone can understand them.

Here are two more examples. Again, notice that the revisions are more specific and interesting:

A store clerk foiled an attempted strong-arm robbery Thursday.

REVISED: A 17-year-old high school student working as a cashier at a drug store slipped out a back door and let the air out of all four tires on a robber's car Thursday.

Police found the robber angrily kicking the car.

A local restaurant is being sued for $350,000 by a man hurt while eating lunch.

REVISED: A minister who required emergency surgery after swallowing a piece of glass in his soup is suing Tony's Restaurant, 940 Michigan Ave., for $350,000.

When you looked at the original leads, were you able to visualize the scenes? Of course not, because the leads were too vague. The revisions, by contrast, mention "a 17-year-old high school student" instead of the vaguer "a store clerk," and "let the air out of all four tires" instead of the vaguer "foiled an attempted strong-arm robbery." Similarly, the second revision mentions "a minister" instead of "a man," "Tony's Restaurant, 940 Michigan Ave." instead of "a local restaurant" and "swallowing a piece of glass in his soup" rather than "hurt while eating lunch."

To make your leads more interesting, also demonstrate their relevance. During the 1930s, one of New York's most famous editors, Stanley Walker, explained that, "A good story is one in which the average reader, whoever he is, can imagine himself, and say, subconsciously, 'Why, that could happen to me!'" Another editor, Frank Caperton, adds that, "Reporters cover a lot of meetings and tell what happens, and that's very important—they need to do that. But they also should be able to transcend that, to tell why the actions are important for their readers."

In many cases, you can demonstrate a story's relevance simply by changing your lead's angle or emphasis:

A statewide study of 8,400 students aged 13 to 19 found that 34 percent had shoplifted.

REVISED: One out of every three teen-agers you know has probably been guilty of shoplifting.

The county commissioners last night voted 7–2 in favor of constructing a sewage plant that will cost $228 million and handle 140 million gallons of sewage each day.

REVISED: The county commissioners last night voted 7–2 in favor of constructing a $228 million sewage plant. To pay for it, the average homeowner's sewer fees will triple to $96 a month.

Avoiding the Obvious and Routine

Public affairs reporters must be careful to avoid emphasizing routine or unimportant details in their leads. Every weekday, Americans file thousands of wills, lawsuits, bankruptcy petitions and other legal documents, and they file all those documents in government offices. Good leads emphasize the documents' content, not the fact that they were filed:

Attorneys for Thomas J. Totten, a real estate agent who died last week, filed his will in Probate Court on Wednesday.

REVISED: Real estate agent Thomas J. Totten has left his entire estate, valued at more than $2 million, to the Salvation Army.

A lawsuit seeking $7.5 million for a 9-year-old girl was filed in Circuit Court today.

REVISED: A lawsuit filed today seeks $7.5 million for a 9-year-old girl shot three times by a hunter who mistook her for a deer.

A local couple Tuesday filed a bankruptcy petition in the U.S. District Court here.

REVISED: A dentist and his wife filed for bankruptcy Tuesday, listing $240,000 in debts and $47 in assets.

Unless reporters are careful, the leads for other common types of public affairs stories may also state the obvious or emphasize the routine:

Due to differences that cannot be worked out, a woman married 17 years has filed for a divorce from her husband.

A police officer who became suspicious during a routine patrol last night found a man's body in a parked car.

Paramedics treated a woman after she was struck by a car while crossing Oregon Avenue today.

Most divorces are caused by "differences that cannot be worked out," and every woman wanting a divorce seeks it "from her husband." Similarly, the police routinely patrol the nation's cities, and paramedics routinely treat people who have been hurt. Thus, all three leads need to be rewritten. The first lead might specify the irreconcilable differences that caused the divorce. The second lead might emphasize the victim's death rather than the discovery of his body during a routine patrol, and the third lead might provide a more specific description of the accident or the severity of the woman's injuries.

Reporters should also avoid leads that contain several names. Especially in large cities, few readers are likely to know the people involved in minor stories. Even if those people are well-known, leads that contain several names are usually complicated and dull. To avoid the problem, emphasize what was said or done, not who was involved:

> E.D. Farnsworth has filed a suit in County Court, charging Majik Rides Inc., with negligence.
> REVISED: A college teacher whose right leg had to be amputated after a Ferris wheel he was riding collapsed is seeking $850,000 in damages.

> Christine Ann Mosher is suing Superintendent of Schools Greg Hubbard, Kennedy High School Principal Thomas R. Burney and Standard Guaranty Insurance Co. in the drowning of her daughter, Margaret.
> REVISED: A mother who charges that her 15-year-old daughter drowned in a high school pool that was left unsupervised has filed a $2.5 million lawsuit against school officials and the company that insures them.

Mistakenly, other reporters begin too many public affairs stories in chronological order. As a consequence, they fail to emphasize the stories' most important details. Normally, the way a story ended—its consequences—is more newsworthy than the way it began:

> An unidentified man called police late Friday night to report a disturbance in a parking lot at 541 Barton Ave.
> REVISED: Three high school students were hospitalized Friday night, and police say a dozen others suffered minor injuries in a fight that started after a basketball game.

> A murder trial began Monday with opening statements by the prosecution and defense.
> REVISED: Prosecutors in the murder trial of Loretta Lorenzo-Perry charged Monday that she fired three shots into her husband's back while he was sleeping, then set fire to his bed.

Before they were revised, both leads emphasized the obvious or unimportant. People normally call the police to quell disturbances, and many refuse to reveal their identities. Leads should emphasize the news (the fight and the injuries it caused), not the fact that an anonymous caller reported the disturbance to police. Similarly, most criminal trials begin with opening statements by attorneys for the prosecution and the defense. A better lead would summarize the attorneys' most newsworthy statements.

Emphasize the Specific, Not the Technical

Beginners tend to place too much emphasis on the technical charges filed against the defendants in criminal cases. News stories should describe the specific crimes involved, not just the legal charges. Because they are less specific, the legal charges often fail to reveal exactly what happened. Moreover, the same legal charges could be repeated in thousands of stories:

> A businessman pleaded guilty Monday to a charge of attempted aggravated battery against his wife and son.
> REVISED: A businessman pleaded guilty Monday to attacking his wife and son with a golf club.

Three people arrested in a church parking lot Sunday morning were charged with petty larceny.

REVISED: Three people arrested in a church parking lot Sunday morning were charged with siphoning gasoline from a car.

Similarly, when defendants appear in court, reporters should provide a specific summary of each day's proceedings. Mistakenly, beginners often emphasize a witness' identity or mention the witness' topic instead of specifically summarizing what the witness said about the topic. If reporters fail to summarize the proceedings, their leads will be much less interesting and, once again, will sound too much alike. Leads usually do not have to reveal whether a witness testified for the state or defense; that can be reported later. The news—a specific summary of the witness' most important remarks—is more important:

A 13-year-old girl testified for the state Wednesday in the murder trial of her mother.

REVISED: A 13-year-old girl testifying at her mother's murder trial Wednesday said she heard her parents arguing, then saw her mother chase her father and stab him with a steak knife.

The trial of William Allen Lee, who is accused of shooting his girlfriend, began Tuesday with the testimony of a prosecution witness who described what he saw on the day of the murder.

REVISED: A neighbor testified Tuesday that he saw William Allen Lee shoot his girlfriend, then carry her body into the house the couple shared at 914 W. 22nd St.

A jury heard opening testimony Tuesday in the trial of a man charged with raping an 11-year-old boy.

REVISED: An 11-year-old boy testified Tuesday that, while spending the night at a friend's house, he was awakened at about 2 a.m. and raped by the friend's uncle.

Stories about wills, lawsuits, bankruptcy petitions and other legal documents should also summarize their specific content. The stories about most lawsuits explain why they were filed: why one person is suing another. Similarly, the stories about most wills describe an estate's value and disposition. However, an estate's recipients do not have to be identified by name in the lead:

The will of Marguerite Vernay, a longtime local resident, was filed in Probate Court on Wednesday.

REVISED: A 73-year-old woman who died last month left more than $160,000 to three neighbors who took her shopping once a week and invited her to their homes on holidays.

A woman who died last year has named her husband as the trustee and personal representative of her estate.

REVISED: A 37-year-old woman who established a chain of 82 restaurants left more than $800,000 to her husband but stipulated that he cannot remarry for at least five years.

In addition to emphasizing the unique content and specific details of a legal document, a lead should report anything unusual about it. The final paragraph in one news story revealed that a young man who robbed a restaurant apologized to the cashier, saying,

"I'm sorry, but my wife is having a baby, and I need your money." That quotation should have been moved to the story's lead. The following leads also emphasize the unusual:

> Two police officers who charged a woman with shoplifting a $6.98 bottle of perfume Monday afternoon found more than $10,000 in cash when they searched her purse.

> The city is threatening to sue more than 700 people, including a member of the City Council and three police officers, because the checks used to pay their property taxes failed to clear their banks.

Again, as all these examples indicate, the best leads tend to be the most specific. They provide a clear summary of each story's unique details, telling readers exactly what was said or done:

> GENERALITY: Beginning Jan. 1, county residents summoned for jury duty will be introduced to a new system.
> REVISED: Beginning Jan. 1, county residents summoned for jury duty will be required to serve only two instead of five days.

> GENERALITY: A local couple has filed a $500,000 lawsuit against Southern Airways Inc., charging the airline with negligence.
> REVISED: A 52-year-old man and his wife have filed a $500,000 lawsuit against Southern Airways Inc., charging that the man was seriously injured when he fell 18 feet from a jetliner to a concrete runway.

> GENERALITY: A suit filed in U.S. District Court charges the Moore Manufacturing Corp. with a violation of the Age Discrimination Employment Act of 1967.
> REVISED: A 58-year-old salesman who says he was fired because of his age has filed a $600,000 lawsuit against Moore Manufacturing Corp.

Each of the following leads contains a number of errors, including generalities, routine details, technical charges and unfamiliar names. Notice how much more interesting the leads become when the errors are corrected:

> Marilyn Curtin of 178 Crestview Circle was charged with one misdemeanor and two felonies following an altercation Friday night.
> REVISED: A woman participating in an amateur topless contest at a local bar was charged with disorderly conduct, kicking a police officer and resisting arrest after she lost the contest Friday night.

> Danny Doss Parker, 28, 122 Lake Sumpter Drive, was acquitted Monday of charges of sexual battery.
> REVISED: After deliberating for two days, a jury found a 28-year-old attorney innocent of charges that he abducted and raped a neighbor.

> Frederick R. Little, Thomas Pohl and Mildred Cress have been charged with grand theft in the second degree.
> REVISED: Police have charged three high school students with stealing $7 in coins and a cassette tape recorder from a parked car.

Remaining Objective

Public affairs reporters must be careful to avoid commenting on the stories they cover. Their comments are unnecessary and likely to confuse rather than clarify:

> Police are resting easier this morning after two bomb threats during the night proved to be hoaxes.

> A shopper learned Wednesday that taking too long to get through a grocery checkout line may lead to violence from those waiting impatiently behind her.

The first example seems to reflect a rather contrived attempt to update the story. But the statement is trite and simplistic. The same statement could be used in most crime and accident stories, since the police are usually happy when a case is resolved. The statement is also likely to be mistaken. Instead of resting after a hoax, the police continue to respond to other calls. The second lead fails to tell readers exactly what happened, and it is subjective (how does the reporter know whether or what the shopper learned?). Here are two more examples:

> A casual shopping trip became a nightmare when a woman fell in a shopping mall Wednesday night.
> REVISED: No one noticed a 54-year-old woman who fell while shopping for a dress in the Colonial Mall Wednesday night. The woman lost consciousness and was locked in the mall overnight, unable to move or call for help.

> An argument over a grade at a high school turned into a tragedy but ended in a heroic display Friday afternoon.
> REVISED: Three high school students surrounded, then tackled a classmate who stabbed a teacher at Kennedy High School Friday afternoon.

Until they were revised, both leads failed to tell what happened: to clearly summarize the stories' primary details.

THE BODIES OF PUBLIC AFFAIRS STORIES

Avoiding Jargon

Public affairs reporters must be especially careful to avoid bureaucratic and technical jargon in the bodies of news stories. While covering the police beat, for example, you are likely to see reports stating that, "One of the perpetrators exited the suspect vehicle and used a crowbar to gain entry to the premises." The reporters covering government agencies gradually learn the jargon's meaning, become accustomed to its use and—if they are not careful—begin to use it in their stories. Yet the jargon is unnecessary and often wordy and redundant. Moreover, readers are unlikely to understand it.

Avoid using words that are not a part of your daily vocabulary. One of your jobs as a reporter is either to eliminate the jargon or to translate it into plain, simple language that your readers can understand.

> By order of her last will and testament, the architect left her entire estate to her daughter.
> REVISED: The architect left her entire estate to her daughter.

The men were released on their own recognizance.
REVISED: The men were released without having to post bail.

He asked the county to rezone the land from R-1AA to P-O and MFR-2.
REVISED: He asked the county to rezone the land from single-family residential (R-1AA) to professional office (P-O) and multiple-family residential (MFR-2).
OR: He asked the county to rezone the land to permit the construction of professional offices and duplexes instead of single-family homes.

Jargon is especially common in lawsuits. Plaintiffs frequently charge that they suffered "great mental and physical pain" and that the defendants "acted in a careless and reckless manner." Other examples of the jargon in lawsuits include:

She charges that she suffered permanent injury to her head, neck, torso, body and nervous sytem.
REVISED: She charges that she was permanently injured.

Mrs. Harris says the sidewalk was slippery, worn, cracked and unsafe to walk on.
REVISED: Mrs. Harris says the sidewalk was unsafe.

While writing about a lawsuit, there's rarely any need to discuss every technical detail: to report that a couple is suing "individually and jointly," for example. If you add that the couple has charged a company "with strict liability, breach of implied warranty and negligence," few readers are likely to understand your story. Look for the specifics: the fact that the couple is upset because they found several bugs in their beer.

Government officials use thousands of other legal and technical terms: "ad valorem taxes," "capital outlays," "declaratory judgments," "percolation ponds," "promissory notes," "rapid infiltration basins," "secured and unsecured debts" and "tangible personal property." All those terms can be replaced by something simpler and more familiar or, often, can simply be deleted. For example, while writing about plans to fix a sewer system, one reporter explained that the repairs were necessary "because of groundwater infiltration." Another reporter explained more clearly that the sewer pipes were so old and cracked that water was leaking into them.

If a legal or technical term is essential to a story, define it:

The store filed for protection under Chapter 11 of the federal bankruptcy laws. Chapter 11 will protect the store from creditors' lawsuits while it tries to reorganize.

Police officers handcuffed the student and committed her to a hospital under the Baker Act. The Baker Act allows authorities to commit people for observation if they seem to be a threat to themselves or others.

Using Quotations and Descriptions

To make your stories more interesting, try to include some quotations and descriptions. Good quotations and descriptions can make even routine stories come alive:

Bryant remained chained and handcuffed throughout the three-week trial.

Harold Picott, 36, told the judge that he had "a few drinks" before police officers stopped him for driving the wrong way on a one-way street.

"But I wasn't drunk," he said. "I just made a wrong turn."

The jury deliberated nearly seven hours before deciding that Zaslow acted in self-defense when he kicked a police officer.

Zaslow waited nervously outside the courtroom. Dressed in a T-shirt and jeans, he paced the hallway, a cigarette in his hand all the while.

Zaslow showed no emotion when the jury announced its verdict. However, when Judge Joseph Miklosi said he was free to go, Zaslow turned to the back of the nearly empty courtroom and smiled at his father. Then he walked out a side door.

ATTRIBUTING CHARGES AND INCLUDING RESPONSES

Many of the issues you cover as a public affairs reporter are likely to be controversial and thus to require attribution. Critically examine all the information you handle, and attribute all statements of opinion you include in your stories. Attribution is especially critical in stories about lawsuits. Lawsuits present only the plaintiff's charges; defendants are likely to deny those charges, and judges may rule (months or even years later) that the charges are unfounded. Thus, you will need to indicate clearly that the charges are the plaintiffs' allegations, not accepted facts. For example:

Because of the accident, Samuelson will require medical care for the rest of his life.

REVISED: Samuelson's lawsuit says he will require medical care for the rest of his life.

The passengers' personal baggage, which had been placed in racks above the seats, was not properly stored and, as a result of the careless driving of the bus driver, a heavy piece of baggage fell from one of the racks and struck Heinrich's head with great force and violence.

REVISED: Heinrich's lawsuit charges that a suitcase fell from an overhead rack and struck his head.

Because of the danger of libel, few newspapers would report the allegation that the bus driver acted carelessly. Consequently, that allegation was deleted when the sentence was revised.

Whenever possible, include the defendants' responses to the charges filed against them. If legal documents do not include the defendants' responses, reporters can often obtain them by calling the defendants or their attorneys. The following example and revision illustrate the inclusion of a defendant's response. They also illustrate the need to condense, to simplify and to attribute the claims made by a plaintiff:

He was caused to slip, trip and fall as a direct result of the negligence and carelessness of the store because of a liquid on the ground. This fall injured his neck, head, body, limbs and nervous system and caused him to be unable to lead a normal life and to lose his normal wages for a prolonged period of time.

REVISED: The suit charges that he slipped and fell on a wet sidewalk outside the store, dislocating his arm and shoulder and tearing several ligaments.

The store's manager responded that, "He was running to get out of the rain and slipped and fell on the wet pavement."

THE PROBLEM OF LIBEL

Because many of the stories they write will harm someone's reputation, reporters covering the police and courts must be especially careful to avoid the problem of libel. As was explained in Chapter 12, reporters can state that a person has been *charged* with a crime. However, reporters cannot say that the person is *guilty*—that the person actually committed the crime—until after that person has been convicted by a judge or jury.

The police, other law enforcement officials and several bystanders may insist that a defendant is guilty. Still, you cannot report their allegations. They may be mistaken or their allegations may be impossible to prove. If so, your paper could lose a million-dollar lawsuit. Even more important, people in our society are presumed innocent and have a right to be tried in a court of law, not by a mob on a street corner nor by their local daily.

No one knows how many crimes occur each year; many are never reported to the police. Statistics compiled in one of the nation's largest states revealed that 803,509 crimes were reported in one year, and that the reports led to 438,222 arrests. Yet few of the arrests led to a trial or conviction. Only 20,020 (4.5 percent) of the cases resulted in a trial, and only 13,213 (3.0 percent) of the defendants who went to trial pleaded or were found guilty.

Remember those statistics the next time you write about a crime. If you libel someone—if you report that a suspect arrested by the police is guilty—you are likely to be wrong. Or, even if you are right, you may be unable to prove the suspect's guilt to a judge and jury.

The following stories do not libel the defendants because they never report that the defendants are guilty of committing a crime. Rather, each of the stories seems to be describing two different people: (1) the defendant and (2) the criminal. The stories never say that the defendant is the criminal, that the defendant actually committed the crime:

> A clerk and two customers tackled a woman who punched the manager of a convenience store on North Avenue Sunday night and snatched $73 from a cash register.
>
> Police say the woman entered the store shortly after 11 p.m., began arguing with the manager, then punched her and took the money.
>
> Two men entering the store witnessed the incident and tackled the woman as she tried to flee. They and a clerk then held the woman until police arrived.
>
> The police charged Anna Diaz, 31, of 709 Stewart Ave. with assault and attempted robbery.

> A 27-year-old woman is suing a downtown hotel because she was raped in the hotel's parking garage on her wedding night.
>
> On Tuesday, the woman filed a suit in Circuit Court, charging that the Grand Hotel failed to adequately protect its guests.
>
> The hotel's general manager, Lillian DeLoy, responded that the hotel's security is adequate.
>
> According to the woman's attorney, James R. Lopez, the rape took place in front of an empty security office—a glassed-in booth with a view of the entire garage.
>
> The attack occurred when the bride returned to her parked car for a suitcase at about 11 p.m. Police arrested a suspect a short time later.
>
> Myron Jaco, 18, of 141 Pine St. has been charged with sexual battery and is scheduled to stand trial next month.

ADDITIONAL GUIDELINES

Reporters must consider several additional guidelines while covering public affairs stories.

1. Reporters should be skeptical of the amounts of money demanded in lawsuits. Plaintiffs can demand any amount they want, even obviously exorbitant amounts. To attract more publicity, some lawyers encourage their clients to demand huge amounts, often hundreds of thousands of dollars, as compensation for minor injuries. The plaintiffs normally settle for much less, often a small fraction of the amounts they originally demanded. Consequently, leads generally should not emphasize any of those amounts.

2. Some reporters use too much attribution. You do not have to attribute uncontested facts provided by government officials, especially not in leads:

> Two women entered the Grand Hotel at noon Monday and robbed it of $640, according to a police report.
> REVISED: Two women entered the Grand Hotel at noon Monday and robbed it of $640.

> Sheriff's deputies reported that one person was killed and three injured when two cars collided on State Route 17 at noon Friday.
> REVISED: One person was killed and three injured when two cars collided on State Route 17 at noon Friday.

You can often avoid excessive attribution by writing a summary lead, then adding a transition such as, "Witnesses gave this account. . . ." After the transition, you may be able to report all the remaining facts without any further attribution.

3. While describing a crime, do not mention that it was committed by an "unidentified" man or woman. Criminals rarely announce their identities, and most crimes are never solved. Thus, most criminals are never "identified." Similarly, if police do not know a criminal's identity, you cannot report that the police are looking for "a suspect." If the police do not know who committed a crime, they have no suspect.

4. Avoid reporting a suspect's race or religion unless it is clearly relevant to your story. The problem of racial discrimination has been especially common in police stories. In the past (and sometimes even today) reporters mentioned only the race of suspects and criminals who were members of minority groups.

Race is relevant, however, in the description of a specific individual, such as:

> Witnesses described the thief as a white male, about 25 and 6 feet tall.
> The thief had a mustache, a scar on his left cheek and was missing several front teeth.

5. People normally "suffer" or "sustain" injuries. They "receive" gifts.

6. Especially while covering the police beat, remember the differences between a robbery, burglary, theft and swindle. Normally, a robbery involves the threat or use of violence. A burglary involves entering a building. A theft involves a larceny without the threat or use of violence. A swindle involves some trickery, not force or violence.

7. Report only what occurred, not what has not occurred. This problem is especially common in police reports, which often state that:

- No one was hurt
- There are no suspects.
- Officers searched the neighborhood but were unable to find the vandals.

A NOTE ABOUT THIS CHAPTER'S EXERCISES

Many of the documents available to a public affairs reporter—lawsuits and police reports, for example—provide all the information needed for minor stories. Examples of such documents are reprinted in this chapter's exercises. Write a news story about each document. Unless the instructions say otherwise, assume that the police reports have been prepared by officers who investigated incidents in your community, and that all the other legal documents have been filed in your city hall, county courthouse or federal building.

Most of the exercises use genuine copies of actual government documents. Even the most unusual police reports are based on actual cases.

SUGGESTED READINGS

The Adversary Press. A Modern Media Institute Ethics Center Seminar. St. Petersburg, Fla., 1983.

Buchanan, Edna. *The Corpse Had a Familiar Face.* New York: Random House, 1987. (Reprinted in paperback by Charter Books.)

Campbell, Don. *Inside the Beltway: A Guide to Washington Reporting.* Ames, IA: Iowa State University Press, 1991.

Dunn, Delmer D. *Public Officials and the Press.* Reading, MA: Addison-Wesley, 1969.

Graber, Doris A. *Mass Media And American Politics.* 3rd ed. Washington, DC: CQ Press, 1989.

Griffin, Robert J., Dayle H. Molen, Clay Schoenfeld, James F. Scotton, with others. *Interpreting Public Issues.* Ames, IA: Iowa State University Press, 1991.

Kelly, Patricia A. *Police and the Media: Bridging Troubled Waters.* Springfield, IL: Thomas, 1987.

Killenberg, George M. *Public Affairs Reporting: Covering the News in the Information Age.* New York: St. Martin's Press, 1992.

Leonard, Thomas C. *The Power of the Press: The Birth of American Political Reporting.* New York: Oxford University Press, 1986.

McIntrye, Bryce T. *Advanced Newsgathering.* New York: Praeger, 1991.

Press, Charles, and Kenneth Verburg. *American Politicians and Journalists.* Glenview, IL: Scott, Foresman/Little Brown, 1988.

Siegal, Leon V. *Reporters and Officials: The Organization and Politics of Newsmaking.* Lexington, MA: Heath, 1973.

Strentz, Herbert. *News Reporters and News Sources: Accomplices in Shaping and Misshaping the News.* 2nd ed. Ames, IA: Iowa State University Press, 1989.

Ward, Hiley H. *Reporting in Depth.* Mountain View, CA: Mayfield, 1991.

QUOTES

It is a newspaper's duty to print the news, and raise hell.

(Wilbur Storey, statement of the aims of the Chicago Times*)*

Never do anything in secret or anything that you wish to hide. For the desire to hide anything means that you are afraid, and fear is a bad thing and unworthy of you. . . . Privacy, of course, we may have and should have, but that is a very different thing from secrecy.

(Jawaharlal Nehru)

Exercise 1

PUBLIC AFFAIRS REPORTING

EVALUATING LEADS

INSTRUCTIONS: Critically evaluate the following leads from public affairs stories. Discuss the leads in class and decide which are most effective, and why. As you evaluate the leads, look for general principles that will help you write better leads. For example: What common problems should you strive to avoid?

1. A man posing as a crime prevention officer tied up and robbed an elderly woman Friday after she let him in to inspect her home.
2. The School Board has voted to grant teachers a 5.8 percent raise but complained that their union protects incompetent teachers and opposes merit pay for outstanding teachers.
3. The city's Crime Prevention Commission has completed its study and announced more than 60 recommendations Monday.
4. A local couple is suing a doctor and a hospital for brain damage suffered by their daughter as a result of improper monitoring during a routine operation.
5. A robbery victim opened testimony Wednesday in the first-degree murder and armed robbery trial of a 19-year-old woman.
6. An ad hoc committee Thursday made recommendations on zoning criteria for foster homes and foster group homes at a workshop session of the county commission.
7. Police say two men have been arrested and charged with burglary to a residence.
8. Two 16-year-old boys who heard burglars break into a neighbor's house Sunday night called the police, then deflated all four tires on the burglars' van.
9. A jury of four men and two women took only 15 minutes Thursday to convict a Montana man of selling 1,000 morphine tablets to undercover agents.
10. The First Federal Bank was evacuated Monday morning as police searched the premises for a bomb.
11. The county's Department of Community Affairs is presently undertaking several ambitious programs designed to benefit residents of the county.
12. A case involving a man who admitted committing three armed robberies may be dismissed because of a technical error.
13. A gunman jumped behind the customer service counter of a local department store Monday afternoon, grabbed a handful of money and ran down a fire escape.
14. A 27-year-old woman who admitted she lied to welfare officials has been ordered to repay $850.
15. A New Jersey manufacturing company is suing a local business and nine of its employees for breach of employment contract.
16. A man on trial in a federal court here sat expressionless as his brother testified against him.
17. An Indiana couple has filed a $1 million lawsuit against two chiropractors they claim are responsible for their son's birth defects.
18. A 24-year-old man convicted of the shooting deaths of his wife and two children was sentenced Thursday to 199 years in prison with no chance of parole.

Exercise 2

PUBLIC AFFAIRS REPORTING

AVOIDING AND DEFINING JARGON

SECTION I: Rewrite the following sentences, providing clear explanations or definitions of the terms that appear in italics.

1. The police *read Lewis his rights*.
2. The jury awarded her $2 million in *punitive damages*.
3. The company's stockholders filed *a class action suit*.
4. The judge sentenced him to two 20-year terms to be served *consecutively*.
5. The judge refused to grant *a change of venue* or to *sequester* the jury.

SECTION II: Rewrite the following sentences, simplifying or eliminating the jargon.

1. She said the car was negligently, carelessly and improperly designed.
2. Police said thieves gained access to the premises by prying open a back door to the restaurant.
3. He says he suffered contusions in and about the head, neck, back, leg, body, spine and nervous system.
4. He says the libelous statements received widespread publicity and caused him extreme humiliation, mental anguish and physical deterioration.
5. Brown charges that he suffered from bodily injury, disability, disfigurement and mental anguish; that he lost his ability to earn a decent living; that he lost the cost of his hospital bills; and, further, that the auto accident aggravated a previous medical condition.

SECTION III: Define the following terms, which frequently appear in public affairs stories. Use "Black's Law Dictionary" and other reference books in your campus and city libraries.

1. ad hoc committee
2. affidavit
3. arraignment
4. common law
5. deposition
6. felony
7. grand jury
8. habeas corpus
9. injunction
10. nolo contendere

Exercise 3

PUBLIC AFFAIRS REPORTING

911 EMERGENCY: A CHILD'S HEROISM

A 6-year-old girl placed the following call to a 911 dispatcher. Assume that the girl placed the call in your city today. She is Laura Burke, the daughter of Lynn and Randy Burke of 412 Wilson Avenue.

Police arrested a neighbor, Andrew Caspinwall of 416 Wilson Avenue, and charged him with raping Mrs. Burke. Bail has been set at $250,000, and Caspinwall, 24, is being held in the county jail.

DISPATCHER: "911 emergency. Hello?"
GIRL: "My mommy needs help."
DISPATCHER: "What's wrong?"
GIRL: "Somebody's hurting my mommy."
DISPATCHER: "Where do you live?"
GIRL: "At home with my mommy and daddy."
DISPATCHER: "No, uh, that's not what I mean. Can you tell me where your house is, your address?"
GIRL: "Wilson Avenue."
DISPATCHER: "Do you know the address, the number?"
GIRL: "Hurry. My mommy's crying."
DISPATCHER: "No, honey, do you know your address?"
GIRL, CRYING: "I gotta think. It's, uh, it's, uh, 4 something, I'm not sure. 412. 412."
DISPATCHER: "OK. I'll send help."
GIRL, CRYING: "Hurry."
DISPATCHER: "What's your name?"
GIRL: "Laura. Laura Anne Burke."
DISPATCHER: "Can you tell me what's wrong, who's hurting your mother?"
GIRL: "A man. He came in the back door and hit my mommy."
DISPATCHER: "Where are you now?"
GIRL: "Upstairs."
DISPATCHER: "Does the man know you're there?"
GIRL: "No. I'm hiding."
DISPATCHER: "Where are you hiding?"
GIRL: "In my mommy and daddy's room. Under the bed."
DISPATCHER: "Can you lock the door?"
GIRL: "I don't know. Maybe."
DISPATCHER: "Don't hang up. Just put the phone down and go lock the door. Then come back, talk to me some more."
GIRL: "My mommy. What'll happen to my mommy?"
DISPATCHER: "We've got three police cars coming. They'll be there in a minute. Now go lock the door, and don't let anyone in until I tell you. OK?"
GIRL: "I guess so."
DISPATCHER: "Hello? Hello? Laura, are you there?"
GIRL: "I locked the door."
DISPATCHER: "How old are you Laura?"
GIRL: "Six."

DISPATCHER: "You're doing a good job, Laura. You have to be brave now to help your mommy. Tell me, is the man armed?"

GIRL: "What's that mean?"

DISPATCHER: "Does he have a gun?"

GIRL: "No. A knife."

DISPATCHER: "OK, a knife. Is the man still there, Laura?"

GIRL, SOBBING: "I don't know. I'm afraid. Will he hurt me too?"

DISPATCHER: "No one will hurt you, Laura. Be brave. The police are outside now. They'll be coming into your house. You may hear some noise, but that's OK. Stay in the bedroom, and don't let anyone in, OK?"

GIRL: "OK."

DISPATCHER: "Your daddy's coming too. We've found your daddy."

GIRL: "Soon?"

DISPATCHER: "The police say they're in your house. They're helping your mommy now. They've found your mommy, and they're going to take her to a doctor, a hospital."

GIRL: "The man?"

DISPATCHER: "He's been caught, arrested. It's OK. It's safe to go downstairs now. There are people there to help you. They want to talk to you, Laura. Can you unlock your door and go downstairs? Laura? Hello? Are you there? Laura? Hello? Laura?"

Exercise 4

PUBLIC AFFAIRS REPORTING

911 EMERGENCY: THE DAHMER TAPES

Police officers in Milwaukee, Wis., found 11 mutilated bodies in an apartment rented by Jeffrey L. Dahmer. Dahmer, 31, confessed to killing a total of 17 people, and pleaded that he was insane. One of Dahmer's victims was a 14-year-old Laotian boy, Konerak Sinthasomphone, whom the police might have saved. When he was finally arrested, Dahmer told police that two officers had been at his apartment two months earlier to investigate a 911 call involving the 14-year-old. The officers left the boy at the apartment, and Dahmer then killed him.

The police later released this transcript of the 911 call. It reveals that a Milwaukee resident named Glenda Cleveland called the police at 2 a.m. the previous May 27. Mrs. Cleveland told a 911 dispatcher that her daughter and a niece had seen the boy on a street corner, and that the boy needed help. In a follow-up call, Mrs. Cleveland, 37, asked the officers if they were certain that the boy was an adult.

A week before the tape's release, the two officers were suspended with pay, but not identified. A lawyer representing the officers said they had seen no evidence at Dahmer's apartment to suggest that anything was wrong. Also, they believed that the naked male was a man living with Dahmer. The officers' lawyer added that they tried to interview the boy, but that he seemed to be seriously intoxicated.

Assume that the Milwaukee police: (1) have already found the bodies and interviewed Dahmer, (2) suspended the officers one week ago and (3) released the transcript today. Write a news story that summarizes the transcript's content. Since this is a verbatim copy of the transcript, you can quote it directly. Include whatever background information seems necessary.

DISPATCHER: "Milwaukee emergency. Operator 71."

WOMAN: "OK. Hi. I am on 25th and State. And there's this young man. He's butt-naked and he has been beaten up. He is very bruised up. He can't stand. He is . . . butt-naked. He has no clothes on. He is really hurt. And I, you know, ain't got no coat on. But I just seen him. He needs some help."

DISPATCHER: "Where is he at?"

WOMAN: "25th and State. The corner of 25th and State."

DISPATCHER: "He's just on the corner of the street?"

WOMAN: "He's in the middle of the street. He (unintelligible). We tried to help him. Some people trying to help him."

DISPATCHER: "OK. And he's unconscious right now?"

WOMAN: "He is getting him up. 'Cause he is bruised up. Somebody must have jumped on him and stripped him or whatever."

DISPATCHER: "OK. Let me put the fire department on the line. They will send an ambulance. Just stay on the phone, OK?"

WOMAN: "OK."

[The dispatcher transferred the call to the fire department and the woman asked for an ambulance, saying a "butt-naked young boy or man or whatever" needed help.]

WOMAN: "He's been beaten up real bad. . . . He can't stand up. . . . He has no clothes on. He is very hurt."

                        FIRE
DEPARTMENT
DISPATCHER: "Is he awake?"
      WOMAN: "He ain't awake. They are trying to get him to walk, but he
                    can't walk straight. He can't even see straight. Any time he
                    stand up he just fall down."
DISPATCHER: "25th and State? All right. OK."

[The woman hung up. The next part of the tape is a police radio transmission of a
dispatcher reporting the woman's call to a street officer.]

DISPATCHER: "36. I got a man down. Caller states there is a man badly
                    beaten and is wearing no clothes, lying in the street, 2-5 and
                    State. Anonymous female caller. Ambulance sent."
      OFFICER: "10-4."

[A Milwaukee emergency operator received information from the sheriff's department,
checking on another call that reported a male dragging a naked male who looked
injured.]

      EMERGENCY
      OPERATOR: "OK. We will get someone out."

[The next conversation involved an officer reporting back to the dispatcher over the
police radio.]

      OFFICER: "36. . . . Intoxicated Asian, naked male. (Laughter.) Was re-
                    turned to his sober boyfriend. (More laughter)."

[An officer advised (C-10) that the assignment was completed (C-18) and the squad
was ready for new duties (10-8). There was a 40-second gap in the tape, then:]

      OFFICER: "Squad 65."
DISPATCHER: "65."
      OFFICER: "Ah, give myself and 64 C-10 and put us 10-8."
DISPATCHER: "10-4 64 and 65."
      OFFICER: "10-4. It will be a minute. My partner is going to get deloused
                    at the station." (Laughter.)
DISPATCHER: "10-4."

[A woman later called Milwaukee Emergency and told the dispatcher that 10 minutes
ago her daughter and niece "flagged down" a policeman after they "walked up on a
young child being molested by a male guy." She said the officers took no information
from the girls, and the boy was naked and bleeding. The woman said further information
"must be needed." The dispatcher asked the location of the incident, and the woman
repeated that her daughter's and niece's names were not taken.]

      WOMAN: "The fact is a crime was being committed. I am sure you must
                    need, you know, some kind of information based on that."

[The call was transferred, and the woman repeated the squad number and the address
of the incident. The women asked if squad car 68 "brought someone in, a child being
molested by an adult that was witnessed by my daughter and niece."]

      WOMAN: "Their names or nothing was taken down and I wonder if this
                    situation was being handled. . . . What it indicated was that
                    this was a male child being raped and molested by an adult."

[The police agent referred the call to another district after getting the address of the incident. The woman repeated her story again to another official. Eventually, she reached an officer who was at the scene.]

> OFFICER: "Hello. This is . . . of the Milwaukee Police."
>
> WOMAN: "Yes. There was a squad car number 68 that was flagged down earlier this evening. About 15 minutes ago."
>
> OFFICER: "That was me."
>
> WOMAN: "Ya, ah, what happened? I mean my daughter and my niece witnessed what was going on. Was anything done about the situation? Do you need their names or information or anything from them?"
>
> OFFICER: "No, not at all."
>
> WOMAN: "You don't?"
>
> OFFICER: "Nope. It's an intoxicated boyfriend of another boyfriend."
>
> WOMAN: "Well, how old was this child?"
>
> OFFICER: "It wasn't a child, it was an adult."
>
> WOMAN: "Are you sure?"
>
> OFFICER: "Yup."
>
> WOMAN: "Are you positive? Because this child doesn't even speak English. My daughter had, you know, dealt with him before, seeing him on the street."
>
> OFFICER: "Hmmm. Yea. No. He's, he's, oh, it's all taken care of, ma'am."
>
> WOMAN: "Are you sure?"
>
> OFFICER: "Ma'am. I can't make it any more clear. It's all taken care of. That's, you know, he's with his boyfriend and, ah, his boyfriend's apartment, where he's got his belongings also. And that is where it is released."
>
> WOMAN: "Isn't this, I mean, what if he's a child and not an adult. I mean are you positive this is an adult?"
>
> OFFICER: "Ma'am. Ma'am. Like I explained to you. It is all taken care of. It's as positive as I can be. OK. I can't do anything about somebody's sexual preferences in life."
>
> WOMAN: "Well, no, I am not saying anything about that, but it appeared to have been a child. This is my concern."
>
> OFFICER: "No. No. He's not."
>
> WOMAN: "He's not a child?"
>
> OFFICER: "No, he's not. OK? And it's a boyfriend-boyfriend thing. And he's got belongings at the house where he came from."
>
> WOMAN: "Hmmmm. Hmmm."
>
> OFFICER: "He has got very . . . pictures of himself and his boyfriend and so forth. So . . . ."
>
> WOMAN: "Oh, I see."
>
> OFFICER: "OK."
>
> WOMAN: "OK. I am just, you know, it appeared to have been a child. That was my concern."
>
> OFFICER: "I understand. No, he is not. Nope."
>
> WOMAN: "Oh. OK. Thank you. 'Bye."

Exercise 5

PUBLIC AFFAIRS REPORTING

Submitting Agency	Sheriff's Dept.			
Descrip- tion Of Victim	**Sex** M	**Descent** Cau.	**Age** 43	**Height** 6'
Weight 180	**Hair** Brown	**Eyes** Blue	**Build** Med.	**Complexion** Tanned

Identifying Marks and Characteristics
Missing tips of two fingers on left hand.

Clothing & Jewelry Worn
Jeans, T-shirt, denim jacket

Victim's Name (last - first - middle) Burmester, Herman Andrew		Comp. No. 867041
Location of Occurrence Holden Rd. one mile north of the city	**Dist.** 23	**Type** Suburban
Date & Time Occurred 9:30 a.m. today	Date & Time Reported To. P.D. 9:32 a.m.	
Type of Premises (loc. of victim) Construction site	Cause of Injury (instr. or means) Fall of about 30 feet	
Reason (Acc.-Ill health, etc.) See narrative below	Extent of Injury (Minor or Serious) Very serious	
Remove To (address) Memorial Hospital	Removed By Alco Ambulance	

Investigative Division or Unit Notified & Person(s) Contacted
Rittmann Engineering Co.

Wife, Sally Burmester

INJURY REPORT   UCR

CODE   R- Person Reporting   D- Person Discovering   W- Witness

	Victim's Occupation Iron worker	Residence Address 1214 S. 23rd St.	City (Yours)	Res. Phone 671-2108	X	Bus. Phone 644-2842	X
	Name R&W Bill McGowin	4842 S. Conway Rd.	(Yours)	671-7022		644-2842	X
	W James Randolph	654 Harrison St.	(Yours)	644-0814		644-2842	X
	W Floyd Leidigh	1218 Dickens Ave.	(Yours)	644-6817		644-2842	X

(1) Reconstruct the circumstances surrounding the injury. (2) Describe physical evidence, location found, & give disposition.

All those persons involved are construction workers and employed by Rittmann

Engineering Co. They were putting up I-beams on the third floor and some steel supports

for the roof of a new warehouse being built on Holden Road, and were working about 30

feet off the ground at the time the accident occurred. Leidigh was operating a crane,

and McGowin and Randolph were up on the third level working with Burmester when there

was a sudden gust of wind while Burmester was standing on a beam, and they report that

he seemed to lose his balance, stumble for a minute and then fall backward, landing on

the structure's concrete base. It rained in the area last night, and everything was

obviously still wet and slippery this morning. There were no rails or safety lines on

the site yet. Only the steel frame for the building has been put up, and the beam

Burmester was standing on measures only 14 inches in width. He was about 8 feet from

the nearest crossbeam. Burmester never lost consciousness, and paramedics in the

ambulance say both his legs are broken. He also seemed to be experiencing some
paralysis of his other extremities. He's being treated in intensive care. Because

of his condition, we were unable to interview him.

Supervisor Approving E.G.	Emp. No. 941	Interviewing Officer(s) Wilcox	Emp. No. 1618	Person Reporting Injury (signature) x Bill McGowin

602-07-23A   **INJURY REPORT**

Exercise 6

PUBLIC AFFAIRS REPORTING

Fire Department Submitting Agency					Name of Deceased (last, first, & middle) Lora Anne and Karen Lynn Dolmovich		Comp. No. 82471
Description Of Deceased	Sex	Descent	Hair	Eyes	Location of Occurrence 714 N. 23rd Street	Dist. 7	Type (Trf, Nat) Accident
Height	Weight	Age	Build	Complexion	Location of Original Illness or Injury 714 N. 23rd Street	Dist. 7	Type Orig. Rpt.

Identifying Marks & Characteristics	Date/Time Original Ill./Inj. 8 p.m. yesterday	Occupation of Deceased None	Date & time Rptd to P.D. 8:05 p.m.
See below	Date/Time Deceased Discovered 8:05 p.m. yesterday	Date/Time Death Occurred 8 p.m. yesterday	Relatives Notified By Were on scene
Clothing and Jewelry Worn None	Removed To (Address) Mercy Hospital		Removed By Paramedics
	Probable Cause of Death Electrocution	Reason (quarrel - illness - revenge - etc.) Accidental	
Deceased's Residence Address 714 N. 23rd Street	Investigation Division or Unit Notified & Persons Contacted Coroner's Office		
Deceased's Business Address None	**DEATH REPORT**		UCR 48-B-8216

CODE:	R- Person Reporting Death	D- Person Discovering Death	I- Person Identifying Deceased	W-Witness	Day Phone ------- X

CODE	Nearest Relative	Relationship I		Address	City I	Phone	X
RDI	Sandra M. Dolmovich	Notified ☐YES ☐NO	Res. Bus.	714 N. 23rd St. 2318 N. Main Street	Yours Yours	824-2791 365-7884	
	Name		Res. Bus.				
			Res. Bus.				

Doctor in Attendance None	Business Address	Phone

Source of Call (How notified & By Whom) Call came from girls' mother. Rescue Squad paramedics dispatched at 8:06 p.m.

Medical Examiner's Name Marlene Stoudnour	Medical Examiner Case No. SD-24-8928

DISPOSITION OF PROPERTY	☒ RELEASED TO M.E.	RECEIPT ☒YES ☐NO	ADDRESS_____
	☐ RELEASED TO RELATIVES	NAME_____	_____

(1) Reconstruct the circumstances surrounding the death. (2) Describe physical evidence, location found & give disposition.

Sandra M. Dolmovich, natural mother of Lora Anne Dolmovich, age 3, and Karen Lynn Dolmovich, age 5, reports that shortly after dinner last night she left her two girls playing in a bathtub as she straightened up the kitchen. After a few minutes, when the mother could not hear the girls splashing around, she went into the bathroom to check. She found both the girls lying face down in the water. A hair dryer, which was plugged in, was also in the water. The victims' mother says she normally kept the hair dryer on a radiator next to the bathtub. She says she immediately pulled the cord and then pulled both girls from the water and called the Fire Department Rescue Squad. The dispatcher received the call at 8:05 p.m. and paramedics Svendsen and Povacz reached the scene at 8:11 p.m. They report finding no heartbeat and immediately administered CPR and oxygen at the scene. Not getting any response, they took the victims to Mercy Hospital, where they were both pronounced dead on arrival at the emergency room. The victims' mother says she used the hair dryer in the bathroom each morning and that her girls sometimes played with it. It has a warning against immersion imprinted in the plastic body of the dryer. Autopsies are scheduled for tomorrow.

If additional space required, use reverse side.

Supervisor Approving Haskell	Emp. No. 1481	Interviewing Officer(s) Svendsen and Povacz	Emp. No.	Person Reporting Death (signature)
				X
				Indexed Yes	Checked Yes

602-07-21 A   **DEATH REPORT**

Exercise 7

PUBLIC AFFAIRS REPORTING

POLICE DEPARTMENT

STOLEN PROPERTY

CR NO. 14	SHIFT NO. 1	CASE NO. 83-4751

| OFFENSE (GRAND OR PETIT) Grand | U.C.R. CLASSIFICATION FR-721-83-4498 | AREA 7 | OCCURRED (DATE & TIME) 11 a.m. yesterday | DAY OF OFF. Yesterday | DISP. 9:07a | ARR. 9:15 | IN SER. 9:40 | DATE OF REP. Today |

NAME AND ADDRESS OF OCCURRENCE
Bert's Shell Station, 4800 Conway Road

OWNER OF PROPERTY Rene J. Firment	AGE - SEX - RACE 19 M W	RESIDENT ADDRESS 2474 Colyer Road	RES. PHONE 350-6974	BUSINESS ADDRESS 4800 Conway Road	BUSINESS PHONE 644-0292

REPORTED BY
Same as above

DISCOVERED BY
Same as above

WITNESSED BY None

OWNERS OCCUPATION
Service station attend.

TYPE OF PREMISES (RES. OR BUS.)
Service Station

METHOD USED TO COMMIT CRIME
Swindle

MODEL NO. - SERIAL NO. - CALIBER			MAKE AND MANUFACTURER	LOCATION OF PROPERTY STOLEN

GENERAL TYPE OF PROPERTY TAKEN Cash		

COST OF PROPERTY (NEW AND AT TIME OF THEFT)
$100

					INSURANCE COMPANY

VEHICLE USED BY OFFENDERS	MAKE	MODEL	YEAR	BODY STYLE	COLOR	LICENSE STATE YEAR		NO. PRIOR THEFTS REPORTED
None seen								

☐ SUBJECT ☐ SUSPECT ☐ JUVENILE	AGE - SEX - RACE	RESIDENCE ADDRESS Unknown		INCARCERATED YES NO No	WHERE	OCCUPATION

KIND OF PROPERTY RECOVERED None	VALUE	PROPERTY RECEIPT		DETECTIVE NOTIFIED -- DATE AND TIME

REMARKS (INCLUDED DETAILED DESCRIPTION OF PROPERTY TAKEN) Firment said a very well dressed young couple, both about 30, walked into the service station at about 11 a.m. yesterday, and the woman asked to use the restroom. While she was in the restroom, the phone rang, and Firment said he answered it in the station office from a man who told him his wife had left her wedding ring on a bathroom sink at the station. The caller said the ring was a genuine diamond worth $2,000 and offered a $200 reward if the ring was found. As Firment was still on the telephone, the woman then walked out of the restroom with a ring, and Firment told her of the offer. The couple said they were on their way to a friend's wedding and couldn't wait for the reward. The caller, who was still on the phone at that point, told Firment to give the couple $100 and said Firment would receive the $200 when he came down to pick up the ring later in the afternoon, so the couple and Firment would split the reward 50-50. Firment said he then proceeded to give the couple the suggested amount, and they left, walking south on Conway Road. The caller never came to the station yesterday, and Firment said he went to a jeweler early today and determined that the ring was a fake and worth only about $6. He called the department at about 9 a.m. today. He was unable to provide clear descriptions of either perpetrator and said he didn't see them get into a vehicle of any kind. Detectives will interview him later today and try to get some kind of description.

REPORTING OFFICER'S SIGNATURE (A) Cullinan	BADGE NO. 42813	AREA	APPROVED BY Forsythe	AREA	PERSON REPORTING CRIME Rene Firment
(B)					STATE TWX MSG. NO.
					LOCAL TWX MSG. NO.

REFERRED TO: Detective Bureau
SUPERVISOR: E. G.

DISPOSITION ☐ CLEARED BY ARREST ☐ EXCEPTIONALLY CLEARED ☐ UNFOUNDED ☐ PENDING

CT 284

Exercise 8

PUBLIC AFFAIRS REPORTING

POLICE DEPARTMENT

STOLEN PROPERTY

CASE NO.	89306411	
SHIFT NO.	2	
CR NO.	11	

U.C.R. CLASSIFICATION	AREA		DISP	ARR	IN SER.	DATE OF REP.
84762.41	7		8:20a	8:32	10:12a	Today

OFFENSE (GRAND OR PETIT)
Grand

NAME AND ADDRESS OF OCCURRENCE
3405 Virginia Ave.

OCCURRED (DATE & TIME)
Sometime in the past week

DAY OF OFF Unknown

OWNER OF PROPERTY

	AGE	SEX	RACE	RESIDENT ADDRESS	RES. PHONE	BUSINESS ADDRESS	BUSINESS PHONE
Dr. William J. Gulas	46	M	B	3405 Virginia Ave.	273-1364	851 Morse Boulevard	442-8090

REPORTED BY
Mrs. Gulas

DISCOVERED BY
Mrs. Gulas and family

WITNESSED BY
No known witnesses

OWNERS OCCUPATION
Medical doctor

TYPE OF PREMISES (RES. OR BUS.)
Residence

MAKE AND MANUFACTURER

LOCATION OF PROPERTY STOLEN

MODEL NO. - SERIAL NO. CALIBER
Checking serial numbers presently

METHOD USED TO COMMIT CRIME
Front door pried open, pry marks found

GENERAL TYPE OF PROPERTY TAKEN
Household furnishings

COST OF PROPERTY (NEW AND AT TIME OF THEFT)
$20,000

MODUS OPERENDI
Used truck to move everything out of home

INSURANCE COMPANY
Prudential

VEHICLE USED BY OFFENDERS MODEL MAKE YEAR BODY STYLE COLOR LICENSE STATE YEAR
Exact vehicle unknown, but probably a large truck

NO. PRIOR THEFTS REPORTED
Two

☐ SUBJECT ☐ SUSPECT ☐ JUVENILE

	AGE	SEX	RACE	RESIDENCE ADDRESS			OCCUPATION
None							

INCARCERATED ☐ YES ☐ NO
DATE AND TIME

DETECTIVE NOTIFIED

KIND OF PROPERTY RECOVERED
None

VALUE

PROPERTY RECEIPT

REMARKS (INCLUDE DETAILED DESCRIPTION OF PROPERTY TAKEN) The family, including four children, had been vacationing in New Orleans for a week and got home at about 8:20 this morning and found the house totally looted. Almost everything is gone. All their furniture, clothes, appliances, yard tools, dishes, etc. Even the rugs were pulled up. About the only thing left were the drapes, so everything looks normal from the outside. Whoever was responsible must have had plenty of time, since they even took food from the kitchen shelves, plus the kitchen stove, refrigerator, a washer and a dryer, and a freezer the family says was half full of meat. Neighbors don't report hearing anything unusual, but the house is isolated on a 1½ acre lot. The house has been robbed twice before, and the family installed a burglar alarm system they say they paid $840 for just before leaving on vacation. It's been tampered with and silenced. Even some interior doors are missing from the home. Because of the previous robberies, much of the property was new, bought as replacements for property stolen earlier. Tire marks are apparent on the front lawn but are too old to make a good impression. We're continuing to interview people in the neighborhood. Because of the previous break-ins, the family hadn't told anyone that they wouldn't be home, and no one was checking the house while they were out of town. The break-in is similar to one of the previous entries, and the same thieves may have returned with a truck. Little was taken in that previous entry.

REPORTING OFFICER'S SIGNATURE
George Oldaker

BADGE NO. 310

AREA 2

APPROVED BY D.N.

PERSON REPORTING CRIME
Mrs. Gulas

STATE TWX MSG. NO.

LOCAL TWX MSG. NO.

REFERRED TO: Detective Bureau
SUPERVISOR: Griffin

DISPOSITION ☐ CLEARED BY ARREST ☐ EXCEPTIONALLY CLEARED ☐ UNFOUNDED ☐ PENDING
(A)
(B)

CT 284

Exercise 9

PUBLIC AFFAIRS REPORTING

POLICE DEPARTMENT

ROBBERY

4A. Offense: Armed robbery

4. U.C.R. Classification: 84-19721
I. Command No. 4
II. CR No. 18
2. Case No. 13817674

10. Address of Occurrence: 1634 Holden Ave.
12. Zone: 8
9. Occurred: 8:40 p.m.
5. Day: Yesterday
6. Disp. On stakeout
7. Arr.
8. In Ser. 10:40 p.m.
3. Date

14. Victim's Name: Thomas A. Golay
Age-Sex-Race: M 57 W
Res. Address: 1203 Texas Avenue
Res. Phone 671-8437
Bus. Address: 1634 Holden Ave.
Bus. Phone 671-4744

15. Reported by: Officers Skinner & Boysie

17. Witnessed By: Officers Skinner & Boysie

49. Owner: Thomas A. Golay

63. Victim's Occupation (14): Liquor store owner
42. Type of Premises: Liquor store
129. Protect. Dev.: Silent alarm
135. Sobriety of Victim: Sober ☒ H.B.D. ☐ Intox. ☐

35. Weapon or Means Used — Serial No.: 2 handguns L4387162 SB8231442
34. Method Used to Commit Crime: Strongarm robbery
37. General Type of Property Taken: Cash
64. Weather: Clear
130. Value: $312

45. Trade Mark or Unusual Event (Modus Operendi) One suspect entered the store when it appeared to be empty, except for the owner, showed a gun and demanded the money.

50. Vehicle Used: Model Mustang Make Ford Year Body Style Sedan 53. Color White 52. license State D812-175 Year 55. Ident. Marks Yes Cur. Badly rusted 47. Storage Receipt 84-3822
136. No. of Offenders: Two

68. What Did Offenders Say "Give me all the money you've got in the register, all of it, and do it fast. This gun is loaded, and I'll shoot."

31. ☐ Subject ☒ Suspect Juv. ☐ Calvin Louis Winkler
Sex-Race-Age: M W 27
Res. Address: Louisville, Kentucky
Incarcerated Where ☐ Yes ☒ No
Occupation: Unknown
95. Condition: Very grave

138. Disguises: Bandana over face
72. How Offender Approached — Flight: Car driven by accomplice
41. Person or Unit Notified — Time: Shift commander 8:45
67. Hospital (14): Memorial

131. Kind of Property Recovered: Cash
132. Value: $312
48. Property Receipt ☒ Yes ☐ No

33. Remarks: We were on a routine stakeout, hiding in a back room in the liquor store when the suspect entered. When he displayed his weapon and grabbed the money we entered the area, identified ourselves and ordered the suspect to drop his weapon. The suspect turned toward us, seemingly pointing his gun at us, and we both opened fire. Skinner fired one shot from a shotgun and Boysie three shots from his service revolver. The shotgun blast struck the suspect in his groin area and one shot from the revolver struck him in the stomach and another in his right arm. The second suspect, who made no attempt to flee, was apprehended outside in their car. He has been identified as Norman F. Piezul, also of Louisville. Winkler is in the hospital's intensive care unit. Piezul is being held in the county jail.

20. Reporting Officer's Signature
(a) Roger Skinner Badge No. 482 87. District 3
(b) Lee Boysie 789 3
19. Approved By R.N.
21. Person Reporting Crime: Skinner and Boysie
22. State TWX Msg. No.
23. Local TWX Msg. No.

Referred To: Detective Bureau and District Attorney
27. Recorded Yes
25. Indexed
29. Statistics

Signature
Assigned To Detective Bureau
Supervisor Griffin

30. Disposition ☒ Cleared by Arrest ☐ Unfounded ☐ Exceptionally Cleared ☐ Pending

Date
Date

C T-78

Exercise 10

PUBLIC AFFAIRS REPORTING

The form (rotated) reads as a Sheriff's Dept. Miscellaneous Incident report:

SHERIFF'S DEPT. — **MISCELLANEOUS INCIDENT**

2. CASE NO. 84761004

- 11. RADIO NO: 42
- 12. ZONE: 15
- 5. DATE: Yesterday
- 6. DISP.: 4:25 p.
- 7. ARR.: 4:31 p.
- 8. IN SERV.: 5:15 p.
- 6A. WEATHER: Clear, sunny

13A. MIRANDA WARNING READ: ☐ YES ☒ NO

- RES: 641-7838
- BUS: 644-2360

14. VICTIM'S NAME: Gregory L. Herwarth
ADDRESS: 4401 Baltimore Avenue (Yours)

- 7A. DATE: 7/11/34

15. REPORTED BY: Unknown caller

4A. NATURE OF INCIDENT: Victim struck by motorboat

10. ADDRESS OF OCCURRENCE: South end of Crystal Lake

9. OCCURRED: Yesterday

50. VEHICLE USED: 18 foot motor boat, 45 horsepower motor
MODEL / MAKE — YEAR — BODY STYLE

53. COLOR: White
52. LICENSE TAG NO.: SB45-721-63 (Yours) STATE

58. IDENT. MARKS (ACCESSORIES, DAMAGE, ETC.)

4. U C R CLASSIFICATION (WHERE APPLICABLE)

31. ☒ SUSPECT
NAME: Vernon Sindelar
OCCUPATION

- RES. PH: 293-5495
- BUS. PH: 644-6648

DOB: 3/28/60
ADDRESS: 4164 Mandar Drive
WHERE: County jail, freed on $1,000 bail at 10 p.m. yesterday

INCARCERATED: ☒ YES ☐ NO

33. NARRATIVE: Herwarth was riding on an innertube being towed by a boat operated by his wife, Ruth. Another couple, Mr. and Mrs. Wayne Morrill of 382 Arlington Circle was in the boat with her. They say the boat operated by Sindelar approached from the west at high speed, suddenly veered straight at Herwarth, its propeller striking him and amputating his right arm at the shoulder. Herwarth was unconscious when we arrived at the scene, and an ambulance took him to St. Nicholas Hospital. His wife and the two Morrills pulled him from the water. They and witnesses allege that Sindelar stopped after the accident but did nothing to help. He appeared to be drunk, and we administered a Breath Analyzer test. He flunked the alcohol in his blood being .14%, and we charged him with operating a power boat while under the influence of alcohol. Doctors at the hospital say Herwarth also suffered a broken collar bone and several broken ribs but is expected to survive.

60. CONTACT INFORMATION: Other witnesses: Darla and Savilla Gould, 4178 N. 11th Ave.

- 19. APPROVED BY: Forsythe
- 13. DISTRICT: 7
- ID NO.: 42813
- 27. RECORDED BY: C.R.
- 25. INDEXED BY: M.A.

21. PERSON REPORTING CRIME: Unknown caller

29. RELEASE REPORT: ☒ YES ☐ NO

38. REPORTING OFFICER'S SIGNATURE (A): Charles Cullinan

28. REFERRED TO: County attorney

30. DISPOSITION (WRITE IN)

RECORDS

PRESS DOWN — YOU ARE MAKING 5 COPIES

Exercise 11

PUBLIC AFFAIRS REPORTING

SHERIFF'S OFFICE

ZONE ___1___ UNIT ___#17___	**COMPLAINT REPORT**	CASE NO. ___131-8864___

GRID ___14___   PAGE ___One___ OF ___One___   OTHER AGCY CASE NO. _____

MESSAGE NUMBER ___131-148___   DATE ___Today___ MONTH   DAY   YR

TIME RECEIVED ___11:35 p.m.___   TIME DISPATCHED ___11:37 p.m.___   TIME ARRIVED ___11:42 p.m.___   TIME IN-SERVICE ___1:20 a.m.___   WEATHER ___OK___

NATURE OF CASE ___Armed Robbery___   CHANGED TO _____   F.S.S. ___   FEL. ___XX___ MISD. ___

LOCATION OF OCCURRENCE (INCL. NAME OF BUSINESS/SCHOOL) ___McDonald's Restaurant   3220 McCoy Road___

VICTIM: ___Taylor___ ___Marsha___ ___Lynn___ AGE ___29___ R/S ___ DOB MO. DAY YR.
(LAST)   (FIRST)   (MIDDLE)

HOME ADDRESS ___2012 Lincoln Avenue___   PHONE ___420-9780___

CITY ___(Yours)___   STATE _____   ZIP _____

BUSINESS ADDRESS ___3220 McCoy Road___   PHONE ___420-6064___

CITY ___About 1 mile south of the city on McCoy Road___   STATE ___   ZIP _____

REPORTER ☐ WITNESS ☐ ___Six other employees, all available at the restaurant___   PHONE ___420-6064___

CITY ___(Yours)___   STATE _____   ZIP _____

PROPERTY MISSING/STOLEN

QUAN.	ITEM	DESCRIPTION - SERIAL NO. - MFG NO. - ETC	EST. VALUE $ STOLEN	RECOVERED
		Approximately $3,700 in cash	$3,700	None

■ MISSING ■ SUSPECT ■ ARRESTED ■ WITNESS ■ OTHER

NAME ___Unknown___ AGE ___ R/S ___ DOB MO. DAY YR.
(LAST)   (FIRST)   (MIDDLE)

ADDRESS _____   PHONE _____

CITY _____   STATE _____   ZIP _____

BUSINESS OR SCHOOL ADDRESS _____

HEIGHT ___ WEIGHT ___ HAIR ___ EYES ___ COMPLEXION ___ OCCUPATION _____

CLOTHING, ETC., _____

VEHICLE INVOLVED

☐ USED   ☐ STOLEN   ☐ TOWED   ☐ DAMAGED   ☐ BURGLARIZED   ☐ WRECKER   ☐ OTHER _____

YEAR ___ MAKE ___ MODEL ___ BODY STYLE ___ COLOR ___ DECAL _____

LICENSE TAG NO. _____   STATE ___ YEAR EXPIRES ___ I.D. OR VIN NO. _____

REMARKS: _____

ENTERED FCIC/NCIC ☐ YES ☐ NO   BOLO ☐ YES ☐ NO   MESSAGE NO. _____

NARRATIVE: Taylor, manager of the restaurant, was taking inventory with two assistant managers in a back room. Four other employees were cleaning the restaurant which had closed at 11 p.m. The front doors were locked, but when an employee opened a back door to take out some trash, three robbers wearing Halloween masks forced their way in. One gunman put a revolver to Taylor's head. Another of the managers was told to round up the other employees in the building. Taylor was forced to open a safe at gunpoint while the other six employees were taken to a small lounge used by employees. The two assistant managers were made to lie face down on the floor, and the other employees were seated at a table and told to put their heads down. Taylor was brought into the room after five cash register drawers in the safe had been emptied of about $3,700. The gunmen then ordered the employees to place their pocketbooks and jewelry on the table and took them as well. The employees then were warned they would be shot if they moved as the men left. The victims waited about five minutes before leaving the room and calling for help.

DISPOSITION: ___Referred to Detective Bureau___

FURTHER POLICE ACTION TAKEN   YES ☐   NO ☐   REFERRED TO ___Detective Bureau___

___Deputy Cullinan___   ___Forsythe___
REPORTING OFFICER'S NAME (PRINT)   I.D. NO. (INITIAL)   APPROVED BY

RECORDS

Exercise 12

PUBLIC AFFAIRS REPORTING

SHERIFF'S OFFICE

COMPLAINT REPORT

ZONE __4__ UNIT __#23__   PAGE __One__ OF __One__   CASE NO. __AR-83-46241__

GRID __2__   OTHER AGCY CASE NO. _____

MESSAGE NUMBER __1-17-486__   DATE __Yesterday__ MONTH DAY YR

TIME RECEIVED __11:15 p.m.__ TIME DISPATCHED __11:17 p.m.__ TIME ARRIVED __11:30 p.m.__ TIME IN-SERVICE __2:15 a.m.__ WEATHER __Good__

NATURE OF CASE __Armed Robbery__ CHANGED TO _____ F.S.S. ___ FEL __XX__ MISD. ___

LOCATION OF OCCURRENCE (INCL. NAME OF BUSINESS/SCHOOL) __Quik Shoppe (Convenience Store)__

VICTIM: __Jimenez__ (LAST) __Edward__ (FIRST) __Carl__ (MIDDLE) AGE __48__ R/S ___ DOB MO. DAY YR.

HOME ADDRESS __3611 N. 31st. Street__ PHONE __365-0038__

CITY __(Yours)__ STATE _____ ZIP _____

BUSINESS ADDRESS __4760 Forest Road__ PHONE __420-5083__

CITY __About 1½ miles south of city__ STATE _____ ZIP _____

REPORTER ☐ WITNESS ☒x __Linda M. Smith, 1814 N. Third Street__ PHONE __422-4562__

CITY __Yes (Yours)__ STATE _____ ZIP _____

PROPERTY MISSING/STOLEN

QUAN.	ITEM	DESCRIPTION - SERIAL NO. - MFG NO. - ETC	EST. VALUE $ STOLEN	RECOVERED
		About $250 in cash	$250	None
		The victim is conducting an inventory. He says he's probably missing several cases of wine, beer and cigarettes. The inventory is due later today.	$400	None

☐ MISSING ☒ SUSPECT ☐ ARRESTED ☐ WITNESS ☐ OTHER

NAME __Unknown__ (LAST) (FIRST) (MIDDLE) AGE __30__ R/S ___ DOB MO. DAY YR.

ADDRESS _____ PHONE _____

CITY _____ STATE _____ ZIP _____

BUSINESS OR SCHOOL ADDRESS _____

HEIGHT __5' 6"__ WEIGHT __220__ HAIR __Black__ EYES __Brown__ COMPLEXION __Bad__ OCCUPATION _____

CLOTHING, ETC. __Green jacket, tan pants, wire-rimmed glasses. No rings or jewelry visible.__

VEHICLE INVOLVED

☐ USED ☐ STOLEN ☐ TOWED ☐ DAMAGED ☐ BURGLARIZED ☐ WRECKER ☐ OTHER _____

YEAR ___ MAKE _____ MODEL _____ BODY STYLE _____ COLOR _____ DECAL _____

LICENSE TAG NO. _____ STATE _____ YEAR EXPIRES _____ I.D. OR VIN NO. _____

REMARKS: __Use and make of vehicle unknown at this time__

ENTERED FCIC/NCIC ☐ YES ☐ NO BOLO ☐ YES ☐ NO MESSAGE NO. _____

NARRATIVE: Last night at approximately 22:50 hours, a white male entered the convenience store at 4760 Forest Road. The suspect moved right to the register and was met by the store manager Jimenez who thought he was a customer. As Jimenez moved to the counter, the suspect pulled up the right side of his coat and produced from the area of his waist band a black hand gun. Holding the gun in his right hand the suspect told Jimenez the manager "let's go into the back room." As Jimenez approached the register, the suspect said "hold it, open the register," which was complied with by Jimenez. The suspect then forced Jimenez into a back storage room of the business where Jimenez was cuffed to the pipes of a sink. The suspect then warned Jimenez to keep quiet and shut the storage room door and went back into the store where Jimenez heard him moving about. A few minutes later, a white female entered the store and upon finding it empty called this department at which time we responded. The suspect's way of exiting the scene and direction of travel are unknown at this time. The fire dept. cut Jimenez free.

DISPOSITION: NOTE: This case resembles a robbery 3 weeks ago, Case #AR-83-46018.

FURTHER POLICE ACTION TAKEN YES ☐ NO ☐ REFERRED TO __Detective Bureau__

__Horan__   __879__   __K. W.__
REPORTING OFFICER'S NAME (PRINT)   I.D. NO. (INITIAL)   APPROVED BY

RECORDS

Exercise 13

PUBLIC AFFAIRS REPORTING

SHERIFF'S OFFICE

COMPLAINT REPORT

ZONE __3__ UNIT __10__

CASE NO. __813-47-C28__

GRID __7__   PAGE __One__ OF __one__

OTHER AGCY CASE NO. __None__

MESSAGE NUMBER __842 - DN__

DATE __Yesterday__
MONTH   DAY   YR

TIME RECEIVED __9:10 p.__ TIME DISPATCHED __9:12 p.__ TIME ARRIVED __9:17 p.__ TIME IN-SERVICE __10:23 p.__ WEATHER ____

NATURE OF CASE __Strongarm robbery__ CHANGED TO ____ F.S.S. ____ FEL. ____ MISD. ____

LOCATION OF OCCURRENCE (INCL. NAME OF BUSINESS/SCHOOL) __Mr. Grocer   4740 Hobson Street__

VICTIM: __Hessling__ (LAST) __Dorothy__ (FIRST) __L.__ (MIDDLE) AGE __27__ R/S __B__ DOB MO. DAY YR.

HOME ADDRESS __8197 Locke Avenue__   PHONE __671-3071__

CITY __Local__   STATE ____ ZIP ____

BUSINESS ADDRESS __4740 Hobson Street__   PHONE __671-1047__

CITY __Local__   STATE ____ ZIP ____

REPORTER ☐
WITNESS ☐   PHONE ____

CITY ____   STATE ____ ZIP ____

PROPERTY MISSING/STOLEN

QUAN.	ITEM	DESCRIPTION - SERIAL NO. - MFG NO. - ETC	EST. VALUE $ STOLEN	RECOVERED
		$1,690 in cash, mostly small bills, nothing larger than a $20. Includes about $100 in loose change.	$1,690	None

■ MISSING ■ SUSPECT ■ ARRESTED ■ WITNESS ■ OTHER

NAME ____ (LAST) ____ (FIRST) ____ (MIDDLE) AGE ____ R/S ____ DOB MO. DAY YR.

ADDRESS ____   PHONE ____

CITY ____   STATE ____ ZIP ____

BUSINESS OR SCHOOL ADDRESS ____

HEIGHT ____ WEIGHT ____ HAIR ____ EYES ____ COMPLEXION ____ OCCUPATION ____

CLOTHING, ETC., ____

VEHICLE INVOLVED

☒ USED   ☐ STOLEN   ☐ TOWED   ☐ DAMAGED   ☐ BURGLARIZED   ☐ WRECKER   ☐ OTHER ____

YEAR __New__ MAKE __Unknown__ MODEL ____ BODY STYLE __Station wagon__ COLOR __White__ DECAL ____

LICENSE TAG NO. ____ STATE ____ YEAR EXPIRES ____ I.D. OR VIN NO. ____

REMARKS: ____

ENTERED FCIC/NCIC ☐ YES ☐ NO   BOLO ☐ YES ☐ NO   MESSAGE NO. ____

NARRATIVE: Hessling said she was carrying the day's bank deposit for the store to her car when she was robbed. Victim reports seeing a man in a white station wagon parked near her car in the parking lot alongside the store. He was described by the victim as in his mid 30s, had a dark beard and something over his head, possibly the hood of a sweatshirt. As the victim opened her car door, the man got out of the station wagon and asked her for directions. When she turned to look at him, he sprayed her in the face with a chemical substance, probably mace. Victim was temporarily blinded and said he grabbed the money from her, and she heard his vehicle exit the parking lot in an apparent easterly direction. Victim states that the perpetrator seemed to know who she was and to be familiar with her routine as he went right for her and the bank receipts whereas he could have robbed any number of customers or other employees leaving the store that night.

DISPOSITION: ____

FURTHER POLICE ACTION TAKEN   YES ☐   NO ☐   REFERRED TO __Detective Squad__

__Henderson, Leon__   __782__   __C.K.__
REPORTING OFFICER'S NAME (PRINT)   I.D. NO. (INITIAL)   APPROVED BY

RECORDS

Exercise 14

PUBLIC AFFAIRS REPORTING

SHERIFF'S OFFICE

COMPLAINT REPORT

ZONE ___3___ UNIT ___10___

CASE NO. ___A874-389224___

GRID ___7___   PAGE ___1___ OF ___1___

OTHER AGCY CASE NO. ___Collier Cty #82411___

MESSAGE NUMBER ___891- DN___

DATE ___Today___
MONTH   DAY   YR.

TIME RECEIVED ___8:50 a.___   TIME DISPATCHED ___8:52 a.___   TIME ARRIVED ___9 a.___   TIME IN-SERVICE ___11:20 a.___   WEATHER _____

NATURE OF CASE ___Apparent hit and run___   CHANGED TO ___Unavoidable accident___ F.S.S.____ FEL.____ MISD.____

LOCATION OF OCCURRENCE (INCL. NAME OF BUSINESS/SCHOOL) ___Called to Allison Ford (service dept.)___

VICTIM: ___Welke___ ___Milan___ ___J___ AGE ___52___ R/S ____   DOB ___ MO. DAY YR.
(LAST)   (FIRST)   (MIDDLE)

HOME ADDRESS ___Unknown. Original case handled by Collier County___   PHONE _____

CITY_____ STATE_____ ZIP_____

BUSINESS ADDRESS_____ PHONE_____

CITY_____ STATE_____ ZIP_____

REPORTER ☒
WITNESS ☐ ___Robert Allen Barlow, mechanic, Allison Ford___   PHONE ___671-0202___

CITY_____ STATE_____ ZIP_____

		PROPERTY MISSING/STOLEN		EST. VALUE $	
QUAN.	ITEM	DESCRIPTION - SERIAL NO. - MFG NO. - ETC		STOLEN	RECOVERED

■ MISSING ■ SUSPECT ■ ARRESTED ■ WITNESS ■ OTHER

NAME ___Mentzer-Meyer___ ___Sonya___ ___M.___ AGE ___47___ R/S ___ DOB ___ MO. DAY YR.
(LAST)   (FIRST)   (MIDDLE)

ADDRESS ___811 Moore Street___   PHONE ___782-8137___

CITY ___Local___ STATE_____ ZIP_____

BUSINESS OR SCHOOL ADDRESS ___None___

HEIGHT ___5'8"___ WEIGHT ___130___ HAIR ___Brown___ EYES ___Brown___ COMPLEXION ___Clear___ OCCUPATION ___Housewife___

CLOTHING, ETC., _____

VEHICLE INVOLVED

☐ USED   ☐ STOLEN   ☐ TOWED   ☒ DAMAGED   ☐ BURGLARIZED   ☐ WRECKER   ☐ OTHER _____

YEAR ___88___ MAKE ___Buick___ MODEL ___LeSabre___ BODY STYLE ___4-door___ COLOR ___Tan___ DECAL ___Yes___

LICENSE TAG NO. _____ STATE_____ YEAR EXPIRES_____ I.D. OR VIN NO. _____

REMARKS: _____

ENTERED FCIC/NCIC ☐ YES ☐ NO   BOLO ☐ YES ☐ NO   MESSAGE NO._____

NARRATIVE: At approx. 8:30 hrs. Robert Barlow, a mechanic for Allison Ford, began work on the Mentzer-Meyer vehicle. Barlow noticed on the undercarriage what appeared to be human hair, blood, flesh, and clothing. At that time he called another mechanic. After they both observed the undercarriage of the vehicle, it was determined that the police should be called. Further investigation and questioning of the owner revealed that she had driven to another part of the state last weekend to visit a daughter at night. Along the way on a dark strip of highway a man tried to flag her down. Afraid she drove around him and continued. After having arrived at her daughter, the woman contacted the local sheriff who said nothing had been reported but he would look into it. The Collier Cty. sheriff confirms the woman's story and says he had trouble getting back to her but intends to do so. After her call he learned the man waving his arms on the highway had hit a pedestrian and was trying to stop the woman for help. She apparently then unknowingly ran over the already-hit pedestrian accidentally. No charges have been filed against anyone. The sheriff says several vehicles hit the deceased, who appears to have been drunk, and it is impossible to determine what vehicle killed him. No further action is contemplated.

DISPOSITION _____

FURTHER POLICE ACTION TAKEN   YES ☐   NO ☒   REFERRED TO _____

REPORTING OFFICER'S NAME (PRINT) ___Henderson, Leon___   I.D. NO. (INITIAL) ___782___   APPROVED BY ___C.K.___

RECORDS

Exercise 15

PUBLIC AFFAIRS REPORTING

TRAFFIC ACCIDENT REPORT

MAIL TO: ACCIDENT RECORDS BUREAU, DEPT. OF HIGHWAY SAFETY & MOTOR VEHICLES

TIME & LOCATION

DATE OF ACCIDENT	Month	Day	Year	DAY OF WEEK	TIME OF DAY	
				Yesterday	11:40 p.	M

COUNTY (Yours)

CITY, TOWN OR COMMUNITY

LOCAL ACCIDENT REPORT NUMBER 34178004

IF ACCIDENT WAS OUTSIDE CITY LIMITS, INDICATE DISTANCE FROM NEAREST TOWN 1½ ☐ Feet ☒ Miles ☐☒☐☐ N S E W of (Your City) City, Village or Township

ROAD ON WHICH ACCIDENT OCCURRED S. R. 17 Use State or County Road Number or Name ☐ Exit Ramp ☐ Entrance R. ☐ At its intersection with ☐ Influenced by intersection Highway Number or Name of Intersecting Street and Node

IF NOT AT INTER-SECTION 400 ☒ Feet ☐ Miles ☐☒☐☐ N S E W of County Road 41 Show nearest intersecting street or highway, bridge, RR crossing, underpass or curve

☐ Feet ☐☐☐☐ Miles N S E W of Node

IS ENGINEERING STUDY NEEDED (if so explain) No

DO NOT WRITE IN SPACE ABOVE

TYPE MOTOR VEHICLE ACCIDENT

OVERTURNING	OTHER NONCOLLISION	PEDESTRIAN	MV IN TRANSPORT	MV ON OTHER ROADWAY	HIT AND RUN
PARKED MV	RAILWAY TRAIN	PEDALCYCLIST	ANIMAL	FIXED OBJECT XXX	OTHER OBJECT	NON-CONTACT

VEHICLE 1

| TOTAL NO. MOTOR Vehicles Involved | YEAR | MAKE Ford | TYPE (Sedan, Truck, Bus, etc.) Sedan | VEHICLE LICENSE PLATE NO. B678-510 | STATE Yes | YEAR Cur. | VEHICLE IDENTIFICATION NO. 811-423084 |

| Area of Vehicle Damage | 1 | 2 | 4 | | Damage Scale 1 | Damage Severity 1 | AMOUNT (Approximate) | Safety Equipment | VEHICLE REMOVED BY Bob's Shell |

NAME OF INSURANCE (Liability or PIP) Allstate

POLICY NO. 963-818-59

Owner ☐ Driver ☒

Owner's Request ☐ Other (Explain) ☐

☒ Rotation List

OWNER (Print or type FULL name) Alton J. Reimer

ADDRESS (Number and street) 2529 Barbados Avenue

CITY and STATE / Zip Code (Yours)

DRIVER (Exactly as on driver's license) Same as above

ADDRESS (Number and street)

CITY and STATE / Zip Code

| OCCUPATION Student | Driver's License Type A | DRIVER'S LICENSE NUMBER 471380059 | STATE Yes | DATE (Month, Day, Year) OF BIRTH Age 17 | RACE W | SEX M | Safety E. | Eject. X | Injury X |

OCCUPANTS	Name	ADDRESS – Number and Street	City and State / Zip Code	AGE	RACE	SEX	Safety E.	Eject.	Injury
Front center	Marlene Anne Guyer	4043 S. 28th Street		17	W	F			X
Front right									
Rear left									
Rear center									
Rear right									

VEHICLE 2 or PEDESTRIAN

| YEAR | MAKE | TYPE (Sedan, Truck, Bus, etc.) | VEHICLE LICENSE PLATE NO. | STATE | YEAR | VEHICLE IDENTIFICATION NO. |

| Area of Vehicle Damage | | | | | Damage Scale | Damage Severity | AMOUNT (Approximate) | Safety Equipment | VEHICLE REMOVED BY |

NAME OF INSURANCE (Liability or PIP)

POLICY NO.

Owner ☐ Driver ☐

Owner's Request ☐ Other (Explain) ☐

☐ Rotation List

OWNER (Print or type FULL name)

ADDRESS (Number and street)

CITY and STATE / Zip Code

DRIVER (Exactly as on driver's license)

ADDRESS (Number and street)

CITY and STATE / Zip Code

| OCCUPATION | Driver's License Type | DRIVER'S LICENSE NUMBER | STATE | DATE (Month, Day, Year) OF BIRTH | RACE | SEX | Safety E. | Eject. | Injury |

OCCUPANTS	Name	ADDRESS – (Number and Street)	City and State Zip Code	AGE	RACE	SEX	Safety E.	Eject.	Injury
Front center									
Front right									
Rear left									
Rear center									
Rear right									

PROPERTY DAMAGED–Other than vehicles Utility pole

AMOUNT $500

OWNER – Name State Power & Light,

ADDRESS – Number and Street 2480 S. Main Street

CITY and STATE / Zip Code

| INVESTIGATOR – Name and rank (Signature) Cpl. Alvarez | BADGE NO. 3814 | I.D. NO. 684172 | DEPARTMENT Highway Patrol ☐ F.H.P. ☒ C.P.D. ☐ S.O. ☐ Other | DATE OF REPORT |

SHEET One OF Two SHEETS

DIAGRAM WHAT HAPPENED – (Number each vehicle and show direction of travel by arrow)

INDICATE NORTH WITH ARROW

POINT OF IMPACT

Vehicle
	1	2	
	☒	☐	Front
	☐	☐	Right front
	☐	☐	Left front
	☐	☐	Right side
	☐	☐	Left side
	☐	☐	Rear
	☐	☐	Right rear
	☐	☐	Left rear

DESCRIBE WHAT HAPPENED – (Refer to vehicles by number)

Reimer was trying to pass a truck driven by J. Vernon Flavell, 827 N. Pigeon Road. Flavell estimates he was traveling about 50 mph and the car was going 60 to 70 mph at the time. Skid marks confirm the car was going 59 mph. Reimer apparently lost control of the car as he pulled alongside Flavell's vehicle and his car ran off the left side of the road, struck a utility pole and stopped, rightside up, in a field 87 feet from the edge of the pavement. Neither occupant was wearing a seat belt, and Reimer was ejected through the windshield, apparently on impact with the utility pole. Guyer remained in the vehicle. Hospital officials say Reimer died of massive head injuries. The girl has been admitted to the hospital's intensive care unit with multiple internal injuries and is listed in serious condition. We were unable to interview either victim at the scene of the accident, Reimer being dead when we arrived at the scene.

*WHAT VEHICLES WERE DOING BEFORE ACCIDENT

VEHICLE No. 1 was traveling ☒☐☐☐ On S.R. 17 .... at 59 M.P.H. Approximately

VEHICLE No. 2 was traveling ☐☐☐☐ On .... at .... M.P.H.

Vehicle 1 2	Vehicle 1 2	Vehicle 1 2	Vehicle 1 2	
☐ ☐ Going straight ahead	☐ ☐ Making right turn	☐ ☐ Slowing or Stopping	☐ ☐ Starting from parked position	
☒☒ Overtaking	☐ ☐ Making left turn	☐ ☐ Changing lanes	☐ ☐ Stopped or parked	
			☐ ☐ Other (explain above)	

*WHAT PEDESTRIAN WAS DOING

☐ Along
PEDESTRIAN was going ☐☐☐☐ ☐ Across or into .... from .... to ....   Color of Clothing ☐ Dark ☐ Light

☐ Crossing at intersection	☐ Stepped into path of Vehicle	☐ Getting on or off Vehicle	☐ Playing in roadway
☐ Crossing not at Intersection	☐ Standing in roadway	☐ Hitching on Vehicle	☐ Other roadway
☐ Walking in roadway - with traffic	☐ Standing in safety zone	☐ Pushing or working on Vehicle	☐ Not in roadway
☐ Walking in roadway - against traffic	☐ Lying or Sitting on roadway	☐ Other working in roadway	☐ Other (explain above)

DRIVERS AND VEHICLES	VEHICLE 1	VEHICLE 2
PHYSICAL DEFECTS (Driver)		
VEHICLE DEFECTS		
CONTRIBUTING CIRCUMSTANCES		

ACCIDENT Characteristics						
LIGHTING CONDITION	Dark	ROAD DEFECTS	None	TRAFFICWAY CHARACTER	Light	CLASS OF TRAFFICWAYS	7
WEATHER	Overc	TRAFFIC CONTROL	None	TRAFFICWAY LANES	Two	TYPE TRAFFICWAY	3
ROAD SURFACE	Dry	TYPE LOCATION	Str.	VISION OBSCURED	No		

WITNESSES other than occupants

NAME	ADDRESS – Number and street	City and State / Zip Code
	J. Vernon Flavell, 827 N. Pigeon Rd.	(Yours)

FIRST AID GIVEN BY
J. Vernon Flavell

| ☐ Doctor or Nurse | ☒ Cert. First Aider |
| ☐ Cert. First Aider (Police) | ☐ Other (Explain) |

INJURED TAKEN TO
Memorial Hospital   BY: Cleary Ambulance

| ☒ Priv. Ambulance | ☐ Other (Explain) |
| ☐ Gov't. Ambulance | |

CHEMICAL TEST: TEST RESULTS:
	YES	NO	
Driver No. 1	☒	☐	Not yet in
Driver No. 2	☐	☐	

ARREST

NAME	CHARGE	Citation No.
NAME	CHARGE	Citation No.

PHOTOGRAPHS TAKEN
☒ Yes ☐ No
☐ Invest. Agency
☐ Other (Explain)

TIME NOTIFIED OF ACCIDENT	TIME ARRIVED AT SCENE	WAS INVESTIGATION MADE AT SCENE (if not where)	IS INVESTIGATION COMPLETE (if not why)
11:44 P.M. 19	12:03 A.M.	Yes	Need to interview surviving passenger

Exercise 16

PUBLIC AFFAIRS REPORTING

TRAFFIC ACCIDENT REPORT

MAIL TO: ACCIDENT RECORDS BUREAU, DEPT. OF HIGHWAY SAFETY & MOTOR VEHICLES,

TIME & LOCATION

DATE OF ACCIDENT	Month	Day	Year	DAY OF WEEK Yesterday	TIME OF DAY 11:35	p. M

COUNTY (Yours) — CITY, TOWN OR COMMUNITY — LOCAL ACCIDENT REPORT NUMBER 34178005

IF ACCIDENT WAS OUTSIDE CITY LIMITS, INDICATE DISTANCE FROM NEAREST TOWN 4 ☐ Feet ☒ Miles N S E W ☐☐☐☒ or (Your city) City, Village or Township

ROAD ON WHICH ACCIDENT OCCURRED U.S. 141 Use State or County Road Number or Name ☐ Exit Ramp ☐ Entrance R. ☐ At its intersection with ☐ Influenced by intersection Highway Number or Name of Intersecting Street and Node

IF NOT AT INTER-SECTION 2 ☐ Feet ☒ Miles N S E W ☐☐☐☒ or State Route 19 Show nearest intersecting street or highway, bridge, RR crossing, underpass or curve
☐ Feet ☐ Miles N S E W of Node
IS ENGINEERING STUDY NEEDED (if so explain) None   DO NOT WRITE IN SPACE ABOVE

TYPE MOTOR VEHICLE ACCIDENT

OVERTURNING	OTHER NONCOLLISION	PEDESTRIAN	MV IN TRANSPORT	MV ON OTHER ROADWAY	HIT AND RUN
PARKED MV xxx	RAILWAY TRAIN	PEDALCYCLIST	ANIMAL	FIXED OBJECT	OTHER OBJECT	NON-CONTACT

VEHICLE 1

TOTAL NO. MOTOR Vehicles Involved

YEAR	MAKE Buick	TYPE (Sedan, Truck, Bus, etc.) Sedan	VEHICLE LICENSE PLATE NO. 7D-8434	STATE Yes	YEAR Cur.	VEHICLE IDENTIFICATION NO. 817-93200745

Area of Vehicle Damage 4 5 6 | Damage Scale 1 | Damage Severity 1 | AMOUNT (Approximate) | Safety Equipment | VEHICLE REMOVED BY Halston Towing |

NAME OF INSURANCE (Liability or PIP) Liberty Mutual POLICY NO. 84-992-8341 Owner ☒ Driver ☐ ☐ Owner's Request ☐ Other (Explain) ☒ Rotation List

OWNER (Print or type FULL name) Mr. and Mrs. Harry Ralph Novogroski ADDRESS (Number and street) 2891 Norris Avenue CITY and STATE/Zip Code (Yours)

DRIVER (Exactly as on driver's license) Harry R. Novogroski ADDRESS (Number and street) 2891 Norris Avenue CITY and STATE/Zip Code (Yours)

OCCUPATION Machinist	Driver's License Type A	DRIVER'S LICENSE NUMBER 74-892-4837	STATE Yes	DATE (Month, Day, Year) OF BIRTH 3/23/27	RACE B	SEX M	Safety E.	Eject.	Injury X

OCCUPANTS

	Name	ADDRESS – Number and Street	City and State/Zip Code	AGE	RACE	SEX	Safety E.	Eject.	Injury
Front center									
Front right									
Rear left	Mary Ruth Novogroski	2891 Norris Ave.		15	B	F			X
Rear center	Margaret Sue Novogroski	2891 Norris Ave.		11	B	F			X
Rear right	Matthew Harold Novogroski	2891 Norris Ave.		9	B	M			X

VEHICLE 2 or PEDESTRIAN

YEAR	MAKE Chevy	TYPE (Sedan, Truck, Bus, etc.) Pickup truck	VEHICLE LICENSE PLATE NO. 7d-3680	STATE Yes	YEAR Cur.	VEHICLE IDENTIFICATION NO. 935-8780341

Area of Vehicle Damage 1 2 3 | Damage Scale 1 | Damage Severity 1 | AMOUNT (Approximate) | Safety Equipment | VEHICLE REMOVED BY Halston Towing |

NAME OF INSURANCE (Liability or PIP) Not yet determined POLICY NO. Owner ☐ Driver ☐ ☐ Owner's Request ☐ Other (Explain) ☒ Rotation List

OWNER (Print or type FULL name) Donald Edward Guerin ADDRESS (Number and street) 1045 Eastview Road CITY and STATE/Zip Code (Yours).

DRIVER (Exactly as on driver's license) Same as above ADDRESS (Number and street) CITY and STATE/Zip Code

OCCUPATION City fireman	Driver's License Type A	DRIVER'S LICENSE NUMBER 62-311-3828	STATE Yes	DATE (Month, Day, Year) OF BIRTH 11/3/56	RACE W	SEX M	Safety E.	Eject.	Injury

OCCUPANTS

	Name	ADDRESS – (Number and Street)	City and State/Zip Code	AGE	RACE	SEX	Safety E.	Eject.	Injury
Front center									
Front right									
Rear left	None								
Rear center									
Rear right									

PROPERTY DAMAGED–Other than vehicles None | AMOUNT | OWNER – Name | ADDRESS – Number and Street | CITY and STATE/Zip Code |

INVESTIGATOR – Name and rank (Signature) Cpl. Alvarez | BADGE NO. 3814 | I.D. NO. 684172 | DEPARTMENT Highway Patrol ☐ F.H.P. ☒ C.P.D. ☐ S.O. ☐ Other | DATE OF REPORT |

SHEET One OF Two SHEETS

DIAGRAM WHAT HAPPENED – (Number each vehicle and show direction of travel by arrow)

INDICATE NORTH WITH ARROW

POINT OF IMPACT

	Vehicle 1	2	
	☐	☒	Front
	☐	☐	Right front
	☐	☐	Left front
	☐	☐	Right side
	☐	☐	Left side
	☒	☐	Rear
	☐	☐	Right rear
	☐	☐	Left rear

#2   #1

DESCRIBE WHAT HAPPENED – (Refer to vehicles by number)

Novogroski had experienced a flat tire and drove onto the shoulder, completely leaving the roadway with his vehicle, to change it. His wife was outside with him, apparently holding a light of some type, when vehicle #2 struck the rear of their car, crushing the couple between the two vehicles, apparently killing them outright. Guerin was not injured and was wearing a seatbelt at the time. Three children in vehicle #1 were injured and taken to Eastbrook Hospital, although the extent of their injuries was not immediately determined. Gasoline ignited, setting both vehicles totally ablaze, burning one of the children who had not yet gotten out of the car. Bystanders helped pull the child out, as did Guerin.

*WHAT VEHICLES WERE DOING BEFORE ACCIDENT

VEHICLE No. 1 was traveling ☐ ☒ ☐ On U.S. 141 at 0 M.P.H. (Approximate)

VEHICLE No. 2 was traveling ☐ ☒ ☐ On U.S. 141 at 50 M.P.H.

								Vehicle 1 2	
☐ ☒	Going straight ahead	☐ ☐	Making right turn	☐ ☐	Slowing or Stopping	☐ ☐	Starting from parked position		
☐ ☐	Overtaking	☐ ☐	Making left turn	☐ ☐	Changing lanes	☒ ☐	Stopped or parked		
						☐ ☐	Other (explain above)		

*WHAT PEDESTRIAN WAS DOING

☐ Along

PEDESTRIAN was going ☐ ☐ ☐ ☐   ☐ Across or into .... from .... to .... | Color of Clothing | ☐ Dark ☐ Light |

☐ Crossing at intersection	☐ Stepped into path of Vehicle	☐ Getting on or off Vehicle	☐ Playing in roadway
☐ Crossing not at intersection	☐ Standing in roadway	☐ Hitching on Vehicle	☐ Other roadway
☐ Walking in roadway - with traffic	☐ Standing in safety zone	☐ Pushing or working on Vehicle	☐ Not in roadway
☐ Walking in roadway - against traffic	☐ Lying or Sitting on roadway	☐ Other working in roadway	☐ Other (explain above)

DRIVERS AND VEHICLES

	VEHICLE 1	VEHICLE 2
PHYSICAL DEFECTS (Driver)		
VEHICLE DEFECTS		
CONTRI- BUTING		
CIRCUM- STANCES		

ACCIDENT Characteristics

LIGHTING CONDITION	Dark	ROAD DEFECTS	None	TRAFFICWAY CHARACTER	Quiet	CLASS OF TRAFFICWAYS 4
WEATHER	Normal	TRAFFIC CONTROL	None	TRAFFICWAY LANES	2 lane	TYPE TRAFFICWAY 2
ROAD SURFACE	Dry	TYPE LOCATION	Hwy.	VISION OBSCURED	No	

WITNESSES other than occupants

NAME	ADDRESS – Number and street	City and State Zip Code
None		

FIRST AID GIVEN BY

Donald Guerin

☐ Doctor or Nurse	☒ Cert. First Aider
☐ Cert. First Aider (Police)	☐ Other (Explain)

CHEMICAL TEST:

	YES	NO
Driver No. 1	☐	☐
Driver No. 2	☒	☐

TEST RESULTS: .... Negative

INJURED TAKEN TO Eastbrook Hospital   BY Cleary Ambulance

☒ Priv. Ambulance	☐ Other (Explain)
☐ Gov't. Ambulance	

ARREST

NAME	CHARGE	Citation No.
Donald Edward Guerin	Manslaughter	8320816
NAME	CHARGE	Citation No.

PHOTOGRAPHS TAKEN ☒ Yes ☐ No

☐ Invest. Agency

☐ Other (Explain)

TIME NOTIFIED OF ACCIDENT	TIME ARRIVED AT SCENE	WAS INVESTIGATION MADE AT SCENE (If not why)	IS INVESTIGATION COMPLETE (If not why)
11:47 19 P. M	11:54 M	Yes	Yes

Exercise 17

PUBLIC AFFAIRS REPORTING

**In the Circuit Court of
The 9th Judicial Circuit
in and for (your) County**

Division: Civil

Case No.: C971-7783

TONY DEWITTE   *Plaintiff,*

vs.

BUDDY RICHBOURG
d/b/a BUDDY'S LOUNGE,   *Defendants.*

C O M P L A I N T

COMES NOW the Plaintiff and sues the Defendant and says:

1. This is an action for damages in the amount of SIX HUNDRED THOUSAND ($600,000) DOLLARS, plus all costs and reasonable attorneys' fees.

2. That at all times material to this cause, Defendant, BUDDY'S LOUNGE, was a business operating in this county.

3. That at all times mentioned herein, the Defendant operated and controlled a bar known as BUDDY'S LOUNGE located in this county, to which the general public was invited for the purpose of obtaining recreation and alcoholic beverages for compensation to be paid to Defendant.

4. On or about December 10 of last year, TONY DEWITTE was a patron in Defendant's bar.

5. At that time and place, and without provocation, a man unknown to the Plaintiff, and others, all in a highly intoxicated condition, willfully and maliciously assaulted and beat TONY DEWITTE and struck him repeatedly, breaking his nose, jaw and arm, and causing him the traumatic loss of several teeth.

6. The assault on TONY DEWITTE was caused by the negligence of Defendant in failing to exercise proper supervision and control over the persons in the bar, when the Defendant knew or should have known that such persons were intoxicated and belligerent and posed a threat to Plaintiff and others.

7. The negligence of Defendant, in addition to that hereinabove alleged, consisted of failing to provide an employee or employees to maintain proper order and exercise reasonable care for the safety of patrons, or the failure of such an employee to perform his duties and prevent injuries sustained by the Plaintiff.

8. The negligence of Defendant, in addition to that hereinabove alleged, consisted of continuing to sell known intoxicants to the assailants long after they had become loud, abusive and argumentative.

9. The negligence of Defendant, in addition to that hereinabove alleged, consisted of failing, once the altercation had commenced, to promptly come to the aid of the Defendant and to seek the assistance of the police and other appropriate law enforcement officials.

10. That as a direct and proximate result of the negligence of the Defendant, TONY DEWITTE sustained a broken nose, jaw and arm, and the traumatic loss of several teeth.

11. At the time of his injuries, the said TONY DEWITTE was of good health, industrious and thrifty, and enjoyed a substantial earning capacity and was acquiring property and resources.

12. As a result of Defendant's negligence, TONY DEWITTE incurred medical expenses, a loss of earnings and a permanent disability as well as pain and suffering, mental anguish, and humiliation and future medical expenses.

WHEREFORE, THE PLAINTIFF sues the Defendant and demands judgment for damages, costs, trial by jury and such other relief as the Court deems just.

Enrique Diaz

Enrique Diaz
208 Baxter Avenue
Attorney for Plaintiff

Exercise 18
PUBLIC AFFAIRS REPORTING

**In the Circuit Court of
The 9th Judicial Circuit
in and for (your) County**

Division: Probate

Case No.: PR 67-1381

IN RE: GUARDIANSHIP
OF PATRICIA JEAN
WILLIAMS, an Incompetent

JOHN RUSSELL
WILLIAMS, as Guardian
of the Person of
PATRICIA JEAN
WILLIAMS,   *Plaintiff,*

vs.

MERCY HOSPITAL;
ROSS R. GRAHAM,
M.D.; RICHARD M.
CESSARINI, M.D.;
RAMON HERNANDEZ,
DISTRICT ATTORNEY,   *Defendants.*

FINAL DECLARATORY JUDGMENT

THIS CAUSE came for hearing upon the Complaint for Declaratory Relief because of the uncertainty of the law by JOHN RUSSELL WILLIAMS as Guardian of the Person of PATRICIA JEAN WILLIAMS, an Incompetent, against MERCY HOSPITAL; ROSS R. GRAHAM, M.D.; RICHARD M. CESSARINI, M.D.; and RAMON HERNANDEZ, DISTRICT ATTORNEY for the city, the Defendants, wherein Plaintiff seeks a Declaratory Judgment as to the following:

Authorization for JOHN RUSSELL WILLIAMS, as Guardian of the Person of PATRICIA JEAN WILLIAMS, an Incompetent, to direct MERCY HOSPITAL; ROSS R. GRAHAM, M.D.; RICHARD M. CESSARINI, M.D.; and all other attending physicians and health care providers to discontinue and to withhold all extraordinary measures such as mechanical ventilators, respirators, antibiotics, cardiovascular or similar type drugs; that these extraordinary measures should not be utilized, but be discontinued or withheld, in that the doctors agree there is no reasonable possibility of the Ward ever recovering from her present, persistent, "vegetative" (coma-like) state, which is irreversible;

That your Petitioner, JOHN RUSSELL WILLIAMS, surviving son; MERCY HOSPITAL; ROSS R. GRAHAM, M.D.; RICHARD M. CESSARINI, M.D.; and all other treating and consulting physicians and health care providers shall not be held civilly or criminally liable for taking the above action; and

That an appropriate restraining order be issued restraining the Defendant, RAMON HERNANDEZ, DISTRICT ATTORNEY, from prosecuting any of the above named individuals and organizations for withdrawing or withholding all extraordinary measures such as mechanical ventilators, respirators, antibiotics, cardiovascular or similar type drugs.

The Court makes the following findings of fact:

1. That this action is properly brought as a suit for declaratory judgment and relief, and that Plaintiff is the proper party to bring this action.

2. That at all times material hereto, the Plaintiff is a resident of the county in which this action is brought, and PATRICIA JEAN WILLIAMS, the Ward, has been maintained at MERCY HOSPITAL since she was involved in a serious motor vehicle accident 73 days prior to the issuance of this order.

3. That the following findings are based upon reasonable medical certainty and derived from the testimony of ROSS R. GRAHAM, M.D.; RICHARD M. CESSARINI, M.D.; and the records of MERCY HOSPITAL:

   (a) That four electroencephalograms, commonly referred to as EEGs, were performed on PATRICIA JEAN WILLIAMS, the Ward. None of the electroencephalograms indicated any cortical response. The only indication was a flat line.

   (b) That the Ward has suffered severe brain damage, which brain damage is totally irreversible and untreatable with no hope of recovery; and that the Ward is in a chronic and persistent "vegetative" (coma-like) state.

   (c) That the testimony of the doctors revealed that it was their respective medical opinion that all measures which are considered extraordinary lifesaving measures should not be utilized with respect to the Ward, but be discontinued or withheld; however, the decision to withdraw or withhold extraordinary lifesaving measures should be made by the Plaintiff and the family of the Ward.

   (d) That PATRICIA JEAN WILLIAMS, the Ward, requires constant care, and will so require IN THE FUTURE.

4. That PATRICIA JEAN WILLIAMS, the Ward, requires constant care, which care invades the Ward's body and violates the Ward's right to privacy as guaranteed by the Constitution of the United States of America and of this State; and that the State does not have an overriding interest it needs to protect, nor is there overriding medical interests that need to be protected.

5. That the son, JOHN RUSSELL WILLIAMS, has determined, subject to the approval of this Court, that all extraordinary lifesaving measures should not be utilized with respect to the Ward, but be discontinued or withheld from the Ward, PATRICIA JEAN WILLIAMS, and that MERCY HOSPITAL has no objection.

It is, therefore, ORDERED AND ADJUDGED:

1. That JOHN RUSSELL WILLIAMS, as the Guardian of the Person of PATRICIA JEAN WILLIAMS, an Incompetent, has full power to make decisions with regard to the identity of the Ward's treating physicians.

2. That MERCY HOSPITAL; ROSS R. GRAHAM, M.D.; AND RICHARD M. CESSARINI, M.D., are authorized to discontinue or to withdraw all extraordinary measures and life-support systems upon written direction of JOHN RUSSELL WILLIAMS, as Guardian of the Person of PATRICIA JEAN WILLIAMS, an Incompetent.

3. That no one shall be held civilly or criminally liable for taking action authorized by this Order.
4. That the Defendant, RAMON HERNANDEZ, as District Attorney for the city, shall be bound by this decision.

DONE AND ORDERED in Chambers.

BY: ___*Randall Pfaff*___

RANDALL PFAFF, Circuit Judge

Exercise 19

PUBLIC AFFAIRS REPORTING

**In the Circuit Court of
The 9th Judicial Circuit
in and for (your) County**

Division: Civil

Case No.: I-78-1439

JOHN H. WARD and
FRANCIS B. WARD,
individually and as next friends
and parents of KAREN
WARD, a minor,   *Plaintiffs,*

vs.

EILEEN BARTON and
BARTON SCHOOL
OF DANCE,   *Defendants.*

C O M P L A I N T

COME NOW the Plaintiffs and sue the Defendants and say:

1. This is an action for damages in the amount of $1,000,000 (One Million Dollars).

2. That at all times material to this cause, the Plaintiffs, JOHN H. WARD and FRANCIS B. WARD, were and are husband and wife residing together in this county, and that KAREN WARD is their natural born daughter.

3. That at all times material to this cause, the Defendants do business in this county and advertise the BARTON SCHOOL OF DANCE as a reputable institution, suitable for the enrollment of young children, and these advertisements further assert that lessons provided by said school will favorably promote the development of children's poise, health, happiness, personality and character.

4. That, to enrich the life of Plaintiff KAREN WARD, a minor and only daughter, Plaintiffs JOHN H. WARD and FRANCIS B. WARD enrolled the child in the BARTON SCHOOL OF DANCE and, at the personal urging of Defendant EILEEN BARTON, kept her in the school for a second year, regularly and at great personal sacrifice to themselves, paying a monthly fee of $128.95 for ballet lessons for Plaintiff KAREN WARD, during the course of both years.

5. That Willis A. Boyette was employed as a janitor by the Defendant, BARTON SCHOOL OF DANCE, and, due to the nature of his work, often came in close proximity to students.

6. That, on at least three separate occasions, Willis A. Boyette took Plaintiff KAREN WARD into a school restroom and violently and without her consent raped her.

7. That Plaintiff KAREN WARD was, at the time in question, only 9 years of age and a fourth-grade student at Croft Elementary School.

8. That the Plaintiff KAREN WARD did not immediately tell anyone of the attacks because of her confusion and shame and because she feared Boyette, who threatened her with further harm.

9. That Plaintiff KAREN WARD contracted a venereal disease and, when she was taken to a doctor for treatment of such disease, confided in that doctor and then in her parents about the attacks.

10. That, as a result of these attacks, the Plaintiff KAREN WARD has and continues to be very traumatized, fearful and unhappy, requiring psychiatric care of a continuing nature.

11. That the Defendants, EILEEN BARTON and BARTON SCHOOL OF DANCE, are solely responsible for the actions of Willis A. Boyette; that Boyette was personally hired by Defendant EILEEN BARTON, who thereupon failed to investigate adequately his background and to provide the proper supervision of his work.

12. That Willis A. Boyette has since been tried, convicted and sentenced to serve three to nine years in prison following his conviction in a criminal trial of carnal knowledge.

WHEREFORE, THE PLAINTIFFS, JOHN H. WARD and FRANCIS B. WARD, individually and as next friends and parents of KAREN WARD, a minor, sue the Defendants, EILEEN BARTON and BARTON SCHOOL OF DANCE, both jointly and severally, for compensatory damages in an amount within the jurisdicational limits of this Court, and demand trial by jury of all issues triable as of right by a jury.

> DAVID CASIO & ASSOCIATES
> 831 Forester Road
> Attorneys for Plaintiffs
>
> BY: *Bruce R. Washington*
>
> BRUCE R. WASHINGTON

Exercise 20

PUBLIC AFFAIRS REPORTING

**In the Circuit Court of
The 9th Judicial Circuit
in and for (your) County**

Division: Civil

Case No.: 1-78-1440

THADDEUS DOWDELL
and LAURA DOWDELL,
individually and as next friends
and parents of JAMES
DOWDELL, a minor,   *Plaintiffs,*

vs.

MARVIN FERRELL,
GREG HUBBARD
and (YOUR CITY'S)
SCHOOL DISTRICT,   *Defendants.*

C O M P L A I N T

COME NOW the Plaintiffs, THADDEUS DOWDELL and LAURA DOWDELL, individually and as next friends and parents of JAMES DOWDELL, a minor, by and through their undersigned counsel, and sue the Defendants, MARVIN FERRELL, GREG HUBBARD, AND (YOUR CITY'S) SCHOOL DISTRICT, jointly and severally, for damages and allege:

1. That this is an action for damages of $500,000, exclusive of interest, costs and further demands.
2. That at all times material to this cause, JAMES DOWDELL was and is the minor son of THADDEUS DOWDELL and LAURA DOWDELL, residing together with them in a family relationship as residents of this county.
3. That at all times material to this cause, the Defendant MARVIN FERRELL held and now holds the position of Principal of Kennedy High School, and that the Defendant GREG HUBBARD held and now holds the position of School Superintendent.
4. That the minor JAMES DOWDELL is and has been a student in Kennedy High School for the past three years and has been told that he will graduate from that school on or about the First Day of next June.
5. That the minor, JAMES DOWDELL, of this date, can barely read or do simple arithmetic and obviously has not learned enough to be graduated from high school or to function successfully in a society as complex as ours.
6. That the problem is not the fault of the minor JAMES DOWDELL, who, according to tests administered by guidance counselors at the high school, enjoys a normal IQ of 94.

7. That the failure of the minor JAMES DOWDELL to master the skills expected of high school students is the fault of the Defendants, MARVIN FERRELL, GREG HUBBARD, and (YOUR CITY'S) SCHOOL DISTRICT, that said defendants failed to employ competent teachers, to maintain discipline, to provide remedial help, and to provide an atmosphere in which learning might take place.

WHEREFORE, the Plaintiffs, THADDEUS DOWDELL and LAURA DOWDELL, individually and as next friends and parents of JAMES DOWDELL, a minor, sue the Defendants MARVIN FERRELL, GREG HUBBARD and (YOUR CITY'S) SCHOOL DISTRICT, jointly and severally, for compensatory damages in the amount of $500,000, exclusive of interest and costs.

FURTHER, the Plaintiffs demand that the minor JAMES DOWDELL be retained in Kennedy High School until he masters the skills expected of a high school graduate.

FURTHER, the Plaintiffs demand trial by jury of all issues triable as of right by a jury.

> PILOTO and HERNDON, Attorneys
> 1048 Westmore Drive
> Attorneys for Plaintiffs
>
> BY: *Kenneth T. Piloto*
> KENNETH T. PILOTO

Exercise 21

PUBLIC AFFAIRS REPORTING

HOUSE BILL 4424: MAKING ENGLISH THE OFFICIAL LANGUAGE

INSTRUCTIONS: Write a news story that summarizes the content of the following speech and bill. This is a verbatim copy of a speech given by Rep. Bill Emerson of Missouri and can be quoted directly. Assume that Rep. Emerson gave the speech today, then immediately introduced the bill.

Introductory Speech

Mr. Speaker, this nation has achieved its greatness through the contributions of the many diverse peoples who have come to settle here. Yet this is an unusual phenomenon which stands out against the background of world history. It is not often that people of so many varying cultures and backgrounds can live together in peace. Human nature often leads us to resist and fear those who are different from us.

What, then, has enabled America to become the country that it is, the "great melting pot" of the world? It is, in large measure, our common bond of the English language. We come from widely varying cultures. We eat a vast variety of foods. We have different cultural norms and different lifestyles. Yet we share a common tongue. We can talk to each other. We can communicate. We can discuss our differences, and each culture can learn to respect the others. If we had no common tongue, we would be little more than isolated islands of communities, lacking a common vision.

I will be introducing legislation to promote and encourage the use of English as the official language of the United States. I am aware that some folks will look at this legislation with a jaundiced eye, however. This legislation will not ask minority groups to give up their various cultures. It will not stifle or prohibit languages other than English. It simply states that English should be the one language that everybody knows and the one language in which all of our official business is conducted.

I am aware that some critics of this legislation may paint it as a subtle form of discrimination. Yet I propose to you that as a second language becomes more prominent in the United States, we will see more, not less, racial and ethnic discrimination. We will see more, not less, strife among the races. We will see more hatred of, and less respect for, our differences.

We need to preserve the common bond of a unifying language in this country. I urge you to join me in supporting efforts to make English the official language of the United States.

The Bill

Mr. EMERSON (for himself, Mr. SKELTON, Mr. SHUMWAY, Mr. BROOMFIELD, Mr. DICKINSON, Mr. IRELAND, Mr. MYERS of Indiana, Mr. PORTER, and Mr. ROGERS) introduced the following bill; which was referred to the Committee on Education and Labor.

A bill to amend title 4, United States Code, to declare English as the official language of the Government of the United States.

Be it enacted by the Senate and House of Representatives of the United States of America in Congress assembled,

SEC. 1. SHORT TITLE.

This Act may be cited as the "Language of Government Act."

SEC. 2. FINDINGS AND PURPOSE.

The Nation has benefited throughout its history by using the common language of English. The Congress finds and declares that English, the language of opportunity, should be recognized in law as the official language of the United States. The purpose of this Act (and the amendments made by this Act) is to maintain the benefits of a single official language of the Government of the United States. There is no intent to discriminate against or restrict the rights of any individual in the United States. Except where an existing law of the United States directly contravenes this Act (or the amendments made by this Act) (such as by requiring the use of a language other than English for an official act of Government of the United States), no implied repeal of existing laws of the United States is intended.

SEC. 3. ENGLISH AS OFFICIAL LANGUAGE.

(a) IN GENERAL.—Title 4, United States Code, is amended by adding at the end the following new chapter:

"CHAPTER 6—LANGUAGE OF THE GOVERNMENT

"Sec.
"161. Declaration of official language.
"162. Preserving official language.
"163. Government activities in English.
"164. Antidiscrimination provisions.
"165. Standing.
"166. Definitions.

"§ 161. Declaration of official language

"The official language of the Government of the United States is English.

"§ 162. Preserving and enhancing the role of the official language

"The Government shall have an affirmative obligation to protect, preserve, and enhance the role of English as the official language of the United States.

"§ 163. Government activities in English

"(a) DENIAL OF SERVICES.—No person shall be denied services, assistance, or facilities, directly or indirectly provided by the Government solely because the person communicates in English.
    "(b) ENTITLEMENT.—Every person in the United States is entitled to—
        "(1) communicate with the Government in English;
        "(2) receive information from or contribute information to the Government in English; and
        "(3) be informed of or be subject to official orders in English.
    "(c) RESTRICTIONS.—No entity to which this chapter applies shall make or enforce an official act that requires the use of a language other than English.

"§ 164. Antidiscrimination provisions

"Any person in the United States discriminated against solely because the person communicates in English shall be considered to have been discriminated against on the basis of national origin, and all lawful remedies available under section 701 of the Civil Rights Act of 1964 (42 U.S.C. 2000e) shall be available to a person so discriminated against.

"§ 165. Standing

"Any resident of the United States (including a corporation) alleging a violation of this chapter shall have standing to sue in the courts of the United States under sections 2201 and 2202 of title 28, United States Code, and for such other relief as may be considered appropriate by the courts (including attorneys fees under section 2412 of title 28, United States Code, or similar statutes).

"§ 166. Definitions

For purposes of this chapter:

"(1) GOVERNMENT.—The term 'Government' means all branches of the Government of the United States and all employees and officials of the Government of the United States while performing official acts.

"(2) OFFICIAL.—The term 'official' means governmental actions, documents, or policies that are enforceable with full weight and authority of the Government, but does not include—

"(A) actions, documents, or policies that are purely informational or educational;

"(B) actions, documents, or policies that are not enforceable in the United States;

"(C) actions that protect the public health or safety;

"(D) actions that protect the rights of victims of crimes or criminal defendants; and

"(E) documents that utilize terms of art or phrases from languages other than English."

(b) CLERICAL AMENDMENT.—The table of chapters for title 4, United States Code, is amended by adding at the end the following new item:

"6. Language of the Government .... 161".

SEC. 4. PREEMPTION.

This Act (and the amendments made by this Act) shall not preempt any law of any State.

SEC. 5. EFFECTIVE DATE.

This Act (and the amendments made by this Act) shall take effect upon the date of the enactment of this Act.

Exercise 22

PUBLIC AFFAIRS REPORTING

INSTRUCTIONS: Write a news story about the following bill. Assume that the state senator for the district in which you live introduced the bill in the State Senate today.

HOUSE BILL 319

An act relating to cable television; providing legislative intent; prohibiting persons from sending, transmitting, or retransmitting by a cable television system any material which is indecent; providing definitions; providing penalties; providing an effective date.

Be It Enacted by the Legislature of the State:

SECTION 1. LEGISLATIVE INTENT.—

(1) It is the intention of the Legislature in adopting this act to apply to cable television the prohibition against indecent programming, which was upheld by the United States Supreme Court in FCC vs. Pacifica Foundation. Subsequent judicial decisions had construed the Communications Act of 1934 as placing in doubt the ability of the federal or state governments to regulate indecency on cable television, as distinguished from radio and over the air television broadcasting. The "Cable Communications Policy Act" has now clarified the right of states to regulate indecent programming on cable television within their state. It is thus the intention of this act to restore the prohibition against indecent programming to cable television.

(2) The violence against and degradation of women and children in our society are increasing. There are many causes of this, but the most powerful communications medium cannot escape responsibility for its part in this phenomenon. Just as cable operators have rights, so have parents, children, women, victims of crime, and society itself. This act seeks to balance and protect all those rights.

SECTION 2.

(1) No person shall send, transmit, or retransmit by a cable television system material which is indecent. For the purposes of this section, material is indecent when, under contemporary community standards for cable television, it is patently offensive and is a representation or verbal description of:
    (a) Ultimate sexual acts, normal or perverted, actual or simulated;
    (b) Masturbation;
    (c) Human sexual or excretory organs or functions; or
    (d) A display, description, or representation in lurid detail of the violent physical torture or dismemberment of a person.

(2) For the purposes of this section, the term "material" includes visual and audible material and "community standards" means standards of the community encompassed within the territorial area covered by the franchise.

(3) Any person who violates the provision of this section is guilty of a misdemeanor of the first degree, punishable by fines of up to $10,000 and 6 months in jail. A person who, after having been convicted of a violation of this section, thereafter violates any of its provisions, is guilty of a felony of the third degree, punishable by fines of up to $25,000 and 15 years in prison.

Exercise 23

PUBLIC AFFAIRS REPORTING

ORDINANCE NO. 20505

An Ordinance of (Your) City, Amending Chapter 31 "Zoning Ordinance" by Repealing Section 31-21, "General Provisions," Paragraph 14, Entitled "Walls and Fences," and Substituting Therefor a New Paragraph Entitled "Walls and Fences."

Be It Enacted by the People of (Your City):

SECTION 1. Pursuant to Section 31-24 thereof, Chapter 31 of the Code of Ordinances of the City is hereby amended and modified by repealing Paragraph 14 of Section 31-21, entitled, "Walls and Fences" and substituting the following therefor:

"14. *Walls and Fences*.

(a) *Permits*. Requests for permits for walls and fences must be accompanied by a site plan and drawings clearly showing the locations and heights for which approval is asked.

(b) *Height*. In front yards, and in side yards with street frontage, walls and fences shall not exceed (3) feet in height above the street curb elevation. In the rear yard of a corner lot, fences in excess of three (3) feet in height above the street curb elevation shall be set back from the street right-of-way the same distance as is prescribed for accessory buildings in the rear yard of corner lots. In all other side and rear yard areas, walls and fences may be a maximum of six (6) feet in height above the ground. Where compliance with these height limits would cause a hardship due to the natural topography of a particular lot, the Administrative Official may permit portions of a fence or wall to be up to eight (8) feet in height in areas where the normal maximum height would be six (6) feet; and where fences are normally limited to three (3) feet in height above the street curb elevation, he may permit the fence height to be measured from the underlying natural ground level rather than the curb. However, no wall or fence shall be permitted which would in any way obstruct the visibility of automobiles at intersections and points of ingress and egress to the public right-of-way.

(c) *Materials Permitted in Residential Districts*. In any single-family residential district, fences in the front yard or in a side yard with street frontage shall be decorative. Chain link, chicken wire or similar type fences shall be prohibited. Barbed wire or electrically charged fences shall not be erected in any residential district. Neither shall any wall, fence, or similar structure erected in any residential district contain any material or substance such as broken glass, spikes, nails, barbs or similar materials designed to inflict pain or injury on any person or animal.

(d) *Designs and Materials Permitted in Non-residential Districts*. In any non-residential districts, barbed wire may be incorporated in or used as a fence above the level of six (6) feet from the ground. Any barbed wire shall be placed so that it does not project outward over any street, sidewalk, public way, or adjacent property.

SECTION 2. This Ordinance shall take effect immediately upon its final passage and adoption.

ADOPTED at a regular meeting of the City Council (last night).

Exercise 24

PUBLIC AFFAIRS REPORTING

ORDINANCE NO. 20732

An Ordinance of the City Enacting Chapter 2A, "Alarm Devices," Relating to Privately Owned General Alarm Devices: Defining Terms; Imposing upon the Owner or Manager of the Premises the Responsibility of Deactivating Alarms upon Notification to Do So; Requiring Corrective Action and the Filing of Reports; Prescribing Fees; Providing for Disconnection of Faulty Alarm Devices; Prohibiting the Installation of Telephone Alarm Devices Connected to the Police Department; and Providing for an Effective Date.

WHEREAS, malfunctions of privately owned alarm devices are causing substantial misuse of the manpower and resources of the Police Department of the City by provoking responses to numerous false alarms; and

WHEREAS, telephone alarm devices regulated or programmed to make connection with the Police Department could seize and hold Police Department telephone lines to the exclusion of other calls; and

WHEREAS, false alarms and use of telephone alarm devices create a threat or potential threat to the health, safety and welfare of the people of the City,

NOW, THEREFORE, BE IT ENACTED BY THE CITY COUNCIL THAT:

SECTION 1. Chapter 2A, "Alarm Devices," of the Code of Ordinances of the City is hereby enacted to read as follows:

Sec. 2A-1. *Definitions.* For purposes of this ordinance, the following terms shall have the following meanings:
  (a) *False alarm*—the activation of a telephone alarm device or general alarm device by other than a forced entry or attempted forced entry to the premises and at a time when no burglary or hold-up is being committed or attempted on the premises, except acts of God.
  (b) *First response*—a response to a false alarm to premises at which no other false alarm has occurred within the preceding six (6) month period.
  (c) *Telephone alarm device*—any device which, when activated, automatically transmits by telephone lines a recorded alarm message or electronic or mechanical alarm signal to any telephone instrument installed in any facility of the Police Department.
  (d) *General alarm device*—any alarm bell, light or other signaling device which, when activated, is designed to indicate a burglary or hold-up.

Sec. 2A-2. *Duty of owner or manager of premises.* Prior to the installation or use of any type of telephone device or general alarm device, the owner or manager of the premises shall furnish to the Police Department information regarding the full names, addresses and telephone numbers of at least two (2) persons who can be reached at all times and who are authorized to enter the premises and deactivate the alarm device. Owners or mangers of premises with telephone alarm devices or general alarm devices already installed shall have thirty (30) days from the effective date of this ordinance to comply with the above notice requirement. If any such person shall fail to appear and reset any such alarm within one (1) hour after being notified by the Police Department to do so, then the owner or manager of the premises shall be charged a fee of twenty dollars ($20.00) for the first such occurrence, and a fee of fifty dollars ($50.00) for each succeeding occurrence within six (6) months of the last failure to appear.

Sec. 2A-3. *Responses to false alarms; corrective action and reports required; fees charged.*

(a) Corrective action and report required. For each response by the Police Department to a false alarm, the owner or manager of the premises involved shall, within three (3) working days after notice to do so, make a written report to the Chief of Police, on forms provided by him, setting forth the cause of the false alarm, the corrective action taken, the name, address and telephone number of the service man, if any, by whom the device has been inspected or repaired, and such other information as the department may reasonably require to determine the cause of the false alarm and what corrective action has been taken or may be necessary.

(b) Fees charged. There shall be no fee charged for a first response to premises or for a second or third response within six (6) months after a first response. For a fourth response to premises within six (6) months after a third response, there shall be a fee of twenty dollars ($20.00), and for all succeeding responses within six (6) months of the last response, a fee of fifty dollars ($50.00) for each such response shall be charged. Upon a failure to pay any such fee within ten (10) days after the notification for which it is charged, the Chief of Police shall be authorized to disconnect or deactivate the alarm device involved.

(c) Authority to disconnect. Upon failure of an owner or manager of premises to pay any fee specified above within ten (10) days after the occurrence for which the fee is charged, or upon a determination by the Chief of Police that any false alarm, other than a false alarm caused by the act of God, to which a first response is made has resulted from a failure on the part of the owner or manager of the premises to take necessary corrective action, the Chief of Police shall be authorized to disconnect the telephone alarm device or general alarm device, and it shall be unlawful to reconnect such telephone alarm device or general alarm device unless and until appropriate corrective action has been taken and such reconnection is authorized by the Chief of Police; provided, however, that no disconnection or deactivation shall be ordered or made as to any premises required by law to have an alarm device in operation.

Sec. 2A-4. *Telephone alarm devices prohibited.* It shall be unlawful for any person, firm, corporation or association to install any telephone alarm device after the effective date of this ordinance.

SECTION 2. All ordinances or parts of ordinances in conflict herewith are hereby repealed.

Exercise 25

PUBLIC AFFAIRS REPORTING
SENATE BILL 143

(legalizing heroin for terminally ill cancer patients)

BACKGROUND: Two U.S. senators, Dennis DeConcini and Daniel Inouye, have introduced Senate Bill 143, which would allow doctors to prescribe parenteral (intravenous) diacetylmorphine (heroin) "to relieve the excruciating pain of terminally ill cancer patients." Although most pain associated with cancer is controllable by drugs such as morphine and dilaudid, estimates are that in the United States 8,000 people a year die in intractable pain from cancer. "For many of these victims, the closing days of their lives are ones of prolonged agony," explains Sen. DeConcini. "They cannot function in a normal way and their families often endure great trauma. Medical studies that have been conducted abroad and in this country suggest that heroin can be used very effectively to control the extreme pain of cancer patients. If there is a beneficial use of the drug, we should not let our normal instincts of aversion to its use unreasonably affect our thinking." This bill proposes an experimental program operating "under the strictest controls of production and distribution." The authors add that, "In five years we will have a solid body of facts and experience upon which to decide whether the program should be extended, modified, or terminated."

S.143

Be It Enacted by the Senate and House of Representatives of the United States of America in Congress Assembled, That This Act May Be Cited as the "Compassionate Pain Relief Act."

Sec. 2. The Congress finds the following:

(1) Cancer is a progressive, degenerative, and often painful disease which afflicts one out of every four Americans and is the second leading cause of death.

(2) In the progression of terminal cancer, a significant number of patients will experience levels of intense and intractable pain which cannot be effectively treated by presently available medication. The effect of the pain often leads to a severe deterioration in the quality of life of the patient and heartbreak for the patient's family.

(3) The therapeutic use of parenteral diacetylmorphine is not permitted in the United States, but extensive clinical research has demonstrated that it is a potent, highly soluble painkilling drug when properly formulated and administered under a physician's supervision.

(4) Making parenteral diacetylmorphine available to patients through controlled channels as a drug for the relief of intractable pain due to terminal cancer is in the public interest. Diacetylmorphine is successfully used in Great Britain and other countries for relief of pain due to cancer.

(5) The availability of parenteral diacetylmorphine for the limited purposes of controlling intractable pain due to terminal cancer will not adversely affect the abuse of illicit drugs or increase the incidence of pharmacy thefts.

(6) The availability of parenteral diacetylmorphine will enhance the ability of physicians to effectively treat and control intractable pain due to terminal cancer.

(7) It is appropriate for the Federal Government to establish a temporary program to permit the use of pharmaceutical dosage forms of parenteral diacetylmorphine for the control of intractable pain due to terminal cancer.

Sec. 3 (a) Not later than three months after the date of the enactment of this Act, the Secretary of Health and Human Services (hereinafter in this Act referred to as the

"Secretary") shall issue regulations establishing a program under which parenteral diacetylmorphine may be made available to hospital pharmacies and other such pharmacies as may be prescribed by the Secretary for dispensing pursuant to written prescriptions of physicians to individuals for the relief of intractable pain due to terminal cancer (hereinafter in this section referred to as "the program"). For purposes of the program, an individual shall be considered to have terminal cancer if there is histologic evidence of a malignancy in the individual and the individual's cancer is generally recognized as a cancer with a high and predictable mortality. It is the intent of Congress that the Secretary primarily utilize hospital pharmacies for the dispensing of parenteral diacetylmorphine under the program, but the Congress recognizes that humanitarian concerns might necessitate the provision of parenteral diacetylmorphine through pharmacies other than hospital pharmacies in cases in which a significant need is shown for such provision and in which adequate protection is available against the diversion of parenteral diacetylmorphine.

(b) The Secretary shall provide for the manufacture of parenteral diacetylmorphine for dispensing under the program using adequate methods in, and adequate facilities and controls for, the manufacturing, processing, and packing of such drug to preserve its identity, strength, quality, and purity.

(c) Under the program parenteral diacetylmorphine may only be made available upon application to pharmacies registered under section 302 of the Controlled Substances Act that also meet such qualifications as the Secretary may by regulation prescribe. An application for parenteral diacetylmorphine shall—

(1) be in such form and submitted in such manner as the Secretary may prescribe, and

(2) contain assurances satisfactory to the Secretary that—

(A) the applicant meets such special requirements as the Secretary may prescribe respecting the storage and dispensing of parenteral diacetylmorphine, and

(B) parenteral diacetylmorphine provided under the application will be dispensed through the applicant upon the written prescription of a physician registered under Section 302 of the Controlled Substances Act to dispense controlled substances in schedule II of such Act.

(d) Requirements prescribed by the Secretary under subsections (b) and (c)(2)(A) shall be designed to protect against the diversion into illicit channels of parenteral diacetylmorphine distributed under the program.

(e) A physician registered under section 302 of the Controlled Substances Act may prescribe parenteral diacetylmorphine for individuals for the relief of intractable pain due to terminal cancer. Any such prescription shall be in writing as prescribed by the Secretary by regulations.

(f) The Federal Food, Drug, and Cosmetic Act and titles II and III of the Comprehensive Drug Abuse Prevention and Control Act of 1970 shall not apply with respect to—

(1) the importing of opium,

(2) the manufacture of parenteral diacetylmorphine, and

(3) the distribution and dispensing of parenteral diacetylmorphine in accordance with the program.

Sec. 4. (a) Not later than the second month beginning after the date of the enactment of this section and every third month thereafter until the program is established under section 3, the Secretary shall report to the Committee on Energy and Commerce of the House of Representatives and the Committee on Labor and Human Resources of the Senate on the activities undertaken to implement the program. Each year after the program is established and while the program is in effect, the Secretary shall report to such committees on the activities under the progam during the period for which the report is submitted.

(b) Upon the expiration of fifty-six months after the date the program is established, the Comptroller General of the United States shall report to the committees referred to in subsection (a) on the activities under the program during such fifty-six month period.

Sec. 5. The program established under section 3 shall terminate upon the expiration of sixty months after the date the program is established.

Sec. 6. The Secretary of Health and Human Services shall transmit a report to the Committee on Energy and Commerce of the House of Representatives and the Committee on Labor and Human Resources of the Senate not later than six months after the date of the enactment of this Act—

(1) describing the extent of research activities on the management of pain which have received funds through the National Institutes of Health,

(2) describing the ways in which the Federal Government supports the training of health personnel in pain management, and

(3) containing recommendations for expanding and improving the training of health personnel in pain management.

Sec. 7. The Secretary may at any time six months after implementation of the program modify or terminate the program if in the Secretary's judgment the program is no longer needed or if modifications or termination is needed to prevent substantial diversion of the diacetylmorphine.

Exercise 26

PUBLIC AFFAIRS REPORTING

CITY BUDGET

WHEREAS, on October 1, the City will start a budget for the next fiscal year; and

WHEREAS, the City Council of the City wishes to adopt a final budget for that fiscal year and that on September 2 at a legally called public hearing the Council did adopt a tentative budget; and

WHEREAS, the City Council made a study of the needs for expenditures in each of the City Departments and determined that this amount for the coming year, including the Federal Revenue Sharing Budget, will be $2,850,777; and, in the same study, the Council has determined that the expected income will be a like amount, including the Federal Revenue Sharing budget; and

WHEREAS, the City Council has set the tax millage rate at 3.99, this being a decrease in the rolled back millage from a rate last year of 4.16,

NOW, THEREFORE, BE IT RESOLVED that the City Council of this City hereby adopts a final budget for next year as follows:

Revenues	Amount
Ad Valorem Taxes	$ 422,609
One-half Cent Sales Tax	262,046
Franchise and Utility Taxes	558,400
Licenses and Permits	42,500
Intergovernmental Revenue	936,031
Service Charges	272,615
Fines and Forfeitures	32,600
Miscellaneous	105,107
Redesignated Capital Improvement Funds	73,761
Federal Revenue Sharing	145,108
TOTAL	$2,850,777

Expenditures	Federal Revenue Sharing	Other Funds	Total
Bond Requirements	—	$ 55,500	$ 55,500
Administration	$ 55,550	243,135	298,135
City Clerk's Office	—	42,518	42,518
Building and Zoning	—	52,416	52,416
Finance & Utility Accounts	—	178,495	178,495
Police Department	—	784,068	784,068
Fire & Ambulance	—	820,464	820,464
General Maintenance	—	33,318	33,318
Street Maintenance	16,700	154,799	171,499
Recreation Department	—	100,961	100,961
Recreation/Special Projects	—	45,052	45,052
Parks and Cemetery	—	116,637	116,637
Garage	—	78,306	78,306
Capital Improvements	73,408	—	73,408
TOTALS	$145,108	$2,705,669	$2,850,777

PASSED AND ADOPTED by the City Council of this City.

CHAPTER 19

STATISTICAL MATERIAL

Much of the information given to newspaper reporters comes in the form of statistics, and reporters must learn how to present those statistics to the public in a form that is both interesting and intelligible. Statistics appear almost daily in news stories concerning budgets, taxes, census data, profits, dividends and annual reports. Other news stories concerning rates of crime, productivity, energy consumption, unemployment and inflation are based largely on statistics.

When you are given a collection of numbers and asked to write a news story about them, critically analyze the data and translate as many of the numbers as possible into words, since readers can understand words more easily than statistics. Thus, instead of simply reporting the statistics, you should explain their significance. Look for and emphasize major trends, record highs and record lows, the unusual and the unexpected. For example:

> The Fire Department's annual report states that last year it responded to the following numbers and types of calls: bomb threats, 60; electrical fires, 201; false alarms, 459; first aid, 1,783; mattress fires, 59; burned pots left on stove, 78; rescues, 18; washdowns, usually of leaking gasoline at the scene of automobile accidents, 227; and water salvage, 46.
>
> REVISED: The Fire Department responded to a total of 5,024 calls last year. According to the department's annual report, calls for first aid were most common, followed by false alarms and washdowns.
>
> The five leading types of calls included, in the order of their frequency: first aid, 1,783; false alarms, 459; washdowns, usually of leaking gasoline at the scene of automobile accidents, 227; electrical fires, 201; and burned pots left on stoves, 78.
>
> Other common types of calls included: bomb threats, 60; mattress fires, 59; water salvage, 46; and rescues, 18.

Go beyond the superficial. If you are writing about a city election, do more than tell your readers who won and the number of votes that each candidate received. Search for additional highlights: for example, did incumbents (or women, blacks, youths or conservatives) tend to win or lose? Did any candidates win by unusually large or small margins? Also, compare the votes cast in different wards and look for significant differences from the outcomes of previous elections.

When you must include some statistics in your news stories, present those statistics as simply as possible. Avoid a series of paragraphs that contains nothing but statistics. Use transitions, explanations and commentary to break up long strings of numbers and to make the information clearer and more interesting for your readers. For example:

> In the races for city council, George McDuff defeated Carl Lasher, 7,614 to 3,581 in the First Ward, Marian V. Fleck defeated David S. DiMassimo

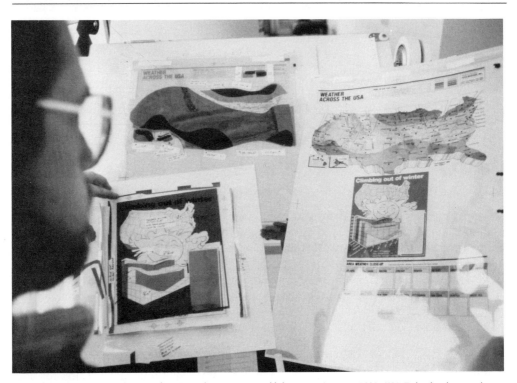

An employee prepares a weather map for USA Today. Since its establishment on Sept. 15, 1982, USA Today has become the second largest daily in the United States, with a circulation of 1.5 million. Signals from its headquarters in Washington, D.C., are transmitted to a satellite 22,300 miles above the Earth, then back to 30 printing plants in the United States and to two abroad (one in Switzerland and one in Singapore).

5,432 to 5,401 in the Second Ward, Michael J. Stewart defeated Kenneth Dunihue 4,802 to 3,781 in the Third Ward, John M. Scroggins defeated Royce R. LaChapelle 7,814 to 1,801 in the Fourth Ward, and Mary M. Tilton defeated Jeffery Pratt 5,041 to 4,014 in the Fifth Ward.

REVISED: All three male incumbents seeking re-election to the City Council were defeated, two of them by women.

In the Second Ward, incumbent David S. DiMassimo was defeated by 31 votes by Marian V. Fleck, 5,432 to 5,401, Another woman, Mary M. Tilton, defeated incumbent Jeffery Pratt in the Fifth Ward by more than 1,000 votes.

The third incumbent, Royce R. LaChapelle of the Fourth Ward, was defeated by John Scroggins, 7,814 to 1,801. Police charged LaChapelle with drunken driving and resisting arrest after he was involved in an automobile accident on Chapman Road last month. He has not yet been tried on the charges.

George McDuff and Michael J. Stewart, who campaigned against higher property taxes, also won.

McDuff defeated Carl Lasher in the First Ward by a vote of 7,614 to 3,581, and Stewart defeated Kenneth Dunihue in the Third Ward by a vote of 4,802 to 3,781.

St. Louis Post-Dispatch

WRITE & WRONG

By **Harry Levins**
Post-Dispatch Writing Coach

Reporters who write about government budgets find themselves working with numbers that stretch way past the experience of most people. In the coming year, for example, Missouri's state government will spend $4.5 billion. Putting that sort of total in perspective is tough; after all, it comes to $1 for every human being on Earth.

Terry Ganey faced the problem recently when he wrote that the state's budget left precious little in reserve. First, he spelled out the situation in the state's terms:

> *The budget . . . includes a $67.6 million operating reserve to maintain cash flow and handle emergencies.*

But raw numbers mean little to the average reader. So Ganey decided to refine the numbers further:

> *While that sounds like a lot, it is less than 1.5 percent of the state's total spending and 2.8 percent of general tax revenue expenditures.*

That helps considerably. Most readers grasp percentages more easily than whole numbers. Even so, Ganey decided to take one more step and put the numbers in terms that almost anybody could see clearly:

> *A comparison to the state's situation would be that of a family with a combined annual income of $30,000 setting a budget for a year that leaves $450 in the bank after all its anticipated bills are paid.*

What a nice touch. Ganey had said in his lede that the state would have "a very thin bank account." And in his comparison with a middle-class family, Ganey drove home just how thin that bank account would be.

Some years back, Eliot Porter turned the same smooth trick in a story on the water supply in the St. Louis area. He mentioned how much water rolled by each day in the Mississippi River and then noted how much water St. Louis needed each day. The numbers were so big that they were, in effect, meaningless. But the next paragraph put the whole thing in focus. Porter wrote words to this effect:

> *In other words, a sightseer standing by the Arch to watch the river roll past need stand there only four minutes and 42 seconds to see all the water St. Louis needs that day.*

The Coach is dredging the passage from memory, and the numbers are guesswork. But what the paragraph accomplished is clear:

1. It reduced big numbers to a total anybody could fit into perspective. Few people can picture millions of gallons of water, but most of us have a close idea of what four minutes and 42 seconds equals.

2. It gave the reader a specific frame for the numbers. Almost all of us have stood at the Arch and watched the river roll by. Porter's use of that image gave us something specific, something

(continued on next page)

concrete to use as an aid to grasping the abstract concepts that we choose to call "numbers."

So good is Porter at this sort of thing that The New York Times lifted his explanation of how to visualize five parts of dioxin for each billion parts of soil:

> *That's the equivalent of five jiggers of vermouth in a thousand railroad tank cars of gin.*

To help people grasp numbers, the people at Dow Chemical have put out a small pamphlet titled "How Big Is 'Small'?" It says:

> *We often find reference to "parts per billion" or "parts per trillion" in our reading or conversations about trace impurities in chemicals.*
>
> *What is a part per billion? How big is a part per trillion? And what about a part per quadrillion? Can we get a fix on these infinitesimally small quantities?*
>
> *Well, if you're a 26-year-old male, for example, your heart beats about 72 times a minute . . . a part per billion is equal to one heartbeat out of all your heartbeats since birth (plus half of your prenatal experience)!*
>
> *Let's start with a part per million, our largest scale . . . that's the equivalent of one automobile in bumper to bumper traffic stretching from Cleveland to San Francisco . . . or one drop of gasoline in a tankful of gas for a full-sized car . . . or one facial tissue in a stack of facial tissues higher than the Empire State Building. It's also one pancake in a stack of pancakes 4 miles high!*

> *Still hungry? How about one 4-inch hamburger in a chain of hamburgers circling the Earth $2\frac{1}{2}$ times at the Equator? That's equal to one part per billion . . . pass the mustard!*
>
> ***Some other comparisons . . . Part per billion***
> *—One silver dollar in a roll of silver dollars stretching from Detroit to Salt Lake City . . .*
> *—One kernel of corn in enough corn to fill a 45-foot silo, 16 feet in diameter . . .*
> *—One sheet in a roll of toilet paper stretching from New York to London . . .*
> *—One second of time in 32 years.*
>
> ***More comparisons . . . Part per trillion:***
> *—One square foot of floor tile on a kitchen floor the size of Indiana . . .*
> *—One drop of detergent in enough dish water to fill a string of railroad tank cars over 10 miles long . . .*
> *—One second of time in the past 32,000 years.*
> *—One mile on a 2-month journey at the speed of light (light travels at 186,000 miles per second).*
>
> ***How about something really small? Part per quadrillion:***
> *—One postage stamp on a "letter" the size of California and Oregon combined . . .*
> *—The palm of one's hand compared to the total land area of the United States . . .*
> *—One human hair out of all the hair on the heads of all the people in the world . . .*
> *—One mile on a journey of 170 light years . . .*

To be sure, Dow has a vested interest in making big numbers look small. But we have our own vested interest: clarity. And in making things clear, we can go beyond Dow's comparisons and come up with our own.

We can use the volume of local landmarks like Busch Stadium; one billion equals a stadium sellout of every home game for almost 247 baseball seasons. For area, we can use the figures for St. Louis (61 square miles, or 39,040 acres), St. Louis County (500 square miles, or 320,000 acres) and Missouri (68,945 square miles, or 44,124,800 acres). Time—when expressed in local terms—is another handy device. For example, more than half a billion seconds have elapsed since the Arch was topped off.

Coming up with your own comparisons involves nothing more than a base figure and a calculator—or, as in Ganey's case, a pencil, a piece of paper and a touch of imagination.

TWO ROADS DIVERGED DEPARTMENT

Here's the lede of a recent story; the emphasis is The Coach's:

> BOSTON   (UPI)—Lead, blamed for various mental and behavioral disorders in children, *has declined in the blood of Americans since unleaded gasoline became widely used, a federal study said today.*

No sentence can serve two ideas: for either it will distract from the one, and overemphasize the other; or else it will weaken the one, and lead the reader astray toward the other. . . .

The lede above is a wearying example of the two-idea sentence. Reading a two-idea sentence can be like listening to a two-headed person when both heads are yakking at once. You get a lot of information, but sorting it out is difficult.

The main point of the UPI story was that Americans had less lead in their blood now that unleaded gasoline was widely used. That's a straightforward notion, simply grasped. So why clutter it up with the secondary information on what lead has been blamed for?

Fixing the lede would have been simple:

> BOSTON (UPI)—*The level of lead in the blood of Americans has declined since unleaded gasoline became widely used, a federal study said today.*
>
> *Lead poisoning has been blamed for various mental and behavioral disorders in children.*

The headline writer had no problem in slicing away the needless clause. The headline said: **Lead in Blood Down Since Fuel Shift.** That says it all—and says it without mentioning mental and behavioral problems in children.

Wire services tend to overload stories with multi-idea sentences. The wire writers are rushed; the editors think that brevity takes priority over clarity. Besides, the wire service people can comfort themselves in the knowledge that editors at the receiving end can unscramble everything if they so choose.

After all, that's how it was done before the Teletype machine. The cable and telegraph editors would get cryptic messages—"Wilson arrive today crowd cheers Southampton"—and translate them into a news story: "President Woodrow Wilson stepped onto British soil at Southampton today to the cheers of a waiting crowd."

Today's wire and copy editors have the same privilege. We're under no obligation to publish two-idea sentences, just because the wire services send them. And reporters here are

(continued on next page)

under no obligation to write two-sentence ideas, even though any edition of the Post-Dispatch carries a dismaying number of precedents.

TYPECAST

A military atrocity has been making its way into our columns recently— the use of "-type" as a suffix. In the Army, a rifle becomes a "shoulder-type weapon." In newspaper writing, we see such examples as "suspension-type bridge," "modern-type architecture" and "office-type furniture." If some sort of extra word is needed— and in all three examples cited, none is—use "style" or "type of."

QUOTES

We are not afraid to entrust the American people with unpleasant facts, foreign ideas, alien philosophies, and competitive values. For a nation that is afraid to let its people judge the truth and falsehood in an open market is afraid of its people.

(John F. Kennedy)

A free press is not a privilege but an organic necessity in a great society. Without criticism and reliable and intelligent reporting, the government cannot govern. For there is no adequate way in which it can keep itself informed about what the people of the country are thinking and doing and wanting.

(Walter Lippmann)

Exercise 1

STATISTICAL MATERIAL

INSTRUCTIONS: Write a news story about the results of the following national opinion poll about certain American presidents, based on a random sample of 2,400 people aged 18 and older. Assume that the interviews were conducted by telephone last week by members of the National Association of Political Scientists, and that the results were announced today. All the figures are percentages.

	Most Loved	Most Powerful	Highest Moral Standards	Did Most to Improve U.S.	Best in Domestic Affairs	Best in Foreign Affairs
Franklin D. Roosevelt	25	24	23	38	30	29
Harry S. Truman	9	9	20	8	7	10
Dwight D. Eisenhower	11	13	14	13	15	16
John F. Kennedy	24	10	6	11	11	14
Lyndon B. Johnson	4	16	2	7	7	4
Richard M. Nixon	3	7	0	2	4	9
Gerald R. Ford	2	3	3	3	6	2
James E. Carter	7	3	17	4	5	3
Ronald Reagan	5	4	4	5	6	3
George Bush	6	7	8	6	7	7
Undecided or no answer	4	4	3	3	2	3

Exercise 2

STATISTICAL MATERIAL

INSTRUCTIONS: Write a news story about the rates of crime in the nation's 52 largest cities. This list includes every U.S. city with 300,000 or more residents last year. The crime rate in each city is based on the number of serious crimes reported per 1,000 residents.

The FBI conducts its Uniform Crime Reporting Study each year. It collects the statistics from local police departments. The results, released today, cover seven types of crime: (1) murder, (2) rape, (3) robbery, (4) aggravated assault, (5) burglary, (6) larceny and theft and (7) motor vehicle theft.

The cities are listed in the order of their overall rate of crime.

Rank and City	Crime Rate Last Year (per 1,000 Residents)	Rank and Crime Rate Two Years Ago	
1. Atlanta	192.4	2.	206.9
2. Miami	190.2	1.	183.8
3. Dallas	155.2	3.	167.3
4. Fort Worth, Texas	149.8	4.	156.9
5. St. Louis	146.7	5.	153.3
6. Kansas City, Mo.	129.5	9.	127.2
7. Seattle	126.0	7.	129.1
8. Charlotte, N.C.	125.9	6.	132.4
9. San Antonio, Texas	124.8	10.	127.2
10. New Orleans	124.4	17.	112.6
11. Detroit	121.9	14.	120.9
12. Tucson, Ariz.	118.8	11.	125.5
13. Boston	118.5	15.	120.7
14. Austin, Texas	117.1	21.	106.7
15. Minneapolis	114.4	13.	121.0
16. Houston	113.4	20.	108.2
17. El Paso, Texas	112.4	22.	106.2
18. Portland, Ore.	111.0	8.	127.5
19. Chicago	110.6	28.	99.6
20. Oakland, Calif.	109.1	12.	125.3
21. Washington, D.C.	107.7	26.	102.8
22. Phoenix, Ariz.	107.6	19.	108.7
23. Oklahoma City	106.1	18.	111.9
24. Baltimore	106.0	33.	93.5
25. Fresno, Calif.	105.3	16.	116.9
26. Jacksonville, Fla.	104.6	24.	103.3
27. Memphis, Tenn.	102.0	37.	88.8
28. Albuquerque, N.M.	100.6	27.	99.7
29. Columbus, Ohio	99.1	23.	103.9
30. New York	97.0	29.	96.7
31. San Francisco	96.6	36.	90.2
32. Toledo, Ohio	96.1	30.	95.4
33. Long Beach, Calif.	95.7	31.	94.1
34. Tulsa, Okla.	95.3	35.	91.8
35. Milwaukee	93.0	39.	87.6
36. Los Angeles	92.3	34.	92.7
37. San Diego	91.5	32.	93.7
38. Sacramento, Calif.	91.3	25.	103.2
39. Cleveland	91.1	42.	83.5
40. Wichita, Kan.	89.3	40.	87.4

ISBN 0-15-500602-9

41.	Buffalo, N.Y.	88.9	41.	85.3	
42.	Pittsburgh	87.6	38.	88.8	
43.	Nashville, Tenn.	78.8	47.	69.7	
44.	Denver	77.6	43.	76.1	
45.	Cincinnati	75.6	44.	74.7	
46.	Philadelphia	71.9	46.	70.0	
47.	Las Vegas, Nev.	71.3	45.	73.9	
48.	Omaha, Neb.	70.5	48.	65.7	
49.	Indianapolis	67.5	49.	65.1	
50.	Honolulu	61.0	50.	62.3	
51.	Virginia Beach, Va.	57.8	51.	56.2	
52.	San Jose, Calif.	48.7	52.	51.4	

Exercise 3

STATISTICAL MATERIAL

UNITED STATES DEPARTMENT OF EDUCATION
WASHINGTON, D.C 20202

UPDATE ON ADULT ILLITERACY

The Source

The English Language Proficiency Survey was commissioned by the U.S. Department of Education and conducted by the Bureau of the Census during the last summer. At that time, simple written tests of English comprehension were administered in the home to a national sample of 3,400 adults, ages 20 and over.

Major Findings

Between 17 and 21 million U.S. adults are illiterate, for an overall rate of nearly 13 percent. In contrast to traditional estimates of illiteracy based on completion of fewer than six years of school, this new study shows that illiterate adults are now much more likely to be located in our major cities, and most are under the age of 50. Immigration and reliance on a non-English language are also major factors; nearly half of all adults using a non-English language at home failed the test of English proficiency. More specifically,

- **OF ALL ADULTS CLASSIFIED AS ILLITERATE:**

— 41 percent live in central cities of metropolitan areas, compared to just 8 percent in rural areas;
— 56 percent are under the age of 50; and
— 37 percent speak a non-English language at home.

- **AMONG NATIVE ENGLISH-SPEAKERS CLASSIFIED AS ILLITERATE:**

— 70 percent did not finish high school;
— 42 percent had no earnings in the previous year; and
— 35 percent are in their twenties and thirties

- **AMONG ILLITERATE ADULTS WHO USE A NON-ENGLISH LANGUAGE:**

— 82 percent were born outside the United States;
— 42 percent live in neighborhoods where exclusive reliance on English is the exception rather than the rule;
— 21 percent had entered the U.S. within the previous six years; and
— About 14 percent are probably literate in their non-English language (judging from their reported education).

The Test and the Definition of Illiteracy

The test employed is called the Measure of Adult English Proficiency (MAEP). The written portion of MAEP consists of 26 questions which test the individual's ability to identify key words and phrases and match these with one of four fixed-choice alternatives. Based on an analysis of the number of questions answered correctly out of 26, a literacy cutoff of 20 was selected as providing the best discrimination between high and low risk groups. Specifically, among native English speakers, less than 1 percent of those completing some college scored below 20, in contrast to a failure rate of more than 50 percent for those with fewer than 6 years of school.

Accuracy of These Estimates

The standard error of our point estimate (18.7 million) is about 1 million. Thus, we can be quite confident (95 chances out of a 100) that the true figure is in the range of 17 to 21 million.

Identification of High-Risk Groups

Six factors were found to be strongly correlated with performance on the written test: age, nativity, recency of immigration for non-natives, race, poverty status, amount of schooling, and reported English speaking ability (of persons who use a non-English language at home).

*Illiteracy Rate Estimates**

	Rate	Inverse Rank		Rate	Inverse Rank
United States	13				
			MISSOURI	12	25
ALABAMA	13	31	MONTANA	8	4
ALASKA	7	2	NEBRASKA	9	9
ARIZONA	12	25	NEVADA	9	9
ARKANSAS	15	40	NEW HAMPSHIRE	9	9
CALIFORNIA	14	33	NEW JERSEY	14	33
COLORADO	8	4	NEW MEXICO	14	33
CONNECTICUT	12	25	NEW YORK	16	47
DELAWARE	11	17	NORTH CAROLINA	14	33
DIST. OF COLUMBIA	16	47	NORTH DAKOTA	12	25
FLORIDA	15	40	OHIO	11	17
GEORGIA	14	33	OKLAHOMA	11	17
HAWAII	15	40	OREGON	8	4
IDAHO	8	4	PENNSYLVANIA	12	25
ILLINOIS	14	33	RHODE ISLAND	15	40
INDIANA	11	17	SOUTH CAROLINA	15	40
IOWA	10	14	SOUTH DAKOTA	11	17
KANSAS	9	9	TENNESSEE	15	40
KENTUCKY	15	40	TEXAS	16	47
LOUISIANA	16	47	UTAH	6	1
MAINE	11	17	VERMONT	10	14
MARYLAND	12	25	VIRGINIA	13	31
MASSACHUSETTS	11	17	WASHINGTON	8	4
MICHIGAN	11	17	WEST VIRGINIA	14	33
MINNESOTA	9	9	WISCONSIN	10	14
MISSISSIPPI	16	47	WYOMING	7	2

*Rates apply to the adult population age 20 and over. All rates have been rounded to the nearest whole percent.

Exercise 4

STATISTICAL MATERIAL

FROM THE OFFICE OF THE GOVERNOR

The annual survey of legislative appropriations for the arts, conducted by the National Assembly of State Arts Agencies, is being released nationwide today. The results show how our state compares to others in the nation.

The complete survey follows:

National Assembly of State Arts Agencies

	Per Capita (¢)		Appropriations ($)		%	% of State General	
	This Year	Last Year	This Year	Last Year	Change	Fund	Rank
Alabama	24.1	26.2	969,020	1,045,000	−7.2	.0374	42
Alaska	420.3	800.2	2,189,800	4,000,000	−45.2	Not available	
Arizona	35.9	33.1	1,144,800	1,010,200	13.3	.0452	37
Arkansas	42.7	35.6	1,006,754	836,226	20.3	.0588	27
California	47.7	46.0	12,589,000	11,793,000	6.7	.0411	40
Colorado	50.8	30.6	1,640,647	971,459	68.8	.0820	17
Connecticut	52.5	46.0	1,666,166	1,479,000	12.6	.0388	41
Delaware	97.1	80.9	603,900	496,000	21.7	.0647	24
Dist. of Columbia	378.3	283.3	2,368,000	1,765,000	34.1	.1032	13
Florida	111.8	88.9	12,710,386	9,761,077	30.2	.1639	5
Georgia	45.0	37.7	2,687,779	2,200,588	22.1	.0506	32
Hawaii	216.5	208.9	2,282,092	2,170,485	5.1	.1230	8
Idaho	13.5	13.3	134,000	131,400	1.9	.0223	49
Illinois	75.9	57.0	8,758,300	6,559,400	33.5	.0857	15
Indiana	33.4	33.3	1,836,923	1,830,576	0.3	.0551	28
Iowa	34.0	18.0	981,590	522,593	87.8	.0452	38
Kansas	24.6	24.5	602,707	596,288	1.0	.0335	45
Kentucky	53.2	42.0	1,983,300	1,564,400	26.7	.0659	23
Louisiana	20.1	27.0	900,000	1,205,431	−25.3	.0212	50
Maine	40.7	36.4	473,503	420,292	12.6	.0456	36
Maryland	108.7	43.9	4,776,096	1,909,382	150.1	.1079	11
Massachusetts	313.7	282.5	18,265,924	16,379,066	11.5	.2738	1
Michigan	125.5	113.4	11,404,000	10,291,500	10.8	.1863	4
Minnesota	65.7	60.1	2,755,083	2,502,961	10.0	.0539	31
Mississippi	15.8	17.9	411,986	465,827	−11.5	.0277	47
Missouri	87.6	137.9	4,403,292	6,904,051	−36.2	.1316	9
Montana	109.2	78.8	901,745	649,068	38.9	.2457	2
Nebraska	36.5	36.3	585,891	582,749	0.5	.0676	22
Nevada	19.1	19.1	178,642	174,270	2.5	.0338	44
New Hampshire	32.6	33.1	325,500	323,000	0.7	.0712	21
New Jersey	177.9	138.3	13,453,000	10,391,000	29.4	.1488	6*
New Mexico	48.2	50.1	698,800	713,500	−2.0	.0481	33
New York	273.2	249.3	48,590,702	44,218,900	9.8	.2081	3
North Carolina	64.8	63.8	4,050,637	3,936,067	2.9	.0734	20
North Dakota	34.8	34.7	238,268	238,268	0.0	.0421	39
Ohio	84.2	69.7	9,050,963	7,493,265	20.7	.0855	16
Oklahoma	46.5	55.2	1,535,253	1,821,462	−15.7	.0900	14
Oregon	18.4	18.2	494,421	487,048	1.5	.0286	46

Pennsylvania	65.6	56.3	7,780,000	6,724,000	15.7	.0805	18
Rhode Island	62.0	46.2	599,854	444,357	34.9	.0539	30
South Carolina	85.7	77.4	2,869,596	2,555,563	12.2	.1039	12
South Dakota	40.5	40.2	286,873	283,912	1.0	.0775	19
Tennessee	29.0	76.7	1,382,500	3,615,800	−61.7	.0476	35
Texas	18.2	30.3	2,983,955	4,846,064	−38.4	.0546	29
Utah	100.1	94.9	1,646,000	1,568,200	4.9	.1242	10
Vermont	49.5	45.8	264,900	242,902	9.0	.0622	26
Virginia	52.2	34.6	2,979,540	1,947,865	52.9	.0637	25
Washington	38.5	43.2	1,697,395	1,879,419	−9.6	.0360	43
West Virginia	115.8	106.5	2,241,793	2,117,238	5.8	.1488	6*
Wisconsin	24.1	24.2	1,148,600	1,151,500	−0.2	.0226	48
Wyoming	33.2	28.3	169,275	144,605	17.0	.0447	34

*New Jersey and West Virginia are tied for sixth.

Exercise 5

STATISTICAL MATERIAL

INSTRUCTIONS: Write a news story based on the following statistics. Assume that the figures were released today by the Office of Institutional Research at your school, summarizing the distribution of grades given during last year's fall term at your school. The statistics are real ones released by a medium-sized university. For two reasons, the statistics do not always add up to 100 percent. First, they do not include grades of "Satisfactory" and "Unsatisfactory." Second, they are rounded off to the nearest tenth.

College and Department	Percentage of Grades							Total No. of Grades
	A	B	C	D	F	WP*	I	
Business Administration								
Accountancy	15.6	29.9	26.1	7.9	7.9	11.9	0.5	949
Economics	19.4	38.5	21.3	6.7	4.4	8.3	1.4	361
Finance	17.6	34.8	24.7	9.3	4.7	8.0	0.9	1,091
Management	15.4	33.4	32.0	7.7	4.9	4.3	2.3	1,489
Marketing	13.6	35.9	37.1	5.0	3.7	4.3	0.4	515
TOTAL	16.1	33.7	28.7	7.7	5.3	7.2	1.2	4,405
Education								
Elementary Education	39.8	35.4	14.2	3.2	2.2	2.6	2.6	1,285
Physical Education	53.2	24.4	8.6	3.0	2.9	3.4	4.5	837
Professional Lab	11.9	6.4	2.2	0.6	0.0	1.2	1.2	328
Secondary Education	39.1	36.4	9.2	1.1	1.5	2.7	10.0	261
Teaching Analysis	41.4	33.6	14.4	1.6	2.4	2.9	3.7	804
TOTAL	40.7	29.7	11.4	2.4	2.1	2.7	3.8	3,515
Engineering								
Civil	20.2	39.4	24.4	4.5	3.8	6.6	1.1	287
Electrical	27.6	32.5	22.7	9.2	3.1	4.3	0.6	163
Engineering Mathematics and Computer Science	21.5	36.6	19.3	11.8	4.3	6.5	—	93
Engineering Core	18.7	31.0	27.3	7.7	4.8	9.5	1.0	1,626
Engineerng Technology	37.0	33.9	15.4	5.6	3.6	3.8	0.7	573
Mechanical	13.4	20.5	40.2	15.2	6.2	3.6	0.9	112
TOTAL	22.9	32.3	24.6	7.5	4.4	7.4	0.9	2,854
Health-Related Professions	38.8	34.1	9.9	1.9	2.4	2.4	3.0	1,338
Humanities and Fine Arts								
Art	31.4	34.8	13.7	2.1	4.6	8.5	4.9	328
English	32.0	35.8	14.1	1.7	5.2	8.2	3.0	696
Foreign Languages	34.0	38.2	13.9	3.5	2.1	4.8	3.5	144
History	10.7	31.3	27.5	10.5	8.4	6.2	5.4	726
Humanities	41.8	29.3	12.0	1.2	3.7	5.8	6.2	242
Music	57.1	22.3	10.9	2.7	2.7	2.3	2.0	615
Theatre	41.3	28.3	15.2	0.0	0.0	6.5	8.7	46
TOTAL	33.0	31.0	16.7	4.3	5.0	6.0	4.0	2,797
Natural Sciences								
Biological Sciences	24.1	33.1	19.7	8.7	8.7	3.8	1.9	366
Chemistry	21.3	23.5	25.6	8.9	12.5	7.0	1.2	328
Computer Science	23.3	29.3	23.3	9.0	6.9	6.0	2.2	1,157

Geology	8.9	26.9	23.9	3.0	11.9	25.4	—	67
Math and Statistics	11.2	17.8	24.3	13.3	15.4	16.8	1.2	1,372
Physics	20.8	36.5	28.0	6.0	2.8	5.3	0.6	318
TOTAL	18.1	25.4	23.9	10.2	10.6	10.3	1.5	3,608

Social Sciences

Air Force ROTC	26.9	45.5	16.7	2.6	5.1	1.9	1.3	156
Communications	21.4	43.5	21.0	4.6	3.9	4.2	1.2	1,115
Political Science	30.3	32.0	19.1	4.2	4.8	6.8	2.8	456
Psychology	35.6	34.4	16.6	4.0	3.2	4.5	1.1	1,185
Public Service Admin.	34.2	29.0	23.1	3.6	2.9	3.4	2.1	1,219
Sociology	27.0	36.0	21.5	4.1	5.1	3.3	2.8	967
TOTAL	29.8	35.5	20.3	4.1	3.8	4.1	1.8	5,098

*Withdraw Passing

Exercise 6

STATISTICAL MATERIAL

INSTRUCTIONS: Write a news story based on the following summary, which was released today by your state's Council of Better Business Bureaus, Inc. It lists the 70 types of complaints that the Better Business Bureaus in your state receive most frequently and the percentage of those complaints that are resolved. All the numbers are authentic; they were provided by an actual Council of Better Business Bureaus.

| Type of Business | Last Year | | | | Two Years Ago | | | |
	Rank	Total	Percent of Total	Percent Settled	Rank	Total	Percent of Total	Percent Settled
TOTAL		369,703	100.00%	71.3%		401,476	100.00%	71.9%
Mail Order Companies	1	76,076	20.57	77.8	1	82,264	20.49	79.5
Franchised Auto Dealers	2	16,461	4.45	82.4	2	18,974	4.72	79.9
Home Furnishing Dealers	3	11,832	3.20	69.6	4	11,643	2.90	70.3
Magazines, Ordered by Mail	4	10,437	2.82	72.4	6	10,379	2.58	77.4
Misc. Home Maintenance Co.'s	5	10,230	2.76	58.3	5	10,672	2.65	55.5
Indep. Auto Repair—Except Transmissions	6	9,713	2.62	64.7	3	13,054	3.25	56.8
Department Stores	7	9,262	2.50	88.5	7	10,306	2.56	89.3
Misc. Automotive	8	8,276	2.23	65.5	8	8,082	2.01	65.9
Television Servicing Co.'s	9	7,028	1.90	70.1	10	7,352	1.83	70.3
Insurance Companies	10	6,797	1.83	82.4	11	7,156	1.78	83.8
Dry Cleaning/Laundry Co.'s	11	6,371	1.72	63.6	12	6,737	1.67	67.0
Home Remodeling Contractors	12	6,131	1.65	58.3	9	7,825	1.94	60.6
Apparel & Accessory Shops	13	5,647	1.52	70.7	14	5,505	1.37	73.3
Appliance Service Co.'s	14	5,537	1.49	63.7	13	6,064	1.51	66.2
Real Estate Sales/Rental Services	15	4,360	1.17	61.9	18	4,339	1.08	63.9
Misc. Health & Personal Services	16	4,345	1.17	67.9	19	4.175	1.03	75.0
Appliance Stores	17	4,215	1.14	70.9	15	5,061	1.26	74.2
Roofing Contractors	18	4,201	1.13	53.7	16	4,557	1.13	54.2
Floor Coverings Stores	19	4,147	1.12	66.1	20	4,142	1.03	66.7
T.V. & Radio/Phone Shops	20	3,989	1.07	71.5	24	3,825	.95	71.2
Heating & Central Air Cond'g Co.'s	21	3,727	1.00	66.6	21	4,111	1.02	70.4
Auto Tire, Battery, Accessory Shops	22	3,369	.91	73.9	22	3,965	.98	72.3
Direct Selling—Magazines	23	3,352	.90	77.5	28	3,452	.85	81.0
Jewelry Stores	24	3,200	.86	74.1	23	3,914	.97	76.2
Gasoline Service Stations	25	3,100	.83	65.3	26	3,587	.89	67.6
Auto Dealers—Used Only	26	2,994	.80	66.6	17	4,519	1.12	74.5
Direct Selling—Misc.	27	2,886	.78	70.7	27	3,498	.87	72.0
Auto Transmission Shops	28	2,758	.74	69.5	35	2,506	.62	69.7
Photographic Studios	29	2,741	.74	69.9	38	2,470	.61	65.1
Moving/Storage Companies	30	2,712	.73	66.7	29	3,321	.82	69.5
Plumbing Contractors	31	2,644	.71	61.7	30	3,121	.77	66.5
House/Apt. Rental—By Indiv.	32	2,486	.67	62.8	25	3,722	.92	54.1
Health Studios	33	2,423	.65	65.4	48	1,931	.48	69.8
Photographic Processing Co.'s	34	2,421	.65	75.7	39	2,437	.60	69.9
Gardening/Nursery Products	35	2,378	.64	68.9	40	2,388	.59	66.3

Vacation Certificate Co.'s	36	2,354	.63	40.3	51	1,853	.46	66.9
Mobile/Modular Home Dealers	37	2,352	.63	69.6	31	3,015	.75	68.3
Banks	38	2,278	.61	87.1	42	2,238	.55	86.3
Misc. Financial	39	2,263	.61	66.3	43	2,256	.56	71.8
Exterminating Service Co.'s	40	2,221	.60	75.1	36	2,504	.62	76.0
Travel Agencies	41	2,187	.59	68.0	37	2,500	.62	68.9
Direct Selling—Photography	42	2,146	.58	67.7	45	1,987	.49	67.3
Credit Card Companies	43	2,116	.57	87.4	41	2,329	.58	88.3
Home Builders—New Construction	44	2,030	.54	65.8	32	2,919	.72	66.8
Utility Companies	45	2,021	.54	84.0	56	1,500	.37	88.3
Advertising Soliciting Orgs.	46	1,971	.53	56.6	47	1,962	.48	58.5
Swimming Pool Companies	47	1,922	.51	66.6	34	2,742	.68	59.0
Credit Collection Companies	48	1,884	.50	77.8	46	1,965	.48	80.1
Waterproofing Companies	49	1,682	.45	57.4	53	1,600	.39	56.0
Reupholstering Shops	50	1,548	.41	54.9	57	1,472	.36	56.1
Carpet & Upholstery Clng. Co.'s	51	1,530	.41	60.8	44	2,202	.54	67.2
Consumer Finance & Loan Co.'s	52	1,489	.40	78.2	52	1,831	.45	80.9
Paving Contractors	53	1,393	.37	50.5	50	1,856	.46	48.3
Homework Companies (Work-at-Home)	54	1,358	.36	51.5	33	2,757	.68	56.2
Buying Clubs/Group Purch.	55	1,321	.35	78.8	60	1,419	.35	66.7
Siding Contractors	56	1,305	.35	63.6	49	1,889	.47	62.7
Trade/Vocational Schools	57	1,283	.34	80.4	62	1,199	.29	77.5
Building Material/Supply Co.'s	58	1,277	.34	75.0	55	1,505	.37	76.9
Employment Services	59	1,270	.34	63.0	58	1,467	.36	69.2
Telephone Companies	60	1,226	.33	82.0	67	894	.22	80.4
Airlines	61	1,190	.32	75.3	59	1,454	.36	80.9
Recreational Vehicle Dealers	62	1,142	.30	65.8	54	1,514	.37	68.4
Hospitals/Clinics	63	1,079	.29	80.9	63	1,079	.26	83.8
Music/Record Stores	64	1,018	.27	72.5	61	1,268	.31	76.0
Alarm Systems Dealers	65	990	.26	67.7	66	919	.22	69.3
Misc. Food Companies	66	887	.23	69.1	65	1,012	.25	66.2
Electrical Contractors	67	790	.21	69.4	64	1,017	.25	68.0
Land Development Co.'s	68	699	.18	77.3	70	741	.18	71.5
Doctors	69	667	.18	81.5	72	712	.17	77.2
Hair Product Improvement Co.'s	70	647	.17	67.9	68	855	.21	64.9

Exercise 7

STATISTICAL MATERIAL

INSTRUCTIONS: Write a news story based on the following returns from the municipal elections that were held yesterday in the suburb of Roseville. "I" stands for "incumbent," "U" means the candidate ran unopposed, and "W" indicates a write-in candidate.

Office	Ward 1	Ward 2	Ward 3	Ward 4	Ward 5	Totals
Mayor						
Alfred Bingston	7,891	3,911	11,824	7,787	9,123	40,536
Thomas Field (I)	6,041	5,886	9,348	4,016	9,007	34,298
Stephen Hamilton (W)	438	521	147	21	86	1,213
City Attorney						
George McCartney	11,121	6,780	9,987	9,987	12,067	49,942
Louis Swanson	3,041	4,844	10,711	1,641	5,291	25,528
City Treasurer						
Joseph Alvito (I, U)	12,942	9,041	21,431	10,039	16,441	69,894
City Clerk						
Henry Wong (I, U)	12,734	9,119	21,402	10,114	16,434	69,803
Superintendent of Schools						
Walter Pfaff	8,824	6,779	13,466	6,004	11,612	46,685
Peter Wilke (I)	5,129	3,412	7,854	4,387	8,941	29,723
Municipal Court Judge						
Frederick Cole	3,824	2,711	6,409	2,878	4,731	20,553
Richard Kernan (I)	9,743	7,443	14,385	8,562	13,862	53,995
Council Member, First Ward						
Mary Hyatt	5,014					
Ralph Issac (I)	8,279					
George Reynolds (W)	482					
Council Member, Second Ward						
Paul Putnam (I)		4,003				
Louis Ramirez		4,019				
Norman Shumate (W)		46				
Council Member, Third Ward						
Alan Kline			10,831			
Jerome Mack			10,176			
Council Member, Fourth Ward						
Howard Elton (I)				8,260		
Leonard Pollard				3,642		
Council Member, Fifth Ward						
Jerry Crum					7,469	
Michael Kelly (I)					8,944	

Exercise 8

STATISTICAL MATERIAL

INSTRUCTIONS: The following budget is an actual copy of the budget for a small town. Assume that the town is Roseville, a suburb of your community, and that the figures for next year's budget were approved today by the Roseville City Council. Write a news story about the budget. The city's revenues are listed on this page, and its expenditures are listed on the following page.

CITY OF ROSEVILLE BUDGET REVENUES

Fiscal Year	Actual Budget Two Years Ago	Actual Budget Last Year	Actual Budget This Year	Adopted Budget for Next Year
Tax Levy Net	1,686,982	1,724,207	1,767,730	1,783,550
Occupational License	140,099	133,358	150,000	150,000
Building Permit Fees	38,137	53,570	60,000	60,000
Registration Fees	8,529	8,054	7,000	7,000
Fines and Forfeitures	169,748	146,333	80,000	120,000
Franchise Taxes	409,187	524,250	550,000	579,900
Interest on Deposits	76,517	68,299	60,000	60,000
Office of Civil Defense	729	475	—	—
Sewer Revenue Funds	732,661	1,024,844	1,080,480	1,083,500
Improvement Rev. Fund	416,107	430,516	391,310	413,500
Cigarette Tax Revenue	164,222	143,527	155,000	155,000
Motor Fuel Tax Revenue	182,454	217,831	201,540	202,000
Other Revenue	90,935	47,016	40,000	45,000
Golf Course	30,000	30,000	30,000	30,000
Total Revenue	4,146,307	4,552,280	4,573,060	4,689,450
Federal Revenue Sharing	389,000	—	379,352	260,700
Prior Year Surplus	—	119,090	164,633	84,300
GRAND TOTAL	4,535,307	4,671,370	5,117,045	5,034,450
Ad Valorem Tax Rate	5.32 mills	5.32 mills	5.5 mills	5.5 mills

CITY OF ROSEVILLE BUDGET EXPENDITURES

Fiscal Year	Actual Budget Two Years Ago	Actual Budget Last Year	Actual Budget This Year	Adopted Budget for Next Year
General Government	101,756	119,131	112,950	93,450
Office of City Manager	56,828	59,893	62,400	74,150
Finance	111,561	127,552	138,850	136,450
Planning	21,982	24,477	21,700	28,650
Building & Zoning	68,485	72,926	74,300	70,550
Administration	68,633	72,989	56,750	65,300
Engineering	102,618	106,474	100,300	107,900
Streets	385,531	396,117	493,652	425,200
Lakes Management	163,747	270,142	252,600	240,700
Public Building Maint.	325,176	366,531	367,500	351,200
Police	1,221,688	1,248,862	1,226,900	1,325,900
Fire	634,116	706,383	826,450	850,300
Civil Defense	5,535	8,520	9,200	—
Parks	384,712	408,085	468,200	444,400
Forestry	96,027	107,231	118,800	117,350
Cemetery	38,662	50,614	48,400	58,800
Recreation	169,034	171,343	115,400	158,600
Community Centers	45,408	41,218	44,600	50,050
Organizational Support	97,922	101,500	182,500	197,700
Transfer to Other Funds	254,411	211,019	311,283	237,800
TOTAL	4,353,832	4,671,007	5,032,735	5,034,450
Personnel	317	310	301	303

CHAPTER 20

FEATURE STORIES

Most news stories describe a recent *event*: a meeting, crime, fire or accident, for example. Earlier chapters have shown that news stories also inform the public about topics that are *important, local* or *unusual*. Many of the topics are *relevant* to people's lives, providing useful information that makes their lives easier and more enjoyable.

Feature stories, by contrast, read more like nonfiction short stories. They have a beginning, a middle and an end. They focus on facts likely to amuse, entertain, inspire or stimulate. Because of that emphasis, they are also called "human interest" and "color" stories.

Magazines as well as newspapers publish features that may describe a person, place or idea rather than an event. So long as the stories appeal to readers, their topics may be less timely, less local and less earthshaking than those of news stories.

There is no single formula of style or writing, such as the inverted pyramid form, that reporters must use for every feature story. In general, however, features explore their topics in greater depth than news stories.

To do this, feature writers may borrow techniques from fiction, often using extensive description, sensory details, quotations and anecdotes. They may use characterization, setting, plot structure and other novelistic elements to dramatize a story's theme and to add more details.

Feature stories, however, are journalistic, not fiction or "creative writing." Nothing is made up. Like news stories, features are factual and original. They are fair and balanced, based on verifiable information. They must also be objective—they are not essays or editorials.

Moreover, reporters must personally gather the facts for their stories. They cannot copy or rewrite stories already published elsewhere.

SELECTING A TOPIC

The crucial step in writing a good feature story is the selection of a topic. Ideally, every topic should be fresh, dramatic, colorful and exciting.

The concept of "universal needs" is useful in choosing a topic. Everyone is interested in ideas relating to the needs we have in common and in satisfying those needs. Food, clothing, shelter, sex, health, approval, belonging, self-esteem, productive work, money, leisure and similar needs are subjects no reader can resist. Glance through any supermarket tabloid's table of contents and see how it uses this concept to grab the reader. Attractive, expensive magazines and reputable newspapers deal with the same needs, although they tend to address them more tastefully.

Feature writers find appropriate topics by being curious and observant. It can be useful to create a grid or graph, writing the universal needs down one side of a piece of paper and current topics from the news, such as AIDS and unemployment, across the top. Then, where each line intersects, write in a "hybrid" topic combining the two, such as AIDS patients' need for emotional contact, or loss of self-esteem among the jobless.

News stories may provide spinoff topics for features. An earthquake, plane crash, international incident or other news event can spark human-interest stories about reactions of victims, heroism in crises and other "people" angles that bring the event into sharper focus. You can explore a local connection with major events or social problems through personal interviews with people who had a relative serving in the war or a friend in the plane crash.

For instance, a college student read several news stories about the street people in her community and noticed that none of the stories quoted the homeless. Instead, reporters relied on the authorities in their community. Police blamed the homeless for a series of minor crimes. Welfare agencies wanted more money to care for the homeless. Church leaders wondered about their responsibilities to the homeless.

The student drove to the area where homeless people congregated, sat on a curb and began to interview one of them. Others gathered around her, so that in an hour she was able to complete a dozen interviews. Her feature story revealed that the homeless were not primarily adult males—or bums and criminals. Rather, families with small children had become homeless. For years, many of the families had lived in their own homes. Then a husband or wife became ill or lost a job, often because a factory closed or moved. The couples came to the city looking for work, but were unable to find new jobs or low-cost housing and ended up living on the streets.

A news story may report that your city is hiring a private business to build or operate its prisons. You might write a feature about the trend. If a criminal's sentence seems too lenient (or too harsh), you might ask how long the average murderer, rapist or robber remains in your state's prisons. If, each week, a local group called "Crime Watch" or "Crime Stoppers" asks the public to help solve a crime, you might ask about the group's success.

Other feature stories are based on reporters' personal experiences—and those of their friends. If, after little or no training, one of your friends is given a gun and hired as a guard, you might ask about the training and qualifications of other "rent-a-cops." In many cities, they outnumber the police. Students have also written about unwed fathers, student suicides, unusual classes and unusual teachers.

After selecting a general topic, reporters must limit it to a manageable size, perhaps by emphasizing a single person, theme or episode. For example: a profile cannot summarize a person's entire life, so reporters might discuss just one aspect: a single experience, trait or achievement that sums up the person's character. If reporters fail to limit their topics, their stories are likely to become too long, disorganized and superficial. They may ramble or skip from one idea to another without providing adequate transitions and without explaining any of the ideas in detail.

While gathering the information for feature stories, reporters normally consult several sources, perhaps a half-dozen or more, to obtain a well-rounded account. Good reporters gather two or three times more information than they can possibly use, then discard all but the most powerful, telling details.

TYPES OF FEATURE STORIES

Profiles or Personality Features

Profiles describe interesting people. The people may have overcome a handicap, pursued an unusual career, achieved success or become famous because of their colorful personalities. To be effective, profiles must do more than list an individual's achievements or important dates in the individual's life. They must reveal the person's character. To gather the necessary information, feature writers often watch their subjects at work; visit them at home; and interview their friends, relatives and business associates. Completed profiles then quote and describe their subjects. The best profiles are so revealing that readers feel as though they actually know and have talked to the people.

Some sources may surprise you by revealing their most personal and embarrassing secrets. However, a few may ask you to keep their identities a secret. Their stories are compelling. But you need *their* stories. Instead of interviewing the police about a drug problem, or faculty members about students who cheat, interview the drug users and cheaters themselves—specific individuals who seem to be representative of a larger problem.

The following profile uses a single individual to reveal the problems of the elderly. Notice how the use of quotations enables the woman to tell much of the story in her own words:

> She is old—86—but doesn't like to admit it. "It's like admitting defeat," Rilla says. "Why does old age have to be such a hardship? It's supposed to give you time to enjoy things."
>
> Rilla was the oldest of 10 children but is the only one still alive. The youngest died three months ago at the age of 72.
>
> "One of the hardest things I've had to face is watching my family and friends die," she says. "Even my own children are middle-aged and in ill health."
>
> Rilla seems reluctant to discuss old age, but considers herself an authority on the subject. "I've been old for a long time now," she explains. "I just see myself get a little older every day. I guess I'm what's kindly referred to as 'fragile.'"
>
> She lives with a daughter and her husband. "I used to have a lot of friends in the neighborhood," she adds, "but they're all dead."
>
> "There's nothing for me to do anymore. I can't see to read. I have such bad arthritis that I can't hardly walk from the living room to the kitchen. My garden has all gone to weeds because I can't bend over far enough to work in it."
>
> Rilla says there are a few benefits to old age: "I don't worry about my figure anymore. I eat as much as I want as often as I want.
>
> "Of course, I've been able to watch my children and grandchildren grow and develop and become good people. And too, there have been times when I've wanted to die."

Historical Features

Historical features commemorate the dates of important events, such as the attack on Pearl Harbor, the bombing of Hiroshima or the assassination of Dr. Martin Luther King Jr. The following story, distributed by the North American Newspaper Alliance, typifies that type of historical feature:

> MATEWAN, W.Va.—The most infamous episode in the annals of Appalachia erupted on Blackberry Creek 100 years ago.
>
> The feud between the Hatfields and McCoys, two powerful mountain clans, lasted for about 15 years. When the fighting finally subsided, more than 100 men, women and children had been killed or wounded, and the region's residents generally were viewed by the rest of the country as a bunch of

murderous moonshine-swilling hillbillies who liked nothing better than to loll about the front porch, picking their toes and taking potshots at each other.

Newspapers also publish historical features on 100th birthdays and on the anniversaries of the births and deaths of famous people. Other historical features are tied to current events that generate interest in their topics. If a tornado, flood or earthquake strikes your city, newspapers are likely to publish feature stories about earlier tornadoes, floods or earthquakes. When President Kennedy was assassinated, newspapers published historical features about the assassinations of Presidents Lincoln, Garfield and McKinley. When the space shuttle exploded, killing seven astronauts, newspapers published features about the astronauts killed in previous accidents. Other historical features describe famous landmarks, pioneers and philosophies; improvements in educational, entertainment, medical and transportation facilities; and changes in an area's racial composition, housing patterns, food, industries, growth, religions and wealth.

Every city (and every school) is likely to have experienced some interesting events at some time in its history. A good feature writer will learn more about those events, perhaps by consulting historical documents or by interviewing the people who witnessed or participated in them.

Adventure Features

Adventure features describe unusual and exciting experiences—perhaps the experiences of someone who survived an airplane crash, climbed a mountain, sailed around the world, served in the Peace Corps or fought in a war. In this type of feature story, too, quotations and descriptions are especially important. After a catastrophe, for example, feature writers often use the survivors' eyewitness accounts to recreate the scene. Many writers begin with the action—their stories' most interesting and dramatic moments. Here are two examples:

Visibility was unlimited as the single-engine Cessna sped westward, climbing to 10,500 feet as it approached the snow-capped Sierra, a rugged mountain range that separates Nevada and California.

Then the airplane's motor stopped: suddenly, completely, without warning.

"After all these years of flying, I'm going to crash," the pilot thought. "And it's going to happen at the worst spot in the United States and at the worst time of year—midwinter in the High Sierra."

"It was the 10th of July, 1969, approximately 5 p.m.," said Steve Jefferson, one of the Vietnam veterans attending classes here. "Myself and two sergeants were driving down the road in a Jeep. Theoretically, we shouldn't have been in this situation. We should have been accompanied by more men in another Jeep, but I always thought that when my time was up, it was up. It was going to happen no matter what.

"There was a white flash and a pop, and the next thing I knew I was lying in the middle of the road.

"I thought we had hit a hole, and that I had flipped out of the Jeep. I always rode kind of haphazardly in the Jeep, with one leg hanging out one side of it. I really thought I had fallen out, and they had kept going without me; you know, as a joke.

"Then I turned and saw the Jeep overturned and on fire by the side of the road. I touched my arm with my good hand, and it was all bloody. It finally dawned on me that it was an ambush. I heard some rifle fire but, at the time, didn't realize they were shooting at me.

"I crawled over to the side of the road, away from the Jeep, and hollered for the other guys. There was no answer. . . ."

Seasonal Features

Reporters are often assigned to write feature stories about seasons and holidays: about Christmas, Easter, St. Patrick's Day, Friday the 13th and the first day of spring. Such stories are difficult to write because, in order to make them interesting, reporters must find a new angle.

A reporter in Madison, Wis., was asked to write about June weddings, and her story was interesting because it went beyond the routine. The reporter learned that the county clerk did issue more wedding licenses in June than during any other month of the year. However, the reporter continued questioning the clerk and also learned that the couples applying for marriage licenses are getting older. Most are in their mid- to late 20s. Applicants under the age of 18 need their parents' consent, but fewer are getting married. As the interview continued, the reporter also learned that, "Not every couple that applies for a marriage license gets as far as the wedding cermony." The county clerk recalled one applicant, a man, who seemed unusually nervous. The next day, he called back and asked whether he could get a refund. He could—and did.

Explanatory Features

Explanatory features are also called "local situation" and "interpretive" features. They attempt to provide a more detailed description or explanation of topics in the news. Explanatory features may examine a specific organization, activity, trend or idea. For example, after news stories describe an act of terrorism, an explanatory feature may examine the terrorists' identity, tactics and goals.

News stories provide the ideas for thousands of other explanatory features. After a bank robbery, an explanatory feature might examine the training that banks give their employees to prepare them for robberies. Or, an explanatory feature might reveal more about a typical bank robber, including the robber's chances of getting caught and probable punishment. If you see several news stories about a new diet, you might ask why so many dieters lose weight but seem unable to keep it off. Or, if you notice that more people are driving pickup trucks—and riding in the back of them—you might ask about the trucks' safety.

One followup won a Pulitzer Prize. In 1947, an explosion killed 111 men in an Illinois mine, and Joseph Pulitzer, editor of the St. Louis Post-Dispatch, asked his staff to thoroughly review the tragedy. Pulitzer wanted to know what was likely to be done to improve mine safety. What would be done for the miners' families? Also, who was responsible for the tragedy, and were they likely to be punished for it? Notice that the story starts with the action. Also notice the reporter's use of specific detail:

> The clock in the office of the Centralia Coal Company's Mine No. 5 ticked toward quitting time on the afternoon of March 25. As the hands registered 3:27 and the 142 men working 540 feet under ground prepared to leave the pit at the end of their shift, an explosion occurred.
>
> The blast originated in one of the work rooms in the northwestern section of the workings. Fed by coal dust, it whooshed through the labyrinth of tunnels underlying the town of Wamac, Ill., on the southern outskirts of Centralia.

Thirty-one men, most of whom happened to be near the shaft at the time, made their way to the cage and were brought out alive, but the remaining 111 were trapped. Fellow-workmen who tried to reach them shortly after the explosion were driven back by poisonous fumes.

An explanatory feature published by the Chicago Tribune examined the problems of young lawyers. A Tribune reporter found that law students look forward to exciting, glamorous careers. But when they actually begin work—often 12 to 14 hours a day—many are disillusioned:

SAN FRANCISCO—They are young, bright and well paid with big futures. They are also very unhappy.

They are the many young lawyer associates who enter the profession out of law school with high hopes of an interesting career and expectations of all the good things life has to offer.

Instead, they find long hours of boring work, often under the thumb of a senior partner who is more a taskmaster than teacher, unwilling to give needed feedback and support.

Some of them drop out of the profession, move to another law firm or end up in a hospital or on a psychiatrist's couch.

How-to-Do-It Features

How-to-do-it features tell readers how to perform some task. They may describe a tangible project like building a bookcase or a house, planting a garden or repairing a lawn mower. They may focus on psychological issues, such as strengthening a marriage or overcoming shyness. Or, they may provide information, showing how newcomers to a city can find a physician or how anyone can organize receipts for tax time.

Inexperienced reporters tend to preach or dictate to readers, presenting their own opinions. Instead, in preparing for a how-to story, professionals should gather facts from several sources, including book and magazine articles. They should interview experts in the field and get tips from people who have done the task or experienced the changes.

Reporters break down the task into simple, clear, easy-to-follow steps. They tell readers what materials are needed and the cost in money and time. Often they conclude such stories with a list or summary of the process, such as "eight ways to build confidence in children."

Behind-the-Scenes Features

Behind-the-scenes stories take readers backstage for an inside view of some everyday event. Reporters often find such ventures fascinating and are able to convey the excitement. As with all features, behind-the-scenes stories are based on personal interviews: with stage managers, rock group "roadies," library catalogers, night street-cleaning crews, caterers, convention decorators and the like.

Reporters look for people who perform jobs out of the public eye but essential to some operation. They interview the source, visit him or her on location and use his or her own words to tell the story. They also include details they observe at the scene, such as atmosphere, hectic or calm working conditions, physical appearance of the person and his or her workspace, specialized terms and conversations between workers.

Behind-the-scenes features convey a sense of immediacy, allowing readers to see, feel, taste, touch, smell and understand the "backstage" work that goes into a public event.

Participatory Features

Participatory features give another kind of inside view, this time through the senses of a reporter who is actually experiencing an event or situation. John Howard Griffin, author of "Black Like Me," was a superb participatory reporter who turned his skin dark with melanin injections and entered a black community to find out about life in the South during the late 1950s and early 1960s.

His experiences are gripping, but a story need not be that all-encompassing to be effective. For instance, a Midwestern student sat up all one rainy night talking with a group of homeless alcoholics in an alley behind a convenience store. He caught a serious case of bronchitis, but his story rang with truth.

If lack of time and money prohibits total immersion in the world of the subject, you might shadow an attorney, a retail clerk, a mother of preschoolers or an elderly man in adult day care for an afternoon.

Reporters usually arrange such experiences with the boss, director or person in charge of an agency, making it clear that they are journalists and will write a newspaper story about the experience. Undercover, cloak-and-dagger approaches, like having yourself arrested so that you can expose jail conditions, are risky and ethically questionable.

Medical Features

Some newspaper and news-service reporters specialize in medical topics. However, general-assignment reporters can find good features in any community. Illness and health are vitally interesting to readers, and subjects abound.

Reporters find ideas by scanning news releases from the community's hospitals. Such releases yield tidbits about new equipment and what it does, support groups, educational workshops for patients with a chronic disease and volunteer programs. Reporters can call and arrange to interview a local participant.

Other topics with endless variations include: the costs of devastating illnesses, new and radical treatments for common ailments, ethical issues surrounding medical advances, pregnancy, child rearing, abortion, mental illness and death and the grief process.

Reporters gather facts from medical experts, people with the condition, relatives and friends. They use quotes, allowing subjects to tell about their experiences and feelings, but define technical terms and translate jargon into plain English.

Often they use vivid comparisons and descriptions to show the reader what is going on. For example, they may explain that the uterus "is about the size and shape of a pear."

When interviewing people dissatisfied with their medical treatment, reporters must be careful not to quote libelous statements. "He probably got his M.D. at Kmart" or "She's obviously a money-grubbing quack" can provoke a lawsuit for the reporter's paper, even if the subject did say it. It's helpful to balance complaints with other points of view from experts.

Business Features

News stories from the business page or small-business entrepreneurs provide topics for lively business features. These stories highlight one person or aspect of local commerce. Reporters find ideas by looking for the human interest in stories of promotions, new businesses in the community, small-business reports, the local economy and even the election of club officers.

Feature writers may pan gold from these seemingly dry stories by being curious, asking themselves, "Who is Zelda Wriggler, the woman who just opened a bellydance-gram service? What's her background? How did she decide there was a market here? What do the customers think? Does she make much money? What's the weirdest thing that's happened since she opened her business?"

A wealth of such stories exists in any town. Fad businesses like balloons and flavored popcorn rise and fall. Dating bureaus, computer software merchants and shopping services for working parents respond to new needs in society. Stories on old, established firms, perhaps focusing on the personality of a founder or dynamic leader, are also of perennial interest.

Unusual Hobby or Occupation Features

Many features about unusual career pursuits contain aspects of another type of feature story, such as business, behind-the-scenes, profile or participatory. The difference is that while all those types may be written about a person in a well-known or everyday job, a feature about an unusual hobby or occupation focuses on a person whose work is anything but humdrum.

Reporters may write about an occupation because it is dangerous, highly skilled and specialized (cleaning up oil spills) or exciting (personal fitness trainer to movie stars). They may pick a boring or exacting job (sorting clothes at Goodwill) that is fulfilling to a handicapped worker because it allows him or her to earn money and live independently.

A reporter might also interview someone on his or her first job, or someone who has changed fields dramatically, such as a college professor quitting to work at a car wash. Or, a reporter might interview workers in occupations traditionally held by the other sex. (However, it's no longer "odd" to write about male nurses or female telephone installers.)

Strange hobbies make good topics, too, because they involve colorful characters. Reporters find collectors and crafts enthusiasts to be passionately involved, often eccentric, quotable and entertaining. Their verve lends momentum to the story.

For ideas, reporters scan their papers' meeting notices for hobby club meetings, senior citizens' activities, church and school events and speeches on unusual topics. They ask people they meet in other contexts what they do to relax. They read the classified ads to seek out magicians, storytellers, psychic readers, basement cleaners and unicycle instructors.

Personal Experience Features

News stories are usually written in the third person, with the reporter a neutral observer or outsider. Feature stories, however, can be written in the first person, with the reporter appearing in the story, or in the second person, with the reporter addressing readers directly. At times, these styles can be extremely effective. Note the following lead, taken from a feature story written by a young woman. During a storm, the woman and three companions tried to swim ashore after their boat sank two miles from the coast of California:

> It felt like an endless battle. I paddled as hard as I could but thought we'd never reach shore. My arms ached and Jip's legs were numb. All I wanted

was to be warm again. Every time a wave splashed over us the chill ran through our bodies.

It was horrible, not really knowing if we were going to make it to shore, or if we should stop trying because we were going to drown anyway.

It is tempting to write about your own experiences because it seems easy; you do not have to interview anyone, spend any time digging for information or do any other research. But you should use the first person cautiously, especially in your first feature stories. While describing your own experiences, you run a greater risk of selecting poor topics and dwelling on insignificant details and dull generalities, as in the following leads, neither of which merits a passing grade:

During the summer, 20 ardent cyclists (I among them) biked through 300 miles of the Canadian Rockies. In the course of our journey, we encountered many exciting experiences.

The clock read 6:30. I was already 30 minutes late for the fishing date. Waking up will never be easy for me, especially when I am to go fishing.

I have never been enthusiastic about fishing. The aversion probably began when I was a boy and every vacation was spent in the same fishing camp. I had decided to give the sport one more chance, however.

The following story is also written in the first person—but is more interesting because it describes a truly unusual experience. Also, the story emphasizes specific details, descriptions and anecdotes. It was written by M. Timothy O'Keefe, a successful free-lancer and one of the first Americans to visit modern China:

Any time any of us walked down a street alone, we drew tremendous interest. If we stopped to talk or eat an ice cream bar, we drew a crowd. If we did something interesting, like change the film in a camera, we drew a horde.

The Chinese paid especially close attention to our feet. Leather shoes are a sign of great wealth among the Chinese, and one of the things the crowds discussed about us was how wealthy we might be. The quality of our shoes was a clue.

If we wanted to talk seriously with the Chinese in a particular city, all we had to do was stand on a street corner near our hotel at dusk when the work day was done. In a short time some young man—never a woman—would stop to talk. Often his English was broken and halting simply because he hadn't had sufficient opportunity to practice. Other times the English was amazingly fluent.

Their questions were direct and blunt. They wanted to know how much money we made, what our sex practices were and, in general, what interested young people in the United States. They were especially interested in our music.

Sometimes the Chinese would make strange requests of us. Several wanted to rub our arms to see if our freckles were permanent or would come off. They also were intrigued about the amount of hair on our arms (the guys', of course). And they were always impressed at our larger size, which they ascribed to our different diet.

TYPES OF FEATURE LEADS

Like news stories, many features begin with summary leads. However, features may also begin with quotations, anecdotes, questions, action, descriptions, shocking facts or a combination of these techniques. Again, the only requirement is that the leads interest readers, luring them into the stories.

As you read the following examples, also notice that a feature lead can be a unit of thought that contains two, three or even four paragraphs.

Summaries

They come seeking excitement: the thrill of toting a gun and flashing a badge. They leave disappointed to find that the job of an auxiliary Highway Patrol officer includes even mundane tasks.

Jared is one of the lucky few. He found a bed in a homeless shelter tonight. But tomorrow night he might not. He might be forced to sleep on the streets.

Quotations

"Hey, Bubba, walk on back here and let me guess your weight," Carla said to a chubby man with two corn dogs in each hand at Nebraska's state fair.

"When it hit me, I was unconscious for three days, and when I came to I couldn't remember a thing. I asked my boy what happened, and he told me, 'You were hit by lightning.' "

(The Orlando Sentinel)

Anecdotes and Examples

NEW YORK—A high school graduate on Long Island sues the local school system because he cannot read above the third-grade level.

The chief of personnel for the Navy reports $250,000 in damage to a diesel engine because a sailor who worked on it could not read the maintenance manual.

The National Assessment of Educational Progress shows a group of 17-year-olds a replica of a traffic ticket, and more than half cannot determine the last day the fine can be paid.

Such anecdotes are being heard with increasing frequency and point to a conclusion that is becoming painfully obvious to employers, educators, politicians and the general public alike: the United States has a serious problem with illiteracy.

(The New York Times)

Martha, a 28-year-old, began to suffer from ulcers, headaches and high blood pressure. A doctor advised her to change jobs and, three days later, she became a travel consultant.

Kim, 32, was divorced with four children to support. To increase her income, she began to sell real estate. She earned $39,000 last year—and expects to earn $50,000 this year.

Allison, 25, disliked taking orders from doctors. Moreover, she thought some doctors were lazy and uncaring. So she returned to college and is studying to become an English professor.

Until last year, all three women were nurses. Like thousands of others, they became frustrated by the job's stress, low pay, hard work and irregular hours.

Questions

How much longer will you live?

What are your chances of becoming a millionaire?

Action or Narratives

Pepper O'Neill can't keep her hands off people. Walking down the streets of Muncie, she sees men and women with bad posture and knotted muscles, the unmistakable signs of stress—and she wants to help them. She needs to knead them. Pepper is a masseuse with a mission.

As the heat of the New Mexico sun beats down, a young boy plays catch with his father in the front yard. The father lobs the ball to the boy, who struggles to catch it with a glove two sizes too big. The boy heaves it back, putting his whole body behind the throw. Passers-by brush past without a glance, taking the scene for granted. But after open-heart surgery, Mike Sullivan, the father, takes nothing for granted.

Shockers

Thousands of the world's children under the age of 5 die each day of illnesses that most Americans shrug off.

Cancer will kill someone in your family.

Descriptions

Chicago resident Aprille Jones once stood on her head with her legs tucked into a yoga position in mid-air while wearing a pair of silk pajamas. While she performed the headstand, she was surrounded by a gaggle of Japanese men clutching cameras. She eventually toppled over, to a remorseful chorus of "ahh's" from the photographers.

Jones, who is a fashion and sales consultant at Petite Clothier on Park Avenue, calls the pajama episode "the weirdest assignment I've ever had."

On Thursday, Jim Donaldson woke up and prepared for work. He took a shower, brushed his teeth and shaved. Jim then put on his makeup: a little blush here and a little eyeliner there. Afterward, he looked to his wife, Lara, for her approval.

Lara inspected her husband. "You need a little more lipstick, honey."

Jim put on some more lipstick while his daughter, Judy, added a bright red bow to her father's hair. That was the perfect touch. His family all agreed that he looked "absolutely marvelous."

Jim kissed his family goodbye, grabbed his bow and arrow and headed off to another day at the office.

As a member of the Activities Committee at Roubidoux Regional Medical Center in Baltimore, Jim has many annual rituals. On Christmas, he's Santa and on Halloween, he's Dracula. On Valentine's Day, he's a tall, dark and handsome Cupid.

THE BODY OF A FEATURE STORY

Like the lead, the body of a feature story can take a number of forms. The inverted pyramid style is most appropriate for some features, and chronological order for many others. Regardless of the form or style of writing you decide on, every feature must be coherent. All the facts must fit together smoothly and logically. Transitions must guide readers from one segment of the story to the next and clearly reveal the relationship between those segments. Transitions should be brief. They may ask a question; shift to a new time or place; or repeat a key word, phrase or idea.

Remember to be concise: never waste your newspaper's space or your readers' time. Emphasize lively details—the action. And provide an occasional change of pace. A good writer rarely composes an entire story of all quotations or all summaries. Instead, you might use several paragraphs of summary, then some quotations to explain an idea, then some description, and then more quotations or summary.

Also be specific. Instead of saying that a person is generous or humorous, give specific examples of the subject's generosity and humor. Instead of simply stating that "President Calvin Coolidge was a taciturn man," it would be better to illustrate his reluctance to speak by quoting Coolidge himself:

A woman meeting President Coolidge for the first time said to him, "My friends bet that I couldn't get you to say three words."

The president replied, "You lose."

Successful feature writers have learned that readers respond well to stories that use techniques from drama and fiction. In this visual age, the people reading newspapers and magazines like stories that show them "scenes," as movies and TV shows do.

Some elements borrowed from fiction are characterization, setting, plot and subplot, conflict, time, dialogue and narrative. Reporters can use these elements, except that instead of making up people, events, actions and conversation, they interview real people and write about what they actually said and did.

Reporters reveal character by using quotations and describing speech patterns, mannerisms, body language, appearance, dress, age, preferences, prejudices, use of personal space and a host of other traits. Reporters can sprinkle small touches of these descriptions throughout a story to show what the subject of an interview is like.

The setting reveals character and puts the reader in a context. Geography shapes physical and mental traits, determines lifespan, influences ways of earning a living. Reporters should tell where a subject grew up, what the person's surroundings are now and how these factors reflect what he or she is.

One way to look at plot is to think of it as a description of the overcoming of obstacles that lie between a person and his or her goal. The solution of conflict (frustration induced by the obstacles) is the theme of every human-interest story. The main plots are human vs. nature, human vs. human, and human vs. the inner self. As reporters interview people and ask them about events in their lives, plots naturally emerge. Often there is a subplot, a secondary line of action that runs in counterpoint to the main action, sometimes helping and sometimes hindering the progress. If reporters listen and identify plot and subplot elements as the subject tells the story, a natural sort of order, suspense and resolution occur. These elements can be used for dramatic effect.

Time can be handled in a variety of ways. While writing some stories, you can use a dramatic episode in the present as an opener, then flash back to the beginning of a story and continue in chronological order. Or, writers can build in a series of flashbacks, arranged in the order in which they actually happened.

Writers can begin in the past, foreshadow the future, flash back to a dramatic event and then continue in chronological order. Whatever form you choose, be sure to use transition words—"now," "then," "in 1969," "however"—to let the reader know when events are taking place.

Dialogue is a vital part of any novel or play. Reporters may use dialogue to show temperament, plot, events, time, customs, color, or continuity. They must be careful to choose only the best, most revealing quotes. Readers do not have to know every word that was said, only those that move the story along.

Narrative is used to weave the whole story together. It summarizes, arranges, creates flow and transitions, links one idea to the next. The reporter's narrative voice should be unobtrusive and subtle, taking care not to insert its own opinions, but faithfully reporting its impressions.

THE ENDING OF A FEATURE STORY

As for the conclusion to feature stories, some writers say that features should end like news stories, by reporting the last solid chunk of information. Other writers, particularly those who work for magazines, say that features should end with a satisfying conclusion, perhaps a quote, anecdote, or key word or phrase repeated in some surprising or meaningful way. In any case, you should avoid ending feature stories with a summary; summary endings are too likely to state the obvious, to be repetitious, to be flat and boring.

After finishing a feature, a professional is likely to edit and rewrite it, perhaps five, six or even 10 times. A professional will also slant the feature for a particular publication and audience, emphasizing its relevance and importance to them.

Newspapers probably publish more features than any other medium, and many editors expect every reporter to write one or two features a week, often for publication in their Sunday editions. Typically, the reporters employed by an afternoon daily will work on feature stories every afternoon, after their papers have been published for that day.

Most reporters enjoy writing features. They can select their own topics, examine the topics in depth and experiment with different styles of writing. Reporters who freelance during their spare time usually write features, submitting them to magazines.

SUGGESTED READINGS

Alexander, Louis. *Beyond the Facts: A Guide to the Art of Feature Writing.* 2d ed. Houston: Gulf, 1982.

Babb, Laura Longley, ed., *Writing in Style.* Washington, DC: The Washington Post Co., 1975.

Barnhart, Helen S. *How to Write and Sell the 8 Easiest Article Types.* Cincinnati: Writer's Digest Books, 1985.

Brooks, Terri. *Words' Worth: A Handbook on Writing and Selling Nonfiction.* New York: St. Martin's Press, 1989.

Cappon, René J. *The Word: An Associated Press Guide to Good News Writing.* New York: The Associated Press, 1982.

Emerson, Connie. *Write on Target.* Cincinnati: Writer's Digest Books, 1981.

Enos, Sondra Forsyth. *Breaking into Article Writing.* Boston: The Writer, 1988.

Fensch, Thomas, ed., *Best Magazine Articles: 1988.* Hillsdale, NJ: Erlbaum, 1989.

Franklin, Jon. *Writing for Story: Craft Secrets of Dramatic Nonfiction by a Two-Time Pulitzer Prize Winner.* New York: Atheneum, 1987.

Friedlander, Edward Jay, and John Lee. *Feature Writing for Newspapers and Magazines: The Pursuit of Excellence.* New York: Harper & Row, 1988.

Garrrison, Bruce. *Professional Feature Writing.* Hillsdale, NJ: Erlbaum, 1989.

Gunther, Max. *Writing the Modern Magazine Article.* Boston: The Writer, 1968.

Harral, Stewart. *The Feature Writer's Handbook.* Norman, OK: University of Oklahoma Press, 1958.

Hennessy, Brendan. *Writing Feature Articles: A Practical Guide to Methods and Markets.* Oxford, England: Heinemann, 1989.

Hughes, Helen McGill. *News and the Human Interest Story.* New Brunswick, NJ: Transaction Books, 1980.

Jacobs, Hayes B. *Writing and Selling Non-Fiction.* Cincinnati: Writer's Digest Books, 1967.

Martindale, David. *How to Be a Freelance Writer: A Guide to Building a Full-Time Career.* New York: Crown, 1982.

Nelson, Roy Paul. *Articles and Features.* Boston: Houghton Mifflin, 1978.

Patterson, Benton Rain. *Write to Be Read: A Practical Guide to Feature Writing.* Ames, IA: Iowa State University Press, 1986.

Rivers, William L., and Alison R. Work. *Free-Lancer and Staff Writer: Newspaper Features and Magazine Articles.* 4th ed. Belmont, CA: Wadsworth, 1986.

Ruehlmann, William. *Stalking the Feature Story.* Cincinnati: Writer's Digest Books, 1977.

Schoenfeld, A. Clay, and Karen S. Diegmueller. *Effective Feature Writing.* New York: Holt, Rinehart and Winston, 1982.

Williamson, Daniel R. *Feature Writing for Newspapers.* New York: Hastings House, 1975.

Yudkin, Marcia. *Freelance Writing for Magazines and Newspapers.* New York: Harper & Row, 1988.

QUOTES

Everybody hates editors. Writers especially. They give editors stuff they can't possibly print the way it is, and when the editors make it printable, the writers curse them instead of thanking them.

(An editor quoted in A Corner of Chicago *by Robert Hardy Andrews)*

Not for its own sake alone, but for the sake of society and good government, the press should be free. Publicity is the strong bond which unites the people and their government. Authority should do no act that will not bear the light.

(James A. Garfield)

Exercise 1

FEATURE STORIES

WRITING YOUR OWN FEATURES

1. GENERATING IDEAS AND SELECTING A TOPIC

A. List some universal needs (such as food, clothing, shelter, sex, love, belong-ing, self-expression) across the top of a piece of paper. Down the left side, list some pressing social issues (concerns of the elderly, health care, AIDS, unem-ployment, teen suicide). Draw lines to form a grid. Fill in the spaces in the grid with story ideas created by meshing the two topics.

B. Pair up with another student. Set a timer and write for 10 minutes, completely free and uncensored, about one or more of the following topics: pet peeves; things I avoid writing about; things I am curious about; favorite places in my hometown; a specific holiday, such as Christmas or Thanksgiving; my biggest problem as a child (or teen-ager). Take turns reading your papers aloud to your partner. Discuss how you could conduct more research and interviews to make a story from one of the ideas each of you generated.

2. STORY TYPES

A. Find and clip an example of each story type described in this chapter. As you read and discuss the various types in class, analyze your examples for strong and weak points.

B. List five story ideas of your own for each type.

3. FEATURE LEADS

A. Critically evaluate the following leads. Decide which topics would interest readers and which leads pull them into the story.

   1.   It may be one of the smallest pieces of real estate that you will ever buy, but chances are that your cemetery plot will also be the most expensive.

        The price of cemetery property goes up at least 10 percent a year, said Robert Neel, president of Woodlawn Memorial Park. The current starting price for a 5-by-10-foot plot is between $1,200 and $1,500 at most ceme-teries.

   2.   There was no hesitation. The bowler picked up his ball and smoothly let it roll down the alley. Nine pins fell, leaving just one standing. Alfred Her-shey took careful aim and knocked that one down too.

        Perfectly ordinary.

        Except that Hershey is blind.

   3.   ''How about if I just sit on the floor with you?'' asked Judge Clarence Du-breff after a child complained that he ''always sits higher than anybody else.''

        The juvenile court judge took off his coat, rolled up his sleeves and sat on the classroom floor.

   4.   Twenty teen-agers plan their own curriculum and live and work at Free-dom House School. All 20 are from welfare families, and most have police records.

   5.   The student governments at most universities in the state are having problems.

6.   Rudy Willging, Rick Kaeppler and Don Zitto aren't foresters and don't diagnose sick trees, and they aren't firefighters in the traditional sense, but are rather a combination, intensively trained to battle forest fires, perhaps the most dangerous fires of all.

7.   Pancho is a short, dark-skinned, curly-haired 20-year-old with flashing black eyes, a bouncing step and a Spanish accent.

B. Find and clip a newspaper or magazine feature lead to illustrate each type of lead discussed in this chapter. Identify what kind each is. Then rewrite it as a different type. Also, evaluate the leads: Which leads are most likely to interest readers?

C. Exchange the feature stories you have written for class with another student. Rewrite each other's leads as different types. Decide which type is better for each lead.

4. PRACTICING FICTION SKILLS TO ENHANCE FEATURES

A. Find and clip an example of these fiction elements used in a newspaper or magazine feature: character revealed through conversation, physical appearance, dress, age, preferences, mannerisms, body language; setting or physical surroundings giving clues to character; plot and subplot; use of flashbacks or foreshadowing; dialogue used to reveal character, setting, plot or time element; narration used to tie a story together.

B. Interview a subject for a feature story. Using your notes, state the theme. Outline three or four scenes as if you were viewing them in a movie or television program, using dialogue, action and other plot elements to make them clear to a reader. Give quotes, anecdotes and examples you will use. Then write the story, tying the scenes together with narration.

5. MISCELLANEOUS EXERCISES

A. Clip five feature stories from a newspaper or magazine and write a two- or three-page paper that critically analyzes the stories' topics, leads and style of writing, particularly their organization and development of color.

B. Rewrite the introductory paragraphs of five news stories as feature leads.

C. Take a feature story you have written and read it to class members or a tape recorder. Make notes of the places where you stumble, run out of breath or become confused about a passage's meaning. Reword these spots, shortening sentences and smoothing awkward passages. Write a one-page paper about what you discovered.

CHAPTER 21

ADVANCED REPORTING EXERCISES

This chapter contains advanced reporting exercises—the most realistic and perhaps the most exciting in this book. Some of the exercises are longer and more complex than the exercises in previous chapters. However, all the exercises involve the types of stories that you are likely to be assigned during your first years of work as a reporter. To do well on these exercises, you will have to apply all the skills you developed in the earlier chapters of this book.

All 10 exercises are genuine; they involve actual letters, statements and other documents. You may remember several of them. The most famous, in Exercise 1, is a letter written by a murderer: John List of Westfield, N.J. In 1971, List murdered his wife, mother and three children. Eighteen years later, the television program "America's Most Wanted" described the murders. List was hiding in another state, and a tip helped the police find him there just a few days later.

Only a few names and dates have been changed. Unless the exercises mention another time and location, assume that each story occurred in your community today. Briefly, the exercises include:

1. A five-page letter that John List wrote to his minister, confessing that he had murdered five members of his family.
2. A policy statement issued by the American Academy of Pediatrics, warning the public about television's effects on children.
3. A statement issued by a university president who decided to accept $150,000 from a club that discriminates against women, blacks and Jews.
4. A complaint filed by the NAACP, charging that a school system discriminates against black students and teachers.
5. A preliminary report that describes a fire and the deaths of two firefighters trying to extinguish it.
6. A statement dictated by a cab driver who was beaten and robbed.
7. A report that describes juvenile shoplifters.
8. A sociological report that describes the families of death row inmates.
9. An extortion note left at a Nevada casino.
10. A booklet that describes the damage San Francisco would suffer in a nuclear attack.

Exercise 1

ADVANCED REPORTING

JOHN LIST'S LETTER

INSTRUCTIONS: In 1971, the police in Westfield, N.J., found five bodies in John List's home. Eighteen years later, the television program "America's Most Wanted" described the murders. The broadcast showed a bust prepared by a forensic sculptor. The bust showed List as he might look 18 years after he had last been seen. Just 10 days later—on June 1, 1989—the police found List in Virginia. He was working as an accountant in Richmond and had changed his name to Robert P. Clark, but looked remarkably like the bust shown on "America's Most Wanted." List waived extradition and was returned to New Jersey to be tried on five counts of first-degree murder. A judge there ruled that prosecutors could use a five-page letter that List had written to his minister.

The letter is reprinted below. Write a news story that summarizes the letter's content. As you write the story, assume that the murders occurred 18 years ago, that List was returned to New Jersey last June, and that the letter was made public today. You can also use the following background information provided by Jill Vejnoska, a prize-winning reporter for The Courier-News in Bridgewater, N.J.

Remember the point at which you are writing your story. List has been captured and returned to New Jersey. Eighteen years after he wrote it, his letter has just been released to the public. List has not yet been convicted, however. Emphasize the contents of the letter, not the background information.

Background Information

On the night of Dec. 7, 1971, in Westfield, N.J., police officers George Zhelesnik and Charles Haller responded to a call of possible prowlers at the List family home, located at 431 Hillside Avenue. List's neighbors had observed lights blazing inside and outside the house for three weeks. In the last few days, the lights had begun burning out. Meanwhile, relatives and friends who hadn't seen or heard from the Lists in weeks had begun calling the police, asking them to check on the house and its occupants. In fact, 46-year-old John List had himself called the police nearly a month earlier with a similar request. List said he wanted police to check on the 19-room mansion periodically while he took an unexpected trip to North Carolina with his wife and three children to visit his sick mother-in-law.

Sometime around 9:30 p.m. on Dec. 7, the Lists' next-door neighbors, William and Shirley Cunnick, saw a battered white Pontiac moving slowly up the long, circular driveway in front of 431 Hillside Avenue. While Shirley Cunnick phoned police, William Cunnick, a physician, walked across the side lawn and met the car's occupants. Edward Iliano and Barbara Sheridan explained they were advisers to the Westfield Drama Club, which Patricia List belonged to. Zhelesnik and Haller arrived soon after and, while Cunnick told them about the lights, the drama teachers conveyed their concerns about the long-absent Lists—particularly John's mother, Alma, 86, who lived in an apartment on the mansion's third floor.

Zhelesnik and Haller found an unlocked window on the first floor and entered the mansion. With Iliano trailing them, they moved cautiously in the dark through the dining room and living room. The air was musty, and mournful organ music played on an audio system somewhere in the house as the two officers approached a huge ballroom at the rear of the house. Switching on a ballroom light, they saw four bodies laid out on sleeping bags. One of the officers ran outside and radioed for assistance.

Cunnick identified the bloated, maggot-infested bodies of John List's wife, Helen, 45, and their three teen-age children: Patricia, 16; John, 15; and Frederick, 13. Helen List wore a nightgown. The three children were clad in heavy overcoats and woolen gloves.

As Zhelesnik and Haller made room-by-room checks of the mansion's three floors for more victims (Alma List's body was found sprawled in the hallway of her apartment a few minutes later), Westfield Police Chief James Moran entered a first-floor office at the opposite end of the house from the ballroom. Some of his men had already found a note taped to a desk drawer, and it directed ''the finder'' to a key to a nearby file cabinet. Opening the file cabinet, Moran found a heavy envelope containing six short notes to friends and relatives, and a five-page letter addressed to List's minister. The Rev. Eugene A. Rehwinkel, pastor of Redeemer Lutheran Church in Westfield, was summoned and given the letter. After reading it three times, Rehwinkel gave it back to Moran. Police would keep the letter for a short time, but it was soon turned over to the Union County Prosecutor's Office, which kept it locked away for nearly 19 years. Neither the authorities nor Rehwinkel would ever discuss the letter, other than to make vague references to it being confessional in nature and to indicate that List had killed his family for religious and financial reasons.

When List finally was arrested after being profiled on the television show ''America's Most Wanted,'' he was 63. The letter List had written to his minister became the focal point of pretrial squabbling. List's lawyer, Elijah L. Miller Jr., wanted its contents suppressed, claiming that police had not had a search warrant to enter the mansion and that it was confidential under the priest-penitent relationship. Prosecutors Eleanor Clark and Brian Gillet disagreed, contending that police fear for the Lists' safety permitted them to enter the house, and that Rehwinkel willingly returned the letter to Moran. Judge William Wertheimer agreed with the prosecution, and the letter was admitted into evidence. With that, its contents were released to the press. The letter was neatly handwritten in blue ink on yellow-lined sheets of legal paper.

The Letter

Dear Pastor Rehwinkel:

I am very sorry to add this additional burden to your work. I know that what has been done is wrong from all that I have been taught and that any reasons that I might give will not make it right. But you are the one person that I know that while not condoning this will at least possibly understand why I felt that I had to do this.

1. I wasn't earning anywhere near enough to support us. Everything I tried seemed to fall to pieces. True, we could have gone bankrupt & maybe gone on welfare.

2. But that brings me to my next point. Knowing the type of location that one would have to live in plus the environment for children, plus the effect on them knowing they were on welfare was just more then I thought they could and should endure. I know that they were willing to cut back but this involved a lot more than that.

3. With Pat being so determined to get into acting, I was also fearful as to what that might do to her continuing to be a Christian. I'm sure it wouldn't have helped.

4. Also, with Helen not going to church, I know that this would harm the children eventually in their attendance. I had continued to hope that she would begin to come to church soon. But when I mentioned to her that Mr. Jutzi wanted to pay her an Elders call, she just blew up & stated that she wanted her name taken off the church rolls. Again, this could only have given an adverse result for the children's continued attendance.

[In the margin here, List wrote: ''This is not a criticism of Ed.'']

So that is the sum of it. If any one of these had been the condition we might have pulled through, but this was just too much; at least I'm certain that all have gone to heaven now. If things had gone on, who knows if that would be the case.

Of course, Mother got involved because doing what I did to my family would have been a tremendous shock to her at this age. Therefore, knowing that she is also a Christian, I felt it best that she be relieved of the troubles of this world that would have hit her.

After it was all over, I said some prayers for them all—from the hymn book. That was the least that I could do.

Now for the final arrangements:

Helen & the children have all agreed that they would prefer to be cremated. Please see to it that the costs are kept low.

For mother, she has a plot at the Frankenmuth Church cemetery. Please contact Mr. Herman Schelhas, Rt. 4, Vasser, Mich. 41768. He's married to a niece of Mothers & knows what arrangements are to be made. She always wanted Rev. Herman Zelinder of Bay City to preach the sermon. But he's not well.

Also, I'm leaving some letters in your care. Please send them on & add whatever comments you think appropriate.

The relationships are as follows:

Mrs. Lydia Meyer—Mother's sister.

Mrs. Eva Morris—Helen's mother.

Jean Syfert—Helen's sister.

Fred & Clara—John's sponsor.

Herb & Ruth—Fred's sponsor.

Marie—Pat's sponsor.

[The last three sets of names were written, then crossed out.)

Also, I don't know what will happen to the books & other personal things. But to the extent possible I'd like for them to be distributed as you see fit. Some books might go to the school or church library.

Originally, I had planned this for Nov. 1—All Saints Day. But travel arrangements were delayed. I thought it would be an appropriate day for them to get to heaven.

As for me, please let me be dropped from the congregation rolls. I leave myself in the hands of Gods <u>Justice</u> & <u>Mercy</u>. I don't doubt that he is able to help us, but apparently he saw fit not to answer my prayers the way I had hoped they would be answered. This makes me think that perhaps it was for the best as far as the children's souls are concerned. I know that many will only look at the additional years that they could have lived, but if finally they were no longer Christians, what would be gained?

Also, I'm sure many will say, "How could anyone do such a horrible thing." My only answer is it isn't easy and was only done after much thought.

Pastor, Mrs. Morris may possibly be reached at

802 Pleasant Hill Drive

Eikin—home of her sister.

One other thing. It may seem cowardly to have always shot from behind, but I didn't want any of them to know even at the last second that I had to do this to them.

John got hurt more because he seemed to struggle longer. The rest were immediately out of pain. John didn't [List had written "probably," then crossed it out and wrote "didn't"] consciously feel anything either.

Please remember me in your prayers. I will need them whether or not the government does its duty as it sees it. I'm only concerned with making my peace with God & of this I am assured because of Christ dying even for me.

P.S. Mother is in the hallway in the attic—third floor. She was too heavy to move. John.

UPDATE: For your information (do not include it in your story), the jury deliberated for nine hours over two days, then found List guilty on five counts of first-degree murder. Judge Wertheimer sentenced List to five life terms, to be served consecutively. He will not be eligible for parole until 2064.

Exercise 2

ADVANCED REPORTING

TELEVISION'S EFFECTS ON CHILDREN

INSTRUCTIONS: This is a verbatim account of a policy statement issued by the American Academy of Pediatrics. Assume that the statement was issued today. Write a news story that summarizes its content.

Policy Statement

In 1984 the American Academy of Pediatrics' Task Force on Children and Television issued a statement that cautioned pediatricians and parents about the potential for television to promote violent and/or aggressive behavior and obesity. The influence of television on early sexual activity, drug and alcohol abuse, school performance, and perpetuation of ethnic stereotypes was also stressed. Advances in our understanding of the effects of television on children have prompted this update of the Academy's policy.

[Last year] the average child in the United States still spent more time watching television than in any other activity except sleeping. According to recent Neilsen data, children aged 2 to 5 years view approximately 25 hours per week, children aged 6 to 11 watch more than 22 hours weekly, and adolescents 12 to 17 years watch 23 hours of television per week. Although the amount of commercial television viewed by children has declined since 1980, the most recent estimates of television viewing do not include VCR use. Therefore, the amount of time that children in our country spend in front of the television set has probably not decreased significantly since 1984.

Television influence on children is a function of the length of time they spend watching and the cumulative effect of what they see. By the time today's child reaches age 70, he or she will have spent approximately seven years watching television. Therefore, television may displace more active experience of the world. For some children, the world shown on television becomes the real world.

In the years since the original statement was released, sufficient data have accumulated to warrant the conclusion that protracted television viewing is one cause of violent or aggressive behavior. Television viewing also contributes substantially to obesity.

Although there is no clear documentation that the relationship between television viewing and sexual activity or the use of alcohol is causal, the frequency of adolescent pregnancy and sexually transmitted diseases, and the prevalence of alcohol-related deaths among adolescents and young adults represent major sources of illness, injury, and death. American teenagers see an estimated 14,000 sexual references and innuendoes per year on television, yet only 150 of these references deal with sexual responsibility, abstinence, or contraception. Therefore, the many implicit and explicit messages on television that promote alcohol consumption and promiscuous or unprotected sexual activity are a cause for concern.

The Committee on Communications therefore makes the following recommendations:

1. Efforts should be developed and intensified to teach pediatricians and parents about the influence of television and furthermore, new initiatives should be developed to promote involvement by parents as well as critical television viewing skills among children.

2. Pediatricians should advise parents to limit their children's television viewing to one to two hours per day. In addition, pediatricians should include advice regarding

the effects of television on children and the importance of limiting television time as part of anticipatory guidance during health maintenance visits. Parents should be encouraged to develop television substitutes such as reading, athletics, and physical conditioning as well as instructive hobbies.

3. Families should participate in the selection of the programs that their children watch. Parents should watch television with their children in order to help interpret what they see. Parents should take advantage of the acceptable programs offered on video cassettes for their children's viewing, if affordable.

4. Pediatricians should continue to support legislation making broadcast of high-quality children's programming a condition of license renewal and seek a revival of legislation mandating at least one hour per day of programs of educational and instructional benefit to children.

5. Pediatricians should continue their efforts to ban toy-based programs, since such programs are designed to sell toys to children and constitute program-length commercials.

6. Pediatricians should continue to urge that sexuality be portrayed responsibly by the media.

7. Pediatricians should support efforts to eliminate alcohol advertising on television and also encourage extensive counter advertising.

8. The Academy should support further research into the effects of television on children; and continue to build coalitions with other groups to monitor and improve television for children.

Exercise 3
ADVANCED REPORTING

CLUB'S CONTROVERSIAL SCHOLARSHIPS

INSTRUCTIONS: The following story and memorandum are genuine. Assume that the president of your school released the memorandum today.

Background

Several hundred prominent businessmen belong to the University Club in your city. The club does not admit women, blacks or Jews. One month ago, the club offered to donate $150,000 ($30,000 a year for five years) to your school for scholarships. During a meeting last Thursday, your school's Faculty Senate adopted the following resolutions:

Resolution 13

It is inappropriate for the University to encourage or support faculty involvement or the involvement of other members of the university community with clubs or other institutions which knowingly engage in discriminatory practices on the basis of race, gender, ethnic or religious preferences.

Resolution 14

It is not appropriate for the university to engage in any activity which may lend support or give credence to any club or private institutions which knowingly engage in discriminatory practices on the basis of race, gender, ethnic or religious preferences.

Memorandum

TO: The Faculty
FROM: School President
SUBJ: University Club

Today I have asked the Faculty Senate to re-consider Resolutions 13 & 14. As written, both are difficult or impractical to implement, yet the principle of nondiscrimination is important to affirm. I intend to meet with the Faculty Senate's leaders to develop new language.

While the Resolutions were general, clearly their purpose was specifically directed to the prospect of the University receiving funds from the University Club for student scholarships. The funds, if accepted, would amount to approximately $150,000 over five years, and are unrestricted in their use at the University. But, well beyond the issue of money is the broader policy question of the University's posture toward donors, and more specifically toward the University Club.

Because of the policy question, and the interest the issue has stirred, I have engaged in broad consultation, on campus and off, to solicit input and to assess the impact of an action either way. I have been impressed with the depth and quality of the discussion this matter has sparked in the community, and by the thoughtful debate which has occurred on campus. John Milton said, "Where there is desire to learn, there of necessity will be much arguing, much writing, many opinions; for opinion in good men is but knowledge in the making."

His words ring true. Knowledge is in the making, and the Faculty Senate's action has shown leadership in bringing an important issue to the public's attention. But, now it is time to decide—based on what is in the best interests of the University.

My decision is to accept the gift for unrestricted scholarship use. The funds will be used consistent with University priorities to recruit and provide assistance to high ability students, minority students and other special talent students. A talented and diverse student body is fundamental to our development. As graduates, they will provide future leadership to the community.

The reasons for my decision are many, but before detailing several of them I must say that this has been a very difficult decision. Discriminatory practices are abhorrent, and this University must be committed in its education and research programs to actions which promote equal opportunity. As we assemble the tools to be able to do so more fully, I am confident that even more progress soon will be evident. My decision now is rooted in my commitment to build the very best university we can. It did not result from votes, loud voices or pressure.

The decision is also difficult because of my belief in the development of a strong Faculty Senate at the University. My preference is to support its work on behalf of the entire faculty, and to affirm the principle of responsible faculty governance. At the same time, we can all recognize the tensions which arise between the expression of transcendent values and life in a vastly imperfect world. Both positions require respect.

It is my judgment that the message conveyed by the Senate's action has been heard clearly throughout the community and in the University Club. I have reason to believe that progress is underway to open up current membership practices, and the Club should be encouraged to move forward with the change process for the good of the community. My hope is that in so doing, its leadership may set an example for all organizations with restrictive practices. This is important to the future of the region. Yet, I also have reason to believe that continued contentiousness from the University at this point will actually impede the progress we all hope will occur.

There may always be differences among reasonable people about the best means to create change, but in this case I believe it will now have to come from within the organization. In the meantime, no moral cause will be advanced by discouraging people with whom we may disagree from doing a good thing.

By accepting funds from the University Club, the University is not lending its support to them. The funds are absolutely unrestricted for scholarship use, and are totally subject to the University's control. The very nature of the gift means that the University is not obligated to do anything except use the funds responsibly. If this were not the case, my decision would be different.

There are other examples in academe where universities separate their actions from those of their donors. They, and we, accept funds from the Ford Foundation even though Henry Ford expressed anti-Semitic views. They, and we, encourage our students to pursue Rhodes Scholarships without fear that we endorse the racial and colonial views of Cecil Rhodes. Members of our faculties do not condone the earlier votes of J. William Fulbright in support of racial segregation by accepting Fulbright Scholarships. While these are not current practices of these organizations, the point is that people and institutions do change over time. The University should be able to exert leadership to help bring it about, but the means to do so will differ in each situation.

The bigger question is the University's relationship to donors generally. The institution is placed in an untenable position if it must begin probing the intentions and character of each donor to assure itself that certain standards of conduct are observed. We do not have standing nor the authority to make such judgments, and in fact, we expose ourselves to legal liability if we were to do so in a manner that would be construed to be defamatory. If this practice were to start, its logical and simple extensions would confound our better judgment about where to draw the line before we accept a gift.

The above does not suggest, however, that no standard at all should be applied. The University will not accept funds acquired through illegal activity, nor from organizations and individuals whose purposes undermine social order or human dignity. The University will not accept funds from benefactors who seek to endanger our most basic academic values. In Justice Frankfurter's words, these include "determining" for ourselves "on academic grounds who may teach, what may be taught, how it shall be taught, and who may be admitted to study." It is not difficult to draw these distinctions and to apply them rigorously.

Our community is on its way to becoming a major U.S. city, and its aspirations for further development are high. A great future is possible here, and part of that depends on the ability of business people to show the leadership necessary to avail themselves of all the talent that is available. Our setting is so competitive that any exclusionary practices undermine the unity that makes good things possible. The University's increasing stature aids this process; our efforts to advance cultural diversity in the faculty, staff and student body will lead by example. Our own diversity agenda is one of our biggest challenges now, and many people rightfully are monitoring our progress closely. We need to get on with that task as we work with the business community to build a better university.

Despite the many other issues involved, and the negative financial impact this situation has already had, we have to finally remember why we are here. Simply put, we are here to educate students. They are the ones who are either helped or hurt by whatever decision we make. My commitment is to aggressively seek support for them, just as it is to bolster support for the faculty. These funds will help a significant number of students get an education who otherwise would not be likely to do so, or at least not here. We owe them that opportunity, secure in the knowledge that education is the best weapon against racism, sexism and other social ills.

I ask for your support as we move forward. The debate is healthy, and reflective of a university that is maturing rapidly. The mere fact that we can deal openly with it affirms the values for which the institution stands. The subject will stay with us as we get on with our other work.

Exercise 4

ADVANCED REPORTING

NAACP COMPLAINT

INSTRUCTIONS: The following complaint is genuine. Assume that your County Branch of the National Association for the Advancement of Colored People filed the complaint today with the superintendent of your local school system. Write a news story that summarizes the complaint.

NAACP Complaint

The County Branch NAACP contends that the School District has ignored educational quality and equity for the black students and black professionals. It appears that the School District is in continuous violation of the Fourteenth Amendent—that is, students are not fully desegregated in the system. Specifically, the NAACP, black parents and concerned citizens have found that:

I. STUDENT CONCERNS

A. Black students are suspended and expelled at a disproportionately higher rate than white students.

B. Black students receive corporal punishment at a far higher rate than white students.

C. Black students are channeled into special education and remedial classes at a far higher rate than white students and are generally kept there.

D. Black students are generally excluded from the gifted classes.

E. Black students are channeled into dead-end programs by counselors in the high schools and are not challenged to enter the discipline courses (biology, chemistry, physics, geometry, trigonometry and calculus).

F. Black students have fewer role models in school-based and central office administration.

G. High potential and gifted black students are recruited by the white schools while the low performing black students are coerced to attend the predominately black schools and,

H. The majority of our black students is not being educated in the School District.

II. PROFESSIONAL CONCERNS

A. Black teachers are denied professional contracts at a far higher rate and percentage than white teachers.

B. Black teachers eligible for retirement are constantly harassed and pushed to leave the profession.

C. After gaining experience in predominately black schools white teachers are recruited from these schools two or three days prior to the opening of schools—thereby reducing the effectiveness of black school faculties.

D. Black teachers that are strong and effective are passed over for promotion to administrative positions.

E. Black principals and black parents are denied participation in the decision making process as related to school operation, programming and personnel selection.

F. Black principals are denied the right to attain deputy or superintendent status regardless of preparation or experience.

G. Black teachers are not retained in the system but shuttled out after two years of performance and,

H. Black teachers are not treated the same as white teachers in the School District.

III. PHYSICAL FACILITIES

A. The buildings at the predominately black schools are not maintained as well as those at predominately white schools.

B. The furnishings in the predominately black schools are not of the same quality as that in predominately white schools.

C. The buildings at the predominately black schools are in dire need of repair while the predominately white schools are highly maintained.

D. Quality materials in predominately black schools are less than that in predominately white schools.

E. The equipment in predominately white schools is greater in number and quality than that in predominately black schools.

F. The landscaping at predominately white schools is far more attractive than that at black schools.

G. The overall facilities at black schools are inferior to those at white schools.

IV. RECOMMENDATIONS

The County Branch NAACP, parents and concerned citizens recommend that:

A. The predominately black schools be brought up to par via construction, materials, equipment and personnel.

B. Teachers' quotas for schools that are predominately black or white be at least fifity percent of the dominant race in the school.

C. The administration respect the predominately black communities by meeting with the parents and teachers, permitting them to select principals and teachers and to have a say so in the operation of the schools.

D. The NAACP Education Committee work with district personnel and parents to study, adjust and/or correct situations that affect the education of black boys and girls in the county, and

E. Further recommendations for effective schooling: The School Board organize each school in the following manner:

   1. *Elementary Schools*
      a. Select one teacher from each grade level to serve on a school-based council for a total of six persons for curriculum reasons.
      b. Select six (6) parents that are interested; have some knowledge of education and are strong supporters of the school. Total six (6) for community services.
      c. Elect six (6) citizens to serve on the Council, four of whom should be business leaders.
      d. Assign an Area Superintendent to work with these councils for communication purposes only.

   2. *Secondary Schools*
      a. Select one teacher from each department to serve on a school council.
      b. Select interested and knowledgeable parents equal to the number of departments in the school to serve on a school council.

  c. Select six citizens with a minimum of four business persons to serve on a school council.

  d. Assign one Associate Superintendent to work with this council for communication purposes and,

  e. Give them the power to employ the school-based management system: the power to set policies and select all their schools' personnel—their teachers and principals.

 3. *Administration*

  a. Select and employ more black administrators at all levels. Administrators that project positive images in black communities.

  b. Require all administrative personnel to acquaint themselves with the citizens of black communities.

  c. Have the district board members work closer with the schools and its personnel so as to improve relations with black communities.

  d. Communicate with the school boards of Chicago, Milwaukee, Los Angeles and Colorado regarding their approach to school-based management.

  e. Build more schools in the inner-city where the majority of blacks is concentrated.

  f. Evaluate and react to the above concerns of black parents, citizens and the County Branch NAACP relative to equality in education for blacks.

The County Branch NAACP, black parents and concerned citizens of the county request that the District School Board respond to the aforementioned concerns regarding assurance of quality and equity in education for blacks via a special work session with the above groups.

Exercise 5

ADVANCED REPORTING

FIREFIGHTERS' DEATHS

INSTRUCTIONS: This is a preliminary report that a fire department issued after the deaths of two of its men. The document is genuine; only a few technical details have been deleted, and the names have been changed. Assume that the firefighters died in your city, and that your fire department released the report today. Write a news story that summarizes its content.

Background

The fire occurred at Sunrise Gifts, 8629 West Palm Parkway. The building was less than one year old, 154 feet long and about 50 feet wide. The gift shop occupied 4,000 square feet, and sold miscellaneous goods, such as towels, clothing, gifts and cards. The fire started in the attic (the loft or volume) above the shop. A restaurant, Joe's Gourmet Deli, occupied the building's remaining 3,000 square feet. Investigators concluded that the fire was probably started by ''heat from an electrical source.'' It burned for some time before anyone noticed it, seriously weakening the structure. The fire was reported at 4:09 p.m., and a highway patrol officer evacuated the building before firefighters arrived.

After the roof collapsed, a second and third alarm were sounded to obtain more manpower to extinguish the fire and to rescue the firefighters trapped inside. The gift store was destroyed. The restaurant sustained only minor damage.

The names of the firefighters are:

FF#1: Tony Salcido
FF#2: Ronald Sheppard
FF#3: Joseph Van Atti

Fire Department Report

[Last] February 24, the engine was staffed with a three man crew. They are designated, Officer FF#2, tailboard man FF#3, and driver FF#4. Rescue 36 was staffed with a two man crew. They are designated driver FF#5, and paramedic FF#1.

While enroute, Engine-36 driver and the officer reviewed actions they believed would be necessary in view of the reports received regarding the alarm.

Smoke was visible as soon as the engine crew entered onto West Palm Parkway. The engine proceeded to the front of the fire building.

The officer's arrival report indicated heavy smoke and fire showing. He elected to attack the fire with engine tank water. Engine-36 carries 750 gallons of water.

Upon stopping in front of the structure, the crew deployed one 1-3/4 inch handline. The crew, fully outfitted in protective gear, proceeded into the interior of the structure to investigate conditions and to verify the occupancy was clear of people. The interior of the structure was notably free of heat and smoke.

After sizing-up the situation, the officer directed the engine firefighter (FF#3) to direct a 1-3/4 inch handline stream into a second story dormer from a position on the ground, approximately 30 feet from the structure. It appears, from still photos taken at the scene, that the fire stream did not significantly affect fire intensity.

The officer then ordered pike poles, a roof ladder, and the same 1-3/4 inch handline into the interior of the structure. At approximately the same time, the officer ordered a 24 foot extension ladder raised to the roof of the building near the dormer issuing flames. A decision was made to again enter the structure. The 24 foot ladder was not used during the fire incident.

There were now three firefighters in the structure. FF#1 firefighter is the firefighter/ paramedic, FF#2 firefighter is the officer, FF#3 firefighter is Engine-36 tailboard man.

The team proceeded down a four foot wide aisle for approximately 15 feet to the area the officer believed to be directly below the dormer issuing flame.

First opening in the gypsum board ceiling was made between truss members at an area about 30 feet from the west wall, 18 feet from the south wall and 14 feet from the south double door. The ceiling was removed in pieces approximately 3 feet by 3 feet. No insulation material was noted above the ceiling by the firefighters. FF#1 and FF#2 stood to the north of the opening.

FF#3 directed a fog pattern from directly underneath the hole in short blasts into the roof volume. The nozzle was then shut down to inspect conditions.

FF#3 observed a slow rolling fire with minimal smoke inside and filling the roof volume. He also observed that the bottom sides of the truss chords were not charred.

FF#2 shifted position to the west of FF#3 to view conditions inside the roof volume to the east. FF#2 saw fire to the east inside the roof volume. He stated that they have fire above them. He directed his crew to back out to the main entrance door, take a position and stop the overhead fire. FF#2 directed FF#3 to hand him the nozzle. FF#3 exchanged a nozzle for a pike pole. FF#3 then began the task of expanding the original hole to the south to ''see what they had.'' FF#2 then again ordered the men to the door.

All three were standing directly under the opening to the roof volume. As they began to move toward the door, the firefighters heard a loud ''pop.'' FF#3 was instantly thrown onto his back. (It is probable that the loud noise was caused by a failure of structure and falling debris.)

FF#3 found himself under a rack of clothing, facing upright. To gain a better view, he spread the clothes above him with his hands. He observed flames and a ''rafter'' above him. Fire was visible in the roof volume above. No ceiling material could be observed from his location, leaving the impression it had fallen to the floor.

The view of FF#3 to the outside was obscured by smoke. He then rolled to his left and observed an area of outside light to the northwest of his location. He crawled to the spot of light, turned around, and lunged backward, using the air tank as a battering ram. After several unsuccessful attempts, he noted that there was a metal bar placed horizontally across the window. It was preventing him from breaking the glass. He followed the window until he found another glass area where he attempted to break out again with air tank. This attempt was also unsuccessful. He then dropped to a lower position, struck the glass three more times with the air tank, finally breaking the glass. He tumbled out to the exterior of the building. After the fire was suppressed, it was determined that exit was made through the bottom side of an exit door glass pane. The door was chained shut with a heavy chain and a padlock and, therefore, he was not able to open the door.

No word was heard from FF#1. It appears FF#1 was trapped by falling debris and hot gases as he attempted escape. Evidence collected indicates that he was struck on the head by falling debris causing a skull fracture. He was found in a face down position. Glass shards, debris, gypsum board, and structural materials were found under his body. His air pack was found at his feet, in line with the body. His helmet lay close by, within one foot of his head, next to the SCBA [breathing apparatus] face piece.

FF#2 was also trapped by falling debris and hot gases as he attempted escape. He was found in the face up position. His helmet was approximately 12 to 13 feet from the body. His SCBA was found approximately 13 feet from the body, in line with the body. The SCBA was found near the end of the hoseline. Glass shards, debris, gypsum board, and structural materials were found under his body. The depth of debris under the body of FF#2 was less than that under FF#1.

FF#3 rejoined two remaining firefighters from the first due engine and rescue companies, and the Assistant Chief, to continue rescue and fire fighting efforts. FF#1 and FF#2 were lost in the fire. The autopsy reports show heat damage to the breathing passages and lungs of the firefighters. Carbon monoxide levels were higher in FF#1 than FF#2.

The above sequence of events took place within approximately eight to nine minutes after arrival on scene.

Exercise 6

ADVANCED REPORTING

CAB DRIVER BEATEN AND ROBBED

INSTRUCTIONS: This is another true story. Two men robbed a cab driver, 20-year-old Jimmy Kirkman, and Kirkman dictated the following statement for this book. Assume that the robbery occurred this morning in your city. Write a news story that summarizes Kirkman's statement. Because this is a verbatim account, you can use direct quotations.

Victim's Statement

It was night—about 3:30 a.m. I was sitting there at Lee Road at the Sheraton Hotel. I was waiting and waiting. I waited about an hour for the next call, and then this call came up and I said it was my last one. It was at the Buckey Bar and, uh, I went and picked up two guys standing out near a phone booth, and they told me they were going to Pine Hills [a suburb of your city]. When they first got in the cab one sat in the back seat and one sat in front. I said, "I'm sorry it took me so long to get here." They said, "Oh, it's all right. We were wondering if we'd get a cab tonight or not." Uh, both of them were white, about my height. They were just a couple of inches taller: 6 feet 1 inch, 6 feet, something like that. They were both more stockier than I am, probably 22 or 21, around my age. They were clean cut—didn't seem like the criminal type, anything like that. They were talking about this girl they had met. By this time I had pulled into the new part of Pine Hills Road, kind of a fourth mile down this road. There are maybe six to seven houses along a mile stretch of the road.

The guy in the back seat grabbed me in like a choke hold and started pulling me from behind, and the guy sitting beside me started hitting me in the face. I was sort of arched over, and the other guy slid on top of my legs and took over control of the cab. My foot was off the gas. Still, at this point, I can't believe this was happening, and then, after I get hit a couple of more times—yeah, it is happening. At first I thought it was a joke because my friends and I used to play rough like that. And then it finally hit me that, hey, I'm getting beat up here, and I'm going to get robbed. And, uh, that's when the cab got stuck. I could feel the back of the cab spinning around. I remember a little sinking in a ditch and then a jolt, like we got in some real soft dirt. I heard them arguing with themselves saying, "We're stuck, now what do we do? How are we going to get home?" or something like that.

They pulled me out. I was kind of like half standing. I was on my feet, but I was kind of crouched down because they were holding me by the neck, and that's when the Coke bottle came. I had a Coke bottle, and they saw that in the front seat, and they took that out and started hitting me over the head three–four times with the bottle. The bottle didn't break. Luckily for me, I'd of had glass in my head.

After that I wasn't unconscious, but I wasn't too sure of what was going on, and they opened up the trunk—flipped to see what was in the trunk—took out the spare tire, took out a crowbar for the tire. I never got hit with that, but I was brought around to the trunk of the car, pushed me around with that, had that on my chest. Then that's when they asked for my money. They were saying something like they wanted $200, and all I had was $105, and they were saying, "You better search good and find more money or you're going to be in more trouble than you are now." I was trying to waggle my way out of something because I did have a couple of friends who lived a couple miles from there, and I said, "We can go up there, and he can give me some money," and they said, "Oh, no, you're lying to us." I remember pleading with them at one time, saying, "Let me go—just take the cab." This is after they got my money—"You got my money. Just take the cab and let me go my way, and you go your way," and they said, "No, we can't do that. You've seen us." At this time my eyes were so filled with mud, and my left eye was almost swelled shut at this time. I never really got a good, clear look at them, but if I see them again, I'll know who they were. I'm sure, if I see them again, if I look at them hard enough, they'd know who I am, too.

So the one said, "Let's take him with us." So they started walking down the road, and one was sort of holding me by the arm and hair at the same time. And, uh, they were both kind of mumbling back and forth to each other—couldn't hear what they were saying. But I heard something like tying me to a tree. As we got toward the other side of the road there was a big six-foot chain link fence. One of the guys started climbing over the fence. The other one was holding me, and I'm sure he was going to start pushing me over the fence. And when the one guy got over the fence and jumped down, that's when I started swinging my hand around and knocked his hand away and started running toward the cab because I thought that was a safe thing, whatever. I didn't bother to look back or anything like that, but I heard the guy who was over the fence say, "Get him! Get him!" and then the other guy saying, "No, I can't," or something like that, so I don't know if he wanted to run after me or if they had something to throw at me—a gun—but I didn't want to take any chances. When I ran down the road I kind of zig-zagged. I just ran as fast as I could and didn't bother to look back to see what's behind me—just wanted to get out of there.

As I got to the cab I noticed it was starting on fire in the front seat area and, uh, there was a house just behind the cab on the opposite side of the street, and I ran to the fence there. They had a big chain link fence with a gate on it and, uh, a German shepherd came up to me and ran away. I came up to the front door—knocked on the front door. A man answered the door with a shotgun and, as soon as he saw me, he put down the shotgun and invited me in—asked me what was happening and called the police, and I had to talk to the police, and then heard an explosion from the car. The gas and engine were exploding, and I told them they needed to get the fire department here. By this time you could see the fire from the house, and the cab and, uh, it took probably about 10 minutes for the fire department to get there, and probably about a couple of minutes for the police to get there, and they had a couple of dogs out to find the trail—they could see where they drug me down the road—I had lost one shoe, and they found my other shoe. They saw where they had jumped the fence, but they couldn't figure out how to get the dogs over the fence to continue the trail, so they kind of left it at that. The police don't know whether the cab caught itself on fire or if they set it on fire. The whole front end was burned. The seats were all burned up. There was nothing left of the seats and carpeting except for wire and stuff.

They got my report and, uh, somehow it wasn't broken or nothing, but I couldn't move my right arm, it was kind of numb. So I got taken to the hospital in an ambulance. It was Mercy Hospital. They x-rayed my head, they x-rayed my hand, my back. My eyes were so filled with dirt and mud that they had to flush those out. They had to clean my face up. It was kind of bloody. Both my eyes were black. They were pretty swollen. They put ice packs on them. By this time, I was going into shock, I guess, because I was getting sort of shaky. I didn't break down or cry or anything like that. But I was really shaky, and getting really cold. And, uh, nothing was broken. The only thing that was really hurt was my face from being hit.

I didn't think I was going to see a sunrise again and, when I was in the hospital, there was a window, and I sat on the hospital bed looking at the sun come up, and it was the most beautiful sunrise I ever saw. I can tell you that. It definitely scared the life out of me. I didn't think I was going to pull through. And, uh, the safety officer from our cab company got there, and he brought his wife to see if there was anything that they could do, and there was nothing they could do. It was about 7 in the morning. My sister got there, and she took me home. I was okay until I got in the car, and that's where I fell to pieces—in there—you know, the family and knowing I was all right now.

Exercise 7

ADVANCED REPORTING

INSTRUCTIONS: Write a news story that summarizes this report about shoplifters. Newspapers received copies of the report exactly as it appears here.

The Juvenile Shoplifter

Shoplifting is the largest monetary crime in the nation. Annual retail losses have been recently estimated at $16 billion nationally and as high as 7.5% of dollar sales. Shoplifting-related costs have been cited as a prime cause in one-third of all bankruptcies in small businesses. Shoplifting losses are on the rise, with a 300 percent increase in the incidence of this crime during the 1970s alone.

Juveniles make up the largest percentage of shoplifters. Several studies have revealed that juvenile shoplifters account for approximately fifty percent of all shoplifting.

To gain further insight into the shoplifting problem, George P. Moschis, Professor of Marketing at Georgia State University, and Professor Judith Powell of the University of Richmond, surveyed 7,379 students ages 7 to 19 in urban, suburban and rural areas using methods that insured anonymity of responses.

Some key findings:

- Approximately one out of three juveniles said they had shoplifted.
- Among teen-agers ages 15 to 19, about 43% had shoplifted.
- Male youths shoplift more than females; approximately 41% of the males and 26% of the females reported having shoplifted at some time.
- A large amount of shoplifting is done by relatively few juveniles. Approximately 14 percent of those who admitted to shoplifting indicated repeat shoplifting behavior.
- In comparison with non-shoplifters, youths who shoplift are more likely to believe that shoplifting is not a crime.
- Motives for shoplifting are primarily social rather than economic, especially among girls.
- A great deal of shoplifting is done because of peer pressure, especially among girls.
- About half of the time shoplifting takes place in the presence of peers. Shoplifting with peers is more common among girls than among boys (61% vs 47%).
- Females show greater tendency to shoplift with others with age than males.
- Females tend to shoplift more frequently in the presence of others with age.
- Boys tend to shoplift more frequently alone (less frequently with others) with age.
- Shoplifting done by juveniles is primarily impulsive; four times out of five it is done on impulse.
- Female juveniles who shoplift are more likely to shoplift on impulse. Approximately 87% of females and 76% of males who admitted they had shoplifted decided to shoplift after they entered the store.
- Older teen-age girls are more likely to shoplift on impulse than older teen-age boys. Older boys tend to plan out shoplifting more than girls.

- There is a decline in impulse shoplifting with age and an increase in planned shoplifting among boys. No decline in impulsive shoplifting behavior is shown for girls.
- Impulsive (unplanned) shoplifting in the presence of others is not only more common among girls but it also becomes more frequent with age. Impulsive shoplifting among boys in the presence of others does not increase with age.

The findings regarding differences in shoplifting behaviors due to age and sex characteristics are expected to apply to other parts of the country, and they are consistent with the results of previous studies.

The authors recommend two broad strategies for reducing shoplifting losses: shoplifting prevention and shoplifting detection. Among shoplifting prevention methods the authors suggest promotional campaigns that would increase awareness of the seriousness of the crime, and methods that would increase the difficulty of shoplifting. Proposed shoplifting detection strategies focus on educating security-detection personnel to be alert to the shoplifter's early warning signals, including knowledge of characteristics of youths most likely to shoplift.

Exercise 8

ADVANCED REPORTING

INSTRUCTIONS: Write a news story that summarizes the content of the following report about the families of death row inmates. The report was written by Michael L. Radelet and Felix M. Berardo of the Department of Sociology at the University of Florida and by Margaret Vandiver of the College of Criminal Justice at Northeastern University.

The Families of Death Row Inmates

Since 1930 more than 4,000 people have been executed in the United States, and the 3,000 people now awaiting execution constitute the largest number of inmates living under a death sentence in the history of the United States. Florida leads the country with over 325 men sentenced to death. This report focuses on the families of death row inmates. Information was obtained from several hundred hours of visiting men sentenced to die in Florida, by weekly correspondence with a dozen of the men, and by discussions with several of the men's family members, friends, and attorneys.

A. THE PSYCHOLOGICAL IMPACT OF THE DEATH SENTENCE

The men sentenced to death in Florida experience a variety of physical constraints beyond those encountered by other prisoners. The condemned men are each housed in a separate 6 × 9 cell, which they usually are permitted to leave only three times per week for brief showers and twice per week for a two-hour exercise period. Men with death sentences are not permitted to visit the prison library or chapel, and no phone calls are allowed except in rare emergencies. More painful than these physical restraints, however, are the psychological consequences of being formally condemned as unfit to live. The men are often seen by outsiders, prison officials, and each other only as condemned murderers, and other aspects of their identity are not regularly recognized or nurtured. The death sentence carries with it an all-encompassing personality label, and there are few opportunities to escape this label. In short, while awaiting physical death the men may experience a slow social death, with various aspects of their self-identity quietly eroding through lack of social outlet and reinforcement.

B. THE IMPORTANCE OF FAMILY CONTACT

It is in relation to this identity struggle that families provide their most valuable functions for the men sentenced to die. Families can respond to the non-deviant aspects of the inmate's personality and encourage him to maintain dignity and self-respect. The family recognizes the man as a person with a unique history and individuality, and thereby draws out aspects of his identity that are dormant in everyday prison interactions. Because some inmates have little or no contact with their relatives, it is not uncommon for close friends and correspondents outside the prison to assume functional importance as quasi-family members.

Families offer not only social release from the identity crisis of a death sentence, but also physical release from the cell through a visit. While less than half of the men sentenced to death receive a visit in a given year, we estimate that this rate is double that of visits to other inmates in the maximum security prison where death row inmates are housed. This higher rate of visits for the condemned may indicate that their families perceive the death sentence as a threat which must be met by the family as well as the condemned man. Visits are held in a large room in which there are 30 four-person tables, and are permitted for up to six hours each holiday and Saturday or Sunday (longer visits are granted for out-of-state visitors). A visit is usually the highlight of the prison stay for the man, for it offers the opportunity to leave the cell, see women and children, and talk in confidence. It also offers the opportunity for the man to assume a different role than that of condemned inmate.

C. THE STRESSES OF THE FAMILY

A major barrier to visits is the time and expense involved in getting to the prison, which is located in a rural area of north Florida some 350 miles from Miami. No public transportation to the prison is available. One inmate's 78-year-old illiterate mother, who suffers from arthritis and a variety of other physical problems, reported that she occasionally would hitchhike the final 15 miles to the prison when rides were unavailable. Nearly all the families of condemned prisoners are poor, and many live in other states. The expenses of travel make visits nearly impossible for many families.

To visit a condemned prisoner requires an initial formal application for placement on the inmate's visiting list, a thorough search when entering the prison, and a tolerance for the noise, heat, smoke and uncomfortable seats in the visiting room. Visits can be emotionally and physically draining, and it is not uncommon for a pattern of visits set early after confinement to gradually taper off. The prisoners are aware of the difficulties of visiting and frequently express concern at the strains their families endure to see them.

A second source of stress for the family members is the uncertainty of their family member's fate. Like the families of those suffering chronic or terminal disabilities, of workers facing unemployment or of those in areas of natural disaster, a great deal of anxiety is produced by the inability to predict and control the future and by the effort to fight despair. There is also outright fear, particularly as legal appeals are exhausted, other inmates are executed, and the family member's execution date is set.

Several other stresses confront the families of death row inmates. Almost all are poor, and the others quickly exhaust their monetary resources on legal expenses. Many do not understand the complex legal issues involved in trying and appealing capital cases, further augmenting their uncertainty. Perhaps most demoralizing is the stigma attached to having a loved one sentenced to die and the knowledge that a majority of the public supports executions. Crank letters and phone calls to families (and those who write about them) are not uncommon, and cries for executions by public officials or in newspaper editorials can have marked impacts on the families. Rather than receiving public sympathy, as do for example the families of the terminally ill, the families of the condemned must face their loss knowing the public actively desires the death of their relatives.

Facing such hardships, some family members resolve their uncertainty by abandoning their condemned relative and terminating visits and correspondence. For the inmate, erosion of this contact can be the most stressful aspect of imprisonment. The diminution in family contact threatens that part of the social identity which the family reinforces. Similarly, part of the inmate is also destroyed when a family member dies or develops a serious illness.

Other family members, however, remain committed and devoted to their loved ones. Part of this devotion can be explained by their strong belief in the injustice of capital punishment. Convinced that capital punishment has no deterrent effect and built-in racial and class disparities, the families are often united to their condemned relatives in their outrage at this form of punishment. They also believe the death penalty is cruel and unusual, and justifiable only as a primitive form of vengeance. Anger at prison officials and regulations is sometimes evident, although most believe that the prison personnel are usually decent. Instead the families direct the brunt of their anger at state officials and a public that they perceive as uninformed about the realities of capital punishment. While most family members insist that their loved one is innocent of the crime, others believe that there are major mitigating circumstances that were not considered by the judge or that their relative was severely sentenced because of an inability to hire a highly skilled lawyer.

Exercise 9

ADVANCED REPORTING

INSTRUCTIONS: A bomb caused extensive damage at Harvey's Resort Casino-Hotel in Stateline, Nev., a plush gambling casino. The casino was being remodeled, and the bomb was planted by two men posing as computer technicians. The bomb was about the size of a desk and supposedly contained 1,000 sticks of dynamite. However, there were no injuries.

The bombers were trying to extort $3 million from the casino and left a three-page letter. An attempt to make the payoff apparently failed when a helicopter pilot, aloft in darkness, failed to see the bombers' prearranged signs at the delivery point. The pilot returned with the money, and the bomb exploded as experts tried to disarm it by remote control.

Assume that the bomb exploded today. Write a news story summarizing the letter's content.

Extortion Note from the Casino Bombers

STERN WARNING TO THE MANAGEMENT AND BOMB SQUAD

Do not move or tilt this bomb, because the mechanism controlling the detonators in it will set it off at a movement of less than .01 on the open-end Richter scale. Don't try to flood or gas the bomb. There is a float switch and an atmospheric switch set at 26.00–33.00. Both are attached to detonators. Do not try to take it apart. The flathead screws are also attached to triggers and as much as 1/4 to 3/4 of a turn will cause an explosion. In other words, this bomb is so sensitive that the slightest movement either inside or outside will cause it to explode.

The bomb can never be dismantled or disarmed without causing an explosion. Not even by the creator. Only by proper instruction can it be moved to a safe place where it can be deliberately exploded, or where the third automatic timer can be allowed to detonate it. There are three automatic timers each set for three different explosion times. Only if you comply with the instructions of this letter will you be given instructions on how to disconnect the first two automatic timers and how to move the bomb to a place where it can be exploded safely.

WARNING

I repeat, do not try to move, disarm or enter this bomb. It will explode.

If exploded this bomb contains enough TNT to severely damage Harrah's across the street. This should give you some idea of the amount of TNT contained within this box. It is full of TNT. It is our advice to cordon off a minimum twelve hundred foot radius and remove all people from that area.

DEMANDS

We demand three million dollars in used one hundred dollar bills. They must be unmarked, unbugged and chemically untreated. If we find anything wrong with the money we will stop all instructions for moving the bomb.

INSTRUCTIONS FOR DELIVERY

The money is to be delivered by helicopter. The helicopter pilot is to park at 2300 hours as close as possible to the LTA building by the light at Lake Tahoe Airport. It is to face the east. The pilot has to be alone and unarmed. The pilot is to get out and stand by chain link fence gate. He is to wait for further instructions which will be delivered by a taxi that will be hired. The driver will know nothing. They may also be delivered by a private telephone or through the nearby public phone at exactly 0010 hours. At 0010 hours the pilot will receive instructions about where to go and what to do.

Before the pilot enters the helicopter, he has to take a strong flashlight and shine it around the inside of the helicopter so that it will light up the entire inside. We must be able to see it from a distance with binoculars. We want to be able to see everything that is inside the helicopter so that we can be sure there is no one hiding inside and that there is no contraband inside.

CONDITIONS OF THE BUSINESS TRANSACTION

These conditions must be followed to the letter. Any deviation from these conditions will leave your casino in a shambles. Also remember that even a very small earthquake will detonate the bomb so do not try to delay the delivery of the money.

(1) All news media, local or nationwide will be kept ignorant of the transactions between us and the casino management until the bomb is removed from the building.

(2) The helicopter will be manned only by the pilot. He must be unarmed and unbugged. We do not want any misunderstanding which might cause us to have to take lives unnecessarily.

(3) Fill the helicopter up completely with gas.

(4) The helicopter pilot after he receives the first instructions cannot communicate with anyone except the necessary instructions given and taken by the tower. All channels from 11.80 to 17.00 will be monitored.

The designer of this bomb will not participate in the exchange. So it will be completely useless to apprehend any person making the exchange because they will not know how it works. They perform their duty for a reward. And again if you don't want to be stuck with a thousand pounds of TNT do not allow any investigation by local agencies, FBI or any other investigative action before the bomb is removed. If the instructions are violated in any way by any authority the secret of the handling of the bomb would definitely not be revealed. If the money is received without any problem, six sets of instructions regarding the removal of the bomb will be given to you at different times. The pilot will receive the first set of instructions. He can carry it back with him. You may receive the remaining five sets of instructions one by one via the Kingsbury Post Office by general delivery, or you may receive them all at once. The extent of your cooperation will make the difference. If you cooperate fully it will insure a very speedy exchange. We don't want to burden your business opportunities or cause more loss of money than is necessary.

ATTENTION

There will be no extension or renegotiation. Demands are firm regardless. The transaction has to take place within 24 hours. If you do not comply we will not contact you again and we will not answer any attempts to contact us. In the event of a double-cross there will be another time sometime in the future when another attempt will be made. We have the ways and means to get another bomb in.

TO THE PILOT

The helicopter has to be filled up with gas. Do not come armed with any weapon. Do not bring a shotgun rider. All radio channels will be monitored. You are to have no communication with anyone after you reach the airport. Do not try to be a hero. Arlington is full of them and they can't even smell the flowers. Follow the orders strictly. You will make five stops, none of which will be at an airfield. You will have ample light for landing. All sites are fairly level. One has about 2 degrees pitch. There will be a clearance of more than two hundred feet radius. We don't want any trouble but we won't run away if you bring it.

HAPPY landings.

Exercise 10

ADVANCED REPORTING

THE NUCLEAR THREAT TO SAN FRANCISCO

INSTRUCTIONS: As a community service, the mayor and Board of Supervisors of San Francisco issued this booklet about the danger of nuclear war. The mayor and board explained that they are responsible for public safety and have a duty "to inform the people of any imminent danger and to take steps to prevent harm from occurring." Their booklet adds that: "The danger is real. The risks are great. You should read this booklet to learn what is at stake. Then you can decide what you wish to do about it."

The mayor and board also issued a proclamation calling for a "temporary suspension of nuclear weapons production, while seeking a permanent international nuclear weapons ban." Assume that the mayor and Board of Supervisors released the booklet today. Write a news story summarizing its content.

1. Nuclear Weapons: How Many? How Powerful?

The United States and Russia have the most weapons. France, Great Britain and China have them as well. India, Pakistan, Israel, South Africa and other nations are trying to get them or may already have them. The United States has about 30,000 nuclear warheads; the former Soviet republics have a total of approximately 20,000. Both the United States and Russia can hit each other with nuclear weapons carried by missiles launched from land or sea or air.

Each nuclear warhead is, of course, extremely powerful. The explosive power of a bomb or warhead is measured in "megatons." One megaton equals a *million* tons of TNT. The bombs which destroyed the Japanese cities of Hiroshima and Nagasaki had the explosive power of "only" 10 to 20 *thousand* tons of TNT. So, a one-megaton bomb—the size of the kind which could hit San Francisco—is 50 to 100 times more powerful.

The United States and Russia have nuclear weapons ranging in size up to 20 megatons. If used, all these weapons would produce nearly a *million* times the explosive power used against Hiroshima. Thus, if a nuclear war were started—by accident or on purpose—the destruction would be beyond anything ever before experienced by the human race. The following sections describe what would happen.

2. Suppose a One-Megaton Bomb Were Exploded Near Ground Level at San Francisco City Hall

Almost every child, every woman and every man would be killed. The Civic Center, the Opera House and most of the elderly housing nearby would disappear as a crater 20 stories deep was formed. A deadly cloud of radioactive soil would be thrown thousands of feet into the air while the blast created winds up to 500 mph. Nothing recognizable would remain from the Old Mint on Mission to St. Mary's Cathedral and Japantown. Little of significance would remain standing from the Mission and Potrero Districts on the south, to Russian Hill on the north, from the Panhandle on the west to the Financial District and Chinatown on the east. This destruction would occur in seconds.

IF YOU WERE FARTHER AWAY FROM CITY HALL (1.5 TO 5.0 MILES FROM THE BOMB BLAST)

Imagine instead you were fortunate enough to be farther from City Hall, driving across a bridge to Marin or the East Bay, shopping at Serramonte or Stonestown, at home in the Sunset or attending a game at Candlestick. The heat from the explosion and the instant burning of clothing would cause third-degree flash burns over much of the body for most people in this area, killing at least half. Brick and wood frame buildings would be destroyed. Vast firestorms could be caused by the intense heat, fanned by 160 mph winds. Such fires would suck up so much air that thousands could die from a lack of oxygen. Even underground shelters, if there were any, would become ovens from the heat. Pressure from the blast would shatter glass and turn it into missiles traveling at over 100 mph. Almost all transportation of any kind would be destroyed or made useless. Emergency medical equipment and supplies would be destroyed.

IF YOU WERE ANYWHERE IN THE EXTENDED BAY AREA (5.0 MILES AND BEYOND)

The intense light from the explosion could cause retinal damage and even blindness to those who see the blast. Among the wounded survivors, many could be deaf because of ruptured eardrums. For up to hundreds of miles away, depending upon wind patterns, the nature of the bomb and other factors, radiation would kill many more. The radiation would be spread by tons and tons of contaminated soils and debris floating and drifting away from the blast area. The deaths may be rapid or slow. Radiation would also affect unborn generations because of its effects on genetic characteristics. For those of us who survive, the recovery would be long and painful, perhaps with permanent disability. The survivors may very well envy the dead.

3. What a Nuclear War Would Do

What we have just described are the effects of a single one-megaton bomb attack on San Francisco. The probability, however, is that an attack would not be limited to one bomb or to San Francisco, but rather would be a part of a full-scale attack on the United States.

In such an all-out attack, over one-half of the population of the United States would be killed or injured. In the long run, millions more people would die from injuries, exposure to radiation, burns, and lack of food, water or adequate shelter. The Bay Area, as a financial center and with a higher than average concentration of military and industrial facilities, unquestionably would be a prime target.

With many hospitals destroyed and many doctors and nurses killed and injured, we would have almost no medical care and few facilities for the hundreds of thousands of people suffering from burns, radiation sickness, blast effects, shock or other injuries. Epidemics of plague, typhus, cholera or other diseases could break out. There would be hundreds of thousands of human corpses to dispose of in San Francisco alone.

Our economic structure would be devastated. There would be drastic food shortages, with foodstuffs largely destroyed and little hope of replacing them quickly. With roads clogged or damaged, there would be a breakdown of transportation. Most communications would be cut off. Basic services such as fire, police, sanitation and water would be disrupted. There would be severe energy shortages. Because of lingering radiation, people would not be able to return to their homes for weeks, months or even years—that is, if their homes were left standing.

THE WORST MAY BE UNKNOWN

It is almost impossible to calculate the effects of a nuclear war on the environment. The oceans, air and land may be too contaminated to sustain life. Entire species of plants and animals may die out. Certain insects and bacteria which are more immune to radiation will multiply.

The effects on the minds of the people who witness this holocaust can only be guessed.

4. What Can We Do?

Being involved in the prevention of a nuclear holocaust is more realistic than trying to deny the danger. After reviewing these facts about nuclear war and the nuclear weapons, the Mayor and the Board of Supervisors felt a responsibility to act. The first step was to endorse this booklet and have it distributed throughout San Francisco to inform you of the risks and dangers we all face.

Here are some steps you can take:

Learn More. There are lots of materials on nuclear weapons, nuclear war and related issues available in our public libraries.

Discuss the Problem. Engage in discussions with your family, friends, at your school, work, club or religious institution. Children too young to participate in activities to prevent nuclear disaster should have the support and reassurance which the involvement of their parents can provide.

Contact Groups in Your Neighborhood. Offer to arrange for a speaker and film presentation on the nuclear weapons issue.

Vote Appropriately. Make sure those persons for whom you vote will do all in their power to promote peace and avoid nuclear war, and actively oppose the nuclear arms race.

Call and Write the News Media. Ask for coverage of the issue. Praise as well as criticize where indicated. The press needs and wants to hear from their viewers/readers.

Write Your Elected Officials Frequently. Elected representatives in Washington, D.C. and Sacramento are YOUR voice. Make sure that *your* voice is heard. Jot two or three sentences on a postcard and uge them to support the reduction and elimination of nuclear stockpiles as well as opposition to the development and deployment of any new nuclear weaponry.

CITY DIRECTORY

Like other city directories, this directory lists only the names of adults (people 18 and older) who live in your community. The directory does not list children under the age of 18, nor adults who live in other cities. Also, city directories (like telephone books) are published only once a year. Thus, they may not list people who moved to your community within the past year.

When it conflicts with information presented in the exercises, always assume that the information in this directory is correct and the exercises are mistaken. You will be expected to correct the exercises' errors. If a name in an exercise is not listed in the directory, assume that the name is used correctly.

As you check the names of people involved in news stories, also check their addresses and occupations, since they may also be erroneous. Sources often make errors while supplying that information to police and other authorities. Also, a person's identity may add to a story's newsworthiness. You will find, for example, that some of the people involved in stories are prominent government officials.

Finally, assume that the people listed as university professors teach at your school.

SECTION I: DIRECTORY OF CITY OFFICIALS

- Belmonte, William. Member, City Council
- Brennan, Rosemary. Director, City Library
- Cycler, Alice. Member, City Council
- Datolli, Sabrina. Mayor
- DeBecker, David. Member, School Board
- Drolshagen, Todd. Director, Code Enforcement Board
- Farci, Allen. City Attorney
- Ferguson, Tony. City Treasurer
- Gandolf, Sandra. Member, City Council
- Graham, Cathleen, M.D. Director, City Health Department
- Hernandez, Ramon. District Attorney
- Hubbard, Gary. Superintendent of Schools
- Kopperud, Barry. Police Chief
- Lieber, Mimi. Member, School Board
- Lo, Roger. Member, City Council
- Lu, Judie. Member, School Board
- Maceda, Diana. Member, School Board
- Nemechek, Anna. Member, School Board
- Nyad, Carole. Member, City Council
- Nyez, Jose. Member, School Board
- Onn, Tom. Director, City Housing Authority

- Plambeck, Emil. Superintendent, City Park Commission
- Ramirez, Luis. Member, City Council
- Stoudnaur, Marlene, M.D. Medical Examiner
- Sullivan, Tony. Fire Chief
- Tribitt, Jane. Member, School Board
- Tuschak, Joseph. Member, City Council
- Vacante, Umberto. Member, School Board

SECTION II: DIRECTORY OF COUNTY OFFICIALS

- Alvarez, Harold. County Administrator
- Chenn, Anne. Member, County Commission
- Dawkins, Kerwin. Director, Public Works
- Dawkins, Valerie. Member, County Commission
- DiCesari, Gus. Sheriff
- Ellis, Faith. Member, County Commission
- Gardez, José. Member, County Commission
- Grauman, Roland. Member, County Commission
- Hedricks, Donald. Assistant County Attorney
- Laybourne, Raymond. Member, County Commission
- McNally, Ronald. County Attorney
- Morsberger, Diedre. Supervisor of Elections
- Shenuski, Anita. Member, County Commission
- Sindelair Vernon. County Treasurer
- Smith, Ronald. County Clerk
- Wehr, Helen. Assistant County Attorney

SECTION III: JUDGES

Municipal Court

Hall, Marci   Kocembra, Edward

Circuit Court

Johnson, Edwin   Ostreicher, Marlene
Kaeppler, JoAnn   Pfaff, Randall
Levine, Bryce R.   Picott, Marilyn
McGregor, Samuel   Stricklan, Julian

SECTION IV: ABBREVIATIONS

acct	accountant	appr	apprentice
admn	administration	apt	apartment
adv	advertising	archt	architect
agcy	agency	asmbl	assembler
agt	agent	assn	association

asst	assistant	ins	insurance
attnd	attendant	insp	inspector
atty	attorney	jr	junior
aud	auditor	jtr	janitor
av	avenue	jwlr	jeweler
bkpr	bookkeeper	la	lane
bldr	builder	lab	laborer
blvd	boulevard	librn	librarian
brklyr	bricklayer	lt	lieutenant
bros	brothers	lwyr	lawyer
capt	captain	mach	machinist
carp	carpenter	mech	mechanic
cash	cashier	med	medical
cc	community college	mfg	manufacturing
ch	church	mgr	manager
chem	chemist	min	minister
chiro	chiropractor	mkt	market
cir	circle/circuit	mstr	master
clk	clerk	mtce	maintenance
clns	cleaners	muncp	municipal
co	company	mus	musician
colm	council member	nat	national
com	commissioner	ofc	office
const	construction	ofer	officer
cpl	corporal	opr	operator
ct	court	optn	optician
ctr	center	pcpl	principal
cty	county	pers	personnel
custd	custodian	pharm	pharmacist
dent	dental/dentist	photog	photographer
dep	deputy	phys	physician
dept	department	pl	place
det	detective	plmb	plumber
dir	director	pntr	painter
dispr	dispatcher	po	post office
dist	district	polof	police officer
dr	drive/driver	pres	president
ele	elementary	prof	professor
electn	electrician	pts	postal
emp	employee	pub	public
eng	engineer	r	resident/roomer
est	estate	rd	road
exec	executive	real est	real estate
facty	factory	recpt	receptionist
fed	federal	rel	relations
formn	foreman	rep	represenatative
gdnr	gardener	repr	repairer
govt	government	restr	restaurant
h	homeowner	retd	retired
hairdrsr	hairdresser	Rev	Reverend
hosp	hospital	sav	savings
hwy	highway	sch	school
inc	incorporated	sec	secretary

secy	security	tel	telephone
sen	senator	ter	terrace
serv	service	treas	treasurer
sgt	sergeant	univ	university
slsp	salesperson	USA	U.S. Army
soc	social	USAF	U.S. Air Force
sq	square	USM	U.S. Marines
sr	senior	USN	U.S. Navy
st	street	vet	veterinarian
stat	station	vp	vice president
studt	student	watr	waiter
supm	supermarket	watrs	waitress
supt	superintendent	wdr	welder
supvr	supervisor	wid	widow
tech	technician	widr	widower
techr	teacher	wrk	worker

SECTION V: SAMPLE ENTRIES

Hurley Carl J & Mary; printer Weisz Printing Co h 140 Kings Point Dr
1   2   3   4   5   6

Hurley Mary ofc sec Roosevelt Ele Sch h 140 Kings Point Dr
7   8   9   10   11

Hurley Ralph studt r 140 Kings Point Dr
12   13   14   15

- 1 = Name of man, last name first
- 2 = First name of wife
- 3 = Husband's occupation
- 4 = Husband's employer
- 5 = Homeowner
- 6 = Home address
- 7 = Woman employed outside home (May be wife also mentioned in family entry)
- 8 = Woman's occupation
- 9 = Woman's employer
- 10 = Homeowner
- 11 = Woman's address
- 12 = Name of roomer or renter 18 years of age or older
- 13 = Roomer/renter's occupation
- 14 = Resident or roomer
- 15 = Address

SECTION VI: ENTRIES

Aaron Betsy retd r410 Hillcrest St Apt 302
Abare Ann recpt Chavez Bros Chevrolet h855 Tichnor Way
Abbondanzio Anthony & Deborah; brklyr Wagnor Bros h473 Geele Av

Abdondanzio Denise pub rel rep Haile Associates r3218 Holbrook Av Apt 832

Adcock George & Lydia; mgr Blackhawk Hotel h141 N Cortez Av

Adcock Lydia soc wkr Catholic Social Services h141 N Cortez Av

Adler Stuart & Sandra; min Ch of Christ r1847 Oakland Blvd

Adles John & Dora; rep Bach & Co h1218 S 23rd St

Ahl Thomas C facty wkr Vallrath Plastics r2634 6th St Apt 382

Ahrons Tommy managing editor The Daily Courier h1097 Leeway Dr

Ahsonn Jeffrey R & Teresa; retd h49 Groveland Av

Albertson Wanda pers dir Vallrath Plastics h529 Adirondack Av

Alicea Carlos cty emp h2930 Leisure Dr

Allen Christopher prof Pierce CC h1810 Collins Av

Allen James D & Margie; mach opr Collins Industries h28 Rio Grande Rd

Allen Margie atty h28 Rio Grande Rd

Allen Michael mech Allison Ford r410 Hillcrest St Apt 82

Allersen Thomas & Alice; acct Mercy Hosp h418 Meridan Av

Alvarez Harold & Tina M; cty administrator r854 Maury Rd Apt 11B

Alvarez Jose cpl state hwy patrol h1982 Elmwood Dr

Alvarez Thomas studt r854 Maury Rd Apt 11B

Alvarez Tina M techr Washington Ele Sch r854 Maury Rd Apt 11B

Amanpor Elton & Effie; technical writer Wirtz Electronics h823 E Pierce Av

Anchall Mildred dir Sunnyview Retirement Home r2202 8th Av Apt 382

Andrews Ira auto mech Allison Ford h561 Tichnor Way

Andrews Paula wid; aud Blackhawk Hotel h4030 New Orleans Av

Aneesa Ahmad univ prof h1184 3rd Av

Aneja David & Tracy; sgt sheriff's dept h488 Tulip Dr

Aneja Tracy carp h488 Tulip Dr

Ansell Herman clk Blackhawk Hotel r2814 Ambassador Dr Apt 61

Arico James K pntr Kalina Painting & Decorating r9950 Turf Way Apt 703C

Baille Maggy wdr Halstini Manufacturing h810 N Ontario Av

Baliet Karen adv exec Baliet & Associates h1440 Walters Av

Baliet Thomas & Karen; pres Republican Bldrs h1440 Walters Av

Ball James studt r1012 Cortez Av Apt 870

Barber Herbert & Irene; vp Denny's Restaurant Group h2440 College Dr

Barlow Janet hairdrsr Lynn's Styling h2868 Moor St

Barlow Kevin polof r3363 Andover Dr

Barlow Raymond & Janet; dir United Way h2868 Moor St

Barlow Robert A mech Allison Ford r112 Hope Cir

Barsch Michael & Margaret; sgt police dept h2489 Hazel La

Barton Eileen owner/mgr Barton Sch of Dance h1012 Treasure Dr

Basa Shannon optn r6718 Fox Creek Dr Apt 1010

Baugh Marcia state consumer advocate h350 Meridan Av

Bealle Denise univ prof h1018 Cortez Av

Beasley Ralph pntr Kalina Painting & Decorating r810 Howard St

Beaumont Edward & Hazel; po wkr h7240 N Ontario Av

Beaumont Roger studt r7240 N Ontario Av

Becker Ricky & Maurine; publisher The Daily Courier h1521 Cole Rd

Belcuor Christine watrs Holiday House Restr h497 Fern Creek Dr

Belcuor Paul & Christine; librn h497 Fern Creek Dr

Belmonte Lucy mus h177 Andover Dr

Belmonte William & Lucy; archt Belmonte & Associates & city colm
   h177 Andover Dr

Berg Mildred univ prof h984 Elmwood Dr

Biagi Allison polof r2634 6th St Apt 906B

Biegel Franklin custd Filko Furniture r782 12th Av

Blanchfield Elaine owner/mgr Elaine's Jewelry r780 Cole Rd Apt 282

Bledsoe Edward & Rosalie; photog The Daily Courier h833 Meridan Av

Blohm Kevin cook North Point Inn r5604 Woodland St

Boyette Willis A jtr Barton Sch of Dance r2121 Biarritz Dr

Boyssie Betty bkpr Allstate Ins h1407 3rd Av

Boyssie Lee & Betty; polof h1407 3rd Av

Brame Don city emp 3402 Virginia Av

Brennan Rosemary dir City Library h1775 Nair Dr

Brookes Oliver & Sunni; univ prof h5402 Andover Dr

Brookes Sunni tech writer Halstini Manufacturing h5402 Andover Dr

Brown Howard slsp Prudential Ins Co h2745 Collins Av

Bulnes Karen atty Sch Board h43 Princeton Pl

Burke Randy & Lynn; capt USA h412 Wilson Av

Burmeister Abraham & Esther; pres First Nat Bank h4439 Harding Av

Burmester Herman A & Sally; const wkr Rittman Eng Co h1412 S 23rd St

Burnes Todd polof r1502 Matador Dr Apt 203

Burnes Tyrone min United Methodist Ch r8430 Wilson Av

Butler Max & Irene; courier First National Bank r444 Jamestown Dr

Cain Fred & Irma; mus r427 Hidden La

Cantrell Michael pres/mgr Mr. Muscles r410 South St

Capiello Ann studt r8210 University Blvd Apt 311

Carey John priest St. John Vianney Catholic Ch r2020 Oak Ridge Rd

Carey Myron univ prof h641 N Highland Dr

Carigg Craig & Susan; min Allen Chapel AME Ch h453 Twisting Pine Cir

Carigg James R studt r453 Twisting Pine Cir

Carter, Deborah counselor Lovell Psychiatric Assn r550 Oak Parkway Apt 821

Caruna Alyce min Howell Presbyterian Ch h423 Charrow La

Carvel Reba techr Colonial Ele Sch r1883 Hope Ter

Casio David & Getta; atty r711 N 31st St Apt 220

Caspinwall Andrew r416 Wilson Av

Caspinwall Nadine phys h416 Wilson Av

Cessarini Maxine univ prof r4184 Cypress Av

Cessarini Richard M & Maxine; phys r4184 Cypress Av

Charlton John city ff r3158 Virginia Av

Cheesbro Marilyn asst public defender r1010 Eastview Rd Apt 3

Chenn Anne cty commissioner r91 Melrose Av

Chenn Steven & Anne; 1t fire dept r91 Melrose Av

Chevez Larry det police dept h4747 Collins Rd

Chmielewski Albert nurse Mercy Hosp r2814 Ambassador Dr Apt 82

Chuey Karen slsp Allison Ford r5710 Michigan Av

Chuey William J & Karen; clk police dept r5710 Michigan Av

Cisneroes Andrew & Lillian; min Redeemer Lutheran Ch r818 Bell Av

Clayton Amy univ pres r820 Twisting Pine Cir

Cohen Abraham & Estelle; asst dir computer srv city sch system
  r1903 Conway Rd

Cohen Estelle pub rel rep Evans Pub Rel Group r1903 Conway Rd

Collin Ronald const wkr Wagnor Development Corp r2814 Ambassador Dr
  Apt 47D

Conaho Henry & Jeanne; supv sales ERA Realty h820 Hope Ter

Conaho Jeanne pres Lake CC h820 Hope Ter

Correia Bobby & Dawn; supvr Delta Airlines h9542 Holbrook Dr

Cortez Manual & Nina; polof r1242 Alton Rd

Cortez Nina bkpr North Point Inn r1242 Alton Rd
Cosby Minnie agt Watson Realty r487 Jamestown Dr
Courhesne Adolph & Gloria; mech Fridley Volkswagen h1186 N Highland Av
Cowles Stephen jtr VFW Post 40 h8217 Cypress Av
Cross Andrea chiro h2 Virginia Av
Cross Lee & Andrea; city acct h2 Virginia Av
Cross Raymond E & Dina; pts wkr r101 Charow La
Cruz Jena atty r48 DeLaney Av
Cullinan Charles A & Susan; sheriff's dep r848 Rio Grande Rd
Cullinan Kyle polof h615 Pennsylvania Av
Cullinan Susan; sheriff's dep r848 Rio Grande Rd
Curtis Sarah sr vp SunBank r663 Harding Av
Cycler Alice city colm r7842 Toucan Dr
Cycler Richard & Alice; atty r7842 Toucan Dr
Daigel Annette hairdrsr Anne's Beauty Salon r431 E Central Blvd
DaRoza Sue studt r410 University Blvd Apt 80
DaRoza Terry & Sue; clk Jiffy Food Store r410 University Blvd Apt 80
Datolli Roger & Sabrina; retd r845 Conway Rd
Datolli Sabrina mayor r845 Conway Rd
Dawkins Kerwin & Agnes; dir cty Dept of Public Works r2203 Coble Dr
Dawkins Ronald & Valerie; brkly r1005 Stratmore Dr
Dawkins Valerie cty com r1005 Stratmore Dr
Dawson Shirley wid; techr Colonial Ele Sch h492 Melrose Av
Deacosti Amy studt r3254 Virginia Av
Deacosti Michael & Peggy; pres Deacosti's Restr h3254 Virginia Av
Deacosti Peggy hostess Deacosti's Restr h3254 Virginia Av
Deboare Ann dir emp rel Rittman Industries r1415 Idaho Av
Deboare Jack R & Ann; mgr Lucky's Supm r1415 Idaho Av
DeCastro Wilma techr Kennedy High Sch h3277 Pine Av
Dees Karen studt r410 University Blvd Apt 52
DeLoy Joseph R phys r280 Lancaster Rd Apt 110
Desaur Roland studt r700 Classics St
DeVitini Brenda asst min Redeemer Lutheran Ch r313 Coble Dr
DeVitini Ronald & Brenda; mach Rittman Industries r313 Coble Dr
DeWitt Tony studt r2230 Cortez Av Apt 828
Deyo Ashley graphic designer r2814 Ambassador Dr Apt 7
Deyo Ralph & Ashley; dent r2814 Ambassador Dr Apt 7
DeZinno Marc & Nancy; asmbl Vallrath Industries h205 Rockingham Ct
Diaz Diane author h1978 Holcroft Av
Diaz Enrique & Lisa; atty r3224 Mt Semonar Av
Diaz Lisa pts wkr r3224 Mt Semonar Av
Diaz Richard & Diane; nurse St. Nicholas Hosp h1978 Holcroft Av
DiCesari Gus & Henrietta; cty sheriff h980 Atlantic Av
Dillan Martha atty Westinghouse Corp h702 S Kirkmann Av
DiLorrento Allison univ prof h666 Texas Av
DiLorrento Anthony executive dir State Press Assn r7800 West Av Apt 477
Dolmovich Sandra M clk Dayton-Hudson h714 N 23rd St
Dow Tammy sgt police dept r2208 17th Av
Dowdell Laura clk Dowdell Jewelry h620 Lexon Av
Dowdell Thaddeus & Laura; jwlr Dowdell Jewelry h620 Lexon Av
Drolshagen Todd & Ilse; dir city Code Enforcement Board h2406 Alabama Av
Dwyer Margaret studt r2047 Princeton Av Apt 405
Dysart Troy studt r724 Aloma Av Apt 24F

Edwards Traci R psychiatrist h3303 Lake Dr
Einhorn Robert & Doris; univ phys h8320 Meadowdale Rd
Eisen Priscilla phys r1118 Bumby Av Apt 204
Ellam Dorothy R techr Madison Ele Sch r2481 Santana Blvd
Ellam Roger A & Dorothy; landscape contractor r2481 Santana Blvd
Ellerbe Robert widr; pres Ellerbe's Boats h3213 Hidalgo Dr
Eulon Harley & Martha; jtr St. Nicholas Hosp h410 E 3rd St
Evans Mark & Trish; cty soc wkr h4232 Stewart Av
Evans Nikki loan ofer First Federal Sav & Loan r806 Apple La
Evans Timothy & Nikki; mgr Allstate Ins r806 Apple La
Evans Trish W owner/mgr Evans Pub Rel Group h4232 Stewart Av
Farci Allen widr; city atty h818 Texas Av
Favata Celia J wid; h9930 Bumby Av
Ferguson Marcia vet h96 West Av
Ferguson Tony & Marcia; city treas h96 West Av
Ferrell Fannie atty h2384 West Av
Ferrell Melvin & Fannie; pcpl Kennedy High Sch h2384 West Av
Firmett Rene J serv stat attnd Bert's Shell Station r4474 Colyer Rd
Flavel Vernon J dr Becker Express h827 N Pigeon Rd
Forlenza Henry custd K Mart r4620 Alabama Av Apt 22
Forsythe Scott cpl sheriff's dept h1414 S 14th Av
Foucault Carmen wid; techr Aloma Ele Sch h1452 Penham Av
Fowler Barbara K polof h88 Eastbrook Av
Fowler Fritz & Barbara; owner Fowler Allstate h88 Eastbrook Av
Fowler Joel studt r2006 Hillcrest St
Franklin Allen sgt USA r840 Apollo Dr Apt 322
Friedmann Leo asst dist atty r2814 Ambassador Dr Apt C2
Gable Jay & Frances; truck dr Becker Express h1701 Woodcrest Dr
Gandolf Sandra wid; city colm h8 Hillcrest Av
Gant Diana univ prof h810 Villae La
Gardepe Ellen serv mgr Derek Chevrolet h210 Lake Dr
Garland Chester & Charlotte; city health insp h2008 N 21st St
Garner David & Cheryl; emp City Recreation Dept r2814 Ambassador Dr Apt 88
Giangelli Marlene P pres Pestfree Inc h214 Lake Dr
Gill Todd watr Fred's Steakhouse r1893 14th Av
Goetz Beryl dent & writer h1010 McLeod Rd
Golay Evelyn cashier Tom's Liquors h1203 Texas Av
Golay Thomas A & Evelyn; owner/mgr Tom's Liquors h1203 Texas Av
Goree Linda exec dir cty Girl Scout Council r2202 8th Av Apt 302
Gould Savilla & Darlene; slsp Anchor Realty Co h4178 N 11th Av
Graham Cathleen dir City Health Dept h710 Harding Av
Graham Ross R & Cathleen; phys h710 Harding Av
Grauman Roland & Tina; cty com r3417 Charnow La
Grauman Samuel & Alice; min First Covenent Ch r610 Eisen Av
Grauman Tina asst supt for pub education r3417 Charnow La
Green Joel atty h604 Michigan Av
Greenhouse Irwin & Trina; administrator Mercy Hosp h9575 Holbrook Dr
Griffin Marlene det police dept h3130 Joyce Dr
Guarino Anne chiro r4100 Conway Rd Apt 611
Guarino Belva retd r84 Lakeland Av
Guarino Gerhard chiro h1813 Texas Av
Guarino Tony A techr Colonial High Sch h6139 Eastland Dr
Guerin Ronald E & Anita; city ff r1045 Eastvue Rd

Guitterman Daniel bartender Jim's Lounge r550 Oak Park Way Apt 7
Gulas Gail studt h3405 Virginia Av
Gulas William J & Gail; phys h3405 Virginia Av
Guyer Joseph & Rita; artist h4043 S 28th St
Guzmann Trina mgr Sports Unlimited r2032 Turf Way Apt 230
Haile Jeffrey polof r2634 6th St Apt 847
Hall Marci muncp ct judge h34 Magee Ct
Halso Beverly pres Halso Publ Rel r879 Tichnor Way
Halso Jeff & Beverly; vet r879 Tichnor Way
Hamill Kimberly mgr Albertson's supm h811 N Cortez Av
Hamill Margaret studt r811 N Cortez Av
Hammar Margaret J secy ofer Macy Dept Store h1181 6th St
Hana Edward & Jena; min Unity Church of Christianity h134 Eisen Av
Hana Kyle custd Unity Church of Christianity r134 Eisen Av
Hanson Lydia atty r880 6th St
Hanson Myron widr; retd h880 6th St
Hariss Jerry R & Jewel; asst mgr House of Pancakes h2245 E Broadway Av
Harmon Rhonda watrs Red Lobster r816 Westwinds Dr Apt 8
Harnish Cheryl supvr sales Cargell Corp h288 Hillcrest St
Harnish David & Cheryl; state sen h288 Hillcrest St
Haselfe Richard & Jennifer; pres Haselfe Development Corp h554 Beloit Av
Haserott Mildred wid; ticket agt Greyhound Lines r411 Wisconsin Av
Haskell Thomas widr; lt fire dept h2482 Elmwood Dr
Hattaway Willie widr; retd r411 Wisconsin Av
Hedricks Donald asst city atty r4320 Elsie Dr Apt 884
Hemphall Loretta dir secy State Alliance Businesspeople h429 Conway Rd
Henderson Leon & Diane; sheriff's dep h902 Patty Way
Hennigen Maggy polof r550 Oak Park Way Apt A3
Henricks Florence techr Risser Ele Sch h423 Marble Rd
Herdon Joyce atty h310 Mill Av
Hermann Andrew J & Jennifer; acct h1888 Hope Ter
Hermann Jennifer teller First Nat Bank h1888 Hope Ter
Hernandez Ramon dist atty h84 Lake Cir
Herrin Raymond W univ prof h410 Park Av
Herwarthe Gregory L & Ruth; pres Knight Realty h4410 Baltimore Av
Herwarthe Ruth asst mgr Harrington & Co Investments h4410 Baltimore Av
Heslinn Allison clk K Mart h8197 Locke Av
Heslinn Burt & Allison; sales rep Prudential Bache h8197 Locke Av
Heslinn Dorothy L mgr Mr. Grocer r8197 Locke Av
Higginbotham Gladies Anne mgr Security Federal Bank h1886 Hope Ter
Hilten Randall J & Virginia; lt fire dept h915 Baxter Dr
Hoequist Thomas owner/pres The Jewelry Shoppe h2418 Collins Av
Hoffmann Vivian wid; clk Quik Shoppe h711 Meadow Creek Dr
Hoffsinger Nora wid; retd r411 Wisconsin Av
Holland George & Tanaka; dr Greyhound Lines h4368 Normandy Dr
Holland Keith studt r410 University Av Apt 11
Holland Maryanne adv exec Wilson Associates h947 Greenbrier Dr
Holman Leonard & Evelyn; phys h4366 Normandy Dr
Holtzclaw Norma J wid; slsp ERA Realty h739 West Av
Horan Roger sheriff's dep r118 Hillside Dr Apt C3
Howe Lynn studt r410 University Av Apt 318
Hubbard Gary & Peggy; supt of schs h384 Hillcrest St
Hyde Marie asst sch supt h1381 Lakeview Dr

Hyde Roger & Marie; slsp Ross Chevrolet h1381 Lakeview Dr
Iacobi Neil atty r6214 Maldren Av
Innis Alvin & Sara; lt police dept h1305 Atlantic Blvd
Jabil Stephen dr Becker Express r800 Crestbrook Loop Apt 314
Jacbos Martha mgr Mom's Donuts r1889 32nd St
Jaco Milan & Robyn; dir Blood Bank h2202 S 8th St
Jacobs Bill & Carol; sgt police dept h2481 Lakeside La
Jacobs Carol dispr Yellow Cab h2481 Lakeside La
Janviere Jeanne techr Colonial Ele Sch r1883 Hope Ter
Jeffreys Michael dir Humane Society h2781 Collins Av
Jimenez Edwin C mgr Quik Shoppe r3611 31st St
Joanakatt Cathy asst dir We Care 2442 Collins Av
Johnson Edwin & Susan; cir ct judge h148 West Av
Johnson Karen asst supt schl dist h2344 S 11th St
Johnson Marc const wkr r2643 Pioneer Rd
Jones Danny & Margaret; min Metro Life Church h1152 Darlington Av
Jones Robyn med tech Mercy Hosp h4216 Winford Cir
Jones Samuel & Lucinda; lt USM h4851 Edmee Cir
Jones Sean & Robyn; capt USN h4216 Winford Cir
Kaeppler JoAnn cir ct judge h2192 West Av
Kaeppler Ronald & Lori; sgt USM h9540 Holbrook Dr
Kalani Andrew mgr Kalani Bros Bakery h2481 Kaley Way
Kalani Charles pres Kalani Bros Bakery h2481 Kaley Way
Kasandra Kelli retd r9847 Eastbrook La
Kasparov Linda univ dietitian r9103 Lake St
Keegan Patrick Jr fed atty h505 Walnut Dr
Keel Sally asmbl Cargell Corp h1413 Griesi Dr
Keel Timothy & Sally; barber Plaza Barber Shop h1413 Griesi Dr
Kehole Marvin mtce wkr Cargell Corp r182 W Broadway Av
Kernan Russell mach Vallrath Industries r168 Lake St
Kindstrom Sarah watrs Steak & Ale h4828 N Vine St
Kirkmann James dr Yellow Cab r816 Westwinds Dr Apt 202
Knapp Erik A cook Frisch's Restr r2314 N 11th St
Kocembra Edward & Heather; muncp ct judge h388 31st St
Koche Ellen Jane atty Neighborhood Law Ofc h4214 Azalea Ct
Kopez Frank & Lisa; cty mech h1067 Eastland Av
Kopp Suzanne wid; retd r4200 S 11th St Quality Trailer Ct
Kopperud Barry widr; chief of police h458 Kaley Way
Kostyn Ralph E & Elizabeth; asst supt for ele education city schs h284 Erie Av
Krueger William & Melody; pres Aladdin Paints h48 Michigan Av
Kubic Marilyn techr North High Sch h1452 N 3rd St
Kubic Ralph & Marilyn; techr North High Sch h1452 N 3rd St
Kunze Robert & Lauren; mach Vallrath Industries r94 Jamestown Dr Apt 318
LaCette Cecil serv stat attnd r2814 Ambassador Dr Apt 61
Lasiter James & Harriet; techr Roosevelt Ele Sch r374 Walnut Dr
Layous Michael E studt r212 N Wisconsin Av
Lee Fred owner/cook Kona Village h1181 24th St
Leforge Ted dent h537 Peterson Pl
Leidigh Floyd & Rose; const wkr Rittman Engineering Co h1812 Dickins Av
Levin Ida mgr Mr. Waterbeds h8521 Shady Glen Dr
Levine Bryce R & Trina; cir ct judge h8521 Shady Glen Dr
Lewis Jacquelin watrs Holiday House h1840 Maldren Av
Lewis Jonnie & Jacquelin; insptr Vallrath Industries h1840 Maldren Av

Linn Eddy & Marie; sgt police dept h6287 Airport Blvd
Linn Ronald studt r6287 Airport Blvd
Lo Roger & Joan; city colm h1993 Collins Av
Logass Jeffrey economist Larco Corp h81 Venetian Way
Lowdes Enrico & Sandra; dir Regional Medical Center h77 Maldren Av
Lowrie Catrina phys Regional Medical Center r118 Hillside Dr Apt 74
Lowrie Cynthia studt r118 Hillside Dr Apt 74
Lozando Marie clinical dir Mercy Hosp r234 E Markham Dr Apt 4
Lucas Frank cpl hwy patrol h2417 County Club Dr
Lydin Charles R mgr LaCorte Printing Co h888 Melrose Av
Macbos Martha dir of nursing Mercy Hosp h1889 32nd St
Macco Alan mus r503 29th St
Madea Ramon exec dir Bon Voyage Travel Agcy r118 Hillside Dr Apt 606
Mahew Arthur mgr Frische's Bowling Alley h1918 Pacific Rd
Majorce Albert & Monica; archt h2882 Ambassador Dr
Marcheese Harvey O & Joyce; min Faith Baptist Ch h1481 Cole Rd
Marcheese Joyce organist Faith Baptist Ch h1481 Cole Rd
Mariston Saundra watrs Freddy's Inn h822 Kentucky Av
Matros Margo univ prof r410 University Av Apt 818
McCauley Melvin & Veronica; truck dr Becker Express h540 Osceola Blvd
McDonald Herbert J & Rosalie; owner/mgr Tastee Popcorn h1842 Hazel La
McDowell William pntr h1429 Highland Dr
McEwen Lonnie & Victoria; techr Washington Jr High Sch h1024 Nancy Cir
McFarland Charlotte nursing supv Sand Lake Hosp h1090 Timberline Trail
McFerren Patrick J widr; U.S. postmaster h1227 Baldwin Dr
McFerren Patti const wkr Rittmann Engineering Co r816 Westwinds Dr Apt 3
McGorwann Karen cc prof r4320 Elsie Dr Apt 6
McGorwin Rosalind maid Hyatt Hotel h4842 S Conway Rd
McGowin Bill & Rosalind; const wkr Rittmann Engineering Co
    h4842 S Conway Rd
McGowin William sheriff's dep h4224 N 21st St
McGrath Sunni jtr Washington Ele Sch h109 19th St
McGregor Carol; mgr trainee Albertsons Supm h1501 Southwest Ct
McGregor Samuel & Carol; cir ct judge h1501 Southwest Ct
McIntry Eugene & Irene; pres McIntry Realty h2552 Post Rd
Meir Sharon pers dir Vallrath Industries r810 Kalani St Apt 2
Mejian Colette pcpl Risser Ele Sch h415 Ivanhoe Blvd
Merrit Jacob & June; eng WTMC-TV h301 Wymore Rd
Meyer Robert & Sonia; sgt USAF h811 Moor St
Meyer Sonia M credit mgr Sears h811 Moor St
Miehee Richard & Margaret; asst U.S. postmaster h1190 Euclid Av
Millan Timothy cook Grande Hotel r1112 Huron Av
Miller Sharon optn LensCrafters h2827 Norwell Av
Minh Stephen retd r410 Hillcrest St Apt 842
Moravchek Albert & Dorothy; city ff h4187 N 14th St
Moravchek Dorothy clk police dept h4187 N 14th St
Morrell Wayne & Cathy; mgr Bon Voyage Travel Agency h382 Arlington Cir
Morsberger Diedre cty supvr elections h898 Hemlock Dr
Muldaur Eddy studt r660 S Conway Rd
Murhana Thomas laborer Cargell Corp r40 W Hillier Av
Murphy Joseph & Kathleen; dir research Collins Industries h114 Conway Rd
Murray Blair & Patricia; mgr Beneficial Finance h1748 N 3rd St
Murray Harold & Marty; atty h1801 Hillcrest St

Murray Marty curriculum resource techr h1801 Hillcrest St
Neely Myron A det police dept h1048 Jennings Rd
Nego Alan polof r1840 Wymore Rd Apt 10
Nicholls Cheryl fed emp h1287 Belgard Av
Noffsinger Nora wid; retd r411 Wisconsin Av
Noonan Jack widr; det police dept h5928 Jody Way
Nouse Sharon pilot Aerial Promotions Inc r4740 Valley View La
Novogreski Harry R & Melba; mach Keller Plastics h2891 Morris Av
Nuñez Roger & Carolynn; eng Keele-Baldwin Corp h2820 Norwell Av
Nunziata Carmen h1410 1st Av
Nyad Carole city colm h850 Sutter Loop
Nyer JoAnne sec Washington Ele Sch r550 Oak Park Way Apt 264
Nyez Diana studt r550 Oak Park Way Apt 264
O'Hara Allison city sec r4729 Texas Av
Oldaker George polof r2117 Wisconsin Av Apt 488
Oldaker Thomas polof r2117 Wisconsin Av Apt 488
Oliver Frankin R & Jeannette; exec Gill Assoc Inc Pub Rel h1121 Elm Blvd
Onn Tom C & Esther; dir City Housing Authority h3869 Jefferson Av
Ortiz Randy & Lynn; brklyr HomeRite Builders r816 Westwinds Dr Apt 78
Ortson Thomas J & Martha; vp Secy First Federal Bank h810 N 14th St
Ostreicher Marlene wid; cir ct judge h449 Ferncreek Cr
Paddock Cynthia credit mgr Belks Dept Store h1736 Hinkley Rd
Paddock Thomas C & Cynthia; mach Cargell Corp h1736 Hinkley Rd
Palomino Ralph R & Molly; vp Genesco Inc h374 Douglas Rd
Patzell Bruce & MaryAnne; carp h915 Bishop Dr
Patzell Larry studt r915 Bishop Dr
Paynick Nina techr Washington Ele Sch h901 2nd St
Paynick Stanley & Nina; owner Paynick's Carpets h901 2nd St
Peerson Marc univ prof h4851 Edmee Cir
Perakiss Michael & Ethel; atty h876 Collins Av
Perez Jason const wkr Wagnor Development Corp r2414 Skan Ct
Perez Joseph & Vicki; city emp h2414 Skan Ct
Perez Vicki lt police dept h2414 Skan Ct
Petchski Pearl asst cashier Morrison's Cafeteria r411 Wisconsin Av
Peters Frederick & Rene; pharm K Mart h484 Sugar Ridge Ct
Peters Rene C pres Humane Society h484 Sugar Ridge Ct
Peterson Sara wid; h1671 Drexel Av
Pfaff Randall cir ct judge h2134 Oak Ridge Rd
Phillips Teresa M clk The Jewlery Shoppe r800 Crestbrook Loop Apt 228
Picardo Marie nurse r510 Concord St Apt 48
Picott Marilyn cir ct judge h901 2nd St
Piloto Claire interior decorator h1472 Bayview Rd
Piloto Kenneth T & Claire; atty Piloto & Herndon h1472 Bayview Rd
Pinccus Jennifer atty Piloto & Herndon r2021 Dyan Way Unit 2
Pinckney Samuel & Terese; retd h976 Grand Av
Ping Louis & Dorothy; plmb Lou's Plumbing h348 Conroy Rd
Plambeck Emil & Dolly; supt City Park Com h6391 Norris Av
Porej Irvin vp for loans First Federal Savings & Loan h112 Anzio St
Povacz Julius city paramedic r210 E King Av Apt 4
Proppes Richard E asst mgr Safeway Supm h1012 2nd St
Pryor Lynne R const wkr Rittmann Engineering Co r2634 6th St Apt 45
Rafelsin Louis lt police dept h934 Old Tree Rd
Ramirez Harriet dental asst h982 Euclid Av

Ramirez Luis & Harriet; city colm h982 Euclid Av
Randolph James const wkr Rittman Engineering Co r654 Harrison St
Reeves Charlton E & Polly; state health ofer h658 Lennox Av
Reimer Maurice & Mildred; acct h2529 Barbados Av
Richards Patricia r42 Tusca Trail
Richardson Thomas E & Inez; polof h5421 Jennings Rd
Richbourg Bud & Kathleen; owner/mgr Buddy's Lounge h1014 Turkey Hollow
Richter Robyn Anne retd h42 Tusca Trail
Riggs Gladies Ann wid; retd r1080 Harvard Rd Apt 4
Rivera Hector phys Medi-First Clinic r800 Crestbrook Loop Apt 38
Robbitzsch John W psychiatrist h1014 Bear Creek Cir
Roehl Cecil & Esther; polof h1228 Euclid Av
Romaine Nickolas H & Gerri; wdr h2876 Post Av
Romansaik Michael const wkr Wagnor Development Corp r118 Hillside Dr Apt 8
Rudnike Harold & Martha; h4825 N Vine St
Rudnike Martha sales mgr Vallrath Industries h4825 N Vine St
Ruffenbach Laura univ prof h6741 Waxwing La
Ruiz George & Lila; polof h263 9th St
Ruiz Guillermo & Harriet; asst cty med examiner h4718 Bell Av
Ruiz Harriet dir public affairs Regional Medical Center h4718 Bell Av
Rybinski Kim owner Kim's Pets r2634 6th St Apt 710
Salcido Tony & Martha; city ff h10 Exeter Ct
Saleeby Henry widr; retd r84 Sunnyvale Rd
Saleeby John & Claire; lt colonel USA h626 N 3rd St
Saleeby Wesley & Olivida; retd h1916 Elizabeth La
Sanchez Gumersinda hairdrsr Lillian's Beauty Salon h173 Burgasse Rd
Satava Kenneth widr; techr Kennedy High Sch h2204 Marcel Av
Saterwaitte Benjamin widr; retd h307 E King Blvd
Sawyer Claire min Christian Redeemer Ch h7400 Southland Blvd
Sawyer Harley & Betty; techr Kennedy High Sch r2032 Turf Way Apt 512
Schifini Destiny vp SunBank h3620 Timber Ter
Schipper Michele studt r4100 Conway Rd Apt 814
Schweitzer Ralph city building insp r816 Westwinds Dr Apt 160
Scott Kerry & Nancy; slsp Kohlerware h4189 Hazel St
Scott Milan & Nancy; techr Kennedy High Sch h20 Magee Ct
Scott Nancy techr Wilson Ele Sch h20 Magee Ct
Shadgott Frank D & Carol; phys h8472 Chestnut Dr
Sharp Lynita L clk Jiffy Foods r5836 Bolling Dr
Shattuck Christina mgr Perkins Restr h532 3rd St
Shattuck Dennis A & Christina; emp city garage h532 3rd St
Shearer Ethel cocktail watrs Melody Lounge r408 Kasper Av Apt 718
Shenuski Anita cty com h1230 Embree Cir
Shenuski Frederic & Anita; dist mgr IRS h1230 Embree Cir
Sheppard Ronald lt fire dept r2024 Vincent Rd Apt 1020
Shisenauntt Arthur & Lillian; secy consultant h1243 Washington Av
Shisenauntt Lillian pharm Walgreen h1243 Washington Av
Shoemaker JoAnn techr Colonial High Sch r6139 Eastland Dr
Silverbach Daniel G & Jill; polof h3166 Wayne Av
Simmens Karen dist dir Greenpeace r708 E Lisa La
Simmons Wayne & Rachel; slsp Prudential Ins h708 E Lisa La
Sindelair Vernon & Elaine; cty treas h4164 Mandar Dr
Skinner Dorothy clk typist Lawton Bros h2080 Washington Av
Skinner Roger & Dorothy; polof h2080 Washington Av

Skurow Melvin widr; carp h4138 Hennessy Ct
Slater David & Carolyn; chiro h8443 Turkey Hollow
Smith Grady r8213 Peach St
Smith Linda M studt h1814 N 3rd St
Smith Ronald & Linda; cty clk h1814 N 3rd St
Smitkins Myron & Marlene; mach Kohlarware h417 Huron Av
Smythe Asa A & Carol; cty emp h4280 Timber Trail
Smythe Terry studt r4280 Timber Trail
Snow Dale & Terri; h4381 Hazel St
Snow Terri nurse Mercy Hosp h4381 Hazel St
Snowdin Elizabeth clk state employment ofce h952 Kasper Av
Snyder Christina dir pub rel Mercy Hosp h711 Broadway Av
Sodergreen Karl & Lillian; phys h788 Timber Trail
Sota Mimi dir Drug Abuse Unit Mercy Hosp h655 Brickell Dr
Stevens Julie Ann mus h624 N 3rd St
Stockdale George & Lillian; capt USM h472 Bolling Dr
Stoudnaur John & Marlene; mgr Rexall Drugs h1350 41st St
Stoudnaur Marlene city med examiner h1350 41st St
Stovall Iris wid; mgr Quikke Clns h7204 Southland Blvd
Straitten Walter & Karen; cty building insptr r4450 Richmond Rd
Stricklan Julian cir ct judge h4268 Wayne Av
Sulenti Allen D studt r800 Crestbrook Loop Apt 1010
Sullivan Tony widr; fire chief h863 Benchwood Ct
Svec Wallace A mech Allison Ford r4320 Elsie Dr Apt 1
Svendson Wayne & Lillian; city paramedic h814 Washington Av
Swaugger Charlotte cc prof h4987 Huron Dr
Swaugger Samuel & Charlotte; reporter The Daily Courier h4987 Huron Dr
Sweers Daniel & Karen; fed emp h108 Eastbrook Av
Sweers Karen det police dept h108 Eastbrook Av
Tai Wendy housekeeper Hilton Hotel r84 Chestnut Dr
Talbertsen Sarah A artist h3214 Riverview Dr
Taylor Fredric C r4828 N Vine St
Taylor Marsha L mgr McDonald's h2012 Lincoln Av
Temple Roger polof r2032 Turf Way Apt 818
Thistell Dirk & Mildred R; eng Rittman Industries h528 Kennedy Blvd
Thistell Mildred R counselor Roosevelt High Sch h528 Kennedy Blvd
Thomas Joseph techr Kennedy High Sch r2848 Santa Av Apt 2
Thompsen Yvonne studt r1012 University Av Apt 812
Tifton Albert & Marsha; capt fire dept r2814 Ambassador Dr Apt 417
Tijoriwalli Cathy owner Cathy's Sandwiches r1320 S Embree Cir
Tiller Julius & Ida; polof h539 Sheridan Blvd
Tilman Randall C & Marion; city health insptr h818 N 41st St
Tontenote Eldred L & Lisa; mech Ace AutoBody r2634 6th St Apt 17
Totmann Gloria dent asst h1818 4th St
Totmann Marvin & Gloria; secy guard Brinks h1818 4th St
Tribitt Jane mgr Colonial Apts r1040 Colonial Way Apt 101
Tuschak Joseph & Arlene; mastr electn & city colm h2094 Byron Av
Ungarient James R & Margaret; atty The Law Office h7314 Byron Av
Ungarient Margaret atty The Law Office h7314 Byron Av
Uosis Michael & Bobbie; retd h4772 E Harrison Av
Vacante Umberto & Mary; tech writer Martin Marietta h3202 Joyce St
Vacanti Carlos & Carol; polof h4910 Magee Ct
Valderama Lynn dir secy J C Penny h1020 Lincoln Av

Van Atti Joseph & Trina; city ff h960 Stratmore Dr
Van Den Shuck Margaret pub serv rep Allstate Ins h7663 Robinhood Dr
VanPelt Audrey W min First United Methodist Ch h420 N Wilkes Rd
VanPelt James & Audrey; serv mgr Lane Toyota h420 N Wilkes Rd
Veit Helen Lynn min First Covenant Ch h184 Nelson Av
Verdugo Maureen pcpl Kennedy High Sch r816 Westwinds Dr Apt 482
Verkler LeeAnn univ prof r800 Crestbrook Loop Apt 10A
Vermell Cathy S dr Yellow Cab r1010 Vermont Av
Vorholt Andrew A owner/mgr Hallmark Cards h10 E Lake Rd
Wagnor Timothy Sr & Kristine; owner/mgr Tim's Coffee Shop r418 N Wilkes Rd
Ward Jon H & Frances; sgt/recruiter USA r3113 DeLaney Av
Ward Lonnie D mtce wkr Colonial Apts r2814 Ambassador Dr Apt 22
Warniky Clara mgr Hertz Car Rentals h418 N Wilkes Rd
Warniky Wayne & Clara; polof h418 N Wilkes Rd
Washington Bruce R atty David Casio & Associates r1104 Esplada Av Apt 19
Waundry James R & Lisa; mgr 2-Hour Clns h5310 Stratmore Dr
Weber Nancy techr Washington Ele Sch h44 E Princeton St
Wehr Helen asst cty atty h1298 Vermont Av
Wei Albert sgt police dept h964 Jody Way
Weinstein Jeanette techr Colonial High Sch h6139 Eastland Dr
Weiskoph Herman asst min John Calvin Presbyterian Ch h4817 Twin Lakes Blvd
Wentilla Reid R & Lorrie; pres Keele-Baldwin Corp h640 Clayton Av
West Billy L asst min John Calvin Presbyterian Ch h452 Central Blvd
Whidden Bonnie sec cty fair h2913 Oak La
White Katherine mgr Blackhawk Hotel h4218 Bell Av
Whitlock Randall vp Wagnor Development Corp h504 Sutter Loop
Wiess Robert A wkr Belks Moving & Storage r2032 Turf Way Apt 338
Wilke James & Laura; sgt police dept h2420 Highland Av
Wilke Laura sheriff's dep h2420 Highland Av
Willging Jurgen & Judy; owner/mgr Choice Video Rentals h2204 S 8th St
Willging Marty & Tessie; dir YMCA h1808 Gadsden Blvd
Williams Jon R tech K107 Radio r814 Harding Av
Williams Patricia J retd h1338 Biarritz Dr
Williams Phyllis nurse Lovell Psychiatric Assn r1220 Jasper Av Apt 56
Wong Phyllis & Steven I; mgr Sears h441 S 28th St
Woods Amy dir State Federation of Independent Businesses h640 Sherwood Dr
Wymann Paul & Barbara; mech Lane Toyota h2020 Lorry La
Yamer Frank studt r118 Hillside Dr Apt 1020
Yapenco Thomas & Nancy; writer h4941 Pine St
Younge Rachel techr Kennedy High Sch r3361 Bolling Dr
Zarrinfair Lois retd r411 Wisconsin Av
Zerwinn Sarah h2021 Dyan Way
Zito Allen and Linda; archt Zito Associates h818 Jamestown Dr
Zito Linda W dir of com and marketing Blood Bank h818 Jamestown Dr
Zito Robert & Nancy; pharm K Mart h328 Winford Cir
Zozulla Wesley polof h5219 Ranch Rd
Zumbaddo Carlos general mgr cty fair h1902 White Av

THE ASSOCIATED PRESS STYLEBOOK

The following pages summarize the most commonly used rules in The Associated Press Stylebook and Libel Manual. These selected rules have been reprinted with the permission of The Associated Press. United Press International, the nation's second major news agency, uses a similar stylebook, and most newspapers in the United States—both dailies and weeklies—follow the rules they recommend.

Complete copies of The Associated Press Stylebook and Libel Manual can be ordered from most bookstores.

SECTION 1: ABBREVIATIONS

1.1 COMPANY. Abbreviate and capitalize *company, corporation, incorporated, limited* and *brothers* when used after the name of a corporate entity. Do not capitalize or abbreviate when used by themselves: *He works for the company.*

1.2 DEGREES. Generally avoid abbreviations for academic degrees. Use instead a phrase such as: *John Jones, who has a doctorate in psychology.* Use an apostrophe in *bachelor's degree, a master's,* etc. Use abbreviations as *B.A., M.A., LL.D.* and *Ph.D.* only when the need to identify many individuals by degree on first reference would make the preferred form cumbersome.

1.3 DO NOT ABBREVIATE: *assistant, association, attorney, building, district, government, president, professor, superintendent* or the days of the week, or use the ampersand (&) in place of *and* in news stories.

1.4 INITIALS. Use the initials of organizations and government agencies that are widely recognized: *NATO, PTA, CIA, FBI* (no periods). The first time you mention other organizations, use their full names. On second reference, use their abbreviations or acronyms only if they would be clear or familiar to most readers.

1.5 JUNIOR/SENIOR. Abbreviate and capitalize *junior* and *senior* after an individual's name: *John Jones Jr.* (no comma).

1.6 MPH/MPG. The abbreviation *mph* (no periods) is acceptable in all references for miles per hour. The abbreviation *mpg* (miles per gallon) is acceptable only on second reference.

1.7 STATES. Do not use postal abbreviations for states. Eight states are never abbreviated: *Alaska, Hawaii, Idaho, Iowa, Maine, Ohio, Texas* and *Utah.* Abbreviations for other states include: *Ala., Ariz., Ark., Calif., Colo., Conn., Del., Fla., Ga., Ill., Ind., Kan., Ky., La., Md., Mass., Mich., Minn., Miss., Mo., Mont., Neb., Nev., N.H., N.J., N.M., N.Y., N.C., N.D., Okla., Ore., Pa., R.I., S.C., S.D., Tenn., Vt., Va., Wash., W. Va., Wis.* and *Wyo.*

1.8 TITLES. Abbreviate the following titles when used before a full name outside direct quotations: *Dr., Lt. Gov., Mr., Mrs., Ms., Sen., the Rev.*, and military titles such as: *Pfc., Cpl., Sgt., 1st Lt., Capt., Maj., Lt. Col., Col., Gen., Cmdr.* and *Adm.* Spell out all except *Dr., Mr., Mrs.* and *Ms.* when used before a name in direct quotations.

1.9 U.N./U.S. Spell out *United Nations* and *United States* when used as nouns. Use *U.N.* and *U.S.* (no space between initials) only as adjectives.

SECTION 2: ADDRESSES

2.1 ADDRESSES. Always use figures for an address number: *9 Morningside Circle.*

2.2 DIRECTIONS. Abbreviate compass points used to indicate directional ends of a street or quadrants of a city in a numbered address: *562 W. 43rd St., 600 K St. N.W.* Do not abbreviate if the number is omitted: *East 42nd Street.*

2.3 STREETS. Spell out and capitalize *First* through *Ninth* when used as street names; use figures with two letters for *10th* and above: *7 Fifth Ave., 100 21st St.*

Use the abbreviations *Ave., Blvd.* and *St.* only with a numbered address: *1600 Pennsylvania Ave.* Spell them out and capitalize when part of a formal street name without a number: *Pennsylvania Avenue.* All similar words (*alley, drive, road, terrace,* etc.) are always spelled out.

SECTION 3: CAPITALIZATION

In general, avoid unnecessary capitals. Use a capital letter only if you can justify it by one of the principles listed here.

3.1 ACADEMIC DEPARTMENTS. When mentioning an academic department, use lowercase except for words that are proper nouns or adjectives: *the department of history, the department of English, the English department.*

3.2 AWARDS/EVENTS/HOLIDAYS/WARS. Capitalize awards (*Medal of Honor, Nobel Prize*), historic events and periods (*the Great Depression, Prohibition*), holidays (*Christmas Eve, Mother's Day*) and wars (*the Civil War, World War II*).

3.3 BIBLE/GOD. Use *Bible* (no quotation marks) and *God* (but lowercase pronouns referring to the deity: *he, his, thee*).

3.4 BRAND NAMES. Capitalize brand names: *Buick, Ford, Mustang.* Lowercase generic terms: *a Volkswagen van.* But use brand names only if they are essential to a story.

3.5 BUILDINGS/ROOMS. Capitalize the proper names of buildings, including the word *building* if it is an integral part of the proper name: *the Empire State Building.* Also capitalize the names of specially designated rooms: *Blue Room, Oval Office.* Use figures and capitalize *room* when used with a figure: *Room 2, Room 211.*

3.6 CAPITOL. Capitalize *U.S. Capitol* and *the Capitol* when referring to the building in Washington, D.C., or to state capitols.

3.7 CONGRESS. Capitalize *U.S. Congress* and *Congress* when referring to the U.S. Senate and House of Representatives. Lowercase when used as a synonym for convention. Lowercase *congressional* unless it is part of a proper name.

3.8 CONSTITUTION. Capitalize references to the *U.S. Constitution*, with or without the *U.S.* modifier. Lowercase *constitutional* in all uses.

Also capitalize *Bill of Rights, First Amendment* (and all other amendments to the Constitution).

3.9 DIRECTIONS/REGIONS. In general, lowercase *north, south, northeast* when they indicate a compass direction; capitalize when they designate geographical regions: *the Atlantic Coast states, Deep South, Sun Belt, Midwest. He drove west. The cold front is moving east. The North was victorious. She has a Southern accent.*

3.10 DO NOT CAPITALIZE: *administration; first lady; first family; government; presidential; presidency; priest;* seasons of the year: *winter, spring, summer, fall;* and years in school: *freshman, sophomore, junior, senior.*

Also lowercase the common noun elements of all names in plural uses: *the Democratic and Republican parties, Main and State streets, lakes Erie and Ontario.*

3.11 EARTH. Generally lowercase *earth*; capitalize when used as the proper name of the planet.

3.12 GOVERNMENT. Capitalize *city, county, state* and *federal* when part of a formal name: *Dade County, the Federal Trade Commission.* Retain capitalization for the name of a specific body when the proper noun is not needed: *the County Commission.* Generally lowercase elsewhere.

Also capitalize *city council, city hall, courthouse, legislature, assembly,* etc., when part of a proper name: *the Boston City Council.* Retain capitalization if the reference is to a specific city council, city hall, etc., but the context does not require the specific name: *The City Council met last night.*

3.13 HIGHWAYS. Use these forms, as appropriate in the context, for highways identified by number: *U.S. Highway 1, U.S. Route 1, Route 1, Illinois 34, Illinois Route 34, State Route 34, Route 34, Interstate Highway 495, Interstate 495.* On second reference only for Interstate: *I-495.* When a letter is appended to a number, capitalize it but do not use a hyphen: *Route 1A.*

3.14 MILITARY. Capitalize names of the U.S. armed forces: *the U.S. Army, the Navy, Marine regulations.* Use lowercase for the forces of other nations.

3.15 NATIONALITIES/RACE. Capitalize the proper names of nationalities, races, tribes, etc.: *Arab, Caucasian, Eskimo.* However, lowercase *black, white, mulatto.* Do *not* use the word ''colored.'' In the United States, the word is considered derogatory.

3.16 PLURALS. To form the plural of a number, add *s* (no apostrophe). To form the plural of a single letter, add *'s.* To form the plural of multiple letters, add only *s: 1920s, Mind your p's and q's. She knows her ABCs.*

3.17 POLITICAL PARTIES. Capitalize both the name of a political party and the word *party*: the *Democratic Party*. Also capitalize *Communist, Conservative, Republican, Socialist*, etc., when they refer to a specific party or to individuals who are members of it. Lowercase when they refer to a political philosophy. After a name, use this short form, set off by commas: *D-Minn, R-Ore*.

3.18 PROPER NOUNS. Capitalize proper nouns that constitute the unique identification for a specific person, place or thing. Lowercase (do not capitalize) common nouns when they stand alone in subsequent references: *the party, the river, the street*.

3.19 SATAN. Capitalize *Satan* but lowercase *devil* and *satanic*.

3.20 TITLES. Capitalize formal titles, including academic titles, when used immediately before a name: *president, chairman, professor*. Lowercase formal titles used after a name, alone or in constructions that set them off from a name by commas. Use lowercase at all times for terms that are job descriptions rather than formal titles: *astronaut John Glenn, movie star John Wayne, peanut farmer Jimmy Carter*.

SECTION 4: NUMERALS

For general purposes, spell out whole numbers below 10, use figures for 10 and above. Exceptions: figures are used for all ages, betting odds, dates, dimensions, percentages, speeds and times. Also, spell out a number at the beginning of a sentence, except for a calendar year.

4.1 AGES. Use figures for all ages. Hyphenate ages expressed as adjectives before a noun or as substitutes for a noun: *a 5-year-old boy*, but *the boy is 5 years old. The boy, 7, has a sister, 10. The woman is in her 30s* (no apostrophe).

4.2 CENTS. Spell out the word *cents* and lowercase, using numerals for amounts less than a dollar: *5 cents, 12 cents*. Use the *$* sign and decimal system for larger amounts: *$1.01*.

4.3 DECADES/CENTURY. Use Arabic figures to indicate decades of history. Use an apostrophe to indicate numbers that are left out; show the plural by adding the letter *s*: *the 1890s, the '90s, the Gay '90s, the mid-1930s*. Lowercase *century* and spell out numbers less than 10: *the first century, the 20th century*.

4.4 DOLLARS. Lowercase *dollars*. Use figures and the *$* sign in all except casual references or amounts without a figure: *The book cost $4. Dollars are flowing overseas*. For amounts of more than $1 million, use the *$* and numerals up to two decimal places: *He is worth $4.35 million. He proposed a $300 million budget*.

4.5 ELECTION RETURNS. For election returns, use the word *to* (not a hyphen) in separating different totals listed together: *Jimmy Carter defeated Gerald Ford 40,287,292 to 39,145,157*.

4.6 FRACTIONS. Spell out amounts less than *1*, using hyphens between the words: *two-thirds, four-fifths, seven-sixteenths*. For precise amounts larger than 1, convert to decimals whenever practical.

4.7 MEASUREMENTS. Use figures and spell out *inches, feet, yards*, etc. Hyphenate adjectival forms before nouns: *He is 5 feet 6 inches tall, the 5-foot-6-inch man. The rug is 9 feet by 12 feet, the 9-by-12 rug*.

4.8 MILLION/BILLION. Do not go beyond two decimals: *7.51 million people, $2.56 billion.* Decimals are preferred where practical: *1.5 million.* Not: *1½ million.*

Do not drop the word *million* or *billion* in the first figure of a range: *He is worth from $2 million to $4 million:* Not *$2 to $4 million,* unless you really mean *$2.*

4.9 NUMBER. Use *No.* as the abbreviation for *number* in conjunction with a figure to indicate position or rank: *No. 1 man, No. 3 choice.*

4.10 ODDS. Use figures and a hyphen for betting odds: *The odds were 5-4, he won despite 3-2 odds against him.*

4.11 PERCENTAGES. Use figures: *1 percent, 2.56 percent.* For amounts less than 1 percent, precede the decimal point with a zero: *The cost of living rose 0.6 percent.* The word "percent" should be spelled out; never use the symbol "%."

4.12 RATIOS. Use figures and a hyphen for ratios: *The ratio was 2-to-1, a ratio of 2-to-1, 2-1 ratio.*

4.13 SCORES. Use figures exclusively for scores, placing a hyphen between the totals of the winning and losing teams: *The Reds defeated the Red Sox 4-1, the Giants scored a 12-6 victory over the Cardinals, the golfer had a 5 on the last hole but finished with a 2-under-par score.*

4.14 TEMPERATURES. Use figures for all temperatures except *zero.* Use a word, not a minus sign, to indicate temperatures below zero.

SECTION 5: PUNCTUATION

5.1 COMMA/AGE. An individual's age is set off by commas: *Phil Taylor, 11, is here.*

5.2 COMMA/CITY-STATE. Place a comma between the city and the state name, and another comma after the state name, unless the state name ends a sentence: *He was traveling from Nashville, Tenn., to Albuquerque, N.M.*

5.3 COMMA/HOMETOWN. Use a comma to set off an individual's hometown when it is placed in apposition to a name: *Mary Richards, Minneapolis, and Maude Findlay, Tuckahoe, N.Y., were there.* However, the use of the word *of* without a comma between the individual's name and the city name is generally preferable: *Mary Richards of Minneapolis and Maude Findlay of Tuckahoe, N.Y., were there.*

5.4 COMMA/QUOTATION. Use a comma to introduce a complete, one-sentence quotation within a paragraph: *Wallace said, "She spent six months in Argentina."* Do not use a comma at the start of an indirect or partial quotation. Always place commas and periods inside quotation marks.

5.6 COMMA/SERIES. Use commas to separate elements in a series, but do not put a comma before the conjunction in a simple series: *The flag is red, white and blue. He would nominate Tom, Dick or Harry.*

5.7 COLON. The most frequent use of a colon is at the end of a sentence to introduce lists, tabulations, texts, etc: *There were three considerations: expense, time and feasibility.*

Use a colon to introduce direct quotations longer than one sentence within a paragraph and to end all paragraphs that introduce a paragraph of quoted material.

5.8 POSSESSIVES. Appendix C contains the rules for forming possessives.

5.9 SEMICOLON. Use a semicolon to separate elements of a series when individual segments contain material that also must be set off by commas: *He leaves a son, John Smith of Chicago; three daughters, Jane Smith of Wichita, Kan., Mary Smith of Denver, and Susan, wife of William Kingsbury of Boston; and a sister, Martha, wife of Robert Warren of Omaha, Neb.* Note that the semicolon is used before the final *and* in such a series.

SECTION 6: PREFERRED SPELLINGS

Adviser
Afterward (Not *afterwards*)
All right (Never *alright*)
Ax (Not *axe*)
Baby-sit, baby-sitting, baby sitter
Backward (Not *backwards*)
Damage (For destruction; *damages* for a court award)
Employee (Not *employe*)
Forward (Not *forwards*)
Goodbye
Gray (Not *grey*)
Kidnapping
Likable (Not *likeable*)
Percent (One word, spelled out)
Teen, teen-ager, teen-age. Do not use *teen-aged*.
Vice president (No hyphen)
Whiskey

SECTION 7: TIME

Use figures except for *noon* and *midnight*. Do not put a *12* in front of them. Use a colon to separate hours from minutes: *11:15 a.m., 1:45 p.m., 3:30 p.m.* Avoid such redundancies as *10 a.m. this morning or 10 p.m. Monday night.* Use *10 a.m. today* or *10 p.m. Monday.* The hour is placed before the day: *a.m.* and *p.m.* are lowercase, with periods.

7.1 DAYS. Use the words *today, this morning, tonight,* etc. in direct quotes, in stories intended for publication in afternoon newspapers on the day in question, and in phrases that do not refer to a specific day: *Customs today are different from those of a century ago.* Use the day of the week in stories intended for publication in morning newspapers and in stories filed for use in either publishing cycle. Use *yesterday* and *tomorrow* only in direct quotations and in phrases that do not refer to a specific day.

7.2 DAYS/DATES. Use *Monday, Tuesday,* etc. for days of the week within seven days before or after the current date. Use the month and a figure for dates beyond this range. Avoid such redundancies as *last Tuesday* or *next Tuesday.*

7.3 MONTHS. Capitalize the names of the months in all uses. When a month is used with a specific date, abbreviate only: *Jan., Feb., Aug., Sept., Oct., Nov.* and *Dec.* Spell out when using alone, or with a year alone. When a phrase lists only a month and a year, do not separate the year with commas. When a phrase refers to a month, day and year, set off the year with commas: *January 1972 was a cold month. Jan. 2 was the coldest day of the month. His birthday is May 15. Feb. 14, 1976, was the target date*. Do not use *st., nd., rd.* or *th* after the date.

SECTION 8: TITLES

Formal titles that appear directly before a name are capitalized and abbreviated. After a name or alone, lowercase and spell out: *The president issued a statement. The pope gave his blessing*. Do not repeat a title the second time you use a person's name: *Sheriff Sam Smith, Smith* (not *Sheriff Smith*).

8.1 BOY/GIRL. The terms *boy* and *girl* are applicable until the age of 18. Use *man, woman, young man* or *young woman* afterward.

8.2 COMPOSITIONS. Capitalize the principal words in titles of books, movies, operas, plays, poems, songs, television programs, lectures, speeches and works of art. Put quotation marks around the names of all such works. Do not underline the titles of any of these works.

8.3 CONGRESSMAN. Use *congressman* and *congresswoman* only in references to members of the U.S. House of Representatives.

8.4 COURTESY TITLES. In general, do not use the courtesy titles *Miss, Mr., Mrs.* or *Ms.* on first reference. Instead, use the first and last names and middle initial of the person.

For a married woman, the preferred form on first reference is to identify her by her own first name and her husband's last name: *Susan Smith*. Use *Mrs.* on the first reference only if a woman requests that her husband's first name be used or if her own first name cannot be determined: *Mrs. John Smith*.

On the second reference, use *Miss, Mrs.* or *Ms.* before the last name of a woman, depending on her preference.

If a woman is divorced or widowed, use *Mrs.* or no title, if she prefers it. But, if a woman returns to the use of her maiden name, use *Miss, Ms.* or no title if she prefers it.

On the second reference, use only the last name of a man. Use *Mr.* only when it is combined with *Mrs.: Mr. and Mrs. John Smith*.

8.5 INITIALS. In general, use middle initials. Particular care should be taken to include middle initials in stories where they help identify a specific individual. Examples include casualty lists and stories naming the accused in a crime.

Use periods and no space when an individual uses initials instead of a first name: *H.L. Mencken*. Do not give a name with a single initital (*J. Jones*) unless it is the individual's preference or the first name cannot be learned.

8.6 MAGAZINES. Capitalize magazine titles but do not place in quotes. Lowercase *magazine* if it is not part of the publication's formal title: *Newsweek magazine*.

8.7 NEWSPAPERS. Capitalize *the* in a newspaper's name if that is the way the publication prefers to be known. If the location is needed but is not part of the official name, use parentheses: *The Huntsville (Ala.) Times*. Do not underline or add quote marks.

8.8 REFERENCE MATERIALS. Capitalize, but do not use quotation marks around, books that are primarily catalogs of reference materials. These rules also apply to almanacs, directories, dictionaries, handbooks and encyclopedias.

8.9 REVEREND. When using the title *Rev.* before a name, precede it with the word *the*.

SECTION 9: WORDS

9.1 INJURIES. Injuries are *suffered* or *sustained,* not *received.*

9.2 INNOCENT/NOT GUILTY. Use *innocent* rather than *not guilty* in describing a defendant's plea or a jury's verdict to guard against the word *not* being dropped inadvertently.

9.3 MASS. It is *celebrated,* not *said.* Always capitalize when referring to the ceremony, but lowercase any preceding adjectives: *high Mass, low Mass, requiem Mass.*

9.4 NOUNS/VERBS. Nouns that denote a unit take singular verbs and pronouns: *class, committee, family, group, herd, jury, team. The committee is meeting to set its agenda. The jury reached its verdict.* When used in the sense of two persons, the word *couple* takes plural verbs and pronouns: *The couple were married Saturday.*

9.5 PERSON/PEOPLE. Use *person* when speaking of an individual. The word *people* is preferred in all plural uses. For example: *Some rich people pay few taxes. There were 17 people in the room.*

9.6 RAISED/REARED. Only humans may be *reared.* Any living thing, including humans, may be *raised.*

9.7 REALTOR. The term *real estate agent* is preferred. Use *Realtor* only if the individual is a member of the National Association of Realtors.

9.8 WORDS TO AVOID. Do not use the following words in news stories: *kids, irregardless, ladies* (as a synonym for *women*), *cop* (except in quoted matter) or *entitled* (when you mean *titled*).

RULES FOR FORMING POSSESSIVES

1. Always begin by writing the correct form of the word that you want to use. This rule applies to both the singular and to the plural form of the word.

2. If the word, regardless of whether it is singular or plural, does not already end in the letter "s," add an apostrophe and "s" to form the possessive. For example:

SINGULAR	man	child	person
SINGULAR POSSESSIVE	man's	child's	person's
PLURAL	men	children	people
PLURAL POSSESSIVE	men's	children's	people's

3. If the word already ends in the letter "s," add only an apostrophe to form the possessive. Note that this rule also applies to proper nouns, such as a person's name.

SINGULAR	fraternity	lady	Ralph	Smith
SINGULAR POSSESSIVE	fraternity's	lady's	Ralph's	Smith's
PLURAL	fraternities	ladies	Ralphs*	Smiths**
PLURAL POSSESSIVE	fraternities'	ladies'	Ralphs'	Smiths'

  * Refers to two different people whose first name is Ralph.

**Refers to two different people whose last name is Smith.

4. If an object is hyphenated, add an apostrophe and the letter "s" to the last word only.

SINGULAR	father-in-law	He is my father-in-law.
SINGULAR POSSESSIVE	father-in-law's	It is my father-in-law's car.
PLURAL	fathers-in-law	They are your fathers-in-law.
PLURAL POSSESSIVE	fathers-in-law's	They are your fathers-in-law's cars.

5. If an object is owned by two or more people, add an apostrophe and the letter "s" to the latter name only.

Mary and Fred's entry won a prize.

My mother and father's home was destroyed by fire.

6. If the objects are not jointly owned—if you are describing separate objects owned or possessed by different people—add an apostrophe and the letter "s" to both nouns.

   Mary's and Fred's entries won a prize.

   My mother's and my father's luggage was lost.

7. Indefinite pronouns such as "everyone" follow the same rules. However, personal pronouns have special forms that never use an apostrophe. The personal pronouns include such words as: "his," "mine," "ours," "theirs," "whose" and "yours."

8. Generally avoid using an apostrophe and the letter "s" for inanimate objects. Instead, try to rewrite the passage, either dropping the apostrophe and the letter "s" or converting the passage to an "of" phrase.

   WRONG: the table's leg
   RIGHT: the table leg   OR: the leg of the table

   WRONG: the book's chapter
   RIGHT: the book chapter   OR: the chapter of the book

9. When mentioning the name of an organization, group or geographical location, always use the common or preferred and official spelling. Some of the names use the possessive case but others, such as Pikes Peak, do not.

10. The word 'it's," spelled with an apostrophe, is a contraction of "it is." The possessive form, "its," does *not* contain an apostrophe.

ANSWER KEYS FOR EXERCISES

CHAPTER 1: THE BASICS: FORMAT, SPELLING AND AP STYLE

Exercise 9

1. Robert j. Curey junior, the Mayor of Eugene, Oregon, sa id the media is to bias d)

2. Sandra Oliver, age six, is four feet Tall, weighs 81 pds, and lives on Elm boulevard.

3. Oliver Brooks, who has a Ph.d., wrote a book entitled Urban Terrorists. (CAUTION: See the city directory. Brookes' name was misspelled.)

4. After serving in the army he obtained a B.A. and became a citizen of the U.S.

5. The girl, an 18 year old blond, sipped a coke, and read Time Magazine

6. The retired col. fought with the united states marines in vietnam during the 1960's.

7. The united states congress will meet at 10:00 A.M. tues. January 4th in the United States capital bludg.

8. Mr. Richard Harris, an Editor AT Newsweek Magazine, will fly north on Mon. Harris, was born in oct., 1942, and began work as a reporter fr the Chicago Tribune.

9. Sen. Andrews, a democrat from New Hampsire, said he will spend about fifty percent of his campaign funds—nearly $18,000,000—on radio and television advertizing.

10. Prof. Myron Carey, of 614 North Highland Dr. is Chairman of THE Dept. of Mathematics and has an office in Rm. 407 of the humanities bldg. (See the city directory. Carey's address was mistaken.)

11. the temperature is zero. She is white; he is, Vietnamese. She earns $278.00 a week and spends fourty percent of her ingincome on food.

12. Prange Incorporated of Columbia, South carolina manufacsre widgets at a cost of fourty seven cents and sells th hem for two dollars. Normaly, about two% are defective.

13. Ruth, who was ~~borg~~born durin~~gg~~ the 1960s will be
    a Sophmore this Fall and wants to join the republican party.

14. (8,000) ~~persons~~ people were killed when a severe hurrican struck south florida during the
    eighteenth century.

15. At ~~10:00 A.M.~~ This morning, the Vice President said, "The Federal (Govt.) is far
    too wasteful."

16. A presidential aide said it's safe to assume that the criteria are so vague that
    neither the republican nor the democratic parties will object to their content.

17. The source said (Eleven) College Students—five ~~boys~~ men and six ~~girls~~ women—are likely to
    attend the city council meeting.

18. (14) members of a Black Congressional delega-tion visited the President in the
    Oval Office to day and demanded that, as his ~~Number One~~ No. 1 Priority, HE solve
    the unemployment problem.

19. ~~Mr.~~ Randolph R. Wilcox (junior) of Columbus, Ohio, a former presidential aide,
    will speak at the university of (N) Carolina at 7:30 P.M. ~~Friday~~ (November) 6.

20. The senator, an alumnus of Harvard, complained that he cannot afford to live in
    the nations capital.

21. He warned that, by the 2020s, the Federal Government will have to transfer
    $14,800,000,000 billion ~~dollars~~ from general tax revenues to save the social security
    system.

22. the retired army sargeant, ~~age~~ 43, lives in Sacramento (california) with his wife and
    three children James, Randolph and Tricia.

23. Timothy Wagnor, ~~age eight,~~ of 418 (Notrh) Wilkes Road ATE some french fries and
    sipped a Coke.

24. A jury awarded ~~Mrs.~~ Sarah Petersen $1,316,400 million after a car was struck and ~~totally~~
    destroyed by a van driven by a drunken driver, killing her husband. (CAUTION:
    See the city directory. Sara Peterson's names were misspelled.)

CHAPTER 1: THE BASICS: FORMAT, SPELLING AND AP STYLE

Exercise 10

1. The consultant was given $125,000 on Feb~~ruary~~ 7th, 1980 in aust in texas.

2. The temperature fell to minus 14 after a blizzard struck Denver (colorado) in december
   1982.

3. Tom Becker, a black born in the south during the 1930s was elected Mayor of the
   City.

4. a senior who will graduate next Spring said "history and english are my favorite subjects"

5. The girls elbow was injured when she fell twelve feat at lincoln park at Noon yesterdy.

6. Susan Majorce, age seven, is five ft. tall and weighs eight-seven lbs.

7. the caddccident Occurred on Interstate 80, about twleve miles West of Reno, Nevada.

8. They moved from 438 North Sunset Drive to 318 Jamestown boulevard last Thurs.

9. Mr. Carl r. zastrow junior, of Columbus, Ohio, a former Presidential aide, will speak at the university Thursday at 7:00 PM. on the 1st of next month.

10. Atty Martha Dillan formerly liglived at 4062 South Eastland DRIVE and works for the Westinghouse corporation (CAUTION: See the city directory. Dillan's name was misspelled.)

11. the companys president said his firm will provide more than $100,000,000 dollars to develokpe an electric car able to travel sixty miles per hour.

12. The youth a high school sophomore, said the temperature in Idaho often falls below 0 during the winter.

13. 50 women who met yesterday morning at 11 am said there children are entitled to use the new park on Vallrath Avenue.

14. The 5 member city council wantkks to canvass the towns voters to determine whether a large group favors the establishment of a civic orchestra.

15. Dist Atty Ramon Hernandez, who was born in Mont during the 1940s graduated from the Univarsity of Nebraska.

16. Mrs. Marie Hyde, Asst Supt for public education for the city, said the 16 year old girls were raised in athens georgia.

17. The lady woman earned her beachelors degree from te university of Kentucky and her masters degree from Indiana University during the 1960s.

18. The suspects were arrested at 1602 North Highland Avenue, 64 East Wilshire Drive and 3492 3rd Street.

19. Chris Repanski, of pocatello idaho will enrollel in the college as a sophmore next fall and hopes to become an attorney.

20. The man, whose who is in his mid 30s, joined the FBI, after recieving a Ph.D. doctorate in computer science.

21. Afterwards, the Vice President sayd he will need $25 to $30 million dollars to win the Presidential Election next Fall.

22. Reverand Andrew Cisneros estimated that 1/3 of his parishioners contribute at least five per cent of their annual income to the church's general revenue fund. (CAUTION: See the city directory. Cisneroes' name was misspelled.)

23. The ~~cops~~ police arrested four ~~kids dirvng~~ youths driving North on Michigan Ave. minutes after the restaurant was robed of $1640.83 ~~last~~ Friday.

24. The Catholic Priest, ~~that~~ who was elected to the city council by a vote of 8,437 to 8,197, said he had expected to lose the ~~elb~~ election.

25. the bill of rights was added to the united states constitution during the eighteenth century.

26. Since the 1940s, he has lived in five States Ws., Ken., Mass., N.Y., & Ca.

CHAPTER 2: NEWSWRITING STYLE

Quiz

1. She was in a ~~quick~~ hurry and warned that~~, in the future,~~ she will seek ~~out~~ textbooks that are sexist and demand that they be ~~totally~~ banned.

2. ~~As it now stands,~~ three ~~separate~~ members of the committee said they will try to prevent the city from closing ~~down~~ the park during the winter ~~months~~.

3. His convertible was ~~totally~~ destroyed and, ~~in order~~ to obtain the money necessary to buy a new car, he ~~now~~ plans to ask a ~~personal~~ friend for a loan ~~to help him along~~.

4. After police found the ~~lifeless~~ body, the ~~medical~~ doctor conducted an autopsy ~~to determine the cause of death~~ and concluded that the youth had been strangled ~~to death~~.

5. ~~In the past,~~ he often met ~~up with~~ the students at the computer lab and, because of their ~~future~~ potential, invited them to ~~attend~~ the convention.

6. Based upon her ~~previous~~ experience as an architect, she warned the committee members that constructing the ~~new~~ hospital ~~facility~~ will be ~~pretty~~ expensive and suggested that they ~~step in and~~ seek ~~out~~ more donors.

7. The two men were hunting in a ~~wooded~~ forest ~~a total of~~ 12 miles ~~away~~ from the nearest hospital ~~in the region~~ when both suffered severe ~~bodily~~ injuries.

8. Based upon several studies ~~conducted in the past~~, he ~~firmly~~ believes that, when ~~first~~ started next year, the two programs should be ~~very~~ selective, similar ~~in nature~~ and conducted only in the morning ~~hours~~.

CHAPTER 2: NEWSWRITING STYLE

Exercise 7

NOTE: Several of the sentences in this exercise can be rewritten many different ways. Thus, the sentences shown here are suggested or model answers—not the only possible answers. You can divide the longer, more complicated sentences into several shorter, simpler sentences.

SECTION I

1. The 15th annual Pre-Law Day is scheduled for Nov. 3 at the Student Center.
2. The woman told the crowd that she favors abortions. (Are the woman's youth and beauty relevant to the story? In the same circumstances, would you mention

a man's youth and beauty? If not, delete both comments. You may want to discuss this problem with your instructor and classmates.)

3. The school has scheduled a banquet to celebrate its 10th anniversay.

SECTION II

1. facts	6. gifts	11. here
2. close	7. to	12. tracked
3. bodies	8. innovation	13. unique
4. dropped	9. history	14. winter
5. began	10. revert	15. child

SECTION III

1. stopped	6. near
2. ignored	7. possesses
3. because	8. investigated
4. before	9. considered
5. soon	10. married

SECTION IV

1. The City Council voted to sue the builders.
2. A pickup truck collided with a car.
3. The sign may be installed later this month.
4. The police found only an empty box, not a bomb.
5. Police found that the assailants had kicked him in the head and neck.

SECTION V

1. He lost his right eye.
2. The debt was smaller then.
3. He called the president inconsistent and unrealistic.
4. The politician thanked his supporters.
5. The article will examine the problems of migrant workers.
6. Before reaching the age of 18, a child will see 20,000 acts of violence on television. (CAUTION: Avoid using the masculine "he" when you are referring to any or every child, both male and female.)
7. Participants in the workshop agree that the governor should decide how to spend the funds.
8. The conference revealed that Israelis dislike the agreement.
9. Lydia Hanson is an expert on criminal law. (Are the woman's parentage, age and marital status revelant to her expertise in criminal law? If not, delete them. Use her name, not just her father's; it is listed in the city directory. Also, why would a woman not look like an expert? You may want to discuss the sentence with your instructor and classmates.)
10. Co-workers planned a party for the day of the librarian's retirement and gave her a trip to Paris.

CHAPTER 3: WORDS

Exercise 8

(NOTE: Several of the sentences in this exercise can be rewritten many different ways. Thus, the sentences shown here are suggested or model answers—not the only possible answers. You can divide the longer, more complicated sentences into several shorter, simpler sentences.)

SECTION I

1. The club president said he plans to quit.
2. She said the student will not graduate soon.
3. The mayor said the city's financial situation is good. OR: The mayor praised the city's financial condition.
4. The bank vice president said she is missing $43,000.
5. The exercise trail is designed for adults who are serious about getting physically fit.

SECTION II

1. The governor wants to raise teachers' salaries. (NOTE: The word ''teachers' '' is a plural possessive.)
2. A boy, about 16, snatched the woman's purse.
3. Other people use the bike path as an exercise track.
4. Their lawsuit complains that the bottle contained an insect.
5. Church officials estimate that the chapel will cost $320,000.

SECTION III

1. His girlfriend, Saundra Mariston, 33, is a waitress at Freddy's Inn, 410 Lakemont Ave., and he was charged with shooting her in the throat. OR: He was charged with shooting his girlfriend, Saundra Mariston, in the throat. Mariston, 33, is a waitress at Freddy's Inn, 410 Lakemont Ave. (CAUTION: See the city directory. Mariston's name was misspelled.)
2. Her high school sweetheart, David Garner, works as a tennis instructor, and she married him in Greenville, N.C., on Jan. 3, 1975.
3. During a speech at the church Sunday evening, she begged her parents and other adults to donate money for the handicapped children's medical care. (CAUTION: Should reporters use the word ''crippled''? You may want to discuss this issue with your instructor and classmates.)
4. The good Samaritan was driving a Honda Civic, and witnesses described him as a white male, about 35 years old and 5 feet, 8 inches tall, with black hair, brown eyes and a bandage on his forehead. (NOTE: The word ''Samaritan'' should be capitalized.)
5. She said the students most likely to drop out of high school have failed two or more subjects, are often absent, have discipline problems, and show signs of low self-esteem, loneliness or stress. (CAUTION: When referring to any or every high school student, avoid using the male pronoun ''he.'' As one solution, you can use the plural ''students.'')

SECTION IV

1. He said it is a good book.
2. The city attorney said the plan is illegal.

3. The teacher is not clear. OR: The teacher cannot communicate effectively. OR: The teacher is hard to understand.
4. The council chair voted against the proposal. (CAUTION: Avoid the word "chairman"—a word that excludes women.)
5. The new program will provide medical services for the poor.
6. The youths did not intend to tell their parents how they obtained the money.
7. The report stated that people of all ages can enjoy water skiing.
8. Participants in the workshop agree that the nurses should receive a raise of 15 to 20 percent.

CHAPTER 3: WORDS

Exercise 9

1. He advised the city to adopt the ordinance.
2. The concept was too elusive to ensure success.
3. Its rules were altered, but the effects were minor.
4. The blond's fiancée said their new home was burglarized.
5. Whose statue was lying near your construction site?
6. Rather than dissenting, he agreed to study their advice.
7. The alumni, all men, said the dissent became too violent.
8. He censured the aides' behavior and ignored their dissent.
9. A prison trusty said it's two miles farther down the road.
10. The council was confident that its advice would ensure success. OR: The counsel was confident that the advice would ensure success. (CAUTION: Avoid assuming that everyone in a position of authority is a male. Thus, avoid using the masculine "his.")
11. The data were placed in envelopes and sent to all the news media.
12. The governor's two aides were given offices in the Capitol.
13. The man was hanged because he incited a riot that caused three deaths.
14. The portrait hung in his brother-in-law's office in the state Capitol.
15. Six of the school's alumni said their children's curriculum should be altered.
16. The principal is liable to lose his students' respect if he blocks their proposal.
17. The phenomena were unusual and affected their son-in-law's role in the family. OR: The phenomenon was unusual. . . .
18. The board is composed of seven alumni rather than seven students or teachers.
19. He cited three precedents and implied that the council's decision could be altered.
20. Thomas Alvarez, a tall blond from California, said the government's data are false.
21. The counselor was confident of victory but said his role in the matter was minor.
22. The church altar lay on its side, less than a dozen feet from the broken statues.
23. His insight, conscience and high principles ensured an excellent performance.
24. The school's principal threatened to censor the newspaper if it tries to publish an article advising students on how to obtain an abortion.
25. Merchants, fearing that they would lose thousands of dollars, complained that the government's criteria are too difficult to implement.

CHAPTER 8: QUOTATIONS AND ATTRIBUTION

Exercise 3

1. ''Our goal is peace,'' the president said. (Use a comma, not a period, before the attribution and place the punctuation mark inside the quotation mark. Transpose the attribution's wording so the subject appears before the verb. Avoid using ''claimed'' as a word of attribution.)

2. Benjamin Franklin said, ''Death takes no bribes.'' (Use a comma, not a colon, before the one-sentence quotation. Because it is a complete sentence, capitalize the first word of the quotation. Place the final period inside the quotation mark.)

3. She said her son calls her literary endeavors ''Mom's writing thing.'' (Condense the attribution and place the period inside the quotation mark. Normally, you do not need a comma before a partial quote.)

4. He is a scuba diver and pilot. He also enjoys skydiving and explains, ''I like challenge, something exciting.'' (Clearly attribute the direct quotation.)

5. President Eisenhower said the dangers of communism could continue for a long time. (The quotation can be paraphrased more clearly and simply. Place the explanation before the paraphrase. Note that ''communism'' is not capitalized.)

6. ''Freedom of the press is not merely freedom to publish the news,'' columnist Jack Anderson said during a speech last night. ''It is also freedom to gather the news. We cannot publish what we cannot gather.'' (Place the attribution near the beginning, not end, of a long quotation, and attribute a direct quotation only once. The attribution should be preceded by a comma, not a period. Quotation marks do not have to be placed around every sentence in a continuing quotation. Use the normal word order in the attribution.)

7. ''I think that America has become too athletic,'' Jesse Owens said. ''From Little League to the pro leagues, sports are no longer recreation. They are big business, and they're drudgery.'' (The attribution ''expressed the opinion that'' is wordy. Do not place quotation marks around every sentence in a continuing quotation. If it remains at the beginning of the quotation, the attribution should be followed by a colon. Attribute a continuing direct quotation only once.)

8. The man smiled and said: ''It's a great deal for me. I expect to double my money.'' (Because the quotation contains more than one sentence, ''said'' should be followed by a colon, not a comma. Do not use ''smiled'' as a word of attribution. Place quotation marks at the beginning and end of the direct quotation, not at the beginning and end of every sentence. Attribute a continuing direct quotation only once.)

9. The woman said she likes her job as a newspaper reporter and explained: ''I'm not paid much, but the work is important. And it's varied and exciting. Also, I like seeing my byline in the paper.'' (Reporters should stress their source's answer to a question, not the question. Attribute a continuing quote only once. Avoid ''grinned'' as a word of attribution. The attribution ''responded by saying'' is wordy.)

10. The librarian said the new building will cost about $4.6 million. (The attribution can be condensed, and, by paraphrasing, you can simplify the quotation. Also, virtually all the news published in newspapers is given to reporters. You do not have to mention that routine detail in every story.)

11. ''Thousands of the poor in the United States die every year of diseases we can easily cure,'' the professor said. ''It's a crime, but no one ever is punished for their deaths.'' (Use the normal word order: ''the profesor said.'' Place the attribution at the beginning or end of a sentence or at a natural break in a sentence. Attribute a direct quotation only once, and place quotation marks at

the beginning and end of the quotation, not at the beginning and end of every sentence.)

12. Thomas said students should never be spanked. He explained that, ''A young boy or girl who gets spanked in front of peers becomes embarrassed and the object of ridicule.'' (Clearly attribute the direct quotation. The city directory reveals that Thomas is a male. Thus, in this case, use of the masculine ''he'' is correct. Do not, however, assume that every public figure or other source is a male.)

13. The lawyer said: ''He ripped the life-sustaining respirator tubes from his throat three times in an effort to die. He is simply a man who rejects medical treatment regardless of the consequences. He wants to die and has a constitutional right to do so.'' (Because the quotation includes more than one sentence, use a colon, not a comma, after ''said.'' Attribute a direct quotation only once.)

14. Bobby Knight, the basketball coach at Indiana University, said: ''Everyone has the will to win. Few have the will to prepare. It is the preparation that counts.'' (Use a colon, not a comma, after ''said,'' because the quotation includes more than one sentence. Attribute a continuing quotation only once. Place quotation marks at the beginning and end of a direct quotation, not at the beginning and end of every sentence.)

15. She said the federal government must do more to help cities support and retrain the chronically unemployed. (Condense the attribution and avoid orphan quotes, quotation marks placed around one or two words.)

CHAPTER 8: QUOTATIONS AND ATTRIBUTION

Exercise 4

1. ''We can't wait any longer,'' he said. (Use a comma, not a period, before the attribution.)

2. He said, ''No one was seriously injured.'' (Use a comma when the attribution precedes a quotation that contains a single sentence. If the quotation is a complete sentence, capitalize the first word. Also, place the final period inside the quotation mark.)

3. Smith said he is not very happy. ''My wife is divorcing me,'' he explained. OR: Smith said he is ''not very happy.'' He explained, ''My wife is divorcing me.'' (Avoid combining a partial and complete quotation. You can either paraphrase the partial quotation or place the attribution between the two to separate them.)

4. He found the plane in a woods a half mile away and saw two people inside, both dead. (Avoid orphan quotes, quotation marks placed around one or two words.)

5. He said, ''At least two and perhaps three people will be charged with fraud.'' (Do not place the attribution within quotation marks. They are your words, not your source's. Also, place the attribution at the beginning or end of a quotation or at the first natural break in it. The attribution should not interrupt a thought.)

6. The girl smiled and said: ''Yes, I'll marry you. I've always loved you.'' (Avoid using ''smiled'' as a word of attribution. Use a colon, not a comma, before quotations that contain two or more sentences. Also, attribute a direct quotation only once.)

7. ''I know I shouldn't smoke,'' the girl said, coughing. ''But I can't help myself.'' (Avoid using ''coughed'' as a word of attribution. Also, you may combine the two sentences.)

8. She said she hates college. ''The teachers make us memorize,'' she explained. ''They don't teach us how to think.'' (Clearly attribute every direct quotation.

Place the final period inside the quotation mark. If you placed the attribution before the quotation, it should be followed by a colon, not a comma, because the quotation contains more than one sentence. Place quotation marks at the beginning and end of a direct quotation, not at the beginning and end of every sentence.)

9. Thompsen received the award as the school's outstanding journalism student and said, "It's the biggest surprise of my life." (Stress your sources' answers, not the questions they are asked. Also, capitalize the first word of a quotation that contains a complete sentence.)

10. The art professor said he will probably teach next year. "I like having a steady income," he explained, "and I haven't been able to earn enough from the sale of my paintings." (Stress your sources' answers, not the questions they are asked. Place the attribution near the beginning, not end, of long quotations. Also, attribute a direct quotation only once. If you placed the attribution before the quotation, it should be followed by a comma, not a period.)

11. The student grinned and said: "I really don't enjoy college, but I don't know what else to do. Perhaps I should just quit school and look for a job." (Do not use "grinned" as a word of attribution. Use a colon, not a comma, when the quotation that follows contains more than one sentence. Also, place quotation marks only at the beginning and end of a direct quotation, not at the beginning and end of every sentence.)

12. The woman said that only a few of her friends are happy as full-time homemakers and that most want to find a job. "They want to make some money and become less dependent on their husbands," she explained. OR: The woman said that only a few of her friends are happy as full-time homemakers and that, "Most want to find a job." She explained, "They want to make some money and become less dependent on their husbands." (Avoid using "claimed" as a word of attribution. It editorializes, implying doubt. Also avoid orphan quotes, and separate partial and complete quotations. As an alternative, paraphrase the partial quotation.)

13. The City Council voted 7 to 2 against a proposal to give police officers a 12 percent raise. "It's just too much," Mayor Sabrina Datolli said. "Policemen are already overpaid. Police officers just aren't worth $25,000 a year." (Attribute a direct quotation only once. CAUTION: Should you use the word "policemen"? Here, it appears in a direct quotation. Still, it excludes women. You may want to discuss this problem with your instructor and classmates.)

14. "My daddy will give me a dime," the girl said as she ran home. (Use a comma, not a period, when the attribution follows a quotation. Also, be certain to use an appropriate word of attribution. A declaration is a formal statement or announcement, not a child's shout.)

15. The governor said it is too early to speculate about whether he will run for another term. (Stress your sources' answers, not the questions they are asked. A paraphrase can simplify this quotation. Attribute a direct quotation only once.)

16. Tests showed that low- or moderate-speed, rear-end collisions involving the car caused massive fuel leaks and fires, the magazine reported. (Avoid orphan quotes. Also avoid another common error: You can always delete the quotation marks around a statement and paraphrase it; however, you cannot place new quotation marks around an entire statement unless you know that every word in the statement is part of an accurate direct quotation, not simply a reporter's summary of the source's remarks.)

CREDITS

AMERICAN ACADEMY OF PEDIATRICS, COMMITTEE ON COMMUNICATIONS POLICY STATEMENT For "Children, Adolescents and Television." *AAP NEWS*, April 1990; 6:7. Copyright 1990 American Academy of Pediatrics. Reprinted with permission.

KNIGHT-RIDDER TRIBUNE NEWS SERVICE "From Desktop to Doorstep" Knight-Ridder Tribune Graphics. Reprinted with permission.

MIAMI HERALD For various article excerpts. Reprinted with permission.

NATIONAL VICTIM CENTER For "Victims Rights." Copyright © by the National Victim Center. Reprinted with permission.

THE NEW YORK TIMES For various article excerpts. Copyright © 1992 by The New York Times Company. Reprinted with permission.

UNITED PRESS INTERNATIONAL For leads and articles. Copyright by United Press International, Inc. Reprinted with permission.

**All other literary permissions are listed within the text.

PHOTO AND COMIC CREDITS

p. 74 Reprinted by permission: Tribune Media Services

p. 86 UNIVERSAL PRESS SYNDICATE

p. 115 AP/Wide World

p. 120 Courtesy of The New-York Historical Society

p. 122 Photo by Chris O'Meara/THE LEDGER

p. 127 UPI/Bettmann Newsphotos

p. 288 Reprinted by permission: Tribune Media Services

p. 387 Zimbel/Monkmeyer

p. 389 © Ellis Herwig/Stock Boston

p. 390 © Alan Carey/The Image Works

p. 392 (left) © Oliver Rebbot 1980/Woodfin Camp & Associates

p. 392 (right) Bob Daemmric/The Image Works

p. 409 Courtesy Gannett Co.

p. 410 Courtesy WALL STREET JOURNAL, Dow Jones & Co., Inc.

p. 424 Reprinted by permission: Tribune Media Services

p. 445 Joe Cavaretta/THE ALBUQUERQUE TRIBUNE/1988 Distinguished Service Award

p. 447 Burk Uzzle/Woodfin Camp & Associates

p. 449 AP/Wide World

p. 463 Courtesy THE BAKERSFIELD CALIFORNIAN

p. 468 (top) Courtesy THE MIAMI HERALD

p. 468 (middle left) AP/Wide World

p. 468 (middle right) UPI/Bettmann Newsphotos

p. 468 (bottom left) Courtesy THE NATIONAL ENQUIRER

p. 468 (bottom right) © Bill Beebe

p. 471 Courtesy Ron Olshwanger

p. 474 Stanley Forman/BOSTON HERALD AMERICAN/Pulitzer Prize 1976

p. 478 AP/Wide World

p. 480 AP/Wide World

p. 483 AP/Wide World

p. 487 AP/Wide World

p. 491 AP/Wide World

p. 492 NEW YORK DAILY NEWS

p. 550 © John Seakwood/Outline

p. 580 Reprinted by permission: Tribune Media Services

p. 710 Courtesy USA TODAY

INDEX

Copyright © 1993 by Harcourt Brace Jovanovich, Inc.
All rights reserved. Printed in the United States of America
ISBN 0-15-500602-9